THE BILLBOARD BOOK OF
TOP 40 HITS
REVISED AND EXPANDED EIGHTH EDITION

JOEL WHITBURN

BILLBOARD BOOKS
An imprint of Watson-Guptill Publications/New York

Executive Editor: Bob Nirkind
Editor: Michelle Bredeson
Editorial Assistant: Shannon Kerner
Designer: Bob Fillie, Graphiti Design, Inc.
Cover design by Spencer Drate and Judith Salavetz
Production Manager: Ellen Greene
Photo Captions: Christopher Feldman
Picture sleeves selected from Joel Whitburn's personal collection.
The principal typefaces used in the composition
of this book were Palatino and Futura.

First published in 2004 by Billboard Books,
an imprint of Watson-Guptill Publications,
a division of VNU Business Media, Inc.,
770 Broadway, New York, NY 10003
www.wgpub.com

Library of Congress Control Number: 2004104967

ISBN: 0-8230-7499-4

Manufactured in the U.S.A.

First printing 2004

3 4 5 6 7 8 9 / 12 11 10 09 08 07 06

Dedicated to

Margaret Ruth Lambrecht
6/25/30–12/5/03

...my wonderful sister, Margaret,
who left this world for a better place
this past December. She was like a
second mother to me, always kind,
gentle, unselfish and loving. I miss
you immensely Marg, but I'll
"see you in the morning."

The author wishes to give thanks to the staff of Record Research.

Top: Jeanne Olynick, Nestor Vidotto, Joel Whitburn, Paul Haney, Bill Hathaway
Middle: Brent Olynick, Fran Whitburn, Kim Bloxdorf
Bottom: Jessica Arbuckle

CONTENTS

AUTHOR'S NOTE

Welcome to the eighth edition of *Top 40 Hits*! This book contains all of the artists and all of their songs that hit between #1 and #40 on *Billboard* magazine's Hot 100 chart. A diverse array of music and a broad span of years are covered in the following pages.

Nineteen hundred and fifty-five marked the beginning of the rock era and was also the year that *Billboard* began publishing the Top 100 chart. This was their first chart to list more than 30 song titles. In 1958, the Top 100 chart evolved into the Hot 100 chart and, like its predecessor, ranked the 100 most popular songs across America. The ranking was based on surveys of radio airplay, jukebox activity and record sales reports. *Billboard*'s charts were reporting on an exciting and explosive time in popular music.

In 1955 I was 15, the prime age to experience the rock and roll revolution. I was hooked and found myself a frequent customer of the Jess Electric store, the local appliance store that had record racks near the front counter. Fueling my passion for music were my subscription to *Billboard* magazine and my radio. I remember surfing the AM dial and when I heard a hit on a pop station, I would put a check mark next to it on the chart.

My passion for cataloging and collecting records continued through many musical styles over the years (and, obviously, still continues today). I followed the records up and down the chart. I made up an index card for each artist and carefully noted for each of their charted hits the debut date, peak position, peak date, weeks on chart, label and number, etc.—much of the same type of information that is found in this book.

In 1970, I typed up the information on those cards and published my first book, *Record Research,* which covered everything that had, up to then, hit the Hot 100. Through my burning desire to have a handy copy of my own research, I found that there were many other record fanatics who also had a keen interest in knowing precisely the who, what, when and how long of each song. That modest little book became the heart of a business and was the granddaddy of my *Top Pop Singles* book and this book.

Much about record collecting and cataloging has changed in the past half century. I have collected every available format of music, from shiny black-grooved 78s to iridescent CDs, and every charted artist from Ellington to Elvis to Evanescence. The formatting of radio has changed greatly, too. Nowadays, it would be quite a feat to check off the Top 40 songs on the Hot 100 in one week. You'd likely burn out your FM radio dial, scanning between stations playing Adult Top 40, R&B Top 40, Mainstream Top 40 and so on.

A lot of musical territory is covered in the pages ahead. If you can recall more than 70 percent of the songs listed herein, you too are a rare breed of chart fanatic. If so, also check out my *Top Pop Singles* book. For the majority of readers of *Top 40 Hits*, music ranks as a pleasant diversion, rather than a fixation. Wherever you're at in this continuum, I hope that this book provides answers to those challenging trivia questions, helps you to remember long-forgotten songs and occasionally puts a smile on your face.

JOEL WHITBURN

RESEARCHING THE CHARTS

The eighth edition of *Top 40 Hits* features America's most popular songs and artists from the beginning of the rock era through 2003. It is a spin-off of Joel Whitburn's *Top Pop Singles* book, which includes all of the songs and artists that hit *Billboard*'s Hot 100 chart. In the pages ahead, you'll rediscover the biggest-selling and most-played hits and recording artists on pop radio from New York to Los Angeles.

The research of *Top 40 Hits* begins with 1955—the year rock 'n' roll scored its first mainstream success with the chart-topping hit "(We're Gonna) Rock Around The Clock" by Bill Haley & His Comets. At that time, *Billboard* magazine published three main pop singles charts: Best Sellers In Stores, Most Played By Jockeys and Most Played In Juke Boxes. The research begins with the issue of *Billboard* dated January 1, 1955, and includes all hits within the Top 40 on the above-mentioned charts, even if they first charted in 1954. In November of 1955, *Billboard* introduced their first 100-position chart, the Top 100. These four charts reported on different aspects of the sales and radio airplay of the hottest singles. Each of these charts are researched in order to impart an intricate picture of popular music of the mid-1950s.

August 4, 1958, marked the first issue of *Billboard* to feature the Hot 100 chart. It was *Billboard*'s first chart to fully integrate the hottest-selling and most-played singles. Ever since, the Hot 100 has stood the test of time as the premiere monitor of the most popular songs in America each week. All songs to make the first 40 positions of this 100-position ranking through 2003 constitute the bulk of this book.

For the Hot 100's first four decades, an essential qualification for a song's placement on the chart was its commercial availability in America as a single. The record industry's practice of releasing singles commercially declined dramatically in the 1990s. More and more radio hits were ineligible to chart on the Hot 100 as they were never released as singles. The Hot 100 Airplay and Hot 100 Singles Sales charts that *Billboard* created in 1984 became valued accompaniments to the Hot 100 chart in providing a thorough picture of each week's biggest hits. For this reason, we have included all Top 40 hits of *Billboard*'s Hot 100 Airplay and Hot 100 Singles Sales charts that did not appear on the Hot 100 chart. *Billboard* has made major adjustments to the compilation of their Hot 100 in order to keep pace with a rapidly changing music marketplace. On December 5, 1998, *Billboard* debuted a completely revised Hot 100, which included, for the first time, songs that were not commercially available in America as singles.

All chart data within *Top 40 Hits* are related to the charts listed below. The beginning dates researched are also the debut dates of most charts, with the exception of Best Sellers, Jockeys and Juke Box charts, all of which debuted prior to 1955. As "# of Positions" indicates, the size of certain charts varied from week to week.

Chart Title	Dates Researched	# of Positions
Best Sellers In Stores	1/1/55–10/13/58*	25–50
Most Played By Jockeys	1/1/55–7/28/58*	20–25
Most Played In Juke Boxes	1/1/55–6/17/57*	20
Top 100	11/12/55–7/28/58*	100
Hot 100	8/4/58–12/27/03	100
Hot 100 Singles Sales	10/20/84–12/27/03	30–75
Hot 100 Airplay	10/20/84–12/27/03	30–75
Top 40 Radio Monitor	12/8/90–7/10/93*	75

* date of final chart

For songs that hit the Top 40 on more than one of these charts, their chart-by-chart breakdowns are listed to the right of these titles.

MULTIPLE POP CHARTS, 1955–1958

The single's "DATE" is taken from the chart on which it first entered the Top 40 if it hit in the Top 40 on more than one of the following Pop singles charts published from 1955-58: Best Sellers In Stores, Most Played By Jockeys, Most Played In Juke Boxes, Top 100 or Hot 100. The date shown is *Billboard*'s actual issue date, and is not taken from the "week ending" dates as shown on the various charts when they were originally published. (The issue and week ending dates were different until January 13, 1962, when *Billboard* began using one date system for both the issue and the charts inside.)

The single's highest position (POS) is taken from the chart on which it achieved its highest ranking.

The single's weeks in Top 40 (WKS) and weeks at positions #1 or #2 are taken from the chart on which it achieved its highest total.

HOT 100 SALES & AIRPLAY, 1984-2003

The data used to compile each week's Hot 100 chart is also used to compile the weekly Hot 100 Singles Sales and Hot 100 Airplay charts. The early Sales chart was compiled from the best-selling records based on reports from record stores, and the early Airplay chart was compiled from the most-played songs based on radio station playlists. From June 8, 1991 through November 23, 1991, the Sales and Airplay charts were not compiled from the same data as the Hot 100. During that period *Billboard* began compiling the Sales and Airplay charts from data provided by BDS and SoundScan. As of November 30, 1991, *Billboard* also began compiling the Hot 100 via BDS and SoundScan; the charts were once again directly related.

The songs that hit the Sales and Airplay charts, but did not hit the Hot 100, are denoted by the superscript letters "A" (Airplay chart) and "S" (Sales chart), in the peak position (POS) column. The Sales and Airplay peak positions of songs that crossed over to the Hot 100 are listed to the right of the song title (e.g., Sales #2 / Airplay #5). If a song peaked at #1, the total weeks charted at #1 are shown in parentheses after the peak position.

As mentioned previously, *Billboard* revamped the Hot 100 on December 5, 1998, and included, for the first time, songs that were not commercially available in America as singles. From this date forward, if a Hot 100 Singles Sales hit did not cross over to the Hot 100, it is listed in this book only if it peaks in the Top 5 of the Hot 100 Singles Sales chart. As record companies discontinued issuing singles in the 1990s, unless a title made the Top 5, its sales totals were too insignificant to climb into the Top 40 ranks.

TOP 40 RADIO MONITOR, 1990-1993

Billboard compiled their Top 40 Radio Monitor chart from actual monitored airplay data provided by Broadcast Data Systems (BDS). From December 8, 1990, through June 1, 1991, *Billboard* published both the Hot 100 Airplay chart (compiled from radio station playlists) and the Top 40 Radio Monitor chart. As of June 8, 1991, *Billboard* dropped the Hot 100 Airplay chart in favor of the Top 40 Radio Monitor chart. On July 17, 1993, the Top 40 Radio Monitor chart was renamed the Hot 100 Airplay chart. During the overlap period of the Top 40 Radio Monitor chart and the early Airplay chart (December 8, 1990 through June 1, 1991), the only Top 40 Radio Monitor chart hits included herein are those that *did not* also make either the Hot 100, Hot 100 Sales or Hot 100 Airplay charts. Songs that hit the Top 40 Radio Monitor chart exclusively appear in the main artist section and are denoted by the superscript letter "A" following their peak position.

THE ARTISTS

LISTS, ALPHABETICALLY BY ARTIST NAME,
EVERY SONG THAT CHARTED IN THE TOP 40
ON *BILLBOARD*'S POP SINGLES CHARTS
FROM JANUARY 1, 1955,
THROUGH DECEMBER 27, 2003.

HOW TO USE
THIS SECTION

Each artist's Top 40 hits are listed in chronological order. A sequential number is shown in front of each song title to indicate that artist's number of Top 40 hits. All Top 10 hits are highlighted in dark type.

EXPLANATION OF COLUMNAR HEADINGS

DATE: Date song debuted in the Top 40

POS: Highest charted (a.k.a. peak) position (highlighted in bold type)

WKS: Total weeks charted in the Top 40

LABEL & NO.: Original label and number of commercially available single when charted. The words "album cut" are shown in the label column for Hot 100 Airplay tracks, and the album from which the track attained its airplay is noted below the title along with its label and number.

EXPLANATION OF SYMBOLS

A   Following the peak position indicates that song peaked on the Hot 100 Airplay chart but did not hit the Hot 100 chart. For a song that hit the Hot 100 Airplay and the Hot 100 charts, its Airplay peak position is listed to the right of the title (e.g., Airplay #7).

S   Following the peak position indicates that single peaked on the Hot 100 Singles Sales chart but did not hit the Hot 100 chart. For a single that hit the Hot 100 Singles Sales and the Hot 100 charts, its Sales peak position is listed to the right of the title (e.g., Sales #3).

(1)   Number in parentheses to the right of a #1 or #2 peak position is the total weeks the single held that position

+	Indicates single peaked in the year after it first charted (symbol shown next to date)
●	Gold single*
▲	Platinum single* (additional million units sold are indicated by a numeral following the symbol)
/	Divides a two-sided hit. Complete chart data (date, peak position, etc.) is shown for both sides if each side achieved its own peak position. If a title was shown only as the B-side (never achieved its own peak position), then only the debut date and the weeks it charted as a "tag along" are listed. When listing chart data to the right of a title (see "Peak Position Designations" below), "flip" is listed as the peak position for "tag-along" hits.
↑	Indicates the weeks charted data is subject to change since the single was still charted as of the 5/22/04 cut-off date

PEAK POSITION DESIGNATIONS

As mentioned previously, before the debut of the Hot 100 chart on August 4, 1958, *Billboard* published four primary weekly pop singles charts (Most Played By Jockeys, Best Sellers In Stores, Most Played in Juke Boxes and the Top 100). The peak position shown in the "POS" column for the pre-Hot 100 pop singles charts is taken from the chart on which it achieved its highest position. No letter designation for the peak's particular chart appears in the "POS" column. The individual peak positions attained on these four pre-Hot 100 pop singles charts are listed to the right of the title, preceded by:

Jockey:	Most Played By Jockeys
Best Seller:	Best Sellers In Stores
Juke Box:	Most Played In Juke Boxes
Top 100:	The Top 100
Hot 100:	Hot 100 (used during transition to the Hot 100 chart)

*The primary source used to determine gold and platinum singles is the Recording Industry Association of America (RIAA), which began certifying gold singles in 1958 and platinum singles in 1976. From 1958 through 1988, RIAA required sales of one million units for a gold single and two million units for a platinum single; however, as of January 1, 1989, RIAA lowered the certification requirements for gold singles to sales of 500,000 units and for platinum to one million units. Please keep in mind that some record labels have never requested RIAA certifications for their hits. In order to fill in the gaps, especially during the period prior to 1958, various other trade publications and reports were used to supplement RIAA's certifications.

The peak positions of Hot 100 Singles Sales and Hot 100 Airplay chart hits that crossed over to the Hot 100 are listed to the right of the title, and preceded by:

Sales: Hot 100 Singles Sales

Airplay: Hot 100 Airplay (and Top 40 Radio Monitor [12/8/90-7/10/93])

Hot 100:   Hot 100 (used for airplay titles that appeared on the 12/5/98 Hot 100 chart [first chart to include airplay-only titles], which achieved a higher peak position on the Hot 100 Airplay chart prior to 12/5/98)

LETTER(S) IN BRACKETS AFTER TITLES

[I]   instrumental recording

[L]   live recording

[N]   novelty recording

[C]   comedy recording

[S]   spoken word recording

[F]   foreign language recording

[X]   Christmas recording

[R]   re-entry, reissue, remix or re-recording of a previous hit by that artist*

*Includes singles that re-entered following an absence of at least six months from the charts, and singles re-issued with a new label and number.

ARTIST & TITLE NOTES

Below each artist name are brief biographical notes about the artist. Directly under some song titles are notes indicating backing vocalists, guest instrumentalists, the title of a movie in which the song was featured, the name of a famous songwriter or producer, etc. Duets and other important name variations are shown in bold capital letters. All titles of movies, TV shows, plays, albums and other major works are shown in italics.

#1 HITS ON OTHER CHARTS

Title notes indicate singles that peaked at #1 on the Adult Contemporary, R&B and Country singles charts, and tracks that peaked at #1 on the Mainstream (Album) Rock and Modern Rock charts.

DATE	POS	WKS	ARTIST–RECORD TITLE	LABEL & NO.

A

AALIYAH

Born Aaliyah Dana Haughton on 1/16/79 in Brooklyn, New York; raised in Detroit, Michigan. Died in a plane crash on 8/25/2001 (age 22). Female R&B singer/actress. Acted in the movies *Romeo Must Die* and *Queen Of The Damned*. Married R. Kelly on 7/31/94 (marriage later annulled).

DATE	POS	WKS	ARTIST–RECORD TITLE	LABEL & NO.
5/7/94	**5**	21	● 1. **Back & Forth** Sales #3 / Airplay #7 #1 R&B hit (3 weeks)	Blackground 42174
9/10/94	**6**	14	● 2. **At Your Best (You Are Love)** Sales #4 / Airplay #11 first recorded by The Isley Brothers in 1976	Blackground 42239
8/31/96	**11**	15	3. If Your Girl Only Knew Sales #7 / Airplay #43 #1 R&B hit (2 weeks)	Blackground 98067
1/25/97	**25** ᴬ	12	4. One In A Million #1 R&B Airplay hit (6 weeks); from the album *One In A Million* on Blackground 92715	album cut
10/4/97	**9**	17	● 5. **The One I Gave My Heart To** Sales #6 / Airplay #41	Blackground 98002
7/25/98	**4** ᴬ	27	6. **Are You That Somebody?** Hot 100 #21 (8 wks) #1 R&B Airplay hit (8 weeks); Timbaland (male rapper); from the movie *Dr. Dolittle* starring Eddie Murphy (soundtrack on Blackground 83113)	album cut
2/26/00	**35**	9	7. I Don't Wanna Airplay #26 from the movie *Next Friday* starring Ice Cube (soundtrack on Priority 23123)	album cut
4/1/00	**1** (1)	29	8. **Try Again** Airplay #1 (9) from the movie *Romeo Must Die* starring Jet Li and Aaliyah	Blackground 38722
9/22/01	**14**	22	9. Rock The Boat Airplay #13	album cut
3/9/02	**25**	18	10. More Than A Woman Airplay #21	album cut
9/7/02	**16**	14	11. I Care 4 U Airplay #15 above 3 from the album *Aaliyah* on Blackground 10082	album cut
12/7/02+	**3**	28	12. **Miss You** Sales #3 / Airplay #3 #1 R&B hit (3 weeks)	Blackground 000384
8/23/03	**32**	7	13. Come Over Airplay #29 from the album *I Care 4 U* on Blackground 060082	album cut

ABBA

Pop group from Stockholm, Sweden: Anni-Frid "Frida" Lyngstad (vocals; see #15 below), Agnetha Fältskog (vocals; see #16 below), Bjorn Ulvaeus (guitar) and Benny Andersson (keyboards). Bjorn and Agnetha were married from 1971-79. Benny and Frida were married from 1978-81. Bjorn and Benny co-wrote the musical *Chess* with Tim Rice.

DATE	POS	WKS	ARTIST–RECORD TITLE	LABEL & NO.
6/22/74	**6**	12	1. **Waterloo** **ABBA (Bjorn, Benny, Anna & Frida)**	Atlantic 3035
10/12/74	**27**	4	2. Honey, Honey	Atlantic 3209
10/11/75	**15**	8	3. SOS only chart hit where both title and artist are palindromes	Atlantic 3265
3/27/76	**15**	8	4. I Do, I Do, I Do, I Do, I Do	Atlantic 3310
6/19/76	**32**	4	5. Mamma Mia	Atlantic 3315
9/25/76	**13**	11	6. Fernando #1 Adult Contemporary hit (2 weeks)	Atlantic 3346
1/22/77	**1** (1)	15	● 7. **Dancing Queen**	Atlantic 3372

DATE	POS	WKS	ARTIST–RECORD TITLE	LABEL & NO.
6/4/77	14	10	8. Knowing Me, Knowing You	Atlantic 3387
1/28/78	12	9	9. The Name Of The Game	Atlantic 3449
5/6/78	3	14	● 10. **Take A Chance On Me**	Atlantic 3457
6/9/79	19	10	11. Does Your Mother Know	Atlantic 3574
12/8/79+	29	6	12. Chiquitita	Atlantic 3629
12/27/80+	8	16	13. **The Winner Takes It All** #1 Adult Contemporary hit (2 weeks)	Atlantic 3776
2/6/82	27	8	14. When All Is Said And Done all of above written and produced by Benny & Bjorn	Atlantic 3889
2/12/83	13	12	15. I Know There's Something Going On **FRIDA** produced by Phil Collins	Atlantic 89984
10/8/83	29	5	16. Can't Shake Loose **AGNETHA FÄLTSKOG**	Polydor 815230

ABBOTT, Gregory

Born on 4/2/54 in Harlem, New York. R&B singer/songwriter. Formerly married to Freda Payne.

DATE	POS	WKS	ARTIST–RECORD TITLE	LABEL & NO.
11/8/86+	1 (1)	16	▲ 1. **Shake You Down**　　　Airplay #1 (1) / Sales #2 #1 R&B hit (2 weeks)	Columbia 06191

ABC

Electro-pop/dance group from Sheffield, Yorkshire, England: Martin Fry (vocals), Mark White (guitar), Stephen Singleton (sax), Mark Lickley (bass) and David Robinson (drums). At the end of 1983, the latter three left, leaving duo of Fry and White.

DATE	POS	WKS	ARTIST–RECORD TITLE	LABEL & NO.
10/30/82+	18	13	1. The Look Of Love (Part One)	Mercury 76168
2/26/83	25	8	2. Poison Arrow	Mercury 810340
9/28/85	9	11	3. **Be Near Me**　　　Sales #10 / Airplay #10	Mercury 880626
2/15/86	20	7	4. (How To Be A) Millionaire　　　Sales #17 / Airplay #26	Mercury 884382
8/1/87	5	12	5. **When Smokey Sings**　　　Sales #5 / Airplay #6 a tribute to Smokey Robinson	Mercury 888604

ABDUL, Paula

Born on 6/19/62 in San Fernando, California. Pop-dance singer/choreographer. Former cheerleader with the NBA's Los Angeles Lakers. Choreographed Janet Jackson's *Control* videos and Tracey Ullman's TV show. Started own Captive label. Married to actor Emilio Estevez from 1992-94. Starred in the 1997 TV movie *Touched By Evil*. One of the judges on TV's *American Idol*.

DATE	POS	WKS	ARTIST–RECORD TITLE	LABEL & NO.
12/24/88+	1 (3)	16	▲ 1. **Straight Up**　　　Airplay #1 (3) / Sales #1 (1)	Virgin 99256
4/1/89	1 (2)	14	● 2. **Forever Your Girl**　　　Airplay #1 (2) / Sales #2	Virgin 99230
7/8/89	1 (1)	15	● 3. **Cold Hearted**　　　Sales #1 (1) / Airplay #1 (1)	Virgin 99196
10/7/89	3	14	4. (It's Just) The Way That You Love Me 　　　Airplay #2 / Sales #4　**[R]** originally charted at #88 in 1988	Virgin 99282
1/6/90	1 (3)	14	● 5. **Opposites Attract**　　　Airplay #1 (4) / Sales #1 (3) **PAULA ABDUL (with The Wild Pair)** Derrick Delite (rap)	Virgin 99158
5/11/91	1 (5)	15	● 6. **Rush, Rush**　　　Airplay #1 (8) / Sales #3 #1 Adult Contemporary hit (5 weeks)	Virgin 98828
7/20/91	1 (1)	13	7. **The Promise Of A New Day**　　　Airplay #5 / Sales #25	Captive/Virgin 98752

DATE	POS	WKS	ARTIST–RECORD TITLE	LABEL & NO.
10/26/91	**6**	14	8. **Blowing Kisses In The Wind** Airplay #5 / Sales #15	Captive/Virgin 98683
2/1/92	**16**	7	9. Vibeology Airplay #16 / Sales #22	Captive/Virgin 98737
4/18/92	**19**	8	10. Will You Marry Me? Airplay #13 / Sales #61	Captive/Virgin 98584
			Stevie Wonder (harmonica); Sandra St. Victor (backing vocal)	
6/17/95	**28**	6	11. My Love Is For Real Sales #24 / Airplay #44	Captive/Virgin 38493
			Ofra Haza (backing vocal)	

AC/DC

Hard-rock group from Sydney, Australia: Brian Johnson (vocals), brothers Angus and Malcolm Young (guitars), Cliff Williams (bass) and Phil Rudd (drums). Original lead singer Bon Scott died of alcohol abuse on 2/19/80 (age 33). By 1990, Chris Slade (of The Firm) had replaced Rudd. Angus and Malcolm are the younger brothers of George Young of The Easybeats. Group inducted into the Rock and Roll Hall of Fame in 2003.

DATE	POS	WKS	ARTIST–RECORD TITLE	LABEL & NO.
10/25/80	**35**	3	1. You Shook Me All Night Long	Atlantic 3761
2/7/81	**37**	5	2. Back In Black	Atlantic 3787
1/26/91	**23**	5	3. Moneytalks Sales #16 / Airplay #30	Atco 98881

ACE

Pub-rock group from Sheffield, Yorkshire, England: Paul Carrack (vocals), Phil Harris and Alan King (guitars), Terry Comer (bass) and Fran Byrne (drums). Disbanded in 1977. Carrack later joined Mike + The Mechanics.

DATE	POS	WKS	ARTIST–RECORD TITLE	LABEL & NO.
4/5/75	**3**	11	1. **How Long**	Anchor 21000

ACE, Johnny

Born John Alexander on 6/9/29 in Memphis, Tennessee. Shot himself playing Russian Roulette backstage at the City Auditorium in Houston, Texas, on 12/24/54; died the following day (age 25). R&B singer/pianist/organist/songwriter.

DATE	POS	WKS	ARTIST–RECORD TITLE	LABEL & NO.
2/19/55	**17**	9	1. Pledging My Love Best Seller #17 / Juke Box #17 / Jockey #19	Duke 136
			#1 R&B hit (10 weeks); Johnny Board (orch.)	

ACE OF BASE

Pop-dance group from Gothenburg, Sweden: vocalists/sisters Jenny and Linn Berggren with keyboardists Jonas "Joker" Berggren (their brother) and Ulf "Buddha" Ekberg.

DATE	POS	WKS	ARTIST–RECORD TITLE	LABEL & NO.
10/9/93	**2 (3)**	30	▲ 1. **All That She Wants** Sales #1 (3) / Airplay #2	Arista 12614
1/22/94	**1 (6)**	33	▲ 2. **The Sign** Airplay #1 (13) / Sales #2	Arista 12653
5/14/94	**4**	28	● 3. **Don't Turn Around** Airplay #1 (2) / Sales #6	Arista 12691
			first recorded by Luther Ingram in 1987	
10/29/94	**20**	13	4. Living In Danger Airplay #16 / Sales #42	Arista 12754
11/11/95	**15**	13	5. Beautiful Life Sales #11 / Airplay #21	Arista 12889
3/30/96	**30**	4	6. Lucky Love Airplay #35 / Sales #38	Arista 12979
7/18/98	**10**	14	● 7. **Cruel Summer** Sales #10 / Airplay #40	Arista 13505

ACKLIN, Barbara

Born on 2/28/42 in Chicago, Illinois. Died of pneumonia on 11/27/98 (age 56). R&B singer/songwriter. Formerly married to Eugene Record of The Chi-Lites.

DATE	POS	WKS	ARTIST–RECORD TITLE	LABEL & NO.
8/10/68	**15**	8	1. Love Makes A Woman	Brunswick 55379

ADAM & THE ANTS — see ANT, Adam

DATE	POS	WKS	ARTIST–RECORD TITLE	LABEL & NO.
			ADAMS, Bryan	
			Born on 11/5/59 in Kingston, Ontario, Canada. Rock singer/songwriter/ guitarist. Lead singer of Sweeney Todd in 1976. Teamed with Jim Vallance in 1977 in songwriting partnership. Cameo appearance in the movie *Pink Cadillac*.	
4/16/83	**10**	11	1. **Straight From The Heart**	A&M 2536
6/25/83	**15**	8	2. Cuts Like A Knife	A&M 2553
10/1/83	**24**	6	3. This Time	A&M 2574
11/24/84+	**6**	12	4. **Run To You** Airplay #6 / Sales #7 #1 Mainstream Rock hit (4 weeks)	A&M 2686
2/23/85	**11**	10	5. Somebody Airplay #10 / Sales #14 #1 Mainstream Rock hit (2 weeks)	A&M 2701
4/27/85	**1 (2)**	14	6. **Heaven** Sales #1 (2) / Airplay #2	A&M 2729
7/13/85	**5**	12	7. **Summer Of '69** Airplay #4 / Sales #5	A&M 2739
9/28/85	**13**	9	8. One Night Love Affair Airplay #10 / Sales #15	A&M 2770
12/7/85+	**15**	9	9. It's Only Love Airplay #14 / Sales #16 **BRYAN ADAMS/TINA TURNER**	A&M 2791
4/11/87	**6**	10	10. **Heat Of The Night** Sales #4 / Airplay #6	A&M 2921
7/4/87	**26**	6	11. Hearts On Fire Sales #23 / Airplay #26	A&M 2948
9/12/87	**32**	5	12. Victim Of Love Sales #29 / Airplay #30	A&M 2964
7/6/91	**1 (7)**	17	▲³ 13. **(Everything I Do) I Do It For You** Sales #1 (17) / Airplay #1 (8) #1 Adult Contemporary hit (8 weeks); from the movie *Robin Hood: Prince Of Thieves* starring Kevin Costner	A&M 1567
9/21/91	**2 (1)**	19	● 14. **Can't Stop This Thing We Started** Sales #11 / Airplay #14	A&M 1576
2/1/92	**31**	4	15. There Will Never Be Another Tonight Airplay #48 / Sales #72	A&M 1588
4/4/92	**13**	13	16. Thought I'd Died And Gone To Heaven Airplay #14 / Sales #24	A&M 1592
8/15/92	**11**	15	17. Do I Have To Say The Words? Airplay #10 / Sales #29	A&M 1611
11/6/93	**7**	26	18. **Please Forgive Me** Airplay #3 / Sales #8	A&M 0422
12/4/93+	**1 (3)**	20	▲ 19. **All For Love** Sales #1 (5) / Airplay #3 **BRYAN ADAMS ROD STEWART STING** from the movie *The Three Musketeers* starring Kiefer Sutherland and Charlie Sheen	A&M 0476
4/22/95	**1 (5)**	20	20. **Have You Ever Really Loved A Woman?** Sales #1 (1) / Airplay #3 #1 Adult Contemporary hit (5 weeks); Paco de Lucia (acoustic guitar); from the movie *Don Juan DeMarco* starring Johnny Depp	A&M 1028
9/21/96	**24**	14	21. Let's Make A Night To Remember Airplay #26 / Sales #28	A&M 1862
11/23/96	**8**	15	● 22. **I Finally Found Someone** Sales #7 / Airplay #20 **BARBRA STREISAND and BRYAN ADAMS** from the movie *The Mirror Has Two Faces* starring Streisand	Columbia 78480
			ADAMS, Johnny	
			Born Lathan John Adams on 1/5/32 in New Orleans, Louisiana. Died of cancer on 9/14/98 (age 66). R&B singer. Nicknamed "The Tan Canary."	
7/26/69	**28**	4	1. Reconsider Me	SSS Int'l. 770
			ADAMS, Oleta	
			Born on 5/4/62 in Seattle, Washington. Female R&B singer/pianist.	
2/9/91	**5**	10	1. **Get Here** Sales #2 / Airplay #13	Fontana 878476

DATE	POS	WKS	ARTIST–RECORD TITLE	LABEL & NO.
			ADDERLEY, "Cannonball"	
			Born Julian Adderley on 9/15/28 in Tampa, Florida. Died of a stroke on 8/8/75 (age 46). Nickname derived from "cannibal" in tribute to his love of eating. Alto saxophonist/leader of own jazz combo.	
1/28/67	11	8	1. Mercy, Mercy, Mercy **[I-L]**	Capitol 5798
			ADDRISI BROTHERS, The	
			Pop singing/songwriting duo from Winthrop, Massachusetts. Dick was born on 7/4/41. Don was born on 12/14/38; died on 11/13/84 (age 45).	
2/26/72	25	7	1. We've Got To Get It On Again	Columbia 45521
5/14/77	20	8	2. Slow Dancin' Don't Turn Me On	Buddah 566
			AD LIBS, The	
			Black doo-wop group from Newark, New Jersey: Mary Ann Thomas (lead), Hugh Harris, Danny Austin, Norman Donegan and Dave Watt.	
2/6/65	8	7	1. **The Boy From New York City**	Blue Cat 102
			ADVENTURES OF STEVIE V	
			Black dance group from Bedfordshire, England. Assembled by producer Stevie Vincent. Includes singer Melodie Washington and multi-instrumentalist Mick Walsh.	
8/25/90	25	8	1. Dirty Cash (Money Talks) Sales #13 / Airplay #31	Mercury 875802
			AEROSMITH	
			Hard-rock group formed in Boston, Massachusetts: Steven Tyler (vocals), Joe Perry (guitar), Brad Whitford (guitar), Tom Hamilton (bass) and Joey Kramer (drums). Group appeared in the movies *Sgt. Pepper's Lonely Hearts Club Band* and *Wayne's World 2*. Tyler's daughter is actress Liv Tyler. Group inducted into the Rock and Roll Hall of Fame in 2001.	
7/12/75	36	3	1. Sweet Emotion	Columbia 10155
2/14/76	6	11	2. **Dream On** **[R]** originally charted at #59 in 1973	Columbia 10278
6/26/76	21	10	3. Last Child	Columbia 10359
12/18/76+	10	11	4. **Walk This Way**	Columbia 10449
5/7/77	38	2	5. Back In The Saddle	Columbia 10516
9/2/78	23	7	6. Come Together from the movie *Sgt. Pepper's Lonely Hearts Club Band* starring Peter Frampton and the Bee Gees	Columbia 10802
11/14/87	14	10	7. Dude (Looks Like A Lady) Sales #10 / Airplay #15	Geffen 28240
2/27/88	3	15	8. **Angel** Sales #2 / Airplay #4	Geffen 28249
7/9/88	17	8	9. Rag Doll Sales #15 / Airplay #20	Geffen 27915
9/16/89	5	11	● 10. **Love In An Elevator** Sales #2 / Airplay #7 #1 Mainstream Rock hit (2 weeks)	Geffen 22845
12/16/89+	4	13	11. **Janie's Got A Gun** Sales #3 / Airplay #7	Geffen 22727
3/31/90	9	10	12. **What It Takes** Sales #7 / Airplay #10 #1 Mainstream Rock hit (1 week)	Geffen 19944
7/21/90	22	7	13. The Other Side Airplay #19 / Sales #24 #1 Mainstream Rock hit (2 weeks)	Geffen 19927
4/24/93	18	11	14. Livin' On The Edge Sales #16 / Airplay #38 #1 Mainstream Rock hit (9 weeks)	Geffen 19149
8/28/93	12	20	● 15. **Cryin'** Sales #9 / Airplay #23 #1 Mainstream Rock hit (6 weeks)	Geffen 19256

DATE	POS	WKS	ARTIST–RECORD TITLE	LABEL & NO.
1/1/94	**24**	16	16. Amazing Sales #24 / Airplay #26 Don Henley (backing vocal)	Geffen 19264
6/18/94	**17**	16	17. Crazy Airplay #18 / Sales #21	Geffen 19267
3/29/97	**35**	4	● 18. Falling In Love (Is Hard On The Knees) Sales #25 #1 Mainstream Rock hit (5 weeks)	Columbia 78499
2/28/98	**27**	6	19. Pink Sales #21 / Airplay #65 #1 Mainstream Rock hit (4 weeks)	Columbia 78830
9/5/98	**1** (4)	14	● 20. **I Don't Want To Miss A Thing** Sales #1 (2) / Airplay #1 (1) from the movie *Armageddon* starring Bruce Willis	Columbia 78952
2/3/01	**7**	17	21. **Jaded** Sales #8 / Airplay #11 #1 Mainstream Rock hit (5 weeks)	Columbia 79555
			AFROMAN	
			Born Joseph Foreman in Los Angeles, California; later based in Hattiesburg, Mississippi. Novelty rapper/songwriter.	
8/25/01	**13**	6	1. Because I Got High Airplay #11 / Sales #56 **[N]** from the movie *Jay And Silent Bob Strike Back* starring Jason Mewes and Kevin Smith	Universal 015310
			AFTERNOON DELIGHTS, The	
			Female studio vocal group from Boston, Massachusetts: Rebecca Hall, Suzanne Boucher, Janet Powell and Robalee Barnes. Group named after Starland Vocal Band's #1 hit from 1976.	
9/12/81	**33**	5	1. General Hospi-Tale **[N]** parody of the TV soap *General Hospital*	MCA 51148
			AFTER 7	
			R&B vocal trio from Indianapolis, Indiana: brothers Kevon Edmonds (see #6 below) and Melvin Edmonds, with Keith Mitchell. Keith is the cousin of L.A. Reid. Kevon and Melvin are the brothers of Babyface.	
4/28/90	**7**	13	● 1. **Ready Or Not** Sales #5 / Airplay #9 #1 R&B hit (2 weeks)	Virgin 98995
8/25/90	**6**	15	● 2. **Can't Stop** Airplay #6 / Sales #10 #1 R&B hit (1 week)	Virgin 98961
1/26/91	**19**	5	3. Heat Of The Moment Airplay #18 / Sales #20 **[R]** originally charted at #74 in 1989	Virgin 99204
7/6/91	**24**	5	4. Nights Like This Sales #36 / Airplay #36 from the movie *The Five Heartbeats* starring Robert Townsend	Virgin 98798
9/2/95	**31**	11	5. 'Til You Do Me Right Sales #20 / Airplay #59	Virgin 38494
12/4/99	**10**	9	● 6. **24/7** Sales #4 / Airplay #45 **KEVON EDMONDS** Shanice, Jason Edwards and IveyGirl (backing vocals)	RCA 65924
			AFTER THE FIRE	
			Rock group from England: Andy Piercy (vocals, bass), John Russell (guitar), Peter Banks (keyboards) and Pete King (drums). Banks was a member of Yes and Flash.	
3/5/83	**5**	14	1. **Der Kommissar** *Kommissar* is German for "detective"	Epic 03559
			AGUILERA, Christina	
			Born on 12/18/80 in Staten Island, New York (of Irish and Ecuadorian descent); raised in Wexford, Pennsylvania. Pop-dance singer/songwriter. Regular on TV's *The Mickey Mouse Club* (1992-93). Won the 1999 Best New Artist Grammy Award.	
7/10/99	**1** (5)	23	▲ 1. **Genie In A Bottle** Sales #1 (4) / Airplay #1 (3)	RCA 65692

DATE	POS	WKS	ARTIST–RECORD TITLE	LABEL & NO.
12/11/99+	**1** (2)	21	● 2. **What A Girl Wants** Sales #1 (2) / Airplay #2	RCA 65960
1/1/00 -	**18**	2	3. The Christmas Song (Chestnuts Roasting On An Open Fire) Sales #6 **[X]**	RCA 65943
4/22/00	**3**	19	4. I Turn To You Sales #1 (1) / Airplay #14	RCA 60251
8/26/00	**1** (4)	16	● 5. **Come On Over Baby (all I want is you)** Sales #1 (6) / Airplay #4	RCA 60341
2/3/01	**13**	13	6. Nobody Wants To Be Lonely Airplay #10 **RICKY MARTIN with CHRISTINA AGUILERA** from Martin's album *Sound Loaded* on Columbia 61394	album cut
4/21/01	**1** (5)	17	7. Lady Marmalade Airplay #1 (6) **CHRISTINA AGUILERA, LIL' KIM, MYA and P!NK** from the movie *Moulin Rouge* starring Nicole Kidman and Ewan McGregor	Interscope 497066
11/30/02+	**2** (1)	24	8. **Beautiful** Airplay #2 #1 Adult Contemporary hit (5 weeks)	RCA 51195
5/3/03	**20**	11	9. Fighter Airplay #19 from the album *Stripped* on RCA 68037	album cut
8/16/03	**12**	15	10. Can't Hold Us Down Airplay #12 **CHRISTINA AGUILERA featuring Lil' Kim**	RCA 54526
12/20/03+	**33**	4	11. The Voice Within Airplay #35 from the album *Stripped* on RCA 68037	album cut
			A-HA	
			Pop trio from Oslo, Norway: Morten Harket (vocals), Pal Waaktaar (guitar) and Magne "Mags" Furuholmen (keyboards).	
8/24/85	**1** (1)	15	1. **Take On Me** Airplay #1 (2) / Sales #3	Warner 29011
1/11/86	**20**	8	2. The Sun Always Shines On T.V. Airplay #17 / Sales #21	Warner 28846
			AHMAD	
			Born Ahmad Lewis on 10/12/75 in Los Angeles. Male rapper.	
6/25/94	**26**	12	● 1. Back In The Day Sales #13 / Airplay #39 samples "Let's Do It Again" by The Staple Singers	Giant 18217
			AIKEN, Clay	
			Born on 11/30/78 in Chapel Hill, North Carolina. White male vocalist. Finished in second place on the second season of TV's *American Idol* in 2003.	
6/28/03	**1** (2)	7	▲ 1. **This Is The Night** Sales #1 (11) the Hot 100 Sales chart also showed the B-side ("Bridge Over Troubled Water")	RCA 51785
			AIR SUPPLY	
			Pop vocal duo formed in Australia: Russell Hitchcock (born on 6/15/49 in Melbourne, Australia) and Graham Russell (born on 6/1/50 in Nottingham, England). Their regular backing band included David Moyse and Rex Goh (guitars), Frank Esler-Smith (keyboards), David Green (bass) and Ralph Cooper (drums).	
3/8/80	**3**	17	1. **Lost In Love** #1 Adult Contemporary hit (6 weeks)	Arista 0479
7/19/80	**2** (4)	17	● 2. **All Out Of Love**	Arista 0520
11/15/80+	**5**	17	3. **Every Woman In The World**	Arista 0564
5/23/81	**1** (1)	14	● 4. **The One That You Love**	Arista 0604
10/3/81	**5**	15	5. **Here I Am (Just When I Thought I Was Over You)** #1 Adult Contemporary hit (3 weeks)	Arista 0626

DATE	POS	WKS	ARTIST–RECORD TITLE	LABEL & NO.
1/9/82	5	15	6. **Sweet Dreams**	Arista 0655
6/26/82	5	13	7. **Even The Nights Are Better** #1 Adult Contemporary hit (4 weeks)	Arista 0692
10/23/82	38	2	8. Young Love	Arista 1005
12/25/82+	38	5	9. Two Less Lonely People In The World	Arista 1004
8/13/83	2 (3)	17	● 10. **Making Love Out Of Nothing At All**	Arista 9056
6/8/85	19	10	11. Just As I Am Sales #16 / Airplay #22	Arista 9353

AKENS, Jewel

Born on 9/12/40 in Houston, Texas. Male R&B singer/producer.

2/6/65	3	12	1. **The Birds And The Bees**	Era 3141

ALABAMA

Country group from Fort Payne, Alabama: Randy Owen (vocals, guitar), Jeff Cook (keyboards, fiddle), Teddy Gentry (bass, vocals) and Mark Herndon (drums, vocals). Randy, Jeff and Teddy are cousins.

7/25/81	20	8	1. Feels So Right #1 Country hit (2 weeks)	RCA 12236
1/16/82	15	10	2. Love In The First Degree #1 Country hit (2 weeks)	RCA 12288
6/5/82	18	8	3. Take Me Down #1 Country hit (1 week); #102 hit for Exile in 1980	RCA 13210
6/4/83	38	3	4. The Closer You Get #1 Country hit (1 week); #103 hit for Rita Coolidge in 1981	RCA 13524
6/12/99	29	11	5. God Must Have Spent A Little More Time On You Airplay #22 / Sales #23 **ALABAMA (featuring *NSYNC)**	RCA 65759

ALBERT, Morris

Born Morris Albert Kaisermann on 9/7/51 in Brazil. Singer/songwriter.

8/23/75	6	16	● 1. **Feelings**	RCA Victor 10279

AL B. SURE!

Born Al Brown in 1969 in Boston, Massachusetts; raised in Mt. Vernon, New York. R&B singer/songwriter.

5/14/88	7	13	1. Nite And Day Sales #6 / Airplay #8 #1 R&B hit (3 weeks)	Warner 28192
4/7/90	31	4	● 2. The Secret Garden (Sweet Seduction Suite) Sales #20 **QUINCY JONES/Al B. Sure!/James Ingram/El DeBarge/Barry White** #1 R&B hit (1 week)	Qwest 19992

ALEXANDER, Arthur

Born on 5/10/40 in Florence, Alabama. Died of a heart attack on 6/9/93 (age 53). R&B singer/songwriter.

3/31/62	24	6	1. You Better Move On	Dot 16309

ALI, Tatyana

Born on 1/24/79 in North Bellmore, Long Island, New York. R&B singer/actress. Played "Ashley Banks" on TV's *The Fresh Prince Of Bel-Air*.

8/8/98	6	16	● 1. **Daydreamin'** Sales #5 / Airplay #43 samples "Black Cow" by Steely Dan	MJJ Music/Work 78855

DATE	POS	WKS	ARTIST–RECORD TITLE	LABEL & NO.
			ALIAS	
			Rock group formed in Los Angeles, California: Freddy Curci (vocals), Steve DeMarchi (guitar), Roger Fisher (guitar), Steve Fossen (bass) and Mike DeRosier (drums). Curci and DeMarchi were members of Sheriff. Fisher, Fossen and DeRosier were members of Heart.	
9/29/90	**2** (1)	15	1. **More Than Words Can Say** Airplay #3 / Sales #4	EMI 50324
2/2/91	**13**	9	2. Waiting For Love Airplay #13 / Sales #20	EMI 50337
			ALICE DEEJAY	
			Techno-dance act from Amsterdam, Netherlands. Featuring Judy (Alice Deejay).	
5/13/00	**27**	8	1. Better Off Alone Airplay #28	Republic 156798
			ALIEN ANT FARM	
			Rock group from Los Angeles, California: Dryden Mitchell (vocals), Terry Corso (guitar), Tye Zamora (bass) and Mike Cosgrove (drums).	
9/29/01	**23**	9	1. Smooth Criminal Airplay #23 #1 Modern Rock hit (4 weeks); from the album *ANThology* on New Noize 450293	album cut
			ALIVE AND KICKING	
			Pop-rock group from Brooklyn, New York: Pepe Cardona (male vocals), Sandy Toder (female vocals), John Parisio (guitar), Bruce Sudano (organ), Thomas "Woody" Wilson (bass) and Vito Albano (drums). Sudano married Donna Summer on 7/16/80 and was a member of Brooklyn Dreams.	
7/4/70	**7**	10	1. **Tighter, Tighter** co-written and co-produced by Tommy James	Roulette 7078
			ALLAN, Davie, And The Arrows	
			Born in Los Angeles, California. Session guitarist. The Arrows consisted of Jared Hendler (keyboards), Drew Bennett (bass) and Larry Brown (drums).	
9/9/67	**37**	3	1. Blue's Theme **[I]** from the movie *The Wild Angels* starring Peter Fonda	Tower 295
			ALLAN, Gary	
			Born Gary Herzberg on 12/5/67 in Montebello, California; raised in La Mirada, California. Country singer/songwriter/guitarist.	
7/20/02	**37**	5	1. The One Airplay #32	album cut
2/15/03	**25**	6	2. Man To Man Airplay #23 #1 Country hit (1 week); above 2 from the album *Alright Guy* on MCA Nashville 70201	album cut
10/11/03	**32**	5	3. Tough Little Boys Airplay #28 #1 Country hit (2 weeks); from the album *See If I Care* on MCA Nashville 000111	album cut
			ALLEN, Deborah	
			Born Deborah Lynn Thurmond on 9/30/53 in Memphis, Tennessee. Country singer/songwriter.	
12/24/83+	**26**	7	1. Baby I Lied	RCA 13600

Aaliyah had the first Airplay-only track to reach #1 on the Hot 100 with her *Romeo Must Die* soundtrack single "Try Again." Sadly, she would not get the chance to try for another—a tragic 2001 plane crash ended her blossoming career.

ABBA were one of the biggest acts of the 1970s, scoring 14 Top 40 hits during their career. However, only one of the Swedish group's songs, "Dancing Queen," danced its way to #1.

Paula Abdul went from cheerleader to video choreographer to pop star during the 1980s, releasing six #1 hits, including "Cold Hearted." She made yet another career move in the 21st century as a celebrity judge on TV's *American Idol*.

Bryan Adams recorded "Heaven" for the soundtrack of the 1983 movie *A Night In Heaven*. However, it was two years later before the song finally reached #1 as the third Top 40 hit from his album *Reckless*.

Christina Aguilera didn't reach the Top 40 with her *Mulan* soundtrack hit, "Reflection," but she definitely cast a spell on pop fans when "Genie in a Bottle" became the first of three chart-toppers from her debut album.

A-ha created one of MTV's most distinctive early videos for the #1 hit "Take On Me." Not surprisingly, the mix of live action and animation resulted in five MTV Video Music Awards for the Norwegian group's only chart-topper.

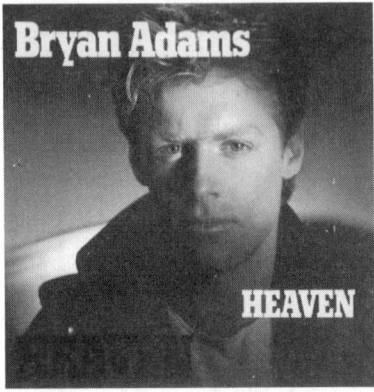

CLAY AIKEN
This Is The Night and Bridge Over Troubled Water

ALL-4-ONE
i swear

AMERICA
HORSE WITH NO NAME

Ashanti
foolish

Patti Austin
Baby Come To Me
(with James Ingram)

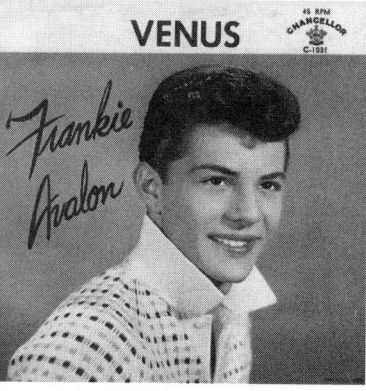

VENUS
Frankie Avalon

Clay Aiken may have finished in second place behind Ruben Studdard on TV's *American Idol,* but he had the last laugh when his #1 hit "This Is The Night" kept Ruben's debut hit, "Flying Without Wings," at #2.

All-4-One topped the charts by recording a pop version of John Michael Montgomery's #1 Country hit "I Swear." They returned to the Top 10 with another #1 Montgomery cover song, "I Can Love You Like That."

America was actually formed in London and took their name from an Americana jukebox. Soon they were the ones being played in jukeboxes, as their debut hit, "A Horse With No Name," quickly rose to #1.

Ashanti scored Top 10 hits singing with Ja Rule, Fat Joe, and Irv Gotti, so it wasn't really foolish for her to expect stardom on her own. The only "Foolish" part about her #1 hit was that the word itself did not appear in the song's lyrics.

Patti Austin got a chart boost for her song "Baby, Come To Me" when it was prominently featured on the ABC daytime drama *General Hospital.* The duet with James Ingram became her only Top 40 hit.

Frankie Avalon earned his first #1 hit in 1959 with "Venus." In 1976, a disco version of the song just missed the Top 40, but it did become Frankie's first #1 hit on the Adult Contemporary chart.

DATE	POS	WKS	ARTIST–RECORD TITLE	LABEL & NO.
			ALLEN, Donna	
			Born in Key West, Florida; raised in Tampa, Florida. R&B singer. Former cheerleader for the NFL's Tampa Bay Buccaneers.	
3/28/87	**21**	9	1. Serious Airplay #19 / Sales #21	21 Records 99497
			ALLEN, Rex	
			Born on 12/31/20 in Willcox, Arizona. Died after being struck by a car on 12/17/99 (age 78). Western singer/guitarist/actor. Starred in numerous western movies in the 1950s. Narrator for numerous Walt Disney documentaries during the 1960s and the 1970s. Own TV series, *Frontier Doctor*, in 1954. His son, Rex Jr., was a top country singer from 1973-87.	
10/6/62	**17**	4	1. Don't Go Near The Indians The Merry Melody Singers (backing vocals)	Mercury 71997
			ALLEN, Steve	
			Born on 12/26/21 in Manhattan, New York; raised in Chicago, Illinois. Died of heart failure on 10/30/2000 (age 78). Comedian/actor/ songwriter/author. In 1954, became the first host of TV's *The Tonight Show*. Played title role in the 1956 movie *The Benny Goodman Story*. Hosted own variety and talk shows, 1956-80. Wrote several books. Married actress Jayne Meadows on 7/31/54.	
12/3/55	**35**	2	1. Autumn Leaves Top 100 #35 **[I]** **STEVE ALLEN with GEORGE CATES And His Orchestra & Chorus**	Coral 61485
			ALL-4-ONE	
			Male interracial vocal group from Los Angeles, California: Jamie Jones, Delious Kennedy, Alfred Nevarez and Tony Borowiak.	
1/22/94	**5**	19	● 1. **So Much In Love** Sales #4 / Airplay #6	Blitzz/Atlantic 87271
4/30/94	**1** (11)	26	▲ 2. **I Swear** Airplay #1 (9) / Sales #1 (7) #1 Country hit for John Michael Montgomery in 1994	Blitzz/Atlantic 87243
6/17/95	**5**	28	● 3. **I Can Love You Like That** Airplay #3 / Sales #10 #1 Country hit for John Michael Montgomery in 1995	Blitzz/Atlantic 87134
7/6/96	**30**	8	● 4. Someday Sales #15 from the animated movie *The Hunchback Of Notre Dame*	Hollywood 64011
			ALLISON, Gene	
			Born on 8/29/34 in Nashville, Tennessee. Died of liver failure on 2/28/2004 (age 69). R&B singer.	
3/10/58	**36**	1	1. You Can Make It If You Try Best Seller #36 / Top 100 #37	Vee-Jay 256
			ALLMAN BROTHERS BAND, The	
			Southern-rock group formed in Macon, Georgia: brothers Duane Allman (guitar) and Gregg Allman (keyboards, vocals, see #2 below), Dickey Betts (guitar, vocals), Berry Oakley (bass), and the drum duo of Butch Trucks and Jai Johnny Johanson. Duane was killed in a motorcycle crash on 10/29/71 (age 24). Oakley died in another cycle accident on 11/11/72 (age 24); replaced by Lamar Williams (died on 1/25/83). Chuck Leavell (keyboards) added in 1972. Lineup from 1979-81: Gregg Allman, Dickey Betts and Butch Trucks, with Dan Toler (guitar) and Rook Goldflies (bass). Group inducted into the Rock and Roll Hall of Fame in 1995.	
9/8/73	**2** (1)	13	1. **Ramblin Man**	Capricorn 0027
1/19/74	**19**	8	2. Midnight Rider **GREGG ALLMAN**	Capricorn 0035
4/7/79	**29**	5	3. Crazy Love	Capricorn 0320
9/19/81	**39**	2	4. Straight From The Heart	Arista 0618

DATE	POS	WKS	ARTIST–RECORD TITLE	LABEL & NO.
			ALL SAINTS	
			Female interracial vocal group from London, England: sisters Natalie and Nicky Appleton, with Shaznay Lewis and Melanie Blatt.	
3/7/98	36	3	1. I Know Where It's At　　　Sales #31 / Airplay #53	London 570112
			samples "The Fez" by Steely Dan	
7/25/98	4	19	2. **Never Ever**　　　Sales #3 / Airplay #12	London 570178
			ALL STAR TRIBUTE — see ARTISTS AGAINST AIDS	
			ALLURE	
			Female R&B vocal group from Long Island, New York: Alia Davis, Akissa Mendez, Lalisha McLean and Linnie Belcher.	
3/15/97	35	5	1. Head Over Heels　　　Sales #32 / Airplay #61	Crave 78522
			ALLURE featuring Nas	
			samples "The Bridge" by MC Shan	
8/30/97	4	24	● 2. All Cried Out　　　Sales #6 / Airplay #8	Crave 78678
			ALLURE featuring 112	
			above 2 co-produced by Mariah Carey	
			ALPERT, Herb, & The Tijuana Brass	
			Born on 3/31/35 in Los Angeles, California. Trumpeter/producer/composer. Played trumpet since age eight. Formed A&M Records with Jerry Moss in 1962. Used studio musicians until early 1965, then formed own band. Alpert and Moss formed the Almo Sounds label in 1994.	
11/10/62	6	11	1. **The Lonely Bull (El Solo Torro)**　　　[I]	A&M 703
			THE TIJUANA BRASS Featuring Herb Alpert	
10/16/65	7	13	2. **Taste Of Honey**　　　[I]	A&M 775
			#1 Adult Contemporary hit (5 weeks)	
1/22/66	11	7	3. **Zorba The Greek /**　　　[I]	
			title song from the movie starring Anthony Quinn	
2/5/66	38	2	4. Tijuana Taxi　　　[I]	A&M 787
4/9/66	24	5	5. What Now My Love /　　　[I]	
4/9/66	27	4	6. Spanish Flea　　　[I]	A&M 792
			theme song from TV's *The Dating Game*	
7/9/66	18	6	7. The Work Song　　　[I]	A&M 805
9/17/66	28	4	8. Flamingo　　　[I]	A&M 813
			#13 hit for Duke Ellington in 1941	
12/3/66	19	6	9. Mame	A&M 823
			title song from the Broadway musical starring Angela Lansbury	
4/1/67	37	2	10. Wade In The Water　　　[I]	A&M 840
4/29/67	27	6	11. Casino Royale　　　[I]	A&M 850
			#1 Adult Contemporary hit (2 weeks); title song from the movie starring David Niven and Peter Sellers	
7/22/67	32	3	12. The Happening　　　[I]	A&M 860
			title song from the movie starring Anthony Quinn	
9/30/67	35	3	13. A Banda (Ah Bahn-da)　　　[I]	A&M 870
			#1 Adult Contemporary hit (2 weeks)	
			HERB ALPERT:	
5/25/68	1 (4)	12	● 14. **This Guy's In Love With You**	A&M 929
			#1 Adult Contemporary hit (10 weeks)	
8/25/79	1 (2)	15	● 15. **Rise**　　　[I]	A&M 2151
			#1 Adult Contemporary hit (1 week)	

DATE	POS	WKS	ARTIST–RECORD TITLE	LABEL & NO.
12/22/79+	30	6	16. Rotation **[I]**	A&M 2202
7/31/82	37	4	17. Route 101 **[I]**	A&M 2422
5/2/87	5	12	18. **Diamonds** Sales #5 / Airplay #7 **HERB ALPERT (with Janet Jackson)** #1 R&B hit (2 weeks)	A&M 2929
8/29/87	35	3	19. Making Love In The Rain Sales #35 / Airplay #39 Lisa Keith (backing vocal, above 2)	A&M 2949
			AMAZING RHYTHM ACES, The	
			Country-rock group from Memphis, Tennessee: Russell Smith (vocals, guitar), Barry Burton (guitar, Dobro), Billy Earhart (keyboards), Jeff Davis (bass) and Butch McDade (drums). McDade died of cancer on 11/29/98 (age 52).	
7/26/75	14	9	1. Third Rate Romance	ABC 12078
			AMBER	
			Born Marie-Claire Cremers in Holland; raised in Germany. Female dance singer/songwriter.	
9/21/96+	24	25	1. This Is Your Night Airplay #14 / Sales #61	Tommy Boy 7735
			AMBOY DUKES, The	
			Hard-rock group from Detroit, Michigan: John Drake (vocals), Ted Nugent and Steve Farmer (guitars), Rick Lorber (keyboards), Bill White (bass) and Dave Palmer (drums). Nugent went solo in 1975.	
7/27/68	16	7	1. Journey To The Center Of The Mind	Mainstream 684
			AMBROSIA	
			Pop group formed in Los Angeles, California: David Pack (vocals, guitar), Joe Puerta (vocals, bass), Christopher North (keyboards) and Burleigh Drummond (drums).	
7/19/75	17	8	1. Holdin' On To Yesterday	20th Century 2207
4/2/77	39	2	2. Magical Mystery Tour featuring the London Symphony Orch. and the Royal Philharmonic Orch.; from the documentary movie *All This And World War II*	20th Century 2327
9/30/78	3	14	3. **How Much I Feel**	Warner 8640
4/19/80	3	14	4. **Biggest Part Of Me**	Warner 49225
8/2/80	13	10	5. You're The Only Woman (You & I)	Warner 49508
			AMERICA	
			Soft-rock trio formed in London, England: Dewey Bunnell, Gerry Beckley and Dan Peek. All played guitars and shared vocals. Met while in school in England (all were sons of American military personnel). Moved back to the U.S. in February 1972. Won the 1972 Best New Artist Grammy Award. Peek left in 1976.	
3/4/72	1 (3)	12	● 1. **A Horse With No Name**	Warner 7555
5/27/72	9	9	2. **I Need You**	Warner 7580
11/4/72	8	9	3. **Ventura Highway**	Warner 7641
2/24/73	35	2	4. Don't Cross The River	Warner 7670
9/21/74	4	11	5. **Tin Man** #1 Adult Contemporary hit (1 week)	Warner 8014
1/18/75	5	10	6. **Lonely People** #1 Adult Contemporary hit (1 week)	Warner 8048
4/26/75	1 (1)	12	7. **Sister Golden Hair**	Warner 8086

DATE	POS	WKS	ARTIST–RECORD TITLE	LABEL & NO.
8/16/75	**20**	7	8. Daisy Jane	Warner 8118
6/12/76	**23**	6	9. Today's The Day	Warner 8212
			#1 Adult Contemporary hit (2 weeks)	
8/21/82	**8**	15	10. **You Can Do Magic**	Capitol 5142
7/16/83	**33**	6	11. The Border	Capitol 5236
			AMERICAN BREED, The	
			Interracial pop-rock group from Chicago, Illinois: Gary Loizzo (vocals, guitar), Al Ciner (guitar), Chuck Colbert (bass) and Lee Graziano (drums). Later members Kevin Murphy (keyboards) and Andre Fischer (drums) went on to form Rufus.	
7/8/67	**24**	4	1. Step Out Of Your Mind	Acta 804
12/16/67+	**5**	12	● 2. **Bend Me, Shape Me**	Acta 811
3/16/68	**39**	3	3. Green Light	Acta 821
			AMERICAN IDOL FINALISTS	
			Group of contestants from season two of the TV talent show *American Idol*: Clay Aiken, Kimberly Caldwell, Corey Clark, Julia Demato, Joshua Gracin, Kimberley Locke, Carmen Rasmusen, Rickey Smith, Ruben Studdard and Trenyce.	
5/3/03	**4**	2	● 1. **God Bless The U.S.A.** Sales #1 (8)	RCA 51780
5/17/03	**4** s	14	2. **What The World Needs Now Is Love**	RCA 52557
			AMERIE	
			Born Amerie Rogers in 1980 in Brooklyn, New York (Korean mother/African-American father); raised in Washington DC. Female R&B singer.	
8/3/02	**23**	6	1. Why Don't We Fall In Love Sales #17 / Airplay #22	Rise/Columbia 79774
			AMERIE (featuring Ludacris)	
1/25/03	**36**	3	2. Paradise Sales #33 / Airplay #36	Def Jam 063820
			LL COOL J feat. Amerie	
			samples "Rising To The Top" by Keni Burke	
			AMES, Ed	
			Born Ed Urick on 7/9/27 in Malden, Massachusetts. Lead singer of The Ames Brothers. Played the Native American "Mingo" on the TV series *Daniel Boone*.	
2/11/67	**8**	10	1. **My Cup Runneth Over**	RCA Victor 9002
			#1 Adult Contemporary hit (4 weeks); from the off-Broadway musical I Do, I Do starring Mary Martin and Robert Preston; title based on Psalms 23:5	
12/30/67+	**19**	4	2. Who Will Answer?	RCA Victor 9400
			AMES BROTHERS, The	
			Pop vocal group from Malden, Massachusetts: brothers Ed, Gene, Joe and Vic Ames. Vic died on 1/23/78 (age 52).	
11/20/54	**3**	15	● 1. **The Naughty Lady Of Shady Lane**	RCA Victor 5897
			Best Seller #3 / Jockey #3 / Juke Box #3	
9/24/55	**11**	11	2. My Bonnie Lassie	RCA Victor 6208
			Best Seller #11 / Top 100 #11 / Jockey #14 / Juke Box #16	
3/24/56	**35**	3	3. Forever Darling Top 100 #35	RCA Victor 6400
			title song from the movie starring Lucille Ball and Desi Arnaz	
5/19/56	**11**	20	4. It Only Hurts For A Little While	RCA Victor 6481
			Juke Box #11 / Top 100 #15 / Jockey #15 / Best Seller #16	

DATE	POS	WKS	ARTIST–RECORD TITLE	LABEL & NO.
7/22/57	5	16	5. **Tammy** Jockey #5 / Best Seller #24 / Top 100 #29 from the movie *Tammy and The Bachelor* starring Debbie Reynolds	RCA Victor 6930
10/7/57	5	14	6. **Melodie D'Amour (Melody of Love)** Jockey #5 / Top 100 #12 / Best Seller #12	RCA Victor 7046
3/31/58	23	2	7. **A Very Precious Love** Jockey #23 / Top 100 #65 from the movie *Marjorie Morningstar* starring Natalie Wood	RCA Victor 7167
9/29/58	17	10	8. Pussy Cat Hot 100 #17 / Best Seller #20	RCA Victor 7315
1/19/59	37	4	9. Red River Rose	RCA Victor 7413
2/22/60	38	2	10. China Doll	RCA Victor 7655

ANDERSON, Bill

Born James William Anderson III on 11/1/37 in Columbia, South Carolina. Country singer/songwriter/actor. Known as "Whispering Bill."

DATE	POS	WKS	ARTIST–RECORD TITLE	LABEL & NO.
5/11/63	8	11	1. **Still** #1 Country hit (7 weeks)	Decca 31458

ANDERSON, Carl — see LORING, Gloria

ANDERSON, Lynn

Born on 9/26/47 in Grand Forks, North Dakota; raised in Sacramento, California. Country singer. Daughter of country singer Liz Anderson.

DATE	POS	WKS	ARTIST–RECORD TITLE	LABEL & NO.
12/19/70+	3	14	● 1. **Rose Garden** #1 Country hit (5 weeks)	Columbia 45252

ANDERSON, Sunshine

Born on 10/26/73 in Charlotte, North Carolina. Female R&B singer.

DATE	POS	WKS	ARTIST–RECORD TITLE	LABEL & NO.
3/24/01	18	13	1. Heard It All Before Airplay #12 / Sales #51 Mikey Dan (male vocal)	Soulife 95524

ANDREWS, Jessica

Born on 12/29/83 in Huntingdon, Tennessee. Country singer.

DATE	POS	WKS	ARTIST–RECORD TITLE	LABEL & NO.
3/3/01	28	11	1. Who I Am Airplay #20 #1 Country hit (3 weeks); from the album *Who I Am* on DreamWorks 50248	album cut

ANDREWS, Lee, And The Hearts

Born Arthur Lee Andrew Thompson in 1938 in Goldsboro, North Carolina; raised in Philadelphia, Pennsylvania. The Hearts consisted of Thomas Curry, Ted Weems, Roy Calhoun and Wendell Calhoun.

DATE	POS	WKS	ARTIST–RECORD TITLE	LABEL & NO.
12/9/57	20	10	1. Tear Drops Best Seller #20 / Top 100 #20 / Jockey #21	Chess 1675
6/16/58	33	1	2. Try The Impossible Best Seller #33 / Top 100 #33	United Artists 123

ANGELICA

Born Angelica Garcia on 5/21/72 in El Monte, California. Latin pop-dance singer.

DATE	POS	WKS	ARTIST–RECORD TITLE	LABEL & NO.
11/30/91+	29	7	1. Angel Baby Sales #19 / Airplay #40	Quality/Ultra 15171

ANGELS, The

Female vocal trio from Orange, New Jersey: sisters Phyllis and Barbara Allbut, with Linda Jansen. Jansen was replaced by Peggy Santiglia in 1962. Also recorded as The Starlets.

DATE	POS	WKS	ARTIST–RECORD TITLE	LABEL & NO.
12/4/61+	14	7	1. 'Til	Caprice 107

DATE	POS	WKS	ARTIST–RECORD TITLE	LABEL & NO.
4/7/62	38	1	2. Cry Baby Cry Hutch Davie (orch., above 2)	Caprice 112
8/10/63	1 (3)	12	3. **My Boyfriend's Back**	Smash 1834
11/9/63	25	5	4. I Adore Him	Smash 1854

ANIMALS, The

Rock group formed in Newcastle, England: Eric Burdon (vocals), Hilton Valentine (guitar), Alan Price (keyboards), Bryan "Chas" Chandler (bass) and John Steel (drums). Price left in May 1965, replaced by Dave Rowberry (died of heart failure on 6/6/2003, age 62). Chandler pursued a management career and discovered Jimi Hendrix in 1966; died in his sleep of an apparent heart attack on 7/17/96 (age 57). Steel left in 1966, replaced by Barry Jenkins. Group inducted into the Rock and Roll Hall of Fame in 1994.

DATE	POS	WKS	ARTIST–RECORD TITLE	LABEL & NO.
8/15/64	1 (3)	10	1. **The House Of The Rising Sun**	MGM 13264
10/17/64	19	6	2. I'm Crying	MGM 13274
3/6/65	15	6	3. Don't Let Me Be Misunderstood	MGM 13311
5/29/65	32	4	4. Bring It On Home To Me	MGM 13339
9/4/65	13	8	5. We Gotta Get Out Of This Place	MGM 13382
12/4/65+	23	8	6. It's My Life	MGM 13414
4/2/66	34	1	7. Inside-Looking Out	MGM 13468
6/4/66	12	8	8. Don't Bring Me Down	MGM 13514

ERIC BURDON & THE ANIMALS:

DATE	POS	WKS	ARTIST–RECORD TITLE	LABEL & NO.
10/1/66	10	7	9. **See See Rider** #14 hit for Ma Rainey in 1925 (as "See See Rider Blues")	MGM 13582
12/31/66	29	4	10. Help Me Girl	MGM 13636
4/22/67	15	6	11. When I Was Young	MGM 13721
8/19/67	9	8	12. **San Franciscan Nights**	MGM 13769
12/30/67+	15	6	13. Monterey	MGM 13868
6/22/68	14	10	14. Sky Pilot (Part One)	MGM 13939

ANIMOTION

Techno-pop group formed in Los Angeles, California: Astrid Plane (female vocals), Bill Wadhams (male vocals, keyboards), Don Kirkpatrick (guitar), Charles Ottavio (bass) and Frenchy O'Brien (drums). Plane and Wadhams left by 1988, replaced by Cynthia Rhodes and Paul Engemann. Rhodes was an actress (in movies *Staying Alive* and *Dirty Dancing*). Engemann was formerly with Device. Rhodes married Richard Marx on 1/8/89. Plane and Ottavio married on 10/13/90.

DATE	POS	WKS	ARTIST–RECORD TITLE	LABEL & NO.
3/2/85	6	14	1. **Obsession** Sales #5 / Airplay #5	Mercury 880266
7/27/85	39	1	2. Let Him Go	Mercury 880737
3/11/89	9	11	3. **Room To Move** Airplay #9 / Sales #12 from the movie *My Stepmother Is An Alien* starring Dan Aykroyd and Kim Basinger	Polydor 871418

ANKA, Paul

Born on 7/30/41 in Ottawa, Ontario, Canada. Singer/songwriter. Performer since age 12. Wrote "She's A Lady" for Tom Jones and the English lyrics to "My Way" for Frank Sinatra. Also wrote theme for TV's *The Tonight Show*. Own TV variety show in 1973. Appeared in the movies *Girls Town* (1959), *The Longest Day* (1962) and *Captain Ron* (1992). Longtime popular entertainer in Las Vegas.

DATE	POS	WKS	ARTIST–RECORD TITLE	LABEL & NO.
7/29/57	1 (1)	18	● 1. **Diana** Best Seller #1 (1) / Top 100 #2 / Jockey #2 #1 R&B hit (2 weeks)	ABC-Paramount 9831

DATE	POS	WKS	ARTIST–RECORD TITLE	LABEL & NO.
2/3/58	7	11	2. **You Are My Destiny** Top 100 #7 / Best Seller #9 / Jockey #9	ABC-Paramount 9880
4/28/58	15	10	3. Crazy Love / Best Seller #15 / Top 100 #19	
4/28/58	16	10	4. Let The Bells Keep Ringing Best Seller #16 / Jockey #18 / Top 100 #30	ABC-Paramount 9907
12/15/58+	29	5	5. The Teen Commandments **[S]** **PAUL ANKA-GEO. HAMILTON IV-JOHNNY NASH** Bill Givens (narrative)	ABC-Paramount 9974
1/5/59	15	13	6. (All of a Sudden) My Heart Sings #7 hit for Johnnie Johnston in 1945	ABC-Paramount 9987
4/20/59	33	3	7. I Miss You So #20 hit for The Cats and the Fiddle in 1940	ABC-Paramount 10011
6/8/59	1 (4)	14	● 8. **Lonely Boy** from the movie *Girls Town* starring Mamie Van Doren and Anka	ABC-Paramount 10022
9/14/59	2 (3)	14	9. **Put Your Head On My Shoulder**	ABC-Paramount 10040
11/30/59	4	12	10. **It's Time To Cry**	ABC-Paramount 10064
3/7/60	2 (2)	11	11. **Puppy Love**	ABC-Paramount 10082
6/6/60	8	9	12. **My Home Town**	ABC-Paramount 10106
8/22/60	23	6	13. Hello Young Lovers / from the musical *The King And I* starring Yul Brynner	
9/12/60	40	1	14. I Love You In The Same Old Way	ABC-Paramount 10132
10/10/60	11	7	15. Summer's Gone	ABC-Paramount 10147
2/6/61	16	5	16. The Story Of My Love	ABC-Paramount 10168
3/27/61	13	8	17. Tonight My Love, Tonight	ABC-Paramount 10194
6/12/61	10	7	18. **Dance On Little Girl**	ABC-Paramount 10220
9/11/61	35	1	19. Kissin' On The Phone	ABC-Paramount 10239
3/17/62	12	9	20. Love Me Warm And Tender	RCA Victor 7977
6/16/62	13	7	21. A Steel Guitar And A Glass Of Wine	RCA Victor 8030
11/24/62	19	5	22. Eso Beso (That Kiss!)	RCA Victor 8097
2/9/63	26	4	23. Love (Makes the World Go 'Round)	RCA Victor 8115
5/25/63	39	1	24. Remember Diana	RCA Victor 8170
2/1/69	27	6	25. Goodnight My Love #7 R&B hit for Jesse Belvin in 1956	RCA Victor 9648
7/27/74	1 (3)	11	● 26. (You're) Having My Baby	United Artists 454
11/30/74+	7	11	27. **One Man Woman/One Woman Man**	United Artists 569
4/5/75	8	10	28. **I Don't Like To Sleep Alone**	United Artists 615
8/16/75	15	8	29. (I Believe) There's Nothing Stronger Than Our Love **PAUL ANKA with Odia Coates** (above 4)	United Artists 685
11/29/75+	7	12	30. **Times Of Your Life** #1 Adult Contemporary hit (1 week); tune adapted from a Kodak jingle	United Artists 737
5/1/76	33	3	31. Anytime (I'll Be There)	United Artists 789
11/18/78	35	3	32. This Is Love	RCA 11395
9/3/83	40	2	33. Hold Me 'Til The Mornin' Comes Peter Cetera (backing vocal)	Columbia 03897
			ANNETTE with the Afterbeats Born Annette Funicello on 10/22/42 in Utica, New York. Became a Mouseketeer in 1955. Acted in several teen movies in the early 1960s. Co-starred with Frankie Avalon in the 1987 movie *Back To The Beach*. Diagnosed with multiple sclerosis in 1987.	
2/2/59	7	9	1. **Tall Paul**	Disneyland 118

DATE	POS	WKS	ARTIST–RECORD TITLE	LABEL & NO.
12/14/59+	**20**	10	2. First Name Initial	Buena Vista 349
3/7/60	**10**	8	3. **O Dio Mio** **ANNETTE**	Buena Vista 354
6/20/60	**36**	3	4. Train Of Love written by Paul Anka	Buena Vista 359
9/5/60	**11**	9	5. Pineapple Princess	Buena Vista 362

ANN-MARGRET

Born Ann-Margret Olsson on 4/28/41 in Valsjöbyn, Jämtland, Sweden; raised in Wilmette, Illinois. Actress/dancer/singer. Starred in many movies and Broadway shows.

DATE	POS	WKS	ARTIST–RECORD TITLE	LABEL & NO.
8/21/61	**17**	6	1. I Just Don't Understand	RCA Victor 7894

ANOTHER BAD CREATION

Pre-teen R&B-rap vocal group from Atlanta, Georgia: Chris Sellers, Dave Shelton, Romell Chapman, with brothers Marliss and Demetrius Pugh. Appeared in the movie *The Meteor Man*.

DATE	POS	WKS	ARTIST–RECORD TITLE	LABEL & NO.
2/2/91	**9**	15	● 1. **Iesha** Sales #2 / Airplay #18 Michael Bivins (rap)	Motown 2070
5/18/91	**10**	10	2. **Playground** Sales #9 / Airplay #27 Boyz II Men (backing vocals, above 2)	Motown 2088

ANT, Adam

Born Stuart Leslie Goddard on 11/3/54 in London, England. Singer/actor. Former leader of Adam & The Ants. Acted in several movies and TV shows.

DATE	POS	WKS	ARTIST–RECORD TITLE	LABEL & NO.
12/11/82+	**12**	14	1. Goody Two Shoes	Epic 03367
4/7/90	**17**	8	2. Room At The Top Sales #15 / Airplay #16	MCA 53679
5/27/95	**39**	2	3. Wonderful Airplay #37 / Sales #69	Capitol 58239

ANTHONY, Marc

Born Marco Antonio Muñiz on 9/16/69 in the Bronx, New York. Latin singer/actor. Starred in Paul Simon's Broadway musical *The Capeman* and in the movie *Bringing Out The Dead*.

DATE	POS	WKS	ARTIST–RECORD TITLE	LABEL & NO.
10/2/99	**3**	34	● 1. **I Need To Know** Sales #4 / Airplay #5	Columbia 79250
3/25/00	**2** (2)	27	2. **You Sang To Me** Sales #1 (3) / Airplay #12 #1 Adult Contemporary hit (7 weeks)	Columbia 79406

ANTHONY, Ray

Born Raymond Antonini on 1/20/22 in Bentleyville, Pennsylvania; raised in Cleveland, Ohio. Big band leader/trumpeter. Own TV series in the 1950s. Appeared in the movie *Daddy Long Legs*. Married to actress Mamie Van Doren from 1955-61.

DATE	POS	WKS	ARTIST–RECORD TITLE	LABEL & NO.
1/22/55	**19**	4	1. Melody Of Love Jockey #19 **FRANK SINATRA and RAY ANTHONY And His Orchestra**	Capitol 3018
1/19/59	**8**	13	2. Peter Gunn [I] title song from the TV series starring Craig Stevens	Capitol 4041

ANTON, Susan — see KNOBLOCK, Fred

APOLLO 100

Studio group from England: Tom Parker, Clem Cattini, Vic Flick, Jim Lawless and Brian Odgers.

DATE	POS	WKS	ARTIST–RECORD TITLE	LABEL & NO.
1/22/72	**6**	10	1. **Joy** [I] based upon Bach's *Jesu, Joy of Man's Desiring*	Mega 0050

DATE	POS	WKS	ARTIST–RECORD TITLE	LABEL & NO.
			APPLE, Fiona	
			Born Fiona Apple Maggart on 9/13/77 in Manhattan, New York. Adult Alternative pop-rock singer/songwriter/pianist. Daughter of singer Diane McAfee and actor Brandon Maggart.	
10/4/97	21	17	1. Criminal Airplay #21 / Sales #25	Clean Slate 78595
			APPLEJACKS, The	
			Studio band led by Dave Appell (born on 3/24/22 in Philadelphia, Pennsylvania).	
9/15/58	16	9	1. Mexican Hat Rock Hot 100 #16 / Best Seller #29 [I]	Cameo 149
1/12/59	38	3	2. Rocka-Conga	Cameo 155
			APRIL WINE	
			Rock group from Montreal, Quebec, Canada: Myles Goodwyn (vocals, guitar), Brian Greenway (guitar), Gary Moffet (guitar), Steve Lang (bass) and Jerry Mercer (drums). Mercer was also a member of Mashmakhan.	
4/29/72	32	5	1. You Could Have Been A Lady	Big Tree 133
4/14/79	34	4	2. Roller	Capitol 4660
3/14/81	21	7	3. Just Between You And Me	Capitol 4975
			AQUA	
			Pop-dance group from Denmark: Lene Grawford Nystrom, Rene Dif, Claus Norreen and Soren Rasted.	
9/6/97	7	6	1. **Barbie Girl** Sales #5 / Airplay #24 [N]	MCA 55392
12/20/97+	23	5	2. Lollipop (Candyman) Sales #18	MCA 55410
			AQUATONES, The	
			White doo-wop group formed in Valley Stream, Long Island, New York: Lynn Nixon and Larry Vannata (lead singers), David Goddard and Eugene McCarthy. Female lead Nixon trained as an operatic soprano.	
5/5/58	21	8	1. You Top 100 #21 / Best Seller #24	Fargo 1001
			ARBORS, The	
			Pop vocal group formed in Ann Arbor, Michigan, by two pairs of brothers: Edward and Fred Farran, and Scott and Tom Herrick. Edward Farran died of kidney failure on 1/2/2003 (age 64).	
4/5/69	20	3	1. The Letter	Date 1638
			ARCADIA	
			Pop-rock trio from England: Duran Duran's Simon LeBon (vocals), Nick Rhodes (keyboards) and Roger Taylor (drums).	
11/2/85	6	12	1. **Election Day** Sales #4 / Airplay #6	Capitol 5501
			Grace Jones (narration)	
3/1/86	33	3	2. Goodbye Is Forever Sales #29	Capitol 5542
			ARCHER, Tasmin	
			Born in 1964 in Bradford, Yorkshire, England (of Jamaican parentage). Black female singer.	
5/29/93	32	5	1. Sleeping Satellite Airplay #29 / Sales #73	SBK 50426

DATE	POS	WKS	ARTIST–RECORD TITLE	LABEL & NO.
			ARCHIES, The	
			Studio group created by Don Kirshner; based on the Saturday morning cartoon TV series. Actual singers included Ron Dante, Andy Kim and Toni Wine. The cartoon characters' names are Archie, Betty, Veronica, Jughead and Reggie.	
11/2/68	**22**	8	1. Bang-Shang-A-Lang	Calendar 1006
8/16/69	**1** (4)	18	● 2. **Sugar, Sugar**	Calendar 1008
12/20/69+	**10**	10	● 3. **Jingle Jangle**	Kirshner 5002
3/28/70	**40**	2	4. Who's Your Baby?	Kirshner 5003
			ARDEN, Jann	
			Born Jann Arden Richards on 3/27/62 in Calgary, Alberta, Canada. Female singer/songwriter.	
4/13/96	**12**	30	1. Insensitive Airplay #8 / Sales #20 from the movie *Bed Of Roses* starring Christian Slater	A&M 1274
			ARDEN, Toni	
			Born Antoinette Aroizzone in Brooklyn, New York. Female singer.	
6/2/58	**13**	11	1. Padre Jockey #13 / Top 100 #18 / Best Seller #19 Jack Pleis (orch.)	Decca 30628
			ARENA, Tina	
			Born Philopina Arena on 11/1/67 in Melbourne, Australia. Female singer.	
5/4/96	**38**	3	1. Chains Airplay #30 / Sales #48	Epic 78281
			ARGENT	
			Rock group from England: Rod Argent (vocals, keyboards), Russ Ballard (guitar), Jim Rodford (bass) and Robert Henrit (drums). Argent was leader of The Zombies. Henrit later joined Charlie. Rodford and Henrit later joined The Kinks.	
7/8/72	**5**	11	1. **Hold Your Head Up**	Epic 10852
			ARMS, Russell	
			Born on 2/3/29 in Berkeley, California. One of the regulars on TV's "Your Hit Parade" (1952-57).	
2/2/57	**22**	8	1. Cinco Robles (Five Oaks) Best Seller #22 / Top 100 #23 / Jockey #23 Pete King (orch.)	Era 1026
			ARMSTRONG, Louis	
			Born Daniel Louis Armstrong on 8/4/01 in New Orleans, Louisiana. Died of heart failure on 7/6/71 (age 69). Legendary singer/trumpet player. Nicknamed "Satchmo." Numerous appearances on radio, TV and in movies. Won Grammy's Lifetime Achievement Award in 1972. Inducted into the Rock and Roll Hall of Fame in 1990.	
2/25/56	**20**	7	1. A Theme From The Threepenny Opera (Mack The Knife) Top 100 #20 **LOUIS ARMSTRONG & HIS ALL-STARS**	Columbia 40587
12/15/56	**29**	1	2. Blueberry Hill Top 100 #29 **LOUIS ARMSTRONG AND GORDON JENKINS AND HIS ORCHESTRA AND CHORUS** #2 hit for Glenn Miller in 1940	Decca 30091

DATE	POS	WKS	ARTIST–RECORD TITLE	LABEL & NO.
2/29/64	**1** (1)	19	3. **Hello, Dolly!** **LOUIS ARMSTRONG AND THE ALL STARS** #1 Adult Contemporary hit (9 weeks); title song from the Broadway musical starring Carol Channing	Kapp 573
3/19/88	**32**	3	4. What A Wonderful World　　　Sales #29 / Airplay #38　**[R]** originally hit #116 in 1968; featured in the movie *Good Morning, Vietnam* starring Robin Williams	A&M 3010

ARNOLD, Eddy

Born Richard Edward Arnold on 5/15/18 in Henderson, Tennessee. Legendary country singer.

DATE	POS	WKS	ARTIST–RECORD TITLE	LABEL & NO.
12/1/56	**22**	1	1. I Wouldn't Know Where To Begin　Jockey #22 / Top 100 #64	RCA Victor 6699
11/13/65	**6**	10	2. **Make The World Go Away** #1 Country hit (3 weeks) / #1 Adult Contemporary hit (4 weeks)	RCA Victor 8679
3/12/66	**36**	5	3. I Want To Go With You #1 Country hit (6 weeks) / #1 Adult Contemporary hit (3 weeks)	RCA Victor 8749
6/18/66	**40**	1	4. The Last Word In Lonesome Is Me	RCA Victor 8818

ARRESTED DEVELOPMENT

Rap group from Atlanta: Todd "Speech" Thomas, Dionne Farris, Aerlee Taree, Tim Barnwell, Montsho Eshe, Rasa Don and Baba Oje. Won the 1992 Best New Artist Grammy Award.

DATE	POS	WKS	ARTIST–RECORD TITLE	LABEL & NO.
4/25/92	**6**	17	● 1. **Tennessee**　　　Sales #4 / Airplay #10 #1 R&B hit (1 week)	Chrysalis 23829
8/29/92	**8**	18	● 2. **People Everyday**　　　Sales #5 / Airplay #10	Chrysalis 50397
1/9/93	**6**	20	● 3. **Mr. Wendal**　　　Airplay #6 / Sales #7	Chrysalis 24810

ARROWS, The — see ALLAN, Davie

ARTISTS AGAINST AIDS

All-star group organized to benefit worldwide AIDS research. Featured performers include Christina Aguilera, Backstreet Boys, Mary J. Blige, Destiny's Child, Eve, Nelly Furtado, Ja Rule, Jagged Edge, Alicia Keys, Lil' Kim, Jennifer Lopez, Nas, Nelly, *NSYNC, P. Diddy, Britney Spears and Usher.

DATE	POS	WKS	ARTIST–RECORD TITLE	LABEL & NO.
10/13/01	**27**	4	1. What's Going On　　　Airplay #26 **ARTISTS AGAINST AIDS Featuring All-Star Lineup** a portion of the proceeds donated to the September 11th Fund of the United Way	Play-Tone 79670

ARTISTS UNITED AGAINST APARTHEID

Benefit group of superstar artists formed to protest the South African apartheid government; proceeds went to political prisoners in South Africa. Organized by Little Steven and Arthur Baker. Featuring Pat Benatar, Bono, Jackson Browne, Jimmy Cliff, Bob Dylan, Peter Gabriel, Bonnie Raitt, Lou Reed, Bruce Springsteen and many others.

DATE	POS	WKS	ARTIST–RECORD TITLE	LABEL & NO.
12/7/85	**38**	3	1. Sun City　　　Sales #25	Manhattan 50017

ART OF NOISE, The

Techno-pop trio from England: Anne Dudley (keyboards), J.J. Jeczalik (keyboards, programmer) and Gary Langan (engineer).

DATE	POS	WKS	ARTIST–RECORD TITLE	LABEL & NO.
9/20/86	**34**	4	1. Paranoimia　　　Airplay #33 / Sales #37 **THE ART OF NOISE with MAX HEADROOM** Max Headroom is a British "computer-generated" celebrity voiced by actor Matt Frewer	China 43002

DATE	POS	WKS	ARTIST–RECORD TITLE	LABEL & NO.
12/24/88+	**31**	6	2. Kiss Sales #23 / Airplay #35 **THE ART OF NOISE Featuring Tom Jones**	China 871038

ASHANTI

Born Ashanti Douglas on 10/13/80 in Glen Cove, Long Island, New York. Female hip-hop singer/songwriter.

DATE	POS	WKS	ARTIST–RECORD TITLE	LABEL & NO.
12/1/01+	**1** (2)	24	1. **Always On Time** Airplay #1 (2) / Sales #27 **JA RULE (feat. Ashanti)** #1 R&B hit (8 weeks)	Def Jam 588795
2/23/02	**2** (7)	25	2. **What's Luv?** Airplay #2 / Sales #20 **FAT JOE Featuring Ashanti**	Atlantic 85233
3/9/02	**1** (10)	26	3. **Foolish** Airplay #1 (10) / Sales #15 #1 R&B hit (10 weeks); samples "Stay With Me" by DeBarge	Murder Inc. 588986
6/29/02	**6**	15	4. **Down 4 U** Airplay #6 **IRV GOTTI PRESENTS THE INC. Featuring Ja Rule,** **Ashanti, Charli Baltimore & Vita** from the album *Irv Gotti Presents The Inc.* on Murder Inc. 062033	album cut
7/13/02	**8**	16	5. **Happy** Airplay #8 / Sales #32 contains an interpolation of "Outstanding" by The Gap Band	Murder Inc. 582935
9/21/02	**15**	13	6. **Baby** Airplay #14 / Sales #61 **ASHANTI feat. Crooked I** samples "Mary Jane" by Scarface	Murder Inc. 063851
1/4/03	**2** (1)	17	7. **Mesmerize** Airplay #2 / Sales #23 **JA RULE feat. Ashanti** samples "Stop, Look, Listen" by The Stylistics	Murder Inc. 063773
5/17/03	**2** (1)	18	8. **Rock Wit U (Awww Baby)** Airplay #2 / Sales #36	Murder Inc. 000540
6/21/03	**4**	24	9. **Into You** Airplay #4 / Sales #71 **FABOLOUS Featuring Ashanti or Tamia** the version with Ashanti is from the Fabolous album *Street Dreams* on Desert Storm 62791	Desert Storm 67452
9/27/03	**7**	12	10. **Rain On Me** Airplay #7 samples "The Look Of Love" by Isaac Hayes	Murder Inc. 001107

ASHFORD & SIMPSON

Husband-and-wife R&B vocal/songwriting duo: Nick Ashford (born on 5/4/43 in Fairfield, South Carolina) and Valerie Simpson (born on 8/26/46 in Brooklyn, New York). Joined staff at Motown and wrote and produced for many of the label's top stars. Valerie recorded solo in 1972. They married in 1974. Valerie's brother, Ray Simpson, was the lead singer of Village People.

DATE	POS	WKS	ARTIST–RECORD TITLE	LABEL & NO.
10/13/79	**36**	2	1. Found A Cure	Warner 8870
1/5/85	**12**	11	2. Solid Sales #8 / Airplay #15 #1 R&B hit (3 weeks)	Capitol 5397

ASHTON, GARDNER & DYKE

Pop trio from England: Tony Ashton (vocals, keyboards), Kim Gardner (bass) and Roy Dyke (drums). Ashton died of cancer on 5/28/2001 (age 55). Gardner died of cancer on 10/24/2001 (age 53).

DATE	POS	WKS	ARTIST–RECORD TITLE	LABEL & NO.
8/7/71	**40**	1	1. Resurrection Shuffle	Capitol 3060

ASIA

Rock supergroup from England: John Wetton (vocals, bass), Steve Howe (guitar), Geoff Downes (keyboards) and Carl Palmer (drums). Wetton was with King Crimson. Howe was with Yes. Downes was with The Buggles and Yes. Palmer was with Emerson, Lake & Palmer.

DATE	POS	WKS	ARTIST–RECORD TITLE	LABEL & NO.
5/1/82	**4**	12	1. **Heat Of The Moment** #1 Mainstream Rock hit (6 weeks)	Geffen 50040

DATE	POS	WKS	ARTIST–RECORD TITLE	LABEL & NO.
8/14/82	**17**	8	2. Only Time Will Tell	Geffen 29970
8/6/83	**10**	11	3. **Don't Cry**	Geffen 29571
			#1 Mainstream Rock hit (1 week)	
11/12/83	**34**	5	4. The Smile Has Left Your Eyes	Geffen 29475

ASSEMBLED MULTITUDE, The

Studio group from Philadelphia, Pennsylvania. Arranged by Tom Sellers (died in a house fire on 3/9/88, age 39).

DATE	POS	WKS	ARTIST–RECORD TITLE	LABEL & NO.
8/1/70	**16**	7	1. Overture From Tommy (A Rock Opera) [I]	Atlantic 2737

ASSOCIATION, The

Pop group from Los Angeles, California: Gary Alexander, Russ Giguere and Jim Yester (guitars), Terry Kirkman (keyboards), Brian Cole (bass) and Ted Bluechel (drums). All shared vocals. Larry Ramos (guitar) joined in 1967. Cole died of a heroin overdose on 8/2/72 (age 29).

DATE	POS	WKS	ARTIST–RECORD TITLE	LABEL & NO.
6/25/66	**7**	8	1. **Along Comes Mary**	Valiant 741
9/3/66	**1** (3)	12	● 2. **Cherish**	Valiant 747
12/17/66	**35**	3	3. Pandora's Golden Heebie Jeebies	Valiant 755
			title refers to the Sunset Strip nightclub Pandora's Box	
6/3/67	**1** (4)	13	● 4. **Windy**	Warner 7041
9/9/67	**2** (2)	11	● 5. **Never My Love**	Warner 7074
2/10/68	**10**	8	6. **Everything That Touches You**	Warner 7163
6/22/68	**39**	2	7. **Time For Livin'**	Warner 7195

ASTLEY, Rick

Born on 2/6/66 in Warrington, England. Pop singer/guitarist.

DATE	POS	WKS	ARTIST–RECORD TITLE	LABEL & NO.
1/23/88	**1** (2)	14	● 1. **Never Gonna Give You Up** Sales #1 (1) / Airplay #1 (1)	RCA 5347
			#1 Adult Contemporary hit (3 weeks)	
4/30/88	**1** (1)	12	2. **Together Forever** Sales #1 (1) / Airplay #1 (1)	RCA 8319
8/6/88	**10**	10	3. **It Would Take A Strong Strong Man**	RCA 8663
			Sales #8 / Airplay #12	
			#1 Adult Contemporary hit (1 week)	
1/7/89	**6**	10	4. **She Wants To Dance With Me** Sales #6 / Airplay #6	RCA 8838
5/27/89	**38**	1	5. Giving Up On Love Sales #34 / Airplay #40	RCA 8872
3/9/91	**7**	12	6. **Cry For Help** Sales #7 / Airplay #7	RCA 2774
			#1 Adult Contemporary hit (1 week)	
10/2/93	**28**	6	7. Hopelessly Airplay #21 / Sales #64	RCA 62597

ATARIS, The

Punk-rock group from Los Angeles, California: Kris Roe (vocals, guitar), John Collura (guitar), Mike Davenport (bass) and Chris Knapp (drums).

DATE	POS	WKS	ARTIST–RECORD TITLE	LABEL & NO.
8/23/03	**20**	8	1. The Boys Of Summer Airplay #22	album cut
			from the album *So Long, Astoria* on Columbia 86184	

ATC

Pop vocal group: Joe (from New Zealand), Sarah (from Australia), Tracey (from England) and Livio (from Italy). ATC: A Touch of Class.

DATE	POS	WKS	ARTIST–RECORD TITLE	LABEL & NO.
2/24/01	**28**	6	1. Around The World (La La La La La) Airplay #29	Republic 158610

DATE	POS	WKS	ARTIST–RECORD TITLE	LABEL & NO.
			ATLANTA RHYTHM SECTION	
			Rock group formed in Doraville, Georgia: Ronnie Hammond (vocals), Barry Bailey and J.R. Cobb (guitars), Dean Daughtry (keyboards), Paul Goddard (bass) and Robert Nix (drums). Daughtry and Nix were with Roy Orbison's band, The Candymen. Cobb, Daughtry and band manager/producer Buddy Buie were with the Classics IV. Nix left in late 1978, replaced by Roy Yeager.	
11/9/74	35	2	1. Doraville	Polydor 14248
2/26/77	7	14	2. **So In To You**	Polydor 14373
3/25/78	7	12	3. **Imaginary Lover**	Polydor 14459
7/8/78	14	7	4. I'm Not Gonna Let It Bother Me Tonight	Polydor 14484
6/16/79	19	9	5. Do It Or Die	Polydor 14568
9/8/79	17	8	6. Spooky	Polydor 2001
10/10/81	29	4	7. Alien	Columbia 02471
			ATLANTIC STARR	
			R&B group from White Plains, New York: brothers David (guitar), Wayne (keyboards) and Jonathan (trumpet) Lewis, with Sharon Bryant (vocals; see #4 below), Cliff Archer (bass) and Porter Carroll (drums). Barbara Weathers replaced Bryant in 1984. Rachel Oliver replaced Weathers in 1991.	
5/15/82	38	3	1. Circles	A&M 2392
1/25/86	3	14	2. **Secret Lovers** Sales #2 / Airplay #2 #1 Adult Contemporary hit (1 week)	A&M 2788
4/25/87	1 (1)	14	3. **Always** Airplay #1 (1) / Sales #2 #1 R&B hit (2 weeks) / #1 Adult Contemporary hit (2 weeks)	Warner 28455
9/30/89	34	4	4. Let Go Sales #32 / Airplay #35 **SHARON BRYANT**	Wing 871722
2/1/92	3	19	● 5. **Masterpiece** Airplay #4 / Sales #6 written by Kenny Nolan	Reprise 19076
			AUDIOSLAVE	
			Group of former Rage Against The Machine members Tom Morello (guitar), Tim Commerford (bass) and Brad Wilk (drums), with Chris Cornell of Soundgarden (vocals).	
4/26/03	31	10	1. Like A Stone Airplay #28 #1 Mainstream Rock hit (12 weeks) / #1 Modern Rock hit (2 weeks); from the album *Audioslave* on Interscope 86968	album cut
			AUGUST, Jan — see HAYMAN, Richard	
			AUSTIN, Patti	
			Born on 8/10/48 in Harlem, New York. R&B-jazz singer.	
12/4/82+	1 (2)	18	● 1. **Baby, Come To Me** **PATTI AUSTIN (with James Ingram)** #1 Adult Contemporary hit (3 weeks)	Qwest 50036
			AUSTIN, Sil	
			Born Sylvester Austin on 9/17/29 in Dunnellon, Florida. Died of cancer on 9/1/2001 (age 71). R&B tenor saxophonist.	
11/24/56	17	7	1. Slow Walk Juke Box #17 / Top 100 #19 / Best Seller #20 **[I]**	Mercury 70963

DATE	POS	WKS	ARTIST–RECORD TITLE	LABEL & NO.
			AUTOGRAPH	
			Hard-rock group from Los Angeles, California: Steve Plunkett (vocals, guitar), Steve Lynch (guitar), Steven Isham (keyboards), Randy Rand (bass) and Keni Richards (drums).	
2/23/85	**29**	5	1. Turn Up The Radio Sales #25	RCA 13953
			AVALON, Frankie	
			Born Francis Avallone on 9/18/39 in Philadelphia, Pennsylvania. Teen idol managed by Bob Marcucci. Singer/trumpet player with Rocco & His Saints in 1956, which included Bobby Rydell. Co-starred in several movies with Annette.	
1/27/58	**7**	11	1. **DeDe Dinah** Top 100 #7 / Best Seller #9 / Jockey #24	Chancellor 1011
7/28/58	**9**	12	2. **Ginger Bread** Hot 100 #9 / Best Seller #11	Chancellor 1021
			The Four Dates (backing vocals)	
11/17/58	**15**	10	3. I'll Wait For You Hot 100 #15	Chancellor 1026
2/23/59	**1** (5)	14	● 4. **Venus**	Chancellor 1031
6/1/59	**8**	10	5. **Bobby Sox To Stockings /**	
6/15/59	**10**	9	6. **A Boy Without A Girl**	Chancellor 1036
9/14/59	**7**	11	7. **Just Ask Your Heart**	Chancellor 1040
12/7/59	**1** (1)	12	8. **Why /**	
1/4/60	**39**	1	9. Swingin' On A Rainbow	Chancellor 1045
3/28/60	**22**	6	10. Don't Throw Away All Those Teardrops	Chancellor 1048
8/1/60	**32**	4	11. Where Are You	Chancellor 1052
10/17/60	**26**	7	12. Togetherness	Chancellor 1056
5/5/62	**26**	4	13. You Are Mine	Chancellor 1107
			AVANT	
			Born Myron Avant on 4/26/76 in Cleveland, Ohio. Male R&B singer.	
5/6/00	**23**	18	1. Separated Sales #2 / Airplay #22	Magic Johnson 155725
			#1 R&B hit (1 week)	
12/2/00	**26**	10	2. My First Love Airplay #21	album cut
			AVANT Featuring Ketara Wyatt	
			from Avant's album *My Thoughts* on Magic Johnson 112069	
2/16/02	**27**	7	3. Nothing In This World Airplay #25	album cut
			KEKE WYATT featuring Avant	
			from Wyatt's album *Soul Sista* on MCA 112609	
4/27/02	**27**	9	4. Makin' Good Love Airplay #27	album cut
			from the album *Ecstasy* on Magic Johnson 112809	
11/15/03+	**13**	20	5. Read Your Mind Sales #2 / Airplay #13	Geffen 001449
			AVANT-GARDE, The	
			Folk duo of Chuck Woolery and Elkin "Bubba" Fowler. Woolery hosted such TV game shows as *Wheel Of Fortune*, *Love Connection* and *Greed*.	
10/26/68	**40**	1	1. Naturally Stoned	Columbia 44590
			AWB (AVERAGE WHITE BAND)	
			White funk group from Scotland: Alan Gorrie (vocals, bass), Onnie McIntyre (guitar, vocals), Hamish Stuart (guitar, vocals), Malcolm Duncan (saxophone), Roger Ball (saxophone, keyboards) and Robbie McIntosh (drums). McIntosh died of a drug overdose on 9/23/74 (age 24); replaced by Steve Ferrone.	
			AWB:	
12/21/74+	**1** (1)	13	● 1. **Pick Up The Pieces** [I]	Atlantic 3229

DATE	POS	WKS	ARTIST–RECORD TITLE	LABEL & NO.
4/26/75	**10**	12	2. **Cut The Cake**	Atlantic 3261
9/27/75	**39**	2	3. If I Ever Lose This Heaven	Atlantic 3285
12/20/75	**33**	3	4. School Boy Crush	Atlantic 3304
			AVERAGE WHITE BAND:	
10/16/76	**40**	1	5. Queen Of My Soul	Atlantic 3354
			AZ	
			Born Anthony Cruz in Brooklyn, New York. Male rapper.	EMI 58407
8/12/95	**25**	13	● 1. **Sugar Hill**　　　　　Sales #11 / Airplay #64 　　missjones (female vocal)	
			AZAR, Steve	
			Born on 4/11/64 in Greenville, Mississippi. Country singer/songwriter/guitarist.	album cut
5/18/02	**35**	6	1. I Don't Have To Be Me ('Til Monday)　Airplay #32 　　from the album *Waitin' On Joe* on Mercury 170269	
			AZ YET	
			R&B vocal group from Philadelphia, Pennsylvania: Dion Allen, Darryl Anthony, Marc Nelson, Shawn Rivera and Kenny Terry.	
9/7/96	**9**	25	● 1. **Last Night**　　　　　Sales #5 / Airplay #40 　　#1 R&B hit (1 week); from the movie *The Nutty Professor* starring 　　Eddie Murphy	LaFace 24181
2/22/97	**8**	32	▲ 2. **Hard To Say I'm Sorry**　　Sales #6 / Airplay #15 　　**AZ YET Featuring Peter Cetera**	LaFace 24223

B

DATE	POS	WKS	ARTIST–RECORD TITLE	LABEL & NO.
			BABY	
			Born Bryan Williams in New Orleans, Louisiana. Member of Big Tymers and Cash Money Millionaires.	
1/4/03	**33**	4	1. Do That...　　　　　Sales #22 / Airplay #33 　　**BABY (AKA DA #1 STUNNA) Featuring P. Diddy**	Cash Money 060079
3/15/03	**17**	12	2. Hell Yeah　　　　　Airplay #17 / Sales #25 　　**GINUWINE (feat. Baby)** 　　written and produced by R. Kelly	Epic 76881
8/9/03	**14**	9	3. Let's Get Down　　　Sales #4 / Airplay #12 　　**BOW WOW (Feat. Baby)**	Columbia 79928
			BABY BASH	
			Born Ronald Bryant in Vallejo, California; raised in Houston, Texas. Latin male rapper.	
9/20/03	**7**	27	1. **Suga Suga**　　　　　Airplay #7 / Sales #8 　　**BABY BASH Feat. Frankie J**	Universal 001055

DATE	POS	WKS	ARTIST–RECORD TITLE	LABEL & NO.
			BABYFACE	
			Born Kenneth Edmonds on 4/10/59 in Indianapolis, Indiana. R&B singer/songwriter/multi-instrumentalist. Formerly with The Deele. Dubbed "Babyface" by Bootsy Collins. Brother of Melvin and Kevon Edmonds of After 7. Formed prolific songwriting partnership with Mark "L.A. Reid" Rooney (The Deele); they co-founded LaFace Records in Atlanta in 1989. Babyface's wife, Tracey, was president of Yab Yum Records.	
9/9/89	7	10	1. **It's No Crime** Airplay #7 / Sales #8 #1 R&B hit (2 weeks)	Solar 68966
12/23/89+	14	9	2. Tender Lover Sales #8 / Airplay #18 #1 R&B hit (1 week); Troop (backing vocals)	Solar 74003
3/17/90	6	11	3. **Whip Appeal** Sales #6 / Airplay #6	Solar 74007
7/21/90	30	5	4. My Kinda Girl Airplay #24 / Sales #38	Solar 74515
8/22/92	29	6	5. Give U My Heart Airplay #29 / Sales #39 **BABYFACE (Featuring Toni Braxton)** from the movie Boomerang starring Eddie Murphy	LaFace 24026
11/27/93+	15	16	6. Never Keeping Secrets Airplay #15 / Sales #18	Epic 77264
4/2/94	21	10	7. And Our Feelings Airplay #26 / Sales #29 After 7 (backing vocals)	Epic 77394
7/9/94	4	30	● 8. **When Can I See You** Airplay #4 / Sales #9	Epic 77550
5/27/95	10	22	● 9. **Someone To Love** Sales #9 / Airplay #16 **JON b featuring BABYFACE** from the movie Bad Boys starring Martin Lawrence and Will Smith (Fresh Prince)	Yab Yum 77895
10/26/96	6	14	▲ 10. **This Is For The Lover In You** Sales #3 / Airplay #37 **BABYFACE Featuring LL Cool J, Howard Hewett, Jody Watley and Jeffrey Daniels** #17 R&B hit for Shalamar in 1981	Epic 78443
2/1/97	6	23	● 11. **Every Time I Close My Eyes** Sales #5 / Airplay #10 Mariah Carey (backing vocal); Sheila E. (percussion); Kenny G (saxophone)	Epic 78485
7/7/01	31	2	12. There She Goes Sales #3	Arista 13988
			BABYS, The	
			Rock group from England: John Waite (vocals), Walt Stocker (guitar), Mike Corby (keyboards) and Tony Brock (drums). In 1978, Jonathan Cain replaced Corby and Ricky Phillips (bass) joined. Cain went on to join Journey. Waite later formed Bad English with Phillips and Cain.	
10/29/77	13	11	1. Isn't It Time	Chrysalis 2173
2/3/79	13	10	2. Every Time I Think Of You	Chrysalis 2279
3/8/80	33	3	3. Back On My Feet Again	Chrysalis 2398
			BACHELORS, The	
			Pop vocal trio from Dublin, Ireland: brothers Declan and Conleth Cluskey, with John Stokes.	
5/16/64	10	8	1. **Diane** #2 hit for the Nat Shilkret Orchestra in 1928	London 9639
8/1/64	33	2	2. I Believe #2 hit for Frankie Laine in 1953	London 9672
1/30/65	27	4	3. No Arms Can Ever Hold You	London 9724
7/3/65	15	7	4. Marie #1 hit for Tommy Dorsey in 1937	London 9762
11/6/65	32	3	5. Chapel In The Moonlight #1 hit for Shep Fields in 1936	London 9793
5/14/66	38	2	6. Love Me With All Of Your Heart	London 9828

DATE	POS	WKS	ARTIST–RECORD TITLE	LABEL & NO.
			BACHMAN, Tal	
			Born on 8/13/69 in Vancouver, British Columbia, Canada. Male rock singer /songwriter/guitarist. Son of Randy Bachman (of Bachman-Turner Overdrive).	
7/24/99	**14**	20	1. She's So High *Airplay #10* from the album *Tal Bachman* on Columbia 67956	album cut
			BACHMAN-TURNER OVERDRIVE	
			Hard-rock group from Vancouver, British Columbia, Canada: brothers Randy (vocals, guitar) and Robbie (drums) Bachman, with C. Fred Turner (vocals, bass) and Blair Thornton (guitar). Randy (father of Tal Bachman) was with The Guess Who; later formed Ironhorse.	
3/23/74	**23**	9	1. Let It Ride	Mercury 73457
6/29/74	**12**	10	2. Takin' Care Of Business	Mercury 73487
10/5/74	**1 (1)**	12	● 3. **You Ain't Seen Nothing Yet /**	
12/7/74		3	4. Free Wheelin' **[I]** dedicated to Duane Allman	Mercury 73622
2/1/75	**14**	7	5. Roll On Down The Highway	Mercury 73656
6/7/75	**21**	7	6. Hey You	Mercury 73683
2/28/76	**33**	3	7. Take It Like A Man Little Richard (backing vocal)	Mercury 73766
			BACKSTREET BOYS	
			"Boy band" formed in Orlando, Florida: Nick Carter (born on 1/28/80 in Jamestown, New York), Howie Dorough (born on 8/22/73 in Orlando, Florida), Brian Littrell (born on 2/20/75 in Lexington, Kentucky), A.J. McLean (born on 1/9/78 in West Palm Beach, Florida) and Kevin Richardson (born on 10/3/71 in Lexington, Kentucky). Carter is the older brother of Aaron Carter.	
6/28/97	**2 (2)**	35	▲ 1. **Quit Playing Games (With My Heart)** *Airplay #2 / Sales #3*	Jive 42453
11/15/97+	**4** ᴬ	45	2. **As Long As You Love Me** from the album *Backstreet Boys* on Jive 41589	album cut
4/18/98	**4**	20	▲ 3. **Everybody (Backstreet's Back)** *Sales #4 / Airplay #27*	Jive 42510
8/1/98	**4** ᴬ	20	4. **I'll Never Break Your Heart** *Hot 100 #35 (2 wks)* #1 Adult Contemporary hit (7 weeks)	Jive 42528
2/6/99	**5**	19	▲ 5. **All I Have To Give** *Sales #3 / Airplay #16*	Jive 42562
5/1/99	**6**	30	6. **I Want It That Way** *Airplay #1 (3)* #1 Adult Contemporary hit (10 weeks)	album cut
10/9/99	**25**	9	7. Larger Than Life *Airplay #20*	album cut
1/22/00	**6**	19	8. **Show Me The Meaning Of Being Lonely** *Airplay #2*	album cut
6/17/00	**30**	4	9. The One *Airplay #30* above 4 from the album *Millennium* on Jive 41672	album cut
10/14/00	**9**	16	10. **Shape Of My Heart** *Airplay #7*	Jive 42758
6/16/01	**27**	7	11. More Than That *Airplay #23* from the album *Black & Blue* on Jive 41743	album cut
11/3/01	**28**	5	12. Drowning *Airplay #33* from the album *The Hits - Chapter One...* on Jive 41779	album cut
			BACKUS, Jim, and Friend	
			Born on 2/25/13 in Cleveland, Ohio. Died of pneumonia on 7/3/89 (age 76). Actor, starred in several movies. Played "Thurston Howell III" on TV's *Gilligan's Island*. Also famous as the voice of "Mr. Magoo" in the cartoon series.	
7/21/58	**40**	2	1. Delicious! *Best Seller #40 / Top 100 #42* **[N]** Appleknocker And His Group (instrumental backing)	Jubilee 5330

DATE	POS	WKS	ARTIST–RECORD TITLE	LABEL & NO.
			BAD COMPANY	
			Rock group from England: Paul Rodgers (vocals), Mick Ralphs (guitar), Raymond "Boz" Burrell (bass) and Simon Kirke (drums). Rodgers and Kirke from Free; Ralphs from Mott The Hoople; Burrell from King Crimson. Rodgers, who left group in late 1984, was a member of The Firm (1984-86). Lead singer Brian Howe joined in 1986. Burrell left in 1987. Group named after a 1972 Jeff Bridges movie.	
8/31/74	**5**	11	1. **Can't Get Enough**	Swan Song 70015
2/8/75	**19**	6	2. Movin' On	Swan Song 70101
5/31/75	**36**	2	3. Good Lovin' Gone Bad	Swan Song 70103
7/26/75	**10**	11	4. **Feel Like Makin' Love**	Swan Song 70106
4/24/76	**20**	7	5. Young Blood	Swan Song 70108
4/14/79	**13**	12	● 6. Rock 'N' Roll Fantasy	Swan Song 70119
1/26/91	**16**	8	7. If You Needed Somebody Airplay #14 / Sales #18	Atco 98914
9/28/91	**28**	5	8. Walk Through Fire Airplay #54	Atco 98748
10/31/92	**38**	2	9. How About That Airplay #55	Atco 98509
			#1 Mainstream Rock hit (6 weeks)	
			BAD ENGLISH	
			Rock supergroup: John Waite (vocals), Neal Schon (guitar), Jonathan Cain (keyboards), Ricky Phillips (bass) and Deen Castronovo (drums). Waite, Phillips and Cain were members of The Babys. Cain and Schon were members of Journey.	
9/30/89	**1** (2)	15	● 1. **When I See You Smile** Sales #1 (2) / Airplay #1 (2)	Epic 69082
1/20/90	**5**	11	2. **Price Of Love** Airplay #5 / Sales #7	Epic 73094
7/14/90	**21**	8	3. Possession Airplay #14 / Sales #34	Epic 73398
			BADFINGER	
			Rock group from Swansea, Wales: Pete Ham and Joey Molland (guitars), Tom Evans (bass) and Mike Gibbins (drums). All but Gibbins shared vocals. Ham committed suicide on 4/23/75 (age 27). Evans committed suicide on 11/23/83 (age 36).	
3/7/70	**7**	11	1. **Come And Get It**	Apple 1815
			written and produced by Paul McCartney; from the movie *The Magic Christian* starring Peter Sellers	
11/21/70	**8**	9	2. **No Matter What**	Apple 1822
12/18/71+	**4**	12	● 3. **Day After Day**	Apple 1841
			George Harrison (guitar, producer); Leon Russell (piano)	
4/8/72	**14**	7	4. Baby Blue	Apple 1844
			produced by Todd Rundgren	
			BADU, Erykah	
			Born Erica Wright on 2/26/71 in Dallas, Texas. R&B singer/songwriter/actress. Played "Rose Rose" in the movie *The Cider House Rules*.	
1/25/97	**12**	11	● 1. On&On Sales #7 / Airplay #58	Kedar/Universal 56002
			#1 R&B hit (2 weeks)	
4/3/99	**39**	2	2. You Got Me Airplay #24	MCA 55539
			THE ROOTS featuring Erykah Badu	
9/30/00	**6**	12	3. **Bag Lady** Sales #3 / Airplay #21	Motown 158326
			#1 R&B hit (7 weeks); samples "Bumpy's Lament" by Isaac Hayes	
11/9/02+	**9**	18	4. **Love Of My Life (An Ode To Hip Hop)** Airplay #9 / Sales #27	Fox/MCA 113987
			ERYKAH BADU Featuring Common	
			#1 R&B hit (4 weeks); from the movie *Brown Sugar* starring Taye Diggs	

DATE	POS	WKS	ARTIST–RECORD TITLE	LABEL & NO.
			BAEZ, Joan	
			Born on 1/9/41 in Staten Island, New York (of British and Mexican parentage). Pre-eminent folk singer/political activist.	
8/28/71	3	13	● 1. **The Night They Drove Old Dixie Down**	Vanguard 35138
			#1 Adult Contemporary hit (5 weeks); first recorded by The Band in 1969	
11/8/75	35	2	2. Diamonds And Rust	A&M 1737
			autobiographical song about Baez and Bob Dylan	
			BAHA MEN	
			R&B group from the Bahamas: Rick Carey and Omerit Hield (vocals), Marvin Prosper (rapper), Herschel Small and Patrick Carey (guitars), Tony Flowers (percussion), Jeff Cher (keyboards), Isaiah Taylor (bass) and Colyn Grant (drums).	
10/21/00	40	1	1. Who Let The Dogs Out Sales #15 / Airplay #35 [N]	S-Curve 751050
3/9/02	5 ˢ	17	2. **Move It Like This**	S-Curve 77687
			BAILEY, Philip	
			Born on 5/8/51 in Denver, Colorado. Co-lead singer of Earth, Wind & Fire.	
12/8/84+	2 (2)	16	● 1. **Easy Lover** Sales #1 (1) / Airplay #2	Columbia 04679
			PHILIP BAILEY (with Phil Collins)	
			BAINBRIDGE, Merril	
			Born on 6/2/68 in Melbourne, Australia. Female singer/songwriter.	
9/28/96	4	25	● 1. **Mouth** Airplay #5 / Sales #9	Universal 56018
			BAIRD, Dan — see GEORGIA SATELLITES	
			BAKER, Anita	
			Born on 12/20/57 in Toledo, Ohio; raised in Detroit, Michigan. R&B/jazz-styled singer.	
9/13/86	8	11	1. **Sweet Love** Sales #6 / Airplay #9	Elektra 69557
2/7/87	37	2	2. Caught Up In The Rapture Sales #37 / Airplay #40	Elektra 69511
10/22/88	3	15	3. **Giving You The Best That I Got** Sales #2 / Airplay #3	Elektra 69371
			#1 R&B hit (2 weeks) / #1 Adult Contemporary hit (1 week)	
2/4/89	14	11	4. Just Because Airplay #11 / Sales #14	Elektra 69327
			#1 R&B hit (1 week)	
9/17/94	36	7	5. Body & Soul Sales #19 / Airplay #52	Elektra 64520
			BAKER, George, Selection	
			Born Johannes Bouwens on 12/9/44 in the Netherlands. His Selection consisted of Jan Hop, Jacobus Greuter, George The and Jan Visser. Female singer Nelleke Brzoskowsky joined in 1975 (heard on "Paloma Blanca").	
4/11/70	21	10	1. Little Green Bag	Colossus 112
1/10/76	26	5	2. Paloma Blanca	Warner 8115
			#1 Adult Contemporary hit (1 week)	
			BAKER, LaVern	
			Born Delores Williams on 11/11/29 in Chicago, Illinois. Died of heart failure on 3/10/97 (age 67). R&B singer. Inducted into the Rock and Roll Hall of Fame in 1991.	
1/15/55	14	11	1. Tweedlee Dee Juke Box #14 / Best Seller #22	Atlantic 1047
			LaVERN BAKER and The Gliders	

DATE	POS	WKS	ARTIST–RECORD TITLE	LABEL & NO.
10/13/56	22	2	2. I Can't Love You Enough *Jockey #22 / Top 100 #48*	Atlantic 1104
12/29/56+	17	14	3. Jim Dandy *Best Seller #17 / Jockey #20 / Top 100 #22*	Atlantic 1116
			LaVERNE BAKER and The Gliders #1 R&B hit (1 week)	
12/28/58+	6	15	● 4. **I Cried A Tear**	Atlantic 2007
6/1/59	33	2	5. I Waited Too Long *written by Neil Sedaka*	Atlantic 2021
5/1/61	37	3	6. Saved	Atlantic 2099
1/5/63	34	3	7. See See Rider *#14 hit for Ma Rainey in 1925 (as "See See Rider Blues")*	Atlantic 2167
			BALANCE	
			Pop-rock trio from the Bronx, New York: Peppy Castro (vocals), Bob Kulick (guitar) and Doug Katsaros (keyboards). Castro was with the Blues Magoos.	
8/15/81	22	9	1. Breaking Away	Portrait 02177
			BALIN, Marty	
			Born Martyn Buchwald on 1/30/42 in Cincinnati. Co-founder of Jefferson Airplane/Jefferson Starship.	
6/13/81	8	13	1. **Hearts**	EMI America 8084
10/10/81	27	5	2. Atlanta Lady (Something About Your Love)	EMI America 8093
			BALL, David	
			Born on 7/9/53 in Rock Hill, South Carolina. Country singer/songwriter/guitarist.	
7/23/94	40	1	1. Thinkin' Problem *Sales #18*	Warner 18250
12/15/01	36	2	2. Riding With Private Malone *Airplay #33* *from the album Amigo on Dualtone 01109*	album cut
			BALL, Kenny, and His Jazzmen	
			Born on 5/22/30 in Ilford, Essex, England. Trumpet player. His Jazzmen consisted of Diz Disley (banjo), Johnny Bennett (trombone), Dave Jones (clarinet), Colin Bates (piano), Vic Pitts (bass) and Ron Bowden (drums).	
2/17/62	2 (1)	12	1. **Midnight In Moscow** **[I]** *#1 Adult Contemporary hit (3 weeks)*	Kapp 442
			BALLARD, Hank, And The Midnighters	
			Born on 11/18/27 in Detroit, Michigan. Died of cancer on 3/2/2003 (age 75). R&B singer. The Midnighters consisted of Henry Booth, Charles Sutton, Lawson Smith and Sonny Woods. Ballard inducted into the Rock and Roll Hall of Fame in 1990.	
7/18/60	7	13	1. **Finger Poppin' Time**	King 5341
8/29/60	28	6	2. The Twist	King 5171
10/17/60	6	11	3. **Let's Go, Let's Go, Let's Go** *#1 R&B hit (3 weeks)*	King 5400
1/16/61	23	4	4. The Hoochi Coochi Coo	King 5430
3/20/61	39	1	5. Let's Go Again (Where We Went Last Night)	King 5459
5/1/61	33	3	6. The Continental Walk	King 5491
7/17/61	26	4	7. The Switch-A-Roo	King 5510

DATE	POS	WKS	ARTIST–RECORD TITLE	LABEL & NO.
			BALLOON FARM, The	
			Psychedelic-rock group from New Jersey: Mike Appel, Ed Schnug, Don Henny and Jay Saks. Appel went on to manage Bruce Springsteen.	
3/16/68	**37**	4	1. A Question Of Temperature	Laurie 3405
			first pressings show last word in title as "Tempature"	
			BALTIMORA	
			Born Jimmy McShane on 5/23/57 in Londonderry, Northern Ireland. Died of AIDS on 3/28/95 (age 37). Pop singer.	
1/11/86	**13**	10	1. Tarzan Boy Sales #11 / Airplay #17	Manhattan 50018
			BALTIMORE, Charli	
			Born Tiffany Lane on 10/11/73 in Philadelphia, Pennsylvania. Female rapper.	
5/11/02	**21**	9	1. Down A** Chick Airplay #20 / Sales #63	Def Jam 063946
			JA RULE feat. Charli "Chuck" Baltimore	
6/29/02	**6**	15	2. **Down 4 U** Airplay #6	album cut
			IRV GOTTI PRESENTS THE INC. Featuring Ja Rule, Ashanti, Charli Baltimore & Vita	
			from the album *Irv Gotti Presents The Inc.* on Murder Inc. 062033	
			BANANARAMA	
			Pop-rock "girl group" from London, England: Sarah Dallin, Keren Woodward and Siobhan Fahey. Group name is a combination of the children's TV show "The Banana Splits" and the Roxy Music song "Pyjamarama." Fahey married David A. Stewart (of Eurythmics) on 8/1/87; later formed the duo Shakespear's Sister.	
8/11/84	**9**	11	1. **Cruel Summer** Sales #17	London 810127
7/19/86	**1** (1)	12	2. **Venus** Sales #1 (2) / Airplay #3	London 886056
8/15/87	**4**	12	3. **I Heard A Rumour** Sales #3 / Airplay #5	London 886165
			from the movie *Disorderlies* starring the Fat Boys and Ralph Bellamy	
			BAND, The	
			Rock group formed in Woodstock, New York: Robbie Robertson (guitar), Levon Helm (vocals, drums), Rick Danko (bass), Richard Manuel and Garth Hudson (keyboards). All hailed from Canada (except Helm from Arkansas). Group's farewell concert on Thanksgiving Day in 1976 was documented in the Martin Scorsese movie *The Last Waltz*. Manuel committed suicide on 3/4/86 (age 42). Group inducted into the Rock and Roll Hall of Fame in 1994.	
11/29/69+	**25**	7	1. Up On Cripple Creek	Capitol 2635
10/14/72	**34**	6	2. Don't Do It [L]	Capitol 3433
			#27 hit in 1964 for Marvin Gaye as "Baby Don't You Do It"	
			BAND AID	
			A benefit recording to assist famine relief in Ethiopia. Organized by Bob Geldof. All-star group also included Bananarama, Phil Collins, Culture Club, Duran Duran, Frankie Goes To Hollywood, Heaven 17, Paul McCartney, Spandau Ballet, Sting, The Style Council, Ultravox, U2, Wham! and Paul Young.	
1/5/85 -	**13**	4	● 1. Do They Know It's Christmas? Sales #6 [X]	Columbia 04749

DATE	POS	WKS	ARTIST–RECORD TITLE	LABEL & NO.
			BANGLES	
			Female pop-rock group from Los Angeles, California: sisters Vicki (guitar) and Debbi (drums) Peterson, Susanna Hoffs (guitar; see #9 below) and Michael Steele (bass). Originally named The Bangs. Steele was previously in The Runaways. Hoffs starred in the 1987 movie *The Allnighter*.	
2/22/86	**2** (1)	14	1. **Manic Monday** Sales #3 / Airplay #4	Columbia 05757
			written by Prince under the pseudonym "Christopher"	
6/14/86	29	5	2. If She Knew What She Wants Airplay #27 / Sales #29	Columbia 05886
11/1/86	**1** (4)	15	● 3. **Walk Like An Egyptian** Sales #1 (4) / Airplay #1 (4)	Columbia 06257
3/14/87	**11**	9	4. Walking Down Your Street Sales #9 / Airplay #10	Columbia 06674
12/5/87+	**2** (1)	14	5. **Hazy Shade Of Winter** Sales #2 / Airplay #3	Def Jam 07630
			from the movie *Less Than Zero* starring Andrew McCarthy	
11/12/88+	**5**	12	6. **In Your Room** Sales #4 / Airplay #9	Columbia 08090
2/11/89	**1** (1)	14	● 7. **Eternal Flame** Airplay #1 (1) / Sales #2	Columbia 68533
			#1 Adult Contemporary hit (2 weeks)	
6/3/89	30	5	8. Be With You Sales #29 / Airplay #29	Columbia 68744
3/2/91	30	4	9. My Side Of The Bed Airplay #28 / Sales #32	Columbia 73529
			SUSANNA HOFFS	
			BANKS, Darrell	
			Born Darrell Eubanks in 1938 in Mansfield, Ohio; raised in Buffalo, New York. Shot to death in March 1970 (age 31) in Detroit, Michigan. R&B singer/songwriter.	
9/10/66	**27**	4	1. Open The Door To Your Heart	Revilot 201
			BARBER('S), Chris, Jazz Band	
			Born on 4/17/30 in Welwyn Garden City, Hertfordshire, England. Trombone player. His Jazz Band featured Monty Sunshine (clarinet).	
2/2/59	**5**	10	● 1. **Petite Fleur (Little Flower)** [I]	Laurie 3022
			BARBOUR, Keith	
			Born on 1/21/41 in New York. Pop singer/songwriter. Formerly with The New Christy Minstrels. Married to TV actress Deidre Hall *(Our House* and *Days of Our Lives)* from 1972-77.	
11/1/69	**40**	2	1. Echo Park	Epic 10486
			BARBUSTERS, The — see JETT, Joan	
			BARCLAY, Eddie, and His Orch.	
			Born on 1/26/21 in Paris, France. Head of the French recording company Compagnie Phonographique Française and own Barclay label.	
7/16/55	**18**	1	1. The Bandit (O'Cangaceiro) Juke Box #18 [I]	Tico 45-249
			theme from the Brazilian movie *O'Cangaceiro*	
			BARDEUX	
			Female dance duo from Los Angeles, California: Stacy "Acacia" Smith and Jaz. Bardeux (pronounced: bar-DO) is plural for Bardot (as in actress Brigitte Bardot).	
5/28/88	**36**	3	1. When We Kiss Airplay #32 / Sales #40	Enigma 75018

DATE	POS	WKS	ARTIST–RECORD TITLE	LABEL & NO.
			BARE, Bobby	
			Born on 4/7/35 in Ironton, Ohio. Country singer/songwriter/guitarist. Drafted by the Army in 1958; left a demo tape of "The All American Boy" with Fraternity Records. The song was released erroneously as by Bill Parsons. Acted in the movie *A Distant Trumpet* in 1964. Hosted own TV series in the mid-1980s.	
12/28/58+	**2** (1)	13	1. **The All American Boy** **[N]** **BILL PARSONS**	Fraternity 835
8/18/62	**23**	7	2. Shame On Me	RCA Victor 8032
6/29/63	**16**	9	3. Detroit City written by Mel Tillis	RCA Victor 8183
10/26/63	**10**	7	4. **500 Miles Away From Home**	RCA Victor 8238
3/7/64	**33**	2	5. Miller's Cave #9 Country hit for Hank Snow in 1960	RCA Victor 8294
			BARENAKED LADIES	
			Alternative-rock group from Toronto, Ontario, Canada: Steven Page (vocals), Ed Robertson (guitar), Kevin Hearn (keyboards), Jim Creeggan (bass) and Tyler Stewart (drums).	
10/3/98	**1** (1)	16	1. **One Week** Airplay #2 / Sales #3 #1 Modern Rock hit (5 weeks)	Reprise 17174
10/14/00	**15**	15	2. Pinch Me Sales #14 / Airplay #17	Reprise 16827
			BAR-KAYS	
			Funk group from Memphis, Tennessee: Jimmy King (guitar), Ronnie Caldwell (organ), Phalon Jones (sax), Ben Cauley (trumpet), James Alexander (bass) and Carl Cunningham (drums). The plane crash that killed Otis Redding (on 12/10/67 in Madison, Wisconsin) also claimed the lives of all the Bar-Kays except Alexander (not on the plane) and Cauley (survived the crash). Alexander re-formed the group with Larry Dodson (vocals), Barry Wilkins (guitar), Harvey Henderson (sax), Winston Stewart (organ) and Willie Hall (drums).	
7/1/67	**17**	9	● 1. Soul Finger **[I]**	Volt 148
12/4/76+	**23**	8	2. Shake Your Rump To The Funk	Mercury 73833
			BARNUM, H.B.	
			Born on 7/15/36 in Houston, Texas; raised in Los Angeles, California. Songwriter/producer/arranger. Member of The Dyna-Sores.	
2/6/61	**35**	1	1. Lost Love **[I]**	Eldo 111
			BARRETTO, Ray	
			Born on 4/29/29 in Brooklyn, New York. Latin percussionist. Member of The Blackout Allstars.	
5/11/63	**17**	7	1. El Watusi **[F-N]**	Tico 419
			BARRY, Joe	
			Born Joe Barrios on 7/13/1939 in Cut Off, Louisiana. Singer/guitarist.	
5/29/61	**24**	5	1. I'm A Fool To Care #6 hit for Les Paul & Mary Ford in 1954	Smash 1702
			BARRY, Len	
			Born Leonard Borisoff on 6/12/42 in Philadelphia, Pennsylvania. Lead singer of The Dovells from 1957-63.	
10/23/65	**2** (1)	10	1. **1-2-3**	Decca 31827

DATE	POS	WKS	ARTIST–RECORD TITLE	LABEL & NO.
1/22/66	27	5	2. Like A Baby	Decca 31889
4/9/66	26	5	3. Somewhere *from the musical West Side Story*	Decca 31923
			BARRY And The TAMERLANES Pop vocal trio from Los Angeles, California: songwriters Barry DeVorzon, Terry Smith and Bodie Chandler.	
11/16/63	21	5	1. I Wonder What She's Doing Tonight	Valiant 6034
			BARTLEY, Chris Born on 4/17/49 in Harlem, New York. Male R&B singer.	
8/19/67	32	2	1. The Sweetest Thing This Side Of Heaven *written and produced by Van McCoy*	Vando 101
			BASIA Born Basia Trzetrzelewska on 9/30/59 in Jaworzno, Poland. Female pop singer.	
9/24/88	26	7	1. Time And Tide Sales #21 / Airplay #28	Epic 07730
5/12/90	29	4	2. Cruising For Bruising Airplay #27 / Sales #34	Epic 73239
			BASIE, Count Born William Basie on 8/21/04 in Red Bank, New Jersey. Died of cancer on 4/26/84 (age 79). Legendary jazz, big-band leader/pianist/organist. Appeared in many movies. Won Grammy's Lifetime Achievement Award in 2002.	
2/4/56	28	3	1. April In Paris Top 100 #28 **[I]**	Clef 89162
			BASIL, Toni Born Antonia Basilotta on 9/22/43 in Philadelphia, Pennsylvania. Choreographer/actress. Worked on TV shows *Shindig* and *Hullabaloo*. Choreographed the movie *American Grafitti*. Appeared in the movie *Easy Rider*.	
10/9/82	1 (1)	18	▲ 1. Mickey *cheering provided by the 1981 Dorsey High School (Los Angeles) cheerleaders*	Chrysalis 2638
			BASS, Fontella Born on 7/3/40 in St. Louis, Missouri. R&B singer/pianist.	
3/27/65	33	3	1. Don't Mess Up A Good Thing **FONTELLA BASS & BOBBY McCLURE**	Checker 1097
10/23/65	4	10	2. **Rescue Me** *#1 R&B hit (4 weeks)*	Checker 1120
1/29/66	37	1	3. Recovery	Checker 1131
			BASSEY, Shirley Born on 1/8/37 in Tiger Bay, Cardiff, Wales. R&B singer.	
2/27/65	8	8	1. **Goldfinger** *John Barry (orch.); title song from the James Bond movie starring Sean Connery*	United Artists 790

DATE	POS	WKS	ARTIST–RECORD TITLE	LABEL & NO.
			BAXTER, Les, his Chorus and Orchestra	
			Born on 3/14/22 in Mexia, Texas. Died of a heart attack on 1/15/96 (age 73). Orchestra leader/arranger.	
4/9/55	**1** (2)	21	1. **Unchained Melody** / Jockey #1 (2) / Best Seller #2 / Juke Box #3 from the movie *Unchained* starring football star Elroy "Crazylegs" Hirsch	
4/30/55		1	2. Medic　　　　　　　　　　　Best Seller: flip **[I]** theme from the TV series *Medic* starring Richard Boone; song also known as "Blue Star"	Capitol 3055
8/13/55	**5**	12	3. **Wake The Town And Tell The People** Jockey #5 / Juke Box #8 / Best Seller #10 / Top 100 #24 The Notables (vocals)	Capitol 3120
2/18/56	**1** (6)	20	● 4. **The Poor People Of Paris** Top 100 #1 (6) / Jockey #1 (6) / Best Seller #1 (4) / Juke Box #1 (3) **[I]**	Capitol 3336
			BAY CITY ROLLERS	
			Pop-rock group from Edinburgh, Scotland: Les McKeown (vocals), brothers Alan (guitar) and Derek (drums) Longmuir, Eric Faulkner (guitar) and Stuart "Woody" Wood (bass). Alan Longmuir left in mid-1976; returned in 1978. Ian Mitchell (guitar) joined briefly in 1976.	
11/8/75+	**1** (1)	12	● 1. **Saturday Night**	Arista 0149
2/14/76	**9**	11	2. **Money Honey**	Arista 0170
5/22/76	**28**	4	3. Rock And Roll Love Letter	Arista 0185
9/18/76	**12**	12	4. I Only Want To Be With You	Arista 0205
6/25/77	**10**	12	5. **You Made Me Believe In Magic**	Arista 0256
11/19/77+	**24**	9	6. The Way I Feel Tonight	Arista 0272
			BAZUKA	
			Instrumental studio group assembled by producer Tony Camillo.	
6/7/75	**10**	11	1. **Dynomite-Part I**　　　　　　　　　**[I]** **Tony Camillo's BAZUKA** song inspired by an exclamation used by Jimmie Walker on the TV series *Good Times*	A&M 1666
			BBMAK	
			Male pop trio from Liverpool, England: Mark Barry, Christian Burns and Steve McNally.	
5/27/00	**13**	24	1. Back Here　　　　　　　Sales #4 / Airplay #11 #1 Adult Contemporary hit (7 weeks)	Hollywood 64040
			B. BUMBLE & THE STINGERS	
			Instrumental group formed in Los Angeles, California: Ernie Freeman (piano), Tommy Tedesco (guitar), Red Callender (bass) and Earl Palmer (drums). All were top session musicians.	
4/24/61	**21**	5	1. **Bumble Boogie**　　　　　　　　　**[I]** adaptation of Rimsky-Korsakov's *Flight Of The Bumble Bee*; #7 hit for Freddy Martin (Jack Fina, piano) in 1946	Rendezvous 140
3/31/62	**23**	7	2. Nut Rocker　　　　　　　　　　　**[I]** adapted from Tchaikovsky's *The Nutcracker* Suite	Rendezvous 166

DATE	POS	WKS	ARTIST–RECORD TITLE	LABEL & NO.
			BEACH BOYS, The	
			Pop-rock group from Hawthorne, California: brothers Brian Wilson (keyboards, bass; see #19 below), Carl Wilson (guitar) and Dennis Wilson (drums); their cousin Mike Love (lead vocals, saxophone) and Al Jardine (guitar). Jardine replaced by David Marks from March 1962 to March 1963. Brian quit touring with group in December 1964;replaced briefly by Glen Campbell until Bruce Johnston (of Bruce & Terry) joined permanently in April 1965. Johnston and Campbell also recorded with the studio band Sagittarius in 1967. Brian continued to write for and produce group; returned to stage in 1983. Daryl Dragon (of Captain & Tennille) was a keyboardist in their stage band. Mike Love formed Celebration in 1978. Dennis Wilson drowned on 12/28/83 (age 39). Carl Wilson died of cancer on 2/6/98 (age 51). Carnie and Wendy Wilson, daughters of Brian Wilson, were members of Wilson Phillips. Group inducted into the Rock and Roll Hall of Fame in 1988. Won Grammy's Lifetime Achievement Award in 2001.	
9/15/62	14	10	1. Surfin' Safari	Capitol 4777
4/13/63	3	14	2. **Surfin' U.S.A.** / also see #28 below	
5/25/63	23	8	3. Shut Down	Capitol 4932
8/17/63	7	11	4. **Surfer Girl** /	
9/7/63	15	7	5. Little Deuce Coupe	Capitol 5009
11/23/63	6	8	6. **Be True To Your School** / featuring cheerleading by The Honeys and the University of Wisconsin "fight" song "On Wisconsin"	
11/30/63	23	6	7. In My Room	Capitol 5069
2/22/64	5	9	8. **Fun, Fun, Fun**	Capitol 5118
6/6/64	1 (2)	13	● 9. **I Get Around** /	
6/27/64	24	6	10. Don't Worry Baby	Capitol 5174
9/19/64	9	8	11. **When I Grow Up (To Be A Man)**	Capitol 5245
11/21/64	8	8	12. **Dance, Dance, Dance**	Capitol 5306
3/13/65	12	6	13. Do You Wanna Dance?	Capitol 5372
5/1/65	1 (2)	11	14. **Help Me, Rhonda**	Capitol 5395
8/7/65	3	9	15. **California Girls**	Capitol 5464
12/11/65+	20	5	16. The Little Girl I Once Knew	Capitol 5540
1/15/66	2 (2)	9	17. **Barbara Ann** Dean Torrence (of Jan & Dean; lead vocals)	Capitol 5561
4/9/66	3	10	18. **Sloop John B** originally a folk song ("The Wreck Of The John B. Sails") from the West Indies in 1927	Capitol 5602
4/23/66	32	3	19. Caroline, No **BRIAN WILSON**	Capitol 5610
8/20/66	8	7	20. **Wouldn't It Be Nice** /	
9/17/66	39	2	21. God Only Knows	Capitol 5706
10/29/66	1 (1)	12	● 22. **Good Vibrations**	Capitol 5676
8/12/67	12	5	23. Heroes And Villains	Brother 1001
11/18/67	31	4	24. Wild Honey	Capitol 2028
1/13/68	19	6	25. Darlin'	Capitol 2068
8/17/68	20	7	26. Do It Again	Capitol 2239
4/5/69	24	6	27. I Can Hear Music	Capitol 2432
9/28/74	36	1	28. Surfin' U.S.A. [R] same version as #2 above	Capitol 3924
6/19/76	5	13	29. **Rock And Roll Music**	Brother/Reprise 1354
9/18/76	29	4	30. It's O.K.	Brother/Reprise 1368
6/9/79	40	1	31. Good Timin'	Caribou 9029

DATE	POS	WKS	ARTIST–RECORD TITLE	LABEL & NO.
8/15/81	**12**	11	32. The Beach Boys Medley _Good Vibrations/Help Me, Rhonda/I Get Around/Shut Down/ Surfin' Safari/Barbara Ann/Surfin' USA/Fun, Fun, Fun_	Capitol 5030
12/19/81+	**18**	8	33. Come Go With Me	Caribou 02633
6/8/85	**26**	7	34. Getcha Back Airplay #24 / Sales #29	Caribou 04913
8/8/87	**12**	11	35. Wipeout Sales #4 / Airplay #20	Tin Pan Apple 885960
			FAT BOYS (with The Beach Boys)	
9/24/88	**1** (1)	15	▲ 36. **Kokomo** Airplay #1 (2) / Sales #1 (1)	Elektra 69385
			from the movie Cocktail starring Tom Cruise	

BEASTIE BOYS

White rap-punk trio from Brooklyn, New York: Adam Horovitz, Adam Yauch and Mike Diamond. Horovitz starred in the movie _Lost Angels_; was married to actress Ione Skye (daughter of Donovan) from 1991-99. Group started own Grand Royal record label.

DATE	POS	WKS	ARTIST–RECORD TITLE	LABEL & NO.
1/24/87	**7**	10	1. **(You Gotta) Fight For Your Right (To Party!)** Sales #4 / Airplay #9	Def Jam 06595
8/26/89	**36**	2	2. Hey Ladies Sales #25	Capitol 44454
8/8/98	**28**	10	3. Intergalactic Airplay #32	Grand R./Cap. 58705
			samples "Prelude C# Minor" by Les Baxter and elements from The Jazz Crusaders' album Powerhouse	

BEATLES, The

The world's #1 rock group was formed in Liverpool, England, in the late 1950s. Known in early forms as The Quarrymen, Johnny & the Moondogs, The Rainbows, and the Silver Beatles. Named The Beatles in 1960. Originally consisted of John Lennon, Paul McCartney, George Harrison (guitars), Stu Sutcliffe (bass) and Pete Best (drums). Sutcliffe left in April 1961 (died of a brain hemorrhage on 4/10/62, age 21); McCartney moved to bass. Best replaced by Ringo Starr in August 1962. Group managed by Brian Epstein (died of a sleeping-pill overdose on 8/27/67) and produced by George Martin. First U.S. tour in February 1964. Won the 1964 Best New Artist Grammy Award. Group starred in the movies _A Hard Day's Night_ (1964), _Help_ (1965), _Magical Mystery Tour_ (1967) and _Let It Be_ (1970); contributed soundtrack to the animated movie _Yellow Submarine_ (1968). Started own Apple label in 1968. McCartney publicly announced group's dissolution on 4/10/70. Won the Grammy's Trustees Award in 1972. Lennon was shot to death on 12/8/80 (age 40). Harrison died of cancer on 11/29/2001 (age 58). Group inducted into the Rock and Roll Hall of Fame in 1988.

DATE	POS	WKS	ARTIST–RECORD TITLE	LABEL & NO.
1/25/64	**1** (7)	14	● 1. **I Want To Hold Your Hand** /	
1/25/64	**14**	8	2. I Saw Her Standing There	Capitol 5112
2/1/64	**1** (2)	14	3. **She Loves You**	Swan 4152
2/22/64	**3**	10	4. **Please Please Me**	Vee-Jay 581
			recorded November 1962	
3/7/64	**26**	2	5. My Bonnie (My Bonnie Lies Over The Ocean)	MGM 13213
			THE BEATLES With TONY SHERIDAN	
3/21/64	**2** (4)	9	6. **Twist And Shout**	Tollie 9001
			song first recorded by the Top Notes in 1961; also see #50 below	
3/28/64	**1** (5)	9	● 7. **Can't Buy Me Love**	Capitol 5150
4/11/64	**2** (1)	9	8. **Do You Want To Know A Secret** /	
4/25/64	**35**	3	9. Thank You Girl	Vee-Jay 587
5/2/64	**1** (1)	11	10. **Love Me Do** /	
5/16/64	**10**	7	11. **P.S. I Love You**	Tollie 9008
			above 2 recorded September 1962 (with Andy White on drums, Ringo on tambourine)	
7/18/64	**1** (2)	12	● 12. **A Hard Day's Night**	Capitol 5222

DATE	POS	WKS	ARTIST–RECORD TITLE	LABEL & NO.
8/1/64	**19**	7	13. Ain't She Sweet	Atco 6308
			recorded May 1961 (Pete Best, Lennon, McCartney, Harrison); #1 hit for Ben Bernie in 1927	
8/8/64	**12**	7	14. And I Love Her	Capitol 5235
8/15/64	**25**	5	15. I'll Cry Instead	Capitol 5234
			#12,14,15: from the movie *A Hard Day's Night*	
9/19/64	**17**	5	16. Matchbox /	
			written and first recorded by Carl Perkins in 1956	
9/26/64	**25**	4	17. Slow Down	Capitol 5255
			written and first recorded by Larry Williams in 1958	
12/5/64	**1 (3)**	11	● 18. **I Feel Fine /**	
12/12/64	**4**	8	19. **She's A Woman**	Capitol 5327
2/27/65	**1 (2)**	9	● 20. **Eight Days A Week /**	
3/20/65	**39**	1	21. **I Don't Want To Spoil The Party**	Capitol 5371
5/1/65	**1 (1)**	9	22. **Ticket To Ride**	Capitol 5407
8/14/65	**1 (3)**	12	● 23. **Help!**	Capitol 5476
			above 2 from the movie *Help!*	
10/2/65	**1 (4)**	9	● 24. **Yesterday**	Capitol 5498
12/18/65+	**1 (3)**	11	● 25. **We Can Work It Out /**	
12/25/65+	**5**	8	26. **Day Tripper**	Capitol 5555
3/5/66	**3**	9	● 27. **Nowhere Man**	Capitol 5587
6/11/66	**1 (2)**	10	● 28. **Paperback Writer /**	
6/25/66	**23**	5	29. **Rain**	Capitol 5651
8/27/66	**2 (1)**	8	● 30. **Yellow Submarine /**	
			title song of The Beatles' animated movie, released in 1968	
9/10/66	**11**	6	31. **Eleanor Rigby**	Capitol 5715
3/4/67	**1 (1)**	9	● 32. **Penny Lane /**	
3/11/67	**8**	7	33. **Strawberry Fields Forever**	Capitol 5810
7/29/67	**1 (1)**	9	● 34. **All You Need Is Love /**	
			intro is from "La Marseillaise" (the French national anthem)	
8/12/67	**34**	2	35. **Baby You're A Rich Man**	Capitol 5964
12/9/67	**1 (3)**	10	● 36. **Hello Goodbye**	Capitol 2056
3/23/68	**4**	10	▲ 37. **Lady Madonna**	Capitol 2138
9/14/68	**1 (9)**	19	▲⁴ 38. **Hey Jude /**	
9/14/68	**12**	11	39. **Revolution**	Apple 2276
5/10/69	**1 (5)**	12	▲² 40. **Get Back /**	
5/10/69	**35**	3	41. **Don't Let Me Down**	Apple 2490
			THE BEATLES with Billy Preston (above 2)	
6/21/69	**8**	8	● 42. **The Ballad Of John And Yoko**	Apple 2531
10/18/69	**1 (1)**	16	▲² 43. **Come Together /**	
10/18/69	**3**	16	44. **Something**	Apple 2654
3/21/70	**1 (2)**	13	▲² 45. **Let It Be**	Apple 2764
			#1 Adult Contemporary hit (4 weeks)	
5/23/70	**1 (2)**	10	▲ 46. **The Long And Winding Road /**	
5/23/70		10	47. **For You Blue**	Apple 2832
			above 3 from The Beatles' documentary movie *Let It Be*	
6/19/76	**7**	11	● 48. **Got To Get You Into My Life**	Capitol 4274
4/10/82	**12**	8	49. **The Beatles' Movie Medley**	Capitol 5107
			Magical Mystery Tour/All You Need Is Love/You've Got To Hide Your Love Away/I Should Have Known Better/A Hard Day's Night/Ticket To Ride/Get Back	

DATE	POS	WKS	ARTIST–RECORD TITLE	LABEL & NO.
8/30/86	**23**	7	50. Twist And Shout Sales #20 / Airplay #29 **[R]** same version as #6 above; revived through inclusion in the movies *Ferris Bueller's Day Off* and *Back To School*	Capitol 5624
12/30/95+	**6**	4	● 51. **Free As A Bird** Sales #5 / Airplay #60	Apple 58497
3/23/96	**11**	3	● 52. Real Love Sales #5 above 2 are original demos recorded by John Lennon in 1977 & 1979, with new vocals and instrumentation added by the other Beatles	Apple 58544
			BEAU, Toby — see TOBY	
			BEAU BRUMMELS, The	
			Rock group from San Francisco, California: Sal Valentino (vocals), Ron Elliott (guitar), Ron Meagher (bass) and John Petersen (drums). Petersen later joined Harpers Bizarre.	
1/30/65	**15**	8	1. Laugh, Laugh	Autumn 8
5/8/65	**8**	9	2. **Just A Little**	Autumn 10
8/28/65	**38**	1	3. You Tell Me Why	Autumn 16
			BECK	
			Born Beck David Campbell (later changed his last name to his mother's maiden name of Hansen) on 7/8/70 in Los Angeles, California. Alternative-rock singer/songwriter/guitarist.	
3/5/94	**10**	15	● 1. **Loser** Sales #3 / Airplay #31 #1 Modern Rock hit (5 weeks); samples "I Walk On Guilded Splinters" by Dr. John	DGC/Bong Load 19270
			BECK, Jeff — see DONOVAN	
			BECKHAM, Bob	
			Born on 7/8/27 in Stratford, Oklahoma. Pop-country singer.	
10/12/59	**32**	10	1. Just As Much As Ever	Decca 30861
2/29/60	**36**	1	2. Crazy Arms	Decca 31029
			BEDINGFIELD, Daniel	
			Born in 1980 in New Zealand; raised in England. Pop singer/songwriter.	
8/17/02	**10**	17	1. **Gotta Get Thru This** Airplay #13	Island 570976
4/19/03	**15**	14	2. If You're Not The One Sales #2 / Airplay #18	Island 000267
			BEE GEES	
			Trio of brothers from Manchester, England: Barry Gibb (born on 9/1/46; see #28, 29 & 33 below) and twins Maurice and Robin Gibb (born on 12/22/49; see #24 & 32 below). Moved to Australia in 1958, performed as the Gibbs, later as BG's, finally the Bee Gees. Returned to England in February 1967, with guitarist Vince Melouney and drummer Colin Peterson. Melouney left in December 1968; Robin left for solo career in 1969. When Peterson left in August 1969, Barry and Maurice went solo. After eight months, the brothers reunited. Maurice married to Lulu from 1969-73. Composed soundtracks for *Saturday Night Fever* and *Staying Alive*. Acted in the movie *Sgt. Pepper's Lonely Hearts Club Band*. Youngest brother, Andy Gibb, was a successful solo singer (died on 3/10/88). Maurice died of heart failure on 1/12/2003 (age 53). Trio inducted into the Rock and Roll Hall of Fame in 1997.	
6/10/67	**14**	4	1. New York Mining Disaster 1941 (Have You Seen My Wife, Mr. Jones)	Atco 6487

DATE	POS	WKS	ARTIST–RECORD TITLE	LABEL & NO.
7/29/67	**17**	7	2. To Love Somebody	Atco 6503
10/21/67	**16**	5	3. Holiday	Atco 6521
11/25/67	**11**	6	4. (The Lights Went Out In) Massachusetts	Atco 6532
2/10/68	**15**	8	5. Words	Atco 6548
9/7/68	**8**	10	6. **I've Gotta Get A Message To You**	Atco 6603
1/4/69	**6**	9	7. **I Started A Joke**	Atco 6639
4/12/69	**37**	3	8. First Of May	Atco 6657
12/26/70+	**3**	10	● 9. **Lonely Days**	Atco 6795
7/3/71	**1 (4)**	14	● 10. **How Can You Mend A Broken Heart**	Atco 6824
2/5/72	**16**	7	11. My World	Atco 6871
8/26/72	**16**	7	12. Run To Me	Atco 6896
12/2/72	**34**	4	13. Alive	Atco 6909
6/28/75	**1 (2)**	12	● 14. **Jive Talkin'**	RSO 510
10/18/75	**7**	13	15. **Nights On Broadway**	RSO 515
1/17/76	**12**	12	16. Fanny (Be Tender With My Love)	RSO 519
7/17/76	**1 (1)**	12	● 17. **You Should Be Dancing**	RSO 853
10/2/76	**3**	16	● 18. **Love So Right**	RSO 859
1/29/77	**12**	9	19. Boogie Child	RSO 867
8/13/77	**26**	5	20. Edge Of The Universe [L]	RSO 880
10/8/77	**1 (3)**	26	● 21. **How Deep Is Your Love**	RSO 882
			#1 Adult Contemporary hit (6 weeks)	
12/24/77+	**1 (4)**	22	▲ 22. **Stayin' Alive**	RSO 885
2/11/78	**1 (8)**	18	▲ 23. **Night Fever**	RSO 889
			above 3 from the movie *Saturday Night Fever* starring John Travolta	
8/19/78	**15**	9	24. Oh! Darling	RSO 907
			ROBIN GIBB	
			from the movie *Sgt. Pepper's Lonely Hearts Club Band* starring Peter Frampton and the Bee Gees; first recorded by The Beatles in 1969	
11/18/78+	**1 (2)**	17	▲ 25. **Too Much Heaven**	RSO 913
2/10/79	**1 (2)**	13	▲ 26. **Tragedy**	RSO 918
4/21/79	**1 (1)**	13	● 27. **Love You Inside Out**	RSO 925
11/15/80+	**3**	15	● 28. **Guilty**	Columbia 11390
2/14/81	**10**	10	29. **What Kind Of Fool**	Columbia 11430
			BARBRA STREISAND & BARRY GIBB (above 2)	
			#1 Adult Contemporary hit (4 weeks)	
10/10/81	**30**	4	30. He's A Liar	RSO 1066
5/28/83	**24**	6	31. The Woman In You	RSO 813173
			from the movie *Staying Alive* starring John Travolta	
7/7/84	**37**	4	32. Boys Do Fall In Love	Mirage 99743
			ROBIN GIBB	
9/29/84	**37**	3	33. Shine Shine	MCA 52443
			BARRY GIBB	
8/12/89	**7**	10	34. **One** Sales #8 / Airplay #9	Warner 22899
			#1 Adult Contemporary hit (2 weeks)	
6/7/97	**28**	9	35. Alone Sales #23 / Airplay #49	Polydor 571006
			BEENIE MAN	
			Born Moses Davis on 8/22/73 in Kingston, Jamaica. Reggae singer/rapper. Beenie is Jamaican slang for little.	
5/23/98	**40**	2	1. Who Am I "Sim Simma" Sales #26 / Airplay #74	VP 6160

DATE	POS	WKS	ARTIST–RECORD TITLE	LABEL & NO.
8/24/02	**28**	4	2. Feel It Boy Sales #12 / Airplay #30 **BEENIE MAN feat. JANET**	Virgin 38846

BEGA, Lou

Born David Lubega on 4/13/75 in Munich, Germany (Sicilian mother/ Ugandan father).

DATE	POS	WKS	ARTIST–RECORD TITLE	LABEL & NO.
9/4/99	**3**	20	1. **Mambo No. 5 (A Little Bit Of...)** Airplay #1 (6) new lyrics added to Perez Prado's 1950 recording (also see "7-11" by the Gone All Stars)	RCA 65842

BEGINNING OF THE END, The

R&B group from the Bahamas: brothers Ray (organ), Roy (guitar) and Frank (drums) Munnings, with Fred Henfield (bass).

DATE	POS	WKS	ARTIST–RECORD TITLE	LABEL & NO.
6/5/71	**15**	10	1. Funky Nassau-Part I	Alston 4595

BELAFONTE, Harry

Born on 3/1/27 in Harlem, New York (of Jamaican and West Indian parentage). Calypso singer/actor. Rode the crest of the calypso craze to worldwide stardom. Starred in several movies. Became UNICEF goodwill ambassador in 1987. Father of actress Shari Belafonte. Won Grammy's Lifetime Achievement Award in 2000.

DATE	POS	WKS	ARTIST–RECORD TITLE	LABEL & NO.
11/24/56+	**14**	16	1. Jamaica Farewell Jockey #14 / Best Seller #17 / Top 100 #17 / Juke Box #17	RCA Victor 6663
12/29/56	**12**	3	2. Mary's Boy Child Best Seller #12 / Jockey #12 / Top 100 #15 **[X]** William Lorin (orch., above 2)	RCA Victor 47-6735
1/12/57	**5**	17	● 3. **Banana Boat (Day-O)** Jockey #5 / Best Seller #5 / Top 100 #5 / Juke Box #5 Tony Scott (orch. and chorus)	RCA Victor 6771
3/23/57	**11**	10	4. Mama Look At Bubu Best Seller #11 / Top 100 #13 / Jockey #14 / Juke Box #18	RCA Victor 6830
7/8/57	**25**	3	5. Cocoanut Woman / Best Seller #25 / Top 100 #48	
7/8/57	**30**	3	6. Island In The Sun Best Seller #30 / Top 100 #42 title song from the movie starring Belafonte; Bob Corman (orch., above 3)	RCA Victor 6885

BELL, Archie, & The Drells

Born on 9/1/44 in Henderson, Texas. R&B singer. The Drells consisted of James Wise, Lee Bell and Willie Parnell.

DATE	POS	WKS	ARTIST–RECORD TITLE	LABEL & NO.
4/13/68	**1 (2)**	13	● 1. **Tighten Up** #1 R&B hit (2 weeks)	Atlantic 2478
8/3/68	**9**	8	2. **I Can't Stop Dancing**	Atlantic 2534
1/4/69	**21**	8	3. There's Gonna Be A Showdown	Atlantic 2583

BELL, Benny

Born Benjamin Samberg on 3/27/06 in Brooklyn, New York. Died on 9/1/99 (age 93). Risque singer/songwriter.

DATE	POS	WKS	ARTIST–RECORD TITLE	LABEL & NO.
4/19/75	**30**	4	1. Shaving Cream **[N]** Paul Wynn (real name: Phil Winston; vocal); first released in 1946; reissued due to heavy airplay on Dr. Demento's radio show	Vanguard 35183

BELL, Madeline

Born on 7/23/42 in Newark, New Jersey. Singer/actress. Moved to England in 1962.

DATE	POS	WKS	ARTIST–RECORD TITLE	LABEL & NO.
3/9/68	**26**	5	1. I'm Gonna Make You Love Me	Philips 40517

DATE	POS	WKS	ARTIST—RECORD TITLE	LABEL & NO.
4/25/70	31	5	**BELL, Vincent** Born Vincent Gambella on 7/28/35 in Brooklyn, New York. Prolific studio guitarist. 　　　1. Airport Love Theme (Gwen And Vern)　　**[I]** 　　　_from the movie Airport starring Burt Lancaster_	Decca 32659
3/12/77	10	9	**BELL, William** Born William Yarborough on 7/16/39 in Memphis, Tennessee. R&B singer. ● 　1. **Tryin' To Love Two** 　　　#1 R&B hit (1 week)	Mercury 73839
3/6/76 7/14/79	1 (1) 39	12 2	**BELLAMY BROTHERS** Country duo from Darby, Florida: brothers Howard (born on 2/2/46) and David (born on 9/16/50) Bellamy. 　　　1. **Let Your Love Flow** 　　　2. **If I Said You Have A Beautiful Body Would You 　　　　　Hold It Against Me** 　　　　　#1 Country hit (3 weeks)	Warner/Curb 8169 Warner/Curb 8790
3/10/79	15	8	**BELL & JAMES** R&B duo of Leroy Bell and Casey James. Began as songwriting team for Bell's uncle, producer Thom Bell. ● 　1. **Livin' It Up (Friday Night)**	A&M 2069
4/14/90 7/21/90 11/10/90 9/28/91 5/30/92 11/28/92+ 10/9/93	3 3 26 37 ᴬ 10 21 38	17 16 5 3 18 8 2	**BELL BIV DeVOE** R&B trio of New Edition members: Ricky Bell (born on 9/18/67), Michael Bivins (born on 8/10/68) and Ronnie DeVoe (born on 11/17/67). ▲ 　1. **Poison**　　　　　　　　Sales #1 (3) / Airplay #3 　　　　#1 R&B hit (2 weeks) 　　　2. **Do Me!**　　　　　　　　Sales #1 (1) / Airplay #4 　　　3. **B.B.D. (I Thought It Was Me)?**　Sales #18 / Airplay #39 　　　　#1 R&B hit (1 week) 　　　4. Word To The Mutha! 　　　　_New Edition (guest vocals); from the album WBBD - Bootcity! The 　　　　Remix Album on MCA 10345_ 　　　5. **The Best Things In Life Are Free**　Airplay #5 / Sales #16 　　　　**LUTHER VANDROSS and JANET JACKSON with BBD and 　　　　Ralph Tresvant** 　　　　#1 R&B hit (1 week); from the movie _Mo' Money_ starring Damon 　　　　Wayans 　　　6. Gangsta　　　　　　　　Sales #10 / Airplay #29 　　　7. Something In Your Eyes　　　Sales #26 / Airplay #54	 MCA 53772 MCA 53848 MCA 53897 album cut Perspective 0010 MCA 54555 MCA 54725
			BELLE, Regina — see BRYSON, Peabo	
4/1/89	14	10	**BELLE STARS, The** Female group from England: Jennie McKeown (vocals), Sarah-Jane Owen and Stella Barker (guitars), Miranda Joyce and Clare Hirst (saxophones), Lesley Shone (bass) and Judy Parsons (drums). 　　　1. Iko Iko　　　　　　　　　Sales #6 / Airplay #18 　　　　_from the movie Rain Man starring Dustin Hoffman and Tom Cruise_	Capitol 44343

DATE	POS	WKS	ARTIST—RECORD TITLE	LABEL & NO.
			BELL NOTES, The	
			Rock and roll group from Long Island, New York: Carl Bonura (vocals, sax), Ray Ceroni (vocals, guitar), Lenny Giamblavo (bass), Peter Kane (piano) and John Casey (drums).	
2/9/59	6	11	1. **I've Had It**	Time 1004
			BELLS, The	
			Pop group from Canada: Jacki Ralph and Cliff Edwards (vocals), Charles Clarke (guitar), Dennis Will (Keyboards), Michael Waye (bass) and Douglas Gravelle (drums).	
3/27/71	7	11	● 1. **Stay Awhile**	Polydor 15023
			BELLUS, Tony	
			Born Anthony Bellusci on 4/17/36 in Chicago, Illinois. Pop singer/accordionist.	
6/29/59	25	11	1. Robbin' The Cradle	NRC 023
			BELMONTS, The	
			Doo-wop trio from the Bronx, New York: Angelo D'Aleo, Fred Milano and Carlo Mastrangelo. Sang with Dion from 1957-60. Frank Lyndon replaced Mastrangelo in May 1962.	
6/19/61	18	6	1. Tell Me Why	Sabrina 500
8/25/62	28	8	2. Come On Little Angel	Sabina 505
			BELVIN, Jesse	
			Born on 12/15/33 in Texarkana, Texas; raised in Los Angeles, California. Died in a car crash on 2/6/60 (age 26). R&B singer/songwriter. Member of The Shields.	
4/13/59	31	9	1. Guess Who Shorty Rogers (orch. and chorus)	RCA Victor 7469
			BENATAR, Pat	
			Born Patricia Andrzejewski on 1/10/53 in Lindenhurst, Long Island, New York. Rock singer/songwriter. Married her producer/guitarist Neil Giraldo on 2/20/82. Acted in the movie *Union City*.	
2/9/80	23	10	1. Heartbreaker	Chrysalis 2395
5/17/80	27	6	2. We Live For Love	Chrysalis 2419
10/18/80	9	15	● 3. **Hit Me With Your Best Shot**	Chrysalis 2464
1/31/81	18	10	4. Treat Me Right	Chrysalis 2487
8/1/81	17	9	5. Fire And Ice	Chrysalis 2529
10/31/81	38	2	6. Promises In The Dark	Chrysalis 2555
11/6/82	13	10	7. Shadows Of The Night	Chrysalis 2647
3/5/83	20	7	8. Little Too Late	Chrysalis 03536
5/21/83	39	3	9. Looking For A Stranger	Chrysalis 42688
10/15/83	5	14	● 10. **Love Is A Battlefield** #1 Mainstream Rock hit (4 weeks)	Chrysalis 42732
11/3/84+	5	14	11. **We Belong** Airplay #2 / Sales #3	Chrysalis 42826
2/9/85	36	3	12. Ooh Ooh Song	Chrysalis 42843
7/27/85	10	11	13. **Invincible** Sales #9 / Airplay #9 theme from the movie *Legend of Billie Jean* starring Helen Slater	Chrysalis 42877
12/14/85+	28	7	14. Sex As A Weapon Airplay #28	Chrysalis 42927
7/30/88	19	8	15. All Fired Up Sales #11 / Airplay #30	Chrysalis 43268

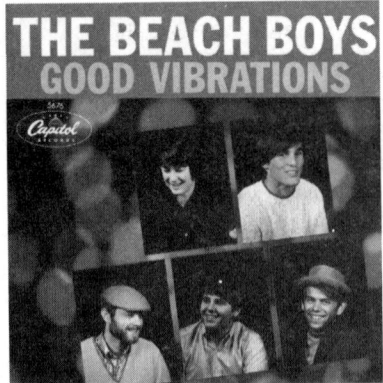

Toni Basil took a very simple approach to the video for her #1 hit "Mickey," filming cheerleaders against a white background. She would later choreograph slightly more complex movements for films like *That Thing You Do!*

The Beach Boys scored their third #1 hit with "Good Vibrations," but the good vibes didn't last forever. A 21st century court battle over the use of the Beach Boys name pitted members Al Jardine and Mike Love against each other.

The Beatles found inspiration close to home for their #1 hit "Hey Jude." Paul McCartney wrote the song for John Lennon's son, Julian, to comfort him during some difficult times between his parents.

The Bee Gees meant it when they named their #1 hit "Stayin' Alive." When their follow-up song from the film *Saturday Night Fever*, "Night Fever," reached #1, "Stayin' Alive" rebounded up the charts spending another month at #2.

The Bellamy Brothers had 26 Top 10 hits on the Country charts, including 10 #1s. Strangely enough, their only #1 pop hit, "Let Your Love Flow," didn't even make the Country Top 10, stalling at #21.

Berlin scored their only #1 hit with the *Top Gun* soundtrack single "Take My Breath Away." Lead singer Terri Nunn would later earn a minor soundtrack hit on the Adult Contemporary charts with her Paul Carrack duet, "Romance," from the movie *Sing*.

Beyoncé proved she could handle a solo career away from Destiny's Child. "Baby Boy," her duet with reggae artist Sean Paul, was the second #1 hit from her solo debut album, *Dangerously in Love*.

BLACKstreet liked to collaborate with other artists on their hits. Two of their singles featured Janet Jackson, and their #1 smash, "No Diggity," included a cameo by rapper/producer Dr. Dre.

Mary J. Blige was an R&B superstar in the 1990s, earning four #1 R&B hits. Her fifth #1 R&B hit, 2001's Dr. Dre–produced "Family Affair," became her first #1 pop hit, spending six weeks at #1 on the Hot 100.

Blondie scored their second #1 hit with 1980's "Call Me," featured in the film *American Gigolo*. Unfortunately for them, their name wasn't called during the 1980 Grammy Award presentation of Best Group Rock Performance, which they lost to Bob Seger and the Silver Bullet Band.

Michael Bolton enjoyed remaking classic hits such as "Georgia On My Mind" and his #1 version of "When A Man Loves A Woman." In 1992, he recorded an entire album of remakes titled *Timeless (The Classics)*.

Bone Thugs-N-Harmony had a much more successful chart career than the man who discovered them, NWA founder Eazy E, who died of AIDS in 1995. The group's #1 hit, "Tha Crossroads," was a tribute to their mentor.

DATE	POS	WKS	ARTIST–RECORD TITLE	LABEL & NO.
			BENÉT, Eric	
			Born Eric Benét Jordan on 10/5/69 in Milwaukee, Wisconsin. R&B singer/songwriter. Married to actress Halle Berry from 2001-2003.	
8/7/99	21	15	● 1. Spend My Life With You Sales #11 / Airplay #34 **ERIC BENÉT featuring Tamia** #1 R&B hit (2 weeks)	Warner 16958
			BENNETT, Boyd, And His Rockets	
			Born on 12/7/24 in Muscle Shoals, Alabama. Died of lung failure on 6/2/2002 (age 77).	
7/9/55	5	17	1. **Seventeen** Best Seller #5 / Juke Box #8 / Jockey #9 / Top 100 #28	King 1470
11/12/55	39	1	2. My Boy-Flat Top Top 100 #39 Joe "Big Moe" Muzey (vocal, above 2)	King 1494
			BENNETT, Joe, and The Sparkletones	
			Teen rock and roll band from Spartanburg, South Carolina: Joe Bennett (vocals, guitar; born in 1941), Howard Childress (guitar), Wayne Arthur (bass) and Irving Denton (drums).	
9/23/57	17	9	1. Black Slacks Top 100 #17 / Best Seller #18 / Jockey #21	ABC-Paramount 9837
			BENNETT, Tony	
			Born Anthony Benedetto on 8/3/26 in Queens, New York. Legendary pop/jazz-styled singer. Appeared in the movie *The Oscar*. Won Grammy's Lifetime Achievement Award in 2001.	
5/5/56	16	11	1. Can You Find It In Your Heart Best Seller #16 / Juke Box #18 / Top 100 #19 / Jockey #20	Columbia 40667
8/18/56	11	7	2. From The Candy Store On The Corner To The Chapel On The Hill / Jockey #11 / Top 100 #33 Lois Winter (female vocal)	
10/6/56	38	2	3. Happiness Street (Corner Sunshine Square) Top 100 #38	Columbia 40726
11/17/56	18	4	4. The Autumn Waltz Jockey #18 / Top 100 #41	Columbia 40770
8/12/57	9	14	5. **In The Middle Of An Island** Best Seller #9 / Top 100 #9 / Jockey #13	Columbia 40965
11/18/57	22	1	6. Ca, C'est L'amour Jockey #22 / Top 100 #96 from the movie *Les Girls* starring Gene Kelly	Columbia 41032
6/30/58	23	1	7. Young And Warm And Wonderful Jockey #23 / Best Seller #42 / Top 100 #57	Columbia 41172
9/22/58	20	8	8. Firefly Hot 100 #20 / Best Seller #45	Columbia 41237
9/29/62	19	10	9. I Left My Heart In San Francisco	Columbia 42332
2/16/63	14	10	10. I Wanna Be Around	Columbia 42634
6/1/63	18	6	11. The Good Life	Columbia 42779
10/31/64	33	6	12. Who Can I Turn To (When Nobody Needs Me) from the Broadway musical *The Roar of the Greasepaint* starring Anthony Newley	Columbia 43141
3/20/65	34	4	13. If I Ruled The World The Will Bronson Chorus (backing vocals); from the Broadway musical *Pickwick* starring Harry Secombe	Columbia 43220
			BENSON, George	
			Born on 3/22/43 in Pittsburgh, Pennsylvania. R&B/jazz-styled singer/guitarist.	
7/17/76	10	11	1. **This Masquerade** first recorded by Leon Russell in 1972; 1976 Grammy winner: Record of the Year	Warner 8209

DATE	POS	WKS	ARTIST–RECORD TITLE	LABEL & NO.
9/3/77	24	7	2. The Greatest Love Of All from the movie *The Greatest* starring Muhammad Ali	Arista 0251
4/22/78	7	10	3. **On Broadway** **[L]**	Warner 8542
3/24/79	18	8	4. Love Ballad	Warner 8759
8/2/80	4	14	5. **Give Me The Night** #1 R&B hit (3 weeks)	Warner 49505
11/21/81+	5	16	6. **Turn Your Love Around** #1 R&B hit (1 week)	Warner 49846
8/27/83	30	6	7. Lady Love Me (One More Time)	Warner 29563
			BENSON, Jo Jo — see SCOTT, Peggy	
			BENTLEY, Dierks	
			Born on 11/20/75 in Phoenix, Arizona. Country singer/songwriter/guitarist.	
8/16/03	22	10	1. What Was I Thinkin' Sales #9 / Airplay #22 #1 Country hit (1 week)	Capitol 77963
			BENTON, Brook	
			Born Benjamin Franklin Peay on 9/19/31 in Camden, South Carolina. Died of spinal meningitis on 4/9/88 (age 56). R&B singer/songwriter.	
2/9/59	3	14	● 1. **It's Just A Matter Of Time** #1 R&B hit (9 weeks)	Mercury 71394
5/4/59	12	9	2. Endlessly /	
6/8/59	38	1	3. So Close	Mercury 71443
8/3/59	16	9	4. Thank You Pretty Baby #1 R&B hit (4 weeks)	Mercury 71478
10/26/59	6	13	5. **So Many Ways** #1 R&B hit (3 weeks)	Mercury 71512
2/8/60	5	12	● 6. **Baby (You've Got What It Takes)** **DINAH WASHINGTON & BROOK BENTON** #1 R&B hit (10 weeks)	Mercury 71565
5/9/60	37	1	7. The Ties That Bind	Mercury 71566
6/6/60	7	10	8. **A Rockin' Good Way (To Mess Around And Fall In Love)** **DINAH WASHINGTON & BROOK BENTON** #1 R&B hit (4 weeks); first recorded by The Spaniels in 1958	Mercury 71629
8/22/60	7	13	9. **Kiddio /** #1 R&B hit (9 weeks); first recorded by Teddy Randazzo in 1957	
8/29/60	16	10	10. The Same One	Mercury 71652
11/21/60	24	7	11. Fools Rush In (Where Angels Fear To Tread) #3 hit for Glenn Miller in 1940	Mercury 71722
2/27/61	11	9	12. Think Twice /	
3/20/61	28	1	13. For My Baby	Mercury 71774
6/5/61	2 (3)	12	14. **The Boll Weevil Song** **[N]** #1 Adult Contemporary hit (3 weeks); The Mike Stewart Singers (backing vocals)	Mercury 71820
9/4/61	20	4	15. Frankie And Johnny	Mercury 71859
12/18/61+	15	5	16. Revenge	Mercury 71903
1/27/62	19	5	17. Shadrack	Mercury 71912
9/15/62	13	6	18. Lie To Me	Mercury 72024
12/8/62+	3	10	19. **Hotel Happiness**	Mercury 72055
4/6/63	28	4	20. I Got What I Wanted	Mercury 72099

DATE	POS	WKS	ARTIST–RECORD TITLE	LABEL & NO.
7/13/63	**22**	4	21. My True Confession	Mercury 72135
10/5/63	**32**	5	22. Two Tickets To Paradise	Mercury 72177
2/15/64	**35**	3	23. Going Going Gone	Mercury 72230
1/31/70	**4**	12	● 24. **Rainy Night In Georgia**	Cotillion 44057
			#1 R&B hit (1 week); written by Tony Joe White	

BERLIN

Electro-pop group from Los Angeles, California: Terri Nunn (vocals), Rick Olsen (guitar), Matt Reid and David Diamond (keyboards), John Crawford (bass) and Rob Brill (drums). Pared down to a trio in 1985 with Nunn, Crawford and Brill.

DATE	POS	WKS	ARTIST–RECORD TITLE	LABEL & NO.
4/7/84	**23**	8	1. No More Words	Geffen 29360
7/19/86	**1** (1)	13	● 2. **Take My Breath Away** Sales #1 (1) / Airplay #2	Columbia 05903
			love theme from the movie *Top Gun* starring Tom Cruise	

BERNARD, Rod

Born on 8/12/40 in Opelousas, Louisiana. Rock and roll singer/guitarist.

DATE	POS	WKS	ARTIST–RECORD TITLE	LABEL & NO.
3/23/59	**20**	9	1. This Should Go On Forever	Argo 5327

BERNSTEIN, Elmer, and Orchestra

Born on 4/4/22 in Manhattan, New York. Composer/conductor for numerous movies.

DATE	POS	WKS	ARTIST–RECORD TITLE	LABEL & NO.
3/24/56	**16**	9	1. "Main Title" From "The Man With The Golden Arm" Best Seller #16 / Top 100 #32 **[I]**	Decca 29869
			Shelly Manne (drums); title song from the movie *The Man With The Golden Arm* starring Frank Sinatra	

BERRY, Chuck

Born on 10/18/26 in St. Louis, Missouri. Highly influential singer/songwriter/guitarist. Appeared in several movies. Won Grammy's Lifetime Achievement Award in 1984. Inducted into the Rock and Roll Hall of Fame in 1986. Movie documentary/concert tribute to Berry, *Hail! Hail! Rock 'N' Roll*, released in 1987.

DATE	POS	WKS	ARTIST–RECORD TITLE	LABEL & NO.
8/20/55	**5**	11	1. **Maybellene** Best Seller #5 / Juke Box #6 / Jockey #13 / Top 100 #42	Chess 1604
			#1 R&B hit (11 weeks)	
6/30/56	**29**	1	2. Roll Over Beethoven Top 100 #29	Chess 1626
			CHUCK BERRY and His Combo (above 2)	
4/20/57	**3**	15	3. **School Day** Best Seller #3 / Top 100 #5 / Jockey #6 / Juke Box #7	Chess 1653
			#1 R&B hit (5 weeks); some pressings show title as "School Day (Ring! Ring! Goes The Bell)"	
11/11/57	**8**	13	4. **Rock & Roll Music** Top 100 #8 / Best Seller #9	Chess 1671
2/24/58	**2** (3)	11	5. **Sweet Little Sixteen** Best Seller #2 / Top 100 #2 / Jockey #5	Chess 1683
			#1 R&B hit (3 weeks)	
5/5/58	**8**	11	6. **Johnny B. Goode** Top 100 #8 / Best Seller #9 / Jockey #16	Chess 1691
9/15/58	**18**	5	7. Carol Hot 100 #18 / Best Seller #29	Chess 1700
4/20/59	**32**	7	8. Almost Grown	Chess 1722
7/13/59	**37**	1	9. Back In The U.S.A.	Chess 1729
4/4/64	**23**	5	10. Nadine (Is It You?)	Chess 1883
6/13/64	**10**	7	11. **No Particular Place To Go**	Chess 1898
8/22/64	**14**	5	12. You Never Can Tell	Chess 1906
9/9/72	**1** (2)	12	● 13. **My Ding-A-Ling** **[L-N]**	Chess 2131
			Average White Band (backing band); first recorded by Berry in 1966 as "My Tambourine"	

DATE	POS	WKS	ARTIST–RECORD TITLE	LABEL & NO.
1/6/73	**27**	7	14. Reelin' & Rockin' [L] above 2 recorded in Coventry, England	Chess 2136
			BETTER THAN EZRA	
			Rock trio from New Orleans, Louisiana: Kevin Griffin (vocals, guitar), Tom Drummond (bass) and Cary Bonnecaze (drums).	
7/1/95	**30**	11	1. Good Airplay #21 / Sales #40 #1 Modern Rock hit (5 weeks)	Elektra 64428
			BEWITCHED — see B*WITCHED	
			BEYONCÉ	
			Born Beyoncé Knowles on 9/4/81 in Houston, Texas. R&B singer/songwriter/actress. Member of Destiny's Child. Acted in the movies *Austin Powers In Goldmember* and *The Fighting Temptations*.	
5/31/03	**1 (8)**	24	1. **Crazy In Love** Airplay #1 (8) / Sales #11 **BEYONCÉ (Featuring Jay-Z)** #1 R&B hit (3 weeks); samples "Are You My Woman? (Tell Me So)" by The Chi-Lites	Columbia 79949
8/23/03	**1 (9)**	26	2. **Baby Boy** Airplay #1 (9) **BEYONCÉ feat. Sean Paul** #1 R&B hit (5 weeks)	Columbia 76867
12/6/03+	**4**	19	3. **Me, Myself And I** Sales #1 (3) / Airplay #4	Columbia 76911
			B-52's, The	
			New-wave dance group from Athens, Georgia: Fred Schneider (vocals, keyboards), Kate Pierson (vocals, organ), Cindy Wilson (vocals, guitar) and Keith Strickland (guitar). Wilson left in 1991. Group appeared as the B.C. 52's in the movie *The Flintstones*. B-52 is slang for the bouffant hairstyle worn by Kate and Cindy.	
9/30/89	**3**	17	● 1. **Love Shack** Sales #2 / Airplay #6 #1 Modern Rock hit (4 weeks)	Reprise 22817
1/20/90	**3**	13	● 2. **Roam** Sales #2 / Airplay #2	Reprise 22667
5/19/90	**30**	4	3. Deadbeat Club Airplay #25	Reprise 19938
7/4/92	**28**	7	4. Good Stuff Airplay #25 / Sales #46 #1 Modern Rock hit (4 weeks)	Reprise 18895
6/11/94	**33**	1	5. (Meet) The Flintstones Airplay #32 / Sales #50 [N] **the B.C. 52's** from the movie *The Flintstones* starring John Goodman (theme song of the TV series)	MCA 54839
			B.G.	
			Born Christopher Dorsey in 1980 in New Orleans, Louisiana. Male rapper. B.G.: Baby Gangsta.	
10/30/99	**36**	5	1. Bling Bling Airplay #25 / Sales #72 **B.G. Feat. Baby, Turk, Mannie Fresh, Juvenile and Lil Wayne**	Cash Money 156483
			BIG AUDIO DYNAMITE II	
			Rock group from England: Mick Jones (vocals, guitar), Nick Hawkins (guitar), Gary Stonadge (bass) and Chris Kavanagh (drums). Jones was co-founder of The Clash; not to be confused with Mick Jones of Foreigner.	
11/2/91	**32**	4	1. Rush Sales #53 / Airplay #75 #1 Modern Rock hit (4 weeks)	Columbia 73987

DATE	POS	WKS	ARTIST–RECORD TITLE	LABEL & NO.
			BIG BOPPER	
			Born Jiles Perry Richardson on 10/24/30 in Sabine Pass, Texas. DJ at KTRM in Beaumont, Texas. Wrote "Running Bear" for Johnny Preston. Died with Buddy Holly and Ritchie Valens in the 2/3/59 plane crash (age 28).	
8/4/58	6	22	1. **Chantilly Lace** Hot 100 #6 / Best Seller #13 **[N]**	Mercury 71343
12/22/58	38	1	2. Big Bopper's Wedding **[N]**	Mercury 71375
			BIG BROTHER & THE HOLDING COMPANY — see JOPLIN, Janis	
			BIG COUNTRY	
			Pop-rock group from Dunfermline, Scotland: Stuart Adamson (vocals, guitar), Bruce Watson (guitar), Tony Butler (bass) and Mark Brzezicki (drums). Adamson committed suicide on 12/16/2001 (age 43).	
11/12/83	17	9	1. In A Big Country	Mercury 814467
			BIG MOUNTAIN	
			Multi-cultural reggae group from San Diego, California: Quino (vocals, guitar), Jerome Cruz (guitar), Manfred Reinke (keyboards), Gregory Blakney (percussion), Lynn Copeland (bass) and Lance Rhodes (drums).	
3/19/94	6	24	● 1. **Baby, I Love Your Way** Airplay #2 / Sales #12 from the movie *Reality Bites* starring Winona Ryder	RCA 62780
			BIG PUNISHER	
			Born Christopher Rios on 11/9/71 in the Bronx, New York. Died of a heart attack on 2/7/2000 (age 28). Male rapper.	
6/13/98	24	19	1. Still Not A Player Airplay #23 **BIG PUNISHER (Featuring Joe)**	Loud/RCA 65478
			BIG TYMERS	
			Rap duo from New Orleans, Louisiana: Mannie Fresh and Bryan "Baby" Williams. Members of Cash Money Millionaires.	
6/1/02	11	17	1. Still Fly Airplay #11 / Sales #28	Cash Money 060072
1/4/03	33	4	2. Do That... Sales #22 / Airplay #33 **BABY (AKA DA #1 STUNNA) Featuring P. Diddy**	Cash Money 060079
			BILK, Mr. Acker	
			Born Bernard Stanley Bilk on 1/28/29 in Pensford, Somerset, England. Clarinet player.	
4/7/62	1 (1)	15	● 1. **Stranger On The Shore** **[I]** #1 Adult Contemporary hit (7 weeks); title song from the British TV show starring Richard Vernon; originally titled "Jenny"	Atco 6217
			BILLY & LILLIE	
			Vocal duo of Billy Ford (born on 3/9/25 in Bloomfield, New Jersey) and Lillie Bryant (born on 2/14/40 in Newburg, New York).	
1/13/58	9	10	1. **La Dee Dah** Top 100 #9 / Best Seller #10 / Jockey #23	Swan 4002
1/5/59	14	8	2. Lucky Ladybug	Swan 4020
			BILLY & THE BEATERS — see VERA, Billy	

DATE	POS	WKS	ARTIST–RECORD TITLE	LABEL & NO.
			BILLY JOE & THE CHECKMATES	
			Born Louis Bideu on 3/21/19 in El Paso, Texas. Worked as a comedian. Hosted own local *Lew Bedell Show* in New York. Dubbed himself Billy Joe Hunter in the early 1960s.	
2/17/62	**10**	7	1. **Percolator (Twist)** [I] based on the "perky" tune used in a Maxwell House coffee jingle	Dore 620
			BINGOBOYS	
			Dance trio of DJs from Vienna, Austria: Klaus Biedermann, Paul Pfab and Helmut Wolfgruber. Princessa is a female rapper from New York.	
3/16/91	**25**	6	1. How To Dance Sales #23 / Airplay #31 **BINGOBOYS Featuring Princessa** samples "Dance, Dance, Dance" by Chic, "Dance (Disco Heat)" by Sylvester and "Kiss" by The Art Of Noise	Atlantic 87756
			BISHOP, Elvin	
			Born on 10/21/42 in Tulsa, Oklahoma. Lead guitarist with The Paul Butterfield Blues Band (1965-68).	
4/3/76	**3**	12	● 1. **Fooled Around And Fell In Love** Mickey Thomas (of Starship; lead vocal)	Capricorn 0252
			BISHOP, Stephen	
			Born on 11/14/51 in San Diego, California. Pop-rock singer/songwriter. Wrote several movie themes. Cameo role as the "Charming Guy With Guitar" in *National Lampoon's Animal House*.	
1/22/77	**22**	7	1. Save It For A Rainy Day Chaka Khan (background vocal); Eric Clapton (guitar solo)	ABC 12232
7/23/77	**11**	15	2. On And On	ABC 12260
10/28/78	**32**	5	3. Everybody Needs Love	ABC 12406
4/2/83	**25**	8	4. It Might Be You #1 Adult Contemporary hit (2 weeks); theme from the movie *Tootsie* starring Dustin Hoffman	Warner 29791
			BIZ MARKIE	
			Born Marcel Hall on 4/8/64 in Harlem. Rapper/actor. Appeared in the movie *The Meteor Man*.	
2/10/90	**9**	11	▲ 1. **Just A Friend** Sales #5 / Airplay #19	Cold Chillin' 22784
			BLACK('S), Bill, Combo	
			Born on 9/17/26 in Memphis, Tennessee. Died of a brain tumor on 10/21/65 (age 39). White bass guitarist/songwriter. Session work in Memphis; backed Elvis Presley (with Scotty Moore, guitar; D.J. Fontana, drums) on most of his early records. Formed own band in 1959. Labeled as "The Untouchable Sound." Larry Rogers and Bob Tucker led group after Black's death; recorded well into the 1970s.	
12/21/59+	**17**	8	● 1. Smokie — Part 2 [I] #1 R&B hit (4 weeks)	Hi 2018
3/21/60	**9**	11	● 2. **White Silver Sands** [I] #1 R&B hit (4 weeks)	Hi 2021
7/4/60	**18**	8	● 3. Josephine [I] #3 hit for Wayne King's Orchestra in 1937	Hi 2022
10/3/60	**11**	9	4. Don't Be Cruel [I] Black played bass on Elvis Presley's original 1956 hit	Hi 2026

DATE	POS	WKS	ARTIST–RECORD TITLE	LABEL & NO.
12/12/60	**16**	7	5. Blue Tango **[I]** #1 hit for Leroy Anderson in 1952	Hi 2027
3/6/61	**20**	4	6. Hearts Of Stone **[I]**	Hi 2028
6/26/61	**25**	4	7. Ole Buttermilk Sky **[I]** written and popularized in 1946 by Hoagy Carmichael	Hi 2036
1/20/62	**26**	4	8. Twist-Her **[I]**	Hi 2042
			BLACK, Cilla	
			Born Priscilla White on 5/27/43 in Liverpool, England.	
7/25/64	**26**	4	1. You're My World	Capitol 5196
			BLACK, Clint	
			Born on 2/4/62 in Long Branch, New Jersey; raised in Houston, Texas. Country singer/guitarist. Married actress Lisa Hartman on 10/20/91.	
11/27/99	**31**	4	1. When I Said I Do Airplay #19 **CLINT BLACK (with Lisa Hartman Black)** #1 Country hit (2 weeks); from the album *D'lectrified* on RCA 67823	album cut
			BLACK, Jeanne	
			Born Gloria Jeanne Black on 10/25/37 in Pomona, California. Country-pop singer.	
5/2/60	**4**	10	● 1. **He'll Have To Stay** answer song to "He'll Have To Go" by Jim Reeves	Capitol 4368
			BLACK BOX	
			Male Italian dance trio of producer Daniele Davoli and musicians Mirko Limoni and Valerio Semplici. Martha Wash is the uncredited lead vocalist on all of the group's hits.	
9/1/90	**8**	12	1. **Everybody Everybody** Sales #5 / Airplay #15	RCA 2628
1/19/91	**23**	4	2. I Don't Know Anybody Else Sales #15	RCA 2735
4/27/91	**8**	12	3. **Strike It Up** Airplay #10 / Sales #14	RCA 2794
			BLACKBYRDS, The	
			R&B group from Washington DC. Core members: Donald Byrd (trumpet), Joe Hall (vocals, bass), Kevin Toney (vocals, keyboards) and Keith Killgo (vocals, drums).	
3/15/75	**6**	12	1. **Walking In Rhythm**	Fantasy 736
4/17/76	**19**	6	2. Happy Music	Fantasy 762
			BLACK CROWES, The	
			Rock group from Atlanta: brothers Chris (vocals) and Rich (guitar) Robinson, with Jeff Cease (guitar), Johnny Colt (bass) and Steve Gorman (drums). Chris Robinson married actress Kate Hudson (daughter of Goldie Hawn) on 12/31/2000.	
4/20/91	**30**	7	1. **She Talks To Angels** Airplay #28 / Sales #33 #1 Mainstream Rock hit (1 week)	Def American 19403
7/20/91	**26**	6	2. Hard To Handle **[R]** #1 Mainstream Rock hit (2 weeks); originally charted at #45 in 1990	Def American 19245

DATE	POS	WKS	ARTIST–RECORD TITLE	LABEL & NO.
			BLACK EYED PEAS	
			Hip-hop group from Los Angeles, California: WIll Adams (will.i.am), Allan Pineda (apl.de.ap), Jaime Gomez (taboo) and Stacey Ferguson (fergie). Ferguson was a member of Wild Orchid.	
6/28/03	8	22	1. **Where Is The Love?** Airplay #9 Justin Timberlake (guest vocal)	A&M 000714
			BLACKFOOT	
			Rock group from Jacksonville, Florida: Rickey Medlocke (vocals, guitar), Charlie Hargrett (guitar), Greg Walker (bass) and Jakson Spires (drums).	
8/4/79	26	6	1. Highway Song	Atco 7104
12/22/79	38	4	2. Train, Train	Atco 7207
			BLACK OAK ARKANSAS	
			Rock group from Black Oak, Arkansas: Jim "Dandy" Mangrum (vocals), Ricky Reynolds, Jimmy Henderson and Stan Knight (guitars), Pat Daugherty (bass) and Wayne Evans (drums).	
1/26/74	25	6	1. Jim Dandy Ruby Starr (female vocal)	Atco 6948
			BLACKOUT ALLSTARS, The	
			All-star Latin group: Ray Barretto, Sheila E, Tito Puente, Tito Nieves, Paquito D'Rivera, Dave Valentin and Grover Washington Jr. Washington died of a heart attack on 12/17/99 (age 56). Puente died of heart failure on 5/31/2000 (age 77).	
1/25/97	25	9	1. I Like It Airplay #26 / Sales #46 recorded for the 1994 movie *I Like It Like That* starring Lauren Velez; renewed popularity due to inclusion in a Burger King commercial	Columbia 78455
			BLACK ROB	
			Born Robert Ross in 1970 in Harlem, New York. Male rapper.	
9/1/01	33	3	1. Bad Boy For Life Airplay #30 / Sales #49 **P. DIDDY, BLACK ROB & MARK CURRY**	Bad Boy 79400
			BLACKstreet	
			R&B/hip-hop group: Teddy Riley, Chauncey Hannibal, Levi Little and David Hollister. Little and Hollister left in late 1995; replaced by Eric Williams and Mark Middleton.	
8/13/94	34	2	1. Booti Call Sales #21 / Airplay #71 samples "Atomic Dog" by George Clinton and "Heartbreaker" by Zapp	Interscope 98255
11/19/94+	7	21	2. **Before I Let You Go** Sales #5 / Airplay #14	Interscope 98211
10/19/96	1 (4)	26	▲ 3. **No Diggity** Sales #1 (6) / Airplay #9 **BLACKstreet (Featuring Dr. Dre)** #1 R&B hit (4 weeks); Queen Pen (female rap); samples "Grandma's Hands" by Bill Withers	Interscope 97007
3/8/97	12 ᴬ	23	4. Don't Leave Me #1 R&B Airplay hit (3 weeks); from the album *Another Level* on Interscope 90071	album cut
5/23/98	3	12	● 5. **I Get Lonely** Sales #2 / Airplay #24 **JANET (Featuring BLACKstreet)** #1 R&B hit (2 weeks)	Virgin 38631

DATE	POS	WKS	ARTIST–RECORD TITLE	LABEL & NO.
12/12/98+	**14**	11	6. Take Me There <div align="right">Airplay #8</div>**BLACKSTREET & MYA featuring MA$E & BLINKY BLINK** samples "I Want You Back" by The Jackson 5; from the animated movie *The RugRats Movie*	album cut
			BLANCHARD, Jack, & Misty Morgan	
			Husband-and-wife country duo. Both born in Buffalo, New York. Jack (born on 5/8/42) plays saxophone and keyboards. Misty (born on 5/23/45) plays keyboards. Met and married while working in Florida.	
3/28/70	23	8	1. Tennessee Bird Walk <div align="right">**[N]**</div>#1 Country hit (2 weeks)	Wayside 010
			BLAND, Billy	
			Born on 4/5/32 in Wilmington, North Carolina. R&B singer.	
3/28/60	7	13	1. **Let The Little Girl Dance**	Old Town 1076
			BLAND, Bobby	
			Born on 1/27/30 in Rosemark, Tennessee. Blues singer/guitarist. Nicknamed "Blue." Inducted into the Rock and Roll Hall of Fame in 1992. Won Grammy's Lifetime Acievement Award in 1997.	
1/20/62	28	3	1. Turn On Your Love Light	Duke 344
2/2/63	22	7	2. Call On Me /	
2/9/63	33	5	3. That's The Way Love Is #1 R&B hit (2 weeks)	Duke 360
3/28/64	20	6	4. Ain't Nothing You Can Do	Duke 375
			BLANE, Marcie	
			Born on 5/21/44 in Brooklyn, New York. Pop singer.	
11/10/62	3	13	1. **Bobby's Girl**	Seville 120
			BLAQUE	
			Female R&B vocal trio from Atlanta, Georgia: Shamari Fears, Natina Reed and Brandi Williams.	
5/8/99	8	15	● 1. **808** <div align="right">Sales #4 / Airplay #22</div>	Track Masters 78857
11/20/99+	5	24	2. **Bring It All To Me** <div align="right">Airplay #4</div>**BLAQUE (Feat. *NSYNC)** from the album *Blaque* on Track Masters 68987	album cut
			BLESSID UNION OF SOULS	
			Interracial Adult Alternative group from Cincinnati, Ohio: Eliot Sloan (vocals, piano), Jeff Pence (guitar), Charly Roth (keyboards), Tony Clark (bass) and Eddie Hedges (drums). Group name taken from a line in the TV show *M*A*S*H*.	
3/25/95	8	23	1. **I Believe** <div align="right">Airplay #3 / Sales #14</div>	EMI 58320
9/23/95	29	10	2. **Let Me Be The One** <div align="right">Airplay #28 / Sales #66</div>	EMI 58443
7/5/97	39	2	3. **I Wanna Be There** <div align="right">Airplay #47 / Sales #55</div>	EMI 58643
8/7/99	33	4	4. **Hey Leonardo (she likes me for me)** <div align="right">Airplay #28</div>from the album *Walking Off The Buzz* on Push 27047	album cut

DATE	POS	WKS	ARTIST–RECORD TITLE	LABEL & NO.
			BLEYER, Archie	
			Born on 6/12/09 in Corona, New York. Died of Parkinson's disease on 3/20/89 (age 79). Arranger/music director for the radio and TV show *Arthur Godfrey and His Friends* from 1949-54. Founded Cadence Records. Married Chordettes member Janet Ertel in 1954.	
12/4/54+	17	6	1. The Naughty Lady Of Shady Lane Jockey #17 / Juke Box #20 / Best Seller #26	Cadence 1254
			BLIGE, Mary J.	
			Born Mary Jane Blige on 1/11/71 in Atlanta, Georgia; raised in Yonkers, New York. R&B singer/songwriter.	
8/1/92	29	6	● 1. You Remind Me Sales #17 / Airplay #37 #1 R&B hit (1 week); from the movie *Strictly Business* starring Tommy Davidson	Uptown/MCA 54327
9/26/92	7	23	● 2. **Real Love** Airplay #4 / Sales #12 #1 R&B hit (2 weeks)	Uptown/MCA 54455
2/20/93	28	9	3. Sweet Thing Airplay #16 / Sales #43	Uptown/MCA 54586
12/3/94	29	8	4. Be Happy Sales #21 / Airplay #48 samples "You're Too Good To Me" by Curtis Mayfield	Uptown/MCA 54927
4/15/95	22	6	5. I'm Goin' Down Sales #11 / Airplay #22	Uptown/MCA 55008
5/13/95	3	13	▲ 6. **I'll Be There For You/You're All I Need To Get By** Sales #1 (1) / Airplay #33 **METHOD MAN featuring Mary J. Blige** #1 R&B hit (3 weeks); medley of 2 songs written by Ashford & Simpson	Def Jam 851878
2/3/96	2 (2)	17	▲ 7. **Not Gon' Cry** Sales #1 (5) / Airplay #19 #1 R&B hit (5 weeks); from the movie *Waiting To Exhale* starring Whitney Houston	Arista 12957
7/26/97	28	6	8. I Can Love You Sales #18 / Airplay #75 samples "Queen Bitch" by Lil' Kim	MCA 55362
9/27/97	24	10	9. Everything Sales #23 / Airplay #40 samples "You Are Everything" by The Stylistics, "The Payback" by James Brown and "Sukiyaki" by A Taste Of Honey	MCA 55353
11/25/00	38	2	10. 911 Airplay #30 / Sales #61 **WYCLEF JEAN Featuring Mary J. Blige** samples "The Payback" by James Brown and "What I Am" by Edie Brickell & New Bohemians	Columbia 79460
8/18/01	1 (6)	36	11. **Family Affair** Airplay #1 (5) / Sales #4 #1 R&B hit (2 weeks)	MCA 155894
1/26/02	15	9	12. No More Drama Airplay #15 / Sales #24 samples "Nadia's Theme (The Young And The Restless)" by Barry DeVorzon & Perry Botkin, Jr.	MCA 155929
4/13/02	12	14	13. Rainy Dayz Airplay #10 / Sales #60 **MARY J. BLIGE Featuring Ja Rule**	MCA 155972
7/19/03	22	6	14. Love @ 1st Sight Sales #5 / Airplay #22 **MARY J. BLIGE featuring Method Man** samples "Hot Sex" by A Tribe Called Quest	Geffen 000954
10/11/03	29	3	15. Ooh! Airplay #27 samples "Singing This Song For My Mother" by Hamilton Bohannon; from the album *Love & Life* on Geffen 95602	album cut

DATE	POS	WKS	ARTIST–RECORD TITLE	LABEL & NO.
			BLIND MELON	
			Male rock group formed in Los Angeles, California: Shannon Hoon (vocals), Rogers Stevens and Christopher Thorn (guitars), Brad Smith (bass) and Glen Graham (drums). Stevens, Smith and Graham are from West Point, Mississippi. Hoon died of a drug overdose on 10/21/95 (age 28).	
10/9/93	**20**	11	1. No Rain Airplay #16 / Sales #66	Capitol 15994
			#1 Mainstream Rock hit (2 weeks) / #1 Modern Rock hit (3 weeks)	
			BLINK-182	
			Punk-rock trio from San Diego, California: Tom DeLonge (vocals, guitar), Mark Hoppus (vocals, bass) and Travis Barker (drums).	
1/22/00	**6**	14	1. **All The Small Things** Sales #5 / Airplay #18	MCA 155606
			#1 Modern Rock hit (8 weeks)	
			BLONDIE	
			New-wave rock group formed in Brooklyn, New York: Debbie Harry (vocals), Chris Stein and Frank Infante (guitars), Jimmy Destri (keyboards), Nigel Harrison (bass) and Clem Burke (drums).	
3/17/79	**1** (1)	14	● 1. **Heart Of Glass**	Chrysalis 2295
6/30/79	**24**	7	2. One Way Or Another	Chrysalis 2336
11/3/79	**27**	6	3. Dreaming	Chrysalis 2379
3/8/80	**1** (6)	19	● 4. **Call Me**	Chrysalis 2414
			theme from the movie *American Gigolo* starring Richard Gere	
6/21/80	**39**	3	5. Atomic	Chrysalis 2410
11/29/80+	**1** (1)	17	● 6. **The Tide Is High**	Chrysalis 2465
2/14/81	**1** (2)	14	● 7. **Rapture**	Chrysalis 2485
6/26/82	**37**	3	8. Island Of Lost Souls	Chrysalis 2603
			BLOODROCK	
			Rock group from Fort Worth, Texas: Jim Rutledge (vocals), Lee Pickens and Nick Taylor (guitars), Stevie Hill (keyboards), Eddie Grundy (bass) and Rick Cobb (drums).	
2/27/71	**36**	2	1. D.O.A.	Capitol 3009
			BLOODSTONE	
			R&B vocal group from Kansas City, Missouri: Charles Love, Willis Draffen, Charles McCormick and Harry Williams. Group starred in the 1975 movie *Train Ride To Hollywood*. Draffen died on 2/8/2002 (age 56).	
6/9/73	**10**	12	▲ 1. **Natural High**	London 1046
4/6/74	**34**	4	2. Outside Woman	London 1052
			BLOOD, SWEAT & TEARS	
			Brassy pop-rock group formed in New York: David Clayton-Thomas (vocals), Steve Katz (guitar), Jim Fielder (bass) and Bobby Colomby (drums).	
3/15/69	**2** (3)	11	● 1. **You've Made Me So Very Happy**	Columbia 44776
6/7/69	**2** (3)	12	● 2. **Spinning Wheel**	Columbia 44871
			#1 Adult Contemporary hit (2 weeks)	
10/25/69	**2** (1)	12	● 3. **And When I Die**	Columbia 45008
			written by Laura Nyro	
8/15/70	**14**	6	4. Hi-De-Ho	Columbia 45204
10/10/70	**29**	6	5. Lucretia Mac Evil	Columbia 45235
8/14/71	**32**	5	6. Go Down Gamblin'	Columbia 45427

DATE	POS	WKS	ARTIST—RECORD TITLE	LABEL & NO.
			BLOOM, Bobby	
10/17/70	8	11	Born in 1945 in Brooklyn, New York. Died from an accidental shooting on 2/28/74 (age 28). Pop singer/songwriter. Much session work in the 1960s. 1. **Montego Bay**	L&R/MGM 157
			BLOW MONKEYS, The	
6/14/86	14	10	Pop-rock group from England: "Dr. Robert" Howard (vocals, guitar), Neville Henry (saxophone), Mick Anker (bass) and Tony Kiley (drums). 1. Digging Your Scene Sales #12 / Airplay #16	RCA 14325
			BLUE-BELLES, The—see LaBELLE, Patti/STARLETS	
			BLUE CHEER	
3/23/68	14	10	Hard-rock trio from San Francisco, California: Dickie Peterson (vocals, bass), Leigh Stephens (guitar) and Paul Whaley (drums). Considered to be the first "heavy metal" band. 1. Summertime Blues	Philips 40516
			BLUE HAZE	
12/23/72+	27	7	Reggae studio group assembled in England by producers Johnny Arthey and Phil Swern. 1. Smoke Gets In Your Eyes #1 hit for Paul Whiteman in 1934	A&M 1357
			BLUE JAYS, The	
9/4/61	31	4	R&B vocal group from Los Angeles, California: Leon Peels, Van Richardson, Alex Manigo and Leonard Davidson. Peels died of cancer on 4/12/99 (age 62). 1. Lover's Island	Milestone 2008
			BLUE MAGIC	
6/8/74	8	15	R&B vocal group from Philadelphia, Pennsylvania: Theodore Mills, Vernon Sawyer, Wendell Sawyer, Keith Beaton and Richard Pratt. ● 1. Sideshow #1 R&B hit (1 week)	Atco 6961
11/23/74	36	2	2. Three Ring Circus	Atco 7004
			BLUE ÖYSTER CULT	
9/4/76	12	14	Hard-rock group from Long Island, New York: Eric Bloom (vocals), Donald "Buck Dharma" Roeser (guitar), Allen Lanier (keyboards), and brothers Joe (bass) and Albert (drums) Bouchard. 1. (Don't Fear) The Reaper	Columbia 10384
10/3/81	40	3	2. Burnin' For You #1 Mainstream Rock hit (2 weeks)	Columbia 02415
			BLUE RIDGE RANGERS — see FOGERTY, John	

DATE	POS	WKS	ARTIST–RECORD TITLE	LABEL & NO.
			BLUES BROTHERS	
			Duo of comedians John Belushi (as "Jake Blues") and Dan Aykroyd (as "Elwood Blues"). Originally created for TV's *Saturday Night Live*. Starred in their own movie. Belushi was born on 1/24/49 in Wheaton, Illinois; died of a drug overdose on 3/5/82 (age 33). Aykroyd was born on 7/1/52 in Ottawa, Ontario, Canada. Backing band included Paul Shaffer, Steve Cropper and Donald "Duck" Dunn.	
1/6/79	**14**	9	1. Soul Man **[L]**	Atlantic 3545
3/31/79	**37**	3	2. Rubber Biscuit **[L-N]**	Atlantic 3564
			first recorded by The Chips in 1956; above 2 recorded at the Universal Ampitheater in Los Angeles	
6/21/80	**18**	8	3. Gimme Some Lovin'	Atlantic 3666
			from the movie *The Blues Brothers*	
1/31/81	**39**	2	4. Who's Making Love	Atlantic 3785
			BLUES IMAGE	
			Rock group from Tampa, Florida: Mike Pinera (vocals, guitar), Frank Konte (keyboards), Joe Lala (percussion), Malcolm Jones (bass) and Manuel Bertematti (drums). Pinera later joined Iron Butterfly.	
5/23/70	**4**	12	● 1. **Ride Captain Ride**	Atco 6746
			BLUES MAGOOS	
			Psychedelic-rock group from the Bronx, New York: Emil "Peppy Castro" Thielhelm (vocals, guitar), Mike Esposito (guitar), Ralph Scala (keyboards), Ronnie Gilbert (bass) and Geoff Daking (drums). Castro later became lead singer of Balance.	
1/7/67	**5**	10	1. **(We Ain't Got) Nothin' Yet**	Mercury 72622
			BLUE STARS	
			Pop-jazz group formed in Paris, France. Lead vocals by Blossom Dearie (born on 4/28/26 in East Durham, New York).	
2/4/56	**16**	7	1. Lullaby Of Birdland	Mercury 70742
			Jockey #16 / Best Seller #20 / Top 100 #20 **[F]**	
			BLUES TRAVELER	
			Blues-rock group formed in New York: John Popper (vocals, harmonica), Chan Kinchla (guitar), Bobby Sheehan (bass) and Brendan Hill (drums). Sheehan died of a drug overdose on 8/20/99 (age 31); replaced by Chan's brother, Tad Kinchla.	
5/20/95	**8**	36	1. **Run-Around** Airplay #3 / Sales #27	A&M 0982
12/30/95+	**23**	18	2. Hook Airplay #18 / Sales #50	A&M 1176
8/31/96	**36** A	3	3. But Anyway **[L]**	album cut
			from the album *Live From The Fall* on A&M 0515	
			BLUE SWEDE	
			Pop group from Sweden: Bjorn Skifs (vocals), Michael Areklew (guitar), Anders Berglund (keyboards), Hinke Ekestubbe (sax), Thomas Berglund (trumpet), Bosse Liljedahl (bass) and Jan Guldback (drums).	
3/2/74	**1** (1)	14	● 1. **Hooked On A Feeling**	EMI 3627
9/7/74	**7**	8	2. **Never My Love**	EMI 3938

DATE	POS	WKS	ARTIST–RECORD TITLE	LABEL & NO.
			BMU (BLACK MEN UNITED)	
			All-star gathering of top R&B singers: R. Kelly, Tevin Campbell, Aaron Hall, Brian McKnight, Boyz II Men, Tony Toni Toné, Silk, Keith Sweat, Stokley, H-Town, Christopher Williams, Portrait, Gerald Levert, Al B. Sure!, Damion Hall, Lil' Joe, Intro, D.R.S., El DeBarge, After 7, Usher, Savory, Joe, D'Angelo and Lenny Kravitz (guitar).	
11/5/94	**28**	6	1. U Will Know Sales #12 from the movie *Jason's Lyric* starring Forest Whitaker	Mercury 856200
			BOBBETTES, The	
			Female R&B vocal group from Harlem, New York: sisters Emma and Jannie Pought, Laura Webb, Helen Gathers and Heather Dixon. Jannie Pought died in a car crash in September 1980 (age 36). Webb died of cancer on 1/8/2001 (age 59).	
8/12/57	**6**	14	1. **Mr. Lee** Top 100 #6 / Jockey #6 / Best Seller #7 #1 R&B hit (4 weeks)	Atlantic 1144
			BOB B. SOXX And The Blue Jeans	
			Vocal trio formed in Los Angeles: Bobby Sheen, Darlene Love and Fanita James. Sheen died of pneumonia on 11/23/2000 (age 58).	
12/8/62+	**8**	9	1. **Zip-A-Dee Doo-Dah** song introduced in the 1947 movie *Song of the South*	Philles 107
3/23/63	**38**	3	2. Why Do Lovers Break Each Other's Heart?	Philles 110
			BoDEANS	
			Folk-rock group from Waukesha, Wisconsin: Sam Llanas and Kurt Neumann (vocals, guitars), Bob Griffin (bass) and Nick Kitsos (drums).	
3/9/96	**16**	15	1. Closer To Free Airplay #6 featured in the TV show *Party Of Five* starring Neve Campbell	Slash 17674
			BOLTON, Michael	
			Born Michael Bolotin on 2/26/53 in New Haven, Connecticut. Adult Contemporary singer/songwriter. First recorded for Epic in 1968. Lead singer of rock group Blackjack in the late 1970s. Began recording as Michael Bolton in 1983.	
11/7/87	**19**	10	1. That's What Love Is All About Airplay #17 / Sales #18	Columbia 7322
2/13/88	**11**	10	2. (Sittin' On) The Dock Of The Bay Sales #7 / Airplay #12	Columbia 07680
8/12/89	**17**	7	3. Soul Provider Sales #18 / Airplay #21	Columbia 68909
11/25/89+	**1 (3)**	16	4. **How Am I Supposed To Live Without You** Airplay #1 (2) / Sales #1 (1) #1 Adult Contemporary hit (2 weeks)	Columbia 73017
3/17/90	**3**	12	5. **How Can We Be Lovers** Airplay #3 / Sales #4	Columbia 73257
6/9/90	**7**	11	6. **When I'm Back On My Feet Again** Airplay #5 / Sales #14 #1 Adult Contemporary hit (3 weeks)	Columbia 73342
10/6/90	**36**	2	7. Georgia On My Mind Airplay #30 / Sales #39 Kenny G (sax solo)	Columbia 73490
4/20/91	**4**	13	8. **Love Is A Wonderful Thing** Airplay #2 / Sales #11 #1 Adult Contemporary hit (4 weeks)	Columbia 73719
7/27/91	**7**	13	9. **Time, Love And Tenderness** Airplay #15 / Sales #39 #1 Adult Contemporary hit (2 weeks)	Columbia 73889
10/19/91	**1 (1)**	16	10. **When A Man Loves A Woman** Airplay #1 (3) / Sales #8 #1 Adult Contemporary hit (4 weeks)	Columbia 74020

DATE	POS	WKS	ARTIST–RECORD TITLE	LABEL & NO.
2/8/92	**12**	12	11. Missing You Now Airplay #10 / Sales #33 **MICHAEL BOLTON Featuring Kenny G** #1 Adult Contemporary hit (3 weeks)	Columbia 74184
5/23/92	**16** A	16	12. Steel Bars written by Bolton and Bob Dylan; from the album *Time, Love & Tenderness* on Columbia 46771	album cut
11/7/92	**11**	14	13. To Love Somebody Airplay #13 / Sales #16 #1 Adult Contemporary hit (5 weeks)	Columbia 74733
11/13/93+	**6**	20	● 14. **Said I Loved You...But I Lied** Airplay #7 / Sales #10 #1 Adult Contemporary hit (12 weeks)	Columbia 77260
4/16/94	**32**	4	15. Completely Airplay #32 / Sales #51	Columbia 77376
7/2/94	**30** A	5	16. Ain't Got Nothing If You Ain't Got Love from the album *The One Thing* on Columbia 53567	album cut
9/9/95	**27**	6	17. Can I Touch You...There? Sales #26 / Airplay #36	Columbia 77991
6/14/97	**24**	11	● 18. Go The Distance Sales #16 / Airplay #62 #1 Adult Contemporary hit (3 weeks); from the animated movie *Hercules*	Columbia 78554
			BOND, Johnny	
			Born Cyrus Bond on 6/1/15 in Enville, Oklahoma. Died of a heart attack on 6/12/78 (age 63). Country singer/songwriter/actor. Acted in several western movies.	
8/22/60	**26**	7	1. Hot Rod Lincoln **[N-S]** #29 hit for Tiny Hill in 1951 (as "Hot Rod Race")	Republic 2005
			BONDS, Gary (U.S.)	
			Born Gary Anderson on 6/6/39 in Jacksonville, Florida; raised in Norfolk, Virginia. Black rock and roll singer/songwriter.	
10/31/60	**6**	11	1. **New Orleans**	Legrand 1003
6/5/61	**1** (2)	12	● 2. **Quarter To Three** **U.S. BONDS** (above 2)	Legrand 1008
7/31/61	**5**	9	3. **School Is Out**	Legrand 1009
11/6/61	**28**	2	4. School Is In	Legrand 1012
1/13/62	**9**	11	5. **Dear Lady Twist**	Legrand 1015
4/7/62	**9**	9	6. **Twist, Twist Senora**	Legrand 1018
7/7/62	**27**	4	7. Seven Day Weekend from the movie *It's Trad-Dad* starring Helen Shapiro	Legrand 1019
5/2/81	**11**	13	8. This Little Girl	EMI America 8079
7/10/82	**21**	9	9. Out Of Work Clarence Clemons (sax solo); above 2 produced by Bruce Springsteen and Miami Steve Van Zandt	EMI America 8117
			BONE CRUSHER	
			Born Wayne Hardnett on 8/23/71 in Atlanta, Georgia. Male rapper.	
5/31/03	**26**	6	1. Never Scared Airplay #24 / Sales #26 **BONE CRUSHER Featuring Killer Mike & T.I.**	Break-Em-Off 50870
			BONE THUGS-N-HARMONY	
			Male rap group from Cleveland, Ohio: Anthony Henderson ("Krayzie Bone"), Steven Howse ("Layzie Bone"), Charles Scruggs ("Wish Bone"), Bryon McCane ("Bizzy Bone") and Stanley Howse ("Flesh-N-Bone"; left in 1996). Mo Thugs Family (see #7 below): Powder, Thug Queen and Felecia.	
10/8/94	**22**	15	● 1. thuggish-ruggish-Bone Sales #10 / Airplay #53 Shatasha Williams (female vocal)	Ruthless 5527

DATE	POS	WKS	ARTIST–RECORD TITLE	LABEL & NO.
9/2/95	**14**	10	● 2. 1st Of Tha Month Sales #9 / Airplay #35	Ruthless 6331
5/11/96	**1** (8)	16	▲² 3. **Tha Crossroads** Sales #1 (9) / Airplay #8	Ruthless 6335
			#1 R&B hit (7 weeks); samples "Make Me Say It Again Girl" by The Isley Brothers	
9/28/96	**39** ᴬ	4	4. Days Of Our Livez	EastWest 64206
			from the movie *Set It Off* starring Jada Pinkett	
6/21/97	**4**	12	▲ 5. **Look Into My Eyes** Sales #2 / Airplay #72	Ruthless 6343
			from the movie *Batman & Robin* starring George Clooney	
10/25/97	**27**	12	● 6. If I Could Teach The World Sales #14	Ruthless 6344
11/21/98+	**15**	12	● 7. Ghetto Cowboy Sales #5	Mo Thugs 1707
			MO THUGS FAMILY AND BONE THUGS N HARMONY	

BONEY M

Vocal group created in Germany by producer/composer Frank Farian. Consisted of Marcia Barrett, Maizie Williams, Liz Mitchell and Bobby Farrell. All were from the West Indies. Farian created Milli Vanilli in 1988.

DATE	POS	WKS	ARTIST–RECORD TITLE	LABEL & NO.
7/22/78	**30**	6	1. Rivers Of Babylon	Sire 1027

BONHAM, Tracy

Born on 3/16/67 in Eugene, Oregon. Female rock singer/songwriter/guitarist.

DATE	POS	WKS	ARTIST–RECORD TITLE	LABEL & NO.
5/11/96	**32** ᴬ	8	1. Mother Mother	album cut
			#1 Modern Rock hit (3 weeks); from the album *The Burdens Of Being Upright* on Island 524187	

BON JOVI

Rock group from Sayreville, New Jersey: Jon Bon Jovi (vocals; born on 3/2/62), Richie Sambora (guitar), Dave Bryan (keyboards), Alec John Such (bass) and Tico Torres (drums). Jon also pursued acting with roles in movies *Moonlight and Valentino* (1995) and *U571* (2000).

DATE	POS	WKS	ARTIST–RECORD TITLE	LABEL & NO.
4/21/84	**39**	1	1. Runaway	Mercury 818309
10/11/86	**1** (1)	14	2. **You Give Love A Bad Name** Sales #1 (2) / Airplay #5	Mercury 884953
1/10/87	**1** (4)	13	3. **Livin' On A Prayer** Airplay #1 (4) / Sales #1 (3)	Mercury 888184
			#1 Mainstream Rock hit (2 weeks)	
4/25/87	**7**	12	4. **Wanted Dead Or Alive** Sales #6 / Airplay #6	Mercury 888467
5/23/87	**28** ᴬ	6	5. Never Say Goodbye	album cut
			from the album *Slippery When Wet* on Mercury 830264	
10/17/87	**38** ᴬ	1	6. Edge Of A Broken Heart	album cut
			from the movie *Disorderlies* starring the Fat Boys (soundtrack album on Polydor 833274)	
10/1/88	**1** (2)	12	7. **Bad Medicine** Sales #2 / Airplay #2	Mercury 870657
12/17/88+	**3**	13	8. **Born To Be My Baby** Airplay #2 / Sales #3	Mercury 872156
3/18/89	**1** (1)	13	9. **I'll Be There For You** Sales #1 (1) / Airplay #1 (1)	Mercury 872564
6/17/89	**7**	11	10. **Lay Your Hands On Me** Sales #7 / Airplay #7	Mercury 874452
10/28/89	**9**	12	11. **Living In Sin** Airplay #9 / Sales #10	Mercury 876070
7/28/90	**1** (1)	14	▲ 12. **Blaze Of Glory** Sales #1 (3) / Airplay #2	Mercury 875896
			#1 Mainstream Rock hit (1 week)	
11/10/90	**12**	11	13. Miracle Sales #11 / Airplay #12	Mercury 878392
			JON BON JOVI (above 2)	
			above 2 from the movie *Young Guns II* starring Emilio Estevez and Kiefer Sutherland	
10/31/92	**29**	9	14. Keep The Faith Sales #31 / Airplay #39	Jambco 864432
			#1 Mainstream Rock hit (1 week)	

DATE	POS	WKS	ARTIST–RECORD TITLE	LABEL & NO.
2/6/93	**10**	15	15. **Bed Of Roses** Sales #10 / Airplay #20	Jambco 864852
5/29/93	**27**	7	16. In These Arms Airplay #27 / Sales #46	Jambco 862088
10/8/94	**4**	29	▲ 17. **Always** Sales #2 / Airplay #3	Mercury 856227
6/10/95	**14**	13	18. This Ain't A Love Song Sales #15 / Airplay #27	Mercury 856824
9/23/00	**33**	7	19. It's My Life Airplay #27	album cut
			from the album *Crush* on Island 542474	

BONNIE LOU

Born Mary Kath on 10/27/24 in Towanda, Illinois. Country singer/guitarist.

11/26/55	**14**	3	1. Daddy-O Juke Box #14 / Best Seller #25 / Top 100 #28	King 4835

BONNIE SISTERS

Doo-wop "girl group" from Brooklyn, New York: Pat, Jean and Sylvia Bonnie. All were nurses at Bellevue Hospital.

2/25/56	**18**	3	1. Cry Baby Best Seller #18 / Top 100 #35	Rainbow 328

BONOFF, Karla

Born on 12/27/51 in Los Angeles, California. Pop singer/songwriter/pianist.

6/5/82	**19**	12	1. Personally	Columbia 02805
			#92 R&B hit for Jackie Moore in 1978	

BOOKER T. & THE MG'S

Interracial R&B band formed in Memphis, Tennessee: Booker T. Jones (keyboards; born on 11/12/44), Steve Cropper (guitar), Donald "Duck" Dunn (bass) and Al Jackson (drums). MG stands for Memphis Group. Jackson was murdered on 10/1/75 (age 39). Cropper and Dunn joined the Blues Brothers band. Group inducted into the Rock and Roll Hall of Fame in 1992.

9/1/62	**3**	12	● 1. **Green Onions** [I]	Stax 127
			#1 R&B hit (4 weeks)	
5/20/67	**37**	3	2. Hip Hug-Her [I]	Stax 211
9/2/67	**21**	7	3. Groovin' [I]	Stax 224
8/3/68	**17**	7	● 4. Soul-Limbo [I]	Stax 0001
12/28/68+	**9**	11	5. **Hang 'Em High** [I]	Stax 0013
			title song from the movie starring Clint Eastwood	
4/5/69	**6**	10	● 6. **Time Is Tight** [I]	Stax 0028
			from the movie *Up Tight* starring Ruby Dee	
7/5/69	**37**	3	7. Mrs. Robinson [I]	Stax 0037
			from the movie *The Graduate* starring Dustin Hoffman	

BOONE, Daniel

Born Peter Lee Stirling on 7/31/42 in Birmingham, England. Pop singer/songwriter.

8/5/72	**15**	11	1. Beautiful Sunday	Mercury 73281

BOONE, Debby

Born on 9/22/56 in Leonia, New Jersey. Daughter of Pat Boone. Won the 1977 Best New Artist Grammy Award. Married Gabriel Ferrer (son of Rosemary Clooney and actor Jose Ferrer) on 9/1/79.

9/17/77	**1** (10)	21	▲ 1. **You Light Up My Life**	Warner/Curb 8455
			#1 Adult Contemporary hit (1 week); title song from the movie starring Didi Conn	

DATE	POS	WKS	ARTIST–RECORD TITLE	LABEL & NO.
			BOONE, Pat	
			Born Charles Eugene Boone on 6/1/34 in Jacksonville, Florida; raised in Nashville, Tennessee. Direct descendant of Daniel Boone. Married Shirley Foley (daughter of country singer Red Foley) on 11/7/53. Hosted own TV show *The Pat Boone-Chevy Showroom* (1957-60). Appeared in several movies. Wrote several books. Recording artist Nick Todd is his younger brother. Pat's trademark: white buck shoes.	
4/2/55	16	12	1. Two Hearts Best Seller #16 / Juke Box #16 #8 R&B hit for The Charms in 1955; Lew Douglas (orch.)	Dot 15338
7/9/55	1 (2)	20	● 2. **Ain't That A Shame** Juke Box #1 (2) / Best Seller #2 / Jockey #2 / Top 100 #21	Dot 15377
10/29/55	7	10	3. **At My Front Door (Crazy Little Mama)** / Top 100 #7 / Juke Box #7 / Best Seller #8 / Jockey #10	
11/19/55	26	5	4. No Other Arms Top 100 #26 / Best Seller: flip / Juke Box: flip tune better known as "No Arms Can Ever Hold You"	Dot 15422
12/24/55+	19	5	5. Gee Whittakers! Juke Box #19 / Top 100 #27 #14 R&B hit for The Five Keys in 1956	Dot 15435
2/4/56	4	18	● 6. **I'll Be Home** / Jockey #4 / Juke Box #4 / Top 100 #5 / Best Seller #6 #5 R&B hit for The Flamingos in 1956	
2/4/56	12	10	7. Tutti' Frutti Top 100 #12 / Juke Box #13 / Best Seller #15 / Jockey #15	Dot 15443
4/28/56	8	9	8. **Long Tall Sally** Juke Box #8 / Top 100 #18 / Best Seller #23 / Jockey #23	Dot 15457
6/9/56	1 (4)	19	● 9. **I Almost Lost My Mind** Juke Box #1 (4) / Top 100 #1 (2) / Best Seller #2 / Jockey #2 #1 R&B hit for Ivory Joe Hunter in 1950	Dot 15472
9/22/56	5	17	● 10. **Friendly Persuasion (Thee I Love)** / Jockey #5 / Top 100 #8 / Juke Box #8 / Best Seller #9 title song from the movie *Friendly Persuasion* starring Gary Cooper and Dorothy McGuire	
9/29/56	10	8	11. **Chains Of Love** Juke Box #10 / Best Seller #15 / Top 100 #20 #2 R&B hit for Joe Turner in 1951	Dot 15490
12/22/56+	1 (1)	19	● 12. **Don't Forbid Me** / Top 100 #1 (1) / Juke Box #1 (1) / Jockey #2 / Best Seller #3	
1/26/57	37	2	13. Anastasia Top 100 #37 / Best Seller: flip title song from the movie starring Ingrid Bergman and Yul Brynner	Dot 15521
3/23/57	5	13	● 14. **Why Baby Why** / Best Seller #5 / Top 100 #6 / Jockey #7 / Juke Box #7	
3/23/57	27	5	15. I'm Waiting Just For You Top 100 #27 / Best Seller: flip / Juke Box: flip #2 R&B hit for Lucky Millinder in 1951	Dot 15545
5/13/57	1 (7)	24	● 16. **Love Letters In The Sand** / Jockey #1 (7) / Best Seller #1 (5) / Top 100 #1 (5) / Juke Box #2 #6 hit for Ted Black & His Orchestra in 1931	
5/20/57	14	13	17. Bernardine Jockey #14 / Top 100 #23 / Best Seller: flip / Juke Box: flip above 2 from the movie *Bernardine* starring Boone and Janet Gaynor	Dot 15570
8/12/57	6	14	● 18. **Remember You're Mine** / Jockey #6 / Best Seller #10 / Top 100 #20	
8/19/57	14	11	19. There's A Gold Mine In The Sky Best Seller #14 / Jockey #20 / Top 100 #28 #5 hit for Horace Heidt in 1938	Dot 15602
10/28/57	1 (6)	19	● 20. **April Love** Jockey #1 (6) / Best Seller #1 (2) / Top 100 #1 (1) title song from the movie starring Boone and Shirley Jones	Dot 15660
2/17/58	4	15	● 21. **A Wonderful Time Up There** / Best Seller #4 / Jockey #7 / Top 100 #10	

DATE	POS	WKS	ARTIST–RECORD TITLE	LABEL & NO.
2/17/58	**4**	15	22. **It's Too Soon To Know** Best Seller #4 / Jockey #11 / Top 100 #13 #1 R&B hit for The Orioles in 1948	Dot 15690
5/12/58	**5**	12	23. **Sugar Moon** Jockey #5 / Best Seller #10 / Top 100 #11	Dot 15750
7/14/58	**7**	10	24. **If Dreams Came True** /Jockey #7 / Best Seller #11 / Hot 100 #12	
8/4/58	**39**	1	25. That's How Much I Love You Hot 100 #39 / Best Seller: flip #10 hit for Frank Sinatra in 1947	Dot 15785
9/22/58	**23**	4	26. For My Good Fortune / Hot 100 #23 / Best Seller #29	
10/6/58	**21**	2	27. Gee, But It's Lonely Best Seller #21 / Hot 100 #31 written by Phil Everly (of The Everly Brothers)	Dot 15825
11/17/58	**34**	5	28. I'll Remember Tonight from the movie *Mardi Gras* starring Boone and Tommy Sands	Dot 15840
1/26/59	**21**	8	29. With The Wind And The Rain In Your Hair #4 hit for Kay Kyser in 1940	Dot 15888
4/6/59	**23**	7	30. For A Penny Billy Vaughn (orch., all of above - except #1)	Dot 15914
6/29/59	**17**	6	31. Twixt Twelve And Twenty also the title of Boone's best-selling book	Dot 15955
9/28/59	**29**	4	32. Fools Hall Of Fame	Dot 15982
3/7/60	**18**	7	33. (Welcome) New Lovers Mort Lindsey (orch.: #31 & 33)	Dot 16048
5/22/61	**1** (1)	12	34. **Moody River**	Dot 16209
9/4/61	**19**	5	35. Big Cold Wind Milt Rogers (orch.)	Dot 16244
12/25/61+	**35**	3	36. Johnny Will	Dot 16284
2/24/62	**32**	3	37. I'll See You In My Dreams #1 hit for Isham Jones in 1925; Billy Vaughn (orch.: #32, #34, #36, #37)	Dot 16312
6/30/62	**6**	10	38. **Speedy Gonzales** [N] featuring the voice of Mel Blanc as "Speedy Gonzales"; Jimmie Haskell (orch.); first recorded by David Dante in 1962	Dot 16368
			BOSTON	
			Rock group from Boston, Massachusetts: Brad Delp (vocals), Tom Scholz (guitar, keyboards), Barry Goudreau (guitar), Fran Sheehan (bass) and Sib Hashian (drums). By 1986, reduced to duo of Scholz and Delp.	
10/16/76	**5**	14	1. **More Than A Feeling**	Epic 50266
2/12/77	**22**	6	2. Long Time	Epic 50329
6/18/77	**38**	2	3. Peace Of Mind	Epic 50381
8/26/78	**4**	10	4. **Don't Look Back**	Epic 50590
12/23/78+	**31**	5	5. A Man I'll Never Be	Epic 50638
10/4/86	**1** (2)	12	6. **Amanda** Airplay #1 (3) / Sales #1 (2) #1 Mainstream Rock hit (3 weeks)	MCA 52756
12/27/86+	**9**	10	7. **We're Ready** Sales #8 / Airplay #9	MCA 52985
3/28/87	**20**	5	8. Can'tcha Say (You Believe In Me)/Still In Love Sales #20 / Airplay #24	MCA 53029
			BOTKIN, Perry Jr. — see DeVORZON, Barry	
			BOUNTY KILLER — see NO DOUBT	

DATE	POS	WKS	ARTIST—RECORD TITLE	LABEL & NO.
			BOURGEOIS TAGG	
			Rock group from Los Angeles, California: Brent Bourgeois (vocals, keyboards; see #2 below), Larry Tagg (vocals, bass), Lyle Workman (guitar), Scott Moon (keyboards) and Michael Urbano (drums).	
12/5/87	**38**	2	1. I Don't Mind At All　　　　　　　　Sales #35	Island 99409
			produced by Todd Rundgren	
6/9/90	**32**	3	2. Dare To Fall In Love　　　　　　　Airplay #25	Charisma 98971
			BRENT BOURGEOIS	
			BOWEN, Jimmy, with the Rhythm Orchids	
			Born on 11/30/37 in Santa Rita, New Mexico. Formed The Rhythm Orchids at West Texas State University with Buddy Knox, Don Lanier and Dave "Dicky Doo" Alldred. Jimmy later became a producer and record executive.	
3/9/57	**14**	12	1. I'm Stickin' With You	Roulette 4001
			Top 100 #14 / Juke Box #15 / Best Seller #16 / Jockey #20	
			BOWIE, David	
			Born David Jones on 1/8/47 in Brixton, London, England. Pop-rock singer/actor. Joined Lindsay Kemp Mime Troupe in 1967. Adopted new personas (Ziggy Stardust, Alladin Sane, Thin White Duke) to accompany several of his musical phases. Married to Angie Barnett, the subject of The Rolling Stones' song "Angie," from 1970-80. Acted in several movies. Starred in *The Elephant Man* on Broadway. Formed the group Tin Machine in 1988. Married Somalian actress/supermodel Iman on 4/24/92. Inducted into the Rock and Roll Hall of Fame in 1996.	
2/24/73	**15**	10	1. Space Oddity	RCA Victor 0876
			first released in 1969	
4/19/75	**28**	4	2. Young Americans	RCA Victor 10152
			Luther Vandross (backing vocal); David Sanborn (saxophone)	
8/2/75	**1 (2)**	14	● 3. **Fame**	RCA Victor 10320
			John Lennon (backing vocal and song's co-writer)	
1/10/76	**10**	16	4. **Golden Years**	RCA Victor 10441
12/5/81+	**29**	8	5. Under Pressure	Elektra 47235
			QUEEN & DAVID BOWIE	
4/9/83	**1 (1)**	14	● 6. **Let's Dance**	EMI America 8158
7/9/83	**10**	11	7. **China Girl**	EMI America 8165
10/1/83	**14**	9	8. Modern Love	EMI America 8177
9/29/84	**8**	10	9. **Blue Jean**　　　　　　Sales #7 / Airplay #10	EMI America 8231
3/9/85	**32**	4	10. This Is Not America　　　　　　Sales #27	EMI America 8251
			DAVID BOWIE/PAT METHENY GROUP	
			theme from the movie *The Falcon And The Snowman* starring Timothy Hutton and Sean Penn	
9/7/85	**7**	9	11. **Dancing In The Street**　　Sales #5 / Airplay #8	EMI America 8288
			MICK JAGGER/DAVID BOWIE	
4/25/87	**21**	7	12. Day-In Day-Out　　　　Sales #17 / Airplay #24	EMI America 8380
9/5/87	**27**	5	13. Never Let Me Down　　　Sales #23 / Airplay #32	EMI America 43031
			BOW WOW — see LIL' BOW WOW	
			BOX TOPS, The	
			Pop-rock group from Memphis, Tennessee: Alex Chilton (vocals), Gary Talley (guitar), John Evans (organ), Bill Cunningham (bass) and Danny Smythe (drums). Cunningham is the brother of B.B. Cunningham of The Hombres.	
8/26/67	**1 (4)**	13	● 1. **The Letter**	Mala 565
12/2/67	**24**	5	2. Neon Rainbow	Mala 580

DATE	POS	WKS	ARTIST–RECORD TITLE	LABEL & NO.
3/16/68	**2** (2)	12	● 3. **Cry Like A Baby**	Mala 593
6/8/68	**26**	6	4. Choo Choo Train	Mala 12005
10/12/68	**37**	1	5. I Met Her In Church	Mala 12017
2/8/69	**28**	9	6. Sweet Cream Ladies, Forward March	Mala 12035
			some pressings show title as just "Sweet Cream Ladies"	
8/23/69	**18**	7	7. Soul Deep	Mala 12040

BOYCE, Tommy, & Bobby Hart

Songwriting/singing/production duo. Boyce was born on 9/29/39 in Charlottesville, Virginia. Died of a self-inflicted gunshot wound on 11/23/94 (age 55). Hart was born on 2/18/39 in Phoenix, Arizona.

DATE	POS	WKS	ARTIST–RECORD TITLE	LABEL & NO.
8/5/67	**39**	2	1. Out & About	A&M 858
1/20/68	**8**	9	2. **I Wonder What She's Doing Tonite**	A&M 893
8/3/68	**27**	6	3. Alice Long (You're Still My Favorite Girlfriend)	A&M 948

BOY GEORGE — see CULTURE CLUB

BOY KRAZY

Female pop vocal group formed in New York: Kimberly Blake, Johnna Lee Cummings, Josselyne Jones and Ruth Ann Roberts.

DATE	POS	WKS	ARTIST–RECORD TITLE	LABEL & NO.
2/13/93	**18**	16	1. That's What Love Can Do *Airplay #11 / Sales #40*	Next Plateau 857024

BOY MEETS GIRL

Songwriting/recording duo from Seattle, Washington: Shannon Rubicam and George Merrill. Married in 1988.

DATE	POS	WKS	ARTIST–RECORD TITLE	LABEL & NO.
5/25/85	**39**	1	1. Oh Girl	A&M 2713
10/15/88	**5**	16	2. **Waiting For A Star To Fall** *Sales #4 / Airplay #6*	RCA 8691
			#1 Adult Contemporary hit (1 week)	

BOYS, The

R&B vocal group from Northridge, California: brothers Khiry, Hakeem, Tajh and Bilal Samad.

DATE	POS	WKS	ARTIST–RECORD TITLE	LABEL & NO.
1/14/89	**13**	9	1. Dial My Heart *Sales #11 / Airplay #17*	Motown 53301
			#1 R&B hit (1 week)	
9/8/90	**29**	8	2. Crazy *Sales #17*	Motown 2053
			#1 R&B hit (1 week)	

BOYS CLUB

Vocal duo from Minneapolis, Minnesota: Gene Hunt and Joe Pasquale. Hunt (real name: Eugene Wolfgramm) was a member of The Jets.

DATE	POS	WKS	ARTIST–RECORD TITLE	LABEL & NO.
11/19/88+	**8**	12	1. **I Remember Holding You** *Sales #6 / Airplay #11*	MCA 53430

BOYS DON'T CRY

Pop-rock group from England: Nick Richards (vocals), Nico Ramsden (guitar), Brian Chatton (keyboards), Mark Smith (bass) and Jeff Seopardi (drums).

DATE	POS	WKS	ARTIST–RECORD TITLE	LABEL & NO.
5/17/86	**12**	9	1. I Wanna Be A Cowboy *Sales #11 / Airplay #11*	Profile 5084

DATE	POS	WKS	ARTIST–RECORD TITLE	LABEL & NO.
			BOYZ II MEN	
			R&B vocal group from Philadelphia, Pennsylvania: Wanya Morris (born on 7/29/74), Michael McCary (born on 12/16/72), Shawn Stockman (born on 9/26/73) and Nathan Morris (born on 6/18/72).	
7/6/91	3	18	▲ 1. **Motownphilly** Sales #2 / Airplay #3 Michael Bivins (rap)	Motown 2090
10/12/91	2 (4)	19	● 2. **It's So Hard To Say Goodbye To Yesterday** Sales #2 / Airplay #5 #1 R&B hit (1 week)	Motown 2136
1/18/92	16	14	3. Uhh Ahh Sales #14 / Airplay #19 #1 R&B hit (1 week)	Motown 2141
7/25/92	1 (13)	28	▲ 4. **End of the Road** Airplay #1 (13) / Sales #1 (12) #1 R&B hit (4 weeks); from the movie *Boomerang* starring Eddie Murphy	Motown 2178
11/28/92+	3	17	▲ 5. **In The Still Of The Nite (I'll Remember)** Airplay #2 / Sales #3 from the TV mini-series *The Jacksons: An American Dream*	Motown 2193
1/8/94 -	32	1	6. Let It Snow Sales #27 / Airplay #40 **[X]** Brian McKnight (guest vocal)	Motown 2218
8/13/94	1 (14)	31	▲ 7. **I'll Make Love To You** Airplay #1 (12) / Sales #1 (11) #1 R&B hit (9 weeks) / #1 Adult Contemporary hit (3 weeks)	Motown 2257
11/19/94	1 (6)	25	▲ 8. **On Bended Knee** Airplay #1 (11) / Sales #2	Motown 0244
3/4/95	21	10	9. Thank You Sales #21 / Airplay #28 samples "La-Di-Da-Di" by Doug E. Fresh	Motown 0274
4/29/95	2 (1)	25	● 10. **Water Runs Dry** Airplay #1 (1) / Sales #8 above 4 from the album *II*	Motown 0358
12/2/95	1 (16)	26	▲² 11. **One Sweet Day** Airplay #1 (13) / Sales #1 (11) **MARIAH CAREY & BOYZ II MEN** #1 Adult Contemporary hit (13 weeks)	Columbia 78074
9/27/97	1 (1)	19	▲ 12. **4 Seasons Of Loneliness** Sales #1 (1) / Airplay #12	Motown 0684
12/13/97+	7	17	▲ 13. **A Song For Mama** Sales #5 / Airplay #30 #1 R&B hit (2 weeks); from the movie *Soul Food* starring Vanessa Williams	Motown 0720
1/30/99	32	4	● 14. I Will Get There Sales #8 from the animated movie *The Prince Of Egypt*	DreamWorks 59018
			BRADLEY, Jan	
			Born Addie Bradley on 7/6/43 in Byhalia, Mississippi; raised in Robbins, Illinois. R&B singer.	
2/2/63	14	9	1. Mama Didn't Lie	Chess 1845
			BRADLEY, Owen, Quintet	
			Born on 10/21/15 in Westmoreland, Tennessee. Died on 1/7/98 (age 82). Top country producer.	
7/29/57	18	4	1. White Silver Sands Jockey #18 / Top 100 #68 Anita Kerr Quartet (vocals)	Decca 30363
			BRAM TCHAIKOVSKY	
			Rock trio from Lincolnshire, England: Peter Bramall (vocals, guitar), Micky Broadbent (bass) and Keith Boyce (drums).	
8/18/79	37	3	1. Girl Of My Dreams	Polydor 14575

DATE	POS	WKS	ARTIST–RECORD TITLE	LABEL & NO.

BRANCH, Michelle

Born on 7/2/83 in Sedona, Arizona. Adult Alternative pop-rock singer/songwriter/guitarist.

DATE	POS	WKS	ARTIST–RECORD TITLE	LABEL & NO.
9/22/01	12	13	1. Everywhere — Airplay #12	album cut
3/23/02	6	21	2. **All You Wanted** — Airplay #6	album cut
10/5/02	21	7	3. Goodbye To You — Airplay #26	album cut
			above 3 from the album The Spirit Room on Maverick 47985	
10/12/02	5	33	4. **The Game Of Love** — Airplay #5 / Sales #19	Arista 15203
			SANTANA featuring Michelle Branch	
			#1 Adult Contemporary hit (4 weeks)	
6/21/03	16	16	5. Are You Happy Now? — Airplay #16 / Sales #54	album cut
			single available only as a paid download; from the album Hotel Paper on Maverick 48426	
12/13/03	36	2	6. Breathe — Sales #24 / Airplay #40	Maverick 42689

BRANDY

Born Brandy Norwood on 2/11/79 in McComb, Mississippi; raised in Los Angeles, California. R&B singer/actress. Star of the TV series *Moesha*. Played "Karla Wilson" in the 1998 movie *I Still Know What You Did Last Summer*. Sister of Ray J.

DATE	POS	WKS	ARTIST–RECORD TITLE	LABEL & NO.
10/8/94	6	25	● 1. **I Wanna Be Down** — Sales #4 / Airplay #10	Atlantic 87225
			#1 R&B hit (4 weeks)	
2/11/95	4	18	▲ 2. **Baby** — Sales #1 (5) / Airplay #19	Atlantic 87173
			#1 R&B hit (4 weeks)	
7/1/95	34	6	3. Best Friend — Sales #25 / Airplay #51	Atlantic 87148
9/9/95	9	14	● 4. **Brokenhearted** — Sales #5 / Airplay #21	Atlantic 87150
			Wanya Morris (of Boyz II Men; male vocal)	
1/6/96	2 (2)	29	▲ 5. **Sittin' Up In My Room** — Sales #2 / Airplay #8	Arista 12929
			from the movie Waiting To Exhale starring Whitney Houston	
9/14/96	25	10	6. Missing You — Sales #15	EastWest 64262
			BRANDY, TAMIA, GLADYS KNIGHT & CHAKA KHAN	
			from the movie Set It Off starring Jada Pinkett and Queen Latifah	
5/30/98	1 (13)	27	▲² 7. **The Boy Is Mine** — Sales #1 (9) / Airplay #2	Atlantic 84089
			BRANDY & MONICA	
			#1 R&B hit (8 weeks)	
12/5/98+	1 (2)	22	8. **Have You Ever?** — Airplay #1 (9) / Sales #3	Atlantic 84198
5/8/99	16	12	9. Almost Doesn't Count — Airplay #7	album cut
			from the album Never S-a-y Never on Atlantic 83039	
2/2/02	7	11	10. **What About Us?** — Airplay #6 / Sales #25	Atlantic 85217
5/25/02	18	10	11. Full Moon — Sales #16 / Airplay #17	Atlantic 85269

BRANIGAN, Laura

Born on 7/3/57 in Brewster, New York. Pop singer/actress. Played "Monica" in the 1984 movie *Delta Pi*.

DATE	POS	WKS	ARTIST–RECORD TITLE	LABEL & NO.
9/4/82	2 (3)	22	▲ 1. **Gloria**	Atlantic 4048
			first recorded by Umberto Tozzi in 1979	
4/2/83	7	13	2. **Solitaire**	Atlantic 89868
8/13/83	12	12	3. How Am I Supposed To Live Without You	Atlantic 89805
			#1 Adult Contemporary hit (3 weeks); written by Michael Bolton	
5/5/84	4	15	4. **Self Control**	Atlantic 89676
8/25/84	20	8	5. The Lucky One	Atlantic 89636
			from the TV movie An Uncommon Love starring Barry Bostwick	
9/7/85	40	2	6. Spanish Eddie	Atlantic 89531
11/28/87+	26	9	7. Power Of Love — Sales #19 / Airplay #32	Atlantic 89191

DATE	POS	WKS	ARTIST–RECORD TITLE	LABEL & NO.
			BRASS CONSTRUCTION	
			Disco group from Brooklyn, New York: Randy Muller (vocals, keyboards), Joe Wong (guitar), Wayne Parris, Morris Price, Jesse Ward and Mickey Grudge (horn section), Sandy Billups (congas), Wade Williamston (bass) and Larry Payton (drums). Muller later formed Skyy.	
5/8/76	14	9	1. Movin' [I] #1 R&B hit (1 week)	United Artists 775
			BRASS RING, The	
			Studio group assembled by producer/arranger/saxophonist Phil Bodner.	
4/16/66	32	4	1. The Phoenix Love Theme (Senza Fine) [I] from the movie The Flight Of The Phoenix starring James Stewart	Dunhill 4023
3/4/67	36	2	2. The Dis-Advantages Of You [I] melody taken from a Benson & Hedges cigarette jingle	Dunhill 4065
			BRAT PACK, The	
			Male dance vocal duo from New Jersey: Patrick Donovan and Ray Frazier.	
3/17/90	36	3	1. You're The Only Woman Airplay #33	Vendetta 1447
			BRAUN, Bob	
			Born Robert Brown on 4/20/29 in Ludlow, Kentucky. Died of Parkinson's disease on 1/15/2001 (age 71). Hosted own TV show in Cincinnati, Ohio.	
8/18/62	26	4	1. Till Death Do Us Part [S]	Decca 31355
			BRAXTON, Toni	
			Born on 10/7/68 in Severn, Maryland. Female R&B singer. Recorded in 1990 with her younger sisters as The Braxtons. Married Keri Lewis (of Mint Condition) on 4/21/2001. Won the 1993 Best New Artist Grammy Award.	
8/22/92	29	6	1. Give U My Heart Airplay #29 / Sales #39 **BABYFACE (Featuring Toni Braxton)**	LaFace 24026
1/9/93	33	2	2. Love Shoulda Brought You Home Sales #25 / Airplay #36 above 2 from the movie Boomerang starring Eddie Murphy	LaFace 24035
8/14/93	7	18	● 3. **Another Sad Love Song** Airplay #8 / Sales #14	LaFace 24047
10/30/93+	3	33	● 4. **Breathe Again** Airplay #1 (1) / Sales #6	LaFace 24054
4/16/94	7	28	● 5. **You Mean The World To Me** Airplay #3 / Sales #14	LaFace 24064
11/26/94+	28	11	6. I Belong To You / Sales #31 / Airplay #35	
11/12/94	35	13	7. How Many Ways Sales #27 / Airplay #54	LaFace 24081
6/8/96	1 (1)	39	▲ 8. **You're Makin' Me High /** Sales #2 / Airplay #6 #1 R&B hit (2 weeks)	
6/8/96		39	9. Let It Flow Sales: flip from the movie Waiting To Exhale starring Whitney Houston	LaFace 24160
10/26/96	1 (11)	37	▲ 10. **Un-Break My Heart** Airplay #1 (2) / Sales #1 (1) #1 Adult Contemporary hit (14 weeks); Shanice Wilson (backing vocal)	LaFace 24200
4/12/97	19	15	● 11. I Don't Want To / Sales #18 / Airplay #34 written and produced by R. Kelly	
4/12/97		15	12. I Love Me Some Him Sales: flip	LaFace 24229
4/8/00	2 (2)	32	● 13. **He Wasn't Man Enough** Sales #1 (5) / Airplay #9 #1 R&B hit (4 weeks)	LaFace 24463
8/26/00	32	6	14. Just Be A Man About It Airplay #19 Dr. Dre (backing vocal)	LaFace 24517

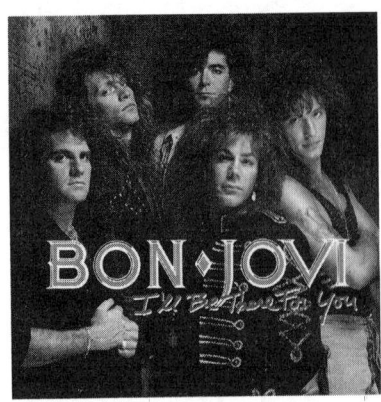

Bon Jovi remembered their roots by titling their 1988 album *New Jersey*. The album generated five Top 10 singles, including the #1 hits "Bad Medicine" and "I'll Be There For You."

Pat Boone reached #1 with the song "I Almost Lost My Mind." Many fans wondered if he had really lost his mind when he decided to record a big band album of heavy metal cover songs in 1997.

The Box Tops, featuring Alex Chilton, hit #1 with the song "The Letter." Years later, Chilton would form the band Big Star and release an album called *#1 Record.* Sadly, it never made the album charts.

Boyz II Men achieved the "End Of The Road" for a longstanding chart record. Their hit spent 13 weeks at #1, surpassing the 11 weeks Elvis Presley spent on top with "Don't Be Cruel/ Hound Dog."

Brandy went down easily with pop music fans, as shown by her #1 hits like "Have You Ever." However, she also found an audience in other fields, including her own TV series *Moesha* and several movie roles.

Toni Braxton won the 1993 Grammy Award for Best New Artist. That proved to be a good choice, as her 1996 album *Secrets* spun off two #1 hits, "You're Makin' Me High" and "Un-Break My Heart."

Bread served up a number of tasty easy-listening hits in the 1970s, including the #1 single, "Make It With You." The Bread sound stayed fresh, as their hits were later covered by artists like Boy George.

Peabo Bryson teamed with Celine Dion for a Top 10 *Beauty And The Beast* hit, and followed it up by pairing with Regina Belle for another Disney movie hit, the chart-topping *Aladdin* single "A Whole New World (Aladdin's Theme)."

B2K had a lot of help on their first #1 hit, "Bump Bump Bump," as P. Diddy provided a cameo rap and R. Kelly co-wrote it. Despite the repetition in their song title, they have yet to repeat their chart-topping feat.

The Byrds covered Bob Dylan's "Mr. Tambourine Man" and scored a #1 hit. Ironically, Dylan songs became #1 Pop, Country, and R&B hits for other artists, but the artist himself never had a #1 hit as a performer.

DATE	POS	WKS	ARTIST–RECORD TITLE	LABEL & NO.
			BREAD	
			Soft-rock group formed in Los Angeles, California: David Gates (vocals, keyboards), James Griffin (guitar), Robb Royer (bass) and Mike Botts (drums). Larry Knechtel replaced Royer in 1971. Disbanded in 1973, reunited briefly in 1976.	
7/11/70	**1** (1)	13	● 1. **Make It With You**	Elektra 45686
10/10/70	**10**	9	2. **It Don't Matter To Me**	Elektra 45701
1/30/71	**28**	4	3. Let Your Love Go	Elektra 45711
4/3/71	**4**	11	4. **If**	Elektra 45720
			#1 Adult Contemporary hit (3 weeks)	
8/14/71	**37**	2	5. Mother Freedom	Elektra 45740
11/6/71	**3**	10	● 6. **Baby I'm - A Want You**	Elektra 45751
			#1 Adult Contemporary hit (1 week)	
2/5/72	**5**	11	7. **Everything I Own**	Elektra 45765
5/6/72	**15**	8	8. Diary	Elektra 45784
8/5/72	**11**	9	9. The Guitar Man	Elektra 45803
			#1 Adult Contemporary hit (1 week)	
11/18/72	**15**	8	10. Sweet Surrender	Elektra 45818
			#1 Adult Contemporary hit (2 weeks)	
2/17/73	**15**	8	11. Aubrey	Elektra 45832
12/4/76+	**9**	13	12. **Lost Without Your Love**	Elektra 45365
			BREAKFAST CLUB	
			Pop-dance group from Manhattan, New York: brothers Dan (vocals) and Eddie (guitar) Gilroy, Gary Burke (bass) and Stephen Bray (drums). Madonna was the group's drummer for a short time in 1979.	
4/11/87	**7**	11	1. **Right On Track** Sales #5 / Airplay #12	MCA 52954
			BREATHE	
			Pop group from London, England: David Glasper (vocals), Marcus Lillington (guitar), Michael Delahunty (bass) and Ian "Spike" Spice (drums). Delahunty left in 1989.	
6/11/88	**2** (2)	16	1. **Hands To Heaven** Sales #1 (2) / Airplay #2	A&M 2991
10/1/88	**3**	16	2. **How Can I Fall?** Sales #1 (1) / Airplay #3	A&M 1224
			#1 Adult Contemporary hit (2 weeks)	
1/28/89	**10**	10	3. **Don't Tell Me Lies** Airplay #9 / Sales #13	A&M 1267
9/15/90	**21**	8	4. Say A Prayer Airplay #15 / Sales #30	A&M 1519
1/5/91	**34**	3	5. Does She Love That Man? Airplay #32	A&M 1535
			BREATHE featuring David Glasper	
			BREMERS, Beverly	
			Born on 3/10/50 in Chicago, Illinois. Pop singer/actress.	
1/22/72	**15**	10	1. Don't Say You Don't Remember	Scepter 12315
7/22/72	**40**	2	2. We're Free	Scepter 12348
			BRENDA & THE TABULATIONS	
			R&B vocal group from Philadelphia, Pennsylvania: Brenda Payton, Jerry Jones, Eddie Jackson and Maurice Coates. Reorganized in 1970 with Payton, Pat Mercer and Deborah Martin. Payton died on 6/14/92.	
3/25/67	**20**	6	1. Dry Your Eyes	Dionn 500
5/1/71	**23**	9	2. Right On The Tip Of My Tongue	Top & Bottom 407

DATE	POS	WKS	ARTIST—RECORD TITLE	LABEL & NO.
			BRENNAN, Walter	
			Born on 7/25/1894 in Swampscott, Massachusetts. Died on 9/21/74 (age 80). Famous character actor. Appeared in several movies and TV shows.	
5/30/60	30	3	1. Dutchman's Gold [S]	Dot 16066
			WALTER BRENNAN With BILLY VAUGHN and his Orchestra	
4/21/62	5	9	2. **Old Rivers** [S]	Liberty 55436
12/1/62	38	1	3. Mama Sang A Song [S]	Liberty 55508
			The Johnny Mann Singers (backing vocals, above 2)	
			BREWER, Teresa	
			Born Theresa Breuer on 5/7/31 in Toledo, Ohio. Pop singer. Appeared in the 1953 movie *Those Redheads From Seattle*.	
12/18/54+	6	12	1. **Let Me Go, Lover!** Juke Box #6 / Jockey #7 / Best Seller #8	Coral 61315
			TERESA BREWER with The Lancers	
3/19/55	17	3	2. Pledging My Love / Jockey #17 / Juke Box #18 / Best Seller #30	
5/7/55		1	3. How Important Can It Be? Juke Box: flip	Coral 61362
6/4/55	20	1	4. Silver Dollar Juke Box #20	Coral 61394
			Jack Pleis (orch., all of above)	
7/30/55	15	4	5. The Banjo's Back In Town Juke Box #15	Coral 61448
3/3/56	5	17	6. **A Tear Fell /** Juke Box #5 / Top 100 #7 / Best Seller #9 / Jockey #9	
			#15 R&B hit for Ivory Joe Hunter in 1956	
3/10/56	17	10	7. Bo Weevil	
			Top 100 #17 / Jockey #20 / Best Seller: flip / Juke Box: flip	Coral 61590
6/16/56	7	16	8. **A Sweet Old Fashioned Girl**	
			Juke Box #7 / Top 100 #9 / Jockey #11 / Best Seller #12	Coral 61636
11/17/56	21	8	9. Mutual Admiration Society	
			Top 100 #21 / Best Seller #24 / Jockey #24	Coral 61737
			from the musical *Happy Hunting* starring Ethel Merman	
4/27/57	13	9	10. Empty Arms Juke Box #13 / Top 100 #18 / Jockey #19 / Best Seller #23	Coral 61805
11/11/57	8	11	11. **You Send Me** Jockey #8 / Best Seller #27 / Top 100 #31	Coral 61898
10/20/58	38	1	12. The Hula Hoop Song Hot 100 #38	Coral 62033
4/6/59	40	1	13. Heavenly Lover	Coral 62084
9/12/60	31	6	14. Anymore	Coral 62219
			Dick Jacobs (orch.: #5-14)	
			BREWER & SHIPLEY	
			Folk-rock duo formed in Los Angeles, California: Mike Brewer (born in 1944 in Oklahoma City, Oklahoma) and Tom Shipley (born in 1942 in Mineral Ridge, Ohio).	
3/13/71	10	10	1. **One Toke Over The Line**	Kama Sutra 516
			Jerry Garcia (of Grateful Dead; steel guitar)	
			BRICK	
			Black disco-jazz group from Atlanta, Georgia: Jimmy Brown (sax), Reggie Hargis (guitar), Don Nevins (keyboards), Ray Ransom (bass) and Eddie Irons (drums). All share vocals.	
11/20/76+	3	15	1. **Dazz**	Bang 727
			#1 R&B hit (4 weeks); title is short for disco-jazz	
10/1/77	18	10	2. Dusic	Bang 734
			title is short for disco-music	

DATE	POS	WKS	ARTIST—RECORD TITLE	LABEL & NO.
			BRICKELL, Edie, & New Bohemians	
			Born on 3/10/66 in Oak Cliff, Texas. Female singer/songwriter. New Bohemians consisted of Kenny Withrow (guitar), Brad Houser (bass) and John Bush (drums). Brickell married Paul Simon on 5/30/92.	
1/14/89	7	10	1. **What I Am** Sales #4 / Airplay #9	Geffen 27696
			BRIDGES, Alicia	
			Born on 7/15/53 in Lawndale, North Carolina. Disco singer/songwriter.	
9/9/78	5	19	● 1. **I Love The Nightlife (Disco 'Round)**	Polydor 14483
			BRIGGS, Lillian	
			Born Lillian Biggs in Allentown, Pennsylvania. Died of cancer on 4/11/98 (age 64). White big band-styled singer. Discovered by Alan Freed while working in Joy Cayler's All-Girl Orchestra.	
9/17/55	18	3	1. I Want You To Be My Baby Jockey #18 / Juke Box #19 / Best Seller #23 / Top 100 #53 O.B. Masingill (orch.); first recorded by Louis Jordan in 1953	Epic 9115
			BRIGHTER SIDE OF DARKNESS	
			R&B vocal group from Chicago, Illinois: Darryl Lamont, Ralph Eskridge, Randolph Murphy and Larry Washington.	
1/6/73	16	8	● 1. Love Jones	20th Century 2002
			BRILEY, Martin	
			Born on 6/10/52 in England. Rock singer/songwriter/guitarist.	
7/16/83	36	3	1. The Salt In My Tears	Mercury 812165
			BRISTOL, Johnny	
			Born on 2/3/39 in Morganton, North Carolina. Died on 3/21/2004 (age 65). R&B singer/songwriter/producer.	
7/20/74	8	13	1. **Hang On In There Baby**	MGM 14715
			BROCK, Chad	
			Born on 7/31/63 in Ocala, Florida. Country singer/songwriter/guitarist.	
4/17/99 5/20/00	39 22	2 10	1. Ordinary Life Airplay #23 / Sales #70 2. Yes! Sales #23 / Airplay #24 #1 Country hit (3 weeks)	Warner 17136 Warner 16876
			B-ROCK & THE BIZZ	
			B-Rock is rap producer Baron Agee from Mobile, Alabama. The Bizz is a studio group assembled by Agee.	
4/19/97	10	11	● 1. **MyBabyDaddy** Sales #3 / Airplay #65 Kitty Thomas (female vocal); samples "Best Of My Love" by The Emotions	Tony Mercedes 24221
			BROOD, Herman	
			Born on 11/5/46 in Zwolle, Netherlands. Committed suicide on 7/11/2001 (age 54). Singer/keyboardist.	
9/1/79	35	3	1. Saturdaynight	Ariola America 7754

DATE	POS	WKS	ARTIST–RECORD TITLE	LABEL & NO.
			BROOKLYN BRIDGE	
			Pop group from Long Island, New York: Johnny Maestro (lead vocals), Fred Ferrara, Les Cauchi and Mike Gregorie (backing vocals), Richie Macioce (guitar), Tom Sullivan and Joe Ruvio (saxophones), Shelly Davis (trumpet), Carolyn Wood (organ), Jimmy Rosica (bass) and Artie Catanzarita (drums). Maestro was lead singer of The Crests.	
1/4/69	3	10	● 1. **Worst That Could Happen**	Buddah 75
			BROOKLYN DREAMS — see SUMMER, Donna	
			BROOKS, Donnie	
			Born John Abahosh in Dallas, Texas; raised in Ventura, California. Pop singer.	
7/11/60	7	15	1. **Mission Bell**	Era 3018
12/26/60	31	3	2. Doll House	Era 3028
			BROOKS, Garth	
			Born Troyal Garth Brooks on 2/7/62 in Luba, Oklahoma; raised in Yukon, Oklahoma. Best-selling country artist of all time. Recorded as alter-ego pop singer "Chris Gaines."	
9/11/99	5	6	1. **Lost In You** Sales #2 **GARTH BROOKS AS CHRIS GAINES**	Capitol 58788
			BROOKS, Meredith	
			Born on 6/12/66 in Oregon City, Oregon. Female rock singer/guitarist.	
5/10/97	2 (4)	25	● 1. **Bitch** Sales #2 / Airplay #6	Capitol 58634
			BROOKS & DUNN	
			Country vocal duo: Kix Brooks (born on 5/12/55 in Shreveport, Louisiana) and Ronnie Dunn (born on 6/1/53 in Coleman, Texas).	
12/12/98	36	2	1. Husbands And Wives Airplay #28 #1 Country hit (1 week); from the album *If You See Her* on Arista Nashville 18865	album cut
4/14/01	25	12	2. Ain't Nothing 'Bout You Airplay #16 #1 Country hit (6 weeks)	album cut
9/29/01	33	7	3. Only In America Airplay #29 #1 Country hit (1 week)	album cut
2/23/02	39	3	4. The Long Goodbye Airplay #35 #1 Country hit (1 week); above 3 from the album *Steers & Stripes* on Arista Nashville 67003	album cut
7/5/03	25	9	5. Red Dirt Road Airplay #24 #1 Country hit (1 week); from the album *Red Dirt Road* on Arista Nashville 67070	album cut
			BROTHER BEYOND	
			Pop group from England: Nathan Moore (vocals), David White (guitar), Carl Fysh (keyboards) and Steve Alexander (drums).	
8/11/90	27	4	1. The Girl I Used To Know Sales #26 / Airplay #28	EMI 50287

DATE	POS	WKS	ARTIST–RECORD TITLE	LABEL & NO.
			BROTHERHOOD OF MAN, The	
			Studio group from England featuring lead singer Tony Burrows (lead singer of Edison Lighthouse, First Class, The Pipkins and White Plains). Actual vocal group formed in 1976: Nicky Stevens, Sandra Stevens, Martin Lee and Lee Sheridan.	
5/23/70	**13**	10	1. United We Stand	Deram 85059
6/19/76	**27**	4	2. Save Your Kisses For Me	Pye 71066
			#1 Adult Contemporary hit (1 week)	
			BROTHERS FOUR, The	
			Folk-pop group formed at the University of Washington: Dick Foley, Bob Flick, John Paine and Mike Kirkland.	
3/21/60	**2** (4)	15	1. **Greenfields**	Columbia 41571
4/24/61	**32**	3	2. Frogg　　　　　　　　　　　　　　　**[N]**	Columbia 41958
			BROTHERS JOHNSON, The	
			R&B duo of brothers from Los Angeles: George (guitar; born on 5/17/53) and Louis (bass; born on 4/13/55). With Billy Preston's band from 1973-75.	
5/22/76	**3**	12	● 1. **I'll Be Good To You**	A&M 1806
			#1 R&B hit (1 week)	
9/18/76	**30**	6	2. Get The Funk Out Ma Face	A&M 1851
7/30/77	**5**	13	● 3. **Strawberry Letter 23**	A&M 1949
			#1 R&B hit (1 week); Lee Ritenour (guitar solo)	
4/12/80	**7**	13	4. **Stomp!**	A&M 2216
			#1 R&B hit (2 weeks)	
			BROWN('S), Al, Tunetoppers featuring Cookie Brown	
			Born on 5/22/30 in Fairmont, West Virginia. Black singer/songwriter/producer.	
5/2/60	**23**	5	1. The Madison	Amy 804
			BROWN, Arthur, The Crazy World Of	
			Born Arthur Wilton on 6/24/44 in Whitby, England. Theatrical rock singer. His band consisted of Sean Nicholas (guitar), Vince Crane (organ) and Carl Palmer (drums). Palmer went on to join Emerson, Lake & Palmer and Asia. Crane committed suicide on 2/14/89 (age 44).	
9/21/68	**2** (1)	11	● 1. **Fire**	Atlantic 2556
			BROWN, Bobby	
			Born on 2/5/69 in Roxbury, Massachusetts. R&B singer. Former member of New Edition. Appeared in the movies *Ghostbusters II, Panther* and *A Thin Line Between Love & Hate*. Married Whitney Houston on 7/18/92.	
8/20/88	**8**	14	● 1. **Don't Be Cruel**　　Sales #3 / Airplay #13	MCA 53327
			#1 R&B hit (2 weeks)	
11/12/88+	**1** (1)	15	● 2. **My Prerogative**　　Sales #1 (1) / Airplay #2	MCA 53383
			#1 R&B hit (2 weeks)	
1/28/89	**3**	11	3. Roni　　　　　　Airplay #3 / Sales #4	MCA 53463
4/15/89	**3**	13	● 4. **Every Little Step**　　Sales #2 / Airplay #3	MCA 53618
			#1 R&B hit (1 week)	
7/1/89	**2** (3)	13	▲ 5. **On Our Own**　　Sales #1 (2) / Airplay #2	MCA 53662
			#1 R&B hit (1 week); from the movie *Ghostbusters II* starring Bill Murray and Dan Aykroyd	

DATE	POS	WKS	ARTIST–RECORD TITLE	LABEL & NO.
9/16/89	7	11	● 6. **Rock Wit'cha** Airplay #6 / Sales #8	MCA 53652
5/26/90	**1** (2)	14	● 7. **She Ain't Worth It** Airplay #1 (3) / Sales #4 **GLENN MEDEIROS Featuring Bobby Brown**	MCA 53831
8/8/92	3	17	● 8. **Humpin' Around** Sales #4 / Airplay #4 #1 R&B hit (2 weeks)	MCA 54342
10/24/92	7	21	● 9. **Good Enough** Airplay #5 / Sales #7 Whitney Houston (backing vocal)	MCA 54517
1/30/93	14	10	10. Get Away Sales #15 / Airplay #18	MCA 54511
11/27/93	32 ᴬ	5	11. Something In Common **BOBBY BROWN With WHITNEY HOUSTON** from Brown's album *Remixes N The Key Of B* on MCA 10974	album cut

BROWN, Boots, And His Blockbusters

			Brown was actually jazz trumpeter Shorty Rogers. Born Milton Rajonsky on 4/14/24 in Lee, Massachusetts. Died of liver failure on 11/7/94 (age 70). Worked with the big bands of Woody Herman and Stan Kenton.	
9/15/58	23	3	1. Cerveza Best Seller #23 / Hot 100 #62 **[I]** title is Spanish for "beer"	RCA Victor 7269

BROWN, Buster

			Born Wayman Glasco on 8/15/11 in Cordele, Georgia. Died on 1/31/76 (age 64). R&B singer/harmonica player.	
3/28/60	38	3	1. Fannie Mae #1 R&B hit (1 week)	Fire 1008

BROWN, Chuck, & The Soul Searchers

			Funk group from Washington DC: Chuck Brown (vocals, guitar), John Buchanan and Curtis Johnson (keyboards), Don Tillery (trumpet), Leroy Fleming (sax), Gregory Gerran (congas), Jerry Wilder (bass) and Ricky Wellman (drums).	
3/17/79	34	5	● 1. Bustin' Loose Part 1 #1 R&B hit (4 weeks)	Source 40967

BROWN, Foxy

			Born Inga Marchand on 9/6/79 in Brooklyn, New York. Female rapper. Took her name from the action movie character played by actress Pam Grier.	
3/22/97	7	11	● 1. I'll Be Sales #2 / Airplay #52 **FOXY BROWN Featuring Jay-Z** samples "I'll Be Good" by Rene & Angela	Violator 574028

BROWN, James

			Born on 5/3/33 in Barnwell, South Carolina; raised in Augusta, Georgia. Acclaimed as one of the most influential "soul" artists of all-time. Various nicknames include "The Godfather of Soul" and "The Hardest Working Man in Show Business." Inducted into the Rock and Roll Hall of Fame in 1986. On 12/15/88, received a six-year prison sentence after leading police on an interstate car chase; released from prison on 2/27/91. Won Grammy's Lifetime Achievement Award in 1992.	
5/30/60	33	2	1. Think #9 R&B hit for The 5 Royales in 1957	Federal 12370
4/3/61	40	2	2. Bewildered #1 R&B hit for Amos Milburn in 1948	King 5442
5/19/62	35	4	3. Night Train #1 R&B hit for Jimmy Forest in 1952	King 5614

DATE	POS	WKS	ARTIST–RECORD TITLE	LABEL & NO.
5/18/63	**18**	7	4. Prisoner Of Love #1 hit for Perry Como in 1946	King 5739
2/15/64	**23**	7	5. Oh Baby Don't You Weep (Part 1)	King 5842
9/12/64	**24**	5	6. Out Of Sight **JAMES BROWN And His Orchestra**	Smash 1919
8/7/65	**8**	9	7. Papa's Got A Brand New Bag Part I #1 R&B hit (8 weeks)	King 5999
11/20/65	**3**	10	8. I Got You (I Feel Good) #1 R&B hit (6 weeks)	King 6015
5/7/66	**8**	8	9. It's A Man's Man's Man's World #1 R&B hit (2 weeks)	King 6035
1/28/67	**29**	4	10. Bring It Up	King 6071
8/12/67	**7**	8	11. **Cold Sweat - Part 1** #1 R&B hit (3 weeks)	King 6110
11/25/67	**40**	1	12. Get It Together (Part 1)	King 6122
12/30/67+	**28**	5	13. I Can't Stand Myself (When You Touch Me) /	
2/17/68	**36**	4	14. There Was A Time	King 6144
3/23/68	**6**	10	15. **I Got The Feelin'** #1 R&B hit (2 weeks)	King 6155
6/1/68	**14**	7	16. Licking Stick - Licking Stick (Part 1) **JAMES BROWN And The Famous Flames (all of above King titles)**	King 6166
9/14/68	**10**	10	17. **Say It Loud - I'm Black And I'm Proud (Part 1)** #1 R&B hit (6 weeks)	King 6187
12/7/68	**31**	2	18. Goodbye My Love	King 6198
2/8/69	**15**	7	19. Give It Up Or Turnit A Loose #1 R&B hit (2 weeks)	King 6213
4/19/69	**20**	6	20. I Don't Want Nobody To Give Me Nothing (Open Up The Door, I'll Get It Myself)	King 6224
6/21/69	**11**	10	21. Mother Popcorn (You Got To Have A Mother For Me) Part 1 #1 R&B hit (2 weeks)	King 6245
6/28/69	**30**	5	22. The Popcorn [I]	King 6240
9/27/69	**37**	2	23. World (Part 1)	King 6258
11/1/69	**21**	5	24. Let A Man Come In And Do The Popcorn Part One	King 6255
12/13/69+	**24**	8	25. Ain't It Funky Now (Part 1) [I]	King 6280
1/24/70	**40**	2	26. Part Two (Let A Man Come In And Do The Popcorn)	King 6275
2/28/70	**32**	6	27. It's A New Day (Part 1) & (Part 2)	King 6292
5/23/70	**32**	2	28. Brother Rapp (Part 1) & (Part 2)	King 6310
8/1/70	**15**	7	29. Get Up (I Feel Like Being Like A) Sex Machine (Part 1)	King 6318
10/17/70	**13**	8	30. Super Bad (Part 1 & Part 2) #1 R&B hit (2 weeks)	King 6329
1/16/71	**34**	5	31. Get Up, Get Into It, Get Involved Pt. 1	King 6347
3/13/71	**29**	6	32. Soul Power Pt. 1	King 6368
6/26/71	**35**	3	33. Escape-ism (Part 1) [S]	People 2500
7/17/71	**15**	9	34. Hot Pants Pt. 1 (She Got To Use What She Got To Get What She Wants) #1 R&B hit (1 week)	People 2501
9/11/71	**22**	6	35. Make It Funky (Part 1) #1 R&B hit (2 weeks)	Polydor 14088
12/4/71	**35**	3	36. I'm A Greedy Man - Part I	Polydor 14100

DATE	POS	WKS	ARTIST–RECORD TITLE	LABEL & NO.
2/26/72	27	4	37. Talking Loud And Saying Nothing - Part I #1 R&B hit (1 week)	Polydor 14109
4/1/72	40	2	38. King Heroin [S]	Polydor 14116
9/9/72	18	8	● 39. Get On The Good Foot-Part 1 #1 R&B hit (4 weeks)	Polydor 14139
2/10/73	27	4	40. I Got Ants In My Pants - Part 1 (and i want to dance)	Polydor 14162
4/13/74	26	9	● 41. The Payback - Part I #1 R&B hit (2 weeks)	Polydor 14223
8/3/74	29	4	42. My Thang #1 R&B hit (2 weeks)	Polydor 14244
9/21/74	31	3	43. Papa Don't Take No Mess Part I #1 R&B hit (1 week)	Polydor 14255
1/11/86	4	11	44. **Living In America** Sales #4 / Airplay #6 from the movie *Rocky IV* starring Sylvester Stallone	Scotti Brothers 05682
			BROWN, Maxine	
			Born on 4/27/32 in Kingstree, South Carolina. R&B singer.	
1/30/61	19	6	1. All In My Mind	Nomar 103
4/24/61	25	5	2. Funny	Nomar 106
12/5/64+	24	7	3. Oh No Not My Baby Dee Dee Warwick (harmony vocal)	Wand 162
			BROWN, Nappy	
			Born Napoleon Brown Culp on 10/12/29 in Charlotte, North Carolina. R&B singer.	
4/30/55	25	4	1. Don't Be Angry Best Seller #25	Savoy 1155
			BROWN, Peter	
			Born on 7/11/53 in Blue Island, Illinois; later based in Miami, Florida. Disco singer/songwriter/keyboardist.	
10/8/77	18	8	1. Do Ya Wanna Get Funky With Me Wildflower (backing vocals)	Drive 6258
5/6/78	8	14	2. **Dance With Me** **PETER BROWN with Betty Wright**	Drive 6269
			BROWN, Polly	
			Born on 4/18/47 in Birmingham, England. White soul singer. Lead singer of Pickettywitch and Sweet Dreams.	
2/8/75	16	7	1. Up In A Puff Of Smoke	GTO 1002
			BROWN, Roy	
			Born on 9/10/25 in New Orleans, Louisiana. Died of a heart attack on 5/25/81 (age 55). Influential R&B singer/pianist.	
7/1/57	29	1	1. Let The Four Winds Blow Best Seller #29 / Top 100 #38	Imperial 5439
			BROWN, Ruth	
			Born Ruth Weston on 1/30/28 in Portsmouth, Virginia. R&B singer/actress. Appeared in several movies and TV shows. Starred in the 1988 musical *Black And Blue*. Inducted into the Rock and Roll Hall of Fame in 1993.	
3/2/57	25	5	1. Lucky Lips Best Seller #25 / Jockey #25 / Top 100 #26	Atlantic 1125

DATE	POS	WKS	ARTIST–RECORD TITLE	LABEL & NO.
10/13/58	24	2	2. This Little Girl's Gone Rockin' Hot 100 #24 King Curtis (sax solo); written by Bobby Darin	Atlantic 1197
			BROWN, Shirley	
			Born on 1/6/47 in West Memphis, Arkansas; raised in St. Louis, Missouri. R&B singer.	
11/23/74	22	6	1. Woman To Woman #1 R&B hit (2 weeks)	Truth 3206
			BROWNE, Jackson	
			Born on 10/9/48 in Heidelberg, Germany (U.S. Army base); raised in Los Angeles, California. Pop-rock singer/songwriter/guitarist/pianist. Worked with the Eagles and Warren Zevon. Wife, Phyllis, committed suicide on 3/25/76. Prominent activist against nuclear power. Inducted into the Rock and Roll Hall of Fame in 2004.	
4/8/72	8	9	1. **Doctor My Eyes**	Asylum 11004
2/19/77	23	6	2. Here Come Those Tears Again Bonnie Raitt (harmony vocal); John Hall (of Orleans; guitar solo)	Asylum 45379
3/4/78	11	12	3. Running On Empty	Asylum 45460
7/8/78	20	7	4. Stay / David Lindley (falsetto vocal); Rosemary Butler (female vocal)	
7/8/78		4	5. The Load-Out	Asylum 45485
7/26/80	19	10	6. Boulevard	Asylum 47003
10/18/80	22	5	7. That Girl Could Sing	Asylum 47036
8/21/82	7	12	8. **Somebody's Baby** from the movie *Fast Times At Ridgemont High* starring Sean Penn and Jennifer Jason Leigh	Asylum 69982
7/16/83	13	12	9. Lawyers In Love	Asylum 69826
10/22/83	25	7	10. Tender Is The Night	Asylum 69791
11/23/85+	18	12	11. You're A Friend Of Mine Airplay #17 / Sales #20 **CLARENCE CLEMONS And Jackson Browne** Daryl Hannah (backing vocals)	Columbia 05660
3/29/86	30	5	12. For America Airplay #27	Asylum 69566
			BROWNS, The	
			Family vocal trio from Sparkman, Arkansas: Jim Edward Brown and his sisters Maxine and Bonnie Brown.	
8/3/59	1 (4)	14	● 1. **The Three Bells** #1 Country hit (10 weeks); #14 hit for Les Compagnons De La Chanson in 1952	RCA Victor 7555
11/23/59	13	9	2. Scarlet Ribbons (For Her Hair) #14 hit for Jo Stafford in 1950	RCA Victor 7614
3/28/60	5	12	3. **The Old Lamplighter** **THE BROWNS featuring Jim Edward Brown** #1 hit for Sammy Kaye's Orchestra in 1946	RCA Victor 7700
			BROWNSTONE	
			Female R&B vocal trio from Los Angeles, California: Monica Doby, Nichole Gilbert and Charmayne Maxwell. Doby left group for health reasons in June 1995; replaced by Kina Cosper.	
1/7/95	8	22	● 1. **If You Love Me** Sales #5 / Airplay #9 samples "Spellbound" by K-Solo	MJJ Music 77732
6/21/97	39	2	2. 5 Miles To Empty Sales #25	MJJ Music 78496

DATE	POS	WKS	ARTIST–RECORD TITLE	LABEL & NO.
			BROWNSVILLE STATION	
			Rock trio from Ann Arbor, Michigan: Michael Lutz (vocals, bass), Michael "Cub" Koda (guitar) and Henry Weck (drums). Koda died of kidney failure on 7/1/2000 (age 51).	
12/8/73+	3	13	● 1. Smokin' In The Boy's Room	Big Tree 16011
10/5/74	31	3	2. Kings Of The Party	Big Tree 16001
			BRUBECK, Dave, Quartet	
			Born on 12/6/20 in Concord, California. Leader of jazz quartet consisting of Brubeck (piano), Paul Desmond (alto sax), Joe Morello (drums) and Eugene Wright (bass). One of America's all-time most popular jazz groups on college campuses. Desmond died on 5/30/77 (age 52). Brubeck won Grammy's Lifetime Achievement Award in 1996.	
9/25/61	25	7	1. Take Five [I]	Columbia 41479
			trend-setting jazz classic played in 5/4 time	
			BRYANT, Anita	
			Born on 3/25/40 in Barnsdale, Oklahoma. Adult Contemporary singer.	
7/27/59	30	7	1. Till There Was You	Carlton 512
			from the Broadway musical The Music Man starring Robert Preston and Shirley Jones	
5/2/60	5	12	2. **Paper Roses**	Carlton 528
			Monty Kelly (orch., above 2)	
8/8/60	10	9	3. **In My Little Corner Of The World**	Carlton 530
12/26/60+	18	6	4. Wonderland By Night	Carlton 537
			Lew Douglas (orch.)	
			BRYANT, Ray, Combo	
			Born Raphael Bryant on 12/24/31 in Philadelphia, Pennsylvania. R&B-jazz pianist/bandleader.	
5/9/60	30	4	1. The Madison Time - Part I [I-S]	Columbia 41628
			Eddie Morrison (dance calls)	
			BRYANT, Sharon — see ATLANTIC STARR	
			BRYSON, Peabo	
			Born Robert Peabo Bryson on 4/13/51 in Greenville, South Carolina. R&B singer/producer. First solo recording for Bang in 1970. Married Juanita Leonard, former wife of boxer Sugar Ray Leonard, in 1992.	
9/3/83	16	15	1. Tonight, I Celebrate My Love	Capitol 5242
			PEABO BRYSON/ROBERTA FLACK	
6/30/84	10	13	2. **If Ever You're In My Arms Again**	Elektra 69728
			#1 Adult Contemporary hit (4 weeks)	
2/22/92	9	14	▲ 3. **Beauty And The Beast** Sales #8 / Airplay #17	Epic 74090
			CELINE DION and PEABO BRYSON	
			title song from the animated movie	
1/2/93	1 (1)	18	● 4. **A Whole New World (Aladdin's Theme)**	
			Airplay #1 (4) / Sales #2	Columbia 74751
			PEABO BRYSON and REGINA BELLE	
			#1 Adult Contemporary hit (6 weeks); from the animated movie Aladdin	
6/19/93	25	7	5. By The Time This Night Is Over Airplay #24 / Sales #57	Arista 12565
			KENNY G with Peabo Bryson	
			#1 Adult Contemporary hit (2 weeks)	

DATE	POS	WKS	ARTIST–RECORD TITLE	LABEL & NO.
			B.T. EXPRESS	
			Disco group from Brooklyn, New York. Core members: Barbara Joyce (female vocals), brothers Louis (vocals, bass) and Bill (sax) Risbrook, Richard Thompson (guitar), Carlos Ward (flute) and Dennis Rowe (congas).	
10/5/74	**2** (2)	14	● 1. **Do It ('Til You're Satisfied)**	Scepter 12395
			#1 R&B hit (1 week)	
2/8/75	**4**	11	● 2. **Express** [I]	Roadshow 7001
			#1 R&B hit (1 week)	
9/13/75	**31**	4	3. Peace Pipe /	
9/6/75	**40**	2	4. Give It What You Got	Roadshow 7003
			B2K	
			Male R&B vocal group from Los Angeles, California: Jarell "J-Boog" Houston, Mario "Raz-B" Thornton, Dreux "Lil Fizz" Frederic and Omari Grandberry. Group starred in the movie *You Got Served.*	
2/23/02	**37**	6	1. Uh Huh Sales #1 (10) / Airplay #41	Epic 79686
6/22/02	**34**	4	2. Gots Ta Be Sales #6 / Airplay #35	Epic 79719
12/14/02+	**1** (1)	19	3. **Bump, Bump, Bump** Airplay #1 (2) / Sales #24	Epic 79842
			B2K & P. DIDDY	
4/19/03	**30**	3	4. Girlfriend Sales #19 / Airplay #31	Epic 76877
			BUBBLE PUPPY, The	
			Psychedelic-rock group from Houston, Texas: Rod Price (vocals), Todd Potter (guitar), Roy Cox (bass) and David Fore (drums).	
3/15/69	**14**	7	1. Hot Smoke & Sasafrass	Int'l. Artists 128
			BUCHANAN & GOODMAN — see GOODMAN, Dickie	
			BUCHANAN BROTHERS—see CASHMAN & WEST	
			BUCKINGHAM, Lindsey	
			Born on 10/3/49 in Palo Alto, California. Rock guitarist/singer/songwriter. Formed Buckingham-Nicks duo with then-girlfriend, Stevie Nicks. Both joined Fleetwood Mac in 1975.	
11/7/81+	**9**	14	1. **Trouble**	Asylum 47223
8/25/84	**23**	9	2. Go Insane	Elektra 69714
			BUCKINGHAMS, The	
			Pop-rock group from Chicago, Illinois: Dennis Tufano (vocals), Carl Giammarese (guitar), Martin Grebb (keyboards), Nick Fortune (bass) and Jon Paulos (drums). Paulos died of a drug overdose on 3/26/80 (age 32).	
1/21/67	**1** (2)	10	1. **Kind Of A Drag**	U.S.A. 860
4/8/67	**6**	10	2. **Don't You Care**	Columbia 44053
7/1/67	**5**	10	3. **Mercy, Mercy, Mercy**	Columbia 44182
9/30/67	**12**	7	4. Hey Baby (They're Playing Our Song)	Columbia 44254
12/23/67+	**11**	10	5. Susan	Columbia 44378
			BUCKNER & GARCIA	
			Novelty duo from Atlanta, Georgia: Jerry Buckner (keyboards) and Gary Garcia (vocals).	
1/30/82	**9**	14	● 1. **Pac-Man Fever** [N]	Columbia 02673
			tribute to the video game	

DATE	POS	WKS	ARTIST–RECORD TITLE	LABEL & NO.
			BUDDEN, Joe	
			Born in 1980 in Jersey City, New Jersey. Male rapper.	
6/28/03	38	1	1. Pump It Up Sales #23 / Airplay #39	Def Jam 000395
			samples "Soul Vibrations" by Kool & The Gang	
11/1/03	39	1	2. Clubbin Airplay #37	album cut
			MARQUES HOUSTON Featuring Joe Budden & Pied Piper	
			written and produced by R. Kelly; from Houston's album *MH* on T.U.G. 62935	
			BUFFALO SPRINGFIELD, The	
			Superstar group formed in Los Angeles, California: Stephen Stills (vocals, guitar), Neil Young and Richie Furay (guitars), Bruce Palmer (bass) and Dewey Martin (drums). Stills and Young later with Crosby, Stills, Nash & Young. Furay later formed Poco. Group inducted into the Rock and Roll Hall of Fame in 1997.	
2/18/67	7	11	1. **For What It's Worth (Stop, Hey What's That Sound)**	Atco 6459
			BUFFETT, Jimmy	
			Born on 12/25/46 in Pascagoula, Mississippi; raised in Mobile, Alabama. Singer/songwriter/guitarist. Settled in Key West, Florida, in 1971. Author of several books. Appeared in the movie *FM*. Faithful fans known as "Parrotheads."	
6/29/74	30	5	1. Come Monday	Dunhill/ABC 4385
5/7/77	8	15	2. **Margaritaville**	ABC 12254
			#1 Adult Contemporary hit (1 week)	
10/22/77	37	3	3. Changes In Latitudes, Changes In Attitudes	ABC 12305
5/27/78	32	4	4. Cheeseburger In Paradise **[N]**	ABC 12358
10/20/79	35	3	5. Fins	MCA 41109
7/19/03	17	15	6. It's Five O'Clock Somewhere Airplay #14	album cut
			ALAN JACKSON & JIMMY BUFFETT	
			#1 Country hit (8 weeks); from Jackson's album *Greatest Hits Volume II and Some Other Stuff* on Arista Nashville 53097	
			BUGGLES, The	
			New-wave duo from England: Geoff Downes and Trevor Horn. Both joined the group Yes in 1980. Downes joined Asia in 1981. Horn became a prolific producer.	
12/15/79	40	1	1. Video Killed The Radio Star	Island 49114
			first video ever played on MTV (August 1, 1981)	
			BULL & THE MATADORS	
			R&B vocal trio from St. Louis, Missouri: JaMell "Bull" Parks (born on 6/7/45), Milton Hardy and James Otis Love.	
11/16/68	39	1	1. The Funky Judge	Toddlin' Town 108
			BULLET	
			Rock duo from London, England: John Cann (vocals) and Paul Hammond (drums).	
12/25/71+	28	5	1. White Lies, Blue Eyes	Big Tree 123

DATE	POS	WKS	ARTIST–RECORD TITLE	LABEL & NO.
			BUOYS, The	
			Rock group from Wilkes-Barre, Pennsylvania: Bill Kelly (vocals), Carl Siracuse (guitar), Fran Brozena (keyboards), Jerry Hludzik (bass) and Chris Hanlon (drums).	
4/17/71	**17**	8	1. Timothy	Scepter 12275
			BURDON, Eric, And War	
			Born on 5/11/41 in Walker, Newcastle, England. After leaving The Animals, Burdon teamed up with the funk band War for two albums. Starred in the movie *Comeback* and made a cameo appearance in *The Doors*.	
7/11/70	**3**	13	● 1. **Spill The Wine**	MGM 14118
			BURKE, Solomon	
			Born on 2/22/36 in Philadelphia, Pennsylvania. R&B singer. Inducted into the Rock and Roll Hall of Fame in 2001.	
11/13/61	**24**	7	1. Just Out Of Reach (Of My Two Open Arms)	Atlantic 2114
5/25/63	**37**	2	2. If You Need Me	Atlantic 2185
5/23/64	**33**	4	3. Goodbye Baby (Baby Goodbye)	Atlantic 2226
4/3/65	**22**	5	4. Got To Get You Off My Mind #1 R&B hit (3 weeks)	Atlantic 2276
7/3/65	**28**	5	5. Tonight's The Night	Atlantic 2288
			BURNETTE, Dorsey	
			Born on 12/28/32 in Memphis, Tennessee. Died of a heart attack on 8/19/79 (age 46). Singer/songwriter/guitarist. Brother of Johnny Burnette. Uncle of Rocky Burnette.	
2/22/60	**23**	9	1. (There Was A) Tall Oak Tree	Era 3012
			BURNETTE, Johnny	
			Born on 3/25/34 in Memphis, Tennessee. Died in a boating accident on 8/1/64 (age 30). Singer/songwriter/guitarist. Brother of Dorsey Burnette. Father of Rocky Burnette.	
8/15/60	**11**	11	1. Dreamin'	Liberty 55258
11/21/60	**8**	11	2. **You're Sixteen**	Liberty 55285
2/20/61	**17**	6	3. Little Boy Sad	Liberty 55298
11/6/61	**18**	4	4. God, Country And My Baby Johnny Mann Singers (backing vocals)	Liberty 55379
			BURNETTE, Rocky	
			Born Jonathan Burnette on 6/12/53 in Memphis, Tennessee. Singer/songwriter/guitarist. Son of Johnny Burnette. Nephew of Dorsey Burnette.	
6/7/80	**8**	12	1. **Tired Of Toein' The Line**	EMI America 8043
			BUSCH, Lou, and His Orchestra	
			Born on 7/18/10 in Louisville, Kentucky. Died on 9/19/79 (age 69). Pianist/orchestra leader. Also recorded as Joe "Fingers" Carr (see #2 below).	
3/24/56	**35**	2	1. 11th Hour Melody　　　　　Top 100 #35	Capitol 3349
6/16/56	**19**	10	2. Portuguese Washerwomen Jockey #19 / Top 100 #25 / Best Seller #25 **[I]** **JOE "FINGERS" CARR**	Capitol 3418

DATE	POS	WKS	ARTIST–RECORD TITLE	LABEL & NO.

BUSH

Rock group from London, England: Gavin Rossdale (vocals, guitar), Nigel Pulsford (guitar), Dave Parsons (bass) and Robin Goodridge (drums). Rossdale married Gwen Stefani (lead singer of No Doubt) on 9/14/2002.

DATE	POS	WKS	ARTIST–RECORD TITLE	LABEL & NO.
3/18/95	40 A	1	1. Everything Zen from the album *Sixteen Stone* on Trauma 92531	album cut
10/14/95	30	7	2. Comedown Airplay #25 / Sales #68 #1 Modern Rock hit (2 weeks)	Trauma 98134
1/27/96	28	7	3. Glycerine Airplay #28 / Sales #33 #1 Modern Rock hit (2 weeks)	Trauma 98088
11/2/96	27 A	12	4. Swallowed #1 Modern Rock hit (7 weeks); from the album *Razorblade Suitcase* on Trauma 90091	album cut

BUSH, Kate

Born on 7/30/58 in Bexleyheath, Kent, England. Singer/songwriter.

DATE	POS	WKS	ARTIST–RECORD TITLE	LABEL & NO.
11/9/85	30	4	1. Running Up That Hill Sales #26	EMI America 8285

BUSTA RHYMES

Born Trevor Smith on 5/20/72 in Brooklyn, New York. Male rapper. Founder of rap group Leaders Of The New School and member of Flipmode Squad. Played "Freddie Harris" in the 2002 movie *Halloween: Resurrection*.

DATE	POS	WKS	ARTIST–RECORD TITLE	LABEL & NO.
3/16/96	8	13	▲ 1. **Woo-Hah!! Got You All In Check /** Sales #5 / Airplay #52 samples "Space" by Galt MacDermot	
4/6/96		10	2. Everything Remains Raw Sales: flip	Elektra 64335
10/25/97	37 A	4	3. Put Your Hands Where My Eyes Could See from the album *When Disaster Strikes...* on Elektra 62064	album cut
1/17/98	9	9	● 4. **Dangerous** Sales #6 / Airplay #60 samples "E.T. Boogie" by Extra T'S	Elektra 64131
3/28/98	19	13	● 5. Victory Sales #11 **PUFF DADDY & THE FAMILY Featuring The Notorious B.I.G. & Busta Rhymes** samples "Alone In The Ring" (from the movie *Rocky*) by Bill Conti	Bad Boy 79155
5/9/98	10	12	● 6. **Turn It Up [Remix]/Fire It Up** Sales #5 samples the theme from TV's *Knight Rider*	Elektra 64104
3/27/99	3	13	● 7. **What's It Gonna Be?!** Sales #2 / Airplay #9 **BUSTA RHYMES Featuring Janet** #1 R&B hit (1 week); Antoinette Roberson (backing vocal)	Elektra 64051
1/5/02	26	8	8. Break Ya Neck Airplay #21 / Sales #39 samples "Give It Away" by Red Hot Chili Peppers	J Records 21061
3/30/02	11	14	9. Pass The Courvoisier Part II Airplay #10 / Sales #14 **BUSTA RHYMES featuring P. Diddy & Pharrell**	J Records 21154
3/15/03	3	22	10. **I Know What You Want** Airplay #3 / Sales #15 **BUSTA RHYMES AND MARIAH CAREY (feat. The Flipmode Squad)**	J Records 21258

BUSTERS, The

Instrumental group from Springfield, Massachusetts: Alan Orkins, John Chappel and Fred Cole (guitars), Al Marczyk (sax), Jack Baker (bass) and Fran Parda (drums).

DATE	POS	WKS	ARTIST–RECORD TITLE	LABEL & NO.
9/28/63	25	5	1. Bust Out [I]	Arlen 735

DATE	POS	WKS	ARTIST–RECORD TITLE	LABEL & NO.
			BUTLER, Jerry	
			Born on 12/8/39 in Sunflower, Mississippi; raised in Chicago, Illinois. R&B singer. Member of The Impressions from 1957-58. Nicknamed "The Ice Man." Hosted the popular PBS TV "Doo Wop" specials.	
6/16/58	11	9	1. For Your Precious Love _Best Seller #11 / Top 100 #11 / Jockey #25_ **JERRY BUTLER and The Impressions**	Abner 1013
11/7/60	7	13	2. **He Will Break Your Heart** _#1 R&B hit (7 weeks)_	Vee-Jay 354
4/3/61	27	4	3. Find Another Girl	Vee-Jay 375
8/7/61	25	4	4. I'm A Telling You	Vee-Jay 390
10/30/61	11	11	5. Moon River _from the movie Breakfast At Tiffany's starring Audrey Hepburn_	Vee-Jay 405
8/18/62	20	4	6. Make It Easy On Yourself	Vee-Jay 451
12/28/63+	31	5	7. Need To Belong	Vee-Jay 567
9/19/64	5	11	8. **Let It Be Me** **BETTY EVERETT & JERRY BUTLER**	Vee-Jay 613
11/25/67	38	2	9. Mr. Dream Merchant	Mercury 72721
6/8/68	20	9	10. Never Give You Up	Mercury 72798
10/5/68	16	8	11. Hey, Western Union Man _#1 R&B hit (1 week)_	Mercury 72850
1/18/69	39	2	12. Are You Happy	Mercury 72876
3/8/69	4	12	● 13. **Only The Strong Survive** _#1 R&B hit (2 weeks)_	Mercury 72898
6/21/69	24	7	14. Moody Woman	Mercury 72929
9/6/69	20	9	15. What's The Use Of Breaking Up	Mercury 72960
2/5/72	21	10	● 16. Ain't Understanding Mellow **JERRY BUTLER and BRENDA LEE EAGER**	Mercury 73255
			BUTLER, Jonathan	
			Born in Capetown, South Africa. R&B singer/songwriter/guitarist.	
8/15/87	27	5	1. Lies _Sales #21 / Airplay #30_	Jive 1038
			BUTTHOLE SURFERS	
			Punk-rock group from San Antonio, Texas: Gibby Haynes (vocals), Paul Leary (guitar), Jeff Pinkus (bass) and King Coffey (drums).	
6/22/96	26 ᴬ	12	1. Pepper _#1 Modern Rock hit (3 weeks); from the album Electriclarryland on Capitol 29842_	album cut
			B*WITCHED	
			Female vocal group from Dublin, Ireland: twin sisters Edele and Keavy Lynch, with Sinead O'Carroll and Lindsay Armaou.	
3/27/99	9	8	● 1. **C'est La Vie** _Sales #4_ _title is French for "That's Life"_	Epic 79084
			BYRD, Charlie — see GETZ, Stan	
			BYRD, Tracy	
			Born on 12/17/66 in Beaumont, Texas; raised in Vidor, Texas. Male country singer/guitarist.	
8/31/02	26	6	1. Ten Rounds With José Cuervo _Airplay #25_ _#1 Country hit (1 week); from the album Ten Rounds on RCA 67009_	album cut

DATE	POS	WKS	ARTIST–RECORD TITLE	LABEL & NO.
			BYRDS, The	
			Folk-rock group formed in Los Angeles, California: Roger McGuinn and David Crosby (guitars), Gene Clark (tambourine, guitar), Chris Hillman (bass) and Mike Clarke (drums). All shared vocals. McGuinn had been with the Chad Mitchell Trio. Gene Clark had been with the New Christy Minstrels; left after "Eight Miles High." Crosby later formed Crosby, Stills & Nash. McGuinn, Clark & Hillman later recorded as a trio. Mike Clarke later joined Firefall. Gene Clark died on 5/24/91 (age 46). Mike Clarke died of liver failure on 12/19/93 (age 49). Group inducted into the Rock and Roll Hall of Fame in 1991.	
6/5/65	1 (1)	10	1. **Mr. Tambourine Man**	Columbia 43271
8/21/65	40	1	2. All I Really Want To Do	Columbia 43332
11/6/65	1 (3)	11	3. **Turn! Turn! Turn! (To Everything There Is A Season)**	Columbia 43424
			lyrics adapted by Pete Seeger from the Book of Ecclesiastes	
4/30/66	14	6	4. Eight Miles High	Columbia 43578
10/22/66	36	2	5. Mr. Spaceman	Columbia 43766
2/18/67	29	3	6. So You Want To Be A Rock 'N' Roll Star	Columbia 43987
4/29/67	30	3	7. My Back Pages	Columbia 44054
			#1, 2 & 7: written by Bob Dylan	
			BYRNES, Edward	
			Born Edward Breitenberger on 7/30/33 in Brooklyn, New York. Played "Kookie" on TV's *77 Sunset Strip*.	
4/27/59	4	11	● 1. **Kookie, Kookie (Lend Me Your Comb)** [N] **EDWARD BYRNES And CONNIE STEVENS**	Warner 5047
			C	
			CADETS, The	
			R&B vocal group from Los Angeles, California: Aaron Collins, Ted Taylor, William "Dub" Jones, Willie Davis and Lloyd McCraw. Jones later joined The Coasters. Collins and Davis later joined The Flares. Collins's sisters, Betty and Rosie, recorded as The Teen Queens. Jones died of heart failure on 1/16/2000 (age 71).	
7/21/56	15	7	1. Stranded In The Jungle	Modern 994
			Best Seller #15 / Jockey #16 / Juke Box #16 / Top 100 #18 [N]	
			CADILLACS, The	
			Black doo-wop group from Harlem, New York: Earl "Speedo" Carroll, LaVerne Drake, Earl Wade, Charles Brooks and Robert Phillips. James Bailey and Robert Spencer replaced Drake and Brooks in 1958. Carroll later joined The Coasters. Spencer later joined Crazy Elephant. Bailey died in 1980 (age 48).	
2/4/56	17	5	1. Speedoo Best Seller #17 / Top 100 #30	Josie 785
			Jesse Powell (orch.)	
1/12/59	28	3	2. Peek-A-Boo	Josie 846
			Osie Johnson (orch.)	
			CAFFERTY, John, And The Beaver Brown Band	
			Rock group from Narragansett, Rhode Island: John Cafferty (vocals, guitar), Gary Gramolini (guitar), Robert Cotoia (keyboards), Michael Antunes (saxophone), Pat Lupo (bass) and Kenny Jo Silva (drums).	
9/15/84	7	11	1. **On The Dark Side** Airplay #6 / Sales #11 [R]	Scotti Brothers 04594
			#1 Mainstream Rock hit (5 weeks); originally charted at #64 in 1983	

DATE	POS	WKS	ARTIST–RECORD TITLE	LABEL & NO.
12/8/84+	**31**	7	2. Tender Years Sales #28 / Airplay #28 **[R]** originally charted at #78 in 1984; above 2 from the movie *Eddie and the Cruisers* starring Tom Berenger	Scotti Brothers 04682
6/1/85	**22**	8	3. Tough All Over Airplay #13 / Sales #26 #1 Mainstream Rock hit (2 weeks)	Scotti Brothers 04891
8/31/85	**18**	8	4. C-I-T-Y Sales #19 / Airplay #19	Scotti Brothers 05452
			CAGE, Athena — see SWEAT, Keith	
			CAGLE, Chris	
			Born Christian Cagle on 11/10/68 in Louisiana; raised in Houston, Texas. Male country singer/songwriter/guitarist.	album cut
4/6/02	**35**	3	1. I Breathe In, I Breathe Out Airplay #34 #1 Country hit (1 week); from the album *Play It Loud* on Capitol 34170	
			CAIN, Tané	
			Born Tané McClure on 6/8/59 in Pacific Palasades, California. Female singer/songwriter. Daughter of actor Doug McClure. Formerly married to Jonathan Cain (of The Babys, Journey, Bad English).	
9/18/82	**37**	3	1. Holdin' On	RCA 13287
			CAIOLA, Al, And His Orchestra	
			Born on 9/7/20 in Jersey City, New Jersey. Prolific studio guitarist.	
1/16/61	**35**	4	1. The Magnificent Seven **[I]** title song from the movie starring Yul Brynner	United Artists 261
5/1/61	**19**	5	2. Bonanza **[I]** title song from the TV series starring Lorne Greene	United Artists 302
			CAKE	
			Rock group from Sacramento, California: John McCrea (vocals, guitar), Greg Brown (guitar), Vince DiFiore (trumpet), Victor Damiani (bass) and Todd Roper (drums).	album cut
11/23/96	**35** ᴬ	3	1. The Distance from the album *Fashion Nugget* on Capricorn 532867	
			CALDWELL, Bobby	
			Born on 8/15/51 in Manhattan, New York; raised in Miami, Florida. Multi-instrumentalist/songwriter.	
2/3/79	**9**	12	1. **What You Won't Do For Love**	Clouds 11
			CALE, J.J.	
			Born Jean Jacques Cale on 12/5/38 in Oklahoma City. Rock singer/songwriter/guitarist.	
3/11/72	**22**	8	1. Crazy Mama	Shelter 7314
			CALLING, The	
			Rock group from Los Angeles, California: Alex Band (vocals), Aaron Kamin and Sean Woolstenhulme (guitars), Billy Mohler (bass) and Nate Wood (drums).	RCA 60518
12/1/01+	**5**	40	1. **Wherever You Will Go** Sales #3 / Airplay #5	

DATE	POS	WKS	ARTIST–RECORD TITLE	LABEL & NO.
			CALLOWAY	
			R&B duo from Cincinnati, Ohio: brothers Reggie and Vincent Calloway. Both were members of Midnight Star.	
3/10/90	**2** (1)	15	● 1. **I Wanna Be Rich** Sales #2 / Airplay #2	Solar 74005
			CAMEO	
			R&B-funk trio from Brooklyn, New York: Larry Blackmon, Tomi Jenkins and Nathan Leftenant.	
10/4/86	**6**	14	1. **Word Up** Sales #2 / Airplay #8 #1 R&B hit (3 weeks)	Atlanta Artists 884933
2/14/87	**21**	7	2. Candy Sales #19 / Airplay #28 #1 R&B hit (2 weeks)	Atlanta Artists 888193
			CAMILLO, Tony — see BAZUKA	
			CAMPBELL, Glen	
			Born on 4/22/36 in Delight, Arkansas. Country singer/songwriter/guitarist. Became prolific studio musician; with The Champs in 1960, The Hondells in 1964, The Beach Boys in 1965 and Sagittarius in 1967. Own TV show *The Glen Campbell Goodtime Hour* (1968-72). Acted in the movies *True Grit*, *Norwood* and *Strange Homecoming*; voice in the animated movie *Rock-A-Doodle*.	
11/25/67	**26**	7	1. By The Time I Get To Phoenix	Capitol 2015
5/25/68	**36**	2	2. I Wanna Live #1 Country hit (3 weeks)	Capitol 2146
8/3/68	**32**	3	3. Dreams Of The Everyday Housewife	Capitol 2224
11/2/68	**39**	1	4. Gentle On My Mind **[R]** originally charted at #62 in 1967	Capitol 5939
11/16/68+	**3**	13	● 5. **Wichita Lineman** #1 Country hit (2 weeks) / #1 Adult Contemporary hit (6 weeks)	Capitol 2302
3/8/69	**36**	1	6. Let It Be Me **GLEN CAMPBELL AND BOBBIE GENTRY**	Capitol 2387
3/15/69	**4**	10	● 7. **Galveston** #1 Country hit (3 weeks) / #1 Adult Contemporary hit (6 weeks)	Capitol 2428
5/17/69	**26**	5	8. Where's The Playground Susie	Capitol 2494
8/23/69	**35**	2	9. True Grit title song from the movie starring John Wayne and Campbell	Capitol 2573
11/1/69	**23**	7	10. Try A Little Kindness #1 Adult Contemporary hit (1 week)	Capitol 2659
1/31/70	**19**	7	11. Honey Come Back	Capitol 2718
3/14/70	**27**	6	12. All I Have To Do Is Dream **BOBBIE GENTRY & GLEN CAMPBELL**	Capitol 2745
5/9/70	**40**	2	13. Oh Happy Day	Capitol 2787
9/26/70	**10**	9	14. **It's Only Make Believe**	Capitol 2905
3/27/71	**31**	4	15. Dream Baby (How Long Must I Dream)	Capitol 3062
6/21/75	**1** (2)	18	● 16. **Rhinestone Cowboy** #1 Country hit (3 weeks) / #1 Adult Contemporary hit (1 week); #24 Adult Contemporary hit for Larry Weiss (song's writer) in 1974	Capitol 4095
11/22/75+	**11**	11	17. Country Boy (You Got Your Feet In L.A.) #1 Adult Contemporary hit (1 week)	Capitol 4155
4/17/76	**27**	5	18. Don't Pull Your Love/Then You Can Tell Me Goodbye #1 Adult Contemporary hit (1 week)	Capitol 4245
3/5/77	**1** (1)	15	● 19. **Southern Nights** #1 Country hit (2 weeks) / #1 Adult Contemporary hit (4 weeks)	Capitol 4376

DATE	POS	WKS	ARTIST–RECORD TITLE	LABEL & NO.
8/13/77	**39**	2	20. Sunflower *#1 Adult Contemporary hit (1 week)*	Capitol 4445
12/9/78	**38**	2	21. Can You Fool	Capitol 4638
			CAMPBELL, Jo Ann	
9/8/62	**38**	3	Born on 7/20/38 in Jacksonville, Florida. Appeared in the movies *Johnny Melody, Go Johnny Go* and *Hey, Let's Twist.* 1. (I'm The Girl On) Wolverton Mountain *answer song to Claude King's "Wolverton Mountain"; some pressings titled as "I'm The Girl From Wolverton Mountain"*	Cameo 223
			CAMPBELL, Tevin	
			Born on 11/12/76 in Waxahachie, Texas. R&B singer. Appeared in the movie *Graffiti Bridge.*	
2/9/91	**12**	13	● 1. Round And Round Airplay #12 / Sales #13 *from the movie Graffiti Bridge starring Prince*	Paisley Park 21740
12/7/91+	**6**	20	● 2. **Tell Me What You Want Me To Do** Airplay #6 / Sales #8 *#1 R&B hit (1 week)*	Qwest 19131
10/23/93+	**9**	23	● 3. **Can We Talk** Sales #9 / Airplay #9 *#1 R&B hit (3 weeks)*	Qwest 18346
3/26/94	**9**	18	4. **I'm Ready** Airplay #8 / Sales #15	Qwest 18264
7/9/94	**20**	10	5. Always In My Heart Airplay #22 / Sales #24	Qwest 18260
			CAM'RON	
			Born Cameron Giles on 2/4/76 in Harlem, New York. Male rapper.	
5/11/02	**4**	18	1. **Oh Boy** Airplay #4 / Sales #17 **CAM'RON feat. Juelz Santana** *#1 R&B hit (5 weeks); samples "I'm Going Down" by Rose Royce*	Roc-A-Fella 582864
9/7/02	**3**	20	2. Hey Ma Airplay #3 / Sales #21 **CAM'RON (feat. Juelz Santana, Freekey Zekey and Toya)**	Roc-A-Fella 063958
5/10/03	**16**	9	3. Snake Airplay #15 / Sales #21 **R. KELLY featuring Cam'ron and Big Tigger**	Jive 40108
			C & C MUSIC FACTORY	
			Dance group led by producers/songwriters Robert Clivilles (percussion) and David Cole (keyboards). Featured vocalists include Freedom Williams, Deborah Cooper and Martha Wash. Cole died of spinal meningitis on 1/24/95 (age 32).	
12/15/90+	**1 (2)**	17	▲ 1. **Gonna Make You Sweat (Everybody Dance Now)** Sales #1 (4) / Airplay #3 **C & C MUSIC FACTORY Featuring Freedom Williams** *#1 R&B hit (1 week)*	Columbia 73604
3/23/91	**3**	14	● 2. Here We Go Sales #3 / Airplay #5 **C + C MUSIC FACTORY Presents Freedom Williams and Zelma Davis**	Columbia 73690
7/27/91	**4**	12	● 3. Things That Make You Go Hmmmm... Airplay #10 / Sales #12 **C + C MUSIC FACTORY featuring Freedom Williams**	Columbia 73687
9/10/94	**40**	2	4. Do You Wanna Get Funky Sales #21 / Airplay #47	Columbia 77582

DATE	POS	WKS	ARTIST–RECORD TITLE	LABEL & NO.
			CANDLEBOX	
			Rock group from Seattle, Washington: Kevin Martin (vocals), Peter Klett (guitar), Bardi Martin (bass) and Scott Mercado (drums).	
9/3/94	**18**	15	1. Far Behind Sales #13 / Airplay #23	Maverick/Sire 18118
			CANDYMAN	
			Born on 6/25/68 in Los Angeles, California. Male rapper.	
10/13/90	**9**	12	▲ 1. **Knockin' Boots** Sales #2 / Airplay #28 samples "Ooh Boy" by Rose Royce and "Tonight Is The Night" by Betty Wright	Epic 73450
			CANIBUS	
			Born Germaine Williams in New Jersey. Male rapper.	
4/11/98	**28**	7	1. Second Round K.O. Sales #18	Universal 56175
			CANNED HEAT	
			Blues-rock group from Los Angeles, California: Bob "The Bear" Hite (vocals, harmonica), Alan "Blind Owl" Wilson (guitar, harmonica, vocals), Henry Vestine (guitar), Larry Taylor (bass) and Adolfo DeLa Parra in 1968. Vestine replaced by Harvey Mandel in 1969. Wilson died of a drug overdose on 9/3/70 (age 27). Hite died of a heart attack on 4/6/81 (age 36). Vestine died of heart failure on 10/20/97 (age 52).	
9/7/68	**16**	7	1. On The Road Again	Liberty 56038
12/21/68+	**11**	9	2. Going Up The Country	Liberty 56077
11/7/70	**26**	6	3. Let's Work Together	Liberty 56151
			CANNIBAL AND THE HEADHUNTERS	
			Latino vocal group from Los Angeles, California: Frankie "Cannibal" Garcia, brothers Robert and Joe Jaramillo, and Richard Lopez. Garcia died on 1/21/96 (age 49). Joe Jaramillo died on 5/24/2000 (age 51).	
4/17/65	**30**	6	1. Land Of 1000 Dances	Rampart 642
			CANNON, Ace	
			Born on 5/4/34 in Grenada, Mississippi. White saxophonist/songwriter. Worked with Bill Black's Combo.	
1/27/62	**17**	10	1. Tuff [I]	Hi 2040
5/19/62	**36**	1	2. Blues (Stay Away From Me) [I] #11 hit for Owen Bradley in 1949	Hi 2051
			CANNON, Freddy	
			Born Frederick Picariello on 12/4/39 in Lynn, Massachusetts. Pop singer. Nickname "Boom Boom" came from big bass drum-sound on his records.	
5/25/59	**6**	10	1. **Tallahassee Lassie**	Swan 4031
12/7/59+	**3**	11	● 2. **Way Down Yonder In New Orleans** **FREDDIE CANNON**	Swan 4043
3/7/60	**34**	3	3. Chattanooga Shoe Shine Boy #1 hit for Red Foley in 1950	Swan 4050
5/30/60	**28**	4	4. Jump Over	Swan 4053
9/4/61	**35**	1	5. Transistor Sister	Swan 4078
5/26/62	**3**	12	6. **Palisades Park** written by Chuck Barris (host of TV's *The Gong Show*)	Swan 4106

DATE	POS	WKS	ARTIST–RECORD TITLE	LABEL & NO.
2/15/64	**16**	6	7. Abigail Beecher	Warner 5409
8/28/65	**13**	6	8. Action from Dick Clark's TV show *Where The Action Is*	Warner 5645

CANNON, Nick

Born on 10/17/80 in San Diego, California. R&B singer/actor. Regular on TV's *All That* (1998-2001). Starred in the movie *Drumline*.

12/27/03+	**24**	14	1. Gigolo Airplay #22 / Sales #70 **NICK CANNON featuring R. Kelly**	Nick/Jive 56646

CANTRELL, Blu

Born Tiffany Cantrell in 1976 in Providence, Rhode Island. Female R&B singer.

7/14/01	**2 (2)**	21	1. **Hit 'Em Up Style (Oops!)** Sales #1 (1) / Airplay #3	Arista 13974

CAPALDI, Jim

Born on 8/24/44 in Evesham, Worcestershire, England. Rock singer/drummer. Member of Traffic.

5/28/83	**28**	5	1. That's Love	Atlantic 89849

CAPITOLS, The

R&B trio from Detroit, Michigan: Sam George (vocals, drums), Donald Storball (guitar) and Richard McDougall (keyboards). George was murdered on 3/17/82 (age 39).

5/21/66	**7**	11	1. **Cool Jerk**	Karen 1524

CAPRIS, The

Doo-wop group from Queens, New York: Nick Santamaria, Mike Mincieli, Frank Reina, Vinny Naccarato and John Apostol.

1/23/61	**3**	10	1. **There's A Moon Out Tonight**	Old Town 1094

CAPTAIN & TENNILLE

Pop duo: Daryl "The Captain" Dragon (born on 8/27/42 in Los Angeles, California) and his wife, Toni Tennille (born on 5/8/43 in Montgomery, Alabama). Dragon is the son of noted conductor Carmen Dragon. Keyboardist with The Beach Boys; nicknamed "The Captain" by Mike Love. Duo had own TV show on ABC from 1976-77.

5/24/75	**1 (4)**	16	● 1. **Love Will Keep Us Together** #1 Adult Contemporary hit (1 week); first recorded by Neil Sedaka in 1974	A&M 1672
10/4/75	**4**	14	● 2. **The Way I Want To Touch You** #1 Adult Contemporary hit (2 weeks)	A&M 1725
2/7/76	**3**	13	● 3. **Lonely Night (Angel Face)** #1 Adult Contemporary hit (1 week); first recorded by Neil Sedaka in 1975	A&M 1782
5/8/76	**4**	12	● 4. **Shop Around** #1 Adult Contemporary hit (1 week)	A&M 1817
10/9/76	**4**	15	● 5. **Muskrat Love** #1 Adult Contemporary hit (4 weeks); first recorded by America in 1973	A&M 1870
4/2/77	**13**	8	6. Can't Stop Dancin' written by Ray Stevens	A&M 1912
9/9/78	**10**	14	7. **You Never Done It Like That** first recorded by Neil Sedaka in 1977	A&M 2063

DATE	POS	WKS	ARTIST–RECORD TITLE	LABEL & NO.
1/27/79	**40**	1	8. You Need A Woman Tonight	A&M 2106
11/10/79+	**1** (1)	22	● 9. **Do That To Me One More Time**	Casablanca 2215
			CAPTAIN HOLLYWOOD PROJECT	
			Captain Hollywood is dance producer Tony Harrison. Born on 8/9/62 in Newark, New Jersey; raised in Detroit, Michigan.	
5/22/93	**17**	12	1. More And More Airplay #12 / Sales #21	Imago 25029
			Nina (lead vocal)	
			CARA, Irene	
			Born Irene Escalera on 3/18/64 in the Bronx, New York. Dance singer/actress/pianist. Appeared in several movies and TV shows.	
7/26/80	**4**	12	1. Fame	RSO 1034
9/27/80	**19**	9	2. Out Here On My Own	RSO 1048
			above 2 from the movie *Fame* starring Cara	
4/16/83	**1** (6)	20	● 3. **Flashdance...What A Feeling**	Casablanca 811440
			from the movie *Flashdance* starring Jennifer Beals	
11/5/83	**13**	10	4. Why Me?	Geffen 29464
1/28/84	**37**	3	5. The Dream (Hold On To Your Dream)	Geffen 29396
			from the movie *D.C. Cab* starring Cara and Mr. T.	
4/14/84	**8**	11	6. **Breakdance**	Geffen 29328
			CARAVELLES, The	
			Female pop vocal duo from England: Andrea Simpson (born on 9/12/45) and Lois Wilkinson (born on 4/3/44).	
11/23/63	**3**	10	1. **You Don't Have To Be A Baby To Cry**	Smash 1852
			#10 Country hit for Ernest Tubb in 1950	
			CARDIGANS, The	
			Pop-rock group from Malmo, Sweden: Nina Persson (vocals), Peter Svensson (guitar), Lars-Olof Johansson (keyboards), Magnus Sveningsson (bass) and Bengt Lagersburg (drums).	
12/14/96+	**2** (8)ᴬ	38	1. **Lovefool**	album cut
			from the album *First Band On The Moon* on Stockholm/Mercury 533117	
			CAREFREES, The	
			Female vocal trio from England: Lyn Cornell, Betty Prescott and Barbara Kay.	
4/11/64	**39**	1	1. We Love You Beatles **[N]**	London Int'l. 10614
			new lyrics to "We Love You Conrad" from the musical *Bye Bye Birdie* starring Chita Rivera	
			CAREY, Mariah	
			Born on 3/27/70 in Greenlawn, Long Island, New York. Her mother is Patricia Carey, former singer with the New York City Opera. Mariah sang backup for Brenda K. Starr. Won the 1990 Best New Artist Grammy Award. Married to Tommy Mottola, president of Sony Music Entertainment, from 1993-98. Starred in the 2001 movie *Glitter*.	
6/16/90	**1** (4)	17	● 1. **Vision Of Love** Airplay #1 (3) / Sales #1 (2)	Columbia 73348
			#1 R&B hit (2 weeks) / #1 Adult Contemporary hit (3 weeks)	
9/29/90	**1** (3)	18	● 2. **Love Takes Time** Sales #1 (2) / Airplay #1 (2)	Columbia 73455
			#1 R&B hit (1 week) / #1 Adult Contemporary hit (1 week)	

DATE	POS	WKS		ARTIST–RECORD TITLE		LABEL & NO.
1/19/91	1 (2)	15	●	3. **Someday**	Airplay #1 (4) / Sales #2	Columbia 73561
4/13/91	1 (2)	14		4. **I Don't Wanna Cry**	Airplay #1 (2) / Sales #3	Columbia 73743
				#1 Adult Contemporary hit (1 week)		
8/31/91	1 (3)	20	●	5. **Emotions**	Airplay #1 (4) / Sales #10	Columbia 73977
				#1 R&B hit (1 week)		
11/23/91+	2 (1)	17		6. **Can't Let Go**	Airplay #2 / Sales #8	Columbia 74088
				#1 Adult Contemporary hit (3 weeks)		
3/7/92	5	16		7. **Make It Happen**	Airplay #2 / Sales #18	Columbia 74239
5/30/92	1 (2)	14		8. **I'll Be There**	Airplay #1 (8) / Sales #3 [L]	Columbia 74330
				#1 Adult Contemporary hit (2 weeks); Trey Lorenz (backing vocal)		
8/7/93	1 (8)	26	▲	9. **Dreamlover**	Airplay #1 (11) / Sales #2	Columbia 77080
				samples "Blind Alley" by The Emotions		
11/6/93	1 (4)	25	▲	10. **Hero**	Airplay #1 (10) / Sales #2	Columbia 77224
2/5/94	3	21	●	11. **Without You /**	Airplay #2 / Sales #3	
2/12/94		20		12. Never Forget You	Sales: flip	Columbia 77358
				Babyface (co-writer and backing vocal)		
6/4/94	12	18		13. Anytime You Need A Friend	Airplay #8 / Sales #19	Columbia 77499
9/10/94	2 (1)	13	●	14. **Endless Love**	Sales #2 / Airplay #5	Columbia 77629
				LUTHER VANDROSS & MARIAH CAREY		
12/24/94	12 ᴬ	3		15. All I Want For Christmas Is You	[X]	album cut
				from the album *Merry Christmas* on Columbia 64222		
9/30/95	1 (8)	23	▲²	16. **Fantasy**	Airplay #1 (7) / Sales #1 (5)	Columbia 78043
				#1 R&B hit (6 weeks); samples "Genius Of Love" by Tom Tom Club		
12/2/95	1 (16)	26	▲²	17. **One Sweet Day**	Airplay #1 (13) / Sales #1 (11)	Columbia 78074
				MARIAH CAREY & BOYZ II MEN		
				#1 Adult Contemporary hit (13 weeks)		
1/6/96 -	35 ᴬ	1		18. All I Want For Christmas Is You	[X-R]	album cut
				from the album *Merry Christmas* on Columbia 64222		
4/6/96	1 (2)	26	▲	19. **Always Be My Baby**	Sales #1 (1) / Airplay #2	Columbia 78276
				#1 R&B hit (1 week)		
7/6/96	9 ᴬ	17		20. **Forever**		album cut
				from the album *Daydream* on Columbia 66700		
1/4/97 -	35 ᴬ	1		21. All I Want For Christmas Is You	[X-R]	album cut
9/13/97	1 (3)	18	▲	22. **Honey**	Sales #1 (3) / Airplay #11	Columbia 78648
				samples "The Body Rock" by Treacherous 3 and "Hey D.J." by Lighter Shade Of Brown		
10/18/97	16 ᴬ	9		23. Butterfly		album cut
				from the album *Butterfly* on Columbia 67835		
5/9/98	1 (1)	18	▲	24. **My All**	Sales #1 (2) / Airplay #15	Columbia 78821
1/23/99	15	7	●	25. When You Believe	Sales #7 / Airplay #38	DreamWorks 59022
				WHITNEY HOUSTON and MARIAH CAREY		
				from the animated movie *The Prince Of Egypt*		
2/27/99	4	12	▲	26. **I Still Believe**	Sales #3 / Airplay #20	Columbia 79093
9/11/99	1 (2)	14	●	27. **Heartbreaker**	Sales #1 (2) / Airplay #8	Columbia 79260
				MARIAH CAREY (Featuring Jay-Z)		
				#1 R&B hit (2 weeks); samples "Attack Of The Name Game" by Stacy Lattisaw		
1/15/00	1 (1)	11	●	28. **Thank God I Found You**	Sales #1 (3) / Airplay #15	Columbia 79338
				MARIAH With Joe & 98°		
				#1 R&B hit (1 week)		
6/24/00	28	2		29. Crybaby	Sales #2	Columbia 79348
				MARIAH CAREY Featuring Snoop Dogg		
				samples "Piece Of My Love" by Guy		

DATE	POS	WKS	ARTIST–RECORD TITLE	LABEL & NO.
8/4/01	**2 (2)**	4	● 30. **Loverboy** Sales #1 (4) / Airplay #50 #1 R&B hit (2 weeks); samples "Candy" by Cameo; from the movie *Glitter* starring Carey	Virgin 38791
3/15/03	**3**	22	31. **I Know What You Want** Airplay #3 / Sales #15 **BUSTA RHYMES AND MARIAH CAREY (feat. The Flipmode Squad)**	J Records 21258
			CAREY, Tony	
			Born on 10/16/52 in Watsonville, California; later settled in West Germany. Rock singer/songwriter/keyboardist.	
3/31/84	**22**	8	1. A Fine Fine Day #1 Mainstream Rock hit (1 week)	MCA 52343
7/14/84	**33**	2	2. The First Day Of Summer	MCA 52388
			CARGILL, Henson	
			Born on 2/5/41 in Oklahoma City, Oklahoma. Country singer.	
1/20/68	**25**	7	1. Skip A Rope #1 Country hit (5 weeks)	Monument 1041
			CARLISLE, Belinda	
			Born on 8/17/58 in Hollywood, California. Lead singer of the Go-Go's. Married Morgan Mason (son of actor James Mason) in 1986.	
6/21/86	**3**	14	1. **Mad About You** Sales #2 / Airplay #4 Andy Taylor (of Duran Duran; guitar solo)	I.R.S. 52815
10/10/87	**1 (1)**	15	2. **Heaven Is A Place On Earth** Sales #1 (2) / Airplay #1 (1)	MCA 53181
1/23/88	**2 (1)**	13	3. **I Get Weak** Sales #1 (1) / Airplay #3	MCA 53242
5/7/88	**7**	10	4. **Circle In The Sand** Sales #6 / Airplay #9	MCA 53308
10/28/89	**11**	10	5. **Leave A Light On** Sales #11 / Airplay #13 George Harrison (slide guitar solo)	MCA 53706
2/17/90	**30**	5	6. Summer Rain Sales #23 / Airplay #35	MCA 53783
			CARLISLE, Bob	
			Born on 9/29/56 in Santa Anna, California. Singer/songwriter/guitarist. Recorded Christian music on the Sparrow label since 1993.	
5/10/97	**10** ᴬ	11	1. **Butterfly Kisses** Sales #65 #1 Adult Contemporary hit (7 weeks); "Limited Edition Collector's CD Gift Box" single available only in Christian bookstores (therefore ineligible for the main *Hot 100* chart)	Diadem 1221
			CARLTON, Carl	
			Born on 10/22/52 in Detroit, Michigan. R&B singer/songwriter.	
10/12/74	**6**	10	1. **Everlasting Love**	Back Beat 27001
9/26/81	**22**	7	● 2. **She's A Bad Mama Jama (She's Built, She's Stacked)**	20th Century 2488
			CARLTON, Larry — see POST, Mike	
			CARLTON, Vanessa	
			Born on 8/16/80 in Milford, Pennsylvania. Adult Contemporary singer/songwriter/pianist.	
3/23/02	**5**	36	1. **A Thousand Miles** Sales #2 / Airplay #5 #1 Adult Contemporary hit (7 weeks)	A&M 497676
9/14/02	**30**	8	2. Ordinary Day Airplay #38	A&M 497761

DATE	POS	WKS	ARTIST–RECORD TITLE	LABEL & NO.
			CARMEN, Eric	
			Born on 8/11/49 in Cleveland, Ohio. Singer/songwriter/pianist. Lead singer of the Raspberries from 1970-74.	
1/17/76	**2** (3)	14	● 1. **All By Myself**	Arista 0165
			interlude based on Rachmaninov's *Piano Concerto No.2*	
5/22/76	**11**	10	2. Never Gonna Fall In Love Again	Arista 0184
			#1 Adult Contemporary hit (1 week); melody based on Rachmaninov's *Second Symphony*	
9/18/76	**34**	3	3. Sunrise	Arista 0200
9/24/77	**23**	8	4. She Did It	Arista 0266
10/28/78	**19**	7	5. Change Of Heart	Arista 0354
2/9/85	**35**	4	6. I Wanna Hear It From Your Lips	Geffen 29118
12/12/87+	**4**	16	7. **Hungry Eyes** Sales #4 / Airplay #4	RCA 5315
			from the movie *Dirty Dancing* starring Patrick Swayze	
6/18/88	**3**	13	8. **Make Me Lose Control** Sales #1 (1) / Airplay #4	Arista 9686
			#1 Adult Contemporary hit (3 weeks)	
			CARNES, Kim	
			Born on 7/20/45 in Los Angeles, California. Singer/songwriter/pianist. Member of The New Christy Minstrels with husband/co-writer Dave Ellingson.	
8/5/78	**36**	3	1. You're A Part Of Me	Ariola America 7704
			GENE COTTON with Kim Carnes	
			#32 Adult Contemporary hit for Kim Carnes (solo) in 1976	
4/12/80	**4**	14	2. **Don't Fall In Love With A Dreamer**	United Artists 1345
			KENNY ROGERS with KIM CARNES	
6/14/80	**10**	15	3. **More Love**	EMI America 8045
4/11/81	**1** (9)	20	● 4. **Bette Davis Eyes**	EMI America 8077
			1981 Grammy winner: Record of the Year	
8/29/81	**28**	6	5. Draw Of The Cards	EMI America 8087
9/11/82	**29**	6	6. Voyeur	EMI America 8127
12/25/82+	**36**	4	7. Does It Make You Remember	EMI America 8147
11/26/83	**40**	2	8. Invisible Hands	EMI America 8181
10/13/84	**15**	9	9. What About Me? Airplay #14 / Sales #16	RCA 13899
			KENNY ROGERS with KIM CARNES and JAMES INGRAM	
			#1 Adult Contemporary hit (2 weeks)	
6/1/85	**15**	9	10. Crazy In The Night (Barking At Airplanes) Sales #14 / Airplay #20	EMI America 8267
			CAROSONE, Renato	
			Born on 1/2/20 in Naples, Italy. Died on 5/20/2001 (age 81). Male singer.	
5/12/58	**18**	9	1. Torero Jockey #18 / Top 100 #19 / Best Seller #20 **[F]**	Capitol 71080
			CARPENTERS	
			Brother-sister duo originally from New Haven, Connecticut: Richard (born on 10/15/46) and Karen (born on 3/2/50) Carpenter. Moved to Downey, California, in 1963. Richard played piano from age nine. Karen played drums in group with Richard and bass player Wes Jacobs in 1965. The trio recorded for RCA in 1966. After a period with the band Spectrum, the Carpenters recorded as a duo for A&M in 1969. Won the 1970 Best New Artist Grammy Award. Karen died of heart failure due to anorexia nervosa on 2/4/83 (age 32).	
6/27/70	**1** (4)	15	● 1. **(They Long To Be) Close To You**	A&M 1183
			#1 Adult Contemporary hit (6 weeks)	

DATE	POS	WKS	ARTIST–RECORD TITLE	LABEL & NO.
10/3/70	2 (4)	14	● 2. **We've Only Just Begun** #1 Adult Contemporary hit (7 weeks); adapted from a commercial jingle for Crocker Bank of California	A&M 1217
2/13/71	3	12	● 3. **For All We Know** #1 Adult Contemporary hit (3 weeks); from the movie *Lovers And Other Strangers* starring Bea Arthur	A&M 1243
5/22/71	2 (2)	11	● 4. **Rainy Days And Mondays** #1 Adult Contemporary hit (4 weeks)	A&M 1260
9/11/71	2 (2)	12	● 5. **Superstar** #1 Adult Contemporary hit (2 weeks)	A&M 1289
1/22/72	2 (2)	11	● 6. **Hurting Each Other** #1 Adult Contemporary hit (2 weeks); first recorded by Jimmy Clanton in 1965	A&M 1322
5/13/72	12	8	7. It's Going To Take Some Time first recorded by Carole King in 1971	A&M 1351
7/22/72	7	9	8. **Goodbye To Love**	A&M 1367
3/10/73	3	11	● 9. **Sing** #1 Adult Contemporary hit (2 weeks); Jimmy Joyce Children's Choir (guest vocals); featured on TV's *Sesame Street*	A&M 1413
6/16/73	2 (1)	12	● 10. **Yesterday Once More** #1 Adult Contemporary hit (3 weeks)	A&M 1446
10/20/73	1 (2)	16	● 11. **Top Of The World**	A&M 1468
4/27/74	11	9	12. I Won't Last A Day Without You #1 Adult Contemporary hit (1 week)	A&M 1521
12/7/74+	1 (1)	12	● 13. **Please Mr. Postman** #1 Adult Contemporary hit (1 week)	A&M 1646
4/12/75	4	9	14. **Only Yesterday** #1 Adult Contemporary hit (1 week)	A&M 1677
8/16/75	17	7	15. Solitaire #1 Adult Contemporary hit (1 week); first recorded by Neil Sedaka in 1974	A&M 1721
3/13/76	12	8	16. There's A Kind Of Hush (All Over The World) #1 Adult Contemporary hit (2 weeks)	A&M 1800
7/4/76	25	5	17. I Need To Be In Love #1 Adult Contemporary hit (1 week)	A&M 1828
6/18/77	35	3	18. All You Get From Love Is A Love Song	A&M 1940
11/5/77	32	4	19. Calling Occupants Of Interplanetary Craft (The Recognized Anthem of World Contact Day)	A&M 1978
7/4/81	16	8	20. Touch Me When We're Dancing #1 Adult Contemporary hit (2 weeks)	A&M 2344
			CARR, Cathy	
4/7/56	2 (1)	18	Born Angela Helen Catherine Cordovano on 6/28/36 in the Bronx, New York. Died in November 1988 (age 52). 1. **Ivory Tower** Juke Box #2 / Top 100 #6 / Best Seller #7 / Jockey #9 Dan Belloc (orch.)	Fraternity 734
			CARR, Joe "Fingers" — see BUSCH, Lou	
6/9/58	19	2	**CARR, Valerie** Born in 1936 in New York. R&B singer. 1. When The Boys Talk About The Girls Jockey #19 / Top 100 #84 Hugo Peretti (orch.)	Roulette 4066

DATE	POS	WKS	ARTIST—RECORD TITLE	LABEL & NO.
			CARR, Vikki	
			Born Florencia Martinez Cardona on 7/19/41 in El Paso, Texas. Regular on TV's *Ray Anthony Show*.	
9/30/67	**3**	11	1. **It Must Be Him**	Liberty 55986
			#1 Adult Contemporary hit (3 weeks)	
1/27/68	**34**	1	2. The Lesson	Liberty 56012
			#1 Adult Contemporary hit (1 week)	
6/28/69	**35**	4	3. With Pen In Hand	Liberty 56092
			written by Bobby Goldsboro	
			CARRACK, Paul	
			Born on 4/22/51 in Sheffield, Yorkshire, England. Lead singer of Ace and Mike + The Mechanics.	
10/30/82	**37**	2	1. I Need You	Epic 03146
			produced by Nick Lowe	
12/19/87+	**9**	13	2. **Don't Shed A Tear** Sales #6 / Airplay #9	Chrysalis 43164
4/23/88	**28**	5	3. One Good Reason Sales #25 / Airplay #25	Chrysalis 43204
11/25/89	**31**	4	4. I Live By The Groove Sales #28 / Airplay #31	Chrysalis 23427
			CARRADINE, Keith	
			Born on 8/8/49 in San Mateo, California. Singer/guitarist/actor. Son of actor John Carradine. Half-brother of actor David Carradine. Acted in several movies.	
6/12/76	**17**	12	1. I'm Easy	ABC 12117
			#1 Adult Contemporary hit (1 week); from the movie *Nashville* starring Carradine	
			CARROLL, David, And His Orchestra	
			Born Nook Schrier on 10/15/13 in Chicago, Illinois. Arranger/conductor.	
1/8/55	**8**	17	1. **Melody Of Love** Jockey #8 / Best Seller #9 / Juke Box #12 **[I]**	Mercury 70516
12/17/55	**20**	1	2. It's Almost Tomorrow Jockey #20 / Top 100 #34	Mercury 70717
			Jack Halloran Singers (vocals)	
			CARS, The	
			Rock group from Boston, Massachusetts: Ric Ocasek (vocals, guitar; see #13 below), Benjamin Orr (bass, vocals; see #14 below), Elliot Easton (guitar), Greg Hawkes (keyboards) and David Robinson (drums). Ocasek appeared in the 1987 movie *Made In Heaven*; married supermodel/actress Paulina Porizkova on 8/23/89. Orr died of cancer on 10/3/2000 (age 53).	
8/12/78	**27**	7	1. Just What I Needed	Elektra 45491
12/9/78	**35**	5	2. My Best Friend's Girl	Elektra 45537
7/28/79	**14**	9	3. Let's Go	Elektra 46063
10/11/80	**37**	3	4. Touch And Go	Elektra 47039
12/12/81+	**4**	17	5. **Shake It Up**	Elektra 47250
3/24/84	**7**	11	6. **You Might Think**	Elektra 69744
			#1 Mainstream Rock hit (3 weeks)	
5/26/84	**12**	11	7. Magic	Elektra 69724
			#1 Mainstream Rock hit (1 week)	
8/11/84	**3**	14	8. **Drive** Sales #3 / Airplay #8	Elektra 69706
			#1 Adult Contemporary hit (3 weeks)	
11/10/84	**20**	10	9. Hello Again Sales #17 / Airplay #17	Elektra 69681
3/9/85	**33**	5	10. Why Can't I Have You Airplay #28	Elektra 69657

DATE	POS	WKS	ARTIST–RECORD TITLE	LABEL & NO.
11/16/85+	7	12	11. **Tonight She Comes** Airplay #7 / Sales #10 #1 Mainstream Rock hit (3 weeks)	Elektra 69589
3/8/86	32	4	12. I'm Not The One Airplay #30 recorded in 1981	Elektra 69569
10/11/86	15	8	13. Emotion In Motion Sales #16 / Airplay #17 **RIC OCASEK** #1 Mainstream Rock hit (1 week) / #1 Modern Rock hit (1 week)	Geffen 28617
1/17/87	24	6	14. Stay The Night Airplay #18 / Sales #26 **BENJAMIN ORR**	Elektra 69506
9/12/87	17	9	15. You Are The Girl Airplay #16 / Sales #19	Elektra 69446

CARSON, Kit

Born Lisa Morrow. Vocalist on Benny Goodman's 1946 #2 hit "Symphony."

DATE	POS	WKS	ARTIST–RECORD TITLE	LABEL & NO.
12/31/55	11	11	1. Band Of Gold Jockey #11 / Top 100 #17 Dick Hyman (orch.)	Capitol 3283

CARSON, Mindy

Born on 7/16/27 in Queens, New York. Sang with Paul Whiteman's band in the 1940s.

DATE	POS	WKS	ARTIST–RECORD TITLE	LABEL & NO.
8/27/55	13	8	1. Wake The Town And Tell The People Jockey #13 / Juke Box #13 / Best Seller #20 / Top 100 #33 Norman Leyden (orch.)	Columbia 40537
1/5/57	34	2	2. Since I Met You Baby Top 100 #34 Ray Conniff (orch.)	Columbia 40789

CARTER, Aaron

Born on 12/7/87 in Tampa, Florida. White teen rapper. Younger brother of Nick Carter of the Backstreet Boys.

DATE	POS	WKS	ARTIST–RECORD TITLE	LABEL & NO.
9/16/00	35	3	● 1. Aaron's Party (Come Get It) Sales #4	Jive 42691

CARTER, Carlene — see ORRALL, Robert Ellis

CARTER, Clarence

Born on 1/14/36 in Montgomery, Alabama. R&B singer/guitarist. Blind since age one. Married for a time to Candi Staton.

DATE	POS	WKS	ARTIST–RECORD TITLE	LABEL & NO.
8/17/68	6	11	● 1. **Slip Away**	Atlantic 2508
11/30/68+	13	11	● 2. **Too Weak To Fight**	Atlantic 2569
3/29/69	31	5	3. Snatching It Back	Atlantic 2605
8/1/70	4	12	● 4. **Patches**	Atlantic 2748

CARTER, June — see CASH, Johnny

CARTER, Mel

Born on 4/22/39 in Cincinnati, Ohio. R&B singer/actor. Acted in several TV shows in the 1970s.

DATE	POS	WKS	ARTIST–RECORD TITLE	LABEL & NO.
7/24/65	8	11	1. **Hold Me, Thrill Me, Kiss Me** #1 Adult Contemporary hit (1 week); #5 hit for Karen Chandler in 1953	Imperial 66113
11/27/65	38	2	2. (All Of A Sudden) My Heart Sings #7 hit for Johnnie Johnston in 1945	Imperial 66138
5/21/66	32	2	3. Band Of Gold #1 Adult Contemporary hit (2 weeks)	Imperial 66165

DATE	POS	WKS	ARTIST–RECORD TITLE	LABEL & NO.
			CASCADES, The	
			Pop group from San Diego, California: John Gummoe (vocals, guitar), Eddie Snyder (piano), David Wilson (sax), David Stevens (bass) and David Zabo (drums). Wilson died of cancer on 11/14/2000 (age 63).	
1/26/63	**3**	13	1. **Rhythm Of The Rain** #1 Adult Contemporary hit (2 weeks)	Valiant 6026
			CASE	
			Born Casey Woodard on 1/10/73 in Harlem, New York. Male R&B singer/songwriter.	
5/25/96	**14**	14	● 1. Touch Me Tease Me Sales #7 / Airplay #50 Mary J. Blige and Foxy Brown (backing vocals); samples "P.S.K. What Does It Mean" by Schooly D; from the movie *The Nutty Professor* starring Eddie Murphy	Def Jam 854620
2/13/99	**10**	9	2. **Faded Pictures** Sales #8 / Airplay #56 **CASE & JOE** from the movie *Rush Hour* starring Jackie Chan	Def Jam 566494
6/12/99	**15**	13	3. Happily Ever After Sales #8 / Airplay #23	Def Jam 566954
4/7/01	**4**	12	4. **Missing You** Sales #3 / Airplay #24 #1 R&B hit (4 weeks)	Def Soul 572839
9/15/01	**6**	23	5. **Livin' It Up** Airplay #6 / Sales #29 **JA RULE (feat. Case)** samples "Do I Do" by Stevie Wonder	Def Jam 588741
			CASH, Alvin, & The Crawlers	
			Born Alvin Welch on 2/15/39 in St. Louis, Missouri. Died on 11/21/99 (age 60). Soul-funk singer/dancer.	
1/30/65	**14**	7	1. Twine Time [I]	Mar-V-Lus 6002
			CASH, Johnny	
			Born J.R. Cash on 2/26/32 in Kingsland, Arkansas. Died of diabetes on 9/12/2003 (age 71). Country singer/songwriter/guitarist. Formed trio with Luther Perkins (guitar) and Marshall Grant (bass) in 1955. Hosted own TV show for ABC from 1969-71. Worked with June Carter from 1961, married her on 3/1/68. Daughter Rosanne Cash and stepdaughter Carlene Carter had successful singing careers. Elected to the Country Music Hall of Fame in 1980. Inducted into the Rock and Roll Hall of Fame in 1992. Won Grammy's Lifetime Achievement Award in 1999.	
10/20/56	**17**	11	1. I Walk The Line Best Seller #17 / Juke Box #17 / Top 100 #19 / Jockey #25 #1 Country hit (6 weeks)	Sun 241
2/10/58	**14**	13	2. Ballad Of A Teenage Queen / Jockey #14 / Best Seller #16 / Top 100 #16 #1 Country hit (10 weeks)	
3/17/58		7	3. Big River Best Seller: flip	Sun 283
6/9/58	**11**	13	4. Guess Things Happen That Way Best Seller #11 / Top 100 #11 / Jockey #18 #1 Country hit (8 weeks)	Sun 295
9/1/58	**24**	6	5. The Ways Of A Woman In Love / Hot 100 #24 / Best Seller #26	
9/8/58		5	6. You're The Nearest Thing To Heaven Best Seller: flip **JOHNNY CASH And The Tennessee Two** (all of above)	Sun 302
11/10/58	**38**	1	7. All Over Again Hot 100 #38	Columbia 41251
2/2/59	**32**	6	8. Don't Take Your Guns To Town #1 Country hit (6 weeks)	Columbia 41313

DATE	POS	WKS	ARTIST–RECORD TITLE	LABEL & NO.
6/22/63	**17**	10	9. Ring Of Fire *#1 Country hit (7 weeks)*	Columbia 42788
3/14/64	**35**	3	10. Understand Your Man *#1 Country hit (6 weeks)*	Columbia 42964
6/29/68	**32**	6	11. Folsom Prison Blues **[L]** *#1 Country hit (4 weeks); recorded at Folsom Prison*	Columbia 44513

8/2/69	**2** (3)	11	● 12. **A Boy Named Sue** **[L-N]**
			  *#1 Country hit (5 weeks) / #1 Adult Contemporary hit (2 weeks);
			  recorded at San Quentin prison*
				Columbia 44944

2/21/70	**36**	2	13. If I Were A Carpenter **JOHNNY CASH & JUNE CARTER**	Columbia 45064
4/25/70	**19**	6	14. What Is Truth **[S]**	Columbia 45134

5/15/76	**29**	3	15. One Piece At A Time **[N]**
			  JOHNNY CASH And The Tennessee Three
			  #1 Country hit (2 weeks)
				Columbia 10321

			CASH, Rosanne	
			Born on 5/24/56 in Memphis, Tennessee. Country singer/songwriter. Daughter of Johnny Cash. Married to Rodney Crowell from 1979-92. Married producer John Leventhal on 4/30/95. Released short-story collection Bodies Of Water in 1996.	
6/13/81	**22**	7	1. Seven Year Ache *#1 Country hit (1 week)*	Columbia 11426
			CASHMAN & WEST	
			Duo of pop record producers/songwriters/singers Dennis "Terry Cashman" Minogue (born on 7/5/41) and Thomas "Tommy West" Picardo (born on 8/17/42). Produced all of Jim Croce's recordings. Also recorded as the Buchanan Brothers (see #1 below).	
5/31/69	**22**	7	1. Medicine Man (Part I) **BUCHANAN BROTHERS**	Event 3302
10/21/72	**27**	7	2. American City Suite *Sweet City Song/All Around The Town/A Friend Is Dying*	Dunhill/ABC 4324
			CASINOS, The	
			Pop vocal group from Cincinnati, Ohio: Gene Hughes, Pete Bolton, Bob Armstrong, Tom Mathews, Ray White, Mickey Denton, Glen Hughes, Joe Patterson and Bill Hawkins. Hughes died of a car crash on 2/3/2004 (age 67).	
1/28/67	**6**	10	1. **Then You Can Tell Me Goodbye**	Fraternity 977
			CASSIDY, David	
			Born on 4/12/50 in Manhattan, New York. Son of actor Jack Cassidy and actress Evelyn Ward. Played "Keith Partridge," the lead singer of TV's The Partridge Family. Married to actress Kay Lenz from 1977-83. Co-starred with his half-brother Shaun Cassidy on Broadway in Blood Brothers in 1993.	
11/13/71	**9**	11	● 1. **Cherish** *#1 Adult Contemporary hit (1 week)*	Bell 45,150
3/25/72	**37**	2	2. Could It Be Forever	Bell 45,187
6/10/72	**25**	5	3. How Can I Be Sure	Bell 45,220
10/14/72	**38**	2	4. Rock Me Baby	Bell 45,260
10/27/90	**27**	5	5. Lyin' To Myself *Sales #26 / Airplay #26*	Enigma 75084

DATE	POS	WKS	ARTIST–RECORD TITLE	LABEL & NO.
			CASSIDY, Shaun	
			Born on 9/27/58 in Los Angeles, California. Son of actor Jack Cassidy and actress Shirley Jones of TV's *The Partridge Family*. Played "Joe Hardy" on TV's *The Hardy Boys*. Co-starred with his half-brother David Cassidy on Broadway in *Blood Brothers* in 1993. Cast member of the TV soap *General Hospital* in 1987. Married to model Ann Pennington from 1979-91.	
6/4/77	**1** (1)	12	● 1. **Da Doo Ron Ron**	Warner/Curb 8365
8/20/77	**3**	15	● 2. **That's Rock 'N' Roll**	Warner/Curb 8423
11/26/77+	**7**	12	● 3. **Hey Deanie**	Warner/Curb 8488
			above 2 written by Eric Carmen	
4/22/78	**31**	5	4. Do You Believe In Magic	Warner/Curb 8533
			CASTAWAYS, The	
			Rock group of teens from St. Paul, Minnesota: Richard Robey (vocals, bass), Robert Folschow and Roy Hensley (guitars), James Donna (keyboards) and Dennis Craswell (drums). Craswell later joined Crow.	
9/18/65	**12**	9	1. Liar, Liar	Soma 1433
			CASTELLS, The	
			Adult Contemporary vocal group from Santa Rosa, California: Bob Ussery, Tom Hicks, Joe Kelly and Chuck Girard (later with The Hondells).	
7/3/61	**20**	7	1. Sacred	Era 3048
5/26/62	**21**	5	2. So This Is Love	Era 3073
			CASTLEMAN, Boomer	
			Born Owen Castleman in Farmers Branch, Texas. Singer/songwriter/guitarist.	
5/31/75	**33**	3	1. Judy Mae	Mums 6038
			CASTOR, Jimmy, Bunch	
			Born on 6/22/43 in the Bronx, New York. R&B singer/saxophonist. The Bunch consisted of Harry Jensen (guitar), Gerry Thomas (keyboards), Lenny Fridie (congas), Doug Gibson (bass) and Bobby Manigault (drums).	
2/4/67	**31**	3	1. Hey, Leroy, Your Mama's Callin' You [I]	Smash 2069
			JIMMY CASTOR	
5/27/72	**6**	10	● 2. **Troglodyte (Cave Man)** [N]	RCA Victor 48-1029
3/22/75	**16**	8	3. The Bertha Butt Boogie-Part 1 [N]	Atlantic 3232
			CATE BROS.	
			White pop/rock duo of twins Ernie (vocals, piano) and Earl (guitar) Cate. Born on 12/26/42 in Fayetteville, Arkansas.	
4/17/76	**24**	8	1. Union Man	Asylum 45294
			CATES, George, And His Orchestra	
			Born on 10/19/11 in Brooklyn, New York. Died on 5/10/2002 (age 90). Conductor/arranger. Musical director of TV's *Lawrence Welk Show*.	
12/3/55	**35**	2	1. Autumn Leaves *Top 100 #35* [I]	Coral 61485
			STEVE ALLEN with GEORGE CATES And His Orchestra & Chorus	
4/21/56	**4**	19	2. **Moonglow And Theme From "Picnic"**	Coral 61618
			Top 100 #4 / Jockey #4 / Best Seller #5 / Juke Box #7 [I] *featuring The Stan Wrightsman Quartet; from the movie* Picnic *starring William Holden*	

DATE	POS	WKS	ARTIST–RECORD TITLE	LABEL & NO.
			CATHY JEAN and THE ROOMMATES	
			Born Cathy Jean Giordano on 9/8/45 in Brooklyn, New York. The Roommates were a vocal quartet from Queens, New York: Steve Susskind, Jack Sailson, Felix Alvarez and Bob Minsky.	
3/6/61	**12**	10	1. Please Love Me Forever	Valmor 007
			CAT MOTHER and The All Night News Boys	
			Rock group from Brooklyn, New York: Larry Packer (guitar), Bob Smith (piano), Charley Chin (banjo), Roy Michaels (bass) and Michael Equine (drums). All shared vocals.	
7/12/69	**21**	6	1. Good Old Rock 'N Roll Sweet Little Sixteen/Long Tall Sally/Chantilly Lace/Whole Lotta Shakin' Goin On/Blue Suede Shoes/Party Doll	Polydor 14002
			CAUSE & EFFECT	
			Pop duo formed in California: Sean Rowley (keyboards) and Robert Rowe (vocals, guitar). Rowley died of asthma-related cardiac arrest on 11/12/92 (age 23).	
5/9/92	**38**	2	1. You Think You Know Her Airplay #33	SRC/Zoo 14025
			CAVALIERE, Felix — see RASCALS, The	
			C COMPANY Featuring TERRY NELSON	
			Group of studio musicians led by DJ/singer Terry Nelson from Russellville, Alabama.	
5/1/71	**37**	3	● 1. Battle Hymn Of Lt. Calley **[S]** Lt. William Calley Jr. was court-martialed for the massacre of unarmed civilians in My Lai, Vietnam, committed by his Army company	Plantation 73
			CELEBRATION featuring MIKE LOVE	
			Pop group formed in Los Angeles, California: Mike Love (vocals), Ron Altback (keyboards), Charles Lloyd (sax) and Dave "Doc" Robinson (bass). Love is lead singer of The Beach Boys. Altback and Robinson were members of King Harvest.	
6/3/78	**28**	4	1. Almost Summer title song from the movie starring Bruno Kirby	MCA 40891
			CERRONE	
			Born Jean-Marc Cerrone in 1952 in St. Michel, France. Dance composer/producer/drummer.	
3/26/77	**36**	3	1. Love In 'C' Minor - Pt. I **[I]**	Cotillion 44215
			CETERA, Peter	
			Born on 9/13/44 in Chicago, Illinois. Lead singer/bass guitarist of Chicago from 1967-85.	
6/21/86	**1 (2)**	14	1. **Glory Of Love** Airplay #1 (2) / Sales #2 #1 Adult Contemporary hit (5 weeks); theme from the movie *The Karate Kid Part II* starring Ralph Macchio	Full Moon 28662
10/11/86	**1 (1)**	15	2. **The Next Time I Fall** Airplay #2 / Sales #3 **PETER CETERA w/AMY GRANT** #1 Adult Contemporary hit (2 weeks)	Full Moon 28597
8/6/88	**4**	13	3. **One Good Woman** Airplay #3 / Sales #6 #1 Adult Contemporary hit (4 weeks)	Full Moon 27824

DATE	POS	WKS	ARTIST–RECORD TITLE	LABEL & NO.
4/1/89	**6**	11	● 4. **After All**　　　Sales #4 / Airplay #9 **CHER and PETER CETERA** #1 Adult Contemporary hit (4 weeks); love theme from the movie *Chances Are* starring Cybill Shepherd and Robert Downey, Jr.	Geffen 27529
8/29/92	35	4	5. Restless Heart　　　Airplay #30 / Sales #48 #1 Adult Contemporary hit (2 weeks)	Warner 18897
2/22/97	**8**	32	▲ 6. **Hard To Say I'm Sorry**　　Sales #6 / Airplay #15 **AZ YET Featuring Peter Cetera**	LaFace 24223
			CHAD & JEREMY	
			Soft-rock duo from London, England: Chad Stuart (born on 12/10/43) and Jeremy Clyde (born on 3/22/44).	
6/13/64	21	6	1. Yesterday's Gone	World Artists 1021
9/19/64	7	9	2. **A Summer Song** **CHAD STUART & JEREMY CLYDE** (above 2)	World Artists 1027
12/12/64+	15	8	3. Willow Weep For Me #1 Adult Contemporary hit (1 week); #2 hit for Paul Whiteman in 1933	World Artists 1034
3/13/65	23	5	4. If I Loved You from the Rodgers & Hammerstein musical *Carousel*	World Artists 1041
5/29/65	17	6	5. Before And After	Columbia 43277
8/28/65	35	3	6. I Don't Wanna Lose You Baby	Columbia 43339
8/13/66	30	2	7. Distant Shores	Columbia 43682
			CHAIRMEN OF THE BOARD	
			R&B vocal group from Detroit, Michigan: General Norman Johnson, Danny Woods, Harrison Kennedy and Eddie Curtis.	
2/7/70	**3**	12	● 1. **Give Me Just A Little More Time**	Invictus 9074
6/6/70	38	2	2. (You've Got Me) Dangling On A String	Invictus 9078
9/12/70	38	2	3. Everything's Tuesday **CHAIRMAN OF THE BOARD**	Invictus 9079
12/12/70+	13	9	4. Pay To The Piper	Invictus 9081
			CHAKACHAS, The	
			Studio group from Belgium. Featuring saxophonist Victor Ingeveld.	
2/19/72	**8**	10	● 1. **Jungle Fever**　　　[I]	Polydor 15030
			CHAMBERLAIN, Richard	
			Born George Richard Chamberlain on 3/31/35 in Beverly Hills, California. Leading movie, theater and TV actor. Played lead role in TV's *Dr. Kildare* from 1961-66.	
6/23/62	**10**	10	1. **Theme From Dr. Kildare (Three Stars Will Shine Shine Tonight)**	MGM 13075
10/27/62	21	5	2. Love Me Tender	MGM 13097
3/9/63	**14**	7	3. All I Have To Do Is Dream	MGM 13121
			CHAMBERS BROTHERS, The	
			Funk-rock group from Lee County, Mississippi: brothers Willie (guitar), Joe (guitar), Lester (harmonica) and George (bass) Chambers, with Brian Keenan (drums).	
9/14/68	**11**	9	1. Time Has Come Today	Columbia 44414

DATE	POS	WKS	ARTIST–RECORD TITLE	LABEL & NO.
12/21/68	37	2	2. I Can't Turn You Loose written by Otis Redding	Columbia 44679

CHAMPAIGN

R&B group from Champaign, Illinois: Pauli Carman and Rena Jones (vocals), Leon Reeder (guitar), Michael Day and Dana Walden (keyboards), Michael Reed (bass) and Rocky Maffit (drums).

DATE	POS	WKS	ARTIST–RECORD TITLE	LABEL & NO.
3/28/81	12	13	1. How 'Bout Us #1 Adult Contemporary hit (2 weeks)	Columbia 11433
5/14/83	23	9	2. Try Again	Columbia 03563

CHAMPS, The

Rock and roll instrumental group from Los Angeles, California: Dave Burgess (rhythm guitar), Buddy Bruce (lead guitar), Chuck Rio (sax), Cliff Hils (bass) and Gene Alden (drums). Shortly after "Tequila" became a hit, Bruce and Hils were replaced by Dale Norris and Joe Burnas. Eight months after recording "Tequila," Rio and Alden left, replaced by Jimmy Seals (sax) and Dash Crofts (drums). Other personnel changes followed; in 1960, guitarist Glen Campbell spent some time in the group. Seals and Crofts later recorded as a duo.

DATE	POS	WKS	ARTIST–RECORD TITLE	LABEL & NO.
3/3/58	**1** (5)	16	● 1. **Tequila**　　　Best Seller #1 (5) / Top 100 #1 (5) / Jockey #1 (2) **[I]** #1 R&B hit (4 weeks)	Challenge 1016
6/2/58	30	5	2. El Rancho Rock　　　　Top 100 #30 / Best Seller #31 **[I]** #6 hit for Bing Crosby in 1939	Challenge 59007
2/8/60	30	5	3. Too Much Tequila　　　　　　　　　　　　　　　　　**[I]**	Challenge 59063
7/14/62	40	1	4. Limbo Rock　　　　　　　　　　　　　　　　　　　　**[I]**	Challenge 9131

CHANDLER, Gene

Born Eugene Dixon on 7/6/40 in Chicago, Illinois. R&B singer/producer.

DATE	POS	WKS	ARTIST–RECORD TITLE	LABEL & NO.
1/27/62	**1** (3)	11	● 1. **Duke Of Earl** #1 R&B hit (5 weeks)	Vee-Jay 416
8/1/64	19	7	2. Just Be True	Constellation 130
11/14/64	39	1	3. Bless Our Love	Constellation 136
1/16/65	40	1	4. What Now	Constellation 141
5/22/65	18	6	5. Nothing Can Stop Me	Constellation 149
8/8/70	12	11	● 6. Groovy Situation	Mercury 73083

CHANGE

European-American dance group formed in Italy by producers Jacques Fred Petrus and Mauro Malavasi.

DATE	POS	WKS	ARTIST–RECORD TITLE	LABEL & NO.
7/19/80	40	1	1. A Lover's Holiday	RFC 49208

CHANGING FACES

Female R&B vocal duo from Brooklyn, New York: Charisse Rose and Cassandra Lucas.

DATE	POS	WKS	ARTIST–RECORD TITLE	LABEL & NO.
8/6/94	3	18	▲ 1. **Stroke You Up**　　　　　　　Sales #2 / Airplay #12	Big Beat 98279
2/4/95	38	2	2. Foolin' Around　　　　　　　　Sales #19 / Airplay #68	Big Beat 98207
5/10/97	8	22	▲ 3. **G.H.E.T.T.O.U.T.**　　　　　　Sales #4 / Airplay #31 #1 R&B hit (4 weeks)	Big Beat 98026

CHANNEL, Bruce

Born on 11/28/40 in Jacksonville, Texas. Pop singer.

DATE	POS	WKS	ARTIST–RECORD TITLE	LABEL & NO.
2/10/62	**1** (3)	12	● 1. **Hey! Baby** Delbert McClinton (harmonica)	Smash 1731

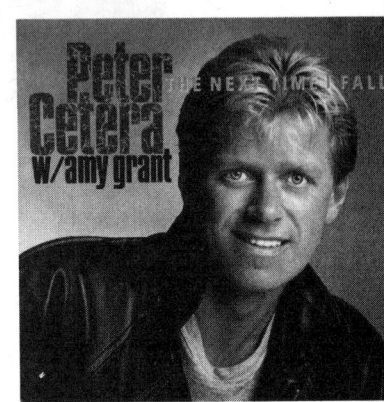

Captain & Tennille left A&M Records in 1979, but the success of their #1 hit "Do That To Me One More Time," their first single on Casablanca Records, proved to the husband-and-wife team that things were the same as ever.

Mariah Carey turned her appearance on *MTV's Unplugged* into her sixth #1 hit, as her remake of the Jackson 5 classic "I'll Be There" quickly topped the chart. Carey would later remake another Motown classic, "Endless Love."

The Carpenters built a strong fan base among Adult Contemporary listeners. Starting with their #1 pop hit, "(They Long To Be) Close To You," The Carpenters had 17 straight songs peak at #1 or #2 on the Adult Contemporary chart.

Shaun Cassidy converted his starring role on TV's *The Hardy Boys* into a boost for his music career. His character would frequently perform his songs, like the #1 hit "Da Doo Ron Ron," during episodes.

Peter Cetera left the band Chicago for a solo career, but still enjoyed performing with other artists from time to time. His duet partners included Cher, *Wings* TV star Crystal Bernard, and Amy Grant, his partner on the #1 hit "The Next Time I Fall."

Gene Chandler took his last name from actor Jeff Chandler. Gene wasn't above character acting himself; when his "Duke of Earl" peaked at #1, he started appearing on stage as the Duke, complete with cape and hat.

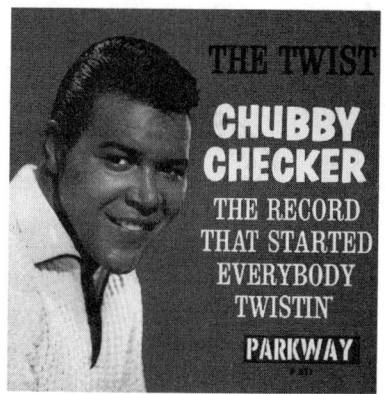

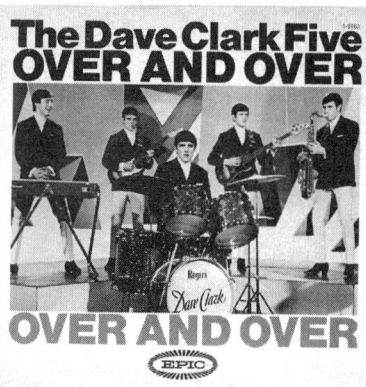

Bruce Channel became a fan favorite with his first single, the chart-topping "Hey! Baby." His follow-up singles failed to reach the Top 40, so it seemed fans had switched Channel off.

Ray Charles had #1 hits on the Pop, Country, Adult Contemporary, and R&B charts. His 1961 #1 hit, "Hit The Road Jack," found yet another audience, as it was used by several NBA teams to serenade players who fouled out during games.

Chubby Checker owed a lot of the success of his chart-topping hit "The Twist" to TV producer Dick Clark. Not only did Clark allow him to appear on *American Bandstand,* several times, but Clark's wife gave the former Ernest Evans his stage name.

Cher endured a decade of bad movie reviews, infomercials, and a duet of "I Got You Babe" with Beavis & Butt-Head during the 1990s before returning with the biggest hit of her music career, the 1999 chart-topping "Believe."

Lou Christie co-wrote his #1 hit, "Lightnin' Strikes," with his clairvoyant friend Twyla Herbert. Even with her supernatural influences, lightning couldn't strike twice, as Christie failed to have another chart-topper.

The Dave Clark Five typically recorded songs written by their leader, Dave Clark. However, their only #1 hit, "Over And Over," was a cover song written by "Rockin' Robin" singer Bobby Day (as Robert Byrd).

DATE	POS	WKS	ARTIST–RECORD TITLE	LABEL & NO.
			CHANSON	
			R&B duo formed in Los Angeles, California: James Jamerson Jr. (born in Detroit, Michigan) and David Williams (born in Newport News, Virginia). Jamerson is the son of the prominent Motown session bassist.	
12/16/78+	**21**	9	1. Don't Hold Back	Ariola America 7717
			CHANTAY'S	
			Teen surf-rock group from Santa Ana, California: Bob Spickard (lead guitar), Brian Carman (rhythm guitar), Rob Marshall (piano), Warren Waters (bass) and Bob Welsh (drums).	
4/6/63	**4**	11	1. **Pipeline** [I]	Dot 16440
			CHANTELS, The	
			Female R&B vocal group from the Bronx, New York: Arlene Smith, Sonia Goring, Rene Minus, Jackie Landry and Lois Harris. Landry died of cancer on 12/23/97 (age 56).	
1/27/58	**15**	12	1. Maybe Top 100 #15 / Best Seller #16	End 1005
4/7/58	**39**	3	2. Every Night (I Pray) Best Seller #39 / Top 100 #40	End 1015
9/11/61	**14**	8	3. Look In My Eyes	Carlton 555
12/11/61	**29**	3	4. Well. I Told You	Carlton 564
			answer to "Hit The Road Jack" by Ray Charles	
			CHAPIN, Harry	
			Born on 12/7/42 in Greenwich Village, New York. Died in a car crash on 7/16/81 (age 38). Folk-rock singer/songwriter/guitarist.	
4/22/72	**24**	9	1. Taxi	Elektra 45770
			also see #4 below	
3/16/74	**36**	2	2. WOLD	Elektra 45874
11/2/74	**1** (1)	12	● 3. **Cat's In The Cradle**	Elektra 45203
11/22/80	**23**	7	4. Sequel	Boardwalk 5700
			sequel to #1 above	
			CHAPMAN, Tracy	
			Born on 3/20/64 in Cleveland, Ohio. Folk-R&B singer/songwriter. Won the 1988 Best New Artist Grammy Award.	
7/16/88	**6**	12	1. **Fast Car** Sales #4 / Airplay #7	Elektra 69412
4/20/96	**3**	34	▲ 2. **Give Me One Reason** Airplay #2 / Sales #5	Elektra 64346
			CHARLENE	
			Born Charlene D'Angelo on 6/1/50 in Hollywood, California. Pop-R&B singer.	
3/27/82	**3**	14	1. **I've Never Been To Me** [R]	Motown 1611
			originally charted at #97 in 1977	
			CHARLES, Jimmy	
			Born in 1942 in Paterson, New Jersey. R&B singer.	
9/5/60	**5**	11	1. **A Million To One**	Promo 1002
			The Revelletts (backing vocals)	

DATE	POS	WKS	ARTIST–RECORD TITLE	LABEL & NO.
			CHARLES, Ray	
			Born Ray Charles Robinson on 9/23/30 in Albany, Georgia; raised in Greenville, Florida. Legendary R&B singer/pianist. Partially blind at age five, completely blind at seven (glaucoma). Studied classical piano and clarinet at State School for Deaf and Blind Children, St. Augustine, Florida, 1937-45. With local Florida bands; moved to Seattle in 1948. Formed the McSon Trio (also known as the Maxim Trio and the Maxine Trio) with Gossady McGhee (guitar) and Milton Garred (bass). First recordings were very much in the King Cole Trio style. Formed own band in 1954. The 1950s female vocal group, The Cookies, became his backing group, The Raeletts. Inducted into the Rock and Roll Hall of Fame in 1986. Won Grammy's Lifetime Achievement Award in 1987. Popular performer, with many TV and movie appearances.	
11/25/57	34	1	1. Swanee River Rock (Talkin' 'Bout That River)	Atlantic 1154
			Best Seller #34 / Top 100 #42	
			Mongo Santamaria (conga drums)	
7/20/59	6	11	2. **What'd I Say (Part I)**	Atlantic 2031
			#1 R&B hit (1 week)	
12/14/59	40	1	3. I'm Movin' On	Atlantic 2043
			#1 Country hit for Hank Snow in 1950	
8/8/60	40	1	4. Sticks And Stones	ABC-Paramount 10118
10/10/60	1 (1)	10	5. **Georgia On My Mind**	ABC-Paramount 10135
			#10 hit for Frankie Trumbauer in 1931	
12/12/60	28	5	6. Ruby	ABC-Paramount 10164
			#3 hit for Richard Hayman in 1953; from the movie Ruby Gentry starring Charlton Heston	
3/27/61	8	9	7. **One Mint Julep** [I]	Impulse! 200
			#1 R&B hit (1 week); #2 R&B hit for The Clovers in 1952	
9/18/61	1 (2)	11	8. **Hit The Road Jack**	ABC-Paramount 10244
			#1 R&B hit (5 weeks)	
12/4/61+	9	10	9. **Unchain My Heart**	ABC-Paramount 10266
			#1 R&B hit (2 weeks)	
4/21/62	20	4	10. Hide 'Nor Hair	ABC-Paramount 10314
5/19/62	1 (5)	14	● 11. **I Can't Stop Loving You**	ABC-Paramount 10330
			#1 R&B hit (10 weeks) / #1 Adult Contemporary hit (5 weeks)	
8/4/62	2 (1)	9	12. **You Don't Know Me**	ABC-Paramount 10345
			#1 Adult Contemporary hit (3 weeks)	
12/1/62	7	9	13. **You Are My Sunshine /**	
			#1 R&B hit (3 weeks); #20 hit for Bing Crosby in 1941	
12/8/62	29	5	14. Your Cheating Heart	ABC-Paramount 10375
			#1 Country hit for Hank Williams in 1953	
3/16/63	20	4	15. Don't Set Me Free	ABC-Paramount 10405
4/27/63	8	8	16. **Take These Chains From My Heart**	ABC-Paramount 10435
			Jack Halloran Singers (backing vocals); #1 Country hit for Hank Williams in 1953	
7/6/63	21	5	17. No One /	
7/6/63	29	4	18. Without Love (There Is Nothing)	ABC-Paramount 10453
9/14/63	4	11	19. **Busted**	ABC-Paramount 10481
			#13 Country hit for Johnny Cash earlier in 1963	
12/21/63+	20	7	20. That Lucky Old Sun	ABC-Paramount 10509
			#1 hit for Frankie Laine in 1949	
3/21/64	38	2	21. My Heart Cries For You /	
			#2 hit for Guy Mitchell in 1951	
3/21/64	39	1	22. Baby, Don't You Cry (The New Swingova Rhythm)	ABC-Paramount 10530
1/15/66	6	9	23. **Crying Time**	ABC-Paramount 10739
			#1 Adult Contemporary hit (3 weeks); Jack Halloran Singers (backing vocals)	

DATE	POS	WKS	ARTIST–RECORD TITLE	LABEL & NO.
4/16/66	**19**	5	24. Together Again *#1 Adult Contemporary hit (3 weeks)*	ABC-Paramount 10785
6/25/66	**31**	4	25. Let's Go Get Stoned *#1 R&B hit (1 week)*	ABC 10808
10/1/66	**32**	2	26. I Chose To Sing The Blues *#4, 8, 9, 13, 15, 17, 23, 25 & 26: The Raeletts (backing vocals)*	ABC 10840
6/10/67	**15**	9	27. Here We Go Again	ABC/TRC 10938
9/23/67	**33**	3	28. In The Heat Of The Night *title song from the movie starring Sidney Poitier*	ABC/TRC 10970
12/2/67	**25**	3	29. Yesterday	ABC/TRC 11009
7/20/68	**35**	3	30. Eleanor Rigby	ABC/TRC 11090
4/17/71	**36**	4	31. Don't Change On Me	ABC/TRC 11291
5/15/71	**36**	2	32. Booty Butt **[I]** **THE RAY CHARLES ORCHESTRA**	Tangerine 1015
12/16/89+	**18**	8	33. I'll Be Good To You *Sales #13 / Airplay #26* **QUINCY JONES Featuring Ray Charles and Chaka Khan** *#1 R&B hit (2 weeks)*	Qwest 22697
			CHARLES, Ray, Singers	
			Born Charles Raymond Offenberg on 9/13/18 in Chicago, Illinois. Arranger/conductor for many TV shows.	
5/2/64	**3**	12	1. **Love Me With All Your Heart (Cuando Calienta El Sol)** *#1 Adult Contemporary hit (4 weeks)*	Command 4046
7/25/64	**29**	4	2. Al-Di-La *from the movie Rome Adventure starring Troy Donahue*	Command 4049
12/19/64+	**32**	5	3. One More Time	Command 4057
			CHARLES, Sonny	
			Born Charles Hemphill on 9/4/40 in Fort Wayne, Indiana. R&B singer. Leader of The Checkmates, Ltd., which included Bobby Stevens (vocals), Harvey Trees (guitar), Bill Van Buskirk (bass) and Marvin Smith (drums).	
5/31/69	**13**	10	1. Black Pearl **SONNY CHARLES and THE CHECKMATES, LTD.**	A&M 1053
1/22/83	**40**	2	2. Put It In A Magazine	Highrise 2001
			CHARLES & EDDIE	
			R&B vocal duo: Charles Pettigrew (from Philadelphia, Pennsylvania) and Eddie Chacon (from Oakland, California). Pettigrew died of cancer on 4/6/2001 (age 37).	
9/19/92	**13**	20	1. Would I Lie To You? *Airplay #14 / Sales #15*	Capitol 44809
			CHARLIE	
			Rock group from England: Terry Slesser (vocals), Terry Thomas (guitar), John Anderson (bass), and Steve Gadd and Bob Henrit (drums). Henrit was a member of Argent; later joined The Kinks.	
8/6/83	**38**	2	1. It's Inevitable	Mirage 99862
			CHARMS, The	
			R&B vocal group from Cincinnati, Ohio: Otis Williams (not to be confused with Otis Williams of The Temptations), Richard Parker, Donald Peak, Joe Penn and Rolland Bradley.	
11/27/54+	**15**	15	1. Hearts Of Stone *Best Seller #15 / Juke Box #15 / Jockey #20* *#1 R&B hit (9 weeks)*	DeLuxe 6062

DATE	POS	WKS	ARTIST–RECORD TITLE	LABEL & NO.
1/15/55	**26**	3	2. Ling, Ting, Tong _Best Seller #26_	DeLuxe 6076
4/14/56	**11**	15	3. Ivory Tower	DeLuxe 6093
			Jockey #11 / Top 100 #12 / Best Seller #13 / Juke Box #19	
			OTIS WILLIAMS And His CHARMS	

CHARTBUSTERS, The

Rock group from Washington DC: Vernon Sandusky (vocals, guitar), Vince Gideon (guitar), John Dubas (bass) and Mitch Corday (drums).

DATE	POS	WKS	ARTIST–RECORD TITLE	LABEL & NO.
8/15/64	**33**	3	1. She's The One	Mutual 502

CHASE

Jazz-rock group organized by trumpeter Bill Chase (born in 1935 in Chicago, Illinois; formerly with Woody Herman and Stan Kenton). Varying lineup. Chase along with bandmates John Emma, Wallace Yohn and Walter Clark were killed in a plane crash on 8/9/74 near Jackson, Minnesota.

DATE	POS	WKS	ARTIST–RECORD TITLE	LABEL & NO.
6/26/71	**24**	8	1. Get It On	Epic 10738

CHASEZ, JC

Born Joshua Chasez on 8/8/76 in Washington DC. Pop singer/songwriter. Member of *NSYNC.

DATE	POS	WKS	ARTIST–RECORD TITLE	LABEL & NO.
2/22/03	**35**	4	1. Blowin' Me Up (With Her Love) _Sales #6 / Airplay #39_	Fox/Jive 40070

CHEAP TRICK

Rock group from Rockford, Illinois: Robin Zander (vocals), Rick Nielsen (guitar), Tom Petersson (bass) and Brad "Bun E. Carlos" Carlson (drums).

DATE	POS	WKS	ARTIST–RECORD TITLE	LABEL & NO.
5/26/79	**7**	13	● 1. **I Want You To Want Me** [L]	Epic 50680
9/15/79	**35**	3	2. Ain't That A Shame [L]	Epic 50743
			above 2 recorded on 4/28/78 at the Budokan concert hall in Japan	
10/27/79	**26**	5	3. Dream Police	Epic 50774
1/19/80	**32**	3	4. Voices	Epic 50814
5/21/88	**1** (2)	14	5. **The Flame** _Airplay #1 (2) / Sales #1 (1)_	Epic 07745
8/20/88	**4**	12	6. **Don't Be Cruel** _Sales #3 / Airplay #4_	Epic 07965
12/17/88	**33**	5	7. Ghost Town _Airplay #32 / Sales #34_	Epic 08097
8/18/90	**12**	7	8. Can't Stop Fallin' Into Love _Airplay #13 / Sales #15_	Epic 73444

CHECKER, Chubby

Born Ernest Evans on 10/3/41 in Andrews, South Carolina; raised in Philadelphia, Pennsylvania. Did impersonations of famous singers. First recorded for Parkway in 1959. Dick Clark's then-wife Bobbie suggested that Evans change his name to Chubby Checker due to his resemblance to a teenage Fats Domino. Cover version of Hank Ballard's "The Twist" started worldwide dance craze. On 4/12/64, married Miss World 1962, Dutch-born Catharina Lodders ("Loddy Lo" written for her). In the movies _Don't Knock The Twist_ and _Twist Around The Clock_.

DATE	POS	WKS	ARTIST–RECORD TITLE	LABEL & NO.
6/15/59	**38**	2	1. The Class [N]	Parkway 804
			imitations of Fats Domino, The Coasters, Elvis Presley, Cozy Cole and The Chipmunks parodying "Mary Had A Little Lamb"	
8/8/60	**1** (1)	15	● 2. **The Twist**	Parkway 811
			also see #8 below	
10/31/60	**14**	9	3. The Hucklebuck	Parkway 813
			#5 hit for Tommy Dorsey in 1949	
1/30/61	**1** (3)	14	4. Pony Time	Parkway 818
			#1 R&B hit (2 weeks)	

DATE	POS	WKS	ARTIST–RECORD TITLE	LABEL & NO.
5/1/61	24	4	5. (Dance The) Mess Around	Parkway 822
7/3/61	8	15	● 6. **Let's Twist Again**	Parkway 824
10/2/61	7	11	7. **The Fly**	Parkway 830
11/20/61+	1 (2)	18	● 8. **The Twist** [R]	Parkway 811
			same version as #2 above	
12/25/61	21	3	9. Jingle Bell Rock [X]	Cameo 205
			BOBBY RYDELL CHUBBY CHECKER	
3/10/62	3	12	10. **Slow Twistin'**	Parkway 835
			CHUBBY CHECKER (with Dee Dee Sharp)	
7/7/62	12	7	11. Dancin' Party	Parkway 842
9/29/62	2 (2)	17	● 12. **Limbo Rock /**	
9/29/62	10	9	13. **Popeye (The Hitchhiker)**	Parkway 849
2/23/63	20	8	14. Let's Limbo Some More /	
3/23/63	15	7	15. Twenty Miles	Parkway 862
6/1/63	12	7	16. Birdland	Parkway 873
8/3/63	25	5	17. Twist It Up	Parkway 879
11/23/63	12	9	18. Loddy Lo /	
1/11/64	17	8	19. Hooka Tooka	Parkway 890
4/4/64	23	5	20. Hey, Bobba Needle	Parkway 907
7/11/64	40	1	21. Lazy Elsie Molly	Parkway 920
5/22/65	40	1	22. Let's Do The Freddie	Parkway 949
7/9/88	16	8	23. The Twist (Yo, Twist!) Sales #12 / Airplay #17 [R]	Tin Pan Apple 887571
			FAT BOYS (with Chubby Checker)	
			CHECKMATES, LTD., The — see CHARLES, Sonny	
			CHEECH & CHONG	
			Duo of comedians Richard "Cheech" Marin (born on 7/13/46 in Watts, California) and Thomas Chong (born on 5/24/38 in Edmonton, Alberta, Canada). Starred in several movies. Chong, the father of actress Rae Dawn Chong, was the guitarist of Bobby Taylor & The Vancouvers. Cheech was a cast member of TV's *Golden Palace* and *Nash Bridges*.	
9/29/73	15	7	1. Basketball Jones Featuring Tyrone Shoelaces [N] parody of "Love Jones" by Brighter Side Of Darkness; all-star band includes George Harrison, Carole King, Billy Preston, Tom Scott, and Darlene Love and Michelle Phillips (The Mamas & The Papas) as cheerleaders	Ode 66038
12/29/73+	24	5	2. Sister Mary Elephant (Shudd-Up!) [C]	Ode 66041
8/31/74	9	8	3. **Earache My Eye (Featuring Alice Bowie)** [C]	Ode 66102
			CHEERS, The	
			Pop vocal trio from Los Angeles, California: Bert Convy, Gil Garfield and Sue Allen. Convy later became a popular TV personality; died of a brain tumor on 7/15/91 (age 58).	
9/24/55	6	11	1. **Black Denim Trousers** Best Seller #6 / Jockey #6 / Top 100 #13 / Juke Box #20 Les Baxter (orch. and chorus)	Capitol 3219

DATE	POS	WKS	ARTIST–RECORD TITLE	LABEL & NO.
			CHER	
			Born Cherilyn Sarkisian on 5/20/46 in El Centro, California. Adopted by stepfather at age 15 and last name changed to La Piere. Worked as backup singer for Phil Spector. Recorded as "Bonnie Jo Mason" and "Cherilyn" in 1964. Recorded with Sonny Bono as "Caesar & Cleo" in 1963, then as Sonny & Cher from 1965-73. Married to Bono from 1963-75. Married to Gregg Allman from 1975-78. Own TV series with Bono from 1971-74, 1976-77. Member of the group Black Rose in 1980. Acclaimed movie actress (won the 1987 Best Actress Oscar for *Moonstruck*).	
8/7/65	15	6	1. All I Really Want To Do written by Bob Dylan	Imperial 66114
11/6/65	25	3	2. Where Do You Go	Imperial 66136
3/26/66	2 (1)	9	3. **Bang Bang (My Baby Shot Me Down)**	Imperial 66160
8/20/66	32	3	4. Alfie title song from the movie starring Michael Caine	Imperial 66192
11/18/67	9	9	5. **You Better Sit Down Kids**	Imperial 66261
10/2/71	1 (2)	14	● 6. **Gypsys, Tramps & Thieves**	Kapp 2146
2/12/72	7	10	7. **The Way Of Love**	Kapp 2158
6/3/72	22	6	8. Living In A House Divided	Kapp 2171
9/1/73	1 (2)	14	● 9. **Half-Breed**	MCA 40102
2/2/74	1 (1)	12	● 10. **Dark Lady**	MCA 40161
6/15/74	27	4	11. Train Of Thought	MCA 40245
3/17/79	8	11	● 12. **Take Me Home**	Casablanca 965
1/16/88	10	12	13. **I Found Someone** Sales #8 / Airplay #11 written and produced by Michael Bolton	Geffen 28191
4/30/88	14	9	14. We All Sleep Alone Airplay #12 / Sales #14 co-written and co-produced by Jon Bon Jovi	Geffen 27986
4/1/89	6	11	● 15. **After All** Sales #4 / Airplay #9 **CHER and PETER CETERA** #1 Adult Contemporary hit (4 weeks); love theme from the movie *Chances Are* starring Cybill Shepherd and Robert Downey, Jr.	Geffen 27529
8/5/89	3	14	● 16. **If I Could Turn Back Time** Sales #2 / Airplay #4 #1 Adult Contemporary hit (1 week)	Geffen 22886
11/18/89	8	11	17. **Just Like Jesse James** Sales #6 / Airplay #11	Geffen 22844
3/24/90	20	6	18. Heart Of Stone Sales #21 / Airplay #27	Geffen 19953
1/19/91	33	2	19. The Shoop Shoop Song (It's In His Kiss) Sales #23 from the movie *Mermaids* starring Cher	Geffen 19659
6/29/91	17	9	20. Love And Understanding Airplay #38 / Sales #45	Geffen 19023
12/21/91+	37	4	21. Save Up All Your Tears Airplay #40 / Sales #59	Geffen 19105
1/23/99	1 (4)	25	▲ 22. **Believe** Sales #1 (4) / Airplay #2	Warner 17119
			CHERI	
			Female dance duo from Montreal, Quebec, Canada: Rosalind Hunt and Lyn Cullerier.	
6/5/82	39	2	1. Murphy's Law **[N]**	Venture 149
			CHERRELLE	
			Born Cheryl Norton on 10/13/58 in Los Angeles, California. R&B singer. Cousin of singer Pebbles.	
3/29/86	26	6	1. Saturday Love Sales #19 **CHERRELLE with ALEXANDER O'NEAL**	Tabu 05767
3/5/88	28	6	2. Never Knew Love Like This Airplay #26 / Sales #28 **ALEXANDER O'NEAL featuring Cherrelle**	Tabu 07646

DATE	POS	WKS	ARTIST–RECORD TITLE	LABEL & NO.
			CHERRY, Don	
			Born on 1/11/24 in Wichita Falls, Texas. Pop singer. Not to be confused with the jazz trumpeter/father of Eagle-Eye and Neneh Cherry.	
12/10/55+	4	18	1. **Band Of Gold** Jockey #4 / Best Seller #5 / Top 100 #5 / Juke Box #5	Columbia 40597
4/14/56	29	6	2. Wild Cherry Top 100 #29	Columbia 40665
8/11/56	22	6	3. Ghost Town Jockey #22 / Top 100 #26	Columbia 40705
			Ray Conniff (orch., above 3)	
			CHERRY, Eagle-Eye	
			Born on 5/7/69 in Stockholm, Sweden. Son of trumpeter Don Cherry. Half-brother of Neneh Cherry.	
12/5/98+	5	25	1. **Save Tonight** Airplay #2	album cut
			from the album *Desireless* on Work 69434	
			CHERRY, Neneh	
			Born on 3/10/63 in Stockholm, Sweden; raised in Brooklyn, New York. Female R&B singer. Stepdaughter of jazz trumpeter Don Cherry. Half-sister of Eagle-Eye Cherry.	
5/6/89	3	14	● 1. **Buffalo Stance** Sales #1 (2) / Airplay #4	Virgin 99231
			from the movie *Slaves Of New York* starring Bernadette Peters	
8/19/89	8	8	2. **Kisses On The Wind** Sales #9 / Airplay #10	Virgin 99183
			CHESNEY, Kenny	
			Born on 3/26/68 in Knoxville, Tennessee; raised in Luttrell, Tennessee. Country singer/songwriter/guitarist.	
3/6/99	27	11	1. How Forever Feels Airplay #17 / Sales #31	BNA 65666
			#1 Country hit (6 weeks)	
8/28/99	34	5	2. You Had Me From Hello Airplay #25	album cut
			#1 Country hit (1 week); from the album *Everywhere We Go* on BNA 67655	
12/16/00	34	3	3. I Lost It Airplay #30	album cut
			Pam Tillis (backing vocal)	
5/5/01	26	9	4. Don't Happen Twice Airplay #20	album cut
			#1 Country hit (1 week); above 2 from the album *Greatest Hits* on BNA 67976	
4/13/02	35	4	5. Young Airplay #33	album cut
7/6/02	22	12	6. The Good Stuff Airplay #20	album cut
			#1 Country hit (7 weeks)	
3/22/03	28	8	7. Big Star Airplay #25	album cut
8/2/03	28	8	8. No Shoes, No Shirt, No Problems Airplay #24	album cut
			above 4 from the album *No Shoes, No Shirt, No Problems* on BNA 67038	
12/13/03	29	10	9. There Goes My Life Airplay #28	album cut
			#1 Country hit (7 weeks); from the album *When The Sun Goes Down* on BNA 56609	
			CHESNUTT, Mark	
			Born on 9/6/63 in Beaumont, Texas. Country singer/guitarist.	
1/2/99	17	12	1. I Don't Want To Miss A Thing Sales #14 / Airplay #21	Decca 72078
			#1 Country hit (2 weeks)	

DATE	POS	WKS	ARTIST–RECORD TITLE	LABEL & NO.
			CHIC	
			R&B-disco group formed in New York by prolific producers Bernard Edwards (bass) and Nile Rodgers (guitar). Featured drummer Tony Thompson and singers Luci Martin and Norma Jean Wright. Wright began solo career in 1978 as Norma Jean; replaced by Alfa Anderson. Rodgers joined The Honeydrippers in 1984. Thompson joined Power Station in 1985 and Edwards became their producer. Edwards died of pneumonia on 4/18/96 (age 43). Thompson died of cancer on 11/12/2003 (age 48).	
12/10/77+	6	17	● 1. **Dance, Dance, Dance (Yowsah, Yowsah, Yowsah)**	Atlantic 3435
6/17/78	38	1	2. Everybody Dance	Atlantic 3469
			Luther Vandross (backing vocal, above 2)	
11/18/78	1 (6)	19	▲ 3. **Le Freak**	Atlantic 3519
			#1 R&B hit (5 weeks)	
3/10/79	7	12	● 4. **I Want Your Love**	Atlantic 3557
7/7/79	1 (1)	14	● 5. **Good Times**	Atlantic 3584
			#1 R&B hit (6 weeks)	
			CHICAGO	
			Jazz-oriented rock group from Chicago, Illinois: Peter Cetera (vocals, bass), Terry Kath (vocals, guitar), Robert Lamm (vocals, keyboards), James Pankow (trombone), Lee Loughnane (trumpet), Walt Parazaider (sax) and Danny Seraphine (drums). Kath died of an accidental self-inflicted gunshot on 1/23/78 (age 31); replaced by Donnie Dacus (guitar, vocals; 1978-80). Bill Champlin (guitar, keyboards, vocals) joined in 1981. Cetera left in 1985, replaced by Jason Scheff (bass, vocals). Seraphine left in 1990.	
4/25/70	9	11	1. **Make Me Smile**	Columbia 45127
8/1/70	4	11	2. **25 Or 6 To 4**	Columbia 45194
11/21/70+	7	11	3. **Does Anybody Really Know What Time It Is?**	Columbia 45264
3/6/71	20	6	4. Free	Columbia 45331
5/29/71	35	4	5. Lowdown	Columbia 45370
7/10/71	7	11	6. **Beginnings /**	
			#1 Adult Contemporary hit (1 week)	
7/10/71		11	7. Colour My World	Columbia 45417
10/30/71	24	6	8. Questions 67 And 68 [R]	Columbia 45467
			originally charted at #71 in 1969	
8/12/72	3	10	● 9. **Saturday In The Park**	Columbia 45657
11/18/72	24	6	10. Dialogue (Part I & II)	Columbia 45717
7/7/73	10	12	11. **Feelin' Stronger Every Day**	Columbia 45880
10/20/73	4	14	● 12. **Just You 'N' Me**	Columbia 45933
4/6/74	9	12	13. **(I've Been) Searchin' So Long**	Columbia 46020
7/13/74	6	8	14. **Call On Me**	Columbia 46062
			#1 Adult Contemporary hit (1 week)	
10/26/74	11	10	15. Wishing You Were Here	Columbia 10049
			#1 Adult Contemporary hit (1 week); Carl Wilson, Dennis Wilson and Al Jardine (of The Beach Boys; backing vocals)	
3/8/75	13	7	16. Harry Truman	Columbia 10092
5/10/75	5	7	17. **Old Days**	Columbia 10131
7/17/76	32	4	18. Another Rainy Day In New York City	Columbia 10360
8/21/76	1 (2)	17	▲ 19. **If You Leave Me Now**	Columbia 10390
			#1 Adult Contemporary hit (1 week)	
10/15/77	4	12	20. **Baby, What A Big Surprise**	Columbia 10620
10/28/78	14	8	21. Alive Again	Columbia 10845
1/13/79	14	9	22. No Tell Lover	Columbia 10879

DATE	POS	WKS	ARTIST–RECORD TITLE	LABEL & NO.
6/26/82	**1 (2)**	18	● 23. **Hard To Say I'm Sorry** #1 Adult Contemporary hit (3 weeks); from the movie *Summer Lovers* starring Daryl Hannah	Full Moon 29979
10/23/82	**22**	8	24. Love Me Tomorrow	Full Moon 29911
5/12/84	**16**	10	25. Stay The Night	Warner/Full M. 29306
8/25/84	**3**	15	26. **Hard Habit To Break** Airplay #2 / Sales #3	Warner/Full M. 29214
12/1/84+	**3**	14	27. **You're The Inspiration** Airplay #1 (1) / Sales #5 #1 Adult Contemporary hit (2 weeks)	Warner/Full M. 29126
3/9/85	**14**	10	28. Along Comes A Woman Airplay #7 / Sales #25	Warner/Full M. 29082
12/27/86+	**3**	13	29. **Will You Still Love Me?** Airplay #2 / Sales #4	Warner/Full M. 28512
4/25/87	**17**	8	30. If She Would Have Been Faithful... Airplay #11 / Sales #22	Warner/Full M. 28424
7/2/88	**3**	13	31. **I Don't Wanna Live Without Your Love** Airplay #2 / Sales #3	Reprise/Full M. 27855
10/15/88	**1 (2)**	16	● 32. **Look Away** Airplay #1 (3) / Sales #1 (1) #1 Adult Contemporary hit (1 week)	Reprise/Full M. 27766
2/4/89	**10**	10	33. **You're Not Alone** Airplay #8 / Sales #13	Reprise/Full M. 27757
12/23/89+	**5**	12	34. **What Kind Of Man Would I Be?** Airplay #4 / Sales #6	Reprise/Full M. 22741
3/9/91	**39**	2	35. Chasin' The Wind Sales #37 / Airplay #38	Reprise 19466

CHICAGO LOOP, The

Rock group from Chicago, Illinois: Bob Slawson and Judy Navy (vocals), John Savanna (guitar), Barry Goldberg (piano), Carmen Riole (bass) and Jack Siomoms (drums).

DATE	POS	WKS	ARTIST–RECORD TITLE	LABEL & NO.
11/26/66	**37**	3	1. (When She Needs Good Lovin') She Comes To Me	DynoVoice 226

CHIFFONS, The

Female R&B vocal group from the Bronx, New York: Judy Craig, Barbara Lee Jones, Patricia Bennett and Sylvia Peterson. Jones died of a heart attack on 5/15/92 (age 44).

DATE	POS	WKS	ARTIST–RECORD TITLE	LABEL & NO.
3/9/63	**1 (4)**	12	1. **He's So Fine** #1 R&B hit (4 weeks)	Laurie 3152
6/8/63	**5**	9	2. **One Fine Day**	Laurie 3179
10/19/63	**40**	1	3. A Love So Fine	Laurie 3195
1/4/64	**36**	1	4. I Have A Boyfriend	Laurie 3212
5/28/66	**10**	7	5. **Sweet Talkin' Guy**	Laurie 3340

CHILD, Desmond

Born John Charles Barrett on 10/28/53 in Miami, Florida. Prolific producer/songwriter.

DATE	POS	WKS	ARTIST–RECORD TITLE	LABEL & NO.
8/17/91	**40**	1	1. Love On A Rooftop Airplay #66	Elektra 64883

CHILD, Jane

Born on 2/15/69 in Toronto, Ontario, Canada. Singer/songwriter/keyboardist.

DATE	POS	WKS	ARTIST–RECORD TITLE	LABEL & NO.
3/3/90	**2 (3)**	14	● 1. **Don't Wanna Fall In Love** Airplay #1 (2) / Sales #3	Warner 19933

CHI-LITES, The

R&B vocal group from Chicago, Illinois: Eugene Record, Robert Lester, Marshall Thompson and Creadel Jones. Record married Barbara Acklin.

DATE	POS	WKS	ARTIST–RECORD TITLE	LABEL & NO.
5/8/71	**26**	6	1. (For God's Sake) Give More Power To The People	Brunswick 55450
10/30/71	**3**	13	2. **Have You Seen Her** #1 R&B hit (2 weeks)	Brunswick 55462

DATE	POS	WKS	ARTIST–RECORD TITLE	LABEL & NO.
4/15/72	**1** (1)	14	3. **Oh Girl** #1 R&B hit (2 weeks)	Brunswick 55471
3/24/73	**33**	5	4. A Letter To Myself	Brunswick 55491
9/1/73	**30**	5	5. Stoned Out Of My Mind	Brunswick 55500
			CHILLIWACK	
			Rock group from Vancouver, British Columbia, Canada: Bill Henderson (vocals, guitar), Brian MacLeod (guitar), Ab Bryant (bass) and Rick Taylor (drums). Bryant was also with Prism. MacLeod died of cancer on 4/25/92.	
10/31/81	**22**	11	1. My Girl (Gone, Gone, Gone)	Millennium 11813
2/27/82	**33**	3	2. I Believe	Millennium 13102
			CHIMES, The	
			Vocal group from Brooklyn, New York: Len Cocco, Pat DePrisco, Richard Mercado, Joe Croce and Pat McGuire.	
1/16/61	**11**	6	1. Once In Awhile #1 hit for Tommy Dorsey in 1937	Tag 444
5/15/61	**38**	1	2. I'm In The Mood For Love #1 hit for Little Jack Little in 1935	Tag 445
			CHINGY	
			Born Howard Bailey on 3/9/80 in St. Louis, Missouri. Male rapper.	
6/21/03	**2** (5)	28	1. **Right Thurr** Airplay #2 / Sales #3	Disturb. Tha P. 77995
10/4/03	**3**	18	2. **Holidae In** Airplay #3 / Sales #42 **CHINGY featuring Ludacris & Snoop Dogg**	Disturb. Tha P. 52816
			CHORDETTES, The	
			Female vocal group from Sheboygan, Wisconsin: Janet Ertel, Carol Buschman, Lynn Evans and Margie Needham. With Arthur Godfrey from 1949-53. Ertel married Cadence record owner Archie Bleyer in 1954; her daughter Jackie was married to Phil Everly of The Everly Brothers. Ertel died of cancer on 11/22/88 (age 75).	
10/30/54	**1** (7)	20	● 1. **Mr. Sandman** Best Seller #1 (7) / Jockey #1 (7) / Juke Box #1 (4)	Cadence 1247
3/10/56	**14**	9	2. Eddie My Love Jockey #14 / Best Seller #17 / Top 100 #18	Cadence 1284
6/2/56	**5**	17	3. **Born To Be With You** Top 100 #5 / Jockey #5 / Juke Box #5 / Best Seller #7	Cadence 1291
10/13/56	**16**	10	4. Lay Down Your Arms Top 100 #16 / Juke Box #16 / Best Seller #18 / Jockey #20	Cadence 1299
9/16/57	**8**	8	5. **Just Between You And Me** Jockey #8 / Best Seller #15 / Top 100 #19	Cadence 1330
3/10/58	**2** (2)	12	6. **Lollipop** Jockey #2 / Best Seller #2 / Top 100 #2	Cadence 1345
5/26/58	**17**	7	7. Zorro Top 100 #17 / Best Seller #18 / Jockey #22 theme from the Disney TV series starring Guy Williams	Cadence 1349
3/30/59	**27**	4	8. No Other Arms, No Other Lips	Cadence 1361
7/3/61	**13**	8	9. Never On Sunday title song from the movie starring Melina Mercouri; Archie Bleyer (orch., all of above)	Cadence 1402
			CHRISTIAN, Chris	
			Born on 2/7/51 in Abilene, Texas. Singer/songwriter/producer. Member of Cotton, Lloyd and Christian.	
11/14/81	**37**	3	1. I Want You, I Need You	Boardwalk 126

DATE	POS	WKS	ARTIST–RECORD TITLE	LABEL & NO.
			CHRISTIE	
			Pop-rock trio from England: Jeff Christie (vocals, bass), Vic Elmes (guitar) and Mike Blakely (drums). Blakely's brother, Alan, was a member of The Tremeloes.	
10/24/70	23	8	1. Yellow River	Epic 10626
			CHRISTIE, Lou	
			Born Lugee Sacco on 2/19/43 in Glen Willard, Pennsylvania. Pop singer/songwriter.	
2/16/63	24	6	1. The Gypsy Cried	Roulette 4457
4/27/63	6	10	2. **Two Faces Have I**	Roulette 4481
1/22/66	**1** (1)	10	● 3. **Lightnin' Strikes**	MGM 13412
4/23/66	16	4	4. Rhapsody In The Rain	MGM 13473
9/13/69	10	9	5. **I'm Gonna Make You Mine**	Buddah 116
			CHRISTOPHER, Gavin	
			Born in Chicago, Illinois. Male R&B singer/songwriter/producer.	
7/12/86	22	7	1. One Step Closer To You Sales #18 / Airplay #27	Manhattan 50028
			CHUMBAWAMBA	
			Post-punk rock group from Leeds, England: Alice Nutter, Lou Watts, Danbert Nubacon, Paul Greco, Jude Abbott, Dunstan Bruce, Neil Ferguson and Harry Hamer.	
10/4/97	6	25	1. **Tubthumping** Airplay #1 (9) / Sales #30 #1 Modern Rock hit (7 weeks)	Republic 56146
			CHURCH, The	
			Folk-rock group from Canberra, Australia: Steve Kilbey (vocals, bass), Peter Koppes and Marty Willson-Piper (guitars), and Richard Ploog (drums).	
5/28/88	24	5	1. Under The Milky Way Sales #19 / Airplay #29	Arista 9673
			CHURCH, Eugene	
			Born on 1/23/38 in St. Louis, Missouri; raised in Los Angeles, California. Died of AIDS on 4/16/93 (age 55). R&B singer/songwriter.	
2/23/59	36	2	1. Pretty Girls Everywhere **EUGENE CHURCH and The Fellows**	Class 235
			CINDERELLA	
			Hard-rock group from Philadelphia, Pennsylvania: Tom Keifer (vocals, guitar), Jeff LaBar (guitar), Eric Brittingham (bass) and Fred Coury (drums).	
1/17/87	13	8	1. Nobody's Fool Sales #11 / Airplay #22	Mercury 884851
10/1/88	12	11	2. Don't Know What You Got (Till It's Gone) Sales #9 / Airplay #16	Mercury 870644
2/25/89	36	2	3. The Last Mile Sales #34 / Airplay #39	Mercury 872148
5/20/89	20	7	4. Coming Home Sales #18 / Airplay #20	Mercury 872982
1/26/91	36	2	5. Shelter Me Airplay #35 / Sales #37	Mercury 878700

DATE	POS	WKS	ARTIST–RECORD TITLE	LABEL & NO.
			CITIZEN KING	
			Rock group from Milwaukee, Wisconsin: Matt Sims (vocals, bass), Kristian Riley (guitar), Malcolm Michiles (DJ), Dave Cooley (keyboards) and DJ Brooks (drums).	
7/3/99	**25**	12	1. Better Days (and the bottom drops out) Airplay #31 / Sales #32	Warner 16965
			CITY BOY	
			Pop-rock group from Birmingham, England: Lol Mason (vocals), Mike Slamer (guitar), Max Thomas (keyboards), Steve Broughton (percussion), Chris Dunn (bass) and Roy Ward (drums).	
9/9/78	**27**	6	1. 5.7.0.5.	Mercury 73999
			CITY HIGH	
			Black hip-hop trio from Willingboro, New Jersey: Claudette Ortiz, Robby Pardlo and Ryan Toby.	
4/7/01	**8**	25	1. **What Would You Do?** Sales #1 (2) / Airplay #9	Booga Basement 497489
11/3/01+	**18**	20	2. Caramel Airplay #18 **CITY HIGH Featuring Eve**	Booga Basement 497608
			C.J. & CO.	
			Disco group from Detroit, Michigan: Cornelius Brown, Curtis Durden, Joni Tolbert, Connie Durden and Charles Clark.	
7/9/77	**36**	2	1. Devil's Gun	Westbound 55400
			CLANTON, Jimmy	
			Born on 9/2/40 in Baton Rouge, Louisiana. Pop singer. Starred in the 1958 movie Go, Johnny, Go!.	
7/21/58	**4**	15	1. **Just A Dream** Best Seller #4 / Hot 100 #4 **JIMMY CLANTON And His Rockets** #1 R&B hit (1 week)	Ace 546
11/17/58	**25**	5	2. A Letter To An Angel /	
12/1/58	**38**	2	3. A Part Of Me	Ace 551
8/17/59	**33**	6	4. My Own True Love melody is "Tara's Theme" from the movie Gone With The Wind starring Clark Gable and Vivien Leigh	Ace 567
12/21/59+	**5**	11	5. **Go, Jimmy, Go**	Ace 575
5/30/60	**22**	6	6. Another Sleepless Night	Ace 585
9/1/62	**7**	10	7. **Venus In Blue Jeans** above 2 written by Neil Sedaka	Ace 8001
			CLAPTON, Eric	
			Born Eric Patrick Clapp on 3/30/45 in Ripley, England. Prolific rock-blues guitarist/vocalist. With The Roosters in 1963, The Yardbirds, 1963-65, and John Mayall's Bluesbreakers, 1965-66. Formed Cream with Jack Bruce and Ginger Baker in 1966. Formed Blind Faith in 1968; worked with John Lennon's Plastic Ono Band, and Delaney & Bonnie. Formed Derek and The Dominos in 1970. After two years of reclusion (1971-72), Clapton performed his comeback concert at London's Rainbow Theatre in January 1973. Began actively recording and touring again in 1974. Nicknamed "Slowhand" in 1964 while with The Yardbirds. Inducted into the Rock and Roll Hall of Fame in 2000.	
11/14/70	**18**	8	1. After Midnight	Atco 6784

DATE	POS	WKS	ARTIST–RECORD TITLE	LABEL & NO.
6/17/72	**10**	10	2. **Layla** [R] **DEREK AND THE DOMINOS** originally charted at #51 in 1971; also see #16 below	Atco 6809
8/3/74	**1 (1)**	10	● 3. **I Shot The Sheriff** Yvonne Elliman (backing vocal); written by Bob Marley	RSO 409
11/23/74	26	5	4. Willie And The Hand Jive	RSO 503
11/13/76	24	6	5. Hello Old Friend	RSO 861
2/4/78	**3**	17	● 6. **Lay Down Sally**	RSO 886
6/10/78	16	7	7. Wonderful Tonight Yvonne Elliman and Marcy Levy (backing vocals, above 3)	RSO 895
			ERIC CLAPTON AND HIS BAND:	
11/25/78+	9	11	8. **Promises /**	
3/24/79	40	2	9. Watch Out For Lucy	RSO 910
7/26/80	30	5	10. Tulsa Time / [L] #1 Country hit for Don Williams in 1978	
7/26/80		5	11. Cocaine [L]	RSO 1039
3/14/81	10	12	12. **I Can't Stand It** #1 Mainstream Rock hit (2 weeks)	RSO 1060
			ERIC CLAPTON:	
2/19/83	18	10	13. I've Got A Rock N' Roll Heart	Duck/Warner 29780
3/30/85	26	6	14. Forever Man Airplay #20 / Sales #30 #1 Mainstream Rock hit (2 weeks)	Duck/Warner 29081
2/15/92	**2 (4)**	23	▲ 15. **Tears In Heaven** Sales #1 (3) / Airplay #3 #1 Adult Contemporary hit (3 weeks); from the movie *Rush* starring Jason Patric; 1992 Grammy winner: Record of the Year	Duck/Reprise 19038
10/17/92	12	14	16. Layla Airplay #12 / Sales #16 **[L-R]** acoustic version of #2 above	Duck/Reprise 18787
7/20/96	5	36	● 17. **Change The World** Airplay #2 / Sales #9 #1 Adult Contemporary hit (13 weeks); from the movie *Phenomenon* starring John Travolta; 1996 Grammy winner: Record of the Year	Reprise 17621
2/28/98	16 ᴬ	20	18. My Father's Eyes from the album *Pilgrim* on Duck 46577	album cut
			CLARK, Claudine	
			Born on 4/26/41 in Macon, Georgia; raised in Philadelphia, Pennsylvania. Female R&B singer/songwriter.	
7/21/62	5	10	1. **Party Lights**	Chancellor 1113
			CLARK, Dave, Five	
			Born on 12/15/42 in London, England. Pop-rock drummer. His group consisted of Mike Smith (vocals, keyboards), Lenny Davidson (guitar), Denny Payton (sax) and Rick Huxley (bass). Group starred in the movie *Having A Wild Weekend* (released abroad as *Catch Us If You Can*) in 1965. Clark co- wrote and produced the 1986 London stage musical *Time*.	
3/7/64	6	11	1. **Glad All Over**	Epic 9656
4/11/64	4	10	2. **Bits And Pieces**	Epic 9671
5/9/64	11	9	3. Do You Love Me	Epic 9678
6/20/64	4	9	4. **Can't You See That She's Mine**	Epic 9692
8/8/64	3	9	5. **Because**	Epic 9704
10/17/64	15	6	6. Everybody Knows (I Still Love You)	Epic 9722
12/5/64+	14	9	7. Any Way You Want It	Epic 9739

DATE	POS	WKS	ARTIST–RECORD TITLE	LABEL & NO.
2/27/65	**14**	6	8. Come Home	Epic 9763
5/8/65	**23**	5	9. Reelin' And Rockin'	Epic 9786
7/10/65	**7**	8	10. **I Like It Like That**	Epic 9811
9/4/65	**4**	9	11. **Catch Us If You Can**	Epic 9833
			from the movie *Having A Wild Weekend* (originally titled *Catch Us If You Can*) starring the Dave Clark Five	
11/20/65	**1 (1)**	11	12. **Over And Over**	Epic 9863
2/19/66	**18**	5	13. At The Scene	Epic 9882
4/23/66	**12**	5	14. Try Too Hard	Epic 10004
7/2/66	**28**	4	15. Please Tell Me Why	Epic 10031
4/15/67	**7**	7	16. **You Got What It Takes**	Epic 10144
7/1/67	**35**	2	17. You Must Have Been A Beautiful Baby	Epic 10179
			#1 hit for Bing Crosby in 1938	

CLARK, Dee

Born Delecta Clark on 11/7/38 in Blytheville, Arkansas; raised in Chicago, Illinois. Died of a heart attack on 12/7/90 (age 62). Male R&B singer.

DATE	POS	WKS	ARTIST–RECORD TITLE	LABEL & NO.
1/12/59	**21**	6	1. Nobody But You	Abner 1019
5/25/59	**18**	9	2. Just Keep It Up	Abner 1026
9/14/59	**20**	9	3. Hey Little Girl	Abner 1029
1/4/60	**33**	5	4. How About That	Abner 1032
3/6/61	**34**	4	5. Your Friends	Vee-Jay 372
5/22/61	**2 (1)**	12	6. **Raindrops**	Vee-Jay 383

CLARK, Petula

Born on 11/15/32 in Epsom, Surrey, England. Pop singer/actress. Hosted own radio and TV shows in England. Starred in several movies including *Finian's Rainbow* and *Goodbye Mr. Chips*.

DATE	POS	WKS	ARTIST–RECORD TITLE	LABEL & NO.
1/2/65	**1 (2)**	13	● 1. **Downtown**	Warner 5494
4/3/65	**3**	9	2. **I Know A Place**	Warner 5612
7/31/65	**22**	5	3. You'd Better Come Home	Warner 5643
10/30/65	**21**	4	4. Round Every Corner	Warner 5661
1/15/66	**1 (2)**	9	5. **My Love**	Warner 5684
4/2/66	**11**	7	6. A Sign Of The Times	Warner 5802
7/30/66	**9**	7	7. **I Couldn't Live Without Your Love**	Warner 5835
			#1 Adult Contemporary hit (1 week)	
10/29/66	**21**	6	8. Who Am I	Warner 5863
12/31/66+	**16**	7	9. Color My World	Warner 5882
3/18/67	**3**	9	10. **This Is My Song**	Warner 7002
			written by Charlie Chaplin; from the movie A Countess From Hong Kong *starring Marlon Brando*	
6/17/67	**5**	7	11. **Don't Sleep In The Subway**	Warner 7049
			#1 Adult Contemporary hit (3 weeks)	
9/16/67	**26**	4	12. The Cat In The Window (The Bird In The Sky)	Warner 7073
12/30/67	**31**	2	13. The Other Man's Grass Is Always Greener	Warner 7097
3/2/68	**15**	9	14. Kiss Me Goodbye	Warner 7170
8/24/68	**37**	1	15. Don't Give Up	Warner 7216

DATE	POS	WKS	ARTIST–RECORD TITLE	LABEL & NO.
			CLARK, Roy	
			Born on 4/15/33 in Meherrin, Virginia. Country singer/guitarist. Co-hosted TV's *Hee Haw*.	
7/12/69	**19**	6	1. Yesterday, When I Was Young	Dot 17246
			CLARK, Sanford	
			Born on 10/24/35 in Tulsa, Oklahoma. Male singer/songwriter/guitarist.	
8/11/56	**7**	15	1. **The Fool** Best Seller #7 / Juke Box #7 / Top 100 #9 / Jockey #16 Al Casey (guitar)	Dot 15481
			CLARK, Terri	
			Born Terri Sauson (Clark is her stepfather's last name) on 8/5/68 in Montreal, Quebec, Canada; raised in Medicine Hat, Alberta, Canada. Female country singer/guitarist.	
12/19/98	**40**	1	1. You're Easy On The Eyes Airplay #30 #1 Country hit (3 weeks); from the album *How I Feel* on Mercury 558211	album cut
1/25/03	**27**	7	2. I Just Wanna Be Mad Airplay #26	Mercury 172262
			CLARKE, Stanley	
			Born on 6/30/51 in Philadelphia, Pennsylvania. R&B-jazz bassist.	
6/13/81	**19**	9	1. Sweet Baby **STANLEY CLARKE/GEORGE DUKE**	Epic 01052
			CLARKE, Tony	
			Born in Harlem, New York; raised in Detroit, Michigan. Died in 1970. R&B singer/songwriter.	
5/8/65	**31**	2	1. The Entertainer	Chess 1924
			CLARKSON, Kelly	
			Born on 4/24/82 in Burleson, Texas. Female pop singer. Winner of TV's first *American Idol* talent series.	
10/5/02	**1 (2)**	11	● 1. **A Moment Like This** Sales #1 (5) / Airplay #8	RCA 60622
5/31/03	**9**	17	2. **Miss Independent** Airplay #10 co-written by Christina Aguilera; from the album *Thankful* on RCA 68159	album cut
			CLASH, The	
			Eclectic new wave rock group from London, England: John "Joe Strummer" Mellor (vocals), Mick Jones (guitar), Paul Simonon (bass) and Nicky "Topper" Headon (drums). Political activists who wrote songs protesting racism and oppression. Jones (not to be confused with Mick Jones of Foreigner) left band in 1984 to form Big Audio Dynamite. Strummer appeared in the 1987 movie *Straight To Hell*. Strummer died of heart failure on 12/22/2002 (age 50). Group inducted into the Rock and Roll Hall of Fame in 2003.	
4/26/80	**23**	7	1. Train In Vain (Stand By Me)	Epic 50851
11/13/82+	**8**	15	2. **Rock The Casbah**	Epic 03245
			CLASSICS, The	
			White doo-wop group from Brooklyn, New York: Emil Stucchio, Johnny Gambale, Tony Victor and Jamie Troy.	
7/20/63	**20**	5	1. Till Then #10 hit for The Hilltoppers in 1954	Musicnote 1116

DATE	POS	WKS	ARTIST–RECORD TITLE	LABEL & NO.
			CLASSICS IV	
			Soft-rock group from Jacksonville, Florida: Dennis Yost (vocals), J.R. Cobb and Wally Eaton (guitars), Joe Wilson (bass) and Kim Venable (drums). Wilson was replaced by Dean Daughtry. Cobb, Daughtry and producer Buddy Buie later joined Atlanta Rhythm Section.	
1/13/68	3	12	1. **Spooky**	Imperial 66259
			CLASSICS IV FEATURING DENNIS YOST:	
11/16/68	5	12	● 2. **Stormy**	Imperial 66328
2/22/69	2 (1)	10	3. **Traces**	Imperial 66352
5/31/69	19	7	4. Everyday With You Girl	Imperial 66378
			DENNIS YOST AND THE CLASSICS IV:	
12/9/72	39	3	5. What Am I Crying For?	MGM South 7002
			CLAY, Judy — see VERA, Billy	
			CLAY, Tom	
			Born Thomas Clague on 8/20/29 in Binghamton, New York. Died of cancer on 11/22/95 (age 66). Was a DJ at KGBS in Los Angeles when he created this recording.	
7/24/71	8	7	1. **What The World Needs Now Is Love/ Abraham, Martin and John** [S] The Blackberries (vocal accompaniment)	Mowest 5002
			CLAYTON, Adam — see U2	
			CLEFTONES, The	
			R&B vocal group from Queens, New York: Herbie Cox, Charlie James, Berman Patterson, William McClain and Warren Corbin.	
6/19/61	18	4	1. Heart And Soul #1 hit for Larry Clinton in 1938	Gee 1064
			CLEMONS, Clarence	
			Born on 1/11/42 in Norfolk, Virginia. Black saxophonist. Member of Bruce Springsteen's E Street Band. Nicknamed the "Big Man."	
11/23/85+	18	12	1. You're A Friend Of Mine Airplay #17 / Sales #20 **CLARENCE CLEMONS And Jackson Browne** Daryl Hannah (backing vocals)	Columbia 05660
			CLEOPATRA	
			Black teen vocal trio from Manchester, England: sisters Cleopatra, Zainam and Yonah Higgins.	
7/18/98	26	8	1. Cleopatra's Theme Sales #14	Maverick 17229
			CLIFF, Jimmy	
			Born James Chambers on 4/1/48 in St. James, Jamaica. Reggae singer/composer. Starred in the movies *The Harder They Come* (1975) and *Club Paradise* (1986).	
12/27/69+	25	7	1. Wonderful World, Beautiful People	A&M 1146
12/4/93+	18	14	2. I Can See Clearly Now Airplay #11 / Sales #33 from the movie *Cool Runnings* starring John Candy	Chaos/Columbia 77207

DATE	POS	WKS	ARTIST–RECORD TITLE	LABEL & NO.
			CLIFFORD, Buzz	
			Born Reese Francis Clifford III on 10/8/42 in Berwyn, Illinois. Teen pop-novelty singer.	
1/30/61	6	10	1. **Baby Sittin' Boogie** [N] babies' voices are by the children (boy & girl) of the producer; originally titled "Baby Sitter Boogie"	Columbia 41876
			CLIFFORD, Mike	
			Born on 11/6/43 in Los Angeles, California. White pop singer/actor. In the 1970s Broadway production of *Grease*.	
10/13/62	12	8	1. Close To Cathy	United Artists 489
			CLIMAX	
			White pop group from Los Angeles, California: Sonny Geraci (vocals), Walter Nims (guitar), Virgil Weber (keyboards), Steve York (bass) and Robert Neilson (drums). Geraci was a member of The Outsiders.	
1/22/72	3	12	● 1. **Precious And Few**	Rocky Road 30055
			CLIMAX BLUES BAND	
			Blues-rock group from Stafford, England: Colin Cooper (vocals, sax), Peter Haycock (guitar, vocals), Derek Holt (bass) and John Cuffley (drums).	
3/26/77	3	14	1. **Couldn't Get It Right**	Sire 736
4/4/81	12	17	2. I Love You	Warner 49669
			CLIMIE FISHER	
			Pop-rock duo. Simon Climie (vocals) was born on 4/7/60 in Fulham, London, England. Rob Fisher (keyboards) was born on 11/5/59 in Cheltenham, Gloucestershire, England; died of complications following stomach surgery on 8/25/99 (age 39). Fisher was a member of Naked Eyes.	
7/2/88	23	6	1. Love Changes (Everything) Sales #22 / Airplay #24	Capitol 44137
			CLINE, Patsy	
			Born Virginia Patterson Hensley on 9/8/32 in Gore, Virginia. Killed in a plane crash on 3/5/63 (age 30) near Camden, Tennessee. Legendary country singer. Jessica Lange portrayed Cline in the 1985 biographical movie *Sweet Dreams*. Won Grammy's Lifetime Achievement Award in 1995.	
3/2/57	12	11	1. Walkin' After Midnight Juke Box #12 / Top 100 #17 / Best Seller #21 / Jockey #22	Decca 30221
7/24/61	12	10	2. I Fall To Pieces #1 Country hit (2 weeks)	Decca 31205
11/6/61	9	7	3. **Crazy** written by Willie Nelson	Decca 31317
2/24/62	14	8	4. She's Got You #1 Country hit (5 weeks)	Decca 31354
			CLIPSE	
			Male rap duo from Virginia Beach, Virginia: brothers Gene "Malice" and Terrance "Pusha T" Thornton.	
7/27/02	30	5	1. Grindin' Sales #11 / Airplay #30	Arista 15078
10/19/02	19	15	2. When The Last Time Sales #18 / Airplay #19	Arista 15154

DATE	POS	WKS	ARTIST–RECORD TITLE	LABEL & NO.
			CLIQUE, The	
			Pop-rock group from Beaumont, Texas: Randy Shaw (vocals), David Dunham, Sid Templeton, Tommy Pena, John Kanesaw and Jerry Cope.	
9/20/69	**22**	7	1. Sugar On Sunday written by Tommy James	White Whale 323
			CLOONEY, Rosemary	
			Born on 5/23/28 in Maysville, Kentucky. Died of cancer on 6/29/2002 (age 74). Sang with her sister Betty in Tony Pastor's orchestra in the late 1940s. Became one of the most popular singers of the early 1950s. Acted in several movies including *White Christmas*. Re-emerged in the late 1970s as a successful jazz and ballad singer and as a TV commercial actress. Married for a time to actor Jose Ferrer; their son Gabriel married Debby Boone. Her nephew, George Clooney, is a popular TV and movie actor. Won Grammy's Lifetime Achievement Award in 2002.	
7/17/54	**1** (6)	27	● 1. **Hey There** / Best Seller #1 (6) / Jockey #1 (5) / Juke Box #1 (4) from the Broadway musical *The Pajama Game* starring John Raitt	
8/7/54	**1** (3)	27	2. **This Ole House** Juke Box #1 (3) / Best Seller #1 (1) / Jockey #5 #2 Country hit for Stuart Hamblen in 1954	Columbia 40266
11/13/54	**9**	0	● 3. **Mambo Italiano** Juke Box #9 / Best Seller #10 / Jockey #13 The Mellomen (backing vocals); Buddy Cole (orch., above 3)	Columbia 40361
3/17/56	**20**	1	4. Memories Of You Juke Box #20 / Top 100 #52 **THE BENNY GOODMAN TRIO with ROSEMARY CLOONEY** from the movie *The Benny Goodman Story* starring Steve Allen (originally from the 1930 all-black revue *Blackbirds*)	Columbia 40616
4/13/57	**10**	9	5. **Mangos** Jockey #10 / Best Seller #23 / Top 100 #25 Frank Comstock (orch.); from the musical revue *Ziegfeld Follies 1957*	Columbia 40835
			CLOVERS, The	
			R&B vocal group from Washington DC: John Bailey, Matthew McQuater, Harold Lucas, Billy Mitchell and Harold Winely, with Bill Harris (guitar). Harris died of cancer on 12/10/88 (age 63). Lucas died of cancer on 1/6/94 (age 61). Mitchell died of a stroke on 11/5/2002 (age 71).	
7/28/56	**30**	3	1. Love, Love, Love Top 100 #30	Atlantic 1094
11/2/59	**23**	5	2. Love Potion No. 9	United Artists 180
			CLUB NOUVEAU	
			R&B group from Sacramento, California: Jay King (producer/owner of King Jay Records; founded the Timex Social Club), Valerie Watson, Samuelle Prater, Denzil Foster and Thomas McElroy. Foster and McElroy formed a prolific production duo and also recorded as FMob.	
2/21/87	**1** (2)	12	● 1. **Lean On Me** Airplay #1 (2) / Sales #1 (1)	King Jay/Warner 28430
7/18/87	**39**	1	2. Why You Treat Me So Bad Sales #37	King Jay/Warner 28360
			COASTERS, The	
			R&B vocal group from Los Angeles, California: Carl Gardner, Leon Hughes, Billy Guy, Bobby Nunn and Cornelius Gunter, with Adolph Jacobs (guitar). Will "Dub" Jones replaced Nunn in late 1958 and is heard on "Charlie Brown" and "Along Came Jones." Earl "Speedoo" Carroll (of the Cadillacs) replaced Gunter in 1961. Bobby Nunn died of a heart attack on 11/5/86 (age 61). Gunter was shot to death on 2/26/90 (age 51) in his car at an intersection in Las Vegas. Jones died on 1/16/2000 (age 71). Guy died of a heart attack on 11/5/2002 (age 66). Group inducted into the Rock and Roll Hall of Fame in 1987.	
5/20/57	**3**	22	● 1. **Searchin'** / Best Seller #3 / Top 100 #5 / Jockey #6 / Juke Box #10 #1 R&B hit (12 weeks)	

DATE	POS	WKS	ARTIST—RECORD TITLE	LABEL & NO.
5/20/57	8	11	2. **Young Blood** Top 100 #8 / Jockey #10 / Juke Box #12 / Best Seller #14 #1 R&B hit (1 week)	Atco 6087
6/9/58	1 (1)	15	● 3. **Yakety Yak** Top 100 #1 (1) / Best Seller #2 / Jockey #2 #1 R&B hit (7 weeks)	Atco 6116
2/9/59	2 (3)	12	● 4. **Charlie Brown** [N] King Curtis (saxophone, above 2)	Atco 6132
6/1/59	9	8	5. **Along Came Jones** [N]	Atco 6141
9/7/59	7	11	● 6. **Poison Ivy /** #1 R&B hit (4 weeks)	
9/21/59	38	1	7. I'm A Hog For You	Atco 6146
1/25/60	36	1	8. Run Red Run	Atco 6153
2/27/61	37	2	9. Wait A Minute written by Bobby Darin and Don Kirshner	Atco 6186
5/29/61	23	6	10. Little Egypt (Ying-Yang) [N] all of above (except #9) written by Leiber and Stoller	Atco 6192

COATES, Odia — see ANKA, Paul

COCHRAN, Eddie

Born on 10/3/38 in Oklahoma City, Oklahoma; raised in Albert Lea, Minnesota. Killed in a car crash on 4/17/60 (age 21) in Chippenham, Wiltshire, England; accident also injured Gene Vincent. Influential rock and roll singer/guitarist. Appeared in movies *The Girl Can't Help It, Untamed Youth* and *Go, Johnny, Go!*. Inducted into the Rock and Roll Hall of Fame in 1987.

DATE	POS	WKS	ARTIST—RECORD TITLE	LABEL & NO.
3/30/57	18	8	1. Sittin' In The Balcony Top 100 #18 / Jockey #18 / Juke Box #20 / Best Seller #22	Liberty 55056
8/25/58	8	12	2. **Summertime Blues** Hot 100 #8 / Best Seller #13	Liberty 55144
1/5/59	35	1	3. C'mon Everybody	Liberty 55166

COCHRANE, Tom

Born on 5/13/53 in Lynn Lake, Manitoba, Canada. Rock singer/songwriter/guitarist.

DATE	POS	WKS	ARTIST—RECORD TITLE	LABEL & NO.
6/6/92	6	20	● 1. **Life Is A Highway** Sales #7 / Airplay #7	Capitol 44815

COCKBURN, Bruce

Born on 5/27/45 in Ottawa, Ontario, Canada. Pop-rock singer/songwriter.

DATE	POS	WKS	ARTIST—RECORD TITLE	LABEL & NO.
5/3/80	21	9	1. Wondering Where The Lions Are	Millennium 11786

COCKER, Joe

Born John Robert Cocker on 5/20/44 in Sheffield, Yorkshire, England. Pop-rock singer.

DATE	POS	WKS	ARTIST—RECORD TITLE	LABEL & NO.
1/10/70	30	7	1. She Came In Through The Bathroom Window written by John Lennon and Paul McCartney	A&M 1147
5/9/70	7	9	2. **The Letter** [L] **JOE COCKER with Leon Russell & The Shelter People**	A&M 1174
10/24/70	11	7	3. Cry Me A River [L] recorded on 3/27/70 at the Fillmore East in New York	A&M 1200
6/19/71	22	6	4. High Time We Went /	
6/19/71		6	5. Black-Eyed Blues	A&M 1258
1/29/72	33	5	6. Feeling Alright [R] originally charted at #69 in 1969	A&M 1063

DATE	POS	WKS	ARTIST–RECORD TITLE	LABEL & NO.
10/7/72	27	5	7. Midnight Rider **JOE COCKER and The Chris Stainton Band**	A&M 1370
2/15/75	5	10	8. **You Are So Beautiful**	A&M 1641
10/2/82	1 (3)	15	▲ 9. **Up Where We Belong** **JOE COCKER and JENNIFER WARNES** love theme from the movie *An Officer And A Gentleman* starring Richard Gere and Debra Winger	Island 99996
12/2/89+	11	11	10. When The Night Comes Airplay #9 / Sales #15	Capitol 44437

COCK ROBIN

Pop group from Los Angeles, California: Peter Kingsbery (vocals, bass), Anna LaCazio (vocals, keyboards), Clive Wright (guitars) and Louis Molino (drums).

DATE	POS	WKS	ARTIST–RECORD TITLE	LABEL & NO.
8/17/85	35	3	1. When Your Heart Is Weak	Columbia 04875

COFFEY, Dennis, And The Detroit Guitar Band

Born in Detroit, Michigan. White session guitarist for Motown.

DATE	POS	WKS	ARTIST–RECORD TITLE	LABEL & NO.
11/13/71+	6	15	● 1. **Scorpio** [I]	Sussex 226
3/11/72	18	8	2. Taurus [I]	Sussex 233

COHN, Marc

Born on 7/5/59 in Cleveland, Ohio. Pop-rock singer/songwriter/pianist. Won the 1991 Best New Artist Grammy Award.

DATE	POS	WKS	ARTIST–RECORD TITLE	LABEL & NO.
5/25/91	13	10	1. Walking In Memphis Airplay #27 / Sales #30	Atlantic 87747

COLDPLAY

Rock group from Edinburgh, Scotland: Chris Martin (vocals), Jon Buckland (guitar), Guy Berryman (bass) and Will Champion (drums). Martin married actress Gwyneth Paltrow on 12/5/2003.

DATE	POS	WKS	ARTIST–RECORD TITLE	LABEL & NO.
4/19/03	29	10	1. Clocks Sales #13 / Airplay #29 2003 Grammy winner: Record of the Year	Capitol 52608

COLE, Cozy

Born William Randolph Cole on 10/17/09 in East Orange, New Jersey. Died of cancer on 1/29/81 (age 71). Lead drummer for many swing bands, including Benny Carter, Willie Bryant, Cab Calloway and Louis Armstrong.

DATE	POS	WKS	ARTIST–RECORD TITLE	LABEL & NO.
9/29/58	3	14	● 1. Topsy II / Hot 100 #3 / Best Seller #10 [I] #1 R&B hit (6 weeks); #14 hit for Benny Goodman in 1938	
10/27/58	27	3	2. Topsy I Hot 100 #27 / Best Seller #45 [I]	Love 5004
12/28/58	36	1	3. Turvy II [I]	Love 5014

COLE, Jude

Born on 6/18/60 in Carbon Cliff, Illinois; raised in East Moline, Illinois. Male singer/guitarist.

DATE	POS	WKS	ARTIST–RECORD TITLE	LABEL & NO.
5/5/90	16	10	1. Baby, It's Tonight Airplay #12 / Sales #21	Reprise 19869
9/22/90	32	4	2. Time For Letting Go Airplay #26	Reprise 19743

DATE	POS	WKS	ARTIST–RECORD TITLE	LABEL & NO.
			COLE, Nat "King"	
			Born Nathaniel Adams Coles on 3/17/19 in Montgomery, Alabama; raised in Chicago, Illinois. Died of cancer on 2/15/65 (age 45). R&B-jazz singer/songwriter/pianist. Father of Natalie Cole. Formed The King Cole Trio in 1939. Long series of top-selling records led to his solo career in 1950. Appeared in several movies. Hosted own TV variety series from 1956-57. Won Grammy's Lifetime Achievement Award in 1990. Inducted into the Rock and Roll Hall of Fame in 2000 as an early influence.	
11/13/54	**14**	7	1. Hajji Baba (Persian Lament) Best Seller #14 / Jockey #16 / Juke Box #19 from the movie *The Adventures of Hajji Baba* starring John Derek	Capitol 2949
3/5/55	**7**	16	2. **Darling Je Vous Aime Beaucoup /** Jockey #7 / Best Seller #10 / Juke Box #14 #21 hit for Hildegarde in 1943 (her theme song)	
3/5/55	**23**	13	3. The Sand And The Sea Best Seller #23 / Juke Box: flip	Capitol 3027
5/7/55	**2 (1)**	20	4. **A Blossom Fell /** Best Seller #2 / Juke Box #2 / Jockey #3	
5/21/55	**8**	10	5. **If I May** Jockey #8 / Best Seller: flip / Juke Box: flip **NAT "KING" COLE and THE FOUR KNIGHTS**	Capitol 3095
7/16/55	**24**	2	6. My One Sin Best Seller #24	Capitol 3136
10/22/55	**13**	8	7. Someone You Love / Best Seller #13 / Jockey #19 / Top 100 #21	
10/22/55	**13**	8	8. Forgive My Heart Best Seller #13 / Top 100 #21	Capitol 3234
3/3/56	**18**	3	9. Ask Me Jockey #18 / Top 100 #25	Capitol 3328
4/21/56	**21**	6	10. Too Young To Go Steady Jockey #21 / Top 100 #31 from the musical *Strip For Action*	Capitol 3390
7/21/56	**16**	12	11. That's All There Is To That Juke Box #16 / Best Seller #17 / Top 100 #18 / Jockey #18 **NAT "KING" COLE and THE FOUR KNIGHTS**	Capitol 3456
11/3/56	**11**	10	12. Night Lights / Jockey #11 / Top 100 #16 / Best Seller #17	
11/10/56	**25**	2	13. To The Ends Of The Earth Best Seller #25 / Jockey #25 / Top 100 #39	Capitol 3551
2/23/57	**18**	5	14. Ballerina Jockey #18 / Top 100 #36 #1 hit for Vaughn Monroe in 1947; Nelson Riddle (orch., all of above)	Capitol 3619
7/1/57	**6**	18	15. **Send For Me /** Best Seller #6 / Top 100 #7 / Jockey #9 #1 R&B hit (2 weeks)	
8/5/57	**21**	2	16. My Personal Possession Jockey #21 / Top 100 #63 / Best Seller: flip **NAT "KING" COLE and THE FOUR KNIGHTS**	Capitol 3737
10/21/57	**30**	4	17. With You On My Mind / Best Seller #30 / Top 100 #33 McCoy's Boys (backing vocals: #15 & 17); Billy May (orch.: #15 & 17)	
11/11/57		3	18. (The Song Of) Raintree County Best Seller: flip from the movie *Raintree County* starring Elizabeth Taylor; Johnny Green (orch.)	Capitol 3782
2/24/58	**33**	3	19. Angel Smile Best Seller #33 / Top 100 #35	Capitol 3860
4/14/58	**5**	16	20. **Looking Back** Best Seller #5 / Top 100 #5 / Jockey #9	Capitol 3939
7/28/58	**38**	2	21. Come Closer To Me (Acercate Mas) Best Seller #38 / Hot 100 #41 Armando Romeu (orch.)	Capitol 4004
2/15/60	**30**	3	22. Time And The River	Capitol 4325
8/18/62	**2 (2)**	13	● 23. **Ramblin' Rose** #1 Adult Contemporary hit (5 weeks)	Capitol 4804
12/1/62	**13**	8	24. Dear Lonely Hearts	Capitol 4870
5/25/63	**6**	9	25. **Those Lazy-Hazy-Crazy Days Of Summer**	Capitol 4965
9/28/63	**12**	9	26. That Sunday, That Summer	Capitol 5027

DATE	POS	WKS	ARTIST–RECORD TITLE	LABEL & NO.
5/16/64	**22**	6	27. I Don't Want To Be Hurt Anymore	Capitol 5155
10/24/64	**34**	4	28. I Don't Want To See Tomorrow	Capitol 5261
7/27/91	**14**	10	● 29. Unforgettable Sales #9 / Airplay #37	Elektra 64875
			NATALIE COLE with Nat "King" Cole	
			Nat's vocals are dubbed in from his 1961 recording; 1991 Grammy winner: Record of the Year	

COLE, Natalie

Born Stephanie Natalie Cole on 2/6/50 in Los Angeles, California. R&B singer. Daughter of Nat "King" Cole. Marriages include Marvin Yancey (her producer) and Andre Fischer (former drummer of Rufus). Won the 1975 Best New Artist Grammy Award. Hosted own syndicated variety TV show *Big Break* in 1990.

DATE	POS	WKS	ARTIST–RECORD TITLE	LABEL & NO.
10/4/75	**6**	11	1. **This Will Be**	Capitol 4109
			#1 R&B hit (2 weeks)	
2/28/76	**32**	5	2. Inseparable	Capitol 4193
			#1 R&B hit (1 week)	
6/26/76	**25**	7	3. Sophisticated Lady (She's A Different Lady)	Capitol 4259
			#1 R&B hit (1 week)	
2/26/77	**5**	14	● 4. **I've Got Love On My Mind**	Capitol 4360
			#1 R&B hit (5 weeks)	
2/11/78	**10**	15	● 5. **Our Love**	Capitol 4509
			#1 R&B hit (2 weeks)	
8/9/80	**21**	9	6. Someone That I Used To Love	Capitol 4869
8/22/87	**13**	10	7. Jump Start Sales #12 / Airplay #16	Manhattan 50073
12/19/87+	**13**	11	8. I Live For Your Love Sales #11 / Airplay #17	Manhattan 50094
3/19/88	**5**	12	9. **Pink Cadillac** Sales #2 / Airplay #6	EMI-Manhattan 50117
			written and recorded by Bruce Springsteen in 1984 (B-side of "Dancing In The Dark")	
5/13/89	**7**	13	10. **Miss You Like Crazy** Sales #5 / Airplay #8	EMI 50185
			#1 R&B hit (1 week) / #1 Adult Contemporary hit (1 week)	
3/31/90	**34**	3	11. Wild Women Do Sales #25	EMI 50275
			from the movie *Pretty Woman* starring Julia Roberts and Richard Gere	
7/27/91	**14**	10	● 12. Unforgettable Sales #9 / Airplay #37	Elektra 64875
			NATALIE COLE with Nat "King" Cole	
			Nat's vocals are dubbed in from his 1961 recording; 1991 Grammy winner: Record of the Year	

COLE, Paula

Born on 4/5/68 in Rockport, Massachusetts. Adult Alternative singer/songwriter. Won the 1997 Best New Artist Grammy Award.

DATE	POS	WKS	ARTIST–RECORD TITLE	LABEL & NO.
4/12/97	**8**	17	1. **Where Have All The Cowboys Gone?** Airplay #6 / Sales #17	Warner 17373
11/1/97+	**11**	46	2. I Don't Want To Wait Airplay #5 / Sales #33	Warner 17318
			used as the theme for the TV series *Dawson's Creek*	
4/18/98	**35** A	6	3. Me	album cut
			from the album *This Fire* on Imago 46424	

COLLECTIVE SOUL

Rock group from Stockbridge, Georgia: brothers Ed (vocals) and Dean (guitar) Roland, with Ross Childress (guitar), Will Turpin (bass) and Shane Evans (drums).

DATE	POS	WKS	ARTIST–RECORD TITLE	LABEL & NO.
6/4/94	**11**	23	● 1. Shine Airplay #8 / Sales #11	Atlantic 87237
			#1 Mainstream Rock hit (8 weeks)	

DATE	POS	WKS	ARTIST–RECORD TITLE	LABEL & NO.
6/3/95	**20**	30	2. December Airplay #11 / Sales #57 #1 Mainstream Rock hit (9 weeks)	Atlantic 87157
12/23/95+	**19**	24	3. The World I Know Airplay #9 / Sales #51 #1 Mainstream Rock hit (4 weeks)	Atlantic 87088
			COLLINS, Dave And Ansil	
			Reggae duo from Jamaica: Dave Barker (vocals) and Ansil Collins (keyboards).	
7/3/71	**22**	8	1. Double Barrel	Big Tree 115
			COLLINS, Dorothy	
			Born Marjorie Chandler on 11/18/26 in Windsor, Ontario, Canada. Died of a heart attack on 7/21/94 (age 67). Star of TV's *Your Hit Parade*.	
12/3/55	**16**	3	1. My Boy - Flat Top Juke Box #16 / Top 100 #22	Coral 61510
2/11/56	**17**	2	2. Seven Days Juke Box #17 / Top 100 #25 Dick Jacobs (orch., above 2)	Coral 61562
			COLLINS, Edwyn	
			Born on 8/23/59 in Edinburgh, Scotland. Pop-rock singer/songwriter.	
11/4/95	**32**	3	1. A Girl Like You Airplay #31 from the movie *Empire Records* starring Anthony LaPaglia	Bar None/A&M 1234
			COLLINS, Judy	
			Born on 5/1/39 in Seattle, Washington. Contemporary folk singer/songwriter. Moved to Los Angeles, then to Denver at age nine, where her father, Chuck Collins, was a radio personality. Stephen Stills wrote "Suite: Judy Blue Eyes" for her. Appeared in the New York Shakespeare Festival's production of *Peer Gynt*. Nominated for a 1974 Academy Award for co-directing *Antonia: A Portrait of the Woman*, a documentary about Judy's former classical mentor and a pioneer female orchestra conductor, Dr. Antonia Brico.	
11/23/68	**8**	9	1. **Both Sides Now** written by Joni Mitchell	Elektra 45639
1/9/71	**15**	11	2. Amazing Grace recorded at St. Paul's Chapel, Columbia University; Rev. John Newton wrote the words in 1779; William Walker composed the melody in 1844	Elektra 45709
3/17/73	**32**	5	3. Cook With Honey	Elektra 45831
7/26/75	**36**	3	4. Send In The Clowns from the Broadway musical *A Little Night Music* starring Glynis Johns	Elektra 45253
10/15/77	**19**	8	5. Send In The Clowns **[R]** above 2 are the same version	Elektra 45253
			COLLINS, Phil	
			Born on 1/31/51 in Chiswick, London, England. Pop singer/songwriter/drummer. Stage actor as a young child; played the "Artful Dodger" in the London production of *Oliver*. Joined Genesis as its drummer in 1970, became lead singer in 1975. Starred in the 1988 movie *Buster* and appeared in *Hook* and *Frauds*. Left Genesis in April 1996.	
4/11/81	**19**	9	1. I Missed Again	Atlantic 3790
7/11/81	**19**	8	● 2. In The Air Tonight	Atlantic 3824
11/27/82+	**10**	16	3. **You Can't Hurry Love**	Atlantic 89933
3/26/83	**39**	3	4. I Don't Care Anymore	Atlantic 89877

DATE	POS	WKS	ARTIST–RECORD TITLE	LABEL & NO.
3/10/84	1 (3)	16	● 5. **Against All Odds (Take A Look At Me Now)** #1 Mainstream Rock hit (1 week); title song from the movie *Against All Odds* starring Jeff Bridges	Atlantic 89700
12/8/84+	2 (2)	16	● 6. **Easy Lover** Sales #1 (1) / Airplay #2 **PHILIP BAILEY (with Phil Collins)**	Columbia 04679
2/23/85	1 (2)	12	● 7. **One More Night** Airplay #1 (2) / Sales #1 (1) #1 Adult Contemporary hit (3 weeks)	Atlantic 89588
5/11/85	1 (1)	14	● 8. **Sussudio** Airplay #1 (4) / Sales #2	Atlantic 89560
7/27/85	4	13	9. **Don't Lose My Number** Airplay #2 / Sales #7	Atlantic 89536
10/12/85	1 (1)	16	10. **Separate Lives** Airplay #1 (2) / Sales #2 **PHIL COLLINS and MARILYN MARTIN** #1 Adult Contemporary hit (3 weeks); love theme from the movie *White Nights* starring Mikhail Baryshnikov	Atlantic 89498
3/29/86	7	11	11. **Take Me Home** Airplay #3 / Sales #10 Peter Gabriel and Sting (backing vocals)	Atlantic 89472
9/17/88	1 (2)	13	● 12. **Groovy Kind Of Love** Airplay #1 (2) / Sales #1 (1) #1 Adult Contemporary hit (3 weeks)	Atlantic 89017
11/26/88+	1 (2)	13	13. **Two Hearts** Airplay #1 (3) / Sales #1 (1) #1 Adult Contemporary hit (5 weeks); above 2 from the movie *Buster* starring Collins	Atlantic 88980
11/11/89	1 (4)	14	● 14. **Another Day In Paradise** Airplay #1 (5) / Sales #2 #1 Adult Contemporary hit (5 weeks); David Crosby (backing vocal); 1990 Grammy winner: Record of the Year	Atlantic 88774
2/17/90	3	11	15. **I Wish It Would Rain Down** Airplay #3 / Sales #4 Eric Clapton (guitar)	Atlantic 88738
5/5/90	4	13	16. **Do You Remember?** Airplay #4 / Sales #9 #1 Adult Contemporary hit (5 weeks)	Atlantic 87955
8/18/90	4	12	17. **Something Happened On The Way To Heaven** Airplay #1 (2) / Sales #10	Atlantic 87885
12/8/90+	23	7	18. Hang In Long Enough Airplay #24 / Sales #26	Atlantic 87800
11/13/93	25	7	19. Both Sides Of The Story Airplay #22	Atlantic 87299
2/12/94	24	13	20. Everyday Airplay #16	Atlantic 87300
7/3/99	21	7	21. You'll Be In My Heart Sales #9 / Airplay #50 #1 Adult Contemporary hit (19 weeks); from the animated movie *Tarzan*	Walt Disney 60025

COLLINS, Tyler

DATE	POS	WKS	ARTIST–RECORD TITLE	LABEL & NO.
			Born in Harlem, New York; raised in Detroit, Michigan. Female R&B singer.	
6/2/90	6	13	1. **Girls Nite Out** Airplay #3 / Sales #9	RCA 2630

COLOR ME BADD

DATE	POS	WKS	ARTIST–RECORD TITLE	LABEL & NO.
			Vocal group from Oklahoma City, Oklahoma: Bryan Abrams, Sam Watters, Mark Calderon and Kevin Thornton.	
4/27/91	2 (4)	16	▲² 1. **I Wanna Sex You Up** Sales #1 (3) / Airplay #2 #1 R&B hit (2 weeks); from the movie *New Jack City* starring Wesley Snipes and Ice-T	Giant 19382
8/10/91	1 (2)	14	● 2. **I Adore Mi Amor** Airplay #1 (3) / Sales #4 #1 R&B hit (1 week)	Giant 19204
11/9/91+	1 (1)	25	● 3. **All 4 Love** Airplay #1 (4) / Sales #4	Giant 19236
2/15/92	16	12	4. Thinkin' Back Airplay #15 / Sales #33	Giant 19074
5/23/92	18	12	5. Slow Motion Airplay #12 / Sales #43 samples "Spinning Wheel" by Blood, Sweat & Tears	Giant 18908
9/26/92	15	10	6. Forever Love Airplay #9 / Sales #16 from the movie *Mo' Money* starring Damon and Marlon Wayans	Giant 18727

DATE	POS	WKS	ARTIST–RECORD TITLE	LABEL & NO.
11/20/93	23	9	7. Time And Chance Sales #19 / Airplay #44 samples "My Philosophy" by Boogie Down Productions	Giant 18339
1/22/94	23	9	8. Choose Airplay #20 / Sales #42	Giant 18270
5/11/96	21	19	9. The Earth, The Sun, The Rain Airplay #20 / Sales #31	Giant 17654
			COLTER, Jessi	
			Born Mirriam Johnson on 5/25/43 in Phoenix, Arizona. Country singer/songwriter. Married to Duane Eddy from 1961-68. Married Waylon Jennings in October 1969.	
4/26/75	4	14	1. **I'm Not Lisa** #1 Country hit (1 week)	Capitol 4009
			COLTRANE, Chi	
			Born on 11/16/48 in Racine, Wisconsin. Female rock singer/pianist. Chi pronounced: shy.	
9/30/72	17	9	1. Thunder And Lightning	Columbia 45640
			COLVIN, Shawn	
			Born Shanna Colvin on 1/10/58 in Vermillion, South Dakota. Female folk singer.	
7/12/97	7	23	1. **Sunny Came Home** Airplay #1 (4) / Sales #29 #1 Adult Contemporary hit (4 weeks); 1997 Grammy winner: Record of the Year	Columbia 78528
			COMMANDER CODY And His Lost Planet Airmen	
			Born George Frayne on 7/19/44 in Boise, Idaho; raised in Brooklyn, New York. Singer/keyboardist. His Lost Planet Airmen consisted of John Tichy, Don Bolton and Bill Kirchen (guitars), Andy Stein (fiddle, sax), Bruce Barlow (bass) and Lance Dickerson (drums). Dickerson died on 11/10/2003 (age 55).	
4/15/72	9	11	1. **Hot Rod Lincoln** **[N]** #29 hit for Tiny Hill in 1951 (as "Hot Rod Race")	Paramount 0146
			COMMODORES	
			R&B group formed in Tuskegee, Alabama: Lionel Richie (vocals, saxophone), Thomas McClary (guitar), William King (trumpet), Milan Williams (keyboards), Ronald LaPread (bass) and Walter "Clyde" Orange (drums). Group appeared in the movie *Thank God It's Friday*. Richie left group in 1982.	
7/6/74	22	6	1. Machine Gun **[I]**	Motown 1307
6/28/75	19	7	2. Slippery When Wet #1 R&B hit (1 week)	Motown 1338
2/14/76	5	14	3. **Sweet Love**	Motown 1381
10/9/76	7	11	4. **Just To Be Close To You** #1 R&B hit (2 weeks)	Motown 1402
2/19/77	39	1	5. Fancy Dancer	Motown 1408
6/25/77	4	13	6. **Easy** #1 R&B hit (1 week)	Motown 1418
9/17/77	5	11	7. **Brick House**	Motown 1425
1/14/78	24	7	8. Too Hot Ta Trot #1 R&B hit (1 week)	Motown 1432
7/8/78	1 (2)	16	9. **Three Times A Lady** #1 R&B hit (2 weeks) / #1 Adult Contemporary hit (3 weeks)	Motown 1443
11/4/78	38	2	10. Flying High	Motown 1452

DATE	POS	WKS	ARTIST–RECORD TITLE	LABEL & NO.
8/18/79	**4**	12	11. **Sail On**	Motown 1466
10/13/79	**1** (1)	15	12. **Still**	Motown 1474
			#1 R&B hit (1 week)	
1/26/80	**25**	6	13. Wonderland	Motown 1479
7/12/80	**20**	11	14. Old-Fashion Love	Motown 1489
7/11/81	**8**	15	15. **Lady (You Bring Me Up)**	Motown 1514
10/10/81	**4**	15	16. **Oh No**	Motown 1527
3/2/85	**3**	13	17. **Nightshift** Sales #3 / Airplay #4	Motown 1773
			#1 R&B hit (4 weeks); a tribute to Marvin Gaye and Jackie Wilson	
			COMMON — see BADU, Erykah	
			COMMUNARDS	
			Dance duo: Jimmy Somerville (vocals) was born on 6/22/61 in Glasgow, Scotland. Richard Coles (keyboards) was born on 6/23/62 in Northampton, England. Somerville was lead singer of Bronski Beat.	
3/7/87	**40**	1	1. Don't Leave Me This Way Sales #31	MCA/London 52928
			COMO, Perry	
			Born Pierino Como on 5/18/12 in Canonsburg, Pennsylvania. Died on 5/12/2001 (age 88). Owned barbershop in hometown. With Freddy Carlone band in 1933; with Ted Weems from 1936-42. Appeared in several movies. Hosted own TV shows from 1948-63. One of the most popular singers of the 20th century. Won Grammy's Lifetime Achievement Award in 2002.	
10/2/54	**4**	18	● 1. **Papa Loves Mambo** Best Seller #4 / Jockey #4 / Juke Box #4	RCA Victor 5857
12/25/54	**8**	3	2. **(There's No Place Like) Home For The Holidays** Jockey #8 / Best Seller #18 **[X]**	RCA Victor 47-5950
			The Fontane Sisters (backing vocals)	
2/5/55	**2** (3)	14	3. **Ko Ko Mo (I Love You So)** Jockey #2 / Best Seller #4 / Juke Box #5	RCA Victor 5994
			#6 R&B hit for Gene & Eunice in 1955	
6/11/55	**12**	5	4. Chee Chee-oo Chee (Sang the Little Bird) / Jockey #12 / Juke Box #14 / Best Seller #24	
6/25/55	**18**	1	5. Two Lost Souls Jockey #18 / Best Seller: flip	RCA Victor 6137
			PERRY COMO and JAYE P. MORGAN (above 2)	
			from the Broadway musical *Damn Yankees* starring Gwen Verdon	
8/13/55	**5**	14	6. **Tina Marie** / Jockey #5 / Best Seller #6 / Juke Box #8 / Top 100 #12	
8/20/55	**20**	1	7. Fooled Jockey #20 / Best Seller: flip	RCA Victor 6192
11/19/55+	**11**	11	8. All At Once You Love Her Jockey #11 / Top 100 #24	RCA Victor 6294
			from the Broadway musical *Pipe Dream* starring Helen Traubel	
3/10/56	**1** (1)	20	● 9. **Hot Diggity (Dog Ziggity Boom)** / Jockey #1 (1) / Top 100 #2 / Best Seller #2 / Juke Box #2	
3/10/56	**10**	10	10. **Juke Box Baby** Top 100 #10 / Jockey #11 / Best Seller: flip / Juke Box: flip	RCA Victor 6427
6/16/56	**4**	14	11. **More** / Best Seller #4 / Juke Box #6 / Jockey #8 / Top 100 #9	
6/23/56	**8**	12	12. Glendora Jockey #8 / Top 100 #14 / Best Seller: flip / Juke Box: flip	RCA Victor 6554
8/25/56	**18**	3	13. Somebody Up There Likes Me Juke Box #18 / Jockey #22 / Top 100 #26	RCA Victor 6590
			title song from the movie starring Paul Newman	
3/2/57	**1** (2)	19	● 14. **Round And Round** Jockey #1 (2) / Best Seller #1 (1) / Top 100 #1 (1) / Juke Box #3	RCA Victor 6815
5/27/57	**13**	6	15. The Girl With The Golden Braids Jockey #13 / Top 100 #15 / Best Seller #26	RCA Victor 6904

DATE	POS	WKS	ARTIST–RECORD TITLE	LABEL & NO.
10/14/57	**12**	14	16. Just Born (To Be Your Baby) / Best Seller #12 / Jockey #13 / Top 100 #19	
10/21/57	**18**	8	17. Ivy Rose Jockey #18 / Top 100 #32 / Best Seller: flip	RCA Victor 7050
1/13/58	**1** (1)	16	● 18. **Catch A Falling Star** / Jockey #1 (1) / Best Seller #3 / Top 100 #9	
1/20/58	**4**	12	19. **Magic Moments** Jockey #4 / Top 100 #27 / Best Seller #42	RCA Victor 7128
4/21/58	**6**	11	20. **Kewpie Doll** / Jockey #6 / Best Seller #12 / Top 100 #12	
5/5/58	**19**	1	21. Dance Only With Me Jockey #19	RCA Victor 7202
			from the Broadway musical *Say Darling* starring David Wayne	
8/4/58	**28**	6	22. Moon Talk Best Seller #28 / Hot 100 #29	RCA Victor 7274
11/17/58	**33**	2	23. Love Makes The World Go 'Round Hot 100 #33	RCA Victor 7353
3/23/59	**29**	3	24. Tomboy	RCA Victor 7464
2/22/60	**22**	6	25. Delaware [N]	RCA Victor 7670
4/28/62	**23**	6	26. Caterina	RCA Victor 8004
7/20/63	**39**	1	27. (I Love You) Don't You Forget It	RCA Victor 8186
			Mitchell Ayres (orch., all of above); Ray Charles Singers (backing vocals, all of above - except #2, 5, 7 & 15)	
5/1/65	**25**	6	28. Dream On Little Dreamer	RCA Victor 8533
5/31/69	**38**	1	29. Seattle	RCA Victor 9722
			from the TV series *Here Come The Brides* starring Bobby Sherman	
12/5/70+	**10**	13	30. **It's Impossible**	RCA Victor 0387
			#1 Adult Contemporary hit (4 weeks)	
5/19/73	**29**	8	31. And I Love You So	RCA Victor 0906
			#1 Adult Contemporary hit (1 week); written by Don McLean	
			COMPANY B	
			Female dance trio from Miami, Florida: Lori L, Lezlee Livrano and Susan Johnson.	
5/9/87	**21**	8	1. Fascinated Sales #17 / Airplay #27	Atlantic 89294
			CONCRETE BLONDE	
			Rock trio from Los Angeles, California: Johnette Napolitano (vocals, bass), James Andrew Mankey (guitar) and Paul Thompson (drums).	
10/6/90	**19**	8	1. Joey Sales #14 / Airplay #30 #1 Modern Rock hit (4 weeks)	I.R.S. 77014
			CON FUNK SHUN	
			Funk group from Vallejo, California: Michael Cooper (vocals, guitar), Danny Thomas (keyboards), Karl Fuller, Paul Harrell and Felton Pilate (horns), Cedric Martin (bass) and Louis McCall (drums).	
1/21/78	**23**	6	1. Ffun #1 R&B hit (2 weeks)	Mercury 73959
2/28/81	**40**	1	2. Too Tight	Mercury 76089
			CONLEY, Arthur	
			Born on 4/1/46 in Atlanta, Georgia. Died of cancer on 11/17/2003 (age 57). R&B singer.	
4/1/67	**2** (1)	11	● 1. **Sweet Soul Music** originally written by Sam Cooke as "Yeah Man"	Atco 6463
7/1/67	**31**	3	2. Shake, Rattle & Roll #1 R&B hit for Joe Turner in 1954	Atco 6494
4/6/68	**14**	9	3. Funky Street	Atco 6563

DATE	POS	WKS	ARTIST–RECORD TITLE	LABEL & NO.
			CONNIFF, Ray	
7/9/66	9	9	Born on 11/6/16 in Attleboro, Massachusetts. Died of a stroke on 10/12/2002 (age 85). Legendary arranger/conductor. 　　1. **Somewhere, My Love** 　　　**RAY CONNIFF And The Singers** 　　　#1 Adult Contemporary hit (4 weeks); "Lara's Theme" from the 　　　movie *Dr. Zhivago* starring Omar Sharif	Columbia 43626
			CONNOR, Chris	
2/16/57	34	3	Born on 11/8/27 in Kansas City, Missouri. Female jazz-styled singer; with Stan Kenton from 1952-53. 　　1. I Miss You So　　　　　　　　　Top 100 #34 　　　#20 hit for The Cats and the Fiddle in 1940	Atlantic 1105
			CONNORS, Norman	
10/2/76	27	10	Born on 3/1/48 in Philadelphia, Pennsylvania. Jazz drummer. 　　1. You Are My Starship 　　　Michael Henderson (vocal)	Buddah 542
			CONTI, Bill	
5/7/77	1 (1)	13	Born on 4/13/42 in Providence, Rhode Island. Composer/conductor for several movies and TV shows. ● 　1. **Gonna Fly Now**　　　　　　　　　　[I] 　　　theme from the movie *Rocky* starring Sylvester Stallone	United Artists 940
			CONTOURS, The	
9/22/62	3	11	R&B vocal group from Detroit: Billy Gordon, Billy Hoggs, Joe Billingslea, Sylvester Potts and Hubert Johnson, with Huey Davis (guitar). Johnson committed suicide on 7/11/81. Davis died on 2/23/2002 (age 63). ● 　1. **Do You Love Me** 　　　#1 R&B hit (3 weeks)	Gordy 7005
7/2/88	11	8	2. Do You Love Me　　　Airplay #7 / Sales #15 [R] 　　　same version as #1 above; featured in the movie *Dirty Dancing* 　　　starring Patrick Swayze	Motown Yesteryear 448
			COOKE, Sam	
10/28/57	1 (3)	17	Born on 1/22/31 in Clarksdale, Mississippi; raised in Chicago, Illinois. Died from a gunshot wound on 12/11/64 (age 33) in Los Angeles; shot by a female motel manager under mysterious circumstances. Son of a Baptist minister. Nephew is singer R.B. Greaves. Inducted into the Rock and Roll Hall of Fame in 1986. Won Grammy's Lifetime Achievement Award in 1999. Revered as the definitive soul singer. ● 　1. **You Send Me**　　Top 100 #1 (3) / Best Seller #1 (2) / Jockey #1 (1) 　　　#1 R&B hit (6 weeks)	Keen 3-4013
12/23/57+	18	10	2. I'll Come Running Back To You Best Seller #18 / Top 100 #22 　　　#1 R&B hit (1 week)	Specialty 619
1/6/58	17	7	3. (I Love You) For Sentimental Reasons 　　　　　　　　Best Seller #17 / Top 100 #43 　　　#1 hit for Nat "King" Cole in 1946	Keen 3-4002
3/24/58	26	5	4. Lonely Island /　　　Best Seller #26 / Top 100 #39	
3/24/58	27	5	5.　You Were Made For Me　Best Seller #27 / Top 100 #39	Keen 3-4009
9/8/58	22	6	6. Win Your Love For Me　　Best Seller #22 / Hot 100 #33	Keen 3-2006

DATE	POS	WKS	ARTIST–RECORD TITLE	LABEL & NO.
12/15/58	26	7	7. Love You Most Of All Bumps Blackwell (orch.: #1, 4, 5 & 7)	Keen 3-2008
3/30/59	31	5	8. Everybody Likes To Cha Cha Cha	Keen 3-2018
7/6/59	28	4	9. Only Sixteen	Keen 3-2022
5/23/60	12	11	10. Wonderful World	Keen 8-2112
8/29/60	2 (2)	13	11. **Chain Gang** Glenn Osser (orch.)	RCA Victor 7783
12/19/60	29	4	12. Sad Mood	RCA Victor 7816
3/20/61	31	4	13. That's It - I Quit - I'm Movin' On Sammy Lowe (orch., above 2)	RCA Victor 7853
6/26/61	17	9	14. Cupid	RCA Victor 7883
2/17/62	9	13	15. **Twistin' The Night Away** #1 R&B hit (3 weeks)	RCA Victor 7983
8/4/62	13	5	16. Bring It On Home To Me /	
6/16/62	17	9	17. Having A Party Lou Rawls (backing vocal, above 2)	RCA Victor 8036
10/20/62	12	8	18. Nothing Can Change This Love	RCA Victor 8088
2/2/63	13	8	19. Send Me Some Lovin'	RCA Victor 8129
5/4/63	10	9	20. **Another Saturday Night** #1 R&B hit (1 week)	RCA Victor 8164
8/17/63	14	7	21. Frankie And Johnny Ralph Burns (orch.)	RCA Victor 8215
11/9/63	11	8	22. Little Red Rooster	RCA Victor 8247
2/15/64	11	7	23. Good News	RCA Victor 8299
6/27/64	11	7	24. Good Times /	
7/4/64	35	4	25. Tennessee Waltz #1 hit for Patti Page in 1950	RCA Victor 8368
10/24/64	31	4	26. Cousin Of Mine	RCA Victor 8426
1/16/65	7	9	27. **Shake** /	
2/13/65	31	4	28. A Change Is Gonna Come written by Sam in response to Bob Dylan's "Blowin' In The Wind"	RCA Victor 8486
8/28/65	32	3	29. Sugar Dumpling	RCA Victor 8631
			COOKIES, The	
			Female R&B vocal trio from Brooklyn, New York: Earl-Jean McCrea (see #4 below), Dorothy Jones and Margaret Ross.	
12/1/62	17	8	1. Chains	Dimension 1002
3/23/63	7	9	2. **Don't Say Nothin' Bad (About My Baby)**	Dimension 1008
1/18/64	33	4	3. Girls Grow Up Faster Than Boys	Dimension 1020
8/8/64	38	1	4. I'm Into Somethin' Good **EARL-JEAN**	Colpix 729
			COOLEY, Eddie, And The Dimples	
			Born in Harlem, New York. R&B singer/songwriter. The Dimples were a black female trio.	
11/24/56	20	8	1. Priscilla Best Seller #20 / Juke Box #20 / Top 100 #26	Royal Roost 621

DATE	POS	WKS	ARTIST–RECORD TITLE	LABEL & NO.

COOLIDGE, Rita

Born on 5/1/44 in Nashville, Tennessee. Pop-rock singer. Did backup work for Delaney & Bonnie, Leon Russell, Joe Cocker and Eric Clapton. With Kris Kristofferson from 1971, married to him from 1973-80. Known as "The Delta Lady," for whom Leon Russell wrote the song of the same name. In the 1983 movie *Club Med*.

DATE	POS	WKS	ARTIST–RECORD TITLE	LABEL & NO.
6/11/77	**2** (1)	17	● 1. **(Your Love Has Lifted Me) Higher And Higher**	A&M 1922
10/15/77	**7**	13	● 2. **We're All Alone**	A&M 1965
			#1 Adult Contemporary hit (1 week); written by Boz Scaggs	
2/4/78	**20**	7	3. The Way You Do The Things You Do	A&M 2004
7/29/78	**25**	6	4. You	A&M 2058
1/5/80	**38**	2	5. I'd Rather Leave While I'm In Love	A&M 2199
8/6/83	**36**	4	6. All Time High	A&M 2551
			#1 Adult Contemporary hit (4 weeks); from the James Bond movie *Octopussy* starring Roger Moore	

COOLIO

Born Artis Ivey on 8/1/63 in Los Angeles, California. Male rapper/actor. Appeared in several movies and TV shows.

DATE	POS	WKS	ARTIST–RECORD TITLE	LABEL & NO.
6/25/94	**3**	21	▲ 1. **Fantastic Voyage** Sales #1 (4) / Airplay #11	Tommy Boy 7617
			rap version of Lakeside's "Fantastic Voyage"	
8/19/95	**1** (3)	36	▲³ 2. **Gangsta's Paradise** Sales #1 (7) / Airplay #7	MCA Sound. 55104
			COOLIO featuring L.V.	
			rap version of "Pastime Paradise" by Stevie Wonder; from the movie *Dangerous Minds* starring Michelle Pfeiffer	
12/16/95+	**24**	5	3. Too Hot Sales #13	Tommy Boy 7718
3/16/96	**5**	15	● 4. **1,2,3,4 (Sumpin' New)** Sales #4 / Airplay #16	Tommy Boy 7721
			samples "Wikka Wrap" by The Evasions and "Thighs High" by Tom Browne	
6/15/96	**29**	6	● 5. It's All The Way Live (Now) Sales #17	Tommy Boy 7731
			from the movie *Eddie* starring Whoopi Goldberg	
7/12/97	**12**	12	● 6. C U When U Get There Sales #6	Tommy Boy 7785
			COOLIO Featuring 40 Thevz	
			contains an interpolation of Pachelbel's "Canon In D Major"; from the movie *Nothing To Lose* starring Martin Lawrence	

COOPER, Alice

Born Vincent Furnier on 2/4/48 in Detroit, Michigan; raised in Phoenix, Arizona. Formed hard-rock band Alice Cooper: Furnier (vocals), Glen Buxton (guitar), Michael Bruce (keyboards), Dennis Dunaway (bass) and Neal Smith (drums). Furnier went on to assume the Alice Cooper name for himself. Band split in 1974. Cooper went solo and became known for his bizarre stage antics. Appeared in the movies *Prince Of Darkness* and *Wayne's World*.

DATE	POS	WKS	ARTIST–RECORD TITLE	LABEL & NO.
3/20/71	**21**	8	1. Eighteen	Warner 7449
6/24/72	**7**	10	2. **School's Out**	Warner 7596
10/21/72	**26**	6	3. Elected	Warner 7631
3/10/73	**35**	3	4. Hello Hurray	Warner 7673
5/12/73	**25**	8	5. No More Mr. Nice Guy	Warner 7691
5/3/75	**12**	11	6. Only Women	Atlantic 3254
10/30/76+	**12**	14	● 7. I Never Cry	Warner 8228
6/11/77	**9**	13	8. **You And Me**	Warner 8349
11/11/78	**12**	11	9. How You Gonna See Me Now	Warner 8695
7/5/80	**40**	1	10. Clones (We're All)	Warner 49204
10/14/89	**7**	10	● 11. **Poison** Sales #5 / Airplay #12	Epic 68958

Petula Clark may have been considered an Adult Contemporary artist, but her #1 hit "Downtown" nonetheless managed to snag Clark the 1964 Grammy Award for Best Rock & Roll Recording, beating Roy Orbison and The Beatles.

Kelly Clarkson beat out Justin Guarini on *American Idol,* but there were no hard feelings. After recording her #1 hit, "A Moment Like This," Clarkson teamed with Guarini for the film *From Justin To Kelly.*

The Coasters didn't merely coast through their chart career. The R&B vocal group created memorable Top 10 hits like "Charlie Brown," "Poison Ivy," "Searchin'," "Young Blood," and their biggest hit, the chart-topping "Yakety Yak."

Phil Collins could take some comfort in the fact that it took 45 of America's biggest music stars to knock his song "One More Night" from the #1 position. He was replaced at the top by the star-studded USA For Africa's "We Are The World."

Color Me Badd helped revive the R&B hip-hop doo-wop sound of the early 1990s, and frequently sang their harmonies a cappella. It must have worked, because "All 4 Love" was their second straight #1 hit.

The Commodores randomly picked their name out of a dictionary, and were thus dangerously close to going through life as The Commodes. Nonetheless, the band flushed out 10 Top 10 hits, including "Three Times A Lady."

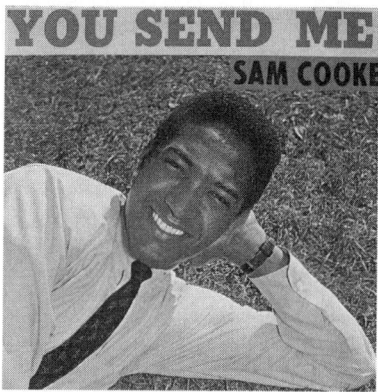

Perry Como had the highest-charting single with the word "diggity" in its title with his 1956 hit, "Hot Diggity (Dog Ziggity Boom)." The record stood for 40 years, until BLACKstreet's "No Diggity" hit #1 in 1996.

Sam Cooke topped the R&B chart four times, but only one of those hits, 1957's "You Send Me," reached #1 on the pop charts. Nonetheless, his overall chart career was impressive enough to earn an invitation to the Rock and Roll Hall of Fame in 1986.

Dave "Baby" Cortez was in danger of typecasting himself after "The Happy Organ" reached #1. His future organ-based hits included "The Whistling Organ" and "Organ Shout," both of which missed the Top 40.

Jim Croce based his first #1 hit, "Bad, Bad Leroy Brown," on an AWOL soldier he observed at Fort Dix, New Jersey. The plane crash that ended his life just two months later was bad news for fans everywhere.

Christopher Cross followed up his 1980 Grammy Award sweep with his Oscar-winning, chart-topping hit "Arthur's Theme (Best That You Can Do)." Unfortunately, Christopher would never cross such peaks again.

Culture Club earned six Top 10 hits, including the #1 "Karma Chameleon," before winning the Grammy Award for 1983's Best New Artist. Ironically, they would score only one more Top 10 hit after that point.

DATE	POS	WKS	ARTIST–RECORD TITLE	LABEL & NO.
			COOPER, Les, and the Soul Rockers	
			Born on 3/15/31 in Norfolk, Virginia. Pianist/arranger.	
11/17/62+	22	11	1. Wiggle Wobble [I]	Everlast 5019
			Joe Grier (former lead singer of The Charts; tenor sax solo)	
			COPELAND, Ken	
			Born on 5/25/37 in Gainesville, Texas. Later became a televangelist with own Kenneth Copeland Ministries.	
4/20/57	12	8	1. Pledge Of Love Jockey #12 / Top 100 #17 / Best Seller #23	Imperial 5432
			COPPOLA, Imani	
			Born in Long Island, New York. Female singer/rapper.	
10/25/97	36	6	1. Legend Of A Cowgirl Sales #41 / Airplay #41	Columbia 78651
			samples "Sunshine Superman" by Donovan	
			COREY, Jill	
			Born Norma Jean Speranza on 9/30/35 in Avonmore, Pennsylvania. Married major league baseball player Don Hoak. Regular on TV's *Your Hit Parade* from 1957-58.	
2/2/57	21	5	1. I Love My Baby (My Baby Loves Me) Jockey #21 / Top 100 #28	Columbia 40794
			#6 hit for Fred Waring in 1926	
8/5/57	11	9	2. Love Me To Pieces Best Seller #11 / Jockey #11 / Top 100 #18	Columbia 40955
			Jimmy Carroll (orch., above 2)	
			CORINA	
			Born Corina Ayala on 10/14/63 in Manhattan, New York. Female dance singer.	
6/22/91	6	13	1. **Temptation** Airplay #2 / Sales #24	Cutting/Atco 98775
			CORNELIUS BROTHERS & SISTER ROSE	
			R&B family trio from Dania, Florida: Edward, Carter and Rose Cornelius. Carter died of a heart attack on 11/7/91 (age 43).	
5/15/71	3	13	● 1. **Treat Her Like A Lady**	United Artists 50721
6/17/72	2 (2)	11	● 2. **Too Late To Turn Back Now**	United Artists 50910
9/23/72	23	7	3. Don't Ever Be Lonely (A Poor Little Fool Like Me)	United Artists 50954
2/3/73	37	2	4. I'm Never Gonna Be Alone Anymore	United Artists 50996
			CORNELL, Don	
			Born Louis Valaro on 4/21/19 in Brooklyn, New York. Died of emphysema on 2/23/2004 (age 84). Popular singer/guitarist. Lead singer with Sammy Kaye's orchestra from 1942-50.	
9/11/54	2 (1)	18	● 1. **Hold My Hand** Jockey #2 / Best Seller #5 / Juke Box #7	Coral 61206
			Jerry Carr (orch.); from the movie *Susan Slept Here* starring Dick Powell and Debbie Reynolds	
5/14/55	14	6	2. Most Of All / Jockey #14 / Best Seller #20	
			#5 R&B hit for The Moonglows in 1955	
5/21/55		2	3. The Door Is Still Open To My Heart Best Seller: flip	Coral 61393
			#4 R&B hit for The Cardinals in 1955	
9/10/55	7	13	4. **The Bible Tells Me So**	Coral 61467
			Best Seller #7 / Juke Box #8 / Jockey #18 / Top 100 #31	

DATE	POS	WKS	ARTIST–RECORD TITLE	LABEL & NO.
11/12/55	25	1	5. Young Abe Lincoln Top 100 #25 Dick Jacobs (orch., above 4)	Coral 61521
11/12/55	26	3	6. Love Is A Many-Splendored Thing Top 100 #26 / Best Seller: flip / Juke Box: flip Carretta (orch.); title song from the movie starring William Holden	Coral 61467

CORONA

Dance duo: Italian producer Francesco Bontempi and Brazilian singer Olga DeSouza.

DATE	POS	WKS	ARTIST–RECORD TITLE	LABEL & NO.
12/17/94+	11	20	1. The Rhythm Of The Night Airplay #10 / Sales #18	EastWest 98192

CORRS, The

Sibling pop group from Ireland: Andrea (lead vocals), Jim (guitar), Sharon (violin) and Caroline (drums) Corr.

DATE	POS	WKS	ARTIST–RECORD TITLE	LABEL & NO.
3/24/01	34	6	1. Breathless Airplay #30 from the album In Blue on 143/Lava 83352	album cut

CORSAIRS Featuring Jay "Bird" Uzzell

R&B vocal group from La Grange, North Carolina: brothers Jay "Bird" (lead), James and "King" Moe Uzzell, with cousin George Wooten.

DATE	POS	WKS	ARTIST–RECORD TITLE	LABEL & NO.
1/27/62	12	10	1. Smoky Places	Tuff 1808

CORTEZ, Dave "Baby"

Born David Cortez Clowney on 8/13/38 in Detroit, Michigan. Black organist.

DATE	POS	WKS	ARTIST–RECORD TITLE	LABEL & NO.
3/30/59	1 (1)	14	1. The Happy Organ [I]	Clock 1009
8/11/62	10	9	2. Rinky Dink [I]	Julia/Chess 1829

COSBY, Bill

Born William Henry Cosby, Jr. on 7/12/38 in Philadelphia, Pennsylvania. Popular black comedian. Starred in several movies and TV shows.

DATE	POS	WKS	ARTIST–RECORD TITLE	LABEL & NO.
9/16/67	4	8	1. Little Ole Man (Uptight-Everything's Alright) [N]	Warner 7072

COSTA, Don, And His Orchestra And Chorus

Born on 6/10/25 in Boston, Massachusetts. Died on 1/19/83 (age 57). Conductor/arranger.

DATE	POS	WKS	ARTIST–RECORD TITLE	LABEL & NO.
6/27/60	27	4	1. Theme From "The Unforgiven"(The Need For Love) [I] from the movie The Unforgiven starring Burt Lancaster and Audrey Hepburn	United Artists 221
8/29/60	19	14	2. Never On Sunday [I] title song from the movie starring Melina Mercouri; originally charted for 11 weeks; re-entered on 5/8/61 (#37)	United Artists 234

COSTELLO, Elvis

Born Declan McManus on 8/25/54 in Paddington, London, England. Leading eclectic rock singer. Changed name to Elvis Costello in 1976 (Costello is his mother's maiden name). The Attractions: Steve "Nieve" Nason (keyboards), Bruce Thomas (bass) and Peter Thomas (drums). Appeared in the 1987 movie Straight To Hell. Married singer Diana Krall on 12/6/2003. Inducted into the Rock and Roll Hall of Fame in 2003.

DATE	POS	WKS	ARTIST–RECORD TITLE	LABEL & NO.
10/15/83	36	2	1. Everyday I Write The Book **ELVIS COSTELLO & THE ATTRACTIONS**	Columbia 04045
5/27/89	19	6	2. Veronica Sales #15 / Airplay #28 #1 Modern Rock hit (2 weeks); Paul McCartney (co-writer, bass guitar)	Warner 22981

DATE	POS	WKS	ARTIST–RECORD TITLE	LABEL & NO.
			COTTON, Gene	
			Born on 6/30/44 in Columbus, Ohio. Pop-rock singer.	ABC 12227
1/22/77	33	3	1. You've Got Me Runnin'	
3/4/78	23	7	2. Before My Heart Finds Out	Ariola America 7675
8/5/78	36	3	3. You're A Part Of Me	Ariola America 7704
			GENE COTTON with Kim Carnes	
11/11/78	40	2	4. Like A Sunday In Salem (The Amos & Andy Song)	Ariola America 7723
			COUGAR, John — see MELLENCAMP	
			COUNT FIVE	
			Psychedelic-garage rock band from San Jose, California: Kenn Ellner (vocals), John Michalski and Sean Byrne (guitars), Roy Chaney (bass) and Craig Atkinson (drums). Atkinson died on 10/13/98 (age 50).	
9/24/66	5	9	1. **Psychotic Reaction**	Double Shot 104
			COUNTING CROWS	
			Rock group from San Francisco, California: Adam Duritz (vocals), David Bryson (guitar), Charlie Gillingham (piano), Matt Malley (bass) and Steve Bowman (drums). Ben Mize replaced Bowman in 1994. Guitarist Dan Vickrey joined in 1996.	
2/26/94	5 ᴬ	38	1. **Mr. Jones**	album cut
7/30/94	31 ᴬ	9	2. Round Here	album cut
			above 2 from the album *August And Everything After* on DGC 24528	
12/14/96+	6 ᴬ	24	3. **A Long December**	album cut
			from the album *Recovering The Satellites* on DGC 24975	
12/11/99+	28	10	4. Hanginaround Airplay #19	album cut
			from the album *This Desert Life* on DGC 490415	
			COVAY, Don	
			Born on 3/24/38 in Orangeburg, South Carolina. R&B singer/songwriter. Formed The Goodtimers in 1960.	
10/3/64	35	5	1. Mercy, Mercy	Rosemart 801
			DON COVAY & THE GOODTIMERS	
			Jimi Hendrix (guitar)	
8/11/73	29	5	2. I Was Checkin' Out She Was Checkin' In	Mercury 73385
			COVEN	
			Pop group from Chicago, Illinois: Jinx Dawson (female vocals), Oz (male vocals), Christopher Nelson (guitar), John Hobbs (keyboards) and Steve Ross (drums).	
10/30/71	26	6	1. One Tin Soldier (The Legend of Billy Jack)	Warner 7509
			from the movie *Billy Jack* starring Tom Laughlin	
			COVER GIRLS, The	
			Female dance trio from the Bronx, New York: Louise Sabater, Caroline Jackson and Sunshine Wright (replaced by Margo Urban in 1989). New 1992 lineup: Jackson, Evelyn Escalera and Michelle Valentine.	
1/30/88	27	8	1. Because Of You Sales #24 / Airplay #28	Fever 1914
5/21/88	40	1	2. Promise Me Sales #33	Fever 1917
10/21/89	38	2	3. My Heart Skips A Beat Sales #36	Capitol 44436

DATE	POS	WKS	ARTIST–RECORD TITLE	LABEL & NO.
1/13/90	8	11	4. **We Can't Go Wrong** Airplay #7 / Sales #9	Capitol 44498
6/6/92	9	14	5. **Wishing On A Star** Airplay #2 / Sales #16	Epic 74343
			COWBOY CHURCH SUNDAY SCHOOL, The	
			Producer Stuart Hamblen's family: his daughters Veeva Susanne (age 18) and Obee Jane "Lisa" (age 16) with his wife Suzy, plus two of the girls' friends. Recorded at 33-1/3 rpm so that the record sounds like children's voices at 45 rpm.	
1/1/55	8	21	1. **Open Up Your Heart (And Let The Sunshine In)** Best Seller #8 / Jockey #18 / Juke Box #19	Decca 29367
			COWSILLS, The	
			Family pop group from Newport, Rhode Island: brothers Bill, Bob, Paul, Barry and John, with their younger sister Susan and mother Barbara Cowsill (died on 1/31/85, age 56). Group was the inspiration for TV's *The Partridge Family.*	
10/21/67	2 (2)	12	● 1. **The Rain, The Park & Other Things**	MGM 13810
2/3/68	21	6	2. We Can Fly	MGM 13886
6/22/68	10	9	3. **Indian Lake**	MGM 13944
3/29/69	2 (2)	13	● 4. **Hair** from the rock musical *Hair* starring Steve Curry	MGM 14026
			COX, Deborah	
			Born on 7/13/74 in Toronto, Ontario, Canada. R&B singer/songwriter.	
10/21/95	27	8	1. Sentimental Sales #9	Arista 12852
3/2/96	17	12	2. Who Do U Love Sales #12 / Airplay #62	Arista 12950
10/10/98	2 (8)	27	▲ 3. **Nobody's Supposed To Be Here** Sales #1 (1) / Airplay #6 #1 R&B hit (14 weeks)	Arista 13550
10/2/99	8	9	4. **We Can't Be Friends** Sales #5 / Airplay #36 **DEBORAH COX with R.L. from Next** #1 R&B hit (2 weeks); Montell Jordan (backing vocal)	Arista 13724
			COZIER, Jimmy	
			Born on 10/15/77 in Brooklyn, New York. R&B singer/songwriter.	
7/7/01	26	7	1. She's All I Got Sales #6 / Airplay #51	J Records 21069
			CRABBY APPLETON	
			Pop-rock group from Los Angeles, California: Michael Fennelly (vocals, guitar), Casey Foutz (keyboards), Felix Falcon (percussion), Hank Harvey (bass) and Phil Jones (drums).	
6/27/70	36	5	1. Go Back	Elektra 45687
			CRADDOCK, Billy "Crash"	
			Born on 6/13/39 in Greensboro, North Carolina. Country-rock singer.	
7/27/74	16	9	1. Rub It In #1 Country hit (2 weeks)	ABC 12013
12/28/74+	33	2	2. Ruby, Baby #1 Country hit (1 week)	ABC 12036

DATE	POS	WKS	ARTIST–RECORD TITLE	LABEL & NO.
			CRAMER, Floyd	
			Born on 10/27/33 in Samti, Louisiana; raised in Huttig, Arkansas. Died of cancer on 12/31/97 (age 64). Legendary country session pianist.	
10/31/60	**2 (4)**	15	● 1. **Last Date** **[I]**	RCA Victor 7775
3/13/61	**4**	11	2. **On The Rebound** **[I]**	RCA Victor 7840
6/26/61	**8**	8	3. **San Antonio Rose** **[I]** written by Bob Wills in 1938	RCA Victor 7893
2/24/62	**36**	2	4. Chattanooga Choo Choo **[I]** #1 hit for Glenn Miller in 1941 (from the movie *Sun Valley Serenade* starring Sonja Henie)	RCA Victor 7978
			CRANBERRIES, The	
			Pop-rock group from Limerick, Ireland: Dolores O'Riordan (vocals), brothers Noel (guitar) and Mike (bass) Hogan, and Fergal Lawler (drums).	
11/20/93+	**8**	19	● 1. **Linger** Airplay #14 / Sales #16	Island 862800
10/22/94	**22** A	16	2. Zombie #1 Modern Rock hit (6 weeks)	album cut
4/15/95	**39** A	2	3. Ode To My Family above 2 from the album *No Need To Argue* on Island 524050	album cut
4/13/96	**21** A	10	4. Salvation #1 Modern Rock hit (4 weeks); from the album *To The Faithful Departed* on Island 524234	album cut
1/11/97	**22**	11	5. When You're Gone Sales #23 / Airplay #50	Island 854802
			CRANE, Les	
			Born on 12/3/35 in San Francisco, California. Hosted TV talk show *ABC's Nightlife* in 1964. Married to actress Tina Louise from 1966-70.	
10/23/71	**8**	10	1. **Desiderata** **[S]** originally a piece of prose written in 1906 by Max Ehrmann	Warner 7520
			CRASH TEST DUMMIES	
			Pop-rock group from Winnipeg, Manitoba, Canada: brothers Brad (vocals) and Dan (bass) Roberts, with Ellen Reid (keyboards), Ben Darvill (harmonica) and Mitch Dorge (drums).	
3/5/94	**4**	18	● 1. **Mmm Mmm Mmm Mmm** Sales #2 / Airplay #15 #1 Modern Rock hit (1 week)	Arista 12654
			CRAWFORD, Johnny	
			Born on 3/26/46 in Los Angeles, California. Teen pop singer/actor. One of the original Mouseketeers. Played "Mark McCain" on TV's *The Rifleman*.	
6/2/62	**8**	9	1. **Cindy's Birthday**	Del-Fi 4178
8/25/62	**14**	6	2. Your Nose Is Gonna Grow	Del-Fi 4181
11/24/62	**12**	7	3. Rumors	Del-Fi 4188
1/26/63	**29**	4	4. Proud	Del-Fi 4193
			CRAWFORD, Randy — see CRUSADERS, The	
			CRAY, Robert, Band	
			Born on 8/1/53 in Columbus, Georgia. Blues-rock singer/guitarist.	
3/21/87	**22**	6	1. Smoking Gun Sales #21 / Airplay #33	Mercury 888343

DATE	POS	WKS	ARTIST–RECORD TITLE	LABEL & NO.
			CRAZY ELEPHANT	
			Bubblegum studio group assembledf by producers Jerry Kasenetz and Jeff Katz. Robert Spencer (of The Cadillacs) on lead vocals. Touring group formed later.	
4/5/69	**12**	8	1. Gimme Gimme Good Lovin'	Bell 763
			CRAZY OTTO	
			Born Fritz Schulz-Reichel on 7/4/12 in Meiningen, Germany. Died on 2/14/90 (age 77). Honky-tonk pianist. Also see Johnny Maddox.	
2/26/55	**19**	5	1. Glad Rag Doll / Best Seller #19 **[I]**	
			#10 hit for Ted Lewis in 1929	
2/26/55	**21**	3	2. Smiles Best Seller #21 **[I]**	Decca 29403
			#1 hit for Joseph C. Smith in 1918	
			CRAZY TOWN	
			White rock-rap group from Los Angeles, California: Seth "Shifty Shellshock" Binzer and Bret "Epic" Mazur (vocals), DJ AM (DJ), Craig Tyler and Anthony Valli (guitars), Doug Miller (bass) and James Bradley (drums).	
2/3/01	**1** (2)	18	1. **Butterfly** Sales #3 / Airplay #4	Columbia 79549
			#1 Modern Rock hit (2 weeks); samples "Pretty Little Ditty" by the Red Hot Chili Peppers	
			CREAM	
			All-star rock trio from England: Eric Clapton (guitar, vocals), Jack Bruce (bass, vocals) and Ginger Baker (drums). Baker and Bruce had been in Alexis Korner's Blues Inc. and the Graham Bond Organization. Clapton and Bruce were in John Mayall's Bluesbreakers. After Cream disbanded, Clapton and Baker formed Blind Faith. Cream inducted into the Rock and Roll Hall of Fame in 1993.	
2/24/68	**5**	12	● 1. **Sunshine Of Your Love**	Atco 6544
10/19/68	**6**	9	2. **White Room**	Atco 6617
2/8/69	**28**	6	3. Crossroads **[L]**	Atco 6646
			recorded at the Fillmore Auditorium in San Francisco	
			CREED	
			Rock group from Tallahassee, Florida: Scott Stapp (vocals), Mark Tremonti (guitar), Brian Marshall (bass) and Scott Phillips (drums).	
4/8/00	**7**	30	1. **Higher** Airplay #6	album cut
			#1 Mainstream Rock hit (17 weeks) / #1 Modern Rock hit (3 weeks); from the album *Human Clay* on Wind-Up 13053	
9/9/00	**1** (1)	29	2. **With Arms Wide Open** Airplay #2 / Sales #13	Wind-Up 18004
			#1 Mainstream Rock hit (4 weeks)	
11/17/01+	**4**	25	3. **My Sacrifice** Airplay #4	album cut
			#1 Mainstream Rock hit (9 weeks)	
8/3/02	**6**	25	4. **One Last Breath** Airplay #5	album cut
			above 2 from the album *Weathered* on Wind-Up 13075	
			CREEDENCE CLEARWATER REVIVAL	
			Rock group formed in El Cerrito, California: brothers John (vocals, guitar) and Tom (guitar) Fogerty, with Stu Cook (keyboards, bass) and Doug "Cosmo" Clifford (drums). Tom Fogerty left for a solo career in 1971 and group disbanded in October 1972. Tom Fogerty died of respiratory failure on 9/6/90 (age 48). Group inducted into the Rock and Roll Hall of Fame in 1993.	
9/28/68	**11**	9	● 1. Suzie Q. (Part One)	Fantasy 616
2/8/69	**2** (3)	12	▲ 2. **Proud Mary**	Fantasy 619
5/17/69	**2** (1)	12	▲ 3. **Bad Moon Rising**	Fantasy 622

DATE	POS	WKS	ARTIST–RECORD TITLE	LABEL & NO.
8/9/69	**2 (1)**	11	● 4. **Green River /**	
8/9/69	30	7	5. Commotion	Fantasy 625
11/8/69	**3**	13	▲ 6. **Down On The Corner /**	
11/8/69	14	13	7. Fortunate Son	Fantasy 634
2/7/70	**2 (2)**	9	▲ 8. **Travelin' Band /**	
2/7/70		9	9. Who'll Stop The Rain	Fantasy 637
5/2/70	**4**	10	● 10. **Up Around The Bend /**	
5/2/70		10	11. Run Through The Jungle	Fantasy 641
8/15/70	**2 (1)**	12	▲ 12. **Lookin' Out My Back Door /**	
8/15/70		12	13. Long As I Can See The Light	Fantasy 645
2/6/71	**8**	9	● 14. **Have You Ever Seen The Rain /**	
2/6/71		4	15. Hey Tonight	Fantasy 655
7/24/71	**6**	8	● 16. **Sweet Hitch-Hiker**	Fantasy 665
5/20/72	25	5	17. Someday Never Comes	Fantasy 676

CRENSHAW, Marshall

Born on 11/11/53 in Detroit, Michigan. Rockabilly singer/guitarist.

8/14/82	36	4	1. Someday, Someway	Warner 29974
			from the movie *Night Shift* starring Michael Keaton and Henry Winkler	

CRESCENDOS, The

White pop vocal group from Nashville, Tennessee: cousins George Lanuis and James Lanuis, Ken Brigham, Tom Fortner and Jim Hall.

1/20/58	5	14	1. **Oh Julie** Top 100 #5 / Best Seller #6 / Jockey #7	Nasco 6005
			Janice Green (female vocal)	

CRESTS, The

Interracial doo-wop group formed in Manhattan, New York: Johnny Maestro (see #6 & 7 below), Harold Torres, Talmadge Gough, J.T. Carter and Patricia Vandross (older sister of Luther Vandross). Maestro later formed Brooklyn Bridge.

12/22/58+	**2 (2)**	14	1. **16 Candles**	Coed 506
4/13/59	28	7	2. Six Nights A Week	Coed 509
9/14/59	22	9	3. The Angels Listened In	Coed 515
4/4/60	14	8	4. Step By Step	Coed 525
7/18/60	20	8	5. Trouble In Paradise	Coed 531
3/20/61	20	5	6. Model Girl	Coed 545
			JOHNNY MASTRO The Voice Of The Crests	
5/22/61	33	4	7. What A Surprise	Coed 549
			JOHNNY MAESTRO The Voice Of The Crests	

CREW-CUTS, The

White pop vocal group from Toronto, Ontario, Canada: brothers John and Ray Perkins, Pat Barrett and Rudi Maugeri.

1/29/55	**3**	13	1. **Earth Angel /** Jockey #3 / Best Seller #8 / Juke Box #8	
1/29/55	6	14	2. **Ko Ko Mo (I Love You So)**	Mercury 70529
			Juke Box #6 / Best Seller #10 / Jockey #11	
			#6 R&B hit for Gene & Eunice in 1955	
4/30/55	14	8	3. Don't Be Angry / Best Seller #14 / Jockey #14 / Juke Box #19	
4/30/55		8	4. Chop Chop Boom Best Seller: flip	Mercury 70597
			#10 R&B hit for The Danderliers in 1955	

DATE	POS	WKS	ARTIST–RECORD TITLE	LABEL & NO.
6/25/55	**16**	7	5. A Story Untold Best Seller #16 #2 R&B hit for The Nutmegs in 1955	Mercury 70634
8/27/55	**10**	8	6. **Gum Drop** Best Seller #10/Jockey #14/Juke Box #20/Top 100 #80	Mercury 70668
12/17/55+	**11**	15	7. Angels In The Sky / Best Seller #11 / Top 100 #13 / Juke Box #13 / Jockey #16	
1/7/56	**31**	8	8. Mostly Martha Top 100 #31 / Best Seller: flip / Juke Box: flip #2 hit for Larry Clinton in 1938	Mercury 70741
2/18/56	**18**	5	9. Seven Days Jockey #18 / Top 100 #20	Mercury 70782
1/26/57	**17**	3	10. Young Love Jockey #17 / Juke Box #17 / Top 100 #24 David Carroll (orch., all of above)	Mercury 71022
			CREWE, Bob	
			Born on 11/12/37 in Newark, New Jersey. Prolific arranger/producer.	
1/21/67	**15**	7	1. Music To Watch Girls By **[I]** Hutch Davie (orch.); tune used in a Diet Pepsi commercial	DynoVoice 229
			CRITTERS, The	
			Pop group from Plainfield, New Jersey: Don Ciccone (vocals, guitar), Jimmy Ryan (guitar), Chris Darway (organ), Kenny Gorka (bass) and Jack Decker (drums). Ciccone later joined The 4 Seasons.	
9/3/66	**17**	8	1. Mr. Dieingly Sad	Kapp 769
8/5/67	**39**	3	2. Don't Let The Rain Fall Down On Me	Kapp 838
			CROCE, Jim	
			Born on 1/10/43 in Philadelphia, Pennsylvania. Killed in a plane crash on 9/20/73 (age 30) in Natchitoches, Louisiana. Singer/songwriter/guitarist. Recorded with wife Ingrid for Capitol in 1968. Lead guitarist on his hits, Maury Muehleisen, was killed in the same crash.	
7/22/72	**8**	10	1. **You Don't Mess Around With Jim**	ABC 11328
11/4/72	**17**	8	2. Operator (That's Not the Way it Feels)	ABC 11335
3/17/73	**37**	3	3. One Less Set Of Footsteps	ABC 11346
6/2/73	**1** (2)	16	● 4. **Bad, Bad Leroy Brown**	ABC 11359
10/13/73	**10**	13	5. **I Got A Name** from the movie *The Last American Hero* starring Jeff Bridges	ABC 11389
12/1/73	**1** (2)	12	● 6. **Time In A Bottle** #1 Adult Contemporary hit (2 weeks)	ABC 11405
3/16/74	**9**	11	7. **I'll Have To Say I Love You In A Song** #1 Adult Contemporary hit (1 week)	ABC 11424
6/29/74	**32**	6	8. Workin' At The Car Wash Blues	ABC 11447
			CROSBY, Bing	
			Born Harry Lillis Crosby on 5/3/03 in Tacoma, Washington. Died of a heart attack on 10/14/77 (age 74). One of the most popular entertainers of the 20th century. Charted over 300 hits from 1931-54. Starred in several movies (won Academy Award for *Going My Way* in 1944). Won Grammy's Lifetime Achievement Award in 1962. Married to actress Dixie Lee from 1930 until her death in 1952; their son Gary began recording in 1950. Married to actress Kathryn Grant from 1957 until his death; their daughter Mary became an actress. Bing's youngest brother, Bob Crosby, was a popular swing-era bandleader.	
12/25/54	**13**	3	● 1. **White Christmas** Jockey #13 / Juke Box #19 / Best Seller #21 **[X-R]** with the Ken Darby Singers and John Scott Trotter's Orchestra; original version hit #1 in October 1942; this version recorded in 1947	Decca 23778

DATE	POS	WKS	ARTIST–RECORD TITLE	LABEL & NO.
12/31/55	7	2	2. **White Christmas** Jockey #7 / Top 100 #18 [X-R]	Decca 23778
10/6/56	3	22	● 3. **True Love** Jockey #3 / Top 100 #4 / Best Seller #5 / Juke Box #6 **BING CROSBY and GRACE KELLY**	Capitol 3507
10/21/57	25	1	4. Around The World Best Seller #25 / Top 100 #54 from the movie *Around The World In 80 Days* starring David Niven	Decca 30262
1/6/58 -	34	2	5. White Christmas Top 100 #34 / Best Seller #36 [X-R]	Decca 23778
12/19/60	26	2	6. White Christmas [X-R]	Decca 23778
12/18/61	12	3	7. White Christmas [X-R]	Decca 23778
12/29/62	38	1	8. White Christmas [X-R]	Decca 23778
			CROSBY, David — see NASH, Graham	

CROSBY, STILLS & NASH

Folk-rock trio formed in Laurel Canyon, California: David Crosby (guitar), Stephen Stills (guitar, keyboards, bass) and Graham Nash (guitar). Crosby had been in The Byrds; Stills had been in The Buffalo Springfield; Nash had been in The Hollies. Won the 1969 Best New Artist Grammy Award. Neil Young (guitar), formerly with The Buffalo Springfield, joined group in 1970, left in 1974. Trio inducted into the Rock and Roll Hall of Fame in 1997.

CROSBY, STILLS & NASH:

DATE	POS	WKS	ARTIST–RECORD TITLE	LABEL & NO.
8/2/69	28	6	1. Marrakesh Express	Atlantic 2652
10/25/69	21	9	2. Suite: Judy Blue Eyes written by Stephen Stills for Judy Collins	Atlantic 2676

CROSBY, STILLS, NASH & YOUNG:

DATE	POS	WKS	ARTIST–RECORD TITLE	LABEL & NO.
4/4/70	11	10	3. Woodstock written by Joni Mitchell about the legendary 1969 rock festival	Atlantic 2723
6/20/70	16	9	4. Teach Your Children Jerry Garcia (of Grateful Dead; steel guitar)	Atlantic 2735
7/11/70	14	7	5. Ohio written by Neil Young after 4 students were killed at Kent State by National Guardsmen during an anti-war demonstration on 5/4/70	Atlantic 2740
10/10/70	30	6	6. Our House	Atlantic 2760

CROSBY, STILLS & NASH:

DATE	POS	WKS	ARTIST–RECORD TITLE	LABEL & NO.
7/2/77	7	12	7. **Just A Song Before I Go**	Atlantic 3401
7/3/82	9	12	8. **Wasted On The Way** with Timothy B. Schmit	Atlantic 4058
10/9/82	18	9	9. Southern Cross	Atlantic 89969

CROSS, Christopher

Born Christopher Geppert on 5/3/51 in San Antonio, Texas. Pop-rock singer/songwriter/guitarist. Won the 1980 Best New Artist Grammy Award.

DATE	POS	WKS	ARTIST–RECORD TITLE	LABEL & NO.
3/1/80	2 (4)	17	1. **Ride Like The Wind** Michael McDonald (backing vocal)	Warner 49184
7/5/80	1 (1)	13	2. **Sailing** 1980 Grammy winner: Record of the Year	Warner 49507
10/25/80	15	12	3. Never Be The Same #1 Adult Contemporary hit (2 weeks)	Warner 49580
4/25/81	20	7	4. Say You'll Be Mine Nicolette Larson (backing vocal)	Warner 49705
8/29/81	1 (3)	17	● 5. **Arthur's Theme (Best That You Can Do)** #1 Adult Contemporary hit (4 weeks); from the movie *Arthur* starring Dudley Moore	Warner 49787

DATE	POS	WKS	ARTIST–RECORD TITLE	LABEL & NO.
1/22/83	**12**	13	6. All Right	Warner 29843
5/21/83	**33**	5	7. No Time For Talk	Warner 29662
12/24/83+	**9**	11	8. **Think Of Laura**	Warner 29658
			#1 Adult Contemporary hit (4 weeks); popularized through play on TV's *General Hospital*	
			CROSS COUNTRY — see TOKENS, The	
			CROW	
			Rock-blues group from Minneapolis, Minnesota: Dave Waggoner (vocals), Dick Weigand (guitar), Kink Middlemist (organ), Larry Weigand (bass) and Denny Craswell (drums). Craswell was a member of The Castaways.	
11/29/69+	**19**	10	1. Evil Woman Don't Play Your Games With Me	Amaret 112
			CROW, Sheryl	
			Born on 2/11/62 in Kennett, Missouri. Adult Alternative rock singer/songwriter/guitarist. Worked as backing singer for Michael Jackson, Don Henley, George Harrison and others. Won the 1994 Best New Artist Grammy Award.	
8/27/94	**2** (6)	27	● 1. **All I Wanna Do** Airplay #2 / Sales #7	A&M 0702
			#1 Adult Contemporary hit (8 weeks)	
1/28/95	**5**	21	2. **Strong Enough** Airplay #2 / Sales #11	A&M 0798
8/5/95	**36**	6	3. Can't Cry Anymore Airplay #30 / Sales #69	A&M 0638
9/28/96+	**10**	25	4. **If It Makes You Happy** Airplay #7 / Sales #17	A&M 1874
3/29/97	**11**	12	5. Everyday Is A Winding Road Airplay #6 / Sales #27	A&M 2032
5/31/97	**19** A	17	6. A Change Would Do You Good	album cut
			from the album *Sheryl Crow* on A&M 0587	
9/19/98	**9** A	21	7. **My Favorite Mistake** Hot 100 #20 (10 wks)	album cut
			from the album *The Globe Sessions* on A&M 540959	
5/18/02	**17**	21	8. Soak Up The Sun Airplay #18	album cut
			from the album *C'mon, C'mon* on A&M 493260	
12/28/02+	**4**	28	● 9. **Picture** Sales #1 (12) / Airplay #6	Universal South 172274
			KID ROCK Featuring ALLISON MOORER or SHERYL CROW commercial single features Moorer; the vast majority of radio stations played the original album version featuring Crow	
12/6/03+	**14**	25↑	10. The First Cut Is The Deepest Airplay #14	album cut
			written by Cat Stevens; from the album *The Very Best Of Sheryl Crow* on A&M 152102	
			CROWDED HOUSE	
			Pop trio from New Zealand: Neil Finn (vocals, guitar, piano), Nick Seymour (bass) and Paul Hester (drums). Finn and Hester were former members of Split Enz.	
2/21/87	**2** (1)	15	1. **Don't Dream It's Over** Sales #2 / Airplay #2	Capitol 5614
5/30/87	**7**	11	2. **Something So Strong** Sales #7 / Airplay #7	Capitol 5695
			CROWELL, Rodney	
			Born on 8/7/50 in Houston, Texas. Country singer/songwriter/guitarist. Married to Rosanne Cash from 1979-92.	
6/28/80	**37**	2	1. Ashes By Now	Warner 49224

DATE	POS	WKS	ARTIST–RECORD TITLE	LABEL & NO.
			CRUCIAL CONFLICT	
			Hip-hop group from Chicago, Illinois: Corey Johnson, Marrico King, Ralph Levertson and Wondosas Martin.	
6/15/96	**18**	10	● 1. Hay Sales #6	Pallas/Universal 56008
			CRUSADERS, The	
			Instrumental jazz-oriented trio from Houston, Texas: Joe Sample (keyboards), Wilton Felder (reeds) and Nesbert "Stix" Hooper (drums).	
10/27/79	**36**	3	1. Street Life Randy Crawford (vocal)	MCA 41054
			CRYSTALS, The	
			Female vocal group from Brooklyn, New York: Barbara Alston, Dee Dee Kennibrew, Mary Thomas, Patricia Wright and Myrna Gerrard. La La Brooks replaced Gerrard in 1962. Thomas left in 1962. Alston died of a heart attack on 5/15/92 (age 48).	
12/11/61+	**20**	7	1. There's No Other (Like My Baby)	Philles 100
4/28/62	**13**	8	2. Uptown Barbara Alston (lead vocal, above 2)	Philles 102
10/6/62	**1** (2)	12	3. **He's A Rebel** written by Gene Pitney	Philles 106
1/19/63	**11**	8	4. He's Sure The Boy I Love Darlene Love (lead vocal); above 2 actually recorded by The Blossoms	Philles 109
5/11/63	**3**	10	5. **Da Doo Ron Ron (When He Walked Me Home)**	Philles 112
8/31/63	**6**	9	6. **Then He Kissed Me** La La Brooks (lead vocal, above 2); all of above produced by Phil Spector	Philles 115
			CUFF LINKS, The	
			Group is actually the overdubbed voice of Ron Dante (of The Archies).	
10/4/69	**9**	9	1. **Tracy**	Decca 32533
			CULTURE BEAT	
			Dance group assembled by Germans Torsten Fenslau (DJ/producer), Juergen Katzmann (composer/guitarist) and Peter Zweier (composer/engineer). Includes British singer Lana Evans and New Jersey rapper Jay Supreme. Fenslau died in a car crash on 11/6/93 (age 29).	
11/27/93+	**17**	13	● 1. Mr. Vain Airplay #17 / Sales #19	550 Music/Epic 77259
			CULTURE CLUB	
			Pop group formed in London, England: George "Boy George" O'Dowd (vocals; see #11 & 12 below), Roy Hay (guitar, keyboards), Michael Craig (bass) and Jon Moss (drums). Won the 1983 Best New Artist Grammy Award.	
1/15/83	**2** (3)	18	1. **Do You Really Want To Hurt Me**	Epic/Virgin 03368
4/30/83	**2** (2)	13	2. **Time (Clock Of The Heart)**	Epic/Virgin 03796
7/16/83	**9**	12	3. **I'll Tumble 4 Ya**	Epic/Virgin 03912
10/29/83	**10**	12	4. **Church Of The Poison Mind**	Epic/Virgin 04144
12/10/83+	**1** (3)	16	● 5. **Karma Chameleon**	Virgin/Epic 04221
3/3/84	**5**	12	6. **Miss Me Blind** Jermaine Stewart (backing vocal)	Virgin/Epic 04388
5/19/84	**13**	8	7. It's A Miracle	Virgin/Epic 04457

DATE	POS	WKS	ARTIST–RECORD TITLE	LABEL & NO.
10/20/84	**17**	7	8. The War Song $\quad$ Sales #18 / Airplay #18	Virgin/Epic 04638
1/12/85	**33**	5	9. Mistake No. 3 $\quad$ Airplay #29	Virgin/Epic 04727
4/19/86	**12**	10	10. Move Away $\quad$ Sales #11 / Airplay #14	Virgin/Epic 05847
			BOY GEORGE:	
2/20/88	**40**	1	11. Live My Life $\quad$ Sales #37 / Airplay #39	Virgin 99390
			from the movie *Hiding Out* starring Jon Cryer	
4/3/93	**15**	9	12. The Crying Game $\quad$ Sales #18 / Airplay #22	SBK 50437
			title song from the movie starring Stephen Rea	
			CUMMINGS, Burton	
			Born on 12/31/47 in Winnipeg, Manitoba, Canada. Lead singer of The Guess Who.	
11/6/76+	**10**	15	● 1. **Stand Tall**	Portrait 70001
10/24/81	**37**	2	2. You Saved My Soul	Alfa 7008
			from the movie *Melanie* starring Glynnis O'Connor	
			CURB, Mike, Congregation	
			Born on 12/24/44 in Savannah, Georgia. Pop music mogul and politician. President of MGM Records from 1969-73. Elected lieutenant governor of California in 1978; served as governor of California in 1980. Formed own company, Sidewalk Records, in 1964; became Curb Records in 1974. Currently resides in Nashville.	
2/27/71	**34**	4	1. Burning Bridges	MGM 14151
			from the movie *Kelly's Heroes* starring Clint Eastwood	
4/15/72	**1** (3)	16	● 2. **The Candy Man**	MGM 14320
			SAMMY DAVIS, Jr. with The Mike Curb Congregation	
			#1 Adult Contemporary hit (2 weeks); from the movie *Willy Wonka & The Chocolate Factory* starring Gene Wilder	
6/3/72	**38**	3	3. Long Haired Lover From Liverpool	MGM 14376
			LITTLE JIMMY OSMOND with The Mike Curb Congregation	
			CURE, The	
			Techno-rock group from England: Robert Smith (vocals, guitar), Porl Thompson (guitar), Laurence "Lol" Tolhurst (keyboards), Simon Gallup (bass) and Boris Williams (drums). Numerous personnel changes with Smith the only constant.	
1/9/88	**40**	1	1. Just Like Heaven $\quad$ Airplay #37	Elektra 69443
8/26/89	**2** (1)	12	2. **Love Song** $\quad$ Sales #3 / Airplay #7	Elektra 69280
6/20/92	**18**	14	3. Friday I'm In Love $\quad$ Airplay #16 / Sales #28	Fiction/Elektra 64742
			#1 Modern Rock hit (4 weeks)	
			CURRY, Mark — see PUFF DADDY	
			CURTIS — see KING CURTIS	
			CUTTING CREW	
			Pop-rock group formed in England: Nick Van Eede (vocals), Kevin MacMichael (guitar), Colin Farley (bass) and Martin Beedle (drums). MacMichael died of cancer on 12/31/2002 (age 51).	
3/21/87	**1** (2)	13	1. **(I Just) Died In Your Arms** $\quad$ Airplay #1 (2) / Sales #2	Virgin 99481
7/18/87	**38**	2	2. One For The Mockingbird $\quad$ Airplay #32	Virgin 99464
10/3/87	**9**	11	3. **I've Been In Love Before** $\quad$ Airplay #8 / Sales #11	Virgin 99425

DATE	POS	WKS	ARTIST–RECORD TITLE	LABEL & NO.
			CYMARRON	
			Male pop vocal trio from Memphis, Tennessee: Richard Mainegra, Rick Yancey and Sherrill Parks.	
7/17/71	**17**	7	1. Rings	Entrance 7500
			CYMBAL, Johnny	
			Born on 2/3/45 in Ochitree, Scotland. Died of a heart attack on 3/16/93 (age 48). Singer/songwriter/producer. Also recorded as Derek (see #2 below).	
3/16/63	**16**	8	1. Mr. Bass Man **[N]** Ronnie Bright (bass singer; member of the Valentines)	Kapp 503
11/23/68+	**11**	11	2. Cinnamon **DEREK**	Bang 558
			CYPRESS HILL	
			Rap trio from Los Angeles, California: Senen "Sen Dog" Reyes, Louis "B-Real" Freese and Lawrence "Mixmaster Muggs" Muggerud. Reyes is the brother of Mellow Man Ace. Group appeared in the movie *The Meteor Man*.	
7/24/93	**19**	15	● 1. Insane In The Brain Sales #10 / Airplay #35	Ruffhouse 77135
			CYRKLE, The	
			Pop group formed in Easton, Pennsylvania: Don Dannemann (vocals, guitar), Mike Losekamp (keyboards), Tom Dawes (bass) and Marty Fried (drums).	
6/4/66	**2** (1)	11	1. **Red Rubber Ball** written by Paul Simon and Bruce Woodley (of The Seekers)	Columbia 43589
8/27/66	**16**	5	2. Turn-Down Day	Columbia 43729
			CYRUS, Billy Ray	
			Born on 8/25/61 in Flatwoods, Kentucky. Country singer. Plays "Dr. Clint Cassidy" on the PAX-TV series *Doc*.	
5/23/92	**4**	22	▲ 1. **Achy Breaky Heart** Sales #2 / Airplay #38 #1 Country hit (5 weeks)	Mercury 866522
			D	
			DA BRAT	
			Born Shawntae Harris on 4/14/74 in Chicago, Illinois. Female rapper/songwriter.	
6/18/94	**6**	17	▲ 1. **Funkdafied** Sales #3 / Airplay #17 samples "Between The Sheets" by The Isley Brothers	So So Def 77532
11/26/94	**37**	4	2. Fa All Y'all Sales #20	So So Def 77594
4/22/95	**26**	11	● 3. Give It 2 You Sales #15 / Airplay #43 Trey Lorenz (backing vocal)	So So Def 77836
10/12/96	**30**	8	● 4. Sittin' On Top Of The World Sales #15 samples "Mary Jane" by Rick James	So So Def 78426
3/22/97	**16**	5	● 5. Ghetto Love Sales #8 **DA BRAT Featuring T-Boz** samples "All This Love" by DeBarge and "Public Enemy No. 1" by Public Enemy	So So Def 78527

DATE	POS	WKS	ARTIST–RECORD TITLE	LABEL & NO.
7/12/97	6	17	▲ 6. **Not Tonight** Sales #3 / Airplay #39 **LIL' KIM Featuring Da Brat, Left Eye, Missy "Misdemeanor" Elliott and Angie Martinez** samples "Ladies Night" by Kool & The Gang; from the movie *Nothing To Lose* starring Martin Lawrence	Undeas/Big Beat 98019
10/25/97	12	15	● 7. Sock It 2 Me Sales #7 / Airplay #36 **MISSY "MISDEMEANOR" ELLIOTT Featuring Da Brat** samples "Ready Or Not Here I Come" by The Delfonics	EastWest 64144
3/7/98	29	9	● 8. The Party Continues Sales #16 **JD & DA BRAT** Usher (backing vocal); samples "She's Strange" by Cameo	So So Def 78807
7/22/00	26	7	9. What'Chu Like Airplay #19 **DA BRAT Featuring Tyrese**	So So Def 79330
			DADDY DEWDROP	
4/10/71	9	11	Born Richard Monda in 1952 in Cleveland, Ohio. Pop singer/songwriter. 1. **Chick-A-Boom (Don't Ya Jes' Love It)** [N]	Sunflower 105
			DADDY-O'S, The	
6/23/58	39	3	Novelty session group produced by guitarist Billy Mure (of The Trumpeteers). 1. Got A Match? Best Seller #39 / Top 100 #40 [I-N]	Cabot 122
			DALE, Alan	
			Born Aldo Sigismondi on 7/9/28 in Brooklyn, New York. Died of heart failure on 4/20/2002 (age 73). Pop singer. Hosted his own TV show in 1951. Starred in the 1956 movie *Don't Knock The Rock*.	
4/30/55	14	7	1. Cherry Pink (And Apple Blossom White) Juke Box #14 / Jockey #19 / Best Seller #27 from the movie *Underwater!* starring Jane Russell	Coral 61373
7/2/55	10	7	2. **Sweet And Gentle** Jockey #10 / Best Seller #12 / Juke Box #14 Dick Jacobs (orch., above 2)	Coral 61435
			DALE & GRACE	
			Pop vocal duo: Dale Houston (from Ferriday, Louisiana) and Grace Broussard (from Prairieville, Louisiana).	
10/26/63	1 (2)	12	1. **I'm Leaving It Up To You** #1 Adult Contemporary hit (2 weeks)	Montel 921
2/8/64	8	7	2. **Stop And Think It Over**	Montel 922
			DALTREY, Roger	
			Born on 3/1/44 in Hammersmith, London, England. Lead singer of The Who. Starred in the movies *Tommy, Lisztomania, The Legacy* and *McVicar*.	
10/25/80	20	8	1. Without Your Love from the movie *McVicar* starring Daltrey	Polydor 2121
			DAMIAN, Michael	
			Born Michael Damian Weir on 4/26/62 in San Diego, California. Pop singer/actor. Played "Danny Romalotti" on the TV soap opera *The Young & The Restless*.	
4/8/89	1 (1)	13	● 1. **Rock On** Airplay #1 (1) / Sales #2 from the movie *Dream A Little Dream* starring Corey Feldman	Cypress 1420
7/29/89	31	4	2. Cover Of Love Airplay #29 / Sales #34	Cypress 1430
12/23/89+	24	9	3. Was It Nothing At All Sales #22 / Airplay #22	Cypress 1451

DATE	POS	WKS	ARTIST—RECORD TITLE	LABEL & NO.
			DAMITA JO	
			Born Damita Jo DuBlanc on 8/5/30 in Austin, Texas. Died on 12/25/98 (age 68). Female singer. Regular on Redd Foxx's TV variety series in 1977.	
11/7/60	**22**	8	1. I'll Save The Last Dance For You Cliff Parman (orch.); answer to "Save The Last Dance For Me" by The Drifters	Mercury 71690
7/17/61	**12**	7	2. I'll Be There Chuck Sagle (orch.); answer to "Stand By Me" by Ben E. King	Mercury 71840
			DAMN YANKEES	
			Superstar rock group: Ted Nugent (guitar), Tommy Shaw (guitar, vocals), Jack Blades (bass, vocals) and Michael Cartellone (drums). Nugent was with the Amboy Dukes. Shaw was with Styx. Blades was with Night Ranger.	
11/3/90+	**3**	18	● 1. **High Enough** Sales #2 / Airplay #4	Warner 19595
11/7/92	**20**	11	2. Where You Goin' Now Airplay #28 / Sales #37	Warner 18728
			DAMON('S), Liz, Orient Express	
			Damon is the leader of the three-woman, six-man vocal/instrumental group from Hawaii.	
1/30/71	**33**	3	1. 1900 Yesterday	White Whale 368
			DAMONE, Vic	
			Born Vito Farinola on 6/12/28 in Brooklyn, New York. Pop singer. Appeared in the movies *Kismet*, *Meet Me In Las Vegas* and *Hell To Eternity*. Hosted own TV series (1956-57). Married to actress Diahann Carroll from 1987-96.	
6/2/56	**4**	16	1. **On The Street Where You Live** Jockey #4 / Top 100 #8 / Best Seller #8 / Juke Box #13 from the Broadway musical *My Fair Lady* starring Julie Andrews	Columbia 40654
9/30/57	**16**	4	2. An Affair To Remember (Our Love Affair) Jockey #16 / Top 100 #35 from the movie *An Affair To Remember* starring Cary Grant and Deborah Kerr	Columbia 40945
5/22/65	**30**	4	3. You Were Only Fooling (While I Was Falling In Love) Ernie Freeman (orch.); #8 hit for the Ink Spots in 1949	Warner 5616
			DANA, Vic	
			Born on 8/26/42 in Buffalo, New York. Pop singer.	
4/25/64	**27**	5	1. Shangri-La	Dolton 92
3/6/65	**10**	8	2. **Red Roses For A Blue Lady** #3 hit for Vaughn Monroe in 1949	Dolton 304
6/4/66	**30**	4	3. I Love You Drops #4 Country hit for Bill Anderson in 1966	Dolton 319
			DANCER, PRANCER AND NERVOUS	
			Novelty production of "The Singing Reindeer" (similar to The Chipmunks).	
12/28/59	**34**	1	1. The Happy Reindeer **[X-N]**	Capitol 4300
			D'ANGELO	
			Born Michael D'Angelo Archer on 2/11/74 in Richmond, Virginia. R&B singer/songwriter.	
7/29/95	**27**	11	1. Brown Sugar Sales #16 / Airplay #63	EMI 58360

DATE	POS	WKS	ARTIST–RECORD TITLE	LABEL & NO.
3/9/96	**10**	11	● 2. **Lady** Sales #7 / Airplay #43	EMI 58543
2/5/00	**25**	9	3. Untitled (How Does It Feel) Airplay #17 from the album *Voodoo* on Virgin 48499	album cut

DANIELS, Charlie, Band

Born on 10/28/36 in Wilmington, North Carolina. Country-rock singer/fiddle player. His band consisted of Tom Crain (guitar), Joe "Taz" DiGregorio (keyboards), Charles Hayward (bass), and James Marshall and Fred Edwards (drums). Group appeared in the movie *Urban Cowboy*.

DATE	POS	WKS	ARTIST–RECORD TITLE	LABEL & NO.
7/21/73	**9**	9	1. **Uneasy Rider** **[N]** **CHARLIE DANIELS**	Kama Sutra 576
3/15/75	**29**	3	2. The South's Gonna Do It	Kama Sutra 598
7/21/79	**3**	12	▲ 3. **The Devil Went Down To Georgia** #1 Country hit (1 week)	Epic 50700
6/28/80	**11**	8	4. In America	Epic 50888
9/27/80	**31**	4	5. The Legend Of Wooley Swamp	Epic 50921
4/17/82	**22**	8	6. Still In Saigon	Epic 02828

DANIELS, Jeffrey — see BABYFACE

DANLEERS, The

Black doo-wop group from Brooklyn, New York: Jimmy Weston, Johnny Lee, Willie Ephraim, Nathaniel McCune and Roosevelt Mays. Weston died on 6/10/93.

DATE	POS	WKS	ARTIST–RECORD TITLE	LABEL & NO.
6/30/58	**7**	10	1. **One Summer Night** Jockey #7 / Best Seller #14 / Hot 100 #16 originally released on AMP-3 2115 in 1958 as by The Dandleers	Mercury 71322

DANNY & THE JUNIORS

Vocal group from Philadelphia: Danny Rapp (born on 5/10/41), David White, Frank Maffei and Joe Terranova. White later joined The Spokesmen. Group appeared in the 1958 movie *Let's Rock*. Rapp committed suicide on 4/5/83 (age 41).

DATE	POS	WKS	ARTIST–RECORD TITLE	LABEL & NO.
12/9/57+	**1 (7)**	18	● 1. **At The Hop** Top 100 #1 (7) / Best Seller #1 (5) / Jockey #1 (3) #1 R&B hit (5 weeks)	ABC-Paramount 9871
3/10/58	**19**	7	2. Rock And Roll Is Here To Stay Best Seller #19 / Top 100 #19	ABC-Paramount 9888
7/21/58	**39**	1	3. Dottie Best Seller #39 / Top 100 #41 Artie Singer (orch., all of above)	ABC-Paramount 9926
10/10/60	**27**	3	4. Twistin' U.S.A. Frank Slay (orch.)	Swan 4060

DANNY WILSON

Pop trio from Dundee, Scotland: brothers Gary (vocals, guitar) and Kit (keyboards, drums) Clark, with Ged Grimes (bass). Group named after the 1952 Frank Sinatra movie *Meet Danny Wilson*.

DATE	POS	WKS	ARTIST–RECORD TITLE	LABEL & NO.
8/1/87	**23**	8	1. Mary's Prayer Sales #22 / Airplay #22	Virgin 99465

DANTÉ and the EVERGREENS

Born Donald Drowty on 9/8/41 in Los Angeles, California. The Evergreens consisted of Bill Young, Tony Moon and Frank Rosenthal.

DATE	POS	WKS	ARTIST–RECORD TITLE	LABEL & NO.
6/13/60	**15**	8	1. Alley-Oop **[N]**	Madison 130

DATE	POS	WKS	ARTIST–RECORD TITLE	LABEL & NO.
			D'ARBY, Terence Trent	
			Born on 3/15/62 in Brooklyn, New York; later based in London, England. R&B-pop singer/songwriter/producer.	
2/27/88	**1** (1)	15	● 1. **Wishing Well** Sales #1 (1) / Airplay #2	Columbia 07675
			#1 R&B hit (1 week)	
6/18/88	**4**	13	2. **Sign Your Name** Sales #4 / Airplay #5	Columbia 07911
10/8/88	**30**	5	3. Dance Little Sister (Part One) Sales #26 / Airplay #30	Columbia 08023
			DARIN, Bobby	
			Born Walden Robert Cassotto on 5/14/36 in the Bronx, New York. Died of heart failure on 12/20/73 (age 37). Pop/rock/swing singer/pianist/ songwriter/entertainer. Won the 1959 Best New Artist Grammy Award. Married to actress Sandra Dee from 1960-67. Appeared in several movies. Inducted into the Rock and Roll Hall of Fame in 1990.	
6/30/58	**3**	13	● 1. **Splish Splash** Hot 100 #3 / Best Seller #4 / Jockey #5	Atco 6117
			#1 R&B hit (2 weeks)	
8/11/58	**24**	5	2. Early In The Morning Hot 100 #24 / Best Seller #24	Atco 6121
			THE RINKY-DINKS	
10/27/58	**9**	14	● 3. **Queen Of The Hop** Hot 100 #9	Atco 6127
2/23/59	**38**	2	4. Plain Jane	Atco 6133
5/4/59	**2** (1)	13	● 5. **Dream Lover**	Atco 6140
9/7/59	**1** (9)	22	● 6. **Mack The Knife**	Atco 6147
			lyrical version of "Moritat" or "Theme From The Threepenny Opera"; 1959 Grammy winner: Record of the Year	
1/25/60	**6**	11	7. **Beyond The Sea**	Atco 6158
			introduced by Benny Goodman in 1948 (from the 1945 French song "La Mer")	
4/4/60	**21**	6	8. Clementine	Atco 6161
			folk tune written in 1884 as "Oh, My Darling Clementine"	
6/20/60	**19**	5	9. Won't You Come Home Bill Bailey	Atco 6167
			#1 hit for Arthur Collins in 1902	
10/17/60	**20**	8	10. Artificial Flowers	Atco 6179
			from the musical *Tenderloin* starring Eileen Rodgers	
2/20/61	**14**	7	11. Lazy River	Atco 6188
			#19 hit for Hoagy Carmichael in 1932	
7/10/61	**40**	1	12. Nature Boy	Atco 6196
			#1 hit for Nat King Cole in 1948	
9/11/61	**5**	9	13. **You Must Have Been A Beautiful Baby**	Atco 6206
			#1 hit for Bing Crosby in 1938	
1/13/62	**15**	8	14. Irresistible You /	
1/20/62	**30**	5	15. Multiplication	Atco 6214
			from the movie *Come September* starring Darin and Sandra Dee	
4/14/62	**24**	5	16. What'd I Say (Part 1)	Atco 6221
7/21/62	**3**	9	17. **Things**	Atco 6229
10/27/62	**32**	3	18. If A Man Answers	Capitol 4837
			title song from the movie starring Darin and Sandra Dee	
2/2/63	**3**	12	19. **You're The Reason I'm Living**	Capitol 4897
5/25/63	**10**	7	20. **18 Yellow Roses**	Capitol 4970
10/8/66	**8**	9	21. **If I Were A Carpenter**	Atlantic 2350
2/11/67	**32**	3	22. Lovin' You	Atlantic 2376

DATE	POS	WKS	ARTIST–RECORD TITLE	LABEL & NO.
			DARREN, James	
			Born James Ercolani on 6/8/36 in Philadelphia, Pennsylvania. Pop singer/ actor. Starred in several movies. Regular on TV's *The Time Tunnel* from 1966-67 and *T.J. Hooker* from 1983-86.	
11/6/61	3	12	1. **Goodbye Cruel World**	Colpix 609
2/17/62	6	8	2. **Her Royal Majesty**	Colpix 622
5/5/62	11	7	3. Conscience	Colpix 630
8/4/62	39	1	4. Mary's Little Lamb	Colpix 644
2/18/67	35	2	5. All	Warner 5874
			from the movie *Run for Your Wife* starring Frankie Randall	
			DARTELLS, The	
			Rock and roll band from Oxnard, California: Doug Phillips (vocals, bass), Dick Burns (guitar), Corky Wilkie and Rich Peil (saxophones), Randy Ray (organ) and Gary Peeler (drums). Phillips died on 5/5/95 (age 50).	
4/27/63	11	9	1. Hot Pastrami	Dot 16453
			DAS EFX	
			Hip-hop duo: Andre Weston (born on 9/9/70 in New Jersey) and Willie Hines (born on 11/27/70 in New York).	
6/6/92	25	12	● 1. They Want EFX Sales #12 / Airplay #35	EastWest 98600
8/7/93	20	10	▲ 2. Check Yo Self Sales #9 / Airplay #47	Priority 53830
			ICE CUBE featuring DAS EFX #1 R&B hit (1 week); samples "The Message" by Grandmaster Flash & The Furious Five	
			DAVID, Craig	
			Born on 5/5/81 in Southampton, England. R&B singer/songwriter.	
6/30/01	15	23	1. Fill Me In Sales #3 / Airplay #17	Wildstar/Atlantic 88101
12/22/01+	10	16	2. **7 Days** Sales #8 / Airplay #10	Wildstar/Atlantic 85232
			DAVID & DAVID	
			Pop-rock duo from Los Angeles, California: David Baerwald and David Ricketts.	
11/15/86	37	3	1. Welcome To The Boomtown Sales #31	A&M 2857
			DAVID & JONATHAN	
			Songwriting/producing/vocal duo from Bristol, England: Roger "David" Greenaway and Roger "Jonathan" Cook. Both later were production team for White Plains. Cook founded Blue Mink. Greenaway also in The Pipkins.	
1/29/66	18	5	1. Michelle	Capitol 5563
			George Martin (orch.); first recorded by The Beatles in 1965	
			DAVIS, Alana	
			Born on 5/6/74 in Manhattan, New York. Female pop-rock singer/ songwriter.	
1/24/98	37	3	1. 32 Flavors Sales #43 / Airplay #52	Elektra 64129

DATE	POS	WKS	ARTIST–RECORD TITLE	LABEL & NO.
			DAVIS, Mac	
			Born on 1/21/42 in Lubbock, Texas. Country-pop singer/songwriter/actor. Hosted own TV series from 1974-76. Appeared in several movies.	
8/5/72	**1** (3)	13	● 1. **Baby Don't Get Hooked On Me** #1 Adult Contemporary hit (3 weeks)	Columbia 45618
5/25/74	**11**	14	2. One Hell Of A Woman	Columbia 46004
9/7/74	**9**	10	3. **Stop And Smell The Roses** #1 Adult Contemporary hit (1 week)	Columbia 10018
12/21/74+	**15**	8	4. Rock N' Roll (I Gave You The Best Years Of My Life)	Columbia 10070
			DAVIS, Paul	
			Born on 4/21/48 in Meridian, Mississippi. Pop-country singer/songwriter/producer.	
12/7/74+	**23**	8	1. Ride 'Em Cowboy	Bang 712
9/11/76	**35**	3	2. Superstar tribute to Elton John, Stevie Wonder, Linda Ronstadt and Joni Mitchell	Bang 726
10/29/77+	**7**	25	3. **I Go Crazy**	Bang 733
10/7/78	**17**	13	4. Sweet Life	Bang 738
4/12/80	**23**	6	5. Do Right	Bang 4808
11/28/81+	**11**	13	6. Cool Night	Arista 0645
3/20/82	**6**	13	7. **'65 Love Affair**	Arista 0661
8/28/82	**40**	2	8. Love Or Let Me Be Lonely	Arista 0697
			DAVIS, Sammy Jr.	
			Born on 12/8/25 in Harlem, New York. Died of cancer on 5/16/90 (age 64). Singer/dancer/actor. Starred in several movies and Broadway shows. Won Grammy's Lifetime Achievement Award in 2001.	
6/4/55	**9**	11	1. **Something's Gotta Give /** Best Seller #9 / Juke Box #16 / Jockey #20 from the movie *Daddy Long Legs* starring Fred Astaire	
5/28/55	**12**	12	2. Love Me Or Leave Me Best Seller #12 / Jockey #20 #2 hit for Ruth Etting in 1929; Sy Oliver (orch., above 2)	Decca 29484
7/2/55	**13**	6	3. That Old Black Magic Jockey #13 / Best Seller #16 / Juke Box #18 Morty Stevens (orch.); #1 hit for Glenn Miller in 1943	Decca 29541
10/6/62	**17**	10	4. What Kind Of Fool Am I Marty Paich (orch.); from the musical *Stop the World–I Want to Get Off* starring Anthony Newley	Reprise 20,048
2/1/64	**17**	9	5. The Shelter Of Your Arms	Reprise 20,216
6/24/67	**37**	4	6. Don't Blame The Children [S]	Reprise 0566
1/18/69	**11**	11	7. I've Gotta Be Me #1 Adult Contemporary hit (7 weeks); from the Broadway musical *Golden Rainbow* starring Steve Lawrence and Eydie Gorme	Reprise 0779
4/15/72	**1** (3)	16	● 8. **The Candy Man** **SAMMY DAVIS, JR. with The Mike Curb Congregation** #1 Adult Contemporary hit (2 weeks); from the movie *Willy Wonka & The Chocolate Factory* starring Gene Wilder	MGM 14320
			DAVIS, Skeeter	
			Born Mary Penick on 12/30/31 in Dry Ridge, Kentucky. Country singer. Married to DJ/TV host Ralph Emery (1960-64) and NRBQ bassist Joey Spampinato (1983-96).	
9/5/60	**39**	1	1. (I Can't Help You) I'm Falling Too answer to "Please Help Me, I'm Falling" by Hank Locklin	RCA Victor 7767

DATE	POS	WKS	ARTIST–RECORD TITLE	LABEL & NO.
1/16/61	**26**	2	2. My Last Date (With You) vocal version of Floyd Cramer's "Last Date"	RCA Victor 7825
2/16/63	**2** (1)	13	3. **The End Of The World** #1 Adult Contemporary hit (4 weeks)	RCA Victor 8098
9/21/63	**7**	11	4. **I Can't Stay Mad At You**	RCA Victor 8219
			DAVIS, Spencer, Group	
			Born on 7/14/41 in Swansea, South Wales. Rock singer/rhythm guitarist. Formed his group in Birmingham, England, in 1963. Featured Steve Winwood (vocals, guitar, keyboards), his brother Muff Winwood (bass) and Pete York (drums). Steve Winwood left in 1967 to form the group Traffic.	
1/28/67	**7**	9	1. **Gimme Some Lovin'**	United Artists 50108
4/8/67	**10**	7	2. **I'm A Man**	United Artists 50144
			DAVIS, Tyrone	
			Born on 5/4/38 in Greenville, Mississippi; raised in Saginaw, Michigan. R&B singer. His younger sister, Jean Davis, was a member of the group Facts Of Life.	
1/4/69	**5**	11	● 1. **Can I Change My Mind** #1 R&B hit (3 weeks)	Dakar 602
4/12/69	**34**	2	2. Is It Something You've Got	Dakar 605
4/4/70	**3**	11	● 3. **Turn Back The Hands Of Time** #1 R&B hit (2 weeks)	Dakar 616
8/25/73	**32**	3	4. There It Is	Dakar 4523
10/30/76	**38**	4	5. Give It Up (Turn It Loose)	Columbia 10388
			DAWN — see ORLANDO, Tony	
			DAY, Bobby	
			Born Robert Byrd on 7/1/30 in Ft. Worth, Texas. Died of cancer on 7/15/90 (age 60). R&B singer/songwriter. Member of The Hollywood Flames.	
8/4/58	**2** (2)	19	● 1. **Rock-in Robin**　　Hot 100 #2 / Best Seller #4 #1 R&B hit (3 weeks)	Class 229
			DAY, Doris	
			Born Doris Kappelhoff on 4/3/22 in Cincinnati, Ohio. Lead singer with Les Brown's big band. Starred in several movies. Star of own TV series from 1968-73. Her husband, Marty Melcher, owned Arwin Records; their son, Terry, was a member of The Rip Chords and Bruce & Terry, and a prolific producer (The Beach Boys).	
9/11/54	**3**	17	1. **If I Give My Heart To You** 　　　　　Juke Box #3 / Best Seller #4 / Jockey #4 The Mellomen (backing vocals)	Columbia 40300
7/23/55	**13**	9	2. I'll Never Stop Loving You 　　　　　Jockey #13 / Best Seller #15 / Top 100 #93 Percy Faith (orch.); from the movie Love Me Or Leave Me starring Day	Columbia 40505
7/7/56	**2** (3)	22	● 3. **Whatever Will Be, Will Be (Que Sera, Sera)** 　　　　　Top 100 #2 / Jockey #2 / Juke Box #3 / Best Seller #3 from the movie The Man Who Knew Too Much starring Day and James Stewart	Columbia 40704
7/21/58	**6**	12	4. **Everybody Loves A Lover** 　　　　　Jockey #6 / Hot 100 #14 / Best Seller #17 Frank DeVol (orch., above 2)	Columbia 41195

DATE	POS	WKS	ARTIST–RECORD TITLE	LABEL & NO.
			DAY, Morris — see TIME, The	
			DAYNE, Taylor	
			Born Leslie Wunderman on 3/7/62 in Baldwin, Long Island, New York. White female dance/pop singer.	
11/14/87+	7	15	● 1. **Tell It To My Heart** Sales #5 / Airplay #10	Arista 9612
3/12/88	7	11	2. **Prove Your Love** Sales #7 / Airplay #9	Arista 9676
7/23/88	3	16	● 3. **I'll Always Love You** Sales #2 / Airplay #5	Arista 9700
11/26/88+	2 (1)	13	4. **Don't Rush Me** Sales #2 / Airplay #2	Arista 9722
11/4/89	5	13	5. **With Every Beat Of My Heart** Airplay #3 / Sales #6	Arista 9895
2/3/90	1 (1)	15	● 6. **Love Will Lead You Back** Airplay #1 (2) / Sales #1 (1) #1 Adult Contemporary hit (4 weeks)	Arista 9938
5/19/90	4	12	7. **I'll Be Your Shelter** Airplay #3 / Sales #9	Arista 2005
8/18/90	12	10	8. Heart Of Stone Airplay #11 / Sales #18	Arista 2057
6/19/93	20	9	9. Can't Get Enough Of Your Love Airplay #17 / Sales #27	Arista 12582
			DAZZ BAND	
			Funk-dance band from Cleveland, Ohio: Skip Martin (vocals), Eric Fearman (guitar), Bobby Harris (sax), Pierre DeMudd (trumpet), Kevin Frederick (keyboards), and brothers Michael (bass) and Isaac (drums) Wiley.	
5/15/82	5	16	1. **Let It Whip** #1 R&B hit (5 weeks)	Motown 1609
			DC TALK	
			Contemporary rock/hip-hop Christian trio from Washington DC: Toby McKeehan, Michael Tait and Kevin Smith.	
11/16/96	29	9	1. Just Between You And Me Airplay #21 / Sales #56	Virgin 38575
			DEADEYE DICK	
			Pop-rock trio from New Orleans, Louisiana: Caleb Guillotte (guitar), Mark Miller (bass) and Billy Landry (drums). All share vocals. Group name taken from a Kurt Vonnegut novel.	
11/5/94+	27	11	● 1. New Age Girl Sales #18 / Airplay #48 from the movie *Dumb And Dumber* starring Jim Carrey	Ichiban 232
			DEAD OR ALIVE	
			Dance group from Liverpool, England: Pete Burns (vocals), Tim Lever (keyboards), Mike Percy (bass) and Steve Coy (drums).	
6/29/85	11	11	1. You Spin Me Round (Like A Record) Airplay #11 / Sales #12	Epic 04894
1/31/87	15	9	2. Brand New Lover Sales #15 / Airplay #15	Epic 06374
			DEAL, Bill, & The Rhondels	
			Brassy-rock group from Virginia Beach, Virginia: Bill Deal (vocals, organ), Bob Fisher (guitar), Mike Kerwin, Jeff Pollard, Ronny Rosenbaum and Ken Dawson (horns), Dan Queinsenburry (bass) and Ammon Tharp (drums). Deal died of a heart attack on 12/10/2003 (age 59).	
3/15/69	39	1	1. May I	Heritage 803
5/31/69	35	3	2. I've Been Hurt	Heritage 812
9/13/69	23	5	3. What Kind Of Fool Do You Think I Am	Heritage 817

DATE	POS	WKS	ARTIST–RECORD TITLE	LABEL & NO.
			### DEAN, Jimmy	
			Born on 8/10/28 in Plainview, Texas. Country singer/pianist/guitarist. Hosted own CBS-TV series (1957-58), ABC-TV series (1963-66). Business interests include a restaurant chain and a line of pork sausage. Married country singer Donna Meade on 10/27/91.	
1/6/58 -	**32**	1	1. Little Sandy Sleighfoot Top 100 #32 / Best Seller #37 **[X-N]** Ray Ellis (orch.)	Columbia 41025
10/9/61	**1 (5)**	13	● 2. **Big Bad John** **[S]** #1 Country hit (2 weeks) / #1 Adult Contemporary hit (10 weeks)	Columbia 42175
2/10/62	**22**	5	3. The Cajun Queen **[S]**	Columbia 42282
1/20/62	**24**	3	4. Dear Ivan **[S]** background music: "Battle Hymn Of The Republic"	Columbia 42259
2/10/62	**26**	5	5. To A Sleeping Beauty **[S]** background music: "Memories"	Columbia 42282
4/14/62	**8**	9	6. P.T. 109 based on the sinking of President John F. Kennedy's torpedo boat on 8/2/43	Columbia 42338
10/6/62	**29**	5	7. Little Black Book	Columbia 42529
5/22/76	**35**	2	● 8. I.O.U. **[S]** an ode of thanks to his mother	Casino 052
			### DEAN AND JEAN	
			Vocal duo from Dayton, Ohio: Welton "Dean" Young and Brenda Lee "Jean" Jones. Jones died of cancer on 8/4/2001 (age 63).	
12/14/63+	**35**	2	1. Tra La La La Suzy	Rust 5067
3/21/64	**32**	3	2. Hey Jean, Hey Dean	Rust 5075
			### DeBARGE/EL DeBARGE	
			R&B family group from Grand Rapids, Michigan: Eldra "El" (male vocals, keyboards), Bunny (female vocals), Mark (horns), James (keyboards) and Randy (bass) DeBarge. Brothers Bobby and Tommy were members of Switch. James was briefly married to Janet Jackson in 1984.	
			DEBARGE:	
3/26/83	**31**	6	1. I Like It	Gordy 1645
5/28/83	**17**	10	2. All This Love #1 Adult Contemporary hit (3 weeks)	Gordy 1660
11/26/83+	**18**	11	3. Time Will Reveal #1 R&B hit (5 weeks)	Gordy 1705
3/9/85	**3**	14	4. **Rhythm Of The Night** Sales #3 / Airplay #3 #1 R&B hit (1 week) / #1 Adult Contemporary hit (1 week); from the movie *The Last Dragon* starring Vanity	Gordy 1770
6/22/85	**6**	12	5. **Who's Holding Donna Now** Airplay #6 / Sales #7 #1 Adult Contemporary hit (3 weeks)	Gordy 1793
5/17/86	**3**	13	6. **Who's Johnny** Airplay #3 / Sales #4 **EL DeBARGE** #1 R&B hit (1 week); theme from the movie *Short Circuit* starring Ally Sheedy	Gordy 1842
4/7/90	**31**	4	● 7. The Secret Garden (Sweet Seduction Suite) Sales #20 **QUINCY JONES/Al B. Sure!/James Ingram/El DeBarge/Barry White** #1 R&B hit (1 week)	Qwest 19992

DATE	POS	WKS	ARTIST–RECORD TITLE	LABEL & NO.
			DeBARGE, Chico	
			Born Jonathan DeBarge on 6/23/66 in Grand Rapids, Michigan. R&B singer. DeBarge sibling, but not a member of the group DeBarge.	
12/27/86+	21	11	1. Talk To Me Airplay #17 / Sales #22	Motown 1858
			DeBURGH, Chris	
			Born Christopher Davidson on 10/15/48 in Buenos Aires, Argentina (Irish parents). Adult Contemporary singer/songwriter. DeBurgh was his mother's maiden name.	
6/11/83	34	4	1. Don't Pay The Ferryman	A&M 2511
4/4/87	3	14	2. **The Lady In Red** Sales #1 (1) / Airplay #4	A&M 2848
			DeCASTRO SISTERS, The	
			Female vocal trio from Cuba: Peggy, Babette and Cherie DeCastro.	
10/9/54+	2 (1)	20	1. **Teach Me Tonight** Juke Box #2 / Jockey #3 / Best Seller #3	Abbott 3001
5/7/55	17	4	2. Boom Boom Boomerang Juke Box #17 / Best Seller #24	Abbott 3003
			Thurl Ravenscroft (bass voice); Skip Martin (orch., above 2)	
			DEE, Joey, & the Starliters	
			Born Joseph DiNicola on 6/11/40 in Passaic, New Jersey. Pop singer/dancer. The Starliters: David Brigati, Carlton Lattimore, Willie Davis, Larry Vernieri and Don Martin. Rogers Freeman replaced Vernieri in July 1962. Group appeared in the movies *Hey, Let's Twist* and *Two Tickets To Paris*. Later members included Brigati's brother Eddie, Felix Cavaliere and Gene Cornish (the future Young Rascals), and touring guitarist Jimmy James (the future Jimi Hendrix).	
12/4/61+	1 (3)	14	● 1. **Peppermint Twist - Part I**	Roulette 4401
			inspired by New York City's Peppermint Lounge club	
3/3/62	20	4	2. Hey, Let's Twist	Roulette 4408
3/31/62	6	9	3. **Shout - Part I**	Roulette 4416
			above 2 from the movie *Hey, Let's Twist!* starring Dee	
9/15/62	18	6	4. What Kind Of Love Is This	Roulette 4438
			from the movie *Two Tickets to Paris*; written by Johnny Nash	
6/1/63	36	1	5. Hot Pastrami With Mashed Potatoes - Part I	Roulette 4488
			DEE, Johnny — see LOUDERMILK, John D.	
			DEE, Kiki	
			Born Pauline Matthews on 3/6/47 in Bradford, Yorkshire, England. Female pop-rock singer.	
10/19/74	12	10	1. I've Got The Music In Me **THE KIKI DEE BAND**	Rocket 40293
7/17/76	1 (4)	15	● 2. **Don't Go Breaking My Heart** **ELTON JOHN and KIKI DEE**	Rocket 40585
			#1 Adult Contemporary hit (1 week)	
			DEE, Lenny	
			Born Leonard DeStoppelaire on 1/5/23 in Chicago, Illinois. Male organist.	
2/12/55	19	15	1. Plantation Boogie Juke Box #19 / Best Seller #23 [I]	Decca 29360

DATE	POS	WKS	ARTIST–RECORD TITLE	LABEL & NO.
			DEE, Tommy	
			Born Thomas Donaldson on 7/15/36 in Vicker, Virginia. DJ at KFXM-San Bernadino at the time of his only hit (first recorded by Eddie Cochran).	
4/13/59	**11**	8	1. Three Stars **[S]**	Crest 1057
			Tommy Dee (narration); Carol Kay and the Teen-Aires (vocals); a tribute to Buddy Holly, Ritchie Valens and the Big Bopper	
			DEEE-LITE	
			Dance trio formed in New York: Super DJ Dmitry Brill (from Kiev, Soviet Union), Jungle DJ Towa "Towa" Tei (from Tokyo, Japan) and vocalist Lady Miss Kier (Kier Kirby from Youngstown, Ohio). Group's name inspired by the tune "It's De-lovely" from the 1936 Cole Porter musical *Red, Hot & Blue*. Brill and Kier are married.	
10/20/90	**4**	13	● 1. **Groove Is In The Heart** Sales #1 (2) / Airplay #6	Elektra 64934
			Bootsy Collins (backing vocal); Q-Tip (rap)	
			DEELE, The	
			R&B group from Cincinnati, Ohio: Darnell Bristol and Carlos Greene (vocals), Stanley Burke, Kenny "Babyface" Edmonds, Mark "L.A. Reid" Rooney and Kevin Roberson. Babyface and L.A. Reid later formed LaFace Records.	
4/2/88	**10**	12	1. **Two Occasions** Airplay #8 / Sales #13	Solar 70015
			DEEP BLUE SOMETHING	
			Pop-rock group from Dallas, Texas: brothers Todd (vocals, bass) and Toby (guitar) Pipes, Kirk Tatom (guitar) and John Kirtland (drums).	
10/14/95+	**5**	26	1. **Breakfast At Tiffany's** Airplay #4 / Sales #15	Interscope 98138
			DEEP PURPLE	
			Hard-rock group from England: Rod Evans (vocals), Ritchie Blackmore (guitar), Jon Lord (keyboards), Nicky Simper (bass) and Ian Paice (drums). Evans and Simper left in 1969, replaced by Ian Gillan (vocals) and Roger Glover (bass).	
8/24/68	**4**	9	1. **Hush**	Tetragrammaton 1503
12/7/68	**38**	3	2. Kentucky Woman	Tetragrammaton 1508
6/16/73	**4**	12	● 3. **Smoke On The Water**	Warner 7710
			inspired by the burning of the Montreux Casino on 12/3/71 during a Frank Zappa show for which Deep Purple opened	
			DEES, Rick, And His Cast Of Idiots	
			Born Rigdon Dees on 3/14/50 in Jacksonville, Florida. DJ working at WMPS-Memphis when he conceived idea for "Disco Duck." Currently one of America's top radio DJs. Host of TV's *Solid Gold* (1984) and his own late-night talk show *Into The Night* (1990).	
9/4/76	**1 (1)**	16	▲ 1. **Disco Duck (Part I)** **[N]**	RSO 857
			DEFAULT	
			Rock group from Vancouver, British Columbia, Canada: Dallas Smith (vocals), Jeremy Hora (guitar), Dave Benedict (bass) and Dan Craig (drums).	
3/30/02	**13**	20	1. Wasting My Time Airplay #13	album cut
			from the album *The Fallout* on TVT 2310	

DATE	POS	WKS	ARTIST–RECORD TITLE	LABEL & NO.

DEF LEPPARD

Hard-rock group from Sheffield, Yorkshire, England: Joe Elliott (vocals), Steve Clark and Pete Willis (guitars), Rick Savage (bass) and Rick Allen (drums). Phil Collen replaced Willis in late 1982. Allen lost his left arm in a car crash on 12/31/84. Clark died of alcohol-related respiratory failure on 1/8/91 (age 30). Guitarist Vivian Campbell (formerly of Whitesnake) joined in April 1992.

DATE	POS	WKS	ARTIST–RECORD TITLE	LABEL & NO.
4/16/83	12	9	1. Photograph #1 Mainstream Rock hit (6 weeks)	Mercury 811215
7/9/83	16	9	2. Rock Of Ages #1 Mainstream Rock hit (1 week)	Mercury 812604
10/8/83	28	5	3. Foolin'	Mercury 814178
11/21/87	19	9	4. Animal Sales #16 / Airplay #24	Mercury 888832
2/13/88	10	10	5. **Hysteria** Sales #10 / Airplay #11	Mercury 870004
5/21/88	2 (1)	15	6. **Pour Some Sugar On Me** Airplay #2 / Sales #3	Mercury 870298
8/20/88	1 (1)	13	7. **Love Bites** Airplay #1 (2) / Sales #2	Mercury 870402
12/3/88+	3	12	8. **Armageddon It** Sales #1 (1) / Airplay #3	Mercury 870692
3/18/89	12	9	9. Rocket Sales #11 / Airplay #13	Mercury 872614
4/11/92	15	11	10. Let's Get Rocked Sales #10 / Airplay #43 #1 Mainstream Rock hit (1 week)	Mercury 866568
7/18/92	36	3	11. Make Love Like A Man Sales #41 / Airplay #57	Mercury 864038
9/5/92	12	15	12. Have You Ever Needed Someone So Bad Sales #14 / Airplay #21	Mercury 864136
1/23/93	34	3	13. Stand Up (Kick Love Into Motion) Airplay #50 #1 Mainstream Rock hit (5 weeks)	Mercury 864604
9/25/93	12	12	14. Two Steps Behind Airplay #17 / Sales #18 from the movie *Last Action Hero* starring Arnold Schwarzenegger	Columbia 77116
1/22/94	39	2	15. Miss You In A Heartbeat Airplay #53 / Sales #54	Mercury 858080

DeFRANCO FAMILY Featuring Tony DeFranco

Family vocal group from Port Colborne, Ontario, Canada: Tony, Merlina, Nino, Marisa and Benny DeFranco.

DATE	POS	WKS	ARTIST–RECORD TITLE	LABEL & NO.
9/29/73	3	14	● 1. **Heartbeat - It's A Lovebeat**	20th Century 2030
1/26/74	32	4	2. Abra-Ca-Dabra	20th Century 2070
5/25/74	18	6	3. Save The Last Dance For Me	20th Century 2088

DeJOHN SISTERS

Pop vocal duo from Chester, Pennsylvania: Julie (born on 3/18/31) and Dux (born on 1/21/33) DeGiovanni.

DATE	POS	WKS	ARTIST–RECORD TITLE	LABEL & NO.
12/25/54+	6	13	1. **(My Baby Don't Love Me) No More** Jockey #6 / Best Seller #8 / Juke Box #11 O.B. Masingill (orch.)	Epic 9085

DEKKER, Desmond, & The Aces

Born Desmond Dacris on 7/16/41 in Kingston, Jamaica. Reggae singer.

DATE	POS	WKS	ARTIST–RECORD TITLE	LABEL & NO.
6/7/69	9	7	1. **Israelites**	Uni 55129

DEL AMITRI

Pop-rock group from Glasgow, Scotland: Justin Currie (vocals, bass), David Cummings and Iain Harvie (guitars), and Brian McDermott (drums).

DATE	POS	WKS	ARTIST–RECORD TITLE	LABEL & NO.
6/30/90	35	3	1. Kiss This Thing Goodbye Sales #31 / Airplay #33	A&M 1485
9/26/92	30	7	2. Always The Last To Know Airplay #31 / Sales #71	A&M 1604
8/26/95	10	26	3. **Roll To Me** Airplay #6 / Sales #50	A&M 1114

DATE	POS	WKS	ARTIST—RECORD TITLE	LABEL & NO.
			DELANEY & BONNIE	
			Folk-rock duo: Delaney Bramlett (born on 7/1/39 in Pontotoc County, Mississippi) and wife Bonnie Lynn Bramlett (born on 11/8/44 in Acton, Illinois). Married from 1967-72. Backing artists (Friends) included, at various times, Leon Russell, Rita Coolidge, Dave Mason, Eric Clapton, Duane Allman and many others. Bonnie (as Bonnie Sheridan) played "Bonnie Watkins" on TV's *Roseanne*.	
6/26/71	**13**	10	1. Never Ending Song Of Love **DELANEY & BONNIE & FRIENDS**	Atco 6804
10/9/71	**20**	7	2. Only You Know And I Know	Atco 6838
			DE LA SOUL	
			Alternative-rap trio from Amityville, Long Island, New York: Kelvin Mercer ("Posdnuos"), David Jolicoeur ("Trugoy The Dove") and Vincent Mason ("Pasemaster Mase").	
7/22/89	**34**	3	● 1. Me Myself And I Sales #21 #1 R&B hit (1 week); samples "(not just) Knee Deep" by Funkadelic	Tommy Boy 7926
			DELEGATES, The	
			Novelty trio of Bob DeCarlo, Nick Cenci and Nick Kousaleous. DeCarlo was a DJ in Tampa. Cenci and Kousaleous owned the Co & Ce record label.	
11/4/72	**8**	6	1. **Convention '72** [N] "break-in" record	Mainstream 5525
			DELFONICS, The	
			R&B vocal trio from Philadelphia, Pennsylvania: brothers William and Wilbert Hart, with Randy Cain.	
2/24/68	**4**	12	1. **La - La - Means I Love You**	Philly Groove 150
10/5/68	**35**	4	2. Break Your Promise	Philly Groove 152
1/25/69	**35**	1	3. Ready Or Not Here I Come (Can't Hide From Love)	Philly Groove 154
10/4/69	**40**	2	4. You Got Yours And I'll Get Mine	Philly Groove 157
2/7/70	**10**	10	● 5. **Didn't I (Blow Your Mind This Time)**	Philly Groove 161
7/25/70	**40**	1	6. Trying To Make A Fool Of Me	Philly Groove 162
			DELINQUENT HABITS	
			Latino hip-hop trio from Los Angeles, California: David "Kemo" Thomas, Ivan "Ives" Martin and Alejandro "O.G. Style" Martinez.	
6/22/96	**35**	4	1. Tres Delinquentes Sales #22 / Airplay #71 samples "The Lonely Bull" by Herb Alpert	Loud/RCA 64526
			DELIVERANCE Soundtrack — see WEISSBERG, Eric	
			DELLS, The	
			R&B vocal group from Harvey, Illinois: Johnny Carter, Marvin Junior, Verne Allison, Mickey McGill and Chuck Barksdale. Carter was a member of The Flamingos. Group inducted into the Rock and Roll Hall of Fame in 2004.	
2/17/68	**20**	7	1. There Is	Cadet 5590
7/20/68	**10**	10	2. **Stay In My Corner** #1 R&B hit (3 weeks)	Cadet 5612
11/2/68	**18**	5	3. Always Together	Cadet 5621
2/8/69	**38**	2	4. Does Anybody Know I'm Here	Cadet 5631
6/21/69	**22**	6	5. I Can Sing A Rainbow/Love Is Blue	Cadet 5641

DATE	POS	WKS	ARTIST–RECORD TITLE	LABEL & NO.
8/23/69	**10**	10	6. **Oh, What A Night** #1 R&B hit (1 week)	Cadet 5649
9/18/71	**30**	6	7. The Love We Had (Stays On My Mind)	Cadet 5683
6/23/73	**34**	2	● 8. Give Your Baby A Standing Ovation	Cadet 5696
			DELL-VIKINGS, The	
			Interracial doo-wop group formed in Pittsburgh, Pennsylvania. Group members at various times: Norman Wright, Krips Johnson, Don Jackson, Clarence Quick, David Lerchey, Gus Backus and William Blakely. Quick died of a heart attack on 5/5/83 (age 46). Johnson died on 6/22/90 (age 57).	
3/2/57	**4**	22	● 1. **Come Go With Me** Best Seller #4 / Top 100 #5 / Juke Box #6 / Jockey #6 first released on Fee Bee 205 in 1956	Dot 15538
7/15/57	**9**	13	2. **Whispering Bells** Top 100 #9 / Best Seller #10 / Jockey #19 **THE DELL-VIKINGS Featuring Kripp Johnson** first released on Fee Bee 214 in 1956	Dot 15592
7/15/57	**12**	1	3. Cool Shake Jockey #12 / Top 100 #46 **DEL VIKINGS featuring Gus Backus**	Mercury 71132
			DEMENSIONS, The	
			Pop vocal group from the Bronx, New York: Lenny Dell, Marisa Martelli, Howard Margolin, and Charlie Peterson.	
8/8/60	**16**	9	1. Over The Rainbow Irv Spice (orch.); introduced by Judy Garland in the 1939 movie *The Wizard Of Oz*	Mohawk 116
			DENNIS, Cathy	
			Born on 3/25/69 in Norwich, Norfolk, England. White dance/pop singer/songwriter. Vocalist for producer Dancin' Danny D's D-Mob.	
1/27/90	**10**	12	1. **C'mon And Get My Love** Airplay #10 / Sales #12 **D MOB Introducing Cathy Dennis** from the movie *She-Devil* starring Meryl Streep and Roseanne Barr	FFRR 886798
12/8/90+	**9**	12	2. **Just Another Dream** Sales #8 / Airplay #8	Polydor 877962
3/23/91	**2** (2)	14	3. **Touch Me (All Night Long)** Airplay #2 / Sales #3 #70 R&B hit for Wish Featuring Fonda Rae in 1985	Polydor 879466
7/27/91	**8**	13	4. **Too Many Walls** Airplay #13 / Sales #35 #1 Adult Contemporary hit (2 weeks)	Polydor 867134
10/3/92	**32**	5	5. You Lied To Me Airplay #25 / Sales #65	Polydor 863452
			DENNY, Martin (The Exotic Sounds of)	
			Born on 4/10/11 in Manhattan, New York. Composer/arranger/pianist. Originated the "Exotic Sounds" in Hawaii, featuring Arthur Lyman and Julius Wechter (Baja Marimba Band) on vibes and marimba.	
4/27/59	**4**	13	● 1. **Quiet Village** [I] first recorded by Les Baxter in 1952	Liberty 55162
11/16/59	**28**	2	2. The Enchanted Sea [I]	Liberty 55212
			DENVER, John	
			Born Henry John Deutschendorf on 12/31/43 in Roswell, New Mexico. Died on 10/12/97 (age 53) at the controls of a light plane that crashed off the California coast. Singer/songwriter/guitarist. With the Chad Mitchell Trio from 1965-68. Wrote "Leaving On A Jet Plane." Starred in the 1977 movie *Oh, God.*	
6/26/71	**2** (1)	14	● 1. **Take Me Home, Country Roads** Fat City (Bill Danoff & Taffy Nivert of Starland Vocal Band; backing vocals)	RCA Victor 0445

DATE	POS	WKS	ARTIST–RECORD TITLE	LABEL & NO.
1/6/73	9	12	2. **Rocky Mountain High**	RCA Victor 0829
2/16/74	1 (1)	13	● 3. **Sunshine On My Shoulders** #1 Adult Contemporary hit (2 weeks)	RCA Victor 0213
6/15/74	1 (2)	11	● 4. **Annie's Song** #1 Adult Contemporary hit (3 weeks); written by Denver for his then-wife Annie Martell (married 1967-83)	RCA Victor 0295
10/5/74	5	10	● 5. **Back Home Again** #1 Country hit (1 week) / #1 Adult Contemporary hit (2 weeks)	RCA Victor 10065
1/11/75	13	8	6. Sweet Surrender **[L]** #1 Adult Contemporary hit (1 week)	RCA Victor 10148
4/5/75	1 (1)	15	● 7. **Thank God I'm A Country Boy** **[L]** #1 Country hit (1 week); above 2 recorded at the Universal City Amphitheater in California	RCA Victor 10239
8/30/75	1 (1)	13	● 8. **I'm Sorry /** #1 Country hit (1 week) / #1 Adult Contemporary hit (2 weeks)	
10/11/75	2 (4)	7	9. **Calypso** dedicated to Jacques Cousteau and his ship "Calypso"	RCA Victor 10353
12/13/75+	13	9	10. Fly Away #1 Adult Contemporary hit (2 weeks); Olivia Newton-John (backing vocal)	RCA Victor 10517
3/20/76	29	4	11. Looking For Space #1 Adult Contemporary hit (1 week)	RCA Victor 10586
10/2/76	36	2	12. Like A Sad Song #1 Adult Contemporary hit (1 week)	RCA 10774
4/30/77	32	3	13. My Sweet Lady recorded in 1971	RCA 10911
9/5/81	36	4	14. Some Days Are Diamonds (Some Days Are Stone)	RCA 12246
4/24/82	31	5	15. Shanghai Breezes #1 Adult Contemporary hit (1 week)	RCA 13071
			DEODATO	
			Born Eumir Deodato on 6/21/42 in Rio de Janeiro, Brazil. Dance keyboardist/producer/arranger.	
2/17/73	2 (1)	10	1. **Also Sprach Zarathustra (2001)** **[I]** theme from the movie *2001: A Space Odyssey*; written by classical composer Richard Strauss in 1896	CTI 12
			DEPECHE MODE	
			All-synthesized electro-pop group formed in Basildon, Essex, England: singer Dave Gahan and synthesizer players Martin Gore, Alan Wilder and Andy Fletcher. Wilder left in 1995. Group name is French for fast fashion.	
6/22/85	13	10	1. People Are People Airplay #11 / Sales #16	Sire 29221
2/10/90	28	6	● 2. Personal Jesus Sales #20	Sire/Reprise 19941
5/26/90	8	12	● 3. **Enjoy The Silence** Airplay #4 / Sales #10 #1 Modern Rock hit (3 weeks)	Sire/Reprise 19885
9/1/90	15	9	4. Policy Of Truth Airplay #11 / Sales #22 #1 Modern Rock hit (1 week)	Sire/Reprise 19842
3/13/93	37	1	● 5. I Feel You Sales #14 / Airplay #59 #1 Modern Rock hit (5 weeks)	Sire/Reprise 18600
5/31/97	38	3	6. It's No Good Airplay #44 / Sales #58	Mute/Reprise 17390
			DEREK — see CYMBAL, Johnny	
			DEREK AND THE DOMINOS—see CLAPTON, Eric	

DATE	POS	WKS	ARTIST—RECORD TITLE	LABEL & NO.
			DERRINGER, Rick	
			Born Richard Zehringer on 8/5/47 in Celina, Ohio. Rock singer/guitarist. Member of The McCoys and the Edgar Winter Group.	
3/2/74	**23**	6	1. Rock And Roll, Hoochie Koo	Blue Sky 2751
			DeSARIO, Teri	
			Born in Miami, Florida. Female dance-pop singer/songwriter.	
12/22/79+	**2 (2)**	16	● 1. **Yes, I'm Ready** **TERI DeSARIO with K.C.** #1 Adult Contemporary hit (2 weeks)	Casablanca 2227
			DeSHANNON, Jackie	
			Born Sharon Myers on 8/21/44 in Hazel, Kentucky. Female singer/prolific songwriter.	
6/19/65	**7**	9	1. **What The World Needs Now Is Love**	Imperial 66110
7/26/69	**4**	10	● 2. **Put A Little Love In Your Heart**	Imperial 66385
12/6/69	**40**	1	3. Love Will Find A Way	Imperial 66419
			DESMOND, Johnny	
			Born Giovanni Desimons on 11/14/20 in Detroit, Michigan. Died on 9/6/85 (age 64). Pop singer. Featured on the *Breakfast Club* radio show and TV's *Your Hit Parade*.	
3/26/55	**6**	11	1. **Play Me Hearts And Flowers (I Wanna Cry)** Jockey #6 / Juke Box #11 / Best Seller #16 Don Jacoby (orch.); introduced by Desmond on 3/6/55 on TV's *Philco Playhouse*	Coral 61379
8/13/55	**3**	16	2. **The Yellow Rose Of Texas** Jockey #3 / Juke Box #4 / Best Seller #6 / Top 100 #16	Coral 61476
12/3/55	**17**	1	3. Sixteen Tons Jockey #17 / Top 100 #50 Dick Jacobs (orch., above 2)	Coral 61529
			DES'REE	
			Born Des'ree Weeks on 11/30/68 in London, England (West Indian parents). Black female singer/songwriter.	
11/19/94+	**5**	30	1. **You Gotta Be** Airplay #2 / Sales #17	550 Music/Epic 77551
			DESTINY'S CHILD	
			Female R&B vocal group from Houston, Texas: Beyoncé Knowles, Kelly Rowland, LaTavia Roberson and LeToya (Toya) Luckett. Roberson and Luckett left in early 2000; replaced by Farrah Franklin and Michelle Williams. Franklin left shortly thereafter, leaving trio of Knowles, Rowland and Williams.	
12/20/97+	**3**	31	▲ 1. **No, No, No Part 2** Sales #1 (1) / Airplay #22 **DESTINY'S CHILD (featuring Wyclef Jean)** #1 R&B hit (1 week)	Columbia 78618
7/3/99	**1 (1)**	16	● 2. **Bills, Bills, Bills** Sales #1 (1) / Airplay #4 #1 R&B hit (9 weeks)	Columbia 79175
10/16/99	**33**	7	3. Bug A Boo Airplay #22 from the album *The Writing's On The Wall* on Columbia 69870	album cut
1/15/00	**1 (3)**	27	● 4. **Say My Name** Sales #1 (2) / Airplay #1 (1) #1 R&B hit (3 weeks)	Columbia 79342
6/24/00	**3**	26	5. **Jumpin', Jumpin'** Airplay #1 (7) / Sales #16	Columbia 79446

DATE	POS	WKS	ARTIST–RECORD TITLE	LABEL & NO.
10/14/00	**1** (11)	25	6. **Independent Women Part I** Airplay #1 (9) / Sales #3 #1 R&B hit (3 weeks); from the movie *Charlie's Angels* starring Drew Barrymore	Columbia 79493
3/24/01	**2** (7)	15	7. **Survivor** Airplay #1 (5) / Sales #3	Columbia 79566
6/23/01	**1** (2)	12	8. **Bootylicious** Sales #2 / Airplay #5 samples "Edge Of Seventeen" by Stevie Nicks; from the TV movie *MTV's Hip Hopera: Carmen* starring Beyoncé Knowles	Columbia 79622
10/13/01	**10**	15	9. **Emotion** Airplay #10	Columbia 79672

DETERGENTS, The

Novelty vocal trio from New York: Ron Dante (of The Archies and The Cuff Links), Tommy Wynn and Danny Jordan.

DATE	POS	WKS	ARTIST–RECORD TITLE	LABEL & NO.
12/19/64+	**19**	6	1. **Leader Of The Laundromat** **[N]** parody of "Leader Of The Pack" by The Shangri-Las	Roulette 4590

DETROIT EMERALDS

R&B vocal trio from Little Rock, Arkansas: brothers Abrim and Ivory Tilmon, with James Mitchell. Abrim Tilmon died of a heart attack in July 1982 (age 37).

DATE	POS	WKS	ARTIST–RECORD TITLE	LABEL & NO.
2/19/72	**36**	4	1. **You Want It, You Got It**	Westbound 192
7/29/72	**24**	7	2. **Baby Let Me Take You (In My Arms)**	Westbound 203

DeVAUGHN, William

Born in 1948 in Washington DC. R&B singer/songwriter/guitarist.

DATE	POS	WKS	ARTIST–RECORD TITLE	LABEL & NO.
5/18/74	**4**	10	● 1. **Be Thankful For What You Got** #1 R&B hit (1 week)	Roxbury 0236

DEVICE

Pop-rock trio from Los Angeles, California: Paul Engemann (vocals), Holly Knight (keyboards, bass) and Gene Black (guitar). Engemann joined Animotion in 1988. Prolific songwriter Knight was also a member of Spider.

DATE	POS	WKS	ARTIST–RECORD TITLE	LABEL & NO.
8/2/86	**35**	4	1. **Hanging On A Heart Attack** Airplay #26 / Sales #37	Chrysalis 42996

DEVO

Robotic rock-dance group from Akron, Ohio: brothers Mark (synthesizers) and Bob (vocals, guitar) Mothersbaugh, brothers Jerry (bass) and Bob (guitar) Casale, and Alan Myers (drums).

DATE	POS	WKS	ARTIST–RECORD TITLE	LABEL & NO.
10/4/80	**14**	15	● 1. **Whip It**	Warner 49550

DeVORZON, Barry, and Perry Botkin, Jr.

Songwriting/producing/arranging duo based in California. DeVorzon was born on 7/31/34 in Brooklyn, New York. Leader of Barry & The Tamerlanes. Botkin was born on 4/16/33 in Manhattan, New York. Son of orchestra leader Perry Botkin, Sr.

DATE	POS	WKS	ARTIST–RECORD TITLE	LABEL & NO.
10/2/76	**8**	16	● 1. **Nadia's Theme (The Young And The Restless)** **[I]** originally written as "Cotton's Dream" for the movie *Bless the Beasts And Children*, then used as the theme song for TV's *The Young and the Restless*, and finally as the music for Romanian gymnast Nadia Comaneci in the 1976 summer Olympics	A&M 1856

DEVOTIONS, The

White doo-wop group from Queens, New York: Ray Sanchez, Bob Weisbrod, Bob Hovorka, and brothers Frank and Joe Pardo.

DATE	POS	WKS	ARTIST–RECORD TITLE	LABEL & NO.
4/4/64	**36**	1	1. **Rip Van Winkle** **[N]**	Roulette 4541

DATE	POS	WKS	ARTIST–RECORD TITLE	LABEL & NO.
			DEXYS MIDNIGHT RUNNERS	
			Pop-rock group from Birmingham, England: Kevin Rowland (vocals), Billy Adams (guitar), Brian Maurice (sax), Paul Speare (flute), Jimmy Patterson (trombone), Micky Billingham (piano), Giorgio Kilkenny (bass) and Seb Shelton (drums). Billingham was later with General Public.	
2/26/83	**1** (1)	14	1. **Come On Eileen**	Mercury 76189
			DeYOUNG, Cliff	
			Born on 2/12/46 in Los Angeles, California. Adult Contemporary singer/actor. Appeared in several movies.	
2/16/74	**17**	8	1. My Sweet Lady written by John Denver; from the TV movie *Sunshine*	MCA 40156
			DeYOUNG, Dennis	
			Born on 2/18/47 in Chicago, Illinois. Lead singer/keyboardist of Styx.	
9/22/84	**10**	12	1. **Desert Moon** Airplay #6 / Sales #12	A&M 2666
			DIAMOND, Leo	
			Born on 6/29/15 in Brooklyn, New York. Died on 9/15/66 (age 51). Harmonica player/arranger.	
2/19/55	**30**	1	1. Melody Of Love Best Seller #30 **[I]**	RCA Victor 5973
			DIAMOND, Neil	
			Born on 1/24/41 in Brooklyn, New York. Pop-rock singer/guitarist/prolific songwriter. Worked as a staff writer at the Brill Building in New York City. Wrote score for the movie *Jonathan Livingston Seagull*. Starred in and composed the music for *The Jazz Singer* in 1980.	
9/10/66	**6**	9	1. **Cherry, Cherry** also see #22 below	Bang 528
11/26/66	**16**	6	2. I Got The Feelin' (Oh No No)	Bang 536
2/11/67	**18**	5	3. You Got To Me	Bang 540
4/29/67	**10**	8	4. **Girl, You'll Be A Woman Soon**	Bang 542
8/5/67	**13**	7	5. I Thank The Lord For The Night Time	Bang 547
10/28/67	**22**	6	6. Kentucky Woman	Bang 551
3/29/69	**22**	7	7. Brother Love's Travelling Salvation Show	Uni 55109
7/12/69	**4**	12	▲ 8. **Sweet Caroline (Good Times Never Seemed So Good)**	Uni 55136
11/15/69	**6**	12	▲ 9. **Holly Holy**	Uni 55175
3/21/70	**24**	8	10. Shilo recorded in 1968	Bang 575
5/16/70	**30**	4	11. Soolaimón (African Trilogy II)	Uni 55224
8/15/70	**21**	7	12. Solitary Man **[R]** originally charted at #55 in 1966	Bang 578
8/29/70	**1** (1)	14	▲ 13. **Cracklin' Rosie**	Uni 55250
11/21/70	**20**	9	14. He Ain't Heavy...He's My Brother	Uni 55264
12/5/70	**36**	5	15. Do It recorded in 1966	Bang 580
4/3/71	**4**	8	16. **I Am...I Said**	Uni 55278
11/27/71	**14**	7	17. Stones /	
1/8/72		1	18. Crunchy Granola Suite	Uni 55310
5/13/72	**1** (1)	12	● 19. **Song Sung Blue** #1 Adult Contemporary hit (7 weeks)	Uni 55326

DATE	POS	WKS	ARTIST–RECORD TITLE	LABEL & NO.
9/2/72	11	7	20. Play Me	Uni 55346
11/25/72	17	8	21. Walk On Water	Uni 55352
4/21/73	31	4	22. "Cherry Cherry" from Hot August Night **[L-R]**	MCA 40017
11/24/73	34	3	23. Be from the movie *Jonathan Livingston Seagull*	Columbia 45942
10/19/74	5	10	24. **Longfellow Serenade** #1 Adult Contemporary hit (1 week)	Columbia 10043
3/1/75	34	2	25. I've Been This Way Before #1 Adult Contemporary hit (1 week)	Columbia 10084
6/26/76	11	8	26. If You Know What I Mean #1 Adult Contemporary hit (2 weeks); produced by Robbie Robertson (of The Band)	Columbia 10366
12/24/77+	16	9	27. Desirée #1 Adult Contemporary hit (1 week)	Columbia 10657
11/4/78	1 (2)	15	▲ 28. **You Don't Bring Me Flowers** **BARBRA & NEIL**	Columbia 10840
2/17/79	20	6	29. Forever In Blue Jeans	Columbia 10897
1/19/80	17	10	30. September Morn'	Columbia 11175
11/1/80+	2 (3)	17	31. **Love On The Rocks**	Capitol 4939
1/31/81	6	12	32. **Hello Again**	Capitol 4960
5/2/81	8	13	33. **America** #1 Adult Contemporary hit (3 weeks); above 3 from the movie *The Jazz Singer* starring Diamond	Capitol 4994
11/14/81+	11	12	34. Yesterday's Songs #1 Adult Contemporary hit (6 weeks)	Columbia 02604
3/6/82	27	5	35. On The Way To The Sky	Columbia 02712
6/19/82	35	4	36. Be Mine Tonight	Columbia 02928
10/2/82	5	11	37. **Heartlight** #1 Adult Contemporary hit (4 weeks); inspired by the movie *E.T.* starring Henry Thomas	Columbia 03219
2/19/83	35	4	38. I'm Alive	Columbia 03503
			DIAMOND RIO Country group formed in Nashville, Tennessee: Marty Roe (vocals), Jimmy Olander (guitar), Gene Johnson (mandolin), Dan Truman (piano), Dana Williams (bass) and Brian Prout (drums).	
2/13/99	36	3	1. Unbelievable Airplay #24 from the album *Unbelievable* on Arista Nashville 18866	album cut
3/3/01	29	8	2. One More Day Airplay #21 #1 Country hit (2 weeks); from the album *One More Day* on Arista Nashville 67999	album cut
9/14/02	28	9	3. Beautiful Mess Airplay #27 #1 Country hit (2 weeks)	album cut
5/24/03	31	4	4. I Believe Airplay #27 #1 Country hit (2 weeks); above 2 from the album *Completely* on Arista Nashville 67046	album cut
			DIAMONDS, The White doo-wop group from Toronto, Ontario, Canada: Dave Somerville, Ted Kowalski, Phil Levitt and Bill Reed. Michael Douglas replaced Levitt in early 1958. Evan Fisher and John Felton replaced Reed and Kowalski in 1959. Felton was killed in a plane crash in 1982.	
3/17/56	12	11	1. Why Do Fools Fall In Love Jockey #12 / Top 100 #16 / Best Seller #18 / Juke Box #19	Mercury 70790

DATE	POS	WKS	ARTIST–RECORD TITLE	LABEL & NO.
5/12/56	**14**	11	2. The Church Bells May Ring Best Seller #14 / Juke Box #15 / Jockey #17 / Top 100 #20	Mercury 70835
7/28/56	**30**	2	3. Love, Love, Love Top 100 #30	Mercury 70889
9/29/56	**34**	1	4. Soft Summer Breeze / Top 100 #34	
9/29/56	**35**	2	5. Ka-Ding-Dong Top 100 #35	Mercury 70934
3/16/57	**2** (8)	21	● 6. **Little Darlin'** Best Seller #2 / Juke Box #2 / Top 100 #2 / Jockey #2	Mercury 71060
7/15/57	**13**	2	7. Words Of Love Jockey #13 / Top 100 #76 written by Buddy Holly	Mercury 71128
9/30/57	**16**	1	8. Zip Zip Jockey #16 / Top 100 #45 David Carroll (orch., all of above)	Mercury 71165
11/4/57	**10**	8	9. **Silhouettes** Jockey #10 / Top 100 #60	Mercury 71197
1/6/58	**4**	14	● 10. **The Stroll** Jockey #4 / Top 100 #5 / Best Seller #7	Mercury 71242
5/19/58	**37**	1	11. High Sign Best Seller #37 / Top 100 #38	Mercury 71291
7/28/58	**16**	1	12. Kathy-O Jockey #16 / Best Seller #41 / Hot 100 #45 title song from the movie starring Patty McCormack	Mercury 71330
11/17/58	**29**	6	13. Walking Along first recorded by The Solitaires in 1957	Mercury 71366
2/9/59	**18**	10	14. She Say (Oom Dooby Doom)	Mercury 71404
8/7/61	**22**	4	15. One Summer Night	Mercury 71831

DIBANGO, Manu

Born on 2/10/34 in Douala, Cameroon, Africa. Jazz-R&B
saxophonist/pianist.

DATE	POS	WKS	ARTIST–RECORD TITLE	LABEL & NO.
7/21/73	**35**	3	1. Soul Makossa **[I]**	Atlantic 2971

DICK AND DEEDEE

Vocal duo formed in Santa Monica, California: Dick Gosting and Deedee
Sperling. Dick died from injuries suffered in a fall on 12/27/2003 (age 63).

DATE	POS	WKS	ARTIST–RECORD TITLE	LABEL & NO.
8/28/61	**2** (2)	10	1. **The Mountain's High**	Liberty 55350
5/12/62	**22**	5	2. Tell Me	Liberty 55412
4/6/63	**17**	6	3. Young And In Love	Warner 5342
12/21/63+	**27**	4	4. Turn Around	Warner 5396
12/12/64+	**13**	10	5. Thou Shalt Not Steal	Warner 5482

DICKENS, "Little" Jimmy

Born on 12/19/20 in Bolt, West Virginia. Country singer/guitarist.

DATE	POS	WKS	ARTIST–RECORD TITLE	LABEL & NO.
11/13/65	**15**	5	1. May The Bird Of Paradise Fly Up Your Nose **[N]** #1 Country hit (2 weeks)	Columbia 43388

DICKY DOO AND THE DON'TS

White vocal group from Brooklyn, New York: Gerry Granahan (vocals), Ray
Gangi (guitar), Al Ways (sax), Harvey Davis (bass) and Dave Alldred
(drums).

DATE	POS	WKS	ARTIST–RECORD TITLE	LABEL & NO.
2/17/58	**28**	6	1. Click-Clack Top 100 #28 / Best Seller #29 **DICKEY DOO And The Don'ts**	Swan 4001
5/12/58	**40**	1	2. Nee Nee Na Na Na Na Nu Nu Top 100 #40 / Best Seller #42 **[I-N]**	Swan 4006

DATE	POS	WKS	ARTIST–RECORD TITLE	LABEL & NO.
			DIDDLEY, Bo	
			Born Otha Ellas Bates McDaniel on 12/30/28 in McComb, Mississippi; raised in Chicago, Illinois. Highly influential singer/songwriter/guitarist. Inducted into the Rock and Roll Hall of Fame in 1987. Won Grammy's Lifetime Achievement Award in 1998.	
10/5/59	20	7	1. Say Man **[N]**	Checker 931
			Diddley trades insults with maracas player Jerome Green	
			DIDO	
			Born Florian Armstrong on 12/25/71 in London, England. Female Adult Alternative pop-rock singer/songwriter.	
2/10/01	3	29	1. **Thankyou** Airplay #3 / Sales #36	Arista 13996
			#1 Adult Contemporary hit (4 weeks)	
11/8/03+	18	29↑	2. White Flag Sales #19 / Airplay #19	Arista 58336
			DIESEL	
			Rock group from the Netherlands: Rob Vunderink (vocals, guitar), Mark Boon (guitar), Frank Papendrecht (bass) and Pim Koopman (drums).	
10/17/81	25	6	1. Sausalito Summernight	Regency 7339
			DIFFIE, Joe	
			Born on 12/28/58 in Tulsa, Okalhoma; raised in Duncan, Oklahoma. Country singer/songwriter/guitarist.	
7/31/99	38	3	1. A Night To Remember Airplay #32 / Sales #46	Epic 79118
			DIGABLE PLANETS	
			Hip-hop trio from Washington DC: Ishmael "Butterfly" Butler, Mary Ann "Ladybug" Vierra and Craig "Doodle Bug" Irving.	
1/30/93	15	13	● 1. Rebirth Of Slick (Cool Like Dat) Sales #5 / Airplay #26	Pendulum 64674
			DIGITAL UNDERGROUND	
			Hip-hop group from Oakland, California: Gregory Jacobs (aka "Humpty-Hump" and "Shock-G"), Ron Brooks (aka "Money B"), Earl Cook (aka "Schmoovy-Schmoov"), James Dight (aka "Chopmaster J") and DJ Fuze. Tupac (2Pac) Shakur was a member in 1991. Group appeared in the movie *Nothing But Trouble*.	
4/14/90	11	14	▲ 1. The Humpty Dance Sales #5 / Airplay #25 **[N]**	Tommy Boy 7944
1/11/92	40	1	● 2. Kiss You Back Sales #23 / Airplay #50	Tommy Boy 993
			samples "(not just) Knee Deep" by Funkadelic	
			DINNING, Mark	
			Born on 8/17/33 in Drury, Oklahoma. Died of a heart attack on 3/22/86 (age 52). Pop singer.	
1/4/60	1 (2)	14	● 1. Teen Angel	MGM 12845
			DINO	
			Born Dino Esposito on 7/20/63 in Encino, California; raised in Hawaii and Connecticut. Pop-dance singer.	
6/24/89	7	14	● 1. I Like It Sales #6 / Airplay #7	4th & B'way 7483
10/14/89	23	6	2. Sunshine Airplay #23 / Sales #25	4th & B'way 7489
9/1/90	6	10	3. **Romeo** Airplay #7 / Sales #8	Island 878012

DATE	POS	WKS	ARTIST–RECORD TITLE	LABEL & NO.
12/22/90+	31	5	4. Gentle Sales #28 / Airplay #38 Delona Tanner (female vocal)	Island 878472
8/7/93	27	11	5. Ooh Child Airplay #16 / Sales #62	EastWest 98398
			DINO, Kenny	
			Born on 9/12/39 in Hicksville, Long Island, New York. Pop singer.	
12/4/61	24	6	1. Your Ma Said You Cried In Your Sleep Last Night	Musicor 1013
			DINO, Paul	
			Born Paul Dino Bertuccini on 3/2/35 in Philadelphia, Pennsylvania. Pop singer.	
4/10/61	38	1	1. Ginnie Bell	Promo 2180
			DINO, DESI & BILLY	
			Vocal trio formed in Los Angeles, California: Dino Martin, Desi Arnaz Jr. and Billy Hinsche. Martin is the son of Dean Martin. Arnaz is the son of Lucille Ball and Desi Arnaz. Dino (formerly married to actress Olivia Hussey and to Olympic skater Dorothy Hamill) was killed on 3/21/87 (age 35) when his Air National Guard jet crashed.	
7/24/65	17	7	1. I'm A Fool	Reprise 0367
10/16/65	25	5	2. Not The Lovin' Kind	Reprise 0401
			DION (Dion and The Belmonts)	
			Born Dion DiMucci on 7/18/39 in the Bronx, New York. Formed doo-wop group, Dion & The Belmonts, in 1958. Consisted of Dion, Angelo D'Aleo, Fred Milano and Carlo Mastrangelo. Named for Belmont Avenue in the Bronx. Angelo was in the Navy in 1959 and missed some recording and picture sessions. Dion went solo in 1960 as did The Belmonts. Dion was inducted into the Rock and Roll Hall of Fame in 1989.	
			DION AND THE BELMONTS:	
5/26/58	22	10	1. I Wonder Why Top 100 #22 / Best Seller #24	Laurie 3013
9/15/58	19	8	2. No One Knows Best Seller #19 / Hot 100 #24	Laurie 3015
1/5/59	40	1	3. Don't Pity Me	Laurie 3021
4/27/59	5	13	4. **A Teenager In Love**	Laurie 3027
1/11/60	3	11	5. **Where Or When** #1 hit for Hal Kemp & His Orchestra in 1937 (from the Rodgers & Hart musical *Babes In Arms* starring Mitzi Green)	Laurie 3044
5/16/60	30	2	6. When You Wish Upon A Star from the Disney animated movie *Pinocchio*; #1 hit for Glenn Miller in 1940	Laurie 3052
8/15/60	38	1	7. In The Still Of The Night the Cole Porter classic; #3 hit for Tommy Dorsey in 1937	Laurie 3059
			DION:	
11/14/60	12	11	8. Lonely Teenager	Laurie 3070
10/2/61	1 (2)	12	● 9. **Runaround Sue**	Laurie 3110
12/18/61+	2 (1)	13	10. **The Wanderer /**	
12/18/61	36	1	11. The Majestic	Laurie 3115
5/5/62	3	9	12. **Lovers Who Wander**	Laurie 3123
7/21/62	8	8	13. **Little Diane**	Laurie 3134
11/24/62	10	9	14. **Love Came To Me**	Laurie 3145

DATE	POS	WKS	ARTIST–RECORD TITLE	LABEL & NO.
1/26/63	**2** (3)	11	15. **Ruby Baby** #10 R&B hit for The Drifters in 1956	Columbia 42662
3/30/63	21	6	16. Sandy	Laurie 3153
5/4/63	21	6	17. This Little Girl	Columbia 42776
7/27/63	31	3	18. Be Careful Of Stones That You Throw first recorded by Hank Williams in 1952	Columbia 42810
9/28/63	6	8	19. **Donna The Prima Donna**	Columbia 42852
11/23/63	6	9	20. **Drip Drop** **DION DI MUCI** (above 2)	Columbia 42917
11/2/68	4	12	● 21. **Abraham, Martin And John** a tribute to Abraham Lincoln, Martin Luther King, Jr. and John and Robert Kennedy	Laurie 3464

DION, Celine

Born on 3/30/68 in Charlemagne, Quebec, Canada. Adult Contemporary singer. Youngest of 14 children. Began performing at age five. Wrote first song at age 12. Married her longtime manager, Rene Angelil, on 12/17/94.

DATE	POS	WKS	ARTIST–RECORD TITLE	LABEL & NO.
1/5/91	4	15	1. **Where Does My Heart Beat Now** Airplay #3 / Sales #9	Epic 73536
6/1/91	35	1	2. (If There Was) Any Other Way Airplay #28	Epic 73665
2/22/92	9	14	▲ 3. **Beauty And The Beast** Sales #8 / Airplay #17 **CELINE DION and PEABO BRYSON** title song from the animated movie	Epic 74090
5/9/92	4	19	4. **If You Asked Me To** Airplay #3 / Sales #11 #1 Adult Contemporary hit (3 weeks)	Epic 74277
9/12/92	29	6	5. Nothing Broken But My Heart Airplay #35 / Sales #49 #1 Adult Contemporary hit (1 week)	Epic 74336
1/23/93	36	3	6. Love Can Move Mountains Airplay #35	Epic 74337
8/28/93	23	7	7. When I Fall In Love Airplay #28 / Sales #31 **CELINE DION · CLIVE GRIFFIN** from the movie *Sleepless In Seattle* starring Tom Hanks and Meg Ryan; #20 hit for Doris Day in 1952	Epic Soundtrax 77021
12/25/93+	**1** (4)	26	▲ 8. **The Power Of Love** Sales #1 (5) / Airplay #2 #1 Adult Contemporary hit (4 weeks)	550 Music/Epic 77230
5/21/94	23	9	9. Misled Airplay #22 / Sales #52	550 Music/Epic 77344
3/9/96	**1** (6)	30	▲ 10. **Because You Loved Me** Airplay #1 (14) / Sales #1 (6) #1 Adult Contemporary hit (19 weeks); theme from the movie *Up Close & Personal* starring Robert Redford	550 Music/Epic 78237
8/17/96	**2** (5)	29	▲ 11. **It's All Coming Back To Me Now** Airplay #1 (2) / Sales #3 #1 Adult Contemporary hit (5 weeks)	550 Music/Epic 78345
3/29/97	4	11	● 12. **All By Myself** Sales #5 / Airplay #7 #1 Adult Contemporary hit (3 weeks)	550 Music/Epic 78529
2/28/98	**1** (2)	16	● 13. **My Heart Will Go On (Love Theme From "Titanic")** Airplay #1 (10) / Sales #1 (2) #1 Adult Contemporary hit (10 weeks); from the movie *Titanic* starring Leonardo DiCaprio; 1998 Grammy winner: Record of the Year	550 Music/Epic 78825
6/13/98	11 ᴬ	19	14. To Love You More #1 Adult Contemporary hit (8 weeks); from the album *Let's Talk About Love* on 550 Music/Epic 68861	album cut
12/5/98	**1** (6)	15	▲ 15. **I'm Your Angel** Sales #1 (6) / Airplay #22 **R. KELLY & CELINE DION** #1 Adult Contemporary hit (12 weeks)	Jive 42557
12/18/99+	6	22	16. **That's The Way It Is** Airplay #2 / Sales #62 #1 Adult Contemporary hit (1 week)	550 Music/Epic 79473
3/30/02	22	9	● 17. A New Day Has Come Sales #16 / Airplay #22 #1 Adult Contemporary hit (21 weeks)	Epic 79728

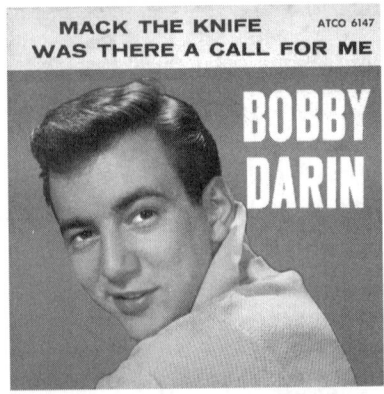

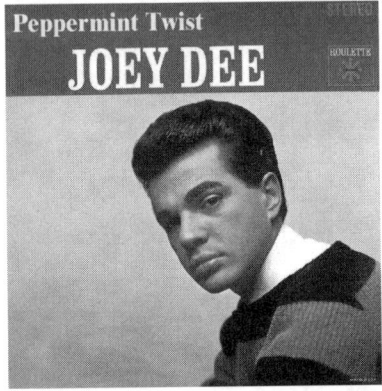

Dale and Grace earned a #1 hit with their Don & Dewey cover song "I'm Leaving It Up To You." After one more Top 10 hit, "Stop And Think It Over," the duo made a graceful exit from the pop charts.

Bobby Darin took "Mack The Knife" to a place where Louis Armstrong, Lawrence Welk, Ella Fitzgerald, and Frank Sinatra couldn't—the top of the Hot 100, and the 1959 Grammy Award for Record of the Year.

Taylor Dayne seemed tailor-made for the late 1980s. Her powerful voice and dance beats translated into seven straight Top 10 hits, including the #1 ballad "Love Will Lead You Back."

Joey Dee & the Starlighters recorded "Peppermint Twist" in tribute to the nation's hot new dance craze and New York's hip Peppermint Lounge. The song obviously had appeal beyond the Big Apple, twisting its way to #1.

John Denver wrote "Annie's Song" in just 10 minutes, but reaped a lifetime of benefits as it became his second #1 hit. Ironically, despite the title, the ode to his wife doesn't actually mention her name in the song.

Destiny's Child gave birth to successful solo projects after "Bootylicious" went to #1. Michelle Williams recorded a gospel album, Beyoncé became a solo star, and Kelly Rowland scared up interest with her role in the film *Freddy Vs. Jason.*

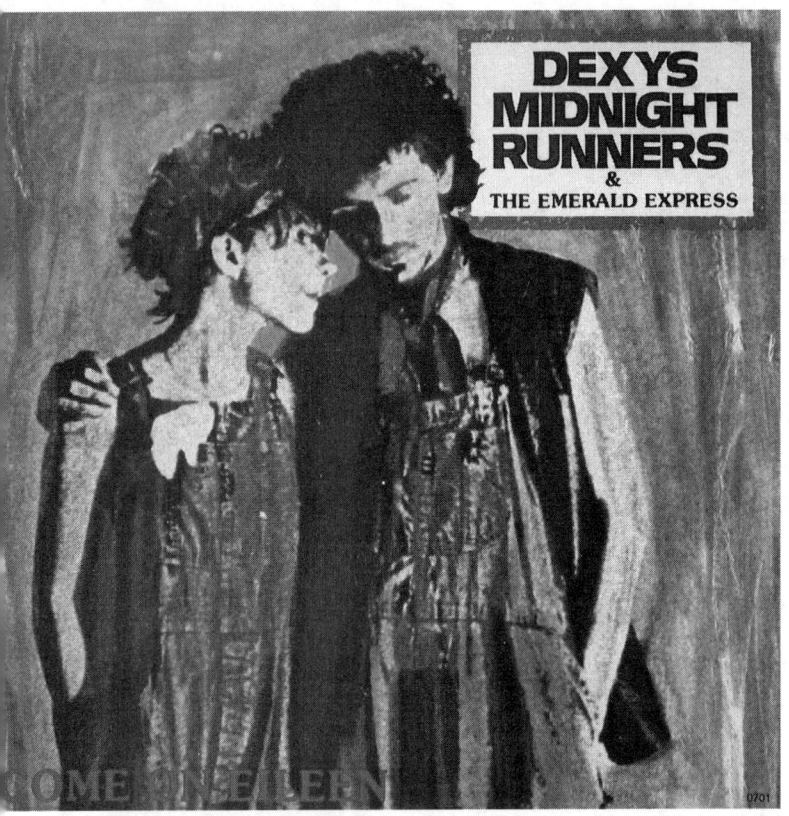

Dexy's Midnight Runners used the expression "too-rye-ay" as both their 1983 album title and a major part of their #1 hit "Come On Eileen." The song both replaced and was replaced by Michael Jackson for the #1 spot.

Neil Diamond songs turned into #1 hits for acts like the Monkees ("I'm A Believer") and UB40 ("Red Red Wine"), but he also found time to write songs for himself. "Cracklin' Rosie" was the first of his three #1 hits as a performer.

Dion married a woman named Sue, but maintained she was not the inspiration for his only #1 hit, "Runaround Sue." The song featured uncredited background vocals by the group the Del Satins.

Celine Dion took "The Power Of Love," a powerful song that had already been recorded by Air Supply, Laura Branigan, and Jennifer Rush, and showed its strength, which turned the song into the first of her four #1 hits.

The Doobie Brothers were one of the few rock bands that were able to successfully replace lead singers. Michael McDonald, who replaced Tom Johnston, was the band's lead voice on "What A Fool Believes," a #1 hit co-written with Kenny Loggins.

The Doors their chart-topping "Light My Fire" on *The Ed Sullivan Show*. Despite assurances they would, the line still made the television broadcast.

DATE	POS	WKS	ARTIST–RECORD TITLE	LABEL & NO.
			DIRE STRAITS	
			Rock group formed in London, England: brothers Mark (vocals, guitar) and David (guitar) Knopfler, with John Illsley (bass) and Pick Withers (drums). Alan Clark (keyboards) joined in 1982. Terry Williams replaced Withers in 1983. Guy Fletcher replaced David Knopfler by 1984.	
2/17/79	**4**	12	1. **Sultans Of Swing**	Warner 8736
8/10/85	**1** (3)	13	2. **Money For Nothing** Airplay #1 (3) / Sales #1 (2)	Warner 28950
			#1 Mainstream Rock hit (3 weeks); Sting (backing vocal, co-writer)	
11/16/85+	**7**	15	3. **Walk Of Life** Airplay #6 / Sales #8	Warner 28878
3/22/86	**19**	7	4. So Far Away Airplay #17 / Sales #26	Warner 28789
			DIRKSEN, Senator Everett McKinley	
			Born on 1/4/1896 in Pekin, Illinois. Died on 9/7/69 (age 73). U.S. senator from Illinois (1950-69).	
1/7/67	**29**	3	1. Gallant Men [S]	Capitol 5805
			John Cacavas (orch.); words written by CBS News Commentator, Charles Osgood	
			DIRT BAND, The—see NITTY GRITTY DIRT BAND	
			DIRTY VEGAS	
			Electronica trio from England: producers Ben Harris, Paul Harris and Steve Smith.	
6/8/02	**14**	9	1. Days Go By Airplay #15 / Sales #26	Capitol 77742
			tune featured in a 2002 Mitsubishi Eclipse TV ad campaign	
			DISCO TEX & HIS SEX-O-LETTES	
			Disco studio group assembled by producer Bob Crewe. Featuring lead voice Sir Monti Rock III (real name: Joseph Montanez).	
12/28/74+	**10**	9	1. **Get Dancin'**	Chelsea 3004
5/17/75	**23**	5	2. I Wanna Dance Wit' Choo (Doo Dat Dance), Part I	Chelsea 3015
			DISHWALLA	
			Pop-rock group from Santa Barbara, California: J.R. Richards (vocals), Rodney Browning (guitar), Scot Alexander (bass) and George Pendergast (drums).	
6/29/96	**15**	33	1. **Counting Blue Cars** Airplay #5 / Sales #41	A&M 1462
			#1 Modern Rock hit (1 week)	
			DIVINE	
			Female R&B vocal trio from New Jersey: Nikki Bratcher, Kia Thornton and Tonia Tash.	
9/12/98	**1** (1)	25	▲ 1. **Lately** Sales #1 (2) / Airplay #8	Red Ant 15316
4/10/99	**29**	3	2. One More Try Sales #15	Red Ant 15330
			DIVINYLS	
			Rock duo from Australia: Christina Amphlett (vocals) and Mark McEntee (guitar).	
3/30/91	**4**	12	1. **I Touch Myself** Sales #2 / Airplay #7	Virgin 98873

DATE	POS	WKS	ARTIST–RECORD TITLE	LABEL & NO.
			DIXIEBELLES, The	
			Black female trio from Memphis, Tennessee: Shirley Thomas, Mary Hunt and Mildred Pratcher.	
10/26/63	9	8	1. **(Down At) Papa Joe's**	Sound Stage 7 2507
2/8/64	15	5	2. Southtown, U.S.A.	Sound Stage 7 2517
			DIXIE CHICKS	
			Female country trio from Lubbock, Texas: sisters Emily Robison (guitar, banjo) and Martie Maguire (fiddle, mandolin), with Natalie Maines (lead vocals). Several radio stations banned their songs after Maines made a controversial statement about President Bush in March 2003.	
8/1/98	36	1	1. There's Your Trouble Sales #23	Monument 78899
			#1 Country hit (2 weeks)	
3/6/99	34	4	2. You Were Mine Airplay #20	album cut
			#1 Country hit (2 weeks); from the album *Wide Open Spaces* on Monument 68195	
10/2/99	39	3	3. Ready To Run Airplay #27	album cut
			from the movie *Runaway Bride* starring Julia Roberts and Richard Gere	
1/15/00	27	8	4. Cowboy Take Me Away Airplay #22	album cut
			#1 Country hit (3 weeks); above 2 from the album *Fly* on Monument 69678	
3/18/00	19	9	● 5. Goodbye Earl Sales #4 / Airplay #60	Monument 79352
12/9/00	31	7	6. Without You Airplay #27	album cut
			#1 Country hit (1 week)	
5/5/01	38	3	7. If I Fall You're Going Down With Me Airplay #31	album cut
			above 2 from the album *Fly* on Monument 69678	
8/3/02	7	7	8. **Long Time Gone** Sales #1 (5) / Airplay #28	Monument 79790
11/2/02+	7	22	9. **Landslide** Sales #3 / Airplay #8	Monument 79857
			#1 Adult Contemporary hit (7 weeks)	
2/22/03	25	5	10. Travelin' Soldier Airplay #23	album cut
			#1 Country hit (1 week); from the album *Home* on Monument 86840	
			DIXIE CUPS, The	
			Black female "girl group" from New Orleans, Louisiana: sisters Barbara Ann and Rosa Lee Hawkins, with their cousin Joan Marie Johnson.	
5/16/64	1 (3)	11	1. **Chapel Of Love**	Red Bird 001
8/1/64	12	7	2. People Say	Red Bird 006
11/21/64	39	1	3. You Should Have Seen The Way He Looked At Me	Red Bird 012
5/1/65	20	5	4. Iko Iko	Red Bird 024
			DIXIE FLYERS, The — see FRANKLIN, Aretha	
			D.J. JAZZY JEFF & THE FRESH PRINCE	
			Rap duo from Philadelphia, Pennsylvania: D.J. Jeff Townes (born on 1/22/65) and rapper/actor Will Smith (born on 9/25/68).	
6/18/88	12	10	● 1. Parents Just Don't Understand Sales #6 / Airplay #19	Jive 1099
8/20/88	15	9	2. A Nightmare On My Street Sales #10 / Airplay #22	Jive 1124
6/29/91	4	13	▲ 3. **Summertime** Sales #2 / Airplay #10	Jive 1465
			#1 R&B hit (1 week); samples "Summer Madness" by Kool & The Gang	
11/2/91	20	6	● 4. Ring My Bell Sales #9 / Airplay #54	Jive 42024

DATE	POS	WKS	ARTIST–RECORD TITLE	LABEL & NO.
8/21/93	**13**	13	● 5. Boom! Shake The Room Sales #3 / Airplay #51 **JAZZY JEFF & FRESH PRINCE** samples "Funky Worm" by the Ohio Players	Jive 42108
3/8/97	**30**	9	**DJ KOOL** Born John Bowman in Washington DC. Male rapper. ● 1. Let Me Clear My Throat Sales #21 **[L]** samples "Hollywood Swinging" by Kool & The Gang and "The 900 Number" by DJ Mark	American 17441
6/29/02	**8**	21	**DJ SAMMY** Born on 10/29/69 in Mallorca, Spain. Electronica dance producer. 1. Heaven Sales #2 / Airplay #12 **DJ SAMMY & YANOU featuring DO**	Robbins 72057
			D MOB — see DENNIS, Cathy	
4/11/98 5/23/98 4/8/00	**17** **39** **27**	11 1 11	**DMX** Born Earl Simmons on 12/18/70 in Yonkers, New York. Male rapper. DMX is short for Dark Man X. ● 1. Money, Power & Respect Sales #10 / Airplay #65 **THE LOX [Feat. DMX & Lil' Kim]** samples "New Beginning" by Dexter Wansel ● 2. Get At Me Dog Sales #28 **DMX (featuring Sheek of The Lox)** samples "Everything Good To You" by B.T. Express 3. Party Up (Up In Here) Airplay #22 / Sales #68	Bad Boy 79156 Def Jam 568862 Def Jam 562605
			D.N.A. — see VEGA, Suzanne	

6/1/59
1/18/60
	3
	25
		16
		8
			DOBKINS, Carl Jr.
			Born on 1/13/41 in Cincinnati, Ohio. Teen pop singer/songwriter.
			     1. My Heart Is An Open Book
			     2. Lucky Devil
				Decca 30803
				Decca 31020

12/11/76+	**27**	8	**DR. BUZZARD'S ORIGINAL SAVANNAH BAND** Big-band swing-disco band formed in Brooklyn, New York: brothers Stony (guitar) and Thomas "August Darnell" (bass) Browder, Cory Daye (vocals), Andy Hernandez (vibraphone), Don Armando Bonilla (percussion) and Mickey Sevilla (drums). 1. Whispering/Cherchez La Femme/Se Si Bon "Whispering" was a #1 hit for Paul Whiteman in 1920; "Se Si Bon" was a #8 hit for Eartha Kitt in 1953 as "C'est Si Bon"	RCA 10827
2/13/93 6/5/93	**2** (1) **8**	24 14	**DR. DRE** Born Andre Young on 2/18/65 in Compton, California. Rapper/producer. Co-founder of N.W.A. and World Class Wreckin' Cru. Produced several artists. Founded Death Row Records in 1992. Half-brother of Warren G. ▲ 1. Nuthin' But A "G" Thang Sales #1 (1) / Airplay #10 #1 R&B hit (2 weeks); samples "I Want'a Do Something Freaky To You" by Leon Haywood ● 2. Dre Day Sales #4 / Airplay #17 **DR. DRE (featuring Snoop Doggy Dogg)** (above 2)	Death Row 53819 Death Row 53827

DATE	POS	WKS	ARTIST–RECORD TITLE	LABEL & NO.
10/9/93	**34**	5	3. Let Me Ride *Sales #26 / Airplay #44* George Clinton (special guest); Val Young (female vocal); samples "Mothership Connection (Star Child)" by Parliament	Death Row 53839
3/25/95	**10**	18	● 4. **Keep Their Heads Ringin'** *Sales #6 / Airplay #31* from the movie *Friday* starring Ice Cube	Priority 53188
6/22/96	**6**	21	5. **California Love** *Sales #3 / Airplay #19* **2 PAC (featuring Dr. Dre and Roger Troutman)** samples "So Ruff So Tuff" by Roger and "Woman To Woman" by Joe Cocker	Death Row 854652
10/19/96	**1 (4)**	26	▲ 6. **No Diggity** *Sales #1 (6) / Airplay #9* **BLACKstreet (Featuring Dr. Dre)** #1 R&B hit (4 weeks); Queen Pen (female rap); samples "Grandma's Hands" by Bill Withers	Interscope 97007
2/12/00	**25**	12	7. Forgot About Dre *Airplay #20* **DR. DRE Featuring Eminem** from the album *2001* on Aftermath 90486	album cut
7/8/00	**23**	8	8. The Next Episode *Airplay #16 / Sales #62* **DR. DRE Featuring Snoop Dogg** Kurupt (backing vocal)	Aftermath 497333
			DR. HOOK	
			Pop-rock group formed in Union City, New Jersey: Ray Sawyer (vocals), Dennis Locorriere (vocals, guitar), George Cummings and Rick Elswit (guitars), William Francis (keyboards), Jance Garfat (bass) and Jay David (drums). John Wolters replaced David in 1973. Bob Henke replaced Cummings in 1976. Rod Smarr replaced Henke in 1980. Wolters died of cancer on 6/16/97 (age 52).	
5/6/72	**5**	10	● 1. **Sylvia's Mother**	Columbia 45562
2/3/73	**6**	11	● 2. **The Cover Of "Rolling Stone"** **[N]** **DR. HOOK AND THE MEDICINE SHOW** (above 2)	Columbia 45732
2/7/76	**6**	14	● 3. **Only Sixteen**	Capitol 4171
7/31/76	**11**	14	4. A Little Bit More	Capitol 4280
10/14/78+	**6**	16	● 5. **Sharing The Night Together**	Capitol 4621
6/2/79	**6**	16	● 6. **When You're In Love With A Beautiful Woman**	Capitol 4705
11/3/79+	**12**	14	7. Better Love Next Time	Capitol 4785
3/15/80	**5**	15	● 8. **Sexy Eyes**	Capitol 4831
11/29/80	**34**	6	9. Girls Can Get It	Casablanca 2314
3/27/82	**25**	6	10. Baby Makes Her Blue Jeans Talk	Casablanca 2347
			DR. JOHN	
			Born Malcolm Rebennack on 11/20/42 in New Orleans, Louisiana. Swamp- rock singer/pianist.	
5/12/73	**9**	13	1. **Right Place Wrong Time**	Atco 6914
			DOGGETT, Bill	
			Born on 2/16/16 in Philadelphia, Pennsylvania. Died on 11/13/96 (age 80). R&B organist/pianist.	
8/25/56	**2 (3)**	22	● 1. **Honky Tonk (Parts 1 & 2)** *Juke Box #2 / Best Seller #2 / Top 100 #2 / Jockey #6* **[I]** #1 R&B hit (13 weeks); Clifford Scott (sax)	King 4950
12/15/56+	**26**	5	2. Slow Walk *Top 100 #26* **[I]**	King 5000
12/2/57	**35**	1	3. Soft *Best Seller #35 / Top 100 #51* **[I]** #3 R&B hit for Tiny Bradshaw in 1953	King 5080

DATE	POS	WKS	ARTIST–RECORD TITLE	LABEL & NO.
			DOGG POUND, Tha — see MACK 10	
			DOG'S EYE VIEW	
			Rock group from Manhattan, New York: Peter Stuart (vocals, guitar), Oren Bloedow (guitar), John Abbey (bass) and Alan Bezozi (drums).	
4/6/96	14 ᴬ	20	1. Everything Falls Apart from the album *Happy Nowhere* on Columbia 66882	album cut
			DOLBY, Thomas	
			Born Thomas Morgan Dolby Robertson on 10/14/58 in Cairo, Egypt (British parents); raised in London, England. New-wave singer/songwriter/keyboardist. Married actress Kathleen Beller (played "Kirby Colby" on TV's *Dynasty*) in 1988.	
3/19/83	5	15	1. **She Blinded Me With Science**	Capitol 5204
			DOMINO	
			Born Shawn Ivy in 1972 in St. Louis, Missouri; raised in Long Beach, California. Male rapper.	
12/18/93+	7	13	● 1. **Getto Jam** Sales #3 / Airplay #27	OutBurst 77298
5/7/94	27	8	2. Sweet Potatoe Pie Sales #18 / Airplay #40	OutBurst 77350
			DOMINO, Fats	
			Born Antoine Domino on 2/26/28 in New Orleans, Louisiana. Legendary R&B singer/songwriter/pianist. Heavily influenced by Fats Waller and Albert Ammons. Joined the Dave Bartholomew band (mid-1940s). Signed to Imperial record label in 1949. Nicknamed "The Fat Man." Heard on many sessions cut by other R&B artists. In the movies *Shake, Rattle And Rock!*, *Jamboree!*, *The Big Beat* and *The Girl Can't Help It*. Inducted into the Rock and Roll Hall of Fame in 1986. Won Grammy's Hall of Fame and Lifetime Achievement Awards in 1987.	
7/16/55	10	13	● 1. **Ain't It A Shame** Juke Box #10 / Best Seller #16 / Top 100 #86 #1 R&B hit (11 weeks)	Imperial 5348
4/7/56	35	1	● 2. Bo Weevil Top 100 #35	Imperial 5375
5/5/56	3	18	● 3. **I'm In Love Again /** Juke Box #3 / Best Seller #4 / Top 100 #5 / Jockey #6 #1 R&B hit (9 weeks)	
5/5/56	19	13	4. **My Blue Heaven** Juke Box #19 / Top 100 #21 / Best Seller: flip #1 hit for both Gene Austin and Paul Whiteman in 1927	Imperial 5386
7/28/56	14	8	5. When My Dreamboat Comes Home Juke Box #14 / Best Seller #21 / Top 100 #22 #3 hit for Guy Lombardo in 1937	Imperial 5396
10/13/56+	2 (3)	21	● 6. **Blueberry Hill** Juke Box #2 / Best Seller #3 / Top 100 #4 / Jockey #7 #1 R&B hit (11 weeks); #2 hit for Glenn Miller in 1940	Imperial 5407
1/12/57	5	12	● 7. **Blue Monday** Juke Box #5 / Best Seller #9 / Top 100 #9 / Jockey #9 #1 R&B hit (8 weeks); from the movie *The Girl Can't Help It* starring Jayne Mansfield	Imperial 5417
3/9/57	4	14	● 8. **I'm Walkin'** Jockey #4 / Juke Box #5 / Best Seller #5 / Top 100 #5 #1 R&B hit (6 weeks)	Imperial 5428
6/24/57	6	6	● 9. **It's You I Love /** Best Seller #6 / Top 100 #22	
5/27/57	8	13	10. **Valley Of Tears** Best Seller #8 / Top 100 #13 / Jockey #13	Imperial 5442
8/26/57	29	2	11. When I See You Best Seller #29 / Top 100 #36 Ann Cole (female vocal)	Imperial 5454

DATE	POS	WKS	ARTIST–RECORD TITLE	LABEL & NO.
10/21/57	23	6	● 12. Wait And See Best Seller #23 / Top 100 #27 from the movie *Jamboree!* starring Kay Medford	Imperial 5467
12/23/57+	26	9	13. The Big Beat / Best Seller #26 / Top 100 #36 title song from the movie starring William Reynolds	
12/30/57+	32	8	14. I Want You To Know Best Seller #32 / Top 100 #48	Imperial 5477
5/5/58	22	7	15. Sick And Tired Best Seller #22 / Top 100 #30 first recorded by Chris Kenner in 1957	Imperial 5515
12/1/58+	6	12	● 16. **Whole Lotta Loving**	Imperial 5553
5/25/59	16	7	17. I'm Ready	Imperial 5585
8/10/59	8	10	18. **I Want To Walk You Home /** #1 R&B hit (1 week)	
8/10/59	17	9	19. I'm Gonna Be A Wheel Some Day first recorded by Bobby Mitchell in 1957	Imperial 5606
11/9/59	8	10	20. **Be My Guest /**	
11/9/59	33	2	21. I've Been Around	Imperial 5629
2/15/60	25	5	22. Country Boy	Imperial 5645
7/4/60	6	11	23. **Walking To New Orleans /**	
7/18/60	21	7	24. Don't Come Knockin'	Imperial 5675
9/12/60	15	9	25. Three Nights A Week	Imperial 5687
11/14/60	14	11	26. My Girl Josephine /	
12/5/60	38	3	27. Natural Born Lover	Imperial 5704
2/6/61	22	6	28. What A Price /	
2/13/61	33	4	29. Ain't That Just Like A Woman #17 hit for Louis Jordan in 1946	Imperial 5723
4/3/61	32	2	30. Fell In Love On Monday /	
4/17/61	32	2	31. Shu Rah	Imperial 5734
6/19/61	23	5	32. It Keeps Rainin'	Imperial 5753
7/31/61	15	6	33. Let The Four Winds Blow	Imperial 5764
10/23/61	22	4	34. What A Party	Imperial 5779
12/25/61+	30	3	35. Jambalaya (On The Bayou) #1 Country hit for Hank Williams in 1952	Imperial 5796
3/17/62	22	5	36. You Win Again #10 Country hit for Hank Williams in 1952	Imperial 5816
10/26/63	35	2	37. Red Sails In The Sunset #1 hit for both Bing Crosby and Guy Lombardo in 1935	ABC-Paramount 10484
			DOMINOES — see WARD, Billy	
			DONALDS, Andru	
			Born in Kingston, Jamaica. Male reggae singer.	
2/4/95	38	2	1. Mishale Airplay #49	Metro Blue 58256
			DONALDSON, Bo, And The Heywoods	
			Pop group from Cincinnati, Ohio: Bo Donaldson (keyboards), Mike Gibbons (vocals), Scott Baker (guitar), Gary Coveyou (reeds), Rick Joswick (percussion), David Krock (bass) and Nicky Brunetti (drums).	
5/11/74	1 (2)	12	● 1. **Billy, Don't Be A Hero**	ABC 11435
8/24/74	15	7	2. Who Do You Think You Are	ABC 12006
12/14/74	39	1	3. The Heartbreak Kid	ABC 12039

DATE	POS	WKS	ARTIST–RECORD TITLE	LABEL & NO.
			DON & JUAN	
			R&B vocal duo from Brooklyn, New York: Roland "Don" Trone and Claude "Juan" Johnson. Don died in May 1982 (age 45). Juan died on 10/31/2002 (age 67).	
2/24/62	**7**	9	1. **What's Your Name**	Big Top 3079
			DONEGAN, Lonnie, And His Skiffle Group	
			Born Anthony Donegan on 4/29/31 in Glasgow, Scotland. Died on 11/3/2002 (age 71). Known as England's "King of Skiffle." Member of Chris Barber's Jazz Band in 1954.	
3/31/56	**8**	11	1. **Rock Island Line** Best Seller #8 / Top 100 #10 / Jockey #10 / Juke Box #13 **THE LONNIE DONEGAN Skiffle Group**	London 1650
8/14/61	**5**	9	2. **Does Your Chewing Gum Lose It's Flavor (On The Bedpost Over Night)** [N] #9 hit for Ernest Hare & Billy Jones in 1924	Dot 15911
			DONNER, Ral	
			Born Ralph Donner on 2/10/43 in Chicago, Illinois. Died of cancer on 4/6/84 (age 41). Pop singer similar in style to Elvis Presley. Narrator for the movie *This Is Elvis*.	
5/1/61	**19**	8	1. **Girl Of My Best Friend** **RAL DONNER & The Starfires** first recorded by Elvis Presley in 1960	Gone 5102
7/24/61	**4**	9	2. **You Don't Know What You've Got (Until You Lose Lose It)**	Gone 5108
11/13/61	**39**	1	3. Please Don't Go	Gone 5114
2/3/62	**18**	4	4. She's Everything (I Wanted You To Be)	Gone 5121
			DONNIE and THE DREAMERS	
			Italian-American doo-wop group from the Bronx, New York: Louis "Donnie" Burgio, Andy Catalano, Frank Furstaci and Pete Vecchiarelli.	
6/12/61	**35**	3	1. **Count Every Star** #4 hit for Ray Anthony in 1950	Whale 500
			DONOVAN	
			Born Donovan Leitch on 5/10/46 in Glasgow, Scotland; raised in London, England. Pop-rock-folk singer/songwriter/guitarist. Appeared in the movies *The Pied Piper Of Hamlin* and *Brother Sun, Sister Moon*. Father of actress Ione Skye and actor Donovan Leitch, Jr.	
6/12/65	**23**	5	1. Catch The Wind	Hickory 1309
8/13/66	**1** (1)	10	2. **Sunshine Superman** Jimmy Page (guitar)	Epic 10045
11/19/66	**2** (3)	10	● 3. **Mellow Yellow** Paul McCartney (whispers)	Epic 10098
2/25/67	**19**	5	4. Epistle To Dippy	Epic 10127
8/26/67	**11**	6	5. There Is A Mountain	Epic 10212
12/9/67	**23**	5	6. Wear Your Love Like Heaven	Epic 10253
3/30/68	**26**	5	7. Jennifer Juniper	Epic 10300
6/29/68	**5**	10	8. **Hurdy Gurdy Man**	Epic 10345
10/19/68	**33**	4	9. Lalena	Epic 10393

DATE	POS	WKS	ARTIST–RECORD TITLE	LABEL & NO.
4/26/69	7	10	10. **Atlantis /** Atlantis: legendary sunken continent in the Atlantic Ocean	
3/1/69	35	2	11. To Susan On The West Coast Waiting	Epic 10434
8/30/69	36	2	12. Goo Goo Barabajagal (Love Is Hot) **DONOVAN (With The Jeff Beck Group)**	Epic 10510

DOOBIE BROTHERS, The

Rock group formed in San Jose, California: Patrick Simmons (vocals, guitar; see #17 below), Tom Johnston (vocals, guitar; see #14 below), Tiran Porter (bass), and John Hartman and Mike Hossack (drums). Keith Knudsen replaced Hossack in 1973. Jeff "Skunk" Baxter (guitar) joined in 1974. Michael McDonald (vocals, keyboards) joined in 1975. Johnston left in 1978. Hartman and Baxter left in 1979; John McFee (guitar), Cornelius Bumpus (sax) and Chet McCracken (drums) joined. Disbanded in 1983. Re-formed in 1988 with Simmons, Johnston, Porter, Hossack and Bobby LaKind (percussion). LaKind died of cancer on 12/24/92 (age 47). Bumpus died of a heart attack on 2/3/2004 (age 58).

DATE	POS	WKS	ARTIST–RECORD TITLE	LABEL & NO.
9/23/72	11	10	1. Listen To The Music	Warner 7619
2/17/73	35	2	2. Jesus Is Just Alright	Warner 7661
5/26/73	8	11	3. **Long Train Runnin'**	Warner 7698
9/15/73	15	8	4. China Grove	Warner 7728
6/1/74	32	2	5. Another Park, Another Sunday	Warner 7795
1/11/75	1 (1)	12	● 6. **Black Water**	Warner 8062
5/17/75	11	9	7. Take Me In Your Arms (Rock Me)	Warner 8092
8/30/75	40	1	8. Sweet Maxine	Warner 8126
5/15/76	13	8	9. Takin' It To The Streets	Warner 8196
1/22/77	37	2	10. It Keeps You Runnin'	Warner 8282
2/10/79	1 (1)	14	● 11. **What A Fool Believes** written by Kenny Loggins and Michael McDonald; 1979 Grammy winner: Record of the Year	Warner 8725
5/19/79	14	9	12. Minute By Minute	Warner 8828
9/15/79	25	6	13. Dependin' On You	Warner 49029
1/12/80	34	2	14. Savannah Nights **TOM JOHNSTON**	Warner 49096
9/6/80	5	11	15. **Real Love**	Warner 49503
12/6/80+	24	7	16. One Step Closer	Warner 49622
4/16/83	30	5	17. So Wrong **PATRICK SIMMONS**	Elektra 69839
6/3/89	9	9	18. **The Doctor** Sales #9 / Airplay #11 #1 Mainstream Rock hit (3 weeks)	Capitol 44376

DO OR DIE

Male rap trio from Chicago, Illinois: Dennis Rounk ("AK"), Anthony Round ("N.A.R.D." - which stands for Niggas Ain't Ready to Die) and Darnell Smith ("Belo Zero").

DATE	POS	WKS	ARTIST–RECORD TITLE	LABEL & NO.
9/7/96	22	13	● 1. Po Pimp Sales #10 **DO OR DIE featuring Twista**	Rap-A-Lot 38559

DATE	POS	WKS	ARTIST–RECORD TITLE	LABEL & NO.
			DOORS, The	
			Rock group formed in Los Angeles, California: Jim Morrison (vocals), Robby Krieger (guitar), Ray Manzarek (keyboards) and John Densmore (drums). Controversial onstage performances by Morrison caused several arrests and cancellations. Morrison left group on 12/12/70; died of heart failure in Paris on 7/31/71 (age 27). Group disbanded in 1973. 1991 movie based on group's career, *The Doors*, starred Val Kilmer as Morrison. Group inducted into the Rock and Roll Hall of Fame in 1993.	
6/24/67	**1** (3)	14	● 1. **Light My Fire**	Elektra 45615
10/7/67	**12**	7	2. People Are Strange	Elektra 45621
12/30/67+	**25**	4	3. Love Me Two Times	Elektra 45624
5/4/68	**39**	3	4. The Unknown Soldier	Elektra 45628
7/13/68	**1** (2)	11	● 5. **Hello, I Love You**	Elektra 45635
1/4/69	**3**	12	● 6. **Touch Me**	Elektra 45646
4/24/71	**11**	9	7. Love Her Madly	Elektra 45726
7/24/71	**14**	9	8. Riders On The Storm	Elektra 45738
			DORE, Charlie	
			Born in 1956 in London, England. Female singer/songwriter.	
3/22/80	**13**	10	1. Pilot Of The Airwaves	Island 49166
			DORMAN, Harold	
			Born on 12/23/26 in Drew, Mississippi; raised in Sledge, Mississippi. Died on 10/8/88 (age 61). Rock and roll singer.	
4/18/60	**21**	9	1. Mountain Of Love	Rita 1003
			DORSEY, Jimmy, Orchestra	
			Born on 2/29/04 in Shenandoah, Pennsylvania. Died of cancer on 6/12/57 (age 53). Esteemed alto sax and clarinet soloist/bandleader. Brother of Tommy Dorsey.	
4/13/57	**2** (4)	26	● 1. **So Rare** Jockey #2 / Top 100 #2 / Best Seller #3 / Juke Box #6 Jimmy Dorsey (sax); #1 hit for Guy Lombardo in 1937	Fraternity 755
9/9/57	**21**	2	2. June Night Jockey #21 / Best Seller #27 / Top 100 #39 cut 5 days after Jimmy's death, under the direction of Lee Castle; Dick Stabile (sax); #2 hit for Ted Lewis in 1924; Arthur Malvin Singers (vocals, above 2)	Fraternity 777
			DORSEY, Lee	
			Born Irving Lee Dorsey on 12/24/24 in New Orleans, Louisiana. Died of emphysema on 12/1/86 (age 61). R&B singer.	
9/25/61	**7**	10	1. **Ya Ya** #1 R&B hit (1 week)	Fury 1053
1/20/62	**27**	5	2. Do-Re-Mi	Fury 1056
7/31/65	**28**	4	3. Ride Your Pony	Amy 927
8/13/66	**8**	9	4. **Working In The Coal Mine**	Amy 958
11/19/66	**23**	5	5. Holy Cow	Amy 965

DATE	POS	WKS	ARTIST–RECORD TITLE	LABEL & NO.
9/15/58	7	14	**DORSEY, Tommy, Orchestra** Born on 11/19/05 in Mahanoy Plane, Pennsylvania. Choked to death on 11/26/56 (age 51). Esteemed trombonist/band leader. Brother of Jimmy Dorsey. Warren Covington fronted band after Tommy's death. ● 1. **Tea For Two Cha Cha** Hot 100 #7 / Best Seller #8 **[I]** **THE TOMMY DORSEY ORCHESTRA STARRING WARREN COVINGTON** "Tea For Two" was a #1 hit for Marion Harris in 1925	Decca 30704
8/9/86	16	9	**DOUBLE** Pop duo from Switzerland: Felix Haug (vocals, guitar) and Kurt Maloo (keyboards). 1. The Captain Of Her Heart Sales #10 / Airplay #19	A&M 2838
11/9/74	1 (2)	12	**DOUGLAS, Carl** Born in 1942 in Jamaica; raised in California. Disco singer. ● 1. **Kung Fu Fighting** #1 R&B hit (1 week)	20th Century 2140
12/21/74+	11	11	**DOUGLAS, Carol** Born Carol Strickland on 4/7/48 in Brooklyn, New York. Disco singer. 1. Doctor's Orders	Midland Int'l. 10113
1/8/66	6	7	**DOUGLAS, Mike** Born Michael Dowd on 8/11/25 in Chicago, Illinois. Singer with Kay Kyser's band from 1945-50. Hosted own TV talk show from 1961-80. 1. **The Men In My Little Girl's Life**	Epic 9876
			DOVE, Ronnie Born on 9/7/35 in Herndon, Virginia; raised in Baltimore, Maryland. Adult Contemporary singer.	
9/26/64	40	1	1. Say You	Diamond 167
11/14/64	14	7	2. Right Or Wrong	Diamond 173
4/10/65	14	7	3. One Kiss For Old Times' Sake	Diamond 179
6/26/65	16	6	4. A Little Bit Of Heaven	Diamond 184
9/18/65	21	5	5. I'll Make All Your Dreams Come True	Diamond 188
11/27/65	25	4	6. Kiss Away	Diamond 191
2/5/66	18	7	7. When Liking Turns To Loving	Diamond 195
5/7/66	20	5	8. Let's Start All Over Again	Diamond 198
7/9/66	27	4	9. Happy Summer Days	Diamond 205
9/24/66	22	5	10. I Really Don't Want To Know #11 hit for Les Paul & Mary Ford in 1954	Diamond 208
12/10/66	18	6	11. Cry #1 hit for Johnnie Ray in 1951	Diamond 214
9/18/61	2 (2)	14	**DOVELLS, The** Rock and roll vocal group from Philadelphia, Pennsylvania: Len Barry, Arnie Silver, Jerry Summers, Mike Dennis and Danny Brooks (left in 1962). 1. **Bristol Stomp** Bristol: town near Philadelphia	Parkway 827

DATE	POS	WKS	ARTIST–RECORD TITLE	LABEL & NO.
3/3/62	37	2	2. (Do The New) Continental	Parkway 833
6/23/62	27	5	3. Bristol Twistin' Annie	Parkway 838
9/15/62	25	7	4. Hully Gully Baby	Parkway 845
5/11/63	3	11	5. **You Can't Sit Down**	Parkway 867

DOWELL, Joe

Born on 1/23/40 in Bloomington, Indiana. Pop singer.

DATE	POS	WKS	ARTIST–RECORD TITLE	LABEL & NO.
7/17/61	1 (1)	12	1. **Wooden Heart** #1 Adult Contemporary hit (3 weeks); first recorded by Elvis Presley in 1960	Smash 1708
7/28/62	23	4	2. Little Red Rented Rowboat Stephen Scott Singers (backing vocals); Jerry Kennedy (orch.)	Smash 1759

DOZIER, Lamont

Born on 6/16/41 in Detroit, Michigan. R&B singer/songwriter/producer. With the brothers Brian and Eddie Holland in highly successful songwriting/ production team for Motown. Trio left Motown in 1968 and formed own Invictus/Hot Wax label. Trio inducted into the Rock and Roll Hall of Fame in 1990.

DATE	POS	WKS	ARTIST–RECORD TITLE	LABEL & NO.
2/16/74	15	9	1. Trying To Hold On To My Woman	ABC 11407
7/6/74	26	6	2. Fish Ain't Bitin'	ABC 11438

DRAKE, Charlie

Born Charles Springall on 6/19/25 in London, England. Actor/comedian.

DATE	POS	WKS	ARTIST–RECORD TITLE	LABEL & NO.
2/17/62	21	6	1. My Boomerang Won't Come Back　　　　**[N]**	United Artists 398

DRAKE, Pete, And His Talking Steel Guitar

Born Roddis Franklin Drake on 10/8/32 in Atlanta, Georgia. Died on 7/29/88 (age 55). Session steel guitarist.

DATE	POS	WKS	ARTIST–RECORD TITLE	LABEL & NO.
4/11/64	25	5	1. Forever	Smash 1867

DRAMATICS, The

R&B vocal group from Detroit, Michigan: Ron Banks, William Howard, Larry Demps, Willie Ford and Elbert Wilkins.

DATE	POS	WKS	ARTIST–RECORD TITLE	LABEL & NO.
7/31/71	9	11	1. **Whatcha See Is Whatcha Get**	Volt 4058
3/4/72	5	11	2. **In The Rain** #1 R&B hit (4 weeks)	Volt 4075

DRAPER, Rusty

Born Farrell Draper on 1/25/25 in Kirksville, Missouri. Died of pneumonia on 3/28/2003 (age 80). Male singer/songwriter/guitarist. Known as "Ol' Redhead."

DATE	POS	WKS	ARTIST–RECORD TITLE	LABEL & NO.
8/20/55	18	4	1. Seventeen　　　　　　　Best Seller #18 / Top 100 #88	Mercury 70651
10/1/55	3	16	2. **The Shifting, Whispering Sands** Juke Box #3 / Best Seller #6 / Top 100 #7 / Jockey #14	Mercury 70696
12/31/55+	11	12	3. Are You Satisfied?　　Best Seller #11 / Juke Box #11 / Top 100 #12	Mercury 70757
9/22/56	20	8	4. In The Middle Of The House　Top 100 #20 / Jockey #24　**[N]** Jack Halloran Singers (backing vocals, above 3); David Carroll (orch., all of above)	Mercury 70921
5/27/57	6	12	5. **Freight Train**　　　Jockey #6 / Top 100 #11 / Best Seller #17 Dick Noel Singers (backing vocals); Carl Stevens (orch.); folk song composed in the early 1900s	Mercury 71102

DATE	POS	WKS	ARTIST–RECORD TITLE	LABEL & NO.
			DREAM	
			Female pop vocal group from Los Angeles, California: Holly Arnstein, Melissa Schuman, Ashley Poole and Diana Ortiz.	
11/11/00	**2** (2)	21	● 1. **He Loves U Not** Sales #1 (4) / Airplay #7	Bad Boy 79338
6/9/01	**39**	1	2. This Is Me Sales #4 / Airplay #44	Bad Boy 79402
			Kain (rap); samples "Take Me To The Mardi Gras" by Paul Simon; produced by Puff Daddy	
			DREAM ACADEMY, The	
			Pop-rock trio from England: Nick Laird-Clowes (guitar, vocals), Gilbert Gabriel (keyboards) and Kate St. John (oboe, vocals).	
1/11/86	**7**	11	1. **Life In A Northern Town** Airplay #4 / Sales #7	Warner 28841
5/31/86	**36**	3	2. The Love Parade Airplay #32	Reprise 28750
			DREAMLOVERS, The	
			R&B vocal group from Philadelphia, Pennsylvania: Tommy Ricks, Cleveland Hammock, Morris Gardner, and brothers Cliff and Ray Dunn. Backup vocal group for most of Chubby Checker's hits.	
8/28/61	**10**	6	1. **When We Get Married**	Heritage 102
			DREAM WEAVERS, The	
			Adult Contemporary vocal group from Miami, Florida: Wade Buff, Gene Adkinson, Lee Turner, Eddie Newson, Sally Sanborn, Mary Carr and Mary Rude.	
11/12/55+	**7**	21	1. **It's Almost Tomorrow** Juke Box #7 / Best Seller #8 / Top 100 #8 / Jockey #10	Decca 29683
			Jack Pleis (orch.)	
5/19/56	**33**	1	2. A Little Love Can Go A Long, Long Way Top 100 #33	Decca 29905
			THE DREAM WEAVERS Featuring Wade Buff	
			Sy Oliver (orch.); from the Goodyear TV Playhouse Production *Joey*	
			DRIFTERS, The	
			R&B vocal group formed in New York: Ben E. King, Charlie Thomas, Doc Green and Elsbearry Hobbs, with Reggie Kimber (guitar). Rudy Lewis replaced King in 1961. Lewis died of a heart attack on 5/20/64 (age 27); replaced by Johnny Moore. Hobbs died on 5/31/96 (age 60). Moore died of respiratory failure on 12/30/98 (age 64). Group inducted into the Rock and Roll Hall of Fame in 1988.	
6/29/59	**2** (1)	14	● 1. **There Goes My Baby** #1 R&B hit (1 week)	Atlantic 2025
11/2/59	**15**	9	● 2. Dance With Me /	
11/23/59	**33**	5	3. (If You Cry) True Love, True Love	Atlantic 2040
3/14/60	**16**	6	4. This Magic Moment	Atlantic 2050
9/19/60	**1** (3)	14	● 5. **Save The Last Dance For Me** #1 R&B hit (1 week)	Atlantic 2071
12/31/60+	**17**	7	6. I Count The Tears	Atlantic 2087
4/10/61	**32**	6	7. Some Kind Of Wonderful	Atlantic 2096
6/26/61	**14**	8	8. Please Stay	Atlantic 2105
9/25/61	**16**	9	9. Sweets For My Sweet	Atlantic 2117
3/24/62	**28**	4	10. When My Little Girl Is Smiling	Atlantic 2134
12/29/62+	**5**	11	11. **Up On The Roof**	Atlantic 2162
4/6/63	**9**	8	12. **On Broadway**	Atlantic 2182

DATE	POS	WKS	ARTIST–RECORD TITLE	LABEL & NO.
10/5/63	25	5	13. I'll Take You Home	Atlantic 2201
7/11/64	4	12	14. **Under The Boardwalk**	Atlantic 2237
10/10/64	33	5	15. I've Got Sand In My Shoes	Atlantic 2253
11/28/64	18	7	16. Saturday Night At The Movies	Atlantic 2260

D.R.S.

Male R&B vocal group from Sacramento, California: Endo, Pic, Jail Bait, Deuce Deuce and Blunt. D.R.S.: Dirty Rotten Scoundrels.

10/30/93	4	15	▲ 1. **Gangsta Lean** Sales #2 / Airplay #13 #1 R&B hit (6 weeks)	Capitol 44958

DRU HILL

Male R&B vocal group from Baltimore, Maryland: Mark "Sisqo" Andrews, James "Woody" Green, Tamir "Nokio" Ruffin and Larry "Jazz" Anthony. Green left in March 1999. Group named after Druid Hill Park in Baltimore.

10/12/96	18	15	● 1. **Tell Me** Sales #10 / Airplay #62 from the movie *Eddie* starring Whoopi Goldberg	Island 854660
1/25/97	4	21	▲ 2. **In My Bed** Sales #3 / Airplay #36 #1 R&B hit (3 weeks)	Island 854854
8/9/97	7	12	● 3. **Never Make A Promise** Sales #3 / Airplay #61 #1 R&B hit (4 weeks)	Island 572082
12/13/97+	13	13	● 4. **We're Not Making Love No More** Sales #8 Babyface (backing vocal, writer and producer); from the movie *Soul Food* starring Vanessa Williams	LaFace 24295
10/10/98	3	17	● 5. **How Deep Is Your Love** Sales #1 (2) / Airplay #16 **DRU HILL Featuring REDMAN** #1 R&B hit (3 weeks)	Island 572424
12/19/98+	21	15	6. These Are The Times Airplay #12 / Sales #15 produced by Babyface	Island 572588
5/22/99	1 (1)	14	● 7. **Wild Wild West** Sales #1 (1) / Airplay #2 **WILL SMITH featuring Dru Hill and Kool Mo Dee** Sales #1(1) / Airplay #2; samples "Wild, Wild West" by Kool Moe Dee and "I Wish" by Stevie Wonder; title song from the movie starring Will Smith and Kevin Kline	Overbrook 79157
12/21/02+	25	9	8. I Should Be... Airplay #22 from the album *Dru World Order* on Def Soul 063377	album cut

DRUSKY, Roy

Born on 6/22/30 in Atlanta, Georgia. Country singer/guitarist.

6/26/61	35	1	1. Three Hearts In A Tangle	Decca 31193

D12

Rap group from Detroit, Michigan: Marshall Mathers ("Eminem"), DeShaun Holton ("Proof"), Denine Porter ("Kon Artis"), Rufus Johnson ("Bizzare"), Oscar Moore ("Swift") and Von Carlisle ("Kuniva"). D-12 is short for Dirty Dozen.

7/14/01	19	9	1. Purple Hills Sales #3 / Airplay #40	Shady 497583

DUALS

Rock and roll instrumental duo from Los Angeles, California: Henry Bellinger and Johnny Lageman.

10/2/61	25	6	1. Stick Shift [I]	Sue 745

DATE	POS	WKS	ARTIST–RECORD TITLE	LABEL & NO.
			DUBS, The	
			R&B vocal group from Harlem, New York: Richard Blandon, Cleveland Still, Bill Carlyle, Tommy Grate and Jim Miller. Blandon died on 12/20/91 (age 57).	
11/18/57	**23**	8	1. Could This Be Magic Best Seller #23 / Top 100 #24	Gone 5011
			DUDLEY, Dave	
			Born David Pedruska on 5/3/28 in Spencer, Wisconsin. Died of a heart attack on 12/22/2003 (age 75). Country singer/guitarist.	
7/20/63	**32**	4	1. Six Days On The Road	Golden Wing 3020
			DUICE	
			Male rap duo: Ira "LA Sno" Brown (from California) and Anthony "Creo-D" Darlington (from Barbados).	
4/10/93	**12**	26	▲² 1. Dazzey Duks Sales #8 / Airplay #18	TMR/Bellmark 72501
			title inspired by the short shorts worn by Daisy Duke of TV's *The Dukes Of Hazzard*	
			DUKE, George — see CLARKE, Stanley	
			DUKE, Patty	
			Born Anna Marie Duke on 12/14/46 in Elmhurst, New York. Movie and TV actress. Married to actor John Astin from 1972-85.	
7/17/65	**8**	8	1. **Don't Just Stand There**	United Artists 875
10/30/65	**22**	4	2. Say Something Funny	United Artists 915
			DULFER, Candy — see STEWART, David A.	
			DUNDAS, David	
			Born on 4/2/45 in Oxford, Oxfordshire, England. Pop singer/actor/commercial jingle writer.	
11/27/76+	**17**	13	1. Jeans On	Chrysalis 2094
			originally a jingle in England for Brutus Jeans	
			DUPREE, Robbie	
			Born Robert Dupuis on 12/23/46 in Brooklyn, New York. Soft-rock singer/songwriter.	
5/3/80	**6**	15	1. **Steal Away**	Elektra 46621
8/9/80	**15**	12	2. Hot Rod Hearts	Elektra 47005
			DUPREES, The	
			Italian-American doo-wop group from Jersey City, New Jersey: Joey Vann, Mike Arnone, Tom Bialablow, Joe Santollo and John Salvato. Santollo died of a heart attack on 6/3/81 (age 37). Vann died on 2/28/84 (age 40).	
8/25/62	**7**	9	1. **You Belong To Me**	Coed 569
			#1 hit for Jo Stafford in 1952	
11/10/62	**13**	6	2. My Own True Love	Coed 571
			melody is "Tara's Theme" from the movie *Gone With The Wind* starring Clark Gable and Vivien Leigh	
9/14/63	**37**	3	3. Why Don't You Believe Me	Coed 584
			#1 hit for Joni James in 1952	
11/30/63	**18**	6	4. Have You Heard	Coed 585
			#4 hit for Joni James in 1953	

DATE	POS	WKS	ARTIST–RECORD TITLE	LABEL & NO.
			DUPRI, Jermaine	
			Born on 9/23/72 in Asheville, North Carolina; raised in Atlanta, Georgia. Rapper/prolific producer.	
3/7/98	29	9	● 1. The Party Continues Sales #16 **JD & DA BRAT** Usher (backing vocal); samples "She's Strange" by Cameo	So So Def 78807
3/2/02	35	4	2. Welcome To Atlanta Airplay #36 **JERMAINE DUPRI • LUDACRIS** from the Dupri album *Instructions* on So So Def 85830 and the Ludacris album *Word Of Mouf* on Def Jam 586446	album cut
11/1/03	17	13	3. Wat Da Hook Gon Be Airplay #16 / Sales #49 **MURPHY LEE Featuring Jermaine Dupri**	Fo' Reel 001451
			DURAN DURAN	
			Synth-pop-dance band from Birmingham, England: Simon LeBon (vocals), Andy Taylor (guitar; see #11 below), Nick Rhodes (keyboards), John Taylor (bass; see #10 below) and Roger Taylor (drums). None of the Taylors are related. Group named after a villain in the Jane Fonda movie *Barbarella*. In 1984, Andy and Roger left the group. In 1985, Andy and John recorded with supergroup The Power Station; Simon, Nick and Roger recorded as Arcadia. Duran Duran reduced to a trio in 1986 of Simon, Nick and John. Expanded to a quintet in 1990 with the addition of guitarist Warren Cuccurullo (of Missing Persons) and drummer Sterling Campbell (left by 1993; joined Soul Asylum in 1995).	
1/22/83	3	16	● 1. **Hungry Like The Wolf** #1 Mainstream Rock hit (3 weeks)	Harvest 5195
4/9/83	14	9	2. Rio	Capitol 5215
6/18/83	4	12	3. **Is There Something I Should Know**	Capitol 5233
11/19/83	3	12	4. **Union Of The Snake**	Capitol 5290
1/28/84	10	10	5. **New Moon On Monday**	Capitol 5309
4/28/84	1 (2)	15	● 6. **The Reflex**	Capitol 5345
11/3/84	2 (4)	14	● 7. **The Wild Boys** Sales #1 (2) / Airplay #2	Capitol 5417
2/16/85	16	8	8. Save A Prayer Airplay #12 / Sales #21 recorded in 1982	Capitol 5438
5/25/85	1 (2)	13	9. **A View To A Kill** Sales #1 (3) / Airplay #2 title song from the James Bond movie starring Roger Moore	Capitol 5475
4/5/86	23	6	10. I Do What I Do...(Theme for 9 1/2 Weeks) Sales #18 / Airplay #26 **John TAYLOR Jonathan ELIAS** from the movie *9 1/2 Weeks* starring Mickey Rourke and Kim Basinger	Capitol 5551
7/5/86	24	7	11. Take It Easy Airplay #23 / Sales #24 **ANDY TAYLOR** from the movie *American Anthem* starring Mitch Gaylord	Atlantic 89414
11/15/86+	2 (1)	13	12. **Notorious** Sales #1 (1) / Airplay #3	Capitol 5648
3/14/87	39	1	13. Skin Trade Sales #30	Capitol 5670
10/22/88	4	13	14. **I Don't Want Your Love** Sales #3 / Airplay #4	Capitol 44237
1/21/89	22	6	15. All She Wants Is Sales #18 / Airplay #25 **DURANDURAN** (above 2)	Capitol 44287
1/23/93	3	18	● 16. **Ordinary World** Airplay #3 / Sales #6	Capitol 44908
5/8/93	7	16	17. **Come Undone** Airplay #6 / Sales #15	Capitol 44918

DATE	POS	WKS	ARTIST–RECORD TITLE	LABEL & NO.
			### DYKE AND THE BLAZERS	
			R&B-funk group from Buffalo, New York: Arlester "Dyke" Christian (vocals), Alvester "Pig" Jacobs (guitar), Bernard Williams and Clarence Towns (saxophones), Alvin Battle (bass) and Willie Earl (drums). Dyke was shot to death on 3/30/71 (age 28).	
7/5/69	35	3	1. We Got More Soul	Original Sound 86
11/1/69	36	1	2. Let A Woman Be A Woman - Let A Man Be A Man	Original Sound 89
			### DYLAN, Bob	
			Born Robert Zimmerman on 5/24/41 in Duluth, Minnesota; raised in Hibbing, Minnesota. Highly influential singer/songwriter/guitarist/harmonica player. Innovator of folk-rock style. Took stage name from poet Dylan Thomas. To New York City in December 1960. Worked Greenwich Village folk clubs. Signed to Columbia Records in October 1961. Motorcycle crash on 7/29/66 led to short retirement. Subject of documentaries *Don't Look Back* (1965) and *Eat The Document* (1969). Acted in movies *Pat Garrett And Billy The Kid* (1973), *Renaldo And Clara* (1978; also directed) and *Hearts Of Fire* (1987). Member of the supergroup Traveling Wilburys. His son Jakob is lead singer of The Wallflowers. Inducted into the Rock and Roll Hall of Fame in 1988. Won Grammy's Lifetime Achievement Award in 1991.	
5/15/65	39	1	1. Subterranean Homesick Blues	Columbia 43242
8/14/65	2 (2)	9	2. **Like A Rolling Stone**	Columbia 43346
10/9/65	7	7	3. **Positively 4th Street**	Columbia 43389
4/23/66	2 (1)	9	4. **Rainy Day Women #12 & 35**	Columbia 43592
7/16/66	20	4	5. I Want You	Columbia 43683
10/1/66	33	3	6. Just Like A Woman	Columbia 43792
8/2/69	7	11	7. **Lay Lady Lay**	Columbia 44926
12/25/71+	33	4	8. George Jackson	Columbia 45516
			Jackson: black militant shot to death in a prison riot at San Quentin on 8/21/71	
9/29/73	12	11	9. Knockin' On Heaven's Door	Columbia 45913
			Roger McGuinn (of The Byrds; guitar); from the movie *Pat Garrett And Billy The Kid* starring Dylan	
3/29/75	31	3	10. Tangled Up In Blue	Columbia 10106
1/3/76	33	3	11. Hurricane (Part I)	Columbia 10245
			true story of boxer Rubin "Hurricane" Carter	
10/6/79	24	6	12. Gotta Serve Somebody	Columbia 11072
			Mark Knopfler (of Dire Straits; guitar)	
			### DYSON, Ronnie	
			Born on 6/5/50 in Washington DC; raised in Brooklyn, New York. Died of heart failure on 11/10/90 (age 40). R&B singer/actor. Appeared in the musical *Hair* and the movie *Putney Swope*.	
7/25/70	8	9	1. **(If You Let Me Make Love To You Then) Why Can't I Touch You?**	Columbia 45110
			from the off-Broadway musical *Salvation* starring Peter Link	
4/7/73	28	4	2. One Man Band (Plays All Alone)	Columbia 45776

DATE	POS	WKS	ARTIST–RECORD TITLE	LABEL & NO.

E

DATE	POS	WKS	ARTIST–RECORD TITLE	LABEL & NO.
			EAGER, Brenda Lee — see BUTLER, Jerry	
			EAGLE-EYE CHERRY — see CHERRY, Eagle-Eye	
			EAGLES	
			Soft-rock group formed in Los Angeles, California: Glenn Frey (vocals, guitar), Don Henley (vocals, drums), Bernie Leadon (guitar) and Randy Meisner (bass). Meisner founded Poco; Leadon had been in the Flying Burrito Brothers; and Frey and Henley were with Linda Ronstadt. Don Felder (guitar) added in 1975. Joe Walsh replaced Leadon in 1976. Timothy B. Schmit replaced Meisner in 1977. Frey and Henley were the only members to play on all recordings. Disbanded in 1982. Henley, Frey, Felder, Walsh and Schmit reunited in 1994. Group inducted into the Rock and Roll Hall of Fame in 1998.	
6/24/72	12	8	1. Take It Easy written by Jackson Browne and Glenn Frey	Asylum 11005
9/30/72	9	10	2. **Witchy Woman**	Asylum 11008
2/3/73	22	6	3. Peaceful Easy Feeling	Asylum 11013
6/22/74	32	3	4. Already Gone	Asylum 11036
12/28/74+	1 (1)	14	5. **Best Of My Love** #1 Adult Contemporary hit (1 week)	Asylum 45218
6/14/75	1 (1)	14	6. **One Of These Nights**	Asylum 45257
9/27/75	2 (2)	11	7. **Lyin' Eyes**	Asylum 45279
1/17/76	4	14	8. **Take It To The Limit**	Asylum 45293
12/25/76+	1 (1)	13	● 9. **New Kid In Town**	Asylum 45373
3/12/77	1 (1)	15	● 10. **Hotel California** 1977 Grammy winner: Record of the Year	Asylum 45386
5/28/77	11	8	11. Life In The Fast Lane	Asylum 45403
12/23/78	18	5	12. Please Come Home For Christmas [X]	Asylum 45555
10/13/79	1 (1)	13	● 13. **Heartache Tonight** written by Bob Seger, J.D. Souther, Don Henley and Glenn Frey	Asylum 46545
12/8/79+	8	12	14. **The Long Run**	Asylum 46569
3/1/80	8	12	15. **I Can't Tell You Why** from the movie *Inside Moves* starring John Savage	Asylum 46608
1/10/81	21	7	16. Seven Bridges Road [L] recorded on 7/28/80 at the Santa Monica Civic Auditorium	Asylum 47100
11/12/94	31	3	17. Get Over It Airplay #40 / Sales #57	Geffen 19376
1/21/95	22 A	18	18. Love Will Keep Us Alive #1 Adult Contemporary hit (3 weeks); from the album *Hell Freezes Over* on Geffen 24725	album cut
			EARL, Stacy	
			Born on 12/28/62 in Boston, Massachusetts. Female dance-pop singer.	
12/21/91+	26	8	1. Love Me All Up Airplay #18	RCA 62116
3/7/92	27	8	2. Romeo & Juliet Airplay #22 / Sales #75 **STACY EARL (Featuring The Wild Pair)**	RCA 62192
			EARL-JEAN — see COOKIES, The	

DATE	POS	WKS	ARTIST–RECORD TITLE	LABEL & NO.
			EARLS, The	
			White doo-wop group from the Bronx, New York: Larry Chance, Bob Del Din, Eddie Harder and Jack Wray.	
1/12/63	24	4	1. Remember Then	Old Town 1130
			EARTH, WIND & FIRE	
			R&B group formed by Maurice White (tenor vocals, drums) in Los Angeles, California. Group generally contained eight to ten members, with frequent personnel shuffling. Core members: Philip Bailey (falsetto vocals), Al McKay (guitar) and Verdine White (bass; brother of Maurice). Group appeared in the movies *That's The Way Of The World* and *Sgt. Pepper's Lonely Hearts Club Band*. Group inducted into the Rock and Roll Hall of Fame in 2000.	
4/27/74	29	7	1. Mighty Mighty	Columbia 46007
10/12/74	33	2	2. Devotion	Columbia 10026
3/22/75	1 (1)	14	● 3. **Shining Star** #1 R&B hit (2 weeks)	Columbia 10090
7/26/75	12	11	4. That's The Way Of The World	Columbia 10172
12/13/75+	5	12	● 5. **Sing A Song** #1 R&B hit (2 weeks)	Columbia 10251
4/24/76	39	2	6. Can't Hide Love	Columbia 10309
8/14/76	12	12	● 7. **Getaway** #1 R&B hit (2 weeks)	Columbia 10373
12/11/76+	21	10	8. Saturday Nite	Columbia 10439
11/26/77+	13	13	9. Serpentine Fire #1 R&B hit (7 weeks)	Columbia 10625
4/1/78	32	5	10. Fantasy	Columbia 10688
8/5/78	9	9	● 11. **Got To Get You Into My Life** #1 R&B hit (1 week); from the movie *Sgt. Pepper's Lonely Hearts Club Band* starring Peter Frampton and the Bee Gees	Columbia 10796
12/16/78+	8	11	● 12. **September** #1 R&B hit (1 week)	ARC 10854
5/26/79	6	12	● 13. **Boogie Wonderland** **EARTH, WIND & FIRE WITH THE EMOTIONS**	ARC 10956
7/28/79	2 (2)	13	● 14. **After The Love Has Gone**	ARC 11033
10/31/81	3	16	● 15. **Let's Groove** #1 R&B hit (8 weeks)	ARC 02536
2/12/83	17	10	16. Fall In Love With Me	Columbia 03375
			EASTON, Sheena	
			Born Sheena Orr on 4/27/59 in Bellshill, Scotland. Pop singer/actress. Won the 1981 Best New Artist Grammy Award. Acted on TV's *Miami Vice*.	
2/28/81	1 (2)	15	● 1. **Morning Train (Nine To Five)** #1 Adult Contemporary hit (2 weeks)	EMI America 8071
6/6/81	18	9	2. Modern Girl	EMI America 8080
8/22/81	4	14	3. **For Your Eyes Only** title song from the James Bond movie starring Roger Moore	Liberty 1418
12/19/81+	15	12	4. You Could Have Been With Me	EMI America 8101
5/8/82	30	6	5. When He Shines	EMI America 8113
1/29/83	6	15	6. **We've Got Tonight** **KENNY ROGERS and SHEENA EASTON** #1 Country hit (1 week)	Liberty 1492
9/10/83	9	14	7. **Telefone (Long Distance Love Affair)**	EMI America 8172

DATE	POS	WKS	ARTIST–RECORD TITLE	LABEL & NO.
2/11/84	**25**	6	8. Almost Over You	EMI America 8186
9/22/84	**7**	15	9. **Strut** Sales #4 / Airplay #10	EMI America 8227
1/19/85	**9**	9	10. **Sugar Walls** Sales #4 / Airplay #12	EMI America 8253
			written by Prince (as Alexander Nevermind)	
11/30/85	**29**	4	11. Do It For Love Sales #27 / Airplay #29	EMI America 8295
12/24/88+	**2** (1)	14	12. **The Lover In Me** Sales #2 / Airplay #4	MCA 53416
12/2/89	**36**	3	13. The Arms Of Orion Airplay #35 / Sales #37	Warner 22757
			PRINCE with Sheena Easton from the movie *Batman* starring Michael Keaton	
4/20/91	**19**	9	14. What Comes Naturally Airplay #18 / Sales #19	MCA 53742

EASYBEATS, The

Rock group formed in Sydney, Australia: Steven Wright (vocals), George Young and Harry Vanda (guitars), Dick Diamonde (bass) and Gordon Fleet (drums). Young is the older brother of AC/DC's Angus and Malcolm Young.

DATE	POS	WKS	ARTIST–RECORD TITLE	LABEL & NO.
4/22/67	**16**	8	1. Friday On My Mind	United Artists 50106

ECHOES, The

White vocal trio from Brooklyn, New York: Tommy Duffy, Harry Doyle and Tom Morrissey.

DATE	POS	WKS	ARTIST–RECORD TITLE	LABEL & NO.
3/27/61	**12**	9	1. Baby Blue	Seg-Way 103

EDDY, Duane

Born on 4/26/38 in Corning, New York; raised in Tucson, Arizona. Highly influential guitarist. Best known for his "twangy" guitar sound. Eddy's backing band, The Rebels, included top sessionmen: Al Casey (guitar), Larry Knechtel (piano) and Plas Johnson (sax). Eddy appeared in the movies *Because They're Young*, *A Thunder Of Drums*, *The Wild Westerners*, *The Savage Seven* and *Kona Coast*. Married to Jessi Colter from 1961-68. Inducted into the Rock and Roll Hall of Fame in 1994.

DATE	POS	WKS	ARTIST–RECORD TITLE	LABEL & NO.
7/7/58	**6**	12	1. **Rebel-'Rouser** Best Seller #6 / Hot 100 #6 / Jockey #14 **[I]**	Jamie 1104
			The Sharps (later known as The Rivingtons, rebel yells)	
9/15/58	**27**	5	2. Ramrod Best Seller #27 / Hot 100 #28 **[I]**	Jamie 1109
11/17/58	**15**	9	3. Cannonball **[I]**	Jamie 1111
2/2/59	**23**	8	4. The Lonely One **[I]**	Jamie 1117
4/20/59	**30**	2	5. "Yep!" **[I]**	Jamie 1122
6/29/59	**9**	11	6. **Forty Miles Of Bad Road** **[I]**	Jamie 1126
10/26/59	**37**	3	7. Some Kind-A Earthquake **[I]**	Jamie 1130
			the shortest (1:17) record to chart in the Top 40	
1/11/60	**26**	5	8. Bonnie Came Back **[I]**	Jamie 1144
			traditional Scottish tune "My Bonnie Lies Over The Ocean"	
6/6/60	**4**	12	9. **Because They're Young** **[I]**	Jamie 1156
			title song from the movie starring Dick Clark and Tuesday Weld	
10/31/60	**27**	4	10. Peter Gunn **[I]**	Jamie 1168
			written by Henry Mancini; title song from the TV series starring Craig Stevens	
1/16/61	**18**	7	11. "Pepe" **[I]**	Jamie 1175
			title song from the movie starring Cantinflas	
4/17/61	**39**	1	12. Theme From Dixie **[I]**	Jamie 1183
			Anita Kerr Singers & The Jordanaires (vocals); written in 1860	
8/11/62	**33**	3	13. The Ballad Of Paladin **[I]**	RCA Victor 8047
			theme from the TV series *Have Gun-Will Travel* starring Richard Boone	

DATE	POS	WKS	ARTIST—RECORD TITLE	LABEL & NO.
11/3/62 2/23/63	**12** **28**	10 5	14. (Dance With The) Guitar Man 15. Boss Guitar Darlene Love & The Blossoms (labeled as The Rebelettes; vocals, above 2)	RCA Victor 8087 RCA Victor 8131
			EDEN'S CRUSH Female pop-dance vocal group: Ana Maria Lombo (from Columbia), Ivette Sosa (from New Jersey), Maile Misajon (from California), Nicole Scherzinger (from Hawaii) and Rosanna Tavarez (from New York). Group assembled for TV series *PopStars*.	
3/31/01	**8**	7	● 1. **Get Over Yourself** Sales #1 (2)	143/London 35063
			EDISON LIGHTHOUSE Studio group from England. Featuring lead singer Tony Burrows (of The Brotherhood Of Man, First Class, The Pipkins and White Plains).	
2/28/70	**5**	12	● 1. **Love Grows (Where My Rosemary Goes)**	Bell 858
			EDMONDS, Kevon — see AFTER 7	
			EDMUNDS, Dave Born on 4/15/44 in Cardiff, Wales. Rock and roll singer/songwriter/guitarist/producer.	
1/16/71	**4**	9	1. **I Hear You Knocking** #2 R&B hit for Smiley Lewis in 1955	MAM 3601
7/30/83	**39**	1	2. Slipping Away written and produced by Jeff Lynne (of ELO)	Columbia 03877
			EDSELS, The Black doo-wop group from Campbell, Ohio: George Jones, Marshall Sewell, James Reynolds, and brothers Larry and Harry Green.	
6/5/61	**21**	5	1. Rama Lama Ding Dong	Twin 700
			EDWARD BEAR Pop trio from Toronto, Ontario, Canada: Larry Evoy (vocals, drums), Roger Ellis (guitar) and Paul Weldon (keyboards). Group took name from a character in *Winnie The Pooh*.	
1/27/73	**3**	12	● 1. **Last Song** #1 Adult Contemporary hit (2 weeks)	Capitol 3452
5/26/73	**37**	2	2. Close Your Eyes	Capitol 3581
			EDWARDS, Bobby Born Robert Moncrief on 1/18/26 in Anniston, Alabama. Country singer.	
10/16/61	**11**	9	1. You're The Reason Four Young Men (backing vocals)	Crest 1075
			EDWARDS, Jonathan Born on 7/28/46 in Aitkin, Minnesota; raised in Virginia. Pop-country singer/songwriter/guitarist.	
12/4/71+	**4**	12	● 1. **Sunshine**	Capricorn 8021

DATE	POS	WKS	ARTIST–RECORD TITLE	LABEL & NO.
			EDWARDS, Tommy	
			Born on 2/17/22 in Richmond, Virginia. Died on 10/23/69 (age 47). Black Adult Contemporary singer/songwriter/pianist.	
8/25/58	**1** (6)	19	● 1. **It's All In The Game** Best Seller #1 (3) / Hot 100 #1 (6) #1 R&B hit (3 weeks); original version by Edwards hit #18 in 1951	MGM 12688
11/17/58	**15**	9	2. Love Is All We Need	MGM 12722
3/2/59	**11**	8	3. Please Mr. Sun / original version by Edwards hit #24 in 1952	
3/23/59	**27**	4	4. The Morning Side Of The Mountain original version by Edwards hit #24 in 1951	MGM 12757
6/8/59	**26**	4	5. My Melancholy Baby #9 hit for Walter Van Brunt in 1915	MGM 12794
6/6/60	**18**	7	6. I Really Don't Want To Know #11 hit for Les Paul & Mary Ford in 1954; LeRoy Holmes (orch., all of above)	MGM 12890
			EELS	
			Rock trio formed in Los Angeles, California: Mark Everett (vocals, guitar), Tommy Walter (bass) and Butch Norton (drums).	
11/2/96	**39** ᴬ	2	1. Novocaine For The Soul #1 Modern Rock hit (2 weeks); from the album *Beautiful Freak* on Dreamworks 50001	album cut
			E-40	
			Born Earl Stevens in Vallejo, California. Male rapper.	
2/15/97	**29**	4	1. Things'll Never Change / Sales #17 **E-40 featuring Bo-Rock** samples "The Way It Is" by Bruce Hornsby	
2/15/97		4	2. Rappers' Ball **E-40 featuring Too $hort and K-Ci** samples "Playboy $hort" by Too $hort	Sick Wid' It/Jive 42436
			EGAN, Walter	
			Born on 7/12/48 in Jamaica, New York. Pop-rock singer/songwriter/guitarist.	
7/1/78	**8**	13	● 1. **Magnet And Steel** Lindsey Buckingham and Stevie Nicks (backing vocals)	Columbia 10719
			EIFFEL 65	
			Male dance trio from Italy: Jeffrey Jay, Maurizio Lobina and Gabry Ponte.	
12/18/99+	**6**	14	1. **Blue (Da Ba Dee)** Airplay #6	Republic 156638
			8TH DAY, The	
			R&B group from Detroit, Michigan: Melvin Davis (male vocals), Lynn Harter (female vocals), Michael Anthony and Bruce Nazarian (guitars), Jerry Paul (percussion), Carole Stallings (electric violin), Anita Sherman (vibes) and Tony Newton (bass).	
6/5/71	**11**	10	● 1. She's Not Just Another Woman	Invictus 9087
10/16/71	**28**	6	2. You've Got To Crawl (Before You Walk)	Invictus 9098

DATE	POS	WKS	ARTIST–RECORD TITLE	LABEL & NO.
			ELBERT, Donnie	
			Born on 5/25/36 in New Orleans, Louisiana; raised in Buffalo, New York. Died on 1/26/89 (age 52). R&B singer.	
11/20/71	**15**	8	1. Where Did Our Love Go	All Platinum 2330
2/12/72	**22**	6	2. I Can't Help Myself (Sugar Pie, Honey Bunch)	Avco 4587
			EL CHICANO	
			Latin group formed in Los Angeles, California. Core members: Mickey Lesperon (guitar), Andre Baeza (congas), Bobby Espinosa (organ), Freddie Sanchez (bass) and Johnny De Luna (drums). Singers included Ersi Arvizu, and brothers Rudy, Steve and Jerry Salas. Rudy and Steve Salas later formed Tierra.	
5/2/70	**28**	5	1. Viva Tirado - Part I [I]	Kapp 2085
12/22/73	**40**	1	2. Tell Her She's Lovely	MCA 40104
			EL DORADOS, The	
			R&B vocal group from Chicago, Illinois: Jewel Jones, Pirkle Lee Moses, Richard Nickens, Arthur Bassett and James Maddox. Moses died of a brain tumor on 12/16/2000 (age 63).	
10/15/55	**17**	6	1. At My Front Door Best Seller #17 / Top 100 #35 #1 R&B hit (1 week)	Vee-Jay 147
			ELECTRIC INDIAN, The	
			Instrumental group assembled from top Philadelphia studio musicians. Some members later joined MFSB.	
8/23/69	**16**	8	1. Keem-O-Sabe [I]	United Artists 50563
			ELECTRIC LIGHT ORCHESTRA	
			Orchestral rock band formed in Birmingham, England. Core members: Jeff Lynne (vocals, guitar), Richard Tandy (keyboards), Kelly Groucutt (bass) and Bev Bevan (drums). Numerous personnel changes. Lynne was also a prolific producer and a member of the supergroup Traveling Wilburys.	
1/25/75	**9**	10	1. **Can't Get It Out Of My Head**	United Artists 573
12/13/75+	**10**	12	2. **Evil Woman**	United Artists/Jet 729
4/10/76	**14**	9	3. Strange Magic	United Artists/Jet 770
11/13/76+	**13**	14	4. Livin' Thing	United Artists/Jet 888
3/5/77	**24**	6	5. Do Ya [R] #93 hit for The Move in 1972 (group evolved into ELO)	United Artists/Jet 939
7/9/77	**7**	16	● 6. **Telephone Line**	United Artists/Jet 1000
12/10/77+	**13**	10	7. Turn To Stone	Jet 1099
3/11/78	**17**	12	8. Sweet Talkin' Woman	Jet 1145
7/29/78	**35**	3	9. Mr. Blue Sky	Jet 5050
6/2/79	**8**	11	10. **Shine A Little Love**	Jet 5057
8/11/79	**4**	11	● 11. **Don't Bring Me Down**	Jet 5060
11/17/79	**37**	2	12. Confusion	Jet 5064
1/26/80	**39**	2	13. Last Train To London	Jet 5067
6/14/80	**16**	8	● 14. I'm Alive	MCA 41246
8/16/80	**13**	9	15. All Over The World	MCA 41289
8/30/80	**8**	10	16. **Xanadu** **OLIVIA NEWTON-JOHN/ELECTRIC LIGHT ORCHESTRA** above 3 from the movie *Xanadu* starring Newton-John	MCA 41285

DATE	POS	WKS	ARTIST–RECORD TITLE	LABEL & NO.
8/8/81	**10**	13	17. **Hold On Tight**	Jet 02408
11/28/81	**38**	2	18. Twilight	Jet 02559
7/9/83	**19**	9	19. Rock 'N' Roll Is King	Jet 03964
			ELO (above 3)	
3/1/86	**18**	7	20. Calling America Sales #19 / Airplay #21	CBS Associated 05766
			ELECTRIC PRUNES, The	
			Psychedelic-rock group from Seattle, Washington: James Lowe (vocals), Ken Williams and James Spagnola (guitars), Mark Tulin (bass) and Preston Ritter (drums).	
1/21/67	**11**	8	1. I Had Too Much To Dream (Last Night)	Reprise 0532
4/22/67	**27**	5	2. Get Me To The World On Time	Reprise 0564
			ELECTRONIC	
			Dance duo from Manchester, England: Bernard Sumner (of New Order) and Johnny Marr (of The Smiths).	
5/19/90	**38**	2	1. Getting Away With It Airplay #33 / Sales #39	Warner 19880
			ELEGANTS, The	
			White doo-wop group from Staten Island, New York: Vito Picone, Arthur Venosa, Frank Tardogna, Carmen Romano and James Moschella.	
7/28/58	**1 (1)**	16	● 1. **Little Star** Hot 100 #1 (0) / Best Seller #2 #1 R&B hit (4 weeks); tune adapted from Mozart's "Twinkle Twinkle Little Star"	Apt 25005
			ELGART, Larry, And His Manhattan Swing Orchestra	
			Born on 3/20/22 in New London, Connecticut. Alto saxophonist.	
7/3/82	**31**	5	1. Hooked On Swing **[I]** In The Mood/Cherokee/American Patrol/Sing, Sing, Sing/Don't Be That Way/Little Brown Jug/Opus #1/Zing Went the Strings of My Heart/String of Pearls	RCA 13219
			ELLEDGE, Jimmy	
			Born on 1/8/43 in Nashville, Tennessee. Country singer/songwriter/pianist.	
12/25/61+	**22**	7	1. Funny How Time Slips Away written by Willie Nelson; produced by Chet Atkins	RCA Victor 7946
			ELLIMAN, Yvonne	
			Born on 12/29/51 in Honolulu, Hawaii. Played "Mary Magdalene" on the concept album and in the rock opera and movie *Jesus Christ Superstar*. Backing singer for Eric Clapton.	
5/22/71	**28**	6	1. I Don't Know How To Love Him from the rock opera *Jesus Christ Superstar*	Decca 32785
11/6/76	**14**	12	2. Love Me	RSO 858
4/16/77	**15**	9	3. Hello Stranger #1 Adult Contemporary hit (4 weeks)	RSO 871
2/25/78	**1 (1)**	16	● 4. **If I Can't Have You** from the movie *Saturday Night Fever* starring John Travolta; #2 & 4: written by the Bee Gees	RSO 884
12/1/79	**34**	3	5. Love Pains	RSO 1007

DATE	POS	WKS	ARTIST–RECORD TITLE	LABEL & NO.
			ELLIOTT, Missy "Misdemeanor"	
			Born on 7/1/71 in Portsmouth, Virginia. Female rapper/singer/songwriter/producer.	
7/12/97	6	17	▲ 1. **Not Tonight** Sales #3 / Airplay #39 **LIL' KIM Featuring Da Brat, Left Eye, Missy "Misdemeanor" Elliott and Angie Martinez** samples "Ladies Night" by Kool & The Gang; from the movie *Nothing To Lose* starring Martin Lawrence	Undeas/Big Beat 98019
10/25/97	12	15	● 2. **Sock It 2 Me** Sales #7 / Airplay #36 **MISSY "MISDEMEANOR" ELLIOTT Featuring Da Brat** samples "Ready Or Not Here I Come" by The Delfonics	EastWest 64144
6/27/98	5	23	● 3. **Make It Hot** Sales #2 / Airplay #39 **NICOLE Featuring Missy "Misdemeanor" Elliott and Mocha**	The Gold Mind 64110
11/7/98+	7	16	● 4. **Trippin'** Sales #6 / Airplay #49 **TOTAL (Feat. Missy Elliott)**	Bad Boy 79185
11/27/99+	5	21	▲ 5. **Hot Boyz** Sales #2 / Airplay #24 **MISSY "MISDEMEANOR" ELLIOTT [featuring NAS, EVE & Q-TIP]** #1 R&B hit (6 weeks); Lil' Mo (vocal ad libs)	The Gold Mind 64029
4/21/01	7	19	6. **Get Ur Freak On** Airplay #6 / Sales #46	Goldmind 67190
8/4/01	15	16	7. **One Minute Man** Airplay #13 **MISSY "MISDEMEANOR" ELLIOTT (featuring Ludacris)** from Elliott's album *Miss E...So Addictive* on Goldmind 62639	album cut
12/8/01	28	5	8. **Son Of A Gun (I Betcha Think This Song Is About You)** Airplay #26 **JANET Featuring Missy Elliott and P. Diddy with Carly Simon** samples "You're So Vain" by Carly Simon	Virgin 46171
9/28/02	2 (10)	22	9. **Work It** Airplay #2 / Sales #10 #1 R&B hit (5 weeks)	Goldmind 67340
1/25/03	8	14	10. **Gossip Folks** Airplay #6 / Sales #11 **MISSY ELLIOTT (Featuring Ludacris)** samples "Double Dutch Bus" by Frankie Smith	Goldmind 67356
10/25/03	27	6	11. **Pass That Dutch** Sales #14 / Airplay #26 **MISSY ELLIOTT** samples "Magic Mountain" by War and "Potholes In My Lawn" by De La Soul	EastWest 67506
			ELLIS, Shirley	
			Born Shirley Elliston in 1941 in the Bronx, New York. R&B singer/songwriter.	
12/7/63+	8	10	1. **The Nitty Gritty**	Congress 202
1/9/65	3	10	2. **The Name Game**	Congress 230
4/3/65	8	7	3. **The Clapping Song (Clap Pat Clap Slap)**	Congress 234
			EMERSON DRIVE	
			Country group from Grande Prairie, Alberta, Canada: Brad Mates (vocals), Danick Dupelle (guitar), Chris Hartman (keyboards), Pat Allingham (fiddle), Jeff Loberg (bass) and Mike Melancon (drums).	
6/1/02	35	3	1. **I Should Be Sleeping** Sales #19 / Airplay #37	DreamWorks 50362
1/25/03	34	4	2. **Fall Into Me** Airplay #34 from the album *Emerson Drive* on DreamWorks 450272	album cut

DATE	POS	WKS	ARTIST–RECORD TITLE	LABEL & NO.
			EMERSON, LAKE & PALMER	
			Classical-oriented rock trio from England: Keith Emerson (keyboards), Greg Lake (vocals, bass, guitar) and Carl Palmer (drums). Palmer later joined Asia.	
10/21/72	39	2	1. From The Beginning	Cotillion 44158
			EMF	
			Techno-funk group from Forest of Dean, Gloucestershire, England: James Atkin (vocals), Ian Dench (guitar), Derry Brownson (keyboards, percussion), Zac Foley (bass) and Mark Decloedt (drums). Foley died of a drug overdose on 1/3/2002 (age 31).	
5/11/91	1 (1)	16	● 1. **Unbelievable** Sales #3 / Airplay #4	EMI 50350
10/26/91	18	5	2. Lies. Airplay #64 / Sales #69	EMI 50363
			EMINEM	
			Born Marshall Mathers III on 10/17/72 in Kansas City, Missouri; raised in Detroit, Michigan. White male rapper/actor. Starred in the 2002 movie *8 Mile*. Member of D-12.	
3/13/99	36	4	1. My Name Is Airplay #23 / Sales #66 **[N]** samples "I Got The" by Labi Siffre; co-written and produced by Dr. Dre	Aftermath 95040
2/12/00	25	12	2. Forgot About Dre Airplay #20 **DR. DRE Featuring Eminem** from the Dr. Dre album *2001* on Aftermath 90486	album cut
5/13/00	4	13	3. **The Real Slim Shady** Airplay #2 / Sales #42	Aftermath 497334
5/18/02	2 (5)	16	4. **Without Me** Airplay #2	album cut
8/10/02	4	13	5. **Cleanin' Out My Closet** Airplay #4 above 2 from the album *The Eminem Show* on Aftermath 10798	album cut
10/12/02	1 (12)	21	6. **Lose Yourself** Airplay #1 (11) / Sales #11 from the movie *8 Mile* starring Eminem	Shady 497815
2/8/03	15	10	7. Superman Airplay #15 Dina Rae (female vocal)	album cut
4/12/03	14	10	8. Sing For The Moment Airplay #14 samples "Dream On" by Aerosmith; above 2 from the album *The Eminem Show* on Aftermath 493290	album cut
			EMOTIONS, The	
			Female R&B vocal trio from Chicago, Illinois: sisters Wanda, Sheila and Jeanette Hutchinson. Jeanette replaced by cousin Theresa Davis in 1970, and later by sister Pamela. Jeanette returned to the group in 1978.	
7/19/69	39	1	1. So I Can Love You	Volt 4010
7/2/77	1 (5)	17	▲ 2. **Best Of My Love** #1 R&B hit (4 weeks)	Columbia 10544
5/26/79	6	12	● 3. **Boogie Wonderland** **EARTH, WIND & FIRE WITH THE EMOTIONS**	ARC 10956
			ENCHANTMENT	
			R&B vocal group from Detroit, Michigan: Ed Clanton, Bobby Green, Davis Banks, Emanuel Johnson and Joe Thomas.	
3/5/77	25	5	1. Gloria	Roadshow/U.A. 912
3/11/78	33	4	2. It's You That I Need #1 R&B hit (1 week)	Roadshow/U.A. 1124

DATE	POS	WKS	ARTIST–RECORD TITLE	LABEL & NO.
			ENGLAND DAN & JOHN FORD COLEY	
			Pop duo from Austin, Texas: Dan Seals (born on 2/8/50) and John Ford Coley (born on 10/13/51). Dan is the brother of Jim Seals (of Seals & Crofts) and cousin of country singers Johnny Duncan, Troy Seals and Brady Seals (of Little Texas). Coley appeared in the 1987 movie *Scenes From The Goldmine*.	
7/10/76	2 (2)	17	● 1. **I'd Really Love To See You Tonight** #1 Adult Contemporary hit (1 week)	Big Tree 16069
10/30/76	10	12	2. **Nights Are Forever Without You**	Big Tree 16079
6/18/77	21	8	3. **It's Sad To Belong** #1 Adult Contemporary hit (5 weeks)	Big Tree 16088
11/5/77	23	6	4. Gone Too Far	Big Tree 16102
3/11/78	9	8	5. **We'll Never Have To Say Goodbye Again** #1 Adult Contemporary hit (6 weeks)	Big Tree 16110
4/7/79	10	10	6. **Love Is The Answer** #1 Adult Contemporary hit (2 weeks); written by Todd Rundgren	Big Tree 16131
			ENGLISH CONGREGATION, The	
			Vocal group from England. Led by singer Brian Keith.	
2/19/72	29	5	1. Softly Whispering I Love You	Atco 6865
			ENIGMA	
			Born Michael Cretu on 5/18/57 in Bucharest, Romania. Dance producer. Moved to Germany in 1975. Worked with Vangelis and The Art Of Noise. Featured vocalist is Cretu's wife, Sandra.	
3/2/91	5	11	● 1. **Sadeness Part 1** Sales #1 (2) / Airplay #6 **[F]** features traditional Gregorian chants backed by a dance rhythm; sadeness (pronounced: sadness) refers to 18th-century French author/libertine, the Marquis de Sade	Charisma 98864
3/26/94	4	21	● 2. **Return To Innocence** Sales #5 / Airplay #7	Charisma 38423
			EN VOGUE	
			Female R&B vocal group from San Francisco, California: Terry Ellis, Dawn Robinson, Cindy Herron and Maxine Jones. Herron married pro baseball player Glenn Braggs in June of 1993 and acted in the movie *Juice*. Robinson left in early 1997 to join Lucy Pearl.	
5/12/90	2 (1)	17	▲ 1. **Hold On** Sales #1 (2) / Airplay #8 #1 R&B hit (2 weeks)	Atlantic 87984
10/13/90	38	1	2. Lies Sales #32 #1 R&B hit (1 week)	Atlantic 87893
4/4/92	2 (3)	22	● 3. **My Lovin' (You're Never Gonna Get It)** Airplay #1 (4) / Sales #6 #1 R&B hit (2 weeks)	EastWest 98586
6/27/92	6	17	● 4. **Giving Him Something He Can Feel** Airplay #4 / Sales #10 #1 R&B hit (1 week); #28 hit for Aretha Franklin in 1976 as "Something He Can Feel"	EastWest 98560
9/26/92	8	16	● 5. **Free Your Mind** Sales #13 / Airplay #14	EastWest 98487
12/26/92+	15	12	6. Give It Up, Turn It Loose Airplay #12 / Sales #47	EastWest 98455
5/15/93	36	3	7. Love Don't Love You Airplay #28	EastWest 98432
1/29/94	3	24	▲ 8. **Whatta Man** Sales #2 / Airplay #4 **SALT 'N' PEPA with En Vogue**	Next Plateau 857390
11/9/96+	2 (4)	33	▲ 9. **Don't Let Go (Love)** Sales #3 / Airplay #3 #1 R&B hit (1 week); from the movie *Set It Off* starring Jada Pinkett and Queen Latifah	EastWest 64231

DATE	POS	WKS	ARTIST–RECORD TITLE	LABEL & NO.
7/19/97	**16**	6	● 10. Whatever Sales #15 / Airplay #20	EastWest 64174
10/25/97	**33**	3	11. Too Gone, Too Long Sales #28 / Airplay #58	EastWest 64150
			ENYA	
			Born Eithne Ni Bhraonain on 5/17/61 in Gweedore, County Donegal, Ireland. Female singer.	
3/11/89	**24**	8	1. Orinoco Flow (Sail Away) Sales #19 / Airplay #28 Orinoco is a river in South America	Geffen 27633
9/1/01	**10**	22	2. **Only Time** Sales #2 / Airplay #9 #1 Adult Contemporary hit (6 weeks); from the movie *Sweet November* starring Keanu Reeves and Charlize Theron	Reprise 42420
			EPPS, Preston	
			Born in 1931 in Oakland, California. Black bongo player.	
6/1/59	**14**	9	1. Bongo Rock **[I]**	Original Sound 4
			EQUALS, The	
			Interracial British-Jamaican rock group: twin brothers Derv (vocals) and Lincoln (guitar) Gordon, with Eddy Grant and Patrick Lloyd (guitars), and John Hall (drums).	
9/28/68	**32**	6	1. Baby, Come Back	RCA Victor 9583
			ERASURE	
			Techno-rock/dance duo formed in England: Andy Bell (vocals) and Vince Clarke (instruments).	
9/10/88	**12**	11	1. Chains Of Love Sales #10 / Airplay #10	Sire 27844
1/21/89	**14**	9	2. A Little Respect Sales #13 / Airplay #14	Sire 27738
6/4/94	**20**	15	3. Always Airplay #17 / Sales #40	Mute/Elektra 64552
			ERIC B. & RAKIM — see WATLEY, Jody	
			ERNIE — see HENSON, Jim	
			ERUPTION	
			Techno-funk/dance group of Jamaican natives based in London, England: Precious Wilson and Lintel (vocals), brothers Gregory and Morgan Petrineau (guitars), Horatio McKay (keyboards), and Eric Kingsley (drums).	
6/10/78	**18**	6	1. I Can't Stand The Rain	Ariola/Hansa 7686
			ESCAPE CLUB, The	
			Rock group formed in London, England: Trevor Steel (vocals), John Holliday (guitar), Johnnie Christo (bass) and Milan Zekavica (drums).	
9/17/88	**1 (1)**	16	● 1. **Wild, Wild West** Sales #1 (1) / Airplay #1 (1)	Atlantic 89048
1/21/89	**28**	5	2. Shake For The Sheik Sales #24 / Airplay #28	Atlantic 88983
6/29/91	**8**	14	● 3. **I'll Be There** Sales #6 / Airplay #14	Atlantic 87683

DATE	POS	WKS	ARTIST—RECORD TITLE	LABEL & NO.
			ESPN Presents	
6/7/97	31	14	ESPN is America's leading cable sports network. The medley below is based on their best-selling series of albums. ● 1. The Jock Jam Sales #25 / Airplay #43 "Let's Get Ready To Rumble" (Michael Buffer), "Everybody Everybody" (Black Box), "This Is Your Night" (Amber), "I Like To Move It" (Reel 2 Real), "Give It Up" (The Goodmen), "The Bomb" (The Bucketheads), "Boom Boom Boom" (The Outhere Brothers), "Get Ready 4 This" (2 Unlimited), "Whoomp! There It Is" (Tag Team), "Strike It Up" (Black Box), "Tootsee Roll" (69 Boyz), "It Takes Two" (Rob Base), "Gonna Make You Sweat" (C&C Music Factory), "Pump Up The Jam" (Technotronic), "YMCA" (Village People), "Twilight Zone" (2 Unlimited and "Rock And Roll Part 2" (Gary Glitter)	Tommy Boy 7780
			ESQUIRES, The	
9/16/67 12/16/67	11 22	10 5	R&B vocal group from Milwaukee, Wisconsin: brothers Gilbert and Alvis Moorer, Millard Edwards, Sam Pace and Shawn Taylor. 1. Get On Up 2. And Get Away	Bunky 7750 Bunky 7752
			ESSEX, The	
6/22/63 9/14/63	1 (2) 12	10 6	R&B vocal group formed in North Carolina: Anita Humes, Walter Vickers, Rodney Taylor, Billy Hill and Rudolph Johnson. 1. **Easier Said Than Done** #1 R&B hit (2 weeks) 2. A Walkin' Miracle **THE ESSEX Featuring Anita Humes**	Roulette 4494 Roulette 4515
			ESSEX, David	
1/12/74	5	14	Born David Cook on 7/23/47 in Plaistow, London, England. Portrayed "Christ" in the London production of *Godspell*. Star of British movies since 1970. ● 1. **Rock On**	Columbia 45940
			ESTEFAN, Gloria/Miami Sound Machine	
			Latin pop/dance group from Miami, Florida: Gloria Estefan (born Gloria Fajardo on 9/1/57 in Havana, Cuba), her husband Emilio Estefan (keyboards), Juan Avila (bass) and Enrique Garcia (drums). Group later grew to nine members. The Estefans married in 1978. On 3/20/90, both were in a serious crash involving their tour bus, in which Gloria suffered a broken vertebra but fully recovered within a year.	
			MIAMI SOUND MACHINE:	
11/23/85+	10	16	● 1. **Conga** Sales #7 / Airplay #12	Epic 05457
3/29/86	8	12	● 2. **Bad Boy** Sales #4 / Airplay #9	Epic 05805
7/26/86	5	13	3. **Words Get In The Way** Sales #5 / Airplay #8 #1 Adult Contemporary hit (2 weeks)	Epic 06120
12/13/86+	25	8	4. Falling In Love (Uh-Oh) Airplay #23 / Sales #27	Epic 06352
			GLORIA ESTEFAN AND MIAMI SOUND MACHINE:	
6/13/87	5	12	5. **Rhythm Is Gonna Get You** Sales #3 / Airplay #6	Epic 07059
10/24/87	36	2	6. Betcha Say That Sales #33 / Airplay #33	Epic 07371
1/16/88	6	11	7. **Can't Stay Away From You** Sales #6 / Airplay #6 #1 Adult Contemporary hit (1 week)	Epic 07641

DATE	POS	WKS	ARTIST–RECORD TITLE	LABEL & NO.
3/26/88	1 (2)	14	● 8. **Anything For You** Sales #1 (2) / Airplay #1 (2) #1 Adult Contemporary hit (3 weeks)	Epic 07759
6/25/88	3	13	9. **1-2-3** Sales #3 / Airplay #5 #1 Adult Contemporary hit (1 week)	Epic 07921
			GLORIA ESTEFAN:	
7/22/89	1 (1)	13	● 10. **Don't Wanna Lose You** Sales #1 (1) / Airplay #1 (1)	Epic 68959
10/21/89	11	8	11. Get On Your Feet Airplay #8 / Sales #13	Epic 69064
1/13/90	6	11	12. **Here We Are** Sales #8 / Airplay #8 #1 Adult Contemporary hit (5 weeks)	Epic 73084
2/2/91	1 (2)	14	13. **Coming Out Of The Dark** Airplay #1 (1) / Sales #3 #1 Adult Contemporary hit (2 weeks); backing vocalists include Jon Secada and Betty Wright	Epic 73666
11/16/91	22	13	14. Live For Loving You Airplay #15 / Sales #61	Epic 73962
10/15/94	13	19	● 15. Turn The Beat Around Airplay #13 / Sales #15 from the movie *The Specialist* starring Sylvester Stallone	Crescent Moon 77630
2/18/95	27	10	16. Everlasting Love Airplay #20 / Sales #59	Epic 77756
1/25/97	40	1	17. I'm Not Giving You Up Airplay #48 / Sales #57	Epic 78464
5/23/98	27	8	18. Heaven's What I Feel Sales #22 / Airplay #56	Epic 78875
10/16/99	2 (1)	5	19. **Music Of My Heart** Sales #1 (1) / Airplay #26 ***NSYNC and GLORIA ESTEFAN** from the movie *Music Of The Heart* starring Meryl Streep	Miramax/Epic 79245
			ESTUS, Deon	
			Born in Detroit, Michigan. R&B singer/bassist.	
3/11/89	5	11	1. **Heaven Help Me** Sales #4 / Airplay #6 **DEON ESTUS (with George Michael)**	Mika 871538
			ETERNAL	
			Female R&B vocal group from London, England: sisters Easther and Vernie Bennett, with Louise Nurding and Kelle Bryan.	
2/5/94	19	11	1. **Stay** Airplay #16 / Sales #24 #6 R&B hit for Glenn Jones in 1990	EMI/1st Avenue 58113
			ETHERIDGE, Melissa	
			Born on 5/29/61 in Leavenworth, Kansas. Adult Alternative pop-rock singer/songwriter/guitarist.	
5/7/94	25	26	1. Come To My Window Airplay #10	Island 858028
10/1/94+	8	29	2. **I'm The Only One** Airplay #5 / Sales #36 #1 Adult Contemporary hit (2 weeks)	Island 854068
2/18/95	16	14	3. If I Wanted To Airplay #18 / Sales #43	Island 854238
2/17/96	22	13	4. I Want To Come Over Airplay #21 / Sales #29	Island 854528
10/12/96	40	3	5. Nowhere To Go Airplay #31 / Sales #65	Island 854664
			E.U.	
			Funk group from Washington DC. Led by singer/bassist Gregory Elliott. E.U.: Experience Unlimited.	
5/14/88	35	4	1. Da'Butt Sales #26 #1 R&B hit (1 week); from the movie *School Daze* starring Spike Lee	EMI-Manhattan 50115

DATE	POS	WKS	ARTIST–RECORD TITLE	LABEL & NO.
			EUROPE	
			Hard-rock group from Stockholm, Sweden: Joey Tempest (vocals), Kee Marcello (guitar), Mic Michaeli (keyboards), John Leven (bass) and Ian Haugland (drums).	
2/21/87	8	9	1. **The Final Countdown** Sales #6 / Airplay #8	Epic 06416
			featured in the movie *Rocky IV* starring Sylvester Stallone	
6/6/87	30	4	2. Rock The Night Sales #30 / Airplay #31	Epic 07091
8/22/87	3	12	3. **Carrie** Airplay #1 (1) / Sales #5	Epic 07282
9/24/88	31	4	4. Superstitious Sales #29 / Airplay #31	Epic 07979
			EURYTHMICS	
			Synth-pop duo: Annie Lennox (vocals, keyboards) and David A. Stewart (guitar). Lennox was born on 12/25/54 in Aberdeen, Scotland. Stewart was born on 9/9/52 in Sunderland, England. Both had been in The Tourists from 1977-80. Stewart was married to Siobhan Fahey of Bananarama from 1987-96. Lennox appeared in TV movie *The Room*.	
6/18/83	1 (1)	17	● 1. **Sweet Dreams (Are Made of This)**	RCA 13533
10/15/83	23	6	2. Love Is A Stranger	RCA 13618
2/4/84	4	14	3. **Here Comes The Rain Again**	RCA 13725
5/19/84	21	7	4. Who's That Girl?	RCA 13800
8/11/84	29	5	5. Right By Your Side	RCA 13695
5/11/85	5	13	6. **Would I Lie To You?** Sales #4 / Airplay #6	RCA 14078
8/17/85	22	7	7. There Must Be An Angel (Playing With My Heart) Sales #20 / Airplay #25	RCA 14160
			Stevie Wonder (harmonica)	
11/2/85	18	8	8. Sisters Are Doin' It For Themselves Sales #16 / Airplay #25	RCA 14214
			EURYTHMICS and ARETHA FRANKLIN	
8/30/86	14	9	9. Missionary Man Sales #13 / Airplay #17	RCA 14414
			#1 Mainstream Rock hit (1 week)	
11/4/89	40	1	10. Don't Ask Me Why Sales #31	Arista 9880
			EVAN AND JARON	
			Pop-rock duo of identical twin brothers: Evan and Jaron Lowenstein. Born on 3/18/74 in Atlanta, Georgia.	
11/25/00+	15	20	1. Crazy For This Girl Sales #7 / Airplay #17	Columbia 79484
			EVANESCENCE	
			Rock group from Little Rock, Arkansas: Amy Lee (vocals), Ben Moody (guitar), Josh LeCompt (bass) and Rocky Gray (drums). Won the 2003 Best New Artist Grammy Award.	
4/5/03	5	28	1. **Bring Me To Life** Airplay #5	album cut
			#1 Modern Rock hit (2 weeks); Paul McCoy (of rock group 12 Stones; guest vocal; from the movie *Daredevil* starring Ben Affleck (soundtrack on Wind-Up 13079); also from their album *Fallen* on Wind-Up 13063	
			EVANS, Faith	
			Born on 6/10/73 in Newark, New Jersey. Female R&B singer/songwriter. Married to rapper The Notorious B.I.G. from 1994-97.	
7/15/95	24	12	● 1. You Used To Love Me Sales #13 / Airplay #58	Bad Boy 79025
			FAITH	
12/9/95+	21	13	● 2. Soon As I Get Home Sales #10 / Airplay #64	Bad Boy 79040

DATE	POS	WKS	ARTIST–RECORD TITLE	LABEL & NO.
6/14/97	1 (11)	29	▲³ 3. **I'll Be Missing You** Sales #1 (9) / Airplay #4 **PUFF DADDY & FAITH EVANS (Featuring 112)** #1 R&B hit (8 weeks); tribute to The Notorious B.I.G.; samples "Every Breath You Take" by The Police	Bad Boy 79097
11/14/98	7	15	● 4. **Love Like This** Sales #9 / Airplay #17 samples "Chic Cheer" by Chic	Bad Boy 79117
2/6/99	2 (3)	21	▲ 5. **Heartbreak Hotel** Sales #2 / Airplay #5 **WHITNEY HOUSTON (Feat. Faith Evans & Kelly Price)** #1 R&B hit (7 weeks)	Arista 13619
3/20/99	9	8	6. **All Night Long** Sales #9 / Airplay #29 **FAITH EVANS (feat. Puff Daddy)** samples "I Hear Music In The Streets" by Unlimited Touch	Bad Boy 79203
9/4/99	17	6	7. Never Gonna Let You Go Sales #7 / Airplay #45 #1 R&B hit (1 week); Babyface, Kenya Ivey, Tavia Ivey (backing vocals)	Bad Boy 79252
2/12/00	34	3	8. Love Is Blind Airplay #26 **EVE Featuring Faith Evans** from Eve's album *Ruff Ryders' First Lady* on Ruff Ryders 490453	album cut
12/8/01	38	1	9. You Gets No Love Airplay #34 / Sales #56	Bad Boy 79438
2/23/02	14	13	10. I Love You Airplay #13 / Sales #35	Bad Boy 79425
			EVANS, Paul	
			Born on 3/5/38 in Brooklyn, New York. Pop singer/songwriter.	
10/5/59	9	11	1. **(Seven Little Girls) Sitting In The Back Seat** [N] with the Curls (female backing duo: Sue Singleton and Sue Terry)	Guaranteed 200
2/15/60	16	7	2. Midnite Special #12 R&B hit for Tiny Grimes in 1948	Guaranteed 205
5/30/60	10	8	3. **Happy-Go-Lucky-Me**	Guaranteed 208
			EVANS, Sara	
			Born on 2/5/71 in Boonville, Missouri; raised in Boonesboro, Missouri. Country singer/songwriter.	
2/20/99	37	3	1. No Place That Far Airplay #27 / Sales #29 #1 Country hit (1 week); Vince Gill (backing vocal)	RCA 65584
12/16/00	34	4	2. Born To Fly Airplay #30 #1 Country hit (1 week)	album cut
6/30/01	35	2	3. I Could Not Ask For More Airplay #30	album cut
9/7/02	35	3	4. I Keep Looking Airplay #32 above 3 from the album *Born To Fly* on RCA 67964	album cut
			EVE	
			Born Eve Jeffers on 11/10/78 in Philadelphia, Pennsylvania. Female rapper/ songwriter. Star of the Fox TV series *The Opposite Sex*.	
8/14/99	29	7	1. What Ya Want Airplay #18 **EVE & NOKIO** from Eve's album *Ruff Ryders' First Lady* on Ruff Ryders 490453	album cut
10/16/99	26	8	2. Gotta Man Airplay #19	Ruff Ryders 97085
11/27/99+	5	21	▲ 3. **Hot Boyz** Sales #2 / Airplay #24 **MISSY "MISDEMEANOR" ELLIOTT [featuring NAS, EVE & Q-TIP]** #1 R&B hit (6 weeks); Lil' Mo (vocal ad libs)	The Gold Mind 64029
2/12/00	34	3	4. Love Is Blind Airplay #26 **EVE Featuring Faith Evans** from Eve's album *Ruff Ryders' First Lady* on Ruff Ryders 490453	album cut

DATE	POS	WKS	ARTIST–RECORD TITLE	LABEL & NO.
5/19/01	**2** (1)	28	5. **Let Me Blow Ya Mind** Airplay #1 (4) / Sales #46 **EVE Featuring Gwen Stefani**	Ruff Ryders 497562
11/3/01+	**18**	20	6. Caramel Airplay #18 **CITY HIGH Featuring Eve**	Booga Basement 497608
7/27/02	**2** (4)	19	7. **Gangsta Lovin'** Airplay #2 / Sales #6 **EVE Feat. Alicia Keys** samples "Don't Stop The Music" by Yarbrough & Peoples	Ruff Ryders 497817
1/4/03	**27**	4	8. Satisfaction Airplay #25 from the album *EVE-Olution* on Ruff Ryders 493381	album cut
			EVERCLEAR	
			Rock trio formed in Portland, Oregon: Art Alexakis (vocals, guitar), Craig Montoya (bass) and Greg Eklund (drums).	
3/2/96	**29** A	14	1. Santa Monica (Watch The World Die) #1 Mainstream Rock hit (3 weeks); from the album *Sparkle And Fade* on Capitol 30929	album cut
5/9/98	**33** A	7	2. I Will Buy You A New Life from the album *So Much For The Afterglow* on Capitol 36503	album cut
7/29/00	**11**	17	3. Wonderful Sales #6 / Airplay #17	Capitol 58870
			EVERETT, Betty	
			Born on 11/23/39 in Greenwood, Mississippi. Died on 8/19/2001 (age 61). R&B singer/pianist.	
3/21/64	**6**	10	1. **The Shoop Shoop Song (It's In His Kiss)**	Vee-Jay 585
9/19/64	**5**	11	2. **Let It Be Me** **BETTY EVERETT & JERRY BUTLER**	Vee-Jay 613
2/15/69	**26**	6	3. There'll Come A Time	Uni 55100
			EVERLAST	
			Born Erik Schrody on 8/18/69 in Valley Stream, New York. White rock-hip-hop singer/songwriter. Former member of House Of Pain. Played "Rhodes" in the movie *Judgment Night*.	
3/13/99	**13**	19	1. What It's Like Airplay #5 #1 Mainstream Rock hit (1 week) / #1 Modern Rock hit (9 weeks); from the album *Whitey Ford Sings The Blues* on Tommy Boy 1236	album cut
			EVERLY BROTHERS, The	
			Rock and roll-pop-country vocal duo/guitarists/songwriters: brothers Don (born Isaac Donald on 2/1/37 in Brownie, Kentucky) and Phil (born on 1/19/39 in Chicago, Illinois). Parents were folk and country singers. Don (beginning at age eight) and Phil (age six) sang with parents through high school. Phil was married for a time to the daughter of Janet Bleyer (of The Chordettes). Duo split up in July 1973 and reunited in September 1983. Inducted into the Rock and Roll Hall of Fame in 1986. Won Grammy's Lifetime Achievement Award in 1997. Don's daughter Erin was married for a short time to Axl Rose of Guns N' Roses in 1990.	
5/27/57	**2** (4)	22	● 1. **Bye Bye Love** /Best Seller #2 / Top 100 #2 / Jockey #2 / Juke Box #9 #1 Country hit (7 weeks)	
7/8/57		1	2. I Wonder If I Care As Much Best Seller: flip	Cadence 1315
9/30/57	**1** (4)	20	● 3. **Wake Up Little Susie** Jockey #1 (4) / Top 100 #1 (2) / Best Seller #1 (1) #1 R&B hit (1 week) / #1 Country hit (8 weeks)	Cadence 1337
2/17/58	**26**	3	4. This Little Girl Of Mine Best Seller #26 / Top 100 #28 #9 R&B hit for Ray Charles in 1955	Cadence 1342

DATE	POS	WKS	ARTIST–RECORD TITLE	LABEL & NO.
4/28/58	**1 (5)**	16	● 5. **All I Have To Do Is Dream /** Jockey #1 (5) / Best Seller #1 (4) / Top 100 #1 (3) #1 R&B hit (5 weeks) / #1 Country hit (3 weeks)	
5/12/58	**30**	2	6. Claudette Top 100 #30 / Best Seller: flip written by Roy Orbison for his wife	Cadence 1348
8/11/58	**1 (1)**	15	● 7. **Bird Dog /** Best Seller #1 (1) / Hot 100 #2 #1 Country hit (6 weeks)	
8/18/58	**10**	11	8. **Devoted To You** Hot 100 #10 / Best Seller: flip	Cadence 1350
11/24/58	**2 (1)**	11	9. **Problems /**	
12/15/58	**40**	1	10. Love Of My Life	Cadence 1355
4/20/59	**16**	8	11. Take A Message To Mary /	
4/20/59	**22**	6	12. Poor Jenny	Cadence 1364
8/24/59	**4**	13	13. **('Til) I Kissed You** The Crickets (backing band)	Cadence 1369
1/25/60	**7**	11	14. **Let It Be Me**	Cadence 1376
5/2/60	**1 (5)**	13	● 15. **Cathy's Clown** #1 R&B hit (1 week)	Warner 5151
6/27/60	**8**	9	16. **When Will I Be Loved**	Cadence 1380
9/12/60	**7**	10	17. **So Sad (To Watch Good Love Go Bad)** /	
9/12/60	**21**	7	18. Lucille	Warner 5163
11/28/60	**22**	4	19. Like Strangers	Cadence 1388
2/13/61	**7**	10	20. **Walk Right Back /**	
2/13/61	**8**	9	21. **Ebony Eyes**	Warner 5199
6/12/61	**27**	3	22. Temptation #3 hit for Bing Crosby in 1934	Warner 5220
10/9/61	**20**	6	23. Don't Blame Me #6 hit for Ethel Waters in 1933; released as 7" E.P. with "Muskrat," "Walk Right Back" and "Lucille"	Warner 5501 (+2)
2/3/62	**6**	9	24. **Crying In The Rain**	Warner 5250
6/2/62	**9**	7	25. **That's Old Fashioned (That's The Way Love Should Be)**	Warner 5273
12/5/64	**31**	2	26. Gone, Gone, Gone	Warner 5478
7/8/67	**40**	2	27. Bowling Green	Warner 7020
			EVERY MOTHERS' SON	
			Pop-rock group from New York: brothers Dennis (vocals) and Larry (guitar) Larden, Bruce Milner (organ), Schuyler Larsen (bass) and Christopher Augustine (drums).	
5/27/67	**6**	12	1. **Come On Down To My Boat**	MGM 13733
			EVERYTHING	
			Ska-rock group from Sperryville, Virginia: Craig Honeycutt (vocals, guitar), Rich Bradley, Wolfe Quinn and Steve Van Dam (horns), David Slankard (bass) and Nate Brown (drums).	
10/24/98	**34** ᴬ	6	1. Hooch Hot 100 #69 (7 wks) from the album *Super Natural* on Blackbird 38003	album cut
			EVERYTHING BUT THE GIRL	
			Pop/dance duo formed in London, England: Tracey Thorn (vocals) and Ben Watt (instruments). Group name taken from a furniture store sign on England's Hull University campus.	
11/11/95+	**2 (1)**	37	● 1. **Missing** Airplay #1 (5) / Sales #12	Atlantic 87124

DATE	POS	WKS	ARTIST–RECORD TITLE	LABEL & NO.
			EVE 6	
			Rock trio from Los Angeles, California: Max Collins (vocals, bass), Jon Siebels (guitar) and Tony Fagenson (drums).	
12/5/98	28	11	1. Inside Out Airplay #21	album cut
			#1 Modern Rock hit (4 weeks); from the album *Eve 6* on RCA 67617	
7/7/01	30	9	2. Here's To The Night Airplay #25	album cut
			from the album *Horrorscope* on RCA 67713	
			EXCITERS, The	
			R&B vocal group from Jamaica, New York: Herb Rooney, his wife Brenda Reid, Carol Johnson and Lillian Walker.	
12/15/62+	4	10	1. **Tell Him**	United Artists 544
			EXILE	
			Pop group formed in Richmond, Kentucky: J.P. Pennington (vocals, guitar), Les Taylor (guitar), Marlon Hargis (keyboards), Sonny Lemaire (bass) and Steve Goetzman (drums). Group had a highly successful country career from 1983-91.	
8/5/78	1 (4)	17	● 1. **Kiss You All Over**	Warner/Curb 8589
2/3/79	40	1	2. You Thrill Me	Warner/Curb 8711
			EXPOSÉ	
			Female dance trio based in Miami, Florida: Ann Curless, Jeanette Jurado and Gioia Bruno. Assembled by producer/songwriter Lewis Martineè. Kelly Moneymaker replaced Bruno in 1992.	
2/14/87	5	12	1. **Come Go With Me** Sales #4 / Airplay #6	Arista 9555
5/30/87	5	11	2. **Point Of No Return** Sales #5 / Airplay #6	Arista 9579
9/5/87	7	13	3. **Let Me Be The One** Sales #4 / Airplay #7	Arista 9617
12/5/87+	1 (1)	16	4. **Seasons Change** Sales #1 (1) / Airplay #2	Arista 9640
			#1 Adult Contemporary hit (1 week)	
6/3/89	8	11	● 5. **What You Don't Know** Sales #8 / Airplay #10	Arista 9836
9/2/89	10	12	6. **When I Looked At Him** Airplay #6 / Sales #11	Arista 9868
12/23/89+	9	11	7. **Tell Me Why** Sales #7 / Airplay #13	Arista 9916
4/14/90	17	9	8. Your Baby Never Looked Good In Blue	
			Airplay #11 / Sales #19	Arista 2011
11/21/92	28	7	9. I Wish The Phone Would Ring Airplay #21 / Sales #56	Arista 12466
5/15/93	8	21	● 10. **I'll Never Get Over You (Getting Over Me)**	Arista 12518
			Airplay #4 / Sales #14	
			#1 Adult Contemporary hit (1 week)	
			EXTREME	
			Rock group from Boston, Massachusetts: Gary Cherone (vocals), Nuno Bettencourt (guitar), Pat Badger (bass) and Paul Geary (drums). Cherone became lead singer of Van Halen in September 1996.	
4/13/91	1 (1)	17	● 1. **More Than Words** Sales #1 (4) / Airplay #3	A&M 1552
8/24/91	4	17	2. **Hole Hearted** Airplay #6 / Sales #19	A&M 1564
			EYE TO EYE	
			Pop duo: singer Deborah Berg (from Seattle, Washington) and pianist Julian Marshall (from England).	
7/17/82	37	3	1. Nice Girls	Warner 50050

The Eagles seemed to constantly shift their lineup, with the exception of mainstays Glenn Frey and Don Henley. After Bernie Leadon's departure in 1976, Joe Walsh was the "New Kid In Town" when that song went to #1.

Sheena Easton turned an appearance on the BBC TV series *The Big Time* into a successful pop career. Her #1 hit, "Morning Train (Nine To Five)," debuted on the Hot 100 a week before Dolly Parton's hit "9 to 5" reached #1.

Eminem found some support among Oscar voters for his first chart-topper, "Lose Yourself." The Detroit rapper's hit from the movie *8 Mile* received the Academy Award for "Best Original Song" in 2003.

Gloria Estefan released three Top 40 hits from her album *Let It Loose,* but it was the fourth, a ballad titled "Anything For You," that became the Miami Sound Machine singer's first #1 hit.

Eurythmics couldn't convert their #1 hit "Sweet Dreams (Are Made Of This)" into a Grammy win for Best New Artist, but singer Annie Lennox offered the stuff dreams are made of by performing on the telecast in an Elvis wig.

Exposé opted for a change from their early dance hits by releasing the ballad "Seasons Change," and watched it become their first #1 hit. Despite several more hit singles, Exposé soon found their career in a winter chill.

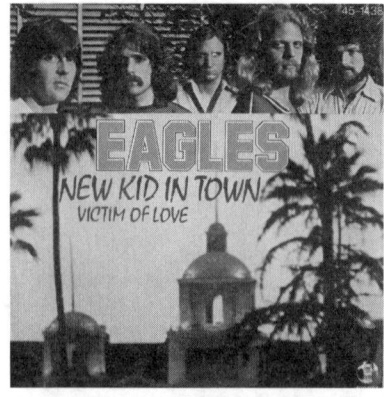

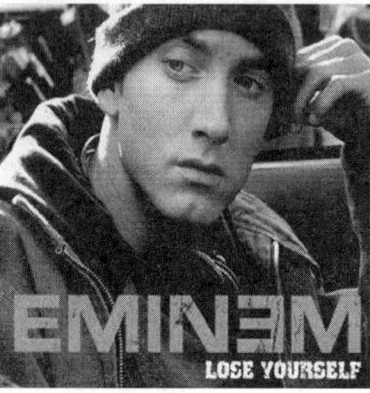

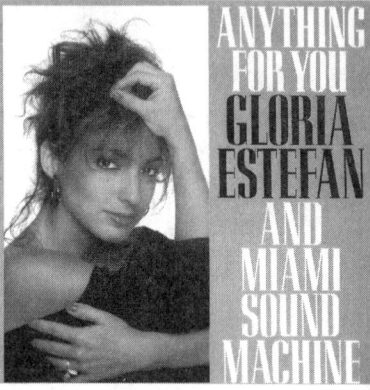

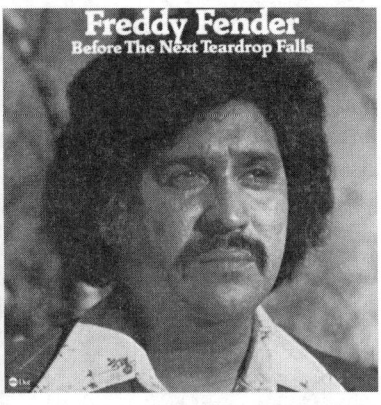

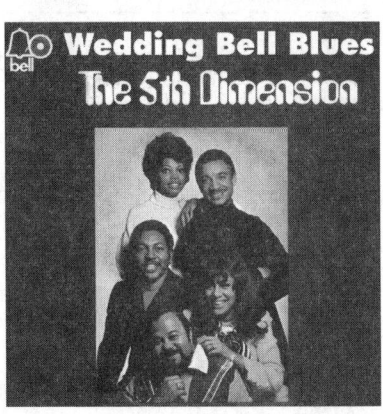

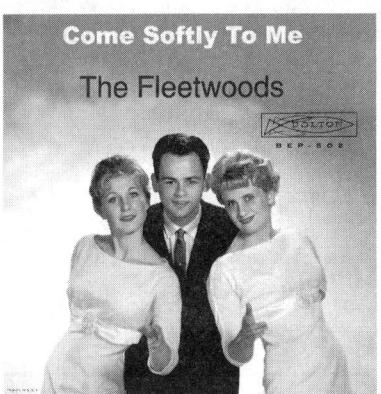

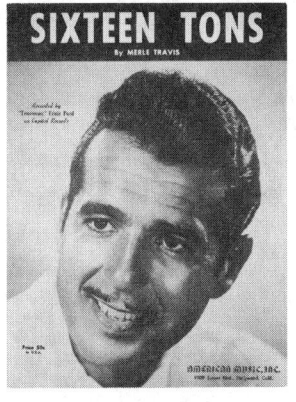

Shelley Fabares followed up her #1 hit "Johnny Angel" with the #21 hit "Johnny Love Me." She eventually starred on the TV show *One Day At A Time* alongside Howard Hesseman, *WKRP*'s Dr. Johnny Fever.

Falco released his chart-topping tribute to Mozart, "Rock Me Amadeus," in 1986, two years after the film based on the composer's life, *Amadeus,* earned an Oscar as Best Picture. To date, Falco's career has not made it to film.

Freddy Fender took his name from a popular style of guitar, but it was his own distinctive guitar style that helped push "Before The Next Teardrop Falls" to #1. The song won the 1975 Country Music Association Award for Single of the Year.

The 5th Dimension did not seem to take the title of their #1 hit "Wedding Bell Blues" to heart. In 1969, group members Marilyn McCoo and Billy Davis, Jr., got married, and another member, Florence LaRue, married their manager.

50 Cent didn't shortchange his fans, as his debut album, *Get Rich or Die Tryin',* spun off #1 hits like "In Da Club." Although Beyoncé's music dominated 2003, her own version of "In Da Club" didn't even reach the Top 40.

The Fireballs already had two Top 40 hits before singer Jimmy Gilmer joined the group, but his voice and arrangements helped push "Sugar Shack" to #1. Sadly, their future hits wouldn't be so sweet.

The Fleetwoods went from a duo to a trio when trumpet player Gary Troxel gave them the missing piece to a song they were working on and joined the group. The end result was their first #1 hit, "Come Softly To Me."

Tennessee Ernie Ford reached #1 with the hit "Sixteen Tons." The next year, he became host of *The Ford Show* on NBC. Coincidentally, the show's name referred to their sponsor, The Ford Motor Company, rather than to the singer.

DATE	POS	WKS	ARTIST–RECORD TITLE	LABEL & NO.

F

FABARES, Shelley

Born Michele Fabares on 1/19/44 in Santa Monica, California. Pop singer/actress. Niece of actress Nanette Fabray. Starred in several movies and TV shows. Married to record producer Lou Adler from 1964-67. Married actor Mike Farrell on 1/31/84.

DATE	POS	WKS	ARTIST–RECORD TITLE	LABEL & NO.
3/17/62	**1** (2)	13	1. **Johnny Angel**	Colpix 621
			The Blossoms (backing vocals)	
6/30/62	21	6	2. Johnny Loves Me	Colpix 636

FABIAN

Born Fabiano Forte on 2/6/43 in Philadelphia, Pennsylvania. Popular teen idol. Acted in several movies.

DATE	POS	WKS	ARTIST–RECORD TITLE	LABEL & NO.
2/2/59	31	3	1. I'm A Man	Chancellor 1029
4/6/59	9	11	2. **Turn Me Loose**	Chancellor 1033
6/22/59	**3**	10	3. **Tiger**	Chancellor 1037
9/28/59	29	3	4. Come On And Get Me	Chancellor 1041
11/30/59	9	11	5. **Hound Dog Man** /	
12/7/59	12	9	6. This Friendly World	Chancellor 1044
			above 2 from the movie *Hound Dog Man* starring Fabian	
3/14/60	31	3	7. About This Thing Called Love /	
3/14/60	39	2	8. String Along	Chancellor 1047
			all of above produced by Peter de Angelis	

FABIAN, Lara

Born Lara Crockaert on 1/9/70 in Bruxelles, Belgium; raised in Italy. Female Adult Contemporary singer/songwriter.

DATE	POS	WKS	ARTIST–RECORD TITLE	LABEL & NO.
7/29/00	32	4	1. I Will Love Again Airplay #35 / Sales #36	Columbia 79375

FABOLOUS

Born John Jackson on 11/18/79 in Brooklyn, New York. Male rapper.

DATE	POS	WKS	ARTIST–RECORD TITLE	LABEL & NO.
5/12/01	11	14	1. Superwoman Pt. II Sales #2 / Airplay #22	EastWest 67171
			LIL MO (Featuring Fabolous)	
9/15/01	25	10	2. Can't Deny It Airplay #24	Desert Storm 67231
			FABOLOUS featuring Nate Dogg	
			Lil' Mo (backing vocal); samples "Ambitionz Az A Ridah" by 2Pac	
2/9/02	33	3	3. Young'n (Holla Back) Airplay #33 / Sales #41	Desert Storm 67265
9/14/02	20	8	4. Trade It All (Part 2) Airplay #13	album cut
			FABOLOUS featuring P. DIDDY & JAGGED EDGE	
			from the movie *Barbershop* starring Ice Cube (soundtrack on Epic 86575)	
10/26/02+	5 ˢ	20	5. **This Is My Party**	Desert Storm 67355
3/22/03	**4**	19	6. **Can't Let You Go** Airplay #4 / Sales #42	Desert Storm 67428
			FABOLOUS featuring Mike Shorey & Lil' Mo	
6/7/03	37	3	7. 4 Ever Sales #33 / Airplay #34	Elektra 67379
			LIL' MO (Featuring Fabolous)	
6/21/03	**4**	24	8. Into You Airplay #4 / Sales #71	Desert Storm 67452
			FABOLOUS Featuring Ashanti or Tamia	
			the version with Tamia is the 12" single above (samples "Fancy Dancer" by the Commodores); the version with Ashanti is from his album *Street Dreams* on Desert Storm 62791 (no sample)	

DATE	POS	WKS	ARTIST—RECORD TITLE	LABEL & NO.
8/25/62	7	12	**FABRIC, Bent, and His Piano** Born Bent Fabricius-Bjerre on 12/7/24 in Copenhagen, Denmark. Male pianist. ● 1. **Alley Cat** **[I]** Danish title: "Omkring et Flygel" ("Around The Piano")	Atco 6226
5/24/86	10	10	**FABULOUS THUNDERBIRDS, The** Male blues-rock group from Austin, Texas: Kim Wilson (vocals, harmonica), Jimmie Vaughan (guitar), Preston Hubbard (bass) and Fran Christina (drums). Vaughan is the older brother of Stevie Ray Vaughan. 1. **Tuff Enuff** Sales #11 / Airplay #12	CBS Associated 05838
11/9/59	28	3	**FACENDA, Tommy** Born on 11/10/39 in Norfolk, Virginia. Pop singer. Nicknamed "Bubba." 1. High School U.S.A. (Area) **[N]** first released as "High School U.S.A. Virginia" on Legrand 1001 (B-side: "Give Me Another Chance"); Atlantic then released 28 different versions of this record, each mentioning the names of high schools in the following areas: Virginia (Atlantic 51), New York City, North & South Carolina, Washington D.C., Philadelphia, Detroit, Pittsburgh, Minneapolis & St. Paul, Florida, Newark, Boston, Cleveland, Buffalo, Hartford, Nashville, Indianapolis, Chicago, New Orleans, St. Louis & Kansas City, Georgia & Alabama, Cincinnati, Memphis, Los Angeles, San Francisco, Texas, Seattle & Portland, Denver, and Oklahoma (Atlantic 78)	Atlantic 51 to 78
			FACES — see SMALL FACES	
7/21/84	38	3	**FACE TO FACE** Rock group from Boston, Massachusetts: Laurie Sargent (vocals), brothers Angelo and Stuart Kimball (guitars), John Ryder (bass) and William Beard (drums). 1. 10-9-8	Epic 04430
4/9/77	31	4	**FACTS OF LIFE** R&B vocal trio: Jean Davis (younger sister of Tyrone Davis), Keith William (of The Flamingos) and Chuck Carter. 1. Sometimes produced by Millie Jackson; #1 Country hit for Bill Anderson & Mary Lou Turner in 1976	Kayvette 5128
10/30/82	26	7	**FAGEN, Donald** Born on 1/10/48 in Passaic, New Jersey. Pop-rock singer/keyboardist. Member of Steely Dan. 1. I.G.Y. (What A Beautiful World) I.G.Y.: International Geophysical Year (Jul '57-Dec '58)	Warner 29900
5/12/73	32	5	**FAIRCHILD, Barbara** Born on 11/12/50 in Knobel, Arkansas. Country singer/songwriter. 1. Teddy Bear Song #1 Country hit (2 weeks)	Columbia 45743
			FAITH — see EVANS, Faith	

DATE	POS	WKS	ARTIST–RECORD TITLE	LABEL & NO.
			FAITH, Adam	
			Born Terence Nelhams on 6/23/40 in Acton, London, England. Died of a heart attack on 3/7/2003 (age 62). Pop singer/actor.	
2/20/65	31	2	1. It's Alright **ADAM FAITH With The Roulettes**	Amy 913
			FAITH, Percy, and his Orchestra	
			Born on 4/7/08 in Toronto, Ontario, Canada. Died of cancer on 2/9/76 (age 67). Conductor/arranger.	
1/25/60	1 (9)	17	● 1. The Theme From "A Summer Place" [I] from the movie starring Troy Donahue and Sandra Dee; 1960 Grammy winner: Record of the Year	Columbia 41490
6/27/60	35	1	2. Theme For Young Lovers [I]	Columbia 41655
			FAITHFULL, Marianne	
			Born on 12/29/46 in Hampstead, London. Singer/actress. Involved in a long, tumultuous relationship with Mick Jagger. Acted in several stage and screen productions.	
12/19/64+	22	6	1. As Tears Go By	London 9697
3/27/65	26	5	2. Come And Stay With Me written by Jackie DeShannon	London 9731
6/26/65	32	5	3. This Little Bird	London 9759
9/4/65	24	5	4. Summer Nights	London 9780
			FAITH NO MORE	
			Rock group from San Francisco, California: Michael "Vlad Dracula" Patton (vocals), Jim Martin (guitar), Roddy Bottum (keyboards), Billy Gould (bass) and Mike Bordin (drums).	
7/14/90	9	13	● 1. Epic Sales #4 / Airplay #19	Slash 19813
			FALCO	
			Born Johann Holzel on 2/19/57 in Vienna, Austria. Died in a car crash on 2/6/98 (age 40). Male singer/songwriter.	
2/22/86	1 (3)	13	1. **Rock Me Amadeus** Sales #1 (3) / Airplay #1 (3) tribute to Wolfgang Amadeus Mozart	A&M 2821
5/17/86	18	8	2. Vienna Calling Airplay #17 / Sales #18	A&M 2832
			FALCON, Billy	
			Born on 7/13/56 in Valley Stream, New York. Rock singer/songwriter/guitarist.	
10/12/91	35	2	1. Power Windows Sales #73 / Airplay #74 co-produced by Jon Bon Jovi	Jambco 868672
			FALCONS, The	
			R&B vocal group from Detroit, Michigan: Eddie Floyd, Mack Rice, Joe Stubbs (brother of Four Tops member Levi Stubbs) and Willie Schofield. Stubbs died of heart failure on 1/19/98 (age 57).	
6/8/59	17	10	1. You're So Fine	Unart 2013

DATE	POS	WKS	ARTIST—RECORD TITLE	LABEL & NO.
			FALTERMEYER, Harold	
			Born on 10/5/52 in Munich, Germany. Keyboardist/songwriter/producer.	
4/13/85	3	12	1. **Axel F** Sales #2 / Airplay #4 **[I]** #1 Adult Contemporary hit (2 weeks); from the movie *Beverly Hills Cop* starring Eddie Murphy (played Axel Foley)	MCA 52536
			FÄLTSKOG, Agnetha — see ABBA	
			FAME, Georgie, And The Blue Flames	
			Born Clive Powell on 6/26/43 in Leigh, Lancashire, England. Began as a pianist with Billy Fury's backup group, The Blue Flames.	
2/27/65 3/2/68	21 7	6 12	1. Yeh, Yeh 2. **The Ballad Of Bonnie And Clyde** inspired by, but not included in, the 1967 movie *Bonnie And Clyde* starring Warren Beatty and Faye Dunaway	Imperial 66086 Epic 10283
			FANCY	
			Pop-rock group from England: Helen Court (vocals), Ray Fenwick (guitar), Alan Hawkshaw (keyboards), Mo Foster (bass) and Henry Spinetti (drums). Court and Spinetti left after "Wild Thing"; replaced by Annie Kavanagh (vocals) and Les Binks (drums).	
8/3/74 11/16/74	14 19	8 4	1. Wild Thing 2. Touch Me	Big Tree 15004 Big Tree 16026
			FANNY	
			Female rock group from Los Angeles, California: sisters June (vocals, guitar) and Jean (vocals, bass) Millington, Nicole Barclay (keyboards) and Alice DeBuhr (drums). Jean Millington and DeBuhr left in 1974, replaced by Patti Quatro (bass; sister of Suzi Quatro) and Brie Howard (drums).	
11/6/71 3/15/75	40 29	1 4	1. Charity Ball 2. Butter Boy	Reprise 1033 Casablanca 814
			FANTASTIC JOHNNY C, The	
			Born Johnny Corley on 4/28/43 in Greenwood, South Carolina. R&B singer.	
11/4/67 8/10/68	7 34	12 2	1. **Boogaloo Down Broadway** 2. Hitch It To The Horse	Phil-L.A. 305 Phil-L.A. 315
			FARDON, Don	
			Born Donald Maughn on 8/19/43 in Coventry, West Midlands, England. Pop singer.	
9/21/68	20	6	1. (The Lament Of The Cherokee) Indian Reservation written by John D. Loudermilk	GNP Crescendo 405
			FARGO, Donna	
			Born Yvonne Vaughan on 11/10/45 in Mount Airy, North Carolina. Country singer/songwriter.	
7/8/72	11	10	● 1. **The Happiest Girl In The Whole U.S.A.** #1 Country hit (3 weeks)	Dot 17409
11/11/72+	5	14	● 2. **Funny Face** #1 Country hit (3 weeks)	Dot 17429

DATE	POS	WKS	ARTIST–RECORD TITLE	LABEL & NO.
			FARRIS, Dionne	
			Born in 1969 in Bordertown, New Jersey. Female R&B singer. Former member of Arrested Development.	
2/11/95	4	29	1. **I Know** Airplay #1 (7) / Sales #22	Columbia 77750
			FASTBALL	
			Rock trio from Austin, Texas: Miles Zuniga (vocals, guitar), Tony Scalzo (vocals, bass) and Joey Shuffield (drums).	
4/4/98	5 ᴬ	35	1. **The Way** #1 Modern Rock hit (7 weeks)	album cut
8/7/99	20	10	2. Out Of My Head Airplay #13 above 2 from the album *All The Pain Money Can Buy* on Hollywood 62130	album cut
			FASTER PUSSYCAT	
			Hard-rock group from Los Angeles, California: Taime Downe (vocals), Greg Steele and Brent Muscat (guitars), Eric Stacy (bass) and Mark Michals (drums). Group name taken from the 1965 action movie *Faster Pussycat! Kill! Kill!*	
4/21/90	28	6	1. House Of Pain Sales #20 / Airplay #39	Elektra 64995
			FAT BOYS	
			Rap trio from Brooklyn, New York: Mark "Prince Markie Dee" Morales, Darren "The Human Beat Box" Robinson and Damon "Kool Rock" Wimbley. Group starred in the 1987 movie *Disorderlies*. Robinson died of heart failure on 12/10/95 (age 28).	
8/8/87	12	11	1. Wipeout Sales #4 / Airplay #20 **FAT BOYS (with The Beach Boys)**	Tin Pan Apple 885960
7/9/88	16	8	2. The Twist (Yo, Twist!) Sales #12 / Airplay #17 **FAT BOYS (with Chubby Checker)**	Tin Pan Apple 887571
			FATBOY SLIM	
			Born Norman Cook on 7/31/63 in Brighton, Sussex, England. Techno-house instrumentalist. Former member of The Housemartins and Beats International.	
5/15/99	36	3	1. Praise You Airplay #36 / Sales #45 samples "Take Yo Praise" by Camille Yarborough	Astralwerks 66254
			FATHER MC	
			Born Timothy Brown in Harlem, New York. Dancehall reggae singer.	
2/16/91	20	8	● 1. I'll Do 4 U Sales #14 / Airplay #32 samples "Got To Be Real" by Cheryl Lynn	Uptown/MCA 53914
2/13/93	37	1	2. Everything's Gonna Be Alright Sales #19 / Airplay #39 samples "Good Times" by Chic	Uptown/MCA 54523
			FAT JOE	
			Born Joseph Cartagena on 3/22/65 in the Bronx, New York. Male rapper.	
12/1/01+	15	13	1. We Thuggin Airplay #15 / Sales #39 **FAT JOE Featuring R. Kelly**	Atlantic 85174
2/23/02	2 (7)	25	2. **What's Luv?** Airplay #2 / Sales #20 **FAT JOE Featuring Ashanti**	Atlantic 85233
7/12/03	22	10	3. I Want You Airplay #23 **THALIA featuring Fat Joe** samples "A Little Bit Of Love" by Brenda Russell	Virgin 47305

DATE	POS	WKS	ARTIST–RECORD TITLE	LABEL & NO.
			FELICIANO, José	
			Born on 9/8/45 in Lares, Puerto Rico; raised in the Bronx, New York. Blind since birth. Singer/guitarist. Won the 1968 Best New Artist Grammy Award.	
8/3/68	**3**	11	1. **Light My Fire**	RCA Victor 9550
10/26/68	**25**	7	2. Hi-Heel Sneakers	RCA Victor 9641
			FENDER, Freddy	
			Born Baldemar Huerta on 6/4/37 in San Benito, Texas. Country singer/guitarist. Acted in the movie *The Milagro Beanfield War*.	
3/8/75	**1** (1)	15	● 1. **Before The Next Teardrop Falls** #1 Country hit (2 weeks)	ABC/Dot 17540
7/19/75	**8**	14	● 2. **Wasted Days And Wasted Nights** #1 Country hit (2 weeks)	ABC/Dot 17558
11/8/75	**20**	6	3. Secret Love #1 Country hit (1 week); #1 hit for Doris Day in 1954	ABC/Dot 17585
3/20/76	**32**	4	4. You'll Lose A Good Thing #1 Country hit (1 week)	ABC/Dot 17607
			FENDERMEN, The	
			Duo of Phil Humphrey (from Stoughton, Wisconsin) and Jim Sundquist (from Niagara, Wisconsin); both were born on 11/26/37.	
6/13/60	**5**	13	1. **Mule Skinner Blues**	Soma 1137
			FERGUSON, Jay	
			Born John Ferguson on 5/10/47 in Burbank, California. Member of Spirit and Jo Jo Gunne.	
1/28/78	**9**	12	1. **Thunder Island**	Asylum 45444
6/9/79	**31**	4	2. Shakedown Cruise	Asylum 46041
			FERGUSON, Johnny	
			Born on 3/22/37 in Nashville, Tennessee. Pop singer.	
4/18/60	**27**	3	1. Angela Jones written by John D. Loudermilk	MGM 12855
			FERGUSON, Maynard	
			Born on 5/4/28 in Verdun, Quebec, Canada. Jazz trumpeter.	
5/28/77	**28**	6	1. Gonna Fly Now (Theme From "Rocky")　　[I] from the movie *Rocky* starring Sylvester Stallone	Columbia 10468
			FERKO STRING BAND	
			String band from Philadelphia, Pennsylvania; directed by William Connors.	
6/18/55	**14**	6	1. Alabama Jubilee　　Juke Box #14 / Best Seller #18　[I] #2 hit for Arthur Collins & Byron Harlan in 1915	Media 1010
			FERRANTE & TEICHER	
			Piano duo: Arthur Ferrante (born on 9/7/21 in Manhattan, New York) and Louis Teicher (born on 8/24/24 in Wilkes-Barre, Pennsylvania). Met as children while attending Manhattan's performing arts academy Juilliard School.	
8/8/60	**10**	15	1. **Theme From The Apartment**　　[I] from the movie starring Jack Lemmon	United Artists 231

DATE	POS	WKS	ARTIST–RECORD TITLE	LABEL & NO.
11/28/60+	**2** (1)	18	● 2. **Exodus** [I] theme from the movie starring Paul Newman	United Artists 274
4/17/61	37	1	3. (Love Theme From) One Eyed Jacks [I] from the movie *One Eyed Jacks* starring Marlon Brando	United Artists 300
11/13/61	8	8	4. **Tonight** [I] from the musical *West Side Story*	United Artists 373
11/29/69+	10	11	5. **Midnight Cowboy** [I] featuring the "water sound" guitar of Vincent Bell; title song from the movie starring Jon Voight and Dustin Hoffman	United Artists 50554
			FERRY, Bryan	
4/16/88	31	3	Born on 9/26/45 in Washington, Tyne & Wear, England. Lead singer of Roxy Music. 1. Kiss And Tell Sales #24 / Airplay #34 from the movie *Bright Lights, Big City* starring Michael J. Fox	Reprise 28117
			FIELD MOB	
2/15/03	18	9	Male rap duo from Albany, Georgia: Darion "Boondox Blax" Crawford and Shawn Kalage. 1. Sick Of Being Lonely Airplay #17 / Sales #75	MCA 000574
			FIELDS, Ernie, Orch.	
10/12/59	4	14	Born on 8/26/05 in Nacogdoches, Texas. Died on 5/11/97 (age 91). Trombonist/pianist/bandleader. 1. **In The Mood** [I] #1 hit for Glenn Miller in 1940	Rendezvous 110
			FIEND — see MASTER P	
			FIESTAS, The	
4/27/59	11	11	R&B vocal group from Newark, New Jersey: Tommy Bullock, Eddie Morris, Sam Ingalls and Preston Lane. 1. So Fine	Old Town 1062
			5TH DIMENSION, The	
			Adult Contemporary-R&B vocal group formed in Los Angeles, California: Marilyn McCoo, Billy Davis Jr., Florence LaRue, Lamont McLemore and Ron Townson. McCoo and Davis were married on 7/26/69 and recorded as a duo since 1976. Townson died of kidney failure on 8/2/2001 (age 68).	
2/4/67	16	7	1. Go Where You Wanna Go	Soul City 753
6/17/67	7	10	2. **Up — Up And Away** above 2 produced by Johnny Rivers (owner of the Soul City label)	Soul City 756
12/9/67	34	1	3. Paper Cup	Soul City 760
2/24/68	29	5	4. Carpet Man above 3 written by Jimmy Webb	Soul City 762
6/22/68	3	12	▲ 5. **Stoned Soul Picnic**	Soul City 766
10/26/68	13	6	6. Sweet Blindness	Soul City 768
1/11/69	25	6	7. California Soul written by Ashford & Simpson	Soul City 770
3/15/69	**1** (6)	16	▲ 8. **Aquarius/Let The Sunshine In (The Flesh Failures)** #1 Adult Contemporary hit (2 weeks); medley from the off-Broadway rock musical *Hair* starring Steve Curry	Soul City 772

DATE	POS	WKS	ARTIST–RECORD TITLE	LABEL & NO.
8/9/69	**20**	7	9. Workin' On A Groovy Thing written by Neil Sedaka	Soul City 776
10/4/69	**1** (3)	14	▲ 10. **Wedding Bell Blues** #1 Adult Contemporary hit (2 weeks)	Soul City 779
1/24/70	**21**	6	11. Blowing Away	Soul City 780
5/2/70	**24**	5	12. Puppet Man written by Neil Sedaka	Bell 880
6/27/70	**27**	5	13. Save The Country	Bell 895
11/21/70	**2** (2)	15	▲ 14. **One Less Bell To Answer** #1 Adult Contemporary hit (1 week)	Bell 940
3/13/71	**19**	8	15. Love's Lines, Angles And Rhymes	Bell 965
10/2/71	**12**	9	16. Never My Love **[L]** #1 Adult Contemporary hit (1 week)	Bell 45,134
1/29/72	**37**	3	17. Together Let's Find Love **[L]**	Bell 45,170
4/22/72	**8**	13	▲ 18. **(Last Night) I Didn't Get To Sleep At All**	Bell 45,195
9/30/72	**10**	12	19. **If I Could Reach You** #1 Adult Contemporary hit (1 week)	Bell 45,261
2/10/73	**32**	4	20. Living Together, Growing Together from the movie *Lost Horizon* starring Peter Finch	Bell 45,310
			FIFTH ESTATE, The Pop group from Stamford, Connecticut: Wayne Wadhams (vocals, keyboards), Rick Engler and Bill Shute (guitars), Doug Ferrara (bass), and Ken Evans (drums).	
6/10/67	**11**	6	1. Ding Dong! The Witch Is Dead song originally appeared in the 1939 movie *The Wizard of Oz* starring Judy Garland	Jubilee 5573
			50 CENT Born Curtis Jackson on 7/6/76 in Jamaica, Queens, New York. Male rapper/songwriter.	
1/11/03	**13**	14	1. Wanksta Airplay #13 / Sales #68 from the movie *8 Mile* starring Eminem	Shady 497816
1/25/03	**1** (9)	26	2. **In Da Club** Airplay #1 (9) / Sales #4 #1 R&B hit (9 weeks)	Shady 497856
4/5/03	**1** (4)	20	3. **21 Questions** Airplay #1 (5) / Sales #13 **50 CENT Feat. Nate Dogg** #1 R&B hit (7 weeks); samples "It's Only Love Doing Its Thing" by Barry White	Shady 080739
5/10/03	**2** (3)	21	4. **Magic Stick** Airplay #1 (1) **LIL' KIM (feat. 50 Cent)** samples "The Thrill Is Gone" by B.B. King; from Lil' Kim's album *La Bella Mafia* on Queen Bee 83572	album cut
6/28/03	**3**	21	5. **P.I.M.P.** Airplay #3 / Sales #30	Shady 000888
			FILTER Industrial rock duo from Cleveland, Ohio: Richard Patrick (vocals, guitar, bass) and Brian Liesegang (keyboards, drums). Both worked with Trent Reznor in Nine Inch Nails.	
12/25/99+	**12**	15	1. Take A Picture Sales #14 / Airplay #14	Reprise 16889

DATE	POS	WKS	ARTIST–RECORD TITLE	LABEL & NO.

FINE YOUNG CANNIBALS

Rock trio formed in Birmingham, England: Roland Gift (vocals), Andy Cox (guitar) and David Steele (bass). Group name taken from the 1960 movie *All The Fine Young Cannibals*. Group appeared in the movie *Tin Men*. Gift acted in the movies *Sammy And Rosie Get Laid* and *Scandal*.

DATE	POS	WKS	ARTIST–RECORD TITLE	LABEL & NO.
2/25/89	**1** (1)	14	● 1. **She Drives Me Crazy**　　Sales #1 (1) / Airplay #2	I.R.S./MCA 53483
5/20/89	**1** (1)	13	2. **Good Thing**　　Airplay #1 (2) / Sales #2	I.R.S./MCA 53639
			from the 1987 movie *Tin Men* starring Richard Dreyfuss and Danny DeVito	
8/26/89	**11**	8	3. Don't Look Back　　Sales #8 / Airplay #18	I.R.S./MCA 53695

FINNEGAN, Larry

Born John Lawrence Finneran on 8/10/38 in Brooklyn, New York. Died of a brain tumor on 7/22/73 (age 34). Pop singer.

DATE	POS	WKS	ARTIST–RECORD TITLE	LABEL & NO.
3/31/62	**11**	8	1. Dear One	Old Town 1113

FIORILLO, Elisa

Born on 2/28/69 in Philadelphia, Pennsylvania. Female dance singer.

DATE	POS	WKS	ARTIST–RECORD TITLE	LABEL & NO.
8/15/87	**16**	8	1. Who Found Who　　Airplay #13 / Sales #14	Chrysalis 43120
			JELLYBEAN/Elisa Fiorillo	
12/8/90+	**27**	6	2. On The Way Up　　Sales #23 / Airplay #36	Chrysalis 23497

FIREBALLS, The

Rock and roll group formed in Raton, New Mexico: Jimmy Gilmer (vocals, piano), George Tomsco (lead guitar), Dan Trammell (rhythm guitar), Stan Lark (bass) and Eric Budd (drums). Doug Roberts replaced Budd in 1962. Roberts died on 11/18/81.

DATE	POS	WKS	ARTIST–RECORD TITLE	LABEL & NO.
10/26/59	**39**	2	1. Torquay　　　　　　　　　　　　　　[I]	Top Rank 2008
2/1/60	**24**	6	2. Bulldog　　　　　　　　　　　　　　[I]	Top Rank 2026
8/7/61	**27**	3	3. Quite A Party　　　　　　　　　　　[I]	Warwick 644
9/28/63	**1** (5)	13	● 4. **Sugar Shack**	Dot 16487
			#1 R&B hit (1 week)	
1/4/64	**15**	8	5. Daisy Petal Pickin'	Dot 16539
			JIMMY GILMER and THE FIREBALLS (above 2)	
1/27/68	**9**	10	6. **Bottle Of Wine**	Atco 6491

FIREFALL

Soft-rock group formed in Boulder, Colorado: Rick Roberts (vocals), Larry Burnett and Jack Bartley (guitars), Mark Andes (bass) and Mike Clarke (drums). David Muse (keyboards) joined in 1977. Andes was a member of Spirit and Jo Jo Gunne; joined Heart in 1980. Clarke was a member of The Byrds; died of liver failure on 12/19/93 (age 49).

DATE	POS	WKS	ARTIST–RECORD TITLE	LABEL & NO.
9/25/76	**9**	15	1. **You Are The Woman**	Atlantic 3335
4/30/77	**34**	3	2. Cinderella	Atlantic 3392
9/17/77	**11**	12	3. Just Remember I Love You	Atlantic 3420
			#1 Adult Contemporary hit (2 weeks); Timothy B. Schmit (backing vocal)	
10/28/78	**11**	10	4. Strange Way	Atlantic 3518
5/10/80	**35**	3	5. Headed For A Fall	Atlantic 3657
2/28/81	**37**	3	6. Staying With It	Atlantic 3791
			Lisa Nemzo (female vocal)	

DATE	POS	WKS	ARTIST–RECORD TITLE	LABEL & NO.
			FIREFLIES	
			White doo-wop group from Philadelphia, Pennsylvania: Ritchie Adams, Gerry Granahan (of Dicky Doo & The Don'ts), Vinnie Reynolds, Paul Giacalone and Johnny Viscelli.	
9/28/59	**21**	10	1. You Were Mine	Ribbon 6901
			FIREHOUSE	
			Pop-rock group from North Carolina: C.J. Snare (vocals), Bill Leverty (guitar), Perry Richardson (bass) and Michael Foster (drums).	
4/20/91	**19**	10	1. Don't Treat Me Bad Sales #11 / Airplay #19	Epic 73676
8/3/91	**5**	16	● 2. **Love Of A Lifetime** Sales #6 / Airplay #10	Epic 73771
9/5/92	**8**	12	3. **When I Look Into Your Eyes** Sales #11 / Airplay #20	Epic 74440
3/18/95	**26**	11	4. I Live My Life For You Sales #27 / Airplay #36	Epic 77812
			FIRM, The	
			All-star rock group from England: Paul Rodgers (vocals), Jimmy Page (guitar), Tony Franklin (bass) and Chris Slade (drums). Rodgers was in Free and Bad Company. Page was in The Yardbirds and Led Zeppelin. Slade later joined AC/DC.	
3/16/85	**28**	6	1. Radioactive Sales #23 / Airplay #28 #1 Mainstream Rock hit (1 week)	Atlantic 89586
			FIRST CHOICE	
			Female R&B-dance vocal trio from Philadelphia, Pennsylvania: Rochelle Fleming, Annette Guest and Joyce Jones.	
4/28/73	**28**	5	1. Armed And Extremely Dangerous	Philly Groove 175
			FIRST CLASS	
			Studio group formed in England: Tony Burrows (lead vocals), John Carter, Del John and Chas Mills (backing vocals), Spencer James (guitar), Robin Shaw (bass) and Eddie Richards (drums). Burrows was also the vocalist on hits by The Brotherhood Of Man, Edison Lighthouse, The Pipkins and White Plains.	
8/17/74	**4**	11	1. **Beach Baby**	UK 49022
			FIRST EDITION, The — see ROGERS, Kenny	
			FISCHER, Lisa	
			Born in Brooklyn, New York. R&B singer.	
6/1/91	**11**	8	1. How Can I Ease The Pain Sales #19 / Airplay #29 #1 R&B hit (2 weeks)	Elektra 64897
			FISHER, Eddie	
			Born Edwin Jack Fisher on 8/10/28 in Philadelphia, Pennsylvania. Pop singer/actor. Married to Debbie Reynolds from 1955-59. Other marriages to Elizabeth Taylor and Connie Stevens. Daughter with Debbie is actress/author Carrie Fisher. Daughters with Connie are singer Tricia Leigh Fisher and actress Joely Fisher. Own *Coke Time* 15-minute TV series (1953-57). Acted in several movies.	
9/4/54	**1** (3)	24	● 1. **I Need You Now** Best Seller #1 (3) / Jockey #1 (2) / Juke Box #1 (2)	RCA Victor 5830
10/30/54+	**5**	15	2. **Count Your Blessings (Instead of Sheep)** Best Seller #5 / Juke Box #9 / Jockey #10 from the movie *White Christmas* starring Bing Crosby	RCA Victor 5871

DATE	POS	WKS	ARTIST–RECORD TITLE	LABEL & NO.
3/5/55	**16**	2	3. A Man Chases A Girl (Until She Catches Him) / *Jockey #16 / Juke Box #20 / Best Seller #27* from the movie *There's No Business Like Show Business* starring Ethel Merman	
4/2/55	**20**	1	4. (I'm Always Hearing) Wedding Bells *Juke Box #20*	RCA Victor 6015
5/14/55	**6**	13	5. **Heart** *Jockey #6 / Juke Box #13 / Best Seller #15* from the Broadway musical *Damn Yankees* starring Gwen Verdon	RCA Victor 6097
8/27/55	**11**	8	6. Song Of The Dreamer / *Juke Box #11 / Best Seller #16 / Jockey #16 / Top 100 #43*	
9/3/55		4	7. Don't Stay Away Too Long *Best Seller: flip / Juke Box: flip*	RCA Victor 6196
12/24/55+	**7**	16	8. **Dungaree Doll** / *Top 100 #7 / Juke Box #7 / Best Seller #8 / Jockey #9*	
12/31/55	**20**	1	9. Everybody's Got A Home But Me *Jockey #20 / Top 100 #41* from the Broadway musical *Pipe Dream* starring Helen Traubel	RCA Victor 6337
6/30/56	**18**	7	10. On The Street Where You Live *Juke Box #18 / Top 100 #28* from the Broadway musical *My Fair Lady* starring Julie Andrews and Rex Harrison	RCA Victor 6529
10/20/56	**10**	17	11. **Cindy, Oh Cindy** *Best Seller #10 / Top 100 #10 / Jockey #10 / Juke Box #10* adapted from a sailor's sea chantey; Hugo Winterhalter (orch., all of above)	RCA Victor 6677
			FISHER, Miss Toni	
			Born in 1931 in Los Angeles, California. Died of a heart attack on 2/12/99 (age 67). Female singer.	
11/23/59	**3**	14	1. **The Big Hurt** first hit recording to feature an electronic "phasing" gimmick	Signet 275
7/14/62	**37**	1	2. West Of The Wall **TONI FISHER** lyrics inspired by the Berlin Wall crisis (8/13/61)	Big Top 3097
			FITZGERALD, Ella	
			Born on 4/25/18 in Newport News, Virginia. Died of diabetes on 6/15/96 (age 78). Legendary jazz singer. Won Grammy's Lifetime Achievement Award in 1967.	
5/30/60	**27**	7	1. Mack The Knife **[L]** recorded in West Berlin with the Paul Smith Quartet; written in 1928 as "Moritat" or "Theme From The Threepenny Opera"	Verve 10209
			FIVE	
			Pop vocal group from England: Rich Neville, Scott Robinson, Richard Breen, Jason Brown and Sean Conlon.	
7/4/98	**10**	22	● 1. **When The Lights Go Out** *Sales #7 / Airplay #41*	Arista 13495
			FIVE AMERICANS, The	
			Rock and roll band from Dallas, Texas: Michael Rabon (vocals), Norman Ezell (guitar), John Durrill (keyboards), James Grant (bass) and James Wright (drums). Wright married Robin of Jon & Robin & The In Crowd in 1970.	
2/12/66	**26**	5	1. I See The Light	HBR 454
3/18/67	**5**	9	2. **Western Union**	Abnak 118
6/17/67	**36**	2	3. Sound Of Love	Abnak 120
9/16/67	**36**	1	4. Zip Code	Abnak 123

DATE	POS	WKS	ARTIST–RECORD TITLE	LABEL & NO.
			FIVE BLOBS, The	
11/3/58	33	3	Group is actually the overdubbed vocals of Bernie Nee (born on 12/4/22; died in February 1974, age 51). 　　1.　The Blob　　　　　　　　　　　　Hot 100 #33 　　　　title song from the movie starring Steve McQueen	Columbia 41250
			FIVE FLIGHTS UP	
10/3/70	37	5	Black male pop group. Featuring lead singer J.B. Bingham. 　　1.　Do What You Wanna Do	T-A 202
			FIVE FOR FIGHTING	
10/27/01	14	22	Group is actually Adult Contemporary singer/songwriter/guitarist John Ondrasik (born in Los Angeles, California). Group name refers to a penalty in hockey. 　　1.　Superman (It's Not Easy)　　　　Airplay #15 　　　　from the album *America Town* on Aware 63759	album cut
			FIVE KEYS, The	
12/25/54	28	2	R&B vocal group from Newport News, Virginia: brothers Rudy and Bernie West, Ripley Ingram, Maryland Pierce and Ramon Loper. Ingram died on 3/23/95 (age 65). Rudy West died of a heart attack on 5/14/98 (age 65). 　　1.　Ling, Ting, Tong　　　　　　Best Seller #28	Capitol 2945
10/6/56	23	6	2.　Out Of Sight, Out Of Mind　Best Seller #23 / Top 100 #27 　　　　Dave Cavanaugh (orch.)	Capitol 3502
1/12/57	35	2	3.　Wisdom Of A Fool　　　　　　Top 100 #35 　　　　Van Alexander (orch.)	Capitol 3597
			FIVE MAN ELECTRICAL BAND	
7/10/71	3	12	Rock group from Ottawa, Ontario, Canada: Les Emmerson (vocals, guitar), Ted Gerow (piano), Brian Rading (bass) and brothers Rick (percussion) and Mike (drums) Belanger. ● 　1.　**Signs**	Lionel 3213
10/30/71	26	6	2.　Absolutely Right	Lionel 3220
			504 BOYZ	
4/22/00	17	6	All-star rap trio from New Orleans, Louisiana: Master P ("Nino Brown"), Silkk The Shocker ("Vito") and Mystikal ("G Money"). 504 is the area code for New Orleans. 　　1.　Wobble Wobble　　　　　Sales #3 / Airplay #56	No Limit 38698
			FIVE SATINS, The	
9/29/56	24	6	R&B vocal group from New Haven, Connecticut: Fred Parris, Al Denby, Jim Freeman and Eddie Martin, with Jessie Murphy (piano). ● 　1.　In The Still Of The Nite　　Best Seller #24 / Top 100 #29	Ember 1005
8/12/57	25	8	2.　To The Aisle　　　　　　Best Seller #25 / Top 100 #25	Ember 1019
			FIVE STAIRSTEPS, The	
6/20/70	8	11	R&B group from Chicago, Illinois: brothers Clarence (vocals), James (guitar), Kenny (bass) and Dennis (drums) Burke, with their sister Alohe (vocals). ● 　1.　**O-o-h Child**	Buddah 165

DATE	POS	WKS	ARTIST–RECORD TITLE	LABEL & NO.
			5000 VOLTS	
			Disco trio from England: Tina Charles, Martin Jay and Tony Eyers.	
11/15/75	26	5	1. I'm On Fire	Philips 40801
			FIXX, The	
			Techno-pop group formed in London, England: Cy Curnin (vocals), Jamie West-Oram (guitar), Rupert Greenall (keyboards), Dan Brown (bass) and Adam Woods (drums).	
7/9/83	20	8	1. Saved By Zero	MCA 52213
9/10/83	4	13	2. **One Thing Leads To Another**	MCA 52264
12/17/83+	32	7	3. The Sign Of Fire	MCA 52316
9/8/84	15	8	4. Are We Ourselves? Sales #13 / Airplay #21	MCA 52444
			#1 Mainstream Rock hit (2 weeks)	
6/28/86	19	6	5. Secret Separation Sales #18 / Airplay #29	MCA 52832
			#1 Mainstream Rock hit (2 weeks)	
5/4/91	35	3	6. How Much Is Enough Sales #35 / Airplay #35	Impact 54028
			FLACK, Roberta	
			Born on 2/10/39 in Asheville, North Carolina; raised in Arlington, Virginia. R&B/jazz-styled singer/pianist.	
7/3/71	29	9	1. You've Got A Friend	Atlantic 2808
			ROBERTA FLACK & DONNY HATHAWAY	
3/25/72	1 (6)	15	● 2. **The First Time Ever I Saw Your Face**	Atlantic 2864
			#1 Adult Contemporary hit (6 weeks); recorded in 1969; featured in the movie *Play Misty For Me* starring Clint Eastwood	
6/24/72	5	11	● 3. **Where Is The Love**	Atlantic 2879
			ROBERTA FLACK & DONNY HATHAWAY	
			#1 R&B hit (1 week) / #1 Adult Contemporary hit (1 week)	
2/3/73	1 (5)	13	● 4. **Killing Me Softly With His Song**	Atlantic 2940
			first recorded by Lori Lieberman in 1972; 1973 Grammy winner: Record of the Year	
10/13/73	30	5	5. Jesse	Atlantic 2982
7/6/74	1 (1)	13	● 6. **Feel Like Makin' Love**	Atlantic 3025
			#1 R&B hit (5 weeks) / #1 Adult Contemporary hit (2 weeks)	
3/18/78	2 (2)	14	● 7. **The Closer I Get To You**	Atlantic 3463
			ROBERTA FLACK with DONNY HATHAWAY	
			#1 R&B hit (2 weeks)	
6/24/78	24	5	8. If Ever I See You Again	Atlantic 3483
			#1 Adult Contemporary hit (3 weeks); title song from the movie starring Joe Brooks	
4/17/82	13	11	9. Making Love	Atlantic 4005
			title song from the movie starring Kate Jackson	
9/3/83	16	15	10. Tonight, I Celebrate My Love	Capitol 5242
			PEABO BRYSON/ROBERTA FLACK	
10/5/91	6	16	11. **Set The Night To Music** Airplay #23 / Sales #25	Atlantic 87607
			ROBERTA FLACK with Maxi Priest	
			FLAMING EMBER, The	
			White R&B-rock group from Detroit, Michigan: Joe Sladich (vocals, guitar), Bill Ellis (piano), Jim Bugnel (bass) and Jerry Plunk (drums).	
11/15/69	26	6	1. Mind, Body and Soul	Hot Wax 6902
6/20/70	24	10	2. Westbound #9	Hot Wax 7003
11/28/70	34	6	3. I'm Not My Brothers Keeper	Hot Wax 7006

DATE	POS	WKS	ARTIST–RECORD TITLE	LABEL & NO.
			FLAMINGOS, The	
			R&B vocal group from Chicago, Illinois: cousins Zeke and Jake Carey, Paul Wilson, Nate Nelson, Tommy Hunt and Terry Johnson. Nelson later joined The Platters. Nelson died of a heart attack on 6/1/84 (age 52). Wilson died in May 1988 (age 53). Jake Carey died of a heart attack on 12/10/97 (age 74). Zeke Carey died of cancer on 12/24/99 (age 66). Group inducted into the Rock and Roll Hall of Fame in 2001.	
6/8/59	11	11	1. I Only Have Eyes For You #2 hit for Ben Selvin in 1934 (from the movie *Dames* starring Joan Blondell)	End 1046
5/23/60	30	3	2. Nobody Loves Me Like You written by Sam Cooke	End 1068
			FLARES, The	
			R&B vocal group from Los Angeles, California: Aaron Collins, Willie Davis, Tommy Miller and George Hollis. Collins and Davis had been in The Cadets.	
10/9/61	25	9	1. Foot Stomping - Part 1	Felsted 8624
			FLASH	
			Rock group from England: Colin Carter (vocals), Peter Banks (guitar), Ray Bennett (bass) and Michael Hough (drums). Banks had been in Yes; later with After The Fire.	
7/29/72	29	6	1. Small Beginnings	Capitol 3345
			FLASH CADILLAC & THE CONTINENTAL KIDS	
			Fifties-styled rock and roll group formed in Colorado: Sam "Flash Cadillac" McFadin (vocals, guitar), Linn "Spike" Phillips (guitar), Kris "Angelo" Moe (keyboards), Dwight "Spider" Bement (sax), Warren "Butch" Knight (bass) and Paul "Wheaty" Wheatbread (drums). Bement and Wheatbread were with Gary Puckett & The Union Gap. Group appeard as the prom band in the movie *American Graffiti*. McFadin died of a heart attack on 8/31/2001 (age 49).	
10/2/76	29	6	1. Did You Boogie (With Your Baby) with spoken interludes by Wolfman Jack (some pressings omit these interludes)	Private Stock 45,079
			FLEETWOOD MAC	
			Pop-rock group formed in England by Mick Fleetwood (drums) and John McVie (bass). Group went through several personnel changes. Christine McVie (vocals, keyboards) joined in August 1970. Americans Lindsey Buckingham (guitar, vocals) and Stevie Nicks (vocals) joined in January 1975. Buckingham left in summer of 1987. Guitarists/vocalists Billy Burnette (son of Dorsey Burnette) and Rick Vito joined in July 1987. The classic lineup of Fleetwood, John and Christine McVie, Buckingham and Nicks reunited in May 1997. Inducted into the Rock and Roll Hall of Fame in 1998.	
12/13/75+	20	7	1. Over My Head	Reprise 1339
4/10/76	11	11	2. Rhiannon (Will You Ever Win)	Reprise 1345
7/31/76	11	13	3. Say You Love Me	Reprise 1356
1/22/77	10	11	4. **Go Your Own Way**	Warner 8304
4/30/77	1 (1)	13	● 5. **Dreams**	Warner 8371
7/23/77	3	14	6. **Don't Stop**	Warner 8413
10/29/77	9	10	7. **You Make Loving Fun**	Warner 8483
10/13/79	8	10	8. **Tusk** **[L]** with U.S.C. Trojan Marching Band; recorded at Dodger Stadium	Warner 49077
12/22/79+	7	11	9. **Sara**	Warner 49150

DATE	POS	WKS	ARTIST–RECORD TITLE	LABEL & NO.
3/29/80	**20**	7	10. Think About Me	Warner 49196
6/19/82	**4**	15	11. **Hold Me**	Warner 29966
9/25/82	**12**	8	12. Gypsy	Warner 29918
12/11/82+	**22**	8	13. Love In Store	Warner 29848
4/11/87	**5**	11	14. **Big Love** Airplay #4 / Sales #6	Warner 28398
7/4/87	**19**	8	15. Seven Wonders Sales #17 / Airplay #17	Warner 28317
9/12/87	**4**	13	16. **Little Lies** Sales #3 / Airplay #5	Warner 28291
			#1 Adult Contemporary hit (4 weeks)	
12/26/87+	**14**	10	17. Everywhere Airplay #12 / Sales #13	Warner 28143
			#1 Adult Contemporary hit (3 weeks)	
4/28/90	**33**	4	18. Save Me Airplay #28 / Sales #33	Warner 19866

FLEETWOODS, The

Pop vocal trio from Olympia, Washington: Gary Troxel, Gretchen Christopher and Barbara Ellis.

DATE	POS	WKS	ARTIST–RECORD TITLE	LABEL & NO.
3/16/59	**1 (4)**	12	● 1. **Come Softly To Me**	Dolphin 1
6/22/59	**39**	1	2. Graduation's Here	Dolton 3
9/14/59	**1 (1)**	17	● 3. **Mr. Blue**	Dolton 5
2/29/60	**28**	3	4. Outside My Window	Dolton 15
6/27/60	**23**	4	5. Runaround	Dolton 22
5/8/61	**10**	8	6. **Tragedy**	Dolton 40
10/2/61	**30**	4	7. (He's) The Great Impostor	Dolton 45
11/24/62	**36**	2	8. Lovers By Night, Strangers By Day	Dolton 62
7/13/63	**32**	4	9. Goodnight My Love	Dolton 75
			#7 R&B hit for Jesse Belvin in 1956	

FLINT, Shelby

Born on 9/17/39 in North Hollywood, California. Female singer/songwriter.

DATE	POS	WKS	ARTIST–RECORD TITLE	LABEL & NO.
2/6/61	**22**	5	1. Angel On My Shoulder	Valiant 6001

FLIPMODE SQUAD — see BUSTA RHYMES

FLIRTATIONS, The

Female R&B vocal trio formed in England: sisters Shirley and Earnestine Pearce (from South Carolina), with Viola Billups (from Alabama).

DATE	POS	WKS	ARTIST–RECORD TITLE	LABEL & NO.
5/24/69	**34**	2	1. Nothing But A Heartache	Deram 85038

FLOATERS, The

R&B vocal group from Detroit, Michigan: brothers Paul and Ralph Mitchell, Charles Clarke and Larry Cunningham.

DATE	POS	WKS	ARTIST–RECORD TITLE	LABEL & NO.
7/30/77	**2 (2)**	11	● 1. **Float On**	ABC 12284
			#1 R&B hit (6 weeks); also see Cheech & Chong's parody "Bloat On"	

FLOCK OF SEAGULLS, A

New-wave group from Liverpool, England: brothers Mike (vocals, keyboards) and Ali (drums) Score, with Paul Reynolds (guitar) and Frank Maudsley (bass).

DATE	POS	WKS	ARTIST–RECORD TITLE	LABEL & NO.
9/4/82	**9**	10	1. **I Ran (So Far Away)**	Jive 102
1/8/83	**30**	7	2. Space Age Love Song	Jive 2003
6/11/83	**26**	7	3. Wishing (If I Had A Photograph Of You)	Jive 2006

DATE	POS	WKS	ARTIST—RECORD TITLE	LABEL & NO.
			FLOETRY	
			Female R&B vocal duo: Marsha Ambrosius (born in London, England) and Natalie Stewart (born in Atlanta, Georgia).	
4/26/03	24	9	1. Say Yes Airplay #21	album cut
			from the album *Floetic* on DreamWorks 450313	
			FLOOD, Dick	
			Born on 11/13/32 in Philadelphia, Pennsylvania. Pop-country singer/songwriter.	
9/14/59	23	4	1. The Three Bells (The Jimmy Brown Story)	Monument 408
			French tune written in 1945 as "Les Trois Cloches"; #14 hit for Les Compagnons De La Chanson in 1952	
			FLOYD, Eddie	
			Born on 6/25/35 in Montgomery, Alabama; raised in Detroit, Michigan. R&B singer/songwriter. Member of The Falcons.	
11/19/66	28	6	● 1. Knock On Wood	Stax 194
			#1 R&B hit (1 week)	
9/7/68	40	2	2. I've Never Found A Girl (To Love Me Like You Do)	Stax 0002
11/16/68	17	9	3. Bring It On Home To Me	Stax 0012
			FLOYD, King	
			Born on 2/13/45 in New Orleans, Louisana. R&B singer/songwriter.	
12/12/70+	6	13	● 1. **Groove Me**	Chimneyville 435
			#1 R&B hit (4 weeks)	
4/3/71	29	7	2. Baby Let Me Kiss You	Chimneyville 437
			FLYING MACHINE, The	
			Studio project of British songwriters/producers Tony MacAuley and Geoff Stephens. Touring group featured Tony Newman as lead vocalist. Not to be confused with James Taylor's group.	
10/18/69	5	12	● 1. **Smile A Little Smile For Me**	Congress 6000
			FOCUS	
			Progressive-rock group formed in Amsterdam, Netherlands: Jan Akkerman (guitar), Thijs van Leer (keyboards, flute), Martin Dresdan (bass) and Hans Cleuver (drums).	
4/21/73	9	11	1. **Hocus Pocus** [I]	Sire 704
			FOGELBERG, Dan	
			Born on 8/13/51 in Peoria, Illinois. Soft-rock singer/songwriter/guitarist.	
3/1/75	31	3	1. Part Of The Plan	Epic 50055
			Graham Nash (harmony vocal); Joe Walsh (lead guitar; producer)	
11/4/78	24	7	2. The Power Of Gold	Full Moon 50606
			DAN FOGELBERG/TIM WEISBERG	
			Don Henley (harmony vocal)	
1/19/80	2 (2)	13	3. **Longer**	Full Moon 50824
			#1 Adult Contemporary hit (1 week)	
4/19/80	21	6	4. Heart Hotels	Full Moon 50862
			Tom Scott (sax solo)	
12/27/80+	9	13	5. **Same Old Lang Syne**	Full Moon 50961

DATE	POS	WKS	ARTIST–RECORD TITLE	LABEL & NO.
9/19/81	7	10	6. **Hard To Say** Glenn Frey (harmony vocal)	Full Moon 02488
12/19/81+	9	16	7. **Leader Of The Band** #1 Adult Contemporary hit (2 weeks)	Full Moon 02647
4/24/82	18	8	8. Run For The Roses	Full Moon 02821
11/13/82	23	9	9. Missing You	Full Moon 03289
3/5/83	29	6	10. Make Love Stay #1 Adult Contemporary hit (1 week)	Full Moon 03525
2/11/84	13	10	11. The Language Of Love	Full Moon 04314
			FOGERTY, John	
			Born on 5/28/45 in Berkeley, California. Rock singer/songwriter/multi-instrumentalist. Leader of Creedence Clearwater Revival. Went solo in 1972 and recorded as The Blue Ridge Rangers.	
1/6/73	16	10	1. Jambalaya (On the Bayou) #1 Country hit for Hank Williams in 1952	Fantasy 689
5/19/73	37	2	2. Hearts Of Stone **THE BLUE RIDGE RANGERS** (above 2)	Fantasy 700
10/4/75	27	6	3. Rockin' All Over The World	Asylum 45274
1/19/85	10	9	4. **The Old Man Down The Road** Airplay #8 / Sales #12 #1 Mainstream Rock hit (3 weeks)	Warner 29100
4/6/85	20	6	5. Rock And Roll Girls Airplay #19 / Sales #21	Warner 29053
			FOGHAT	
			Rock group formed in England: "Lonesome" Dave Peverett (vocals, guitar), Rod Price (guitar), Craig MacGregor (bass) and Roger Earl (drums). Peverett died of pneumonia on 2/7/2000 (age 57).	
1/10/76	20	12	1. Slow Ride	Bearsville 0306
12/25/76+	34	4	2. Drivin' Wheel	Bearsville 0313
10/15/77	33	3	3. I Just Want To Make Love To You **[L-R]** studio version hit #83 in 1972	Bearsville 0319
6/24/78	36	2	4. Stone Blue	Bearsville 0325
12/8/79+	23	10	5. Third Time Lucky (First Time I Was A Fool)	Bearsville 49125
			FOLDS, Ben, Five	
			Born on 9/12/66 in Winston-Salem, North Carolina. Singer/songwriter/pianist. His trio included Robert Sledge (bass) and Darren Jessee (drums).	
1/24/98	19 ᴬ	15	1. Brick from the album *Whatever And Ever Amen* on 550 Music 67762	album cut
			FOLK IMPLOSION	
			Rock duo from San Francisco, California: Lou Barlow (vocals, bass) and John Davis (guitar, drums).	
1/13/96	29	7	1. Natural One Sales #32 / Airplay #33 from the movie *Kids* starring Leo Fitzpatrick	London 0430
			FONTANA, Wayne — see MINDBENDERS, The	

DATE	POS	WKS	ARTIST–RECORD TITLE	LABEL & NO.
			FONTANE SISTERS, The	
			Female vocal trio from New Milford, New Jersey: sisters Marge, Bea and Geri Rosse.	
12/11/54+	**1** (3)	20	● 1. **Hearts Of Stone** Juke Box #1 (3) / Best Seller #1 (1) / Jockey #2	Dot 15265
2/26/55	**13**	8	2. Rock Love Juke Box #13 / Best Seller #19	Dot 15333
6/4/55	**13**	6	3. Rollin' Stone / Juke Box #13	
			#8 R&B hit for The Marigolds in 1955	
6/18/55		2	4. Playmates Juke Box: flip	Dot 15370
			#2 hit for Kay Kyser in 1940	
8/20/55	**3**	15	5. **Seventeen** Juke Box #3 / Best Seller #6 / Jockey #7 / Top 100 #15	Dot 15386
11/26/55	**11**	11	6. Daddy-O Top 100 #11 / Juke Box #11 / Best Seller #13 / Jockey #18	Dot 15428
12/31/55	**36**	1	7. Nuttin' For Christmas Top 100 #36 **[X-N]**	Dot 15434
3/17/56	**11**	11	8. Eddie My Love	Dot 15450
			Juke Box #11 / Top 100 #12 / Jockey #13 / Best Seller #15	
7/14/56	**38**	1	9. I'm In Love Again Top 100 #38	Dot 15462
1/12/57	**13**	10	10. The Banana Boat Song Jockey #13 / Juke Box #14 / Top 100 #22	Dot 15527
4/28/58	**12**	9	11. Chanson D'Amour (Song Of Love)	
			Jockey #12 / Top 100 #68	Dot 15736
			Billy Vaughn (orch., all of above)	
			FOO FIGHTERS	
			Rock group formed in Seattle, Washington: Dave Grohl (vocals, guitar), Pat Smear (guitar), Nate Mendel (bass) and William Goldsmith (drums). Taylor Hawkins replaced Goldsmith in 1997. Franz Stahl replaced Smear in 1998. Grohl was drummer for Nirvana. Group name taken from the fiery UFO-like apparitions seen by U.S. pilots during World War II.	
7/15/95	**35** A	6	1. This Is A Call	album cut
3/16/96	**13** A	13	2. Big Me	album cut
			above 2 from the album *Foo Fighters* on Roswell/Capitol 34027	
12/4/99+	**19**	12	3. Learn To Fly Airplay #13	album cut
			#1 Modern Rock hit (1 week); from the album *There Is Nothing Left To Lose* on Roswell/RCA 67892	
			FORBERT, Steve	
			Born in 1954 in Meridian, Mississippi. Singer/songwriter/guitarist.	
1/5/80	**11**	12	1. Romeo's Tune	Nemperor 7525
			FORCE M.D.'S	
			R&B vocal group from Staten Island, New York: brothers Stevie and Antoine Lundy, Jesse Daniels, Trisco Pearson and Charles Nelson. Nelson died of a heart attack on 3/10/95 (age 30). Antoine Lundy died of ALS on 1/18/98 (age 33). M.D.: Musical Diversity.	
3/1/86	**10**	11	1. **Tender Love** Airplay #7 / Sales #12	Warner 28818
			from the all-rap musical movie *Krush Groove* starring Sheila E.	
			FORD, Frankie	
			Born Frank Guzzo on 8/4/39 in Gretna, Louisiana. Appeared in the movie *American Hot Wax*.	
3/9/59	**14**	12	1. Sea Cruise	Ace 554
			Huey "Piano" Smith (orch.)	

DATE	POS	WKS	ARTIST–RECORD TITLE	LABEL & NO.
			FORD, Lita	
			Born on 9/23/59 in London, England; raised in Los Angeles, California. Rock singer/guitarist. Member of The Runaways from 1975-79.	
5/14/88	12	10	1. Kiss Me Deadly Sales #8 / Airplay #14	RCA 6866
4/22/89	8	12	● 2. **Close My Eyes Forever** Sales #4 / Airplay #13 **LITA FORD (with Ozzy Osbourne)**	RCA 8899
			FORD, "Tennessee" Ernie	
			Born on 2/13/19 in Bristol, Tennessee. Died of liver failure on 10/17/91 (age 72). Legendary country singer. Hosted own TV variety show from 1955-65. Known as "The Old Pea Picker."	
3/19/55	5	17	1. **Ballad Of Davy Crockett** Juke Box #5/ Best Seller #6/ Jockey #7 Cliffie Stone (orch.); from the ABC-TV *Disneyland* series, which featured three "Davy Crockett" segments	Capitol 3058
11/12/55	1 (8)	19	● 2. **Sixteen Tons** Juke Box #1 (8) / Best Seller #1 (7) / Top 100 #1 (6) / Jockey #1 (6) #1 Country hit (10 weeks)	Capitol 3262
3/10/56	17	1	3. That's All Jockey #17 / Top 100 #44	Capitol 3343
9/23/57	23	1	4. In The Middle Of An Island Jockey #23 / Top 100 #56 Jack Fascinato (orch., above 3)	Capitol 3762
			FORD, Willa	
			Born Amanda Lee Williford on 1/22/81 in Tampa, Florida. Female pop singer.	
7/7/01	22	11	1. I Wanna Be Bad Sales #6 / Airplay #34	Lava/Atlantic 85103
			FOREIGNER	
			British-American rock group formed in New York: Lou Gramm (vocals), Mick Jones (guitar), Ian McDonald (guitar, keyboards), Al Greenwood (keyboards), Ed Gagliardi (bass) and Dennis Elliott (drums). Rick Wills replaced Gagliardi in 1979. Greenwood and McDonald left in 1980. Jones not to be confused with Mick Jones of The Clash and Big Audio Dynamite II.	
4/23/77	4	13	1. **Feels Like The First Time**	Atlantic 3394
8/13/77	6	15	2. **Cold As Ice**	Atlantic 3410
1/14/78	20	8	3. Long, Long Way From Home	Atlantic 3439
7/8/78	3	14	● 4. **Hot Blooded**	Atlantic 3488
9/30/78	2 (2)	12	● 5. **Double Vision**	Atlantic 3514
1/20/79	15	8	6. Blue Morning, Blue Day	Atlantic 3543
9/22/79	12	9	7. Dirty White Boy	Atlantic 3618
11/24/79	14	9	8. Head Games	Atlantic 3633
7/11/81	4	17	9. **Urgent** #1 Mainstream Rock hit (4 weeks); Jr. Walker (sax solo)	Atlantic 3831
10/17/81	2 (10)	19	● 10. **Waiting For A Girl Like You** #1 Mainstream Rock hit (1 week)	Atlantic 3868
3/6/82	26	6	11. Juke Box Hero	Atlantic 4017
6/5/82	26	6	12. Break It Up	Atlantic 4044
12/15/84+	1 (2)	16	● 13. **I Want To Know What Love Is** Airplay #1 (2) / Sales #1 (1) #1 Mainstream Rock hit (1 week); New Jersey Mass Choir and Jennifer Holliday (backing vocals)	Atlantic 89596
3/23/85	12	10	14. That Was Yesterday Airplay #12 / Sales #17	Atlantic 89571
12/26/87+	6	12	15. **Say You Will** Sales #5 / Airplay #8 #1 Mainstream Rock hit (4 weeks)	Atlantic 89169
4/9/88	5	11	16. **I Don't Want To Live Without You** Airplay #4 / Sales #6 #1 Adult Contemporary hit (1 week)	Atlantic 89101

DATE	POS	WKS	ARTIST–RECORD TITLE	LABEL & NO.
			FORTUNES, The	
			Pop group formed in England: Glen Dale and Barry Pritchard (vocals, guitars), David Carr (keyboards), Rod Allen (bass) and Andy Brown (drums). Shel MacRae replaced Dale in 1966. Pritchard died of heart failure on 1/12/99 (age 54).	
9/11/65	7	8	1. **You've Got Your Troubles**	Press 9773
11/27/65	27	4	2. Here It Comes Again	Press 9798
6/19/71	15	9	3. Here Comes That Rainy Day Feeling Again	Capitol 3086
			FOSTER, David	
			Born in 1950 in Victoria, British Columbia, Canada. Prolific producer/keyboardist. Former member of Skylark.	
10/5/85	15	10	1. Love Theme From St. Elmo's Fire Sales #14 / Airplay #15 **[I]** from the movie *St. Elmo's Fire* starring Rob Lowe and Demi Moore	Atlantic 89528
			FOUNDATIONS, The	
			R&B-pop group formed in England: Clem Curtis (vocals), Alan Warner (guitar), Eric Allendale, Pat Burke and Michael Elliott (horns), Anthony Gomez (keyboards), Peter McBeth (bass) and Tim Harris (drums). Colin Young replaced Curtis in 1968. Group disbanded in 1970.	
1/13/68	11	10	1. Baby, Now That I've Found You	Uni 55038
1/18/69	3	13	● 2. **Build Me Up Buttercup**	Uni 55101
			FOUNTAINS OF WAYNE	
			Pop-rock duo from New York: Chris Collingwood (vocals, guitar) and Adam Schlesinger (keyboards, drums).	
10/18/03	21	8	1. Stacy's Mom Airplay #25 from the album *Welcome Interstate Managers* on S-Curve 90875	album cut
			FOUR ACES Featuring Al Alberts	
			White vocal group from Chester, Pennsylvania: Al Alberts, Dave Mahoney, Sol Vaccaro and Lou Silvestri.	
11/27/54+	5	14	1. **Mister Sandman** Jockey #5 / Juke Box #6 / Best Seller #9	Decca 29344
1/15/55	3	21	2. **Melody Of Love** Juke Box #3 / Jockey #9 / Best Seller #11	Decca 29395
5/28/55	13	6	3. Heart Jockey #13 / Juke Box #20 / Best Seller #23 from the Broadway musical *Damn Yankees* starring Gwen Verdon	Decca 29476
8/27/55	1 (6)	21	● 4. **Love Is A Many-Splendored Thing** Jockey #1 (6) / Top 100 #1 (3) / Juke Box #1 (3) / Best Seller #1 (2) title song from the movie starring William Holden and Jennifer Jones	Decca 29625
12/3/55	14	12	5. A Woman In Love Jockey #14 / Top 100 #19 / Best Seller #20 from the movie *Guys and Dolls* starring Marlon Brando	Decca 29725
8/4/56	22	5	6. I Only Know I Love You Jockey #22 / Top 100 #35	Decca 29989
10/20/56	20	2	7. You Can't Run Away From It Jockey #20 / Top 100 #70 title song from the movie starring Jack Lemmon and June Allyson; Jack Pleis (orch., all of above)	Decca 30041
			FOUR COINS, The	
			White vocal group from Canonsburg, Pennsylvania: brothers Michael and George Mahramas, George Mantalis and Jim Gregorakis.	
1/15/55	28	1	1. I Love You Madly Best Seller #28 first recorded by Charlie & Ray in 1954	Epic 9082

DATE	POS	WKS	ARTIST–RECORD TITLE	LABEL & NO.
12/10/55	22	8	2. Memories Of You Best Seller #22 / Top 100 #28 from the movie *The Benny Goodman Story* starring Steve Allen; Don Costa (orch., above 2)	Epic 9129
6/17/57	11	13	3. Shangri-La Jockey #11 / Best Seller #22 / Top 100 #23	Epic 9213
10/14/57	28	4	4. My One Sin Best Seller #28 / Top 100 #29	Epic 9229
11/17/58	21	8	5. The World Outside Marion Evans (orch., above 3)	Epic 9295
			FOUR ESQUIRES, The	
			White vocal group from Boston, Massachusetts: Bill Courtney, Frank Mahoney, Wally Gold and Bob Golden. Gold died of heart failure on 6/7/98 (age 70).	
12/16/57	25	1	1. Love Me Forever Jockey #25 / Best Seller #44 / Top 100 #51 Sid Bass (orch.)	Paris 509
11/3/58	21	6	2. Hideaway Hot 100 #21 Richard Hayman (orch.)	Paris 520
			FOUR FRESHMEN, The	
			White vocal group from Indianapolis, Indiana: brothers Ross and Don Barbour, their cousin Bob Flanigan and Ken Albers. Don Barbour died in a car crash on 10/5/61 (age 32).	
6/9/56	17	7	1. Graduation Day Jockey #17 / Best Seller #25 / Top 100 #27 Dick Reynolds (orch.)	Capitol 3410
			FOUR JACKS AND A JILL	
			Pop group from South Africa: Glenys "Jill" Lynne (vocals), Bruce Bark (guitar), Till Hannamann (keyboards), Clive Harding (bass) and Anthony Hughes (drums).	
5/18/68	18	7	1. Master Jack	RCA Victor 9473
			FOUR KNIGHTS, The — see COLE, Nat "King"	
			FOUR LADS, The	
			White vocal group from Toronto, Ontario, Canada: Bernard Toorish, James Arnold, Frank Busseri and Connie Codarini.	
9/3/55	2 (6)	25	● 1. **Moments To Remember** Jockey #2 / Best Seller #3 / Top 100 #3 / Juke Box #4	Columbia 40539
1/28/56	2 (4)	19	● 2. **No, Not Much!** Jockey #2 / Top 100 #3 / Best Seller #4 / Juke Box #4	Columbia 40629
4/28/56	3	18	3. **Standing On The Corner /** Jockey #3 / Top 100 #3 / Best Seller #3 / Juke Box #3 from the Broadway musical *The Most Happy Fella* starring Robert Weede	
4/28/56	22	12	4. My Little Angel Best Seller #22 / Jockey #24 / Top 100 #30 / Juke Box: flip	Columbia 40674
9/15/56	16	6	5. A House With Love In It / Best Seller #16 / Jockey #20 / Top 100 #23	
9/15/56	17	6	6. The Bus Stop Song (A Paper Of Pins) Jockey #17 / Best Seller #22 / Top 100 #23 from the movie *Bus Stop* starring Marilyn Monroe	Columbia 40736
2/2/57	9	15	7. **Who Needs You** Jockey #9 / Best Seller #13 / Top 100 #14 / Juke Box #17	Columbia 40811
5/20/57	17	4	8. I Just Don't Know Jockey #17 / Top 100 #22	Columbia 40914

DATE	POS	WKS	ARTIST–RECORD TITLE	LABEL & NO.
12/9/57+	8	9	9. **Put A Light In The Window** *Jockey #8 / Top 100 #35 / Best Seller #39*	Columbia 41058
4/7/58	10	7	10. **There's Only One Of You** *Jockey #10 / Top 100 #41 / Best Seller #43*	Columbia 41136
7/14/58	12	6	11. Enchanted Island *Jockey #12 / Hot 100 #29 / Best Seller #32* Ray Ellis (orch., all of above)	Columbia 41194
11/24/58	32	3	12. The Mocking Bird **[R]** Joe Mele (orch.); new version of group's 1952 (#23) and 1956 (#67) hit	Columbia 41266

4 NON BLONDES

Pop/rock group from San Francisco, California: Linda Perry (vocals), Roger
Rocha (guitar), Christa Hillhouse (bass) and Dawn Richardson (drums).

DATE	POS	WKS	ARTIST–RECORD TITLE	LABEL & NO.
6/5/93	14	17	● 1. What's Up *Sales #10 / Airplay #30*	Interscope 98430

4 P.M.

R&B vocal group from Baltimore, Maryland: brothers Rene and Roberto Pena,
Larry McFarland and Marty Ware.

DATE	POS	WKS	ARTIST–RECORD TITLE	LABEL & NO.
11/12/94+	8	23	● 1. **Sukiyaki** *Sales #10 / Airplay #10*	Next Plateau 857736

FOUR PREPS, The

White vocal group from Hollywood, California: Bruce Belland, Ed Cobb,
Marvin Inabnett and Glen Larson. Inabnett died of a heart attack on 3/7/99
(age 60). Cobb died of leukemia on 9/19/99 (age 61).

DATE	POS	WKS	ARTIST–RECORD TITLE	LABEL & NO.
1/20/58	2 (3)	14	● 1. **26 Miles (Santa Catalina)** *Jockey #2 / Top 100 #4 / Best Seller #5*	Capitol 3845
5/5/58	3	12	2. **Big Man** *Jockey #3 / Top 100 #5 / Best Seller #6*	Capitol 3960
9/1/58	21	6	3. Lazy Summer Night / *Hot 100 #21 / Best Seller #34* from the movie *Andy Hardy Comes Home* starring Mickey Rooney	
9/1/58		3	4. Summertime Lies *Best Seller: flip*	Capitol 4023
1/11/60	13	11	5. Down By The Station	Capitol 4312
5/16/60	24	3	6. Got A Girl **[N]**	Capitol 4362
9/11/61	17	4	7. More Money For You And Me **[L-N]** medley: Mr. Blue/Alley Oop/Smoke Gets In Your Eyes/In This Whole Wide World/A Worried Man/Tom Dooley/A Teenager In Love; Lincoln Mayorga (orch., all of above)	Capitol 4599

4 SEASONS, The

Vocal group formed in Newark, New Jersey: Frankie Valli, Bob Gaudio, Nick
Massi and Tommy DeVito. In 1965, Nick Massi was replaced by Charlie
Calello and then by Joe Long. Group disbanded in the early 1970s. Re-formed
in 1975: Valli (vocals), Gerry Polci (vocals, drums), John Pavia (guitar), Lee
Shapiro (keyboards) and Don Ciccone (bass; formerly with The Critters). Massi
died of cancer on 12/24/2000 (age 73). Group inducted into the Rock and
Roll Hall of Fame in 1990. Also recorded as The Wonder Who?.

DATE	POS	WKS	ARTIST–RECORD TITLE	LABEL & NO.
9/1/62	1 (5)	12	● 1. **Sherry** #1 R&B hit (1 week)	Vee-Jay 456
10/27/62	1 (5)	14	● 2. **Big Girls Don't Cry** #1 R&B hit (3 weeks)	Vee-Jay 465
12/22/62	23	2	3. Santa Claus Is Coming To Town **[X]** #12 hit for George Hall in 1934	Vee-Jay 478
1/26/63	1 (3)	12	4. **Walk Like A Man**	Vee-Jay 485
5/4/63	22	6	5. Ain't That A Shame!	Vee-Jay 512

DATE	POS	WKS	ARTIST–RECORD TITLE	LABEL & NO.
7/20/63	**3**	10	6. **Candy Girl /**	
8/10/63	**36**	3	7. Marlena	Vee-Jay 539
11/2/63	**36**	2	8. New Mexican Rose	Vee-Jay 562
2/8/64	**3**	11	9. **Dawn (Go Away)**	Philips 40166
3/7/64	**16**	8	10. Stay	Vee-Jay 582
4/18/64	**6**	8	11. **Ronnie**	Philips 40185
6/27/64	**1 (2)**	11	● 12. **Rag Doll**	Philips 40211
6/27/64	**28**	5	13. Alone	Vee-Jay 597
9/5/64	**10**	6	14. **Save It For Me**	Philips 40225
11/21/64	**20**	5	15. Big Man In Town	Philips 40238
1/30/65	**12**	6	16. Bye, Bye, Baby (Baby, Goodbye)	Philips 40260
7/10/65	**30**	3	17. Girl Come Running	Philips 40305
10/30/65	**3**	12	18. **Let's Hang On!**	Philips 40317
11/27/65	**12**	8	19. Don't Think Twice	Philips 40324
			THE WONDER WHO?	
2/12/66	**9**	6	20. **Working My Way Back To You**	Philips 40350
5/28/66	**13**	7	21. Opus 17 (Don't You Worry 'Bout Me)	Philips 40370
9/17/66	**9**	8	22. **I've Got You Under My Skin**	Philips 40393
			written by Cole Porter; from the movie *Born To Dance* starring James Stewart; #3 hit in 1936 for Ray Noble	
12/24/66+	**10**	8	23. **Tell It To The Rain**	Philips 40412
3/18/67	**16**	7	24. Beggin'	Philips 40433
6/17/67	**9**	8	25. **C'mon Marianne**	Philips 40460
11/18/67	**30**	4	26. Watch The Flowers Grow	Philips 40490
3/9/68	**24**	5	27. Will You Love Me Tomorrow	Philips 40523
			all of above The 4 Seasons' Phillips records (except "Dawn") labeled as: Featuring the "sound" of Frankie Valli	
9/20/75	**3**	12	28. **Who Loves You**	Warner/Curb 8122
1/31/76	**1 (3)**	15	● 29. **December, 1963 (Oh, What a Night)**	Warner/Curb 8168
7/4/76	**38**	2	30. Silver Star	Warner/Curb 8203
9/17/94	**14**	20	31. December 1963 (Oh, What A Night) Airplay #8/Sales #30 **[R]**	Curb 76917
			dance remix version of #29 above	

FOUR TOPS

Legendary R&B vocal group from Detroit, Michigan: Levi Stubbs (lead singer), Renaldo "Obie" Benson, Lawrence Payton and Abdul "Duke" Fakir. Stubbs is the older brother of Joe Stubbs (of 100 Proof Aged In Soul). Stubbs was the voice of the killer plant in the 1986 movie *Little Shop of Horrors*. Payton died of cancer on 6/20/97 (age 59). Group inducted into the Rock and Roll Hall of Fame in 1990.

DATE	POS	WKS	ARTIST–RECORD TITLE	LABEL & NO.
8/29/64	**11**	10	1. Baby I Need Your Loving	Motown 1062
2/20/65	**24**	6	2. Ask The Lonely	Motown 1073
5/22/65	**1 (2)**	13	3. **I Can't Help Myself**	Motown 1076
			#1 R&B hit (9 weeks)	
8/7/65	**5**	8	4. **It's The Same Old Song**	Motown 1081
11/20/65	**19**	6	5. Something About You	Motown 1084
3/12/66	**18**	6	6. Shake Me, Wake Me (When It's Over)	Motown 1090
9/17/66	**1 (2)**	12	● 7. **Reach Out I'll Be There**	Motown 1098
			#1 R&B hit (2 weeks)	
12/24/66+	**6**	9	8. **Standing In The Shadows Of Love**	Motown 1102
3/18/67	**4**	8	9. **Bernadette**	Motown 1104

DATE	POS	WKS	ARTIST–RECORD TITLE	LABEL & NO.
6/3/67	**14**	6	10. 7 Rooms Of Gloom	Motown 1110
9/30/67	**19**	5	11. You Keep Running Away	Motown 1113
2/17/68	**14**	6	12. Walk Away Renee	Motown 1119
5/11/68	**20**	6	13. If I Were A Carpenter	Motown 1124
5/30/70	**24**	8	14. It's All In The Game	Motown 1164
9/26/70	**11**	10	15. Still Water (Love)	Motown 1170
12/12/70+	**14**	8	16. River Deep - Mountain High	Motown 1173
			THE SUPREMES & FOUR TOPS	
2/27/71	**40**	2	17. Just Seven Numbers (Can Straighten Out My Life)	Motown 1175
10/2/71	**38**	3	18. MacArthur Park (Part II)	Motown 1189
12/2/72+	**10**	9	19. **Keeper Of The Castle**	Dunhill/ABC 4330
2/24/73	**4**	12	● 20. **Ain't No Woman (Like The One I've Got)**	Dunhill/ABC 4339
7/28/73	**15**	8	21. Are You Man Enough	Dunhill/ABC 4354
			from the movie *Shaft In Africa* starring Richard Roundtree	
11/17/73	**33**	3	22. Sweet Understanding Love	Dunhill/ABC 4366
9/19/81	**11**	11	23. When She Was My Girl	Casablanca 2338
			#1 R&B hit (2 weeks)	
10/1/88	**35**	2	24. Indestructible Sales #31 / Airplay #38	Arista 9706
			tune used by NBC-TV for the 1988 Summer Olympics	
			FOUR VOICES, The	
			Male vocal group: Allan Chase, Frank Fosta, Sal Mayo and Bill McBride.	
3/17/56	**20**	4	1. Lovely One Best Seller #20 / Top 100 #30	Columbia 40643
			Ray Conniff (orch.)	
			FOX, Samantha	
			Born on 4/15/66 in London, England. Dance singer. Former topless model.	
12/20/86+	**4**	13	1. **Touch Me (I Want Your Body)** Sales #3 / Airplay #6	Jive 1006
4/2/88	**3**	14	2. **Naughty Girls (Need Love Too)** Sales #2 / Airplay #5	Jive 1089
12/17/88+	**8**	12	● 3. **I Wanna Have Some Fun** Sales #4 / Airplay #11	Jive 1154
4/29/89	**31**	4	4. I Only Wanna Be With You Sales #24 / Airplay #38	Jive 1192
			FOXX, Inez	
			Born on 9/9/42 in Greensboro, North Carolina. Female R&B singer. Accompanied vocally by her brother Charlie Foxx. Charlie died of leukemia on 9/18/98 (age 68).	
8/3/63	**7**	10	1. **Mockingbird**	Symbol 919
			INEZ FOXX with Charlie Foxx	
			adapted from the same traditional folk lyrics as was the song "Bo Diddley"	
			FOXX, Jamie — see TWISTA	
			FOXY	
			Latin dance group from Miami, Florida: Ish "Angel" Ledesma (vocals, guitar), Richie Puente (percussion), Charlie Murciano (keyboards), Arnold Pasiero (bass) and Joe Galdo (drums). Puente is the son of famous bandleader Tito Puente. Ledesma later formed Oxo.	
8/26/78	**9**	13	1. **Get Off**	Dash 5046
			#1 R&B hit (2 weeks); Wildflower (background vocals)	
4/28/79	**21**	9	2. Hot Number	Dash 5050

DATE	POS	WKS	ARTIST–RECORD TITLE	LABEL & NO.
			FRAMPTON, Peter	
			Born on 4/22/50 in Beckenham, Kent, England. Rock singer/songwriter/guitarist. Former member of Humble Pie. Played "Billy Shears" in the 1978 movie *Sgt. Pepper's Lonely Hearts Club Band*.	
3/13/76	6	14	1. **Show Me The Way** [L]	A&M 1795
7/17/76	12	11	2. **Baby, I Love Your Way** [L]	A&M 1832
10/9/76	10	10	3. **Do You Feel Like We Do** [L]	A&M 1867
6/11/77	2 (3)	13	4. **I'm In You**	A&M 1941
9/10/77	18	10	5. Signed, Sealed, Delivered (I'm Yours)	A&M 1972
6/9/79	14	9	6. I Can't Stand It No More	A&M 2148
			FRANCIS, Connie	
			Born Concetta Rosa Maria Franconero on 12/12/38 in Newark, New Jersey. Pop singer/actress. Appeared in the movies *Where The Boys Are*, *Follow The Boys*, *Looking For Love* and *When The Boys Meet The Girls*. Pop music's top female vocalist from 1958-64.	
3/3/58	4	13	● 1. **Who's Sorry Now** Top 100 #4 / Best Seller #5 / Jockey #6 #3 hit for Isham Jones in 1923	MGM 12588
6/9/58	36	2	2. **I'm Sorry I Made You Cry** Top 100 #36 / Best Seller #39 #1 hit for Henry Burr in 1918	MGM 12647
8/4/58	14	11	3. Stupid Cupid Best Seller #14 / Hot 100 #17	MGM 12683
11/17/58	30	1	4. Fallin' Hot 100 #30 above 2 written by Neil Sedaka	MGM 12713
12/15/58+	2 (2)	14	● 5. **My Happiness** #2 hit for Jon & Sondra Steele in 1948	MGM 12738
3/30/59	22	4	6. If I Didn't Care #2 hit for the Ink Spots in 1939	MGM 12769
6/1/59	5	12	7. **Lipstick On Your Collar** /	
6/1/59	9	11	8. **Frankie** written by Neil Sedaka	MGM 12793
9/21/59	34	4	9. You're Gonna Miss Me	MGM 12824
12/7/59	7	11	● 10. **Among My Souvenirs** / #1 hit for Paul Whiteman in 1928	
12/21/59	36	2	11. God Bless America written by Irving Berlin and popularized by Kate Smith in 1939; Ray Ellis (orch., above 6)	MGM 12841
3/14/60	8	9	● 12. **Mama** Italian song written in 1941 (English lyrics added in 1946)	
3/28/60	17	6	13. Teddy written by Paul Anka	MGM 12878
5/16/60	1 (2)	16	● 14. **Everybody's Somebody's Fool** /	
6/6/60	19	8	15. Jealous Of You (Tango Della Gelosia) [F]	MGM 12899
8/22/60	1 (2)	14	16. **My Heart Has A Mind Of Its Own**	MGM 12923
11/21/60	7	10	● 17. **Many Tears Ago**	MGM 12964
1/30/61	4	12	● 18. **Where The Boys Are** / written by Neil Sedaka; title song from the movie starring George Hamilton	
2/20/61	34	2	19. No One	MGM 12971
4/24/61	7	9	20. **Breakin' In A Brand New Broken Heart**	MGM 12995
7/3/61	6	9	● 21. **Together** #1 Adult Contemporary hit (1 week); #1 hit for Paul Whiteman in 1928	MGM 13019
10/9/61	14	7	22. (He's My) Dreamboat	MGM 13039

DATE	POS	WKS	ARTIST–RECORD TITLE	LABEL & NO.
12/4/61+	10	9	23. **When The Boy In Your Arms** **(Is The Boy In Your Heart) /**	
1/6/62 -	26	1	24. Baby's First Christmas [X]	MGM 13051
2/24/62	1 (1)	10	25. **Don't Break The Heart That Loves You** #1 Adult Contemporary hit (4 weeks); Don Costa (orch., above 3)	MGM 13059
5/19/62	7	7	26. **Second Hand Love**	MGM 13074
8/11/62	9	6	27. **Vacation**	MGM 13087
11/3/62	24	4	28. I Was Such A Fool (To Fall In Love With You)	MGM 13096
1/5/63	18	6	29. I'm Gonna' Be Warm This Winter	MGM 13116
3/16/63	17	7	30. Follow The Boys title song from the movie starring Francis	MGM 13127
6/8/63	23	5	31. If My Pillow Could Talk	MGM 13143
8/31/63	36	3	32. Drownin' My Sorrows	MGM 13160
11/9/63	28	4	33. Your Other Love	MGM 13176
3/7/64	24	6	34. Blue Winter	MGM 13214
5/30/64	25	5	35. Be Anything (But Be Mine) #7 hit for Eddy Howard in 1952	MGM 13237
			FRANKE & THE KNOCKOUTS	
			Soft-rock group from New Brunswick, New Jersey: Franke Previte (vocals), Billy Elworthy (guitar), Blake Levinsohn (keyboards), Leigh Foxx (bass) and Claude LeHenaff (drums).	
3/28/81	10	14	1. **Sweetheart**	Millennium 11801
8/1/81	27	5	2. You're My Girl	Millennium 11808
5/8/82	24	7	3. Without You (Not Another Lonely Night)	Millennium 13105
			FRANKIE GOES TO HOLLYWOOD	
			Dance-rock group from Liverpool, England: William "Holly" Johnson and Paul Rutherford (vocals), Brian Nash (guitar), Mark O'Toole (bass) and Peter Gill (drums). Group's name inspired by publicity recounting Frank Sinatra's move into the movie industry.	
2/2/85	10	10	● 1. **Relax** Sales #9 / Airplay #10 **[R]** originally charted at #67 in 1984	Island 99805
			FRANKIE J	
			Born Francis Jay Bautista in Tijuana, Mexico; raised in San Diego, California. Latino singer/songwriter/producer.	
5/17/03	19	12	1. Don't Wanna Try Sales #7 / Airplay #22	Columbia 79872
9/20/03	7	27	2. **Suga Suga** Airplay #7 / Sales #8 **BABY BASH Feat. Frankie J**	Universal 001055
			FRANKLIN, Aretha	
			Born on 3/25/42 in Memphis, Tennessee; raised in Detroit, Michigan. Legendary R&B singer/songwriter/pianist. Known as "The Queen of Soul." Daughter of famous gospel preacher Rev. Cecil L. Franklin, pastor of Detroit's New Bethel Baptist Church. Signed to Columbia Records in 1960 as a jazz-styled singer. Dramatic turn in style and success after signing with Atlantic in 1966 and working with producer Jerry Wexler. Married to her manager/co-writer Ted White (1961-69) and actor Glynn Turman (1978-84). Appeared in the 1980 movie The Blues Brothers. Inducted into the Rock and Roll Hall of Fame in 1987. Won Grammy's Lifetime Achievement Award in 1994.	
11/20/61	37	2	1. Rock-A-Bye Your Baby With A Dixie Melody #1 hit for Al Jolson in 1918	Columbia 42157

DATE	POS	WKS	ARTIST–RECORD TITLE	LABEL & NO.
3/18/67	**9**	9	● 2. **I Never Loved A Man (The Way I Love You)** #1 R&B hit (7 weeks)	Atlantic 2386
5/6/67	**1 (2)**	11	● 3. **Respect** #1 R&B hit (8 weeks); King Curtis (sax); written by Otis Redding	Atlantic 2403
8/5/67	**4**	8	● 4. **Baby I Love You** #1 R&B hit (2 weeks)	Atlantic 2427
10/7/67	**8**	8	5. **A Natural Woman (You Make Me Feel Like)**	Atlantic 2441
12/16/67+	**2 (2)**	11	● 6. **Chain Of Fools** #1 R&B hit (4 weeks); Joe Smith (guitar intro)	Atlantic 2464
3/2/68	**5**	12	● 7. **(Sweet Sweet Baby) Since You've Been Gone /** #1 R&B hit (3 weeks)	
4/13/68	**16**	7	8. Ain't No Way	Atlantic 2486
5/25/68	**7**	9	● 9. **Think** #1 R&B hit (3 weeks)	Atlantic 2518
8/24/68	**6**	8	● 10. **The House That Jack Built /**	
8/24/68	**10**	10	11. I Say A Little Prayer	Atlantic 2546
11/23/68	**14**	8	● 12. See Saw /	
12/28/68+	**31**	2	13. My Song	Atlantic 2574
3/1/69	**19**	6	14. The Weight Duane Allman (slide guitar)	Atlantic 2603
4/26/69	**28**	6	15. I Can't See Myself Leaving You	Atlantic 2619
8/9/69	**13**	9	16. Share Your Love With Me #1 R&B hit (5 weeks)	Atlantic 2650
11/15/69	**17**	7	17. Eleanor Rigby	Atlantic 2683
2/28/70	**13**	9	18. Call Me #1 R&B hit (2 weeks)	Atlantic 2706
6/13/70	**23**	5	19. Spirit In The Dark	Atlantic 2731
8/22/70	**11**	8	● 20. **Don't Play That Song** #1 R&B hit (3 weeks)	Atlantic 2751
12/19/70	**37**	2	21. Border Song (Holy Moses) /	
12/19/70		1	22. You And Me **ARETHA FRANKLIN With The Dixie Flyers** (#19, 20 & 22)	Atlantic 2772
3/6/71	**19**	7	23. You're All I Need To Get By	Atlantic 2787
4/24/71	**6**	11	● 24. **Bridge Over Troubled Water /** #1 R&B hit (2 weeks)	
6/12/71		4	25. Brand New Me	Atlantic 2796
8/7/71	**2 (2)**	11	● 26. **Spanish Harlem** #1 R&B hit (3 weeks); Dr. John (keyboards)	Atlantic 2817
11/6/71	**9**	8	● 27. **Rock Steady**	Atlantic 2838
3/25/72	**5**	11	● 28. **Day Dreaming** #1 R&B hit (2 weeks)	Atlantic 2866
6/17/72	**26**	6	29. All The King's Horses	Atlantic 2883
3/10/73	**33**	5	30. Master Of Eyes (The Deepness Of Your Eyes)	Atlantic 2941
7/21/73	**20**	10	31. Angel #1 R&B hit (2 weeks)	Atlantic 2969
12/15/73+	**3**	17	● 32. **Until You Come Back To Me** **(That's What I'm Gonna Do)** #1 R&B hit (1 week); co-written by Stevie Wonder	Atlantic 2995
5/4/74	**19**	8	33. I'm In Love #1 R&B hit (2 weeks); all of above on Atlantic (except #30 & 31) produced by Jerry Wexler	Atlantic 2999
7/10/76	**28**	6	34. Something He Can Feel #1 R&B hit (4 weeks); written and produced by Curtis Mayfield	Atlantic 3326

DATE	POS	WKS	ARTIST–RECORD TITLE	LABEL & NO.
9/11/82	**24**	6	35. Jump To It #1 R&B hit (4 weeks); written and produced by Luther Vandross	Arista 0699
7/6/85	**3**	13	36. **Freeway Of Love** Sales #2 / Airplay #5 #1 R&B hit (5 weeks)	Arista 9354
10/12/85	**7**	13	37. **Who's Zoomin' Who** Sales #6 / Airplay #7	Arista 9410
11/2/85	**18**	8	38. Sisters Are Doin' It For Themselves Sales #16 / Airplay #25 **EURYTHMICS and ARETHA FRANKLIN**	RCA 14214
2/15/86	**22**	7	39. Another Night Sales #19 / Airplay #24	Arista 9453
10/11/86	**21**	6	40. Jumpin' Jack Flash Sales #14 / Airplay #25 produced by Keith Richards; title song from the movie starring Whoopi Goldberg	Arista 9528
1/24/87	**28**	4	41. Jimmy Lee Sales #23 / Airplay #34	Arista 9546
3/7/87	**1** (2)	12	42. **I Knew You Were Waiting (For Me)** Sales #1 (2) / Airplay #1 (1) **ARETHA FRANKLIN AND GEORGE MICHAEL**	Arista 9559
4/29/89	**16**	7	43. Through The Storm Sales #13 / Airplay #19 **ARETHA FRANKLIN AND ELTON JOHN**	Arista 9809
7/2/94	**26**	8	44. Willing To Forgive Sales #16 / Airplay #57	Arista 12680
3/21/98	**26**	9	● 45. A Rose Is Still A Rose Sales #14 samples "What I Am" by Edie Brickell & New Bohemians; written and produced by Lauryn Hill	Arista 13465
			FRASER, Wendy — see SWAYZE, Patrick	
			FREAK NASTY	
			Born Carlito Timmons in Puerto Rico; raised in New Orleans, Louisiana. Male rapper.	
2/15/97	**15**	25	▲ 1. Da' Dip Sales #12 / Airplay #35	Power 0112
			FREBERG, Stan	
			Born on 8/7/26 in Pasadena, California. Top pop music satirist. Did several cartoon voices. Later had a highly successful advertising career.	
10/22/55	**16**	2	1. The Yellow Rose Of Texas Jockey #16 / Top 100 #47 **[C]** Jud Conlon's Rhythmaires (vocal backing); Alvin Stoller (Yankee Snare Drumming)	Capitol 3249
4/27/57	**25**	1	2. Banana Boat (Day-O) Best Seller #25 / Top 100 #43 **[C]** Peter Leeds (interruptions)	Capitol 3687
11/18/57	**32**	3	3. Wun'erful, Wun'erful! (Sides uh-one & uh-two) Best Seller #32 / Top 100 #36 **[C]** Lawrence Welk parody featuring a medley of tunes: Bubbles In The Wine/Thank You/Louise/Please/Moonlight and Shadows; featuring The Lemon Sisters, Peggy Taylor and Daws Butler; Billy May (orch., all of above)	Capitol 3815
			FRED, John, & His Playboy Band	
			Born John Fred Gourrier on 5/8/41 in Baton Rouge, Louisiana. Pop-rock singer/songwriter.	
12/16/67+	**1** (2)	13	● 1. **Judy In Disguise (With Glasses)** parody of "Lucy In The Sky With Diamonds" by The Beatles	Paula 282
			FREDDIE AND THE DREAMERS	
			Pop group from Manchester, England: Freddie Garrity (vocals; born on 11/14/40), Derek Quinn and Roy Crewsdon (guitars), Peter Birrell (bass) and Bernie Dwyer (drums). Dwyer died of cancer on 12/4/2002 (age 62).	
3/27/65	**1** (2)	8	1. **I'm Telling You Now**	Tower 125

DATE	POS	WKS	ARTIST–RECORD TITLE	LABEL & NO.
4/24/65	36	2	2. I Understand (Just How You Feel) #6 hit for The Four Tunes in 1954	Mercury 72377
5/15/65	18	5	3. Do The Freddie	Mercury 72428
5/15/65	21	5	4. You Were Made For Me	Tower 127
			FREE	
			Rock group formed in England: Paul Rodgers (vocals), Paul Kossoff (guitar), Andy Fraser (bass) and Simon Kirke (drums). Rodgers and Kirke formed Bad Company in 1974. Kossoff died of drug-induced heart failure on 3/19/76 (age 25). Rodgers formed The Firm in 1984.	
9/5/70	4	13	1. **All Right Now**	A&M 1206
			FREEMAN, Bobby	
			Born on 6/13/40 in San Francisco, California. R&B singer.	
5/26/58	5	12	1. **Do You Want To Dance** Top 100 #5 / Best Seller #6 / Jockey #11	Josie 835
8/18/58	37	1	2. Betty Lou Got A New Pair Of Shoes Hot 100 #37 / Best Seller #40	Josie 841
9/26/60	37	3	3. (I Do The) Shimmy Shimmy	King 5373
7/25/64	5	10	4. **C'mon And Swim**	Autumn 2
			FREEMAN, Ernie	
			Born on 8/16/22 in Cleveland, Ohio. Died of a heart attack on 5/16/81 (age 58). Pianist/arranger/producer. Recorded with B. Bumble & The Stingers.	
11/18/57	4	12	1. **Raunchy** Jockey #4 / Best Seller #11 / Top 100 #12 **[I]** #1 R&B hit (2 weeks)	Imperial 5474
			FREE MOVEMENT, The	
			R&B vocal group from Los Angeles, California: brothers Adrian and Claude Jefferson, Godoy Colbert, Cheryl Conley, Jennifer Gates and Josephine Brown.	
9/18/71	5	11	1. **I've Found Someone Of My Own**	Decca 32818
			FREHLEY, Ace — see KISS	
			FRENCH, Nicki	
			Born in Carlisle, England. Female dance singer.	
5/6/95	2 (1)	21	● 1. **Total Eclipse Of The Heart** Airplay #2 / Sales #6	Critique 15539
			FREY, Glenn	
			Born on 11/6/48 in Detroit, Michigan. Singer/songwriter/guitarist. Founding member of the Eagles. Appeared in episodes of TV's *Miami Vice* and *Wiseguy*; starred in the 1993 TV series *South Of Sunset*.	
7/17/82	31	5	1. I Found Somebody	Asylum 47466
9/11/82	15	11	2. The One You Love	Asylum 69974
7/14/84	20	9	3. Sexy Girl	MCA 52413
1/19/85	2 (1)	13	4. **The Heat Is On** Sales #1 (1) / Airplay #4 from the movie *Beverly Hills Cop* starring Eddie Murphy	MCA 52512
5/4/85	12	11	5. Smuggler's Blues Sales #7 / Airplay #16	MCA 52546
9/28/85	2 (2)	13	6. **You Belong To The City** Sales #1 (2) / Airplay #3 #1 Mainstream Rock hit (3 weeks); above 2 from TV's *Miami Vice* soundtrack	MCA 52651
9/10/88	13	9	7. True Love Sales #12 / Airplay #15	MCA 53363

DATE	POS	WKS	ARTIST–RECORD TITLE	LABEL & NO.
			FRIDA — see ABBA	
			FRIEDMAN, Dean	
			Born on 4/21/55 in Paramus, New Jersey. Pop singer/songwriter/pianist.	
5/21/77	**26**	10	1. Ariel	Lifesong 45022
			FRIEND AND LOVER	
			Husband-and-wife vocal duo: Jim (from Houston, Texas) and Cathy (from Chicago, Illinois) Post.	
6/1/68	**10**	11	1. **Reach Out Of The Darkness**	Verve Forecast 5069
			FRIENDS OF DISTINCTION, The	
			R&B vocal group from Los Angeles, California: Floyd Butler, Harry Elston, Jessica Cleaves and Barbara Jean Love. Butler died of a heart attack on 4/29/90 (age 49).	
4/26/69	**3**	13	● 1. **Grazing In The Grass**	RCA Victor 0107
10/11/69	**15**	12	● 2. Going In Circles	RCA Victor 0204
3/21/70	**6**	11	3. **Love Or Let Me Be Lonely**	RCA Victor 0319
			FRIJID PINK	
			Male rock group from Detroit, Michigan: Kelly Green (vocals), Gary Thompson (guitar), Tom Beaudry (bass) and Rich Stevens (drums).	
2/21/70	**7**	11	● 1. **House Of The Rising Sun**	Parrot 341
			FROST, Max, And The Troopers	
			Studio group assembled by producer Mike Curb. Paul Wybier was the lead singer.	
9/28/68	**22**	9	1. Shape Of Things To Come	Tower 419
			from the movie *Wild In The Streets* starring Christopher Jones (as Max Frost)	
			FUEL	
			Rock group from Harrisburg, Pennsylvania: Brett Scallions (vocals), Carl Bell (guitar), Jeff Abercrombie (bass) and Kevin Miller (drums).	
12/23/00+	**30**	12	1. Hemorrhage (In My Hands) Airplay #24	album cut
			#1 Modern Rock hit (12 weeks); from the album *Something Like Human* on 550 Music 69436	
			FUGEES	
			Hip-hop trio from East Orange, New Jersey: Lauryn Hill, Wyclef Jean and Pras Michel. Fugees is short for refugees.	
2/10/96	**29**	10	● 1. Fu-Gee-La Sales #16 / Airplay #66	Ruffhouse 78195
			samples "Ooh La La La" by Teena Marie	
3/23/96	**2 (3)ᴬ**	30	2. **Killing Me Softly**	album cut
			#1 R&B Airplay hit (5 weeks)	
7/13/96	**38 ᴬ**	4	3. No Woman, No Cry	album cut
			first recorded by Bob Marley in 1975; above 2 from the album *The Score* on Ruffhouse 67147	
10/4/97	**35**	3	4. Avenues Sales #24	Arista 13411
			REFUGEE CAMP ALL-STARS Featuring Pras (With Ky-Mani) from the movie *Money Talks* starring Chris Tucker; rap version of "Electric Avenue" by Eddy Grant	

DATE	POS	WKS	ARTIST–RECORD TITLE	LABEL & NO.
			FULLER, Bobby, Four	
			Born on 10/22/43 in Baytown, Texas. Died mysteriously of asphyxiation in Los Angeles on 7/18/66 (age 22). Rock singer/guitarist. His group included his brother Randy Fuller (bass), Jim Reese (guitar) and DeWayne Quirico (drums).	
2/12/66	9	8	1. **I Fought The Law**	Mustang 3014
5/7/66	26	3	2. Love's Made A Fool Of You	Mustang 3016
			written in 1958 by Buddy Holly	
			FULL FORCE — see LISA LISA AND CULT JAM	
			FUNKADELIC — see PARLIAMENT/FUNKADELIC	
			FUQUA, Harvey — see MOONGLOWS, The	
			FURAY, Richie	
			Born on 5/9/44 in Yellow Springs, Ohio. Member of Buffalo Springfield, Poco, and the Souther, Hillman, Furay Band.	
12/15/79	39	3	1. I Still Have Dreams	Asylum 46534
			FURTADO, Nelly	
			Born on 12/2/78 in Victoria, British Columbia, Canada (Portugese parents). Female singer/songwriter.	
4/7/01	9	17	1. **I'm Like A Bird** Airplay #9	album cut
			from the album *Whoa, Nelly* on DreamWorks 450217	
9/15/01	5	20	2. **Turn Off The Light** Airplay #5	DreamWorks 459093
			FU-SCHNICKENS with Shaquille O'Neal (Shaq-Fu)	
			Hip-hop trio from Brooklyn, New York: Larry "Poc-Fu" Maturine, Rod "Chip-Fu" Roachford and James "Moc-Fu" Jones.	
8/14/93	39	1	● 1. What's Up Doc? (Can We Rock?) Sales #21 / Airplay #66	Jive 42164
			FUZZ, The	
			Female R&B vocal trio from Washington DC: Sheila Young, Barbara Gilliam and Val Williams.	
4/17/71	21	8	1. I Love You For All Seasons	Calla 174

G

DATE	POS	WKS	ARTIST–RECORD TITLE	LABEL & NO.
			GABRIEL, Peter	
			Born on 2/13/50 in Woking, Surrey, England. Pop-rock singer/songwriter. Lead singer of Genesis from 1966-75.	
12/4/82+	29	10	1. Shock The Monkey	Geffen 29883
			#1 Mainstream Rock hit (2 weeks)	
5/31/86	1 (1)	14	2. **Sledgehammer** Sales #1 (1) / Airplay #2	Geffen 28718
			#1 Mainstream Rock hit (2 weeks)	
9/27/86	26	7	3. In Your Eyes Sales #26 / Airplay #27	Geffen 28622
			#1 Mainstream Rock hit (1 week)	
1/24/87	8	11	4. **Big Time** Airplay #4 / Sales #8	Geffen 28503
			Stewart Copeland (of The Police; drums)	
1/23/93	32	5	5. Steam Airplay #33 / Sales #73	Geffen 19145
			#1 Modern Rock hit (5 weeks)	

DATE	POS	WKS	ARTIST–RECORD TITLE	LABEL & NO.
			GABRIELLE	
			Born Louise Gabrielle Bobb on 4/16/70 in London, England. Female dance singer.	
12/18/93+	**26**	17	1. Dreams Sales #24 / Airplay #26	Go!/London 857298
			GADABOUTS, The	
			R&B vocal group from Chicago, Illinois: Johnnie Barr, Eddie Hayes, Larry Craig and Bill Putnam.	
8/4/56	**39**	1	1. Stranded In The Jungle Top 100 #39 **[N]**	Mercury 70898
			GAINES, Chris — see BROOKS, Garth	
			GALE, Sunny	
			Born Selma Segal on 2/20/27 in Clayton, New Jersey; raised in Philadelphia, Pennsylvania. Pop singer. Formerly with Hal McIntyre's band.	
1/8/55	**17**	1	1. Let Me Go, Lover! Jockey #17 Hugo Winterhalter (orch.)	RCA Victor 5952
			GALLERY	
			Pop group from Detroit, Michigan: Jim Gold (vocals), Brent Anderson and Cal Freeman (guitars), Bill Nova (percussion), Dennis Korvarik (bass) and Danny Brucato (drums).	
4/29/72	**4**	13	● 1. **Nice To Be With You**	Sussex 232
10/7/72	**22**	8	2. I Believe In Music written by Mac Davis	Sussex 239
2/10/73	**23**	8	3. Big City Miss Ruth Ann	Sussex 248
			GALLOP, Frank	
			Born on 6/30/1900 in Brooklyn, New York. Died in May 1988 (age 87). Best known as the announcer on Perry Como's TV shows during the 1950s.	
5/7/66	**34**	5	1. The Ballad Of Irving **[C-L]** parody of "Ringo" by Lorne Greene	Kapp 745
			GAP BAND, The	
			Funk trio of brothers from Tulsa, Oklahoma: Ronnie (vocals, horns, keyboards), Robert (vocals, bass) and Charlie (vocals, drums) Wilson. Named for three streets in Tulsa: Greenwood, Archer and Pine.	
7/3/82	**24**	6	1. Early In The Morning #1 R&B hit (3 weeks)	Total Experience 8201
9/11/82	**31**	7	2. You Dropped A Bomb On Me	Total Experience 8203
			GARBAGE	
			Rock group formed in Madison, Wisconsin: Shirley Manson (vocals, guitar; native of Edinburgh, Scotland), Doug Erikson (guitar, bass, keyboards), Steve Marker (guitar) and Butch Vig (drums). Vig produced albums for Nirvana, Soul Asylum, Sonic Youth and Smashing Pumpkins.	
8/3/96	**24**	10	1. Stupid Girl Airplay #26 / Sales #33 samples "Train In Vain" by The Clash	Almo Sounds 89004
12/7/96+	**29** ᴬ	10	2. #1 Crush #1 Modern Rock hit (4 weeks); from the movie *Romeo & Juliet* starring Leonardo DiCaprio and Claire Danes (soundtrack on Capitol 37715)	album cut

DATE	POS	WKS	ARTIST–RECORD TITLE	LABEL & NO.
			GARDNER, Dave	
			Born on 6/11/26 in Jackson, Tennessee. Died of a heart attack on 9/22/83 (age 57). Pop singer. Recorded several comedy albums as "Brother Dave."	
7/22/57	22	4	1. White Silver Sands Best Seller #22 / Top 100 #28	OJ 1002
			GARDNER, Don, and Dee Dee Ford	
			R&B vocal duo from Philadelphia, Pennsylvania.	
7/7/62	20	7	1. I Need Your Loving	Fire 508
			GARFUNKEL, Art	
			Born on 11/5/41 in Forest Hills, New York. Half of Simon & Garfunkel duo. Appeared in the movies *Catch 22*, *Carnal Knowledge* and *Bad Timing*.	
			GARFUNKEL:	
10/6/73	9	10	1. **All I Know** #1 Adult Contemporary hit (4 weeks)	Columbia 45926
2/9/74	38	1	2. I Shall Sing written by Van Morrison	Columbia 45983
10/19/74	34	3	3. Second Avenue	Columbia 10020
			ART GARFUNKEL:	
9/27/75	18	12	4. I Only Have Eyes For You #1 Adult Contemporary hit (1 week); from the movie musical *Dames* starring Joan Blondell; #2 hit for Ben Selvin in 1934	Columbia 10190
1/31/76	39	2	5. Break Away #1 Adult Contemporary hit (1 week); David Crosby and Graham Nash (backing vocals)	Columbia 10273
2/11/78	17	7	6. (What A) Wonderful World **ART GARFUNKEL with JAMES TAYLOR & PAUL SIMON** #1 Adult Contemporary hit (5 weeks)	Columbia 10676
			GARI, Frank	
			Born on 4/1/42 in Brooklyn, New York. Teen pop singer.	
2/13/61	27	5	1. Utopia	Crusade 1020
5/15/61	23	6	2. Lullaby Of Love	Crusade 1021
8/14/61	30	3	3. Princess	Crusade 1022
			GARNETT, Gale	
			Born on 7/17/42 in Auckland, New Zealand. Female singer/songwriter.	
9/5/64	4	13	1. **We'll Sing In The Sunshine** #1 Adult Contemporary hit (7 weeks)	RCA Victor 8388
			GARRETT, Leif	
			Born on 11/8/61 in Hollywood, California. Pop singer/actor. Acted in several movies.	
9/17/77	20	8	1. Surfin' USA	Atlantic 3423
12/3/77+	13	9	2. Runaround Sue	Atlantic 3440
12/9/78+	10	15	3. **I Was Made For Dancin'**	Scotti Brothers 403

DATE	POS	WKS	ARTIST–RECORD TITLE	LABEL & NO.
			GATES, David	
			Born on 12/11/40 in Tulsa, Oklahoma. Pop singer/songwriter. Lead singer of Bread.	
2/15/75	29	5	1. Never Let Her Go	Elektra 45223
2/18/78	15	12	2. Goodbye Girl	Elektra 45450
			title song from the Neil Simon movie starring Richard Dreyfuss	
10/7/78	30	5	3. Took The Last Train	Elektra 45500
			GAYE, Marvin	
			Born Marvin Pentz Gay, Jr. on 4/2/39 in Washington DC. R&B singer/songwriter/producer. Fatally shot by his father after a quarrel on 4/1/84 (one day before his 45th birthday) in Los Angeles, California. Sang in his father's Apostolic church. In vocal groups the Rainbows and Marquees. Joined Harvey Fuqua in the re-formed Moonglows. Moved to Detroit in 1960. Session work as a drummer at Motown; married to Berry Gordy's sister Anna (1961-75). First recorded under own name for Tamla in 1961. Inducted into the Rock and Roll Hall of Fame in 1987. Won Grammy's Lifetime Achievement Award in 1996.	
3/2/63	30	3	1. Hitch Hike	Tamla 54075
6/15/63	10	10	2. **Pride And Joy**	Tamla 54079
			Martha & The Vandellas (backing vocals, above 2)	
11/23/63	22	10	3. Can I Get A Witness	Tamla 54087
3/28/64	15	7	4. You're A Wonderful One	Tamla 54093
			The Supremes (backing vocals, above 2)	
6/13/64	17	6	5. What's The Matter With You Baby /	
5/23/64	19	6	6. Once Upon A Time	Motown 1057
			MARVIN GAYE & MARY WELLS (above 2)	
6/27/64	15	8	7. Try It Baby	Tamla 54095
			The Temptations (backing vocals)	
10/10/64	27	6	8. Baby Don't You Do It	Tamla 54101
12/12/64+	6	11	9. **How Sweet It Is To Be Loved By You**	Tamla 54107
4/10/65	8	8	10. **I'll Be Doggone**	Tamla 54112
			#1 R&B hit (1 week)	
7/24/65	25	5	11. Pretty Little Baby	Tamla 54117
10/23/65	8	9	12. **Ain't That Peculiar**	Tamla 54122
			#1 R&B hit (1 week)	
3/12/66	29	4	13. One More Heartache	Tamla 54129
			#10, 12 & 13: produced by Smokey Robinson	
2/4/67	14	7	14. It Takes Two	Tamla 54141
			MARVIN GAYE & KIM WESTON	
6/3/67	19	9	15. Ain't No Mountain High Enough	Tamla 54149
			MARVIN GAYE & TAMMI TERRELL	
7/22/67	33	3	16. Your Unchanging Love	Tamla 54153
9/30/67	5	10	17. **Your Precious Love**	Tamla 54156
12/16/67+	10	9	18. **If I Could Build My Whole World Around You**	Tamla 54161
			MARVIN GAYE & TAMMI TERRELL (above 2)	
2/3/68	34	3	19. You	Tamla 54160
4/27/68	8	11	20. **Ain't Nothing Like The Real Thing**	Tamla 54163
			#1 R&B hit (1 week)	
8/10/68	7	10	21. **You're All I Need To Get By**	Tamla 54169
			MARVIN GAYE & TAMMI TERRELL (above 2)	
			#1 R&B hit (5 weeks)	
10/19/68	24	6	22. Keep On Lovin' Me Honey	Tamla 54173
			MARVIN GAYE & TAMMI TERRELL	

DATE	POS	WKS	ARTIST–RECORD TITLE	LABEL & NO.
10/19/68	**32**	4	23. Chained	Tamla 54170
11/23/68	**1** (7)	15	24. **I Heard It Through The Grapevine** #1 R&B hit (7 weeks)	Tamla 54176
2/15/69	**30**	4	25. Good Lovin' Ain't Easy To Come By **MARVIN GAYE & TAMMI TERRELL**	Tamla 54179
5/10/69	**4**	13	26. **Too Busy Thinking About My Baby** #1 R&B hit (6 weeks)	Tamla 54181
9/13/69	**7**	9	27. **That's The Way Love Is**	Tamla 54185
7/11/70	**40**	2	28. The End Of Our Road	Tamla 54195
3/6/71	**2** (3)	13	29. **What's Going On** #1 R&B hit (5 weeks)	Tamla 54201
7/17/71	**4**	10	30. **Mercy Mercy Me (The Ecology)** #1 R&B hit (2 weeks)	Tamla 54207
10/16/71	**9**	8	31. **Inner City Blues (Make Me Wanna Holler)** #1 R&B hit (2 weeks)	Tamla 54209
12/30/72+	**7**	9	32. **Trouble Man** title song from the movie starring Robert Hooks	Tamla 54228
7/28/73	**1** (2)	17	33. **Let's Get It On** #1 R&B hit (6 weeks)	Tamla 54234
10/13/73	**12**	10	34. You're A Special Part Of Me **DIANA ROSS & MARVIN GAYE**	Motown 1280
11/17/73	**21**	8	35. Come Get To This	Tamla 54241
3/30/74	**19**	10	36. My Mistake (Was To Love You) **DIANA ROSS & MARVIN GAYE**	Motown 1269
10/26/74	**28**	3	37. Distant Lover [L]	Tamla 54253
5/8/76	**15**	9	38. I Want You #1 R&B hit (1 week)	Tamla 54264
4/23/77	**1** (1)	15	39. **Got To Give It Up (Pt. I)** [L] #1 R&B hit (5 weeks); recorded at the London Palladium	Tamla 54280
11/20/82+	**3**	15	▲ 40. **Sexual Healing** #1 R&B hit (10 weeks)	Columbia 03302
6/16/01	**22**	10	41. Music Airplay #17 / Sales #31 **ERICK SERMON featuring MARVIN GAYE** samples Marvin Gaye's "Turn On Some Music" from his 1982 *Midnight Love* album; from the movie *What's The Worst That Could Happen?* starring Martin Lawrence	NY.LA 497578
			GAYLE, Crystal	
			Born Brenda Gail Webb on 1/9/51 in Paintsville, Kentucky; raised in Wabash, Indiana. Country singer. Youngest sister of Loretta Lynn.	
9/24/77	**2** (3)	18	● 1. **Don't It Make My Brown Eyes Blue** #1 Country hit (4 weeks)	United Artists 1016
9/2/78	**18**	11	2. Talking In Your Sleep #1 Country hit (2 weeks)	United Artists 1214
11/3/79	**15**	10	3. Half The Way	Columbia 11087
11/13/82+	**7**	21	4. **You And I** **EDDIE RABBITT with CRYSTAL GAYLE** #1 Country hit (1 week)	Elektra 69936
			GAYNOR, Gloria	
			Born Gloria Fowles on 9/7/49 in Newark, New Jersey. Disco singer.	
12/7/74+	**9**	10	1. **Never Can Say Goodbye**	MGM 14748
1/20/79	**1** (3)	17	▲ 2. **I Will Survive**	Polydor 14508

DATE	POS	WKS	ARTIST–RECORD TITLE	LABEL & NO.
			G-CLEFS, The	
			R&B vocal group from Roxbury, Massachusetts: brothers Teddy, Chris, Timmy and Arnold Scott, with Ray Gibson.	
9/15/56	24	1	1. Ka-Ding Dong　　　　　　Best Seller #24 / Top 100 #53	Pilgrim 715
			Freddy Cannon (lead guitar)	
10/16/61	9	11	2. **I Understand (Just How You Feel)**	Terrace 7500
			#6 hit for The Four Tunes in 1954	
			GEDDES, David	
			Born on 7/1/50 in Michigan. Pop singer.	
8/23/75	4	9	1. **Run Joey Run**	Big Tree 16044
11/22/75	18	6	2. The Last Game Of The Season	
			(A Blind Man In The Bleachers)	Big Tree 16052
			GEILS, J., Band	
			Rock group from Boston, Massachusetts: Jerome Geils (guitar), Peter Wolf (vocals), Magic Dick Salwitz (harmonica), Seth Justman (keyboards), Danny Klein (bass) and Stephen Jo Bladd (drums).	
1/15/72	39	2	1. Looking For A Love	Atlantic 2844
5/26/73	30	6	2. Give It To Me	Atlantic 2953
11/23/74+	12	7	3. Must Of Got Lost	Atlantic 3214
1/20/79	35	3	4. One Last Kiss	EMI America 8007
3/8/80	32	5	5. Come Back	EMI America 8032
5/24/80	38	3	6. Love Stinks	EMI America 8039
11/28/81+	1 (6)	20	● 7. **Centerfold**	EMI America 8102
			#1 Mainstream Rock hit (3 weeks)	
3/6/82	4	12	● 8. **Freeze-Frame**	EMI America 8108
7/3/82	40	2	9. Angel In Blue	EMI America 8100
12/11/82+	24	7	10. I Do　　　　　　　　　　　　　[L]	EMI America 8148
			GENE & DEBBE	
			Vocal duo: Gene Thomas and Debbe Neville.	
3/9/68	17	12	1. Playboy	TRX 5006
			GENERAL PUBLIC	
			Pop group formed in Birmingham, England: Dave Wakeling (vocals, guitar), Ranking Roger (vocals, keyboards), Kevin White (guitar), Micky Billingham (keyboards), Horace Panter (bass) and Stoker (drums). Wakeling and Roger had been in English Beat. Billingham was with Dexys Midnight Runners. General Public disbanded in March 1987. Wakeling and Roger reunited in 1994.	
1/26/85	27	5	1. Tenderness　　　　　Sales #20 / Airplay #26	I.R.S. 9934
4/30/94	22	13	2. I'll Take You There　　Airplay #19 / Sales #46	Epic Soundtrax 77452
			from the movie *Threesome* starring Lara Flynn Boyle and Stephen Baldwin	

DATE	POS	WKS	ARTIST–RECORD TITLE	LABEL & NO.

GENESIS

Pop-rock group formed in England. Early members included Peter Gabriel (vocals; left in 1975) and Steve Hackett (guitar; left in 1977 to form GTR). Reduced to a trio in 1977: Phil Collins (vocals, drums), Mike Rutherford (guitar, bass) and Tony Banks (keyboards). Added touring members Daryl Stuermer (guitar) and Chester Thompson (drums). Rutherford also formed Mike + The Mechanics.

DATE	POS	WKS	ARTIST–RECORD TITLE	LABEL & NO.
6/3/78	23	5	1. Follow You Follow Me	Atlantic 3474
6/21/80	14	11	2. Misunderstanding	Atlantic 3662
11/7/81	29	6	3. No Reply At All	Atlantic 3858
			features the Earth, Wind & Fire horn section	
1/23/82	26	6	4. Abacab	Atlantic 3891
5/8/82	40	2	5. Man On The Corner	Atlantic 4025
7/24/82	32	5	6. Paperlate	Atlantic 4053
12/10/83+	6	14	7. **That's All!**	Atlantic 89724
6/7/86	1 (1)	12	8. **Invisible Touch** Airplay #1 (3) / Sales #4	Atlantic 89407
			#1 Mainstream Rock hit (3 weeks)	
8/23/86	4	12	9. **Throwing It All Away** Airplay #2 / Sales #7	Atlantic 89372
			#1 Adult Contemporary hit (2 weeks) / #1 Mainstream Rock hit (3 weeks)	
11/15/86+	4	15	10. **Land Of Confusion** Airplay #3 / Sales #5	Atlantic 89336
2/21/87	3	10	11. **Tonight, Tonight, Tonight** Sales #3 / Airplay #3	Atlantic 89290
5/2/87	3	12	12. **In Too Deep** Sales #3 / Airplay #3	Atlantic 89316
			#1 Adult Contemporary hit (3 weeks)	
11/9/91+	12	16	13. No Son Of Mine Airplay #10 / Sales #31	Atlantic 87571
2/15/92	7	14	14. **I Can't Dance** Airplay #11 / Sales #13	Atlantic 87532
5/16/92	12	14	15. Hold On My Heart Airplay #9 / Sales #41	Atlantic 87481
			#1 Adult Contemporary hit (5 weeks)	
8/15/92	23	9	16. Jesus He Knows Me Airplay #21 / Sales #72	Atlantic 87454
12/12/92+	21	9	17. Never A Time Airplay #22	Atlantic 87411

GENTRY, Bobbie

Born Roberta Streeter on 7/27/44 in Chickasaw County, Mississippi; raised in Greenwood, Mississippi. Singer/songwriter. Won the 1967 Best New Artist Grammy Award. Married to Jim Stafford (1978-79).

DATE	POS	WKS	ARTIST–RECORD TITLE	LABEL & NO.
8/12/67	1 (4)	12	● 1. **Ode To Billie Joe**	Capitol 5950
3/8/69	36	1	2. Let It Be Me	Capitol 2387
			GLEN CAMPBELL AND BOBBIE GENTRY	
1/31/70	31	4	3. Fancy	Capitol 2675
3/14/70	27	6	4. All I Have To Do Is Dream	Capitol 2745
			BOBBIE GENTRY & GLEN CAMPBELL	

GENTRYS, The

Garage-rock band from Memphis, Tennessee: Larry Raspberry, Jimmy Hart and Bruce Bowles (vocals), Bobby Fisher (guitar), Jimmy Johnson (trumpet), Pat Neal (bass) and Larry Wall (drums). Hart later became a professional wrestling manager, known as "The Mouth of The South."

DATE	POS	WKS	ARTIST–RECORD TITLE	LABEL & NO.
9/25/65	4	11	1. **Keep On Dancing**	MGM 13379

GEORGE, Barbara

Born on 8/16/42 in New Orleans, Louisiana. R&B singer/songwriter.

DATE	POS	WKS	ARTIST–RECORD TITLE	LABEL & NO.
12/18/61+	3	11	1. **I Know (You Don't Love Me No More)**	A.F.O. 302
			#1 R&B hit (4 weeks); Melvin Lastie (cornet solo)	

DATE	POS	WKS	ARTIST–RECORD TITLE	LABEL & NO.
			GEORGIA SATELLITES	
			Rock group from Atlanta, Georgia: Dan Baird (vocals, guitar; see #2 below), Rick Richards (guitar), Rich Price (bass) and Mauro Magellan (drums).	
12/20/86+	2 (1)	14	1. **Keep Your Hands To Yourself** Sales #1 (1) / Airplay #6	Elektra 69502
1/16/93	26	5	2. I Love You Period. Sales #36 / Airplay #46 **DAN BAIRD**	Def American 18724
			GERARDO	
			Born Gerardo Mejia on 4/16/65 in Guayaquil, Ecuador; raised in Glendale, California. Rapper/actor. Raps in Spanglish (half Spanish, half English). Appeared in the movies *Can't Buy Me Love* and *Colors*.	
3/2/91	7	10	● 1. **Rico Suave** Sales #5 / Airplay #15	Interscope 98871
5/25/91	16	6	2. We Want The Funk Sales #22 / Airplay #26 samples "Tear The Roof Off The Sucker (Give Up The Funk)" by Parliament	Interscope 98815
			GERRY AND THE PACEMAKERS	
			Pop group from Liverpool, England: brothers Gerry (vocals, guitar; born on 9/24/42) and Freddie (drums) Marsden, with Leslie Maguire (piano) and John Chadwick (bass).	
6/6/64	4	9	1. **Don't Let The Sun Catch You Crying**	Laurie 3251
8/8/64	9	7	2. **How Do You Do It?**	Laurie 3261
10/17/64	17	6	3. I Like It	Laurie 3271
1/9/65	14	5	4. I'll Be There written by Bobby Darin	Laurie 3279
2/13/65	6	9	5. **Ferry Cross The Mersey**	Laurie 3284
4/24/65	23	5	6. It's Gonna Be Alright above 2 from the movie *Ferry Cross The Mersey* starring Gerry And The Pacemakers	Laurie 3293
10/8/66	28	4	7. Girl On A Swing	Laurie 3354
			GETO BOYS, The	
			Rap group from Houston, Texas: Richard "Bushwick Bill" Shaw, William "Willie D" Dennis, Brad "Scarface" Jordan and "Big Mike" Barnett.	
11/2/91+	23	11	● 1. Mind Playing Tricks On Me Sales #6	Rap-A-Lot 7241
6/12/93	40	1	2. Six Feet Deep Sales #20 / Airplay #49 samples "Easy" by the Commodores and "What's Going On" by Marvin Gaye	Rap-A-Lot 53823
			GET WET	
			Pop group featuring lead singer Sherri Beachfront.	
5/23/81	39	2	1. Just So Lonely	Boardwalk 02018
			GETZ, Stan	
			Born Stan Gayetzsky on 2/2/27 in Philadelphia, Pennsylvania. Died of cancer on 6/6/91 (age 64). Jazz saxophonist.	
10/27/62	15	10	1. Desafinado [I] **STAN GETZ/CHARLIE BYRD**	Verve 10260
6/20/64	5	10	2. **The Girl From Ipanema** **GETZ/GILBERTO** #1 Adult Contemporary hit (2 weeks); 1964 Grammy winner: Record of the Year	Verve 10323

DATE	POS	WKS	ARTIST–RECORD TITLE		LABEL & NO.
			GHOST TOWN DJ'S		
			DJ duo from Atlanta, Georgia: Rodney Terry and Carlton Mahoney.		
9/21/96	**31**	16	1. My Boo	Airplay #13	So So Def 78358
			GIANT		
			Rock group formed in Nashville, Tennessee: brothers Dan (vocals, guitar) and David (drums) Huff, with Alan Pasqua (keyboards) and Mike Brignardello (bass).		
5/5/90	**20**	8	1. I'll See You In My Dreams	Airplay #18 / Sales #22	A&M 1495
			GIANT STEPS		
			Duo from England: Campsie (vocals) and George McFarlane (instruments).		
10/1/88	**13**	10	1. Another Lover	Airplay #12 / Sales #13	A&M 1226
			GIBB, Andy		
			Born on 3/5/58 in Manchester, England. Died of heart failure on 3/10/88 (age 30). Pop singer/songwriter. Youngest brother of Barry, Robin and Maurice Gibb (Bee Gees). Hosted TV's *Solid Gold* from 1981-82.		
5/28/77	**1 (4)**	23	● 1. **I Just Want To Be Your Everything**		RSO 872
12/10/77+	**1 (2)**	22	● 2. **(Love Is) Thicker Than Water**		RSO 883
4/22/78	**1 (7)**	19	▲ 3. **Shadow Dancing**		RSO 893
7/22/78	**5**	13	● 4. **An Everlasting Love**		RSO 904
11/4/78	**9**	13	● 5. **(Our Love) Don't Throw It All Away**		RSO 911
2/2/80	**4**	12	6. **Desire**		RSO 1019
4/19/80	**12**	8	7. I Can't Help It		RSO 1026
			ANDY GIBB AND OLIVIA NEWTON-JOHN		
12/6/80+	**15**	11	8. Time Is Time		RSO 1059
4/11/81	**40**	1	9. Me (Without You)		RSO 1056
			GIBB, Barry — see BEE GEES		
			GIBB, Robin — see BEE GEES		
			GIBBS, Georgia		
			Born Fredda Gibbons on 8/17/20 in Worcester, Massachusetts. Female pop singer. Nicknamed "Her Nibs, Miss Gibbs."		
1/29/55	**2 (1)**	19	● 1. **Tweedle Dee**	Jockey #2 / Best Seller #3 / Juke Box #3	Mercury 70517
3/26/55	**1 (3)**	20	● 2. **Dance With Me Henry (Wallflower)**	Juke Box #1 (3) / Best Seller #2 / Jockey #3	Mercury 70572
			#1 R&B hit for Etta James in 1955		
7/9/55	**12**	4	3. Sweet And Gentle	Jockey #12	Mercury 70647
9/17/55	**14**	4	4. I Want You To Be My Baby	Jockey #14 / Best Seller #22 / Top 100 #48	Mercury 70685
			first recorded by Louis Jordan in 1953		
4/14/56	**36**	1	5. Rock Right	Top 100 #36	Mercury 70811
5/26/56	**30**	4	6. Kiss Me Another	Top 100 #30	Mercury 70850
8/25/56	**20**	8	7. Happiness Street	Jockey #20 / Top 100 #25	Mercury 70920
12/22/56	**24**	1	8. Tra La La	Jockey #24 / Top 100 #39	Mercury 70998
			from the movie *Rock, Rock, Rock* starring Tuesday Weld; Glenn Osser (orch.: #1 & 6-8)		
10/20/58	**32**	1	9. The Hula Hoop Song	Hot 100 #32 / Best Seller #42	Roulette 4106
			Hugo Peretti (of Hugo & Luigi; orch.: #2-5 & 9)		

DATE	POS	WKS	ARTIST-RECORD TITLE	LABEL & NO.
			GIBBS, Terri	
			Born on 6/15/54 in Miami, Florida; raised in Augusta, Georgia. Female country singer/pianist. Blind since birth.	
2/28/81	**13**	12	1. Somebody's Knockin'	MCA 41309
			GIBSON, Debbie	
			Born on 8/31/70 in Brooklyn, New York; raised in Merrick, Long Island, New York. Pop singer/songwriter/pianist/actress. Began playing piano at age five and songwriting at age six. Acted in the Broadway shows *Les Misérables* and *Grease*.	
6/27/87	**4**	16	● 1. **Only In My Dreams** Sales #3 / Airplay #3	Atlantic 89322
10/24/87	**4**	15	2. **Shake Your Love** Sales #4 / Airplay #4	Atlantic 89187
2/6/88	**3**	13	3. **Out Of The Blue** Sales #3 / Airplay #3	Atlantic 89129
5/7/88	**1** (1)	14	4. **Foolish Beat** Airplay #1 (2) / Sales #1 (1)	Atlantic 89109
9/3/88	**22**	6	5. Staying Together Sales #19 / Airplay #26	Atlantic 89034
1/28/89	**1** (3)	12	● 6. **Lost In Your Eyes** Airplay #1 (3) / Sales #1 (2)	Atlantic 88970
4/15/89	**11**	8	● 7. Electric Youth Sales #8 / Airplay #12	Atlantic 88919
7/8/89	**17**	7	8. No More Rhyme Sales #15 / Airplay #17	Atlantic 88885
12/15/90+	**26**	6	9. Anything Is Possible Airplay #26 / Sales #28	Atlantic 87793
			GIBSON, Don	
			Born on 4/3/28 in Shelby, North Carolina. Died on 11/17/2003 (age 75). Country singer/songwriter/guitarist.	
3/31/58	**7**	17	1. **Oh Lonesome Me** Best Seller #7 / Top 100 #8 / Jockey #10 #1 Country hit (8 weeks)	RCA Victor 7133
7/14/58	**20**	8	2. Blue Blue Day Jockey #20 / Hot 100 #32 / Best Seller #32 #1 Country hit (2 weeks)	RCA Victor 7010
3/28/60	**29**	6	3. Just One Time	RCA Victor 7690
7/10/61	**21**	8	4. Sea Of Heartbreak	RCA Victor 7890
			GILBERTO, Astrud — see GETZ, Stan	
			GILDER, Nick	
			Born on 11/7/51 in London, England; raised in Vancouver, British Columbia, Canada. Pop singer/songwriter.	
8/5/78	**1** (1)	18	▲ 1. **Hot Child In The City**	Chrysalis 2226
			GILKYSON, Terry, and The Easy Riders	
			Folk trio: Terry Gilkyson, Rich Dehr and Frank Miller. Gilkyson died of an aneurysm on 10/15/99 (age 83).	
2/9/57	**4**	14	1. **Marianne** Juke Box #4 / Top 100 #5 / Jockey #5 / Best Seller #6	Columbia 40817
			GILL, Johnny	
			Born on 5/22/66 in Washington DC. R&B singer. Joined New Edition in 1988.	
5/26/90	**3**	16	● 1. **Rub You The Right Way** Airplay #2 / Sales #4 #1 R&B hit (1 week)	Motown 2045
8/18/90	**10**	10	2. **My, My, My** Sales #9 / Airplay #13 #1 R&B hit (2 weeks); After 7 (backing vocals)	Motown 2033
11/24/90	**28**	6	3. Fairweather Friend Sales #23 / Airplay #33	Motown 2049
5/16/92	**31**	5	4. Silent Prayer Airplay #29 / Sales #33 **SHANICE featuring Johnny Gill**	Motown 2165

DATE	POS	WKS	ARTIST–RECORD TITLE	LABEL & NO.
1/2/93	33	2	● 5. Slow And Sexy Sales #14 / Airplay #63 **SHABBA RANKS (featuring Johnny Gill)**	Epic 74741
			GILL, Vince — see GRANT, Amy	
			GILLETTE — see 20 FINGERS	
			GILLEY, Mickey	
			Born on 3/9/36 in Natchez, Mississippi; raised in Ferriday, Louisiana. Country singer/pianist. First cousin to both Jerry Lee Lewis and TV evangelist Jimmy Swaggart. Owner of Gilleys nightclub in Pasadena, Texas. Gilley and the club were featured in the movie *Urban Cowboy*. The club closed in 1989.	
6/28/80	22	9	1. Stand By Me #1 Country hit (1 week); from the movie *Urban Cowboy* starring John Travolta and Debra Winger	Full Moon 46640
			GILMAN, Billy	
			Born on 5/24/88 in Westerly, Rhode Island; raised in Hope Valley, Rhode Island. Country singer (age 12 in 2000).	
9/2/00	38	2	1. One Voice Sales #8	Epic 79396
			GILMER, Jimmy — see FIREBALLS	
			GILREATH, James	
			Born on 11/14/39 in Prairie, Mississippi. Singer/guitarist/songwriter.	
4/27/63	21	6	1. Little Band Of Gold	Joy 274
			GINA G	
			Born Gina Gardiner in 1971 in Australia. Female dance singer.	
12/21/96+	12	25	1. Ooh Aah...Just A Little Bit Airplay #10 / Sales #22	Eternal/Warner 17455
			GIN BLOSSOMS	
			Pop-rock group from Tempe, Arizona: Robin Wilson (vocals), Jesse Valenzuela and Scott Johnson (guitars), Bill Leen (bass) and Phillip Rhodes (drums). Early guitarist Doug Hopkins, writer of "Hey Jealousy" and "Found Out About You," died of a self-inflicted gunshot wound on 12/5/93 (age 32).	
9/11/93	25	11	1. Hey Jealousy Sales #28 / Airplay #31	A&M 0242
1/1/94	25	17	2. Found Out About You Airplay #14 #1 Modern Rock hit (1 week)	A&M 0418
6/18/94	21 A	19	3. Until I Fall Away	album cut
11/19/94	24 A	12	4. Allison Road above 2 from the album *New Miserable Experience* on A&M 5403	album cut
2/10/96	9	33	5. **Follow You Down /** Airplay #7 / Sales #45	
2/10/96	11	33	6. Til I Hear It From You Airplay #8 / Sales #49 from the movie *Empire Records* starring Anthony LaPaglia	A&M 1380
			GINO & GINA	
			Brother-and-sister vocal duo from Brooklyn, New York: Aristedes and Irene Giosasi.	
6/9/58	20	1	1. (It's Been A Long Time) Pretty Baby Jockey #20 / Top 100 #34 / Best Seller #39	Mercury 71283

DATE	POS	WKS	ARTIST–RECORD TITLE	LABEL & NO.
			GINUWINE	
			Born Elgin Lumpkin on 10/15/75 in Washington DC. Male R&B singer/songwriter.	
10/5/96	6	21	▲ 1. **Pony** Sales #4 / Airplay #24 #1 R&B hit (2 weeks)	550 Music 78373
7/31/99	16	13	2. So Anxious Airplay #10 Playa (backing vocals); from the album *100 Percent Ginuwine* on 550 Music 69598	album cut
8/25/01	4	26	3. **Differences** Airplay #4 / Sales #63 #1 R&B hit (4 weeks)	Epic 79711
6/15/02	4	22	4. **I Need A Girl (Part Two)** Airplay #4 / Sales #17 **P. DIDDY AND GINUWINE Featuring Loon, Mario Winans & Tammy Ruggeri**	Bad Boy 79441
9/7/02	33	6	5. Stingy Airplay #32 / Sales #37 from the movie *Barbershop* starring Ice Cube	Epic 79772
3/15/03	17	12	6. Hell Yeah Airplay #17 / Sales #25 **GINUWINE (feat. Baby)** written and produced by R. Kelly	Epic 76881
6/28/03	8	14	7. **In Those Jeans** Airplay #7 from the album *The Senior* on Epic 86960	album cut
			GIUFFRIA	
			Rock group from California: Gregg Giuffria (keyboards), David Glen Eisley (vocals), Craig Goldy (guitar), Chuck Wright (bass) and Alan Krigger (drums).	
1/5/85	15	7	1. Call To The Heart Sales #12 / Airplay #25	MCA/Camel 52497
			GLAHÉ, Will, and His Orchestra	
			Born on 2/12/02 in Elberfeld, Germany. Died on 11/21/89 (age 87). Accordionist/composer/conductor.	
11/25/57	16	15	1. Liechtensteiner Polka Best Seller #16 / Jockey #18 / Top 100 #19 **[F]**	London 1755
			GLASS BOTTLE, The	
			Pop group from New Jersey: Gary Criss (male vocals), Carol Denmark (female vocals), Dennis Dees (guitar), Charles Moore (keyboards) and Jon Melia (drums).	
9/18/71	36	3	1. I Ain't Got Time Anymore produced by novelty artist Dickie Goodman	Avco Embassy 4575
			GLASS TIGER	
			Pop-rock group from Canada: Alan Frew (vocals), Al Connelly (guitar), Sam Reid (keyboards), Wayne Parker (bass) and Michael Hanson (drums).	
8/9/86	2 (1)	14	1. **Don't Forget Me (When I'm Gone)** Sales #1 (1) / Airplay #6 Bryan Adams (response vocal)	Manhattan 50037
11/29/86+	7	13	2. **Someday** Sales #7 / Airplay #7	Manhattan 50048
3/21/87	34	5	3. I Will Be There Airplay #28 / Sales #37	Manhattan 50066
5/7/88	31	5	4. I'm Still Searching Sales #26 / Airplay #30	EMI-Manhattan 50116

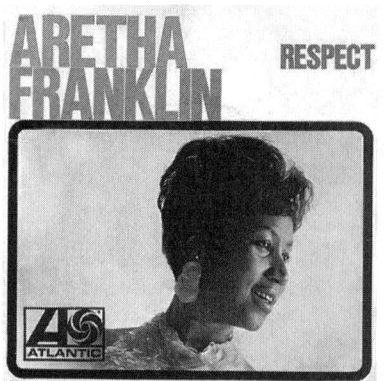

Connie Francis recorded her #1 hit "Don't Break The Heart That Loves You" at the urging of her father. As he had also urged her to record her first hit, "Who's Sorry Now," she couldn't resist his suggestion.

Aretha Franklin placed 20 songs at #1 on the R&B charts, confirming her nickname as "The Queen Of Soul." In that context, it was a bit disrespectful that only one of those soul hits, "Respect," also topped the pop charts.

John Fred and his Playboy Band turned a misheard lyric on a Beatles song into a #1 hit with his parody of "Lucy In The Sky With Diamonds," titled "Judy In Disguise (With Glasses)." Ironically, the song replaced The Beatles' "Hello Goodbye" at #1.

Marvin Gaye released his version of "I Heard It Through The Grapevine" a year after Gladys Knight took her version to #2. Marvin did one better, reaching the top spot. Thanks to the movie *The Big Chill*, the song made a 1980s comeback.

Gloria Gaynor created a disco anthem with her #1 hit "I Will Survive." Although Gloria's career faded, the song lived on into the 1990s through remakes by Safire and Chantay Savage.

Bobbie Gentry took "Ode To Billie Joe" to #1 in 1967. When a movie based on the song was released in 1976, Bobbie found her original song competing against her newly recorded theme version. Unfortunately, both missed the Top 40.

I Just Want To Be Your Everything

Words and Music by
BARRY GIBB
Recorded by ANDY GIBB
on RSO Records

Debbie Gibson
LOST IN YOUR EYES

GOO GOO DOLLS
"Iris"

BUTTERFLY

Words and Music by ANTHONY SEPTEMBER

Recorded by
CHARLIE GRACIE
on Cameo Records

PRICE
50c

Recorded by LESLEY GORE on MERCURY RECORDS

IT'S MY PARTY

Words and Music by HERB WIENER, WALLY GOLD, and JOHN GLUCK, JR.

AL GREEN
LET'S STAY TOGETHER

RINGO

Words by HAL BLAIR and DON ROBERTSON
Music by DON ROBERTSON
Recorded on RCA VICTOR by LORNE GREENE
Produced by Joe Reisman

EDWIN H. MORRIS & CO., LTD.

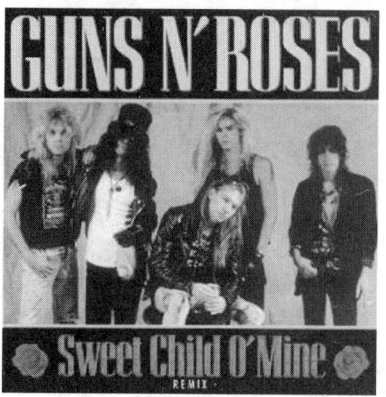

GUNS N' ROSES

Sweet Child O' Mine
REMIX

Andy Gibb scored the first of three consecutive #1 hits with "I Just Want To Be Your Everything." Willing to try everything, Andy also took to the stage in *The Pirates Of Penzance* and hosted TV's *Solid Gold.*

Debbie Gibson had four Top 10 hits from her debut album, *Out Of The Blue,* but the album never reached #1. Her follow-up album, *Electric Youth,* reached the top but only generated one Top 10 hit, the #1 ballad "Lost In Your Eyes."

The Goo Goo Dolls watched "Iris" spend over four months as radio's most popular song. However, because album cuts weren't allowed to reach the Hot 100 until late 1998, the song only managed an "official" Hot 100 peak of #9.

Lesley Gore was only 17 when "It's My Party" went to #1. Although she didn't write her only chart-topper, Lesley would go on to compose songs for the popular movie *Fame* with her brother, Michael.

Charlie Gracie released his hit "Butterfly" just as Andy Williams was releasing his own version. While radio favored Andy's version, Charlie's "Butterfly" proved to be more popular on jukeboxes and with record buyers, and quickly flew to the top of the charts.

Al Green sent over a dozen soulful hits onto the Top 40, including his #1 single, "Let's Stay Together," but his background was in gospel music. Appropriately, most of his Grammy Awards came from the gospel categories.

Lorne Greene spent 14 seasons playing Ben Cartwright on the TV series *Bonanza.* The time obviously made an impression on him, as the B-side of his #1 hit, "Ringo," was a song titled "Bonanza."

Guns N' Roses topped the charts with their first hit, "Sweet Child O' Mine." Things weren't so rosy for the band in the late 1990s, however, as all the original members except Axl Rose had moved on to other projects.

DATE	POS	WKS	ARTIST–RECORD TITLE	LABEL & NO.
			GLAZER, Tom, And The Do-Re-Mi Children's Chorus	
			Born on 9/3/14 in Philadelphia, Pennsylvania. Died on 2/21/2003 (age 88). Folk singer. Hosted own ABC radio program (1945-47).	
6/15/63	14	7	1. On Top Of Spaghetti [N] parody of the traditional folk song "On Top Of Old Smokey"	Kapp 526
			GLENCOVES, The	
			Folk trio from Mineola, Long Island, New York: Brian Bolger, Bill Byrne and Don Connors.	
7/27/63	38	2	1. Hootenanny	Select 724
			GLITTER, Gary	
			Born Paul Gadd on 5/8/44 in Banbury, Oxfordshire, England. Glam-rock singer.	
8/5/72	7	9	1. **Rock And Roll Part 2** [I] tune has become "The Sports Anthem" ("The Hey Song") across the USA	Bell 45,237
12/2/72	35	3	2. I Didn't Know I Loved You (Till I Saw You Rock And Roll)	Bell 45,276
			GODLEY & CREME	
			Duo from Manchester, England: Kevin Godley (born on 10/7/45) and Lol Creme (born on 9/19/47). Both were members of Hotlegs and 10cc.	
8/17/85	16	10	1. Cry　　　　　　　Airplay #15 / Sales #16	Polydor 881786
			GODSPELL	
			The original cast from the Broadway rock musical *Godspell*.	
6/24/72	13	9	1. Day By Day original cast member Robin Lamont (lead vocal)	Bell 45,210
			GO-GO'S	
			Female rock group formed in Los Angeles, California: Belinda Carlisle (vocals), Jane Wiedlin and Charlotte Caffey (guitars), Kathy Valentine (bass) and Gina Schock (drums).	
10/24/81	20	13	1. Our Lips Are Sealed	I.R.S. 9901
2/13/82	2 (3)	15	● 2. **We Got The Beat**	I.R.S. 9903
7/17/82	8	9	3. **Vacation**	I.R.S. 9907
3/31/84	11	10	4. Head Over Heels	I.R.S. 9926
7/14/84	32	5	5. Turn To You	I.R.S. 9928
			GOLD, Andrew	
			Born on 8/2/51 in Burbank, California. Pop-rock singer/songwriter. Son of conductor Ernest Gold and singer Marni Nixon.	
4/16/77	7	13	1. **Lonely Boy** Linda Ronstadt (backing vocal)	Asylum 45384
3/4/78	25	9	2. Thank You For Being A Friend song later adapted as the theme for the TV series *The Golden Girls* starring Bea Arthur and Betty White	Asylum 45456

DATE	POS	WKS	ARTIST–RECORD TITLE	LABEL & NO.
			GOLDEN EARRING	
			Rock group from The Hague, Netherlands: Barry Hay (vocals), George Kooymans (guitar), Rinus Gerritsen (bass) and Cesar Zuiderwijk (drums).	
6/22/74	13	10	1. Radar Love	Track/MCA 40202
1/22/83	10	15	2. **Twilight Zone**	21 Records 103
			#1 Mainstream Rock hit (1 week)	
			GOLDSBORO, Bobby	
			Born on 1/18/41 in Marianna, Florida. Singer/songwriter/guitarist. Hosted own TV variety show from 1972-75.	
2/15/64	9	8	1. **See The Funny Little Clown**	United Artists 672
5/23/64	39	2	2. Whenever He Holds You	United Artists 710
2/20/65	13	8	3. Little Things	United Artists 810
6/5/65	27	6	4. Voodoo Woman	United Artists 862
3/12/66	23	5	5. It's Too Late	United Artists 980
1/14/67	35	3	6. Blue Autumn	United Artists 50087
3/30/68	1 (5)	13	● 7. **Honey**	United Artists 50283
			#1 Country hit (3 weeks) / #1 Adult Contemporary hit (2 weeks); written by Bobby Russell	
7/13/68	19	7	8. Autumn Of My Life	United Artists 50318
11/30/68	36	2	9. The Straight Life	United Artists 50461
1/9/71	11	11	10. Watching Scotty Grow	United Artists 50727
			#1 Adult Contemporary hit (6 weeks); written by Mac Davis	
10/6/73	21	8	11. Summer (The First Time)	United Artists 251
			GOMM, Ian	
			Born on 3/17/47 in Ealing, London, England. Pop-rock singer/songwriter/guitarist.	
10/6/79	18	5	1. Hold On	Stiff/Epic 50747
			GONE ALL STARS	
			Studio group assembled by George Goldner.	
3/3/58	30	4	1. "7-11" Best Seller #30 / Top 100 #31 **[I]**	Gone 5016
			rock version of the Perez Prado tune "Mambo No. 5"	
			GONZALEZ	
			Disco group formed in London, England: Linda Taylor and Alan Marshall (vocals), Jim Cansfield (guitar), Roy Davies (keyboards), Bobby Stignac (percussion), Mick Eve, Chris Mercer, Bud Beadle, Colin Jacas, Ron Carthy and Martin Drover (horn section), Hugh Bullen (bass) and Sergio Castillo (drums).	
2/10/79	26	5	1. Haven't Stopped Dancing Yet	Capitol 4674
			GOOD CHARLOTTE	
			Rock group from Waldorf, Maryland: twin brothers Joel (vocals) and Benji (guitar) Madden, with Billy Martin (guitar), Paul Thomas (bass) and Aaron (drums).	
1/18/03	20	7	1. Lifestyles Of The Rich And Famous	album cut
			Airplay #20 / Sales: flip	
			from the album *The Young And The Hopeless* on Daylight 86486	

DATE	POS	WKS	ARTIST–RECORD TITLE	LABEL & NO.
			GOODIE MOB	
			Male rap group from Atlanta, Georgia: Cee-Lo, Khujo, T-Mo and Big Gipp.	
11/18/95	**39**	3	1. Cell Therapy Sales #14	LaFace 24113
			GOODMAN, Benny — see CLOONEY, Rosemary	
			GOODMAN, Dickie	
			Born Richard Goodman on 4/19/34 in Brooklyn, New York. Died of a self-inflicted gunshot wound on 11/6/89 (age 55). Goodman and partner Bill Buchanan originated the novelty "break-in" recordings featuring bits of the original versions of Top 40 hits interwoven throughout the recording. Buchanan died of cancer on 8/1/96 (age 66).	
			BUCHANAN AND GOODMAN:	
8/11/56	**3**	10	● 1. **The Flying Saucer (Parts 1 & 2)** Best Seller #3 / Top 100 #7 / Jockey #9 / Juke Box #9 **[N]** originally titled "Back To Earth"	Luniverse 101
7/29/57	**18**	8	2. Flying Saucer The 2nd Best Seller #18 / Top 100 #19 **[N]**	Luniverse 105
12/30/57	**32**	2	3. Santa And The Satellite (Parts I & II) Top 100 #32 / Best Seller #36 **[X-N]** Paul Sherman (narration)	Luniverse 107
			DICKIE GOODMAN:	
2/23/74	**33**	4	4. Energy Crisis '74 **[N]**	Rainy Wednesday 206
9/13/75	**4**	7	● 5. **Mr. Jaws** **[N]**	Cash 451
			GOO GOO DOLLS	
			Rock trio from Buffalo, New York: Johnny Rzeznik (vocals, guitar), Robby Takac (bass) and Mike Malinin (drums).	
10/14/95+	**5**	33	1. **Name** Airplay #2 / Sales #31 #1 Mainstream Rock hit (5 weeks) / #1 Modern Rock hit (4 weeks)	Warner 17758
5/2/98	**1** (18)ᴬ	45	2. **Iris** Hot 100 #9 (14 wks) #1 Modern Rock hit (5 weeks); from the movie *City Of Angels* starring Nicolas Cage (soundtrack on Warner Sunset 46867)	album cut
12/5/98+	**8**	34	3. **Slide** Airplay #1 (1) #1 Modern Rock hit (2 weeks); from the album *Dizzy Up The Girl* on Warner 47058	album cut
8/21/99	**16**	22	4. Black Balloon Airplay #18 / Sales #22	Warner 16946
5/20/00	**24**	8	5. Broadway Airplay #24 from the album *Dizzy Up The Girl* on Warner 47058	album cut
4/6/02	**18**	10	6. Here Is Gone Airplay #18 from the album *Gutterflower* on Warner 48206	album cut
			GORDON, Barry	
			Born on 12/21/48 in Brookline, Massachusetts. Acted in several TV shows.	
12/17/55	**6**	4	● 1. **Nuttin' For Christmas** Best Seller #6 / Top 100 #7 / Juke Box #9 / Jockey #10 **[X-N]** **ART MOONEY And His ORCHESTRA with Barry Gordon**	MGM 12092
			GORE, Lesley	
			Born on 5/2/46 in Manhattan, New York; raised in Tenafly, New Jersey. Pop singer. Appeared in the movies *Girls On The Beach*, *Ski Party* and *The T.A.M.I. Show*.	
5/18/63	**1** (2)	11	1. **It's My Party** #1 R&B hit (3 weeks)	Mercury 72119

DATE	POS	WKS	ARTIST–RECORD TITLE	LABEL & NO.
7/20/63	5	9	2. **Judy's Turn To Cry** sequel to "It's My Party"	Mercury 72143
10/19/63	5	11	3. **She's A Fool**	Mercury 72180
1/11/64	2 (3)	10	4. **You Don't Own Me**	Mercury 72206
4/4/64	12	7	5. That's The Way Boys Are	Mercury 72259
6/20/64	37	1	6. I Don't Wanna Be A Loser	Mercury 72270
8/15/64	14	6	7. Maybe I Know	Mercury 72309
1/23/65	27	5	8. Look Of Love	Mercury 72372
7/17/65	13	7	9. Sunshine, Lollipops And Rainbows from the movie *Ski Party* starring Frankie Avalon	Mercury 72433
10/9/65	32	3	10. My Town, My Guy And Me all of above produced by Quincy Jones	Mercury 72475
3/4/67	16	9	11. California Nights	Mercury 72649

GORME, Eydie

Born on 8/16/31 in the Bronx, New York. Vocalist with the big bands of Tommy Tucker and Tex Beneke in the late 1940s. Featured on Steve Allen's *Tonight Show*. Married Steve Lawrence on 12/29/57.

DATE	POS	WKS	ARTIST–RECORD TITLE	LABEL & NO.
6/16/56	39	1	1. Too Close For Comfort Top 100 #39 from the Broadway musical *Mr. Wonderful* starring Sammy Davis Jr.	ABC-Paramount 9684
9/1/56	34	3	2. Mama, Teach Me To Dance Top 100 #34 Sid Feller (orch.)	ABC-Paramount 9722
12/30/57	24	1	3. Love Me Forever Jockey #24 / Top 100 #86 Bernie Glow (trumpet solo)	ABC-Paramount 9863
5/26/58	11	9	4. You Need Hands Jockey #11 / Best Seller #32 / Top 100 #32 Don Costa (orch., all of above - except #2)	ABC-Paramount 9925
2/9/63	7	11	5. **Blame It On The Bossa Nova** The Cookies (backing vocals)	Columbia 42661
8/24/63	28	5	6. I Want To Stay Here **STEVE & EYDIE**	Columbia 42815
1/25/64	35	3	7. I Can't Stop Talking About You **STEVE And EYDIE** Marion Evans (orch., above 3)	Columbia 42932

GOULET, Robert

Born on 11/26/33 in Lawrence, Massachusetts. Singer/actor. Launched career as Sir Lancelot in the hit Broadway musical *Camelot*. Won the 1962 Best New Artist Grammy Award.

DATE	POS	WKS	ARTIST–RECORD TITLE	LABEL & NO.
11/28/64+	16	9	1. My Love, Forgive Me (Amore, Scusami)	Columbia 43131

GO WEST

Pop-rock duo from England: Peter Cox (vocals) and Richard Drummie (guitar, vocals).

DATE	POS	WKS	ARTIST–RECORD TITLE	LABEL & NO.
9/26/87	39	2	1. Don't Look Down - The Sequel Airplay #37 new version of song first recorded in 1985	Chrysalis 43141
6/23/90	8	13	2. **King Of Wishful Thinking** Airplay #4 / Sales #15 from the movie *Pretty Woman* starring Richard Gere and Julia Roberts	EMI 50307
12/5/92+	14	13	3. Faithful Airplay #13 / Sales #47	EMI 50411

DATE	POS	WKS	ARTIST–RECORD TITLE	LABEL & NO.
			GQ	
			Disco group from the Bronx, New York: Emmanuel LeBlanc (vocals, guitar), Herb Lane (keyboards), Keith Crier (bass) and Paul Service (drums).	
4/14/79	**12**	11	● 1. Disco Nights (Rock-Freak)	Arista 0388
			#1 R&B hit (2 weeks)	
8/11/79	**20**	8	2. I Do Love You	Arista 0426
			GRACIE, Charlie	
			Born Charles Graci on 5/14/36 in Philadelphia, Pennsylvania. Pop singer/guitarist.	
2/23/57	**1** (2)	14	● 1. **Butterfly** Juke Box #1 (2) / Best Seller #3 / Top 100 #7 / Jockey #13	Cameo 105
5/20/57	**16**	6	2. Fabulous Best Seller #16 / Top 100 #26	Cameo 107
			Bernie Lowe (orch., above 2)	
			GRAHAM, Larry	
			Born on 8/14/46 in Beaumont, Texas; raised in Oakland, California. Bassist with Sly & The Family Stone from 1966-72. Formed Graham Central Station in 1973.	
9/13/75	**38**	2	1. Your Love	Warner 8105
			GRAHAM CENTRAL STATION	
			#1 R&B hit (1 week)	
8/9/80	**9**	9	● 2. **One In A Million You**	Warner 49221
			#1 R&B hit (2 weeks)	
			GRAMM, Lou	
			Born Lou Grammatico on 5/2/50 in Rochester, New York. Lead singer of Foreigner.	
2/28/87	**5**	11	1. **Midnight Blue** Sales #6 / Airplay #6	Atlantic 89304
			#1 Mainstream Rock hit (5 weeks)	
11/18/89+	**6**	14	2. **Just Between You And Me** Airplay #3 / Sales #9	Atlantic 88781
3/31/90	**40**	1	3. True Blue Love Airplay #35	Atlantic 88768
			GRAMMER, Billy	
			Born on 8/28/25 in Benton, Illinois. Country singer/guitarist.	
12/8/58+	**4**	15	1. **Gotta Travel On**	Monument 400
			GRANAHAN, Gerry	
			Born on 6/17/39 in Pittston, Pennsylvania. Pop singer. Formed Dicky Doo & The Don'ts and The Fireflies.	
6/16/58	**23**	8	1. No Chemise, Please Top 100 #23 / Best Seller #25 [N]	Sunbeam 102
			Arnie Goland (vocal)	
			GRANATA, Rocco, and the International Quintet	
			Born on 8/16/38 in Figline Vigliaturo, Italy. Singer/songwriter/accordionist.	
11/23/59	**31**	7	1. Marina [F]	Laurie 3041

DATE	POS	WKS	ARTIST–RECORD TITLE	LABEL & NO.
			GRAND FUNK RAILROAD	
			Hard-rock group formed in Flint, Michigan: Mark Farner (guitar), Mel Schacher (bass) and Don Brewer (drums). All share vocals. Craig Frost (keyboards) added in 1973. Group name shortened to Grand Funk in 1973.	
9/5/70	22	8	1. Closer To Home	Capitol 2877
2/5/72	29	5	2. Footstompin' Music	Capitol 3255
11/4/72	29	6	3. Rock 'N Roll Soul	Capitol 3363
			GRAND FUNK:	
8/18/73	1 (1)	13	● 4. **We're An American Band**	Capitol 3660
12/29/73+	19	6	5. Walk Like A Man	Capitol 3760
3/30/74	1 (2)	14	● 6. **The Loco-Motion**	Capitol 3840
7/20/74	11	8	7. Shinin' On	Capitol 3917
			above 4 produced by Todd Rundgren	
12/21/74+	3	12	8. **Some Kind Of Wonderful**	Capitol 4002
4/19/75	4	12	9. **Bad Time**	Capitol 4046
			GRANT, Amy	
			Born on 11/25/60 in Augusta, Georgia. Pop singer/songwriter. Began career as a top Contemporary Christian singer. Married to singer/songwriter Gary Chapman from 1982-99. Married country singer Vince Gill on 3/10/2000.	
7/6/85	29	6	1. Find A Way *Airplay #28*	A&M 2734
10/11/86	1 (1)	15	2. **The Next Time I Fall** *Airplay #2 / Sales #3*	Full Moon 28597
			PETER CETERA w/AMY GRANT	
			#1 Adult Contemporary hit (2 weeks)	
3/9/91	1 (2)	16	3. **Baby Baby** *Airplay #1 (4) / Sales #1 (1)*	A&M 1549
			#1 Adult Contemporary hit (3 weeks)	
6/22/91	2 (1)	15	4. **Every Heartbeat** *Airplay #2 / Sales #20*	A&M 1557
10/12/91	7	18	5. **That's What Love Is For** *Airplay #9 / Sales #31*	A&M 1566
			#1 Adult Contemporary hit (3 weeks)	
1/25/92	8	17	6. **Good For Me** *Airplay #6 / Sales #62*	A&M 1573
5/16/92	20	12	7. I Will Remember You *Airplay #25 / Sales #37*	A&M 1600
8/27/94	18	11	8. Lucky One *Airplay #17 / Sales #30*	A&M 0724
2/18/95	37	4	9. House Of Love *Sales #38 / Airplay #41*	A&M 0802
			AMY GRANT with Vince Gill	
10/4/97	21 ᴬ	15	10. Takes A Little Time	album cut
			from the album Behind The Eyes on A&M 0760	
			GRANT, Earl	
			Born on 1/2/31 in Idabelle, Oklahoma. Died in a car crash on 6/10/70 (age 39). Singer/songwriter/pianist.	
9/29/58	7	13	1. **The End** *Hot 100 #7 / Best Seller #26*	Decca 30719
			GRANT, Eddy	
			Born Edmond Grant on 3/5/48 in Plaisance, Guyana; raised in London, England. Rock-reggae singer. Member of The Equals.	
5/21/83	2 (5)	15	▲ 1. **Electric Avenue**	Portrait 03793
6/30/84	26	6	2. Romancing The Stone	Portrait 04433
			written for, but not included in, the movie	

DATE	POS	WKS	ARTIST–RECORD TITLE	LABEL & NO.
			GRANT, Gogi	
			Born Audrey Arinsberg on 9/20/24 in Philadelphia, Pennsylvania. Female pop singer.	
10/1/55	9	10	● 1. **Suddenly There's A Valley** Jockey #9 / Best Seller #14 / Top 100 #14 / Juke Box #19	Era 1003
5/5/56	1 (8)	22	● 2. **The Wayward Wind** Jockey #1 (8) / Top 100 #1 (7) / Best Seller #1 (6) / Juke Box #1 (4) Buddy Bregman (orch., above 2)	Era 1013
			GRANT, Janie	
			Born Rose Marie Casilli on 9/27/44 in Jersey City, New Jersey. Teen pop singer/songwriter.	
5/15/61	29	5	1. Triangle	Caprice 104
			GRASS ROOTS, The	
			Pop-rock group formed in San Francisco, California: Rob Grill (vocals, bass), Warren Entner and Creed Bratton (guitars), and Rick Coonce (drums). New lineup in 1971 included Grill, Entner, Reed Kailing and Virgil Webber (guitars), and Joel Larson (drums).	
7/16/66	28	4	1. Where Were You When I Needed You	Dunhill 4029
6/3/67	8	9	2. **Let's Live For Today**	Dunhill 4084
9/2/67	23	4	3. Things I Should Have Said	Dunhill 4094
9/21/68	5	12	● 4. **Midnight Confessions**	Dunhill/ABC 4144
1/11/69	28	2	5. Bella Linda	Dunhill/ABC 4162
5/17/69	31	5	6. The River Is Wide	Dunhill/ABC 4187
8/9/69	15	10	7. I'd Wait A Million Years	Dunhill/ABC 4198
11/22/69	24	7	8. Heaven Knows	Dunhill/ABC 4217
6/13/70	35	3	9. Baby Hold On	Dunhill/ABC 4237
2/13/71	15	11	10. Temptation Eyes	Dunhill/ABC 4263
6/19/71	9	9	11. **Sooner Or Later**	Dunhill/ABC 4279
10/30/71	16	8	12. Two Divided By Love	Dunhill/ABC 4289
3/18/72	34	3	13. Glory Bound	Dunhill/ABC 4302
7/22/72	39	2	14. The Runway	Dunhill/ABC 4316
			GRATEFUL DEAD	
			Legendary rock group formed in San Francisco, California. Numerous personnel changes throughout the years. The 1987 lineup: Jerry Garcia (vocals, guitar), Bob Weir (guitar), Brent Mydland (keyboards), Phil Lesh (bass), and Bill Kreutzmann and Mickey Hart (drums). Mydland was a member of Silver; died of a drug overdose on 7/26/90 (age 37). Garcia died of a heart attack on 8/9/95 (age 53). Incessant touring band with faithful followers known as "Deadheads." Group inducted into the Rock and Roll Hall of Fame in 1994.	
8/15/87	9	9	1. **Touch Of Grey** Sales #8 / Airplay #15 #1 Mainstream Rock hit (3 weeks)	Arista 9606
			GRAY, Dobie	
			Born Lawrence Darrow Brown on 7/26/40 in Brookshire, Texas. Black singer/songwriter.	
1/23/65	13	7	1. The "In" Crowd	Charger 105
3/31/73	5	15	● 2. **Drift Away**	Decca 33057
2/10/79	37	2	3. You Can Do It	Infinity 50,003

DATE	POS	WKS	ARTIST–RECORD TITLE	LABEL & NO.
5/3/03	9	28	**4. Drift Away** Airplay #9 **[R]** **UNCLE KRACKER Featuring Dobie Gray** #1 Adult Contemporary hit (28 weeks); from Uncle Kracker's album *No Stranger To Shame* on Lava 83542	album cut
			GRAY, Macy	

3/11/00	5	23	Born Natalie McIntyre on 9/9/70 in Canton, Ohio. Female R&B singer/songwriter.
			    1. I Try Airplay #4
			        from the album *On How Life Is* on Epic 69490
				album cut

			GREAN, Charles Randolph, Sounde	

7/5/69	13	8	Born on 10/1/13 in Manhattan, New York. Died of heart failure on 12/20/2003 (age 90). Conductor/arranger. Married singer Betty Johnson.
			    1. Quentin's Theme **[I]**
			        from the cult daytime TV serial *Dark Shadows*
				Ranwood 840

			GREAT WHITE	
6/17/89	5	14	Hard-rock group formed in Los Angeles, California: Jack Russell (vocals), Mark Kendall (guitar), Michael Lardie (keyboards), Teddy Cook (bass) and Audie Desbrow (drums). Many personnel changes since 1991. The band's pyrotechnic show during a Rhode Island club set off a fire that killed nearly 100 people on 2/21/03, including the band's guitarist, Ty Longley. ● **1. Once Bitten Twice Shy** Sales #4 / Airplay #6 first recorded by Ian Hunter in 1975	Capitol 44366
11/18/89	30	4	2. The Angel Song Sales #27 / Airplay #35	Capitol 44449
			GREAVES, R.B.	
10/25/69	2 (1)	13	Born Ronald Bertram Greaves on 11/28/44 at the U.S. Air Force base in Georgetown, British Guyana. R&B singer. Nephew of Sam Cooke. ● **1. Take A Letter Maria**	Atco 6714
2/14/70	27	5	2. Always Something There To Remind Me	Atco 6726
			GRECCO, Cyndi	

6/12/76	25	5	Born on 5/19/52 in Manhattan, New York. Pop singer.
			    1. Making Our Dreams Come True
			        theme from the TV series *LaVerne & Shirley* starring Penny Marshall and Cindy Williams
				Private Stock 45,086

			GREEN, Al	
8/21/71	11	15	Born on 4/13/46 in Forrest City, Arkansas. R&B singer/songwriter. Began career as a gospel singer; returned to gospel music in 1980. Inducted into the Rock and Roll Hall of Fame in 1995. Won Grammy's Lifetime Achievement Award in 2002. ● **1. Tired Of Being Alone**	Hi 2194
12/11/71+	1 (1)	15	● **2. Let's Stay Together** #1 R&B hit (9 weeks)	Hi 2202
4/8/72	4	11	● **3. Look What You Done For Me**	Hi 2211
7/15/72	3	11	● **4. I'm Still In Love With You** #1 R&B hit (2 weeks)	Hi 2216
11/4/72	3	12	● **5. You Ought To Be With Me** #1 R&B hit (1 week)	Hi 2227
3/3/73	10	9	● **6. Call Me (Come Back Home)**	Hi 2235

DATE	POS	WKS	ARTIST–RECORD TITLE	LABEL & NO.
7/21/73	**10**	12	● 7. **Here I Am (Come And Take Me)**	Hi 2247
12/22/73+	**19**	8	8. Livin' For You	Hi 2257
			#1 R&B hit (1 week)	
5/11/74	**32**	3	9. Let's Get Married	Hi 2262
11/2/74	**7**	11	● 10. **Sha-La-La (Make Me Happy)**	Hi 2274
3/22/75	**13**	8	11. L-O-V-E (Love)	Hi 2282
			#1 R&B hit (2 weeks)	
11/29/75	**28**	6	12. Full Of Fire	Hi 2300
			#1 R&B hit (1 week)	
12/18/76+	**37**	4	13. Keep Me Cryin'	Hi 2319
12/3/88+	**9**	10	14. **Put A Little Love In Your Heart**　　　Airplay #8 / Sales #11	A&M 1255
			ANNIE LENNOX & AL GREEN	
			from the movie *Scrooged* starring Bill Murray	
			GREEN, Garland	
			Born Garfield Green on 6/24/42 in Leland, Mississippi. R&B singer/pianist.	Uni 55143
10/18/69	**20**	4	1. Jealous Kind Of Fella	
			GREEN, Pat	
			Born on 4/5/72 in San Antonio, Texas; raised in Waco, Texas. Male country singer/songwriter/guitarist.	album cut
11/29/03	**39**	2	1. Wave On Wave　　　　　　　　　Airplay #36	
			from the album *Wave On Wave* on Republic 000562	
			GREEN, Vivian	
			Born in 1979 in Philadelphia, Pennsylvania. R&B singer/songwriter.	Columbia 79858
3/29/03	**39**	1	1. Emotional Rollercoaster　　　Sales #5 / Airplay #45	
			GREENBAUM, Norman	
			Born on 11/20/42 in Malden, Massachusetts. Pop-rock singer/songwriter.	Reprise 0885
3/7/70	**3**	14	● 1. **Spirit In The Sky**	
			GREEN DAY	
			Punk-rock trio formed in Berkeley, California: Billie Joe Armstrong (vocals, guitar), Mike Dirnt (bass) and Frank "Tre Cool" Wright (drums).	
6/18/94	**36** ᴬ	2	1. Long View	album cut
			#1 Modern Rock hit (1 week)	
9/3/94	**26** ᴬ	21	2. Basket Case	album cut
			#1 Modern Rock hit (5 weeks)	
12/10/94+	**6** ᴬ	34	3. **When I Come Around**	album cut
			#1 Modern Rock hit (7 weeks); above 3 from the album *Dookie* on Reprise 45529	
7/29/95	**22** ᴬ	9	4. J.A.R. (Jason Andrew Relva)	album cut
			#1 Modern Rock hit (1 week); from the movie *Angus* starring George C. Scott (soundtrack album on Reprise 45960)	
10/7/95	**27** ᴬ	6	5. Geek Stink Breath	album cut
2/17/96	**35** ᴬ	6	6. Brain Stew/Jaded	album cut
			above 2 from the album *Insomniac* on Reprise 46046	
12/20/97+	**11** ᴬ	39	7. Good Riddance (Time Of Your Life)	album cut
			from the album *Nimrod* on Reprise 46794	

DATE	POS	WKS	ARTIST–RECORD TITLE	LABEL & NO.
			GREENE, Lorne	
			Born on 2/12/14 in Ottawa, Ontario, Canada. Died of heart failure on 9/11/87 (age 73). Acted in several movies. Starred in TV's *Bonanza* and *Battlestar Galactica*.	
11/7/64	**1** (1)	10	1. **Ringo** [S] #1 Adult Contemporary hit (6 weeks)	RCA Victor 8444
			GREEN JELLY	
			Novelty hard-rock group formed in Kenmore, New York: Moronic Dicktator (lead vocals), Joey Blowey, Rootin', Jesus Quisp, Coy Roy, Sadistica, Hotsy Menshot, Tin Titty, Sven Seven, Reason Clean, Mother Eucker, Roof D.H. and Daddy Longlegs.	
4/24/93	**17**	12	● 1. Three Little Pigs Sales #5 [N] originally released as by Green Jellö	Zoo 14088
			GREENWOOD, Lee	
			Born on 10/27/42 in Los Angeles, California. Country singer/songwriter/multi-instrumentalist.	
6/8/91	**30** ˢ	5	1. God Bless The USA #7 Country hit in 1984; re-popularized due to the Gulf War	MCA 52386
9/29/01	**16**	2	2. God Bless The USA Sales #1 (3) / Airplay #14 [R] new version recorded in response to the 9/11 terrorist attacks	Curb 73128
			GREGG, Bobby, and His Friends	
			Born Robert Grego in Philadelphia, Pennsylvania. Jazz drummer.	
4/14/62	**29**	5	1. The Jam - Part 1 [I] Roy Buchanan (guitar)	Cotton 1003
			GRIFFIN, Clive — see DION, Celine	
			GRIFFITH, Andy	
			Born on 6/1/26 in Mount Airy, North Carolina. Actor/comedian. Starred in several movies and Broadway shows. Star of TV's *The Andy Griffith Show* and *Matlock*.	
4/2/55	**26**	1	1. Make Yourself Comfortable Best Seller #26 [C] Jean Wilson (vocal); Burt Massengale (orch.)	Capitol 3057
			GRIGGS, Andy	
			Born on 8/13/73 in Monroe, Louisiana. Country singer/songwriter/guitarist.	
5/8/99	**28**	6	1. You Won't Ever Be Lonely Airplay #22 / Sales #69	RCA 65646
6/10/00	**37**	1	2. She's More Airplay #33 from the album *You Won't Ever Be Lonely* on RCA 67596	album cut
			GROCE, Larry	
			Born on 4/22/48 in Dallas, Texas. Pop-folk singer/songwriter.	
2/7/76	**9**	9	1. **Junk Food Junkie** [L-N] recorded at McCabe's guitar shop in Santa Monica, California	Warner/Curb 8165
			GROOVE THEORY	
			Male/female R&B duo: Bryce Wilson and Amel Larrieux.	
9/23/95	**5**	25	● 1. **Tell Me** Sales #4 / Airplay #10 Trey Lorenz (backing vocal)	Epic 77961

DATE	POS	WKS	ARTIST–RECORD TITLE	LABEL & NO.
			GROSS, Henry	
			Born on 4/1/51 in Brooklyn, New York. Pop-rock singer/songwriter/ guitarist.	
4/3/76	6	13	● 1. **Shannon**	Lifesong 45002
			song is a tale about the death of a pet dog	
8/21/76	37	2	2. Springtime Mama	Lifesong 45008
			above 2 produced by Terry Cashman & Tommy West	
			GTR	
			Rock group formed in England: Max Bacon (vocals), Steve Hackett and Steve Howe (guitars), Phil Spalding (bass) and Jonathan Mover (drums). Hackett was with Genesis. Howe was with Yes and Asia. Group name is short for guitar.	
5/31/86	14	10	1. When The Heart Rules The Mind Sales #9 / Airplay #19	Arista 9470
			GUARALDI, Vince, Trio	
			Born on 7/17/32 in San Francisco, California. Died of a heart attack on 2/6/76 (age 43). Jazz pianist. Wrote the music for the *Peanuts* TV specials.	
2/9/63	22	6	1. Cast Your Fate To The Wind **[I]**	Fantasy 563
			GUESS WHO, The	
			Rock group formed in Winnipeg, Manitoba, Canada: Chad Allan (vocals, guitar), Randy Bachman (guitar), Bob Ashley (piano), Jim Kale (bass) and Garry Peterson (drums). Recorded as Chad Allan & The Expressions. Ashley replaced by new lead singer Burton Cummings in 1966. Allan left shortly thereafter. Bachman left in 1970 to form Bachman-Turner Overdrive; replaced by Kurt Winter and Greg Leskiw. Leskiw and Kale left in 1972, replaced by Don McDougall and Bill Wallace. Domenic Troiano replaced both Winter and McDougall in 1973. Winter died of a bleeding ulcer on 12/14/97 (age 51).	
6/5/65	22	7	1. Shakin' All Over	Scepter 1295
			GUESS WHO?	
			group is actually Chad Allan & The Expressions	
4/26/69	6	11	● 2. **These Eyes**	RCA Victor 0102
7/26/69	10	9	● 3. **Laughing /**	
11/8/69	22	6	4. Undun	RCA Victor 0195
1/17/70	5	10	5. **No Time**	RCA Victor 0300
3/28/70	1 (3)	14	● 6. **American Woman /**	
4/4/70		13	7. No Sugar Tonight	RCA Victor 0325
			all of above include Randy Bachman before his departure	
8/8/70	17	8	8. Hand Me Down World	RCA Victor 0367
11/7/70	10	8	9. **Share The Land**	RCA Victor 0388
6/12/71	29	4	10. Albert Flasher	RCA Victor 0458
9/4/71	19	8	11. Rain Dance	RCA Victor 0522
4/20/74	39	1	12. Star Baby	RCA Victor 0217
8/10/74	6	11	13. **Clap For The Wolfman**	RCA Victor 0324
			featuring bits of dialogue by Wolfman Jack	
12/14/74+	28	4	14. Dancin' Fool	RCA Victor 10075
			GUIDRY, Greg	
			Born on 1/23/50 in St. Louis, Missouri. Died on 7/28/2003 (age 53). Pop singer/songwriter/pianist.	
3/20/82	17	10	1. Goin' Down	Columbia 02691

DATE	POS	WKS	ARTIST–RECORD TITLE	LABEL & NO.
			GUITAR, Bonnie	
4/27/57	6	10	Born Bonnie Buckingham on 3/25/23 in Seattle, Washington. Singer/guitarist. Owner of Dolphin/Dolton Records. 1. **Dark Moon** Jockey #6 / Top 100 #8 / Best Seller #10 / Juke Box #11	Dot 15550
			GUNHILL ROAD	
6/2/73	40	1	Pop-rock trio: Glenn Leopold, Gil Roman and Steven Goldrich. 1. Back When My Hair Was Short	Kama Sutra 569
			G-UNIT	
11/15/03	13	10	Male rap trio from Jamaica, Queens, New York: Curtis "50 Cent" Jackson, Christopher Lloyd "Banks" and David "Young Buck" Brown. 1. **Stunt 101** Airplay #13 / Sales #27	G-Unit 001601
			GUNS N' ROSES	
			Hard-rock group formed in Los Angeles, California: William "Axl Rose" Bailey (vocals), Saul "Slash" Hudson and Jeffrey "Izzy Stradlin" Isbell (guitars), Michael "Duff" McKagan (bass) and Steven Adler (drums). Rose married Erin Everly (daughter of Don Everly of The Everly Brothers) briefly in 1990. Matt Sorum replaced Adler in 1990. Keyboardist Dizzy Reed joined in 1990. Gilby Clarke replaced Stradlin in 1991. Slash was married to model Renee Surran from 1992-97.	
7/23/88	1 (2)	14	● 1. **Sweet Child O' Mine** Sales #1 (2) / Airplay #1 (2)	Geffen 27963
11/5/88	7	12	2. **Welcome To The Jungle** Sales #3 / Airplay #11	Geffen 27759
1/28/89	5	11	3. **Paradise City** Sales #5 / Airplay #5	Geffen 27570
4/22/89	4	10	● 4. **Patience** Sales #3 / Airplay #5	Geffen 22996
7/20/91	29	8	● 5. You Could Be Mine Sales #2 from the movie *Terminator 2-Judgment Day* starring Arnold Schwarzenegger	Geffen 19039
10/5/91	10	17	● 6. **Don't Cry** Sales #5 / Airplay #52	Geffen 19027
2/8/92	33	4	7. Live And Let Die Sales #19 title song from the James Bond movie starring Roger Moore	Geffen 19114
6/27/92	3	20	● 8. **November Rain** Sales #4 / Airplay #12	Geffen 19067
			GUTHRIE, Arlo	
9/9/72	18	9	Born on 7/10/47 in Brooklyn, New York. Folk singer/songwriter. Son of Woody Guthrie. Starred as himself in the 1969 movie *Alice's Restaurant*, which was based on his 1967 song "Alice's Restaurant Massacree." 1. The City Of New Orleans	Reprise 1103
			GUY	
12/25/99+	19	4	R&B vocal trio from Harlem, New York: brothers Aaron and Damion Hall, with Teddy Riley. Riley also formed BLACKstreet. 1. Dancin' Sales #12	MCA 155657
			GUY, Jasmine	
10/19/91	34	3	Born on 3/10/64 in Boston, Massachusetts; raised in Atlanta, Georgia. R&B singer/actress. Played "Whitley Gilbert" on TV's *A Different World*. 1. Just Want To Hold You Airplay #34 / Sales #52	Warner 19330

DATE	POS	WKS	ARTIST–RECORD TITLE	LABEL & NO.

H

HADDAWAY

Born Nester Haddaway on 1/9/65 in Tobago, West Indies; raised in Chicago, Illinois. Black dance singer/choreographer.

DATE	POS	WKS	ARTIST–RECORD TITLE	LABEL & NO.
10/2/93	11	19	● 1. What Is Love Airplay #11 / Sales #13	Arista 12575

HAGAR, Sammy

Born on 10/13/47 in Monterey, California. Rock singer/songwriter/guitarist. Lead singer of Van Halen from 1985-96. Known as "The Red Rocker."

DATE	POS	WKS	ARTIST–RECORD TITLE	LABEL & NO.
12/25/82+	13	13	1. Your Love Is Driving Me Crazy	Geffen 29816
8/18/84	38	3	2. Two Sides Of Love	Geffen 29246
10/27/84	26	6	3. I Can't Drive 55 Airplay #26 / Sales #27	Geffen 29173
8/1/87	23	7	4. Give To Live Sales #23 / Airplay #23	Geffen 28314
			#1 Mainstream Rock hit (3 weeks)	

HAGGARD, Merle

Born on 4/6/37 in Bakersfield, California. Country singer/songwriter/guitarist.

DATE	POS	WKS	ARTIST–RECORD TITLE	LABEL & NO.
1/5/74 -	28	3	1. If We Make It Through December [X]	Capitol 3746
			#1 Country hit (4 weeks)	

HAILEY, K-Ci — see K-CI & JOJO / JODECI

HAIRCUT ONE HUNDRED

Pop-rock group from Beckenham, Kent, England: Nick Heyward (vocals), Graham Jones (guitar), Phil Smith (sax), Mark Fox (percussion), Les Nemes (bass) and Blair Cunningham (drums).

DATE	POS	WKS	ARTIST–RECORD TITLE	LABEL & NO.
7/17/82	37	4	1. Love Plus One	Arista 0672

HALEY, Bill, And His Comets

Born on 7/6/25 in Highland Park, Michigan. Died of a heart attack on 2/9/81 (age 55). Began career as a country singer. His Comets consisted of Danny Cedrone (lead guitar), Joey D'Ambrose (sax), Billy Williamson (steel guitar), Johnny Grande (piano), Marshall Lytle (bass) and Billy Guesack (drums). D'Ambrose, Richards and Lytle left in September 1955 to form the Jodimars. Comets lineup on subsequent recordings included Williamson, Grande, Frank Beecher (lead guitar), Rudy Pompilli (sax), Al Rex (bass) and Ralph Jones (drums). Cedrone died of a heart attack on 7/10/54. Pompilli died on 2/5/76 (age 47). Group inducted into the Rock and Roll Hall of Fame in 1987. The Comets also recorded as The Kingsmen (see #16 below).

DATE	POS	WKS	ARTIST–RECORD TITLE	LABEL & NO.
8/21/54	7	27	● 1. Shake, Rattle And Roll Best Seller #7 / Juke Box #8 / Jockey #9	Decca 29204
			#1 R&B hit for Joe Turner in 1954	
11/20/54+	11	15	2. Dim, Dim The Lights (I Want Some Atmosphere) Best Seller #11 / Jockey #16 / Juke Box #16	Decca 29317
3/19/55	17	2	3. Birth Of The Boogie / Juke Box #17 / Best Seller #26	Decca 29418
3/5/55	18	8	4. Mambo Rock Best Seller #18 / Juke Box: flip	
5/14/55	1 (8)	24	● 5. (We're Gonna) Rock Around The Clock Best Seller #1 (8) / Juke Box #1 (7) / Jockey #1 (6) / Top 100 #56	Decca 29124
			featured in the movie *Blackboard Jungle* starring Glenn Ford; also see #17 below	

DATE	POS	WKS	ARTIST–RECORD TITLE	LABEL & NO.
7/23/55	15	4	6. Razzle-Dazzle / Best Seller #15	
7/23/55		2	7. Two Hound Dogs Best Seller: flip	Decca 29552
11/19/55+	9	13	8. **Burn That Candle /** Juke Box #9 / Best Seller #16 / Top 100 #20	
11/19/55	23	7	9. Rock-A-Beatin' Boogie	
			Best Seller #23 / Top 100 #41 / Juke Box: flip	Decca 29713
			first recorded by the Esquire Boys in 1953	
1/14/56	6	15	● 10. **See You Later, Alligator**	
			Best Seller #6 / Top 100 #6 / Jockey #6 / Juke Box #6	Decca 29791
			#14 R&B hit for Bobby Charles in 1955	
4/7/56	16	5	11. R-O-C-K / Juke Box #16 / Best Seller #20 / Top 100 #29	
			featured in the movie *Rock Around The Clock* starring Alan Freed	
4/7/56	18	5	12. The Saints Rock 'N Roll	
			Best Seller #18 / Top 100 #42 / Juke Box: flip	Decca 29870
			rock version of the spiritual "When The Saints Go Marching In"	
9/1/56	25	4	13. Rip It Up Best Seller #25 / Top 100 #30	Decca 30028
11/24/56	34	3	14. Rudy's Rock Top 100 #34 **[I]**	Decca 30085
			named for Haley's saxophonist Rudy Pompilli	
4/21/58	22	6	15. Skinny Minnie Top 100 #22 / Best Seller #24	Decca 30592
9/22/58	35	2	16. Week End Best Seller #35 / Hot 100 #84 **[I]**	East West 115
			THE KINGSMEN	
5/25/74	39	1	17. (We're Gonna) Rock Around The Clock **[R]**	MCA 60025
			re-popularized as the original opening theme of TV's *Happy Days*	

HALL, Aaron

Born on 8/10/64 in Brooklyn, New York. Member of Guy.

DATE	POS	WKS	ARTIST–RECORD TITLE	LABEL & NO.
6/18/94	14	15	● 1. I Miss You Sales #8 / Airplay #20	Silas/MCA 54847
10/17/98	26	11	2. All The Places (I Will Kiss You) Sales #12	MCA 55473

HALL, Daryl

Born Daryl Franklin Hohl on 10/11/48 in Philadelphia, Pennsylvania. Half of Hall & Oates duo.

DATE	POS	WKS	ARTIST–RECORD TITLE	LABEL & NO.
8/16/86	5	11	1. **Dreamtime** Airplay #4 / Sales #5	RCA 14387
11/15/86	33	5	2. Foolish Pride Airplay #30 / Sales #37	RCA 5038

HALL, Daryl, & John Oates

Daryl Hall (see previous entry) and John Oates (born on 4/7/49 in Brooklyn, New York) met while students at Temple University in 1967. Hall sang backup for many top soul groups before teaming up with Oates in 1972. They passed The Everly Brothers as the #1 charting duo of the rock era.

DATE	POS	WKS	ARTIST–RECORD TITLE	LABEL & NO.
4/3/76	4	17	● 1. **Sara Smile**	RCA Victor 10530
			written for Hall's girlfriend Sara Allen	
8/14/76	7	16	2. **She's Gone** **[R]**	Atlantic 3332
			originally charted at #60 in 1974	
12/25/76	39	3	3. Do What You Want, Be What You Are	RCA 10808
2/5/77	1 (2)	14	● 4. **Rich Girl**	RCA 10860
5/28/77	28	4	5. Back Together Again	RCA 10970
9/30/78	20	7	6. It's A Laugh	RCA 11371
12/1/79+	18	10	7. Wait For Me	RCA 11747
8/30/80	30	4	8. How Does It Feel To Be Back	RCA 12048
10/11/80	12	14	9. You've Lost That Lovin' Feeling	RCA 12103
2/14/81	1 (3)	17	● 10. **Kiss On My List**	RCA 12142

DATE	POS	WKS	ARTIST–RECORD TITLE	LABEL & NO.
5/16/81	**5**	14	11. **You Make My Dreams**	RCA 12217
9/12/81	**1** (2)	17	● 12. **Private Eyes**	RCA 12296
11/21/81+	**1** (1)	17	● 13. **I Can't Go For That (No Can Do)**	RCA 12357
			#1 R&B hit (1 week)	
4/3/82	**9**	11	14. **Did It In A Minute**	RCA 13065
7/24/82	**33**	5	15. Your Imagination	RCA 13252
11/6/82	**1** (4)	17	● 16. **Maneater**	RCA 13354
2/5/83	**7**	15	17. **One On One**	RCA 13421
5/7/83	**6**	12	18. **Family Man**	RCA 13507
			DARYL HALL JOHN OATES:	
10/29/83	**2** (4)	15	19. **Say It Isn't So**	RCA 13654
2/25/84	**8**	11	20. **Adult Education**	RCA 13714
10/6/84	**1** (2)	16	21. **Out Of Touch** Airplay #1 (3) / Sales #3	RCA 13916
1/5/85	**5**	11	22. **Method Of Modern Love** Airplay #5 / Sales #7	RCA 13970
3/30/85	**18**	8	23. Some Things Are Better Left Unsaid Airplay #16 / Sales #17	RCA 14035
6/15/85	**30**	6	24. Possession Obsession Airplay #29	RCA 14098
9/15/85	**20**	7	25. A Nite At The Apollo Live! The Way You Do The Things You Do/My Girl Sales #21 / Airplay #23 **[L]**	RCA 14178
			DARYL HALL JOHN OATES with David Ruffin & Eddie Kendrick	
			recorded at the reopening of New York's Apollo Theatre	
4/23/88	**3**	11	26. **Everything Your Heart Desires** Sales #4 / Airplay #4	Arista 9684
8/6/88	**29**	5	27. Missed Opportunity Sales #29 / Airplay #29	Arista 9727
10/29/88	**31**	3	28. Downtown Life Airplay #32 / Sales #33	Arista 9753
10/20/90	**11**	9	29. So Close Airplay #11 / Sales #14	Arista 2085
			co-written and co-produced by Jon Bon Jovi	
			HALL, Jimmie — see WET WILLIE	
			HALL, Larry	
			Born on 6/30/40 in Hamlett, Ohio. Died of cancer on 9/24/97 (age 57). Teen rock and roll singer.	
12/7/59+	**15**	11	1. Sandy	Strand 25007
			HALL, Tom T.	
			Born on 5/25/36 in Olive Hill, Kentucky. Country singer/songwriter/guitarist.	
1/19/74	**12**	9	1. I Love	Mercury 73436
			#1 Country hit (2 weeks)	
			HALOS, The	
			R&B vocal group from Harlem, New York: Harold Johnson, Al Cleveland, Phil Johnson and Arthur Crier.	
8/28/61	**25**	4	1. "Nag"	7 Arts 709
			HAMBLEN, Stuart	
			Born Carl Stuart Hamblen on 10/20/08 in Kellyville, Texas. Died on 3/8/89 (age 80). Singer/songwriter/actor. Acted in several western movies.	
11/13/54	**26**	4	1. This Ole House Best Seller #26	RCA Victor 5739

DATE	POS	WKS	ARTIST–RECORD TITLE	LABEL & NO.
			HAMILTON, Bobby	
			Born Robert Caristo on 10/5/39 in Locust Valley, Long Island, New York. Rock and roll singer/songwriter.	
8/4/58	**40**	1	1. Crazy Eyes For You Hot 100 #40	Apt 25002
			HAMILTON, George IV	
			Born on 7/19/37 in Winston-Salem, North Carolina. Country singer/songwriter/guitarist. Hosted own TV series in 1959.	
11/17/56	**6**	14	● 1. **A Rose And A Baby Ruth** Top 100 #6 / Best Seller #7 / Jockey #7 / Juke Box #8	ABC-Paramount 9765
3/9/57	**33**	4	2. Only One Love Top 100 #33	ABC-Paramount 9782
12/9/57+	**10**	12	3. **Why Don't They Understand** Jockey #10 / Top 100 #17 / Best Seller #19	ABC-Paramount 9862
4/7/58	**25**	1	4. Now And For Always Jockey #25 / Best Seller #37 / Top 100 #37	ABC-Paramount 9898
12/15/58+	**29**	5	5. The Teen Commandments [S] **PAUL ANKA-GEO. HAMILTON IV-JOHNNY NASH** inspirational talk from the three ABC-Paramount artists; Bill Givens (narrative); Don Costa (orch., all of above)	ABC-Paramount 9974
7/20/63	**15**	7	6. Abilene #1 Country hit (4 weeks)	RCA Victor 8181
			HAMILTON, Roy	
			Born on 4/16/29 in Leesburg, Georgia. Died of a stroke on 7/20/69 (age 40). R&B singer.	
4/23/55	**6**	16	1. **Unchained Melody** Jockey #6 / Juke Box #6 / Best Seller #9 #1 R&B hit (3 weeks); O.B. Masingill (orch.); from the movie *Unchained* starring football great Elroy "Crazylegs" Hirsch	Epic 9102
1/27/58	**13**	11	2. Don't Let Go Top 100 #13 / Best Seller #14 / Jockey #16 Jesse Stone (orch.)	Epic 9257
2/13/61	**12**	7	3. You Can Have Her Sammy Lowe (orch.)	Epic 9434
			HAMILTON, Russ	
			Born Ronald Hulme in 1934 in Liverpool, England. Pop singer/songwriter.	
8/5/57	**4**	17	● 1. **Rainbow** Jockey #4 / Best Seller #7 / Top 100 #7 Johnny Gregory (orch.)	Kapp 184
			HAMILTON, JOE FRANK & REYNOLDS	
			Pop vocal trio: Dan Hamilton, Joe Frank Carollo and Tommy Reynolds. All were members of The T-Bones. Reynolds left group in 1972 and was replaced by Alan Dennison. Although Reynolds had left, group still recorded as Hamilton, Joe Frank & Reynolds until July 1976. Hamilton died on 12/23/94 (age 48).	
6/12/71	**4**	11	● 1. **Don't Pull Your Love**	Dunhill/ABC 4276
7/19/75	**1** (1)	12	● 2. **Fallin' In Love** #1 Adult Contemporary hit (1 week)	Playboy 6024
12/13/75+	**21**	8	3. Winners And Losers	Playboy 6054
			HAMLISCH, Marvin	
			Born on 6/2/44 in Brooklyn, New York. Pianist/composer/conductor. Won the 1974 Best New Artist Grammy Award.	
4/20/74	**3**	12	● 1. **The Entertainer** [I] #1 Adult Contemporary hit (1 week); written in 1902 by Scott Joplin; featured in the movie *The Sting* starring Paul Newman and Robert Redford	MCA 40174

DATE	POS	WKS	ARTIST–RECORD TITLE	LABEL & NO.
			HAMMER — see M.C. HAMMER	
			HAMMER, Jan	MCA 52666
			Born on 4/17/48 in Prague, Czechoslovakia. Male jazz-rock keyboardist.	
9/21/85	**1** (1)	13	1. **Miami Vice Theme** Sales #1 (3) / Airplay #2 **[I]**	
			from the TV series starring Don Johnson	
			HAMMOND, Albert	
			Born on 5/18/42 in London, England; raised in Gibraltar, Spain. Pop-rock singer/songwriter.	
11/4/72	**5**	13	● 1. **It Never Rains In Southern California**	Mums 6011
4/13/74	**31**	4	2. I'm A Train	Mums 6026
			HANSON	
			Teen pop-rock trio of brothers from Tulsa, Oklahoma: Isaac (age 16 in 1997; guitar), Taylor (age 14; keyboards) and Zac (age 11; drums) Hanson. All share vocals.	
5/3/97	**1** (3)	20	▲ 1. **MMMBop** Airplay #1 (4) / Sales #1 (3)	Mercury 574261
8/2/97	**27** ᴬ	6	2. Where's The Love	album cut
			from the album *Middle Of Nowhere* on Mercury 534615	
11/29/97	**9**	12	● 3. **I Will Come To You** Sales #4 / Airplay #43	Mercury 568132
4/22/00	**20**	3	● 4. This Time Around Sales #2	Island 562716
			HAPPENINGS, The	
			White vocal group from Paterson, New Jersey: Bob Miranda, Tom Giuliano, Ralph DiVito and Dave Libert.	
7/30/66	**3**	11	1. **See You In September**	B.T. Puppy 520
10/22/66	**12**	5	2. Go Away Little Girl	B.T. Puppy 522
4/29/67	**3**	9	3. **I Got Rhythm**	B.T. Puppy 527
			written in 1930 by George & Ira Gershwin for the musical *Girl Crazy* starring Ginger Rogers	
7/22/67	**13**	6	4. My Mammy	B.T. Puppy 530
			Al Jolson's theme song; written in 1920	
			HARDCASTLE, Paul	
			Born on 12/10/57 in London, England. Keyboardist/producer.	
6/22/85	**15**	8	1. 19 Sales #12 / Airplay #19	Chrysalis 42860
			title refers to the average age of U.S. soldiers in Vietnam	
			HARNELL, Joe, And His Orchestra	
			Born on 8/2/24 in the Bronx, New York. Conductor/arranger.	
1/26/63	**14**	8	1. Fly Me To The Moon - Bossa Nova **[I]**	Kapp 497
			first recorded in 1954 by Kaye Ballard as "In Other Words"	
			HARNEN, Jimmy — see SYNCH	

DATE	POS	WKS	ARTIST–RECORD TITLE	LABEL & NO.
			HARPERS BIZARRE	
			White vocal group from Santa Cruz, California: Ted Templeman, Eddie James, Dick Yount, John Petersen and Dick Scoppettone. Petersen was a member of The Beau Brummels. Templeman later produced many albums for The Doobie Brothers and Van Halen.	
3/18/67	13	7	1. The 59th Street Bridge Song (Feelin' Groovy) written by Paul Simon; arranged by Leon Russell	Warner 5890
6/17/67	37	3	2. Come To The Sunshine	Warner 7028
			HARPO, Slim	
			Born James Moore on 1/11/24 in Lobdell, Louisiana. Died of a heart attack on 1/31/70 (age 46). Blues singer/harmonica player.	
7/10/61	34	2	1. Rainin' In My Heart featuring blues guitarist Lightnin' Slim (Otis Hicks)	Excello 2194
3/5/66	16	7	2. Baby Scratch My Back **[I]** #1 R&B hit (2 weeks)	Excello 2273
			HARRIET	
			Born Harriet Roberts in 1966 in Sheffield, Yorkshire, England. Female dance singer.	
4/13/91	39	1	1. Temple Of Love Sales #37 / Airplay #38	EastWest 98863
			HARRIS, Betty	
			Born in 1943 in Orlando, Florida. R&B singer.	
10/26/63	23	6	1. Cry To Me	Jubilee 5456
			HARRIS, Eddie	
			Born on 10/20/36 in Chicago, Illinois. Died of cancer on 11/5/96 (age 60). Jazz tenor saxophonist.	
5/29/61	36	3	1. Exodus **[I]** jazz version of the main theme from the Otto Preminger movie starring Paul Newman	Vee-Jay 378
			HARRIS, Emmylou	
			Born on 4/2/47 in Birmingham, Alabama. Country singer/songwriter/guitarist.	
4/11/81	37	3	1. Mister Sandman solo version; album version featured harmony vocals by Dolly Parton and Linda Ronstadt	Warner 49684
			HARRIS, Major	
			Born on 2/9/47 in Richmond, Virginia. R&B singer.	
4/19/75	5	14	● 1. **Love Won't Let Me Wait** #1 R&B hit (1 week)	Atlantic 3248
			HARRIS, Richard	
			Born on 10/1/30 in Limerick, Ireland. Died of cancer on 10/25/2002 (age 72). Began prolific acting career in 1958. Portrayed "King Arthur" in the long-running stage production and movie version of *Camelot*.	
5/25/68	2 (1)	10	1. **MacArthur Park**	Dunhill 4134

DATE	POS	WKS	ARTIST–RECORD TITLE	LABEL & NO.
			HARRIS, Rolf	
			Born on 3/30/30 in Perth, Australia. Played piano from age nine. Moved to England in the mid-1950s. Developed his unique "wobble board sound" out of a sheet of masonite. Own BBC-TV series from 1970.	
6/22/63	**3**	9	1. **Tie Me Kangaroo Down, Sport** [N] #1 Adult Contemporary hit (3 weeks)	Epic 9596
			HARRIS, Sam	
			Born on 6/4/61 in Cushing, Oklahoma. Pop singer/actor.	
11/3/84	**36**	3	1. Sugar Don't Bite	Motown 1743
			HARRIS, Thurston	
			Born on 7/11/31 in Indianapolis, Indiana. Died of a heart attack on 4/14/90 (age 58). Black singer/songwriter.	
10/28/57	**6**	13	1. **Little Bitty Pretty One** Best Seller #6 / Top 100 #6 / Jockey #12 The Sharps (later The Rivingtons, backing vocals)	Aladdin 3398
			HARRISON, George	
			Born on 2/24/43 in Liverpool, England. Died of cancer on 11/29/2001 (age 58). Singer/songwriter/guitarist. Lead guitarist of The Beatles. Formed own Dark Horse record label. Member of the Traveling Wilburys. Recipient of *Billboard*'s Century Award in 1992. Inducted into the Rock and Roll Hall of Fame in 2004.	
12/5/70	**1 (4)**	13	● 1. **My Sweet Lord /** a 1976 court ruling found this tune plagerized "He's So Fine" by The Chiffons	
12/5/70		13	2. Isn't It A Pity	Apple 2995
3/6/71	**10**	8	3. **What Is Life**	Apple 1828
8/28/71	**23**	5	4. Bangla-Desh /	
9/11/71		3	5. Deep Blue	Apple 1836
5/26/73	**1 (1)**	11	6. **Give Me Love - (Give Me Peace On Earth)**	Apple 1862
12/14/74+	**15**	6	7. Dark Horse	Apple 1877
2/1/75	**36**	2	8. Ding Dong; Ding Dong	Apple 1879
10/11/75	**20**	6	9. You	Apple 1884
12/11/76+	**25**	7	10. This Song song refers to the plagiarism case involving "My Sweet Lord" and "He's So Fine"	Dark Horse 8294
2/12/77	**19**	7	11. Crackerbox Palace	Dark Horse 8313
3/31/79	**16**	8	12. Blow Away	Dark Horse 8763
5/23/81	**2 (3)**	11	13. **All Those Years Ago** #1 Adult Contemporary hit (1 week); tribute to John Lennon; assisted by Ringo Starr and Paul and Linda McCartney	Dark Horse 49725
11/14/87+	**1 (1)**	15	14. **Got My Mind Set On You** Sales #1 (2) / Airplay #1 (1) #1 Adult Contemporary hit (4 weeks); first recorded by James Ray in 1962	Dark Horse 28178
2/27/88	**23**	6	15. When We Was Fab Sales #18 / Airplay #31	Dark Horse 28131
			HARRISON, Wilbert	
			Born on 1/5/29 in Charlotte, North Carolina. Died of a stroke on 10/26/94 (age 65). R&B singer.	
4/27/59	**1 (2)**	12	● 1. **Kansas City** #1 R&B hit (7 weeks); first recorded by Little Willie Littlefield in 1952	Fury 1023
1/24/70	**32**	4	2. Let's Work Together (Part 1) first recorded by Harrison as "Let's Stick Together" in 1962	Sue 11

DATE	POS	WKS	ARTIST–RECORD TITLE	LABEL & NO.
			HART, Bobby — see BOYCE, Tommy	
			HART, Corey	
			Born on 5/31/62 in Montreal, Quebec, Canada; raised in Malaga, Spain and Mexico City, Mexico. Male singer/songwriter/keyboardist.	
6/23/84	**7**	15	1. **Sunglasses At Night**	EMI America 8203
10/20/84	**17**	9	2. It Ain't Enough Airplay #17 / Sales #18	EMI America 8236
6/22/85	**3**	14	3. **Never Surrender** Sales #1 (1) / Airplay #3	EMI America 8268
10/5/85	**26**	6	4. Boy In The Box Sales #26 / Airplay #26	EMI America 8287
12/28/85+	**30**	7	5. Everything In My Heart Sales #26 / Airplay #30	EMI America 8300
10/11/86	**18**	7	6. I Am By Your Side Sales #14 / Airplay #22	EMI America 8348
1/31/87	**24**	5	7. Can't Help Falling In Love Sales #18 / Airplay #34	EMI America 8368
7/23/88	**38**	2	8. In Your Soul Airplay #39	EMI-Manhattan 50134
4/21/90	**37**	2	9. A Little Love Airplay #35 / Sales #39	EMI 50239
			HART, Freddie	
			Born Fred Segrest on 12/21/26 in Lochapoka, Alabama. Country singer/songwriter/guitarist.	
9/25/71	**17**	12	● 1. Easy Loving #1 Country hit (3 weeks)	Capitol 3115
			HARTMAN, Dan	
			Born on 12/8/50 in Harrisburg, Pennsylvania. Died of a brain tumor on 3/22/94 (age 43). Pop-disco singer/songwriter/producer/multi-instrumentalist. Member of the Edgar Winter Group from 1972-76.	
12/2/78+	**29**	7	● 1. Instant Replay	Blue Sky 2772
6/2/84	**6**	16	2. **I Can Dream About You** from the movie *Streets of Fire* starring Michael Pare	MCA 52378
11/3/84	**25**	9	3. We Are The Young Sales #21	MCA 52471
3/23/85	**39**	2	4. Second Nature	MCA 52519
			HARVEY & THE MOONGLOWS — **see MOONGLOWS**	
			HARVEY DANGER	
			Rock group from Seattle, Washington: Sean Nelson (vocals), Jeff Lin (guitar), Aaron Huffman (bass) and Evan Sult (drums).	
8/15/98	**38** ᴬ	6	1. Flagpole Sitta from the album *Where Have All The Merrymakers Gone* on Slash 556000	album cut
			HATHAWAY, Donny	
			Born on 10/1/45 in Chicago, Illinois; raised in St. Louis, Missouri. Committed suicide on 1/13/79 (age 33). R&B singer/songwriter/keyboardist.	
			ROBERTA FLACK & DONNY HATHAWAY:	
7/3/71	**29**	9	1. You've Got A Friend	Atlantic 2808
6/24/72	**5**	11	● 2. **Where Is The Love** #1 R&B hit (1 week) / #1 Adult Contemporary hit (1 week)	Atlantic 2879
3/18/78	**2** (2)	14	● 3. **The Closer I Get To You** #1 R&B hit (2 weeks)	Atlantic 3463

DATE	POS	WKS	ARTIST–RECORD TITLE	LABEL & NO.
4/24/71	**16**	9	**HAVENS, Richie** Born on 1/21/41 in Brooklyn, New York. Black folk singer/guitarist. 1. Here Comes The Sun first recorded by The Beatles in 1969	Stormy Forest 656
9/7/91	**10**	14	**HAWKES, Chesney** Born on 9/22/71 in Windsor, Berkshire, England. Pop-rock singer. Son of Len "Chip" Hawkes of The Tremeloes. 1. **The One And Only** Airplay #28 / Sales #53	Chrysalis 23730
7/1/57 10/13/58	**27** **32**	5 3	**HAWKINS, Dale** Born Delmar Hawkins on 8/22/38 in Goldmine, Louisiana. Rockabilly singer/guitarist. First cousin to Ronnie Hawkins. 1. Susie-Q Best Seller #27 / Top 100 #29 2. La-Do-Dada Hot 100 #32 / Best Seller #44	Checker 863 Checker 900
5/3/69 5/16/70	**4** **6**	9 14	**HAWKINS, Edwin, Singers, The** Born in August 1943 in Oakland, California. Formed gospel group with Betty Watson in 1967 as the Northern California State Youth Choir. Member Dorothy Morrison went on to a solo career. ● 1. **Oh Happy Day** **THE EDWIN HAWKINS' SINGERS Featuring Dorothy Combs Morrison** recorded by the Northern California State Youth Choir in a Church of God; Pavilion reissued it from their original master tape 2. **Lay Down (Candles In The Rain)** **MELANIE with The Edwin Hawkins Singers**	Pavilion 20001 Buddah 167
9/21/59	**26**	7	**HAWKINS, Ronnie** Born on 1/10/35 in Huntsville, Arkansas. Formed The Hawks in 1952. Moved to Canada in 1958. Assembled group later known as The Band. First cousin to Dale Hawkins. 1. Mary Lou **RONNIE HAWKINS and The Hawks** first recorded by Young Jessie in 1955	Roulette 4177
4/25/92 8/12/95	**5** **6**	17 30	**HAWKINS, Sophie B.** Born Sophie Ballantine Hawkins on 11/1/67 in Manhattan, New York. Female singer/songwriter. 1. **Damn I Wish I Was Your Lover** Sales #6 / Airplay #6 2. **As I Lay Me Down** Airplay #4 / Sales #25 #1 Adult Contemporary hit (6 weeks)	Columbia 74164 Columbia 77801
7/4/60	**29**	5	**HAWLEY, Deane** Born William Dean Hawley in Los Angeles, California. Pop singer. 1. Look For A Star from the movie *Circus Of Horrors* starring Donald Pleasence	Dore 554

DATE	POS	WKS	ARTIST–RECORD TITLE	LABEL & NO.
			HAYES, Bill	
			Born on 6/5/26 in Harvey, Illinois. Singer/actor. Regular on TV's *Your Show of Shows*. Played "Doug Williams" on the TV soap opera *Days Of Our Lives*.	
2/26/55	**1** (5)	20	● 1. **The Ballad Of Davy Crockett** Best Seller #1 (5) / Jockey #1 (3) / Juke Box #1 (3) Archie Bleyer (orch.); from the ABC-TV *Disneyland* series, which featured three "Davy Crockett" segments	Cadence 1256
2/16/57	**33**	3	2. Wringle, Wrangle Top 100 #33 Don Costa (orch.); from the movie *Westward Ho, The Wagons* starring Fess Parker	ABC-Paramount 9785
			HAYES, Isaac	
			Born on 8/20/42 in Covington, Tennessee. R&B singer/songwriter/ keyboardist/actor. Session musician for the Stax label. Teamed with songwriter David Porter to write many classic songs. Acted in several movies. Supplies the voice of "Chef" on TV's *South Park*. Inducted into the Rock and Roll Hall of Fame in 2002.	
9/27/69	**37**	4	1. By The Time I Get To Phoenix /	
10/18/69	**30**	5	2. Walk On By	Enterprise 9003
6/12/71	**22**	5	3. Never Can Say Goodbye	Enterprise 9031
10/23/71	**1** (2)	12	● 4. **Theme From Shaft** the Bar-Kays (instrumental backing); from the movie *Shaft* starring Richard Roundtree	Enterprise 9038
3/25/72	**30**	5	5. Do Your Thing	Enterprise 9042
12/2/72	**38**	2	6. Theme From The Men **[I]** from the ABC-TV series *The Men* starring Robert Conrad	Enterprise 9058
1/12/74	**30**	5	7. "Joy" Pt. I	Enterprise 9085
12/8/79+	**18**	12	8. Don't Let Go	Polydor 2011
			HAYMAN, Richard	
			Born on 3/27/20 in Cambridge, Massachusetts. Conductor/arranger/harmonica player.	
2/11/56	**11**	11	1. (A Theme from) The Three Penny Opera (Moritat) **[I]** Jockey #11 / Top 100 #12 / Best Seller #13 / Juke Box #13 **RICHARD HAYMAN and JAN AUGUST** (August died on 1/17/76)	Mercury 70781
			HAYWOOD, Leon	
			Born on 2/11/42 in Houston, Texas. R&B singer/songwriter/keyboardist.	
11/1/75	**15**	8	1. I Want'a Do Something Freaky To You	20th Century 2228
			HAZLEWOOD, Lee — see SINATRA, Nancy	
			HEAD, Murray	
			Born on 3/5/46 in London, England. Pop singer/actor. Appeared in many movies.	
5/8/71	**14**	8	1. Superstar **[R]** **MURRAY HEAD With The Trinidad Singers** originally hit #74 in 1970; from the rock opera *Jesus Christ* *Superstar*	Decca 32603
3/23/85	**3**	13	2. **One Night In Bangkok** Sales #2 / Airplay #4 from the musical project *Chess*	RCA 13988

DATE	POS	WKS	ARTIST–RECORD TITLE	LABEL & NO.
			HEAD, Roy	
			Born on 9/1/41 in Three Rivers, Texas. Rock-country singer/guitarist.	
9/18/65	**2** (2)	9	1. **Treat Her Right**	Back Beat 546
			ROY HEAD And The Traits	
12/4/65	**39**	1	2. Just A Little Bit	Scepter 12116
12/18/65	**32**	2	3. Apple Of My Eye	Back Beat 555
			ROY HEAD And The Traits	
			HEALEY, Jeff, Band	
			Born on 3/25/66 in Toronto, Ontario, Canada. Blues-rock singer/guitarist. Blind since age one. Formed own group with Joe Rockman (bass) and Tom Stephen (drums). Group appeared in the 1989 movie *Road House*.	
7/22/89	**5**	13	1. **Angel Eyes**　　　　　Sales #4 / Airplay #7	Arista 9808
			HEART	
			Rock group formed in Seattle, Washington: sisters Ann (vocals; see #10 & #18 below) and Nancy (guitar) Wilson, brothers Roger and Mike Fisher (guitars), Steve Fossen (bass) and Mike DeRosier (drums). The Fishers left in 1979. Howard Leese (guitar) joined in 1980. Fossen and DeRosier left by 1982, replaced by Mark Andes (of Spirit, Jo Jo Gunne and Firefall) and Denny Carmassi. In 1990, former members Fossen, DeRosier and Roger Fisher joined Alias. Andes left by 1993. Carmassi left in 1994 to join Whitesnake. Nancy married movie director Cameron Crowe on 7/27/86.	
5/29/76	**35**	2	1. Crazy On You	Mushroom 7021
9/4/76	**9**	14	2. **Magic Man**	Mushroom 7011
7/2/77	**11**	12	3. Barracuda	Portrait 70004
5/13/78	**24**	7	4. Heartless	Mushroom 7031
			recorded in 1976	
10/28/78	**15**	10	5. Straight On	Portrait 70020
3/17/79	**34**	3	6. Dog & Butterfly	Portrait 70025
3/15/80	**33**	4	7. Even It Up	Epic 50847
11/29/80+	**8**	11	8. **Tell It Like It Is**	Epic 50950
6/19/82	**33**	4	9. This Man Is Mine	Epic 02925
5/19/84	**7**	13	10. **Almost Paradise...Love Theme From Footloose**	Columbia 04418
			MIKE RENO and ANN WILSON	
			#1 Adult Contemporary hit (1 week); co-written by Eric Carmen; from the movie *Footloose* starring Kevin Bacon and Lori Singer	
6/29/85	**10**	12	11. **What About Love?**　　　　　Sales #8 / Airplay #14	Capitol 5481
10/5/85	**4**	14	12. **Never**　　　　　Sales #3 / Airplay #5	Capitol 5512
2/1/86	**1** (1)	13	13. **These Dreams**　　　Sales #1 (1) / Airplay #1 (1)	Capitol 5541
			#1 Adult Contemporary hit (3 weeks)	
5/3/86	**10**	10	14. **Nothin' At All**　　　　　Sales #9 / Airplay #10	Capitol 5572
5/23/87	**1** (3)	15	15. **Alone**　　　　Sales #1 (2) / Airplay #1 (2)	Capitol 44002
8/29/87	**7**	11	16. **Who Will You Run To**　　　Sales #6 / Airplay #6	Capitol 44040
11/28/87+	**12**	11	17. There's The Girl　　　　Sales #10 / Airplay #14	Capitol 44089
1/21/89	**6**	10	18. **Surrender To Me**　　　　Sales #5 / Airplay #8	Capitol 44288
			ANN WILSON AND ROBIN ZANDER	
			co-written by Richard Marx; love theme from the movie *Tequila Sunrise* starring Mel Gibson and Michelle Pfeiffer	
4/14/90	**2** (2)	13	● 19. **All I Wanna Do Is Make Love To You**　Sales #3/Airplay #3	Capitol 44507
7/14/90	**23**	7	20. I Didn't Want To Need You　　　Sales #24 / Airplay #25	Capitol 44553
10/20/90	**13**	13	21. **Stranded**　　　　Airplay #8 / Sales #19	Capitol 44621
2/12/94	**39**	2	22. Will You Be There (In The Morning)　　Airplay #42 / Sales #63	Capitol 58041

DATE	POS	WKS	ARTIST–RECORD TITLE	LABEL & NO.
			HEATHERTON, Joey	
			Born Johanna Heatherton on 9/14/44 in Rockville Centre, Long Island, New York. Movie/TV actress.	MGM 14387
7/15/72	**24**	7	1. Gone	
			HEATWAVE	
			Multi-national, interracial group formed in Germany. Core members: brothers Johnnie and Keith Wilder (vocals), Eric Johns and William Jones (guitars), Rod Temperton and Calvin Duke (keyboards), Derek Brambiz (bass) and Ernest Berger (drums).	
8/27/77	**2** (2)	17	▲ 1. **Boogie Nights**	Epic 50370
2/4/78	**18**	11	▲ 2. Always And Forever	Epic 50490
6/3/78	**7**	11	▲ 3. **The Groove Line**	Epic 50524
			HEAVY D & THE BOYZ	
			Born Dwight Meyers on 5/24/67 in Jamaica; raised in Mt. Vernon, New York. Male rapper. Former president of Uptown Records. Played "Peaches" in the movie *The Cider House Rules*. The Boyz consisted of Glen Parrish, Troy Dixon and Edward Ferrell. Dixon died on 7/15/90 (age 22) from an accidental fall in Indianapolis, Indiana.	
7/20/91	**11**	15	● 1. Now That We Found Love Sales #5 / Airplay #12	Uptown/MCA 54090
			Aaron Hall (backing vocal)	
1/11/92	**32**	6	2. Is It Good To You Airplay #27 / Sales #28	Uptown/MCA 54200
4/23/94	**20**	13	3. Got Me Waiting Sales #11 / Airplay #28	Uptown/MCA 54815
			samples "Don't You Know That" by Luther Vandross	
9/3/94	**40**	1	4. Nuttin' But Love Sales #28 / Airplay #40	Uptown/MCA 54865
3/8/97	**18**	12	● 5. Big Daddy Sales #10 / Airplay #70	Uptown/Universal 56039
			HEAVY D	
			HEBB, Bobby	
			Born on 7/26/41 in Nashville, Tennessee. R&B singer/songwriter.	
7/23/66	**2** (2)	11	● 1. **Sunny**	Philips 40365
			written by Hebb after his brother Hal was killed in a mugging	
11/5/66	**39**	1	2. A Satisfied Mind	Philips 40400
			#1 Country hit for Porter Wagoner in 1955	
			HEFTI, Neal	
			Born on 10/29/22 in Hastings, Nebraska. Conductor/trumpeter.	
3/5/66	**35**	4	1. Batman Theme [I]	RCA Victor 8755
			original theme from the *Batman* TV series starring Adam West and Burt Ward	
			HEIGHTS, The	
			Band made up of cast members from the Fox-TV network prime time TV show of the same name: Jamie Walters (born on 6/13/69 in Boston, Massachusetts; see #2 below) and Shawn Thompson (vocals), Alex Desert, Ken Garito, Cheryl Pollack, Charlotte Ross, Zachary Throne and Tarisa Valenza. Show was based on fictional adventures featuring the band.	
10/10/92	**1** (2)	16	● 1. **How Do You Talk To An Angel** Sales #3 / Airplay #3	Capitol 44890
3/4/95	**16**	20	2. Hold On Airplay #12 / Sales #34	Atlantic 87240
			JAMIE WALTERS	

Bill Haley is credited with ushering in the rock and roll era with his #1 hit "Rock Around The Clock." The song was revived in the mid-1970s as the original theme song of the TV series *Happy Days*.

Daryl Hall and John Oates scored their third #1 hit with "Private Eyes," and almost replaced themselves at #1 with "I Can't Go For That (No Can Do)." The only song standing between them was Olivia Newton-John's "Physical."

Hanson earned a Grammy Award nomination for Best New Artist in 1997, but lost to Paula Cole. Their chart-topping breakout hit, "MMMBop," was also nominated for Record of the Year, but lost to Shawn Colvin's "Sunny Came Home."

George Harrison had the unique distinction of having his first chart hit be the same song as his last chart hit. "My Sweet Lord" reached #1 in 1970, and a re-release of the song stalled at #94 in 2002.

Wilbert Harrison had to overcome a lot to reach #1 with "Kansas City." The song entered the chart at #100, and had to compete against alternate versions by Hank Ballard, Little Richard, and Rocky Olson on its way to the top.

Heart earned their second #1 hit with the 1987 song "Alone." Lead singer Ann Wilson didn't fare so well when she was alone; her solo hit "The Best Man In The World," from the movie *The Golden Child*, failed to reach the Top 40.

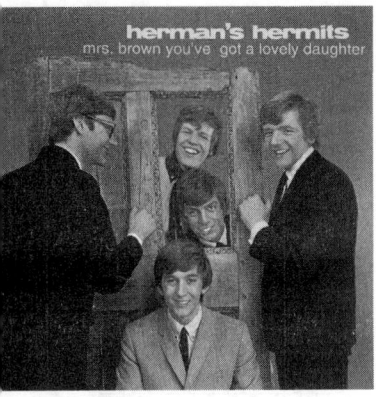

Herman's Hermits certainly weren't shy about releasing hits. In 18 months between 1965 and 1966, they had nine straight Top 10 singles, including the #1 hit "Mrs. Brown You've Got A Lovely Daughter."

Hi-Five were deserving of congratulations after sending their single, "I Like The Way (The Kissing Game)," to #1. The R&B group's singer, Tony Thompson, was only 15 years old when the song was recorded.

Lauryn Hill just missed having a #1 hit as part of the Fugees, but made up for it when her solo hit "Doo Wop (That Thing)," a song she wrote, produced, and performed, debuted on the Hot 100 at #1.

The Hollywood Argyles had a #1 hit with "Alley-Oop," which came out at the same time as competing versions by Dante & The Evergreens and The Dyna-Sores. Although each act had some success with the comic-strip caveman song, after 1960 all three groups were basically extinct.

Whitney Houston set a record by having seven straight singles go to #1. Although the streak was broken in 1988, future #1 hits like "All The Man That I Need" proved she was still needed by pop music fans.

Tab Hunter was climbing the charts with "Young Love" at the same time as Sonny James's own version of the song. Although James's version was a bigger hit among Country fans, Tab's was the bigger pop hit, reaching #1.

DATE	POS	WKS	ARTIST–RECORD TITLE	LABEL & NO.
			HELMS, Bobby	
			Born on 8/15/35 in Bloomington, Indiana. Died of emphysema on 6/19/97 (age 61). Country singer/guitarist.	
10/14/57	7	15	● 1. **My Special Angel** Best Seller #7 / Top 100 #7 / Jockey #8 #1 Country hit (4 weeks); The Anita Kerr Singers (backing vocals)	Decca 30423
10/14/57	36	2	2. Fraulein Top 100 #36 / Best Seller #46 #1 Country hit (4 weeks)	Decca 30194
12/23/57	6	6	● 3. **Jingle Bell Rock** Top 100 #6 / Best Seller #7 / Jockey #11 **[X]**	Decca 30513
12/29/58	35	1	4. Jingle Bell Rock **[X-R]**	Decca 30513
12/26/60	36	1	5. Jingle Bell Rock **[X-R]**	Decca 30513
			HENDERSON, Joe	
			Born in 1937 in Como, Mississippi; raised in Gary, Indiana. Died on 10/24/64 (age 27). R&B singer.	
6/2/62	8	10	1. **Snap Your Fingers**	Todd 1072
			HENDRICKS, Bobby	
			Born on 2/22/38 in Columbus, Ohio. R&B singer.	
9/1/58	25	4	1. Itchy Twitchy Feeling Hot 100 #25 / Best Seller #35 The Coasters (backing vocals); Jimmy Oliver (orch.)	Sue 706
			HENDRIX, Jimi	
			Born on 11/27/42 in Seattle, Washington. Died of a drug overdose on 9/18/70 (age 27). Legendary psychedelic-blues guitarist. Began career as a studio guitarist. Created The Jimi Hendrix Experience with Noel Redding (bass; died on 5/12/2003, age 57) and Mitch Mitchell (drums). The Jimi Hendrix Experience was inducted into the Rock and Roll Hall of Fame in 1992. Won Grammy's Lifetime Achievement Award in 1992.	
9/28/68	20	8	1. All Along The Watchtower **THE JIMI HENDRIX EXPERIENCE** first recorded by Bob Dylan in 1968	Reprise 0767
			HENHOUSE FIVE PLUS TOO — see STEVENS, Ray	
			HENLEY, Don	
			Born on 7/22/47 in Gilmer, Texas. Rock singer/songwriter/drummer. Member of the Eagles. Married model Sharon Summerall on 5/20/95.	
11/7/81+	6	15	1. **Leather And Lace** **STEVIE NICKS (with DON HENLEY)** written for Waylon Jennings and Jessi Colter	Modern 7341
11/13/82+	3	14	● 2. **Dirty Laundry** #1 Mainstream Rock hit (3 weeks); Joe Walsh and Steve Lukather (Toto) (guitar solos)	Asylum 69894
12/8/84+	5	14	3. **The Boys Of Summer** Airplay #5 / Sales #7 #1 Mainstream Rock hit (5 weeks)	Geffen 29141
3/16/85	9	11	4. **All She Wants To Do Is Dance** Airplay #8 / Sales #12 #1 Mainstream Rock hit (2 weeks); Martha Davis of The Motels and Patty Smyth (harmony vocals)	Geffen 29065
7/6/85	34	5	5. Not Enough Love In The World Airplay #30	Geffen 29012
9/21/85	22	8	6. Sunset Grill Airplay #15 / Sales #27 Patty Smyth (harmony vocal)	Geffen 28906
7/8/89	8	12	7. **The End Of The Innocence** Airplay #7 / Sales #9 #1 Mainstream Rock hit (4 weeks)	Geffen 22925

DATE	POS	WKS	ARTIST–RECORD TITLE	LABEL & NO.
11/11/89	21	8	8. The Last Worthless Evening Sales #19 / Airplay #22	Geffen 22771
3/24/90	21	8	9. The Heart Of The Matter Airplay #20 / Sales #21	Geffen 19898
8/29/92	2 (6)	20	● 10. **Sometimes Love Just Ain't Enough** Sales #3 / Airplay #3 **PATTY SMYTH with Don Henley** #1 Adult Contemporary hit (4 weeks)	MCA 54403

HENRY, Clarence

Born on 3/19/37 in Algiers, Louisiana. R&B singer/pianist/trombonist. Nicknamed "Frog Man" from his hit "Ain't Got No Home."

DATE	POS	WKS	ARTIST–RECORD TITLE	LABEL & NO.
1/12/57	20	3	1. Ain't Got No Home Best Seller #20 / Top 100 #30 **[N]** **CLARENCE HENRY "FROG MAN"**	Argo 5259
3/20/61	4	11	2. **But I Do**	Argo 5378
5/29/61	12	7	3. You Always Hurt The One You Love #1 hit in 1944 for The Mills Brothers	Argo 5388

HENSON, Jim

Born on 9/24/36 in Greenville, Mississippi. Died of a sudden virus on 5/16/90 (age 53). Creator of The Muppets. Henson was the voice for both Ernie and Kermit.

DATE	POS	WKS	ARTIST–RECORD TITLE	LABEL & NO.
8/29/70	16	7	1. Rubber Duckie **[N]** **ERNIE (JIM HENSON)**	Columbia 45207
10/20/79	25	7	2. Rainbow Connection **KERMIT (JIM HENSON)** from *The Muppet Movie*	Atlantic 3610

HERMAN'S HERMITS

Pop group formed in Manchester, England: Peter "Herman" Noone (vocals; born on 11/5/47), Derek Leckenby and Keith Hopwood (guitars), Karl Green (bass) and Barry Whitwam (drums). Group name derived from cartoon character "Sherman" of TV's *The Bullwinkle Show*. Leckenby died of cancer on 6/4/94 (age 48).

DATE	POS	WKS	ARTIST–RECORD TITLE	LABEL & NO.
11/14/64	13	9	1. I'm Into Something Good	MGM 13280
2/20/65	2 (2)	11	2. **Can't You Hear My Heartbeat**	MGM 13310
4/17/65	1 (3)	11	● 3. **Mrs. Brown You've Got A Lovely Daughter**	MGM 13341
4/17/65	5	10	4. **Silhouettes**	MGM 13332
6/5/65	4	8	5. **Wonderful World**	MGM 13354
7/10/65	1 (1)	8	● 6. **I'm Henry VIII, I Am** written in 1911; popularized in England by Harry Champion	MGM 13367
9/25/65	7	8	7. **Just A Little Bit Better**	MGM 13398
1/1/66	8	8	8. **A Must To Avoid**	MGM 13437
2/26/66	3	7	9. **Listen People** from the movie *When the Boys Meet the Girls* starring Connie Francis	MGM 13462
4/16/66	9	7	10. **Leaning On The Lamp Post** #8 & 10: from the movie *Hold On!* starring Herman's Hermits	MGM 13500
7/23/66	12	5	11. This Door Swings Both Ways	MGM 13548
10/15/66	5	8	12. **Dandy** written by Ray Davies of The Kinks	MGM 13603
12/24/66	27	5	13. East West	MGM 13639
3/4/67	4	9	● 14. **There's A Kind Of Hush /**	MGM 13681
3/18/67	35	4	15. No Milk Today	
7/8/67	18	4	16. Don't Go Out Into The Rain (You're Going To Melt)	MGM 13761

DATE	POS	WKS	ARTIST–RECORD TITLE	LABEL & NO.
9/16/67	**39**	2	17. Museum *written by Donovan*	MGM 13787
2/3/68	**22**	6	18. I Can Take Or Leave Your Loving *all of above produced by Mickie Most*	MGM 13885

HERNANDEZ, Patrick

Born on 4/6/49 in Paris, France. Disco singer/songwriter.

8/4/79	**16**	11	● 1. Born To Be Alive	Columbia 10986

HERNDON, Ty

Born Boyd Tyrone Herndon on 5/2/62 in Meridian, Mississippi; raised in Butler, Alabama. Country singer/songwriter/guitarist.

12/5/98	**38**	2	1. It Must Be Love *Airplay #28* *#1 Country hit (1 week); from the album Big Hopes on Epic 68167*	album cut

HESITATIONS, The

R&B vocal group from Cleveland, Ohio: brothers George "King" and Charles Scott, Fred Deal, Robert Sheppard, Arthur Blakely, Phillip Dorroh and Leonard Veal. George Scott was accidentally shot to death in February 1968 (age 38).

2/17/68	**38**	2	1. Born Free *title song from the movie starring Virginia McKenna*	Kapp 878

HEWETT, Howard — see BABYFACE

HEYWOOD, Eddie

Born on 12/4/15 in Atlanta, Georgia. Died on 1/2/89 (age 73). Jazz pianist.

7/21/56	**11**	18	1. Soft Summer Breeze *Best Seller #11 / Top 100 #12 / Juke Box #13 / Jockey #14* **[I]**	Mercury 70863
7/28/56	**2 (2)**	23	● 2. **Canadian Sunset** *Jockey #2 / Top 100 #2 / Best Seller #3 / Juke Box #3* **[I]** **HUGO WINTERHALTER and his Orchestra with EDDIE HEYWOOD**	RCA Victor 6537

HIBBLER, Al

Born on 8/16/15 in Tyro, Mississippi. Died on 4/24/2001 (age 85). Blind since birth. R&B singer.

4/9/55	**3**	19	1. **Unchained Melody** *Jockey #3 / Juke Box #3 / Best Seller #5* *#1 R&B hit (1 week); from the movie Unchained starring football great Elroy "Crazylegs" Hirsch*	Decca 29441
10/1/55	**4**	22	2. **He** *Best Seller #4 / Top 100 #7 / Jockey #7 / Juke Box #8*	Decca 29660
2/25/56	**21**	5	3. 11th Hour Melody *Top 100 #21*	Decca 29789
7/14/56	**22**	2	4. Never Turn Back *Jockey #22 / Top 100 #48*	Decca 29950
8/25/56	**10**	12	5. **After The Lights Go Down Low** *Jockey #10 / Juke Box #14 / Top 100 #15 / Best Seller #20* *Jack Pleis (orch., all of above)*	Decca 29982

HI-FIVE

R&B vocal group from Waco, Texas: Tony Thompson, Rod Clark, Russell Neal, Marcus Sanders and Toriano Easley. Treston Irby replaced Easley in late 1991.

3/16/91	**1 (1)**	17	● 1. **I Like The Way (The Kissing Game)** *Sales #1 (2) / Airplay #4* *#1 R&B hit (2 weeks)*	Jive 1424

DATE	POS	WKS	ARTIST–RECORD TITLE	LABEL & NO.
7/13/91	8	13	2. **I Can't Wait Another Minute** Airplay #4 / Sales #15 #1 R&B hit (1 week)	Jive 1445
8/15/92	5	16	3. **She's Playing Hard To Get** Airplay #6 / Sales #8	Jive 42067
1/23/93	38	2	4. Quality Time Sales #18 / Airplay #54 written, produced and backing vocal by R. Kelly	Jive 42109
11/20/93	30	10	5. Never Should've Let You Go Sales #27 / Airplay #40 from the movie *Sister Act II: Back In The Habit* starring Whoopi Goldberg	Jive 42178
			HIGGINS, Bertie	
			Born Elbert Higgins on 12/8/44 in Tarpon Springs, Florida. Soft-rock singer/songwriter.	
1/16/82	8	17	● 1. **Key Largo** #1 Adult Contemporary hit (2 weeks); inspired by the movie starring Humphrey Bogart and Lauren Bacall	Kat Family 02524
			HIGH INERGY	
			Female R&B vocal group from Pasadena, California: sisters Vernessa and Barbara Mitchell, with Linda Howard and Michelle Rumph.	
11/19/77	**12**	11	1. You Can't Turn Me Off (In The Middle Of Turning Me On)	Gordy 7155
			HIGHLIGHTS, The	
			White vocal group from Chicago, Illinois: brothers Frank and Tony Calzaretta, Frank Pizani, Bill Melshimer and Jerry Oleski.	
11/10/56	**19**	5	1. City Of Angels Best Seller #19 / Top 100 #30	Bally 1016
			HIGHWAYMEN, The	
			Folk group formed in Middletown, Connecticut: Dave Fisher, Bob Burnett, Chan Daniels, Steve Trott and Steve Butts. Daniels died of pneumonia on 8/2/75 (age 35).	
7/31/61	**1 (2)**	11	● 1. **Michael** #1 Adult Contemporary hit (5 weeks); 19th-century folk song ("Michael Row The Boat Ashore")	United Artists 258
12/25/61+	**13**	13	2. Cotton Fields traditional American ballad, copyrighted in 1850	United Artists 370
			HILL, Bunker	
			Born David Walker on 5/5/41 in Washington DC. R&B singer.	
10/13/62	**33**	3	1. Hide & Go Seek, Part I	Mala 451
			HILL, Dan	
			Born on 6/3/54 in Toronto, Ontario, Canada. Adult Contemporary singer/songwriter.	
12/24/77+	**3**	15	● 1. **Sometimes When We Touch**	20th Century 2355
7/25/87	**6**	13	2. **Can't We Try** Sales #4 / Airplay #9 **DAN HILL (with Vonda Sheppard)**	Columbia 07050

DATE	POS	WKS	ARTIST–RECORD TITLE	LABEL & NO.
			HILL, Faith	
			Born on 9/21/67 in Jackson, Mississippi. Country singer. Adopted at less than a week old and raised as Audrey Faith Perry in Star, Mississippi. Married Tim McGraw on 10/6/96.	
5/17/97	**7**	17	▲ 1. **It's Your Love** Sales #3	Curb 73019
			TIM McGRAW with Faith Hill	
			#1 Country hit (6 weeks)	
5/16/98	**7**	37	▲ 2. **This Kiss** Airplay #12 / Sales #13	Warner 17247
			#1 Country hit (3 weeks)	
12/5/98	**33**	3	3. Let Me Let Go Airplay #24	album cut
			#1 Country hit (1 week); from the album *Faith* on Warner 46790	
12/11/99+	**2 (5)**	42	● 4. **Breathe** Airplay #2 / Sales #3	Warner 16884
			#1 Country hit (6 weeks) / #1 Adult Contemporary hit (17 weeks)	
5/20/00+	**6**	34	5. **The Way You Love Me** Sales #6 / Airplay #9	Warner 16818
			#1 Country hit (4 weeks)	
4/14/01	**39**	1	6. If My Heart Had Wings Airplay #29	album cut
			from the album *Breathe* on Warner 47373	
6/2/01	**10**	9	7. **There You'll Be** Airplay #8	album cut
			#1 Adult Contemporary hit (12 weeks); from the movie *Pearl Harbor* starring Ben Affleck (soundtrack on Hollywood 48113)	
9/28/02	**33**	6	8. Cry Airplay #31	album cut
			#1 Adult Contemporary hit (11 weeks); from the album *Cry* on Warner 48001	
			HILL, Jessie	
			Born on 12/9/32 in New Orleans, Louisiana. Died of heart failure on 9/17/96 (age 63). R&B singer/pianist/drummer.	
5/9/60	**28**	4	1. Ooh Poo Pah Doo - Part II **[I]**	Minit 607
			HILL, Lauryn	
			Born on 5/25/75 in South Orange, New Jersey. Black singer/actress. Member of The Fugees. Acted on TV's *As The World Turns* and in the movie *Sister Act 2*.	
3/23/96	**2 (3)**ᴬ	30	1. **Killing Me Softly**	album cut
			FUGEES (feat. Lauryn Hill)	
			#1 R&B Airplay hit (5 weeks); from the album *The Score* on Ruffhouse 67147	
8/15/98	**35** ᴬ	12	2. Can't Take My Eyes Off Of You	album cut
			from the movie *Conspiracy Theory* starring Mel Gibson; from the album *The Miseducation of Lauryn Hill* on Ruffhouse 69035	
11/14/98	**1 (2)**	16	● 3. **Doo Wop (That Thing)** Sales #1 (1) / Airplay #2	Ruffhouse 78868
2/13/99	**21**	16	4. Ex-Factor Airplay #11	album cut
			samples "Can It All Be So Simple" by Wu-Tang Clan; from the album *The Miseducation of Lauryn Hill* on Ruffhouse 69035	
7/24/99	**35**	3	● 5. Everything Is Everything Sales #18 / Airplay #50	Ruffhouse 79206
			HILLSIDE SINGERS, The	
			Pop vocal group: Lori Ham, Mary Mayo, Joelle Marino, Bill Marino, Frank Marino, Laura Marino, Rick Shaw, Ron Shaw and Susan Wiedinman. The Marinos are siblings. Mary Mayo was the wife of producer Al Ham; Lori Ham is their daughter. Rick and Ron Shaw are brothers.	
12/11/71+	**13**	10	1. I'd Like To Teach The World To Sing	
			(In Perfect Harmony)	Metromedia 231
			adapted from a Coca-Cola jingle	

DATE	POS	WKS	ARTIST–RECORD TITLE	LABEL & NO.

HILLTOPPERS, The

White vocal group formed in Bowling Green, Kentucky: Jimmy Sacca, Don McGuire, Seymour Spiegelman and Billy Vaughn. Vaughn left for own conducting career in 1955; replaced by Chuck Schrouder. Spiegelman died on 2/13/87 (age 56). Vaughn died of cancer on 9/26/91 (age 72).

THE HILLTOPPERS FEATURING JIMMY SACCA:

DATE	POS	WKS	ARTIST–RECORD TITLE	LABEL & NO.
7/30/55	20	4	1. The Kentuckian Song *Best Seller #20* from the movie *The Kentuckian* starring Burt Lancaster	Dot 15375
11/12/55	8	13	2. **Only You (And You Alone)** *Jockey #8 / Top 100 #9 / Juke Box #10 / Best Seller #15*	Dot 15423
1/21/56	31	1	3. My Treasure *Top 100 #31*	Dot 15437
10/6/56	38	2	4. Ka-Ding-Dong *Top 100 #38*	Dot 15489
			THE HILLTOPPERS Featuring Chuck Schrouder	
2/9/57	3	13	5. **Marianne** *Juke Box #3 / Jockey #6 / Top 100 #8 / Best Seller #12* adapted from a Bahamian folk song	Dot 15537
11/25/57	22	4	6. The Joker (That's What They Call Me) *Jockey #22 / Best Seller #34 / Top 100 #37*	Dot 15662

HINTON, Joe

Born on 11/15/29 in Evansville, Indiana. Died of cancer on 8/13/68 (age 38). R&B singer.

DATE	POS	WKS	ARTIST–RECORD TITLE	LABEL & NO.
9/5/64	13	9	1. Funny written by Willie Nelson	Back Beat 541

HIPSWAY

Pop group from Scotland: Graham Skinner (vocals), Pim Jones (guitar), John McElhone (bass) and Harry Travers (drums).

DATE	POS	WKS	ARTIST–RECORD TITLE	LABEL & NO.
3/14/87	19	6	1. The Honeythief *Sales #16 / Airplay #21*	Columbia 06579

HIRT, Al

Born on 11/7/22 in New Orleans, Louisiana. Died of liver failure on 4/27/99 (age 76). Legendary trumpet player.

DATE	POS	WKS	ARTIST–RECORD TITLE	LABEL & NO.
1/25/64	4	13	1. **Java** [I] #1 Adult Contemporary hit (4 weeks)	RCA Victor 8280
5/2/64	15	8	2. Cotton Candy [I]	RCA Victor 8346
8/1/64	30	4	3. Sugar Lips [I]	RCA Victor 8391

HODGES, Eddie

Born on 3/5/47 in Hattiesburg, Mississippi. Pop singer/actor. Appeared in many movies and TV shows.

DATE	POS	WKS	ARTIST–RECORD TITLE	LABEL & NO.
7/24/61	12	8	1. I'm Gonna Knock On Your Door first recorded by The Isley Brothers in 1959	Cadence 1397
7/7/62	14	8	2. (Girls, Girls, Girls) Made To Love first recorded by The Everly Brothers in 1960	Cadence 1421

HOFFS, Susanna — see BANGLES

HOKU

Born Hoku Ho on 6/10/81 in Oahu, Hawaii. Teen pop-rock singer. Daughter of singer/actor Don Ho.

DATE	POS	WKS	ARTIST–RECORD TITLE	LABEL & NO.
3/11/00	27	6	1. Another Dumb Blonde *Sales #5* from the movie *Snow Day* starring Chris Elliott	Geffen 497246

DATE	POS	WKS	ARTIST–RECORD TITLE	LABEL & NO.
			HOLDEN, Ron	
			Born on 8/7/39 in Seattle, Washington. Died of a heart attack on 1/22/97 (age 57). R&B singer.	
4/25/60	7	13	1. **Love You So** **RON HOLDEN with The Thunderbirds**	Donna 1315
			HOLLAND, Amy	
			Pop singer. Daughter of country singer Esmereldy and opera singer Harry Boersma. Married to Michael McDonald.	
9/13/80	22	6	1. How Do I Survive produced by Michael McDonald	Capitol 4884
			HOLLAND, Eddie	
			Born on 10/30/39 in Detroit, Michigan. Singer/songwriter/producer. Member of Motown's hit production trio with brother Brian Holland and Lamont Dozier; wrote many of Motown's greatest hits. Co-founder of the Invictus/Hot Wax label. Holland-Dozier-Holland were inducted into the Rock and Roll Hall of Fame in 1990.	
3/10/62	30	4	1. Jamie	Motown 1021
			HOLLIDAY, Jennifer	
			Born on 10/19/60 in Riverside, Texas. R&B singer/actress. Appeared in several Broadway musicals.	
7/31/82	22	7	1. And I Am Telling You I'm Not Going #1 R&B hit (4 weeks); from the Broadway musical *Dreamgirls* starring Holliday	Geffen 29983
			HOLLIES, The	
			Pop-rock group from Manchester, England: Allan Clarke (vocals), Graham Nash and Tony Hicks (guitars), Eric Haydock (bass) and Bobby Elliott (drums). Haydock left in 1966, replaced by Bernie Calvert (first heard on "Bus Stop"). Nash left in December 1968 to join David Crosby and Stephen Stills in new trio; replaced by Terry Sylvester, formerly in The Swinging Blue Jeans. Shuffling personnel since then. Clarke, Nash, Hicks and Elliott regrouped briefly in 1983.	
1/8/66	32	4	1. Look Through Any Window	Imperial 66134
8/20/66	5	9	2. **Bus Stop**	Imperial 66186
11/12/66	7	7	3. **Stop Stop Stop**	Imperial 66214
4/15/67	11	9	4. On A Carousel	Imperial 66231
6/24/67	28	3	5. Pay You Back With Interest	Imperial 66240
7/8/67	9	10	6. **Carrie-Anne** written for Marianne Faithfull	Epic 10180
5/18/68	40	1	7. Jennifer Eccles	Epic 10298
2/7/70	7	11	8. **He Ain't Heavy, He's My Brother**	Epic 10532
7/8/72	2 (2)	13	▲ 9. **Long Cool Woman (In A Black Dress)**	Epic 10871
12/2/72	26	5	10. Long Dark Road	Epic 10920
6/8/74	6	11	● 11. **The Air That I Breathe** first recorded by Albert Hammond in 1972	Epic 11100
7/2/83	29	6	12. Stop In The Name Of Love	Atlantic 89819

DATE	POS	WKS	ARTIST–RECORD TITLE	LABEL & NO.
			HOLLISTER, Dave	
			Born in Chicago, Illinois. R&B/hip-hop singer/songwriter. Former member of BLACKstreet.	Def Squad 59019
5/29/99	39	2	1. My Favorite Girl Sales #9	
1/12/02	5 ˢ	11	2. **That Was Then**	Body Head/EMI 74767
			ROY JONES JR. feat. Dave Hollister, Perion & Hahz The Rippa	
			HOLLOWAY, Brenda	
			Born on 6/21/46 in Atascadero, California. R&B singer/songwriter.	
5/23/64	13	6	1. Every Little Bit Hurts	Tamla 54094
3/27/65	25	5	2. When I'm Gone	Tamla 54111
			written and produced by Smokey Robinson	
11/4/67	39	1	3. You've Made Me So Very Happy	Tamla 54155
			HOLLOWAY, Loleatta — see MARKY MARK	
			HOLLY, Buddy/The Crickets	
			Born Charles Hardin Holley on 9/7/36 in Lubbock, Texas. One of rock and roll's most original and innovative performers. Began recording western and pop demos with Bob Montgomery in 1954. Signed to Decca label in January 1956 and recorded in Nashville as Buddy Holly & The Three Tunes (Sonny Curtis, lead guitar; Don Guess, bass; and Jerry Ivan Allison, drums). In February 1957, Holly assembled his backing group, The Crickets (Allison; Niki Sullivan, rhythm guitar; and Joe B. Mauldin, bass), for recordings at Norman Petty's studio in Clovis, New Mexico. Signed to Brunswick and Coral labels (subsidiaries of Decca Records). Because of contract arrangements, all Brunswick records were released as The Crickets, and all Coral records were released as Buddy Holly. Holly split from The Crickets in the fall of 1958. Holly (age 22), Ritchie Valens and the Big Bopper were killed in a plane crash near Mason City, Iowa, on 2/3/59. Gary Busey starred in the 1978 biographical movie *The Buddy Holly Story*. Holly was inducted into the Rock and Roll Hall of Fame in 1986. Won Grammy's Lifetime Achievement Award in 1997.	
8/19/57	1 (1)	16	● 1. **That'll Be The Day** Best Seller #1 (1) / Top 100 #3 / Jockey #3 **THE CRICKETS**	Brunswick 55009
11/11/57	3	16	● 2. **Peggy Sue** Top 100 #3 / Best Seller #3 / Jockey #3	Coral 61885
12/2/57+	10	13	3. Oh, Boy! Top 100 #10 / Best Seller #11 / Jockey #20	Brunswick 55035
3/10/58	17	8	4. Maybe Baby Jockey #17 / Best Seller #18 / Top 100 #18 **THE CRICKETS** (above 2)	Brunswick 55053
6/9/58	37	2	5. Rave On Top 100 #37 / Best Seller #41	Coral 61985
8/4/58	27	4	6. Think It Over Hot 100 #27 / Best Seller #38 **THE CRICKETS**	Brunswick 55072
8/11/58	32	4	7. Early In The Morning Hot 100 #32 / Best Seller #45 The Helen Way Singers (backing vocals); written by Bobby Darin	Coral 62006
3/9/59	13	9	8. It Doesn't Matter Anymore written by Paul Anka; Dick Jacobs (orch.)	Coral 62074
			HOLLYWOOD ARGYLES	
			Gary Paxton recorded "Alley-Oop" as a solo artist; since he was still under contract to Brent Records, where he recorded as Flip of "Skip & Flip," he made up the name, Hollywood Argyles. After the song was a hit, Paxton assembled a Hollywood Argyles group. Formed Garpax Records.	
6/13/60	1 (1)	12	● 1. **Alley-Oop** [N] written by Dallas Frazier; based on the comic strip character	Lute 5905

DATE	POS	WKS	ARTIST–RECORD TITLE	LABEL & NO.
			HOLLYWOOD FLAMES	
			R&B vocal group from Los Angeles, California: Bobby Day, Earl Nelson, David Ford, Clyde Tillis and Curtis Williams (of The Penguins). Day died on 7/15/90 (age 60).	
12/2/57+	**11**	12	1. Buzz-Buzz-Buzz / Top 100 #11 / Best Seller #12	
12/16/57 -		1	2. Crazy Best Seller: flip	Ebb 119
			HOLMAN, Eddie	
			Born on 6/3/46 in Norfolk, Virginia. R&B singer/songwriter.	
1/10/70	**2** (1)	12	● 1. **Hey There Lonely Girl**	ABC 11240
			HOLMES, Clint	
			Born on 5/9/46 in Bournemouth, Dorset, England; raised in Farnham, New York. Pop singer.	
5/5/73	**2** (2)	15	● 1. **Playground In My Mind**
Phillip Vance (child vocal)	Epic 10891
			HOLMES, Rupert	
			Born on 2/24/47 in Northwich, Cheshire, England; raised in Manhattan, New York. Pop singer/songwriter. Member of Street People. Wrote the Broadway musical *Drood*.	
11/10/79	**1** (3)	16	● 1. **Escape (The Pina Colada Song)**	Infinity 50,035
2/9/80	6	12	2. **Him**	MCA 41173
6/14/80	32	3	3. Answering Machine	MCA 41235
			HOLY, Steve	
			Born on 2/23/72 in Dallas, Texas. Country singer/songwriter.	
12/29/01+	**29**	9	1. Good Morning Beautiful Airplay #27
#1 Country hit (5 weeks); from the album *Blue Moon* on Curb 77972; from the movie *Angel Eyes* starring Jennifer Lopez	album cut
			HOMBRES, The	
			Rock group from Memphis, Tennessee: B.B. Cunningham (vocals, organ), Gary McEwen (guitar), Jerry Masters (bass) and Johnny Hunter (drums). Hunter committed suicide in February 1976 (age 34). Cunningham's brother, Bill, was a member of The Box Tops.	
10/7/67	**12**	10	1. Let It Out (Let It All Hang Out)	Verve Forecast 5058
			HOMER AND JETHRO	
			Country comedy duo from Knoxville, Tennessee. Henry "Homer" Haynes was born on 7/27/20; died of a heart attack on 8/7/71 (age 51). Kenneth "Jethro" Burns was born on 3/10/20; died of cancer on 2/4/89 (age 68).	
9/14/59	**14**	7	1. The Battle Of Kookamonga **[N]**
parody of "The Battle Of New Orleans" by Johnny Horton	RCA Victor 7585
			HONDELLS, The	
			Producer Gary Usher recorded various studio musicians in Southern California under different group names. "Little Honda" featured Usher, Chuck Girard (vocals), Glen Campbell and Richie Podolor (guitars), Hal Blaine (drums) and Ritchie Burns (backing vocals). Usher died of cancer on 5/25/90 (age 51).	
10/3/64	**9**	9	1. **Little Honda**
written by Brian Wilson of The Beach Boys	Mercury 72324

DATE	POS	WKS	ARTIST–RECORD TITLE	LABEL & NO.
			HONEYCOMBS, The	
			Rock and roll band from London, England: Dennis D'ell (vocals), Allan Ward and Martin Murray (guitars), John Lantree (bass) and his sister Ann "Honey" Lantree (drums).	
10/10/64	5	9	1. **Have I The Right?**	Interphon 7707
			HONEY CONE, The	
			R&B vocal trio from Los Angeles, California: Carolyn Willis, Edna Wright (sister of Darlene Love) and Shellie Clark.	
5/1/71	**1** (1)	13	● 1. **Want Ads**	Hot Wax 7011
			#1 R&B hit (3 weeks)	
8/21/71	**11**	10	● 2. Stick-Up	Hot Wax 7106
			#1 R&B hit (2 weeks)	
12/11/71+	**15**	8	3. One Monkey Don't Stop No Show Part I	Hot Wax 7110
3/25/72	**23**	6	4. The Day I Found Myself	Hot Wax 7113
			HONEYDRIPPERS, The	
			All-star rock group: Robert Plant (vocals), Jimmy Page and Jeff Beck (guitars), and Nile Rodgers (bass). Plant and Page from Led Zeppelin and Rodgers from Chic.	
10/27/84+	**3**	14	1. **Sea Of Love** Airplay #3 / Sales #4	Es Paranza 99701
			#1 Adult Contemporary hit (1 week)	
1/26/85	**25**	6	2. Rockin' At Midnight Airplay #25 / Sales #27	Es Paranza 99686
			#2 R&B hit for Roy Brown in 1949	
			HONEYMOON SUITE	
			Rock group from Toronto, Ontario, Canada: Johnnie Dee (vocals), Dermot Grehan (guitar), Ray Coburn (keyboards), Garry Lalonde (bass) and Dave Betts (drums).	
4/26/86	**34**	3	1. Feel It Again Airplay #30	Warner 28779
			HOOTERS	
			Pop-rock group from Philadelphia, Pennsylvania: Eric Bazilian (vocals, guitar), Rob Hyman (vocals, keyboards), John Lilley (guitar), Andy King (bass) and David Uosikkinen (drums).	
9/28/85	**21**	8	1. And We Danced Sales #19 / Airplay #23	Columbia 05568
2/1/86	**18**	7	2. Day By Day Sales #15 / Airplay #36	Columbia 05730
5/24/86	**38**	1	3. Where Do The Children Go Airplay #36	Columbia 05854
			Patty Smyth (backing vocal)	
			HOOTIE & THE BLOWFISH	
			Pop-rock group formed in South Carolina: Darius Rucker (vocals), Mark Bryan (guitar), Dean Felber (bass) and Jim Sonefeld (drums). Won the 1995 Best New Artist Grammy Award.	
12/10/94+	**10**	34	1. **Hold My Hand** Airplay #2 / Sales #41	Atlantic 87230
			David Crosby (backing vocal)	
4/15/95	**9**	25	2. **Let Her Cry** Airplay #5 / Sales #32	Atlantic 87231
8/5/95	**6**	29	3. **Only Wanna Be With You** Airplay #2 / Sales #38	Atlantic 87132
12/2/95+	**14**	20	4. Time Airplay #4	Atlantic 87095
4/27/96	**13**	12	5. Old Man & Me (When I Get To Heaven)	Atlantic 87074
			Airplay #7 / Sales #57	
8/17/96	**38**	5	6. Tucker's Town Airplay #23	Atlantic 87051

DATE	POS	WKS	ARTIST–RECORD TITLE	LABEL & NO.
10/5/96	13 ᴬ	30	7. I Go Blind from the TV soundtrack album *Friends* on Reprise 46008	album cut
9/5/98	18 ᴬ	10	8. I Will Wait from the album *Musical Chairs* on Atlantic 83136	album cut

HOPKIN, Mary

Born on 5/3/50 in Pontardawe, Glamorganshire, Wales. Pop singer. Married to producer Tony Visconti from 1971-81.

DATE	POS	WKS	ARTIST–RECORD TITLE	LABEL & NO.

10/12/68	2 (3)	12	● 1. **Those Were The Days**
			    #1 Adult Contemporary hit (6 weeks); melody based on the
			    traditional Russian folk song "Dear For Me"
				Apple 1801

5/3/69	13	7	2. Goodbye
			    written by John Lennon and Paul McCartney; above 2 produced by
			    Paul McCartney
				Apple 1806

3/28/70	39	2	3. Temma Harbour	Apple 1816

HORNE, Jimmy "Bo"

Born on 9/28/49 in West Palm Beach, Florida. R&B singer.

DATE	POS	WKS	ARTIST–RECORD TITLE	LABEL & NO.
6/24/78	38	1	1. Dance Across The Floor written and produced by Harry "KC" Casey	Sunshine Sound 1003

HORNE, Lena

Born on 6/30/17 in Brooklyn, New York. Singer/actress. Starred in several movies and Broadway shows. Won Grammy's Lifetime Achievement Award in 1989.

DATE	POS	WKS	ARTIST–RECORD TITLE	LABEL & NO.

7/9/55	19	1	1. Love Me Or Leave Me Top 100 #19 / Jockey #19
			    Lennie Hayton (orch.); #2 hit in 1929 for Ruth Etting, and title song
			    of Etting's 1955 biopic starring Doris Day
				RCA Victor 6073

HORNSBY, Bruce, And The Range

Born on 11/23/54 in Williamsburg, Virginia. Singer/songwriter/pianist. The Range: George Marinelli and David Mansfield (guitars), Joe Puerta (bass) and John Molo (drums). Puerta was a member of Ambrosia. Hornsby later toured as a member of the Grateful Dead. Won 1986 Best New Artist Grammy Award.

DATE	POS	WKS	ARTIST–RECORD TITLE	LABEL & NO.
10/18/86	1 (1)	15	1. **The Way It Is** Airplay #1 (2) / Sales #2 #1 Adult Contemporary hit (2 weeks)	RCA 5023
1/31/87	4	12	2. **Mandolin Rain** Airplay #2 / Sales #5 #1 Adult Contemporary hit (3 weeks)	RCA 5087
5/30/87	14	9	3. Every Little Kiss Airplay #12 / Sales #15 **[R]** original mix hit #72 in 1986	RCA 5165

5/14/88	5	11	4. **The Valley Road** Sales #5 / Airplay #6
			    #1 Adult Contemporary hit (1 week) / #1 Mainstream Rock hit (3
			    weeks)
				RCA 7645

8/27/88	35	2	5. Look Out Any Window Sales #34 / Airplay #38	RCA 8678

7/21/90	18	7	6. Across The River Airplay #17 / Sales #23
			    #1 Mainstream Rock hit (1 week); Jerry Garcia (of the Grateful
			    Dead; guitar)
				RCA 2621

HORTON, Johnny

Born on 4/30/25 in Los Angeles, California; raised in Tyler, Texas. Died in a car crash on 11/5/60 (age 35). Country singer.

DATE	POS	WKS	ARTIST–RECORD TITLE	LABEL & NO.

5/4/59	1 (6)	18	● 1. **The Battle Of New Orleans**
			    #1 Country hit (10 weeks); original melody written in celebration of
			    the final battle of the War of 1812
				Columbia 41339

DATE	POS	WKS	ARTIST–RECORD TITLE	LABEL & NO.
3/14/60	3	13	2. **Sink The Bismarck** inspired by the movie starring Kenneth More, which is based on the sinking of the German battleship in World War II on 5/27/41	Columbia 41568
10/17/60	4	18	3. **North To Alaska** #1 Country hit (5 weeks); title song from the movie starring John Wayne	Columbia 41782

HOT

Interracial female vocal trio from Los Angeles, California: Gwen Owens, Cathy Carson and Juanita Curiel.

DATE	POS	WKS	ARTIST–RECORD TITLE	LABEL & NO.
4/2/77	6	19	● 1. **Angel In Your Arms**	Big Tree 16085

HOT BUTTER

Group is actually Stan Free (Moog synthesizer player).

DATE	POS	WKS	ARTIST–RECORD TITLE	LABEL & NO.
8/19/72	9	12	1. **Popcorn** [I]	Musicor 1458

HOT CHOCOLATE

Interracial rock-soul group formed in London, England: Errol Brown (vocals), Harvey Hinsley (guitar), Larry Ferguson (keyboards), Patrick Olive (bass) and Tony Connor (drums).

DATE	POS	WKS	ARTIST–RECORD TITLE	LABEL & NO.
3/8/75	8	9	1. **Emma**	Big Tree 16031
7/5/75	28	4	2. Disco Queen	Big Tree 16038
12/6/75+	3	15	● 3. **You Sexy Thing**	Big Tree 16047
8/13/77	31	5	4. So You Win Again	Big Tree 16096
12/2/78+	6	13	● 5. **Every 1's A Winner**	Infinity 50,002

HOTLEGS

Pop-rock trio from Manchester, England: Eric Stewart, Kevin Godley and Lol Creme. Graham Gouldman joined the group later on tour. Group evolved into 10cc.

DATE	POS	WKS	ARTIST–RECORD TITLE	LABEL & NO.
9/5/70	22	6	1. Neanderthal Man	Capitol 2886

HOUSE OF PAIN

White hip-hop group from Los Angeles, California: Erik Schrody, Dan O'Connor and Leor DiMant. Schrody later recorded solo as Everlast.

DATE	POS	WKS	ARTIST–RECORD TITLE	LABEL & NO.
7/25/92	3	25	▲ 1. **Jump Around** Sales #2 / Airplay #29 samples "Harlem Shuffle" by Bob & Earl and "Jump" by Kris Kross	Tommy Boy 7526

HOUSTON, David

Born on 12/9/38 in Bossier City, Louisiana. Died of a brain aneurysm on 11/30/93 (age 54). Country singer/songwriter/guitarist.

DATE	POS	WKS	ARTIST–RECORD TITLE	LABEL & NO.
8/27/66	24	8	1. Almost Persuaded #1 Country hit (9 weeks)	Epic 10025

HOUSTON, Marques

Born on 8/4/81 in Los Angeles, California. R&B singer. Member of Immature.

DATE	POS	WKS	ARTIST–RECORD TITLE	LABEL & NO.
11/1/03	39	1	1. Clubbin Airplay #37 **MARQUES HOUSTON Featuring Joe Budden & Pied Piper** written and produced by R. Kelly; from the album *MH* on T.U.G. 62935	album cut

DATE	POS	WKS	ARTIST–RECORD TITLE	LABEL & NO.
			HOUSTON, Thelma	
			Born on 5/7/46 in Leland, Mississippi. R&B singer/actress.	
1/29/77	**1** (1)	17	1. **Don't Leave Me This Way** #1 R&B hit (1 week)	Tamla 54278
5/19/79	**34**	3	2. Saturday Night, Sunday Morning	Tamla 54297
			HOUSTON, Whitney	
			Born on 8/9/63 in Newark, New Jersey. R&B singer/actress. Daughter of Cissy Houston and cousin of Dionne Warwick. Former fashion model. Married Bobby Brown on 7/18/92. Starred in the movies *The Bodyguard*, *Waiting To Exhale* and *The Preacher's Wife*.	
6/1/85	**3**	13	● 1. **You Give Good Love** Sales #2 / Airplay #5 #1 R&B hit (1 week)	Arista 9274
8/24/85	**1** (1)	15	● 2. **Saving All My Love For You** Sales #1 (2) / Airplay #3 #1 R&B hit (1 week) / #1 Adult Contemporary hit (3 weeks)	Arista 9381
12/28/85+	**1** (2)	16	● 3. **How Will I Know** Airplay #1 (2) / Sales #1 (1) #1 R&B hit (1 week) / #1 Adult Contemporary hit (1 week); Cissy Houston (backing vocal)	Arista 9434
4/5/86	**1** (3)	14	● 4. **Greatest Love Of All** Airplay #1 (2) / Sales #1 (1) #1 Adult Contemporary hit (5 weeks)	Arista 9466
5/16/87	**1** (2)	14	▲ 5. **I Wanna Dance With Somebody (Who Loves Me)** Airplay #1 (3) / Sales #1 (2) #1 Adult Contemporary hit (3 weeks)	Arista 9598
8/8/87	**1** (2)	13	6. **Didn't We Almost Have It All** Sales #1 (2) / Airplay #1 (1) #1 Adult Contemporary hit (3 weeks)	Arista 9616
11/7/87+	**1** (1)	14	● 7. **So Emotional** Sales #1 (2) / Airplay #2	Arista 9642
3/5/88	**1** (2)	13	8. **Where Do Broken Hearts Go** Sales #1 (2) / Airplay #1 (1) #1 Adult Contemporary hit (3 weeks)	Arista 9674
7/9/88	**9**	11	9. **Love Will Save The Day** Sales #8 / Airplay #9	Arista 9720
9/24/88	**5**	11	10. **One Moment In Time** Sales #3 / Airplay #7 #1 Adult Contemporary hit (2 weeks); tune used by NBC-TV for the 1988 Summer Olympics	Arista 9743
10/27/90	**1** (1)	14	● 11. **I'm Your Baby Tonight** Airplay #1 (1) / Sales #3 #1 R&B hit (2 weeks)	Arista 2108
1/5/91	**1** (2)	15	● 12. **All The Man That I Need** Sales #1 (1) / Airplay #1 (1) #1 R&B hit (2 weeks) / #1 Adult Contemporary hit (4 weeks); Kenny G (sax solo); first recorded by Sister Sledge in 1982	Arista 2156
3/9/91	**20**	7	● 13. **The Star Spangled Banner** Sales #3 **[L]** recorded at Super Bowl XXV (1/27/91); also see #32 below	Arista 2207
4/27/91	**9**	9	14. **Miracle** Sales #8 / Airplay #13	Arista 2222
8/10/91	**20**	6	15. My Name Is Not Susan Airplay #33 / Sales #44	Arista 12259
11/14/92	**1** (14)	24	▲⁴ 16. **I Will Always Love You** Sales #1 (14) / Airplay #1 (11) #1 R&B hit (11 weeks) / #1 Adult Contemporary hit (5 weeks); written by Dolly Parton in 1974; 1993 Grammy winner: Record of the Year	Arista 12490
1/23/93	**4**	19	● 17. **I'm Every Woman** Airplay #2 / Sales #11 written by Ashford & Simpson	Arista 12519
3/6/93	**4**	16	● 18. **I Have Nothing** Airplay #1 (6) / Sales #7 #1 Adult Contemporary hit (2 weeks)	Arista 12527
7/17/93	**31**	6	19. Run To You Airplay #26 / Sales #41	Arista 12570
11/27/93	**32** ᴬ	5	20. Something In Common **BOBBY BROWN With WHITNEY HOUSTON** from Brown's album *Remixes N The Key Of B* on MCA 10974	album cut

DATE	POS	WKS	ARTIST–RECORD TITLE	LABEL & NO.
2/19/94	36 ᴬ	1	21. Queen Of The Night above 6 (except #20) from the movie *The Bodyguard* starring Houston and Kevin Costner (soundtrack on Arista 18699)	album cut
11/25/95	1 (1)	20	▲ 22. **Exhale (Shoop Shoop)** Sales #1 (1) / Airplay #4 #1 R&B hit (8 weeks)	Arista 12885
3/23/96	8	15	● 23. **Count On Me** Sales #5 / Airplay #29 **WHITNEY HOUSTON & CECE WINANS**	Arista 12976
8/10/96	26	8	24. Why Does It Hurt So Bad Sales #19 / Airplay #69 above 3 from the movie *Waiting To Exhale* starring Houston	Arista 13213
12/28/96+	4	14	▲ 25. **I Believe In You And Me** Sales #3 / Airplay #29	Arista 13293
3/15/97	15	7	● 26. Step By Step Sales #16 / Airplay #39 written by Annie Lennox; above 2 from the movie *The Preacher's Wife* starring Houston	Arista 13312
1/23/99	15	7	● 27. When You Believe Sales #7 / Airplay #38 **WHITNEY HOUSTON and MARIAH CAREY** from the animated movie *The Prince Of Egypt*	DreamWorks 59022
2/6/99	2 (3)	21	▲ 28. **Heartbreak Hotel** Sales #2 / Airplay #5 **WHITNEY HOUSTON (Feat. Faith Evans & Kelly Price)** #1 R&B hit (7 weeks)	Arista 13619
6/5/99	4	15	● 29. **It's Not Right But It's Okay** Sales #4 / Airplay #13	Arista 13681
9/25/99+	4	24	▲ 30. **My Love Is Your Love** Sales #3 / Airplay #8 Family Friends Community Choir (backing vocals); co-written and co-produced by Wyclef Jean	Arista 13730
3/11/00	27	5	31. I Learned From The Best Sales #8 / Airplay #71 Sue Ann Carwell (backing vocal)	Arista 13790
10/20/01	6	4	▲ 32. **The Star Spangled Banner** Sales #1 (6) / Airplay #45 **[L-R]** re-charted due to the 9/11 terrorist attacks	Arista 15054

HOWARD, Adina

Born on 11/14/74 in Grand Rapids, Michigan. Female R&B singer.

DATE	POS	WKS	ARTIST–RECORD TITLE	LABEL & NO.
2/25/95	2 (2)	27	▲ 1. **Freak Like Me** Sales #2 / Airplay #9 samples "I'd Rather Be With You" by Bootsy Collins	EastWest 64484
9/28/96	32	4	2. What's Love Got To Do With It Sales #15 **WARREN G featuring Adina Howard** from the movie *Supercop* starring Jackie Chan	Interscope 97008

H-TOWN

R&B vocal trio from Houston, Texas: brothers Shazam and Keven "Dino" Conner, with Darryl Jackson. Keven Connor died in a car crash on 1/28/2003 (age 28).

DATE	POS	WKS	ARTIST–RECORD TITLE	LABEL & NO.
5/1/93	3	20	▲ 1. **Knockin' Da Boots** Sales #1 (2) / Airplay #5 #1 R&B hit (4 weeks)	Luke 161
4/27/96	37	2	● 2. A Thin Line Between Love & Hate Sales #19 Shirley Murdock (female vocal); title song from the movie starring Martin Lawrence	Jac-Mac/Warner 17699
11/1/97	35	8	3. They Like It Slow Sales #20 Sales #20; Roger (talk box)	Relativity 1642

HUDSON BROTHERS

Pop vocal trio from Portland, Oregon: Bill, Brett and Mark Hudson. Hosted own TV variety show during the summer of 1974; also hosted kiddie TV show *The Hudson Brothers Razzle Dazzle Comedy Show*. Bill was married to actress Goldie Hawn from 1976-79 (their daughter is actress Kate Hudson).

DATE	POS	WKS	ARTIST–RECORD TITLE	LABEL & NO.
10/26/74	21	5	1. So You Are A Star	Casablanca 0108
8/2/75	26	4	2. Rendezvous	Rocket 40417

DATE	POS	WKS	ARTIST–RECORD TITLE	LABEL & NO.
			HUES CORPORATION, The	
			R&B-disco vocal trio formed in Los Angeles, California: St. Clair Lee, Fleming Williams (died in 1992) and Ann Kelly. Williams replaced by Tommy Brown after "Rock The Boat." Group named after Howard Hughes.	
6/15/74	**1** (1)	10	● 1. **Rock The Boat**	RCA Victor 0232
10/26/74	**18**	5	2. Rockin' Soul	RCA Victor 10066
			HUGH, Grayson	
			Born in Connecticut. Blue-eyed soul singer/songwriter/pianist.	
8/5/89	**19**	8	1. Talk It Over Sales #15 / Airplay #24	RCA 8802
			HUGHES, Fred	
			Born in Arkansas. R&B singer/songwriter.	
6/19/65	**23**	6	1. Oo Wee Baby, I Love You	Vee-Jay 684
			HUGHES, Jimmy	
			Born in Florence, Alabama. Died of cancer on 4/1/97 (age 62). R&B singer. Cousin of Percy Sledge.	
7/11/64	**17**	9	1. Steal Away	Fame 6401
			HUGO & LUIGI	
			Producers/songwriters/label executives Hugo Peretti (born on 12/6/16; died on 5/1/86, age 69) and Luigi Creatore (born on 12/21/20). Owned record labels Roulette and Avco/Embassy.	
1/4/60	**35**	3	1. Just Come Home	RCA Victor 7639
			HUMAN BEINZ, The	
			Rock group from Youngstown, Ohio: Dick Belly (vocals, guitar), Joe Markulin (guitar), John Pachuta (bass) and Mike Tatum (drums).	
1/6/68	**8**	11	1. **Nobody But Me** first recorded by The Isley Brothers in 1962	Capitol 5990
			HUMAN LEAGUE, The	
			Electro-pop trio from Sheffield, Yorkshire, England: lead singer/synthesist Philip Oakey, with female vocalists Joanne Catherall and Susanne Sulley.	
4/10/82	**1** (3)	21	● 1. **Don't You Want Me**	A&M/Virgin 2397
7/2/83	**8**	13	2. **(Keep Feeling) Fascination**	A&M/Virgin 2547
10/29/83	**30**	5	3. Mirror Man	A&M/Virgin 2587
9/27/86	**1** (1)	15	4. **Human** Sales #1 (1) / Airplay #1 (1)	A&M/Virgin 2861
11/3/90	**32**	3	5. Heart Like A Wheel Airplay #31 / Sales #35	A&M/Virgin 1520
4/15/95	**31**	5	6. Tell Me When Airplay #29 / Sales #75	EastWest 64443
			HUMPERDINCK, Engelbert	
			Born Arnold Dorsey on 5/2/36 in Madras, India; raised in Leicester, England. Pop singer. Hosted own TV series in 1970.	
4/29/67	**4**	10	1. **Release Me (And Let Me Love Again)** #5 Country hit for Jimmy Heap in 1954	Parrot 40011
7/15/67	**20**	4	2. There Goes My Everything	Parrot 40015
10/14/67	**25**	5	3. The Last Waltz	Parrot 40019

DATE	POS	WKS	ARTIST–RECORD TITLE	LABEL & NO.
1/6/68	18	7	4. Am I That Easy To Forget *#1 Adult Contemporary hit (1 week); #9 Country hit for Carl Belew in 1959*	Parrot 40023
6/1/68	19	5	5. A Man Without Love (Quando M'innamoro)	Parrot 40027
11/23/68	31	3	6. Les Bicyclettes De Belsize	Parrot 40032
9/27/69	38	1	7. I'm A Better Man	Parrot 40040
1/3/70	16	8	8. Winter World Of Love	Parrot 40044
11/20/76+	8	14	● 9. **After The Lovin'** *#1 Adult Contemporary hit (2 weeks)*	Epic/MAM 50270

HUMPHREY, Paul, & The Cool Aid Chemists

Born on 10/12/35 in Detroit, Michigan. Jazz drummer. The Cool Aid Chemists were Clarence MacDonald, David T. Walker and Bill Upchurch.

DATE	POS	WKS	ARTIST–RECORD TITLE	LABEL & NO.
5/15/71	29	7	1. Cool Aid [I]	Lizard 21006

HUNTER, Ivory Joe

Born on 10/10/14 in Kirbyville, Texas. Died cancer on 11/8/74 (age 60). R&B singer/songwriter/pianist.

DATE	POS	WKS	ARTIST–RECORD TITLE	LABEL & NO.
12/1/56	12	15	● 1. Since I Met You Baby Best Seller #12 / Top 100 #12 / Jockey #14 / Juke Box #14 *#1 R&B hit (3 weeks)*	Atlantic 1111

HUNTER, John

Born in Chicago, Illinois. Rock singer/keyboardist/songwriter.

DATE	POS	WKS	ARTIST–RECORD TITLE	LABEL & NO.
2/16/85	39	2	1. Tragedy	Private I 04643

HUNTER, Tab

Born Arthur Gelien on 7/11/31 in Brooklyn, New York. Singer/actor. Starred in several movies.

DATE	POS	WKS	ARTIST–RECORD TITLE	LABEL & NO.
1/19/57	1 (6)	17	● 1. **Young Love** Top 100 #1 (6) / Jockey #1 (6) / Juke Box #1 (5) / Best Seller #1 (4)	Dot 15533
3/30/57	11	8	2. Ninety-Nine Ways Top 100 #11 / Jockey #11 / Best Seller #12 / Juke Box #17 *written by Charlie Gracie; Billy Vaughn (orch., above 2)*	Dot 15548
2/23/59	31	4	3. (I'll Be With You In) Apple Blossom Time *Don Ralke (orch.); #2 hit for Charles Harrison in 1920*	Warner 5032

HUSKY, Ferlin

Born on 12/3/25 in Flat River, Missouri. Country singer/songwriter/guitarist.

DATE	POS	WKS	ARTIST–RECORD TITLE	LABEL & NO.
3/9/57	4	19	1. **Gone** Jockey #4 / Juke Box #4 / Top 100 #4 / Best Seller #5 *#1 Country hit (10 weeks)*	Capitol 3628
12/26/60+	12	13	2. Wings Of A Dove *#1 Country hit (10 weeks)*	Capitol 4406

HYLAND, Brian

Born on 11/12/43 in Queens, New York. Teen pop singer.

DATE	POS	WKS	ARTIST–RECORD TITLE	LABEL & NO.
7/11/60	1 (1)	13	● 1. **Itsy Bitsy Teenie Weenie Yellow Polkadot Bikini[N]** *Trudy Packer (female spoken voice)*	Leader 805
9/4/61	20	5	2. Let Me Belong To You	ABC-Paramount 10236
4/7/62	21	6	3. Ginny Come Lately	ABC-Paramount 10294
6/30/62	3	11	4. **Sealed With A Kiss**	ABC-Paramount 10336

DATE	POS	WKS	ARTIST–RECORD TITLE	LABEL & NO.
10/13/62	25	4	5. Warmed Over Kisses (Left Over Love) Stan Applebaum (orch., above 4)	ABC-Paramount 10359
8/6/66	20	8	6. The Joker Went Wild	Philips 40377
11/26/66	25	3	7. Run, Run, Look And See	Philips 40405
10/24/70	3	13	● 8. **Gypsy Woman** produced by Del Shannon	Uni 55240

HYMAN, Dick

Born on 3/8/27 in Manhattan, New York. Pianist/conductor/arranger.

| 1/28/56 | 8 | 15 | ● 1. **Moritat (A Theme from "The Three Penny Opera")**
Jockey #8 / Top 100 #9 / Best Seller #10 / Juke Box #14 **[I]**
THE "UNFORGETTABLE" SOUND OF THE DICK HYMAN TRIO
written in 1928; known later as "Mack The Knife" | MGM 12149 |
| 7/5/69 | 38 | 2 | 2. The Minotaur **[I]**
DICK HYMAN & HIS ELECTRIC ECLECTICS | Command 4126 |

HYNDE, Chrissie— see PRETENDERS, The/UB40

I

IAN, Janis

Born Janis Eddy Fink on 4/7/51 in Brooklyn, New York. Contemporary-folk singer/songwriter/pianist/guitarist.

| 6/17/67 | 14 | 8 | 1. Society's Child (Baby I've Been Thinking) | Verve 5027 |
| 7/12/75 | 3 | 14 | 2. **At Seventeen**
#1 Adult Contemporary hit (2 weeks) | Columbia 10154 |

ICE CUBE

Born O'Shea Jackson on 6/15/69 in Los Angeles, California. Male rapper/actor. Former member of N.W.A. Acted in several movies.

6/29/91	36	3	1. You Can't Play With My Yo-Yo Sales #17 **YO-YO Featuring Ice Cube**	EastWest 98831
3/20/93	15	16	● 2. It Was A Good Day Sales #7 / Airplay #32 samples "Sexy Mama" by The Moments and "Footsteps In The Dark" by The Isley Brothers	Priority 53817
8/7/93	20	10	▲ 3. Check Yo Self Sales #9 / Airplay #47 **ICE CUBE featuring DAS EFX** #1 R&B hit (1 week); samples "The Message" by Grandmaster Flash & The Furious Five	Priority 53830
4/2/94	30	8	4. You Know How We Do It Sales #20 / Airplay #46 samples "The Show Is Over" by Evelyn "Champagne" King	Priority 53847
8/27/94	23	11	● 5. Bop Gun (One Nation) Sales #12 / Airplay #34 **ICE CUBE featuring George Clinton** rap version of "One Nation Under A Groove" by Funkadelic	Priority 53155
11/7/98+	26	6	● 6. Pushin' Weight Sales #13 **ICE CUBE Featuring Mr. Short Khop**	Priority 53456
1/8/00	35	2	7. You Can Do It Sales #7 **ICE CUBE Feat. Mack 10** Ms. Toi (female vocal); samples "Planet Rock" by Afrika Bambaataa; from the movie *Next Friday* starring Ice Cube	Priority 53562

DATE	POS	WKS	ARTIST–RECORD TITLE	LABEL & NO.
			ICEHOUSE	
			Rock group formed in Sydney, Australia: Iva Davies (vocals, guitar), Anthony Smith (keyboards), Keith Welsh (bass) and John Lloyd (drums). Numerous personnel changes through the 1980s, with Davies the only constant. Group name is Australian slang for an insane asylum.	
12/5/87+	14	11	1. Crazy Sales #11 / Airplay #21	Chrysalis 43156
3/19/88	7	13	2. **Electric Blue** Sales #5 / Airplay #10	Chrysalis 43201
			co-written by John Oates (of Hall & Oates)	
			ICICLE WORKS	
			Rock trio from Liverpool, England: Robert Ian McNabb (vocals, guitar), Chris Layhe (bass) and Chris Sharrock (drums).	
5/26/84	37	4	1. Whisper To A Scream (Birds Fly)	Arista 9155
			IDEAL	
			R&B vocal group from Houston, Texas: J-Dante, Maverick, PZ and Swab.	
9/25/99	13	16	1. Get Gone Sales #9 / Airplay #35	Noontime 38666
			IDES OF MARCH, The	
			Rock group from Chicago, Illinois: Jim Peterik (vocals, guitar), Ray Herr (guitar), Larry Millas (keyboards), John Larson and Chuck Soumar (horns), Bob Bergland (bass), and Mike Borch (drums). Group named after a line in Shakespeare's *Julius Caesar.* Peterik later played keyboards for Survivor.	
4/11/70	2 (1)	10	1. **Vehicle**	Warner 7378
			IDOL, Billy	
			Born William Broad on 11/30/55 in Stanmore, Middlesex, England. Leader of punk group Generation X from 1977-81. Appeared in the movies *The Doors* and *The Wedding Singer.*	
8/7/82	23	9	1. Hot In The City	Chrysalis 2605
6/25/83	36	3	2. White Wedding	Chrysalis 42697
5/19/84	4	14	3. **Eyes Without A Face**	Chrysalis 42786
9/15/84	29	6	4. Flesh For Fantasy Airplay #29	Chrysalis 42809
10/25/86	6	13	5. **To Be A Lover** Sales #5 / Airplay #9	Chrysalis 43024
			#45 hit for William Bell in 1969 as "I Forgot To Be Your Lover"	
2/28/87	37	2	6. Don't Need A Gun Sales #32 / Airplay #34	Chrysalis 43087
5/30/87	20	7	7. Sweet Sixteen Sales #16 / Airplay #25	Chrysalis 43114
9/26/87	1 (1)	12	8. **Mony Mony "Live"** Sales #1 (1) / Airplay #2 **[L]**	Chrysalis 43161
6/2/90	2 (1)	16	● 9. **Cradle Of Love** Sales #2 / Airplay #5	Chrysalis 23509
			#1 Mainstream Rock hit (2 weeks); from the movie *The Adventures Of Ford Fairlane* starring Andrew Dice Clay	
			IFIELD, Frank	
			Born on 11/30/37 in Coventry, Warwickshire, England; raised in New South Wales, Australia. Pop singer.	
9/22/62	5	8	1. **I Remember You**	Vee-Jay 457
			#1 Adult Contemporary hit (1 week); #9 hit for Jimmy Dorsey in 1942	

DATE	POS	WKS	ARTIST–RECORD TITLE	LABEL & NO.
			IGLESIAS, Enrique	
			Born on 5/8/75 in Madrid, Spain; raised in Miami, Florida. Latin singer. Son of Julio Iglesias.	
7/24/99	**1** (2)	16	1. **Bailamos** Sales #2 / Airplay #6 from the movie *Wild Wild West* starring Will Smith; title is Spanish for "we dance"	Overbrook 97122
1/8/00	**32**	5	2. Rhythm Divine Airplay #25	Interscope 497226
4/15/00	**1** (3)	18	3. **Be With You** Sales #1 (3) / Airplay #3	Interscope 490366
10/6/01	**3**	26	4. **Hero** Airplay #3 #1 Adult Contemporary hit (15 weeks)	album cut
3/9/02	**12**	14	5. Escape Airplay #10 above 2 from the album *Escape* on Interscope 493148	album cut
			IGLESIAS, Julio	
			Born on 9/23/43 in Madrid, Spain. Latin singer. Father of Enrique Iglesias.	
3/31/84	**5**	12	▲ 1. **To All The Girls I've Loved Before** **JULIO IGLESIAS & WILLIE NELSON** #1 Country hit (2 weeks)	Columbia 04217
8/4/84	**19**	8	2. All Of You **JULIO IGLESIAS & DIANA ROSS**	Columbia 04507
			IKETTES, The	
			Female R&B vocal trio formed for the Ike & Tina Turner Revue. Atco group consisted of Delores Johnson, Eloise Hester and "Joshie" Jo Armstead. Modern group consisted of Vanetta Fields, Robbie Montgomery and Jessie Smith.	
2/3/62	**19**	8	1. I'm Blue (The Gong-Gong Song) Tina Turner (backing vocal)	Atco 6212
4/10/65	**36**	4	2. Peaches "N" Cream	Modern 1005
			ILLUSION, The	
			Rock group from Long Island, New York: John Vinci (vocals), Richie Cerniglia (guitar), Mike Maniscalco (keyboards), Chuck Adler (bass) and Mike Ricciardella (drums).	
8/23/69	**32**	6	1. Did You See Her Eyes	Steed 718
			IMAJIN	
			Male R&B vocal group: Jamal Hampton, Talib Kareem, Olamide Faison and John Fitch.	
6/13/98	**25**	7	1. Shorty (You Keep Playin' With My Mind) Sales #18 **IMAJIN Featuring Keith Murray** samples "Dance With Me" by Peter Brown	Jive 42525
			IMBRUGLIA, Natalie	
			Born on 2/4/75 in Sydney, Australia. Alternative pop-rock singer/songwriter. Married Daniel Johns (lead singer of SIlverchair) on 12/31/2003.	
2/21/98	**1** (11)ᴬ	43	1. **Torn** Hot 100 #42 (2 wks)	album cut
8/1/98	**25** ᴬ	11	2. Wishing I Was There above 2 from the album *Left Of The Middle* on RCA 67634	album cut

DATE	POS	WKS	ARTIST–RECORD TITLE	LABEL & NO.
			IMMATURE	
			Teen male R&B vocal trio from Los Angeles, California: Marques Houston, Jerome Jones and Kelton Kessee.	
8/20/94	**5**	21	● 1. **Never Lie** Sales #2 / Airplay #13	MCA 54850
12/24/94+	**16**	13	● 2. **Constantly** Sales #8 / Airplay #40	MCA 54948
2/24/96	**37**	1	3. We Got It Sales #18	MCA 55148
			Smooth (rap); samples "Girl Callin'" by Chocolate Milk	
5/18/96	**36**	3	4. Please Don't Go Sales #17	MCA 55158
2/15/97	**32**	4	5. Watch Me Do My Thing Sales #19	Loud/RCA 64737
			IMMATURE Featuring Smooth and Ed From Good Burger from the Nickelodeon TV show *All That*	
11/6/99+	**23**	10	6. Stay The Night Sales #9 **IMx**	MCA 155630
			IMPALAS, The	
			Doo-wop group from Brooklyn, New York: Joe Frazier, Richard Wagner, Lenny Renda and Tony Carlucci.	
4/13/59	**2** (2)	11	● 1. **Sorry (I Ran All the Way Home)**	Cub 9022
			IMPRESSIONS, The	
			R&B vocal group from Chicago, Illinois: Jerry Butler, Curtis Mayfield, Sam Gooden and brothers Arthur and Richard Brooks. Butler left for a solo career in 1958, replaced by Fred Cash. The Brooks brothers left in 1962, leaving Mayfield as the trio's leader. Mayfield left in 1970 for a solo career, replaced by Leroy Hutson. In 1973, Hutson was replaced by Reggie Torian and Ralph Johnson. Group inducted into the Rock and Roll Hall of Fame in 1991.	
6/16/58	**11**	9	1. For Your Precious Love Best Seller #11 / Top 100 #11 / Jockey #25 **JERRY BUTLER and The Impressions**	Abner 1013
11/20/61	**20**	8	2. Gypsy Woman	ABC-Paramount 10241
10/12/63	**4**	11	3. **It's All Right** #1 R&B hit (2 weeks)	ABC-Paramount 10487
1/25/64	**12**	7	4. Talking About My Baby	ABC-Paramount 10511
4/18/64	**14**	9	5. I'm So Proud	ABC-Paramount 10544
6/27/64	**10**	10	6. **Keep On Pushing**	ABC-Paramount 10554
9/19/64	**15**	8	7. You Must Believe Me	ABC-Paramount 10581
12/12/64+	**7**	7	8. **Amen** [X]	ABC-Paramount 10602
			featured in the 1963 movie *Lilies Of The Field* starring Sidney Poitier	
3/6/65	**14**	5	9. People Get Ready	ABC-Paramount 10622
4/24/65	**29**	4	10. Woman's Got Soul	ABC-Paramount 10647
1/1/66	**33**	2	11. You've Been Cheatin'	ABC-Paramount 10750
2/3/68	**14**	8	12. We're A Winner	ABC 11022
			#1 R&B hit (1 week); Johnny Pate (orch.: #4-12)	
10/5/68	**22**	7	13. Fool For You	Curtom 1932
12/28/68+	**25**	6	14. This Is My Country	Curtom 1934
7/12/69	**21**	9	15. Choice Of Colors	Curtom 1943
			#1 R&B hit (1 week)	
6/13/70	**28**	8	16. Check Out Your Mind	Curtom 1951
6/29/74	**17**	6	17. Finally Got Myself Together (I'm A Changed Man)	Curtom 1997
			#1 R&B hit (2 weeks)	

DATE	POS	WKS	ARTIST–RECORD TITLE	LABEL & NO.
			INC., The	
			All-star rap group assembled by producer Irv Gotti. Featuring Ja Rule, Ashanti, Charli Baltimore and Vita.	
6/29/02	**6**	15	1. **Down 4 U** Airplay #6	album cut
			IRV GOTTI PRESENTS THE INC. Featuring Ja Rule, Ashanti, Charli Balitimore & Vita	
			from the album *Irv Gotti Presents The Inc.* on Murder Inc. 062033	
			INCUBUS	
			Hard-rock group from Calabasas, California: Brandon Boyd (vocals), Mike Einziger (guitar), Chris Kilmore (DJ), Alex Katunich (bass) and Jose Pasillas (drums).	
5/19/01	**9**	23	1. **Drive** Airplay #7	album cut
			#1 Modern Rock hit (8 weeks); from the album *Make Yourself* on Epic/Immortal 63652	
			INDECENT OBSESSION	
			Pop group from Brisbane, Australia: David Dixon (vocals), Andrew Coyne (guitar), Michael Szumowski (keyboards) and Darryl Simms (drums).	
9/1/90	**31**	5	1. **Tell Me Something** Sales #28 / Airplay #32	MCA 53830
			INDEPENDENTS, The	
			R&B vocal group from Chicago, Illinois: Chuck Jackson, Maurice Jackson, Helen Curry and Eric Thomas. Chuck Jackson, not to be confused with the same-named solo singer, is the brother of civil rights leader Jesse Jackson.	
4/28/73	**21**	9	● 1. **Leaving Me**	Wand 11252
			#1 R&B hit (1 week)	
			INFORMATION SOCIETY	
			Techno-dance group from Minneapolis, Minnesota: Kurt Valaquen (singer), Paul Robb (songwriter), Amanda Kramer (keyboards) and Jack Cassidy (bass). Kramer left in early 1990.	
8/27/88	**3**	14	● 1. **What's On Your Mind (Pure Energy)** Sales #4 / Airplay #4	Tommy Boy 27826
1/7/89	**9**	10	2. **Walking Away** Airplay #7 / Sales #10	Tommy Boy 27736
11/10/90	**28**	5	3. Think Sales #24 / Airplay #30	Tommy Boy 19591
			INGMANN, Jorgen, & His Guitar	
			Born Jorgen Ingmann-Pedersen on 4/26/25 in Copenhagen, Denmark. Male guitarist.	
2/20/61	**2** (2)	13	1. **Apache** [I]	Atco 6184
			INGRAM, James	
			Born on 2/16/56 in Akron, Ohio. R&B singer/songwriter/pianist.	
9/19/81	**17**	10	1. Just Once	A&M 2357
			QUINCY JONES Featuring JAMES INGRAM	
2/13/82	**14**	11	2. One Hundred Ways	A&M 2387
			QUINCY JONES Featuring JAMES INGRAM	
12/4/82+	**1** (2)	18	● 3. **Baby, Come To Me**	Qwest 50036
			PATTI AUSTIN (with James Ingram)	
			#1 Adult Contemporary hit (3 weeks)	
1/14/84	**19**	9	4. Yah Mo B There	Qwest 29394
			JAMES INGRAM (with Michael McDonald)	

DATE	POS	WKS	ARTIST—RECORD TITLE	LABEL & NO.
10/13/84	**15**	9	5. What About Me? _Airplay #14 / Sales #16_ **KENNY ROGERS with KIM CARNES and JAMES INGRAM** _#1 Adult Contemporary hit (2 weeks)_	RCA 13899
1/24/87	**2** (1)	12	● 6. **Somewhere Out There** _Sales #1 (2) / Airplay #7_ **LINDA RONSTADT AND JAMES INGRAM** _from the animated movie An American Tail_	MCA 52973
4/7/90	**31**	4	● 7. The Secret Garden (Sweet Seduction Suite) _Sales #20_ **QUINCY JONES/Al B. Sure!/James Ingram/El DeBarge/Barry White** _#1 R&B hit (1 week)_	Qwest 19992
9/8/90	**1** (1)	15	8. **I Don't Have The Heart** _Airplay #1 (2) / Sales #2_	Warner 19911
			INGRAM, Luther	
			Born on 11/30/44 in Jackson, Tennessee. R&B singer/songwriter.	
6/24/72	**3**	13	1. **(If Loving You Is Wrong) I Don't Want To Be Right** _#1 R&B hit (4 weeks)_	KoKo 2111
1/20/73	**40**	2	2. I'll Be Your Shelter (In Time Of Storm)	KoKo 2113
			INNER CIRCLE	
			Reggae group formed in Kingston, Jamaica: Calton Coffie (vocals), Touter Harvey, Lancelot Hall, brothers Ian and Roger Lewis, and Lester Adderly.	
5/15/93	**8**	12	● 1. **Bad Boys** _Sales #6 / Airplay #15_ _theme from the Fox TV series Cops_	Big Beat 98426
9/11/93	**16**	16	2. Sweat (A La La La La Long) _Sales #16 / Airplay #17_	Big Beat 98429
			INNOCENCE, The — see TRADE WINDS, The	
			INNOCENTS, The — see YOUNG, Kathy	
			INOJ	
			Born Ayanna Porter on 11/27/76 in Madison, Wisconsin. Female R&B singer. Given pet name of Joni, spelled backwards is Inoj. Pronounced: i-no-jay.	
2/7/98	**25**	10	1. Love You Down _Airplay #26 / Sales #30_	So So Def 78801
8/22/98	**6**	15	● 2. **Time After Time** _Sales #11 / Airplay #29_	So So Def 79016
			INSTANT FUNK	
			Dance-funk group from Philadelphia, Pennsylvania: James Carmichael (vocals), brothers Kim (guitar) and Scotty (drums) Miller, George Bell (guitar), Dennis Richardson (keyboards), Charles Williams (percussion), Larry Davis (trumpet), Johnny Onderline (sax) and Raymond Earl (bass).	
3/31/79	**20**	8	● 1. I Got My Mind Made Up (You Can Get It Girl) _#1 R&B hit (3 weeks)_	Salsoul 2078
			INTRIGUES, The	
			R&B vocal group from Philadelphia, Pennsylvania: Alfred Brown, Ronald Hamilton, James Harris and James Lee.	
10/4/69	**31**	4	1. In A Moment	Yew 1001
			INTRO	
			R&B vocal trio from Brooklyn, New York: Kenny Greene, Clinton Wike and Jeff Sanders.	
10/23/93	**33**	5	1. Come Inside _Sales #21 / Airplay #38_ _Sebrina Morrison (female voice)_	Atlantic 87317

DATE	POS	WKS	ARTIST–RECORD TITLE	LABEL & NO.
			INTRUDERS, The	
			R&B vocal group from Philadelphia, Pennsylvania: Sam Brown, Eugene Daughtry, Phil Terry and Robert Edwards. Daughtry died on 12/25/94 (age 55).	
4/6/68	6	11	● 1. **Cowboys To Girls**	Gamble 214
			#1 R&B hit (1 week)	
8/10/68	26	4	2. (Love Is Like A) Baseball Game	Gamble 217
6/30/73	36	6	3. I'll Always Love My Mama (Part I)	Gamble 2506
			INXS	
			Rock group from Sydney, Australia: Michael Hutchence (vocals), Kirk Pengilly (guitar, saxophone), Garry Beers (bass) and brothers Tim (guitar), Andy (keyboards, guitar) and Jon (drums) Farriss. Hutchence starred in the movies *Dogs In Space* and *Frankenstein Unbound*. Jon Farriss married actress Leslie Bega (TV's *Head Of The Class*) on 2/14/92. Hutchence committed suicide on 11/22/97 (age 37).	
5/14/83	30	5	1. The One Thing	Atco 99905
2/15/86	5	14	2. **What You Need** Airplay #3 / Sales #7	Atlantic 89460
11/21/87+	1 (1)	17	3. **Need You Tonight** Sales #1 (1) / Airplay #1 (1)	Atlantic 89188
2/27/88	2 (2)	12	4. **Devil Inside** Sales #2 / Airplay #2	Atlantic 89144
5/28/88	3	12	5. **New Sensation** Sales #2 / Airplay #4	Atlantic 89080
9/17/88	7	11	6. **Never Tear Us Apart** Airplay #6 / Sales #8	Atlantic 89038
9/22/90	9	9	● 7. **Suicide Blonde** Airplay #9 / Sales #12	Atlantic 87860
			#1 Mainstream Rock hit (4 weeks) / #1 Modern Rock hit (1 week)	
12/22/90+	8	12	8. **Disappear** Airplay #9 / Sales #11	Atlantic 87784
9/12/92	28	7	9. Not Enough Time Airplay #34 / Sales #52	Atlantic 87437
4/5/97	27 A	7	10. Elegantly Wasted	album cut
			from the album *Elegantly Wasted* on Mercury 534531	
			IRIS, Donnie	
			Born Dominic Ierace on 2/28/47 in Beaver Falls, Pennsylvania. Rock singer/songwriter/guitarist. Former member of The Jaggerz.	
2/7/81	29	6	1. Ah! Leah!	MCA/Carousel 51025
2/13/82	37	2	2. Love Is Like A Rock	MCA/Carousel 51223
5/1/82	25	6	3. My Girl	MCA/Carousel 52031
			IRISH ROVERS, The	
			Irish-born folk group formed in Calgary, Alberta, Canada: Jimmy Ferguson (vocals), brothers Will (vocals, guitar) and George (guitar) Millar, their cousin Joe Millar (bass) and Wilcil McDowell (accordian). Ferguson died in October 1997 (age 57).	
4/6/68	7	9	1. **The Unicorn**	Decca 32254
4/18/81	37	4	2. Wasn't That A Party	Epic 51007
			THE ROVERS	
			IRON BUTTERFLY	
			Hard-rock group from San Diego, California: Doug Ingle (vocals, keyboards), Erik Braunn (guitar), Lee Dorman (bass) and Ron Bushy (drums). Braunn died of heart failure on 7/25/2003 (age 52).	
9/28/68	30	7	1. In-A-Gadda-Da-Vida	Atco 6606

DATE	POS	WKS	ARTIST–RECORD TITLE	LABEL & NO.
			IRONHORSE	
			Rock group from Canada: Randy Bachman (vocals, guitar), Tom Sparks (guitar), John Pierce (bass) and Mike Baird (drums). Bachman was a member of Guess Who and Bachman-Turner Overdrive.	
4/21/79	**36**	3	1. Sweet Lui-Louise	Scotti Brothers 406
			IRWIN, Big Dee	
			Born Difosco Erwin on 8/4/39 in Harlem, New York. Died of heart failure on 8/27/95 (age 56). R&B singer. Former lead singer of The Pastels.	
7/13/63	**38**	2	1. Swinging On A Star **BIG DEE IRWIN (with Little Eva)** #1 hit for Bing Crosby in 1944	Dimension 1010
			IRWIN, Russ	
			Born in 1968 in Huntington Hills, Long Island, New York. Pop-rock singer/songwriter.	
10/19/91	**28**	5	1. My Heart Belongs To You Sales #74	SBK 07363
			ISAAK, Chris	
			Born on 6/26/56 in Stockton, California. Rockabilly singer/songwriter/guitarist. Attended college in Japan. Acted in several movies; starred in own TV show.	
1/19/91	**6**	11	● 1. **Wicked Game** Sales #3 / Airplay #17 featured in the movie *Wild at Heart* starring Laura Dern and Nicolas Cage	Reprise 19704
			ISLANDERS, The	
			Pop instrumental duo of Randy Starr (guitar) and Frank Metis (accordion).	
10/19/59	**15**	8	1. The Enchanted Sea **[I]**	Mayflower 16
			ISLEY BROTHERS, The	
			R&B vocal trio of brothers from Cincinnati, Ohio: O'Kelly, Ronald and Rudolph Isley. Added their younger brothers Ernie (guitar, drums) and Marvin (bass, percussion) Isley and brother-in-law Chris Jasper (keyboards) in September 1969. Formed own T-Neck label the same year. O'Kelly died of a heart attack on 3/31/86 (age 48). Ronald later became the featured member and created his alter-ego "Mr. Biggs"; married singer Angela Winbush in 1993 (later divorced). Group inducted into the Rock and Roll Hall of Fame in 1992.	
6/30/62	**17**	11	1. Twist And Shout first recorded by the Top Notes in 1961	Wand 124
3/19/66	**12**	8	2. This Old Heart Of Mine (Is Weak For You) also see #12 below	Tamla 54128
3/29/69	**2** (1)	12	● 3. **It's Your Thing** #1 R&B hit (4 weeks)	T-Neck 901
6/21/69	**23**	7	4. I Turned You On	T-Neck 902
7/3/71	**18**	9	5. Love The One You're With	T-Neck 930
8/19/72	**24**	7	6. Pop That Thang	T-Neck 935
8/18/73	**6**	15	● 7. **That Lady (Part 1)**	T-Neck 2251
7/12/75	**4**	13	● 8. **Fight The Power Part 1** #1 R&B hit (3 weeks)	T-Neck 2256
11/22/75	**22**	9	9. For The Love Of You (Part 1&2)	T-Neck 2259
8/6/77	**40**	1	10. Livin' In The Life	T-Neck 2264

DATE	POS	WKS	ARTIST–RECORD TITLE	LABEL & NO.
5/24/80	39	2	11. Don't Say Goodnight (It's Time For Love) (Parts 1 & 2) #1 R&B hit (4 weeks)	T-Neck 2290
4/7/90	10	10	12. **This Old Heart Of Mine (1989 Version)** Airplay #7 / Sales #15 **[R]** **ROD STEWART (with Ronald Isley)** #1 Adult Contemporary hit (5 weeks)	Warner 19983
3/2/96	4	16	▲ 13. **Down Low (Nobody Has To Know)** Sales #2 / Airplay #32 **R. KELLY (featuring Ronald Isley and Ernie Isley)** #1 R&B hit (7 weeks)	Jive 42373
6/28/97	35	5	14. Smokin' Me Out Sales #21 **WARREN G Featuring Ronald Isley** samples "Coolin' Me Out" by The Isley Brothers	Def Jam 571024
8/4/01	19	11	15. Contagious Airplay #16 **THE ISLEY BROTHERS Featuring RONALD ISLEY aka MR. BIGGS** written and produced by R. Kelly; additional vocals by Chanté Moore; from the album *Eternal* on DreamWorks 50291	album cut

IVES, Burl

Born on 6/14/09 in Huntington Township, Illinois. Died of cancer on 4/14/95 (age 85). Folk singer/actor. Own CBS radio show *The Wayfaring Stranger* in 1944. Appeared in several movies. Narrated the animated TV classic *Rudolph The Red-Nosed Reindeer*.

DATE	POS	WKS	ARTIST–RECORD TITLE	LABEL & NO.
1/6/62	9	11	1. **A Little Bitty Tear** #1 Adult Contemporary hit (1 week)	Decca 31330
4/21/62	10	8	2. **Funny Way Of Laughin'**	Decca 31371
8/11/62	19	4	3. Call Me Mr. In-Between	Decca 31405
12/8/62	39	1	4. Mary Ann Regrets	Decca 31433

IVY THREE, The

Pop vocal trio formed in Long Island, New York: Charles Koppelman, Art Berkowitz and Don Rubin.

DATE	POS	WKS	ARTIST–RECORD TITLE	LABEL & NO.
8/29/60	8	7	1. **Yogi** **[N]** inspired by the Yogi Bear character from TV's animated *Huckleberry Hound* show	Shell 720

J

JACKS, Terry

Born on 3/29/44 in Winnipeg, Manitoba, Canada. Pop singer/songwriter/guitarist. Recorded with his then-wife Susan Jacks as The Poppy Family.

DATE	POS	WKS	ARTIST–RECORD TITLE	LABEL & NO.
2/9/74	1 (3)	15	● 1. **Seasons In The Sun** #1 Adult Contemporary hit (1 week); first recorded by The Kingston Trio in 1963	Bell 45,432

JACKSON, Alan

Born on 10/17/58 in Newnan, Georgia. Country singer/songwriter/guitarist.

DATE	POS	WKS	ARTIST–RECORD TITLE	LABEL & NO.
9/25/99	39	1	1. Little Man Airplay #29 from the album *High Mileage* on Arista Nashville 18864	album cut

DATE	POS	WKS	ARTIST–RECORD TITLE	LABEL & NO.
8/12/00	37	6	2. It Must Be Love _Airplay #28_ #1 Country hit (1 week); #1 Country hit for Don Williams in 1979; from the album _Under The Influence_ on Arista Nashville 18892	album cut
9/29/01	34	5	3. Where I Come From _Airplay #29_ #1 Country hit (3 weeks); from the album _When Somebody Loves You_ on Arista Nashville 69335	album cut
12/8/01+	28	10	4. Where Were You (When The World Stopped Turning) _Airplay #26_ #1 Country hit (5 weeks)	album cut
4/27/02	28	11	5. Drive (For Daddy Gene) _Airplay #27_ #1 Country hit (4 weeks)	album cut
11/9/02	35	2	6. Work In Progress _Airplay #32_	album cut
3/15/03	29	8	7. That'd Be Alright _Airplay #28_ above 4 from the album _Drive_ on Arista Nashville 67039	album cut
7/19/03	17	15	8. It's Five O'Clock Somewhere _Airplay #14_ **ALAN JACKSON & JIMMY BUFFETT** #1 Country hit (8 weeks); from Jackson's album _Greatest Hits Volume 2_ on Arista Nashville 53097	album cut
			JACKSON, Chuck	
			Born on 7/22/37 in Latta, South Carolina; raised in Pittsburgh, Pennsylvania. R&B singer. Member of The Dell-Vikings from 1957-59.	
3/13/61	36	2	1. I Don't Want To Cry arranged by Carole King	Wand 106
6/2/62	23	6	2. Any Day Now (My Wild Beautiful Bird)	Wand 122
			JACKSON, Deon	
			Born on 1/26/46 in Ann Arbor, Michigan. R&B singer.	
2/19/66	11	9	1. Love Makes The World Go Round	Carla 2526
			JACKSON, Freddie	
			Born on 10/2/56 in Harlem, New York. R&B singer/songwriter.	
7/13/85	18	8	1. Rock Me Tonight (For Old Times Sake) _Sales #18 / Airplay #20_ #1 R&B hit (6 weeks)	Capitol 5459
10/5/85	12	11	2. You Are My Lady _Sales #7 / Airplay #12_ #1 R&B hit (2 weeks)	Capitol 5495
1/25/86	25	6	3. He'll Never Love You (Like I Do) _Sales #23 / Airplay #28_	Capitol 5535
8/15/87	32	3	4. Jam Tonight _Sales #25 / Airplay #38_ #1 R&B hit (1 week)	Capitol 44037
			JACKSON, J.J.	
			Born Jerome Louis Jackson on 4/8/41 in Brooklyn, New York. R&B singer/songwriter. Not to be confused with the former MTV VJ.	
11/5/66	22	7	1. But It's Alright	Calla 119
			JACKSON, Janet	
			Born on 5/16/66 in Gary, Indiana. R&B singer/actress. Sister of The Jacksons (youngest of nine children). Regular on TV's _Good Times, Diff'rent Strokes_ and _Fame._ Co-starred in the movies _Poetic Justice_ and _Nutty Professor 2: The Klumps._ Married to James DeBarge (of DeBarge) from 1984-85. Secretly married to producer Rene Elizondo from 1991-2000.	
3/22/86	4	13	● 1. **What Have You Done For Me Lately** _Sales #3 / Airplay #8_ #1 R&B hit (2 weeks)	A&M 2812

DATE	POS	WKS		ARTIST–RECORD TITLE		LABEL & NO.
6/7/86	3	11	●	2. **Nasty** — Sales #1 (1) / Airplay #5 #1 R&B hit (2 weeks)		A&M 2830
8/23/86	1 (2)	13	●	3. **When I Think Of You** — Airplay #1 (2) / Sales #2		A&M 2855
11/22/86+	5	13	●	4. **Control** — Sales #4 / Airplay #4 #1 R&B hit (1 week)		A&M 2877
2/7/87	2 (1)	11		5. **Let's Wait Awhile** — Sales #3 / Airplay #4 #1 R&B hit (1 week)		A&M 2906
5/2/87	5	12		6. **Diamonds** — Sales #5 / Airplay #7 **HERB ALPERT (with Janet Jackson)** #1 R&B hit (2 weeks); Lisa Keith (backing vocal)		A&M 2929
6/20/87	14	10		7. The Pleasure Principle — Airplay #13 / Sales #17 #1 R&B hit (1 week)		A&M 2927
9/9/89	1 (4)	13	▲	8. **Miss You Much** — Sales #1 (3) / Airplay #1 (3) #1 R&B hit (2 weeks)		A&M 1445
11/18/89+	2 (2)	12	●	9. **Rhythm Nation** — Sales #2 / Airplay #2 #1 R&B hit (1 week)		A&M 1455
1/20/90	1 (3)	14	●	10. **Escapade** — Airplay #1 (4) / Sales #1 (2) #1 R&B hit (1 week)		A&M 1490
4/14/90	4	12	●	11. **Alright** — Airplay #2 / Sales #8		A&M 1479
7/14/90	2 (2)	11		12. **Come Back To Me** — Airplay #1 (2) / Sales #7 #1 Adult Contemporary hit (3 weeks)		A&M 1475
9/15/90	1 (1)	12	●	13. **Black Cat** — Sales #2 / Airplay #2 Vernon Reid (of Living Colour; lead guitar)		A&M 1477
12/1/90+	1 (1)	15	●	14. **Love Will Never Do (Without You)** Airplay #1 (3) / Sales #6		A&M 1538
2/16/91	5 ᴬ	11		15. **State Of The World** from the album *Janet Jackson's Rhythm Nation 1814* on A&M 3920		album cut
5/30/92	10	18		16. **The Best Things In Life Are Free** — Airplay #5 / Sales #16 **LUTHER VANDROSS and JANET JACKSON with BBD and Ralph Tresvant** #1 R&B hit (1 week); from the movie *Mo' Money* starring Damon Wayans		Perspective 0010
5/1/93	1 (8)	20	▲	17. **That's The Way Love Goes** — Airplay #1 (10) / Sales #1 (5) #1 R&B hit (4 weeks); samples "Papa Don't Take No Mess" by James Brown		Virgin 12650
6/26/93	30 ᴬ	19		18. Where Are You Now from the album *janet.* on Virgin 87825		album cut
7/31/93	4	21	●	19. **If** — Airplay #3 / Sales #5 samples "Someday We'll Be Together" by Diana Ross & The Supremes		Virgin 12676
10/23/93	1 (2)	22	▲	20. **Again** — Airplay #1 (4) / Sales #2 from the movie *Poetic Justice* starring Jackson and 2 Pac		Virgin 38404
1/29/94	10	16		21. **Because Of Love** — Airplay #6 / Sales #29		Virgin 38422
5/28/94	2 (1)	19	●	22. **Any Time, Any Place /** — Airplay #3 / Sales #5 #1 R&B hit (10 weeks)		Virgin 38435
5/28/94		19		23. And On And On — Airplay #38 samples "Family Affair" by Sly & The Family Stone		
10/29/94	8	19	●	24. **You Want This /** — Airplay #9 / Sales #12 MC Lyte (rap)		Virgin 38455
11/5/94		17		25. 70's Love Groove #26 & 28: previously unreleased bonus tracks		
6/17/95	5	9	▲	26. **Scream** — Sales #3 / Airplay #12 **MICHAEL JACKSON & JANET JACKSON**		Epic 78000
9/16/95	3	22	●	27. **Runaway** — Sales #3 / Airplay #3		A&M 1194

DATE	POS	WKS	ARTIST–RECORD TITLE	LABEL & NO.
			JANET:	
9/13/97	36 A	3	28. Got 'Til It's Gone **JANET Featuring Q-Tip and Joni Mitchell** samples "Big Yellow Taxi" by Joni Mitchell; from the album *The Velvet Rope* on Virgin 44762	album cut
12/20/97+	1 (2)	34	● 29. **Together Again** Sales #3 / Airplay #8	Virgin 38623
5/23/98	3	12	● 30. **I Get Lonely** Sales #2 / Airplay #24 **JANET (Featuring BLACKstreet)** #1 R&B hit (2 weeks)	Virgin 38631
7/25/98	28 A	16	31. Go Deep from the album *The Velvet Rope* on Virgin 44762	album cut
3/27/99	3	13	● 32. **What's It Gonna Be?!** Sales #2 / Airplay #9 **BUSTA RHYMES Featuring Janet** #1 R&B hit (1 week); Antoinette Roberson (backing vocal)	Elektra 64051
7/8/00	1 (3)	20	● 33. **Doesn't Really Matter** Sales #1 (2) / Airplay #2 from the movie *Nutty Professor 2: The Klumps* starring Eddie Murphy and Janet Jackson	Def Jam 562846
3/17/01	1 (7)	20	34. **All For You** Sales #1 (4) / Airplay #1 (2) #1 R&B hit (2 weeks); samples "The Glow Of Love" by Change	Virgin 97522
6/30/01	3	17	35. **Someone To Call My Lover** Sales #1 (3) / Airplay #9 samples "Ventura Highway" by America	Virgin 38799
12/8/01	28	5	36. Son Of A Gun (I Betcha Think This Song Is About You) Airplay #26 **JANET Featuring Missy Elliott and P. Diddy with Carly Simon** samples "You're So Vain" by Carly Simon	Virgin 46171
8/24/02	28	4	37. Feel It Boy Sales #12 / Airplay #30 **BEENIE MAN feat. JANET**	Virgin 38846
			JACKSON, Jermaine	
			Born on 12/11/54 in Gary, Indiana. Fourth eldest of The Jacksons. Vocalist/bassist of The Jackson 5 until group left Motown in 1976. Married to Hazel Gordy (daughter of Berry Gordy) from 1973-87. Rejoined The Jacksons in 1984 for the group's *Victory* album and tour.	
1/13/73	9	13	1. **Daddy's Home**	Motown 1216
5/3/80	9	14	2. **Let's Get Serious** #1 R&B hit (6 weeks)	Motown 1469
8/30/80	34	4	3. You're Supposed To Keep Your Love For Me above 2 written, produced and arranged by Stevie Wonder	Motown 1490
8/21/82	18	7	4. Let Me Tickle Your Fancy Devo (backing vocals)	Motown 1628
8/4/84	15	10	5. Dynamite	Arista 9190
11/17/84+	13	12	6. Do What You Do Airplay #12 / Sales #14 #1 Adult Contemporary hit (3 weeks)	Arista 9279
3/15/86	16	9	7. I Think It's Love Sales #16 / Airplay #16	Arista 9444
			JACKSON, Joe	
			Born on 8/11/55 in Burton-on-Trent, Staffordshire, England. Singer/songwriter/pianist.	
7/7/79	21	8	1. Is She Really Going Out With Him?	A&M 2132
10/16/82	6	15	2. **Steppin' Out**	A&M 2428
2/5/83	18	10	3. Breaking Us In Two	A&M 2510
5/5/84	15	9	4. You Can't Get What You Want (Till You Know What You Want)	A&M 2628

DATE	POS	WKS	ARTIST–RECORD TITLE	LABEL & NO.
			JACKSON, Michael	
			Born on 8/29/58 in Gary, Indiana. Self-proclaimed "King of Pop." Lead singer of The Jackson 5. Played "The Scarecrow" in the 1978 movie musical *The Wiz*. Starred in the 15-minute movie *Captain Eo*, which was shown exclusively at Disneyland and Disneyworld. His 1988 autobiography, *Moonwalker*, became a movie the same year. Won Grammy's Living Legends Award in 1993. Married to Elvis Presley's daughter, Lisa Marie, from 1994-96. Inducted into the Rock and Roll Hall of Fame in 2001.	
11/6/71	4	13	1. **Got To Be There**	Motown 1191
3/18/72	2 (2)	11	2. **Rockin' Robin**	Motown 1197
6/10/72	16	9	3. I Wanna Be Where You Are	Motown 1202
9/9/72	1 (1)	11	4. **Ben**	Motown 1207
			title song from the movie starring Lee Montgomery	
7/12/75	23	6	5. Just A Little Bit Of You	Motown 1349
9/1/79	1 (1)	12	▲ 6. **Don't Stop 'Til You Get Enough**	Epic 50742
			#1 R&B hit (5 weeks)	
11/24/79+	1 (4)	19	▲ 7. **Rock With You**	Epic 50797
			#1 R&B hit (6 weeks)	
2/23/80	10	11	● 8. **Off The Wall**	Epic 50838
5/10/80	10	11	● 9. **She's Out Of My Life**	Epic 50871
11/13/82+	2 (3)	14	● 10. **The Girl Is Mine**	Epic 03288
			MICHAEL JACKSON/PAUL McCARTNEY	
			#1 R&B hit (3 weeks) / #1 Adult Contemporary hit (4 weeks)	
1/29/83	1 (7)	17	▲ 11. **Billie Jean**	Epic 03509
			#1 R&B hit (9 weeks)	
3/19/83	1 (3)	18	▲ 12. **Beat It**	Epic 03759
			#1 R&B hit (1 week); Eddie Van Halen (lead guitar); 1983 Grammy winner: Record of the Year	
6/4/83	5	11	13. **Wanna Be Startin' Somethin'**	Epic 03914
7/30/83	7	11	14. **Human Nature**	Epic 04026
			also see "Right Here/Human Nature" by SWV	
10/15/83	1 (6)	18	▲ 15. **Say Say Say**	Columbia 04168
			PAUL McCARTNEY AND MICHAEL JACKSON	
10/22/83	10	9	16. **P.Y.T. (Pretty Young Thing)**	Epic 04165
2/11/84	4	9	▲ 17. **Thriller**	Epic 04364
6/23/84	38	3	18. Farewell My Summer Love	Motown 1739
			remix of a recording from 8/31/73	
8/8/87	1 (1)	11	● 19. **I Just Can't Stop Loving You** Sales #1 (1) / Airplay #1 (1)	Epic 07253
			#1 R&B hit (1 week) / #1 Adult Contemporary hit (3 weeks); Siedah Garrett (backing vocal)	
9/19/87	1 (2)	11	20. **Bad** Sales #1 (2) / Airplay #1 (2)	Epic 07418
			#1 R&B hit (3 weeks); Jimmy Smith (organ solo)	
11/28/87+	1 (1)	13	21. **The Way You Make Me Feel** Sales #2 / Airplay #3	Epic 07645
			#1 R&B hit (1 week)	
2/13/88	1 (2)	13	22. **Man In The Mirror** Airplay #1 (3) / Sales #1 (2)	Epic 07668
			#1 R&B hit (1 week); Siedah Garrett, Winans and Andrae Crouch Choir (backing vocals)	
5/14/88	1 (1)	11	23. **Dirty Diana** Sales #1 (1) / Airplay #3	Epic 07739
			featuring Steve Stevens (Billy Idol's guitarist)	
8/6/88	11	8	24. **Another Part Of Me** Sales #8 / Airplay #10	Epic 07962
			#1 R&B hit (1 week)	
11/26/88+	7	11	25. **Smooth Criminal** Sales #5 / Airplay #9	Epic 08044
11/23/91	1 (7)	15	▲ 26. **Black Or White** Sales #1 (4) / Airplay #1 (4)	Epic 74100
			Bill Bottrell (rap); Slash (of Guns N' Roses; guitar)	

DATE	POS	WKS	ARTIST–RECORD TITLE	LABEL & NO.
2/1/92	3	16	● 27. **Remember The Time** — Airplay #1 (2) / Sales #5 #1 R&B hit (2 weeks)	Epic 74200
5/2/92	6	11	● 28. **In The Closet** — Airplay #5 / Sales #15 #1 R&B hit (1 week); features the "Mystery Girl" vocal (Princess Stephanie of Monaco)	Epic 74266
7/18/92	26	9	29. Jam — Sales #19 / Airplay #21 Heavy D (rap)	Epic 74333
2/27/93	27	8	30. Heal The World — Sales #18 / Airplay #24	Epic 74708
4/17/93	14	10	31. Who Is It — Airplay #14 / Sales #26	Epic 74406
7/31/93	7	15	● 32. **Will You Be There** — Airplay #6 / Sales #12 from the movie *Free Willy* starring Jason James Richter	Epic 77060
6/17/95	5	9	▲ 33. **Scream /** — Sales #3 / Airplay #12 **MICHAEL JACKSON & JANET JACKSON**	
6/17/95		9	34. Childhood — Sales: flip theme from the movie *Free Willy 2* starring Jason James Richter	Epic 78000
9/2/95	1 (1)	14	▲ 35. **You Are Not Alone** — Sales #2 / Airplay #2 #1 R&B hit (4 weeks); written and produced by R. Kelly	Epic 78002
6/8/96	30	5	36. They Don't Care About Us — Sales #12	Epic 78264
9/8/01	10	8	37. **You Rock My World** — Airplay #9	album cut
12/1/01+	14	16	38. Butterflies — Airplay #14 above 2 from the album *Invincible* on Epic 69400	album cut
			JACKSON, Millie	
			Born on 7/15/44 in Thomson, Georgia. R&B singer/songwriter.	
5/13/72	27	6	1. Ask Me What You Want	Spring 123
9/29/73	24	8	2. Hurts So Good from the movie *Cleopatra Jones* starring Tamara Dobson	Spring 139
			JACKSON, Rebbie	
			Born Maureen Jackson on 5/29/50 in Gary, Indiana. Eldest of the nine-sibling Jackson family.	
11/17/84	24	8	● 1. Centipede — Sales #22 written and produced by Michael Jackson	Columbia 04547
			JACKSON, Stonewall	
			Born on 11/6/32 in Emerson, North Carolina. Country singer/guitarist/pianist.	
6/8/59	4	12	1. **Waterloo** #1 Country hit (5 weeks)	Columbia 41393
			JACKSON, Wanda	
			Born on 10/20/37 in Maud, Oklahoma. Country-rockabilly singer/songwriter/guitarist.	
10/10/60	37	1	1. Let's Have A Party	Capitol 4397
8/14/61	29	3	2. Right Or Wrong	Capitol 4553
11/27/61	27	3	3. In The Middle Of A Heartache	Capitol 4635

DATE	POS	WKS	ARTIST–RECORD TITLE	LABEL & NO.
			## JACKSON 5, The	
			Group of brothers from Gary, Indiana: Michael, Jermaine, Marlon, Tito and Jackie Jackson. Known as The Jackson 5 from 1968-75, then changed name to The Jacksons. Brother Randy replaced Jermaine in 1976. Jermaine rejoined the group for 1984's highly publicized *Victory* album and tour. Sisters Janet and Rebbie had own hits. Group inducted into the Rock and Roll Hall of Fame in 1997.	
			THE JACKSON 5:	
12/6/69+	**1** (1)	16	▲ 1. **I Want You Back** #1 R&B hit (4 weeks)	Motown 1157
3/21/70	**1** (2)	12	2. **ABC** #1 R&B hit (4 weeks)	Motown 1163
6/6/70	**1** (2)	12	3. **The Love You Save /** #1 R&B hit (6 weeks)	
8/1/70		4	4. I Found That Girl	Motown 1166
9/19/70	**1** (5)	16	5. **I'll Be There** #1 R&B hit (6 weeks)	Motown 1171
2/6/71	**2** (2)	9	6. **Mama's Pearl**	Motown 1177
4/10/71	**2** (3)	11	7. **Never Can Say Goodbye** #1 R&B hit (3 weeks)	Motown 1179
7/31/71	**20**	6	8. Maybe Tomorrow	Motown 1186
12/25/71+	**10**	8	9. **Sugar Daddy**	Motown 1194
4/29/72	**13**	8	10. Little Bitty Pretty One	Motown 1199
7/29/72	**16**	8	11. Lookin' Through The Windows	Motown 1205
11/18/72	**18**	8	12. Corner Of The Sky from the Broadway musical *Pippin* starring Ben Vereen	Motown 1214
4/14/73	**28**	4	13. Hallelujah Day	Motown 1224
9/22/73	**28**	7	14. Get It Together	Motown 1277
3/30/74	**2** (2)	16	15. **Dancing Machine** #1 R&B hit (1 week)	Motown 1286
11/30/74	**38**	2	16. Whatever You Got, I Want	Motown 1308
2/22/75	**15**	7	17. I Am Love (Parts I & II)	Motown 1310
			THE JACKSONS:	
12/11/76+	**6**	15	▲ 18. **Enjoy Yourself**	Epic/Phil. Int. 50289
5/7/77	**28**	3	19. Show You The Way To Go	Epic/Phil. Int. 50350
3/31/79	**7**	14	▲ 20. **Shake Your Body (Down To The Ground)**	Epic 50656
10/11/80	**12**	9	21. Lovely One	Epic 50938
1/10/81	**22**	8	22. Heartbreak Hotel	Epic 50959
6/30/84	**3**	11	● 23. **State Of Shock** Mick Jagger (guest vocalist)	Epic 04503
8/25/84	**17**	8	24. Torture	Epic 04575
			## JACOBS, Dick, And His Orchestra	
			Born on 3/29/18 in Brooklyn, New York. Died of cancer on 5/20/88 (age 70). Music director of TV's *Your Hit Parade* from 1957-58. A&R director for Coral and Brunswick Records. Author of *Who Wrote That Song*.	
4/7/56	**22**	7	1. "Main Title" And "Molly-O" Jockey #22 / Top 100 #26 from the movie *The Man With The Golden Arm* starring Frank Sinatra	Coral 61606
11/3/56	**16**	9	2. Petticoats Of Portugal Jockey #16 / Top 100 #20 / Juke Box #20 / Best Seller #23	Coral 61724

DATE	POS	WKS	ARTIST–RECORD TITLE	LABEL & NO.
9/16/57	**17**	4	3. Fascination Jockey #17 / Top 100 #52 from the movie *Love In The Afternoon* starring Gary Cooper and Audrey Hepburn	Coral 61864
			JADAKISS — see LOPEZ, Jennifer	
			JADE	
			Female R&B vocal trio: Joi Marshall and Tonya Kelly (both born in Chicago, Illinois) and Di Reed (born in Houston, Texas).	
8/22/92	**16**	13	1. I Wanna Love You Airplay #10 / Sales #27 from the movie *Class Act* starring Kid 'N Play	Giant 18950
1/30/93	**4**	27	● 2. **Don't Walk Away** Airplay #2 / Sales #10	Giant 18686
7/10/93	**22**	8	3. One Woman Airplay #17 / Sales #37	Giant 18606
12/3/94+	**20**	19	4. Every Day Of The Week Airplay #20 / Sales #30	Giant 17988
			JAGGED EDGE	
			Male R&B vocal group from Atlanta, Georgia: identical twin brothers Brian and Brandon Casey, with Richard Wingo and Kyle Norman.	
8/15/98	**23**	6	1. Gotta Be Sales #16	So So Def 79010
12/18/99+	**15**	13	● 2. He Can't Love U Sales #4 / Airplay #43	So So Def 79146
6/3/00	**11**	18	3. Let's Get Married Sales #8 / Airplay #15 #1 R&B hit (3 weeks)	So So Def 79437
1/27/01	**9**	15	4. **Promise** Sales #6 / Airplay #11 #1 R&B hit (2 weeks); samples "I Need Love" by LL Cool J	So So Def 79545
6/23/01	**3**	25	5. **Where The Party At** Sales #1 (3) / Airplay #4 **JAGGED EDGE featuring Nelly** #1 R&B hit (3 weeks)	So So Def 79626
9/14/02	**20**	8	6. Trade It All (Part 2) Airplay #13 **FABOLOUS featuring P. DIDDY & JAGGED EDGE** from the movie *Barbershop* starring Ice Cube (soundtrack on Epic 86575)	album cut
11/16/02	**8**	21	7. **Don't Mess With My Man** Sales #1 (1) / Airplay #8 **NIVEA Featuring Brian & Brandon Casey Of Jagged Edge**	Jive 40041
10/4/03	**6**	22	8. **Walked Outta Heaven** Sales #2 / Airplay #6	So So Def 76974
			JAGGER, Mick	
			Born Michael Phillip Jagger on 7/26/43 in Dartford, Kent, England. Lead singer of The Rolling Stones. Appeared in the movies *Ned Kelly* and *Freejack*. Married to model Bianca Jagger from 1971-80. Married to actress/model Jerry Hall from 1990-99.	
2/16/85	**12**	10	1. Just Another Night Airplay #9 / Sales #12 #1 Mainstream Rock hit (2 weeks)	Columbia 04743
5/25/85	**38**	3	2. Lucky In Love	Columbia 04893
9/7/85	**7**	9	3. **Dancing In The Street** Sales #5 / Airplay #8 **MICK JAGGER/DAVID BOWIE**	EMI America 8288
10/24/87	**39**	1	4. Let's Work Sales #37 / Airplay #39	Columbia 07306
			JAGGERZ, The	
			Pop-rock group from Pittsburgh, Pennsylvania: Donnie Iris (vocals, trumpet), Jimmy Ross (vocals, trombone), Billy Maybray (vocals, bass), Benny Faiella (guitar), Thom Davis (organ) and Jim Pugliano (drums).	
2/14/70	**2 (1)**	11	● 1. **The Rapper**	Kama Sutra 502

DATE	POS	WKS	ARTIST–RECORD TITLE	LABEL & NO.
			JAHEIM	
			Born Jaheim Hoagland in 1979 in New Brunswick, New Jersey. Male rapper.	
2/17/01	26	7	1. Could It Be Sales #4	Warner 16791
4/6/02	28	9	2. Anything Airplay #25	album cut
			JAHEIM Featuring Next	
			from the album *Ghetto Love* on Warner 47452	
12/14/02+	28	9	3. Fabulous Airplay #26	album cut
			JAHEIM Featuring Tha Rayne	
			samples "Wake Up Everybody" by Harold Melvin & The Blue Notes	
4/19/03	20	11	4. Put That Woman First Airplay #19	album cut
			samples "I Forgot To Be Your Lover" by William Bell; above 2 from the album *Still Ghetto* on Warner 48214	
			JAMES, Etta	
			Born Jamesetta Hawkins on 1/25/38 in Los Angeles, California. R&B singer. Nicknamed "Miss Peaches." Inducted into the Rock and Roll Hall of Fame in 1993.	
6/6/60	33	4	1. All I Could Do Was Cry	Argo 5359
11/21/60	34	2	2. My Dearest Darling	Argo 5368
4/3/61	30	4	3. Trust In Me	Argo 5385
			#4 hit for Mildred Bailey in 1937	
9/4/61	39	2	4. Don't Cry, Baby	Argo 5393
3/31/62	37	4	5. Something's Got A Hold On Me	Argo 5409
9/8/62	34	2	6. Stop The Wedding	Argo 5418
5/11/63	25	6	7. Pushover	Argo 5437
12/30/67+	23	7	8. Tell Mama	Cadet 5578
			written by Clarence Carter	
4/6/68	35	4	9. Security	Cadet 5594
			written by Otis Redding	
			JAMES, Joni	
			Born Giavanna Carmello Babbo on 9/22/30 in Chicago, Illinois. White pop singer.	
2/19/55	2 (1)	16	● 1. **How Important Can It Be?**	
			Jockey #2 / Juke Box #6 / Best Seller #8 MGM 11919	
			Ray Charles Singers (backing vocals)	
10/22/55	6	10	2. **You Are My Love** Jockey #6 / Top 100 #15 / Best Seller #18	MGM 12066
8/11/56	30	2	3. Give Us This Day Top 100 #30	MGM 12288
			David Terry (orch., above 3)	
10/20/58	19	8	4. There Goes My Heart Hot 100 #19 / Best Seller #45	MGM 12706
			#13 hit for Enric Madriguera in 1934	
2/16/59	33	4	5. There Must Be A Way	MGM 12746
			#9 hit for both Johnnie Johnston and Charlie Spivak in 1945	
1/25/60	35	3	6. Little Things Mean A Lot	MGM 12849
			#1 hit for Kitty Kallen in 1954	
1/23/61	38	1	7. My Last Date (With You)	MGM 12933
			lyric version of Floyd Cramer's "Last Date"; Tony Acquaviva (orch., above 4)	

DATE	POS	WKS	ARTIST–RECORD TITLE	LABEL & NO.
			JAMES, Rick	
			Born James Johnson on 2/1/48 in Buffalo, New York. Funk-rock singer/songwriter/guitarist/producer.	
8/5/78	**13**	10	1. You And I	Gordy 7156
			#1 R&B hit (2 weeks)	
7/18/81	**40**	2	2. Give It To Me Baby	Gordy 7197
			#1 R&B hit (5 weeks)	
9/5/81	**16**	10	3. Super Freak (Part I)	Gordy 7205
			The Temptations (backing vocals)	
9/24/83	**40**	1	4. Cold Blooded	Gordy 1687
			#1 R&B hit (6 weeks)	
8/18/84	**36**	3	5. 17	Gordy 1730
			JAMES, Sonny	
			Born James Loden on 5/1/29 in Hackleburg, Alabama. Country singer/songwriter/guitarist. Nicknamed "The Southern Gentleman."	
1/5/57	**1 (1)**	17	● 1. **Young Love** Jockey #1(1)/ Best Seller #2/ Top 100 #2/ Juke Box #4	Capitol 3602
			#1 Country hit (9 weeks)	
4/20/57	**25**	1	2. First Date, First Kiss, First Love Jockey #25 / Top 100 #39	Capitol 3674
			JAMES, Tommy, And The Shondells	
			Born Thomas Jackson on 4/29/47 in Dayton, Ohio; raised in Niles, Michigan. Pop-rock singer/songwriter. The Shondells consisted of Eddie Gray (guitar), Ronnie Rosman (organ), Mike Vale (bass) and Pete Lucia (drums).	
6/18/66	**1 (2)**	10	● 1. **Hanky Panky**	Roulette 4686
8/20/66	**21**	5	2. Say I Am (What I Am)	Roulette 4695
12/10/66	**31**	4	3. It's Only Love	Roulette 4710
3/11/67	**4**	12	4. **I Think We're Alone Now**	Roulette 4720
5/6/67	**10**	8	5. **Mirage**	Roulette 4736
7/15/67	**25**	5	6. I Like The Way	Roulette 4756
9/2/67	**18**	6	7. Gettin' Together	Roulette 4762
5/4/68	**3**	13	8. **Mony Mony**	Roulette 7008
11/23/68	**38**	2	9. Do Something To Me	Roulette 7024
12/21/68+	**1 (2)**	15	10. **Crimson And Clover**	Roulette 7028
4/5/69	**7**	8	11. **Sweet Cherry Wine**	Roulette 7039
6/28/69	**2 (3)**	12	12. **Crystal Blue Persuasion**	Roulette 7050
10/25/69	**19**	5	13. Ball Of Fire	Roulette 7060
12/20/69+	**23**	7	14. She	Roulette 7066
			TOMMY JAMES:	
6/26/71	**4**	11	15. **Draggin' The Line**	Roulette 7103
10/23/71	**40**	1	16. I'm Comin' Home	Roulette 7110
			The Stephentown Singers (backing vocals)	
2/23/80	**19**	9	17. Three Times In Love	Millennium 11785
			#1 Adult Contemporary hit (1 week)	
			JAMIES, The	
			White vocal group from Dorchester, Massachusetts: Tom Jameson, his sister Serena Jameson, Jeannie Roy and Arthur Blair.	
9/15/58	**26**	4	1. Summertime, Summertime Hot 100 #26 / Best Seller #28	Epic 9281
8/4/62	**38**	1	2. Summertime, Summertime **[R]**	Epic 9281
			above 2 are the same version	

Enrique Iglesias broke out as part of the Latin music explosion of the late 1990s, along with Ricky Martin and Jennifer Lopez. The son of crooner Julio Iglesias went to #1 with his debut hit, "Bailamos."

Natalie Imbruglia must have been "Torn" by the #42 Hot 100 peak of her biggest hit. Due to a chart quirk, her #1 Airplay hit was unable to reach the Hot 100 until late 1998, when its popularity was already on the decline.

Terry Jacks nearly had a #1 hit as part of the Poppy Family with their #2 hit, "Which Way You Goin' Billy?" Showing that less is sometimes more, he finally topped the charts with his solo debut, "Seasons In The Sun."

Janet Jackson spun five #1 R&B hits from her album *Control.* Interestingly, the one song that didn't hit #1 on the R&B charts, "When I Think Of You," was the only song from the album to hit #1 on the pop charts.

Michael Jackson scored his first #1 hit with the title song to the movie *Ben.* A live version of the song, recorded with his brothers, appeared on Michael's 2003 hits collection, *Number Ones.*

Tommy James And The Shondells recorded the chart-topping "Hanky Panky," a former B-side to a Raindrops hit, in 1963. After being discovered two years later by a Pittsburgh DJ, it became the first of eight Top 10 hits for them.

Ja Rule had a substantial chart career as a solo rapper, but his biggest hits came courtesy of duets. He was featured as a guest on a pair of Jennifer Lopez chart-toppers, and featured Ashanti on his #1 hit "Always On Time."

Elton John provided backing vocals for labelmate Neil Sedaka's #1 hit "Bad Blood." Hopefully there was no bad blood between them when Elton replaced Neil at #1 with his own hit, "Island Girl."

Robert John remade other's popular songs for most of his chart hits, but achieved his only #1 with a song he wrote for himself, "Sad Eyes." Its follow-up, "Lonely Eyes," missed the Top 40, which made his eyes even sadder.

Janis Joplin never lived to see her remake of Kris Kristofferson's hit "Me And Bobby McGee" reach #1. She died of a heroin overdose in October of 1970, five months before the song reached its peak.

Montell Jordan was a big fan of rapper Slick Rick. Not only did he sample his track "Children's Story" for his #1 hit "This Is How We Do It," but he also featured the rapper on his 1996 hit "I Like."

DATE	POS	WKS	ARTIST–RECORD TITLE	LABEL & NO.
			JAN & DEAN	
			Surf-rock male vocal duo from Los Angeles, California: Jan Berry (born on 4/3/41) and Dean Torrence (born on 3/10/40). Jan & Dean and Arnie Ginsburg recorded "Jennie Lee" in Jan's garage. Dean left for a six-month Army Reserve stint, whereupon Jan signed with Arwin and released the record as by Jan & Arnie. Upon Dean's return from the service, Arnie (not to be confused with the famed DJ of the same name) joined the Navy, and Jan & Dean signed with the Dore label. Dean sang lead on "Barbara Ann" by The Beach Boys. Jan was critically injured in a car crash on 4/12/66. Duo made a comeback in 1978, after their biographical movie *Dead Man's Curve* aired on TV. Jan died of a seizure on 3/26/2004 (age 62).	
5/26/58	8	11	1. **Jennie Lee** Best Seller #8 / Top 100 #8 / Jockey #17 **JAN & ARNIE** Don Ralke (orch.)	Arwin 108
8/10/59	10	9	2. **Baby Talk**	Dore 522
7/10/61	25	4	3. Heart And Soul #1 hit for Larry Clinton in 1938	Challenge 9111
4/20/63	28	5	4. Linda #1 hit for Buddy Clark in 1947	Liberty 55531
6/22/63	1 (2)	11	5. **Surf City** Brian Wilson (backing vocal)	Liberty 55580
9/21/63	11	8	6. Honolulu Lulu	Liberty 55613
12/21/63+	10	9	7. **Drag City**	Liberty 55641
3/28/64	8	11	8. **Dead Man's Curve /**	
4/4/64	37	4	9. The New Girl In School	Liberty 55672
7/4/64	3	10	10. **The Little Old Lady (From Pasadena)**	Liberty 55704
10/10/64	16	5	11. Ride The Wild Surf title song from the movie starring Tab Hunter and Fabian	Liberty 55724
11/21/64	25	5	12. Sidewalk Surfin'	Liberty 55727
6/26/65	27	4	13. You Really Know How To Hurt A Guy	Liberty 55792
11/13/65	30	2	14. I Found A Girl	Liberty 55833
6/18/66	21	6	15. Popsicle	Liberty 55886
			JANKOWSKI, Horst	
			Born on 1/30/36 in Berlin, Germany. Died of cancer on 6/29/98 (age 62). Jazz pianist.	
6/5/65	12	9	1. A Walk In The Black Forest [I] #1 Adult Contemporary hit (2 weeks)	Mercury 72425
			JARMELS, The	
			R&B vocal group from Richmond, Virginia: Nathaniel Ruff, Ray Smith, Paul Burnett, Tom Eldridge and Earl Christian. Eldridge died on 6/19/2000 (age 59). Burnett died on 3/21/2001 (age 55).	
8/28/61	12	6	1. A Little Bit Of Soap	Laurie 3098
			JARREAU, Al	
			Born on 3/12/40 in Milwaukee, Wisconsin. R&B/jazz-styled singer.	
9/12/81	15	11	1. We're In This Love Together	Warner 49746
4/23/83	21	6	2. Mornin' **JARREAU**	Warner 29720
7/4/87	23	5	3. Moonlighting (Theme) Sales #13 / Airplay #37 #1 Adult Contemporary hit (1 week); theme from the TV series starring Bruce Willis and Cybill Shepherd	MCA 53124

DATE	POS	WKS	ARTIST–RECORD TITLE	LABEL & NO.
			JARS OF CLAY	
			Christian pop group formed in Illinois: Dan Haseltine (vocals), Steve Mason and Matt Odmark (guitars), and Charlie Lowell (keyboards).	
6/1/96	**37**	5	1. Flood Airplay #32 / Sales #48 produced by Adrian Belew	Silvertone 42375
			JA RULE	
			Born Jeffrey Atkins on 2/29/76 in Queens, New York. Male rapper/actor. Appeared in the movies *The Fast And The Furious* and *Half Past Dead*.	
6/5/99	**35**	7	1. Holla Holla Sales #13 / Airplay #46	Def Jam 566959
10/7/00	**11**	15	2. Between Me And You Airplay #7 **JA RULE (Featuring Christina Milian)**	Def Jam 562890
1/20/01	**8**	22	3. Put It On Me Airplay #4 / Sales #62 **JA RULE (feat. Lil' Mo and Vita)**	Def Jam 572751
6/16/01	**40**	2	4. I Cry Airplay #34 **JA RULE (Feat. Lil' Mo)** samples "Cry Together" by The O'Jays	Def Jam 572856
7/14/01	**1 (5)**	29	5. I'm Real Airplay #1 (6) / Sales #31 **JENNIFER LOPEZ featuring Ja Rule** samples "All Night Long" by the Mary Jane Girls	Epic 79639
9/15/01	**6**	23	6. Livin' It Up Airplay #6 / Sales #29 **JA RULE (feat. Case)** samples "Do I Do" by Stevie Wonder	Def Jam 588741
12/1/01+	**1 (2)**	24	7. Always On Time Airplay #1 (2) / Sales #27 **JA RULE (feat. Ashanti)** #1 R&B hit (8 weeks)	Def Jam 588795
1/19/02	**1 (6)**	23	8. Ain't It Funny Airplay #1 (6) **JENNIFER LOPEZ featuring Ja Rule** samples "Flava In Ya Ear" by Craig Mack; from the album *J.Lo* on Epic 85965	album cut
4/13/02	**12**	14	9. Rainy Dayz Airplay #10 / Sales #60 **MARY J. BLIGE Featuring Ja Rule**	MCA 155972
5/11/02	**21**	9	10. Down A** Chick Airplay #20 / Sales #63 **JA RULE feat. Charli "Chuck" Baltimore**	Def Jam 063946
6/29/02	**6**	15	11. Down 4 U Airplay #6 **IRV GOTTI PRESENTS THE INC. Featuring Ja Rule, Ashanti, Charli Baltimore & Vita** from the album *Irv Gotti Presents The Inc.* on Murder Inc. 062033	album cut
1/4/03	**2 (1)**	17	12. Mesmerize Airplay #2 / Sales #23 **JA RULE feat. Ashanti** samples "Stop, Look, Listen" by The Stylistics	Murder Inc. 063773
			JAY & THE AMERICANS	
			Vocal group formed in New York: John "Jay" Traynor, Sandy Yaguda, Kenny Vance and Howie Kane, with Marty Sanders (guitar). Traynor left after "She Cried" and was replaced by lead singer Jay Black (born David Blatt on 11/2/41).	
4/7/62	**5**	11	1. **She Cried**	United Artists 415
9/21/63	**25**	4	2. Only In America	United Artists 626
10/3/64	**3**	11	3. **Come A Little Bit Closer**	United Artists 759
1/16/65	**11**	7	4. Let's Lock The Door (And Throw Away The Key)	United Artists 805
6/19/65	**4**	11	5. **Cara, Mia**	United Artists 881
9/25/65	**13**	6	6. Some Enchanted Evening #1 hit for Perry Como in 1949; from the musical *South Pacific*	United Artists 919

DATE	POS	WKS	ARTIST–RECORD TITLE	LABEL & NO.
12/4/65	**18**	6	7. Sunday And Me *written by Neil Diamond*	United Artists 948
6/11/66	**25**	4	8. Crying	United Artists 50016
1/25/69	**6**	10	● 9. **This Magic Moment**	United Artists 50475
1/17/70	**19**	7	10. Walkin' In The Rain	United Artists 50605
			JAY AND THE TECHNIQUES	
			Interracial R&B-rock group from Allentown, Pennsylvania: Jay Proctor (born on 10/28/40), Karl Landis, Ronnie Goosly, John Walsh, George Lloyd, Chuck Crowl and Dante Dancho.	
8/19/67	**6**	11	1. **Apples, Peaches, Pumpkin Pie**	Smash 2086
11/11/67	**14**	9	2. Keep The Ball Rollin'	Smash 2124
2/10/68	**39**	2	3. Strawberry Shortcake	Smash 2142
			JAYE, Jerry	
			Born Gerald Jaye Hatley on 10/19/37 in Manila, Arkansas.	
5/6/67	**29**	6	1. My Girl Josephine	Hi 2120
			JAYHAWKS, The — see VIBRATIONS, The	
			JAYNETTS, The	
			Female R&B vocal group from the Bronx, New York: Ethel Davis, Mary Sue Wells, Yvonne Bushnell and Ada Ray.	
9/7/63	**2 (2)**	9	1. **Sally, Go 'Round The Roses**	Tuff 369
			JAY-Z	
			Born Shawn Carter on 12/4/69 in Brooklyn, New York. Male rapper/songwriter. Founded the Roc-A-Fella record label. Appeared in the movie *State Property*.	
3/22/97	**7**	11	● 1. **I'll Be** Sales #2 / Airplay #52 **FOXY BROWN Featuring Jay-Z** samples "I'll Be Good" by Rene & Angela	Violator 574028
11/14/98+	**15**	16	● 2. Hard Knock Life (Ghetto Anthem) Sales #5 / Airplay #23 samples "Hard Knock Life" by The Original Broadway Cast of *Annie*	Roc-A-Fella 566977
11/14/98+	**19**	23	3. Can I Get A... Airplay #9 **JAY-Z (featuring Amil of Major Coinz) and Ja** from the movie *Rush Hour* starring Jackie Chan	Def Jam 567683
9/4/99	**28**	4	4. Jigga My Nigga Sales #10 / Airplay #47	Roc-A-Fella 562201
9/11/99	**1 (2)**	14	● 5. **Heartbreaker** Sales #1 (2) / Airplay #8 **MARIAH CAREY (Featuring Jay-Z)** #1 R&B hit (2 weeks); samples "Attack Of The Name Game" by Stacy Lattisaw	Columbia 79260
5/6/00	**18**	16	6. Big Pimpin' Airplay #13 **JAY-Z (featuring UGK)**	Roc-A-Fella 562670
11/11/00	**11**	19	7. I Just Wanna Love U (Give It 2 Me) Airplay #7 / Sales #34 #1 R&B hit (3 weeks); samples "Give It To Me Baby" by Rick James and "The World Is Filled..." by The Notorious B.I.G.	Roc-A-Fella 572666
4/28/01	**6**	15	8. **Fiesta Remix** Sales #4 / Airplay #12 **R. KELLY (Featuring Jay-Z and Boo & Gotti)** #1 R&B hit (5 weeks)	Jive 42904
8/4/01	**8**	17	9. Izzo (H.O.V.A.) Airplay #7 / Sales #19 samples "I Want You Back" by The Jackson 5	Roc-A-Fella 588701

DATE	POS	WKS	ARTIST–RECORD TITLE	LABEL & NO.
11/3/01	**17**	8	10. Girls, Girls, Girls Airplay #15 / Sales #32 Q-Tip, Slick Rick and Biz Markie (backing vocals); samples "I Love You More And More Every Time" performed by Tom Brock	Roc-A-Fella 588793
11/2/02	**4**	21	11. **'03 Bonnie & Clyde** Airplay #4 / Sales #15 **JAY-Z Featuring Beyoncé Knowles** samples "If I Was Your Girlfriend" by Prince	Roc-A-Fella 063843
2/22/03	**8**	13	12. **Excuse Me Miss** Airplay #8 / Sales #14 #1 R&B hit (1 week)	Roc-A-Fella 063717
5/10/03	**33**	2	13. Beware Of The Boys (Mundian To Bach Ke) Sales #7 / Airplay #36 **PAN'JABI MC Featuring JAY-Z** Indian vocals by Labh Janjua; samples the theme from TV's *Knight Rider*	Sequence 8012
5/31/03	**1 (8)**	24	14. **Crazy In Love** Airplay #1 (8) / Sales #11 **BEYONCÉ (Featuring Jay-Z)** #1 R&B hit (3 weeks); samples "Are You My Woman (Tell Me So)" by The Chi-Lites	Columbia 79949
7/26/03	**5**	16	15. **Frontin'** Airplay #5 / Sales #7 **PHARRELL Featuring Jay-Z** #1 R&B hit (6 weeks)	Star Trak 58647
11/22/03	**10**	11	16. **Change Clothes** Airplay #12 / Sales #14 Danne Doty (additional vocals)	Roc-A-Fella 001651
			JAZZY JEFF — see D.J. JAZZY JEFF	
			JB's, The Funk group led by Fred Wesley. Backing group for James Brown.	
6/23/73	**22**	6	● 1. Doing It To Death **FRED WESLEY & THE J.B's** #1 R&B hit (2 weeks); written, produced and arranged by James Brown	People 621
			JD — see DUPRI, Jermaine	
			JEAN, Wyclef Born on 10/17/72 in Croix Des Bouquets, Haiti; raised in Brooklyn, New York. Hip-hop singer/songwriter/guitarist/producer. Member of The Fugees.	
12/20/97+	**3**	31	▲ 1. **No, No, No Part 2** Sales #1 (1) / Airplay #22 **DESTINY'S CHILD (featuring Wyclef Jean)** #1 R&B hit (1 week)	Columbia 78618
2/7/98	**7**	18	▲ 2. **Gone Till November** Sales #4 / Airplay #48 R. Kelly (backing vocal)	Ruffhouse 78752
11/25/00	**38**	2	3. 911 Airplay #30 / Sales #61 **WYCLEF JEAN Featuring Mary J. Blige** samples "The Payback" by James Brown and "What I Am" by Edie Brickell & New Bohemians	Columbia 79460
8/3/02	**28**	6	4. Two Wrongs Sales #1 (3) / Airplay #46 **WYCLEF JEAN feat. Claudette Ortiz of City High**	Columbia 79776
			JEFFERSON Born Geoff Turton on 3/11/44 in Birmingham, England. Male singer.	
1/24/70	**23**	6	1. Baby Take Me In Your Arms	Janus 106

DATE	POS	WKS	ARTIST—RECORD TITLE	LABEL & NO.
			JEFFERSON AIRPLANE/STARSHIP	
			Rock group formed as Jefferson Airplane in San Francisco, California: Marty Balin and Grace Slick (vocals), Paul Kantner (vocals, guitar), Jorma Kaukonen (guitar), Jack Casady (bass) and Spencer Dryden (drums). Group changed name to Jefferson Starship in 1974: Balin, Slick, Kantner, Craig Chaquico (guitar), Pete Sears (keyboards), David Freiberg (bass) and John Barbata (drums). Papa John Creach (violin) sat in occasionally (he died on 2/22/94, age 76). Slick left group from June 1978 to January 1981. Balin and Barbata left in 1979, replaced by Mickey Thomas (sang lead on Elvin Bishop's "Fooled Around And Fell In Love") and Aynsley Dunbar (former drummer for Frank Zappa). Dunbar left in early 1982, replaced by Don Baldwin. Kantner left in late 1984 and, due to legal difficulties, band's name was shortened to Starship, whose lineup included Slick, Thomas, Sears, Chaquico and Baldwin. Slick left in early 1988. Continuing as Starship were Thomas, Chaquico, Baldwin, Brett Bloomfield (bass) and Mark Morgan (keyboards). Starship disbanded in 1990. Jefferson Airplane was inducted into the Rock and Roll Hall of Fame in 1996.	
			JEFFERSON AIRPLANE:	
5/6/67	5	9	1. **Somebody To Love**	RCA Victor 9140
7/1/67	8	9	2. **White Rabbit**	RCA Victor 9248
			JEFFERSON STARSHIP:	
9/13/75	3	13	3. **Miracles**	Grunt 10367
8/14/76	12	11	4. With Your Love	Grunt 10746
3/25/78	8	11	5. **Count On Me**	Grunt 11196
6/24/78	12	8	6. Runaway	Grunt 11274
11/24/79+	14	10	7. Jane	Grunt 11750
5/2/81	29	6	8. Find Your Way Back	Grunt 12211
11/13/82	28	6	9. Be My Lady	Grunt 13350
3/19/83	38	2	10. Winds Of Change	Grunt 13439
6/9/84	23	8	11. No Way Out #1 Mainstream Rock hit (1 week)	Grunt 13811
			STARSHIP:	
9/28/85	1 (2)	15	● 12. **We Built This City** Airplay #1 (2) / Sales #2 #1 Mainstream Rock hit (1 week); Les Garland (DJ voice)	Grunt 14170
1/18/86	1 (1)	13	13. **Sara** Sales #1 (1) / Airplay #1 (1) #1 Adult Contemporary hit (3 weeks)	Grunt 14253
4/26/86	26	6	14. Tomorrow Doesn't Matter Tonight Airplay #25 / Sales #27	Grunt 14332
2/14/87	1 (2)	15	● 15. **Nothing's Gonna Stop Us Now** Airplay #1 (3) / Sales #1 (2) #1 Adult Contemporary hit (2 weeks); from the movie *Mannequin* starring Kim Catrall and Andrew McCarthy	Grunt 5109
7/18/87	9	10	16. **It's Not Over ('Til It's Over)** Sales #9 / Airplay #13	RCA/Grunt 5225
8/26/89	12	9	17. It's Not Enough Airplay #11 / Sales #15	RCA 9032
			JEFFREY, Joe, Group	
			Born in Buffalo, New York. R&B singer/guitarist.	
7/5/69	14	8	1. My Pledge Of Love	Wand 11200
			JELLYBEAN	
			Born John Benitez on 11/7/57 in the Bronx, New York. Renowned club DJ/remixer/producer.	
12/21/85+	18	9	1. **Sidewalk Talk** Sales #15 / Airplay #19 Catherine Buchanan (lead vocal); written and background vocal by Madonna	EMI America 8297

DATE	POS	WKS	ARTIST–RECORD TITLE	LABEL & NO.
8/15/87	**16**	8	2. Who Found Who　　　　　Airplay #13 / Sales #14 **JELLYBEAN/Elisa Fiorillo**	Chrysalis 43120

JELLY BEANS, The

R&B vocal group from Jersey City, New Jersey: sisters Elyse and Maxine Herbert, Alma Brewer, Diane Taylor and Charles Thomas.

DATE	POS	WKS	ARTIST–RECORD TITLE	LABEL & NO.
7/18/64	**9**	7	1. **I Wanna Love Him So Bad**	Red Bird 10-003

JENKINS, Gordon — see ARMSTRONG, Louis

JENNINGS, Waylon

Born on 6/15/37 in Littlefield, Texas. Died of diabetes on 2/13/2002 (age 64). Legendary country singer/songwriter/guitarist. Bass player for Buddy Holly on the fateful "Winter Dance Party" tour in 1959 (gave up his plane seat to the Big Bopper). Established himself in the mid-1970s as a leader of the "outlaw" movement in country music. Married to Jessi Colter since 1969. Narrator for TV's *The Dukes Of Hazzard*.

DATE	POS	WKS	ARTIST–RECORD TITLE	LABEL & NO.
3/6/76	**25**	5	1. Good Hearted Woman　　　　　　**[L]** **WAYLON & WILLIE** #1 Country hit (3 weeks)	RCA Victor 10529
6/11/77	**25**	7	2. Luckenbach, Texas (Back to the Basics of Love) #1 Country hit (6 weeks); Willie Nelson (ending vocal)	RCA 10924
11/1/80	**21**	10	● 3. Theme From The Dukes Of Hazzard (Good Ol' Boys) #1 Country hit (1 week)	RCA 12067

JENSEN, Kris

Born Peter Jensen on 4/4/42 in New Haven, Connecticut. Pop singer/guitarist.

DATE	POS	WKS	ARTIST–RECORD TITLE	LABEL & NO.
10/6/62	**20**	6	1. Torture written by John D. Loudermilk	Hickory 1173

JESUS JONES

Alternative pop-rock group formed in London, England: Mike Edwards (vocals, guitar), Jerry DeBorg (guitar), Iain Baker (keyboards), Al Jaworski (bass) and Simon Matthews (drums).

DATE	POS	WKS	ARTIST–RECORD TITLE	LABEL & NO.
5/25/91	**2 (1)**	15	1. **Right Here, Right Now**　　　Airplay #3 / Sales #9 #1 Modern Rock hit (5 weeks)	SBK/Food 07345
9/14/91	**4**	10	2. **Real, Real, Real**　　　　　Airplay #30 / Sales #67	SBK/Food 07364

JETHRO TULL

Progressive-rock group formed in Blackpool, England: Ian Anderson (vocals, flute), Martin Barre (guitar), John Evan (keyboards), Jeffrey Hammond-Hammond (bass) and Barriemore Barlow (drums). Group named after 18th-century agriculturist/inventor of seed drill.

DATE	POS	WKS	ARTIST–RECORD TITLE	LABEL & NO.
11/25/72+	**11**	10	1. Living In The Past	Chrysalis 2006
11/30/74+	**12**	10	2. Bungle In The Jungle	Chrysalis 2101

JETS, The

Family group from Minneapolis, Minnesota: siblings Leroy, Eddie, Eugene, Haini, Rudy, Kathi, Elizabeth and Moana Wolfgramm. Their parents are from the South Pacific country of Tonga. All members play at least two instruments. Eugene left group and formed duo Boys Club in 1988.

DATE	POS	WKS	ARTIST–RECORD TITLE	LABEL & NO.
5/3/86	**3**	13	1. **Crush On You**　　　　　Sales #3 / Airplay #4	MCA 52774
1/17/87	**3**	12	2. **You Got It All**　　　　　Sales #3 / Airplay #3 #1 Adult Contemporary hit (2 weeks)	MCA 52968

DATE	POS	WKS	ARTIST–RECORD TITLE	LABEL & NO.
6/27/87	7	11	3. **Cross My Broken Heart** Sales #7 / Airplay #8 from the movie *Beverly Hills Cop II* starring Eddie Murphy	MCA 53123
11/14/87	20	6	4. I Do You Sales #15 / Airplay #21	MCA 53193
2/13/88	6	13	5. **Rocket 2 U** Sales #4 / Airplay #7	MCA 53254
5/7/88	4	13	6. **Make It Real** Sales #2 / Airplay #4 #1 Adult Contemporary hit (3 weeks)	MCA 53311

JETT, Joan, & The Blackhearts

Born Joan Larkin on 9/22/58 in Philadelphia, Pennsylvania. Rock singer/guitarist. Member of The Runaways from 1975-78. The Blackhearts consisted of Ricky Byrd (guitar), Gary Ryan (bass) and Lee Crystal (drums). Kasim Sulton (of Utopia) and Thommy Price replaced Ryan and Crystal in 1987. Jett starred in the 1987 movie *Light Of Day* as the leader of a rock band called The Barbusters.

DATE	POS	WKS	ARTIST–RECORD TITLE	LABEL & NO.
2/13/82	1 (7)	16	▲ 1. **I Love Rock 'N Roll** #1 Mainstream Rock hit (5 weeks)	Boardwalk 135
5/15/82	7	10	2. **Crimson And Clover**	Boardwalk 144
8/28/82	20	7	3. Do You Wanna Touch Me (Oh Yeah)	Boardwalk 150
7/30/83	35	4	4. Fake Friends	Blackheart/MCA 52240
10/15/83	37	2	5. Everyday People	Blackheart/MCA 52272
3/21/87	33	5	6. Light Of Day Sales #25 **THE BARBUSTERS (JOAN JETT AND THE BLACKHEARTS)** written by Bruce Springsteen; title song from the movie starring Michael J. Fox and Michael McKean	Blackheart 06692
8/13/88	8	12	7. **I Hate Myself For Loving You** Sales #4 / Airplay #11	Blackheart 07919
12/10/88+	19	10	8. Little Liar Sales #15 / Airplay #17	Blackheart 08095
3/3/90	36	2	9. Dirty Deeds Airplay #37 / Sales #39 **JOAN JETT** first recorded by AC/DC in 1976	Blackheart 73215

JEWEL

Born Jewel Kilcher on 5/23/74 in Payson, Utah; raised in Homer, Alaska. Adult Alternative singer/songwriter/guitarist. Wrote own book of poetry. Played "Sue Lee Shelley" in the movie *Ride With The Devil*.

DATE	POS	WKS	ARTIST–RECORD TITLE	LABEL & NO.
6/1/96	11	27	1. Who Will Save Your Soul Airplay #4 / Sales #17	Atlantic 87151
12/21/96+	2 (2)	60	▲ 2. **You Were Meant For Me /** Airplay #1 (9) / Sales #6 #1 Adult Contemporary hit (1 week)	
9/13/97	7	22	3. **Foolish Games** Airplay #1 (3) / Sales #39 from the movie *Batman & Robin* starring George Clooney	Atlantic 87021
12/5/98+	6	15	4. **Hands** Airplay #3 from the album *Spirit* on Atlantic 82950	album cut
12/29/01+	25	11	5. Standing Still Airplay #29 from the album *This Way* on Atlantic 83519	album cut
6/7/03	20	12	6. Intuition Sales #3 / Airplay #22	Atlantic 88108

JEWELL, Buddy

Born on 4/2/61 in Lepanto, Arkansas. Country singer/songwriter. Winner of TV's first *Nashville Star* talent series.

DATE	POS	WKS	ARTIST–RECORD TITLE	LABEL & NO.
9/13/03	29	5	1. Help Pour Out The Rain (Lacey's Song) Sales #3 / Airplay #27 produced by Clint Black	Columbia 79885

DATE	POS	WKS	ARTIST–RECORD TITLE	LABEL & NO.
			JIGSAW	
			Pop group from England: Des Dyer (vocals, drums), Tony Campbell (guitar), Clive Scott (keyboards) and Barrie Bernard (bass).	
10/11/75	3	14	1. **Sky High**	Chelsea 3022
			from the movie The Dragon Flies starring George Lazenby	
3/13/76	30	5	2. Love Fire	Chelsea 3037
			JIMENEZ, Jose	
			Born William Szathmary on 10/5/24 in Quincy, Massachusetts. Stage name: Bill Dana. Head comedy writer for TV's *Steve Allen Show*. Star of own TV series from 1963-65.	
9/18/61	19	4	1. The Astronaut (Parts 1 & 2) [C-L]	Kapp 409
			interviewed by Don Hinckley	
			JIMMY EAT WORLD	
			Rock group from Mesa, Arizona: Jim Adkins (vocals), Tom Linton (guitar), Rick Burch (bass) and Zach Lind (drums).	
4/20/02	5	26	1. **The Middle** Airplay #5	album cut
			#1 Modern Rock hit (4 weeks); from the album Jimmy Eat World (originally titled Bleed American) on DreamWorks 450334	
			JIVE BOMBERS, The	
			R&B vocal group from Harlem, New York: Clarence Palmer, Earl Johnson, Al Tinney and William Tinney. Al Tinney died of cancer on 12/11/2002 (age 81).	
3/16/57	36	1	1. Bad Boy Top 100 #36	Savoy 1508
			written and recorded by Lil Armstrong as "Brown Gal" in 1936 on Decca 1092 ($50)	
			JIVE BUNNY AND THE MASTERMIXERS	
			Dance group from England: DJ Les Hemstock and mixers John Pickles, his son Andy Pickles and Ian Morgan.	
11/25/89+	11	11	● 1. Swing The Mood Sales #2 / Airplay #27	Music Fac./Atco 99140
			medley: Let's Twist Again/In The Mood/Rock Around The Clock/Rock-A-Beatin' Boogie/Tutti Fruitti/Wake Up Little Susie/C'mon Everybody/Hound Dog/Shake, Rattle & Roll/All Shook Up/Jailhouse Rock/At The Hop	
			JIVE FIVE, The	
			R&B vocal group from Brooklyn, New York: Eugene Pitt, Jerome Hanna, Billy Prophet, Norman Johnson and Richard Harris. Johnson died in 1970.	
8/14/61	3	12	1. **My True Story**	Beltone 1006
			#1 R&B hit (3 weeks)	
9/11/65	36	3	2. I'm A Happy Man	United Artists 853
			JIVE FIVE (featuring Eugene Pitt)	
			J.J. FAD	
			Female rap trio from Los Angeles, California: Juana Burns, Dania Birks and Michelle Franklin. J.J. Fad stands for Just Jammin' Fresh And Def.	
6/11/88	30	4	● 1. Supersonic Sales #20	Ruthless 99328

DATE	POS	WKS	ARTIST–RECORD TITLE	LABEL & NO.
			JoBOXERS	
			Pop group formed in London, England: Dig Wayne (vocals), Rob Marche (guitar), Dave Collard (keyboards), Chris Bostock (bass) and Sean McLusky (drums).	
11/5/83	36	4	1. Just Got Lucky	RCA 13601
			JODECI	
			R&B vocal group. Two pairs of brothers from Charlotte, North Carolina: Joel "JoJo" and Cedric "K-Ci" Hailey, with Dalvin and Donald "DeVante Swing" DeGrate. The Haileys later recorded as K-Ci & JoJo.	
11/16/91	25	12	1. Forever My Lady Sales #12 / Airplay #29 #1 R&B hit (2 weeks)	Uptown/MCA 54197
5/23/92	11	21	● 2. Come & Talk To Me Sales #9 / Airplay #10 #1 R&B hit (2 weeks)	Uptown/MCA 54175
6/19/93	4	22	● 3. **Lately** Sales #4 / Airplay #9 **[L]** #1 R&B hit (4 weeks); from MTV's *Unplugged* series; written by Stevie Wonder	Uptown/MCA 54652
12/11/93+	15	17	● 4. Cry For You Sales #9 / Airplay #23 #1 R&B hit (4 weeks)	Uptown/MCA 54723
4/2/94	25	8	5. Feenin' Sales #19 / Airplay #37 samples "Get Off My Bandwagon" by EPMD	Uptown/MCA 54798
6/17/95	14	15	● 6. Freek 'n You Sales #5 / Airplay #56	Uptown/MCA 55023
11/18/95+	31	8	7. Love U 4 Life Sales #17 / Airplay #59	Uptown/MCA 55133
6/1/96	22	9	8. Get On Up Sales #12 / Airplay #62 samples "Velas" by Quincy Jones	MCA 55123
			JOE	
			Born Joseph Thomas in 1972 in Cuthbert, Georgia. R&B singer/songwriter/guitarist.	
2/24/96	11	15	● 1. All The Things (Your Man Won't Do) Sales #6 / Airplay #49 from the movie *Don't Be A Menace* starring Marlon Wayans	Island 854530
5/10/97	21	11	● 2. Don't Wanna Be A Player Sales #13 from the movie *Booty Call* starring Jamie Foxx	Jive 42450
6/13/98	24	19	3. **Still Not A Player** Airplay #23 **BIG PUNISHER (Featuring Joe)**	Loud/RCA 65478
2/13/99	10	9	4. **Faded Pictures** Sales #8 / Airplay #56 **CASE & JOE** from the movie *Rush Hour* starring Jackie Chan	Def Jam 566494
1/15/00	1 (1)	11	● 5. Thank God I Found You Sales #1 (3) / Airplay #15 **MARIAH With Joe & 98°** #1 R&B hit (1 week); Trey Lorenz (backing vocal)	Columbia 79338
2/5/00	4	38	6. **I Wanna Know** Airplay #2 from the movie *The Wood* starring Taye Diggs (soundtrack on Jive 41686)	album cut
1/20/01	1 (4)	23	● 7. **Stutter** Sales #1 (5) / Airplay #5 **JOE (featuring Mystikal)** #1 R&B hit (5 weeks); samples "Passin' Me By" by The Pharcyde; from the movie *Double Take* starring Eddie Griffin	Jive 42870

DATE	POS	WKS	ARTIST–RECORD TITLE	LABEL & NO.
			JOEL, Billy	
			Born William Martin Joel on 5/9/49 in the Bronx, New York; raised in Hicksville, Long Island, New York. Pop-rock singer/songwriter/pianist. Member of rock bands The Echoes and The Hassles, and duo Attila in 1960s. Signed solo to Columbia in 1973. In a serious motorcycle accident in Long Island in 1982. Married to supermodel Christie Brinkley from 1985-94. Recipient of Grammy's Living Legends Award in 1990 and *Billboard's* Century Award in 1994. Inducted into the Rock and Roll Hall of Fame in 1999.	
4/6/74	25	4	1. Piano Man	Columbia 45963
12/28/74+	34	5	2. The Entertainer	Columbia 10064
12/10/77+	3	18	● 3. **Just The Way You Are**	Columbia 10646
			#1 Adult Contemporary hit (4 weeks); 1978 Grammy winner: Record of the Year	
4/15/78	17	8	4. Movin' Out (Anthony's Song)	Columbia 10708
6/17/78	24	5	5. Only The Good Die Young	Columbia 10750
9/9/78	17	9	6. She's Always A Woman	Columbia 10788
11/11/78+	3	16	▲ 7. **My Life**	Columbia 10853
			Peter Cetera (backing vocal); later used as the theme song to TV's *Bosom Buddies* starring Tom Hanks	
3/3/79	14	6	8. Big Shot	Columbia 10913
5/12/79	24	4	9. Honesty	Columbia 10959
3/22/80	7	11	10. **You May Be Right**	Columbia 11231
			later used as the theme song to the CBS-TV sitcom *Dave's World* starring Harry Anderson	
5/24/80	1 (2)	19	▲ 11. **It's Still Rock And Roll To Me**	Columbia 11276
8/16/80	19	9	12. Don't Ask Me Why	Columbia 11331
			#1 Adult Contemporary hit (2 weeks)	
11/1/80	36	3	13. Sometimes A Fantasy	Columbia 11379
9/26/81	17	8	14. Say Goodbye To Hollywood　　　[L]	Columbia 02518
			recorded at the Milwaukee Arena; written for Ronnie Spector	
12/12/81+	23	9	15. She's Got A Way　　　[L]	Columbia 02628
			recorded at the Paradise Club in Boston	
10/16/82	20	8	16. Pressure	Columbia 03244
12/18/82+	17	16	17. Allentown	Columbia 03413
7/30/83	1 (1)	15	● 18. **Tell Her About It**	Columbia 04012
			#1 Adult Contemporary hit (2 weeks)	
10/8/83	3	16	● 19. **Uptown Girl**	Columbia 04149
1/7/84	10	11	20. **An Innocent Man**	Columbia 04259
			#1 Adult Contemporary hit (1 week)	
4/7/84	14	11	21. The Longest Time	Columbia 04400
			#1 Adult Contemporary hit (2 weeks)	
8/4/84	27	7	22. Leave A Tender Moment Alone	Columbia 04514
			#1 Adult Contemporary hit (2 weeks)	
2/9/85	18	10	23. Keeping The Faith　　　Airplay #14 / Sales #21	Columbia 04681
7/20/85	9	11	24. **You're Only Human (Second Wind)** Sales #8 / Airplay #9	Columbia 05417
10/26/85	34	3	25. The Night Is Still Young	Columbia 05657
6/21/86	10	9	26. **Modern Woman**　　　Sales #10 / Airplay #10	Epic 06118
			from the movie *Ruthless People* starring Danny DeVito and Bette Midler	
9/6/86	10	10	27. **A Matter Of Trust**　　　Sales #9 / Airplay #17	Columbia 06108
12/20/86+	18	9	28. This Is The Time　　　Sales #14 / Airplay #23	Columbia 06526
			#1 Adult Contemporary hit (3 weeks)	
10/21/89	1 (2)	15	● 29. **We Didn't Start The Fire** Sales #1 (3) / Airplay #1 (1)	Columbia 73021
1/27/90	6	11	30. **I Go To Extremes**　　　Airplay #6 / Sales #8	Columbia 73091

DATE	POS	WKS	ARTIST–RECORD TITLE	LABEL & NO.
11/24/90	37	3	31. And So It Goes Airplay #32 / Sales #36	Columbia 73602
8/7/93	3	24	32. **The River Of Dreams** Airplay #2 / Sales #7	Columbia 77086
			#1 Adult Contemporary hit (12 weeks)	
11/27/93	29	9	33. All About Soul Airplay #24	Columbia 77254
			Color Me Badd (guest vocals)	

JOE PUBLIC

R&B vocal group from Buffalo, New York: Kevin Scott, Joe Carter, Joe Sayles and Dwight Wyatt.

DATE	POS	WKS	ARTIST–RECORD TITLE	LABEL & NO.
3/28/92	4	18	1. **Live And Learn** Airplay #3 / Sales #9	Columbia 74012

JOHN, Elton

Born Reginald Kenneth Dwight on 3/25/47 in Pinner, Middlesex, England. Pop-rock singer/songwriter/pianist. Formed his first group Bluesology. Took the name of Elton John from the first names of Bluesology members Elton Dean and John Baldry. Teamed up with lyricist Bernie Taupin beginning in 1967. Formed Rocket Records in 1973. Played the "Pinball Wizard" in the movie version of *Tommy*. Elton was the #1 pop artist of the 1970s. Inducted into the Rock and Roll Hall of Fame in 1994.

DATE	POS	WKS	ARTIST–RECORD TITLE	LABEL & NO.
12/19/70+	8	11	1. **Your Song**	Uni 55265
4/10/71	34	4	2. Friends	Uni 55277
			title song from the British movie starring Sean Bury	
1/1/72	24	7	3. Levon	Uni 55314
5/27/72	6	12	4. **Rocket Man**	Uni 55328
8/26/72	8	7	5. **Honky Cat**	Uni 55343
12/23/72+	1 (3)	14	▲ 6. **Crocodile Rock**	MCA 40000
4/21/73	2 (1)	12	● 7. **Daniel**	MCA 40046
			#1 Adult Contemporary hit (2 weeks)	
8/11/73	12	9	8. Saturday Night's Alright For Fighting	MCA 40105
11/3/73	2 (3)	14	▲ 9. **Goodbye Yellow Brick Road**	MCA 40148
3/2/74	1 (1)	16	▲ 10. **Bennie And The Jets**	MCA 40198
7/6/74	2 (2)	9	● 11. **Don't Let The Sun Go Down On Me**	MCA 40259
			also see #49 below	
9/21/74	4	9	● 12. **The Bitch Is Back**	MCA 40297
			Dusty Springfield (backing vocal)	
12/7/74+	1 (2)	10	● 13. **Lucy In The Sky With Diamonds**	MCA 40344
			with the Reggae guitars of Dr. Winston O'Boogie (John Lennon); song first recorded by The Beatles in 1967	
3/15/75	1 (2)	17	▲ 14. **Philadelphia Freedom**	MCA 40364
			THE ELTON JOHN BAND	
			inspired by tennis star Billie Jean King and her team, the Philadelphia Freedoms	
7/12/75	4	10	● 15. **Someone Saved My Life Tonight**	MCA 40421
10/18/75	1 (3)	12	▲ 16. **Island Girl**	MCA 40461
1/31/76	14	5	17. Grow Some Funk Of Your Own /	
1/31/76		5	18. I Feel Like A Bullet (In The Gun Of Robert Ford)	MCA 40505
			Ford: the man who shot outlaw Jesse James	
7/17/76	1 (4)	15	● 19. **Don't Go Breaking My Heart**	Rocket 40585
			ELTON JOHN and KIKI DEE	
			#1 Adult Contemporary hit (1 week)	
11/20/76	6	11	● 20. **Sorry Seems To Be The Hardest Word**	MCA/Rocket 40645
			#1 Adult Contemporary hit (1 week)	
2/26/77	28	3	21. Bite Your Lip (Get up and dance!)	MCA/Rocket 40677

DATE	POS	WKS	ARTIST–RECORD TITLE	LABEL & NO.
4/29/78	34	4	22. Ego	MCA 40892
11/18/78	22	7	23. Part-Time Love	MCA 40973
6/23/79	9	14	● 24. **Mama Can't Buy You Love** #1 Adult Contemporary hit (1 week)	MCA 41042
10/27/79	31	4	25. Victim Of Love	MCA 41126
5/10/80	3	17	● 26. **Little Jeannie** #1 Adult Contemporary hit (2 weeks)	MCA 41236
9/20/80	39	2	27. (Sartorial Eloquence) Don't Ya Wanna Play This Game No More?	MCA 41293
5/30/81	21	6	28. Nobody Wins	Geffen 49722
9/5/81	34	3	29. Chloe	Geffen 49788
4/17/82	13	10	30. Empty Garden (Hey Hey Johnny) tribute to John Lennon	Geffen 50049
8/14/82	12	10	31. Blue Eyes #1 Adult Contemporary hit (2 weeks)	Geffen 29954
5/14/83	12	12	32. I'm Still Standing	Geffen 29639
8/20/83	25	8	33. Kiss The Bride	Geffen 29568
11/19/83+	4	15	34. **I Guess That's Why They Call It The Blues** Stevie Wonder (harmonica solo)	Geffen 29460
6/16/84	5	13	35. **Sad Songs (Say So Much)**	Geffen 29292
9/15/84	16	10	36. Who Wears These Shoes? Airplay #10 / Sales #27	Geffen 29189
1/12/85	38	3	37. In Neon	Geffen 29111
11/2/85	20	10	38. Wrap Her Up Airplay #16 / Sales #27 George Michael (backing vocal)	Geffen 28873
11/23/85+	1 (4)	17	● 39. **That's What Friends Are For** Sales #1 (5) / Airplay #1 (3) **DIONNE & FRIENDS: Elton John, Gladys Knight and Stevie Wonder** #1 R&B hit (3 weeks) / #1 Adult Contemporary hit (2 weeks); first recorded by Rod Stewart in 1982	Arista 9422
2/8/86	7	11	40. **Nikita** Airplay #6 / Sales #8 George Michael (backing vocal)	Geffen 28800
7/4/87	36	3	41. Flames Of Paradise Sales #32 / Airplay #34 **JENNIFER RUSH (with Elton John)**	Epic 07119
11/28/87+	6	12	42. **Candle In The Wind** Sales #6 / Airplay #7 **[L]** recorded with The Melbourne Symphony Orchestra; tribute to Marilyn Monroe; also see #57 below	MCA 53196
7/2/88	2 (1)	13	43. **I Don't Wanna Go On With You Like That** Sales #2 / Airplay #3 #1 Adult Contemporary hit (1 week)	MCA 53345
10/15/88	19	6	44. A Word In Spanish Sales #15 / Airplay #27	MCA 53408
4/29/89	16	7	45. Through The Storm Sales #13 / Airplay #19 **ARETHA FRANKLIN AND ELTON JOHN**	Arista 9809
9/16/89	13	9	46. Healing Hands Sales #8 / Airplay #20 #1 Adult Contemporary hit (1 week)	MCA 53692
2/10/90	18	9	47. Sacrifice Sales #14 / Airplay #25	MCA 53750
6/9/90	28	5	48. Club At The End Of The Street Sales #26 / Airplay #34	MCA 53818
12/14/91+	1 (1)	16	● 49. **Don't Let The Sun Go Down On Me** Sales #4 / Airplay #4 **[L-R]** #1 Adult Contemporary hit (2 weeks)	Columbia 74086
7/11/92	9	18	50. **The One** Airplay #8 / Sales #17 #1 Adult Contemporary hit (6 weeks)	MCA 54423
11/28/92	23	9	51. The Last Song Airplay #27 / Sales #30	MCA 54510
4/3/93	30	7	52. Simple Life Airplay #26 / Sales #69 #1 Adult Contemporary hit (3 weeks)	MCA 54581

DATE	POS	WKS	ARTIST–RECORD TITLE	LABEL & NO.
6/4/94	4	23	● 53. **Can You Feel The Love Tonight** Airplay #2 / Sales #6 #1 Adult Contemporary hit (8 weeks); Kiki Dee and Rick Astley (backing vocals)	Hollywood 64543
9/17/94	18	11	54. Circle Of Life Airplay #15 / Sales #34 above 2 from the Disney animated movie *The Lion King*	Hollywood 64516
3/18/95	13	16	55. Believe Airplay #14 / Sales #19 #1 Adult Contemporary hit (2 weeks)	Rocket 856014
12/2/95	34	7	56. Blessed Airplay #31 / Sales #46	Rocket 852394
10/11/97	1 (14)	28	▲11 57. **Candle In The Wind 1997 /** Sales #1 (14) / Airplay #21 **[R]** produced by George Martin; song was originally written about Marilyn Monroe; this is a new version with new lyrics honoring Princess Diana who died in a car crash in France on 8/31/97 (age 36)	Rocket 856014
10/11/97		28	58. Something About The Way You Look Tonight Airplay #18 #1 Adult Contemporary hit (10 weeks); *Billboard*'s policy stated that whichever side of a single has the most airplay will be listed first – "Candle In The Wind 1997" was shown as the A-side for the first three weeks, then "Something About The Way You Look Tonight" was shown as the A-side for the remaining weeks on the chart; due to the special nature and record sales of "Candle In The Wind 1997," we are showing it as the A-side for the entire chart run	Rocket 568108
3/13/99	29	4	● 59. Written In The Stars Sales #13 **ELTON JOHN & LEANN RIMES** from Elton John and Tim Rice's musical interpretation of the stage show *Aida*	Rocket/Curb 566918
			JOHN, Little Willie	
			Born William Edgar John on 11/15/37 in Cullendale, Arkansas; raised in Detroit, Michigan. Died of a heart attack in Washington State Prison on 5/26/68 (age 30). R&B singer. Convicted of manslaughter in 1966. Inducted into the Rock and Roll Hall of Fame in 1996.	
7/14/56	24	9	1. Fever Best Seller #24 / Top 100 #27 #1 R&B hit (5 weeks)	King 4935
4/21/58	20	7	2. Talk To Me, Talk To Me Top 100 #20 / Best Seller #22	King 5108
7/25/60	38	1	3. Heartbreak (It's Hurtin' Me)	King 5356
10/10/60	13	10	4. Sleep #1 hit for Fred Waring's Pennsylvanians in 1924	King 5394
			JOHN, Robert	
			Born Robert John Pedrick on 1/3/46 in Brooklyn, New York. Pop singer.	
1/29/72	3	13	● 1. **The Lion Sleeps Tonight** #14 hit for The Weavers in 1952 (as "Wimoweh")	Atlantic 2846
6/30/79	1 (1)	19	● 2. **Sad Eyes**	EMI America 8015
8/23/80	31	4	3. Hey There Lonely Girl	EMI America 8049
			JOHN & ERNEST	
			R&B novelty duo: John Free and Ernest Smith.	
5/12/73	31	4	1. Super Fly Meets Shaft **[N]** "break-in" record; written and produced by Dickie Goodman	Rainy Wednesday 201
			JOHNNIE & JOE	
			R&B vocal duo from the Bronx, New York: Johnnie Louise Richardson and Joe Rivers. Richardson died of a stroke on 10/25/88.	
5/27/57	8	15	1. **Over The Mountain; Across The Sea** Top 100 #8 / Best Seller #9 / Juke Box #17	Chess 1654

DATE	POS	WKS	ARTIST–RECORD TITLE	LABEL & NO.
			JOHNNY AND THE HURRICANES	
			Rock and roll instrumental group from Toledo, Ohio: leader Johnny "Paris" Pocisk (saxophone), Paul Tesluk (organ), Dave Yorko (guitar), Lionel "Butch" Mattice (bass) and Tony Kaye (drums). Bo Savich replaced Kaye in late 1959. Savich died of cancer on 1/4/2002 (age 62).	
6/1/59	23	6	1. Crossfire [I]	Warwick 502
8/17/59	5	13	2. **Red River Rock** [I]	Warwick 509
			rock version of "Red River Valley"	
11/16/59	25	6	3. Reveille Rock [I]	Warwick 513
			rock version of the Army bugle call "Reveille"	
2/22/60	15	10	4. Beatnik Fly [I]	Warwick 520
			rock version of "Blue Tail Fly"	
			JOHNNY HATES JAZZ	
			Pop trio formed in England: Clark Datchler (vocals), Calvin Hayes (keyboards, drums) and Mike Nocito (guitar, bass). Hayes is the son of producer Mickie Most.	
4/2/88	2 (3)	13	1. **Shattered Dreams** Airplay #2 / Sales #3	Virgin 99383
			#1 Adult Contemporary hit (1 week)	
8/13/88	31	5	2. I Don't Want To Be A Hero Airplay #28 / Sales #33	Virgin 99304
			JOHNS, Sammy	
			Born on 2/7/46 in Charlotte, North Carolina. Pop singer/songwriter/guitarist.	
3/1/75	5	12	● 1. **Chevy Van**	GRC 2046
			JOHNSON — see BROTHERS JOHNSON	
			JOHNSON, Betty	
			Born on 3/16/29 in Burlington, North Carolina. Pop singer. Married to musical conductor Charles Randolph Grean.	
12/15/56+	9	18	1. **I Dreamed** Jockey #9 / Top 100 #12 / Juke Box #15 / Best Seller #22	Bally 1020
			Lew Douglas (orch.); featured on an episode of NBC-TV's Modern Romances	
6/24/57	25	1	2. Little White Lies Jockey #25 / Top 100 #40	Bally 1033
			#1 hit for Fred Waring's Pennsylvanians in 1930	
2/24/58	17	11	3. The Little Blue Man	Atlantic 1169
			Jockey #17 / Top 100 #19 / Best Seller #20 [N]	
			voice of the Little Blue Man: Fred Ebb (the song's co-writer)	
6/30/58	19	1	4. Dream Jockey #19 / Top 100 #58	Atlantic 1186
			#1 hit for the Pied Pipers in 1945; Charles Randolph Grean (orch., above 3)	
			JOHNSON, Don	
			Born on 12/15/49 in Flatt Creek, Missouri. Actor/singer. Played "Sonny Crockett" on TV's Miami Vice and title role on TV's Nash Bridges. Starred in several movies. Twice married to and divorced from actress Melanie Griffith.	
9/6/86	5	10	1. **Heartbeat** Sales #3 / Airplay #6	Epic 06285
11/12/88	25	5	2. Till I Loved You Sales #22 / Airplay #32	Columbia 08062
			BARBRA STREISAND AND DON JOHNSON	
			love theme from the Broadway musical Goya	

DATE	POS	WKS	ARTIST–RECORD TITLE	LABEL & NO.
			JOHNSON, Marv	
			Born on 10/15/38 in Detroit, Michigan. Died on 5/16/93 (age 54). R&B singer/songwriter/pianist.	
4/20/59	30	6	1. Come To Me	United Artists 160
11/16/59+	10	16	2. **You Got What It Takes**	United Artists 185
3/21/60	9	10	3. **I Love The Way You Love**	United Artists 208
10/10/60	20	4	4. (You've Got To) Move Two Mountains	United Artists 241
			The Rayber Voices (female backing singers, all of above)	
			JOHNSON, Michael	
			Born on 8/8/44 in Alamosa, Colorado; raised in Denver, Colorado. Singer/guitarist.	
5/27/78	12	10	1. Bluer Than Blue	EMI America 8001
			#1 Adult Contemporary hit (3 weeks)	
9/23/78	32	5	2. Almost Like Being In Love	EMI America 8004
			first recorded by Frank Sinatra in 1947	
9/29/79	19	9	3. This Night Won't Last Forever	EMI America 8019
			JOHNSTON, Tom — see DOOBIE BROTHERS, The	
			JO JO GUNNE	
			Rock group from Los Angeles, California: Jay Ferguson (vocals, keyboards), brothers Matthew (guitar) and Mark (bass) Andes, and Curly Smith (drums). Both Ferguson and Mark Andes had been in Spirit. Group named after the 1958 Chuck Berry hit. Mark Andes was later with Firefall and Heart.	
4/15/72	27	6	1. Run Run Run	Asylum 11003
			JOLI, France	
			Born in 1963 in Montreal, Quebec, Canada. Female dance singer.	
9/29/79	15	8	1. Come To Me	Prelude 8001
			JOMANDA	
			Female R&B vocal trio from New Jersey: Joanne Thomas, Cheri Williams and Renee Washington.	
8/31/91	40	1	1. Got A Love For You Airplay #26 / Sales #54	Big Beat 5031
			JON & ROBIN and The In Crowd	
			Duo of Jon Abnor and Javonne "Robin" Braga. Braga married James Wright of The Five Americans in 1970.	
5/27/67	18	6	1. Do It Again A Little Bit Slower	Abnak 119
			JON B	
			Born Jonathan Buck on 11/11/74 in Rhode Island. R&B singer/songwriter.	
5/27/95	10	22	● 1. **Someone To Love** Sales #9 / Airplay #16	Yab Yum 77895
			JON b featuring BABYFACE	
			from the movie *Bad Boys* starring Martin Lawrence and Will Smith (Fresh Prince)	
10/14/95	25	10	2. Pretty Girl Sales #27 / Airplay #39	Yab Yum 77813
5/23/98	7	14	▲ 3. **They Don't Know /** Sales #5 / Airplay #54	
1/31/98	29	4	4. Are U Still Down	Yab Yum 78793
			co-written and produced by 2Pac	

DATE	POS	WKS	ARTIST–RECORD TITLE	LABEL & NO.
			JONES, Donell	
			Born on 5/22/73 in Chicago, Illinois. R&B singer/songwriter.	
10/23/99	7	18	● 1. **U Know What's Up**　　　　　Sales #7 / Airplay #12	Untouchables 24420
			#1 R&B hit (8 weeks)	
6/3/00	29	9	2. Where I Wanna Be　　　　　　Airplay #23	Untouchables 24481
			JONES, Etta	
			Born on 11/25/28 in Aiken, South Carolina. Died of cancer on 10/16/2001 (age 72). Jazz singer with Earl Hines from 1949-52.	
12/12/60	36	1	1. Don't Go To Strangers	Prestige 180
			first recorded by Al Martino in 1954	
			JONES, Howard	
			Born on 2/23/55 in Southampton, Hampshire, England. Pop singer/songwriter/keyboardist.	
2/25/84	27	6	1. New Song	Elektra 69766
6/2/84	33	4	2. What Is Love?	Elektra 69737
4/20/85	5	14	3. **Things Can Only Get Better**　　Airplay #4 / Sales #8	Elektra 69651
8/3/85	19	8	4. Life In One Day　　　　　　Airplay #16 / Sales #20	Elektra 69631
5/3/86	4	14	5. **No One Is To Blame**　　　　Airplay #2 / Sales #6	Elektra 69549
			#1 Adult Contemporary hit (1 week); Phil Collins (drums, backing vocal, producer)	
11/8/86	17	10	6. You Know I Love You...Don't You?　Airplay #12 / Sales #20	Elektra 69512
4/8/89	12	11	7. Everlasting Love　　　　　　Airplay #10 / Sales #12	Elektra 69308
			#1 Adult Contemporary hit (2 weeks)	
8/12/89	30	4	8. The Prisoner　　　　　　　Airplay #28 / Sales #34	Elektra 69288
5/23/92	32	5	9. Lift Me Up　　　　　　　　Airplay #26	Elektra 64779
			JONES, Jack	
			Born on 1/14/38 in Los Angeles, California. Pop singer. Son of actress Irene Hervey and actor/singer Allan Jones. Performed the theme for TV's *Love Boat*. Married to actress Jill St. John from 1967-69.	
11/30/63+	14	10	1. Wives And Lovers	Kapp 551
			inspired by the movie starring Janet Leigh	
12/26/64+	30	5	2. Dear Heart	Kapp 635
			title song from the movie starring Glenn Ford	
3/20/65	15	7	3. The Race Is On	Kapp 651
			#1 Adult Contemporary hit (1 week)	
7/16/66	35	4	4. The Impossible Dream (The Quest)	Kapp 755
			#1 Adult Contemporary hit (1 week); from the musical *Man Of La Mancha* starring Richard Kiley	
3/25/67	39	2	5. Lady	Kapp 800
			#1 Adult Contemporary hit (4 weeks)	
			JONES, Jimmy	
			Born on 6/2/37 in Birmingham, Alabama. R&B singer.	
1/18/60	2 (1)	14	● 1. **Handy Man**	Cub 9049
5/9/60	3	10	● 2. **Good Timin'**	Cub 9067

DATE	POS	WKS	ARTIST–RECORD TITLE	LABEL & NO.
			JONES, Joe	
			Born on 8/12/26 in New Orleans, Louisiana. R&B singer/songwriter/pianist.	
10/10/60	**3**	9	1. **You Talk Too Much**	Roulette 4304
			JONES, Linda	
			Born on 1/14/44 in Newark, New Jersey. Died of diabetes on 3/14/72 (age 28). R&B singer.	
7/22/67	**21**	7	1. Hypnotized	Loma 2070
			JONES, Norah	
			Born on 3/30/79 in Manhattan, New York; raised in Dallas, Texas. Jazz-styled singer/pianist. Daughter of legendary sitar player Ravi Shankar. Won the 2002 Best New Artist Grammy Award.	

3/8/03	**30**	6	1. Don't Know Why Airplay #29
			        from the album *Come Away With Me* on Blue Note 32088; 2002
			        Grammy winner: Record of the Year
				album cut

12/20/03	**2** (1)ˢ	20	2. **Turn Me On** first recorded by Nina Simone in 1967	Blue Note 53475
			JONES, Oran "Juice"	
			Born on 3/28/57 in Houston, Texas; raised in Harlem, New York. R&B singer/rapper.	
10/11/86	**9**	9	● 1. **The Rain** Sales #8 / Airplay #10 #1 R&B hit (2 weeks)	Def Jam 06209
			JONES, Quincy	
			Born on 3/14/33 in Chicago, Illinois; raised in Seattle, Washington. Composer/producer/conductor/arranger. Began as a jazz trumpeter with Lionel Hampton (1950-53). Music director for Mercury Records in 1961, then vice president in 1964. Wrote scores for many movies. Scored TV series *Roots* in 1977. Arranger/producer for hundreds of successful singers and orchestras. Produced Michael Jackson's mega-albums *Off The Wall*, *Thriller* and *Bad*. Established own Qwest label in 1981. Married to actress Peggy Lipton (TV's *Mod Squad*) from 1974-89. Won the Grammy's Trustees Award in 1989. Won Grammy's Living Legends Award in 1990. His biographical movie *Listen Up: The Lives Of Quincy Jones* was released in 1990.	
7/22/78	**21**	7	1. Stuff Like That #1 R&B hit (1 week); Ashford & Simpson and Chaka Khan (vocals)	A&M 2043
5/9/81	**28**	5	2. Ai No Corrida (I-No-Ko-ree-da) Dune (vocals); first recorded by Chas Jankel in 1980	A&M 2309
9/19/81	**17**	10	3. Just Once **QUINCY JONES Featuring JAMES INGRAM**	A&M 2357
2/13/82	**14**	11	4. One Hundred Ways **QUINCY JONES Featuring JAMES INGRAM**	A&M 2387

12/16/89+	**18**	8	5. I'll Be Good To You Sales #13 / Airplay #26
			        QUINCY JONES Featuring Ray Charles and Chaka Khan
			        #1 R&B hit (2 weeks)
				Qwest 22697

4/7/90	**31**	4	● 6. The Secret Garden (Sweet Seduction Suite) Sales #20
			        QUINCY JONES/Al B. Sure!/James Ingram/El
			        DeBarge/Barry White
			        #1 R&B hit (1 week)
				Qwest 19992

DATE	POS	WKS	ARTIST–RECORD TITLE	LABEL & NO.
			JONES, Rickie Lee	
			Born on 11/8/54 in Chicago, Illinois. Female singer/songwriter. Won the 1979 Best New Artist Grammy Award.	
5/12/79	4	12	1. **Chuck E.'s In Love**	Warner 8825
9/1/79	40	1	2. Young Blood	Warner 49018
			JONES, Roy Jr.	
			Born on 1/16/69 in Pensacola, Florida. R&B singer/rapper/songwriter. Won boxing's WBA heavyweight championship on 3/2/2003. Owner of Body Head Records.	
1/12/02	5 ˢ	11	1. **That Was Then**	Body Head/EMI 74767
			JONES, Shirley — see PARTRIDGE FAMILY, The	
			JONES, Tom	
			Born Thomas Jones Woodward on 6/7/40 in Pontypridd, South Wales. Dynamic pop singer. Won the 1965 Best New Artist Grammy Award. Host of own TV musical variety series from 1969-71. Had a successful country career from 1976-85.	
5/1/65	10	9	1. **It's Not Unusual**	Parrot 9737
7/3/65	3	10	2. **What's New Pussycat?** title song from the movie starring Peter Sellers and Peter O'Toole	Parrot 9765
9/18/65	27	5	3. With These Hands #7 hit for Eddie Fisher in 1953	Parrot 9787
1/1/66	25	6	4. Thunderball title song from the James Bond movie starring Sean Connery	Parrot 9801
1/21/67	11	7	5. Green, Green Grass Of Home #4 Country hit for Porter Wagoner in 1965	Parrot 40009
4/1/67	27	4	6. Detroit City	Parrot 40012
4/13/68	15	11	7. Delilah	Parrot 40025
10/5/68	35	2	8. Help Yourself	Parrot 40029
6/7/69	13	9	9. Love Me Tonight	Parrot 40038
8/9/69	6	14	● 10. **I'll Never Fall In Love Again** [R] #1 Adult Contemporary hit (1 week); originally charted at #49 in 1967	Parrot 40018
1/3/70	5	10	● 11. **Without Love (There Is Nothing)** #1 Adult Contemporary hit (1 week)	Parrot 40045
5/9/70	13	7	12. Daughter Of Darkness #1 Adult Contemporary hit (1 week)	Parrot 40048
8/29/70	14	7	13. I (Who Have Nothing)	Parrot 40051
11/28/70	25	7	14. Can't Stop Loving You	Parrot 40056
2/20/71	2 (1)	12	● 15. **She's A Lady** written by Paul Anka	Parrot 40058
6/12/71	26	6	16. Puppet Man / co-written by Neil Sedaka	
7/3/71	38	3	17. Resurrection Shuffle	Parrot 40064
2/12/77	15	10	18. Say You'll Stay Until Tomorrow #1 Country hit (1 week)	Epic/MAM 50308
12/24/88+	31	6	19. Kiss Sales #23 / Airplay #35 **THE ART OF NOISE Featuring Tom Jones**	China 871038

DATE	POS	WKS	ARTIST–RECORD TITLE	LABEL & NO.
			JONES GIRLS, The	
			R&B vocal trio from Detroit, Michigan: sisters Shirley, Brenda and Valorie Jones. Valorie died on 12/2/2001 (age 45).	
8/18/79	38	1	● 1. You Gonna Make Me Love Somebody Else	Philadelphia I. 3680
			JOPLIN, Janis	
			Born on 1/19/43 in Port Arthur, Texas. Died of a heroin overdose on 10/4/70 (age 27). White blues-rock singer. Nicknamed "Pearl." Moved to San Francisco in 1966; joined Big Brother & The Holding Company. Left band to go solo in 1968. The Bette Midler movie *The Rose* was inspired by Joplin's life. Inducted into the Rock and Roll Hall of Fame in 1995.	
9/28/68	12	8	1. Piece Of My Heart	Columbia 44626
			BIG BROTHER AND THE HOLDING COMPANY	
2/20/71	1 (2)	12	2. **Me And Bobby McGee**	Columbia 45314
			#12 Country hit for Roger Miller in 1969	
			JORDAN, Jeremy	
			Born Don Henson on 9/19/73 in Hammond, Indiana; raised in Calumet City, Illinois.	
2/20/93	14	12	1. The Right Kind Of Love Airplay #11 / Sales #20	Giant 18718
			co-written and co-produced by Robbie Nevil; from the TV soundtrack album *Beverly Hills, 90210*	
6/5/93	28	6	2. Wannagirl Airplay #20	Giant 18548
			JORDAN, Montell	
			Born on 12/3/68 in Los Angeles, California. R&B singer/songwriter.	
3/11/95	1 (7)	24	▲ 1. **This Is How We Do It** Sales #1 (8) / Airplay #5	PMP/RAL 851468
			#1 R&B hit (7 weeks); samples "Children's Story" by Slick Rick	
8/19/95	21	6	● 2. Somethin' 4 Da Honeyz Sales #12 / Airplay #63	PMP/RAL 856962
			samples "Summer Madness" by Kool & The Gang	
7/6/96	28	9	3. I Like Sales #14	Def Jam/RAL 575046
			MONTELL JORDAN FEATURING SLICK RICK	
			samples "I Get Lifted" by KC & The Sunshine Band; from the movie *The Nutty Professor* starring Eddie Murphy	
10/26/96	18	13	● 4. Falling Sales #12	Def Jam 575648
			samples "Streiht Up Menace" by MC Eiht	
3/1/97	21	12	● 5. What's On Tonight Sales #14	Def Jam 574032
3/28/98	2 (2)	17	▲ 6. **Let's Ride** Sales #1 (1) / Airplay #55	Def Jam 568475
			MONTELL JORDAN Featuring Master P & Silkk "The Shocker"	
			#1 R&B hit (3 weeks)	
9/12/98	14	10	● 7. I Can Do That Sales #2	Def Jam 566106
12/18/99+	4	23	● 8. **Get It On...Tonite** Sales #2 / Airplay #12	Def Soul 562622
			#1 R&B hit (3 weeks); samples "Love For The Sake Of Love" by Claudja Barry	
			JOURNEY	
			Rock group formed in San Francisco, California: Steve Perry (vocals), Neal Schon (guitar), Gregg Rolie (keyboards), Ross Valory (bass) and Steve Smith (drums). Schon and Rolie had been in Santana. Jonathan Cain (of The Babys) replaced Rolie in 1981. In 1986 group pared down to a three-man core: Perry, Schon and Cain. Schon and Cain formed Bad English in 1989. Smith, Valory and Rolie formed The Storm in 1991. Reunion in 1996 of Perry, Schon, Cain, Valory and Smith.	
8/25/79	16	12	● 1. Lovin', Touchin', Squeezin'	Columbia 11036

DATE	POS	WKS	ARTIST–RECORD TITLE	LABEL & NO.
3/29/80	23	6	2. Any Way You Want It	Columbia 11213
7/5/80	32	4	3. Walks Like A Lady	Columbia 11275
4/4/81	34	4	4. The Party's Over (Hopelessly In Love)	Columbia 60505
8/1/81	4	14	● 5. **Who's Crying Now**	Columbia 02241
11/7/81	9	13	● 6. **Don't Stop Believin'**	Columbia 02567
1/23/82	2 (6)	14	● 7. **Open Arms**	Columbia 02687
6/12/82	19	9	8. Still They Ride	Columbia 02883
2/5/83	8	16	9. **Separate Ways (Worlds Apart)** #1 Mainstream Rock hit (4 weeks)	Columbia 03513
4/30/83	12	11	10. Faithfully	Columbia 03840
7/23/83	23	8	11. After The Fall	Columbia 04004
10/22/83	23	7	12. Send Her My Love	Columbia 04151
2/2/85	9	11	13. **Only The Young** Airplay #6 / Sales #20 from the movie *Vision Quest* starring Matthew Modine	Geffen 29090
4/19/86	9	10	14. **Be Good To Yourself** Sales #7 / Airplay #10	Columbia 05869
7/12/86	17	7	15. Suzanne Sales #16 / Airplay #19	Columbia 06134
9/20/86	17	8	16. Girl Can't Help It Sales #17 / Airplay #17	Columbia 06302
1/24/87	14	9	17. I'll Be Alright Without You Airplay #11 / Sales #12	Columbia 06301
10/26/96	12	21	● 18. When You Love A Woman Airplay #9 / Sales #17 #1 Adult Contemporary hit (3 weeks)	Columbia 78428
			J-SHIN	
			Born in Miami, Florida. Male R&B singer.	
2/19/00	34	3	1. One Night Stand Sales #9 / Airplay #75 **J-SHIN Featuring LaTocha Scott Of Xscape**	Slip n Slide 84489
			JT MONEY — see MONEY, JT	
			JUMP 'N THE SADDLE	
			Country-pop group from Chicago, Illinois: Peter Quinn (vocals, harmonica), T.C. Furlong and Barney Schwartz (guitars), Tom Trinka (sax), Rick Gorley (bass) and Vincent Dee (drums).	
12/24/83+	15	7	1. The Curly Shuffle [N] a Three Stooges tribute	Atlantic 89718
			JUNIOR	
			Born Norman Giscombe on 11/10/61 in London, England. R&B singer/songwriter.	
4/10/82	30	3	1. Mama Used To Say	Mercury 76132
			JUNIOR M.A.F.I.A.	
			Gathering of four rap acts: Lil' Kim, Klepto, Snakes (Trife & Larceny) and The Sixes (Little Caesar, Chico & Nino Brown). Proteges of The Notorious B.I.G. M.A.F.I.A.: Masters At Finding Intelligent Attitudes.	
7/29/95	13	11	● 1. Player's Anthem Sales #7 / Airplay #47 samples "Ladi Dadi" by Doug E. Fresh	Undeas/Big Beat 98149
2/24/96	17	8	▲ 2. Get Money Sales #9 / Airplay #57 The Notorious B.I.G. (guest rapper); samples "You Can't Turn Me Away" by Sylvia Striplin	Undeas/Big Beat 98087

DATE	POS	WKS	ARTIST–RECORD TITLE	LABEL & NO.
			JUSTIS, Bill	
			Born on 10/14/26 in Birmingham, Alabama. Died on 7/15/82 (age 55). Session saxophonist.	
11/18/57	**2** (1)	14	● 1. **Raunchy** Best Seller #2 / Top 100 #3 / Jockey #5 **[I]**	Phillips 3519
			#1 R&B hit (1 week); Bill Justis (sax); Sid Manker (guitar)	
			JUST US	
			White vocal duo from New York: Chip Taylor and Al Gorgoni.	
5/7/66	**34**	2	1. I Can't Grow Peaches On A Cherry Tree	Colpix 803
			JUVENILE	
			Born Terius Gray in 1975 in New Orleans, Louisiana. Male rapper.	
9/4/99	**19**	22	1. Back That Azz Up Airplay #9 / Sales #64	Cash Money 156482
			JUVENILE Feat. Mannie Fresh and Lil' Wayne	
10/30/99	**36**	5	2. Bling Bling Airplay #25 / Sales #72	Cash Money 156483
			B.G. Feat. Baby, Turk, Mannie Fresh, Juvenile and Lil Wayne	

K

DATE	POS	WKS	ARTIST–RECORD TITLE	LABEL & NO.
			KADISON, Joshua	
			Born on 2/8/63 in Los Angeles, California. Adult Contemporary singer/songwriter/pianist.	
12/25/93+	**26**	8	1. Jessie Airplay #21 / Sales #30	SBK 50429
5/14/94	**19**	15	2. Beautiful In My Eyes Airplay #22 / Sales #26	SBK 58099
			KAEMPFERT, Bert, And His Orchestra	
			Born on 10/16/23 in Hamburg, Germany. Died on 6/21/80 (age 56). Multi-instrumentalist/bandleader.	
11/21/60+	**1** (3)	15	● 1. **Wonderland By Night** **[I]**	Decca 31141
4/10/61	**31**	4	2. Tenderly **[I]**	Decca 31236
			#17 hit for Rosemary Clooney in 1952	
2/13/65	**11**	10	3. Red Roses For A Blue Lady **[I]**	Decca 31722
			#3 hit for Vaughn Monroe in 1949	
5/29/65	**33**	3	4. Three O'Clock In The Morning **[I]**	Decca 31778
			#1 hit for Paul Whiteman in 1922	
			KAJAGOOGOO	
			Pop-synth group formed in Leighton Buzzard, Hertfordshire, England: Chris "Limahl" Hamill (vocals), Steve Askew (guitar), Stuart Neale (keyboards), Nick Beggs (bass) and Jez Strode (drums).	
5/21/83	**5**	12	1. **Too Shy**	EMI America 8161
			KALIN TWINS	
			Pop vocal duo: twins Herbert and Harold Kalin. Born on 2/16/34 in Port Jervis, New York.	
6/30/58	**5**	13	● 1. **When** Hot 100 #5 / Best Seller #7 / Jockey #8	Decca 30642
			#1 R&B hit (1 week)	
10/20/58	**12**	9	2. Forget Me Not Hot 100 #12	Decca 30745

DATE	POS	WKS	ARTIST—RECORD TITLE	LABEL & NO.
			KALLEN, Kitty	
			Born on 5/25/22 in Philadelphia, Pennsylvania. Big band singer with Jack Teagarden, Jimmy Dorsey, Harry James and Artie Shaw.	
2/11/56	**39**	1	1. Go On With The Wedding Top 100 #39 **KITTY KALLEN and GEORGIE SHAW** Jack Pleis (orch.)	Decca 29776
11/9/59	**34**	3	2. If I Give My Heart To You Milton De Lugg (orch.); #3 hit for Doris Day in 1954	Columbia 41473
1/12/63	**18**	6	3. My Coloring Book Ray Ellis (orch.)	RCA Victor 8124
			KAMOZE, Ini	
			Born on 10/9/57 in Jamaica. Male reggae singer.	
10/15/94	**1 (2)**	23	▲ 1. **Here Comes The Hotstepper** Sales #1 (8) / Airplay #3 samples "Hot Pants-I'm Coming" by Bobby Byrd and "Heartbeat" by Taana Gardner; incorporates "Land Of 1000 Dances"; recorded in 1992; later included in the movie *Ready To Wear (Prêt-À-Porter)* starring Julia Roberts	Columbia 77614
			KANDI	
			Born Kandi Burruss on 5/17/76 in Atlanta, Georgia. Female R&B singer/songwriter. Former member of Xscape.	
9/16/00	**24**	17	1. Don't Think I'm Not Sales #23 / Airplay #25 samples "Ike's Mood" by Isaac Hayes	Columbia 79450
			KANE, Big Daddy	
			Born Antonio Hardy on 9/10/68 in Brooklyn, New York. Male rapper. Acted in the movies *The Meteor Man* and *Posse*.	
9/4/93	**31**	8	1. Very Special Sales #30 / Airplay #31 Spinderella, Laree Williams and Karen Anderson (vocals and rap)	Cold Chillin' 18437
			KANE GANG, The	
			Soul-styled pop trio formed in England: singers Martin Brammer and Paul Woods with guitarist David Brewis. Band's name derived from the movie *Citizen Kane*.	
12/19/87	**36**	3	1. Motortown Sales #32 / Airplay #40	Capitol 44062
			KANSAS	
			Pop-rock group from Topeka, Kansas: Steve Walsh (vocals, keyboards), Kerry Livgren (guitar, keyboards), Rich Williams (guitar), Robby Steinhardt (violin), Dave Hope (bass) and Phil Ehart (drums). John Elefante replaced Walsh in 1981. Revised lineup in 1986: Walsh, Williams, Ehart, Steve Morse (guitar) and Billy Greer (bass).	
2/5/77	**11**	13	● 1. Carry On Wayward Son	Kirshner 4267
12/17/77+	**28**	6	2. Point Of Know Return	Kirshner 4273
2/18/78	**6**	15	● 3. **Dust In The Wind**	Kirshner 4274
6/23/79	**23**	8	4. People Of The South Wind	Kirshner 4284
11/8/80	**40**	1	5. Hold On	Kirshner 4291
5/29/82	**17**	9	6. Play The Game Tonight	Kirshner 02903
11/29/86+	**19**	10	7. All I Wanted Sales #18 / Airplay #21	MCA 52958

DATE	POS	WKS	ARTIST–RECORD TITLE	LABEL & NO.
			KASENETZ-KATZ SINGING ORCHESTRAL CIRCUS	
			Bubblegum group assembled by producers Jerry Kasenetz and Jeff Katz. Features members from The 1910 Fruitgum Co./The Ohio Express/The Music Explosion.	
11/9/68	25	6	1. Quick Joey Small (Run Joey Run) Joey Levine (lead singer; Ohio Express, Reunion)	Buddah 64
			KATRINA AND THE WAVES	
			Pop-rock group formed in London, England: Katrina Leskanich (vocals; born in Topeka, Kansas), Kimberley Rew (guitar), Vince Dela Cruz (bass) and Alex Cooper (drums).	
4/20/85	9	13	1. **Walking On Sunshine** Sales #4 / Airplay #10	Capitol 5466
9/7/85	37	2	2. Do You Want Crying	Capitol 5450
8/19/89	16	6	3. That's The Way Sales #14 / Airplay #26	SBK 07303
			KAYE, Sammy, And His Orchestra	
			Born on 3/13/10 in Rocky River, Ohio. Died of cancer on 6/2/87 (age 77). Leader of popular "sweet" dance band with the slogan "Swing and Sway with Sammy Kaye." Also played clarinet and alto sax.	
5/2/64	36	2	1. Charade **[I]** title song from the movie starring Cary Grant and Audrey Hepburn	Decca 31589
			KC AND THE SUNSHINE BAND	
			Disco group from Hialeah, Florida. Formed by Harry Wayne "KC" Casey (vocals, keyboards; born on 1/31/51) and Richard Finch (bass). Other members included Jerome Smith (guitar), Fermin Coytisolo (congas), Robert Johnson (drums), and Ronnie Smith, Denvil Liptrot, James Weaver, and Charles Williams (horn section).	
8/2/75	1 (1)	9	1. **Get Down Tonight** #1 R&B hit (1 week)	T.K. 1009
11/1/75	1 (2)	13	2. **That's The Way (I Like It)** #1 R&B hit (1 week)	T.K. 1015
7/31/76	1 (1)	16	3. **(Shake, Shake, Shake) Shake Your Booty** #1 R&B hit (4 weeks)	T.K. 1019
1/29/77	37	2	4. I Like To Do It	T.K. 1020
4/2/77	1 (1)	16	5. **I'm Your Boogie Man**	T.K. 1022
8/13/77	2 (3)	14	6. **Keep It Comin' Love** #1 R&B hit (1 week)	T.K. 1023
3/25/78	35	3	7. Boogie Shoes originally released as the B-side of #3 above; re-released due to inclusion on the *Saturday Night Fever* soundtrack	T.K. 1025
6/24/78	35	2	8. It's The Same Old Song	T.K. 1028
9/29/79+	1 (1)	18	9. **Please Don't Go**	T.K. 1035
12/22/79+	2 (2)	16	● 10. **Yes, I'm Ready** **TERI DeSARIO with K.C.** #1 Adult Contemporary hit (2 weeks)	Casablanca 2227
2/4/84	18	10	11. Give It Up **KC**	Meca 1001

DATE	POS	WKS	ARTIST–RECORD TITLE	LABEL & NO.
			K-CI & JOJO	
			Brothers Cedric "K-Ci" and Joel "JoJo" Hailey from Charlotte, North Carolina. K-Ci was born on 9/2/69; JoJo was born on 6/10/71. Both were founding members of the R&B vocal group Jodeci.	
2/25/95	**17**	8	1. If You Think You're Lonely Now Sales #7 / Airplay #33 **K-Ci HAILEY of Jodeci** from the movie *Jason's Lyric* starring Forest Whitaker	Mercury 856572
6/22/96	**1** (2)	21	▲² 2. **How Do U Want It** Sales #1 (4) / Airplay #68 **2 PAC (featuring KC and JoJo)** #1 R&B hit (3 weeks); samples "Body Heat" by Quincy Jones	Death Row 854652
2/15/97	flip	4	3. Rappers' Ball **E-40 Featuring Too $hort and K-Ci** samples "Playboy $hort" by Too $hort	Sick Wid' It/Jive 42436
6/14/97	**26**	8	4. You Bring Me Up Sales #16	MCA 55346
3/28/98	**1** (3)	34	5. **All My Life** Sales #1 (2) / Airplay #3 #1 R&B hit (2 weeks)	MCA 55420
6/19/99	**2** (1)	16	6. **Tell Me It's Real** Sales #2 / Airplay #12	MCA 55551
11/20/99	**25**	4	7. Will 2K Airplay #20 **WILL SMITH (Featuring K-Ci)** samples "Rock The Casbah" by The Clash	Columbia 79287
12/30/00+	**11**	21	8. Crazy Airplay #8 from the album *X* on MCA 112398	album cut
			K-DOE, Ernie	
			Born Ernest Kador on 2/22/36 in New Orleans, Louisiana. Died on 7/5/2001 (age 65). R&B singer/songwriter.	
4/3/61	**1** (1)	12	1. **Mother-In-Law** #1 R&B hit (5 weeks); Benny Spellman (bass vocal)	Minit 623
			KEEDY	
			Born Kelly Keedy on 7/26/65 in Abilene, Texas. Female dance singer.	
4/6/91	**15**	8	1. Save Some Love Sales #13 / Airplay #15	Arista 2153
			KEITH	
			Born James Barry Keefer on 5/7/49 in Philadelphia, Pennsylvania. Pop singer/songwriter.	
11/12/66	**39**	1	1. Ain't Gonna Lie	Mercury 72596
1/7/67	**7**	9	2. **98.6** The Tokens (backing vocals, above 2)	Mercury 72639
4/8/67	**37**	2	3. Tell Me To My Face first recorded by The Hollies in 1967	Mercury 72652
			KEITH, Lisa	
			Born in Minneapolis, Minnesota. Singer/songwriter.	
10/30/93	**36**	3	1. Better Than You Airplay #33	Perspective 7430
			KEITH, Toby	
			Born Toby Keith Covel on 7/8/61 in Clinton, Oklahoma; raised in Moore, Oklahoma. Country singer/songwriter/guitarist. Former rodeo hand, oil field worker and semi-pro football player.	
3/18/00	**31**	8	1. How Do You Like Me Now?! Airplay #24 / Sales #29 #1 Country hit (5 weeks)	DreamWorks 50932

DATE	POS	WKS	ARTIST–RECORD TITLE	LABEL & NO.
2/17/01	**32**	7	2. You Shouldn't Kiss Me Like This Airplay #25 #1 Country hit (3 weeks); from the album *How Do You Like Me Now?!* on DreamWorks 50209	album cut
8/11/01	**27**	7	3. I'm Just Talkin' About Tonight Airplay #24 #1 Country hit (1 week)	album cut
11/24/01	**28**	7	4. I Wanna Talk About Me Airplay #26 #1 Country hit (5 weeks)	album cut
4/6/02	**26**	9	5. My List Airplay #26 #1 Country hit (5 weeks); above 3 from the album *Pull My Chain* on DreamWorks 450297	album cut
7/13/02	**25**	7	6. Courtesy Of The Red, White And Blue (The Angry American) Airplay #24 #1 Country hit (1 week)	album cut
11/23/02	**22**	9	7. Who's Your Daddy? Airplay #20 #1 Country hit (1 week)	album cut
5/31/03	**22**	12	8. Beer For My Horses Airplay #18 **TOBY KEITH with Willie Nelson** #1 Country hit (6 weeks); above 3 from Keith's album *Unleashed* on DreamWorks 450254	album cut
10/25/03	**26**	9	9. I Love This Bar Airplay #21 #1 Country hit (5 weeks); from the album *Shock'n Y'all* on DreamWorks 450435	album cut

KELIS

Born Kelis Rogers in Harlem, New York. Female R&B singer.

DATE	POS	WKS	ARTIST–RECORD TITLE	LABEL & NO.
12/11/99	**33**	6	1. Got Your Money Airplay #20 / Sales #26 **OL' DIRTY BASTARD featuring Kelis**	Elektra 67022
11/15/03	**3**	16	2. **Milkshake** Airplay #3 / Sales #8	Star Trak 58648

KELLER, Jerry

Born on 6/20/37 in Fort Smith, Arkansas; raised in Tulsa, Oklahoma. Pop singer/songwriter.

DATE	POS	WKS	ARTIST–RECORD TITLE	LABEL & NO.
7/20/59	**14**	8	1. Here Comes Summer	Kapp 277

KELLY, Grace — see CROSBY, Bing

KELLY, Monty, And His Orchestra

Born on 6/8/10 in Modesto, California. Died on 3/15/71 (age 60). Conductor/arranger. Trumpeter with Paul Whiteman in the early 1940s.

DATE	POS	WKS	ARTIST–RECORD TITLE	LABEL & NO.
4/4/60	**30**	3	1. Summer Set **[I]** written by Mr. Acker Bilk	Carlton 527

KELLY, R.

Born Robert Kelly on 1/8/67 in Chicago, Illinois. R&B singer/songwriter/producer/multi-instrumentalist. Public Announcement was his backing vocal group.

DATE	POS	WKS		ARTIST–RECORD TITLE	LABEL & NO.
7/18/92	**39**	1		1. Honey Love Sales #30 / Airplay #42 #1 R&B hit (2 weeks)	Jive 42031
4/24/93	**31**	7		2. Dedicated Airplay #18 / Sales #55 **R. KELLY AND PUBLIC ANNOUNCEMENT** (above 2)	Jive 42115
11/13/93	**20**	10	●	3. Sex Me (Parts I & II) Sales #9 / Airplay #55	Jive 42161
2/19/94	**1** (4)	23	▲	4. **Bump N' Grind** Sales #1 (10) / Airplay #7 #1 R&B hit (12 weeks)	Jive 42207
5/28/94	**13**	15	●	5. Your Body's Callin' Sales #6 / Airplay #17	Jive 42220

DATE	POS	WKS	ARTIST–RECORD TITLE		LABEL & NO.
11/18/95	4	11	▲ 6. **You Remind Me Of Something** #1 R&B hit (1 week)	Sales #2 / Airplay #47	Jive 42344
3/2/96	4	16	▲ 7. **Down Low (Nobody Has To Know)** **R. KELLY (featuring Ronald Isley and Ernie Isley)** #1 R&B hit (7 weeks)	Sales #2 / Airplay #32	Jive 42373
7/13/96	5	18	▲ 8. **I Can't Sleep Baby (If I)** #1 R&B hit (2 weeks)	Sales #4 / Airplay #14	Jive 42377
12/14/96	2 (4)	31	▲ 9. **I Believe I Can Fly** #1 R&B hit (6 weeks); from the movie *Space Jam* starring Michael Jordan	Sales #1 (7) / Airplay #9	Jive 42422
7/19/97	9	10	● 10. **Gotham City** from the movie *Batman & Robin* starring George Clooney	Sales #5 / Airplay #37	Jive 42473
5/30/98	32 ▲	7	11. Be Careful **SPARKLE featuring R. Kelly** #1 R&B Airplay hit (6 weeks); from the album *Sparkle* on Rock Land 90149		album cut
12/5/98	1 (6)	15	▲ 12. **I'm Your Angel** **R. KELLY & CELINE DION** #1 Adult Contemporary hit (12 weeks)	Sales #1 (6) / Airplay #22	Jive 42557
1/23/99	22	13	13. When A Woman's Fed Up from the album *R.* on Jive 41625	Airplay #12	album cut
6/12/99	27	6	14. Did You Ever Think **R. KELLY (featuring Nas)**	Sales #16 / Airplay #40	Jive 42604
10/9/99	12	7	● 15. If I Could Turn Back The Hands Of Time Sparkle and Bruce Kelly (backing vocals)	Sales #4 / Airplay #46	Jive 42623
10/23/99	2 (3)	10	● 16. **Satisfy You** **PUFF DADDY (Featuring R. KELLY)** #1 R&B hit (2 weeks); samples "Why You Treat Me So Bad" by Club Nouveau	Sales #1 (3) / Airplay #13	Bad Boy 79283
10/21/00+	14	17	17. I Wish #1 R&B hit (2 weeks)	Airplay #10	Jive 42740
4/28/01	6	15	18. Fiesta Remix **R. KELLY (Featuring Jay-Z and Boo & Gotti)** #1 R&B hit (5 weeks)	Sales #4 / Airplay #12	Jive 42904
10/6/01	36	3	19. Feelin' On Yo Booty	Airplay #35	Jive 42946
12/1/01+	15	13	20. We Thuggin **FAT JOE (Featuring R. Kelly)**	Airplay #15 / Sales #39	Atlantic 85174
2/9/02	34	2	21. The World's Greatest from the movie *Ali* starring Will Smith (soundtrack on Interscope 493172)	Airplay #38	album cut
12/21/02+	2 (5)	32	22. **Ignition**	Sales #2 / Airplay #2	Jive 40065
5/10/03	16	9	23. Snake **R. KELLY featuring Cam'ron and Big Tigger**	Airplay #15 / Sales #21	Jive 40108
8/9/03	13	14	24. Thoia Thoing	Airplay #12 / Sales #30	Jive 54283
10/4/03	9	21	25. **Step In The Name Of Love** #1 R&B hit (2 weeks)	Airplay #8 / Sales #67	Jive 55572
12/27/03+	24	14	26. Gigolo **NICK CANNON featuring R. Kelly**	Airplay #22 / Sales #70	Nick/Jive 56646
			KEMP, Johnny Born in Nassau, Bahamas; raised in Harlem, New York. R&B singer/dancer/actor/songwriter.		
6/25/88	10	11	● 1. **Just Got Paid** #1 R&B hit (2 weeks)	Sales #9 / Airplay #12	Columbia 07744

DATE	POS	WKS	ARTIST—RECORD TITLE	LABEL & NO.
4/15/89	36	3	2. Birthday Suit Airplay #33 / Sales #36 *from the movie* Sing *starring Lorraine Bracco*	Columbia 68569
			KEMP, Tara	
			Born on 5/11/64 in San Francisco, California. R&B singer/songwriter/ pianist.	
2/9/91	3	15	● 1. **Hold You Tight** Airplay #3 / Sales #7	Giant 19458
6/8/91	7	11	2. **Piece Of My Heart** Airplay #9 / Sales #48	Giant 19364
			KENDRICKS, Eddie	
			Born on 12/17/39 in Union Springs, Alabama; raised in Birmingham, Alabama. Died of cancer on 10/5/92 (age 52). R&B singer. Lead singer of The Temptations from 1960-71. Kendricks later dropped letter "s" from his last name.	
9/15/73	1 (2)	16	1. **Keep On Truckin' (Part 1)** #1 R&B hit (2 weeks)	Tamla 54238
1/26/74	2 (2)	13	2. **Boogie Down** #1 R&B hit (3 weeks)	Tamla 54243
6/1/74	28	4	3. Son Of Sagittarius	Tamla 54247
4/5/75	18	10	4. **Shoeshine Boy** #1 R&B hit (1 week)	Tamla 54257
3/20/76	36	3	5. He's A Friend	Tamla 54266
9/15/85	20	7	6. A Nite At The Apollo Live! The Way You Do The Things You Do/My Girl Sales #21 / Airplay #23 **[L]** **DARYL HALL JOHN OATES with David Ruffin & Eddie Kendrick** *recorded at the reopening of New York's Apollo Theatre*	RCA 14178
			KENNEDY, Joyce — see OSBORNE, Jeffrey	
			KENNER, Chris	
			Born on 12/25/29 in Kenner, Louisiana. Died of a heart attack on 1/28/76 (age 46). R&B singer/songwriter.	
7/3/61	2 (3)	10	1. **I Like It Like That, Part 1**	Instant 3229
			KENNY G	
			Born Kenny Gorelick on 7/6/56 in Seattle, Washington. Soprano/tenor saxophonist. Joined Barry White's Love Unlimited Orchestra at age 17. The #1 instrumentalist of the 1990s.	
5/16/87	4	12	1. **Songbird** Sales #4 / Airplay #5 **[I]**	Arista 9588
9/26/87	15	9	2. Don't Make Me Wait For Love Sales #14 / Airplay #18 Lenny Williams (vocal)	Arista 9625
11/19/88+	13	10	3. Silhouette Sales #10 / Airplay #17 **[I]**	Arista 9751
2/8/92	12	12	4. Missing You Now Airplay #10 / Sales #33 **MICHAEL BOLTON Featuring Kenny G** #1 Adult Contemporary hit (3 weeks)	Columbia 74184
2/13/93	18	13	5. Forever In Love Airplay #13 / Sales #21 **[I]** #1 Adult Contemporary hit (2 weeks)	Arista 12482
6/19/93	25	7	6. By The Time This Night Is Over Airplay #24 / Sales #57 **KENNY G with Peabo Bryson** #1 Adult Contemporary hit (2 weeks)	Arista 12565
1/8/00	7	2	7. **Auld Lang Syne (The Millennium Mix)** Sales #4 / Airplay #31 **[I-S]**	Arista 13769

DATE	POS	WKS	ARTIST–RECORD TITLE	LABEL & NO.
11/23/02+	2 (1)ˢ	12	8. **Auld Lang Syne (Freedom Mix)** [I-S-R] new mix of #7 above; above 2 contain different audioclips from dozens of historical events	Arista 15215
			KENTON, Stan	
11/17/62	32	4	Born on 2/19/12 in Wichita, Kansas. Died of a stroke on 8/25/79 (age 67). Legendary jazz bandleader/pianist. 1. Mama Sang A Song [S] Ralph Carmichael (orch.)	Capitol 4847
			KERMIT — see HENSON, Jim	
			KEYS, Alicia	
7/21/01	1 (6)	29	Born Alicia Cook on 1/25/81 in Manhattan, New York. R&B singer/ songwriter/keyboardist. Won the 2001 Best New Artist Grammy Award. 1. **Fallin'** Airplay #1 (6) / Sales #34 #1 R&B hit (4 weeks)	J Records 21041
12/8/01+	7	14	2. **A Woman's Worth** Airplay #6 / Sales #72	J Records 21112
7/27/02	2 (4)	19	3. **Gangsta Lovin'** Airplay #2 / Sales #6 **EVE Feat. Alicia Keys** samples "Don't Stop The Music" by Yarbrough & Peoples	Ruff Ryders 497817
11/22/03+	3	18	4. **You Don't Know My Name** Airplay #3 #1 R&B hit (9 weeks); samples "Let Me Prove My Love To You" by The Main Ingredient	J Records 56599
			KHAN, Chaka (Rufus)	
			Born Yvette Marie Stevens on 3/23/53 in Great Lakes, Illinois. Became lead singer of Rufus in 1972. Rufus members Andre Fischer and Kevin Murphy were with The American Breed. **RUFUS:**	
7/13/74	3	12	● 1. **Tell Me Something Good**	ABC 11427
			RUFUS FEATURING CHAKA KHAN:	
11/2/74	11	11	2. You Got The Love #1 R&B hit (1 week)	ABC 12032
3/8/75	10	7	3. **Once You Get Started**	ABC 12066
2/14/76	5	12	● 4. **Sweet Thing** #1 R&B hit (2 weeks)	ABC 12149
6/12/76	39	1	5. Dance Wit Me	ABC 12179
3/12/77	30	6	6. At Midnight (My Love Will Lift You Up) #1 R&B hit (2 weeks)	ABC 12239
6/4/77	32	3	7. Hollywood	ABC 12269
5/27/78	38	3	8. Stay	ABC 12349
11/18/78	21	8	9. I'm Every Woman **CHAKA KHAN** #1 R&B hit (3 weeks); written by Ashford & Simpson	Warner 8683
1/19/80	30	4	10. Do You Love What You Feel #1 R&B hit (3 weeks)	MCA 41131
11/12/83	22	8	11. Ain't Nobody #1 R&B hit (1 week)	Warner 29555

DATE	POS	WKS	ARTIST–RECORD TITLE	LABEL & NO.
			CHAKA KHAN:	
9/29/84	3	17	● 12. **I Feel For You** Sales #2 / Airplay #2	Warner 29195
			#1 R&B hit (3 weeks); with Grandmaster Melle Mel (rap) and Stevie Wonder (harmonica); written by Prince	
12/16/89+	18	8	13. I'll Be Good To You Sales #13 / Airplay #26	Qwest 22697
			QUINCY JONES Featuring Ray Charles and Chaka Khan	
			#1 R&B hit (2 weeks)	
9/14/96	25	10	14. Missing You Sales #15	EastWest 64262
			BRANDY, TAMIA, GLADYS KNIGHT & CHAKA KHAN	
			from the movie *Set It Off* starring Jada Pinkett and Queen Latifah	
			## KID ROCK	
			Born Robert Ritchie on 1/17/71 in Romeo, Michigan. White hip-hop/rock singer.	
3/11/00	19	12	1. Only God Knows Why Airplay #18	album cut
			from the album *Devil Without A Cause* on Lava/Atlantic 83119	
12/28/02+	4	28	● 2. **Picture** Sales #1 (12) / Airplay #6	Universal South 172274
			KID ROCK Featuring ALLISON MOORER or SHERYL CROW	
			commerical single features Moorer; the vast majority of radio stations played the original album version featuring Crow	
			## KIHN, Greg, Band	
			Born on 7/10/50 in Baltimore, Maryland. Rock singer/songwriter/guitarist. His band consisted of Dave Carpender (guitar), Gary Phillips (keyboards), Steve Wright (bass) and Larry Lynch (drums). Greg Douglass replaced Carpender in late 1982.	
7/11/81	15	13	1. The Breakup Song (They Don't Write 'Em)	Beserkley 47149
3/5/83	2 (1)	14	2. **Jeopardy**	Beserkley 69847
3/23/85	30	4	3. Lucky Sales #25	EMI America 8255
			GREG KIHN	
			## KILGORE, Theola	
			Born in Shreveport, Louisiana; raised in Oakland, California. Female gospel-blues singer.	
5/11/63	21	8	1. The Love Of My Man	Serock 2004
			## KILLER MIKE — see BONE CRUSHER	
			## KIM, Andy	
			Born Androwis Jovakim on 12/5/52 in Montreal, Quebec, Canada. Pop singer/songwriter.	
6/1/68	21	8	1. How'd We Ever Get This Way	Steed 707
10/19/68	31	3	2. Shoot'em Up, Baby	Steed 710
6/21/69	9	12	● 3. **Baby, I Love You**	Steed 716
11/8/69	36	1	4. So Good Together	Steed 720
11/28/70	17	8	5. Be My Baby	Steed 729
7/20/74	1 (1)	13	● 6. **Rock Me Gently**	Capitol 3895
11/23/74	28	4	7. Fire, Baby I'm On Fire	Capitol 3962

DATE	POS	WKS	ARTIST–RECORD TITLE	LABEL & NO.
			KIMBERLY, Adrian	
			Artist is actually a Don Everly (Everly Brothers) production, recorded on Don's own label.	
7/10/61	**34**	1	1. The Graduation Song... Pomp And Circumstance **[I]**	Calliope 6501
			written in 1902 for the coronation of King Edward VII; song also known as "Land Of Hope And Glory"	
			KING, B.B.	
			Born Riley King on 9/16/25 in Itta Bena, Mississippi. Legendary blues singer/guitarist. His guitar named "Lucille." Moved to Memphis in 1946. Own radio show on WDIA-Memphis, 1949-50, where he was dubbed "The Beale Street Blues Boy," later shortened to "Blues Boy," then simply "B.B." Inducted into the Rock and Roll Hall of Fame in 1987. Won Grammy's Lifetime Achievement Award in 1987. Appeared in the movies *Into The Night* and *Amazon Women On The Moon*.	
6/13/64	**34**	3	1. Rock Me Baby	Kent 393
5/25/68	**39**	1	2. Paying The Cost To Be The Boss	BluesWay 61015
1/31/70	**15**	8	3. The Thrill Is Gone	BluesWay 61032
			#6 R&B hit for Roy Hawkins in 1951	
4/3/71	**40**	1	4. Ask Me No Questions	ABC 11290
9/22/73	**38**	2	5. To Know You Is To Love You	ABC 11373
			co-written by Stevie Wonder	
2/9/74	**28**	6	6. I Like To Live The Love	ABC 11406
			KING, Ben E.	
			Born Benjamin Earl Nelson on 9/23/38 in Henderson, North Carolina; raised in New York City. Lead singer of The Drifters from 1959-60.	
1/30/61	**10**	10	1. **Spanish Harlem**	Atco 6185
5/22/61	**4**	24	2. **Stand By Me**	Atco 6194
			#1 R&B hit (4 weeks); also see #7 below	
8/21/61	**18**	5	3. Amor	Atco 6203
			#2 hit for Bing Crosby in 1944	
5/19/62	**11**	7	4. Don't Play That Song (You Lied)	Atco 6222
8/3/63	**29**	6	5. I (Who Have Nothing)	Atco 6267
3/8/75	**5**	9	6. **Supernatural Thing - Part I**	Atlantic 3241
			#1 R&B hit (1 week)	
11/1/86	**9**	13	7. **Stand By Me** Sales #7 / Airplay #12 **[R]**	Atlantic 89361
			title song from the movie starring River Phoenix; same version as #2 above	
			KING, Carole	
			Born Carole Klein on 2/9/42 in Brooklyn, New York. Singer/songwriter/pianist. Married to songwriting partner Gerry Goffin from 1958-68. One of the most successful female songwriters of the rock era. She and Goffin were inducted as a songwriting team into the Rock and Roll Hall of Fame in 1990.	
9/22/62	**22**	4	1. It Might As Well Rain Until September	Dimension 2000
5/22/71	**1** (5)	15	● 2. **It's Too Late /**	
			#1 Adult Contemporary hit (5 weeks)	
6/12/71		12	3. I Feel The Earth Move	Ode 66015
9/4/71	**14**	9	4. So Far Away /	
			James Taylor (acoustic guitar)	
9/4/71		9	5. Smackwater Jack	Ode 66019
2/5/72	**9**	8	6. **Sweet Seasons**	Ode 66022

DATE	POS	WKS	ARTIST–RECORD TITLE		LABEL & NO.
12/9/72+	**24**	7	7. Been To Canaan #1 Adult Contemporary hit (1 week)		Ode 66031
8/11/73	**28**	5	8. Believe In Humanity		Ode 66035
12/8/73	**37**	2	9. Corazón	**[F]**	Ode 66039
9/14/74	**2** (1)	12	10. **Jazzman** Tom Scott (sax solo)		Ode 66101
1/18/75	**9**	8	11. **Nightingale** #1 Adult Contemporary hit (1 week)		Ode 66106
3/6/76	**28**	6	12. Only Love Is Real #1 Adult Contemporary hit (1 week)		Ode 66119
8/20/77	**30**	5	13. Hard Rock Cafe		Capitol 4455
6/14/80	**12**	10	14. One Fine Day		Capitol 4864

KING, Claude

Born on 2/5/33 in Shreveport, Louisiana. Country singer/songwriter/guitarist.

DATE	POS	WKS	ARTIST–RECORD TITLE	LABEL & NO.
6/16/62	**6**	11	● 1. **Wolverton Mountain** #1 Country hit (9 weeks)	Columbia 42352

KING, Diana

Born on 11/8/70 in St. Catherine, Jamaica. Reggae singer.

DATE	POS	WKS	ARTIST–RECORD TITLE		LABEL & NO.
5/27/95	**13**	20	● 1. Shy Guy	Sales #10 / Airplay #22	Work 77678
			from the movie *Bad Boys* starring Martin Lawrence and Will Smith		
9/20/97	**38**	1	2. I Say A Little Prayer	Sales #48 / Airplay #53	Work 78596
			from the movie *My Best Friend's Wedding* starring Julia Roberts		

KING, Evelyn "Champagne"

Born on 6/29/60 in the Bronx, New York; raised in Philadelphia, Pennsylvania. Black disco singer.

DATE	POS	WKS	ARTIST–RECORD TITLE	LABEL & NO.
7/22/78	**9**	10	● 1. **Shame**	RCA 11122
3/3/79	**23**	8	● 2. I Don't Know If It's Right	RCA 11386
9/12/81	**40**	2	3. I'm In Love #1 R&B hit (1 week)	RCA 12243
10/2/82	**17**	8	4. Love Come Down **EVELYN KING** (above 2) #1 R&B hit (5 weeks)	RCA 13273

KING, Freddy

Born Freddie Christian on 9/3/34 in Gilmer, Texas. Died of a heart attack on 12/28/76 (age 42). Blues singer/guitarist.

DATE	POS	WKS	ARTIST–RECORD TITLE		LABEL & NO.
4/3/61	**29**	4	1. Hide Away	**[I]**	Federal 12401
			titled after Mel's Hide Away Lounge in Chicago		

KING, Jonathan

Born Kenneth King on 12/6/44 in London, England. Pop singer/songwriter/producer. Formed U.K. Records in 1972.

DATE	POS	WKS	ARTIST–RECORD TITLE	LABEL & NO.
10/23/65	**17**	7	1. Everyone's Gone To The Moon	Parrot 9774

DATE	POS	WKS	ARTIST–RECORD TITLE	LABEL & NO.
			KING, Peggy	
			Born on 2/16/30 in Greensburg, Pennsylvania. Pop singer. Regular on TV's *The George Gobel Show* (1954-56). Appeared in the 1957 movie *Zero Hour*.	
2/5/55	**30**	1	1. Make Yourself Comfortable Top 100 #30 / Best Seller #30 Percy Faith (orch.)	Columbia 40363
			KING, Teddi	
			Born Theodora King on 9/18/29 in Boston, Massachusetts. Died on 11/18/77 (age 48). Female jazz-styled singer.	
3/3/56	**18**	2	1. Mr. Wonderful Jockey #18 / Top 100 #32 from the Broadway musical starring Sammy Davis Jr.	RCA Victor 6392
			KING CURTIS	
			Born Curtis Ousley on 2/7/34 in Fort Worth, Texas. Stabbed to death on 8/13/71 (age 37). Prolific R&B session saxophonist.	
4/7/62	**17**	8	1. Soul Twist **[I]** **KING CURTIS and THE NOBLE KNIGHTS** #1 R&B hit (2 weeks)	Enjoy 1000
9/23/67	**33**	4	2. Memphis Soul Stew **[I]**	Atco 6511
10/7/67	**28**	4	3. Ode To Billie Joe **[I]** **THE KINGPINS**	Atco 6516
			KING HARVEST	
			Pop-rock group from Olcott, New York: Ron Altback (vocals, piano), Eddie Tuleja (guitar), Rod Novack (sax), Dave Robinson (trombone), Tony Cahill (bass) and David Montgomery (drums). Altback and Robinson later joined Celebration.	
1/6/73	**13**	11	1. Dancing In The Moonlight	Perception 515
			KINGPINS, The — see KING CURTIS	
			KINGSMEN, The — see HALEY, Bill	
			KINGSMEN, The	
			Rock and roll band from Portland, Oregon: Jack Ely (vocals, guitar), Mike Mitchell (guitar), Don Gallucci (keyboards), Bob Nordby (bass) and Lynn Easton (drums). After release of "Louie Louie" (featuring lead vocal by Ely), Easton took over leadership of band and replaced Ely as lead singer.	
11/30/63	**2 (6)**	13	1. **Louie Louie** first recorded by Richard Berry in 1957	Wand 143
4/4/64	**16**	8	2. Money	Wand 150
1/30/65	**4**	9	3. **The Jolly Green Giant** same tune (different lyrics) as The Olympics' "Big Boy Pete"; lyrics inspired by the "Green Giant" vegetable commercials	Wand 172
			KINGSTON TRIO, The	
			Folk trio formed in San Francisco, California: Dave Guard, Bob Shane and Nick Reynolds. John Stewart replaced Guard in 1961. Originators of the folk music craze of the 1960s. Guard died of lymphoma on 3/22/91 (age 56).	
10/6/58	**1 (1)**	18	● 1. **Tom Dooley** Hot 100 #1 (0) / Best Seller #22 traditional American folk song written in 1868 as "Tom Dula"	Capitol 4049
3/30/59	**12**	9	2. The Tijuana Jail	Capitol 4167

DATE	POS	WKS	ARTIST–RECORD TITLE	LABEL & NO.
6/29/59	**15**	6	3. M.T.A. M.T.A.: Metropolitan Transit Authority; protest song written in 1948; melody based on the traditional folk song "The Wreck Of The Old 97"	Capitol 4221
9/21/59	**20**	8	4. A Worried Man adapted from the traditional American folk song "Worried Man Blues" (#14 hit for the Carter Family in 1930)	Capitol 4271
3/14/60	**32**	5	5. El Matador	Capitol 4338
8/8/60	**37**	2	6. Bad Man Blunder **[N]**	Capitol 4379
3/3/62	**21**	7	7. Where Have All The Flowers Gone written by folk legend Pete Seeger	Capitol 4671
2/23/63	**21**	5	8. Greenback Dollar	Capitol 4898
4/20/63	**8**	8	9. **Reverend Mr. Black** chorus is from the traditional folk song "Lonesome Valley" (#15 hit for the Carter Family in 1931)	Capitol 4951
8/31/63	**33**	4	10. Desert Pete	Capitol 5005

KINKS, The

Rock group formed in London, England: brothers Ray (vocals, guitar) and Dave (guitar) Davies, Pete Quaife (bass) and Mick Avory (drums). John Dalton replaced Quaife in 1969. Andy Pyle replaced Dalton in 1976. Jim Rodford (of Argent) replaced Pyle in 1978. Ian Gibbons (keyboards) joined in 1979. Group inducted into the Rock and Roll Hall of Fame in 1990.

DATE	POS	WKS	ARTIST–RECORD TITLE	LABEL & NO.
10/24/64	**7**	10	1. **You Really Got Me**	Reprise 0306
1/16/65	**7**	9	2. **All Day And All Of The Night**	Reprise 0334
3/27/65	**6**	8	3. **Tired Of Waiting For You**	Reprise 0347
7/10/65	**23**	4	4. Set Me Free	Reprise 0379
9/4/65	**34**	3	5. Who'll Be The Next In Line	Reprise 0366
1/8/66	**13**	9	6. A Well Respected Man	Reprise 0420
6/18/66	**36**	1	7. Dedicated Follower Of Fashion	Reprise 0471
8/27/66	**14**	7	8. Sunny Afternoon	Reprise 0497
9/12/70	**9**	12	9. **Lola**	Reprise 0930
8/19/78	**30**	5	10. A Rock 'N' Roll Fantasy	Arista 0342
5/28/83	**6**	12	11. **Come Dancing**	Arista 1054
9/17/83	**29**	4	12. Don't Forget To Dance	Arista 9075

KISS

Hard-rock group formed in New York: Paul Stanley (vocals, guitar), Gene Simmons (vocals, bass), Ace Frehley (guitar; see #8 below) and Peter Criss (drums). Noted for elaborate makeup and highly theatrical stage shows. Eric Carr replaced Criss in 1981. Vinnie Vincent replaced Frehley in 1982. Mark St. John replaced Vincent in 1984. Bruce Kulick, brother of Bob Kulick of Balance, replaced St. John in 1985. Carr died of cancer on 11/25/91 (age 41), replaced by Eric Singer. The original group reunited in 1996.

DATE	POS	WKS	ARTIST–RECORD TITLE	LABEL & NO.
11/29/75+	**12**	10	1. Rock And Roll All Nite **[L-R]** studio version charted at #68 earlier in 1975	Casablanca 850
4/17/76	**31**	4	2. Shout It Out Loud	Casablanca 854
9/25/76	**7**	13	● 3. **Beth**	Casablanca 863
1/15/77	**15**	8	4. Hard Luck Woman	Casablanca 873
4/9/77	**16**	8	5. Calling Dr. Love	Casablanca 880
7/30/77	**25**	7	6. Christine Sixteen	Casablanca 889
4/15/78	**39**	2	7. Rocket Ride	Casablanca 915

DATE	POS	WKS	ARTIST–RECORD TITLE	LABEL & NO.
12/2/78+	**13**	12	8. New York Groove **ACE FREHLEY**	Casablanca 941
6/16/79	**11**	11	● 9. I Was Made For Lovin' You	Casablanca 983
2/24/90	**8**	11	10. **Forever**　　　　　　Sales #5 / Airplay #9	Mercury 876716
			KISSOON, Mac And Katie	
			Brother-and-sister pop duo from Port-of-Spain, Trinidad. Mac was born Gerald Farthing on 11/11/43. Katie was born Kathleen Farthing on 11/3/51. Moved to England in the late 1950s.	
9/4/71	**20**	9	1. Chirpy Chirpy Cheep Cheep	ABC 11306
			KIX	
			Hard-rock group from Hagerstown, Maryland: Steve Whiteman (vocals), Ronnie Younkins and Brian Forsythe (guitars), Donnie Purnell (bass) and Jimmy Chalfant (drums).	
10/21/89	**11**	13	● 1. Don't Close Your Eyes　　　Sales #8 / Airplay #14	Atlantic 88902
			KLF, The	
			Dance duo formed in England: Bill Drummond and Jim Cauty. KLF: Kopyright Liberation Front.	
7/13/91	**5**	12	● 1. 3 A.M. Eternal　　　　Sales #5 / Airplay #28	Arista 2230
2/15/92	**11**	12	2. Justified & Ancient　　Sales #10 / Airplay #12 **THE KLF (Featuring Tammy Wynette)**	Arista 12401
			KLYMAXX	
			Female R&B group from Los Angeles, California: Lorena "Lungs" Porter (vocals), Cheryl Cooley (guitar), Lynn Malsby and Robbin Grider (keyboards), Joyce "Fenderella" Irby (bass) and Bernadette Cooper (drums). All shared vocals.	
10/26/85	**5**	17	1. **I Miss You**　　　　　Sales #3 / Airplay #6	Constellation 52606
8/2/86	**15**	8	2. Man Size Love　　　　Sales #12 / Airplay #19 from the movie *Running Scared* starring Gregory Hines and Billy Crystal	MCA 52841
6/20/87	**18**	9	3. I'd Still Say Yes　　　Sales #14 / Airplay #19	Constellation 53028
			KNACK, The	
			Rock group formed in Los Angeles, California: Doug Fieger (vocals, guitar), Berton Averre (guitar), Prescott Niles (bass) and Bruce Gary (drums).	
7/21/79	**1 (6)**	16	● 1. **My Sharona**	Capitol 4731
9/22/79	**11**	11	2. Good Girls Don't	Capitol 4771
3/8/80	**38**	2	3. Baby Talks Dirty	Capitol 4822
			KNICKERBOCKERS, The	
			Rock and roll band formed in Bergenfield, New Jersey: Buddy Randell (vocals, sax), brothers Beau (guitar) and Johnny (bass) Charles, and Jimmy Walker (drums). Randell was a member of The Royal Teens.	
1/1/66	**20**	9	1. Lies	Challenge 59321
			KNIGHT, Frederick	
			Born on 8/15/44 in Alabama. R&B singer/producer.	
5/27/72	**27**	9	1. I've Been Lonely For So Long	Stax 0117

Ini Kamoze had a bit of something for everybody in his #1 hit "Here Comes The Hotstepper." The song featured reggae chants, current dancehall beats, and even a chorus borrowed from the classic hit "Land Of 1000 Dances."

KC And The Sunshine Band repeated the chart-topping peaks of their hits "Get Down Tonight" and "That's The Way (I Like It)" with their repetitively titled #1 hit, "(Shake, Shake, Shake) Shake Your Booty."

R. Kelly went to #1 with "Bump N' Grind," a song that was originally planned to be part of the *Menace II Society* soundtrack. It didn't make the cut, but R. Kelly did supply soundtrack tunes to the films *Space Jam*, *Ali*, and *Batman & Robin*.

Alicia Keys gave J Records, the label created by former Arista executive Clive Davis, its first #1 hit with "Fallin'." The track also helped Alicia win the 2001 Grammy Award for Best New Artist.

Carole King pulled off the triple crown at the 1971 Grammy Awards. She won Album of the Year for *Tapestry*, Record of the Year for its first single, "It's Too Late," and Song of the Year for "You've Got A Friend," a hit recorded by James Taylor.

The Knack brought a power pop sound reminiscent of The Beatles to radio in 1979 with their #1 hit "My Sharona." The song returned to the charts in 1994 after being featured in the movie *Reality Bites*.

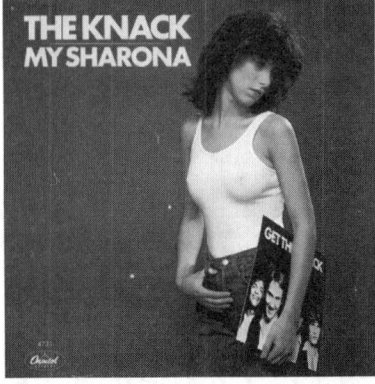

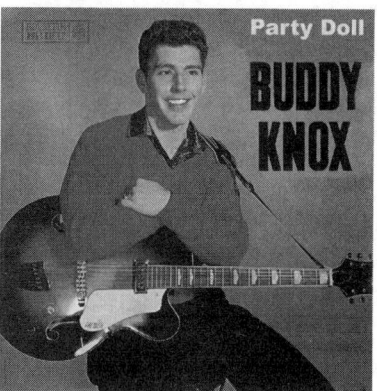

Gladys Knight & The Pips scored their first #1 hit with "Midnight Train To Georgia," a song originally titled "Midnight Plane To Georgia." By being grounded, the song took flight—and earned a Grammy for Best R&B Vocal Performance.

Buddy Knox invited fans to buy his self-penned #1 hit "Party Doll," but immediately found his chart party dampened by an uninvited guest: a competing version of the song by Steve Lawrence.

Kool and the Gang earned their only #1 pop hit with "Celebration." One-word titles seemed to fit the band, as they sent seven straight songs with one-word titles into the Top 40 in the mid-1980s.

Kris Kross attempted to make wearing clothes backwards a fashion trend, but it didn't catch on as well as their music. Their first single, "Jump," lived up to its name, reaching #1 in just four weeks.

LaBelle helped pop fans learn a little bit of French with the line "Voulez-vous coucher avec moi ce soir?" from their #1 hit "Lady Marmalade." The song was remade by current pop stars in 2001 for the movie *Moulin Rouge*.

Cyndi Lauper created a modern classic with her first #1 hit, "Time After Time." The one-time "girl who just wanted to have fun" went back in time in 2003 to record an album of pop standards titled *At Last*.

DATE	POS	WKS	ARTIST–RECORD TITLE	LABEL & NO.

KNIGHT, Gladys, & The Pips

R&B family vocal group from Atlanta, Georgia: Gladys Knight (born on 5/28/44), her brother Merald "Bubba" Knight, and cousins William Guest and Edward Patten. Named "Pips" for their manager, cousin James "Pip" Woods. Due to legal problems, Gladys could not record with the Pips from 1977-80. Gladys was a cast member of the 1985 TV series *Charlie & Co.* Group inducted into the Rock and Roll Hall of Fame in 1996.

DATE	POS	WKS	ARTIST–RECORD TITLE	LABEL & NO.
6/5/61	6	10	1. **Every Beat Of My Heart** **PIPS** #1 R&B hit (1 week)	Vee-Jay 386
1/20/62	19	6	2. Letter Full Of Tears written by Don Covay	Fury 1054
7/4/64	38	1	3. Giving Up	Maxx 326
8/19/67	39	2	4. Everybody Needs Love	Soul 35034
11/4/67	2 (3)	14	5. **I Heard It Through The Grapevine** #1 R&B hit (6 weeks)	Soul 35039
2/17/68	15	8	6. The End Of Our Road	Soul 35042
7/6/68	40	1	7. It Should Have Been Me	Soul 35045
8/9/69	19	8	8. The Nitty Gritty	Soul 35063
11/15/69	17	10	9. Friendship Train	Soul 35068
4/4/70	25	5	10. You Need Love Like I Do (Don't You)	Soul 35071
12/19/70+	9	12	11. **If I Were Your Woman** #1 R&B hit (1 week)	Soul 35078
6/19/71	17	9	12. I Don't Want To Do Wrong	Soul 35083
1/8/72	27	5	13. Make Me The Woman That You Go Home To	Soul 35091
4/8/72	33	6	14. Help Me Make It Through The Night	Soul 35094
2/17/73	2 (2)	12	15. **Neither One Of Us (Wants To Be The First** **To Say Goodbye)** #1 R&B hit (4 weeks)	Soul 35098
6/2/73	19	8	16. Daddy Could Swear, I Declare	Soul 35105
7/7/73	28	7	17. Where Peaceful Waters Flow	Buddah 363
9/15/73	1 (2)	16	● 18. **Midnight Train To Georgia** #1 R&B hit (4 weeks)	Buddah 383
12/8/73+	4	13	● 19. **I've Got To Use My Imagination** #1 R&B hit (1 week)	Buddah 393
3/9/74	3	13	● 20. **Best Thing That Ever Happened To Me** #1 R&B hit (2 weeks)	Buddah 403
6/1/74	5	11	● 21. **On And On** written and produced by Curtis Mayfield; from the movie *Claudine* starring Diahann Carroll	Buddah 423
11/16/74	21	9	22. I Feel A Song (In My Heart) #1 R&B hit (2 weeks)	Buddah 433
5/24/75	11	12	23. The Way We Were/Try To Remember	Buddah 463
11/29/75	22	7	24. Part Time Love	Buddah 513
11/23/85+	1 (4)	17	● 25. **That's What Friends Are For** Sales #1 (5) / Airplay #1 (3) **DIONNE & FRIENDS: Elton John, Gladys Knight and Stevie Wonder** #1 R&B hit (3 weeks) / #1 Adult Contemporary hit (2 weeks); first recorded by Rod Stewart in 1982	Arista 9422
1/30/88	13	9	26. Love Overboard Sales #11 / Airplay #20 #1 R&B hit (1 week)	MCA 53210
9/14/96	25	10	27. Missing You Sales #15 **BRANDY, TAMIA, GLADYS KNIGHT & CHAKA KHAN** from the movie *Set It Off* starring Jada Pinkett and Queen Latifah	EastWest 64262

DATE	POS	WKS	ARTIST–RECORD TITLE	LABEL & NO.
			KNIGHT, Jean	
			Born on 1/26/43 in New Orleans, Louisiana. Female R&B singer.	
6/19/71	**2** (2)	13	▲² 1. **Mr. Big Stuff** #1 R&B hit (5 weeks)	Stax 0088
			KNIGHT, Jordan — see NEW KIDS ON THE BLOCK	
			KNIGHT, Robert	
			Born on 4/21/45 in Franklin, Tennessee. R&B singer.	
10/28/67	**13**	8	1. Everlasting Love	Rising Sons 705
			KNIGHT, Sonny	
			Born Joseph Smith on 5/17/34 in Maywood, Illinois. Died on 9/5/98 (age 64). R&B singer/songwriter/pianist.	
11/24/56	**17**	9	1. Confidential Juke Box #17 / Best Seller #19 / Top 100 #20 Jack Collier (orch.)	Dot 15507
			KNOBLOCK, Fred	
			Born J. Fred Knobloch on 4/28/53 in Jackson, Mississippi. Pop-country singer/songwriter.	
7/26/80	**18**	7	1. Why Not Me #1 Adult Contemporary hit (2 weeks)	Scotti Brothers 518
12/27/80+	**28**	9	2. Killin' Time **FRED KNOBLOCK AND SUSAN ANTON**	Scotti Brothers 609
			KNOWLES, Beyoncé — see JAY-Z	
			KNOX, Buddy, with the Rhythm Orchids	
			Born on 7/20/33 in Happy, Texas. Died of cancer on 2/14/99 (age 65). Rockabilly singer/guitarist. The Rhythm Orchids consisted of Don Lanier (guitar), Jimmy Bowen (bass) and Dave "Dicky Doo" Alldred (drums).	
3/2/57	**1** (1)	15	● 1. **Party Doll** Best Seller #1 (1) / Juke Box #2 / Top 100 #2 / Jockey #5	Roulette 4002

6/3/57	**17**	7	2. Rock Your Little Baby To Sleep
			       Jockey #17 / Best Seller #23 / Top 100 #23
			      Lieutenant BUDDY KNOX With The Rhythm Orchids
				Roulette 4009

9/9/57	**9**	15	3. **Hula Love** Jockey #9 / Top 100 #12 / Best Seller #13 featured in the movie *Jamboree!* starring Kay Medford	Roulette 4018
8/4/58	**22**	11	4. Somebody Touched Me Hot 100 #22 / Best Seller #32 first recorded by Ruth Brown in 1954	Roulette 4082

1/9/61	**25**	4	5. Lovey Dovey
			      BUDDY KNOX
			       #2 R&B hit for The Clovers in 1954
				Liberty 55290

			KOFFMAN, Moe, Quartette	
			Born Morris Koffman on 12/28/28 in Toronto, Ontario, Canada. Died of cancer on 3/28/2001 (age 72). Saxophonist.	
2/10/58	**23**	5	1. The Swingin' Shepherd Blues Jockey #23 / Best Seller #36 / Top 100 #36 **[I]**	Jubilee 5311

DATE	POS	WKS	ARTIST–RECORD TITLE	LABEL & NO.
			KOKOMO	
			Born James Wisner on 12/8/31 in Philadelphia, Pennsylvania. Record producer/pianist.	
3/6/61	8	11	1. **Asia Minor** [I] adapted from Grieg's *Piano Concerto In A Minor*	Felsted 8612
			KON KAN	
			Dance duo from Toronto, Ontario, Canada: Kevin Wynne (vocals) and Barry Harris (instruments).	
2/4/89	15	9	1. I Beg Your Pardon Sales #12 / Airplay #16 includes several lines from Lynn Anderson's "Rose Garden"; samples "Disco Nights (Rock-Freak)" by GQ	Atlantic 88969
			KOOL & THE GANG	
			R&B group formed in Jersey City, New Jersey. Nucleus of group: Robert "Kool" Bell (bass), his brother Ronald Bell (sax), Claydes Smith (guitar), Rick Westfield (keyboards), Dennis Thomas (sax), Robert Mickens (trumpet) and George Brown (drums). Added lead singer James "J.T." Taylor in 1978. Earl Toon replaced Westfield in 1978.	
10/6/73	29	6	1. Funky Stuff	De-Lite 557
1/5/74	4	16	● 2. **Jungle Boogie**	De-Lite 559
5/18/74	6	11	● 3. **Hollywood Swinging** #1 R&B hit (1 week)	De-Lite 561
10/12/74	37	2	4. Higher Plane #1 R&B hit (1 week)	De-Lite 1562
6/28/75	35	3	5. Spirit Of The Boogie / #1 R&B hit (1 week)	
6/28/75		3	6. Summer Madness [I]	De-Lite 1567
11/10/79+	8	14	● 7. **Ladies Night** #1 R&B hit (3 weeks)	De-Lite 801
2/9/80	5	13	● 8. **Too Hot**	De-Lite 802
11/22/80+	1 (2)	21	▲ 9. **Celebration** #1 R&B hit (6 weeks)	De-Lite 807
6/27/81	39	2	10. Jones Vs. Jones	De-Lite 813
11/7/81	17	12	11. Take My Heart (You Can Have It If You Want It) #1 R&B hit (1 week)	De-Lite 815
4/3/82	10	9	● 12. **Get Down On It**	De-Lite 818
9/11/82	21	7	13. Big Fun	De-Lite 822
12/4/82+	30	7	14. Let's Go Dancin' (Ooh La, La, La)	De-Lite 824
12/3/83+	2 (1)	16	● 15. **Joanna** #1 R&B hit (2 weeks)	De-Lite 829
3/17/84	13	10	16. Tonight	De-Lite 830
1/5/85	10	13	17. **Misled** Sales #8 / Airplay #10	De-Lite 880431
4/20/85	9	11	18. **Fresh** Sales #6 / Airplay #12 #1 R&B hit (1 week)	De-Lite 880623
7/27/85	2 (3)	15	● 19. **Cherish** Sales #1 (1) / Airplay #2 #1 R&B hit (1 week) / #1 Adult Contemporary hit (6 weeks)	De-Lite 880869
11/23/85	18	8	20. Emergency Sales #17 / Airplay #19	De-Lite 884199
11/22/86+	10	12	21. **Victory** Sales #6 / Airplay #13	Mercury 888074
3/14/87	10	10	22. **Stone Love** Sales #8 / Airplay #16	Mercury 888292

DATE	POS	WKS	ARTIST–RECORD TITLE	LABEL & NO.
			KOOL MOE DEE — see SMITH, Will	
			KORGIS, The	
			Pop trio formed in England: James Warren (vocals, bass), Stuart Gordon (guitar) and Andy Davis (drums).	
11/8/80	**18**	11	1. Everybody's Got To Learn Sometime	Asylum 47055
			KORN	
			Hard-rock group from Huntington Beach, California: Jonathan Davis (vocals), Brian Welch and James Munkey (guitars), Reggie Fieldy Arvizu (bass) and David Silveria (drums).	
8/9/03	**38**	1	1. Did My Time Sales #2	Epic/Immortal 79977
			from the move *Lara Croft Tomb Raider: The Cradle Of Life* starring Angelina Jolie (not on soundtrack album)	
			K.P. & ENVYI	
			Female rap duo: Kia "K.P." Philips and Susan "Envyi" Hedgepeth.	
1/31/98	**6**	13	● 1. **Swing My Way** Sales #5 / Airplay #34	EastWest 64135
			KRAFTWERK	
			Progressive-rock group formed in Dusseldorf, Germany: Ralf Hutter (keyboards), Florian Schneider (woodwinds), Klaus Roeder (guitar) and Wolfgang Flur (drums).	
4/12/75	**25**	5	1. Autobahn [I]	Vertigo 203
			KRAMER, Billy J., With The Dakotas	
			Born William Ashton on 8/19/43 in Bootle, Merseyside, England. Pop singer. The Dakotas consisted of Mike Maxfield and Robin McDonald (guitars), Ray Jones (bass) and Tony Mansfield (drums).	
5/2/64	**7**	12	1. **Little Children /**	
6/13/64	**9**	8	2. **Bad To Me**	Imperial 66027
8/15/64	**30**	3	3. I'll Keep You Satisfied	Imperial 66048
9/19/64	**23**	5	4. From A Window	Imperial 66051
			above 3 written by John Lennon and Paul McCartney	
			KRAUSS, Alison — see ROGERS, Kenny	
			KRAVITZ, Lenny	
			Born on 5/26/64 in Brooklyn, New York. R&B-rock singer/songwriter/guitarist. Married to actress Lisa Bonet (played "Denise Huxtable" on TV's *The Cosby Show*) from 1987-93. Son of actress Roxie Roker (played "Helen Willis" on TV's *The Jeffersons*).	
6/22/91	**2** (1)	14	1. **It Ain't Over 'Til It's Over** Airplay #8 / Sales #16	Virgin 98795
1/23/99	**12**	22	2. Fly Away Airplay #10	album cut
			#1 Mainstream Rock hit (3 weeks) / #1 Modern Rock hit (2 weeks); from the album *Five* on Virgin 45605	
12/9/00+	**4**	28	3. **Again** Airplay #2	album cut
			from the album *Greatest Hits* on Virgin 50316	
11/24/01	**31**	7	4. Dig In Airplay #31	album cut
			from the album *Lenny* on Virgin 11233	

DATE	POS	WKS	ARTIST–RECORD TITLE	LABEL & NO.
			KRIS KROSS	
			Rap duo from Atlanta, Georgia: Chris "Mack Daddy" Kelly (born on 5/1/78) and Chris "Daddy Mack" Smith (born on 1/10/79). Appeared in the movie *Who's The Man?*	
4/11/92	**1** (8)	18	▲² 1. **Jump** Sales #1 (9) / Airplay #4	Ruffhouse 74197
6/27/92	**13**	13	● 2. Warm It Up Sales #4 / Airplay #28	Ruffhouse 74376
7/31/93	**19**	10	● 3. Alright Sales #9 / Airplay #36	Ruffhouse 77103
			Super Cat (guest vocal); samples "Just A Touch Of Love" by Slave	
12/16/95+	**12**	15	● 4. Tonite's Tha Night Sales #4 / Airplay #50	Ruffhouse 78092
			Trey Lorenz (backing vocal)	
			KRISTOFFERSON, Kris	
			Born on 6/22/36 in Brownsville, Texas. Country singer/songwriter/actor. Starred in several movies. Married to Rita Coolidge from 1973-80.	
10/2/71	**26**	6	1. Loving Her Was Easier (Than Anything I'll Ever Do Again)	Monument 8525
7/7/73	**16**	19	● 2. Why Me	Monument 8571
			#1 Country hit (1 week)	
			KROEGER, Chad	
			Born on 11/15/74 in Hanna, Alberta, Canada. Lead singer of Nickelback.	
6/1/02	**3**	19	1. **Hero** Airplay #3	album cut
			CHAD KROEGER Featuring Josey Scott	
			#1 Mainstream Rock hit (2 weeks) / #1 Modern Rock hit (3 weeks); from the movie *Spider-Man* starring Tobey Maguire and Kirsten Dunst (soundtrack on Columbia 86402)	
8/30/03	**8**	29	2. **Why Don't You & I** Airplay #8	album cut
			SANTANA Featuring Alex Band or Chad Kroeger	
			the Chad Kroeger (of Nickelback) version is from Santana's album *Shaman* on Arista 14737; the Alex Band (of The Calling) version is available as a promo single only (Arista 53233)	
			K7	
			Born Louis Sharpe on 8/25/69 in Harlem, New York. Male rapper/dancer.	
10/16/93	**18**	14	● 1. Come Baby Come Sales #17 / Airplay #30	Tommy Boy 7572
			KUBAN, Bob, And The In-Men	
			Pop-rock group from St. Louis, Missouri: Bob Kuban (drums), Walter Scott (vocals), Ray Schulte (guitar), Greg Hoeltzel (keyboards), Pat Hixton (trumpet), Harry Simon (sax), Skip Weisser (trombone) and Mike Krenski (bass). Scott disappeared on 12/27/83; his ex-wife and her husband were charged with Scott's murder after his body was found three years later with a gunshot wound to the back.	
2/19/66	**12**	7	1. The Cheater	Musicland 20,001
			KUT KLOSE	
			Female R&B vocal trio from Atlanta, Georgia: Tabitha Duncan, Athena Cage and LaVonn Battle.	
6/10/95	**34**	3	1. I Like Sales #18 / Airplay #60	Keia/Elektra 64486
			K.W.S.	
			Dance trio from Nottingham, England: Chris King, Winnie Williams and Meg St. Joseph.	
8/8/92	**6**	16	● 1. **Please Don't Go** Airplay #4 / Sales #15	Next Plateau 339

DATE	POS	WKS	ARTIST–RECORD TITLE	LABEL & NO.

KYPER

Born Randall Kyper in Baton Rouge, Louisiana. Male rapper.

| 8/4/90 | 14 | 12 | ● 1. Tic-Tac-Toe   Sales #7 / Airplay #31 | Atlantic 87910 |

borrows guitar riffs from "Owner Of A Lonely Heart" by Yes

L

LaBELLE, Patti

Born Patricia Holt on 5/24/44 in Philadelphia, Pennsylvania. Formed female R&B vocal group The Blue Belles: Nona Hendryx, Sarah Dash and Cindy Birdsong. Birdsong left in 1967 to join The Supremes. Group continued as a trio. In 1971, group shortened its name to LaBelle. In 1977, group disbanded and Patti recorded solo.

| 5/12/62 | 15 | 7 | 1. I Sold My Heart To The Junkman | Newtown 5000 |

THE BLUE-BELLES

vocal group is actually The Starlets

| 11/2/63 | 37 | 3 | 2. Down The Aisle (Wedding Song) | Newtown 5777 |
| 2/8/64 | 34 | 1 | 3. You'll Never Walk Alone | Parkway 896 |

PATTI LaBELLE And Her Blue Belles (above 2)

from the Broadway musical *Carousel*

| 2/1/75 | 1 (1) | 13 | ● 4. **Lady Marmalade** | Epic 50048 |

LaBELLE

#1 R&B hit (1 week)

| 4/6/85 | 17 | 9 | 5. New Attitude   Sales #13 / Airplay #24 | MCA 52517 |

from the movie *Beverly Hills Cop* starring Eddie Murphy

| 4/19/86 | 1 (3) | 15 | ● 6. **On My Own**   Sales #1 (5) / Airplay #1 (2) | MCA 52770 |

PATTI LaBELLE AND MICHAEL McDONALD

#1 R&B hit (4 weeks)

| 8/23/86 | 29 | 3 | 7. Oh, People   Sales #26 | MCA 52877 |

LA BOUCHE

Black male/female dance duo: Lane McCray and Melanie Thornton. Thornton died in a plane crash on 11/24/2001 (age 34); replaced by Kayo Shekoni. La Bouche is French for "mouth."

12/16/95+	6	26	● 1. **Be My Lover** Sales #6 / Airplay #9	RCA 64446
4/27/96	13	25	2. Sweet Dreams Airplay #15 / Sales #22	RCA 64505
11/9/96	35 A	4	3. Fallin' In Love	Logic 59018

LADD, Cheryl

Born Cheryl Stoppelmoor on 7/2/51 in Huron, South Dakota. Actress/singer. Portrayed "Kris Monroe" on TV's *Charlie's Angels*.

| 8/26/78 | 34 | 3 | 1. Think It Over | Capitol 4599 |

LADY FLASH

Female R&B vocal trio: Lorraine Mazzola, Monica Burruss and Debra Byrd. Backing vocal group for Barry Manilow.

| 8/14/76 | 27 | 6 | 1. Street Singin' | RSO 852 |

written, produced and arranged by Barry Manilow

DATE	POS	WKS	ARTIST–RECORD TITLE	LABEL & NO.
			L.A. GUNS	
			Hard-rock group from Los Angeles, California: Philip Lewis (vocals), Tracii Guns and Mick Cripps (guitar), Kelly Nickels (bass), and Steve Riley (drums).	
6/16/90	33	4	1. The Ballad of Jayne *Sales #22*	Vertigo 876984
			LAI, Francis, And His Orchestra	
			Born on 4/26/32 in Nice, France. Male composer/conductor.	
2/27/71	31	4	1. Theme From Love Story **[I]** Georges Pludermacher (piano solo); theme from the movie *Love Story* starring Ali McGraw and Ryan O'Neal	Paramount 0064
			LAID BACK	
			Synth-pop duo from Denmark: Tim Stahl (keyboards) and John Guldberg (guitar).	
4/28/84	26	4	1. White Horse	Sire 29346
			LAINE, Frankie	
			Born Frank LoVecchio on 3/30/13 in Chicago, Illinois. Dynamic pop singer.	
9/3/55	17	3	1. Humming Bird *Juke Box #17* Jimmy Carroll (orch.)	Columbia 40526
12/17/55	19	10	2. A Woman In Love *Best Seller #19 / Top 100 #24* Percy Faith (orch.); from the movie *Guys And Dolls* starring Marlon Brando	Columbia 40583
12/8/56+	3	18	● 3. **Moonlight Gambler** *Top 100 #3 / Juke Box #3 / Jockey #4 / Best Seller #5* Ray Conniff (orch.)	Columbia 40780
4/20/57	10	8	4. **Love Is A Golden Ring** *Jockey #10 / Best Seller #22 / Top 100 #23* **FRANKIE LAINE with The Easy Riders**	Columbia 40856
3/4/67	39	2	5. I'll Take Care Of Your Cares first recorded by Franklyn Baur in 1927	ABC 10891
5/6/67	35	3	6. Making Memories Peter DeAngelis (orch., above 2)	ABC 10924
3/1/69	24	7	7. You Gave Me A Mountain #1 Adult Contemporary hit (2 weeks); written by Marty Robbins; Jimmy Bowen (orch. and chorus)	ABC 11174
			LaMOND, George	
			Born George Garcia on 2/25/67 in Washington DC; raised in the Bronx, New York. Pop singer.	
6/23/90	25	6	1. Bad Of The Heart *Airplay #23 / Sales #25*	Columbia 73339
			LANCE, Major	
			Born on 4/4/42 in Chicago, Illinois. Died of heart disease on 9/3/94 (age 52). R&B singer.	
8/10/63	8	10	1. **The Monkey Time**	Okeh 7175
11/2/63	13	8	2. Hey Little Girl	Okeh 7181
1/11/64	5	10	3. **Um, Um, Um, Um, Um, Um**	Okeh 7187
4/11/64	20	6	4. The Matador	Okeh 7191
9/19/64	24	5	5. Rhythm	Okeh 7203
4/3/65	40	1	6. Come See all of above (except #4) written by Curtis Mayfield	Okeh 7216

DATE	POS	WKS	ARTIST–RECORD TITLE	LABEL & NO.
			LANCERS, The — see BREWER, Teresa	
			LANE, Mickey Lee	
			Born Mickey Lee Schreiber in 1945 in Rochester, New York. Rock and roll singer/songwriter.	
11/28/64	38	1	1. Shaggy Dog	Swan 4183
			lang, k.d.	
			Born Kathryn Dawn Lang on 11/2/61 in Consort, Alberta, Canada. Eclectic singer/songwriter.	
10/3/92	38	3	1. Constant Craving Airplay #33 / Sales #65	Sire 18942
			LANSON, Snooky	
			Born Roy Landman on 3/27/14 in Memphis, Tennessee. Died of cancer on 7/2/90 (age 76). Star of TV's *Your Hit Parade* (1950-57).	
12/3/55	20	6	1. It's Almost Tomorrow Top 100 #20 / Jockey #20 / Juke Box #20	Dot 15424
			LARKS, The	
			R&B vocal trio from Los Angeles, California: Don Julian, Ted Walters and Charles Morrison. Julian died of pneumonia on 11/6/98 (age 61).	
11/28/64+	7	11	1. **The Jerk**	Money 106
			LaROSA, Julius	
			Born on 1/2/30 in Brooklyn, New York. Pop singer. Regular on *Arthur Godfrey And His Friends* TV show until he was fired on the air on 10/19/53. Popular DJ in New York (WNEW) for many years.	
7/23/55	13	7	1. Domani (Tomorrow) Best Seller #13 / Juke Box #13 / Jockey #15	Cadence 1265
10/8/55	20	5	2. Suddenly There's A Valley Jockey #20 / Best Seller #22 / Top 100 #29 Archie Bleyer (orch., above 2)	Cadence 1270
2/18/56	15	7	3. Lipstick And Candy And Rubbersole Shoes Jockey #15 / Top 100 #21 Joe Reisman (orch.)	RCA Victor 6416
6/16/58	21	1	4. Torero Jockey #21 Nick Perito (orch. and chorus)	RCA Victor 7227
			LARSEN-FEITEN BAND	
			Top session musicians Neil Larsen (keyboards) and Buzz Feiten (guitar).	
9/13/80	29	6	1. Who'll Be The Fool Tonight	Warner 49282
			LARSON, Nicolette	
			Born on 7/17/52 in Helena, Montana; raised in Kansas City, Missouri. Died of a cerebral edema on 12/16/97 (age 45). Former session singer.	
12/23/78+	8	14	1. **Lotta Love** #1 Adult Contemporary hit (1 week); written by Neil Young	Warner 8664
2/16/80	35	3	2. Let Me Go, Love duet with Michael McDonald	Warner 49130

DATE	POS	WKS	ARTIST–RECORD TITLE	LABEL & NO.
			LaSALLE, Denise	
			Born Denise Craig on 7/16/39 in LeFlore County, Mississippi. R&B singer/songwriter.	
9/25/71	13	9	● 1. Trapped By A Thing Called Love #1 R&B hit (1 week)	Westbound 182
			LASGO	
			Dance trio from Belgium: Evi Griffin, Peter Luts and David Vervoort.	
2/1/03	35	1	1. Something Airplay #40 / Sales #47	Robbins 72056
			LASLEY, David	
			Born on 8/20/47 in Sault St. Marie, Michigan. Singer/songwriter.	
4/24/82	36	3	1. If I Had My Wish Tonight	EMI America 8111
			LAST, James, Band	
			Born on 4/17/29 in Bremen, Germany. Producer/arranger/conductor.	
4/26/80	28	6	1. The Seduction (Love Theme) **[I]** from the movie *American Gigolo* starring Richard Gere	Polydor 2071
			LATIMORE	
			Born Benjamin Latimore on 9/7/39 in Charleston, Tennessee. R&B singer/songwriter.	
11/23/74	31	3	1. Let's Straighten It Out #1 R&B hit (2 weeks)	Glades 1722
3/26/77	37	2	2. Somethin' 'Bout 'Cha	Glades 1739
			LaTOUR	
			Born William LaTour in Chicago, Illinois. Techno-dance artist.	
5/4/91	35	4	1. People Are Still Having Sex Sales #25 / Airplay #38	Smash 879666
			LATTIMORE, Kenny	
			Born on 4/10/70 in Washington DC. R&B singer. Married Chanté Moore on 1/1/2002.	
5/3/97	33	6	1. For You Sales #20	Columbia 78456
			LATTISAW, Stacy	
			Born on 11/25/66 in Washington DC. Female R&B singer.	
10/4/80	21	10	1. Let Me Be Your Angel	Cotillion 46001
8/1/81	26	7	2. Love On A Two Way Street	Cotillion 46015
10/22/83	40	1	3. Miracles	Cotillion 99855
			LAUPER, Cyndi	
			Born on 6/22/53 in Queens, New York. Pop-rock singer. Won the 1984 Best New Artist Grammy Award. Acted in the movies *Vibes* and *Life With Mikey*. Married actor David Thornton on 11/24/91.	
1/28/84	2 (2)	14	▲ 1. **Girls Just Want To Have Fun**	Portrait 04120
4/21/84	1 (2)	14	● 2. **Time After Time** #1 Adult Contemporary hit (3 weeks)	Portrait 04432
7/28/84	3	14	● 3. **She Bop** Sales #16 / Airplay #24	Portrait 04516

DATE	POS	WKS	ARTIST–RECORD TITLE	LABEL & NO.
10/13/84	**5**	14	4. **All Through The Night** Airplay #4 / Sales #9	Portrait 04639
1/12/85	**27**	6	5. Money Changes Everything Airplay #23 / Sales #28	Portrait 04737
6/1/85	**10**	9	6. **The Goonies 'R' Good Enough** Sales #10 / Airplay #10	Portrait 04918
			from the movie *The Goonies* starring Sean Astin	
9/13/86	**1** (2)	12	7. **True Colors** Airplay #1 (2) / Sales #2	Portrait 06247
12/13/86+	**3**	13	8. **Change Of Heart** Sales #2 / Airplay #5	Portrait 06431
			The Bangles (guest vocals)	
3/21/87	**12**	10	9. What's Going On Sales #10 / Airplay #12	Portrait 06970
5/20/89	**6**	10	10. **I Drove All Night** Sales #5 / Airplay #7	Epic 68759
			LAUREN, Rod	
			Born Roger Lawrence Strunk on 3/26/40 in Tracy, California. Pop singer. Acted in several low-budget movies.	
1/11/60	**31**	5	1. If I Had A Girl	RCA Victor 7645
			Shorty Rogers (orch. and chorus)	
			LAURIE SISTERS, The	
			Vocal group; similar in style to The Andrews Sisters.	
4/16/55	**30**	1	1. Dixie Danny Best Seller #30	Mercury 70548
			Hugo Peretti (of Hugo & Luigi; orch.)	
			LAVIGNE, Avril	
			Born on 9/30/84 in Napanee, Ontario, Canada. Teen pop-rock female singer/songwriter.	
6/22/02	**2** (2)	27	1. **Complicated** Airplay #2 / Sales #25	Arista 15185
12/14/02+	**4**	24	▲ 2. **I'm With You /** Airplay #5 / Sales #11	
9/28/02	**10**	13	3. **Sk8er Boi** Airplay #10	Arista 51024
			LAWRENCE, Billy – see RAMPAGE	
			LAWRENCE, Eddie	
			Born Lawrence Eisler on 3/2/19 in Brooklyn, New York. Comedian/actor/author/playwright.	
9/1/56	**34**	1	1. The Old Philosopher Top 100 #34 **[C]**	Coral 61671
			The Sentimental Four (musical accompaniment); background music: "Beautiful Dreamer"	
			LAWRENCE, Joey	
			Born on 4/20/76 in Montgomery, Pennsylvania. Actor/singer. Regular on TV's *Gimme A Break* (1983-87) and *Blossom* (1991-94).	
3/20/93	**19**	13	1. Nothin' My Love Can't Fix Sales #20 / Airplay #22	Impact/MCA 54562
			LAWRENCE, Steve	
			Born Sidney Leibowitz on 7/8/35 in Brooklyn, New York. Pop singer. Regular performer on Steve Allen's *Tonight Show* for five years. Married singer Eydie Gorme on 12/29/57.	
1/19/57	**18**	8	1. The Banana Boat Song Jockey #18 / Top 100 #30	Coral 61761
3/9/57	**5**	12	2. **Party Doll** Jockey #5 / Top 100 #10 / Juke Box #11 / Best Seller #12	Coral 61792
			Dick Jacobs (orch., above 2)	
12/14/59+	**9**	13	3. **Pretty Blue Eyes**	ABC-Paramount 10058
3/28/60	**7**	9	4. **Footsteps**	ABC-Paramount 10085

DATE	POS	WKS	ARTIST–RECORD TITLE	LABEL & NO.
4/3/61	9	10	5. **Portrait Of My Love** Don Costa (orch., above 3)	United Artists 291
12/8/62+	1 (2)	12	● 6. **Go Away Little Girl** #1 Adult Contemporary hit (6 weeks)	Columbia 42601
3/30/63	26	6	7. Don't Be Afraid, Little Darlin'	Columbia 42699
6/15/63	27	3	8. Poor Little Rich Girl	Columbia 42795
8/24/63	28	5	9. I Want To Stay Here **STEVE And EYDIE**	Columbia 42815
11/9/63	26	4	10. Walking Proud	Columbia 42865
1/25/64	35	3	11. I Can't Stop Talking About You **STEVE And EYDIE** Marion Evans (orch., above 6)	Columbia 42932
			LAWRENCE, Tracy	
			Born on 1/27/68 in Atlanta, Texas; raised in Foreman, Arkansas. Male country singer/songwriter/guitarist.	
4/8/00	40	2	1. Lessons Learned Airplay #32 from the album *Lessons Learned* on Atlantic 83269	album cut
			LAWRENCE, Vicki	
			Born on 5/26/49 in Inglewood, California. Regular on Carol Burnett's CBS-TV series from 1967-78. Also starred in TV's *Mama's Family* from 1982-87. Married to songwriter/singer Bobby Russell from 1972-74.	
3/17/73	1 (2)	14	● 1. **The Night The Lights Went Out In Georgia**	Bell 45,303
			LAYNE, Joy	
			Born in 1941 in Chicago, Illinois. Female pop singer.	
2/16/57	20	5	1. Your Wild Heart Juke Box #20 / Top 100 #30 Carl Stevens (orch.)	Mercury 71038
			LEAPY LEE	
			Born Lee Graham on 7/2/42 in Eastbourne, England. Male singer/actor.	
11/9/68	16	8	1. Little Arrows	Decca 32380
			LEAVES, The	
			Garage-rock group from Northridge, California: Robert Arlin (vocals), John Beck and Robert Lee Reiner (guitars), Jim Pons (bass), and Tom Ray (drums). Pons was later a brief member of The Turtles.	
6/18/66	31	4	1. Hey Joe	Mira 222
			LeBLANC & CARR	
			Soft-rock duo: Lenny LeBlanc (born on 6/17/51 in Leominster, Massachusetts) and Pete Carr (born on 4/22/50 in Daytona Beach, Florida).	
2/4/78	13	10	1. Falling	Big Tree 16100
			LE CLICK	
			Male/female techno-dance duo: Robert Haynes and Kayo Shekoni.	
6/14/97	35	5	1. Call Me Sales #36 / Airplay #44	Logic 45726

DATE	POS	WKS	ARTIST–RECORD TITLE	LABEL & NO.
			LED ZEPPELIN	
			Hard-rock group formed in England: Robert Plant (vocals), Jimmy Page (guitar), John Paul Jones (bass, keyboards) and John Bonham (drums). First known as the New Yardbirds. Page had been in The Yardbirds from 1966-68. Plant and Bonham had been in a group called Band Of Joy. Group formed own Swan Song label in 1974. In concert movie *The Song Remains The Same* in 1976. Bonham died of asphyxiation on 9/25/80 (age 33). Group disbanded in December 1980. Plant and Page formed The Honeydrippers in 1984. Page also with The Firm (1984-86). Bonham's son Jason formed group Bonham in 1989. Led Zeppelin's most famous recording, "Stairway To Heaven" (on album *Led Zeppelin IV*), was never released as a commercial single. Group inducted into the Rock and Roll Hall of Fame in 1995.	
12/6/69+	4	13	● 1. **Whole Lotta Love**	Atlantic 2690
12/12/70+	16	10	2. **Immigrant Song**	Atlantic 2777
1/15/72	15	8	3. **Black Dog**	Atlantic 2849
11/24/73	20	8	4. **D'yer Mak'er**	Atlantic 2986
5/17/75	38	2	5. **Trampled Under Foot**	Swan Song 70102
1/12/80	21	8	6. **Fool In The Rain**	Swan Song 71003
			LEE, Brenda	
			Born Brenda Mae Tarpley on 12/11/44 in Lithonia, Georgia. Professional singer since age six. Signed to Decca Records in 1956. Became known as "Little Miss Dynamite." Successful country singer from 1971-85. Inducted into the Rock and Roll Hall of Fame in 2002.	
2/15/60	4	15	1. **Sweet Nothin's**	Decca 30967
6/6/60	1 (3)	18	● 2. **I'm Sorry /**	
6/20/60	6	9	3. **That's All You Gotta Do** written by Jerry Reed	Decca 31093
9/19/60	1 (1)	13	4. **I Want To Be Wanted /**	
10/31/60	40	1	5. Just A Little	Decca 31149
12/19/60	14	3	● 6. Rockin' Around The Christmas Tree [X]	Decca 30776
1/16/61	7	9	7. **Emotions /**	
2/6/61	33	2	8. I'm Learning About Love	Decca 31195
4/3/61	6	10	9. **You Can Depend On Me** #4 hit for Louis Armstrong in 1932	Decca 31231
6/26/61	4	10	10. **Dum Dum**	Decca 31272
10/9/61	3	12	11. **Fool #1 /**	
10/16/61	31	3	12. Anybody But Me	Decca 31309
1/20/62	4	11	13. **Break It To Me Gently**	Decca 31348
4/28/62	6	8	14. **Everybody Loves Me But You**	Decca 31379
7/21/62	15	7	15. Heart In Hand /	
7/21/62	29	4	16. It Started All Over Again	Decca 31407
10/6/62	3	12	17. **All Alone Am I** #1 Adult Contemporary hit (5 weeks)	Decca 31424
2/16/63	32	3	18. Your Used To Be	Decca 31454
4/20/63	6	10	19. **Losing You**	Decca 31478
7/27/63	24	6	20. My Whole World Is Falling Down /	
7/27/63	25	5	21. I Wonder #1 R&B hit for Pvt. Cecil Gant in 1945	Decca 31510
10/12/63	17	5	22. The Grass Is Greener	Decca 31539
12/28/63+	12	8	23. As Usual	Decca 31570
3/28/64	25	5	24. Think	Decca 31599

DATE	POS	WKS	ARTIST–RECORD TITLE	LABEL & NO.
10/31/64	**17**	7	25. Is It True	Decca 31690
6/26/65	**13**	8	26. Too Many Rivers	Decca 31792
11/13/65	**33**	3	27. Rusty Bells	Decca 31849
10/29/66	**11**	8	28. Coming On Strong	Decca 32018
2/11/67	**37**	2	29. Ride, Ride, Ride	Decca 32079
			#36 Country hit for Lynn Anderson in 1966	
			### LEE, Curtis	
			Born on 10/28/41 in Yuma, Arizona. Pop singer/songwriter.	
7/17/61	**7**	8	1. **Pretty Little Angel Eyes**	Dunes 2007
			The Halos (backing vocals); produced by Phil Spector	
			### LEE, Dickey	
			Born Dickey Lipscomb on 9/21/36 in Memphis. Pop-country singer/ songwriter.	
9/8/62	**6**	11	1. **Patches**	Smash 1758
12/29/62+	**14**	8	2. I Saw Linda Yesterday	Smash 1791
6/19/65	**14**	7	3. Laurie (Strange Things Happen)	TCF Hall 102
			### LEE, Jackie	
			Born Earl Nelson on 9/8/28 in Lake Charles, Louisiana. R&B singer. One-half of Bob & Earl duo. Sang lead on "Buzz-Buzz-Buzz" by The Hollywood Flames.	
12/18/65+	**14**	9	1. The Duck	Mirwood 5502
			### LEE, Johnny	
			Born John Lee Ham on 7/3/46 in Texas City, Texas; raised in Alta Loma, Texas. Country singer/songwriter. Married to actress Charlene Tilton from 1982-84.	
8/2/80	**5**	13	● 1. **Lookin' For Love**	Full Moon 47004
			#1 Country hit (3 weeks); from the movie *Urban Cowboy* starring John Travolta and Debra Winger	
			### LEE, Laura	
			Born Laura Lee Rundless on 3/9/45 in Chicago, Illinois. R&B singer/ songwriter.	
10/16/71	**36**	4	1. Women's Love Rights	Hot Wax 7105
			### LEE, Leapy — see LEAPY LEE	
			### LEE, Murphy	
			Born Tohri Harper in St. Louis, Missouri. Male rapper. Member of St. Lunatics.	
7/12/03	**1** (4)	27	1. **Shake Ya Tailfeather** Airplay #1 (4) **NELLY/P. DIDDY/MURPHY LEE** from the movie *Bad Boys II* starring Will Smith and Martin Lawrence (soundtrack on Bad Boy 000716)	album cut
11/1/03	**17**	13	2. Wat Da Hook Gon Be Airplay #16 / Sales #49 **MURPHY LEE Featuring Jermaine Dupri**	Fo' Reel 001451

DATE	POS	WKS	ARTIST–RECORD TITLE	LABEL & NO.
			LEE, Peggy	
			Born Norma Jean Egstrom on 5/26/20 in Jamestown, North Dakota. Died of a heart attack on 1/21/2002 (age 81). Jazz singer with Jack Wardlow (1936-40), Will Osborne (1940-41) and Benny Goodman (1941-43). Went solo in March 1943. In movies *Mister Music* (1950), *The Jazz Singer* (1953) and *Pete Kelly's Blues* (1955). Co-wrote many songs with husband Dave Barbour (married from 1943-52). Awarded nearly $4 million in court for her singing in the animated movie *Lady And The Tramp*. Won Grammy's Lifetime Achievement Award in 1995.	
3/24/56	**14**	10	1. Mr. Wonderful Jockey #14 / Top 100 #23 / Best Seller #25 Sy Oliver (orch.); from the Broadway musical starring Sammy Davis Jr.	Decca 29834
7/21/58	**8**	13	2. **Fever** Hot 100 #8 / Best Seller #9 / Jockey #10 Jack Marshall (orch.)	Capitol 3998
10/11/69	**11**	8	3. Is That All There Is #1 Adult Contemporary hit (2 weeks); arranged and conducted by Randy Newman	Capitol 2602
			LEFEVRE, Raymond, and His Orchestra	
			Born in 1922 in Paris, France. Conductor/pianist/flutist.	
11/3/58	**30**	5	1. The Day The Rains Came [I]	Kapp 231
4/6/68	**37**	5	2. Ame Caline (Soul Coaxing) [I]	4 Corners 147
			LEFT BANKE, The	
			Rock group from Brooklyn, New York: Steve Martin (vocals), Rick Brand (guitar), Michael Brown (piano), Tom Finn (bass) and George Cameron (drums). Brown later joined Stories.	
9/24/66	**5**	10	1. **Walk Away Renee**	Smash 2041
2/4/67	**15**	6	2. Pretty Ballerina	Smash 2074
			LEFT EYE — see LIL' KIM	
			LEMON PIPERS, The	
			Pop-rock group from Oxford, Ohio: Ivan Browne (vocals, guitar), Bill Bartlett (guitar), R.G. Nave (organ), Steve Walmsley (bass) and Bill Albaugh (drums). Bartlett later joined Ram Jam. Albaugh died on 1/20/99 (age 53).	
12/23/67+	**1 (1)**	12	● 1. **Green Tambourine**	Buddah 23
			LEN	
			Rock group from Toronto, Ontario, Canada: Marc Costanzo (vocals), his sister Sharon Costanzo, D. Rock, DJ Moves, Planet Pea and Drunkness Monster.	
9/11/99	**9**	21	1. **Steal My Sunshine** Airplay #5 samples "More More More" by Andrea True Connection; from the movie *Go* starring Katie Holmes (soundtrack on Work 69851)	album cut
			LENNON, John	
			Born on 10/9/40 in Liverpool, England. Shot to death on 12/8/80 (age 40) in New York City. Founding member of The Beatles. Married to Cynthia Powell from 8/23/62 to 11/8/68; their son is Julian Lennon. Met Yoko Ono in 1966; married her on 3/20/69. Formed Plastic Ono Band in 1969. To New York City in 1971. Fought deportation from the U.S. (1972-76) until he was granted a permanent visa. Won Grammy's Lifetime Achievement Award in 1991. Inducted into the Rock and Roll Hall of Fame in 1994.	
8/9/69	**14**	6	1. Give Peace A Chance recorded in a hotel suite in Montreal	Apple 1809

DATE	POS	WKS	ARTIST–RECORD TITLE	LABEL & NO.
12/13/69+	**30**	7	2. Cold Turkey **PLASTIC ONO BAND** (above 2) Eric Clapton (guitar)	Apple 1813
3/7/70	**3**	12	● 3. **Instant Karma (We All Shine On)** **JOHN ONO LENNON** George Harrison (guitar) and Billy Preston (keyboards)	Apple 1818
4/10/71	**11**	8	4. Power To The People **JOHN LENNON/PLASTIC ONO BAND**	Apple 1830
10/23/71	**3**	9	5. **Imagine** **JOHN LENNON PLASTIC ONO BAND** above 3 co-produced by Phil Spector	Apple 1840
12/1/73	**18**	8	6. Mind Games	Apple 1868
10/5/74	**1** (1)	11	7. **Whatever Gets You Thru The Night** **JOHN LENNON with THE PLASTIC ONO NUCLEAR BAND** Elton John (backing vocal)	Apple 1874
1/11/75	**9**	8	8. #9 Dream	Apple 1878
4/5/75	**20**	5	9. Stand By Me	Apple 1881
11/1/80	**1** (5)	19	● 10. **(Just Like) Starting Over**	Geffen 49604
1/17/81	**2** (3)	17	● 11. **Woman**	Geffen 49644
4/11/81	**10**	10	12. **Watching The Wheels**	Geffen 49695
1/21/84	**5**	11	13. **Nobody Told Me** above 4 recorded in 1980	Polydor 817254
			LENNON, Julian	
			Born John Charles Julian Lennon on 4/8/63 in Liverpool, England. Pop-rock singer/songwriter/keyboardist. Son of Cynthia and John Lennon.	
11/10/84+	**9**	12	1. **Valotte** Sales #7 / Airplay #7	Atlantic 89609
2/2/85	**5**	12	2. **Too Late For Goodbyes** Airplay #4 / Sales #7 #1 Adult Contemporary hit (2 weeks)	Atlantic 89589
4/27/85	**21**	8	3. Say You're Wrong Airplay #18 / Sales #27	Atlantic 89567
4/26/86	**32**	4	4. Stick Around #1 Mainstream Rock hit (3 weeks)	Atlantic 89437
			LENNON SISTERS, The — see WELK, Lawrence	
			LENNOX, Annie	
			Born on 12/25/54 in Aberdeen, Scotland. Lead singer of the Eurythmics. Appeared in the movie *Edward II* and TV movie *The Room*. Recipient of *Billboard*'s Century Award in 2002.	
12/3/88+	**9**	10	1. **Put A Little Love In Your Heart** Airplay #8 / Sales #11 **ANNIE LENNOX & AL GREEN** from the movie *Scrooged* starring Bill Murray	A&M 1255
7/11/92	**34**	3	2. Why Airplay #38 / Sales #52	Arista 12419
10/3/92	**14**	19	3. Walking On Broken Glass Airplay #12 / Sales #24	Arista 12452
4/15/95	**23**	13	4. No More "I Love You's" Sales #22 / Airplay #25	Arista 12804
			LEONETTI, Tommy	
			Born on 9/10/29 in Bergen, New Jersey. Died of cancer on 9/15/79 (age 50). Vocalist with Charlie Spivak and other bands. Featured singer on TV's *Your Hit Parade* (1957-58).	
7/7/56	**23**	2	1. Free Jockey #23 / Top 100 #40 Neal Hefti (orch. and chorus)	Capitol 3442

DATE	POS	WKS	ARTIST–RECORD TITLE	LABEL & NO.
			LE ROUX	
			Rock group from Louisiana: Jeff Pollard (vocals), Tony Haseldon (guitar), Rod Roddy (piano), Bobby Campo (horns), Leon Medica (bass) and David Peters (drums).	
3/20/82	**18**	6	1. Nobody Said It Was Easy (Lookin' For The Lights)	RCA 13059
			LESTER, Ketty	
			Born Revoyda Frierson on 8/16/34 in Hope, Arkansas. R&B singer/actress.	
3/10/62	**5**	11	1. **Love Letters**	Era 3068
			#11 hit for Dick Haymes in 1945 (title song from the movie starring Jennifer Jones)	
			LETTERMEN, The	
			Adult Contemporary vocal trio formed in Los Angeles, California: Tony Butala, Jim Pike and Bob Engemann. Gary Pike (Jim's brother) replaced Engemann in 1968.	
9/25/61	**13**	9	1. The Way You Look Tonight	Capitol 4586
			#1 hit for Fred Astaire in 1936 (from the movie *Swing Time*)	
12/4/61+	**7**	11	2. **When I Fall In Love**	Capitol 4658
			#1 Adult Contemporary hit (1 week); #20 hit for Doris Day in 1952	
3/10/62	**17**	7	3. Come Back Silly Girl	Capitol 4699
			first recorded by Steve Lawrence in 1960	
7/17/65	**16**	5	4. Theme From "A Summer Place"	Capitol 5437
			from the 1959 movie *A Summer Place* starring Sandra Dee and Troy Donahue; Jimmie Haskell (orch., all of above)	
1/6/68	**7**	11	5. **Goin' Out Of My Head/Can't Take My Eyes Off You**	Capitol 2054
8/16/69	**12**	10	6. Hurt So Bad	Capitol 2482
			LEVEL 42	
			Pop-rock group formed in Manchester, England: Mark King (vocals, bass), brothers Boon (guitar) and Phil (drums) Gould, and Mike Lindup (keyboards).	
4/5/86	**7**	14	1. **Something About You** Sales #4 / Airplay #8	Polydor 883362
5/16/87	**12**	10	2. Lessons In Love Sales #7 / Airplay #13	Polydor 883956
			LEVERT, Gerald	
			Born on 7/13/66 in Cleveland, Ohio. R&B singer/songwriter. Member of Levert (with brother Sean Levert and Marc Gordon). Son of Eddie Levert (of The O'Jays).	
9/5/87	**5**	12	● 1. **Casanova** Sales #5 / Airplay #6	Atlantic 89217
			LEVERT	
3/21/92	**37**	1	2. Baby Hold On To Me Sales #20 / Airplay #60	EastWest 98639
			GERALD LEVERT (with Eddie Levert)	
			#1 R&B hit (1 week)	
8/20/94	**28**	8	3. I'd Give Anything Sales #16 / Airplay #42	EastWest 98244
			#4 Country hit for Boy Howdy in 1994 as "She'd Give Anything"	
9/5/98	**12**	9	● 4. Thinkin' Bout It Sales #2	EastWest 64091
1/30/99	**11**	8	● 5. Taking Everything Sales #4	EastWest 64061
			LEWIS, Barbara	
			Born on 2/9/43 in South Lyon, Michigan. R&B singer/songwriter.	
5/25/63	**3**	10	1. **Hello Stranger**	Atlantic 2184
			#1 R&B hit (2 weeks); The Dells (backing vocals)	

DATE	POS	WKS	ARTIST–RECORD TITLE	LABEL & NO.
3/14/64	**38**	1	2. Puppy Love	Atlantic 2214
7/17/65	**11**	9	3. Baby, I'm Yours	Atlantic 2283
10/9/65	**11**	8	4. Make Me Your Baby	Atlantic 2300
8/13/66	**28**	4	5. Make Me Belong To You	Atlantic 2346
			LEWIS, Bobby	
			Born on 2/17/33 in Indianapolis, Indiana; raised in Detroit, Michigan. R&B singer/songwriter.	
5/29/61	**1** (7)	17	1. **Tossin' And Turnin'** #1 R&B hit (10 weeks)	Beltone 1002
9/11/61	**9**	7	2. **One Track Mind** Joe Rene (orch., above 2)	Beltone 1012
			LEWIS, Donna	
			Born in Cardiff, Wales. White Adult Contemporary singer/songwriter.	
7/20/96	**2** (9)	35	● 1. **I Love You Always Forever** Airplay #1 (13) / Sales #4	Atlantic 87072
			LEWIS, Gary, And The Playboys	
			Born Gary Levitch on 7/31/45 in Brooklyn, New York. Pop singer/drummer. Son of comedian Jerry Lewis. The Playboys consisted of Al Ramsey and John West (guitars), David Walker (keyboards), and David Costell (bass).	
1/23/65	**1** (2)	11	● 1. **This Diamond Ring**	Liberty 55756
4/17/65	**2** (2)	9	2. **Count Me In**	Liberty 55778
7/17/65	**2** (1)	9	3. **Save Your Heart For Me** #1 Adult Contemporary hit (3 weeks); first recorded by Brian Hyland in 1963	Liberty 55809
10/9/65	**4**	8	4. **Everybody Loves A Clown**	Liberty 55818
12/18/65+	**3**	11	5. **She's Just My Style**	Liberty 55846
3/19/66	**9**	7	6. **Sure Gonna Miss Her**	Liberty 55865
5/21/66	**8**	7	7. **Green Grass**	Liberty 55880
8/13/66	**13**	5	8. My Heart's Symphony	Liberty 55898
10/22/66	**15**	6	9. (You Don't Have To) Paint Me A Picture	Liberty 55914
1/7/67	**21**	6	10. Where Will The Words Come From	Liberty 55933
6/10/67	**39**	2	11. Girls In Love	Liberty 55971
7/27/68	**19**	9	12. Sealed With A Kiss first recorded by The Four Voices in 1960	Liberty 56037
			LEWIS, Glenn	
			Born in Toronto, Ontario, Canada. R&B singer/songwriter.	
3/2/02	**30**	5	1. Don't You Forget It Airplay #28	Red Star/Epic 79649
			LEWIS, Huey, and The News	
			Born Hugh Cregg III on 7/5/50 in New York; raised in Danville, California. Pop-rock singer/songwriter. Formed the News in San Francisco, California: Chris Hayes (guitar), Sean Hopper (keyboards), Johnny Colla (sax), Mario Cipollina (bass) and Bill Gibson (drums). Lewis acted in the movies *Back To The Future* and *Short Cuts*.	
2/20/82	**7**	13	1. **Do You Believe In Love**	Chrysalis 2589
6/12/82	**36**	4	2. Hope You Love Me Like You Say You Do	Chrysalis 2604
10/8/83	**8**	13	3. **Heart And Soul** #1 Mainstream Rock hit (1 week)	Chrysalis 42726

DATE	POS	WKS	ARTIST–RECORD TITLE	LABEL & NO.
1/28/84	6	13	● 4. **I Want A New Drug**	Chrysalis 42766
4/28/84	6	14	5. **The Heart Of Rock & Roll**	Chrysalis 42782
7/28/84	6	13	6. **If This Is It** Sales #20	Chrysalis 42803
10/27/84	18	10	7. Walking On A Thin Line Airplay #12 / Sales #28	Chrysalis 42825
7/6/85	1 (2)	15	● 8. **The Power Of Love** Airplay #1 (3) / Sales #1 (1)	Chrysalis 42876
			#1 Mainstream Rock hit (2 weeks); from the movie *Back To The Future* starring Michael J. Fox	
8/9/86	1 (3)	13	9. **Stuck With You** Airplay #1 (3) / Sales #1 (2)	Chrysalis 43019
			#1 Adult Contemporary hit (3 weeks)	
10/25/86	3	12	10. **Hip To Be Square** Sales #1 (1) / Airplay #3	Chrysalis 43065
			#1 Mainstream Rock hit (1 week)	
1/17/87	1 (1)	12	11. **Jacob's Ladder** Airplay #1 (1) / Sales #2	Chrysalis 43097
			written by Bruce Hornsby	
4/11/87	9	10	12. **I Know What I Like** Sales #10 / Airplay #10	Chrysalis 43108
8/1/87	6	11	13. **Doing It All For My Baby** Airplay #5 / Sales #9	Chrysalis 43143
7/23/88	3	12	14. **Perfect World** Airplay #1 (1) / Sales #3	Chrysalis 43265
10/29/88	25	6	15. Small World Sales #25 / Airplay #26	Chrysalis 43306
5/11/91	11	9	16. Couple Days Off Airplay #16 / Sales #25	EMI 50346
8/17/91	21	6	17. It Hit Me Like A Hammer Airplay #37	EMI 50364
8/14/93	37 A	3	18. It's Alright	album cut
			from the various artists album *People Get Ready: A Tribute To Curtis Mayfield* on Shanachie 9004	

LEWIS, Jerry

Born Joseph Levitch on 3/16/25 in Newark, New Jersey. Comedian/actor. Father of Gary Lewis. Formed comedy duo with Dean Martin in 1946. Starred in several movies.

DATE	POS	WKS	ARTIST–RECORD TITLE	LABEL & NO.
11/24/56	10	15	● 1. **Rock-A-Bye Your Baby With A Dixie Melody** Best Seller #10 / Top 100 #12 / Juke Box #13 / Jockey #17 Buddy Bregman (orch.); #1 hit for Al Jolson in 1918	Decca 30124

LEWIS, Jerry Lee

Born on 9/29/35 in Ferriday, Louisiana. Rock and roll singer/pianist. Appeared in the movie *Jamboree!* in 1957. Career waned in 1958 after marriage to 13-year-old cousin, Myra Gale Brown, daughter of his bass player. Made comeback in country music beginning in 1968. Nicknamed "The Killer." Cousin to country singer Mickey Gilley and former TV evangelist Jimmy Swaggart. Inducted into the Rock and Roll Hall of Fame in 1986. Jerry's early career is documented in the 1989 movie *Great Balls Of Fire* starring Dennis Quaid.

DATE	POS	WKS	ARTIST–RECORD TITLE	LABEL & NO.
7/15/57	3	20	● 1. **Whole Lot Of Shakin' Going On** Best Seller #3 / Top 100 #3 / Jockey #9 #1 R&B hit (2 weeks) / #1 Country hit (2 weeks); first recorded by Big Maybelle in 1955	Sun 267
12/2/57+	2 (4)	13	● 2. **Great Balls Of Fire** Top 100 #2 / Best Seller #2 / Jockey #9 #1 Country hit (2 weeks)	Sun 281
3/10/58	7	9	3. **Breathless** Top 100 #7 / Best Seller #9 / Jockey #23	Sun 288
6/2/58	21	8	4. High School Confidential Top 100 #21 / Best Seller #22 title song from the movie starring Russ Tamblyn (song introduced by Lewis in the movie)	Sun 296
4/24/61	30	4	5. What'd I Say **JERRY LEE LEWIS And His Pumping Piano** (above 4)	Sun 356
1/15/72	40	1	6. Me And Bobby McGee	Mercury 73248

DATE	POS	WKS	ARTIST–RECORD TITLE	LABEL & NO.
			LEWIS, Ramsey, Trio	
			Born on 5/27/35 in Chicago, Illinois. R&B-jazz pianist. His trio included Eldee Young (bass) and Isaac "Red" Holt (drums). Disbanded in 1965. Young and Holt then formed The Young-Holt Trio. Lewis re-formed his trio with Cleveland Eaton (bass) and Maurice White (drums). White later founded Earth, Wind & Fire.	
8/21/65	5	12	1. The "In" Crowd [I-L]	Argo 5506
11/27/65	11	6	2. Hang On Sloopy [I-L]	Cadet 5522
2/5/66	29	4	3. A Hard Day's Night [I-L]	Cadet 5525
8/20/66	19	6	4. Wade In The Water [I]	Cadet 5541
			RAMSEY LEWIS	
			LFO	
			White pop vocal trio from Orlando, Florida: Rich Cronin, David Brian and Brad Young. Brian and Young left in 1999; replaced by Brad Fischetti and Devin Lima.	
7/24/99	3	13	▲ 1. **Summer Girls** Sales #1 (6) / Airplay #71	Logic/Arista 13692
11/27/99	10	11	● 2. **Girl On TV** Sales #2	Logic/Arista 13756
			LIFEHOUSE	
			Rock trio from Malibu, California: Jason Wade (vocals, guitar), Sergio Andrade (bass) and Rick Woolstenhulme (drums).	
3/10/01	2 (4)	45	1. **Hanging By A Moment** Airplay #1 (1) #1 Modern Rock hit (3 weeks); from the album *No Name Face* on DreamWorks 50231	album cut
			LIGHTER SHADE OF BROWN	
			Hispanic rap duo from Riverside, California: Robert Gutierrez and Bobby Ramirez.	
2/8/92	39	1	1. On A Sunday Afternoon Sales #24 / Airplay #39 featuring Shiro and Huggy Boy	Pump 15186
			LIGHTFOOT, Gordon	
			Born on 11/17/38 in Orillia, Ontario, Canada. Folk-pop singer/ songwriter/guitarist.	
1/23/71	5	11	1. **If You Could Read My Mind** #1 Adult Contemporary hit (1 week)	Reprise 0974
5/11/74	1 (1)	11	● 2. **Sundown** #1 Adult Contemporary hit (2 weeks)	Reprise 1194
10/5/74	10	7	3. **Carefree Highway** #1 Adult Contemporary hit (1 week)	Reprise 1309
5/3/75	26	4	4. Rainy Day People #1 Adult Contemporary hit (1 week)	Reprise 1328
9/25/76	2 (2)	13	5. **The Wreck Of The Edmund Fitzgerald** true story of an ore vessel, named after a Milwaukee civic leader, that sank in Lake Superior on 11/10/75	Reprise 1369
3/25/78	33	3	6. The Circle Is Small (I Can See It In Your Eyes)	Warner 8518

DATE	POS	WKS	ARTIST—RECORD TITLE	LABEL & NO.
			LIGHTHOUSE	
			Rock group from Toronto, Ontario, Canada: Bob McBride (vocals), Ralph Cole (guitar), Paul Hoffert (keyboards), Howard Shore (sax), Don Dinovo (viola), Dick Armin (cello), Louie Yacknin (bass) and Skip Prokop (drums). Shore went on to become the original musical director of TV's *Saturday Night Live*. McBride died on 2/20/98 (age 51).	
10/9/71	24	8	1. One Fine Morning	Evolution 1048
11/25/72	34	5	2. Sunny Days	Evolution 1069
			LIGHTNING SEEDS, The	
			Group is actually singer/producer Ian Broudie (born on 8/4/58 in Liverpool, England).	
7/7/90	31	6	1. Pure Sales #24 / Airplay #38	MCA 53816
			LIL — also see LITTLE	
			LIL BOW WOW	
			Born Shad Moss on 3/9/87 in Columbus, Ohio. Teen male rapper. Starred in the movie *Like Mike*.	
8/26/00	20	12	1. Bounce With Me Sales #7 / Airplay #29 **LIL BOW WOW (featuring Xscape)** #1 R&B hit (1 week); from the movie *Big Momma's House* starring Martin Lawrence	So So Def 79476
1/6/01	21	7	2. Bow Wow (That's My Name) Sales #2 / Airplay #26	So So Def 79556
8/9/03	14	9	3. Let's Get Down Sales #4 / Airplay #12 **BOW WOW (Feat. Baby)**	Columbia 79928
			LIL JON & THE EAST SIDE BOYZ	
			Black hip-hop group led by Jonathan "Lil Jon" Smith. The East Side Boyz are: Lil Bo, Big Sam and Playa Poncho.	
6/28/03	2 (1)	36	1. Get Low Airplay #2 / Sales #21 **LIL JON & THE EAST SIDE BOYZ Featuring Ying Yang Twins**	BME 2377
9/6/03	4	25	2. Damn! Airplay #4 / Sales #40 **YOUNGBLOODZ Featuring Lil' Jon**	So So Def 52215
12/27/03+	9	19	3. Salt Shaker Airplay #8 / Sales #14 **YING YANG TWINS Feat. LIL JON & The EAST SIDE BOYZ**	Collipark 2485
			LIL' KIM	
			Born Kimberly Jones on 7/11/75 in Brooklyn, New York. Female rapper. Member of Junior M.A.F.I.A.	
11/30/96+	18	13	● 1. No Time Sales #7 **LIL' KIM Featuring Puff Daddy** samples "Take Me Just As I Am" by Lyn Collins	Undeas/Big Beat 98044
7/12/97	6	17	▲ 2. Not Tonight Sales #3 / Airplay #39 **LIL' KIM Featuring Da Brat, Left Eye, Missy "Misdemeanor" Elliott and Angie Martinez** samples "Ladies Night" by Kool & The Gang; from the movie *Nothing To Lose* starring Martin Lawrence	Undeas/Big Beat 98019
12/6/97+	2 (2)	6	▲ 3. It's All About The Benjamins Sales #2 / Airplay #62 **PUFF DADDY & THE FAMILY Feat. The Notorious B.I.G., Lil' Kim, The Lox, Dave Grohl, Perfect, FuzzBubble & Rob Zombie** samples "I Did It For Love" by Love Unlimited Orchestra	Bad Boy 79130

DATE	POS	WKS	ARTIST–RECORD TITLE	LABEL & NO.
4/11/98	**17**	11	● 4. Money, Power & Respect Sales #10 / Airplay #65 **THE LOX [Feat. DMX & Lil' Kim]** samples "New Beginning" by Dexter Wansel	Bad Boy 79156
4/21/01	**1** (5)	17	5. Lady Marmalade Airplay #1 (6) **CHRISTINA AGUILERA, LIL' KIM, MYA and P!NK** co-produced by Missy "Misdemeanor" Elliott; from the movie *Moulin Rouge* starring Nicole Kidman and Ewan McGregor	Interscope 497066
6/30/01	**30**	5	6. Wait A Minute Airplay #27 / Sales #55 **RAY-J Featuring Lil' Kim**	Atlantic 85066
3/8/03	**17**	11	7. The Jump Off Sales #11 / Airplay #16 **LIL' KIM (featuring Mr. Cheeks)** samples "Jeeps, Lex Coups, Bimaz & Benz" by Lost Boyz	Queen Bee 88036
5/10/03	**2** (3)	21	8. Magic Stick Airplay #1 (1) **LIL' KIM (feat. 50 Cent)** samples "The Thrill Is Gone" by B.B. King; from the album *La Bella Mafia* on Queen Bee 83572	album cut
8/16/03	**12**	15	9. Can't Hold Us Down Airplay #12 **CHRISTINA AGUILERA featuring Lil' Kim**	RCA 54526
			LIL' MO	
			Born Cynthia Loving on 3/10/76 in Long Island, New York. Female R&B singer.	
1/20/01	**8**	22	1. Put It On Me Airplay #4 / Sales #62 **JA RULE (feat. Lil' Mo and Vita)**	Def Jam 572751
5/12/01	**11**	14	2. Superwoman Pt. II Sales #2 / Airplay #22 **LIL' MO (Featuring Fabolous)**	EastWest 67171
6/16/01	**40**	2	3. I Cry Airplay #34 **JA RULE (Feat. Lil' Mo)** samples "Cry Together" by The O'Jays	Def Jam 572856
8/24/02	**15**	15	4. If I Could Go! Airplay #14 / Sales #55 **ANGIE MARTINEZ (Featuring Lil' Mo & Sacario)**	Elektra 67311
3/22/03	**4**	19	5. Can't Let You Go Airplay #4 / Sales #42 **FABOLOUS featuring Mike Shorey & Lil' Mo**	Desert Storm 67428
6/7/03	**37**	3	6. 4 Ever Sales #33 / Airplay #34 **LIL' MO (Featuring Fabolous)**	Elektra 67379
			LIL' ROMEO	
			Born Percy Romeo Miller on 8/19/89 in New Orleans, Louisiana. Pre-teen male rapper. Son of Master P.	
5/19/01	**3**	10	1. My Baby Sales #1 (6) / Airplay #52 #1 R&B hit (1 week); Ms. Peaches (female vocal); an adaptation of "I Want You Back" by The Jackson 5	Soulja 50202
			LIL WAYNE	
			Born Wayne Carter on 9/27/83 in New Orleans, Louisiana. Male rapper.	
9/4/99	**19**	22	1. Back That Azz Up Airplay #9 / Sales #64 **JUVENILE Feat. Mannie Fresh and Lil' Wayne**	Cash Money 156482
10/30/99	**36**	5	2. Bling Bling Airplay #25 / Sales #72 **B.G. Feat. Baby, Turk, Mannie Fresh, Juvenile and Lil Wayne**	Cash Money 156483

DATE	POS	WKS	ARTIST–RECORD TITLE	LABEL & NO.
			LIL' ZANE	
			Born Zane Copeland Jr. on 7/11/82 in Yonkers, New York; raised in Atlanta, Georgia. Male rapper.	
4/17/99	**15**	18	1. Anywhere _Airplay #7_	Bad Boy 79214
			112 Featuring Lil' Z	
8/19/00	**21**	4	2. Callin' Me _Sales #3_	Priority 53582
			LIL' ZANE Feat. 112	
			LIMAHL	
			Born Christopher Hamill on 12/19/58 in England. Former lead singer of Kajagoogoo.	
5/4/85	**17**	9	1. Never Ending Story _Sales #14 / Airplay #19_	EMI America 8230
			from the movie _The Never Ending Story_ starring Barret Oliver	
			LIND, Bob	
			Born on 11/25/44 in Baltimore, Maryland. Folk-rock singer/songwriter.	
2/12/66	**5**	9	1. **Elusive Butterfly**	World Pacific 77808
			LINDEN, Kathy	
			Born in Moorestown, New Jersey. Female pop singer.	
3/31/58	**7**	11	1. **Billy** _Jockey #7 / Top 100 #12 / Best Seller #14_	Felsted 8510
			introduced by the American Quartet in 1911 on Victor 16965	
4/27/59	**11**	10	2. Goodbye Jimmy, Goodbye	Felsted 8571
			Joe Leahy (orch., above 2)	
			LINDISFARNE	
			Folk-rock group from Newcastle, England: Alan Hull (vocals), Ray Jackson (guitar), Simon Crowe (mandolin), Rod Clements (bass) and Ray Laidlaw (drums). Hull died of a heart attack on 11/18/95 (age 50).	
11/25/78	**33**	4	1. Run For Home	Atco 7093
			LINDSAY, Mark	
			Born on 3/9/42 in Eugene, Oregon. Pop singer/songwriter. Lead singer of Paul Revere & The Raiders.	
1/10/70	**10**	11	● 1. **Arizona**	Columbia 45037
7/11/70	**25**	5	2. Silver Bird	Columbia 45180
			LINEAR	
			Pop trio from Miami, Florida: Charlie Pennachio (vocals), Wyatt Pauley (guitar) and Joey Restivo (percussion).	
3/31/90	**5**	16	● 1. **Sending All My Love** _Sales #6 / Airplay #7_	Atlantic 87961
5/30/92	**30**	6	2. T.L.C. _Airplay #20 / Sales #65_	Atlantic 87484
			LINES, Aaron	
			Born in 1978 in Fort McMurray, Alberta, Canada. Country singer/ songwriter/guitarist.	
2/15/03	**38**	3	1. You Can't Hide Beautiful _Airplay #35_	album cut
			from the album _Living Out Loud_ on RCA 67057	

Vicki Lawrence could thank Sonny Bono for her music career. After he turned down a song written by her husband, Bobby Russell, Vicki turned "The Night The Lights Went Out In Georgia" into a #1 hit.

Brenda Lee earned her second #1 hit with "I Want To Be Wanted," but one of her most enduring hits never reached the Top 10: the Christmas classic "Rockin' Around The Christmas Tree."

John Lennon made a deal with Elton John, who sang background on "Whatever Gets You Thru The Night." If the song went to #1, he agreed to appear at an Elton John concert. Lennon paid up during a 1974 concert at New York City's Madison Square Garden.

Huey Lewis and The News scored their third #1 hit with "Jacob's Ladder." The song shared time in the Top 10 with the song's writer, Bruce Hornsby, who charted with "Mandolin Rain."

Lisa Lisa and Cult Jam earned back to back #1 hits with "Head To Toe" and "Lost In Emotion." Their production team, Full Force, also produced hits for LaToya Jackson and Samantha Fox.

Little Eva was still a teenager when she recorded the #1 hit "The Loco-Motion." She received the dance song while working as a babysitter for its writers, Carole King and Gerry Goffin.

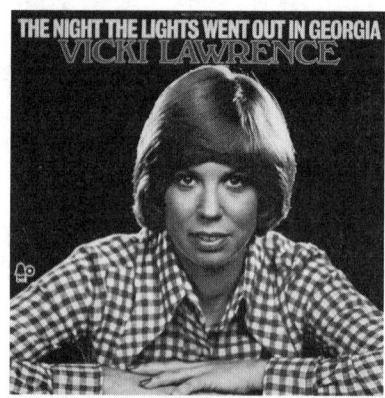

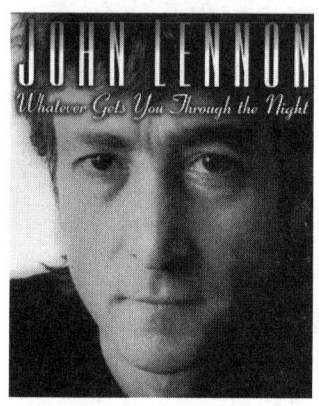

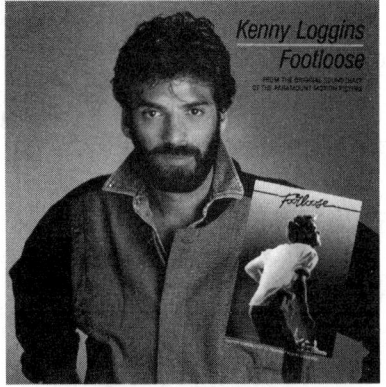

Lisa Loeb & Nine Stories were in a unique position of having a major hit but no record deal. Thanks to reaching #1 with "Stay (I Missed You)," from the movie *Reality Bites,* that situation didn't continue for long.

Kenny Loggins recorded Top 40 hits for the soundtracks of such films as *Caddyshack, Top Gun, Over the Top,* and *Caddyshack II,* but his only #1 pop hit came from the title song to the movie *Footloose.*

Lonestar had two Country #1 hits by 1999, but must have been "Amazed" when their third hit returned Country music to the top of the pop charts. Their crossover ballad was the first Country hit to reach #1 on the pop charts in 17 years.

Jennifer Lopez recorded a Latin-tinged dance number called "Ain't It Funny" for her album *J.Lo.* However, the remix that reached #1, featuring rapper Ja Rule, bore almost no resemblance to the original.

Jim Lowe was working as a DJ at a New York radio station when he released the chart-topping song "The Green Door." The song was a big hit across the country, except in New York, where rival radio stations were naturally reluctant to play it.

Ludacris scored his first #1 hit with 2003's "Stand Up," which featured Shawnna. That same year, Ludacris had to stand up to TV talk show host Bill O'Reilly, who criticized his endorsement deal for a popular soft drink.

DATE	POS	WKS	ARTIST–RECORD TITLE	LABEL & NO.
			LINK	
			Born Lincoln Browder on 10/12/64 in Dallas, Texas. Male rapper.	
6/20/98	**23**	8	1. Whatcha Gone Do? Sales #22	Relativity 1691
			LINKIN PARK	
			Alternative hard-rock/hip-hop group from Los Angeles, California: Chester Bennington (vocals), Mike Shinoda (rap vocals), Joseph "Mr. Hahn" (DJ), Brad Delson (guitar), David "Phoenix" Farrell (bass) and Rob Bourdon (drums).	
12/15/01+	**2** (1)	30	1. **In The End** Airplay #2 #1 Modern Rock hit (5 weeks); from the album *Hybrid Theory* on Warner 47755	album cut
3/29/03	**32**	9	2. Somewhere I Belong Airplay #29 #1 Mainstream Rock hit (1 week) / #1 Modern Rock hit (5 weeks)	album cut
12/13/03+	**11**	24↑	3. Numb Airplay #11 #1 Mainstream Rock hit (3 weeks) / #1 Modern Rock hit (12 weeks); above 2 from the album *Meteora* on Warner 48186	album cut
			LIPPS, INC.	
			Funk-dance project from Minneapolis, Minnesota. Formed by white producer/songwriter/multi-instrumentalist Steven Greenberg. Vocals by black singer Cynthia Johnson. Pronounced: lip-synch.	
4/19/80	▲ **1** (4)	15	1. **Funkytown**	Casablanca 2233
			LISA LISA AND CULT JAM	
			R&B trio from Harlem, New York: Lisa Velez (vocals; born on 1/15/67), Alex Moseley (guitar) and Mike Hughes (drums). Assembled and produced by Full Force.	
8/3/85	**34**	6	● 1. I Wonder If I Take You Home Sales #27	Columbia 04886
8/30/86	**8**	13	● 2. **All Cried Out** Sales #8 / Airplay #8 **LISA LISA AND CULT JAM WITH FULL FORCE** (above 2)	Columbia 05844
5/2/87	**1** (1)	14	● 3. **Head To Toe** Sales #1 (1) / Airplay #1 (1) #1 R&B hit (2 weeks)	Columbia 07008
8/22/87	**1** (1)	13	● 4. **Lost In Emotion** Sales #1 (1) / Airplay #1 (1) #1 R&B hit (1 week)	Columbia 07267
5/13/89	**29**	4	5. Little Jackie Wants To Be A Star Sales #25 / Airplay #36	Columbia 68674
8/3/91	**37**	1	● 6. Let The Beat Hit 'Em Sales #19 / Airplay #38 #1 R&B hit (1 week)	Columbia 73847
			LITTLE — also see LIL	
			LITTLE ANTHONY AND THE IMPERIALS	
			R&B vocal group from Brooklyn, New York: Anthony Gourdine (born on 1/8/40), Ernest Wright, Tracy Lord, Glouster Rogers and Clarence Collins. Sammy Strain, who joined group in 1964, left in 1975 to join The O'Jays.	
8/18/58	**4**	14	1. **Tears On My Pillow** Hot 100 #4 / Best Seller #5	End 1027
1/18/60	**24**	7	2. Shimmy, Shimmy, Ko-Ko-Bop	End 1060
9/5/64	**15**	8	3. I'm On The Outside (Looking In)	DCP 1104
11/21/64	**6**	12	4. **Goin' Out Of My Head**	DCP 1119
2/13/65	**10**	8	5. **Hurt So Bad**	DCP 1128
7/17/65	**16**	7	6. Take Me Back	DCP 1136
11/6/65	**34**	1	7. I Miss You So The 101 Strings (orchestral backing); #20 hit for The Cats and the Fiddle in 1940	DCP 1149

DATE	POS	WKS	ARTIST–RECORD TITLE	LABEL & NO.
			LITTLE CAESAR and The Romans	
			R&B vocal group from Los Angeles, California: Carl "Little Caesar" Burnett, David Johnson, Early Harris, Leroy Sanders and Johnny Simmons.	
5/29/61	9	9	1. **Those Oldies But Goodies (Remind Me Of You)**	Del-Fi 4158
			LITTLE DIPPERS, The	
			One-time studio session recording produced by Buddy Killen; featuring Floyd Cramer (piano), Bob Moore (bass), Hank Garland (lead guitar), Kelso Herston (rhythm guitar), Buddy Harmon (drums) and the Anita Kerr Singers (vocals). Killen later formed a quartet to lip-synch the song on the Dick Clark show.	
2/8/60	9	10	1. **Forever**	University 210
			LITTLE EVA	
			Born Eva Narcissus Boyd on 6/29/45 in Belhaven, North Carolina. Died of cancer on 4/10/2003 (age 57). Discovered by songwriters Carole King and Gerry Goffin while babysitting their daughter Louise Goffin.	
7/21/62	1 (1)	12	● 1. **The Loco-Motion** #1 R&B hit (3 weeks); Carole King (backing vocal)	Dimension 1000
11/24/62	12	8	2. Keep Your Hands Off My Baby	Dimension 1003
2/23/63	20	6	3. Let's Turkey Trot	Dimension 1006
7/13/63	38	2	4. Swinging On A Star **BIG DEE IRWIN (with Little Eva)** #1 hit for Bing Crosby in 1944	Dimension 1010
			LITTLE JOE & THE THRILLERS	
			R&B vocal group from Harlem, New York: Joe Cook, Farris Hill, Richard Frazier, Donald Burnett and Harry Pascle.	
10/7/57	22	9	1. Peanuts Best Seller #22 / Top 100 #23 Leroy Kirkland (orch.)	Okeh 7088
			LITTLE JOEY And The Flips	
			R&B vocal group from Philadelphia, Pennsylvania: Joey Hall, James Meagher, John Smith, Jeff Leonard and Fred Gerace. Hall died in 1972.	
7/14/62	33	3	1. Bongo Stomp	Joy 262
			LITTLE MILTON	
			Born James Milton Campbell on 9/7/34 in Inverness, Mississippi. Blues singer/guitarist.	
4/24/65	25	7	1. We're Gonna Make It #1 R&B hit (3 weeks)	Checker 1105
			LITTLE RICHARD	
			Born Richard Wayne Penniman on 12/5/32 in Macon, Georgia. R&B-rock and roll singer/pianist. Nicknamed the "Georgia Peach." Appeared in the movies *Don't Knock The Rock*, *The Girl Can't Help It*, *Mister Rock 'n' Roll* and *Down And Out In Beverly Hills*. Earned theology degree in 1961 and was ordained a minister. Left R&B for gospel music, 1959-62, and again in the mid-1970s. One of the key figures in the transition from R&B to rock and roll. Inducted into the Rock and Roll Hall of Fame in 1986. Won Grammy's Lifetime Achievement Award in 1993.	
1/28/56	17	5	1. Tutti-Frutti Juke Box #17 / Best Seller #18 / Top 100 #21	Specialty 561
4/7/56	6	12	● 2. **Long Tall Sally /** Best Seller #6 / Top 100 #13 / Juke Box #14 / Jockey #16 #1 R&B hit (8 weeks)	

DATE	POS	WKS	ARTIST–RECORD TITLE	LABEL & NO.
6/30/56	33	1	3. Slippin' And Slidin' (Peepin' And Hidin') Top 100 #33 / Best Seller: flip	Specialty 572
7/14/56	17	7	4. Rip It Up Best Seller #17 / Top 100 #27 #1 R&B hit (2 weeks)	Specialty 579
4/6/57	21	7	5. Lucille Best Seller #21 / Top 100 #27 #1 R&B hit (2 weeks)	Specialty 598
6/24/57	10	13	6. **Jenny, Jenny** Best Seller #10 / Top 100 #14	Specialty 606
10/7/57	8	12	7. **Keep A Knockin'** Top 100 #8 / Best Seller #9 / Jockey #24 from the movie *Mister Rock 'n' Roll* starring Alan Freed	Specialty 611
2/24/58	10	10	8. **Good Golly, Miss Molly** Top 100 #10 / Best Seller #13	Specialty 624
6/23/58	31	3	9. Ooh! My Soul Best Seller #31 / Top 100 #35	Specialty 633

LITTLE RIVER BAND

Pop-rock group formed in Australia: Glenn Shorrock (vocals), Rick Formosa, Beeb Birtles and Graham Goble (guitars), Roger McLachlan (bass) and Derek Pellicci (drums). George McArdle replaced McLachlan in 1977. David Biggs replaced Formosa in 1978. John Farnham and Steve Housden replaced Shorrock and Briggs in 1983.

DATE	POS	WKS	ARTIST–RECORD TITLE	LABEL & NO.
11/6/76	28	6	1. It's A Long Way There	Harvest 4318
9/24/77	14	11	2. Help Is On Its Way	Harvest 4428
1/21/78	16	9	3. Happy Anniversary	Harvest 4524
8/12/78	3	14	4. **Reminiscing**	Harvest 4605
1/27/79	10	14	5. **Lady**	Harvest 4667
8/4/79	6	14	6. **Lonesome Loser**	Capitol 4748
11/10/79+	10	13	7. **Cool Change**	Capitol 4789
9/5/81	6	14	8. **The Night Owls**	Capitol 5033
12/26/81+	10	15	9. **Take It Easy On Me**	Capitol 5057
5/1/82	14	8	10. Man On Your Mind	Capitol 5061
12/4/82+	11	13	11. The Other Guy	Capitol 5185
5/28/83	22	6	12. We Two	Capitol 5231
8/27/83	35	3	13. You're Driving Me Out Of My Mind	Capitol 5256

LITTLE SISTER

Female R&B vocal trio formed by Sly Stone: Vanetta Stewart (Sly's sister), Mary Rand and Elva Melton.

DATE	POS	WKS	ARTIST–RECORD TITLE	LABEL & NO.
3/28/70	22	6	1. You're The One-Part I	Stone Flower 9000
1/30/71	32	3	2. Somebody's Watching You	Stone Flower 9001

LIVE

Rock group from York, Pennsylvania: Edward Kowalczyk (vocals), Chad Taylor (guitar), Patrick Dahlheimer (bass) and Chad Gracey (drums).

DATE	POS	WKS	ARTIST–RECORD TITLE	LABEL & NO.
1/7/95	38 [A]	2	1. I Alone	album cut
2/25/95	12 [A]	25	2. Lightning Crashes #1 Mainstream Rock hit (10 weeks) / #1 Modern Rock hit (9 weeks)	album cut
7/8/95	33 [A]	6	3. All Over You above 3 from the album *Throwing Copper* on Radioactive 10997	album cut
2/1/97	35 [A]	5	4. Lakini's Juice #1 Modern Rock hit (1 week); from the album *Secret Samadhi* on Radioactive 11590	album cut

DATE	POS	WKS	ARTIST–RECORD TITLE	LABEL & NO.
			LIVING COLOUR	
			Black rock group from Brooklyn, New York: Corey Glover (vocals), Vernon Reid (guitar), Muzz Skillings (bass) and William Calhoun (drums). Glover played "Francis" in the movie *Platoon*.	
4/1/89	**13**	9	1. Cult Of Personality Sales #7 / Airplay #17	Epic 68611
10/14/89	**31**	3	2. Glamour Boys Airplay #28 / Sales #32	Epic 68548
			Mick Jagger (producer; backing vocal)	
			LIVING IN A BOX	
			Soul-styled pop-dance trio from Sheffield, Yorkshire, England: Richard Darbyshire (vocals), Marcus Vere (keyboards) and Anthony Critchlow (drums).	
7/25/87	**17**	7	1. Living In A Box Sales #13 / Airplay #20	Chrysalis 43104
			LL COOL J	
			Born James Todd Smith on 8/16/68 in Queens, New York. Male rapper/actor. Stage name is abbreviation for Ladies Love Cool James. Has appeared in several movies and TV shows.	
8/15/87	**14**	8	1. I Need Love Sales #11 / Airplay #13	Def Jam 07350
			#1 R&B hit (1 week)	
3/26/88	**31**	5	● 2. Going Back To Cali Sales #26 / Airplay #32	Def Jam 07679
			from the movie *Less Than Zero* starring Robert Downey, Jr.	
7/8/89	**15**	8	● 3. I'm That Type Of Guy Sales #9 / Airplay #28	Def Jam 68902
1/5/91	**9**	15	● 4. **Around The Way Girl** Sales #5 / Airplay #19	Def Jam 73609
5/11/91	**17**	9	● 5. Mama Said Knock You Out Sales #5 / Airplay #47	Def Jam 73706
11/18/95	**3**	20	▲ 6. **Hey Lover** Sales #2 / Airplay #17	Def Jam 577494
			Boyz II Men (backing vocals); based on the song "The Lady In My Life" by Michael Jackson	
3/9/96	**9**	14	● 7. **Doin It** Sales #6 / Airplay #46	Def Jam 576120
			LeShaun Williams (guest vocal); samples "My Jamaican Guy" by Grace Jones	
7/13/96	**3**	23	▲ 8. **Loungin** Sales #2 / Airplay #24	Def Jam 575062
			Total (guest vocals); samples "Who Do You Love" by Bernard Wright	
10/26/96	**6**	14	▲ 9. **This Is For The Lover In You** Sales #3 / Airplay #37	Epic 78443
			BABYFACE Featuring LL Cool J, Howard Hewett, Jody Watley and Jeffrey Daniels	
			#17 R&B hit for Shalamar in 1981	
1/31/98	**18**	8	10. Father Sales #7	Def Jam 568332
			samples "Father Figure" by George Michael	
9/28/02	**4**	17	11. **Luv U Better** Airplay #3 / Sales #14	Def Jam 063956
			#1 R&B hit (4 weeks); Marc Dorsey (additional vocals)	
12/28/02+	**1 (4)**	20	12. **All I Have** Airplay #1 (4)	album cut
			JENNIFER LOPEZ Featuring LL Cool J	
			from the album *This Is Me...Then* on Epic 86231	
1/25/03	**36**	3	13. Paradise Sales #33 / Airplay #36	Def Jam 063820
			LL COOL J feat. Amerie	
			samples "Rising To The Top" by Keni Burke	
			LOBO	
			Born Roland Kent Lavoie on 7/31/43 in Tallahassee, Florida. Pop singer/songwriter/guitarist.	
4/24/71	**5**	10	1. **Me And You And A Dog Named Boo**	Big Tree 112
			#1 Adult Contemporary hit (2 weeks)	
10/14/72	**2 (2)**	10	● 2. **I'd Love You To Want Me**	Big Tree 147
			#1 Adult Contemporary hit (1 week)	

DATE	POS	WKS	ARTIST–RECORD TITLE	LABEL & NO.
1/13/73	8	10	3. **Don't Expect Me To Be Your Friend** *#1 Adult Contemporary hit (2 weeks)*	Big Tree 158
5/5/73	27	5	4. It Sure Took A Long, Long Time	Big Tree 16001
7/21/73	22	8	5. How Can I Tell Her	Big Tree 16004
5/11/74	37	2	6. Standing At The End Of The Line	Big Tree 15001
4/26/75	27	4	7. Don't Tell Me Goodnight	Big Tree 16033
9/8/79	23	8	8. Where Were You When I Was Falling In Love *#1 Adult Contemporary hit (2 weeks)*	MCA/Curb 41065
			LOCKLIN, Hank	
			Born Lawrence Hankins Locklin on 2/15/18 in McLellan, Florida. Country singer/songwriter/guitarist.	
6/13/60	8	15	1. **Please Help Me, I'm Falling** *#1 Country hit (14 weeks)*	RCA Victor 7692
			LOEB, Lisa, & Nine Stories	
			Born on 3/11/68 in Bethesda, Maryland; raised in Dallas, Texas. Singer/songwriter/guitarist. Nine Stories consisted of Tim Bright (guitar), Joe Quigley (bass) and Jonathan Feinberg (drums).	
5/28/94	1 (3)	25	● 1. **Stay (I Missed You)** Airplay #1 (4) / Sales #2 *from the movie Reality Bites starring Winona Ryder*	RCA 62870
9/30/95	18	12	2. Do You Sleep? Airplay #23 / Sales #24	Geffen 19388
11/15/97+	17	18	3. I Do Airplay #13 / Sales #34 **LISA LOEB**	Geffen 19416
			LOGGINS, Dave	
			Born on 11/10/47 in Mountain City, Tennessee. Pop-country singer/songwriter. Cousin of Kenny Loggins.	
7/13/74	5	10	1. **Please Come To Boston** *#1 Adult Contemporary hit (1 week)*	Epic 11115
			LOGGINS, Kenny	
			Born on 1/7/48 in Everett, Washington; raised in Alhambra, California. Pop-rock singer/songwriter/guitarist. Cousin of Dave Loggins. Half of Loggins & Messina duo.	
8/19/78	5	15	1. **Whenever I Call You "Friend"** Stevie Nicks (harmony vocal)	Columbia 10794
11/24/79+	11	16	2. This Is It Michael McDonald (backing vocal)	Columbia 11109
4/5/80	36	2	3. Keep The Fire	Columbia 11215
8/23/80	7	12	4. **I'm Alright** Eddie Money (backing vocal); theme from the movie *Caddyshack* starring Ted Knight and Rodney Dangerfield	Columbia 11317
9/25/82	17	6	5. Don't Fight It **KENNY LOGGINS with Steve Perry**	Columbia 03192
12/11/82+	15	13	6. Heart To Heart Michael McDonald (backing vocal)	Columbia 03377
4/2/83	24	7	7. Welcome To Heartlight *inspired by the writings of children from Heartlight School*	Columbia 03555
2/11/84	1 (3)	16	▲ 8. **Footloose**	Columbia 04310
6/23/84	22	8	9. I'm Free (Heaven Helps The Man) *above 2 from the movie Footloose starring Kevin Bacon*	Columbia 04452

DATE	POS	WKS	ARTIST–RECORD TITLE	LABEL & NO.
4/13/85	**29**	4	10. Vox Humana — *Airplay #25*	Columbia 04849
7/20/85	**40**	1	11. Forever	Columbia 04931
6/7/86	**2** (1)	13	12. **Danger Zone** — *Sales #1 (1) / Airplay #3*	Columbia 05893
			from the movie *Top Gun* starring Tom Cruise	
4/25/87	**11**	12	13. Meet Me Half Way — *Airplay #10 / Sales #11*	Columbia 06690
			from the movie *Over The Top* starring Sylvester Stallone	
7/30/88	**8**	11	14. **Nobody's Fool** — *Airplay #6 / Sales #10*	Columbia 07971
			theme from the movie *Caddyshack II* starring Jackie Mason and Chevy Chase	

LOGGINS & MESSINA

Pop-rock duo of Kenny Loggins (see above bio) and Jim Messina (born on 12/5/47 in Maywood, California). Messina was a member of Buffalo Springfield and Poco.

DATE	POS	WKS	ARTIST–RECORD TITLE	LABEL & NO.
12/2/72+	**4**	13	● 1. **Your Mama Don't Dance** **KENNY LOGGINS AND JIM MESSINA**	Columbia 45719
4/28/73	**18**	8	2. Thinking Of You	Columbia 45815
11/24/73	**16**	8	3. My Music	Columbia 45952

LO-KEY?

Funk group from Minneapolis, Minnesota: Prof T and Dre (vocals), Lance Alexander (keyboards), T-Bone (bass) and "D" (drums).

DATE	POS	WKS	ARTIST–RECORD TITLE	LABEL & NO.
12/26/92+	**27**	9	1. I Got A Thang 4 Ya! — *Sales #20 / Airplay #31* #1 R&B hit (1 week)	Perspective 0008

LOLITA

Born Ditta Zuza Einzinger on 1/17/31 in St. Poelten, Austria. Female singer.

DATE	POS	WKS	ARTIST–RECORD TITLE	LABEL & NO.
11/14/60	**5**	14	1. **Sailor (Your Home Is The Sea)** [F]	Kapp 349

LONDON, Julie

Born Julie Peck on 9/26/26 in Santa Rosa, California. Died of a stroke on 10/18/2000 (age 74). Singer/actress. Played "Dixie McCall" on TV's *Emergency*. Married to Jack Webb from 1945-53.

DATE	POS	WKS	ARTIST–RECORD TITLE	LABEL & NO.
12/3/55	**9**	13	● 1. **Cry Me A River** *Jockey #9 / Top 100 #13 / Juke Box #14 / Best Seller #23* Barney Kessel (guitar); Ray Leatherwood (bass)	Liberty 55006

LONDON, Laurie

Born on 1/19/44 in London, England. Teen male singer.

DATE	POS	WKS	ARTIST–RECORD TITLE	LABEL & NO.
3/24/58	**1** (4)	14	● 1. **He's Got The Whole World (In His Hands)** *Jockey #1 (4) / Best Seller #2 / Top 100 #2* Geoff Love (orch.); traditional Afro-American gospel song	Capitol 3891

LONDONBEAT

R&B-pop group based in England. Vocal trio of Americans Jimmy Helms and George Chandler, with Trinidad native Jimmy Chambers. Backed by British producer/multi-instrumentalist Willy M.

DATE	POS	WKS	ARTIST–RECORD TITLE	LABEL & NO.
2/16/91	**1** (1)	14	● 1. **I've Been Thinking About You** — *Airplay #1 (2) / Sales #1 (1)*	Radioactive 54005
6/8/91	**18**	7	2. A Better Love — *Airplay #31*	Radioactive 54101

LONDON SYMPHONY ORCHESTRA — see WILLIAMS, John

DATE	POS	WKS	ARTIST–RECORD TITLE	LABEL & NO.
			LONESTAR	
			Country group from Nashville, Tennessee: Richie McDonald (vocals, guitar), Michael Britt (guitar), Dean Sams (keyboards) and Keech Rainwater (drums).	
6/26/99+	**1** (2)	43	● 1. **Amazed** Sales #3 / Airplay #5 #1 Country hit (8 weeks)	BNA 65957
2/12/00	**39**	2	2. Smile Airplay #32 #1 Country hit (1 week)	album cut
7/29/00	**30**	8	3. What About Now Airplay #23 #1 Country hit (4 weeks)	album cut
2/10/01	**39**	1	4. Tell Her Airplay #33 #1 Country hit (2 weeks); above 3 from the album *Lonely Grill* on BNA 67762	album cut
6/2/01	**24**	11	5. I'm Already There Airplay #19 #1 Country hit (6 weeks)	album cut
7/13/02	**36**	3	6. Not A Day Goes By Airplay #35 above 2 from the album *I'm Already There* on BNA 67011	album cut
5/31/03	**23**	13	7. My Front Porch Looking In Airplay #19 #1 Country hit (1 week); from the album *From There To Here: Greatest Hits* on BNA 67076	album cut
			LONG, Shorty	
			Born Frederick Long on 5/20/40 in Birmingham, Alabama. Drowned in a boating accident on the Detroit River on 6/29/69 (age 29). R&B singer/songwriter.	
6/15/68	**8**	8	1. **Here Comes The Judge** [N] title inspired by a recurrent gag line on TV's *Laugh-In*; Judge: Pervis Jackson of the Spinners	Soul 35044
			LOOKING GLASS	
			Pop-rock group formed in New Jersey: Elliot Lurie (vocals, guitar), Larry Gonsky (keyboards), Piet Sweval (bass) and Jeff Grob (drums). Sweval (who later joined Starz) died on 1/23/90 (age 51).	
7/1/72	**1** (1)	14	● 1. **Brandy (You're A Fine Girl)**	Epic 10874
9/29/73	**33**	3	2. Jimmy Loves Mary-Anne	Epic 11001
			LOPEZ, Denise	
			Born in Queens, New York. Female dance singer.	
8/6/88	**31**	5	1. Sayin' Sorry (Don't Make It Right) Sales #22	Vendetta 7200
			LOPEZ, Jennifer	
			Born on 7/24/70 in the Bronx, New York (of Puerto Rican parents). Singer/actress/dancer. In 1990 was a "Fly Girl" dancer on TV's *In Living Color*. Movie break came as the star of *Selena* in 1997; other movies include *Out Of Sight*, *The Cell*, *The Wedding Planner*, *Enough* and *Maid In Manhattan*. Married to professional dancer Cris Judd briefly in 2001. Engaged to actor Ben Affleck from 2002-2004.	
5/29/99	**1** (5)	20	▲ 1. **If You Had My Love** Sales #1 (5) / Airplay #3	Epic/Work 79163
10/23/99	**8**	16	2. **Waiting For Tonight** Airplay #4	Epic/Work 79292
12/16/00+	**3**	19	3. **Love Don't Cost A Thing** Airplay #1 (2) / Sales #10	Epic 79547
4/21/01	**18**	10	4. Play Airplay #15 Christina Millian (backing vocal); from the album *J.Lo* on Epic 63786	album cut

DATE	POS	WKS	ARTIST–RECORD TITLE	LABEL & NO.
7/14/01	**1** (5)	29	5. **I'm Real** Airplay #1 (6) / Sales #31 **JENNIFER LOPEZ featuring Ja Rule** samples "All Night Long" by the Mary Jane Girls	Epic 79639
1/19/02	**1** (6)	23	6. **Ain't It Funny** Airplay #1 (6) **JENNIFER LOPEZ featuring Ja Rule** samples "Flava In Ya Ear" by Craig Mack; from the album *J.Lo* on Epic 63786	album cut
5/11/02	**10**	20	7. **I'm Gonna Be Alright** Sales #7 / Airplay #10 **JENNIFER LOPEZ Featuring Nas** samples "Why You Treat Me So Bad" by Club Nouveau	Epic 79759
10/19/02	**3**	18	8. **Jenny From The Block** Airplay #3 / Sales #16 **JENNIFER LOPEZ Featuring Jadakiss & Styles** samples "South Bronx" by Boogie Down Productions and "Hijack" by Herbie Mann	Epic 79825
12/28/02+	**1** (4)	20	9. **All I Have** Airplay #1 (4) **JENNIFER LOPEZ Featuring LL Cool J** from the album *This Is Me...Then* on Epic 86231	album cut
5/24/03	**32**	5	10. **I'm Glad** Sales #12 / Airplay #33 samples "P.S.K. What Does It Mean?" by Schooly D	Epic 79868
			LOPEZ, Trini	
			Born Trinidad Lopez III on 5/15/37 in Dallas, Texas. Pop-folk singer/guitarist. Played "Pedro Jiminez" in the movie *The Dirty Dozen*.	
8/10/63	**3**	11	1. **If I Had A Hammer** [L]	Reprise 20,198
12/14/63+	**23**	6	2. **Kansas City** [L]	Reprise 20,236
2/6/65	**20**	5	3. **Lemon Tree**	Reprise 0336
5/7/66	**39**	3	4. **I'm Comin' Home, Cindy**	Reprise 0455
			LORAIN, A'Me	
			Born in Simi Valley, California. White female pop-dance singer.	
2/24/90	**9**	12	1. **Whole Wide World** Sales #9 / Airplay #11 from the movie *True Love* starring Annabella Sciorra	RCA 9099
			LORBER, Jeff	
			Born on 11/4/52 in Philadelphia, Pennsylvania. Jazz–fusion keyboardist.	
2/7/87	**27**	5	1. **Facts Of Love** Airplay #27 / Sales #29 **JEFF LORBER Featuring Karyn White**	Warner 28588
			LORD TARIQ & PETER GUNZ	
			Rap duo from Brooklyn, New York: Sean Hamilton ("Lord Tariq") and Peter Panky ("Peter Gunz").	
2/7/98	**9**	18	▲ 1. **Deja Vu (Uptown Baby)** Sales #5 / Airplay #42 samples "Black Cow" by Steely Dan	Columbia 78755
			LORENZ, Trey	
			Born on 1/19/69 in Florence, South Carolina. Male R&B singer. Also see "I'll Be There" by Mariah Carey.	
10/17/92	**19**	10	1. **Someone To Hold** Sales #21 / Airplay #27 co-written and co-produced by Mariah Carey	Epic 74482

DATE	POS	WKS	ARTIST–RECORD TITLE	LABEL & NO.
			LORING, Gloria	

8/2/86	**2** (2)	14	Born on 12/10/46 in Manhattan, New York. Played "Liz Curtis" on the TV soap *Days Of Our Lives*. Married to actor Alan Thicke from 1970-83.
			1. **Friends And Lovers** Sales #1 (1) / Airplay #2
			     GLORIA LORING & CARL ANDERSON
			     #1 Adult Contemporary hit (2 weeks); popularized due to exposure on TV's *Days Of Our Lives*
				USA Carrere 06122

			LOS BRAVOS	
9/10/66	**4**	8	Rock group formed in Spain: Mike Kogel (vocals; born in Germany), Tony Martinez (guitar), Manuel Fernandez (organ), Miguel Danus (bass) and Pablo Gomez (drums). 1. **Black Is Black**	Press 60002
			LOS DEL RIO	

5/18/96
 	
8/24/96
	1 (14)
	
	23
		37
		
		9
			Flamenco guitar duo from Seville, Spain: Antonio Romero Monge and Rafael Ruiz Perdigones. Formed duo in the 1960s. In 1993, they wrote and recorded "Macarena," which became a worldwide dance craze after it was remixed by the Miami production team of The Bayside Boys.
			▲⁴ 1. **Macarena (bayside boys mix)** Sales #1 (13) / Airplay #7 **[F]**
			     female vocal sung in English, male chorus sung in Spanish
			2. Macarena (non stop) Sales #13 **[F]**
			     the original Spanish version
				RCA 64407
				
				BMG/U.S. Latin 39227

			LOS INDIOS TABAJARAS	
10/12/63	**6**	10	Indian guitar instrumental duo from Ceara, Brazil: brothers Natalicio (born Musiperi) and Antenor (born Herundy) Lima. 1. **Maria Elena** **[I]** recorded in 1958; #1 hit for Jimmy Dorsey in 1941	RCA Victor 8216
			LOS LOBOS	
7/18/87 10/17/87	**1** (3) **21**	14 7	Hispanic-American rock group from East Los Angeles, California: David Hildago (vocals), Cesar Rosas (guitar), Steve Berlin (sax), Conrad Lozano (bass) and Louie Perez (drums). 1. **La Bamba** Sales #1 (3) / Airplay #1 (3) **[F]** 2. Come On, Let's Go Airplay #18 / Sales #24 above 2 from *La Bamba*, the Ritchie Valens' biographical movie starring Lou Diamond Phillips	Slash 28336 Slash 28186
			LOST BOYZ	
4/13/96	**33**	7	Rap group from Queens, New York: Spigg Nice, Mr. Cheeks, Freekie Tah and Pretty Lou. Freekie Tah (real name: Raymond Rogers) was shot to death on 3/29/99 (age 28). ● 1. Renee Sales #16 / Airplay #72 from the movie *Don't Be A Menace* starring Marlon Wayans	Island 854584
			LOST GENERATION, The	
8/1/70	**30**	5	R&B vocal group from Chicago, Illinois: brothers Lowrell and Fred Simon, with Larry Brownlee and Jesse Dean. Brownlee died in 1978. 1. The Sly, Slick, And The Wicked	Brunswick 55436
			LOU, Bonnie — see BONNIE LOU	

DATE	POS	WKS	ARTIST–RECORD TITLE	LABEL & NO.
			LOUDERMILK, John D.	
			Born on 3/31/34 in Durham, North Carolina. Pop-country singer/songwriter/multi-instrumentalist.	
4/6/57	38	1	1. Sittin' In The Balcony　　　　Top 100 #38 **JOHNNY DEE** Joe Tanner (guitar)	Colonial 430
12/4/61	32	3	2. Language Of Love	RCA Victor 7938
			LOUIE LOUIE	
			Born Louis Cordero in Los Angeles, California. Dance singer/songwriter. Played Madonna's boyfriend in her "Borderline" video.	
5/26/90	19	8	1. Sittin' In The Lap Of Luxury　　Airplay #15 / Sales #18	WTG 73266
			LOVE	
			Rock group from Los Angeles, California. Core members from 1966-68: Arthur Lee (vocals), John Echols and Bryan MacLean (guitars), and Ken Forssi (bass). Forssi died of cancer on 1/5/98 (age 63). MacLean died of a heart attack on 12/25/98 (age 52).	
9/10/66	33	3	1. 7 And 7 Is	Elektra 45605
			LOVE, Darlene	
			Born Darlene Wright on 7/26/38 in Los Angeles, California. Lead singer of The Blossoms. Sang lead on two songs by The Crystals and with Bob B. Soxx & The Blue Jeans. Her sister, Edna Wright, was a member of The Honey Cone. Starred in the off-Broadway show *Leader of The Pack*. Played Danny Glover's wife in all three *Lethal Weapon* movies.	
5/11/63	39	1	1. (Today I Met) The Boy I'm Gonna Marry	Philles 111
8/24/63	26	4	2. Wait Til' My Bobby Gets Home above 2 produced by Phil Spector	Philles 114
			LOVE, Mike — see CELEBRATION	
			LOVE, Monie	
			Born Simone Johnson on 7/2/70 in London, England; raised in Brooklyn, New York. Black dance club singer/songwriter.	
4/20/91	26	6	1. It's A Shame (My Sister)　　Sales #21 / Airplay #31 rap version of the Spinners' 1970 hit "It's A Shame"	Warner 19515
			LOVE AND KISSES	
			Disco studio group assembled by European producer Alec Costandinos. Singers included Don Daniels, Elaine Hill, Dianne Brooks and Jean Graham.	
6/24/78	22	6	1. Thank God It's Friday title song from the movie starring Jeff Goldblum	Casablanca 925
			LOVE AND ROCKETS	
			Pop-rock trio formed in England: Daniel Ash (guitar, vocals), David Jay (bass) and Kevin Haskins (drums).	
6/17/89	3	12	1. **So Alive**　　　　Sales #3 / Airplay #5 #1 Modern Rock hit (5 weeks)	RCA 8956

DATE	POS	WKS	ARTIST–RECORD TITLE	LABEL & NO.
			LOVERBOY	
			Rock group formed in Canada: Mike Reno (vocals; see #6 below), Paul Dean (guitar), Doug Johnson (keyboards), Scott Smith (bass) and Matt Frenette (drums). Smith drowned on 11/30/2000 (age 45).	
3/21/81	35	6	1. Turn Me Loose	Columbia 11421
1/9/82	29	8	2. Working For The Weekend	Columbia 02589
5/15/82	26	6	3. When It's Over	Columbia 02814
			Nancy Nash (backing vocal)	
7/2/83	11	11	4. Hot Girls In Love	Columbia 03941
10/29/83	34	3	5. Queen Of The Broken Hearts	Columbia 04096
5/19/84	7	13	6. **Almost Paradise...Love Theme From Footloose**	Columbia 04418
			MIKE RENO and ANN WILSON	
			#1 Adult Contemporary hit (1 week); co-written by Eric Carmen; from the movie *Footloose* starring Kevin Bacon and Lori Singer	
9/14/85	9	11	7. **Lovin' Every Minute Of It** Sales #8 / Airplay #11	Columbia 05569
2/15/86	10	10	8. **This Could Be The Night** Airplay #9 / Sales #13	Columbia 05765
8/23/86	12	11	9. Heaven In Your Eyes Airplay #10 / Sales #13	Columbia 06178
			from the movie *Top Gun* starring Tom Cruise	
10/10/87	38	3	10. Notorious Airplay #33	Columbia 07324
			LOVE UNLIMITED	
			Female R&B vocal trio from San Pedro, California: sisters Glodean and Linda James, with Diane Taylor. Glodean was married to Barry White from 1974-88.	
5/6/72	14	9	● 1. Walkin' In The Rain With The One I Love	Uni 55319
			featuring Barry White's voice on the telephone	
1/4/75	27	7	2. I Belong To You	20th Century 2141
			#1 R&B hit (1 week); above 2 written and produced by Barry White	
			LOVE UNLIMITED ORCHESTRA	
			Disco studio orchestra conducted and arranged by Barry White. Formed to back Love Unlimited; also heard on some of White's solo hits. Kenny G was a member at age 17.	
12/22/73+	1 (1)	16	● 1. **Love's Theme** [I]	20th Century 2069
			#1 Adult Contemporary hit (2 weeks)	
3/15/75	22	5	2. Satin Soul [I]	20th Century 2162
			LOVIN' SPOONFUL, The	
			Jug-band rock group formed in New York: John Sebastian (vocals, guitar, harmonica), Zalman Yanovsky (guitar), Steve Boone (bass) and Joe Butler (drums). Sebastian and Yanovsky were members of the Mugwumps with Cass Elliot and Denny Doherty (later with The Mamas & The Papas). Jerry Yester (keyboards) replaced Yanovsky in 1967. Disbanded in 1968. Yanovsky died of a heart attack on 12/13/2002 (age 57). Inducted into the Rock and Roll Hall of Fame in 2000.	
9/18/65	9	8	1. **Do You Believe In Magic**	Kama Sutra 201
12/11/65+	10	9	2. **You Didn't Have To Be So Nice**	Kama Sutra 205
3/12/66	2 (2)	10	3. **Daydream**	Kama Sutra 208
5/14/66	2 (2)	9	4. **Did You Ever Have To Make Up Your Mind?**	Kama Sutra 209
7/23/66	1 (3)	10	● 5. **Summer In The City**	Kama Sutra 211
10/22/66	10	8	6. **Rain On The Roof**	Kama Sutra 216
12/31/66+	8	8	7. **Nashville Cats**	Kama Sutra 219

DATE	POS	WKS	ARTIST–RECORD TITLE	LABEL & NO.
2/25/67	15	5	8. Darling Be Home Soon *from the movie* You're a Big Boy Now *starring Peter Kastner*	Kama Sutra 220
5/20/67	18	5	9. Six O'Clock	Kama Sutra 225
11/11/67	27	3	10. She Is Still A Mystery	Kama Sutra 239

LOWE, Jim

Born on 5/7/27 in Springfield, Missouri. Singer/songwriter/pianist.

DATE	POS	WKS	ARTIST–RECORD TITLE	LABEL & NO.
9/29/56	1 (3)	22	● 1. **The Green Door** Top 100 #1 (3) / Juke Box #1 (3) / Best Seller #2 / Jockey #2 High Fives (backing vocals); Hutch Davie (piano)	Dot 15486
5/13/57	15	6	2. Four Walls/ Juke Box #15 / Jockey #16 / Best Seller #19/Top 100 #20	
5/13/57	15	5	3. Talkin' To The Blues Juke Box #15 / Jockey #20 / Top 100 #21 / Best Seller: flip from the TV production *Modern Romances*; Hutch Davie (orch., above 2)	Dot 15569

LOWE, Nick

Born on 3/25/49 in Walton, Surrey, England. Pop-rock singer/songwriter/guitarist. Married to Carlene Carter from 1979-90.

DATE	POS	WKS	ARTIST–RECORD TITLE	LABEL & NO.
8/18/79	12	10	1. Cruel To Be Kind	Columbia 11018

LOX, The

Rap trio from Yonkers, New York: David Styles, Shawn Jacobs and Jayson "Jadakiss" Phillips.

DATE	POS	WKS	ARTIST–RECORD TITLE	LABEL & NO.
12/6/97+	2 (2)	6	▲ 1. **It's All About The Benjamins** Sales #2 / Airplay #62 **PUFF DADDY & THE FAMILY Feat. The Notorious B.I.G.,** **Lil' Kim, The Lox, Dave Grohl, Perfect, FuzzBubble & Rob** **Zombie** samples "I Did It For Love" by Love Unlimited Orchestra	Bad Boy 79130
2/14/98	30	5	2. If You Think I'm Jiggy Sales #16 samples "Da Ya Think I'm Sexy?" by Rod Stewart	Bad Boy 79115
4/11/98	17	11	● 3. Money, Power & Respect Sales #10 / Airplay #65 **THE LOX [Feat. DMX & Lil' Kim]** samples "New Beginning" by Dexter Wansel	Bad Boy 79156

LSG

All-star R&B trio: Gerald Levert, Keith Sweat and Johnny Gill.

DATE	POS	WKS	ARTIST–RECORD TITLE	LABEL & NO.
11/1/97	4	18	▲ 1. **My Body** Sales #2 / Airplay #36 #1 R&B hit (7 weeks)	EastWest 64132

L.T.D.

R&B-funk group from Greensboro, North Carolina: brothers Jeffrey (vocals, drums) and Billy (keyboards) Osborne, with John McGhee (guitar), Abraham Miller and Lorenzo Carnegie (saxophones), Jimmie Davis (keyboards), Carle Vickers (trumpet), Jake Riley (trombone), Henry Davis (bass) and Alvino Bennett (drums). The Osborne brothers left in 1980. Leslie Wilson and Andre Ray joined as vocalists. L.T.D.: Love, Togetherness and Devotion.

DATE	POS	WKS	ARTIST–RECORD TITLE	LABEL & NO.
11/6/76	20	9	1. Love Ballad #1 R&B hit (2 weeks)	A&M 1847
11/12/77	4	12	● 2. **(Every Time I Turn Around) Back In Love Again** #1 R&B hit (2 weeks)	A&M 1974
1/31/81	40	1	3. Shine On	A&M 2283

DATE	POS	WKS	ARTIST–RECORD TITLE	LABEL & NO.
			LUCAS	
			Born Lucas Secon in 1970 in Copenhagen, Denmark. Male rapper/producer.	
10/22/94	29	7	1. Lucas With The Lid Off Sales #22 / Airplay #46 Junior Dangerous (ragga vocal)	Big Beat 98219
			LUCY PEARL	
			All-star R&B trio: Raphael Saadiq (of Tony Toni Toné), Dawn Robinson (of En Vogue) and Ali Shaheed Muhammad (of A Tribe Called Quest). Joi replaced Robinson in 2001.	
7/15/00	36	3	1. Dance Tonight Airplay #30 from the movie *Love & Basketball* starring Omar Epps (soundtrack on Pookie/Beyond 9001)	album cut
			LUDACRIS	
			Born Christopher Bridges on 9/11/78 in Atlanta, Georgia. Male rapper.	
11/4/00	21	15	1. What's Your Fantasy Airplay #17 / Sales #73 **LUDACRIS (Featuring Shawna)**	Def Jam 562944
2/10/01	23	9	2. Southern Hospitality Airplay #17 / Sales #50	Def Jam 572749
8/4/01	15	16	3. One Minute Man Airplay #13 **MISSY "MISDEMEANOR" ELLIOTT (featuring Ludacris)** from Elliott's album *Miss E...So Addictive* on Goldmind 62639	album cut
8/18/01	24	6	4. Area Codes Airplay #21 / Sales #55 **LUDACRIS (Feat. Nate Dogg)** samples "Do It ('Til You're Satisfied)" by B.T. Express; from the movie *Rush Hour 2* starring Jackie Chan	Def Jam 588671
12/29/01+	17	13	5. Rollout (My Business) Airplay #17 / Sales #60	Def Jam 588792
3/2/02	35	4	6. Welcome To Atlanta Airplay #36 **JERMAINE DUPRI • LUDACRIS** from the Dupri album *Instructions* on So So Def 85830 and the Ludacris album *Word Of Mouf* on Def Jam 586446	album cut
4/6/02	22	8	7. Saturday (Oooh! Ooooh!) Airplay #22 / Sales #34 **LUDACRIS (featuring Sleepy Brown)**	Def Jam 588875
8/3/02	10	15	8. Move B***h Airplay #9 / Sales #20 **LUDACRIS feat. Mystikal and Infamous 2.0**	Def Jam 063949
8/3/02	23	6	9. Why Don't We Fall In Love Sales #17 / Airplay #22 **AMERIE (featuring Ludacris)**	Rise/Columbia 79774
1/25/03	8	14	10. Gossip Folks Airplay #6 / Sales #11 **MISSY ELLIOTT Featuring Ludacris** samples "Double Dutch Bus" by Frankie Smith	Goldmind 67356
7/5/03	32	2	11. Act A Fool Airplay #30 / Sales #31 from the movie *2 Fast 2 Furious* starring Paul Walker and Tyrese	Def Jam S. 000539
9/20/03	1 (1)	25	12. Stand Up Airplay #1 (1) / Sales #24 **LUDACRIS featuring Shawnna** #1 R&B hit (5 weeks)	Def Jam S. 001183
10/4/03	3	18	13. Holidae In Airplay #3 / Sales #42 **CHINGY featuring Ludacris & Snoop Dogg**	Disturb. Tha P. 52816
			LUKE, Robin	
			Born on 3/19/42 in Los Angeles, California. Male teen rock and roll singer/songwriter/guitarist.	
8/18/58	5	15	● 1. Susie Darlin' Hot 100 #5 / Best Seller #6	Dot 15781
			LUKE — see 2 LIVE CREW	

DATE	POS	WKS	ARTIST–RECORD TITLE	LABEL & NO.
			LULU	
			Born Marie Lawrie on 11/3/48 in Glasgow, Scotland. Pop singer/actress. Married to Maurice Gibb (of the Bee Gees) from 1969-73. Appeared in the 1967 movie *To Sir With Love*.	
9/23/67	**1** (5)	15	● 1. **To Sir With Love**	Epic 10187
			title song from the movie starring Sidney Poitier	
1/6/68	**32**	3	2. Best Of Both Worlds	Epic 10260
2/7/70	**22**	8	3. Oh Me Oh My (I'm A Fool For You Baby)	Atco 6722
8/22/81	**18**	10	4. I Could Never Miss You (More Than I Do)	Alfa 7006
			LUMAN, Bob	
			Born on 4/15/37 in Nacogdoches, Texas. Died on 12/27/78 (age 41). Country-rockabilly singer/songwriter/guitarist.	
9/26/60	**7**	9	1. **Let's Think About Living** [N]	Warner 5172
			written in response to the "death-song" fad of 1960	
			LUMIDEE	
			Born Lumidee Cedeno in Harlem, New York (Puerto Rican parents). Female singer/rapper/songwriter.	
6/21/03	**3**	16	1. **Never Leave You - Uh Oooh, Uh Oooh!**	Universal 000652
			Airplay #3 / Sales #17	
			LUNDBERG, Victor	
			Born on 9/2/23 in Grand Rapids, Michigan. Died on 2/14/90 (age 66). News reader at WMAX in Grand Rapids.	
11/25/67	**10**	4	1. **An Open Letter To My Teenage Son** [S]	Liberty 55996
			LUNIZ	
			Rap duo from Oakland, California: Jerold "Yukmouth" Ellis and Garrick "Knumskull" Husband.	
7/8/95	**8**	20	▲ 1. **I Got 5 On It** Sales #4 / Airplay #36	Noo Trybe 38474
			samples material by Kool & The Gang	
			LUSCIOUS JACKSON	
			Female pop-rock group from Manhattan, New York: Jill Cunniff (vocals, bass), Gabrielle Glaser (vocals, guitar), Vivian Trimble (keyboards) and Kate Schellenbach (drums). Named after the former pro basketball player.	
3/22/97	**36**	10	1. Naked Eye Airplay #31 / Sales #44	Grand Royal 58619
			LV — see COOLIO	
			LYMAN, Arthur, Group	
			Born on 2/2/32 in Kauai, Hawaii. Died of cancer on 2/24/2002 (age 70). Played vibraphone, guitar, piano and drums. Formerly with the Martin Denny Trio.	
6/12/61	**4**	10	1. **Yellow Bird** [I]	Hi Fi 5024
			adapted from a West Indian folk song	

DATE	POS	WKS	ARTIST–RECORD TITLE	LABEL & NO.
			LYMON, Frankie, and The Teenagers	
			R&B vocal group from the Bronx, New York. Lead singer Lymon was born on 9/30/42; died of a drug overdose on 2/28/68 (age 25). Other members included Herman Santiago, Jimmy Merchant, Joe Negroni (died on 9/5/78, age 37) and Sherman Garnes (died on 2/26/77, age 36). Group appeared in the movies *Rock, Rock, Rock* and *Mister Rock 'n' Roll*. Inducted into the Rock and Roll Hall of Fame in 1993.	
2/18/56	6	16	● 1. **Why Do Fools Fall In Love** Best Seller #6 / Top 100 #7 / Juke Box #8 / Jockey #9 **THE TEENAGERS Featuring FRANKIE LYMON** #1 R&B hit (5 weeks)	Gee 1002
5/12/56	13	11	2. I Want You To Be My Girl Best Seller #13 / Top 100 #17 / Juke Box #20 / Jockey #25	Gee 1012
8/26/57	20	7	3. Goody Goody Best Seller #20 / Jockey #21 / Top 100 #22 #1 hit for Benny Goodman in 1936; Jimmy Wright (orch., all of above)	Gee 1039
			LYNN, Barbara	
			Born Barbara Lynn Ozen on 1/16/42 in Beaumont, Texas. R&B singer/ songwriter/guitarist.	
7/14/62	8	8	1. **You'll Lose A Good Thing** #1 R&B hit (3 weeks)	Jamie 1220
			LYNN, Cheryl	
			Born Cheryl Lynn Smith on 3/11/57 in Los Angeles, California. R&B singer.	
1/6/79	12	12	▲ 1. **Got To Be Real** #1 R&B hit (1 week)	Columbia 10808
			LYNNE, Gloria	
			Born Gloria Alleyne on 11/23/31 in Harlem, New York. Black jazz-styled singer.	
2/29/64	28	4	1. I Wish You Love French song written and recorded by Charles Trenet in 1943	Everest 2036
			LYNYRD SKYNYRD	
			Southern-rock group formed in Jacksonville, Florida: Ronnie Van Zant (vocals), Gary Rossington and Allen Collins (guitars), Billy Powell (piano), Leon Wilkeson (bass) and Artimus Pyle (drums). Ed King (of the Strawberry Alarm Clock) was guitarist from 1973-74. Steve Gaines (guitar) joined in 1976. Group named after their gym teacher Leonard Skinner. Plane crash on 10/20/77 in Gillsburg, Mississippi, killed Ronnie Van Zant, Steve Gaines and his sister Cassie Gaines. Collins (paralyzed in a car accident in 1986) died of pneumonia on 1/23/90 (age 37). Wilkeson died on 7/27/2001 (age 49).	
8/24/74	8	11	1. **Sweet Home Alabama** answer song to Neil Young's "Alabama" and "Southern Man"	MCA 40258
1/4/75	19	5	2. Free Bird tribute to Duane Allman of The Allman Brothers Band	MCA 40328
7/19/75	27	3	3. Saturday Night Special	MCA 40416
1/8/77	38	2	4. Free Bird **[L-R]** studio version on #2 above	MCA 40665
1/7/78	13	11	5. What's Your Name	MCA 40819

DATE	POS	WKS	ARTIST–RECORD TITLE	LABEL & NO.
			M	
			M	
			Born Robin Scott on 4/1/47 in England. Male new-wave singer.	
8/25/79	**1** (1)	20	● 1. **Pop Muzik**	Sire 49033
			MABLEY, Moms	
			Born Loretta Mary Aiken on 3/19/1894 in Brevard, North Carolina. Died on 5/23/75 (age 81). Black comedian.	
7/19/69	35	2	1. **Abraham, Martin And John**	Mercury 72935
			a tribute to Abraham Lincoln, Martin Luther King, Jr.,and John and Robert Kennedy	
			MacGREGOR, Byron	
			Born Gary Mack in 1948 in Calgary, Alberta, Canada. Died on 1/3/95 (age 46). News director at CKLW-Detroit when he did the narration for "Americans." Narration was originally written and delivered as an editorial by Gordon Sinclair for CFRB-Toronto on 6/5/73.	
1/12/74	4	9	● 1. **Americans** [S]	Westbound 222
			background music: "America The Beautiful"	
			MacGREGOR, Mary	
			Born on 5/6/48 in St. Paul, Minnesota. Pop singer.	
12/25/76+	**1** (2)	16	● 1. **Torn Between Two Lovers**	Ariola America 7638
			#1 Adult Contemporary hit (2 weeks); written and produced by Peter Yarrow (Peter, Paul & Mary)	
10/6/79	39	2	2. **Good Friend**	RSO 938
			from the movie *Meatballs* starring Bill Murray	
			MACK, Craig	
			Born in Long Island, New York. Male rapper.	
9/3/94	9	20	▲ 1. **Flava In Ya Ear** Sales #3 / Airplay #44	Bad Boy 79001
3/18/95	38	2	● 2. **Get Down** Sales #15	Bad Boy 79012
			MACK, Lonnie	
			Born Lonnie McIntosh on 7/18/41 in Aurora, Indiana. Rockabilly guitarist.	
6/22/63	5	10	1. **Memphis** [I]	Fraternity 906
			first recorded by Chuck Berry in 1959	
9/21/63	24	4	2. **Wham!** [I]	Fraternity 912
			MACK 10	
			Born Dedrick Rolison on 8/9/71 in Inglewood, California. Male rapper. Member of Westside Connection. Married T-Boz (of TLC) on 8/19/2000.	
1/11/97	38	5	1. **Nothin' But The Cavi Hit** Sales #22	Priority 53263
			MACK 10 & THA DOGG POUND	
			from the rap documentary movie *Rhyme & Reason*	
9/20/97	37	6	2. **Backyard Boogie** Sales #25	Priority 53282

DATE	POS	WKS	ARTIST–RECORD TITLE	LABEL & NO.
10/2/99	**23**	9	● 3. I Want It All Sales #7 **WARREN G Featuring Mack 10** samples "I Like It" by DeBarge	G-Funk 73721
1/8/00	**35**	2	4. You Can Do It Sales #7 **ICE CUBE Feat. Mack 10** Ms. Toi (female vocal); samples "Planet Rock" by Afrika Bambaataa; from the movie *Next Friday* starring Ice Cube	Priority 53562
			MacKENZIE, Gisele	
			Born Gisele LaFleche on 1/10/27 in Winnipeg, Manitoba, Canada. Died of cancer on 9/5/2003 (age 76). Star of TV's *Your Hit Parade* from 1953-57.	
6/4/55	**4**	19	1. **Hard To Get** Jockey #4 / Juke Box #5 / Best Seller #5 / Top 100 #84 introduced by MacKenzie on a 5/12/55 episode of the NBC-TV drama series *Justice*	"X" 0137
			MacRAE, Gordon	
			Born on 3/12/21 in East Orange, New Jersey. Died of cancer on 1/24/86 (age 64). Sang with Horace Heidt (1942-43) and recorded numerous duets with Jo Stafford in the late 1940s. Starred in the movie musicals *Oklahoma!* and *Carousel*. Actresses Sheila and Meredith were his wife and daughter, respectively.	
10/6/58	**18**	6	1. The Secret Hot 100 #18 Van Alexander (orch.)	Capitol 4033
			MAD COBRA	
			Born Ewart Everton Brown on 3/31/68 in Kingston, Jamaica; raised in St. Mary's, Jamaica. Reggae rapper.	
11/14/92+	**13**	10	● 1. Flex Sales #9 / Airplay #38	Columbia 74373
			MADDOX, Johnny, and The Rhythmasters	
			Born on 8/4/29 in Gallatin, Tennessee. Honky-tonk pianist.	
2/5/55	**2 (7)**	20	● 1. **The Crazy Otto** Juke Box #2 / Best Seller #2 / Jockey #7 **[I]** medley of German tunes inspired by honky-tonk pianist Crazy Otto	Dot 15325
			MADIGAN, Betty	
			Born in Washington DC. Adult Contemporary singer.	
9/8/58	**31**	3	1. Dance Everyone Dance Best Seller #31 / Hot 100 #34 based on the Israeli harvest song "Hava Nagila"; Dick Jacobs (orch.)	Coral 62007
			MADNESS	
			Ska-rock group formed in London, England: Graham McPherson (vocals), Chris Foreman (guitar), Mike Barson (keyboards), Carl Smyth (trumpet), Lee Thompson (sax), Mark Bedford (bass) and Dan Woodgate (drums).	
5/28/83	**7**	13	1. **Our House**	Geffen 29668
9/17/83	**33**	5	2. It Must Be Love	Geffen 29562

DATE	POS	WKS	ARTIST–RECORD TITLE	LABEL & NO.
			MADONNA	
			Born Madonna Louise Ciccone on 8/16/58 in Bay City, Michigan. Moved to New York in the late 1970s; performed with the Alvin Ailey dance troupe. Member of the Breakfast Club in 1979. Formed her own band, Emmy, in 1980. Married to actor Sean Penn from 1985-89. Acted in such movies as *Desperately Seeking Susan, Dick Tracy, A League Of Their Own, Body Of Evidence* and *Evita*. Appeared in Broadway's *Speed-The-Plow*. Released concert tour documentary movie *Truth Or Dare* in 1991. Released adults-only picture book *Sex* in 1992. Married British movie director Guy Ritchie on 12/22/2000.	
12/10/83+	16	11	1. Holiday	Sire 29478
4/14/84	10	15	● 2. **Borderline**	Sire 29354
9/1/84	4	12	3. **Lucky Star** Airplay #3 / Sales #6	Sire 29177
11/24/84	1 (6)	14	● 4. **Like A Virgin** Airplay #1 (5) / Sales #1 (4)	Sire 29210
2/16/85	2 (2)	12	5. **Material Girl** Airplay #2 / Sales #3	Sire 29083
3/16/85	1 (1)	14	● 6. **Crazy For You** Airplay #1 (1) / Sales #2	Geffen 29051
			from the movie *Vision Quest* starring Matthew Modine	
5/11/85	5	12	7. **Angel** Airplay #4 / Sales #9	Sire 29008
8/17/85	5	11	8. **Dress You Up** Airplay #3 / Sales #12	Sire 28919
4/19/86	1 (1)	13	9. **Live To Tell** Airplay #1 (3) / Sales #2	Sire 28717
			#1 Adult Contemporary hit (3 weeks); from the movie *At Close Range* starring Sean Penn	
7/5/86	1 (2)	13	● 10. **Papa Don't Preach** Sales #1 (3) / Airplay #1 (2)	Sire 28660
10/4/86	3	12	● 11. **True Blue** Airplay #3 / Sales #4	Sire 28591
12/13/86+	1 (1)	14	12. **Open Your Heart** Airplay #1 (2) / Sales #2	Sire 28508
3/28/87	4	12	13. **La Isla Bonita** Sales #3 / Airplay #3	Sire 28425
			#1 Adult Contemporary hit (1 week)	
7/18/87	1 (1)	11	14. **Who's That Girl** Airplay #1 (2) / Sales #1 (1)	Sire 28341
9/19/87	2 (3)	11	15. **Causing A Commotion** Sales #2 / Airplay #2	Sire 28224
			above 2 from the movie *Who's That Girl* starring Madonna	
1/16/88	32 ᴬ	5	16. Spotlight	album cut
			from the album *You Can Dance* on Sire 25535	
3/18/89	1 (3)	12	▲ 17. **Like A Prayer** Sales #1 (3) / Airplay #1 (3)	Sire 27539
6/10/89	2 (2)	11	● 18. **Express Yourself** Sales #2 / Airplay #3	Sire 22948
8/19/89	2 (2)	12	19. **Cherish** Sales #2 / Airplay #2	Sire 22883
			#1 Adult Contemporary hit (2 weeks)	
11/25/89+	20	8	20. Oh Father Sales #16 / Airplay #22	Sire 22723
2/17/90	8	9	● 21. **Keep It Together** Sales #7 / Airplay #7	Sire 19986
4/14/90	1 (3)	16	▲² 22. **Vogue** Airplay #1 (3) / Sales #1 (2)	Sire 19863
6/30/90	10	7	● 23. **Hanky Panky** Airplay #11 / Sales #13	Sire 19789
			music inspired by the movie *Dick Tracy* starring Madonna and Warren Beatty	
11/24/90+	1 (2)	13	▲ 24. **Justify My Love** Sales #1 (5) / Airplay #2	Sire 19485
			co-written and produced by Lenny Kravitz	
3/2/91	9	6	● 25. **Rescue Me** Airplay #5 / Sales #11	Sire 19490
7/4/92	1 (1)	14	● 26. **This Used To Be My Playground** Airplay #2 / Sales #3	Sire 18822
			from the movie *A League Of Their Own* starring Madonna and Tom Hanks	
10/17/92	3	9	● 27. **Erotica** Airplay #2 / Sales #4	Maverick/Sire 18782
			samples "Jungle Boogie" by Kool & The Gang	
12/5/92+	7	13	28. **Deeper And Deeper** Airplay #8 / Sales #15	Maverick/Sire 18639
3/20/93	36	3	29. Bad Girl Sales #36 / Airplay #44	Maverick/Sire 18650
7/31/93	14	14	30. Rain Airplay #11 / Sales #31	Maverick/Sire 18505

DATE	POS	WKS	ARTIST–RECORD TITLE	LABEL & NO.
4/2/94	2 (4)	24	● 31. **I'll Remember** Sales #2 / Airplay #2 #1 Adult Contemporary hit (4 weeks); theme from the movie *With Honors* starring Joe Pesci	Maverick/Sire 18247
10/8/94	3	20	● 32. **Secret** Airplay #3 / Sales #11	Maverick/Sire 18035
12/24/94+	1 (7)	27	● 33. **Take A Bow** Airplay #1 (9) / Sales #4 #1 Adult Contemporary hit (9 weeks)	Maverick/Sire 18000
12/9/95	6	14	● 34. **You'll See** Sales #6 / Airplay #10	Maverick/Sire 17719
11/16/96	18	14	● 35. **You Must Love Me** Sales #14 / Airplay #25	Warner 17495
2/22/97	8	7	36. **Don't Cry For Me Argentina** Airplay #5 / Sales #11 above 2 from the movie *Evita* starring Madonna	Warner 43809
3/21/98	2 (1)	16	● 37. **Frozen** Airplay #7 / Sales #10	Maverick 17244
7/11/98	5	11	● 38. **Ray Of Light** Sales #5 / Airplay #26	Maverick 17206
10/17/98	11	10	39. **The Power Of Good-Bye** Sales #13 / Airplay #26	Maverick 17160
6/26/99	19	9	40. **Beautiful Stranger** Airplay #11 from the movie *Austin Powers: The Spy Who Shagged Me* starring Mike Myers (soundtrack on Maverick 47348)	album cut
2/26/00	29	6	41. **American Pie** Airplay #23 from the movie *The Next Best Thing* starring Madonna (soundtrack on Maverick 47595)	album cut
8/19/00	1 (4)	22	▲ 42. **Music** Sales #1 (4) / Airplay #3	Maverick 16826
12/23/00+	4	18	● 43. **Don't Tell Me** Sales #1 (1) / Airplay #10	Maverick 16825
5/19/01	23	4	44. **What It Feels Like For A Girl** Sales #9 / Airplay #36	Maverick 42372
10/26/02	8	10	45. **Die Another Day** Sales #1 (11) / Airplay #15 title song from the James Bond movie starring Pierce Brosnan	Warner 42492
4/26/03	37	1	46. **American Life** Sales #2 / Airplay #61	Maverick 16658
7/26/03	4 ˢ	14	47. **Hollywood**	Maverick 42638
11/8/03	35	4	48. **Me Against The Music** Sales #3 / Airplay #38 **BRITNEY SPEARS featuring Madonna**	Jive 58215
12/27/03	1 (1)ˢ	12	49. **Nothing Fails**	Maverick 42682
			MAESTRO, Johnny — see CRESTS, The	
			MAGGARD, Cledus, And The Citizen's Band	
1/24/76	19	9	Born Jay Huguely in Quick Sand, Kentucky. Recorded "The White Knight" while working at the Leslie Advertising agency in Greenville, South Carolina. 1. The White Knight **[N]** #1 Country hit (1 week)	Mercury 73751
			MAGIC LANTERNS	
11/30/68	29	5	Rock group from Manchester, England: Jimmy Bilsbury (vocals), Peter Shoesmith (guitar), Ian Moncur (bass) and Allan Wilson (drums). 1. Shame, Shame	Atlantic 2560
			MAGOO — see TIMBALAND	
			MAHARIS, George	
5/26/62	25	5	Born on 9/1/28 in Astoria, New York. Actor/singer. Played "Buz Murdock" on TV's *Route 66*. 1. Teach Me Tonight	Epic 9504

DATE	POS	WKS	ARTIST–RECORD TITLE	LABEL & NO.
			MAIN INGREDIENT, The	
			R&B vocal trio from the Bronx, New York: Cuba Gooding, Luther Simmons and Tony Sylvester. Gooding's son, Cuba Jr., is a prominent movie actor.	
9/2/72	3	10	● 1. **Everybody Plays The Fool**	RCA Victor 0731
3/16/74	10	14	● 2. **Just Don't Want To Be Lonely**	RCA Victor 0205
8/10/74	35	2	3. Happiness Is Just Around The Bend	RCA Victor 0305
			MAJORS, The	
			R&B vocal group from Philadelphia, Pennsylvania: Ricky Cordo, Eugene Glass, Frank Troutt, Ronald Gathers and Idella Morris.	
9/8/62	22	5	1. A Wonderful Dream	Imperial 5855
			MAKEBA, Miriam	
			Born Zensi Miriam Makeba on 3/4/32 in Johannesburg, South Africa. Black folk singer. Married to Hugh Masekela from 1964-66.	
10/28/67	12	8	1. Pata Pata **[F]**	Reprise 0606
			MALO	
			Latin-rock group from San Francisco, California. Core members: Arcelio Garcia (vocals), Jorge Santana (guitar), Richard Kermode (keyboards) and Pablo Tellez (bass). Santana is the brother of Carlos Santana.	
4/1/72	18	8	1. Suavecito	Warner 7559
			MALTBY, Richard, and his Orchestra	
			Born on 6/26/14 in Chicago, Illinois. Died on 8/19/91 (age 77). Trumpeter/composer/bandleader.	
3/31/56	14	8	1. (Themes From) "The Man With The Golden Arm" Top 100 #14 / Best Seller #15 / Juke Box #19 / Jockey #20 **[I]** title song from the movie *The Man With The Golden Arm* starring Frank Sinatra	Vik 0196
			MAMA CASS	
			Born Ellen Naomi Cohen on 9/19/41 in Baltimore, Maryland. Died of a heart attack (despite rumors, she did not choke to death on a ham sandwich) on 7/29/74 (age 32). Member of The Mamas & The Papas.	
7/27/68	12	8	1. Dream A Little Dream Of Me **MAMA CASS with The Mamas & The Papas** #1 hit for Wayne King in 1931	Dunhill 4145
8/2/69	30	7	2. It's Getting Better	Dunhill/ABC 4195
11/15/69	36	3	3. Make Your Own Kind Of Music **MAMA CASS ELLIOT**	Dunhill/ABC 4214
			MAMAS & THE PAPAS, The	
			Folk-pop group formed in Los Angeles, California: John Phillips (see #11 below), Michelle Phillips, Denny Doherty and Cass Elliot (see Mama Cass above). Disbanded in 1968, reunited briefly in 1971. John and Michelle were married from 1962-70; their daughter is Chynna Phillips of the Wilson Phillips trio. John is also the father of actress MacKenzie Phillips. Michelle Phillips became a successful actress; briefly married to Dennis Hopper in 1970. Mama Cass died of a heart attack on 7/29/74 (age 32). John Phillips died of heart failure on 3/18/2001 (age 65). Inducted into the Rock and Roll Hall of Fame in 1998.	
2/5/66	4	13	● 1. **California Dreamin'**	Dunhill 4020

DATE	POS	WKS	ARTIST–RECORD TITLE	LABEL & NO.
4/16/66	1 (3)	10	● 2. **Monday, Monday**	Dunhill 4026
7/9/66	5	8	3. **I Saw Her Again**	Dunhill 4031
11/5/66	24	4	4. Look Through My Window	Dunhill 4050
12/17/66+	5	9	5. **Words Of Love**	Dunhill 4057
3/4/67	2 (3)	9	6. **Dedicated To The One I Love**	Dunhill 4077
5/13/67	5	7	7. **Creeque Alley**	Dunhill 4083
			name of the street on which the group lived in the Virgin Islands; a musical biography of the group members	
9/2/67	20	5	8. Twelve Thirty (Young Girls Are Coming To The Canyon)	Dunhill 4099
11/4/67	26	5	9. Glad To Be Unhappy	Dunhill 4107
			from the 1936 Rodgers & Hart musical *On Your Toes*; all of above produced by Lou Adler	
7/27/68	12	8	10. Dream A Little Dream Of Me	Dunhill 4145
			MAMA CASS with The Mamas & The Papas	
			#1 hit for Wayne King in 1931	
6/20/70	32	7	11. Mississippi	Dunhill/ABC 4236
			JOHN PHILLIPS	
			MANCHESTER, Melissa	
			Born on 2/15/51 in the Bronx, New York. Pop singer/songwriter/pianist.	
6/14/75	6	11	1. **Midnight Blue**	Arista 0116
			#1 Adult Contemporary hit (2 weeks)	
10/18/75	30	5	2. Just Too Many People	Arista 0146
2/28/76	27	4	3. Just You And I	Arista 0168
1/6/79	10	14	4. **Don't Cry Out Loud**	Arista 0373
11/24/79	39	2	5. Pretty Girls	Arista 0456
4/5/80	32	5	6. Fire In The Morning	Arista 0485
7/10/82	5	15	7. **You Should Hear How She Talks About You**	Arista 0676
			MANCINI, Henry, And His Orchestra	
			Born on 4/16/24 in Cleveland, Ohio; raised in Aliquippa, Pennsylvania. Died of cancer on 6/14/94 (age 70). Leading movie and TV composer/arranger/conductor. Won Grammy's Lifetime Achievement Award in 1995.	
4/18/60	21	8	1. Mr. Lucky [I]	RCA Victor 7705
			title song from the TV series starring John Vivyan	
11/13/61	11	16	2. Moon River	RCA Victor 7916
			from the movie *Breakfast At Tiffany's* starring Audrey Hepburn	
3/2/63	33	10	3. Days Of Wine And Roses	RCA Victor 8120
			title song from the movie starring Jack Lemmon and Lee Remick; 1963 Grammy winner: Record of the Year	
1/25/64	36	4	4. Charade	RCA Victor 8256
			title song from the movie starring Cary Grant and Audrey Hepburn	
5/9/64	31	2	5. The Pink Panther Theme [I]	RCA Victor 8286
			Johnny Beecher (sax); from the first of the *Pink Panther* movies starring Peter Sellers	
5/24/69	1 (2)	12	● 6. **Love Theme From Romeo & Juliet** [I]	RCA Victor 0131
			#1 Adult Contemporary hit (8 weeks); from the 1968 movie *Romeo & Juliet* starring Leonard Whiting and Olivia Hussey	
2/6/71	13	8	7. (Theme From) Love Story [I]	RCA Victor 9927
			from the movie *Love Story* starring Ali McGraw and Ryan O'Neal	

DATE	POS	WKS	ARTIST—RECORD TITLE	LABEL & NO.
			MANDRELL, Barbara	
			Born on 12/25/48 in Houston, Texas; raised in Oceanside, California. Country singer. Host of own TV variety series from 1980-82.	
5/12/79	**31**	5	1. (If Loving You Is Wrong) I Don't Want To Be Right	MCA 12451
			#1 Country hit (1 week)	
			MANFRED MANN	
			Born Michael Lubowitz on 10/21/40 in Johannesburg, South Africa. Formed pop-rock group in England: Mann (keyboards), Paul Jones (vocals), Michael Vickers (guitar), Tom McGuinnes (bass) and Mike Hugg (drums). Mike D'Abo replaced Jones in 1967. Manfred Mann formed his new Earth Band in 1971: Mann, Chris Thompson (vocals), Colin Pattenden (bass) and Chris Slade (drums). Pat King replaced Pattenden in June 1977. Thompson formed the group Night in 1979. Earth Band lineup in 1984: Mann, Mick Rogers (vocals), Steve Waller (guitar), Matt Irving (bass) and Geoff Britton (drums).	
9/12/64	**1** (2)	12	1. **Do Wah Diddy Diddy**	Ascot 2157
11/28/64+	**12**	9	2. Sha La La	Ascot 2165
7/23/66	**29**	5	3. Pretty Flamingo	United Artists 50040
3/9/68	**10**	10	4. **Mighty Quinn (Quinn The Eskimo)**	Mercury 72770
			written by Bob Dylan	
			MANFRED MANN'S EARTH BAND:	
12/18/76+	**1** (1)	15	● 5. **Blinded By The Light**	Warner 8252
6/4/77	**40**	1	6. Spirit In The Night **[R]**	Warner 8355
			original version (with Mick Rogers on lead vocal) hit #97 in 1976; this version features Chris Thompson on lead vocal; above 2 written by Bruce Springsteen	
2/18/84	**22**	8	7. Runner	Arista 9143
			MANGIONE, Chuck	
			Born on 11/29/40 in Rochester, New York. Flugelhorn player.	
3/18/78	**4**	16	1. **Feels So Good** **[I]**	A&M 2001
			#1 Adult Contemporary hit (1 week)	
2/16/80	**18**	9	2. Give It All You Got **[I]**	A&M 2211
			#1 Adult Contemporary hit (3 weeks); featured song by ABC Sports for the 1980 Winter Olympics	
			MANHATTANS, The	
			R&B vocal group from Jersey City, New Jersey: Gerald Alston, Winfred Lovett, Edward Bivins, Richard Taylor and Ken Kelly. Taylor left in 1976; died on 12/7/87 (age 47).	
2/15/75	**37**	2	1. Don't Take Your Love	Columbia 10045
5/29/76	**1** (2)	17	▲ 2. **Kiss And Say Goodbye**	Columbia 10310
			#1 R&B hit (1 week)	
5/31/80	**5**	14	▲ 3. **Shining Star**	Columbia 11222
			MANHATTAN TRANSFER, The	
			Versatile vocal harmony group formed in Manhattan, New York: Tim Hauser, Alan Paul, Laurel Masse and Janis Siegel. Cheryl Bentyne replaced Masse in 1979.	
11/1/75	**22**	5	1. Operator	Atlantic 3292
5/31/80	**30**	4	2. Twilight Zone/Twilight Tone	Atlantic 3649
			"Twilight Zone" was the theme from the Rod Serling TV series	
6/13/81	**7**	13	3. **Boy From New York City**	Atlantic 3816
11/5/83	**40**	2	4. Spice Of Life	Atlantic 89786

DATE	POS	WKS	ARTIST–RECORD TITLE	LABEL & NO.
			MANILOW, Barry	
			Born Barry Alan Pincus on 6/17/46 in Brooklyn, New York. Pop singer/songwriter/pianist. Studied at New York's Juilliard School. Music director for the WCBS-TV series *Callback*. Worked at New York's Continental Baths bathhouse/nightclub in New York as Bette Midler's accompanist in 1972; later produced her first two albums. First recorded solo as Featherbed. Wrote and performed numerous commercial jingles.	
12/7/74+	**1** (1)	12	● 1. **Mandy**	Bell 45,613
			#1 Adult Contemporary hit (2 weeks); #91 hit for Scott English in 1972 (as "Brandy")	
3/29/75	**12**	8	2. It's A Miracle	Arista 0108
			#1 Adult Contemporary hit (1 week)	
7/26/75	**6**	13	3. **Could It Be Magic**	Arista 0126
			first released by Featherbed Featuring Barry Manilow in 1971; inspired by Chopin's *Prelude in C Minor*	
11/22/75+	**1** (1)	16	● 4. **I Write The Songs**	Arista 0157
			#1 Adult Contemporary hit (2 weeks); written by Bruce Johnston (of The Beach Boys)	
4/10/76	**10**	10	5. **Tryin' To Get The Feeling Again**	Arista 0172
			#1 Adult Contemporary hit (1 week)	
10/9/76	**29**	5	6. This One's For You	Arista 0206
			#1 Adult Contemporary hit (1 week)	
12/25/76+	**10**	13	7. **Weekend In New England**	Arista 0212
			#1 Adult Contemporary hit (1 week)	
5/28/77	**1** (1)	13	● 8. **Looks Like We Made It**	Arista 0244
			#1 Adult Contemporary hit (3 weeks)	
10/22/77	**23**	5	9. Daybreak [L]	Arista 0273
2/18/78	**3**	16	● 10. **Can't Smile Without You**	Arista 0305
			#1 Adult Contemporary hit (2 weeks)	
6/10/78	**19**	4	11. Even Now	Arista 0330
			#1 Adult Contemporary hit (3 weeks)	
7/8/78	**8**	9	● 12. **Copacabana (At The Copa)**	Arista 0339
10/7/78	**11**	10	13. Ready To Take A Chance Again	Arista 0357
			above 2 from the movie *Foul Play* starring Goldie Hawn and Chevy Chase	
1/6/79	**9**	10	14. **Somewhere In The Night**	Arista 0382
10/20/79	**9**	11	15. **Ships**	Arista 0464
2/2/80	**20**	7	16. When I Wanted You	Arista 0481
			#1 Adult Contemporary hit (1 week)	
5/17/80	**36**	4	17. I Don't Want To Walk Without You	Arista 0501
			#2 hit for Harry James in 1942 (from the movie *Sweater Girl* starring Eddie Bracken)	
12/6/80+	**10**	11	18. **I Made It Through The Rain**	Arista 0566
10/17/81	**15**	10	19. The Old Songs	Arista 0633
			#1 Adult Contemporary hit (3 weeks)	
1/23/82	**21**	7	20. Somewhere Down The Road	Arista 0658
			#1 Adult Contemporary hit (2 weeks)	
4/24/82	**32**	3	21. Let's Hang On	Arista 0675
9/18/82	**38**	2	22. Oh Julie	Arista 0698
1/15/83	**39**	2	23. Memory	Arista 1025
			theme from Andrew Lloyd Webber's musical *Cats* starring Betty Buckley	
4/9/83	**26**	7	24. Some Kind Of Friend	Arista 1046
11/26/83+	**18**	10	25. Read 'Em And Weep	Arista 9101
			#1 Adult Contemporary hit (6 weeks)	

DATE	POS	WKS	ARTIST–RECORD TITLE	LABEL & NO.
			MANN, Barry	
			Born Barry Iberman on 2/9/39 in Brooklyn, New York. Pop singer/ songwriter. One of pop music's most prolific songwriters in a partnership with wife Cynthia Weil.	
8/21/61	7	9	1. **Who Put The Bomp (In The Bomp, Bomp, Bomp)** [N]	ABC-Paramount 10237
			MANN, Carl	
			Born on 8/24/42 in Huntingdon, Tennessee. Rockabilly singer/pianist.	
7/27/59	25	6	1. Mona Lisa #1 hit for Nat "King" Cole in 1950	Phillips 3539
			MANN, Gloria	
			Born in Philadelphia, Pennsylvania. Pop-rock and roll singer. Her son, Bob Rosenberg, is the leader of Will To Power.	
2/12/55	18	2	1. Earth Angel (Will You Be Mine) Juke Box #18 / Best Seller #24	Sound 109
12/24/55+	19	8	2. Teen Age Prayer Best Seller #19 / Top 100 #21 Sid Bass (orch.)	Sound 126
			MANN, Herbie	
			Born Herbert Jay Solomon on 4/16/30 in Brooklyn, New York. Died of cancer on 7/1/2003 (age 73). Jazz flutist.	
4/26/75	14	6	1. Hijack	Atlantic 3246
3/17/79	26	6	2. Superman	Atlantic 3547
			MANN, Manfred — see MANFRED MANN	
			MANSON, Marilyn	
			Born Brian Warner on 1/5/69 in Canton, Ohio. Hard-rock singer/ songwriter. Noted for his controversial stage performances. His band includes: Scott "Daisy Berkowitz" Putesky (guitar), Steve "Madonna Wayne Gacy" Bier (keyboards), Jeordi "Twiggy Ramirez" White (bass) and Ken "Ginger Fish" Wilson (drums).	
5/10/03	5 ˢ	4	1. **mOBSCENE**	Nothing 000372
			MANTOVANI And His Orchestra	
			Born Annunzio Paolo Mantovani on 11/15/05 in Venice, Italy. Died on 3/29/80 (age 74). Classical violin player/orchestra leader.	
8/14/54	10	18	● 1. **Cara Mia** Best Seller #10 / Jockey #17 **DAVID WHITFIELD with MANTOVANI His Orchestra and Chorus**	London 1486
7/22/57	12	14	2. Around The World Jockey #12 / Best Seller #23 / Top 100 #25 [I] Stan Newsome (trumpet solo); from the movie Around The World In 80 Days starring David Niven	London 1746
1/23/61	31	2	3. Main Theme from Exodus (Ari's Theme) [I] from the movie Exodus starring Paul Newman and Eva Marie Saint	London 1953
			MARATHONS, The	
			The Olympics' Arvee label needed a new single, but since The Olympics were on tour, the label brought in The Vibrations, who were under contract with the Chess/Checker label. The Vibrations recorded "Peanut Butter" and Arvee released it as by The Marathons. Chess discovered the fraud and stopped the Arvee release, and then released a re-recorded version on their subsidiary label, Argo. Arvee followed up with a new song by The Marathons, recorded by an unknown non-Vibrations group.	
5/22/61	20	7	1. Peanut Butter	Arvee 5027

DATE	POS	WKS	ARTIST–RECORD TITLE	LABEL & NO.
			MARCELS, The	
			R&B vocal group from Pittsburgh, Pennsylvania: Cornelius Harp, Ronald Mundy, Gene Bricker, Richard Knauss and Fred Johnson. Allen Johnson and Walt Maddox replaced Bricker and Knauss in mid-1961. Mundy left in late 1961. Allen Johnson died of cancer on 9/28/95.	
3/20/61	**1** (3)	11	1. **Blue Moon**	Colpix 186
			#1 R&B hit (2 weeks); #1 hit for Glen Gray in 1935	
10/30/61	7	8	2. **Heartaches**	Colpix 612
			#1 hit for Ted Weems in 1947	
			MARCH, Little Peggy	
			Born Margaret Battivio on 3/8/48 in Lansdale, Pennsylvania. Pop singer.	
4/6/63	**1** (3)	11	1. **I Will Follow Him**	RCA Victor 8139
			#1 R&B hit (1 week); adapted from the French song "Chariot"	
6/29/63	32	3	2. I Wish I Were A Princess	RCA Victor 8189
9/28/63	26	4	3. Hello Heartache, Goodbye Love	RCA Victor 8221
			MARCHAN, Bobby	
			Born Oscar James Gibson on 4/30/30 in Youngstown, Ohio. Died on 12/5/99 (age 69). R&B singer. Sang with Huey "Piano" Smith & The Clowns.	
7/11/60	31	4	1. There's Something On Your Mind (Part 2) **[N]**	Fire 1022
			#1 R&B hit (1 week)	
			MARCY PLAYGROUND	
			Rock trio from Manhattan, New York: John Wozniak (vocals, guitar), Dylan Keefe (bass) and Dan Reiser (drums).	
4/11/98	8	22	1. **Sex and Candy** Airplay #4 / Sales #21	Capitol 58695
			#1 Modern Rock hit (15 weeks)	
			MARDONES, Benny	
			Born on 11/9/48 in Cleveland, Ohio. Pop singer/songwriter.	
7/12/80	**11**	12	1. Into The Night	Polydor 2091
6/3/89	20	7	2. Into The Night Sales #17 / Airplay #25 **[R]**	Polydor 889368
			above 2 are the same version	
			MARESCA, Ernie	
			Born on 4/21/39 in the Bronx, New York. Singer/songwriter.	
4/21/62	6	9	1. **Shout! Shout! (Knock Yourself Out)**	Seville 117
			Del Satins (backing vocals); Billy Mure (orch.)	
			MARIE, Teena	
			Born Mary Christine Brockert on 3/5/56 in Santa Monica, California; raised in Venice, California. White dance singer/songwriter.	
1/17/81	37	3	1. I Need Your Lovin'	Gordy 7189
2/2/85	4	13	2. **Lovergirl** Airplay #4 / Sales #5	Epic 04619
			MARIO	
			Born Mario Barrett in 1987 in Baltimore, Maryland; raised in Teaneck, New Jersey. Teen R&B singer/rapper.	
6/29/02	4	15	1. **Just A Friend 2002** Airplay #5 / Sales #22	J Records 21219

DATE	POS	WKS	ARTIST–RECORD TITLE	LABEL & NO.
			MARKETTS, The	
			Surf-rock instrumental group formed in Hollywood, California: Ben Benay (guitar), Mike Henderson (sax), Richard Hobriaco (keyboards), Ray Pohlman (bass) and Gene Pello (drums).	
2/17/62	31	3	1. Surfer's Stomp [I] **THE MAR-KETS**	Liberty 55401
12/28/63+	3	11	2. **Out Of Limits** [I] opening riff is similar to *The Twilight Zone* TV series theme song (not from the *Outer Limits* TV series, although first pressings issued as "Outer Limits")	Warner 5391
2/26/66	17	5	3. Batman Theme [I] from the hit TV series starring Adam West and Burt Ward	Warner 5696
			MAR-KEYS	
			Instrumental group formed in Memphis, Tennessee: Steve Cropper and Charlie Freeman (guitars), Jerry Lee Smith (piano), Charles Axton, Wayne Jackson and Don Nix (horns), Donald "Duck" Dunn (bass) and Terry Johnson (drums). Staff musicians at Stax/Volt. Cropper and Dunn later joined Booker T. & The MG's. Axton died in January 1974 (age 32).	
7/17/61	3	12	1. **Last Night** [I]	Satellite 107
			MARKHAM, Pigmeat	
			Born Dewey Markham on 4/18/04 in Durham, North Carolina. Died of a stroke on 12/13/81 (age 77). Black comedian. Regular on TV's *Laugh-In* (1968-69).	
7/6/68	19	4	1. Here Comes The Judge [N] title inspired by a recurrent gag line originated by Markham on TV's *Laugh-In*	Chess 2049
			MARK IV, The	
			Pop-rock and roll group from Chicago, Illinois.	
2/9/59	24	7	1. I Got A Wife [N] written by Eddie & Dutch	Mercury 71403
			MARKY MARK And The Funky Bunch	
			Born Mark Wahlberg on 6/5/71 in Dorchester, Massachusetts. Singer/rapper/actor. Starred in several movies. Younger brother of Donnie Wahlberg of New Kids On The Block. The Funky Bunch is DJ Terry Yancey and three male and two female dancers.	
8/10/91	1 (1)	15	● 1. Good Vibrations Sales #2 / Airplay #6 **MARKY MARK And The Funky Bunch Featuring Loleatta Holloway** samples "Love Sensation" by Loleatta Holloway	Interscope 98764
11/23/91	10	12	● 2. **Wildside** Sales #5 / Airplay #30 samples "Walk On The Wild Side" by Lou Reed	Interscope 98673
			MARLEY, Ziggy, And The Melody Makers	
			Family reggae group from Kingston, Jamaica. Children of the legendary reggae singer Bob Marley: David "Ziggy" (vocals, guitar), Stephen, Sharon and Cedella Marley.	
7/9/88	39	1	1. Tomorrow People Sales #37 / Airplay #40	Virgin 99347

DATE	POS	WKS	ARTIST–RECORD TITLE	LABEL & NO.
			MARLOWE, Marion	
			Born on 3/7/29 in St. Louis, Missouri. Featured singer on *Arthur Godfrey And His Friends* from 1950-55.	
7/16/55	**14**	2	1. The Man In The Raincoat Jockey #14 / Juke Box #18 Archie Bleyer (orch.)	Cadence 1266
			MARMALADE, The	
			Pop group from Scotland: Thomas "Dean Ford" McAleese (vocals), Junior Campbell (guitar), Patrick Fairley (piano), Graham Knight (bass) and Alan Whitehead (drums).	
4/4/70	**10**	11	1. **Reflections Of My Life**	London 20058
			MAROON5	
			Alternative pop-rock group from Los Angeles, California: Adam Levine (vocals, guitar), James Valentine (guitar), Jesse Carmichael (keyboards), Mickey Madden (bass) and Ryan Dusick (drums).	
9/27/03	**18**	14	1. Harder To Breathe Airplay #18 from the album *Songs About Jane* on Octone 50001	album cut
			M/A/R/R/S	
			Electro-funk group from England featuring two pairs of brothers: Martyn and Steve Young, with Alex and Rudi Kane. Includes mixers Chris Mackintosh and Dave Dorrell.	
1/16/88	**13**	11	● 1. Pump Up The Volume Sales #11 / Airplay #13	4th & B'way 7452
			MARSHALL TUCKER BAND, The	
			Southern-rock group from South Carolina: Doug Gray (vocals), brothers Toy (guitar) and Tommy (bass) Caldwell, George McCorkle (guitar), Jerry Eubanks (sax, flute) and Paul Riddle (drums). Tommy Caldwell died in a car crash on 4/28/80 (age 30). Toy Caldwell died of respiratory failure on 2/25/93 (age 45). Marshall Tucker was the owner of the band's rehearsal hall.	
12/20/75	**38**	2	1. Fire On The Mountain Charlie Daniels (fiddle)	Capricorn 0244
4/16/77	**14**	13	2. Heard It In A Love Song	Capricorn 0270
			MARTERIE, Ralph, And His Orchestra	
			Born on 12/24/14 in Naples, Italy; raised in Chicago, Illinois. Died on 10/8/78 (age 63). Trumpet player/bandleader.	
3/30/57	**25**	3	1. Tricky Jockey #25 / Top 100 #37 [I]	Mercury 71050
5/13/57	**10**	6	2. **Shish-Kebab** Jockey #10 / Top 100 #29 [I]	Mercury 71092
			MARTHA & THE VANDELLAS	
			Female R&B vocal trio from Detroit, Michigan: Martha Reeves (born on 7/18/41), Annette Beard and Rosalind Ashford. Betty Kelly replaced Beard in 1964. Group inducted into the Rock and Roll Hall of Fame in 1995.	
5/18/63	**29**	8	1. Come And Get These Memories	Gordy 7014
8/17/63	**4**	11	2. **Heat Wave** #1 R&B hit (4 weeks)	Gordy 7022
12/7/63+	**8**	9	3. **Quicksand**	Gordy 7025
9/5/64	**2** (2)	11	● 4. **Dancing In The Street**	Gordy 7033
12/26/64+	**34**	4	5. Wild One	Gordy 7036
3/13/65	**8**	8	6. **Nowhere To Run**	Gordy 7039

DATE	POS	WKS	ARTIST–RECORD TITLE	LABEL & NO.
9/11/65	**36**	2	7. You've Been In Love Too Long	Gordy 7045
2/19/66	**22**	7	8. My Baby Loves Me	Gordy 7048
11/12/66	**9**	7	9. **I'm Ready For Love**	Gordy 7056
3/18/67	**10**	10	10. **Jimmy Mack**	Gordy 7058
			#1 R&B hit (1 week)	
9/9/67	**25**	6	11. Love Bug Leave My Heart Alone	Gordy 7062
12/2/67	**11**	9	12. Honey Chile	Gordy 7067
			MARTHA REEVES & THE VANDELLAS	

MARTIKA

Born Marta Marrero on 5/18/69 in Whittier, California. Latin singer/actress. Starred on TV's *Kids, Incorporated*. Appeared in the 1982 movie musical *Annie*.

DATE	POS	WKS	ARTIST–RECORD TITLE	LABEL & NO.
2/18/89	**18**	8	1. More Than You Know Sales #17 / Airplay #18	Columbia 08103
6/10/89	**1** (2)	13	● 2. **Toy Soldiers** Airplay #1 (1) / Sales #2	Columbia 68747
9/30/89	**25**	5	3. I Feel The Earth Move Sales #27 / Airplay #27	Columbia 68996
9/7/91	**10**	9	4. **Love...Thy Will Be Done** Sales #24 / Airplay #31	Columbia 73853
			written by Prince	

MARTIN, Bobbi

Born Barbara Martin on 11/29/38 in Brooklyn, New York; raised in Baltimore, Maryland. Died of cancer on 5/2/2000 (age 61). Adult Contemporary singer/songwriter.

DATE	POS	WKS	ARTIST–RECORD TITLE	LABEL & NO.
1/2/65	**19**	7	1. Don't Forget I Still Love You	Coral 62426
4/11/70	**13**	10	2. For The Love Of Him	United Artists 50602
			#1 Adult Contemporary hit (2 weeks)	

MARTIN, Dean

Born Dino Crocetti on 6/7/17 in Steubenville, Ohio. Died of respiratory failure on 12/25/95 (age 78). Pop singer/actor. Teamed with comedian Jerry Lewis in 1946. Starred in several movies. Hosted own TV series from 1965-74. His son Dino was in Dino, Desi & Billy.

DATE	POS	WKS	ARTIST–RECORD TITLE	LABEL & NO.
12/3/55+	**1** (6)	19	● 1. **Memories Are Made Of This**	Capitol 3295
			Jockey #1 (6) / Best Seller #1 (5) / Top 100 #1 (5) / Juke Box #1 (4) The Easy Riders (backing vocals)	
4/7/56	**27**	4	2. Innamorata Top 100 #27	Capitol 3352
			from the movie *Artists And Models* starring Martin and Jerry Lewis	
5/26/56	**22**	6	3. Standing On The Corner Jockey #22 / Top 100 #29	Capitol 3414
			from the Broadway musical *The Most Happy Fella* starring Robert Weede; Dick Stabile (orch., above 2)	
4/7/58	**4**	18	4. **Return To Me** Jockey #4 / Best Seller #4 / Top 100 #4	Capitol 3894
8/4/58	**30**	3	5. Angel Baby Hot 100 #30 / Best Seller #43	Capitol 3988
8/11/58	**12**	10	6. Volare (Nel Blu Dipinto Di Blu) Best Seller #12 / Hot 100 #15	Capitol 4028
			Gus Levene (orch., above 3)	
7/11/64	**1** (1)	13	● 7. **Everybody Loves Somebody**	Reprise 0281
			#1 Adult Contemporary hit (8 weeks); first recorded by Frank Sinatra in 1948	
10/17/64	**6**	8	8. **The Door Is Still Open To My Heart**	Reprise 0307
			#1 Adult Contemporary hit (1 week); #4 R&B hit for The Cardinals in 1955	
1/9/65	**25**	5	9. You're Nobody Till Somebody Loves You	Reprise 0333
			#1 Adult Contemporary hit (1 week); #14 hit for Russ Morgan in 1946	
3/13/65	**22**	5	10. Send Me The Pillow You Dream On	Reprise 0344

DATE	POS	WKS	ARTIST–RECORD TITLE	LABEL & NO.
6/12/65	32	3	11. (Remember Me) I'm The One Who Loves You *#2 Country hit for Stuart Hamblen in 1950*	Reprise 0369
8/21/65	21	7	12. Houston	Reprise 0393
11/13/65	10	8	13. **I Will**	Reprise 0415
3/5/66	32	4	14. Somewhere There's A Someone	Reprise 0443
6/11/66	35	1	15. Come Running Back	Reprise 0466
7/22/67	25	4	16. In The Chapel In The Moonlight *#1 Adult Contemporary hit (3 weeks); #1 hit for Shep Fields in 1936*	Reprise 0601
9/9/67	38	2	17. Little Ole Wine Drinker, Me	Reprise 0608

MARTIN, Marilyn

Born in Louisville, Kentucky. Former session singer.

DATE	POS	WKS	ARTIST–RECORD TITLE	LABEL & NO.
10/12/85	1 (1)	16	1. **Separate Lives** Airplay #1 (2) / Sales #2 **PHIL COLLINS and MARILYN MARTIN** *#1 Adult Contemporary hit (3 weeks); love theme from the movie White Nights starring Mikhail Baryshnikov*	Atlantic 89498
2/22/86	28	6	2. Night Moves Airplay #21	Atlantic 89465

MARTIN, Moon

Born John Martin in 1950 in Oklahoma. Rock and roll singer/songwriter/guitarist.

DATE	POS	WKS	ARTIST–RECORD TITLE	LABEL & NO.
9/22/79	30	4	1. Rolene	Capitol 4765

MARTIN, Ricky

Born Enrique Martin Morales on 12/24/71 in San Juan, Puerto Rico. Latin singer/actor. Member of Menudo from 1984-89. Acted on the TV soap *General Hospital* and on Broadway in *Les Misérables*.

DATE	POS	WKS	ARTIST–RECORD TITLE	LABEL & NO.
4/24/99	1 (5)	17	▲ 1. **Livin' La Vida Loca** Sales #1 (4) / Airplay #1 (4)	C2/Columbia 79124
8/28/99	2 (2)	12	● 2. **She's All I Ever Had** Sales #2 / Airplay #7	C2/Columbia 79259
12/11/99+	22	7	3. Shake Your Bon-Bon Sales #6 / Airplay #31	C2/Columbia 79333
10/7/00	12	12	4. She Bangs Airplay #8	album cut
2/3/01	13	13	5. Nobody Wants To Be Lonely Airplay #10 **RICKY MARTIN with CHRISTINA AGUILERA** *above 2 from the album Sound Loaded on Columbia 61394*	album cut

MARTIN, Steve

Born on 6/8/45 in Waco, Texas; raised in Garden Grove, California. Popular TV and movie comedian/actor.

DATE	POS	WKS	ARTIST–RECORD TITLE	LABEL & NO.
7/8/78	17	7	● 1. King Tut [N] **STEVE MARTIN and the Toot Uncommons** *Toot Uncommons is actually The Dirt Band; Tut: ancient Egyptian King Tutankhamen (1355 B.C.)*	Warner 8577

MARTIN, Tony

Born Alvin Morris on 12/25/12 in San Francisco, California. Singer/actor. Appeared in several movies. Hosted own TV show from 1954-56. Married actress/dancer Cyd Charisse in 1948.

DATE	POS	WKS	ARTIST–RECORD TITLE	LABEL & NO.
5/26/56	10	11	1. **Walk Hand In Hand** *Top 100 #10 / Jockey #13 / Juke Box #16 / Best Seller #21*	RCA Victor 6493

DATE	POS	WKS	ARTIST–RECORD TITLE	LABEL & NO.
			MARTIN, Trade	
			Born on 11/19/43 in Union City, New Jersey. Teen pop singer.	Coed 570
11/17/62	28	4	1. That Stranger Used To Be My Girl	
			MARTIN, Vince	
			Born on 3/17/37 in Brooklyn, New York. Teen folk singer.	
10/13/56	9	15	1. **Cindy, Oh Cindy**	Glory 247
			Juke Box #9 / Best Seller #12 / Top 100 #12 / Jockey #12	
			VINCE MARTIN With The Tarriers	
			adapted from a sailor's sea chantey	
			MARTINDALE, Wink	
			Born Winston Martindale on 12/4/33 in Jackson, Tennessee. Worked as a DJ and hosted several TV game shows.	Dot 15968
9/28/59	7	12	● 1. **Deck Of Cards** [S]	
			#2 Country hit for T. Texas Tyler in 1948	
			MARTINEZ, Angie	
			Born in the Bronx, New York (of Puerto Rican parents). Female rapper. Radio personality at Hot 97 in New York City.	
7/12/97	6	17	▲ 1. **Not Tonight** Sales #3 / Airplay #39	Undeas/Big Beat 98019
			LIL' KIM Featuring Da Brat, Left Eye, Missy "Misdemenaor" Elliott and Angie Martinez	
			samples "Ladies Night" by Kool & The Gang; from the movie *Nothing To Lose* starring Martin Lawrence	
8/24/02	15	15	2. If I Could Go! Airplay #14 / Sales #55	Elektra 67311
			ANGIE MARTINEZ (Featuring Lil' Mo & Sacario)	
			MARTINEZ, Nancy	
			Born on 8/26/60 in Quebec City, Quebec, Canada. Dance singer/actress.	Atlantic 89371
12/6/86	32	7	1. For Tonight Sales #29	
			MARTINO, Al	
			Born Alfred Cini on 10/7/27 in Philadelphia, Pennsylvania. Pop singer. Portrayed singer "Johnny Fontane" in the 1972 movie *The Godfather*.	
5/4/63	3	11	1. **I Love You Because**	Capitol 4930
			#1 Adult Contemporary hit (2 weeks); #1 Country hit for Leon Payne in 1950	
8/17/63	15	8	2. Painted, Tainted Rose	Capitol 5000
11/16/63	22	6	3. Living A Lie	Capitol 5060
2/15/64	9	8	4. **I Love You More And More Every Day**	Capitol 5108
5/30/64	20	6	5. Tears And Roses	Capitol 5183
9/12/64	33	4	6. Always Together	Capitol 5239
12/18/65+	15	9	7. Spanish Eyes	Capitol 5542
			#1 Adult Contemporary hit (4 weeks)	
4/2/66	30	4	8. Think I'll Go Somewhere And Cry Myself To Sleep	Capitol 5598
			#26 Country hit for Charlie Louvin in 1965	
6/17/67	27	5	9. Mary In The Morning	Capitol 5904
			#1 Adult Contemporary hit (2 weeks)	
2/8/75	17	8	10. To The Door Of The Sun (Alle Porte Del Sole)	Capitol 3987
12/6/75	33	4	11. Volare	Capitol 4134

DATE	POS	WKS	ARTIST–RECORD TITLE	LABEL & NO.
			MARVELETTES, The	
			Female R&B vocal group from Inkster, Michigan: Gladys Horton, Georgeanna Tillman Gordon (married Billy Gordon of The Contours), Wanda Young (married Bobby Rogers of The Miracles), Katherine Anderson and Juanita Cowart. Young and Horton both sang lead. Cowart left in 1962. Gordon left in 1965; died of lupus on 1/6/80 (age 35). Horton left in 1967, replaced by Anne Bogan (later a member of Love, Peace & Happiness and New Birth). Disbanded in 1969. Also recorded as The Darnells.	
10/16/61	**1** (1)	15	● 1. **Please Mr. Postman** #1 R&B hit (7 weeks); first #1 pop hit on a Motown label	Tamla 54046
3/3/62	34	1	2. Twistin' Postman	Tamla 54054
5/26/62	7	11	3. **Playboy**	Tamla 54060
9/1/62	17	7	4. Beechwood 4-5789	Tamla 54065
12/5/64+	25	8	5. Too Many Fish In The Sea	Tamla 54105
7/3/65	34	1	6. I'll Keep Holding On	Tamla 54116
1/29/66	7	8	7. **Don't Mess With Bill**	Tamla 54126
2/18/67	13	7	8. The Hunter Gets Captured By The Game	Tamla 54143
5/20/67	23	5	9. When You're Young And In Love	Tamla 54150
1/6/68	17	8	10. My Baby Must Be A Magician opening male voice: Melvin Franklin of The Temptations; #7, 8 & 10: written and produced by Smokey Robinson	Tamla 54158
			MARVELOWS, The	
			R&B vocal group from Chicago, Illinois: Melvin Mason, Willie Stevenson, Frank Paden, Johnny Paden and Jesse Smith.	
7/3/65	37	1	1. I Do Johnny Pate (orch.)	ABC-Paramount 10629
			MARX, Richard	
			Born on 9/16/63 in Chicago, Illinois. Pop-rock singer/songwriter. Married Cynthia Rhodes (of Animotion) on 1/8/89.	
7/11/87	3	12	1. **Don't Mean Nothing** Sales #4 / Airplay #4 #1 Mainstream Rock hit (1 week)	Manhattan 50079
10/17/87	3	13	2. **Should've Known Better** Sales #3 / Airplay #4 Fee Waybill (of The Tubes) and Timothy B. Schmit (backing vocals)	Manhattan 50083
1/30/88	**2** (2)	15	3. **Endless Summer Nights** Sales #2 / Airplay #2	EMI-Manhattan 50113
6/11/88	**1** (1)	14	4. **Hold On To The Nights** Sales #1 (1) / Airplay #1 (1)	EMI-Manhattan 50106
5/6/89	**1** (1)	13	5. **Satisfied** Airplay #1 (2) / Sales #3	EMI 50189
7/15/89	**1** (3)	13	▲ 6. **Right Here Waiting** Airplay #1 (5) / Sales #1 (1) #1 Adult Contemporary hit (6 weeks)	EMI 50219
10/21/89	4	11	7. **Angelia** Sales #4 / Airplay #4	EMI 50218
1/27/90	12	9	8. Too Late To Say Goodbye Airplay #10 / Sales #14	EMI 50234
5/12/90	13	10	9. Children Of The Night Airplay #8 / Sales #17	EMI 50288
11/9/91	12	13	10. Keep Coming Back Airplay #10 / Sales #43 #1 Adult Contemporary hit (4 weeks)	Capitol 44753
3/7/92	9	16	11. **Hazard** Sales #10 / Airplay #11 #1 Adult Contemporary hit (1 week)	Capitol 44796
6/27/92	20	13	12. Take This Heart Airplay #14 / Sales #42	Capitol 44782
1/29/94	7	23	13. **Now and Forever** Airplay #5 / Sales #10 #1 Adult Contemporary hit (11 weeks)	Capitol 58005
7/23/94	20	11	14. The Way She Loves Me Airplay #20 / Sales #30	Capitol 58167

DATE	POS	WKS	ARTIST–RECORD TITLE	LABEL & NO.
			MARY JANE GIRLS	
			Black female funk-dance vocal group formed in Los Angeles, California: Joanne "JoJo" McDuffie, Candice "Candi" Ghant, Kim "Maxi" Wuletich and Yvette "Corvette" Marina. Formed and produced by Rick James.	
4/27/85	7	12	1. **In My House** Sales #5 / Airplay #9	Gordy 1741
			MARYMARY	
			Black female gospel vocal duo from Inglewood, California: sisters Erica and Tina Atkins.	
4/29/00	28	7	1. Shackles (Praise You) Sales #6 / Airplay #58	C2/Columbia 79303
			MASE	
			Born Mason Betha on 3/24/70 in Jacksonville, Florida; raised in Harlem, New York. Male rapper. In 2000 became a pastor and leader of Sane Ministries in Atlanta, Georgia.	
1/25/97	1 (6)	26	▲² 1. **Can't Nobody Hold Me Down** Sales #1 (7) / Airplay #25 **PUFF DADDY Featuring Mase** #1 R&B hit (6 weeks); samples "The Message" by Grandmaster Flash and "Break My Stride" by Matthew Wilder	Bad Boy 79083
8/2/97	1 (2)	28	▲ 2. **Mo Money Mo Problems** Sales #1 (4) / Airplay #12 **THE NOTORIOUS B.I.G. Featuring Puff Daddy & Mase** samples "I'm Coming Out" by Diana Ross	Bad Boy 79100
9/13/97	17	11	3. You Should Be Mine (Don't Waste Your Time) Sales #9 / Airplay #69 **BRIAN McKNIGHT Featuring Mase** samples "I Got Ants In My Pants" by James Brown	Mercury 574760
11/1/97	5	17	▲ 4. **Feel So Good** Sales #3 / Airplay #25 samples "Hollywood Swinging" by Kool & The Gang and "Bad Boy" by Miami Sound Machine; from the movie *Money Talks* starring Chris Tucker; Kelly Price (female vocal, above 3)	Bad Boy 79122
1/17/98	4	12	▲ 5. **Been Around The World** Sales #1 (2) / Airplay #58 **PUFF DADDY & THE FAMILY Featuring The Notorious B.I.G. & Mase** samples "Let's Dance" by David Bowie and "All Around The World" by Lisa Stansfield	Bad Boy 79130
1/31/98	6	20	● 6. **What You Want** Sales #6 / Airplay #26 **MASE (FEATURING TOTAL)** samples "Right On For The Darkness" by Curtis Mayfield	Bad Boy 79141
7/25/98	8	16	● 7. **Lookin' At Me** Sales #5 / Airplay #69 **MA$E Featuring Puff Daddy**	Bad Boy 79176
10/24/98	17	13	● 8. Love Me Sales #8 **112 featuring MA$E** samples "Don't You Know That?" by Luther Vandross	Bad Boy 79184
12/12/98+	14	11	9. Take Me There Airplay #8 **BLACKSTREET & MYA featuring MA$E & BLINKY BLINK** samples "I Want You Back" by The Jackson 5; from the animated movie *The RugRats Movie* (soundtrack on Interscope 90181)	album cut
			MASEKELA, Hugh	
			Born on 4/4/39 in Wilbank, South Africa. Trumpeter/bandleader/arranger. Married to Miriam Makeba from 1964-66.	
6/22/68	1 (2)	10	● 1. **Grazing In The Grass** [I] #1 R&B hit (4 weeks)	Uni 55066

Madonna had a much better track record with movie soundtrack singles than starring roles. The chart-topping "Crazy For You," from the movie *Vision Quest*, was the first of many Top 40 soundtrack hits for the pop star.

Henry Mancini was one of the most successful film composers in history, sending many of his movie efforts onto the pop charts. However, his #1 pop hit, "Love Theme From Romeo & Juliet," was composed by someone else, Nino Rota.

The Manhattans had 16 Top 40 hits on the R&B chart before ever reaching the pop Top 40. Nonetheless, the first #1 hit on either chart for the New Jersey group was 1976's "Kiss And Say Goodbye."

Barry Manilow wrote songs that made the whole world sing, but his three #1 hits as a performer were written by others: "Mandy" (Scott English & Richard Kerr), "I Write The Songs" (Bruce Johnston), and "Looks Like We Made It" (Will Jennings & Richard Kerr).

The Marcels updated the chart-topping 1935 hit by Glen Gray & The Casa Loma Orchestra, "Blue Moon," and brought the classic Rodgers and Hart doo-wop song back to #1 in 1961.

Little Peggy March may have been less than five feet tall when she recorded her hit "I Will Follow Him," but when the song reached #1, she was standing tall.

MADONNA
CRAZY FOR YOU

FROM THE ORIGINAL SOUND TRACK OF THE WARNER BROS. MOTION PICTURE VISION QUEST

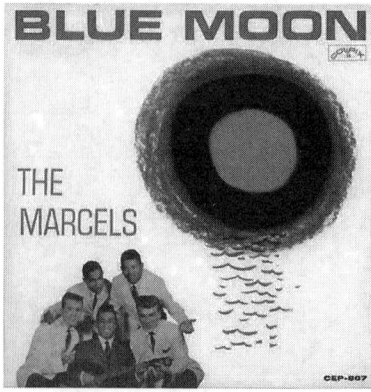

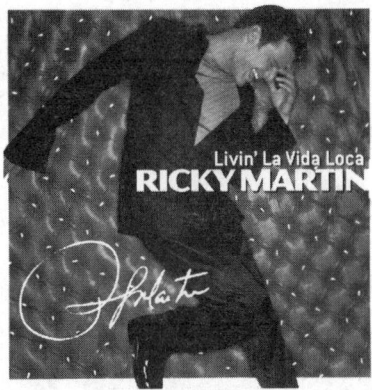

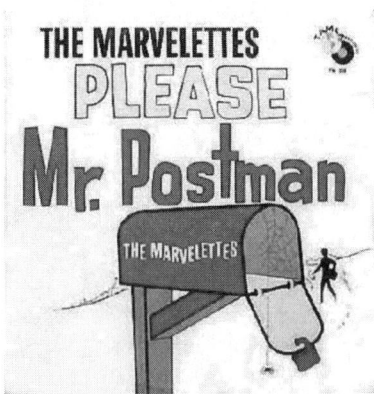

bent

matchbox
T W E N T Y

CD single

Ricky Martin became an overnight sensation after performing "The Cup Of Life" at the 1998 Grammy Awards. The former Menudo singer translated that buzz into his #1 hit, "Livin' La Vida Loca."

The Marvelettes became the first act to give Berry Gordy a #1 hit when "Please Mr. Postman" topped the charts in 1961. The song would reach the top again in 1975 as a remake by the Carpenters.

Matchbox Twenty hoped their fans weren't "Bent" out of shape when they decided to spell out the "20" in their name before releasing the album *Mad Season*. Since its first song, "Bent," reached #1, it's safe to say all was well.

Paul McCartney had nine #1 hits after leaving The Beatles, but none were actually solo hits. He recorded one with Stevie Wonder, one with Michael Jackson, six with Wings, and one, "Uncle Albert/Admiral Halsey," with his wife, Linda.

The McGuire Sisters were regulars on the TV series *Arthur Godfrey And His Friends* during the mid-1950s. The exposure helped their song "Sincerely" spend over two months at the top of the charts.

Meat Loaf and collaborator Jim Steinman reunited for a sequel to their classic album, *Bat Out Of Hell*. The first release from that album, "I'd Do Anything For Love (But I Won't Do That)," became the reheated Meat Loaf's first #1 hit.

DATE	POS	WKS	ARTIST–RECORD TITLE	LABEL & NO.
			MASHMAKHAN	
			Rock group from Montreal, Quebec, Canada: Pierre Senecal (vocals, keyboards), Rayburn Blake (guitar), Brian Edwards (bass) and Jerry Mercer (drums). Mercer later joined April Wine.	
11/7/70	31	4	1. As The Years Go By	Epic 10634
			MASON, Barbara	
			Born on 8/9/47 in Philadelphia, Pennsylvania. R&B singer/songwriter.	
6/12/65	5	10	1. **Yes, I'm Ready**	Arctic 105
9/4/65	27	5	2. Sad, Sad Girl	Arctic 108
2/24/73	31	5	3. Give Me Your Love	Buddah 331
			written and produced by Curtis Mayfield	
12/28/74+	28	4	4. From His Woman To You	Buddah 441
			MASON, Dave	
			Born on 5/10/46 in Worcester, England. Soft-rock singer/songwriter/guitarist. Member of Traffic.	
10/8/77	12	10	1. We Just Disagree	Columbia 10575
7/8/78	39	2	2. Will You Still Love Me Tomorrow	Columbia 10749
			MASTA ACE INCORPORATED	
			Masta Ace is a rapper from Brownsville, New York. His posse includes Lord Digga and rap trio Eyceurokk (Master Eyce, Uneek and Diesalrokk). Member of the trio The Crooklyn Dodgers.	
4/2/94	23	9	1. Born To Roll Sales #21 / Airplay #35	Delicious Vinyl 98315
			MASTER P	
			Born Percy Miller on 4/29/70 in New Orleans, Louisiana. Male rapper. Member of Tru. Founder of the No Limit record label. Played professional basketball for the CBA's Fort Wayne Fury in 1998. Brother of Silkk The Shocker. Father of Lil' Romeo.	
9/6/97	25	13	● 1. I Miss My Homies Sales #15	No Limit 53290
			MASTER P Featuring Pimp C, The Shocker, Mo B. Dick, O'Dell, Sons of Funk and Mercedes	
2/7/98	16	25	▲ 2. Make Em' Say Uhh! Sales #9	No Limit 53302
			MASTER P Featuring Fiend, Silkk (The Shocker), Mia X and Mystikal	
3/28/98	2 (2)	17	▲ 3. Let's Ride Sales #1 (1) / Airplay #55	Def Jam 568475
			MONTELL JORDAN Featuring Master P & Silkk "The Shocker"	
			#1 R&B hit (3 weeks)	
4/18/98	16	17	● 4. I Got The Hook Up! Sales #11	No Limit 53311
			MASTER P Featuring: Sons Of Funk	
			title song from the movie starring Master P	
8/22/98	27	7	5. Goodbye To My Homies Sales #17	No Limit 53326
			MASTER P Featuring Silkk the Shocker, Sons of Funk and Mo B. Dick	
			samples "It's So Hard To Say Goodbye To Yesterday" by Boyz II Men	
			MATCHBOX TWENTY	
			Pop-rock group from Orlando, Florida: Rob Thomas (vocals), Kyle Cook and Adam Gaynor (guitars), Brian Yale (bass) and Paul Doucette (drums).	
6/28/97	5 ᴬ	46	1. **Push**	album cut
			#1 Modern Rock hit (1 week)	

DATE	POS	WKS	ARTIST–RECORD TITLE	LABEL & NO.
11/22/97+	3 ᴬ	54	2. **3 AM**	album cut
5/16/98	9 ᴬ	30	3. **Real World** Hot 100 #38 (2 wks)	album cut
2/20/99	24	19	4. Back 2 Good Airplay #15	album cut
			MATCHBOX 20 (above 4) all of above from the album *Yourself Or Someone Like You* on Lava/Atlantic 92721	
5/6/00	1 (1)	37	● 5. **Bent** Sales #1 (1) / Airplay #2	Lava/Atlantic 84704
11/4/00+	5	34	6. **If You're Gone** Airplay #4	album cut
			#1 Adult Contemporary hit (2 weeks); from the album *Mad Season* on Lava/Atlantic 83339	
11/23/02	29	6	7. Disease Airplay #30	album cut
4/12/03	5	42	8. **Unwell** Airplay #4	album cut
			#1 Adult Contemporary hit (2 weeks)	
11/8/03	23	11	9. Bright Lights Airplay #22	album cut
			above 3 from the album *More Than You Think You Are* on Atlantic 83612	
			MATHEWS, Tobin, & Co.	
			Born Willy Henson in Calumet City, Illinois. Rock and roll singer/guitarist.	Chief 7022
11/14/60	30	4	1. Ruby Duby Du **[I]**	
			from the movie *Key Witness* starring Jeffrey Hunter	
			MATHIS, Johnny	
			Born on 9/30/35 in San Francisco, California. Legendary smooth ballad singer. One of the top album artists of the rock era.	
5/6/57	14	20	1. **Wonderful! Wonderful!**	Columbia 40784
			Jockey #14 / Top 100 #17 / Best Seller #18	
5/20/57	5	23	● 2. **It's Not For Me To Say** Top 100 #5 / Jockey #5 / Best Seller #6	Columbia 40851
			from the movie *Lizzie* starring Eleanor Parker	
9/16/57	1 (1)	22	● 3. **Chances Are /** Jockey #1 (1) / Best Seller #4 / Top 100 #5	
10/14/57	9	14	4. **The Twelfth Of Never**	Columbia 40993
			Jockey #9 / Top 100 #51 / Best Seller: flip	
12/16/57	22	7	5. Wild Is The Wind / Jockey #22 / Best Seller #30 / Top 100 #37	
			title song from the movie starring Anthony Quinn	
1/6/58	21	1	6. No Love (But Your Love) Jockey #21 / Best Seller #37 / Top 100 #48	Columbia 41060
			Ray Conniff (orch., all of above - except #5)	
2/10/58	22	1	7. Come To Me Jockey #22 / Best Seller #40 / Top 100 #43	Columbia 41082
			from the 12/4/57 Kraft TV Theater production of *Come To Me*	
5/5/58	21	7	8. All The Time / Jockey #21 / Best Seller #30 / Top 100 #42	
			from the Broadway musical *Oh Captain!* starring Tony Randall	
5/19/58	21	7	9. Teacher, Teacher Jockey #21 / Best Seller #30 / Top 100 #43	Columbia 41152
7/14/58	14	11	10. A Certain Smile Jockey #14 / Top 100 #19 / Best Seller #21	Columbia 41193
			title song from the movie starring Joan Fontaine	
10/20/58	21	8	11. Call Me Hot 100 #21	Columbia 41253
5/4/59	35	3	12. Someone	Columbia 41355
			#5 & 7-12: Ray Ellis (orch.)	
7/20/59	20	8	13. Small World	Columbia 41410
			from the Broadway musical *Gypsy* starring Ethel Merman	
10/19/59	12	12	14. Misty	Columbia 41483
			first recorded by Erroll Garner in 1954	
3/28/60	25	5	15. Starbright	Columbia 41583
			Glenn Osser (orch., above 3)	
10/13/62	6	9	16. **Gina**	Columbia 42582

DATE	POS	WKS	ARTIST—RECORD TITLE	LABEL & NO.
2/9/63	9	10	17. **What Will Mary Say**	Columbia 42666
6/8/63	30	4	18. Every Step Of The Way	Columbia 42799
4/22/78	**1** (1)	11	● 19. **Too Much, Too Little, Too Late**	Columbia 10693
			JOHNNY MATHIS/DENIECE WILLIAMS	
			#1 R&B hit (4 weeks) / #1 Adult Contemporary hit (1 week)	
5/29/82	38	3	20. Friends In Love	Arista 0673
			DIONNE WARWICK AND JOHNNY MATHIS	
			MATTHEWS, Dave, Band	
			Born on 1/9/67 in Johannesburg, South Africa; raised in New York. Adult Alternative rock singer/songwriter/guitarist. His band: Leroi Moore (sax), Boyd Tinsley (violin), Stefan Lessard (bass) and Carter Beauford (drums).	
4/29/95	22 ᴬ	13	1. What Would You Say Bubbling Under #115	album cut
9/30/95	21 ᴬ	9	2. Ants Marching	album cut
			above 2 from the album *Under The Table And Dreaming* on RCA 66449	
6/8/96	39 ᴬ	1	3. Too Much	album cut
3/15/97	19 ᴬ	39	4. Crash Into Me	album cut
			above 2 from the album *Crash* on RCA 66904	
7/7/01	22	14	5. The Space Between Airplay #20	album cut
			from the album *Everyday* on RCA 67988	
9/14/02	39	2	6. Where Are You Going Airplay #38	album cut
			from the movie *Mr. Deeds* starring Adam Sandler (soundtrack on RCA 68118)	
			MATTHEWS, Ian	
			Born Ian Matthews MacDonald on 6/16/46 in Scunthorpe, Lincolnshire, England. Pop-rock singer.	
4/24/71	23	9	1. Woodstock	Decca 32774
			written by Joni Mitchell about the legendary 1969 rock festival	
12/16/78+	13	12	2. Shake It	Mushroom 7039
			MAURIAT, Paul, and His Orchestra	
			Born on 3/4/25 in Marseilles, France. Orchestra leader.	
1/27/68	**1** (5)	15	● 1. **Love Is Blue** [I]	Philips 40495
			#1 Adult Contemporary hit (11 weeks); French song "L'Amour Est Bleu"	
			MAXWELL	
			Born Maxwell Musze on 5/23/73 in Brooklyn, New York. R&B singer/songwriter/producer.	
9/28/96	36	5	● 1. Ascension (Don't Ever Wonder) Sales #24	Columbia 78372
5/8/99	4	21	● 2. **Fortunate** Sales #2 / Airplay #14	Rock Land 79135
			#1 R&B hit (8 weeks); from the movie *Life* starring Eddie Murphy	
10/27/01	22	6	3. Lifetime Sales #11 / Airplay #21	Columbia 79640
			MAXWELL, Robert, His Harp And Orchestra	
			Born on 4/19/21 in Brooklyn, New York. Jazz harpist. Also recorded as Mickey Mozart.	
6/8/59	30	6	1. Little Dipper [I]	Roulette 4148
			THE MICKEY MOZART QUINTET	
4/18/64	15	7	2. Shangri-La [I]	Decca 25622

DATE	POS	WKS	ARTIST–RECORD TITLE	LABEL & NO.
			MAYER, John	
			Born on 10/16/77 in Fairfield, Connecticut; later based in Atlanta, Georgia. Adult Alternative pop-rock singer/songwriter/guitarist.	
7/6/02	**13**	18	1. No Such Thing Airplay #12	album cut
11/16/02+	**18**	25	2. Your Body Is A Wonderland Airplay #20	album cut
			above 2 from the album Room For Squares *on Aware 85293*	
10/11/03	**33**	5	3. Bigger Than My Body Airplay #38	album cut
			from the album Heavier Things *on Aware 86185*	
			MAYER, Nathaniel	
			Born on 2/10/44 in Detroit, Michigan. R&B singer/songwriter.	
5/26/62	**22**	6	1. Village Of Love **NATHANIEL MAYER And The Fabulous Twilights**	Fortune 449
			MAYFIELD, Curtis	
			Born on 6/3/42 in Chicago, Illinois. Died on 12/26/99 (age 57). R&B singer/songwriter/producer. Leader of The Impressions from 1957-70. Started own Curtom record label in 1968. Paralyzed from the chest down when a stage lighting tower fell on him before a concert on 8/13/90. Won Grammy's Lifetime Achievement Award in 1995. Inducted into the Rock and Roll Hall of Fame in 1999.	
1/2/71	**29**	4	1. (Don't Worry) If There's A Hell Below We're All Going To Go	Curtom 1955
9/23/72	**4**	11	● 2. **Freddie's Dead (Theme From "Superfly")**	Curtom 1975
11/25/72+	**8**	13	● 3. **Superfly**	Curtom 1978
			above 2 from the movie Superfly *starring Ron O'Neal*	
8/25/73	**39**	2	4. Future Shock	Curtom 1987
8/3/74	**40**	1	5. Kung Fu	Curtom 1999
			MC BRAINS	
			Born James Davis in 1975 in Cleveland, Ohio. Male rapper.	
2/22/92	**21**	10	● 1. Oochie Coochie Sales #6 / Airplay #66	Motown 2146
			M.C. HAMMER	
			Born Stanley Kirk Burrell on 3/30/63 in Oakland, California. Male rapper. Billed as Hammer from 1991-94.	
4/28/90	**8**	13	1. **U Can't Touch This** Airplay #2 / Sales #18	Capitol 15571
			#1 R&B hit (1 week); samples "Super Freak" by Rick James	
7/21/90	**4**	12	● 2. **Have You Seen Her** Airplay #4 / Sales #5	Capitol 44573
10/6/90	**2** (2)	11	● 3. **Pray** Sales #3 / Airplay #5	Capitol 44609
			samples "When Doves Cry" by Prince	
			HAMMER:	
11/23/91+	**5**	17	▲ 4. **2 Legit 2 Quit** Sales #1 (3) / Airplay #37	Capitol 44785
			Sonja "Saja" Moore (female vocal)	
12/14/91+	**7**	12	● 5. **Addams Groove** Sales #3 / Airplay #36	Capitol 44794
			from the movie The Addams Family *starring Anjelica Huston*	
5/7/94	**26**	7	● 6. Pumps And A Bump Sales #11 / Airplay #74	Giant 18218
			samples "Atomic Dog" by George Clinton	

DATE	POS	WKS	ARTIST–RECORD TITLE	LABEL & NO.

MC LYTE

Born Lana Moorer on 10/11/71 in Queens, New York. Female rapper.

DATE	POS	WKS		LABEL & NO.
9/18/93	35	4	● 1. RuffNeck Sales #24 / Airplay #45	First Priority 98401
4/27/96	10	11	● 2. **Keep On, Keepin' On** Sales #4 / Airplay #42	Flavor Unit 64302
			MC LYTE Featuring Xscape	
			samples "Liberian Girl" by Michael Jackson; from the movie *Sunset Park* starring Rhea Perlman	
12/21/96+	11	15	● 3. Cold Rock A Party Sales #6 / Airplay #53	EastWest 64212
			samples "Upside Down" by Diana Ross	

McANALLY, Mac

Born Lyman McAnally on 7/15/57 in Red Bay, Alabama. Singer/songwriter/guitarist.

DATE	POS	WKS		LABEL & NO.
8/13/77	37	2	1. It's A Crazy World	Ariola America 7665

McBRIDE, Martina

Born Martina Schiff on 7/29/66 in Medicine Lodge, Kansas; raised in Sharon, Kansas. Country singer.

DATE	POS	WKS		LABEL & NO.
1/23/99	36	1	1. Wrong Again Airplay #26	RCA 65456
			#1 Country hit (1 week)	
6/19/99	37	5	2. Whatever You Say Airplay #26	album cut
			from the album *Evolution* on RCA 67516	
10/2/99	24	11	3. I Love You Airplay #15	album cut
			#1 Country hit (5 weeks); featured in the movie *Runaway Bride* starring Julia Roberts and Richard Gere; from the album *Emotion* on RCA 67824	
3/30/02	31	3	4. Blessed Airplay #28	album cut
			#1 Country hit (2 weeks); from the album *Greatest Hits* on RCA 67012	
10/18/03	39	2	5. This One's For The Girls Airplay #37	album cut
			backing vocalists include Faith Hill, Carolyn Dawn Johnson and McBride's daughters Delaney and Emma; from the album *Martina* on RCA 54207	

McCAIN, Edwin

Born on 1/20/70 in Greenville, South Carolina. Adult Alternative pop-rock singer/songwriter/guitarist.

DATE	POS	WKS		LABEL & NO.
9/26/98	5	21	1. **I'll Be** Airplay #4 / Sales #27	Lava/Atlantic 84191
8/14/99	37	3	2. I Could Not Ask For More Airplay #31	album cut
			from the album *Messenger* on Lava/Atlantic 83197	

McCALL, C.W.

Born William Fries on 11/15/28 in Audubon, Iowa. The character "C.W. McCall" was created for the Mertz Bread Company. Fries was its advertising man. Elected mayor of Ouray, Colorado, in the early 1980s.

DATE	POS	WKS		LABEL & NO.
3/22/75	40	1	1. Wolf Creek Pass [N]	MGM 14764
12/13/75+	1 (1)	11	● 2. Convoy [N]	MGM 14839
			#1 Country hit (6 weeks); jargon-laced CB radio conversation	

McCANN, Peter

Born on 1/29/50 in Bridgeport, Connecticut. Pop singer/songwriter/pianist.

DATE	POS	WKS		LABEL & NO.
5/21/77	5	16	● 1. **Do You Wanna Make Love**	20th Century 2335

DATE	POS	WKS	ARTIST–RECORD TITLE	LABEL & NO.

McCARTNEY, Paul/Wings

Born James Paul McCartney on 6/18/42 in Liverpool, England. Founding member/bass guitarist of The Beatles. Married Linda Eastman on 3/12/69. First solo album in 1970. Formed group Wings in 1971 with Linda (keyboards, backing vocals), Denny Laine of The Moody Blues (guitar) and Denny Seiwell (drums). Henry McCullough (guitar) joined in 1972. Seiwell and McCullough left in 1973. In 1975, Joe English (drums) and Jimmy McCulloch of Thunderclap Newman (guitar) joined. McCulloch died of heart failure on 9/27/79 (age 26). Both English and McCulloch left in 1977. Wings officially disbanded in April 1981. McCartney starred in own movie *Give My Regards To Broad Street* (1984). Won Grammy's Lifetime Achievement Award in 1990. Knighted by Queen Elizabeth II in 1997. Inducted into the Rock and Roll Hall of Fame in 1999. Linda died of cancer on 4/17/98 (age 55). Paul married ex-model Heather Mills on 6/11/2002.

DATE	POS	WKS	ARTIST–RECORD TITLE	LABEL & NO.
3/13/71	5	11	1. **Another Day** /	
3/27/71		9	2. Oh Woman Oh Why **PAUL McCARTNEY** (above 2)	Apple 1829
8/21/71	1 (1)	12	● 3. **Uncle Albert/Admiral Halsey** **PAUL & LINDA McCARTNEY**	Apple 1837
			WINGS:	
3/25/72	21	6	4. Give Ireland Back To The Irish	Apple 1847
7/8/72	28	4	5. Mary Had A Little Lamb /	
7/8/72		4	6. Little Woman Love	Apple 1851
12/30/72+	10	9	7. **Hi, Hi, Hi**	Apple 1857
			PAUL MCCARTNEY & WINGS:	
4/28/73	1 (4)	15	● 8. **My Love** #1 Adult Contemporary hit (3 weeks)	Apple 1861
7/21/73	2 (3)	12	● 9. **Live And Let Die** title song from the James Bond movie starring Roger Moore	Apple 1863
12/8/73+	10	10	10. **Helen Wheels**	Apple 1869
2/23/74	7	10	11. **Jet**	Apple 1871
5/4/74	1 (1)	13	● 12. **Band On The Run**	Apple 1873
11/23/74+	3	10	13. **Junior's Farm** /	
12/14/74+	17	8	14. Sally G	Apple 1875
			WINGS:	
6/7/75	1 (1)	11	● 15. **Listen To What The Man Said**	Capitol 4091
10/25/75	39	2	16. Letting Go	Capitol 4145
11/15/75	12	6	17. Venus And Mars Rock Show	Capitol 4175
4/17/76	1 (5)	15	● 18. **Silly Love Songs** #1 Adult Contemporary hit (1 week)	Capitol 4256
7/17/76	3	11	● 19. **Let 'Em In** #1 Adult Contemporary hit (1 week)	Capitol 4293
2/19/77	10	11	20. **Maybe I'm Amazed** [L]	Capitol 4385
12/24/77+	33	5	21. Girls' School	Capitol 4504
4/8/78	1 (2)	12	22. **With A Little Luck**	Capitol 4559
7/15/78	25	5	23. I've Had Enough	Capitol 4594
10/14/78	39	2	24. London Town	Capitol 4625
3/31/79	5	13	● 25. **Goodnight Tonight**	Columbia 10939
6/30/79	20	6	26. Getting Closer	Columbia 11020
9/22/79	29	4	27. Arrow Through Me	Columbia 11070

DATE	POS	WKS	ARTIST–RECORD TITLE	LABEL & NO.
5/10/80	1 (3)	16	● 28. **Coming Up (Live At Glasgow)** [L] **PAUL McCARTNEY & WINGS** recorded on 12/17/79 at the Glasgow Apollo in Scotland	Columbia 11263
4/10/82	1 (7)	15	● 29. **Ebony And Ivory** **PAUL McCARTNEY (with Stevie Wonder)** #1 Adult Contemporary hit (5 weeks)	Columbia 02860
7/17/82	10	11	30. **Take It Away** **PAUL McCARTNEY**	Columbia 03018
11/13/82+	2 (3)	14	● 31. **The Girl Is Mine** **MICHAEL JACKSON/PAUL McCARTNEY** #1 R&B hit (3 weeks) / #1 Adult Contemporary hit (4 weeks)	Epic 03288
10/15/83	1 (6)	18	▲ 32. **Say Say Say**	Columbia 04168
			PAUL McCARTNEY:	
1/7/84	23	8	33. **So Bad**	Columbia 04296
10/20/84	6	14	34. **No More Lonely Nights** Airplay #5 / Sales #9 from the movie *Give My Regards To Broad Street* starring McCartney	Columbia 04581
12/14/85+	7	11	35. **Spies Like Us** Sales #6 / Airplay #8 title song from the movie starring Chevy Chase and Dan Aykroyd	Capitol 5537
8/23/86	21	6	36. Press Sales #17 / Airplay #32	Capitol 5597
6/17/89	25	5	37. **My Brave Face** Sales #20 / Airplay #33 co-written by Elvis Costello	Capitol 44367
			McCLAIN, Alton, & Destiny Female R&B vocal trio: Alton McClain, Delores Warren and Robyrda Stiger. Warren died in a car crash on 2/22/85 (age 32).	
5/19/79	32	4	1. **It Must Be Love**	Polydor 14532
			McCLINTON, Delbert Born on 11/4/40 in Lubbock, Texas. Played harmonica on Bruce Channel's hit "Hey Baby." Leader of The Ron-Dels.	
12/20/80+	8	14	1. **Giving It Up For Your Love**	MSS/Capitol 4948
			McCLURE, Bobby — see BASS, Fontella	
			McCOO, Marilyn, & Billy Davis, Jr. Husband-and-wife vocal duo. McCoo was born on 9/30/43 in Jersey City, New Jersey. Davis was born on 6/26/39 in St. Louis, Missouri. Both were members of The 5th Dimension. Married on 7/26/69. Duo hosted own summer variety TV series in 1977. McCoo co-hosted TV's *Solid Gold* from 1981-84.	
10/23/76+	1 (1)	18	● 1. **You Don't Have To Be A Star (To Be In My Show)** #1 R&B hit (1 week)	ABC 12208
4/2/77	15	8	2. Your Love	ABC 12262
			McCOY, Van Born on 1/6/40 in Washington DC. Died of a heart attack on 7/6/79 (age 39). Disco songwriter/producer.	
5/31/75	1 (1)	12	● 1. **The Hustle** [I] #1 R&B hit (1 week); The Soul City Symphony (orch.)	Avco 4653

DATE	POS	WKS	ARTIST–RECORD TITLE	LABEL & NO.
			McCOYS, The	
			Pop-rock group from Union City, Indiana: brothers Rick (vocals, guitar) and Randy (drums) Zehringer, Randy Hobbs (bass) and Ronnie Brandon (keyboards). Rick later recorded as Rick Derringer. Hobbs died on 8/5/93 (age 45).	
9/4/65	**1** (1)	11	1. **Hang On Sloopy**	Bang 506
11/27/65	7	8	2. **Fever**	Bang 511
5/14/66	22	6	3. Come On Let's Go	Bang 522
			McCRACKLIN, Jimmy	
			Born James Walker on 8/13/21 in Helena, Arkansas. R&B singer/harmonica player.	
3/3/58	7	10	1. **The Walk** Top 100 #7 / Best Seller #11 / Jockey #23 **JIMMY McCRACKLIN And his Band**	Checker 885
			McCRAE, George	
			Born on 10/19/44 in West Palm Beach, Florida. Disco singer. Married to Gwen McCrae from 1967-77.	
6/15/74	**1** (2)	10	1. **Rock Your Baby** #1 R&B hit (2 weeks)	T.K. 1004
3/1/75	37	2	2. I Get Lifted	T.K. 1007
			McCRAE, Gwen	
			Born on 12/21/43 in Pensacola, Florida. Disco singer. Married to George McCrae from 1967-77.	
6/21/75	9	8	1. **Rockin' Chair** #1 R&B hit (1 week); George McCrae (backing vocal)	Cat 1996
			McDANIELS, Gene	
			Born on 2/12/35 in Kansas City, Missouri; raised in Omaha, Nebraska. R&B singer. Appeared in the 1962 movie *It's Trad, Dad*.	
4/3/61	3	12	1. **A Hundred Pounds Of Clay**	Liberty 55308
8/7/61	31	2	2. A Tear	Liberty 55344
10/16/61	5	10	3. **Tower Of Strength**	Liberty 55371
2/10/62	10	7	4. **Chip Chip**	Liberty 55405
9/1/62	21	5	5. Point Of No Return	Liberty 55480
12/15/62	31	2	6. Spanish Lace The Johnny Mann Singers (backing vocals, all of above)	Liberty 55510
			McDEVITT, Chas., Skiffle Group	
			Born on 12/4/34 in Glasgow, Scotland. Skiffle singer/guitarist.	
6/10/57	40	1	1. Freight Train Top 100 #40 Nancy Whiskey (vocal); folk song composed in the early 1900s	Chic 1008
			McDONALD, Michael	
			Born on 2/12/52 in St. Louis, Missouri. Pop-rock singer/songwriter/keyboardist. Former lead singer of The Doobie Brothers. Married to singer Amy Holland.	
8/28/82	4	13	1. **I Keep Forgettin' (Every Time You're Near)**	Warner 29933
1/14/84	19	9	2. Yah Mo B There **JAMES INGRAM (with Michael McDonald)**	Qwest 29394

DATE	POS	WKS	ARTIST–RECORD TITLE	LABEL & NO.
8/31/85	34	4	3. No Lookin' Back Airplay #30 co-written by Kenny Loggins	Warner 28960
4/19/86	1 (3)	15	● 4. **On My Own** Sales #1 (5) / Airplay #1 (2) **PATTI LaBELLE AND MICHAEL McDONALD** #1 R&B hit (4 weeks)	MCA 52770
7/12/86	7	13	5. **Sweet Freedom** Sales #6 / Airplay #7 theme from the movie *Running Scared* starring Billy Crystal and Gregory Hines	MCA 52857
			McDOWELL, Ronnie	
			Born on 3/26/50 in Portland, Tennessee. Country singer/songwriter.	
9/17/77	13	9	● 1. The King Is Gone a tribute to Elvis Presley after his death on 8/16/77	Scorpion 135
			McENTIRE, Reba	
			Born on 3/28/54 in Chockie, Oklahoma. Country singer/actress. Acted in several movies and starred in own TV sitcom *Reba*.	
1/22/00	31	3	1. What Do You Say Airplay #25 from the album *So Good Together* on MCA Nashville 170119	album cut
			McFADDEN, Bob, And Dor	
			Born on 1/19/23 in East Liverpool, Ohio. Died on 1/7/2000 (age 76). Began career in 1950 as a singing emcee for a special Navy show called *The Bob McFadden Show*. Appeared on the comedy albums *The First Family* and *You Don't Have To Be Jewish*. Dor is poet/singer/songwriter/actor Rod McKuen.	
9/14/59	39	1	1. The Mummy [N] Jack Hansen (orch.); inspired by the 1959 movie of the same title starring Peter Cushing	Brunswick 55140
			McFADDEN & WHITEHEAD	
			R&B duo from Philadelphia, Pennsylvania: Gene McFadden and John Whitehead. Wrote numerous hit songs.	
6/2/79	13	11	▲ 1. Ain't No Stoppin' Us Now #1 R&B hit (1 week)	Philadelphia I. 3681
			McFERRIN, Bobby	
			Born on 3/11/50 in Manhattan, New York. Unaccompanied, jazz-styled improvisation vocalist.	
8/13/88	1 (2)	13	● 1. **Don't Worry Be Happy** Sales #1 (3) / Airplay #2 featured in the movie *Cocktail* starring Tom Cruise; 1988 Grammy winner: Record of the Year	EMI-Manhattan 50146
			McGOVERN, Maureen	
			Born on 7/27/49 in Youngstown, Ohio. Adult Contemporary singer. Acted in the Broadway show *Pirates Of Penzance*.	
7/14/73	1 (2)	11	● 1. **The Morning After** love theme from the movie *The Poseidon Adventure* starring Gene Hackman	20th Century 2010
8/11/79	18	9	2. Different Worlds #1 Adult Contemporary hit (2 weeks); theme from the TV series *Angie* starring Donna Pescow	Warner/Curb 8835

DATE	POS	WKS	ARTIST–RECORD TITLE	LABEL & NO.
			McGRAW, Tim	
			Born on 5/1/67 in Delhi, Louisiana. Country singer. Son of ex-professional baseball pitcher Tug McGraw. Married Faith Hill on 10/6/96.	
3/19/94	**15**	10	● 1. Indian Outlaw Sales #4	Curb 76920
5/28/94	**17**	13	● 2. Don't Take The Girl Sales #3	Curb 76925
			#1 Country hit (2 weeks)	
9/9/95	**25**	6	● 3. I Like It, I Love It Sales #8	Curb 76961
			#1 Country hit (5 weeks)	
5/17/97	**7**	17	▲ 4. **It's Your Love** Sales #3	Curb 73019
			TIM McGRAW with Faith Hill	
			#1 Country hit (6 weeks)	
2/6/99	**37**	2	5. For A Little While Airplay #24	album cut
			from the album *Everywhere* on Curb 77886	
4/10/99	**10**	16	6. **Please Remember Me** Sales #15 / Airplay #17	Curb 73080
			#1 Country hit (5 weeks)	
9/18/99	**28**	9	7. Something Like That Airplay #20	album cut
			#1 Country hit (5 weeks)	
1/22/00	**29**	9	8. My Best Friend Airplay #23	album cut
			#1 Country hit (2 weeks)	
11/25/00	**27**	11	9. My Next Thirty Years Airplay #21	album cut
			#1 Country hit (5 weeks); above 3 from the album *A Place In The Sun* on Curb 77942	
4/28/01	**25**	10	10. Grown Men Don't Cry Airplay #17	album cut
			#1 Country hit (1 week)	
9/15/01	**38**	3	11. Angry All The Time Airplay #31	album cut
			#1 Country hit (2 weeks); above 2 from the album *Set This Circus Down* on Curb 78711	
2/23/02	**36**	4	12. Bring On The Rain Airplay #34	album cut
			JO DEE MESSINA with Tim McGraw	
			#1 Country hit (1 week); from Messina's album *Burn* on Curb 77977	
3/2/02	**33**	5	13. The Cowboy In Me Airplay #30	album cut
			#1 Country hit (1 week)	
8/17/02	**26**	5	14. Unbroken Airplay #24	album cut
			#1 Country hit (1 week); above 2 from the album *Set This Circus Down* on Curb 78711	
12/14/02	**40**	2	15. Red Rag Top Airplay #38	album cut
3/29/03	**27**	9	16. She's My Kind Of Rain Airplay #25	album cut
8/30/03	**27**	8	17. Real Good Man Airplay #23	album cut
			#1 Country hit (2 weeks); above 3 from the album *Tim McGraw and the Dancehall Doctors* on Curb 78746	
			McGRIFF, Jimmy	
			Born on 4/3/36 in Philadelphia, Pennsylvania. Jazz organist.	
10/27/62	**20**	7	1. I've Got A Woman (Part I) **[I]**	Sue 770
			#1 R&B hit for Ray Charles in 1955	
			McGUINN, CLARK & HILLMAN	
			Pop-rock trio: Roger McGuinn, Gene Clark and Chris Hillman. All were founding members of The Byrds. Clark died on 5/24/91 (age 46).	
4/28/79	**33**	4	1. Don't You Write Her Off	Capitol 4693

DATE	POS	WKS	ARTIST–RECORD TITLE	LABEL & NO.
			McGUIRE, Barry	
			Born on 10/15/37 in Oklahoma City, Oklahoma. Folk-rock singer. Member of The New Christy Minstrels (1962-65).	
8/28/65	**1** (1)	10	1. **Eve Of Destruction**	Dunhill 4009
			backing by the original members of The Grass Roots	
			McGUIRE SISTERS, The	
			Vocal trio from Middletown, Ohio: sisters Phyllis (born on 2/14/31), Christine (born on 7/30/29) and Dorothy (born on 2/13/26) McGuire. Replaced The Chordettes on *Arthur Godfrey And His Friends* TV show in 1953.	
1/8/55	**1** (10)	21	● 1. **Sincerely /** Jockey #1 (10) / Juke Box #1 (7) / Best Seller #1 (6)	
1/29/55	**17**	6	2. No More Jockey #17 / Juke Box #17 / Best Seller #23	Coral 61323
3/26/55	**11**	7	3. It May Sound Silly / Jockey #11 / Juke Box #14 / Best Seller #23	
			#14 R&B hit for Ivory Joe Hunter in 1955	
4/16/55		2	4. Doesn't Anybody Love Me? Juke Box: flip	Coral 61369
6/4/55	**5**	14	5. **Something's Gotta Give /**	
			Jockey #5 / Best Seller #6 / Juke Box #6	
			from the movie *Daddy Long Legs* starring Fred Astaire	
6/25/55		2	6. Rhythm 'N' Blues (Mama's Got The Rhythm -	
			Papa's Got The Blues) Best Seller: flip / Juke Box: flip	Coral 61423
10/29/55	**10**	13	7. **He** Juke Box #10 / Best Seller #12 / Top 100 #12 / Jockey #16	Coral 61501
5/19/56	**13**	12	8. Picnic / Top 100 #13 / Jockey #14 / Best Seller #15 / Juke Box #18	
			based on the theme from the movie starring William Holden; lyrics written by Steve Allen	
6/2/56	**37**	1	9. Delilah Jones Top 100 #37 / Best Seller: flip	Coral 61627
			based on the "Main Title" theme from the movie *The Man With The Golden Arm* starring Frank Sinatra	
8/11/56	**32**	3	10. Weary Blues Top 100 #32	Coral 61670
			THE McGUIRE SISTERS and LAWRENCE WELK And His Champagne Music	
			traditional tune first recorded in 1923 by The New Orleans Rhythm Kings	
10/27/56	**37**	3	11. Ev'ry Day Of My Life Top 100 #37	Coral 61703
12/22/56+	**32**	3	12. Goodnight My Love, Pleasant Dreams Top 100 #32	Coral 61748
			#7 R&B hit for Jesse Belvin in 1956	
1/6/58	**1** (4)	19	● 13. **Sugartime** Jockey #1 (4) / Top 100 #5 / Best Seller #7	Coral 61924
6/9/58	**25**	1	14. Ding Dong Jockey #25 / Top 100 #43 / Best Seller #44	Coral 61991
			Neal Hefti (orch.: #4, 13 & 14)	
1/19/59	**11**	12	15. May You Always	Coral 62059
4/17/61	**20**	7	16. Just For Old Time's Sake	Coral 62249
			Dick Jacobs (orch.: #1-3,5-9,11-12,15-16)	
			McINTYRE, Joey — see NEW KIDS ON THE BLOCK	
			McKENNITT, Loreena	
			Born on 2/17/57 in Morden, Manitoba, Canada. Adult Alternative singer/songwriter/harpist.	
3/7/98	**18**	8	1. The Mummers' Dance Airplay #11 / Sales #36	Warner 17241

DATE	POS	WKS	ARTIST–RECORD TITLE	LABEL & NO.
			McKENZIE, Bob & Doug	
			The McKenzie brothers are actually Canadian comedians Rick "Bob" Moranis (born on 4/18/54) and Dave "Doug" Thomas (born on 5/20/49) of SCTV. Both featured (as the McKenzie brothers) in the movie *Strange Brew*. Thomas is the brother of singer Ian Thomas.	
2/20/82	**16**	9	1. Take Off **[N]** Geddy Lee (of Rush; vocal)	Mercury 76134
			McKENZIE, Scott	
			Born Philip Blondheim on 1/10/39 in Jacksonville, Florida; raised in Virginia. Folk singer/songwriter.	
6/10/67	**4**	10	1. **San Francisco (Be Sure To Wear Flowers In Your Hair)**	Ode 103
11/11/67	**24**	3	2. Like An Old Time Movie above 2 written and produced by John Phillips	Ode 105
			McKNIGHT, Brian	
			Born on 6/5/69 in Buffalo, New York. R&B singer/songwriter.	
3/6/93	**3**	20	1. **Love Is** Airplay #2 / Sales #13 **VANESSA WILLIAMS and BRIAN McKNIGHT** #1 Adult Contemporary hit (3 weeks); from the album *Beverly Hills, 90210 - The Soundtrack*	Giant 18630
7/3/93	**13**	18	2. One Last Cry Airplay #12 / Sales #18	Mercury 862404
9/13/97	**17**	11	3. You Should Be Mine (Don't Waste Your Time) Sales #9 / Airplay #69 **BRIAN McKNIGHT Featuring Mase** Kelly Price (female vocal); samples "I Got Ants In My Pants" by James Brown	Mercury 574760
2/21/98	**6** A	35	4. **Anytime** #1 R&B Airplay hit (4 weeks); from the album *Anytime* on Mercury 536215	album cut
1/2/99	**35**	2	5. Hold Me Sales #9 **BRIAN McKNIGHT (featuring Tone & Kobe Bryant)** samples "Sugar Free" by Juicy	Motown 860885
9/18/99	**2** (8)	33	6. **Back At One** Airplay #1 (6)	Motown 156501
			McLACHLAN, Sarah	
			Born on 1/28/68 in Halifax, Nova Scotia, Canada. Adult Alternative folk-pop singer/songwriter/pianist/guitarist.	
9/6/97	**13**	19	1. Building A Mystery Airplay #9 / Sales #27	Arista 13395
2/14/98	**28**	3	2. Sweet Surrender Airplay #22 / Sales #46	Arista 13453
5/30/98	**3**	27	● 3. **Adia** Sales #5 / Airplay #13	Arista 13497
11/14/98+	**4**	27	4. **Angel** Airplay #2 / Sales #5 #1 Adult Contemporary hit (12 weeks); from the movie *City Of Angels* starring Nicolas Cage	Arista 13621
6/19/99	**14**	15	5. I Will Remember You Airplay #7 **[L-R]** studio version hit #65 in 1996; from the album *Mirrorball* on Arista 19049	album cut
			McLAIN, Tommy	
			Born on 3/15/40 in Jonesville, Louisiana. White "swamp-pop" singer/songwriter.	
7/23/66	**15**	7	1. Sweet Dreams	MSL 197

DATE	POS	WKS	ARTIST–RECORD TITLE	LABEL & NO.
			McLEAN, Don	
			Born on 10/2/45 in New Rochelle, New York. Adult Contemporary singer/songwriter/guitarist.	
12/4/71+	**1** (4)	17	● 1. **American Pie - Parts I & II**	United Artists 50856
			#1 Adult Contemporary hit (3 weeks); inspired by the death of Buddy Holly	
4/1/72	**12**	10	2. Vincent /	
			a tribute to artist Vincent Van Gogh	
4/22/72		7	3. Castles In The Air	United Artists 50887
			also see #7 below	
1/20/73	**21**	8	4. Dreidel	United Artists 51100
1/24/81	**5**	15	5. **Crying**	Millennium 11799
5/2/81	**23**	6	6. Since I Don't Have You	Millennium 11804
12/12/81	**36**	5	7. Castles In The Air [R]	Millennium 11819
			new version of #3 above	
			McLEAN, Phil	
			Born in Detroit, Michigan. Veteran DJ on Cleveland's WERE radio station.	
12/18/61+	**21**	6	1. Small Sad Sam [N-S]	Versatile 107
			a parody of "Big Bad John"	
			McNAMARA, Robin	
			Born in Boston, Massachusetts. Male pop singer. One of the original cast members of *Hair*.	
7/18/70	**11**	8	1. Lay A Little Lovin' On Me	Steed 724
			cast of *Hair* (backing vocals)	
			McPHATTER, Clyde	
			Born on 11/15/32 in Durham, North Carolina. Died of a heart attack on 6/13/72 (age 39). R&B singer. Member of The Dominoes from 1950-53. Member of The Drifters in 1954. Inducted into the Rock and Roll Hall of Fame in 1987.	
6/9/56	**16**	12	1. Treasure Of Love Best Seller #16 / Juke Box #18 / Top 100 #22	Atlantic 1092
			#1 R&B hit (1 week)	
2/23/57	**19**	2	2. Without Love (There Is Nothing) Jockey #19 / Top 100 #38	Atlantic 1117
7/8/57	**26**	3	3. Just To Hold My Hand Best Seller #26 / Top 100 #30	Atlantic 1133
10/20/58+	**6**	20	● 4. **A Lover's Question** Hot 100 #6	Atlantic 1199
			#1 R&B hit (1 week)	
8/3/59	**38**	2	5. Since You've Been Gone	Atlantic 2028
			written by Neil Sedaka	
8/22/60	**23**	5	6. Ta Ta	Mercury 71660
3/24/62	**7**	10	7. **Lover Please**	Mercury 71941
			written by Billy Swan	
6/30/62	**25**	5	8. Little Bitty Pretty One	Mercury 71987
			The Merry Melody Singers (backing vocals)	
			McVIE, Christine	
			Born Christine Perfect on 7/12/43 in Birmingham, England. Singer/keyboardist with Fleetwood Mac since 1970. Married to Fleetwood Mac bassist John McVie from 1968-77.	
2/4/84	**10**	11	1. **Got A Hold On Me**	Warner 29372
			#1 Adult Contemporary hit (4 weeks) / #1 Mainstream Rock hit (2 weeks); Steve Winwood (synthesizer)	
5/12/84	**30**	6	2. Love Will Show Us How	Warner 29313

DATE	POS	WKS	ARTIST–RECORD TITLE	LABEL & NO.
			MEAD, Sister Janet	
			Born in 1938 in Adelaide, Australia. Nun at the Sisters of Mercy convent. Gained prominence through her weekly cathedral rock masses and weekly radio programs.	
3/9/74	4	11	● 1. **The Lord's Prayer** [X] Les Sands (orch.); Biblical text with new music by Arnold Strals	A&M 1491
			MEAT LOAF	
			Born Marvin Lee Aday on 9/27/47 in Dallas, Texas. Pop-rock singer. Sang lead vocals on Ted Nugent's 1976 *Free-For-All* album. Played "Eddie" in the Los Angeles production and movie of *The Rocky Horror Picture Show*. Appeared in several other movies.	
4/29/78	11	13	● 1. Two Out Of Three Ain't Bad	Cleveland I./Epic 50513
9/16/78	39	2	2. Paradise By The Dashboard Light [N] Ellen Foley (female vocal); Phil Rizzuto (baseball announcer)	Cleveland I./Epic 50588
1/20/79	39	1	3. You Took The Words Right Out Of My Mouth	Cleveland I./Epic 50634
10/2/93	1 (5)	18	▲ 4. **I'd Do Anything For Love (But I Won't Do That)** Sales #1 (7) / Airplay #4 Patti Russo (female vocal)	MCA 54626
2/5/94	13	13	5. Rock And Roll Dreams Come Through Sales #11 / Airplay #24	MCA 54757
5/28/94	38	3	6. Objects In The Rear View Mirror May Appear Closer Than They Are Sales #31 / Airplay #67	MCA 54848
10/21/95	13	11	● 7. I'd Lie For You (And That's The Truth) Sales #6 / Airplay #43	MCA 55134
			MECO	
			Born Domenico Monardo on 11/29/39 in Johnsonburg, Pennsylvania. Disco producer.	
8/27/77	1 (2)	13	▲ 1. **Star Wars Theme/Cantina Band** [I]	Millennium 604
1/21/78	25	6	2. Theme From Close Encounters [I]	Millennium 608
10/21/78	35	3	3. Themes From The Wizard Of Oz [N]	Millennium 620
7/5/80	18	8	4. Empire Strikes Back (Medley) [I] Darth Vader/Yoda's Theme; all of above inspired by movie themes	RSO 1038
4/3/82	35	3	5. Pop Goes The Movies (Part I) [I] medley: 20th Century Fox Trademark/Tara's Theme/The Magnificent Seven/The James Bond Theme/Goldfinger/The Good, The Bad And The Ugly/Theme From The Apartment/Theme From The High & The Mighty	Arista 0660
			MEDEIROS, Glenn	
			Born on 6/24/70 in Lihue, Kauai, Hawaii (of Portugese parents). Pop singer.	
4/4/87	12	13	1. Nothing's Gonna Change My Love For You Sales #6 / Airplay #17	Amherst 311
5/26/90	1 (2)	14	● 2. **She Ain't Worth It** Airplay #1 (3) / Sales #4 **GLENN MEDEIROS Featuring Bobby Brown**	MCA 53831
9/22/90	32	4	3. All I'm Missing Is You Sales #29 / Airplay #29 **GLENN MEDEIROS Featuring Ray Parker Jr.**	MCA 53886

DATE	POS	WKS	ARTIST–RECORD TITLE	LABEL & NO.
			MEDLEY, Bill	
			Born on 9/19/40 in Santa Ana, California. Half of The Righteous Brothers duo.	
10/10/87	**1 (1)**	15	● 1. **(I've Had) The Time Of My Life** Airplay #1 (2) / Sales #1 (1) **BILL MEDLEY AND JENNIFER WARNES** #1 Adult Contemporary hit (4 weeks); love theme from the movie *Dirty Dancing* starring Patrick Swayze and Jennifer Grey	RCA 5224
			MEISNER, Randy	
			Born on 3/8/46 in Scottsbluff, Nebraska. Pop-rock singer/bassist. Member of Poco (1968-69), Rick Nelson & The Stone Canyon Band (1969-71) and the Eagles (1971-77).	
11/8/80	22	7	1. Deep Inside My Heart Kim Carnes (backing vocal)	Epic 50939
2/7/81	19	9	2. Hearts On Fire	Epic 50964
8/28/82	28	6	3. Never Been In Love	Epic 03032
			MEL AND TIM	
			R&B vocal duo from Holly Springs, Mississippi: cousins Mel Hardin and Tim McPherson.	
11/8/69	10	11	● 1. **Backfield In Motion** produced by Gene Chandler	Bamboo 107
9/16/72	19	9	2. Starting All Over Again	Stax 0127
			MELANIE	
			Born Melanie Safka on 2/3/47 in Queens, New York. Folk-pop singer/songwriter.	
5/16/70	6	14	1. **Lay Down (Candles In The Rain)** **MELANIE with The Edwin Hawkins Singers**	Buddah 167
9/5/70	32	4	2. Peace Will Come (According To Plan)	Buddah 186
11/27/71	1 (3)	14	● 3. **Brand New Key**	Neighborhood 4201
2/19/72	31	5	4. Ring The Living Bell	Neighborhood 4202
2/26/72	35	3	5. The Nickel Song	Buddah 268
4/7/73	36	2	6. Bitter Bad	Neighborhood 4210
			MELENDEZ, Lisette	
			Born in Harlem, New York. Female dance singer.	
3/16/91	35	4	1. Together Forever Airplay #21 / Sales #33	Fever/RAL 73629
			MELLENCAMP, John Cougar	
			Born on 10/7/51 in Seymour, Indiana. Rock singer/songwriter/guitarist. Given name Johnny Cougar by David Bowie's manager, Tony DeFries. First recorded for MCA in 1976. Directed and starred in the 1992 movie *Falling From Grace*. Married model Elaine Irwin on 9/5/92. **JOHN COUGAR:**	
11/10/79	28	8	1. I Need A Lover	Riva 202
11/8/80	27	7	2. This Time	Riva 205
3/14/81	17	12	3. Ain't Even Done With The Night	Riva 207
5/22/82	2 (4)	22	● 4. **Hurts So Good** #1 Mainstream Rock hit (1 week)	Riva 209

DATE	POS	WKS	ARTIST–RECORD TITLE	LABEL & NO.
8/7/82	**1** (4)	17	● 5. **Jack & Diane**	Riva 210
11/27/82+	**19**	11	6. Hand To Hold On To	Riva 211
			JOHN COUGAR MELLENCAMP:	
10/22/83	**9**	11	7. **Crumblin' Down**	Riva 214
12/17/83+	**8**	11	8. **Pink Houses**	Riva 215
3/31/84	**15**	9	9. Authority Song	Riva 216
8/24/85	**6**	13	10. **Lonely Ol' Night** Sales #5 / Airplay #5 #1 Mainstream Rock hit (5 weeks)	Riva 880984
11/16/85	**6**	13	11. **Small Town** Airplay #4 / Sales #6	Riva 884202
2/15/86	**2** (1)	11	12. **R.O.C.K. In The U.S.A. (A Salute To 60's Rock)** Airplay #2 / Sales #3	Riva 884455
5/17/86	**21**	6	13. Rain On The Scarecrow Sales #18 / Airplay #26	Riva 884635
8/2/86	**28**	4	14. Rumbleseat Sales #23 / Airplay #36	Riva 884856
8/29/87	**9**	10	15. **Paper In Fire** Sales #9 / Airplay #9 #1 Mainstream Rock hit (5 weeks)	Mercury 888763
11/14/87+	**8**	12	16. **Cherry Bomb** Sales #6 / Airplay #13 #1 Mainstream Rock hit (1 week)	Mercury 888934
2/27/88	**14**	9	17. Check It Out Sales #14 / Airplay #14	Mercury 870126
5/13/89	**15**	7	18. Pop Singer Sales #12 / Airplay #22	Mercury 874012
			JOHN MELLENCAMP:	
10/19/91	**14**	7	19. Get A Leg Up Airplay #58 / Sales #75 #1 Mainstream Rock hit (3 weeks)	Mercury 867890
2/29/92	**36**	4	20. Again Tonight Airplay #40 #1 Mainstream Rock hit (2 weeks)	Mercury 866414
6/18/94	**3**	33	21. **Wild Night** Airplay #3 / Sales #6 **JOHN MELLENCAMP ME'SHELL NDEGÉOCELLO** #1 Adult Contemporary hit (8 weeks)	Mercury 858738
9/7/96	**14**	21	22. Key West Intermezzo (I Saw You First) Airplay #15 / Sales #23	Mercury 578398
			MELLO-TONES, The	
			R&B vocal group from Detroit, Michigan, featuring lead singer Jerry Carr (composed "Rosie Lee").	
5/13/57	**24**	1	1. Rosie Lee Best Seller #24 / Top 100 #60 Hank Ivory (orch.)	Gee 1037
			MELLOW MAN ACE	
			Born Ulpiano Sergio Reyes on 4/12/67 in Havana, Cuba; raised in Southgate, California. Male rapper. His brother Senen is a member of Cypress Hill.	
6/9/90	**14**	13	● 1. Mentirosa Sales #5 / Airplay #28 samples Santana's "Evil Ways" and "No One To Depend On"	Capitol 44533
			MELVIN, Harold, And The Blue Notes	
			Born on 6/25/39 in Philadelphia, Pennsylvania. Died of a stroke on 3/24/97 (age 57). R&B singer. The Blue Notes: Teddy Pendergrass (lead vocals), Lawrence Brown, Jerry Cummings and Bernard Wilson.	
10/28/72	**3**	11	● 1. **If You Don't Know Me By Now** #1 R&B hit (2 weeks)	Philadelphia I. 3520

DATE	POS	WKS	ARTIST–RECORD TITLE	LABEL & NO.
10/20/73	7	12	● 2. **The Love I Lost (Part 1)** #1 R&B hit (2 weeks)	Philadelphia I. 3533
5/3/75	15	10	3. Bad Luck (Part 1)	Philadelphia I. 3562
12/20/75+	12	12	4. Wake Up Everybody (Part 1) #1 R&B hit (2 weeks)	Philadelphia I. 3579

MEN AT LARGE

R&B vocal duo from Cleveland, Ohio: David Tolliver and Jason Champion.

DATE	POS	WKS	ARTIST–RECORD TITLE	LABEL & NO.
4/10/93	31	4	1. So Alone Sales #25 / Airplay #37	EastWest 98459

MEN AT WORK

Pop-rock group from Melbourne, Australia: Colin Hay (vocals, guitar), Ron Strykert (guitar), Greg Ham (sax, keyboards), John Rees (bass) and Jerry Speiser (drums). Won the 1982 Best New Artist Grammy Award.

DATE	POS	WKS	ARTIST–RECORD TITLE	LABEL & NO.
8/7/82	1 (1)	17	1. **Who Can It Be Now?**	Columbia 02888
11/27/82+	1 (4)	19	▲ 2. **Down Under** #1 Mainstream Rock hit (5 weeks)	Columbia 03303
4/9/83	3	13	3. **Overkill**	Columbia 03795
7/9/83	6	12	4. **It's A Mistake**	Columbia 03959
10/8/83	28	5	5. **Dr. Heckyll & Mr. Jive**	Columbia 04111

MENDES, Sergio, & Brasil '66

Born on 2/11/41 in Niteroi, Brazil. Pianist/bandleader. Brasil '66 consisted of Lani Hall and Janis Hansen (vocals), Joses Soares (percussion), Bob Matthews (bass) and Jao Palma (drums). Hall married Herb Alpert.

DATE	POS	WKS	ARTIST–RECORD TITLE	LABEL & NO.
6/1/68	4	11	1. **The Look Of Love** from the movie *Casino Royale* starring David Niven and Peter Sellers	A&M 924
8/24/68	6	10	2. **The Fool On The Hill** #1 Adult Contemporary hit (6 weeks); first recorded by The Beatles in 1967	A&M 961
12/7/68	16	6	3. **Scarborough Fair**	A&M 986
			SERGIO MENDES:	
5/14/83	4	16	4. **Never Gonna Let You Go** #1 Adult Contemporary hit (4 weeks); Joe Pizzulo and Leza Miller (Lise Miller) (vocals)	A&M 2540
7/7/84	29	7	5. Alibis Joe Pizzulo (vocal)	A&M 2639

MEN WITHOUT HATS

Techno-rock group from Montreal, Quebec, Canada: brothers Ivan (vocals), Stefan (guitar) and Colin (keyboards) Doroschuk, with Allan McCarthy (drums).

DATE	POS	WKS	ARTIST–RECORD TITLE	LABEL & NO.
7/30/83	3	16	1. **The Safety Dance**	Backstreet 52232
12/19/87+	20	10	2. Pop Goes The World Sales #16 / Airplay #25	Mercury 888859

MERCEDES — see MASTER P

MERCHANT, Natalie

Born on 10/26/63 in Jamestown, New York. Alternative-rock singer/songwriter. Lead singer of 10,000 Maniacs from 1981-93.

DATE	POS	WKS	ARTIST–RECORD TITLE	LABEL & NO.
8/26/95	10	26	1. **Carnival** Airplay #6 / Sales #54	Elektra 64413

DATE	POS	WKS	ARTIST–RECORD TITLE	LABEL & NO.
1/20/96	**20**	26	2. Wonder Airplay #7 / Sales #62	Elektra 64376
7/6/96	**23**	14	3. Jealousy Airplay #12	Elektra 64301
5/23/98	**18** ᴬ	18	4. Kind & Generous	album cut
			from the album Ophelia on Elektra 62196	

MERCY

Adult Contemporary group from Florida: James Marvell, Ronnie Caudill, Roger Fuentes, Buddy Good, Debbie Lewis and Brenda McNish.

5/3/69	**2** (2)	10	● 1. **Love (Can Make You Happy)**	Sundi 6811

MESSINA, Jim — see LOGGINS & MESSINA

MESSINA, Jo Dee

Born on 8/25/70 in Framingham, Massachusetts; raised in Holliston, Massachusetts. Country singer.

1/23/99	**34**	4	1. Stand Beside Me Airplay #20	album cut
			#1 Country hit (3 weeks)	
7/3/99	**28**	11	2. Lesson In Leavin' Airplay #15	album cut
			#1 Country hit for Dottie West in 1980; above 2 from the album *I'm Alright* on Curb 77904	
8/5/00	**25**	10	3. That's The Way Sales #21 / Airplay #25	Curb 73106
			#1 Country hit (4 weeks)	
2/23/02	**36**	4	4. Bring On The Rain Airplay #34	album cut
			JO DEE MESSINA with Tim McGraw	
			#1 Country hit (1 week); from Messina's album *Burn* on Curb 77977	

METALLICA

Hard-rock group formed in Los Angeles, California: James Hetfield (vocals, guitar), Kirk Hammett (guitar), Jason Newsted (bass) and Lars Ulrich (drums). Original bassist Cliff Burton was killed in a bus crash on 9/27/86 (age 24).

3/25/89	**35**	4	● 1. One Sales #18	Elektra 69329
8/31/91	**16**	16	● 2. Enter Sandman Sales #3	Elektra 64857
1/11/92	**35**	1	3. The Unforgiven Sales #16	Elektra 64814
4/25/92	**34**	3	4. Nothing Else Matters Sales #18	Elektra 64770
6/8/96	**10**	10	● 5. **Until It Sleeps** Sales #3	Elektra 64276
			#1 Mainstream Rock hit (8 weeks)	
11/29/97	**28**	4	6. The Memory Remains Sales #16	Elektra 64126
			Marianne Faithfull (guest vocal)	

METERS, The

R&B instrumental group formed in New Orleans, Louisiana: Art Neville (keyboards), Leo Nocentelli (guitar), George Porter (bass) and Joseph Modeliste (drums). Neville is the brother of Aaron Neville.

3/22/69	**34**	1	1. Sophisticated Cissy [I]	Josie 1001
5/24/69	**23**	3	2. Cissy Strut [I]	Josie 1005

METHENY, Pat, Group — see BOWIE, David

DATE	POS	WKS	ARTIST—RECORD TITLE	LABEL & NO.
			METHOD MAN	
			Born Clifford Smith on 4/1/71 in Staten Island, New York. Male rapper. Member of Wu-Tang Clan.	
5/13/95	3	13	▲ 1. I'll Be There For You/You're All I Need To Get By Sales #1 (1) / Airplay #33 **METHOD MAN featuring Mary J. Blige** #1 R&B hit (3 weeks); medley of 2 songs written by Ashford & Simpson	Def Jam 851878
7/22/95	flip	3	2. The What Sales: flip **THE NOTORIOUS B.I.G. and METHOD MAN**	Bad Boy 79031
9/2/95	13	8	● 3. How High Sales #7 / Airplay #64 **REDMAN/METHOD MAN** samples "I Am Woman" by The Cover Girls; from the rap concert movie *The Show!*	Def Jam 579924
7/19/03	22	6	4. Love @ 1st Sight Sales #5 / Airplay #22 **MARY J. BLIGE featuring Method Man** samples "Hot Sex" by A Tribe Called Quest	Geffen 000954
			MFSB	
			Group of studio musicians based at Sigma Sound Studios in Philadelphia, Pennsylvania. MFSB: Mother, Father, Sister, Brother.	
3/16/74	1 (2)	14	● 1. TSOP (The Sound Of Philadelphia) [I] **MFSB featuring The Three Degrees** #1 R&B hit (1 week) / #1 Adult Contemporary hit (2 weeks); theme from the TV show "Soul Train"	Philadelphia I. 3540
			MIAMI SOUND MACHINE— see ESTEFAN, Gloria	
			MIA X — see MASTER P	
			MICHAEL, George/Wham!	
			Born Georgios Kyriacos Panayiotou on 6/25/63 in Bushey, England. Wham!, formed in early 1980s, centered around Michael's vocals and songwriting, and included Andrew Ridgeley (born on 1/26/63 in Bushey, England) on guitar. Their association ended in 1986.	
			WHAM!:	
10/6/84	1 (3)	14	▲ 1. Wake Me Up Before You Go-Go Sales #1 (3) / Airplay #1 (3)	Columbia 04552
12/22/84+	1 (3)	17	▲ 2. Careless Whisper Sales #1 (3) / Airplay #1 (3) **WHAM! Featuring George Michael** #1 Adult Contemporary hit (5 weeks)	Columbia 04691
4/6/85	1 (2)	14	● 3. Everything She Wants Sales #1 (2) / Airplay #1 (2)	Columbia 04840
8/3/85	3	12	4. Freedom Sales #3 / Airplay #5	Columbia 05409
12/14/85+	3	12	5. I'm Your Man Sales #3 / Airplay #3	Columbia 05721
5/10/86	7	10	6. A Different Corner Sales #5 / Airplay #8 **GEORGE MICHAEL**	Columbia 05888
7/19/86	10	8	7. The Edge Of Heaven Sales #8 / Airplay #10	Columbia 06182
3/7/87	1 (2)	12	8. I Knew You Were Waiting (For Me) Sales #1 (2) / Airplay #1 (1) **ARETHA FRANKLIN AND GEORGE MICHAEL**	Arista 9559
			GEORGE MICHAEL:	
6/20/87	2 (1)	14	▲ 9. I Want Your Sex Sales #1 (2) / Airplay #5 from the movie *Beverly Hills Cop II* starring Eddie Murphy	Columbia 07164
10/31/87	1 (4)	15	● 10. Faith Airplay #1 (5) / Sales #1 (1)	Columbia 07623

DATE	POS	WKS	ARTIST–RECORD TITLE	LABEL & NO.
1/23/88	**1** (2)	13	11. **Father Figure** Airplay #1 (4) / Sales #1 (1)	Columbia 07682
4/16/88	**1** (3)	14	● 12. **One More Try** Airplay #1 (4) / Sales #1 (3) #1 R&B hit (1 week) / #1 Adult Contemporary hit (3 weeks)	Columbia 07773
7/16/88	**1** (2)	12	13. **Monkey** Sales #1 (2) / Airplay #1 (2)	Columbia 07941
10/15/88	**5**	10	14. **Kissing A Fool** Sales #3 / Airplay #6 #1 Adult Contemporary hit (1 week)	Columbia 08050
3/11/89	**5**	11	15. **Heaven Help Me** Sales #4 / Airplay #6 **DEON ESTUS (with George Michael)**	Mika 871538
9/8/90	**1** (1)	10	16. **Praying For Time** Airplay #1 (2) / Sales #3	Columbia 73512
11/3/90	**8**	12	● 17. **Freedom** Sales #7 / Airplay #9 different tune from #4 above	Columbia 73559
2/9/91	**27**	5	18. Waiting For That Day Airplay #24 / Sales #28	Columbia 73663
12/14/91+	**1** (1)	16	● 19. **Don't Let The Sun Go Down On Me** Sales #4 / Airplay #4 **[L]** **GEORGE MICHAEL/ELTON JOHN** #1 Adult Contemporary hit (2 weeks)	Columbia 74086
6/20/92	**10**	12	● 20. **Too Funky** Airplay #6 / Sales #17	Columbia 74353
5/22/93	**30**	4	21. Somebody To Love Airplay #25 / Sales #72 **[L]** **GEORGE MICHAEL And QUEEN** recorded at Wembly Stadium for the Freddie Mercury Tribute Concert	Hollywood 64647
2/24/96	**7**	5	● 22. **Jesus To A Child** Sales #3 / Airplay #40	DreamWorks 59000
5/11/96	**8**	12	● 23. **Fastlove** Sales #7 / Airplay #18 contains an interpolation of "Forget Me Nots" by Patrice Rushen	DreamWorks 59001
			MICHAELS, Lee	
			Born on 11/24/45 in Los Angeles, California. Rock singer/songwriter/keyboardist.	
9/4/71	**6**	12	1. **Do You Know What I Mean**	A&M 1262
12/25/71	**39**	1	2. Can I Get A Witness	A&M 1303
			MICHEL, Pras	
			Born Prakazrel Michael on 10/19/72 in Harlem, New York. Member of The Fugees.	
10/4/97	**35**	3	1. Avenues Sales #24 **REFUGEE CAMP ALL-STARS Featuring Pras (With Ky-Mani)** rap version of Eddy Grant's "Electric Avenue"; from the movie *Money Talks* starring Chris Tucker	Arista 13411
6/27/98	**15**	16	2. Ghetto Supastar (That Is What You Are) Airplay #11 **PRAS MICHEL featuring OL' DIRTY BASTARD &** **introducing MYA** samples "Get Up, Get Into It, Get Involved" by James Brown and contains an interpolation of "Islands In The Stream"; from the movie *Bulworth* starring Warren Beatty	Interscope 95021
			MICHEL'LE	
			Born Michel'le Toussant in Los Angeles, California. R&B-dance singer.	
1/20/90	**7**	14	● 1. **No More Lies** Sales #4 / Airplay #14	Ruthless 99149
5/26/90	**29**	5	2. Nicety Sales #21 / Airplay #35	Ruthless 98980
3/2/91	**31**	5	3. Something In My Heart Sales #23 / Airplay #61	Ruthless 98885

DATE	POS	WKS	ARTIST–RECORD TITLE	LABEL & NO.
			MICKEY and SYLVIA	
			R&B-rock and roll vocal duo: McHouston "Mickey" Baker (born on 10/15/25 in Louisville, Kentucky) and Sylvia Vanderpool (born on 5/29/36 in Queens, New York).	
1/12/57	**11**	14	1. Love Is Strange Best Seller #11 / Jockey #11 / Top 100 #13 / Juke Box #17 #1 R&B hit (2 weeks)	Groove 0175
			MIDLER, Bette	
			Born on 12/1/45 in Paterson, New Jersey; raised in Honolulu, Hawaii. Adult Contemporary singer/actress. In the Broadway show *Fiddler On The Roof* from 1967-70. Won the 1973 Best New Artist Grammy Award. Barry Manilow was her arranger/accompanist in early years. Starred in several movies.	
1/20/73	**17**	11	1. Do You Want To Dance?	Atlantic 2928
6/9/73	**8**	11	2. **Boogie Woogie Bugle Boy** #1 Adult Contemporary hit (2 weeks); #15 hit for The Andrews Sisters in 1941	Atlantic 2964
11/10/73	**40**	1	3. Friends above 2 produced by Barry Manilow	Atlantic 2980
7/7/79	**40**	2	4. Married Men	Atlantic 3582
3/1/80	**35**	3	5. When A Man Loves A Woman [L]	Atlantic 3643
4/26/80	**3**	16	● 6. **The Rose** #1 Adult Contemporary hit (5 weeks); above 2 from the movie *The Rose* starring Midler	Atlantic 3656
1/17/81	**39**	2	7. My Mother's Eyes [L] from the Bette Midler concert movie *Divine Madness*; #8 hit for George Jessel in 1929	Atlantic 3771
4/15/89	**1** (1)	15	▲ 8. **Wind Beneath My Wings** Sales #1 (1) / Airplay #2 from the movie *Beaches* starring Midler; song also known as "Hero"; 1989 Grammy winner: Record of the Year	Atlantic 88972
10/20/90	**2** (1)	19	▲ 9. **From A Distance** Sales #1 (1) / Airplay #3 #1 Adult Contemporary hit (6 weeks)	Atlantic 87820
			MIDNIGHTERS, The — see BALLARD, Hank	
			MIDNIGHT OIL	
			Rock group formed in Sydney, Australia: Peter Garrett (vocals), Martin Rotsey (guitar), James Moginie (keyboards), Dwayne Hillman (bass) and Rob Hirst (drums).	
5/21/88	**17**	9	1. Beds Are Burning Sales #11 / Airplay #22	Columbia 07433
			MIDNIGHT STAR	
			Funk group from Louisville, Kentucky: Belinda Lipscomb (vocals), brothers Reggie and Vince Calloway (horns), Jeff Cooper (guitar), Ken Gant (keyboards), Melvin Gentry (bass) and Bill Simmons (drums). The Calloway brothers later formed Calloway.	
1/12/85	**18**	8	1. Operator Airplay #17 / Sales #18 #1 R&B hit (5 weeks)	Solar 69684
			MIGHTY MIGHTY BOSSTONES, The	
			Ska-rock group from Boston, Massachusetts: Dicky Barrett (vocals), Nate Albert (guitar), Ben Carr (dancer), Kevin Lenear, Tim Burton and Dennis Brockenborough (horns), Joe Gittleman (bass) and Joe Sirois (drums).	
6/7/97	**23** ^A	26	1. The Impression That I Get #1 Modern Rock hit (1 week)	album cut

DATE	POS	WKS	ARTIST–RECORD TITLE	LABEL & NO.
			MIKAILA	
			Born Mikaila Enriquez on 12/15/86 in Edmond, Oklahoma; raised in Dallas, Texas. Female teen pop singer.	
12/30/00+	25	3	1. So In Love With Two *Sales #4*	Island 572664
			MIKE + THE MECHANICS	
			Pop-rock group formed in England: Mike Rutherford (bass), Paul Carrack and Paul Young (vocals), Adrian Lee (keyboards) and Peter Van Hooke (drums). Rutherford (born on 10/2/50 in Guildford, Surrey, England) is a member of Genesis. Carrack was with Ace. Young, not to be confused with the same-named solo singer, died of a heart attack on 7/17/2000 (age 53).	
1/18/86	6	11	1. **Silent Running (On Dangerous Ground)** *Airplay #5 / Sales #7* #1 Mainstream Rock hit (5 weeks)	Atlantic 89488
4/12/86	5	12	2. **All I Need Is A Miracle** *Airplay #5 / Sales #8*	Atlantic 89450
8/2/86	32	5	3. Taken In *Airplay #24 / Sales #37*	Atlantic 89404
1/21/89	1 (1)	14	4. **The Living Years** *Sales #1 (2) / Airplay #1 (1)* #1 Adult Contemporary hit (4 weeks)	Atlantic 88964
			MILES, Garry	
			Born James Cason on 11/27/39 in Nashville, Tennessee. Also recorded as Buzz Cason.	
7/18/60	16	9	1. Look For A Star from the movie *Circus Of Horrors* starring Donald Pleasence	Liberty 55261
			MILES, John	
			Born on 4/23/49 in Jarrow, England. Rock singer/guitarist/keyboardist. Guest vocalist with the Alan Parsons Project.	
5/14/77	34	5	1. Slowdown	London 20092
			MILES, Robert	
			Born Roberto Concina on 11/3/69 in Venice, Italy. DJ/musician.	
5/25/96	21	16	1. Children *Sales #20 / Airplay #25* **[I]**	Arista 13006
			MILESTONE	
			All-star R&B group: brothers Kenneth ("Babyface"), Kevon and Melvin Edmonds (both from After 7), with K-Ci & JoJo.	
9/20/97	23	13	● 1. I Care 'Bout You *Sales #13* from the movie *Soul Food* starring Vanessa Williams	LaFace 24264
			MILIAN, Christina	
			Born Christina Flores on 9/26/81 in Jersey City, New Jersey; raised in Waldorf, Maryland. R&B singer/songwriter.	
10/7/00	11	15	1. Between Me And You *Airplay #7* **JA RULE (Featuring Christina Milian)**	Def Jam 562890
9/29/01	27	7	2. AM To PM *Sales #1 (1) / Airplay #70*	Def Soul 588775
			MILLER, Chuck	
			Born in California. Boogie-woogie singer/pianist.	
6/18/55	9	14	1. **The House Of Blue Lights** *Best Seller #9 / Jockey #18 / Juke Box #19* #8 hit for Freddie Slack in 1946	Mercury 70627

DATE	POS	WKS	ARTIST–RECORD TITLE	LABEL & NO.
			MILLER, Jody	
			Born Myrna Joy Brooks on 11/29/41 in Phoenix, Arizona; raised in Blanchard, Oklahoma. Country singer.	
5/15/65	**12**	5	1. Queen Of The House	Capitol 5402
			answer song to Roger Miller's "King Of The Road"	
9/25/65	**25**	5	2. Home Of The Brave	Capitol 5483
			MILLER, Mitch, & his Orch. and Chorus	
			Born on 7/4/11 in Rochester, New York. Producer/conductor/arranger. A&R executive for both Columbia and Mercury Records. Best known for his sing-along albums and TV show (1961-64). Won Grammy's Lifetime Achievement Award in 2000.	
8/6/55	**1** (6)	19	● 1. **The Yellow Rose Of Texas**	Columbia 40540
			Best Seller #1 (6) / Jockey #1 (6) / Juke Box #1 (6) / Top 100 #4 adaptation of a Civil War campfire song	
2/18/56	**19**	3	2. Lisbon Antigua (In Old Lisbon) Jockey #19 / Top 100 #30 **[I]**	Columbia 40635
8/11/56	**8**	12	3. **Theme Song From ("Song For A Summer Night") (Parts I & II)** Jockey #8 / Best Seller #9 / Top 100 #10 / Juke Box #10 **[I]**	Columbia 40730
			Part I: instrumental version; Part II: vocal version; from the 7/8/56 *Studio One* TV production "Song For A Summer Night"	
1/27/58	**20**	11	4. March From The River Kwai and Colonel Bogey	Columbia 41066
			Jockey #20 / Best Seller #21 / Top 100 #21 **[I]** from the movie *The Bridge On The River Kwai* starring Alec Guinness and William Holden; "March" written for the movie; "Bogey" is a 1916 traditional march	
1/26/59	**16**	10	5. The Children's Marching Song (Nick Nack Paddy Whack)	Columbia 41317
			with the children from the Broadway musical "Flower Drum Song"	
			MILLER, Ned	
			Born Henry Ned Miller on 4/12/25 in Rains, Utah. Country singer/songwriter.	
1/26/63	**6**	8	1. **From A Jack To A King**	Fabor 114
			original version released on Dot 15601 in 1957 ($40)	
			MILLER, Roger	
			Born on 1/2/36 in Fort Worth, Texas; raised in Erick, Oklahoma. Died of cancer on 10/25/92 (age 56). Country singer/songwriter/guitarist. Hosted own TV show in 1966. Songwriter of 1985's Broadway musical *Big River*.	
7/4/64	**7**	8	1. Dang Me **[N]**	Smash 1881
			#1 Country hit (6 weeks)	
10/3/64	**9**	8	2. **Chug-A-Lug** **[N]**	Smash 1926
1/2/65	**31**	3	3. Do-Wacka-Do **[N]**	Smash 1947
2/6/65	**4**	12	● 4. **King Of The Road**	Smash 1965
			#1 Country hit (5 weeks) / #1 Adult Contemporary hit (10 weeks)	
5/22/65	**7**	7	5. **Engine Engine #9**	Smash 1983
8/7/65	**34**	2	6. One Dyin' And A Buryin'	Smash 1994
10/2/65	**31**	3	7. Kansas City Star **[N]**	Smash 1998
11/27/65	**8**	8	8. **England Swings**	Smash 2010
			#1 Adult Contemporary hit (1 week)	
3/5/66	**26**	5	9. Husbands And Wives	Smash 2024
7/23/66	**40**	1	10. You Can't Roller Skate In A Buffalo Herd **[N]**	Smash 2043
5/6/67	**37**	1	11. Walkin' In The Sunshine	Smash 2081
3/16/68	**39**	6	12. Little Green Apples	Smash 2148

DATE	POS	WKS	ARTIST–RECORD TITLE	LABEL & NO.
			MILLER, Steve, Band	
			Born on 10/5/43 in Milwaukee, Wisconsin; raised in Dallas, Texas. Rock singer/songwriter/guitarist. Formed band in high school, The Marksmen, which included Boz Scaggs. Moved to San Francisco in 1966; formed the Steve Miller Band, which featured a fluctuating lineup.	
11/17/73+	**1** (1)	16	● 1. **The Joker**	Capitol 3732
6/5/76	**11**	9	2. Take The Money And Run	Capitol 4260
9/4/76	**1** (1)	14	3. **Rock'n Me**	Capitol 4323
1/8/77	**2** (2)	15	● 4. **Fly Like An Eagle**	Capitol 4372
			STEVE MILLER (above 3)	
5/14/77	**8**	13	5. **Jet Airliner**	Capitol 4424
9/3/77	**23**	7	6. Jungle Love	Capitol 4466
11/12/77	**17**	9	7. Swingtown	Capitol 4496
11/14/81	**24**	9	8. Heart Like A Wheel	Capitol 5068
6/19/82	**1** (2)	19	● 9. **Abracadabra**	Capitol 5126
			MILLI VANILLI	
			Euro-pop act formed in Germany by producer Frank Farian (creator of Boney M). Originally thought to be Rob Pilatus (from Germany) and Fabrice Morvan (from France). Duo was stripped of the 1989 Best New Artist Grammy Award when it was revealed that they didn't sing on their debut album. Actual vocalists are Charles Shaw, John Davis and Brad Howe. Pilatus died of a drug overdose on 4/2/98 (age 32).	
2/4/89	**2** (1)	15	▲ 1. **Girl You Know It's True** Sales #1 (2) / Airplay #4	Arista 9781
5/20/89	**1** (1)	14	● 2. **Baby Don't Forget My Number** Sales #1 (1) / Airplay #2	Arista 9832
8/12/89	**1** (2)	14	● 3. **Girl I'm Gonna Miss You** Airplay #1 (3) / Sales #1 (1)	Arista 9870
10/21/89	**1** (2)	14	▲ 4. **Blame It On The Rain** Airplay #1 (2) / Sales #1 (1)	Arista 9904
1/13/90	**4**	10	5. **All Or Nothing** Airplay #4 / Sales #6	Arista 9923
			MILLS, Frank	
			Born on 6/27/42 in Toronto, Ontario, Canada. Pianist/producer/arranger.	
3/3/79	**3**	12	● 1. **Music Box Dancer** [I]	Polydor 14517
			MILLS, Garry	
			Born on 10/13/41 in West Wickham, Kent, England. Pop singer.	
7/4/60	**26**	6	1. Look For A Star - Part I	Imperial 5674
			from the movie *Circus Of Horrors* starring Donald Pleasence	
			MILLS, Hayley	
			Born on 4/18/46 in London, England. Singer/actress. Daughter of actor John Mills. Starred in several movies.	
9/18/61	**8**	11	1. **Let's Get Together**	Buena Vista 385
			HAYLEY MILLS and HAYLEY MILLS	
			from the movie *The Parent Trap* starring Mills	
4/14/62	**21**	6	2. Johnny Jingo	Buena Vista 395
			MILLS, Stephanie	
			Born on 3/22/57 in Brooklyn, New York. R&B singer/actress. Played "Dorothy" in Broadway's *The Wiz*. Briefly married to Jeffrey Daniels of Shalamar in 1980.	
9/1/79	**22**	6	1. What Cha Gonna Do With My Lovin'	20th Century 2403

DATE	POS	WKS	ARTIST–RECORD TITLE	LABEL & NO.
8/30/80	6	16	● 2. **Never Knew Love Like This Before**	20th Century 2460
7/4/81	40	2	3. Two Hearts	20th Century 2492
			STEPHANIE MILLS Featuring Teddy Pendergrass	

MILLS BROTHERS, The

Legendary black family vocal group from Piqua, Ohio: father John Mills (died on 12/8/67, age 78), with sons Herbert (died on 4/12/89, age 77), Harry (died on 6/28/82, age 68) and Donald (died on 11/13/99, age 84) Mills. Won Grammy's Lifetime Achievement Award in 1998.

DATE	POS	WKS	ARTIST–RECORD TITLE	LABEL & NO.
6/17/57	39	1	1. Queen Of The Senior Prom Top 100 #39	Decca 30299
3/3/58	21	2	2. Get A Job Jockey #21	Dot 15695
			Milton Rodgers (orch.)	
3/2/68	23	10	3. Cab Driver	Dot 17041
			Sy Oliver (orch.: #1 & 3)	

MILSAP, Ronnie

Born on 1/16/43 in Robbinsville, North Carolina. Country singer/songwriter/pianist. Blind since birth.

DATE	POS	WKS	ARTIST–RECORD TITLE	LABEL & NO.
8/27/77	16	10	1. It Was Almost Like A Song	RCA 10976
			#1 Country hit (3 weeks)	
1/24/81	24	9	2. Smoky Mountain Rain	RCA 12084
			#1 Country hit (1 week) / #1 Adult Contemporary hit (1 week)	
7/11/81	5	15	3. **(There's) No Gettin' Over Me**	RCA 12264
			#1 Country hit (2 weeks)	
11/28/81+	20	11	4. I Wouldn't Have Missed It For The World	RCA 12342
			#1 Country hit (1 week)	
5/29/82	14	9	5. Any Day Now	RCA 13216
			#1 Country hit (1 week) / #1 Adult Contemporary hit (5 weeks)	
4/23/83	23	8	6. Stranger In My House	RCA 13470

MIMMS, Garnet, & The Enchanters

Born Garrett Mimms on 11/16/33 in Ashland, Kentucky. R&B singer. The Enchanters: Zola Pearnell, Sam Bell and Charles Boyer.

DATE	POS	WKS	ARTIST–RECORD TITLE	LABEL & NO.
9/7/63	4	11	1. **Cry Baby**	United Artists 629
			#1 R&B hit (3 weeks)	
12/21/63+	26	5	2. For Your Precious Love /	
12/7/63	30	4	3. Baby Don't You Weep	United Artists 658
5/7/66	30	3	4. I'll Take Good Care Of You	United Artists 995
			GARNET MIMMS	

MINDBENDERS, The

Pop-rock group from Manchester, England: Wayne Fontana (vocals), Eric Stewart (guitar, vocals), Bob Lang (bass) and Ric Rothwell (drums). Fontana left in October 1965. Stewart later formed Hotlegs and 10cc.

DATE	POS	WKS	ARTIST–RECORD TITLE	LABEL & NO.
3/27/65	1 (1)	10	1. **Game Of Love**	Fontana 1509
			WAYNE FONTANA & THE MINDBENDERS	
4/30/66	2 (2)	10	2. **A Groovy Kind Of Love**	Fontana 1541

DATE	POS	WKS	ARTIST–RECORD TITLE	LABEL & NO.
			MINEO, Sal	
			Born Salvatore Mineo on 1/10/39 in the Bronx, New York. Stabbed to death on 2/12/76 (age 37). Singer/actor. Starred in several movies and Broadway shows.	
5/20/57	9	13	1. **Start Movin' (In My Direction) /** Best Seller #9 / Top 100 #10 / Jockey #16 / Juke Box #18 introduced by Mineo on the 5/1/57 Kraft TV Theater production of *Drummer Man*	
6/24/57		5	2. Love Affair Best Seller: flip Ray Ellis (orch., above 2)	Epic 9216
9/23/57	27	3	3. Lasting Love / Best Seller #27 / Top 100 #35	
9/30/57		1	4. You Shouldn't Do That Best Seller: flip Mark Ellis (orch., above 2)	Epic 9227
			MINOGUE, Kylie	
			Born on 5/28/68 in Melbourne, Australia. Dance singer/actress. Regular on the Australian soap opera *Neighbours*.	
7/2/88	28	4	1. I Should Be So Lucky Sales #27 / Airplay #32	Geffen 27922
9/17/88	3	13	● 2. **The Loco-Motion** Sales #1 (1) / Airplay #4	Geffen 27752
2/4/89	37	2	3. It's No Secret Sales #35 / Airplay #37	Geffen 27651
2/9/02	7	14	4. **Can't Get You Out Of My Head** Airplay #8 / Sales #72	Capitol 77685
8/17/02	23	5	5. Love At First Sight Airplay #26	Capitol 77724
			MINT CONDITION	
			R&B group from Minneapolis, Minnesota: Stokley Williams (vocals, drums), Homer O'Dell (guitar), Larry Waddell and Keri Lewis (keyboards), Jeff Allen (sax) and Ricky Kinchen (bass). Lewis married Toni Braxton on 4/21/2001.	
2/8/92	6	16	● 1. **Breakin' My Heart (Pretty Brown Eyes)** Airplay #6 / Sales #9	Perspective 0004
3/19/94	33	2	2. U Send Me Swingin' Sales #26 / Airplay #47	Perspective 7439
10/19/96	17	17	● 3. What Kind Of Man Would I Be Sales #12 / Airplay #46	Perspective 7558
4/12/97	32	5	4. You Don't Have To Hurt No More Sales #22	Perspective 7564
11/20/99	30	5	5. If You Love Me Sales #9 / Airplay #68	Elektra 64027
			MIRACLES, The	
			R&B vocal group from Detroit, Michigan: Smokey Robinson, Claudette Rogers, Bobby Rogers, Ronnie White and Warren Moore. Claudette Rogers (future wife of Smokey Robinson) retired in 1964. Bobby Rogers married Wanda Young of The Marvelettes. Robinson went solo in 1972; replaced by Billy Griffin. White died of leukemia on 8/26/95 (age 56).	
12/31/60+	2 (1)	13	1. **Shop Around** **THE MIRACLES (featuring Bill "Smokey" Robinson)** #1 R&B hit (8 weeks)	Tamla 54034
2/17/62	35	2	2. What's So Good About Good-by	Tamla 54053
6/30/62	39	1	3. I'll Try Something New	Tamla 54059
1/12/63	8	10	4. **You've Really Got A Hold On Me** #1 R&B hit (1 week)	Tamla 54073
5/4/63	31	3	5. A Love She Can Count On	Tamla 54078
8/31/63	8	9	6. **Mickey's Monkey**	Tamla 54083
1/4/64	35	3	7. I Gotta Dance To Keep From Crying	Tamla 54089
7/25/64	27	4	8. I Like It Like That	Tamla 54098
10/10/64	35	1	9. That's What Love Is Made Of	Tamla 54102

DATE	POS	WKS	ARTIST–RECORD TITLE	LABEL & NO.
4/17/65	**16**	7	10. Ooo Baby Baby	Tamla 54113
8/7/65	**16**	8	11. The Tracks Of My Tears	Tamla 54118
11/6/65	**14**	6	12. My Girl Has Gone	Tamla 54123
1/22/66	**11**	7	13. Going To A Go-Go	Tamla 54127
11/26/66	**17**	6	14. (Come 'Round Here) I'm The One You Need	Tamla 54140
			SMOKEY ROBINSON & THE MIRACLES:	
3/11/67	**20**	7	15. The Love I Saw In You Was Just A Mirage	Tamla 54145
7/8/67	**23**	8	16. More Love	Tamla 54152
11/25/67	**4**	12	17. **I Second That Emotion** #1 R&B hit (1 week)	Tamla 54159
3/9/68	**11**	10	18. If You Can Want	Tamla 54162
6/29/68	**31**	3	19. Yester Love	Tamla 54167
8/31/68	**26**	6	20. Special Occasion	Tamla 54172
1/25/69	**8**	11	21. **Baby, Baby Don't Cry**	Tamla 54178
7/19/69	**32**	4	22. Doggone Right	Tamla 54183
7/19/69	**33**	2	23. Abraham, Martin And John a tribute to Abraham Lincoln, Martin Luther King, Jr., and John and Robert Kennedy	Tamla 54184
10/4/69	**37**	3	24. Here I Go Again	Tamla 54183
12/27/69+	**37**	4	25. Point It Out	Tamla 54189
10/31/70	**1 (2)**	14	26. **The Tears Of A Clown** #1 R&B hit (3 weeks); recorded in 1967	Tamla 54199
4/17/71	**18**	8	27. I Don't Blame You At All	Tamla 54205
			THE MIRACLES:	
9/14/74	**13**	9	28. Do It Baby	Tamla 54248
12/13/75+	**1 (1)**	19	29. **Love Machine (Part 1)**	Tamla 54262
			MR. BIG Rock group from San Francisco, California: Eric Martin (vocals), Paul Gilbert (guitar), Billy Sheehan (bass) and Pat Torpey (drums).	
1/25/92	**1 (3)**	17	● 1. **To Be With You** Sales #2 / Airplay #3	Atlantic 87580
5/9/92	**16**	11	2. Just Take My Heart Airplay #25 / Sales #26	Atlantic 87509
11/6/93	**27**	7	3. Wild World Sales #35 / Airplay #36	Atlantic 87308
			MR. CHEEKS Born Terrance Kelly in Queens, New York. Male rapper. Former member of Lost Boyz.	
12/15/01+	**14**	20	1. Lights, Camera, Action! Sales #1 (2) / Airplay #22 #1 R&B hit (1 week); samples "Keep On Truckin'" by Eddie Kendricks	Universal 156257
3/8/03	**17**	11	2. The Jump Off Sales #11 / Airplay #16 **LIL' KIM (featuring Mr. Cheeks)** samples "Jeeps, Lex Coups, Bimaz & Benz" by Lost Boyz	Queen Bee 88036
			MR. MISTER Pop-rock group formed in Los Angeles: Richard Page (vocals, bass), Steve Farris (guitar), Steve George (keyboards) and Pat Mastelotto (drums).	
10/19/85	**1 (2)**	15	1. **Broken Wings** Sales #1 (2) / Airplay #1 (1)	RCA 14136

DATE	POS	WKS	ARTIST–RECORD TITLE	LABEL & NO.
1/11/86	**1** (2)	13	2. **Kyrie** Sales #1 (2) / Airplay #1 (2) #1 Mainstream Rock hit (1 week)	RCA 14258
4/12/86	**8**	11	3. **Is It Love** Airplay #7 / Sales #14	RCA 14313
9/19/87	**29**	5	4. Something Real (Inside Me/Inside You) Sales #25 / Airplay #30	RCA 5273

MR. PRESIDENT

Dance group consisting of German-born singers T-Seven and Lady Danii with British-born rapper DJ Lazy Dee.

DATE	POS	WKS	ARTIST–RECORD TITLE	LABEL & NO.
8/9/97	**21**	11	1. Coco Jamboo Sales #26 / Airplay #36	Warner 17331

MITCHELL, Guy

Born Al Cernik on 2/27/27 in Detroit, Michigan. Died on 7/1/99 (age 72). Pop singer/actor. Appeared in the movies *Those Redheads From Seattle* and *Red Garters*.

DATE	POS	WKS	ARTIST–RECORD TITLE	LABEL & NO.
2/25/56	**23**	4	1. Ninety Nine Years (Dead Or Alive) Top 100 #23 Jimmy Carroll (orch.)	Columbia 40631
11/3/56	**1** (10)	22	● 2. **Singing The Blues** Juke Box #1 (10) / Best Seller #1 (9) / Top 100 #1 (9) / Jockey #1 (9)	Columbia 40769
2/2/57	**16**	8	3. Knee Deep In The Blues Top 100 #16 / Juke Box #16 / Jockey #17 / Best Seller #21 Ray Conniff (orch., above 2)	Columbia 40820
4/13/57	**10**	12	4. **Rock-A-Billy** Best Seller #10 / Top 100 #13 / Juke Box #14 / Jockey #15 Jimmy Carroll (orch.)	Columbia 40877
10/19/59	**1** (2)	16	5. **Heartaches By The Number** Joe Sherman (orch.)	Columbia 41476

MITCHELL, Joni

Born Roberta Joan Anderson on 11/7/43 in Fort McLeod, Alberta, Canada; raised in Saskatoon, Saskatchewan, Canada. Singer/songwriter guitarist/pianist. Married to her producer/bassist, Larry Klein, from 1982-94. Recipient of *Billboard*'s Century Award in 1995. Inducted into the Rock and Roll Hall of Fame in 1997. Won Grammy's Lifetime Achievement Award in 2002.

DATE	POS	WKS	ARTIST–RECORD TITLE	LABEL & NO.
12/30/72+	**25**	8	1. You Turn Me On, I'm A Radio Graham Nash (harmonica)	Asylum 11010
4/20/74	**7**	11	2. **Help Me** #1 Adult Contemporary hit (1 week)	Asylum 11034
8/24/74	**22**	7	3. Free Man In Paris David Crosby and Graham Nash (backing vocals); Larry Carlton and Jose Feliciano (guitars)	Asylum 11041
1/25/75	**24**	4	4. Big Yellow Taxi [L-R] studio version hit #67 in 1970	Asylum 45221
9/13/97	**36** A	3	5. Got 'Til It's Gone **JANET Featuring Q-Tip and Joni Mitchell** samples "Big Yellow Taxi" by Joni Mitchell; from Janet's album *The Velvet Rope* on Virgin 44762	album cut

MITCHELL, Willie

Born on 1/3/28 in Ashland, Mississippi; raised in Memphis, Tennessee. R&B keyboardist/arranger/producer. Led house band and later became president of Hi Records.

DATE	POS	WKS	ARTIST–RECORD TITLE	LABEL & NO.
10/3/64	**31**	5	1. 20-75 [I] title refers to the record's label number	Hi 2075
4/13/68	**23**	10	2. Soul Serenade [I]	Hi 2140

Melanie was somewhat surprised when some radio stations banned her hit "Brand New Key," because they felt the song's images were too suggestive. The Woodstock-era singer nonetheless unlocked a #1 hit.

John Cougar Mellencamp released "Jack And Diane" while his previous hit "Hurts So Good" was still climbing the charts. The two songs from his #1 album, *American Fool,* were simultaneously in the Top 10.

Men At Work put in overtime in 1982. They followed their #1 hit "Who Can It Be Now?" with another chart-topper, "Down Under," and capped it off with a Grammy Award for Best New Artist.

George Michael sent "Father Figure," from his album *Faith,* all the way to #1. Although the song did not earn the 1988 Grammy Award for Best Male Pop Vocal Performance, George did win in an even more impressive category: Album of the Year.

The Steve Miller Band earned the first of three #1 hits with "The Joker." Proving that not everyone gets a joke at the same time, the song reached #1 in Great Britain 16 years later.

Milli Vanilli may have tried to "Blame It On The Rain," but the revelation that they did not actually sing on their debut album resulted in their having to return their Best New Artist Grammy Award and proved they had no one to blame but themselves.

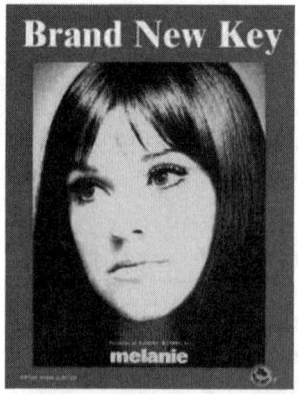

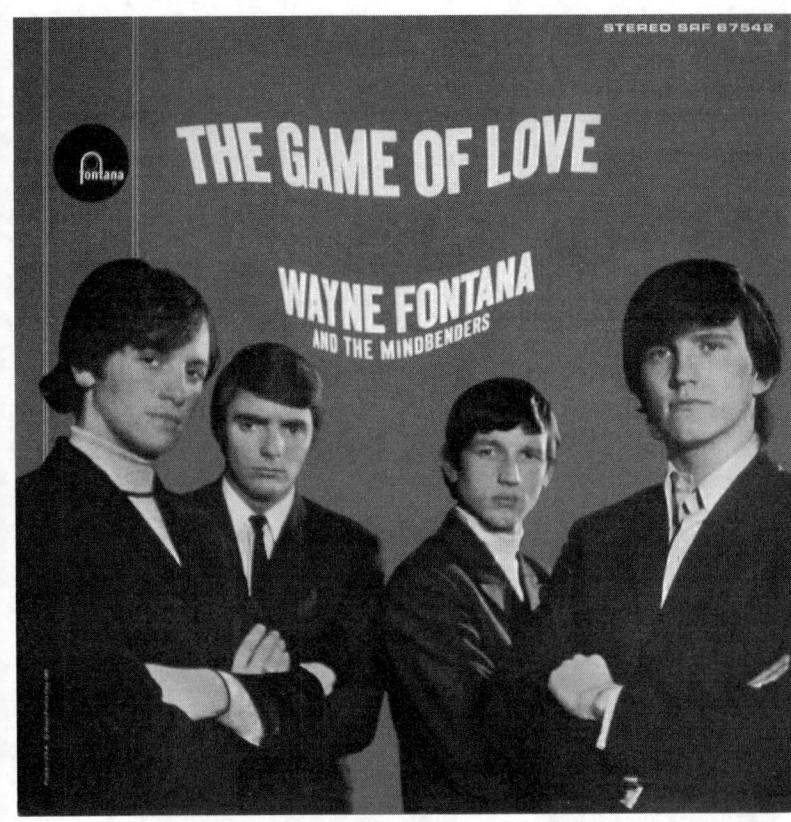

STEREO SAF 67542

THE GAME OF LOVE

WAYNE FONTANA
AND THE MINDBENDERS

MR. BIG

TO BE WITH YOU

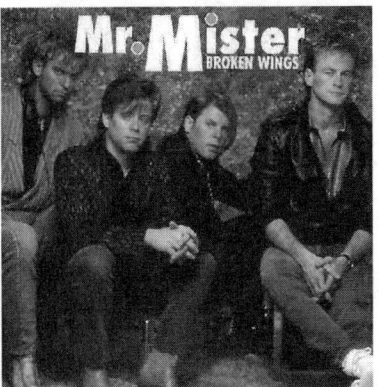

YOU NEEDED ME
ANNE MURRAY

The Mindbenders seemed to have all the rules down for "The Game Of Love," their first #1 hit. Even though lead singer Wayne Fontana left in 1965, the group returned to the Top 10 the following year with "A Groovy Kind Of Love."

Mr. Big had a lot of rock credibility, as bassist Billy Sheehan had played with the likes of David Lee Roth and Yngwie Malmsteen. Nonetheless, it was an acoustic ballad, "To Be With You," that brought them to #1.

Mr. Mister had no problem repeating themselves, as they followed up their first #1 hit, "Broken Wings," with another, "Kyrie." Lead singer Richard Page nearly had another chart-topper as writer of Madonna's #2 hit, "I'll Remember."

Monica almost replaced herself at #1. The only song between her duet with Brandy, "The Boy Is Mine," and her follow-up, "The First Night," was Aerosmith's "I Don't Want To Miss A Thing."

The Monkees enjoyed a career revival in the mid-1980s thanks to a marathon of their television show reruns on MTV. As a result, their 1967 #1 hit, "Daydream Believer," returned to the charts, peaking at #79.

Anne Murray felt very needed by Grammy voters after her #1 hit, "You Needed Me," earned nominations for Record of the Year and Song of the Year, and won for Best Female Pop Vocal Performance.

DATE	POS	WKS	ARTIST–RECORD TITLE	LABEL & NO.
			MO B. DICK — see MASTER P	
			MOBY	
			Born Richard Melville Hall on 9/11/65 in Harlem, New York; raised in Darien, Connecticut. Techno-dance singer/musician/producer/remixer.	
1/6/01	**14**	26	1. South Side Sales #7 / Airplay #15 **MOBY Featuring Gwen Stefani**	V2 27665
			MOCEDADES	
			Vocal group from Bilbao, Spain: siblings Amaya, Izaskum and Roberto Amezaga, with Jose Urien, Carlos Uribarri and Javier Barrenechea.	
2/16/74	**9**	11	1. Eres Tu (Touch The Wind) [F]	Tara 100
			MODELS	
			Pop-rock group formed in Melbourne, Australia: Sean Kelly (vocals, guitar), Roger Mason (keyboards), James Valentine (sax), James Freud (bass) and Barton Price (drums).	
6/7/86	**37**	4	1. Out Of Mind Out Of Sight Airplay #34 / Sales #36	Geffen 28762
			MODUGNO, Domenico	
			Born on 1/9/28 in Polignano a Mare, Italy. Died of a heart attack on 8/6/94 (age 66). Singer/actor.	
8/4/58	**1** (5)	13	● 1. **Nel Blu Dipinto Di Blu (Volaré)** Best Seller #1 (5) / Hot 100 #1 (0) [F] title is Italian for "In The Blue Sky Painted Blue (To Fly)"; 1958 Grammy winner: Record of the Year	Decca 30677
			MOJO MEN, The	
			Rock group from San Francisco, California: Jimmy Alaimo (vocals, guitar), Paul Curcio (guitar), Don Metchick (organ) and Dennis DeCarr (drums). Alaimo died of heart failure on 6/30/92 (age 53).	
3/18/67	**36**	3	1. Sit Down, I Think I Love You written by Stephen Stills	Reprise 0539
			MOKENSTEF	
			Female R&B vocal trio from Los Angeles, California: Monifa, Kenya and Stephanie.	

7/15/95	**7**	18	● 1. He's Mine Sales #5 / Airplay #19
			     contains interpolations of "Be Alright" by Zapp and "Do Me Baby"
			     by Prince
				OutBurst 851704

			MOMENTS, The	
			R&B vocal trio from Hackensack, New Jersey: Harry Ray, Al Goodman and Billy Brown. Changed group name to Ray, Goodman & Brown in 1978. Ray died of a stroke on 10/1/92 (age 45).	
4/18/70	**3**	14	● 1. Love On A Two-Way Street #1 R&B hit (5 weeks); produced by Sylvia (Robinson)	Stang 5012
2/2/74	**17**	9	2. Sexy Mama	Stang 5052
8/2/75	**39**	3	3. Look At Me (I'm In Love) #1 R&B hit (1 week)	Stang 5060

2/16/80	**5**	14	● 4. Special Lady
			     RAY, GOODMAN & BROWN
			     #1 R&B hit (1 week)
				Polydor 2033

DATE	POS	WKS	ARTIST–RECORD TITLE	LABEL & NO.
			MONEY, Eddie	
			Born Edward Mahoney on 3/2/49 in Brooklyn, New York. Pop-rock singer.	
4/8/78	11	11	1. Baby Hold On	Columbia 10663
7/29/78	22	8	2. Two Tickets To Paradise	Columbia 10765
2/24/79	22	8	3. Maybe I'm A Fool	Columbia 10900
7/24/82	16	12	4. Think I'm In Love	Columbia 02964
			#1 Mainstream Rock hit (3 weeks)	
9/27/86	4	12	5. **Take Me Home Tonight** Airplay #4 / Sales #5	Columbia 06231
			#1 Mainstream Rock hit (2 weeks); Ronnie Spector (The Ronettes) sings the lead line from "Be My Baby"	
1/24/87	14	10	6. I Wanna Go Back Airplay #10 / Sales #17	Columbia 06569
5/30/87	21	7	7. Endless Nights Sales #19 / Airplay #20	Columbia 07035
10/22/88	9	13	8. **Walk On Water** Airplay #8 / Sales #10	Columbia 08060
2/11/89	24	7	9. The Love In Your Eyes Airplay #20 / Sales #27	Columbia 68532
			#1 Mainstream Rock hit (1 week)	
12/23/89+	11	9	10. Peace In Our Time Sales #9 / Airplay #9	Columbia 73047
1/25/92	21	10	11. I'll Get By Airplay #23 / Sales #39	Columbia 74109
			MONEY, JT	
			Born Jeff Tompkins in Florida. Male rapper.	
4/24/99	5	12	● 1. **Who Dat** Sales #2 / Airplay #47	Tony Mercedes 53469
			JT MONEY Featuring Solé	
12/11/99	21	5	● 2. **4,5,6** Sales #7	DreamWorks 59029
			SOLÉ Featuring J.T. Money and Kandi	
			MONICA	
			Born Monica Arnold on 10/24/80 in Atlanta, Georgia. R&B singer.	
5/13/95	2 (3)	27	▲ 1. **Don't Take It Personal (just one of dem days)**	Rowdy 35040
			Sales #1 (1) / Airplay #9	
			#1 R&B hit (2 weeks); samples "Back Seat (Of My Jeep)" by L.L. Cool J	
10/28/95	7	24	▲ 2. **Before You Walk Out Of My Life /** Sales #5 / Airplay #28	
			#1 R&B hit (2 weeks)	
10/28/95		24	3. Like This And Like That	Rowdy 35052
			Mr. Malik (guest rapper); samples "Spoonin' Rap" by Sugarhill Gang	
6/8/96	9	16	● 4. **Why I Love You So Much /** Sales #5 / Airplay #46	
6/15/96		15	5. Ain't Nobody	Rowdy 35072
			features Naughty By Nature; contains portions of "Poverty's Paradise" by 24 Karat Black	
3/15/97	4	30	▲ 6. **For You I Will** Airplay #4 / Sales #5	Warner Sunset 87003
			from the movie *Space Jam* starring Michael Jordan	
5/30/98	1 (13)	27	▲² 7. **The Boy Is Mine** Sales #1 (9) / Airplay #2	Atlantic 84089
			BRANDY & MONICA	
			#1 R&B hit (8 weeks)	
8/15/98	1 (5)	23	▲ 8. **The First Night** Sales #1 (6) / Airplay #18	Arista 13522
			#1 R&B hit (6 weeks); samples "Love Hangover" by Diana Ross	
12/26/98+	1 (4)	26	▲ 9. **Angel Of Mine** Sales #1 (4) / Airplay #1 (2)	Arista 13590
5/17/03	10	17	10. **So Gone** Airplay #8 / Sales #41	J Records 21260
			#1 R&B hit (5 weeks); written and produced by Missy Elliott; samples "You Are Number One" by The Whispers	

DATE	POS	WKS	ARTIST–RECORD TITLE	LABEL & NO.
			MONIFAH	
			Born Monifah Carter on 1/28/68 in Harlem, New York. Female R&B singer/actress.	
5/11/96	**32**	7	● 1. You Sales #14	Uptown/Univ. 56001
			written and produced by Heavy D	
9/5/98	**9**	21	2. **Touch It** Sales #11 / Airplay #22	Uptown/Univ. 56207
			samples "White Horse" by Laid Back	
			MONKEES, The	
			Pop group formed in Los Angeles, California. Members chosen from over 400 applicants for new Columbia TV series. Consisted of Davy Jones (vocals), Mike Nesmith (guitar, vocals), Peter Tork (bass, vocals) and Micky Dolenz (drums, vocals). Jones (born on 12/30/45 in Manchester, England) had appeared in London musicals *Oliver* and *Pickwick*. Nesmith (born on 12/30/42 in Houston, Texas) had done session work for Stax/Volt. Tork (born on 2/13/44 in Washington DC) had been in the Phoenix Singers. Dolenz (born on 3/8/45 in Tarzana, California) had starred in the 1956 TV series *Circus Boy*. Group starred in the movie *Head* (1968) and 58 episodes of *The Monkees* TV show (1966-68). Tork left in 1968. Group disbanded in 1969. Re-formed (minus Nesmith) in 1986 and again (with Nesmith) in 1996.	
9/24/66	**1** (1)	12	● 1. **Last Train To Clarksville**	Colgems 1001
12/17/66	**1** (7)	13	● 2. **I'm A Believer /**	
			written by Neil Diamond	
12/31/66+	**20**	6	3. (I'm Not Your) Steppin' Stone	Colgems 1002
			first recorded by Paul Revere & The Raiders in 1966	
3/25/67	**2** (1)	10	● 4. **A Little Bit Me, A Little Bit You /**	
			written by Neil Diamond	
4/15/67	**39**	1	5. The Girl I Knew Somewhere	Colgems 1004
7/29/67	**3**	9	● 6. **Pleasant Valley Sunday /**	
8/5/67	**11**	7	7. Words	Colgems 1007
11/18/67	**1** (4)	12	● 8. **Daydream Believer**	Colgems 1012
3/9/68	**3**	7	● 9. **Valleri /**	
3/30/68	**34**	1	10. Tapioca Tundra	Colgems 1019
6/22/68	**19**	6	11. D. W. Washburn	Colgems 1023
8/2/86	**20**	7	12. That Was Then, This Is Now Sales #16 / Airplay #28	Arista 9505
			MONOTONES, The	
			R&B vocal group from Newark, New Jersey: Charles Patrick, brothers John and Warren Ryanes, Warren Davis, George Malone and Frank Smith. John Ryanes died on 5/30/72 (age 31). Warren Ryanes died in June 1982 (age 45). Smith died of cancer on 11/26/2000 (age 61).	
4/7/58	**5**	12	1. **Book Of Love** Top 100 #5 / Best Seller #6 / Jockey #9	Argo 5290
			MONRO, Matt	
			Born Terrence Parsons on 12/1/32 in London, England. Died of cancer on 2/7/85 (age 52). Pop singer.	
6/26/61	**18**	9	1. My Kind Of Girl	Warwick 636
12/26/64+	**23**	5	2. Walk Away	Liberty 55745
			Johnnie Spence (orch., above 2)	
			MONROE, Vaughn	
			Born on 10/7/11 in Akron, Ohio. Died on 5/21/73 (age 61). Pop singer known for his very deep voice.	
11/12/55	**38**	1	1. Black Denim Trousers And Motorcycle Boots Top 100 #38	RCA Victor 6260

DATE	POS	WKS	ARTIST–RECORD TITLE	LABEL & NO.
2/18/56	38	1	2. Don't Go To Strangers Top 100 #38 first recorded by Al Martino in 1954	RCA Victor 6358
9/8/56	11	8	3. In The Middle Of The House Jockey #11 / Top 100 #21 [N] Joe Reisman (orch.)	RCA Victor 6619
			MONTE, Lou	
			Born on 4/2/17 in Lyndhurst, New Jersey. Died on 6/12/89 (age 72). Italian-styled novelty singer/guitarist.	
3/17/58	12	11	1. Lazy Mary (Luna Mezzo Mare) Best Seller #12 / Top 100 #12 / Jockey #22 [F] Italian song also known as "The Butcher Boy"; #5 hit for Rudy Vallee in 1938	RCA Victor 7160
12/15/62+	5	9	● 2. **Pepino The Italian Mouse** [N] Joe Reisman (orch., above 2)	Reprise 20,106
			MONTENEGRO, Hugo, His Orchestra And Chorus	
			Born on 9/2/25 in Brooklyn, New York. Died of emphysema on 2/6/81 (age 55). Conductor/composer/arranger.	
4/6/68	2 (1)	14	1. **The Good, The Bad And The Ugly** [I] #1 Adult Contemporary hit (3 weeks); title song from the movie starring Clint Eastwood	RCA Victor 9423
			MONTEZ, Chris	
			Born Ezekiel Christopher Montanez on 1/17/43 in Los Angeles, California. Pop-rock singer.	
9/8/62	4	9	1. **Let's Dance**	Monogram 505
2/12/66	22	5	2. Call Me	A&M 780
5/28/66	16	7	3. The More I See You #7 hit for Dick Haymes in 1945 (from the movie *Billy Rose's Diamond Horseshoe* starring Betty Grable)	A&M 796
9/10/66	33	2	4. There Will Never Be Another You #19 hit for Sammy Kaye in 1943 (from the movie *Iceland* starring Sonja Henie)	A&M 810
12/3/66	36	2	5. Time After Time #16 hit for Frank Sinatra in 1947 (from the movie *It Happened In Brooklyn*); #2,3,5: produced by Herb Alpert	A&M 822
			MONTGOMERY, John Michael	
			Born on 1/20/65 in Danville, Kentucky. Country singer/guitarist. Younger brother of Eddie of Montgomery Gentry.	
2/20/99	33	3	1. Hold On To Me Airplay #32 / Sales #46	Atlantic 84197
10/28/00	35	4	2. The Little Girl Airplay #22 #1 Country hit (3 weeks); from the album *Brand New Me* on Atlantic 83378	album cut
			MONTGOMERY, Melba	
			Born on 10/14/38 in Iron City, Tennessee; raised in Florence, Alabama. Country singer/guitarist/fiddler.	
6/8/74	39	1	1. No Charge #1 Country hit (1 week)	Elektra 45883

DATE	POS	WKS	ARTIST–RECORD TITLE	LABEL & NO.
			MONTGOMERY GENTRY	
			Country vocal duo of Eddie Montgomery and Troy Gentry. Montgomery is the older brother of John Michael Montgomery.	
6/30/01	**37**	7	1. She Couldn't Change Me Sales #28 / Airplay #29	Columbia 79540
11/23/02	**40**	1	2. My Town Airplay #36	album cut
			from the album *My Town* on Columbia 86520	
			MOODY BLUES, The	
			Art-rock group formed in Birmingham, England: Denny Laine (guitar, vocals), Ray Thomas (flute, vocals), Mike Pinder (keyboards, vocals), Clint Warwick (bass) and Graeme Edge (drums). Laine and Warwick left in the summer of 1966, replaced by Justin Hayward (vocals, guitar) and John Lodge (vocals, bass). Laine joined Wings in 1971. Switzerland-born Patrick Moraz (former keyboardist of Yes) replaced Pinder in 1978.	
3/27/65	**10**	8	1. **Go Now!**	London 9726
			first recorded by Bessie Banks in 1964	
8/24/68	**24**	6	2. Tuesday Afternoon (Forever Afternoon)	Deram 85028
5/30/70	**21**	8	3. Question	Threshold 67004
9/4/71	**23**	7	4. The Story In Your Eyes	Threshold 67006
5/13/72	**29**	7	5. Isn't Life Strange	Threshold 67009
9/2/72	● **2** (2)	14	6. **Nights In White Satin**	Deram 85023
			recorded in 1968 with the London Festival Orchestra	
2/17/73	**12**	8	7. I'm Just A Singer (In A Rock And Roll Band)	Threshold 67012
9/2/78	**39**	2	8. Steppin' In A Slide Zone	London 270
6/13/81	**12**	9	9. Gemini Dream	Threshold 601
8/15/81	**15**	11	10. The Voice	Threshold 602
			#1 Mainstream Rock hit (4 weeks)	
9/17/83	**27**	6	11. Sitting At The Wheel	Threshold 604
5/24/86	**9**	12	12. **Your Wildest Dreams** Sales #8 / Airplay #13	Polydor 883906
			#1 Adult Contemporary hit (2 weeks)	
7/23/88	**30**	4	13. I Know You're Out There Somewhere	Polydor 887600
			Sales #27 / Airplay #36	
			MOONEY, Art, And His Orchestra	
			Born on 1/26/13 in Lowell, Massachusetts. Died on 9/9/93 (age 80). Orchestra leader.	
4/23/55	● **6**	17	1. **Honey-Babe** Best Seller #6 / Juke Box #6 / Jockey #10	MGM 11900
12/17/55	● **6**	4	2. **Nuttin' For Christmas**	MGM 12092
			Best Seller #6 / Top 100 #7 / Juke Box #9 / Jockey #10 **[X-N]**	
			ART MOONEY And His ORCHESTRA with Barry Gordon	
			MOONGLOWS, The	
			R&B vocal group from Louisville, Kentucky: Harvey Fuqua, Bobby Lester, Alexander Graves and Prentiss Barnes, with Billy Johnson (guitar). Lester died on 10/15/80 (age 50). Johnson died on 4/29/87 (age 63). Inducted into the Rock and Roll Hall of Fame in 2000.	
3/26/55	**20**	1	1. Sincerely Juke Box #20	Chess 1581
			#1 R&B hit (2 weeks)	
10/13/56	**25**	1	2. See Saw Best Seller #25 / Top 100 #28	Chess 1629
10/20/58	**22**	4	3. Ten Commandments Of Love Hot 100 #22 / Best Seller #39	Chess 1705
			HARVEY and The Moonglows	

DATE	POS	WKS	ARTIST–RECORD TITLE	LABEL & NO.
			MOORE, Bob, and His Orch.	
9/11/61	7	10	Born on 11/30/32 in Nashville, Tennessee. Top session bassist. 1. **Mexico** [I] #1 Adult Contemporary hit (1 week)	Monument 446
			MOORE, Bobby, & The Rhythm Aces	
7/30/66	27	4	R&B group from Montgomery, Alabama: Bobby Moore (tenor sax), Chico Jenkins (vocals), Larry Moore, Joe Frank, Clifford Laws, Marion Sledge and John Baldwin. 1. Searching For My Love	Checker 1129
			MOORE, Chanté	
5/22/99	10	11	Born on 2/17/67 in San Francisco, California. Female R&B singer. Married to actor Kadeem Hardison from 1996-2000. Married Kenny Lattimore on 1/1/2002. ● 1. **Chanté's Got A Man** Sales #6 / Airplay #25 samples "One Bad Apple" by The Osmonds	Silas/MCA 55544
			MOORE, Dorothy	
4/10/76	3	16	Born on 10/13/47 in Jackson, Mississippi. R&B singer. 1. **Misty Blue** #4 Country hit for Wilma Burgess in 1966	Malaco 1029
9/10/77	27	7	2. I Believe You written by The Addrisi Brothers	Malaco 1042
			MOORE, Jackie	
1/23/71	30	7	Born in 1946 in Jacksonville, Florida. Female R&B singer. ● 1. Precious, Precious	Atlantic 2681
			MOORE, Mandy	
7/29/00	24	4	Born Amanda Moore on 4/10/84 in Nashua, New Hampshire. Pop singer/actress. Starred in the movies *A Walk To Remember* and *Chasing Liberty*. 1. I Wanna Be With You Airplay #23 from the movie *Center Stage* starring Amanda Schull (soundtrack on Epic 63969)	album cut
			MOORER, Allison — see KID ROCK	
			MORALES, Michael	
6/10/89	15	10	Born on 4/25/63 in San Antonio, Texas. Pop singer/songwriter. 1. Who Do You Give Your Love To? Airplay #14 / Sales #16	Wing 887743
9/9/89	28	6	2. What I Like About You Airplay #21 / Sales #30	Wing 889678
			MORGAN, Debelah	
10/14/00+	8	17	Born in Detroit, Michigan. Female R&B singer. ● 1. **Dance With Me** Sales #3 / Airplay #20 melody is from "Hernando's Hideaway" by Archie Bleyer (#2 hit in 1954)	Atlantic 84783

DATE	POS	WKS	ARTIST–RECORD TITLE	LABEL & NO.
			MORGAN, Jane	
			Born Jane Currier in 1920 in Boston, Massachusetts; raised in Florida. Pop singer.	
9/9/57	7	21	● 1. **Fascination** Jockey #7 / Top 100 #11 / Best Seller #12 **JANE MORGAN and The Troubadors** from the movie *Love In The Afternoon* starring Gary Cooper and Audrey Hepburn	Kapp 191
10/13/58	21	10	2. The Day The Rains Came Hot 100 #21 Vic Schoen (orch.)	Kapp 235
8/31/59	39	1	3. With Open Arms Frank Hunter (orch.)	Kapp 284
			MORGAN, Jaye P.	
			Born Mary Margaret Morgan on 12/3/31 in Mancos, Colorado. Sang with Frank DeVol's band from 1950-53. Regular on TV's *The Gong Show*.	
11/27/54+	3	21	1. **That's All I Want From You** Jockey #3 / Best Seller #5 / Juke Box #5	RCA Victor 5896
3/12/55	12	8	2. Danger! Heartbreak Ahead / Jockey #12 / Juke Box #13 / Best Seller #18	
4/9/55		1	3. Softly, Softly Best Seller: flip	RCA Victor 6016
6/11/55	12	5	4. Chee Chee-oo Chee (Sang the Little Bird) / Jockey #12 / Juke Box #14 / Best Seller #24	
6/25/55	18	1	5. Two Lost Souls Jockey #18 / Best Seller: flip **PERRY COMO and JAYE P. MORGAN** (above 2) from the Broadway musical *Damn Yankees* starring Gwen Verdon; Mitchell Ayres (orch., above 2)	RCA Victor 6137
8/20/55	6	14	6. **The Longest Walk /** Jockey #6 / Juke Box #7 / Best Seller #13 / Top 100 #19	
10/8/55		1	7. Swanee Juke Box: flip #1 hit for Al Jolson in 1920	RCA Victor 6182
11/12/55+	14	8	8. Pepper-Hot Baby / Juke Box #14 / Top 100 #21 Joe Thomas (orch.)	
12/3/55	12	3	9. If You Don't Want My Love Juke Box #12 / Top 100 #40 Hugo Winterhalter (orch., all of above - except #4, 5 & 8)	RCA Victor 6282
			MORGAN, Russ, And His Orchestra	
			Born on 4/29/04 in Scranton, Pennsylvania. Died on 8/8/69 (age 65). Trombonist/orchestra leader.	
11/12/55	30	4	1. Dogface Soldier Top 100 #30 from the movie *To Hell And Back* starring Audie Murphy	Decca 29703
3/17/56	19	3	2. The Poor People Of Paris Juke Box #19 / Jockey #23 / Top 100 #26 **[I]**	Decca 29835
			MORISSETTE, Alanis	
			Born on 6/1/74 in Ottawa, Ontario, Canada. Adult Alternative rock singer/songwriter. At age 12, she acted on the Nickelodeon cable-TV kids series *You Can't Do That On Television*. Played God in the 1999 movie *Dogma*.	
7/1/95	13 A	24	1. You Oughta Know #1 Modern Rock hit (5 weeks); also see #5 below	album cut
9/16/95	15 A	22	2. Hand In My Pocket #1 Modern Rock hit (1 week); above 2 from the album *Jagged Little Pill* on Maverick/Sire 45901	album cut

DATE	POS	WKS	ARTIST–RECORD TITLE	LABEL & NO.
3/16/96	4	29	● 3. **Ironic** Airplay #2 / Sales #10 #1 Modern Rock hit (3 weeks)	Maverick/Sire 17698
7/27/96	6	29	4. **You Learn** / Airplay #1 (5) / Sales #30	
7/27/96		29	5. You Oughta Know Sales: flip **[L-R]** recorded on 2/28/96 at the Grammy Awards in Los Angeles	Maverick/Sire 17644
9/7/96	3 ᴬ	35	6. **Head Over Feet** from the album *Jagged Little Pill* on Maverick/Sire 45901	album cut

4/25/98	4 ᴬ	24	7. **Uninvited**
			       from the movie *City Of Angels* starring Nicolas Cage (soundtrack on
			       Warner Sunset 46867)
				album cut

10/10/98	2 (1)ᴬ	15	8. **Thank U** Hot 100 #17 (11 wks)
			       from the album *Supposed Former Infatuation Junkie* on Maverick
			       47094
				album cut

2/16/02	23	10	9. Hands Clean Airplay #24 from the album *Under Rug Swept* on Maverick 47988	album cut
			MORMON TABERNACLE CHOIR, The	

9/21/59	13	11	Popular 375-voice choir directed by Richard Condie (died on 12/22/85).
			   1. Battle Hymn Of The Republic
			       with the Philadelphia Orchestra, Eugene Ormandy, conductor;
			       written in 1862; #1 hit for The Columbia Stellar Quartet in 1918
				Columbia 41459

			MORODER, Giorgio	

3/10/79	33	4	Born on 4/26/40 in Ortisei, Italy. Electronic composer/conductor/producer.
			   1. Chase **[I]**
			       from the movie *Midnight Express* starring Brad Davis
				Casablanca 956

			MORRISON, Mark	
3/8/97	2 (1)	33	Born on 5/12/74 in Hanover, Germany; raised in Leicester, England. R&B singer. ▲ 1. **Return Of The Mack** Sales #5 / Airplay #5 samples "N.T." by Kool & The Gang	Atlantic 84868
			MORRISON, Van	
			Born George Ivan Morrison on 8/31/45 in Belfast, Ireland. "Blue-eyed soul"- rock singer/songwriter. Leader of Them. Inducted into the Rock and Roll Hall of Fame in 1993.	
8/19/67	10	10	1. **Brown Eyed Girl**	Bang 545
4/25/70	39	2	2. Come Running	Warner 7383
12/5/70+	9	9	3. **Domino**	Warner 7434
3/6/71	23	8	4. Blue Money	Warner 7462
11/20/71	28	4	5. Wild Night	Warner 7518
			MOSS-SCOTT, Brandy	
6/22/02	5 ˢ	26	Born in Los Angeles, California. Female R&B singer. 1. **I Don't Really Know**	Heavenly 2004
			MOTELS, The	
5/29/82	9	15	Pop-rock group formed in Los Angeles, California: Martha Davis (vocals), Guy Perry (guitar), Marty Jourard (keyboards), Michael Goodroe (bass) and Brian Glascock (drums). Scott Thurston (guitar) joined in 1983. 1. **Only The Lonely**	Capitol 5114

DATE	POS	WKS	ARTIST–RECORD TITLE	LABEL & NO.
9/17/83	9	13	2. **Suddenly Last Summer** #1 Mainstream Rock hit (2 weeks)	Capitol 5271
1/14/84	36	3	3. Remember The Nights	Capitol 5246
8/10/85	21	7	4. Shame Sales #22 / Airplay #22	Capitol 5497

MOTHERLODE

Pop-rock group from Canada: William Smith (vocals, keyboards), Ken Marco (guitar), Steve Kennedy (sax) and Wayne Stone (drums). Smith died of a heart attack on 12/1/97 (age 53).

DATE	POS	WKS	ARTIST–RECORD TITLE	LABEL & NO.
9/13/69	18	7	1. When I Die	Buddah 131

MO THUGS FAMILY — see BONE THUGS-N-HARMONY

MÖTLEY CRÜE

Hard-rock group from Los Angeles, California: Vince Neil (vocals; born Vince Wharton), Mick Mars (guitar; born Bob Deal), Nikki Sixx (bass; born Frank Ferranna) and Tommy Lee (drums; born Thomas Bass). Sixx married actress Donna D'Errico on 12/23/96. Lee was married to actress Heather Locklear from 1986-93; married to actress Pamela Anderson from 1995-98.

DATE	POS	WKS	ARTIST–RECORD TITLE	LABEL & NO.
8/3/85	16	9	1. Smokin' In The Boys Room Sales #15 / Airplay #15	Elektra 69625
6/13/87	12	9	2. Girls, Girls, Girls Sales #9 / Airplay #14	Elektra 69465
9/23/89	6	9	● 3. **Dr. Feelgood** Sales #5 / Airplay #12	Elektra 69271
1/6/90	27	6	4. Kickstart My Heart Sales #19 / Airplay #31	Elektra 69248
3/17/90	8	10	5. **Without You** Sales #6 / Airplay #9	Elektra 64985
6/30/90	19	7	6. Don't Go Away Mad (Just Go Away) Airplay #16 / Sales #18	Elektra 64962
1/4/92	37	3	7. Home Sweet Home '91 Sales #42 / Airplay #61 **[R]** remix of group's 1985 hit (#89)	Elektra 64818

MOTT THE HOOPLE

Glitter-rock group formed in England: Ian Hunter (vocals), Mick Ralphs (guitar), Pete Watts (bass) and Dale Griffin (drums). Group name taken from a Willard Manus novel. Ralphs later joined Bad Company.

DATE	POS	WKS	ARTIST–RECORD TITLE	LABEL & NO.
11/4/72	37	3	1. All The Young Dudes David Bowie (producer, rhythm guitar, backing vocal)	Columbia 45673

MOUNTAIN

Power-rock group formed in New York: Leslie West (vocals, bass), Felix Pappalardi (guitar), Steve Knight (keyboards) and Corky Laing (drums). Pappalardi was shot to death on 4/17/83 (age 44).

DATE	POS	WKS	ARTIST–RECORD TITLE	LABEL & NO.
6/13/70	21	9	1. Mississippi Queen	Windfall 532

MOUTH & MACNEAL

Pop vocal duo from the Netherlands: Willem "Mouth" Duyn and Maggie MacNeal (real name: Sjoukje Van't Spijker).

DATE	POS	WKS	ARTIST–RECORD TITLE	LABEL & NO.
6/17/72	8	12	● 1. **How Do You Do?**	Philips 40715

MOVING PICTURES

Pop group from Sydney, Australia: Alex Smith (vocals), Garry Frost (guitar), Andrew Thompson (sax), Charlie Cole (keyboards), Ian Lees (bass) and Paul Freeland (drums).

DATE	POS	WKS	ARTIST–RECORD TITLE	LABEL & NO.
11/27/82+	29	13	1. What About Me	Network 69952

DATE	POS	WKS	ARTIST–RECORD TITLE	LABEL & NO.
			MOYET, Alison	
			Born Genevieve Alison-Jane Moyet on 6/18/61 in Basildon, Essex, England. Female singer.	
5/4/85	31	6	1. Invisible Airplay #28	Columbia 04781
			MOZART, Mickey — see MAXWELL, Robert	
			M PEOPLE	
			Dance trio formed in England: Michael Pickering, Heather Small and Paul Heard.	
6/18/94	34	3	1. Moving On Up Airplay #30 / Sales #75	Epic 77392
			MRAZ, Jason	
			Born on 10/20/72 in Mechanicsville, Virginia. Singer/songwriter/guitarist.	
8/2/03	15	14	1. The Remedy (I Won't Worry) Airplay #15 from the album *Waiting For My Rocket To Come* on Elektra 62829	album cut
			M2M	
			Female pop vocal duo from Lorenskog, Norway: Marion Ravn and Marit Larsen.	
1/1/00	21	2	● 1. Don't Say You Love Me Sales #5 from the animated movie *Pokémon - The First Movie*	Atlantic 84551
			MULDAUR, Maria	
			Born Maria D'Amato on 9/12/43 in the Bronx, New York. Female jazz-styled singer.	
4/13/74	6	14	1. **Midnight At The Oasis**	Reprise 1183
1/25/75	12	8	2. I'm A Woman	Reprise 1319
			MULLEN, Larry — see U2	
			MULLINS, Shawn	
			Born on 3/8/68 in Atlanta, Georgia. Male Adult Alternative pop-rock singer/songwriter/guitarist.	
12/5/98+	7	16	1. **Lullaby** Airplay #1 (2) from the album *Soul's Core* on Columbia 69637	album cut
			MUMBA, Samantha	
			Born on 1/18/83 in Dublin, Ireland. R&B singer.	
10/7/00	4	18	1. **Gotta Tell You** Sales #1 (1) / Airplay #16	Wild Card 497408
			MUNGO JERRY	
			Skiffle group formed in England: Ray Dorset (vocals, guitar), Colin Earl (piano), Paul King (banjo) and Mike Cole (bass).	
7/25/70	3	11	● 1. **In The Summertime**	Janus 125
			MURDOCK, Shirley	
			Born in Toldeo, Ohio. Female R&B singer.	
2/28/87	23	7	1. As We Lay Sales #17 / Airplay #34	Elektra 69518

DATE	POS	WKS	ARTIST–RECORD TITLE	LABEL & NO.
			MURMAIDS, The	
			Teen "girl group" from Los Angeles, California: sisters Carol and Terry Fischer, with Sally Gordon.	
12/7/63+	3	11	1. **Popsicles And Icicles** *written by David Gates of Bread*	Chattahoochee 628
			MURPHEY, Michael	
			Born on 3/14/45 in Oak Cliff, Texas. Progressive-country singer/songwriter. Appeared in the movie *Hard Country*.	
10/7/72	37	2	1. Geronimo's Cadillac	A&M 1368
5/3/75	3	13	▲ 2. **Wildfire** *#1 Adult Contemporary hit (1 week)*	Epic 50084
9/13/75	21	7	3. Carolina In The Pines	Epic 50131
2/21/76	39	2	4. Renegade	Epic 50184
8/28/82	19	11	5. What's Forever For *#1 Country hit (1 week)*	Liberty 1466
			MURPHY, Eddie	
			Born on 4/3/61 in Brooklyn, New York. Comedian/actor. Former cast member of TV's *Saturday Night Live*. Starred in several movies. Married model Nicole Mitchell on 3/18/93.	
11/9/85	2 (3)	14	▲ 1. **Party All The Time** Sales #2 / Airplay #2 *written, produced and arranged by Rick James*	Columbia 05609
8/19/89	27	4	2. Put Your Mouth On Me Sales #23 / Airplay #40	Columbia 68897
			MURPHY, Walter	
			Born on 12/19/52 in Manhattan, New York. Studied classical and jazz piano at Manhattan School of Music. Former arranger for Doc Severinsen and *The Tonight Show* orchestra.	
7/4/76	1 (1)	22	● 1. **A Fifth Of Beethoven** [I] **WALTER MURPHY & THE BIG APPLE BAND** *based on Beethoven's Fifth Symphony*	Private Stock 45,073
			MURRAY, Anne	
			Born Morna Anne Murray on 6/20/45 in Springhill, Nova Scotia, Canada. Country-pop singer. Regular on Glen Campbell's *Goodtime Hour* TV series.	
8/22/70	8	11	● 1. **Snowbird** *#1 Adult Contemporary hit (6 weeks)*	Capitol 2738
2/10/73	7	13	2. **Danny's Song** *#1 Adult Contemporary hit (2 weeks); first recorded by Loggins & Messina in 1972*	Capitol 3481
1/19/74	12	10	3. Love Song *#1 Adult Contemporary hit (1 week); first recorded by Loggins & Messina earlier in 1973*	Capitol 3776
5/25/74	8	10	4. **You Won't See Me** *#1 Adult Contemporary hit (2 weeks); first recorded by The Beatles in 1965*	Capitol 3867
8/19/78	1 (1)	17	● 5. **You Needed Me**	Capitol 4574
2/10/79	12	12	6. I Just Fall In Love Again *#1 Country hit (3 weeks) / #1 Adult Contemporary hit (4 weeks)*	Capitol 4675
6/23/79	25	7	7. Shadows In The Moonlight *#1 Country hit (1 week) / #1 Adult Contemporary hit (3 weeks)*	Capitol 4716
10/20/79	12	11	8. Broken Hearted Me *#1 Country hit (1 week) / #1 Adult Contemporary hit (5 weeks)*	Capitol 4773

DATE	POS	WKS	ARTIST–RECORD TITLE	LABEL & NO.
1/19/80	**12**	11	9. Daydream Believer #1 Adult Contemporary hit (1 week)	Capitol 4813
10/18/80	**33**	4	10. Could I Have This Dance #1 Country hit (1 week); from the movie *Urban Cowboy* starring John Travolta and Debra Winger	Capitol 4920
5/2/81	**34**	4	11. Blessed Are The Believers #1 Country hit (1 week)	Capitol 4987
			MURRAY, Keith — see IMAJIN	
			MUSICAL YOUTH	
			Pop-reggae group from Birmingham, England: Dennis Seaton (vocals), with brothers Kelvin (guitar) and Michael (keyboards) Grant, and Patrick (bass) and Junior (drums) Waite. Patrick Waite died on 2/18/93 (age 24).	
1/15/83	**10**	10	1. **Pass The Dutchie**	MCA 52149
			MUSIC EXPLOSION, The	
			Rock and roll band from Mansfield, Ohio: James Lyons (vocals), Don Atkins and Richard Nesta (guitars), Burton Stahl (bass) and Bob Avery (drums).	
5/27/67	**2** (2)	13	● 1. **Little Bit O' Soul**	Laurie 3380
			MUSIC MACHINE, The	
			Rock group from Los Angeles, California: Sean Bonniwell (vocals, guitar), Mark Landon (guitar), Doug Rhodes (organ), Keith Olsen (bass) and Ron Edgar (drums). Olsen became a top record producer in the 1980s.	
12/10/66+	**15**	8	1. Talk Talk	Original Sound 61
			MUSIQ	
			Born Taalib Johnson on 9/16/77 in Philadelphia, Pennsylvania. Male R&B singer/songwriter. Also recorded as Musiq Soulchild.	
12/16/00	**31**	5	1. Just Friends (Sunny) Airplay #27 samples "Sunny" by Bobby Hebb; from the movie *Nutty Professor II: The Klumps* starring Eddie Murphy and Janet Jackson	Def Jam 562902
3/24/01	**24**	13	2. Love Airplay #18 **MUSIQ Soulchild** from the album *AIJUSWANASEING (I Just Want To Sing)* on Def Soul 548289	album cut
5/4/02	**16**	18	3. halfcrazy Airplay #14 / Sales #70 samples "Live For Life" by Francis Lai	Def Soul 588989
10/12/02	**17**	16	4. dontchange Airplay #13	Def Soul 063790
			MYA	
			Born Mya Harrison on 10/10/79 in Washington DC. Female R&B singer/songwriter/dancer.	
4/11/98	**6**	14	● 1. **It's All About Me** Sales #5 / Airplay #50 **MYA With Special Guest SISQO** samples "Moments In Love" by The Art Of Noise	University 97024
6/27/98	**15**	16	2. Ghetto Supastar (That Is What You Are) Airplay #11 **PRAS MICHEL featuring OL' DIRTY BASTARD & introducing MYA** samples "Get Up, Get Into It, Get Involved" by James Brown and contains an interpolation of "Islands In The Stream"; from the movie *Bulworth* starring Warren Beatty	Interscope 95021
9/12/98	**34**	10	3. Movin' On Airplay #38 **MYA featuring Silkk the Shocker**	University 95032

DATE	POS	WKS	ARTIST–RECORD TITLE	LABEL & NO.
12/12/98+	**14**	11	4. Take Me There Airplay #8 **BLACKSTREET & MYA featuring MA$E & BLINKY BLINK** samples "I Want You Back" by The Jackson 5; from the animated movie *The RugRats Movie* (soundtrack on Interscope 90181)	album cut
4/17/99	**28**	2	5. My First Night With You Sales #14	University 97049
9/23/00	**2** (3)	25	6. **Case Of The Ex (Whatcha Gonna Do)** Sales #1 (3) / Airplay #5	University 97457
4/21/01	**1** (5)	17	7. **Lady Marmalade** Airplay #1 (6) **CHRISTINA AGUILERA, LIL' KIM, MYA and PINK** co-produced by Missy "Misdemeanor" Elliott; from the movie *Moulin Rouge* starring Nicole Kidman and Ewan McGregor	Interscope 497066
8/9/03	**13**	13	8. My Love Is Like...WO Sales #5 / Airplay #14	A&M 000768

MYERS, Billie

Born on 6/14/70 in Coventry, England. Adult Alternative pop-rock singer.

DATE	POS	WKS	ARTIST–RECORD TITLE	LABEL & NO.
1/17/98	**15**	18	1. Kiss The Rain Airplay #12 / Sales #29 produced by Desmond Child	Universal 56140

MYLES, Alannah

Born on 12/25/55 in Toronto, Ontario, Canada; raised in Buckhorn, Ontario, Canada. Female pop-rock singer.

DATE	POS	WKS	ARTIST–RECORD TITLE	LABEL & NO.
2/3/90	**1** (2)	15	● 1. **Black Velvet** Sales #1 (3) / Airplay #2 #1 Mainstream Rock hit (2 weeks)	Atlantic 88742
6/16/90	**36**	4	2. Love Is Airplay #28	Atlantic 87945

MYLES, Billy

Born in Harlem, New York. R&B singer/songwriter.

DATE	POS	WKS	ARTIST–RECORD TITLE	LABEL & NO.
11/25/57	**25**	6	1. The Joker (That's What They Call Me) Best Seller #25 / Top 100 #30	Ember 1026

MYSTICS, The

White doo-wop group from Brooklyn, New York: Phil Cracolici, Bob Ferrante, George Galfo, Albee Cracolici and Allie Contrera.

DATE	POS	WKS	ARTIST–RECORD TITLE	LABEL & NO.
6/15/59	**20**	9	1. Hushabye	Laurie 3028

MYSTIKAL

Born Michael Tyler on 9/22/75 in New Orleans, Louisiana. Male rapper/ songwriter.

DATE	POS	WKS	ARTIST–RECORD TITLE	LABEL & NO.
2/7/98	**16**	25	▲ 1. Make Em' Say Uhh! Sales #9 **MASTER P Featuring Fiend, Silkk The Shocker, Mia X and Mystikal**	No Limit 53302
3/6/99	**18**	8	2. It Ain't My Fault 2 Sales #8 **SILKK THE SHOCKER And Mystikal**	No Limit 53470
9/9/00	**13**	14	3. Shake Ya Ass Airplay #6 / Sales #60	Jive 42721
12/30/00+	**14**	15	4. Danger (Been So Long) Airplay #11 / Sales #50 **MYSTIKAL Featuring Nivea** #1 R&B hit (1 week)	Jive 42860
1/20/01	**1** (4)	23	● 5. **Stutter** Sales #1 (5) / Airplay #5 **JOE (featuring Mystikal)** #1 R&B hit (5 weeks); samples "Passin' Me By" by The Pharcyde; from the movie *Double Take* starring Eddie Griffin	Jive 42870
1/5/02	**37**	4	6. Bouncin' Back (Bumpin' Me Against The Wall) Airplay #35 / Sales #42	Jive 42992

DATE	POS	WKS	ARTIST–RECORD TITLE	LABEL & NO.
8/3/02	**10**	15	7. **Move B***h** Airplay #9 / Sales #20 **LUDACRIS feat. Mystikal and Infamous 2.0**	Def Jam 063949

N

NAKED EYES

			Synth-pop duo from England: Pete Byrne (vocals) and Rob Fisher (keyboards, synthesizer). Fisher later formed Climie Fisher. Fisher died on 8/25/99 (age 39).	
4/23/83	**8**	13	1. **Always Something There To Remind Me**	EMI America 8155
8/13/83	**11**	12	2. Promises, Promises	EMI America 8170
12/17/83	**37**	3	3. When The Lights Go Out	EMI America 8183
9/29/84	**39**	2	4. (What) In The Name Of Love	EMI America 8219

NAPOLEON XIV

			Born Jerry Samuels in 1938 in Brooklyn, New York. Novelty singer/songwriter.	
7/30/66	**3**	5	1. **They're Coming To Take Me Away, Ha-Haaa!** [N]	Warner 5831

NAPPY ROOTS

			Rap group formed in Bowling Green, Kentucky: Brian "B. Stille" Scott, Melvin "Scales" Adams, William "Skinny DeVille" Hughes, Vito "Big V" Tisdale, Ken "R. Prophet" Anthony and Ron "Clutch" Wilson.	
9/28/02	**21**	11	1. Po' Folks Airplay #20 **NAPPY ROOTS Featuring Anthony Hamilton**	Atlantic 85323

NAS

			Born Nasir Jones on 9/14/73 in Long Island, New York. Male rapper.	
11/9/96+	**22**	11	● 1. Street Dreams Sales #15 contains an interpolation of "Sweet Dreams" by Eurythmics; samples "Never Gonna Stop" by Linda Clifford	Columbia 78409
3/15/97	**35**	5	2. Head Over Heels Sales #32 / Airplay #61 **ALLURE featuring Nas** samples "The Bridge" by MC Shan; co-produced by Mariah Carey	Crave 78522
6/12/99	**27**	6	3. Did You Ever Think Sales #16 / Airplay #40 **R. KELLY (featuring Nas)**	Jive 42604
11/27/99+	**5**	21	▲ 4. Hot Boyz Sales #2 / Airplay #24 **MISSY "MISDEMEANOR" ELLIOTT [featuring NAS, EVE & Q-TIP]** #1 R&B hit (6 weeks); Lil' Mo (vocal ad libs)	The Gold Mind 64029
3/31/01	**26**	9	5. Oochie Wally Sales #13 / Airplay #19 **QB FINEST Featuring NAS And Bravehearts** Shelene Thomas (female vocal)	Columbia 79586
5/11/02	**10**	20	6. **I'm Gonna Be Alright** Sales #7 / Airplay #10 **JENNIFER LOPEZ Featuring Nas** samples "Why You Treat Me So Bad" by Club Nouveau	Epic 79759
12/28/02+	**32**	6	7. Made You Look Airplay #31 / Sales #69 from the album *God's Son* on Columbia 86930	album cut
3/8/03	**12**	13	8. I Can Airplay #11 / Sales #31 backing vocals by a children's chorus; melody is Beethoven's "Für Elise"	Columbia 79941

DATE	POS	WKS	ARTIST–RECORD TITLE	LABEL & NO.
			NASH, Graham	
			Born on 2/2/42 in Blackpool, Lancashire, England. Pop-rock singer/ songwriter/guitarist. Former member of The Hollies. Formed Crosby, Stills & Nash in 1968.	
7/10/71	35	4	1. Chicago	Atlantic 2804
6/10/72	36	4	2. Immigration Man **GRAHAM NASH & DAVID CROSBY**	Atlantic 2873
			NASH, Johnny	
			Born on 8/19/40 in Houston, Texas. Singer/guitarist/actor. Appeared on local TV from age 13. With Arthur Godfrey's TV and radio shows from 1956-63. In the movie *Take A Giant Step* in 1959. Own JoDa label in 1965.	
2/3/58	23	1	1. A Very Special Love Jockey #23 / Best Seller #45 / Top 100 #46	ABC-Paramount 9874
12/15/58+	29	5	2. The Teen Commandments [S] **PAUL ANKA-GEO. HAMILTON IV-JOHNNY NASH** Bill Givens (narrative); inspirational talk from the three ABC-Paramount artists	ABC-Paramount 9974
10/5/68	5	12	3. **Hold Me Tight**	JAD 207
1/24/70	39	1	4. Cupid	JAD 220
10/7/72	● 1 (4)	14	5. **I Can See Clearly Now** #1 Adult Contemporary hit (4 weeks); Bob Marley's Wailers (backing band)	Epic 10902
3/3/73	12	10	6. Stir It Up written by Bob Marley	Epic 10949
			NASHVILLE TEENS, The	
			Rock group from Weybridge, Surrey, England: Arthur Sharp (vocals), John Allen (guitar), Ray Phillips (harmonica), John Hawkes (keyboards), Pete Shannon (bass) and Barry Jenkins (drums). Jenkins joined the Animals in 1966.	
10/10/64	14	6	1. Tobacco Road	London 9689
			NATE DOGG	
			Born Nathan Hale in 1969 in Los Angeles, California. Male rapper. Former partner of Warren G. Cousin of Snoop Doggy Dogg.	
5/7/94	▲ 2 (3)	18	1. **Regulate** Sales #1 (2) / Airplay #15 **WARREN G. & NATE DOGG** samples "I Keep Forgettin'" by Michael McDonald; from the movie *Above The Rim* starring 2Pac and Duane Martin	Death Row 98280
11/23/96	33	7	2. Never Leave Me Alone Sales #23 **NATE DOGG featuring Snoop Doggy Dogg** Val Young (female vocal); samples "Where Is The Love" by Roberta Flack & Donny Hathaway	Death Row 97012
7/18/98	18	9	3. Nobody Does It Better Sales #10 **NATE DOGG featuring WARREN G** samples "Let's Get Closer" by Atlantic Starr	Breakaway 4000
8/18/01	24	6	4. Area Codes Airplay #21 / Sales #55 **LUDACRIS (Feat. Nate Dogg)** samples "Do It ('Til You're Satisfied)" by B.T. Express; from the movie *Rush Hour 2* starring Jackie Chan	Def Jam 588671
9/15/01	25	10	5. Can't Deny It Airplay #24 **FABOLOUS featuring Nate Dogg** Lil' Mo (background vocal); samples "Ambitionz Az A Ridah" by 2Pac	Desert Storm 67231

DATE	POS	WKS	ARTIST–RECORD TITLE	LABEL & NO.
4/5/03	**1** (4)	20	6. **21 Questions** Airplay #1 (5) / Sales #13 **50 CENT Feat. Nate Dogg** #1 R&B hit (7 weeks); samples "It's Only Love Doing Its Thing" by Barry White	Shady 080739
			NATURAL FOUR	
2/9/74	**31**	4	R&B vocal group from San Francisco, California: Chris James, Darryl Canady, Steve Striplin and Delmos Whitley. 1. Can This Be Real	Curtom 1990
			NATURAL SELECTION	
8/24/91	**2** (2)	19	Funk duo from Minneapolis, Minnesota: Elliott Erickson (keyboards) and Frederick Thomas (vocals). 1. **Do Anything** Airplay #3 / Sales #5 **NATURAL SELECTION featuring Niki Haris**	EastWest 98724
1/25/92	**28**	4	2. Hearts Don't Think (They Feel)! Airplay #32	EastWest 98652
			NAUGHTON, David	
5/12/79	**5**	16	Born on 2/13/52 in Hartford, Connecticut. Singer/dancer/actor. Starred in the 1981 movie *An American Werewolf In London* and TV shows *Makin' It* and *My Sister Sam*. ● 1. **Makin' It** from the movie *Meatballs* starring Bill Murray	RSO 916
			NAUGHTY BY NATURE	
9/28/91	**6**	18	Black hip-hop trio from East Orange, New Jersey: Anthony "Treach" Criss, Vincent Brown and Kier Gist. Appeared in the movies *The Meteor Man* and *Who's The Man*. Treach was married to Sandra "Pepa" Denton (of Salt-N- Pepa) from 1999-2001. ▲² 1. **O.P.P.** Sales #1 (1) / Airplay #24 O.P.P.: Other People's Property; samples "ABC" by The Jackson 5	Tommy Boy 988
2/6/93	**8**	20	▲ 2. **Hip Hop Hooray** Sales #2 / Airplay #11 #1 R&B hit (1 week)	Tommy Boy 554
6/24/95	**17**	11	● 3. Feel Me Flow Sales #8 / Airplay #40 samples "Find Yourself" by The Meters	Tommy Boy 7682
7/17/99	**10**	10	● 4. Jamboree Sales #4 / Airplay #58 **NAUGHTY BY NATURE (Feat. Zhané)** samples "I'm Always Dancin' To The Music" by Benny Golson	Arista 13712
			NAZARETH	
1/3/76	**8**	14	Hard-rock group formed in Dunfermline, Fife, Scotland: Dan McCafferty (vocals), Manny Charlton (guitar), Pete Agnew (bass) and Darrell Sweet (drums). Sweet died of a heart attack on 4/30/99 (age 51). ● 1. **Love Hurts** first recorded by The Everly Brothers in 1960	A&M 1671
			NDEGÉOCELLO, Me'Shell — see **MELLENCAMP, John**	
			NEELY, Sam	
10/7/72	**29**	6	Born on 8/22/48 in Cuero, Texas. Pop-country singer/songwriter/guitarist. 1. Loving You Just Crossed My Mind	Capitol 3381
11/9/74	**34**	2	2. You Can Have Her	A&M 1612

DATE	POS	WKS	ARTIST–RECORD TITLE	LABEL & NO.
			NEIGHBORHOOD, The	
			Seven-man, two-woman pop vocal group.	
8/8/70	29	4	1. Big Yellow Taxi	Big Tree 102
			NELLY	
			Born Cornell Haynes on 11/2/74 in Travis, Texas; raised in St. Louis, Missouri. Male rapper. Member of St. Lunatics.	
6/3/00	7	28	1. **(Hot S**t) Country Grammar** Sales #2 / Airplay #3	Fo' Reel 156800
10/28/00+	15	17	2. E.I. Airplay #10	album cut
3/17/01	3	26	3. **Ride Wit Me** Airplay #3	album cut
			NELLY (Featuring City Spud)	
			samples "I Like It" by DeBarge; above 2 from the album *Country Grammar* on Fo' Reel 157743	
6/23/01	3	25	4. **Where The Party At** Sales #1 (3) / Airplay #4	So So Def 79626
			JAGGED EDGE featuring Nelly	
			#1 R&B hit (3 weeks)	
11/17/01	22	12	5. #1 Airplay #20	album cut
			from the movie *Training Day* starring Denzel Washington (soundtrack on Priority 50213)	
2/23/02	5	17	6. **Girlfriend** Sales #1 (14) / Airplay #9	Jive 40013
			*NSYNC featuring Nelly	
5/11/02	1 (7)	25	7. **Hot In Herre** Airplay #1 (7) / Sales #5	Fo' Reel 019279
			#1 R&B hit (6 weeks); samples "Bustin' Loose" by Chuck Brown & The Soul Searchers	
7/20/02	1 (10)	27	8. **Dilemma /** Airplay #1 (12) / Sales #17	
			NELLY Featuring Kelly Rowland	
			#1 R&B hit (9 weeks); samples "Love, Need And Want You" by Patti LaBelle	
11/16/02+	3	18	9. **Air Force Ones** Airplay #3 / Sales: flip	Fo' Reel 019509
			NELLY Featuring Kyjuan, Ali and Murphy Lee	
7/12/03	1 (4)	27	10. **Shake Ya Tailfeather** Airplay #1 (4)	album cut
			NELLY/P. DIDDY/MURPHY LEE	
			from the movie *Bad Boys II* starring Will Smith and Martin Lawrence (soundtrack on Bad Boy 000716)	
			NELSON	
			Pop-rock duo from Los Angeles, California: Gunnar (vocals, bass) and Matthew (vocals, guitar) Nelson. The identical twin sons (born on 9/20/67) of Ricky Nelson.	
8/11/90	1 (1)	14	● 1. **(Can't Live Without Your) Love And Affection** Sales #1 (1) / Airplay #4	DGC 19689
12/1/90+	6	14	2. **After The Rain** Sales #4 / Airplay #6	DGC 19667
4/6/91	14	9	3. **More Than Ever** Airplay #12 / Sales #14	DGC 19002
7/27/91	28	5	4. **Only Time Will Tell** Airplay #42 / Sales #51	DGC 19014
			NELSON, Marc	
			Born in Philadelphia, Pennsylvania. R&B singer/songwriter.	
12/4/99	27	3	1. 15 Minutes Sales #10	Columbia 79220

DATE	POS	WKS	ARTIST–RECORD TITLE	LABEL & NO.
			NELSON, Ricky	
			Born Eric Hilliard Nelson on 5/8/40 in Teaneck, New Jersey. Died in a plane crash on 12/31/85 (age 45) in DeKalb, Texas. Son of bandleader Ozzie Nelson and vocalist Harriet Hilliard. Rick and brother David appeared on Nelson's radio show from March 1949, later on TV, 1952-66. Formed own Stone Canyon Band in 1969. In movies *Rio Bravo*, *The Wackiest Ship In The Army* and *Love And Kisses*. Married to Kristin Harmon (sister of actor Mark Harmon) from 1963-82. Their daughter Tracy is a movie/TV actress. Their twin sons began recording as Nelson in 1990. Ricky was one of the first teen idols of the rock era. Inducted into the Rock and Roll Hall of Fame in 1987.	
5/13/57	2 (1)	15	● 1. **A Teenager's Romance** / Best Seller #2 / Top 100 #8 / Jockey #8 / Juke Box #12	
5/6/57	4	15	2. **I'm Walking** Best Seller #4 / Juke Box #16 / Top 100 #17	Verve 10047
9/16/57	14	7	3. You're My One And Only Love / Best Seller #14 / Top 100 #16 Gloria Wood (female vocal)	
9/16/57		5	4. Honey Rock Best Seller: flip **[I]** Barney Kessel (orch., all of above)	Verve 10070
10/7/57	3	18	● 5. **Be-Bop Baby** / Best Seller #3 / Top 100 #5 / Jockey #10	
10/28/57	29	3	6. Have I Told You Lately That I Love You? Top 100 #29 / Best Seller: flip #24 hit for Bing Crosby & The Andrews Sisters in 1950	Imperial 5463
12/30/57+	2 (3)	14	● 7. **Stood Up** / Best Seller #2 / Top 100 #5 / Jockey #5	
12/30/57+	18	9	8. Waitin' In School Top 100 #18 / Jockey #24 / Best Seller: flip	Imperial 5483
4/7/58	4	10	● 9. **Believe What You Say** / Best Seller #4 / Top 100 #8 / Jockey #20	
4/7/58	12	10	10. My Bucket's Got A Hole In It Best Seller #12 / Top 100 #18 / Jockey #25 #2 Country hit for Hank Williams in 1949	Imperial 5503
7/7/58	1 (2)	15	● 11. **Poor Little Fool** Best Seller #1 (2) / Hot 100 #1 (2) / Jockey #2	Imperial 5528
10/20/58	7	16	● 12. **Lonesome Town** /	
10/20/58	10	13	13. **I Got A Feeling** Hot 100 #10	Imperial 5545
3/9/59	6	12	● 14. **Never Be Anyone Else But You** /	
3/16/59	9	10	15. **It's Late**	Imperial 5565
7/13/59	9	9	16. **Just A Little Too Much** /	
7/13/59	9	8	17. **Sweeter Than You**	Imperial 5595
12/7/59	20	8	18. I Wanna Be Loved /	
12/21/59	38	1	19. Mighty Good	Imperial 5614
5/9/60	12	9	20. Young Emotions	Imperial 5663
9/19/60	27	4	21. I'm Not Afraid /	
9/26/60	34	2	22. Yes Sir, That's My Baby #1 hit for Gene Austin in 1925	Imperial 5685
1/9/61	25	4	23. You Are The Only One	Imperial 5707
5/1/61	1 (2)	15	● 24. **Travelin' Man** /	
5/8/61	9	13	25. **Hello Mary Lou**	Imperial 5741
			RICK NELSON:	
10/9/61	11	9	26. A Wonder Like You /	
10/9/61	16	8	27. Everlovin'	Imperial 5770
3/17/62	5	10	28. **Young World**	Imperial 5805
8/25/62	5	9	29. **Teen Age Idol**	Imperial 5864
12/29/62+	6	9	30. **It's Up To You**	Imperial 5901
6/15/63	25	5	31. String Along	Decca 31495
10/5/63	12	9	32. Fools Rush In #3 hit for Glenn Miller in 1940	Decca 31533

DATE	POS	WKS	ARTIST–RECORD TITLE	LABEL & NO.
1/11/64	6	9	33. **For You** *#1 Adult Contemporary hit (2 weeks); first recorded by Glen Gray in 1933*	Decca 31574
5/9/64	26	5	34. The Very Thought Of You	Decca 31612
			RICK NELSON & THE STONE CANYON BAND:	
1/3/70	33	6	35. She Belongs To Me	Decca 32550
9/16/72	6	12	● 36. **Garden Party** *#1 Adult Contemporary hit (2 weeks); inspired by Nelson's experience during a Madison Square Garden concert*	Decca 32980
			NELSON, Sandy	
			Born Sander Nelson on 12/1/38 in Santa Monica, California. Male session drummer.	
9/14/59	4	12	1. **Teen Beat** [I]	Original Sound 5
11/20/61	7	12	2. **Let There Be Drums** [I]	Imperial 5775
3/3/62	29	4	3. Drums Are My Beat [I]	Imperial 5809
			NELSON, Willie	
			Born on 4/30/33 in Abbott, Texas. Legendary country singer/songwriter. Played bass for Ray Price. Moved to Nashville in 1960. Moved back to Texas in 1970. Pioneered the "outlaw" country movement. Appeared in several movies including *The Electric Horseman* (1979), *Honeysuckle Rose* (1980) and *Barbarosa* (1982). Won Grammy's Lifetime Achievement Award in 2000.	
10/11/75	21	9	1. Blue Eyes Crying In The Rain *#1 Country hit (2 weeks); written in 1945 by Fred Rose*	Columbia 10176
3/6/76	25	5	2. Good Hearted Woman [L] *#1 Country hit (3 weeks)*	RCA Victor 10529
9/27/80	20	10	3. On The Road Again *#1 Country hit (1 week); from the movie* Honeysuckle Rose *starring Nelson and Dyan Cannon*	Columbia 11351
4/10/82	5	15	▲ 4. **Always On My Mind** *#1 Country hit (2 weeks); #45 Country hit for Brenda Lee in 1972*	Columbia 02741
9/18/82	40	3	5. Let It Be Me	Columbia 03073
3/31/84	5	12	▲ 6. **To All The Girls I've Loved Before** **JULIO IGLESIAS & WILLIE NELSON** *#1 Country hit (2 weeks)*	Columbia 04217
5/31/03	22	12	7. Beer For My Horses *Airplay #18* **TOBY KEITH with Willie Nelson** *#1 Country hit (6 weeks); from Keith's album* Unleashed *on DreamWorks 450254*	album cut
			NENA	
			Rock group formed in Berlin, Germany: Gabriele "Nena" Kerner (vocals), Carlo Karges (guitar), Uwe Fahrenkrog-Petersen (keyboards), Jurgen Demel (bass) and Rolf Brendel (drums). Karges died of liver failure on 1/30/2002 (age 50).	
1/21/84	2 (1)	13	● 1. **99 Luftballons** [F]	Epic 04108
			NEON PHILHARMONIC, The	
			Chamber-sized orchestra of Nashville Symphony Orchestra musicians. Project headed by Tupper Saussy (composer) and Don Gant (vocals). Gant died on 3/6/87 (age 44).	
5/10/69	17	7	1. Morning Girl	Warner 7261

DATE	POS	WKS	ARTIST—RECORD TITLE	LABEL & NO.
			NERO, Peter	
			Born Bernard Nierow on 5/22/34 in Brooklyn, New York. Pop-jazz-classical pianist. Won the 1961 Best New Artist Grammy Award.	
11/20/71	21	8	1. Theme From "Summer Of '42" **[I]** title song from the movie starring Jennifer O'Neill	Columbia 45399
			NERVOUS NORVUS	
			Born James Drake on 5/13/12 in Nashville, Tennessee. Died of liver failure on 7/24/68 (age 56). Novelty singer/songwriter.	
6/9/56	8	9	1. **Transfusion** Best Seller #8 / Top 100 #13 / Jockey #14 / Juke Box #18 **[N]**	Dot 15470
8/11/56	24	4	2. Ape Call Best Seller #24 / Top 100 #28 **[N]** Red Blanchard (ape calls)	Dot 15485
			NESMITH, Michael, & The First National Band	
			Born on 12/30/42 in Houston, Texas. Pop-rock singer/songwriter/guitarist. Member of The Monkees.	
9/5/70	21	7	1. Joanne	RCA Victor 0368
			NEVIL, Robbie	
			Born on 10/2/60 in Los Angeles, California. Pop singer/songwriter/guitarist.	
11/15/86+	2 (2)	16	1. **C'est La Vie** Sales #1 (1) / Airplay #3 title is French for "That's Life"	Manhattan 50047
3/14/87	14	9	2. Dominoes Airplay #13 / Sales #14	Manhattan 50053
6/27/87	10	9	3. **Wot's It To Ya** Sales #8 / Airplay #16	Manhattan 50075
1/7/89	34	3	4. Back On Holiday Sales #31 / Airplay #32	EMI-Manhattan 50152
8/3/91	25	6	5. Just Like You Airplay #43	EMI 50356
			NEVILLE, Aaron	
			Born on 1/24/41 in New Orleans, Louisiana. R&B singer. Brother of Art Neville (of The Meters). Father of Ivan Neville.	
12/17/66+	2 (1)	11	1. **Tell It Like It Is** #1 R&B hit (5 weeks)	Par-Lo 101
10/28/89	2 (2)	16	● 2. **Don't Know Much** Sales #1 (2) / Airplay #4 #1 Adult Contemporary hit (5 weeks)	Elektra 69261
2/24/90	11	9	3. All My Life Sales #10 / Airplay #14 **LINDA RONSTADT (featuring Aaron Neville) (above 2)** #1 Adult Contemporary hit (3 weeks)	Elektra 64987
8/24/91	8	12	4. **Everybody Plays The Fool** Airplay #19 / Sales #47 #1 Adult Contemporary hit (1 week)	A&M 1563
			NEVILLE, Ivan	
			Born on 7/23/65 in New Orleans, Louisiana. Rock singer/bassist. Son of Aaron Neville.	
11/12/88	26	6	1. Not Just Another Girl Sales #27 / Airplay #28	Polydor 887814
			NEWBEATS, The	
			Pop vocal trio: Larry Henley (from Arp, Texas), with brothers Dean and Marc Mathis (from Hahira, Georgia).	
8/22/64	2 (2)	11	1. **Bread And Butter**	Hickory 1269
11/7/64	16	7	2. Everything's Alright	Hickory 1282

DATE	POS	WKS	ARTIST–RECORD TITLE	LABEL & NO.
2/20/65	40	1	3. Break Away (From That Boy)	Hickory 1290
10/30/65	12	9	4. Run, Baby Run (Back Into My Arms)	Hickory 1332
			NEW BIRTH, The	
			R&B group from Louisville, Kentucky. Consisted of 17 members with two vocal groups (The New Birth and Love, Peace & Happiness) and band (The Nite-Liters). Band consisted of Tony Churchill, Austin Lander, James Baker, Robert Jackson, Leroy Taylor and Robin Russell. Vocal groups consisted of Ann Bogan, Melvin Wilson, Leslie Wilson, Bobby Downs, Londee Loren and Alan Frye. Bogan was a former member of The Marvelettes.	
9/11/71	39	1	1. K-Jee [I] **THE NITE-LITERS**	RCA Victor 0461
5/5/73	35	4	2. I Can Understand It	RCA Victor 0912
8/23/75	36	2	3. Dream Merchant #1 R&B hit (1 week)	Buddah 470
			NEWBURY, Mickey	
			Born Milton Newbury on 5/19/40 in Houston, Texas. Died on 9/28/2002 (age 62). Pop-country singer/songwriter/guitarist.	
12/4/71+	26	7	1. An American Trilogy Dixie/Battle Hymn Of The Republic/All My Trials	Elektra 45750
			NEW CHRISTY MINSTRELS, The	
			Folk group named after the Christy Minstrels (formed in 1842 by Edwin "Pop" Christy). Group founded and led by Randy Sparks, and featured Barry McGuire (1963), Kenny Rogers (1966) and Kim Carnes (1968).	
7/27/63	14	7	1. Green, Green Barry McGuire (lead vocal)	Columbia 42805
11/16/63	29	3	2. Saturday Night	Columbia 42887
5/16/64	17	9	3. Today from the movie Advance To The Rear starring Glenn Ford	Columbia 43000
			NEW COLONY SIX, The	
			Soft-rock group from Chicago, Illinois: Ray Graffia (vocals), Gerald Van Kollenburg (guitar), Patrick McBride (harmonica), Ronnie Rice (organ), Les Kummel (bass) and Chic James (drums). Kummel died in a car crash on 12/18/78 (age 33).	
5/11/68	22	6	1. I Will Always Think About You	Mercury 72775
2/15/69	16	9	2. Things I'd Like To Say	Mercury 72858
			NEW EDITION	
			R&B vocal group from Boston, Massachusetts: Ralph Tresvant, Ronnie DeVoe, Michael Bivins, Ricky Bell and Bobby Brown. Johnny Gill replaced Brown in 1986. Bell, Bivins and DeVoe recorded as Bell Biv DeVoe in 1990. All six members reunited in 1996.	
10/27/84+	4	14	● 1. **Cool It Now** Sales #1 (1) / Airplay #9 #1 R&B hit (1 week)	MCA 52455
1/26/85	12	8	2. Mr. Telephone Man Sales #7 / Airplay #13 #1 R&B hit (3 weeks); written and produced by Ray Parker, Jr.	MCA 52484
4/27/85	35	4	3. Lost In Love Sales #26	MCA 52553
4/12/86	38	2	4. A Little Bit Of Love (Is All It Takes) Sales #26	MCA 52768
9/20/86	21	6	5. Earth Angel Sales #18 / Airplay #32 featured in the movie The Karate Kid Part II starring Ralph Macchio	MCA 52905
7/30/88	7	13	6. **If It Isn't Love** Sales #5 / Airplay #8	MCA 53264

DATE	POS	WKS	ARTIST–RECORD TITLE		LABEL & NO.
8/31/96	3	8	● 7. **Hit Me Off**	Sales #2 / Airplay #44	MCA 55210
			#1 R&B hit (3 weeks); samples "I Got Cha Opin" by Black Moon and "Storm King" by Bob James		
11/9/96+	7	19	● 8. **I'm Still In Love With You**	Sales #7 / Airplay #17	MCA 55264

NEW ENGLAND

Rock group formed in New York: John Fannon (vocals, guitar), Jimmy Waldo (keyboards), Gary Shea (bass) and Hirsh Gardner (drums).

DATE	POS	WKS	ARTIST–RECORD TITLE		LABEL & NO.
6/16/79	40	1	1. Don't Ever Wanna Lose Ya		Infinity 50,013

NEW KIDS ON THE BLOCK

Pop vocal group from Boston, Massachusetts: Joey McIntyre (see #11 below), Donnie Wahlberg, Danny Wood and brothers Jon and Jordan Knight (see #12 below). Wahlberg is the brother of Marky Mark (actor Mark Wahlberg). Shortened group name to NKOTB (see #10 below) in 1992. McIntyre played teacher "Colin Flynn" on TV's *Boston Public*.

DATE	POS	WKS	ARTIST–RECORD TITLE		LABEL & NO.
8/13/88	10	12	1. **Please Don't Go Girl**	Sales #9 / Airplay #13	Columbia 07700
1/14/89	3	13	● 2. **You Got It (The Right Stuff)**	Sales #2 / Airplay #5	Columbia 08092
4/22/89	1 (1)	14	● 3. **I'll Be Loving You (Forever)**	Airplay #1 (2) / Sales #1 (1)	Columbia 68671
7/22/89	1 (1)	12	▲ 4. **Hangin' Tough /**	Sales #1 (1) / Airplay #3	Columbia 68960
9/30/89	8	10	5. **Didn't I (Blow Your Mind)**	Sales #8 / Airplay #8	
9/23/89	2 (1)	10	● 6. **Cover Girl**	Sales #2 / Airplay #3	Columbia 69088
11/25/89	7	10	● 7. **This One's For The Children**	Sales #6 / Airplay #12 **[X]**	Columbia 73064
5/26/90	1 (3)	11	▲ 8. **Step By Step**	Sales #1 (3) / Airplay #1 (1)	Columbia 73343
8/4/90	7	8	9. **Tonight**	Sales #6 / Airplay #8	Columbia 73461
3/7/92	16	6	10. If You Go Away	Sales #8 / Airplay #22	Columbia 74255
			NKOTB		
2/27/99	10	11	● 11. **Stay The Same**	Sales #8 / Airplay #62	C2/Columbia 79103
			JOEY McINTYRE		
4/17/99	10	13	● 12. **Give It To You**	Sales #3 / Airplay #54	Interscope 97048
			JORDAN KNIGHT		

NEWMAN, Jimmy

Born on 8/27/27 in High Point, Louisiana. Country singer/guitarist.

DATE	POS	WKS	ARTIST–RECORD TITLE		LABEL & NO.
7/22/57	23	1	1. A Fallen Star	Jockey #23 / Top 100 #42	Dot 15574

NEWMAN, Randy

Born on 11/28/43 in New Orleans, Louisiana. Singer/songwriter/pianist. Nephew of composers Alfred, Emil and Lionel Newman. Scored several movies.

DATE	POS	WKS	ARTIST–RECORD TITLE		LABEL & NO.
12/10/77+	2 (3)	13	● 1. **Short People**	**[N]**	Warner 8492
			Glenn Frey, J.D. Souther and Timothy B. Schmit (backing vocals)		

NEWMAN, Thunderclap — see THUNDERCLAP NEWMAN

NEW ORDER

Techno-dance group formed in Manchester, England: Bernard Sumner (vocals, guitar), Gillian Gilbert (keyboards), Peter Hook (bass) and Stephen Morris (drums). Sumner also recorded with Electronic.

DATE	POS	WKS	ARTIST–RECORD TITLE		LABEL & NO.
12/5/87	32	8	1. True Faith	Airplay #28 / Sales #35	Qwest 28271
6/5/93	28	8	2. Regret	Airplay #21 / Sales #73	Qwest 18586
			#1 Modern Rock hit (6 weeks)		

DATE	POS	WKS	ARTIST–RECORD TITLE	LABEL & NO.
			NEW RADICALS	
			Group is actually solo rock singer/musician Gregg Alexander.	
1/16/99	**36**	4	1. You Get What You Give — Airplay #30 from the album *Maybe You've Been Brainwashed Too* on MCA 11858	album cut
			NEW SEEKERS, The	
			British-Australian pop group formed by Keith Potger after disbandment of The Seekers in 1969. Consisted of Eve Graham, Lyn Paul, Peter Doyle, Marty Kristian and Paul Layton. Doyle died of cancer on 10/13/2001 (age 52).	
9/19/70	**14**	9	1. Look What They've Done To My Song Ma **THE NEW SEEKERS featuring Eve Graham** written by Melanie	Elektra 45699
12/18/71+	**7**	9	● 2. **I'd Like To Teach The World To Sing (In Perfect Harmony)** adapted from a Coca-Cola jingle	Elektra 45762
4/14/73	**29**	4	3. Pinball Wizard/See Me, Feel Me from the rock opera *Tommy*	MGM/Verve 10709
			NEWTON, Juice	
			Born Judy Kay Cohen on 2/18/52 in Lakehurst, New Jersey; raised in Virginia Beach, Virginia. Pop-country singer/guitarist.	
3/7/81	**4**	16	● 1. **Angel Of The Morning** #1 Adult Contemporary hit (3 weeks)	Capitol 4976
6/20/81	**2 (2)**	19	● 2. **Queen Of Hearts**	Capitol 4997
11/7/81+	**7**	18	3. **The Sweetest Thing (I've Ever Known)** #1 Country hit (1 week) / #1 Adult Contemporary hit (1 week); first recorded by Newton in 1975	Capitol 5046
5/22/82	**7**	13	4. **Love's Been A Little Bit Hard On Me** Andrew Gold (guitar)	Capitol 5120
9/11/82	**11**	10	5. Break It To Me Gently #1 Adult Contemporary hit (2 weeks)	Capitol 5148
12/18/82+	**25**	10	6. Heart Of The Night	Capitol 5192
9/3/83	**27**	5	7. Tell Her No	Capitol 5265
			NEWTON, Wayne	
			Born on 4/3/42 in Roanoke, Virginia. Singer/multi-instrumentalist. Top Las Vegas entertainer. Began singing career with regular appearances on Jackie Gleason's TV variety series in 1962. Appeared in the 1989 James Bond movie *License To Kill* and the 1990 movie *The Adventures Of Ford Fairlane*.	
8/3/63	**13**	8	1. Danke Schoen written by Bert Kaempfert	Capitol 4989
3/27/65	**23**	5	2. Red Roses For A Blue Lady #3 hit for Vaughn Monroe in 1949	Capitol 5366
6/10/72	**4**	13	● 3. **Daddy Don't You Walk So Fast**	Chelsea 0100
3/22/80	**35**	3	4. Years	Aries II 108
			NEWTON-JOHN, Olivia	
			Born on 9/26/48 in Cambridge, England; raised in Melbourne, Australia. Pop-rock-country singer. Granddaughter of Nobel Prize-winning German physicist Max Born. Starred in the movies *Grease*, *Xanadu* and *Two Of A Kind*. Married to actor Matt Lattanzi from 1984-95.	
7/17/71	**25**	10	1. If Not For You #1 Adult Contemporary hit (3 weeks); first recorded by Bob Dylan in 1970	Uni 55281

DATE	POS	WKS	ARTIST–RECORD TITLE	LABEL & NO.
12/15/73+	6	14	● 2. **Let Me Be There**	MCA 40101
5/11/74	5	12	● 3. **If You Love Me (Let Me Know)**	MCA 40209
8/24/74	1 (2)	10	● 4. **I Honestly Love You**	MCA 40280
			#1 Adult Contemporary hit (3 weeks)	
2/8/75	1 (1)	11	● 5. **Have You Never Been Mellow**	MCA 40349
			#1 Adult Contemporary hit (1 week)	
6/21/75	3	12	● 6. **Please Mr. Please**	MCA 40418
			#1 Adult Contemporary hit (3 weeks)	
10/11/75	13	7	7. Something Better To Do	MCA 40459
			#1 Adult Contemporary hit (3 weeks)	
1/3/76	30	4	8. Let It Shine /	
			#1 Adult Contemporary hit (2 weeks)	
1/3/76		4	9. He Ain't Heavy...He's My Brother	MCA 40495
4/17/76	23	6	10. Come On Over	MCA 40525
			#1 Adult Contemporary hit (1 week); written by Barry and Robin Gibb	
9/4/76	33	4	11. Don't Stop Believin'	MCA 40600
			#1 Adult Contemporary hit (1 week)	
2/19/77	20	9	12. Sam	MCA 40670
			#1 Adult Contemporary hit (2 weeks)	
4/8/78	1 (1)	16	▲ 13. **You're The One That I Want**	RSO 891
			JOHN TRAVOLTA AND OLIVIA NEWTON-JOHN	
7/22/78	3	15	● 14. **Hopelessly Devoted To You**	RSO 903
8/19/78	5	12	● 15. **Summer Nights**	RSO 906
			JOHN TRAVOLTA, OLIVIA NEWTON-JOHN & CAST	
			above 3 from the movie *Grease* starring Newton-John and Travolta	
12/9/78+	3	17	● 16. **A Little More Love**	MCA 40975
5/5/79	11	8	17. Deeper Than The Night	MCA 41009
4/19/80	12	8	18. I Can't Help It	RSO 1026
			ANDY GIBB AND OLIVIA NEWTON-JOHN	
6/14/80	1 (4)	16	● 19. **Magic**	MCA 41247
			#1 Adult Contemporary hit (5 weeks)	
8/30/80	8	10	20. Xanadu	MCA 41285
			OLIVIA NEWTON-JOHN/ELECTRIC LIGHT ORCHESTRA	
11/22/80+	20	11	21. Suddenly	MCA 51007
			OLIVIA NEWTON-JOHN AND CLIFF RICHARD	
			above 3 from the movie *Xanadu* starring Newton-John	
10/17/81	1 (10)	21	▲ 22. **Physical**	MCA 51182
2/27/82	5	10	● 23. **Make A Move On Me**	MCA 52000
9/25/82	3	13	24. **Heart Attack**	MCA 52100
2/19/83	38	3	25. Tied Up	MCA 52155
11/12/83+	5	14	26. **Twist Of Fate**	MCA 52284
2/25/84	31	5	27. Livin' In Desperate Times	MCA 52341
			above 2 from the movie *Two Of A Kind* starring Newton-John and Travolta	
10/26/85	20	7	28. Soul Kiss Sales #12 / Airplay #25	MCA 52686
11/30/96	25 ᴬ	10	29. The Grease Megamix	album cut
			JOHN TRAVOLTA & OLIVIA NEWTON-JOHN	
			medley: Greased Lightnin'/You're The One That I Want/Summer Nights; from the various artists album *Pure Disco* on Polydor 535877	

DATE	POS	WKS	ARTIST-RECORD TITLE	LABEL & NO.
			NEW VAUDEVILLE BAND, The	
			Studio creation of songwriter/record producer Geoff Stephens (born on 10/1/34 in London, England). Arrangements similar to Rudy Vallee's hits during the 1930s.	
11/5/66	**1** (3)	13	● 1. **Winchester Cathedral**	Fontana 1562
			#1 Adult Contemporary hit (4 weeks)	
			NEW YORK CITY	
			R&B vocal group from Harlem, New York: Tim McQueen, John Brown, Ed Shell and Claude Johnston.	
4/28/73	**17**	12	1. I'm Doin' Fine Now	Chelsea 0113
			NEXT	
			R&B vocal trio from Minneapolis, Minnesota: Robert Lavelle "R.L." Hugger, with brothers Raphael "Tweety" Brown and Terry "T-Low" Brown.	
9/27/97	**16**	19	● 1. Butta Love — Sales #8	Arista 13407
2/21/98	**1** (5)	49	▲ 2. **Too Close** — Sales #1 (4) / Airplay #4	Arista 13456
			#1 R&B hit (3 weeks); Koffee Brown (vocals); samples "X-mas Rappin'" by Kurtis Blow	
8/15/98	**14**	17	● 3. I Still Love You — Sales #7 / Airplay #63	Arista 13509
			contains resung elements of "Two Occasions" by The Deele	
6/17/00	**7**	18	4. **Wifey** — Sales #5 / Airplay #13	Arista 13881
			#1 R&B hit (1 week); Lil' Mo (female vocal)	
4/6/02	**28**	9	5. Anything — Airplay #25	album cut
			JAHEIM Featuring Next	
			from Jaheim's album *Ghetto Love* on Divine Mill 47452	
			NICHOLAS, Paul	
			Born Paul Beuselinck on 12/3/45 in Peterborough, Cambridgeshire, England. Singer/actor. Played "Dougie Shears" in the 1978 movie *Sgt. Pepper's Lonely Hearts Club Band*.	
9/17/77	**6**	16	● 1. **Heaven On The 7th Floor**	RSO 878
			NICHOLS, Joe	
			Born on 11/26/76 in Rogers, Arkansas. Country singer/songwriter.	
9/7/02	**29**	6	1. The Impossible — Sales #11 / Airplay #29	Universal South 172241
3/1/03	**27**	8	2. Brokenheartsville — Airplay #26 / Sales #48	Universal South 000782
			#1 Country hit (1 week)	
			NICKELBACK	
			Rock group from Vancouver, British Columbia, Canada: brothers Chad (vocals, guitar) and Mike (bass) Kroeger, with Ryan Peake (guitar) and Ryan Vikedal (drums).	
10/20/01	**1** (4)	40	1. **How You Remind Me** — Sales #1 (3) / Airplay #2	Roadrunner 612053
			#1 Mainstream Rock hit (13 weeks) / #1 Modern Rock hit (13 weeks)	
10/18/03+	**7**	32↑	2. **Someday** — Airplay #7	album cut
			from the album *The Long Road* on Roadrunner 618390	

DATE	POS	WKS	ARTIST–RECORD TITLE	LABEL & NO.
			NICKS, Stevie	
			Born Stephanie Nicks on 5/26/48 in Phoenix, Arizona; raised in San Francisco, California. Pop-rock singer/songwriter. Teamed up with Lindsey Buckingham in 1973. Both joined Fleetwood Mac in 1975.	
8/1/81	3	15	1. **Stop Draggin' My Heart Around** **STEVIE NICKS (with Tom Petty and The Heartbreakers)**	Modern 7336
11/7/81+	6	15	2. **Leather And Lace** **STEVIE NICKS (with DON HENLEY)** written for Waylon Jennings and Jessi Colter	Modern 7341
3/6/82	11	10	3. Edge Of Seventeen (Just Like The White Winged Dove)	Modern 7401
6/12/82	32	4	4. After The Glitter Fades	Modern 7405
6/18/83	5	14	5. **Stand Back**	Modern 99863
9/24/83	14	9	6. If Anyone Falls	Modern 99832
1/21/84	33	4	7. Nightbird **STEVIE NICKS (with Sandy Stewart)**	Modern 99799
11/30/85+	4	13	8. **Talk To Me** Airplay #4 / Sales #5 #1 Mainstream Rock hit (2 weeks)	Modern 99582
3/1/86	37	2	9. Needles And Pins **[L]** **TOM PETTY and the HEARTBREAKERS with STEVIE NICKS** recorded at the Wiltern Theater in Los Angeles	MCA 52772
3/8/86	16	8	10. I Can't Wait Airplay #14 / Sales #21	Modern 99565
6/3/89	16	7	11. Rooms On Fire Sales #14 / Airplay #18 #1 Mainstream Rock hit (1 week)	Modern 99216
			NICOLE	
			Born Nicole Wray in Salinas, California; raised in Portsmouth, Virginia. R&B-dance singer.	
6/27/98	5	23	● 1. **Make It Hot** Sales #2 / Airplay #39 **NICOLE Featuring Missy "Misdemeanor" Elliott and Mocha**	The Gold Mind 64110
			NIELSEN/PEARSON	
			Pop duo from Sacramento, California: singers/guitarists Reed Nielsen and Mark Pearson.	
11/15/80	38	2	1. If You Should Sail	Capitol 4910
			NIGHT	
			Pop-rock group: Stevie Lange (female vocals), Chris Thompson (male vocals), Robbie McIntosh (guitar), Nicky Hopkins (piano), Billy Kristian (bass) and Rick Marotta (drums). Thompson was lead singer of Manfred Mann's Earth Band. McIntosh later joined The Pretenders and Paul McCartney's backing band.	
8/4/79	18	8	1. Hot Summer Nights written by Walter Egan	Planet 45903
10/20/79	17	8	2. If You Remember Me **CHRIS THOMPSON & NIGHT** from the movie *The Champ* starring Jon Voight and Ricky Schroder	Planet 45904
			NIGHTINGALE, Maxine	
			Born on 11/2/52 in Wembly, England. Acted in productions of *Hair*, *Jesus Christ Superstar*, *Godspell* and *Savages*.	
3/13/76	2 (2)	15	● 1. **Right Back Where We Started From**	United Artists 752
7/7/79	5	14	● 2. **Lead Me On** #1 Adult Contemporary hit (7 weeks)	Windsong 11530

DATE	POS	WKS	ARTIST–RECORD TITLE	LABEL & NO.
			NIGHT RANGER	
			Rock group formed in San Francisco, California: Jack Blades (vocals, bass), Kelly Keagy (vocals, drums), Jeff Watson and Brad Gillis (guitars), and Alan Fitzgerald (keyboards). Blades and Gillis were members of Rubicon. Blades later joined Damn Yankees.	
2/26/83	40	3	1. Don't Tell Me You Love Me	Boardwalk 171
4/21/84	5	12	2. **Sister Christian**	MCA/Camel 52350
8/4/84	14	11	3. When You Close Your Eyes Sales #26	MCA/Camel 52420
6/8/85	8	11	4. **Sentimental Street** Sales #5 / Airplay #9	MCA/Camel 52591
9/21/85	19	6	5. Four In The Morning (I Can't Take Any More) Sales #20 / Airplay #23	MCA/Camel 52661
12/7/85+	17	10	6. Goodbye Sales #14 / Airplay #23	MCA/Camel 52729
			NIKKI	
			Born Nikki Lee in Okinawa, Japan; raised in Dayton, Ohio. American male singer/multi-instrumentalist.	
6/9/90	21	6	1. Notice Me Airplay #19 / Sales #23	Geffen 19946
			NILSSON	
			Born Harry Nelson on 6/15/41 in Brooklyn, New York. Died of a heart attack on 1/15/94 (age 52). Pop singer/songwriter.	
9/6/69	6	9	1. **Everybody's Talkin'** theme song from the movie *Midnight Cowboy* starring Dustin Hoffman and Jon Voight	RCA Victor 0161
11/29/69	34	2	2. I Guess The Lord Must Be In New York City written for, but not included in, the movie *Midnight Cowboy*	RCA Victor 0261
5/8/71	34	4	3. Me And My Arrow from Nilsson's animated TV special *The Point*	RCA Victor 0443
1/15/72	1 (4)	14	● 4. **Without You** #1 Adult Contemporary hit (5 weeks); Gary Wright (piano); written by Badfinger's Pete Ham and Tom Evans	RCA Victor 0604
4/8/72	27	6	5. Jump Into The Fire	RCA Victor 0673
7/8/72	8	10	6. **Coconut**	RCA Victor 0718
10/14/72	23	6	7. Spaceman Peter Frampton (guitar)	RCA Victor 0788
5/25/74	39	2	8. Daybreak from the movie *Son Of Dracula* starring Nilsson and Ringo Starr (drums); Peter Frampton (guitar); George Harrison (cowbell)	RCA Victor 0246
			NINEDAYS	
			Rock group from New York: John Hampson (vocals, guitar), Brian Desveaux (vocals, guitar), Jeremy Dean (keyboards), Nick Dimichino (bass) and Vincent Tattanelli (drums).	
6/3/00	6	21	1. **Absolutely (Story Of A Girl)** Airplay #5 from the album *The Madding Crowd* on 550 Music 63634	album cut
			NINE INCH NAILS	
			Group is actually industrial rock musician Trent Reznor (born on 5/17/65 in Mercer, Pennsylvania).	
8/7/99	17	1	1. The Day The World Went Away Sales #5	Nothing 97026

DATE	POS	WKS	ARTIST–RECORD TITLE	LABEL & NO.
			1910 FRUITGUM CO.	
			Bubblegum group from New Jersey: Mark Gutkowski (vocals), Floyd Marcus, Pat Karwan, Steve Mortkowitz and Frank Jeckell.	
2/10/68	4	11	● 1. **Simon Says**	Buddah 24
8/10/68	5	11	● 2. **1, 2, 3, Red Light**	Buddah 54
			The Trade Winds (backing vocals)	
12/7/68	37	3	3. Goody Goody Gumdrops	Buddah 71
			Billy Carl (lead vocal)	
2/8/69	5	11	● 4. **Indian Giver**	Buddah 91
6/14/69	38	2	5. Special Delivery	Buddah 114
			98°	
			White teen pop vocal group from Cincinnati, Ohio: brothers Drew and Nick Lachey, with Jeff Timmons and Justin Jeffre. Nick Lachey married Jessica Simpson on 10/26/2002.	
8/2/97	12	20	● 1. Invisible Man Sales #12 / Airplay #23	Motown 860650
10/3/98	3	19	▲ 2. **Because Of You** Sales #4 / Airplay #38	Motown 860830
4/24/99	5	19	● 3. **The Hardest Thing** Sales #5 / Airplay #12	Universal 156246
8/21/99	13	16	4. I Do (Cherish You) Airplay #9	album cut
			from the album 98° And Rising on Motown 530956	
1/15/00	1 (1)	11	● 5. **Thank God I Found You** Sales #1 (3) / Airplay #15	Columbia 79338
			MARIAH With Joe & 98°	
			#1 R&B hit (1 week); Trey Lorenz (backing vocal)	
8/26/00	2 (2)	13	● 6. **Give Me Just One Night (Una Noche)**	Universal 153296
			Sales #2 / Airplay #14	
			Deetah (female vocal)	
1/20/01	34	5	7. My Everything Airplay #34	album cut
			from the album Revelation on Universal 159354	
			95 SOUTH	
			Hip-hop/bass group formed in Florida: male rappers Artice "AB" Bartley and Carlos "Daddy Black" Spencer, female rapper K-Knock, dancers Bootyman and P-Body. Produced by Nathaniel "C.C. Lemonhead" Orange and Johnny "Jay Ski" McGowan. Orange and McGowan also produced 69 Boyz and formed own Quad City DJ's group.	
6/19/93	11	16	▲ 1. Whoot, There It Is Sales #5 / Airplay #44	Wrap/Toy 162
			samples "Looking For The Perfect Beat" by Afrika Bambaataa	
			NIRVANA	
			Grunge-rock trio from Aberdeen, Washington: Kurt Cobain (vocals, guitar), Krist Novoselic (bass) and Dave Grohl (drums). Cobain married Courtney Love (lead singer of Hole) on 2/24/92. Cobain died of a self-inflicted gunshot on 4/5/94 (age 27). Grohl formed Foo Fighters in 1995.	
12/7/91+	6	19	▲ 1. **Smells Like Teen Spirit** Sales #1 (2) / Airplay #41	DGC 19050
			#1 Modern Rock hit (1 week)	
4/18/92	32	5	2. Come As You Are Sales #27 / Airplay #62	DGC 19120
10/22/94	22 ᴬ	11	3. About A Girl [L]	album cut
			#1 Modern Rock hit (1 week)	
3/11/95	39 ᴬ	1	4. The Man Who Sold The World [L]	album cut
			written and recorded by David Bowie in 1970; above 2 from the album MTV Unplugged In New York on DGC 24727	
			NITE-LITERS, The — see NEW BIRTH, The	

Nelly definitely heated up radios in the summer of 2002. After spending seven weeks at #1 with his first chart-topper, "Hot In Herre," he replaced himself at #1 for another ten weeks with "Dilemma."

Nelson carried on the musical legacy of their father, Rick, with hits like the chart-topping "(Can't Live Without Your) Love and Affection." Meanwhile, their sister Tracy inherited her father's acting genes, appearing on TV's *Father Dowling Mysteries.*

New Kids On The Block found that their #1 hit "I'll Be Loving You Forever" was taken to heart by their die-hard fans. Although the group stopped charting in 1994, both Jordan Knight and Joey McIntire had Top 10 solo hits in 1999.

Olivia Newton-John could have made a career out of just her #1 song "I Honestly Love You." The 1974 Grammy Award winner for Record of the Year returned to the pop charts in 1977, and again in 1998.

No Doubt used the video to their chart-topping Airplay hit "Don't Speak" to comment about the extra press coverage given to singer Gwen Stefani. Nonetheless, the song helped send No Doubt's album *Tragic Kingdom* to multi-platinum status.

The Notorious B.I.G. never had a #1 hit while he was alive, but after he was killed on March 9, 1997, two tracks from his album *Life After Death,* "Hypnotize" and "Mo Money Mo Problems," reached the top.

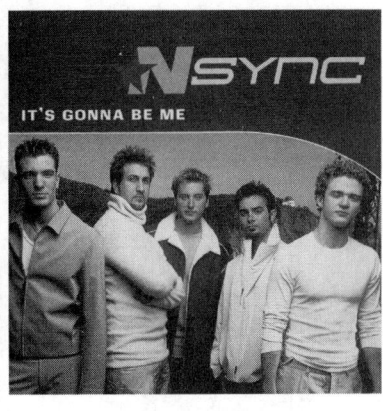

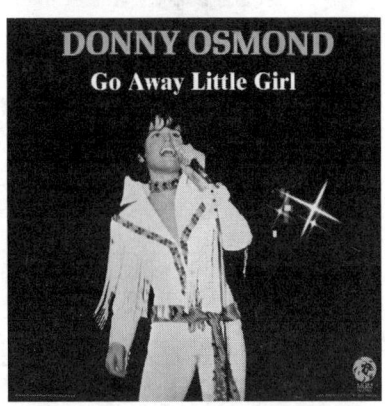

*NSYNC earned their first #1 hit with "It's Gonna Be Me." Appropriately enough, the group members decided to try solo projects in 2002, ranging from singing and acting to Lance Bass's desire to join the space program.

Billy Ocean tried to be inclusive with his #1 hit "Caribbean Queen (No More Love On The Run)." Originally titled "European Queen," it was later remade as "African Queen" to appeal to more listeners.

Sinead O'Connor found more notoriety on *Saturday Night Live* than from her #1 hit "Nothing Compares 2 U." She backed out of a 1990 episode to protest host Andrew Dice Clay, then tore a picture of the Pope during her performance in 1992.

Roy Orbison started his recording career at the legendary Sun studios along with acts like Elvis Presley, Jerry Lee Lewis, and Johnny Cash. However, he didn't get his first #1 hit, "Running Scared," until he moved to Monument Records.

Donny Osmond remade Steve Lawrence's #1 hit, "Go Away Little Girl," and reached the top spot himself. Donny found later success remaking a television classic as well, becoming host of TV's revamped *Pyramid* game show.

OutKast was a welcome sight for pop fans in late 2003. Their hits "Hey Ya!" and "The Way You Move," which both appeared on the same single, held down the top two spots on the Hot 100 for over a month.

DATE	POS	WKS	ARTIST–RECORD TITLE	LABEL & NO.
			NITEFLYTE	
			R&B/disco group formed in Los Angeles, California: Howard Johnson (vocals), Sandy Torano (guitar), George Blitzer (keyboards), Jeff Kirk (sax), Frank Cornelius (bass) and Joe Galdo (drums).	
11/24/79	37	2	1. If You Want It	Ariola America 7747
			NITTY GRITTY DIRT BAND	
			Country-folk-rock group from Long Beach, California. Led by Jeff Hanna (vocals, guitar) and John McEuen (banjo, mandolin). Numerous personnel changes.	
1/2/71	9	13	1. **Mr. Bojangles**	Liberty 56197
			prologue: Uncle Charlie And His Dog Teddy	
			THE DIRT BAND:	
1/12/80	13	11	2. An American Dream	United Artists 1330
			Linda Ronstadt (harmony vocal)	
7/12/80	25	9	3. Make A Little Magic	United Artists 1356
			Nicolette Larson (backing vocal)	
			NITZSCHE, Jack	
			Born Bernard Nitzsche on 4/22/37 in Chicago, Illinois. Died of heart failure on 8/25/2000 (age 63). Arranger/producer/composer/keyboardist.	
9/7/63	39	2	1. The Lonely Surfer **[I]**	Reprise 20,202
			NIVEA	
			Born Nivea Hamilton in 1981 in Atlanta, Georgia. Female R&B singer.	
11/16/02	8	21	1. **Don't Mess With My Man** Sales #1 (1) / Airplay #8	Jive 40041
			NIVEA Featuring Brian & Brandon Casey Of Jagged Edge	
			NKOTB — see NEW KIDS ON THE BLOCK	
			NOBLE, Nick	
			Born Nicholas Valkan on 6/21/36 in Chicago, Illinois. Pop singer.	
8/20/55	22	3	1. The Bible Tells Me So Best Seller #22 / Top 100 #61	Wing 90003
			Lew Douglas (orch.)	
3/24/56	27	6	2. To You, My Love Top 100 #27	Mercury 70821
			Jack Halloran Choir (backing vocals, above 2)	
7/15/57	20	1	3. A Fallen Star Jockey #20	Mercury 71124
			Dick Noel Singers (backing vocals)	
9/30/57	37	1	4. Moonlight Swim Top 100 #37	Mercury 71169
			Carl Stevens (orch., above 3)	
			NOBLES, Cliff, & Co.	
			Born in 1944 in Mobile, Alabama. R&B bandleader/singer.	
6/8/68	2 (3)	12	● 1. **The Horse** **[I]**	Phil-L.A. 313
			NO DOUBT	
			New wave-ska band from Anaheim, California: Gwen Stefani (vocals), Tom Dumont (guitar), Tony Kanal (bass) and Adrian Young (drums). Stefani married Gavin Rossdale (lead singer of Bush) on 9/14/2002.	
4/13/96	23	9	1. Just A Girl Sales #21 / Airplay #32	Trauma 98116

DATE	POS	WKS	ARTIST–RECORD TITLE	LABEL & NO.
7/6/96	18 ^A	30	2. Spiderwebs	album cut
11/2/96	1 (16)^A	52	3. **Don't Speak**	album cut
			above 2 from the album Tragic Kingdom on Trauma 92580	
7/8/00	38	4	4. Simple Kind Of Life Sales #5 / Airplay #73	Trauma 490365
12/22/01+	5	16	5. **Hey Baby** Airplay #5	album cut
			NO DOUBT Featuring Bounty Killer	
4/27/02	13	15	6. Hella Good Airplay #14	album cut
			above 2 from the album Rock Steady on Interscope 493158	
9/14/02	3	26	7. **Underneath It All** Airplay #4 / Sales #64	Interscope 497768
11/15/03+	10	21	8. **It's My Life** Airplay #10	album cut
			from the album The SIngles 1992-2003 on Interscope 000149	

NO GOOD

Male rap duo from Miami, Florida: Derrick Hill and Tracy Lattimer.

DATE	POS	WKS	ARTIST–RECORD TITLE	LABEL & NO.
3/23/02	3 ^S	21	1. **Ballin' Boy**	Artistdirect 01022

NOGUEZ, Jacky, And His Orchestra

Born in Paris, France. Male orchestra leader.

DATE	POS	WKS	ARTIST–RECORD TITLE	LABEL & NO.
7/27/59	24	5	1. Ciao, Ciao Bambina (Chiow, Chiow, Bambeena) **[I]**	Jamie 1127
			original Italian title: "Piove"	

NOKIO — see EVE

NOLAN, Kenny

Born in Los Angeles, California. Pop singer/songwriter.

DATE	POS	WKS	ARTIST–RECORD TITLE	LABEL & NO.
12/11/76+	3	20	● 1. **I Like Dreamin'**	20th Century 2287
5/7/77	20	11	2. Love's Grown Deep	20th Century 2331

NO MERCY

Male techno-dance trio: brothers Ariel and Gabriel Hernandez (from Florida), with Marty Cintron (from New York).

DATE	POS	WKS	ARTIST–RECORD TITLE	LABEL & NO.
8/3/96	5	34	● 1. **Where Do You Go** Airplay #3 / Sales #10	Arista 13225
2/22/97	21	8	2. Please Don't Go Sales #21 / Airplay #41	Arista 13304

NONCHALANT

Born Tanya Pointer in Washington DC. Female singer/rapper/songwriter.

DATE	POS	WKS	ARTIST–RECORD TITLE	LABEL & NO.
4/20/96	24	6	● 1. 5 O'Clock Sales #14	MCA 55075

N.O.R.E. (Noreaga)

Born Victor Santiago in Queens, New York. Male rapper. Half of Capone-N-Noreaga duo.

DATE	POS	WKS	ARTIST–RECORD TITLE	LABEL & NO.
10/3/98	36	6	1. SuperThug (What What) Sales #27	Penalty 0237
			NOREAGA	
			Tammy Lucas and The Neptunes (backing vocals); samples "Heart Of Glass" by Blondie	
7/13/02	10	17	2. **Nothin'** Airplay #8 / Sales #12	Def Jam 582914
			N.O.R.E.	

NORMAN, Chris — see QUATRO, Suzi / SMOKIE

DATE	POS	WKS	ARTIST—RECORD TITLE	LABEL & NO.
			NORTH, Freddie	
			Born on 5/28/39 in Nashville, Tennessee. R&B singer/songwriter/guitarist.	
11/27/71	39	1	1. She's All I Got	Mankind 12004
			NOTORIOUS B.I.G., The	
			Born Christopher Wallace on 5/21/72 in Brooklyn, New York. Shot to death on 3/9/97 (age 24). Male rapper. Also known as Biggy Smallz. Married to singer Faith Evans from 1994-97.	
9/17/94	27	10	● 1. Juicy / Sales #13 / Airplay #50	
9/17/94		10	2. Unbelievable	Bad Boy 79004
1/28/95	6	20	▲ 3. **Big Poppa** / Sales #2 / Airplay #37 samples "Between The Sheets" by The Isley Brothers	
1/28/95		20	4. Warning Sales: flip samples "Walk On By" by Isaac Hayes	Bad Boy 79015
4/22/95	13	14	● 5. Can't You See Sales #9 / Airplay #28 **TOTAL featuring The Notorious B.I.G.** samples "The Payback" by James Brown; from the movie *New Jersey Drive* starring Sharron Corley	Tommy Boy 7676
6/24/95	2 (3)	17	▲ 6. **One More Chance/Stay With Me** /Sales #1 (5) / Airplay #24 #1 R&B hit (9 weeks); Faith Evans (backing vocal); samples "Stay With Me" by DeBarge	
7/22/95		3	7. The What Sales: flip **THE NOTORIOUS B.I.G. and METHOD MAN**	Bad Boy 79031
4/26/97	1 (3)	14	▲ 8. **Hypnotize** Sales #1 (3) / Airplay #23 #1 R&B hit (3 weeks); Pam Long (female vocal); samples "La Di Da Di" by Slick Rick and "Rise" by Herb Alpert	Bad Boy 79092
8/2/97	1 (2)	28	▲ 9. **Mo Money Mo Problems** Sales #1 (4) / Airplay #12 **THE NOTORIOUS B.I.G. Featuring Puff Daddy & Mase** Kelly Price (female vocal); samples "I'm Coming Out" by Diana Ross	Bad Boy 79100
12/6/97+	2 (2)	6	▲ 10. **It's All About The Benjamins** Sales #2 / Airplay #62 **PUFF DADDY & THE FAMILY Feat. The Notorious B.I.G., Lil' Kim, The Lox, Dave Grohl, Perfect, FuzzBubble & Rob Zombie** samples "I Did It For Love" by Love Unlimited Orchestra	Bad Boy 79130
12/27/97+	26	5	▲ 11. Going Back To Cali Sales #19	Bad Boy 79131
1/17/98	4	12	▲ 12. **Been Around The World** Sales #1 (2) / Airplay #58 **PUFF DADDY & THE FAMILY Featuring The Notorious B.I.G. & Mase** samples "Let's Dance" by David Bowie and "All Around The World" by Lisa Stansfield	Bad Boy 79130
3/28/98	19	13	● 13. Victory Sales #11 **PUFF DADDY & THE FAMILY Featuring The Notorious B.I.G. & Busta Rhymes** samples "Alone In The Ring" (from the movie *Rocky*) by Bill Conti	Bad Boy 79155
11/15/03	19	11	14. Runnin (Dying To Live) Airplay #17 / Sales #24 **TUPAC Featuring The Notorious B.I.G.** new mix (produced by Eminem) of their #81 hit in 1997	Amaru 001670
			NOVA, Aldo	
			Born Aldo Scarporuscio in Montreal, Quebec, Canada. Rock singer/songwriter/guitarist.	
5/1/82	23	7	1. Fantasy	Portrait 02799

DATE	POS	WKS	ARTIST–RECORD TITLE	LABEL & NO.
			*NSYNC	
			Male teen vocal group formed in Orlando, Florida: Chris Kirkpatrick, Josh "JC" Chasez, Joey Fatone, Justin Timberlake and Lance Bass. Timberlake and Chasez were regulars on TV's *The Mickey Mouse Club*. Fatone appeared in the 2002 movie *My Big Fat Greek Wedding*.	
3/7/98	13	21	● 1. I Want You Back Sales #15 / Airplay #20	RCA 65348
7/25/98	15 ^	19	2. Tearin' Up My Heart Hot 100 #59 (1 wks)	album cut
			from the album **NSYNC* on RCA 67613	
12/26/98+	8	17	3. **(God Must Have Spent) A Little More Time On You**	RCA 65685
			Sales #9 / Airplay #12	
6/12/99	29	11	4. God Must Have Spent A Little More Time On You	RCA 65759
			Airplay #22 / Sales #23	
			ALABAMA (featuring *NSYNC)	
10/16/99	2 (1)	5	5. **Music Of My Heart** Sales #1 (1) / Airplay #26	Miramax/Epic 79245
			*NSYNC and GLORIA ESTEFAN	
			from the movie *Music Of The Heart* starring Meryl Streep	
11/20/99+	5	24	6. **Bring It All To Me** Airplay #4	album cut
			BLAQUE Featuring *NSYNC	
			from the album *Blaque* on Track Masters 68987	
2/5/00	4	22	7. **Bye Bye Bye** Airplay #1 (5)	Jive 42681
5/27/00	1 (2)	21	● 8. **It's Gonna Be Me** Sales #1 (1) / Airplay #3	Jive 42664
10/7/00	5	23	9. **This I Promise You** Airplay #4	Jive 42746
			#1 Adult Contemporary hit (13 weeks); written and produced by Richard Marx	
6/2/01	19	7	10. Pop Airplay #17	Jive 42933
10/27/01	11	18	11. Gone Airplay #11	album cut
			from the album *Celebrity* on Jive 41758	
2/23/02	5	17	12. **Girlfriend** Sales #1 (14) / Airplay #9	Jive 40013
			N2DEEP	
			White rap duo from Vallejo, California: Jay Trujillo and T.L. Lyon.	
8/22/92+	14	22	● 1. Back To The Hotel Sales #5 / Airplay #44	Profile 5367
			NIIU	
			Male R&B vocal group from New Jersey: Chuck Howard, Chris Herbert, Don Carlis and Craig Hill.	
1/21/95	22	11	1. I Miss You Sales #16 / Airplay #44	Arista 12768
			NU FLAVOR	
			R&B vocal group from Long Beach, California: Jacob Ceniceros, Anthony Dacosta, Rico Luna and Frank Pangelinan.	
11/22/97+	27	15	1. Heaven Sales #32 / Airplay #32	Reprise 17408
			NUGENT, Ted	
			Born on 12/13/48 in Detroit, Michigan. Hard-rock singer/guitarist. Leader of The Amboy Dukes. Later joined Damn Yankees. An avid game hunter and an active supporter of the National Rifle Association.	
9/10/77	30	6	1. Cat Scratch Fever	Epic 50425
			NUMAN, Gary	
			Born Gary Webb on 3/8/58 in Hammersmith, England. Synthesized techno-rock artist.	
3/29/80	9	17	1. **Cars**	Atco 7211

DATE	POS	WKS	ARTIST–RECORD TITLE	LABEL & NO.
			NU SHOOZ	
			Husband-and-wife duo from Portland, Oregon: John Smith and Valerie Day.	
4/5/86	3	15	● 1. **I Can't Wait** Sales #3 / Airplay #3	Atlantic 89446
9/6/86	28	8	2. Point Of No Return Sales #21 / Airplay #39	Atlantic 89392
			NU TORNADOS, The	
			String band from Philadelphia, Pennsylvania: Eddie Dono, Phil Dale, Tom Dell, Mike Perna and Louie Mann.	
12/15/58	26	6	1. Philadelphia U.S.A.	Carlton 492
			NUTTY SQUIRRELS, The	
			Creators and voices: Don Elliot (from Sommerville, New Jersey) and Alexander "Sascha" Burland (from Brooklyn, New York).	
11/30/59	14	7	1. Uh! Oh! Part 2 [N]	Hanover 4540
			NYLONS, The	
			Acappella group formed in Toronto, Ontario, Canada: Marc Connors, Paul Cooper, Claude Morrison and Arnold Robinson. Connors died on 3/25/91 (age 41).	
6/13/87	12	10	1. Kiss Him Goodbye Sales #10 / Airplay #12	Open Air 0022

DATE	POS	WKS	ARTIST–RECORD TITLE	LABEL & NO.
			OAK	
			Pop-rock group from Maine: Rick Pinette (vocals), Scott Weatherspoon (guitar), David Stone (keyboards), John Foster (bass) and Daniel Caron (drums).	
7/12/80	36	3	1. King Of The Hill **RICK PINETTE AND OAK**	Mercury 76049
			OAK RIDGE BOYS	
			Country vocal group formed in Oak Ridge, Tennessee: Duane Allen, Joe Bonsall, Richard Sterban and William Lee Golden.	
6/6/81	5	14	▲ 1. **Elvira** #1 Country hit (1 week)	MCA 51084
2/13/82	12	9	2. Bobbie Sue #1 Country hit (1 week)	MCA 51231
			OASIS	
			Rock group from Manchester, England: brothers Liam (vocals) and Noel (guitar) Gallagher, Paul Arthurs (guitar), Paul McGuigan (bass) and Tony McCarroll (drums). Alan White replaced McCarroll in 1995.	
1/28/95	39 A	2	1. Live Forever from the album *Definitely Maybe* on Epic 66431	album cut
1/27/96	8	14	2. **Wonderwall** Airplay #8 / Sales #13 #1 Modern Rock hit (10 weeks)	Epic 78216
3/30/96	20 A	19	3. Champagne Supernova #1 Modern Rock hit (5 weeks); from the album *(What's The Story) Morning Glory?* on Epic 67351	album cut
10/25/97	35 A	5	4. Don't Go Away from the album *Be Here Now* on Epic 68530	album cut

DATE	POS	WKS	ARTIST–RECORD TITLE	LABEL & NO.
			O'BANION, John	
			Born on 4/28/56 in Kokomo, Indiana. Pop singer.	
4/18/81	**24**	7	1. Love You Like I Never Loved Before	Elektra 47125
			OCASEK, Ric — see CARS, The	
			OCEAN	
			Pop group from London, Ontario, Canada: Janice Morgan (vocals), David Tamblyn (guitar), Greg Brown (keyboards), Jeff Jones (bass) and Charles Slater (drums).	
3/27/71	**2** (1)	12	● 1. **Put Your Hand In The Hand**	Kama Sutra 519
			OCEAN, Billy	
			Born Leslie Sebastian Charles on 1/21/50 in Trinidad, West Indies; raised in England. R&B-pop singer.	
5/1/76	**22**	6	1. Love Really Hurts Without You	Ariola America 7621
9/8/84	**1** (2)	15	● 2. **Caribbean Queen (No More Love On The Run)** Sales #1 (2) / Airplay #2	Jive 9199
			#1 R&B hit (4 weeks)	
12/8/84+	**2** (1)	15	3. **Loverboy** Sales #2 / Airplay #4	Jive 9284
4/13/85	**4**	13	4. **Suddenly** Sales #3 / Airplay #3	Jive 9323
			#1 Adult Contemporary hit (2 weeks)	
7/27/85	**24**	8	5. Mystery Lady Sales #19 / Airplay #21	Jive 9374
12/21/85+	**2** (1)	14	6. **When The Going Gets Tough, The Tough Get Going** Sales #2 / Airplay #2	Jive 9432
			from the movie *The Jewel Of The Nile* starring Michael Douglas and Kathleen Turner	
5/3/86	**1** (1)	14	7. **There'll Be Sad Songs (To Make You Cry)** Sales #1 (1) / Airplay #1 (1)	Jive 9465
			#1 R&B hit (2 weeks) / #1 Adult Contemporary hit (1 week)	
8/9/86	**10**	11	8. **Love Zone** Sales #9 / Airplay #11	Jive 9510
			#1 R&B hit (1 week)	
11/15/86	**16**	11	9. Love Is Forever Sales #13 / Airplay #18	Jive 9540
			#1 Adult Contemporary hit (3 weeks)	
2/20/88	**1** (2)	14	10. **Get Outta My Dreams, Get Into My Car** Sales #1 (2) / Airplay #1 (2)	Jive 9678
			#1 R&B hit (1 week)	
6/25/88	**17**	8	11. The Colour Of Love Sales #13 / Airplay #17	Jive 9707
11/11/89	**32**	2	12. Licence To Chill Sales #26 / Airplay #38	Jive 1283
			O'CONNOR, Sinéad	
			Born on 12/8/66 in Dublin, Ireland. Female singer/songwriter.	
3/24/90	**1** (4)	15	▲ 1. **Nothing Compares 2 U** Airplay #1 (4) / Sales #1 (3)	Ensign/Chrysalis 23488
			#1 Modern Rock hit (1 week); written by Prince	
			O'DAY, Alan	
			Born on 10/3/40 in Hollywood, California. Singer/songwriter/pianist.	
5/7/77	**1** (1)	17	● 1. **Undercover Angel**	Pacific 001
			O'DELL — see MASTER P	

DATE	POS	WKS	ARTIST–RECORD TITLE	LABEL & NO.
			O'DELL, Kenny	
			Born Kenneth Gist in 1942 in Oklahoma. Pop singer/songwriter/guitarist.	
12/16/67	38	2	1. Beautiful People	Vegas 718
			ODYSSEY	
			Disco vocal trio from the Bronx, New York: Manilla-born Tony Reynolds, with sisters Lillian and Louise Lopez, originally from the Virgin Islands.	
12/17/77+	21	12	1. Native New Yorker	RCA 11129
			OFFSPRING, The	
			Punk-rock group from Garden Grove, California: Brian "Dexter" Holland (vocals), Kevin "Noodles" Wasserman (guitar), Greg Kriesel (bass) and Ron Welty (drums).	
8/6/94	38 A	2	1. Come Out And Play #1 Modern Rock hit (2 weeks); from the album *Smash* on Epitaph 86432	album cut
			OHIO EXPRESS	
			Bubblegum group from Mansfield, Ohio: Joey Levine (vocals), Dale Powers and Doug Grassel (guitars), Jim Pflayer (keyboards), Dean Krastan (bass) and Tim Corwin (drums). Levine was lead singer with several studio groups.	
11/18/67	29	5	1. Beg, Borrow And Steal	Cameo 483
5/18/68	4	11	● 2. **Yummy Yummy Yummy**	Buddah 38
8/31/68	33	5	3. Down At Lulu's	Buddah 56
11/2/68	15	10	● 4. **Chewy Chewy**	Buddah 70
4/26/69	30	4	5. Mercy	Buddah 102
			OHIO PLAYERS	
			R&B-funk group from Dayton, Ohio: Leroy "Sugarfoot" Bonner (vocals, guitar), Walter "Junie" Morrison (vocals, keyboards), Marvin Pierce and Ralph "Pee Wee" Middlebrooks (trumpets), Andrew Noland (sax), Norman Napier (trumpet), Marshall "Rock" Jones (bass) and Greg Webster (drums). Morrison, Noland, Napier and Webster left in early 1974, replaced by Clarence "Satch" Satchell (vocals, sax), Billy Beck (keyboards) and James "Diamond" Williams (drums). Satchell died of a brain aneurysm on 12/30/95 (age 55).	
4/14/73	15	9	● 1. Funky Worm **[N]** #1 R&B hit (1 week)	Westbound 214
9/22/73	31	6	2. Ecstasy	Westbound 216
9/14/74	13	7	● 3. Skin Tight	Mercury 73609
12/28/74+	1 (1)	12	● 4. **Fire** #1 R&B hit (2 weeks)	Mercury 73643
10/11/75	33	3	5. Sweet Sticky Thing #1 R&B hit (1 week)	Mercury 73713
11/22/75+	1 (1)	14	● 6. **Love Rollercoaster** #1 R&B hit (1 week)	Mercury 73734
3/27/76	30	5	7. Fopp	Mercury 73775
7/31/76	18	10	8. Who'd She Coo? #1 R&B hit (1 week)	Mercury 73814

DATE	POS	WKS	ARTIST–RECORD TITLE	LABEL & NO.
			O'JAYS, The	
			R&B vocal trio from Canton, Ohio: Eddie Levert, Walter Williams and William Powell. Named after Cleveland DJ, Eddie O'Jay (died on 4/10/98). Sammy Strain (of Little Anthony & The Imperials) replaced Powell in 1975. Powell died of cancer on 5/26/77 (age 35). Levert's sons Gerald and Sean are members of Levert.	
8/12/72	**3**	12	● 1. **Back Stabbers** #1 R&B hit (1 week)	Philadelphia I. 3517
1/27/73	**1** (1)	13	● 2. **Love Train** #1 R&B hit (4 weeks)	Philadelphia I. 3524
6/30/73	33	2	3. Time To Get Down	Philadelphia I. 3531
1/12/74	**10**	11	4. **Put Your Hands Together**	Philadelphia I. 3535
5/4/74	**9**	10	● 5. **For The Love Of Money**	Philadelphia I. 3544
11/15/75+	**5**	14	● 6. **I Love Music (Part 1)** #1 R&B hit (1 week)	Philadelphia I. 3577
3/27/76	20	6	7. Livin' For The Weekend #1 R&B hit (2 weeks)	Philadelphia I. 3587
6/3/78	**4**	11	● 8. **Use Ta Be My Girl** #1 R&B hit (5 weeks)	Philadelphia I. 3642
1/5/80	28	5	9. Forever Mine	Philadelphia I. 3727
			O'KAYSIONS, The	
			White pop-rock group from Wilson, North Carolina: Donny Weaver (vocals, organ), Wayne Pittman (guitar), Ron Turner (trumpet), Jim Speidel (sax), Jimmy Hennant (bass) and Bruce Joyner (drums).	
9/7/68	**5**	11	● 1. **Girl Watcher**	ABC 11094
			O'KEEFE, Danny	
			Born in 1943 in Wenatchee, Washington. Pop singer/songwriter.	
9/23/72	**9**	10	1. **Good Time Charlie's Got The Blues**	Signpost 70006
			OLDFIELD, Mike	
			Born on 5/15/53 in Reading, Berkshire, England. Classical-rock, multi-instrumentalist/composer.	
3/30/74	**7**	10	1. **Tubular Bells** [I] theme from the movie *The Exorcist* starring Linda Blair	Virgin 55100
			OL' DIRTY BASTARD	
			Born Russell Jones on 11/15/68 in Brooklyn, New York. Male rapper. Member of Wu-Tang Clan.	
6/27/98	**15**	16	1. Ghetto Supastar (That Is What You Are) Airplay #11 **PRAS MICHEL featuring OL' DIRTY BASTARD & introducing MYA** samples "Get Up, Get Into It, Get Involved" by James Brown and contains an interpolation of "Islands In The Stream"; from the movie *Bulworth* starring Warren Beatty	Interscope 95021
12/11/99	33	6	2. Got Your Money Airplay #20 / Sales #26 **OL' DIRTY BASTARD featuring Kelis**	Elektra 67022

DATE	POS	WKS	ARTIST–RECORD TITLE	LABEL & NO.
			OLIVER	
			Born William Oliver Swofford on 2/22/45 in North Wilkesboro, North Carolina. Died of cancer on 2/12/2000 (age 54). Adult Contemporary singer.	
6/7/69	3	11	1. **Good Morning Starshine** from the off-Broadway musical *Hair* starring Steve Curry	Jubilee 5659
8/30/69	2 (2)	12	● 2. **Jean** #1 Adult Contemporary hit (4 weeks); written by Rod McKuen; from the movie *The Prime Of Miss Jean Brodie* starring Maggie Smith	Crewe 334
12/20/69	35	2	3. Sunday Mornin' above 3 produced by Bob Crewe	Crewe 337
			OLIVIA	
			Born Olivia Longott in 1980 in Brooklyn, New York; raised in Queens, New York. R&B singer/rapper.	
4/7/01	15	6	1. Bizounce Sales #2 / Airplay #73	J Records 21026
			OLLIE & JERRY	
			R&B vocal duo: Ollie Brown and Jerry Knight (former member of Raydio).	
6/16/84	9	11	1. **Breakin'...There's No Stopping Us** from the movie *Breakin'* starring break-dancers Adolfo Quinones and Michael Chambers	Polydor 821708
			OL SKOOL	
			R&B group from St. Louis, Missouri: Pookie (vocals), Tony Love (guitar), Curtis Jefferson (bass) and Bobby Crawford (drums).	
2/14/98	31	3	1. Am I Dreaming Sales #16 **OL SKOOL [Featuring Keith Sweat and Xscape]**	Universal 56163
			OLSSON, Nigel	
			Born on 2/10/49 in Merseyside, England. Drummer for Elton John's band from 1971-76.	
1/27/79	18	9	1. Dancin' Shoes	Bang 740
5/19/79	34	4	2. Little Bit Of Soap	Bang 4800
			OLYMPICS, The	
			R&B vocal group from Compton, California: Walter Ward, Eddie Lewis, Charles Fizer, Melvin King and Walter Hammond. Fizer was killed during a race riot on 8/14/65 (age 25).	
8/4/58	8	11	1. **Western Movies** Hot 100 #8 / Best Seller #11 **[N]**	Demon 1508
6/8/63	40	2	2. The Bounce	Tri Disc 106
			OMC	
			Born Pauly Fuemana on 2/8/69 in Otara, New Zealand. Singer/songwriter. OMC stands for Otara Millionaires Club.	
5/24/97	4 ^A	36	1. **How Bizarre** from the album *How Bizarre* on Mercury 533435	album cut

DATE	POS	WKS	ARTIST–RECORD TITLE	LABEL & NO.
			O'NEAL, Alexander	
			Born on 11/15/53 in Natchez, Mississippi; raised in Minneapolis, Minnesota. R&B singer.	
3/29/86	26	6	1. Saturday Love Sales #19 **CHERRELLE with ALEXANDER O'NEAL**	Tabu 05767
9/5/87	25	6	2. Fake Sales #24 / Airplay #27 #1 R&B hit (2 weeks)	Tabu 07100
3/5/88	28	6	3. Never Knew Love Like This Airplay #26 / Sales #28 **ALEXANDER O'NEAL featuring Cherrelle**	Tabu 07646
			O'NEAL, Jamie	
			Born Jamie Murphy on 6/3/68 in Sydney, Australia; raised in Hawaii and Nevada. Female country singer.	
2/10/01	40	3	1. There Is No Arizona Airplay #33 #1 Country hit (1 week)	album cut
8/4/01	35	3	2. When I Think About Angels Airplay #26 #1 Country hit (1 week)	album cut
			O'NEAL, Shaquille	
			Born on 3/6/72 in Newark, New Jersey. Male rapper/actor. Professional basketball player with the NBA's Orlando Magic and Los Angeles Lakers. Starred in the movies *Blue Chips*, *Kazaam* and *Steel*.	
8/14/93	39	1	● 1. What's Up Doc? (Can We Rock?) Sales #21 / Airplay #66 **FU-SCHNICKENS with Shaquille O'Neal (Shaq-Fu)**	Jive 42164
11/13/93	35	10	● 2. (I Know I Got) Skillz Sales #15 samples "Snake Eyes" by Main Source	Jive 42177
			100 PROOF AGED IN SOUL	
			R&B vocal trio from Detroit, Michigan: Clyde "Steve Mancha" Wilson, Joe Stubbs and Eddie "Holiday" Anderson. Stubbs, brother of Levi Stubbs of the Four Tops, was also a member of The Contours.	
10/3/70	8	10	● 1. **Somebody's Been Sleeping**	Hot Wax 7004
			ONE 2 MANY	
			Pop trio from Norway: Camilla Griehsel (vocals), Jan Gisle Ytterdal (guitar) and Dag Kolsrud (keyboards).	
5/6/89	37	4	1. Downtown Airplay #31	A&M 1272
			112	
			R&B group from Atlanta, Georgia: Daron Jones (keyboards), Marvin Scandrick (strings), Mike Keith (keyboards) and Quinnes Parker (drums). All share lead vocals. Name pronounced: one-twelve.	
6/15/96	13	23	● 1. Only You Sales #8 / Airplay #32 samples "I Get Lifted" by KC & The Sunshine Band	Bad Boy 79060
12/14/96+	33	6	2. Come See Me Sales #22	Bad Boy 79073
3/22/97	13	24	▲ 3. Cupid Sales #10 / Airplay #33	Bad Boy 79087
6/14/97	1 (11)	29	▲³ 4. I'll Be Missing You Sales #1 (9) / Airplay #4 **PUFF DADDY & FAITH EVANS (Featuring 112)** #1 R&B hit (8 weeks); "tribute to The Notorious B.I.G."; samples "Every Breath You Take" by The Police	Bad Boy 79097
8/30/97	4	24	● 5. All Cried Out Sales #6 / Airplay #8 **ALLURE featuring 112**	Crave 78678

DATE	POS	WKS	ARTIST–RECORD TITLE	LABEL & NO.
10/24/98	**17**	13	● 6. Love Me _Sales #8_ **112 featuring MA$E** samples "Don't You Know That?" by Luther Vandross	Bad Boy 79184
4/17/99	**15**	18	7. Anywhere _Airplay #7_ **112 [Feat. Lil' Z]**	Bad Boy 79214
8/19/00	**21**	4	8. Callin' Me _Sales #3_ **LIL' ZANE feat. 112**	Priority 53582
2/24/01	**6**	8	9. It's Over Now _Sales #1 (2) / Airplay #31_ #1 R&B hit (2 weeks); contains an interpolation of "White Lines" by Grandmaster & Melle Mel	Bad Boy 79366
5/5/01	**4**	25	10. **Peaches & Cream** _Airplay #2 / Sales #58_	Bad Boy 79387
10/27/01	**39**	2	11. Dance With Me _Airplay #34_	Bad Boy 79413
			ONYX	
			Rap group from Jamaica, Queens, New York: Fredro "Starr" Scruggs, Kirk "Sticky Fingaz" Jones, Marlon "Big D.S." Fletcher and Suave Sonny Caesar. Fredro Starr went on to act in several movies. Fletcher left in 1995; died of cancer on 5/22/2003 (age 30).	
6/26/93	**4**	14	▲ 1. **Slam** _Sales #3 / Airplay #23_	JMJ/RAL 77053
			OPUS	
			Pop-rock group from Austria: Herwig Rudisser (vocals), Ewald Pfleger (guitar), Kurt Rene Plisnier (keyboards), Niki Gruber (bass) and Gunter Grasmuck (drums).	
3/15/86	**32**	5	1. Live Is Life _Sales #23_ **[L]**	Polydor 883730
			ORBISON, Roy	
			Born on 4/23/36 in Vernon, Texas. Died of a heart attack on 12/6/88 (age 52). Pop-rock singer/songwriter/guitarist. Wife Claudette killed in a motorcycle accident on 6/7/66; two sons died in a fire in 1968. Inducted into the Rock and Roll Hall of Fame in 1987. Won Grammy's Lifetime Achievement Award in 1998. Member of the Traveling Wilburys.	
6/20/60	**2** (1)	15	1. **Only The Lonely (Know How I Feel)**	Monument 421
10/17/60	**9**	8	2. **Blue Angel**	Monument 425
12/31/60+	**27**	3	3. I'm Hurtin'	Monument 433
4/24/61	**1** (1)	15	4. **Running Scared**	Monument 438
8/28/61	**2** (1)	14	5. **Crying /**	
10/9/61	**25**	5	6. Candy Man	Monument 447
3/3/62	**4**	9	7. **Dream Baby (How Long Must I Dream)**	Monument 456
6/23/62	**26**	6	8. The Crowd	Monument 461
10/27/62	**25**	5	9. Léah /	
10/27/62	**33**	4	10. Workin' For The Man Bob Moore (orch., all of above)	Monument 467
2/23/63	**7**	10	11. **In Dreams**	Monument 806
6/22/63	**22**	5	12. Falling	Monument 815
9/28/63	**5**	10	13. **Mean Woman Blues /** #11 R&B and Country hit for Elvis Presley in 1957 (from the Elvis movie _Loving You_)	
10/12/63	**29**	5	14. Blue Bayou	Monument 824
12/21/63	**15**	5	15. Pretty Paper **[X]** written by Willie Nelson	Monument 830
4/25/64	**9**	9	16. **It's Over**	Monument 837

DATE	POS	WKS	ARTIST–RECORD TITLE	LABEL & NO.
9/5/64	**1** (3)	14	● 17. **Oh, Pretty Woman**	Monument 851
			ROY ORBISON And The Candy Men	
2/20/65	**21**	6	18. Goodnight	Monument 873
8/7/65	**39**	2	19. (Say) You're My Girl	Monument 891
9/18/65	**25**	5	20. Ride Away	MGM 13386
2/12/66	**31**	4	21. Breakin' Up Is Breakin' My Heart	MGM 13446
5/21/66	**39**	2	22. Twinkle Toes	MGM 13498
2/18/89	**9**	11	23. **You Got It** Sales #6 / Airplay #15	Virgin 99245
			#1 Adult Contemporary hit (2 weeks); written by Orbison, Jeff Lynne and Tom Petty; first released with "Crying" as the B-side	
			ORCHESTRAL MANOEUVRES IN THE DARK	
			Electro-pop group formed in England: keyboardists/vocalists Andrew McCluskey and Paul Humphreys, multi-instrumentalist Martin Cooper and drummer Malcolm Holmes. Humphreys left in 1989.	
10/12/85	**26**	7	1. So In Love Sales #23 / Airplay #23	A&M 2746
4/5/86	**4**	13	2. **If You Leave** Airplay #3 / Sales #5	A&M 2811
			from the movie *Pretty In Pink* starring Molly Ringwald	
11/1/86	**19**	7	3. (Forever) Live And Die Sales #18 / Airplay #23	A&M 2872
4/16/88	**16**	9	4. Dreaming Sales #15 / Airplay #15	A&M 3002
			ORIGINAL CASTE, The	
			Pop group from Canada: Dixie Lee Innes (lead vocals), Bruce Innes, Graham Bruce, Joseph Cavender and Bliss Mackie.	
2/7/70	**34**	2	1. One Tin Soldier	T·A 186
			version by Coven became the theme for the 1971 movie *Billy Jack* starring Tom Laughlin	
			ORIGINALS, The	
			R&B vocal group from Detroit, Michigan: Fred Gorman, Crathman Spencer, Henry Dixon and Walter Gaines.	
10/18/69	**14**	13	1. Baby, I'm For Real	Soul 35066
			#1 R&B hit (5 weeks)	
3/7/70	**12**	9	2. The Bells	Soul 35069
			above 2 written and produced by Marvin Gaye	
			ORLANDO, Tony (& DAWN)	
			Born Michael Anthony Orlando Cassavitis on 4/3/44 in Manhattan, New York. At age 16 was discovered by producer Don Kirshner. In 1967, became manager of April-Blackwood Music publishing company. Lead singer of New York studio group Wind in 1969. In 1971, teamed with session singers Telma Hopkins (from Louisville, Kentucky) and Joyce Vincent (from Detroit, Michigan) to form Dawn. Trio hosted weekly TV variety show *Tony Orlando & Dawn* from 1974-76. Group split in 1977. Orlando continued solo career. Hopkins acted on TV's *Bosom Buddies*, *Gimme A Break* and *Family Matters*.	
			TONY ORLANDO:	
5/29/61	**39**	2	1. Halfway To Paradise	Epic 9441
9/4/61	**15**	7	2. Bless You	Epic 9452
			above 2 arranged by Carole King	
10/4/69	**28**	4	3. Make Believe	Life 200
			WIND	
			B-side charted in 1970 as by Cool Heat	

DATE	POS	WKS	ARTIST–RECORD TITLE	LABEL & NO.
			DAWN:	
8/29/70	**3**	13	● 4. **Candida**	Bell 903
12/5/70+	**1** (3)	16	● 5. **Knock Three Times**	Bell 938
4/10/71	**25**	5	6. I Play And Sing	Bell 970
7/10/71	**33**	6	7. Summer Sand	Bell 45,107
			DAWN FEATURING TONY ORLANDO:	
11/13/71	**39**	1	8. What Are You Doing Sunday	Bell 45,141
3/17/73	**1** (4)	17	● 9. **Tie A Yellow Ribbon Round The Ole Oak Tree**	Bell 45,318
			#1 Adult Contemporary hit (2 weeks)	
7/28/73	**3**	13	● 10. **Say, Has Anybody Seen My Sweet Gypsy Rose**	Bell 45,374
			#1 Adult Contemporary hit (3 weeks)	
			TONY ORLANDO & DAWN:	
12/1/73	**27**	7	11. Who's In The Strawberry Patch With Sally	Bell 45,424
9/7/74	**7**	9	12. **Steppin' Out (Gonna Boogie Tonight)**	Bell 45,601
1/11/75	**11**	8	13. Look In My Eyes Pretty Woman	Bell 45,620
3/29/75	**1** (3)	10	● 14. **He Don't Love You (Like I Love You)**	Elektra 45240
			#1 Adult Contemporary hit (1 week)	
7/12/75	**14**	6	15. Mornin' Beautiful	Elektra 45260
9/20/75	**34**	3	16. You're All I Need To Get By	Elektra 45275
2/21/76	**22**	6	17. Cupid	Elektra 45302
			ORLEANS	
			Pop-rock group formed in New York: John Hall (guitar), brothers Lawrence (vocals, guitar) and Lance (bass) Hoppen, Jerry Marotta (keyboards), and Wells Kelly (drums). Hall and Marotta left in 1977, replaced by Bob Leinback (keyboards) and R.A. Martin (horns). Kelly died on 10/29/84 (age 35).	
8/30/75	**6**	11	● 1. **Dance With Me**	Asylum 45261
8/14/76	**5**	12	● 2. **Still The One**	Asylum 45336
4/7/79	**11**	9	3. Love Takes Time	Infinity 50,006
			ORLONS, The	
			R&B vocal group from Philadelphia, Pennsylvania: Rosetta Hightower, Marlena Davis, Shirley Brickley and Steve Caldwell. Brickley was shot to death on 10/13/77 (age 32).	
6/23/62	**2** (2)	11	1. **The Wah Watusi**	Cameo 218
11/3/62	**4**	11	2. **Don't Hang Up**	Cameo 231
3/2/63	**3**	10	3. **South Street**	Cameo 243
7/6/63	**12**	7	4. Not Me	Cameo 257
10/19/63	**19**	5	5. Cross Fire!	Cameo 273
			ORR, Benjamin — see CARS, The	
			ORRALL, Robert Ellis	
			Born on 5/4/55 in Winthrop, Massachusetts. Country-pop singer/songwriter/pianist.	
5/7/83	**32**	3	1. I Couldn't Say No	RCA 13431
			ROBERT ELLIS ORRALL WITH CARLENE CARTER	

DATE	POS	WKS	ARTIST–RECORD TITLE	LABEL & NO.
			ORRICO, Stacie	
			Born on 3/3/86 in Seattle, Washington. Christian pop singer/songwriter.	
11/15/03	30	7	1. (there's gotta be) More To Life　　Sales #15 / Airplay #32	Virgin/ForeFront 52925
			OSBORNE, Jeffrey	
			Born on 3/9/48 in Providence, Rhode Island. R&B singer/songwriter/drummer. Lead singer of L.T.D. until 1980.	
8/14/82	39	2	1. I Really Don't Need No Light	A&M 2410
11/20/82	29	7	2. On The Wings Of Love	A&M 2434
8/20/83	25	6	3. Don't You Get So Mad	A&M 2561
12/17/83+	30	8	4. Stay With Me Tonight	A&M 2591
10/6/84	40	2	5. The Last Time I Made Love	A&M 2656
			JOYCE KENNEDY & JEFFREY OSBORNE	
3/2/85	38	2	6. The Borderlines	A&M 2695
6/28/86	13	11	7. You Should Be Mine (The Woo Woo Song)　　Sales #13 / Airplay #16	A&M 2814
7/25/87	12	9	8. Love Power　　Sales #7 / Airplay #14	Arista 9567
			DIONNE WARWICK & JEFFREY OSBORNE #1 Adult Contemporary hit (1 week)	
			OSBORNE, Joan	
			Born on 7/8/62 in Anchorage, Kentucky. Adult Alternative singer/songwriter/guitarist.	
12/9/95+	4	21	● 1. **One Of Us**　　Sales #5 / Airplay #5	Blue Gorilla 852368
			OSBOURNE, Ozzy	
			Born John Osbourne on 12/3/48 in Birmingham, England. Former lead singer of Black Sabbath. Appeared in the 1986 movie *Trick Or Treat*. MTV began airing *The Osbournes*, a reality show based on his family's home life, in 2002.	
4/22/89	8	12	● 1. **Close My Eyes Forever**　　Sales #4 / Airplay #13	RCA 8899
			LITA FORD (with Ozzy Osbourne)	
3/21/92	28	7	2. Mama, I'm Coming Home　　Sales #17 / Airplay #75	Epic Associated 74093
			OSMOND, Donny	
			Born on 12/9/57 in Ogden, Utah. Lead singer of The Osmonds. Starred in the stage musical *Joseph And The Amazing Technicolor Dreamcoat*. Co-hosted musical variety series and daytime talk show with sister Marie.	
5/1/71	7	11	● 1. **Sweet And Innocent**	MGM 14227
			DONNY OSMOND of The Osmonds first recorded by Roy Orbison in 1958	
8/21/71	1 (3)	13	● 2. **Go Away Little Girl**	MGM 14285
12/4/71+	9	9	● 3. **Hey Girl** /	
12/4/71+		9	4. I Knew You When	MGM 14322
3/4/72	3	10	● 5. **Puppy Love**	MGM 14367
6/17/72	13	8	6. Too Young	MGM 14407
			#1 hit for Nat "King" Cole in 1951	
9/16/72	13	9	7. Why /	
9/16/72		9	8. Lonely Boy	MGM/Kolob 14424
3/24/73	8	9	● 9. **The Twelfth Of Never**	MGM/Kolob 14503

DATE	POS	WKS	ARTIST–RECORD TITLE	LABEL & NO.
8/4/73	23	7	10. A Million To One /	
8/4/73	25	7	11. Young Love	MGM/Kolob 14583
12/15/73+	14	8	12. Are You Lonesome Tonight #4 hit for Vaughn Deleath in 1927	MGM/Kolob 14677
7/24/76	38	3	13. C'mon Marianne	Polydor/Kolob 14320
4/15/89	2 (1)	11	14. **Soldier Of Love** Sales #1 (1) / Airplay #4	Capitol 44369
7/15/89	13	9	15. Sacred Emotion Airplay #11 / Sales #15	Capitol 44379
11/3/90	21	9	16. My Love Is A Fire Airplay #18 / Sales #28	Capitol 44634

OSMOND, Donny And Marie

Brother-and-sister co-hosts of own musical/variety TV series and later of own daytime talk show. Starred in the movie *Goin' Coconuts*.

DATE	POS	WKS	ARTIST–RECORD TITLE	LABEL & NO.
7/27/74	4	10	● 1. **I'm Leaving It (All) Up To You** #1 Adult Contemporary hit (1 week); first recorded by Don & Dewey in 1957	MGM/Kolob 14735
12/14/74+	8	10	2. **Morning Side Of The Mountain** #1 Adult Contemporary hit (1 week); #16 hit for Paul Weston in 1951	MGM/Kolob 14765
1/24/76	14	13	3. Deep Purple #1 hit for Larry Clinton in 1939	MGM/Kolob 14840

DONNY & MARIE:

DATE	POS	WKS	ARTIST–RECORD TITLE	LABEL & NO.
12/25/76+	21	8	4. Ain't Nothing Like The Real Thing	Polydor/Kolob 14363
1/7/78	38	3	5. (You're My) Soul And Inspiration	Polydor/Kolob 14439
11/18/78	38	2	6. On The Shelf	Polydor/Kolob 14510

OSMOND, Little Jimmy

Born on 4/16/63 in Canoga Park, California. Youngest member of the Osmonds Family.

DATE	POS	WKS	ARTIST–RECORD TITLE	LABEL & NO.
6/3/72	38	3	1. Long Haired Lover From Liverpool **LITTLE JIMMY OSMOND with The Mike Curb Congregation**	MGM 14376

OSMOND, Marie

Born Olive Marie Osmond on 10/13/59 in Ogden, Utah. Co-hosted musical variety series and daytime talk show with brother Donny. Co-hosted the TV series *Ripley's Believe It Or Not*. Starred in 1995 TV series *Maybe This Time*.

DATE	POS	WKS	ARTIST–RECORD TITLE	LABEL & NO.
10/6/73	5	12	● 1. **Paper Roses** #1 Country hit (2 weeks) / #1 Adult Contemporary hit (1 week)	MGM/Kolob 14609
4/5/75	40	2	2. Who's Sorry Now #3 hit for Isham Jones in 1923; above 2 produced by Sonny James	MGM/Kolob 14786
6/4/77	39	1	3. This Is The Way That I Feel	Polydor/Kolob 14385

OSMONDS, The

Family group from Ogden, Utah: Alan (born on 6/22/49), Wayne (born on 8/28/51), Merrill (born on 4/30/53), Jay (born on 3/2/55) and Donny (born on 12/9/57) Osmond. Regulars on Andy Williams's TV show from 1962-67.

DATE	POS	WKS	ARTIST–RECORD TITLE	LABEL & NO.
1/23/71	1 (5)	12	● 1. **One Bad Apple**	MGM 14193
5/29/71	14	7	2. Double Lovin'	MGM 14259
9/18/71	3	12	● 3. **Yo-Yo** written by Joe South; #117 hit for Billy Joe Royal in 1966	MGM 14295

DATE	POS	WKS	ARTIST–RECORD TITLE	LABEL & NO.
1/29/72	**4**	12	● 4. **Down By The Lazy River**	MGM 14324
7/8/72	**14**	7	5. Hold Her Tight	MGM 14405
11/11/72	**14**	8	6. Crazy Horses	MGM/Kolob 14450
7/7/73	**36**	2	7. Goin' Home	MGM/Kolob 14562
10/6/73	**36**	3	8. Let Me In	MGM/Kolob 14617
9/21/74	**10**	7	9. **Love Me For A Reason**	MGM/Kolob 14746
8/23/75	**22**	6	10. The Proud One	MGM/Kolob 14791
			#1 Adult Contemporary hit (1 week)	
			O'SULLIVAN, Gilbert	
			Born Raymond O'Sullivan on 12/1/46 in Waterford, Ireland. Adult Contemporary singer/songwriter.	
7/1/72	**1** (6)	15	● 1. **Alone Again (Naturally)**	MAM 3619
			#1 Adult Contemporary hit (6 weeks)	
11/11/72	**2** (2)	14	● 2. **Clair**	MAM 3626
			#1 Adult Contemporary hit (3 weeks)	
4/7/73	**17**	8	3. Out Of The Question	MAM 3628
7/14/73	**7**	11	● 4. **Get Down**	MAM 3629
11/10/73	**25**	4	5. Ooh Baby	MAM 3633
			OTHER ONES, The	
			Pop-rock group consisting of Australian siblings Jayney (vocals), Alf (vocals) and Johnny (bass) Klimek, and Germans Andreas Schwarz-Ruszczynski (guitar), Stephen Gottwald (keyboards) and Uwe Hoffmann (drums).	
10/10/87	**29**	4	1. Holiday Airplay #28 / Sales #32	Virgin 99428
			OTIS, Johnny, Show	
			Born John Veliotes on 12/8/21 in Vallejo, California. R&B bandleader/composer. Inducted into the Rock and Roll Hall of Fame in 1994.	
6/30/58	**9**	15	1. **Willie And The Hand Jive** Hot 100 #9 / Best Seller #14 / Jockey #17	Capitol 3966
			OTIS & CARLA — see REDDING, Otis/ THOMAS, Carla	
			O-TOWN	
			Male teen pop vocal group from Orlando, Florida: Trevor Penick, Jacob Underwood, Ashley Parker Angel, Erik-Michael Estrada and Dan Miller. Group was put together while auditioning for the TV series *Making The Band*.	
12/23/00+	**10**	10	● 1. **Liquid Dreams** Sales #1 (1)	J Records 21001
6/23/01	**3**	16	2. **All Or Nothing** Sales #4 / Airplay #10	J Records 21056
			OUTFIELD, The	
			Pop-rock trio formed in London, England: Tony Lewis (vocals, bass), John Spinks (guitar) and Alan Jackman (drums).	
3/22/86	**6**	12	1. **Your Love** Sales #6 / Airplay #6	Columbia 05796
7/12/86	**19**	7	2. All The Love In The World Airplay #17 / Sales #21	Columbia 05894
7/25/87	**31**	5	3. Since You've Been Gone Airplay #31 / Sales #32	Columbia 07170
4/29/89	**25**	6	4. Voices Of Babylon Sales #23 / Airplay #25	Columbia 68601
12/1/90+	**21**	9	5. For You Sales #21 / Airplay #22	MCA 53935

DATE	POS	WKS	ARTIST–RECORD TITLE	LABEL & NO.

OUTKAST

Male rap duo from Atlanta, Georgia: "Andre 3000" Benjamin and Antoine "Big Boi" Patton.

DATE	POS	WKS	ARTIST–RECORD TITLE	LABEL & NO.
4/9/94	37	5	● 1. Player's Ball Sales #15	LaFace 24060
7/27/96	12	13	● 2. Elevators (me & you) Sales #5	LaFace 24177
			Debra Killins and Sleepy Brown (background vocals)	
12/28/96+	35	3	3. ATLiens Sales #23	LaFace 24196
11/18/00+	1 (1)	21	4. **Ms. Jackson** Sales #2 / Airplay #3	LaFace 24525
			#1 R&B hit (2 weeks)	
4/28/01	30	7	5. So Fresh, So Clean Airplay #24 / Sales #64	LaFace 24537
1/5/02	19	15	6. The Whole World Airplay #17 / Sales #46	LaFace 24550
			OUTKAST Featuring Killer Mike & Joi	
11/1/03	1 (9)	28	▲ 7. **Hey Ya!** / Airplay #1 (9)	
10/11/03+	1 (1)	33↑	8. **The Way You Move** Airplay #2 / Sales #3	Arista 54962
			OUTKAST Featuring Sleepy Brown	

OUTLAWS

Southern-rock group formed in Tampa, Florida: Henry Paul (vocals, guitar), Hughie Thomasson and Billy Jones (guitars), Frank O'Keefe (bass) and Monte Yoho (drums). By 1981, Freddie Salem, Rick Cua and David Dix had replaced Paul, O'Keefe and Yoho. Jones died on 2/7/95 (age 45). O'Keefe died of a drug overdose on 2/26/95 (age 44).

DATE	POS	WKS	ARTIST–RECORD TITLE	LABEL & NO.
10/11/75	34	3	1. There Goes Another Love Song	Arista 0150
2/14/81	31	4	2. (Ghost) Riders In The Sky	Arista 0582
			#1 hit for Vaughn Monroe in 1949	

OUTSIDERS, The

Rock group from Cleveland, Ohio: Sonny Geraci (vocals), Tom King and Bill Bruno (guitars), Mert Madsen (bass), and Rick Baker (drums). Geraci later formed Climax.

DATE	POS	WKS	ARTIST–RECORD TITLE	LABEL & NO.
3/26/66	5	10	1. **Time Won't Let Me**	Capitol 5573
6/4/66	21	5	2. Girl In Love	Capitol 5646
8/20/66	15	6	3. Respectable	Capitol 5701
			written by The Isley Brothers	
12/10/66	37	2	4. Help Me Girl	Capitol 5759

OWEN, Reg, And His Orchestra

Born in 1928 in England. Orchestra leader.

DATE	POS	WKS	ARTIST–RECORD TITLE	LABEL & NO.
12/22/58+	10	13	1. **Manhattan Spiritual** [I]	Palette 5005

OWENS, Buck

Born Alvis Edgar Owens on 8/12/29 in Sherman, Texas; raised in Mesa, Arizona. Country singer/songwriter/guitarist. Co-host of TV's *Hee Haw* (1969-86). Backing group: The Buckaroos.

DATE	POS	WKS	ARTIST–RECORD TITLE	LABEL & NO.
2/13/65	25	5	1. **I've Got A Tiger By The Tail**	Capitol 5336
			#1 Country hit (5 weeks)	

OWENS, Donnie

Born on 10/30/38 in Pennsylvania. Accidentally shot to death on 10/27/94 (age 55). Pop singer/guitarist.

DATE	POS	WKS	ARTIST–RECORD TITLE	LABEL & NO.
11/3/58	25	8	1. Need You Hot 100 #25	Guyden 2001
			The Ben Denton Singers (backing vocals); Duane Eddy (acoustic guitar)	

DATE	POS	WKS	ARTIST–RECORD TITLE	LABEL & NO.
			OXO	
			Pop-rock group from Miami, Florida: Ish Ledesma (vocals), Orlando (guitar), Frank Garcia (bass) and Freddy Alwag (drums). Ledesma was a member of Foxy.	
4/2/83	28	6	1. Whirly Girl	Geffen 29765
			OZARK MOUNTAIN DAREDEVILS	
			Country-rock group from Springfield, Missouri: Larry Lee (vocals, drums), John Dillon (guitar), Steve Cash (harmonica) and Michael Granda (bass).	
6/8/74	25	5	1. If You Wanna Get To Heaven	A&M 1515
3/22/75	3	12	2. **Jackie Blue**	A&M 1654
			P	
			PABLO, Petey	
			Born Moses Barrett in Greenville, North Carolina. Male rapper/songwriter.	
10/6/01	25	11	1. Raise Up Sales #3 / Airplay #24	Jive 42937
			PABLO CRUISE	
			Pop-rock group from San Francisco, California: Dave Jenkins (vocals, guitar), Cory Lerios (keyboards), Bud Cockrell (bass) and Stephen Price (drums). Bruce Day replaced Cockrell in 1977. John Pierce replaced Day, and Angelo Rossi (guitar) joined in 1980.	
6/11/77	6	14	1. **Whatcha Gonna Do?**	A&M 1920
7/1/78	6	12	2. **Love Will Find A Way**	A&M 2048
10/21/78	21	8	3. Don't Want To Live Without It	A&M 2076
11/10/79	19	10	4. I Want You Tonight	A&M 2195
7/25/81	13	11	5. Cool Love	A&M 2349
			PACIFIC GAS & ELECTRIC	
			Blues-rock group from California: Charles Allen (vocals), Glenn Schwartz and Tom Marshall (guitars), Brent Block (bass) and Frank Cook (drums). Allen died on 5/7/90 (age 48).	
6/20/70	14	9	1. Are You Ready? The Blackberries (backing vocals)	Columbia 45158
			PAGE, Jimmy — see PUFF DADDY	
			PAGE, Martin	
			Born on 9/23/59 in Southampton, Hampshire, England. Pop singer/songwriter.	
2/4/95	14	26	1. In The House Of Stone And Light Airplay #4 / Sales #55 #1 Adult Contemporary hit (4 weeks)	Mercury 858940
			PAGE, Patti	
			Born Clara Ann Fowler on 11/8/27 in Muskogee, Oklahoma; raised in Tulsa, Oklahoma. Pop singer. Used multi-voice effect on her recordings. Own TV series The Patti Page Show (1955-58) and The Big Record (1957-58). Acted in the 1960 movie Elmer Gantry.	
12/18/54	8	7	1. **Let Me Go, Lover!** Jockey #8 / Juke Box #12 / Best Seller #24	Mercury 70511

DATE	POS	WKS	ARTIST–RECORD TITLE	LABEL & NO.
11/12/55	16	8	2. Croce Di Oro (Cross Of Gold) Top 100 #16 / Juke Box #16 / Jockey #17 / Best Seller #20	Mercury 70713
1/14/56	11	8	3. Go On With The Wedding Top 100 #11 / Juke Box #12 / Jockey #16 / Best Seller #17 Jack Rael (orch., all of above)	Mercury 70766
6/16/56	2 (2)	22	● 4. **Allegheny Moon** Juke Box #2 / Top 100 #2 / Jockey #2 / Best Seller #5	Mercury 70878
11/3/56	11	12	5. Mama From The Train Top 100 #11 / Jockey #12 / Juke Box #12 / Best Seller #17	Mercury 70971
3/23/57	14	6	6. A Poor Man's Roses (Or A Rich Man's Gold) Jockey #14 / Top 100 #27	Mercury 71059
6/3/57	3	17	7. **Old Cape Cod /** Jockey #3 / Top 100 #7 / Best Seller #8	
6/3/57	12	5	8. Wondering Jockey #12 / Top 100 #35 / Best Seller: flip	Mercury 71101
11/11/57	23	3	9. I'll Remember Today Jockey #23 / Best Seller #31 / Top 100 #32	Mercury 71189
2/10/58	13	8	10. Belonging To Someone Jockey #13 / Best Seller #32 / Top 100 #34	Mercury 71247
5/5/58	20	1	11. Another Time, Another Place Jockey #20 / Top 100 #81 title song from the movie starring Lana Turner	Mercury 71294
6/30/58	9	10	12. **Left Right Out Of Your Heart (Hi Lee Hi Lo** **Hi Lup Up Up)** Jockey #9 / Hot 100 #13 / Best Seller #14	Mercury 71331
10/20/58	39	1	13. Fibbin' Hot 100 #39 Vic Schoen (orch., above 10)	Mercury 71355
7/4/60	31	5	14. One Of Us (Will Weep Tonight)	Mercury 71639
5/12/62	27	4	15. Most People Get Married	Mercury 71950
5/22/65	8	9	16. **Hush, Hush, Sweet Charlotte** title song from the movie starring Bette Davis	Columbia 43251
			PAGE, Tommy	
			Born on 5/24/69 in West Caldwell, New Jersey. Pop singer/songwriter.	
4/15/89	29	6	1. A Shoulder To Cry On Airplay #27 / Sales #30	Sire 27645
2/24/90	1 (1)	13	● 2. **I'll Be Your Everything** Sales #1 (1) / Airplay #2 backing vocals by 3 members of New Kids On The Block	Sire 19959
			PAIGE, Jennifer	
			Born on 9/3/75 in Marietta, Georgia. Pop singer.	
7/18/98	3	23	● 1. **Crush** Sales #3 / Airplay #4	Edel America 64024
			PAIGE, Kevin	
			Born on 10/10/66 in Memphis, Tennessee. Pop singer/songwriter.	
10/14/89	18	10	1. Don't Shut Me Out Sales #15 / Airplay #20	Chrysalis 23389
2/24/90	29	5	2. Anything I Want Airplay #28 / Sales #31	Chrysalis 23444
			PAISLEY, Brad	
			Born on 10/28/72 in Glen Dale, West Virginia. Country singer/songwriter/ guitarist. Married actress Kimberly Williams on 3/15/2003.	
12/11/99	30	4	1. He Didn't Have To Be Airplay #20 #1 Country hit (1 week)	album cut
11/25/00	29	5	2. We Danced Airplay #25 #1 Country hit (2 weeks); above 2 from the album *Who Needs* *Pictures* on Arista 18871	album cut
2/9/02	35	4	3. Wrapped Around Airplay #31	album cut

DATE	POS	WKS	ARTIST–RECORD TITLE	LABEL & NO.
6/8/02	**29**	7	4. I'm Gonna Miss Her (The Fishin' Song) Airplay #26 **[N]** #1 Country hit (2 weeks); above 2 from the album *Part II* on Arista 67008	album cut
7/26/03	**31**	6	5. Celebrity Airplay #28 from the album *Mud On The Tires* on Arista Nashville 50605	album cut

PALMER, Robert

Born Alan Palmer on 1/19/49 in Batley, Yorkshire, England; raised on the Mediterranean island of Malta. Died of a heart attack on 9/26/2003 (age 54). Pop-rock singer. Lead singer of The Power Station.

DATE	POS	WKS	ARTIST–RECORD TITLE	LABEL & NO.
5/6/78	**16**	9	1. Every Kinda People	Island 100
8/11/79	**14**	10	2. Bad Case Of Loving You (Doctor, Doctor)	Island 49016
3/8/86	**1 (1)**	14	● 3. **Addicted To Love** Sales #1 (2) / Airplay #2 #1 Mainstream Rock hit (2 weeks)	Island 99570
6/28/86	**33**	5	4. Hyperactive Sales #29 / Airplay #36	Island 99545
9/13/86	**2 (1)**	13	5. **I Didn't Mean To Turn You On** Sales #2 / Airplay #2	Island 99537
7/16/88	**2 (2)**	14	6. **Simply Irresistible** Sales #2 / Airplay #2 #1 Mainstream Rock hit (3 weeks)	EMI-Manhattan 50133
11/12/88	**19**	9	7. Early In The Morning Airplay #18 / Sales #19	EMI-Manhattan 50157
12/22/90+	**28**	5	8. You're Amazing Sales #21 / Airplay #36	EMI 50338
3/2/91	**16**	10	9. Mercy Mercy Me (The Ecology)/I Want You Airplay #10 / Sales #21	EMI 50344

PAN'JABI MC

Born Rajinder Rai in 1975 in Coventry, England (Indian parents). Male DJ. Employs the "Bhangra" style of East Indian chants and beats combined with Western dance music.

DATE	POS	WKS	ARTIST–RECORD TITLE	LABEL & NO.
5/10/03	**33**	2	1. Beware Of The Boys (Mundian To Bach Ke) Sales #7 / Airplay #36 **PAN'JABI MC Featuring JAY-Z** Indian vocals by Labh Janjua; samples the theme from TV's *Knight Rider*	Sequence 8012

PAPERBOY

Born Mitchell Johnson in Los Angeles, California. Male rapper.

DATE	POS	WKS	ARTIST–RECORD TITLE	LABEL & NO.
1/9/93	**10**	25	▲ 1. **Ditty** Sales #4 / Airplay #21 samples "Doo Wa Ditty (Blow That Thing)" by Zapp (Roger)	Next Plateau 357012

PAPER LACE

Pop-rock group formed in England: Phil Wright (vocals, drums), Michael Vaughan and Chris Morris (guitars), and Cliff Fish (bass).

DATE	POS	WKS	ARTIST–RECORD TITLE	LABEL & NO.
7/13/74	**1 (1)**	11	● 1. **The Night Chicago Died**	Mercury 73492

PARADE, The

Pop-rock trio from Los Angeles, California: Jerry Riopelle, Murray MacLeod and Smokey Roberds.

DATE	POS	WKS	ARTIST–RECORD TITLE	LABEL & NO.
5/6/67	**20**	5	1. Sunshine Girl	A&M 841

PARADONS, The

R&B vocal group from Bakersfield, California: West Tyler, Chuck Weldon, Billy Myers and William Powers.

DATE	POS	WKS	ARTIST–RECORD TITLE	LABEL & NO.
9/26/60	**18**	7	1. Diamonds And Pearls	Milestone 2003

DATE	POS	WKS	ARTIST–RECORD TITLE	LABEL & NO.
			PARIS SISTERS, The	
			Female vocal trio from San Francisco, California: Albeth, Priscilla and Sherrell Paris.	
10/2/61	5	11	1. **I Love How You Love Me**	Gregmark 6
3/3/62	34	3	2. He Knows I Love Him Too Much	Gregmark 10
			above 2 produced by Phil Spector	
			PARKER, Fess	
			Born on 8/16/27 in Fort Worth, Texas. Singer/actor. Starred in the movie *Davy Crockett* and TV's *Daniel Boone* (1964-70).	
3/12/55	5	17	1. **Ballad Of Davy Crockett** Best Seller #5 / Jockey #10	Columbia 40449
			introduced by Parker in the 12/15/54 *Disneyland* TV episode "Davy Crockett Indian Fighter"	
2/9/57	12	6	2. Wringle Wrangle Best Seller #12 / Top 100 #21	Disneyland 43
			Camarata (orch.); from the movie *Westward Ho, The Wagons!* starring Parker	
			PARKER, Graham	
			Born on 11/18/50 in London, England. Pop-rock singer/songwriter/guitarist.	
6/15/85	39	3	1. Wake Up (Next To You)	Elektra 69654
			GRAHAM PARKER AND THE SHOT	
			PARKER, Ray Jr./Raydio	
			Born on 5/1/54 in Detroit, Michigan. R&B singer/songwriter/guitarist. Prominent session guitarist in California; worked with Stevie Wonder, Barry White and others. Formed group Raydio in 1977 with Arnell Carmichael, Jerry Knight, Larry Tolbert, Darren Carmichael and Charles Fearing. Parker went solo in 1982. Knight later recorded in duo Ollie & Jerry.	
			RAYDIO:	
2/11/78	8	16	● 1. **Jack And Jill**	Arista 0283
6/9/79	9	14	2. **You Can't Change That**	Arista 0399
			RAY PARKER JR. & RAYDIO:	
6/7/80	30	5	3. Two Places At The Same Time	Arista 0494
4/25/81	4	15	4. **A Woman Needs Love (Just Like You Do)**	Arista 0592
			#1 R&B hit (2 weeks)	
8/8/81	21	6	5. That Old Song	Arista 0616
			RAY PARKER JR.:	
4/10/82	4	14	6. **The Other Woman**	Arista 0669
8/21/82	38	3	7. Let Me Go	Arista 0695
1/15/83	35	4	8. Bad Boy	Arista 1030
12/10/83+	12	11	9. I Still Can't Get Over Loving You	Arista 9116
6/30/84	1 (3)	14	● 10. **Ghostbusters**	Arista 9212
			#1 R&B hit (2 weeks); title song from the movie starring Bill Murray	
12/1/84+	14	11	11. Jamie Airplay #11 / Sales #18	Arista 9293
10/26/85	34	4	12. Girls Are More Fun	Arista 9352
9/22/90	32	4	13. All I'm Missing Is You Sales #29 / Airplay #29	MCA 53886
			GLENN MEDEIROS Featuring Ray Parker Jr.	

DATE	POS	WKS	ARTIST–RECORD TITLE	LABEL & NO.
			PARKER, Robert	
5/21/66	7	9	Born on 10/14/30 in Crescent City, Louisiana. R&B singer/saxophonist. 1. **Barefootin'**	Nola 721
			PARKS, Michael	
3/28/70	20	8	Born on 4/4/38 in Corona, California. Singer/actor. Appeared in several movies. Played "Jim Bronson" in the 1969 TV series Then Came Bronson. 1. Long Lonesome Highway	MGM 14104
			PARLIAMENT/FUNKADELIC	
			R&B-funk group formed by singer/songwriter/producer George Clinton. Started as vocal group The Parliaments: Clinton, Raymond Davis, Calvin Simon, Clarence "Fuzzy" Haskins and Grady Thomas. Evolved into Parliament (more pop oriented) and Funkadelic (more experimental). Both groups shared the same personnel. Core members: brothers Phelps "Catfish" Collins (guitar) and William "Bootsy" Collins (bass), Bernie Worrell (keyboards), Maceo Parker and Fred Wesley (horns), and Frank "Kash" Waddy (drums). Most had also played in James Brown's backing band. Inducted into the Rock and Roll Hall of Fame in 1997.	
8/5/67	20	7	1. (I Wanna) Testify **THE PARLIAMENTS**	Revilot 207
6/12/76	15	10	● 2. Tear The Roof Off The Sucker (Give Up The Funk)	Casablanca 856
2/25/78	16	12	● 3. Flash Light **PARLIAMENT** (above 2) #1 R&B hit (3 weeks)	Casablanca 909
11/4/78	28	5	● 4. One Nation Under A Groove - Part I **FUNKADELIC** #1 R&B hit (6 weeks)	Warner 8618
8/27/94	23	11	● 5. Bop Gun (One Nation) Sales #12 / Airplay #34 **ICE CUBE featuring George Clinton**	Priority 53155
			PARR, John	
2/2/85	23	8	Born on 11/18/54 in Nottingham, Nottinghamshire, England. Pop-rock singer/songwriter. 1. Naughty Naughty Airplay #22 / Sales #25	Atlantic 89612
7/20/85	1 (2)	14	2. **St. Elmo's Fire (Man In Motion)** Sales #1 (2) / Airplay #1 (1) from the movie St. Elmo's Fire starring Emilio Estevez and Rob Lowe	Atlantic 89541
			PARSONS, Alan, Project	
			Born on 12/20/49 in London, England. Guitarist/keyboardist/producer. Engineered Abbey Road by The Beatles and Dark Side Of The Moon by Pink Floyd. Project features various musicians and vocalists. Eric Woolfson (vocals, keyboards) contributes most of the lyrics.	
9/11/76	37	2	1. (The System Of) Doctor Tarr And Professor Fether John Miles (vocal)	20th Century 2297
9/24/77	36	3	2. I Wouldn't Want To Be Like You **ALAN PARSONS**	Arista 0260
11/17/79	27	8	3. Damned If I Do	Arista 0454
1/24/81	16	10	4. Games People Play Lenny Zakatek (vocal, above 2)	Arista 0573
6/6/81	15	12	5. Time	Arista 0598
7/31/82	3	17	6. **Eye In The Sky**	Arista 0696
3/24/84	15	8	7. Don't Answer Me	Arista 9160
6/23/84	34	3	8. Prime Time	Arista 9208

DATE	POS	WKS	ARTIST—RECORD TITLE	LABEL & NO.
			PARSONS, Bill — see BARE, Bobby	
			PARTLAND BROTHERS	
			Rock duo from Colgan, Ontario, Canada: Chris (vocals, guitars) and G.P. (vocals, percussion) Partland.	Manhattan 50065
6/6/87	27	5	1. Soul City　　　　　　　Sales #26 / Airplay #27	
			PARTNERS IN KRYME	
			Hip-hop duo formed in Syracuse, New York: DJ James Alpern and rapper Richard Usher. KRYME: Keeping Rhythm Your Motivating Energy.	SBK 07325
5/12/90	13	8	● 1. Turtle Power!　　　　　　Sales #12 / Airplay #17 from the movie *Teenage Mutant Ninja Turtles* starring Elias Koteas	
			PARTON, Dolly	
			Born on 1/19/46 in Locust Ridge, Tennessee. Country singer/songwriter/actress. Regular on Porter Wagoner's TV show (1967-74). Starred in the movies *9 To 5*, *The Best Little Whorehouse In Texas*, *Steel Magnolias* and *Straight Talk*. In 1986, opened Dollywood theme park in the Smoky Mountains. Hosted own TV variety show in 1987.	
11/12/77+	3	13	● 1. **Here You Come Again** #1 Country hit (5 weeks)	RCA 11123
4/8/78	19	8	2. Two Doors Down	RCA 11240
9/23/78	37	4	3. Heartbreaker #1 Country hit (3 weeks)	RCA 11296
1/13/79	25	7	4. Baby I'm Burnin'	RCA 11420
5/3/80	36	3	5. Starting Over Again #1 Country hit (1 week)	RCA 11926
12/20/80+	1 (2)	18	● 6. **9 To 5** #1 Country hit (1 week) / #1 Adult Contemporary hit (2 weeks); title song from the movie starring Parton and Jane Fonda	RCA 12133
9/10/83	1 (2)	18	▲ 7. **Islands In The Stream** **KENNY ROGERS with Dolly Parton** #1 Country hit (2 weeks) / #1 Adult Contemporary hit (4 weeks); written by the Bee Gees	RCA 13615
			PARTRIDGE FAMILY, The	
			Popularized through *The Partridge Family* TV series, broadcast from 1970-74. Recordings by series stars David Cassidy (lead singer) and real-life stepmother Shirley Jones (backing vocals). David, son of actor Jack Cassidy, was born on 4/12/50 in New York; raised in California. Shirley, born on 3/31/34 in Smithton, Pennsylvania, starred in the movie musicals *Oklahoma* and *The Music Man*; married to David's father from 1956-74. **THE PARTRIDGE FAMILY STARRING SHIRLEY JONES FEATURING DAVID CASSIDY:**	
10/31/70	1 (3)	16	● 1. **I Think I Love You**	Bell 910
2/20/71	6	11	● 2. **Doesn't Somebody Want To Be Wanted**	Bell 963
5/15/71	9	8	3. **I'll Meet You Halfway**	Bell 996
8/21/71	13	10	4. I Woke Up In Love This Morning	Bell 45,130
1/1/72	20	6	5. It's One Of Those Nights (Yes Love)	Bell 45,160
7/29/72	28	4	6. Breaking Up Is Hard To Do	Bell 45,235
1/27/73	39	2	7. Looking Through The Eyes Of Love	Bell 45,301

DATE	POS	WKS	ARTIST–RECORD TITLE	LABEL & NO.
			PARTY, The	
			Pop-dance group from Florida: Tiffini Hale, Albert Fields, Chase Hampton, Damon Pampolina and Deedee Magno. All were cast members of TV's *The Mickey Mouse Club* in 1988.	
1/25/92	**34**	2	1. In My Dreams Airplay #30 / Sales #54	Hollywood 64832
			PASTELS, The	
			R&B vocal group formed at the U.S. Air Force base in Narsarssuak, Greenland: Big Dee Irwin, Richard Travis, Tony Thomas and Jimmy Willingham. Irwin died of heart failure on 8/27/95 (age 63).	
3/3/58	**24**	3	1. Been So Long Top 100 #24 / Best Seller #25	Argo 5287
			PASTEL SIX, The	
			Pop group from California: Bob Toten (lead vocals), Tony Stealman, Rick Rodriguez, Erick Fickert, Lynn Hamm, Bill Myers, Dave Cadison.	
1/19/63	**25**	5	1. The Cinnamon Cinder (It's A Very Nice Dance)	Zen 102
			PATIENCE & PRUDENCE	
			White vocal duo from Los Angeles, California: sisters Patience and Prudence McIntyre.	
8/25/56	**4**	17	● 1. **Tonight You Belong To Me** Best Seller #4 / Juke Box #4 / Jockey #5 / Top 100 #6 #1 hit for Gene Austin in 1927	Liberty 55022
12/1/56	**11**	12	2. Gonna Get Along Without Ya Now Jockey #11 / Best Seller #12 / Top 100 #12 / Juke Box #16 #25 hit for Teresa Brewer in 1952; Mack McIntyre (orch., above 2)	Liberty 55040
			PATTON, Robbie	
			Born in England. Pop-rock singer/songwriter.	
8/1/81	**26**	6	1. Don't Give It Up co-produced by Christine McVie (of Fleetwood Mac)	Liberty 1420
			PATTY & THE EMBLEMS	
			R&B vocal group from Camden, New Jersey: Patty Russell, Eddie Watts, Vance Walker and Alexander Wilde. Russell died of leukemia on 9/5/98 (age 56). Wilde died of kidney failure on 11/13/98 (age 60).	
8/15/64	**37**	3	1. Mixed-Up, Shook-Up, Girl	Herald 590
			PAUL, Billy	
			Born Paul Williams on 12/1/34 in Philadelphia. R&B singer.	
11/18/72	**1** (3)	14	● 1. **Me And Mrs. Jones** #1 R&B hit (4 weeks)	Philadelphia I. 3521
4/20/74	**37**	3	2. Thanks For Saving My Life	Philadelphia I. 3538
			PAUL, Les, and Mary Ford	
			Paul was born Lester Polsfuss on 6/9/15 in Waukesha, Wisconsin. Ford was born Colleen Summers on 7/7/24 in Pasadena, California; died on 9/30/77 (age 53). Les Paul was an innovator in electric guitar and multi-track recordings. Married to vocalist Mary Ford from 1949-63. Les Paul won the Grammy's Trustees Award in 1983 and he was inducted into the Rock and Roll Hall of Fame in 1988.	
7/9/55	**7**	13	1. **Hummingbird** Juke Box #7 / Best Seller #8 / Jockey #8	Capitol 3165

DATE	POS	WKS	ARTIST–RECORD TITLE	LABEL & NO.
11/12/55	**38**	2	2. Amukiriki (The Lord Willing) Top 100 #38	Capitol 3248
2/23/57	**35**	2	3. Cinco Robles (Five Oaks) Top 100 #35	Capitol 3612
9/8/58	**32**	4	4. Put A Ring On My Finger Hot 100 #32 / Best Seller #44	Columbia 41222
7/3/61	**37**	1	5. Jura (I Swear I Love You)	Columbia 41994

PAUL, Sean

Born Sean Paul Henriques on 1/8/75 in Kingston, Jamaica. Reggae singer.

DATE	POS	WKS	ARTIST–RECORD TITLE	LABEL & NO.
10/12/02	**7**	15	1. **Gimme The Light** Sales #5 / Airplay #7	VP 6400
3/15/03	**1** (3)	27	2. **Get Busy** Airplay #1 (3) / Sales #12 #1 R&B hit (1 week)	VP/Atlantic 88020
7/12/03	**13**	11	3. Like Glue Airplay #13 / Sales #60	VP/Atlantic 88145
8/23/03	**1** (9)	26	4. **Baby Boy** Airplay #1 (9) **BEYONCÉ feat. Sean Paul** #1 R&B hit (5 weeks); Sean Paul is featured on the CD promo single (does NOT appear on the commerical 12" single)	Columbia 76867

PAUL & PAULA

Pop vocal duo. Ray "Paul" Hildebrand was born on 12/21/40 in Joshua, Texas. Jill "Paula" Jackson was born on 5/20/42 in McCaney, Texas.

DATE	POS	WKS	ARTIST–RECORD TITLE	LABEL & NO.
1/12/63	**1** (3)	12	● 1. **Hey Paula** #1 R&B hit (2 weeks)	Philips 40084
3/23/63	**6**	8	2. **Young Lovers**	Philips 40096
6/22/63	**27**	4	3. First Quarrel	Philips 40114

PAVONE, Rita

Born on 8/23/45 in Turin, Italy. Pop singer.

DATE	POS	WKS	ARTIST–RECORD TITLE	LABEL & NO.
7/4/64	**26**	4	1. Remember Me Teacho Wiltshire (orch.)	RCA Victor 8365

PAYNE, Freda

Born on 9/19/45 in Detroit, Michigan. R&B singer. Sister of Scherrie Payne (of The Supremes). Formerly married to R&B singer Gregory Abbott.

DATE	POS	WKS	ARTIST–RECORD TITLE	LABEL & NO.
5/30/70	**3**	15	● 1. **Band Of Gold**	Invictus 9075
10/10/70	**24**	8	2. Deeper & Deeper	Invictus 9080
6/26/71	**12**	10	● 3. Bring The Boys Home	Invictus 9092

PEACHES & HERB

R&B vocal duo from Washington DC: Francine "Peaches" Barker and Herb Fame. Re-formed with Fame and Linda "Peaches" Greene in 1977.

DATE	POS	WKS	ARTIST–RECORD TITLE	LABEL & NO.
2/25/67	**21**	6	1. Let's Fall In Love #1 hit for Eddy Duchin in 1934	Date 1523
4/15/67	**8**	9	2. **Close Your Eyes** written by Chuck Willis; #5 R&B hit for The Five Keys in 1955	Date 1549
7/8/67	**20**	5	3. For Your Love	Date 1563
10/14/67	**13**	7	4. Love Is Strange	Date 1574
1/13/68	**31**	3	5. Two Little Kids co-written by Barbara Acklin	Date 1586
1/27/79	**5**	13	● 6. **Shake Your Groove Thing**	Polydor/MVP 14514
3/31/79	**1** (4)	15	▲ 7. **Reunited** #1 R&B hit (4 weeks)	Polydor/MVP 14547
3/15/80	**19**	8	8. I Pledge My Love	Polydor/MVP 2053

DATE	POS	WKS	ARTIST–RECORD TITLE	LABEL & NO.
			PEACH UNION	
			Pop trio from England: Lisa Lamb, Pascal Gabriel and Paul Statham.	
10/11/97	**39**	3	1. On My Own Airplay #39 / Sales #73	Mute/Epic 78666
			PEARL, Leslie	
			Born on 7/26/52 in Pennsylvania. Pop singer/songwriter.	
7/10/82	**28**	7	1. If The Love Fits Wear It	RCA 13235
			PEARL JAM	
			Rock group formed in Seattle, Washington: Eddie Vedder (vocals), Stone Gossard and Mike McCready (guitars), Jeff Ament (bass), and Dave Abbruzzese (drums). Gossard and Ament were members of Mother Love Bone. All recorded with Temple Of The Dog. Band appeared in the movie *Singles* as Matt Dillon's band, Citizen Dick. Jack Irons replaced Abbruzzese in 1994. Matt Cameron replaced Irons in 1999.	
11/26/94	**18**	2	1. Tremor Christ Sales #13 / Airplay #69	Epic 77771
12/17/94+	**13** ᴬ	26	2. Better Man	album cut
			#1 Mainstream Rock hit (8 weeks); from the album *Vitalogy* on Epic 66900	
12/23/95	**7**	9	● 3. I Got Id / Sales #5 / Airplay #34	
12/23/95		9	4. Long Road	Epic 78199
			Neil Young (guitar, above 2)	
8/17/96	**31**	3	5. Who You Are Airplay #27 / Sales #29	Epic 78389
			#1 Modern Rock hit (1 week)	
1/24/98	**21**	3	6. Given To Fly Sales #19 / Airplay #46	Epic 78797
			#1 Mainstream Rock hit (6 weeks)	
6/26/99	**2** (1)	15	7. **Last Kiss** Sales #1 (1) / Airplay #7	Epic 79197
3/1/03	**4** ˢ	8	8. **Save You**	Epic 79844
			PEBBLES	
			Born Perri McKissack on 8/29/65 in Oakland, California. R&B-dance singer. Nicknamed "Pebbles" by her family for her resemblance to cartoon character Pebbles Flintstone. Formerly married to singer/songwriter/producer L.A. Reid (of The Deele). Cousin of Cherrelle. Assembled/managed TLC.	
2/27/88	**5**	12	1. **Girlfriend** Sales #4 / Airplay #6	MCA 53185
			#1 R&B hit (2 weeks)	
5/28/88	**2** (2)	11	2. **Mercedes Boy** Sales #1 (1) / Airplay #3	MCA 53279
			#1 R&B hit (1 week)	
9/8/90	**4**	13	3. **Giving You The Benefit** Sales #5 / Airplay #5	MCA 53891
			#1 R&B hit (3 weeks)	
1/12/91	**13**	9	4. Love Makes Things Happen Sales #7 / Airplay #26	MCA 53973
			#1 R&B hit (2 weeks)	
			PEEBLES, Ann	
			Born on 4/27/47 in St. Louis, Missouri. R&B singer/songwriter.	
12/22/73	**38**	1	1. **I Can't Stand The Rain**	Hi 2248
			produced by Willie Mitchell	

DATE	POS	WKS	ARTIST–RECORD TITLE	LABEL & NO.
			PEEPLES, Nia	
			Born on 12/10/61 in Hollywood, California. R&B singer/actress. Played "Nicole Chapman" on TV's *Fame*. Hosted *Top Of The Pops* TV show and own syndicated music video dance TV program, *Party Machine*. Married to Howard Hewett from 1989-93.	
7/2/88	35	3	1. Trouble Sales #29	Mercury 870154
10/26/91	12	10	2. Street Of Dreams Airplay #11 / Sales #65	Charisma 98690
			PENDERGRASS, Teddy	
			Born on 3/26/50 in Philadelphia, Pennsylvania. R&B singer. Lead singer of Harold Melvin & The Blue Notes from 1970-76. Acted in the 1982 movie *Soup For One*. Auto accident on 3/18/82 left him partially paralyzed.	
8/12/78	25	6	● 1. Close The Door	Philadelphia I. 3648
			#1 R&B hit (2 weeks)	
7/4/81	40	2	2. Two Hearts	20th Century 2492
			STEPHANIE MILLS Featuring Teddy Pendergrass	
			PENGUINS, The	
			R&B vocal group from Los Angeles, California: Cleveland Duncan, Dexter Tisby, Bruce Tate and Curtis Williams.	
12/25/54+	8	15	● 1. **Earth Angel (Will You Be Mine)**	DooTone 348
			Best Seller #8 / Juke Box #10 / Jockey #13	
			#1 R&B hit (3 weeks)	
			PENISTON, Ce Ce	
			Born on 9/6/69 in Dayton, Ohio; raised in Phoenix, Arizona. R&B-dance singer/songwriter.	
11/9/91+	5	22	● 1. **Finally** Airplay #4 / Sales #9	A&M 1586
			MC Lethal (rap)	
2/29/92	20	11	2. We Got A Love Thang Airplay #11 / Sales #37	A&M 1594
			Kym Sims (backing vocal)	
6/20/92	15	15	3. Keep On Walkin' Airplay #9 / Sales #18	A&M 1598
2/26/94	32	4	4. I'm In The Mood Airplay #27 / Sales #44	A&M 0460
			PENN, Michael	
			Born on 8/1/58 in Manhattan, New York. Pop-rock singer/songwriter/guitarist. Brother of actors Sean and Christopher Penn. Son of actor/director Leo Penn and actress Eileen Ryan. Married Aimee Mann (of 'Til Tuesday) on 12/29/97.	
2/3/90	13	10	1. No Myth Sales #10 / Airplay #18	RCA 9111
			PEOPLE	
			Pop-rock group from San Jose, California: Gene Mason and Larry Norman (vocals), Jeff Levin (guitar), Albert Ribisi (keyboards), Robb Levin (bass) and Denny Friedkin (drums).	
5/25/68	14	10	1. I Love You	Capitol 2078
			PEOPLE'S CHOICE	
			R&B group from Philadelphia, Pennsylvania: Frankie Brunson (vocals), Guy Fiske and Donell Jordan (guitars), Donald Ford (keyboards), Roger Andrews (bass) and David Thompson (drums).	
9/4/71	38	2	1. I Likes To Do It [I]	Phil-L.A. 349

DATE	POS	WKS	ARTIST–RECORD TITLE	LABEL & NO.
9/13/75	**11**	11	● 2. Do It Any Way You Wanna **[I]** #1 R&B hit (1 week)	TSOP 4769
4/12/69	**32**	5	**PEPPERMINT RAINBOW, The** Pop group from Baltimore, Maryland: sisters Bonnie and Pat Lamdin (vocals), Doug Lewis (guitar), Skip Harris (bass) and Tony Corey (drums). 1. Will You Be Staying After Sunday	Decca 32410
3/1/03	**20**	15	**PEREZ, Amanda** Born in Fort Wayne, Indiana. R&B-dance singer/songwriter. 1. Angel Sales #6 / Airplay #20	Virgin 47265
4/28/90	**10**	9	**PERFECT GENTLEMEN** R&B vocal trio from Boston, Massachusetts: Corey Blakely, Maurice Starr Jr. and Tyrone Sutton. Starr's father managed and produced New Edition and New Kids On The Block. 1. **Ooh La La (I Can't Get Over You)** Sales #11 / Airplay #11	Columbia 73211
6/9/62	**6**	10	**PERICOLI, Emilio** Born on 1/7/28 in Cesenatico, Italy. Adult Contemporary singer/actor. 1. **Al Di La'** **[F]** Giampiero Boneschi (orch.); from the movie soundtrack *Rome* *Adventure* starring Troy Donahue	Warner 5259
3/10/56	**2 (4)**	17	**PERKINS, Carl** Born on 4/9/32 in Tiptonville, Tennessee. Died of a stroke on 1/19/98 (age 65). Rockabilly singer/songwriter/guitarist. Member of Johnny Cash's touring troupe from 1965-75. Appeared in the 1985 movie *Into The Night*. Inducted into the Rock and Roll Hall of Fame in 1987. 1. **Blue Suede Shoes** Juke Box #2 / Best Seller #3 / Top 100 #4 / Jockey #5 #1 Country hit (3 weeks)	Sun 234
10/7/57	**24**	1	**PERKINS, Tony** Born on 4/14/32 in Manhattan, New York. Died of AIDS on 9/12/92 (age 60). Actor/singer. Starred in several movies. 1. Moon-Light Swim Jockey #24 / Top 100 #43 Frank DeVol (orch.)	RCA Victor 7020
			PERRY, Steve Born on 1/22/49 in Hanford, California. Lead singer of Journey.	
9/25/82	**17**	6	1. Don't Fight It **KENNY LOGGINS with Steve Perry**	Columbia 03192
4/14/84	**3**	13	2. **Oh Sherrie** #1 Mainstream Rock hit (2 weeks)	Columbia 04391
7/7/84	**21**	8	3. She's Mine	Columbia 04496
10/27/84	**40**	1	4. Strung Out	Columbia 04598
12/22/84+	**18**	11	5. Foolish Heart Airplay #12 / Sales #16	Columbia 04693
7/30/94	**29**	7	6. You Better Wait Airplay #25	Columbia 77580

DATE	POS	WKS	ARTIST–RECORD TITLE	LABEL & NO.
			PERSUADERS, The	
			R&B vocal group formed in Harlem, New York: Doug Scott, Willie Holland, James Barnes and Charles Stodghill.	
9/18/71	**15**	9	● 1. Thin Line Between Love & Hate	Atco 6822
			#1 R&B hit (2 weeks)	
12/8/73	**39**	3	2. Some Guys Have All The Luck	Atco 6943
			PETER AND GORDON	
			Pop vocal duo formed in London, England: Peter Asher (born on 6/22/44 in London, England) and Gordon Waller (born on 6/4/45 in Braemar, Scotland). Asher later went into production and management, including work with Linda Ronstadt, James Taylor and 10,000 Maniacs.	
5/16/64	**1 (1)**	11	1. **A World Without Love**	Capitol 5175
7/11/64	**12**	6	2. Nobody I Know	Capitol 5211
10/24/64	**16**	6	3. I Don't Want To See You Again	Capitol 5272
1/23/65	**9**	9	4. **I Go To Pieces**	Capitol 5335
			written by Del Shannon	
5/8/65	**14**	8	5. True Love Ways	Capitol 5406
			written by Buddy Holly and Norman Petty	
7/24/65	**24**	5	6. To Know You Is To Love You	Capitol 5461
			same song as "To Know Him, Is To Love Him" by The Teddy Bears	
3/12/66	**14**	8	7. Woman	Capitol 5579
			#1-3 & 7 written by Paul McCartney	
11/5/66	**6**	10	8. **Lady Godiva**	Capitol 5740
1/14/67	**15**	5	9. Knight In Rusty Armour	Capitol 5808
4/15/67	**31**	3	10. Sunday For Tea	Capitol 5864
			PETER, PAUL & MARY	
			Folk trio formed in New York: Peter Yarrow (born on 5/31/38 in Brooklyn, New York), Paul Stookey (born on 12/30/37 in Baltimore, Maryland; see #13 below) and Mary Travers (born on 11/7/37 in Louisville, Kentucky).	
6/9/62	**35**	2	1. Lemon Tree	Warner 5274
9/8/62	**10**	8	2. **If I Had A Hammer (The Hammer Song)**	Warner 5296
			written as "The Hammer Song" by Pete Seeger & Lee Hays of The Weavers in 1958	
3/30/63	**2 (1)**	11	3. **Puff (The Magic Dragon)**	Warner 5348
			#1 Adult Contemporary hit (2 weeks)	
7/13/63	**2 (1)**	12	4. **Blowin' In The Wind**	Warner 5368
			#1 Adult Contemporary hit (5 weeks)	
9/28/63	**9**	8	5. **Don't Think Twice, It's All Right**	Warner 5385
			above 2 written by Bob Dylan	
12/28/63	**35**	2	6. Stewball	Warner 5399
			based on the 1822 ballad "Skewbald"	
4/4/64	**33**	3	7. Tell It On The Mountain	Warner 5418
			adapted from the Christmas spiritual "Go Tell It On The Mountain"	
2/13/65	**30**	4	8. For Lovin' Me	Warner 5496
			written by Gordon Lightfoot	
9/2/67	**9**	8	9. **I Dig Rock And Roll Music**	Warner 7067
12/23/67	**35**	2	10. Too Much Of Nothing	Warner 7092
			written by Bob Dylan	
5/17/69	**21**	7	11. Day Is Done	Warner 7279
11/8/69	**1 (1)**	15	● 12. **Leaving On A Jet Plane**	Warner 7340
			#1 Adult Contemporary hit (3 weeks); written by John Denver; recorded in 1967	

DATE	POS	WKS	ARTIST–RECORD TITLE	LABEL & NO.
9/4/71	**24**	9	13. Wedding Song (There Is Love) **PAUL STOOKEY**	Warner 7511
			PETERS, Bernadette	
			Born Bernadette Lazzara on 2/28/48 in Queens, New York. Actress/singer. Appeared in several movies and Broadway shows.	
5/10/80	**31**	5	1. Gee Whiz	MCA 41210
			PETERSEN, Paul	
			Born on 9/23/45 in Glendale, California. Pop singer/actor. Member of Disney's "Mouseketeers" and played "Jeff Stone" on TV's *Donna Reed Show* (1958-66). Became a paperback novelist in the 1970s.	
3/31/62	**19**	7	1. She Can't Find Her Keys	Colpix 620
12/15/62+	**6**	10	2. **My Dad**	Colpix 663
			PETERSON, Ray	
			Born on 4/23/39 in Denton, Texas. Rock and roll singer. Formed own Dunes record label in 1960.	
6/15/59	**25**	7	1. The Wonder Of You Shorty Rogers (orch.)	RCA Victor 7513
6/27/60	**7**	11	2. **Tell Laura I Love Her**	RCA Victor 7745
12/19/60+	**9**	9	3. **Corinna, Corinna** produced by Phil Spector; #2 R&B hit for Joe Turner in 1956	Dunes 2002
9/25/61	**29**	3	4. Missing You #7 Country hit for Webb Pierce in 1957	Dunes 2006
			PETS, The	
			Session group assembled by Joe Lubin. Included Plas Johnson (sax) and Earl Palmer (drums).	
6/9/58	**34**	1	1. Cha-Hua-Hua Top 100 #34 / Best Seller #38 **[I]**	Arwin 109
			PET SHOP BOYS	
			Synth-pop/dance duo formed in England: Neil Tennant (vocals) and Chris Lowe (keyboards).	
3/15/86	**1 (1)**	14	1. **West End Girls** Sales #1 (2) / Airplay #1 (2)	EMI America 8307
6/21/86	**10**	9	2. **Opportunities (Let's Make Lots Of Money)** Sales #10 / Airplay #11	EMI America 8330
9/26/87	**9**	10	3. **It's A Sin** Sales #5 / Airplay #10	EMI America 43027
12/26/87+	**2 (2)**	13	4. **What Have I Done To Deserve This?** Sales #1(1) /Airplay #4 **PET SHOP BOYS (and Dusty Springfield)**	EMI-Manhattan 50107
4/9/88	**4**	10	5. **Always On My Mind** Sales #2 / Airplay #6	EMI-Manhattan 50123
11/5/88	**18**	6	6. Domino Dancing Sales #15 / Airplay #23 The Voice In Fashion (backing vocals)	EMI-Manhattan 50161
			PETTY, Tom, And The Heartbreakers	
			Born on 10/20/50 in Gainesville, Florida. Rock singer/songwriter/guitarist. Formed The Heartbreakers in Los Angeles, California: Mike Campbell (guitar), Benmont Tench (keyboards), Ron Blair (bass) and Stan Lynch (drums). Howie Epstein (died of a drug overdose on 2/23/2003, age 47) replaced Blair in 1982; Blair returned in 2002. Petty appeared in the movies *FM* and *Made In Heaven*. Member of the Traveling Wilburys. Group inducted into the Rock and Roll Hall of Fame in 2002.	
2/18/78	**40**	1	1. Breakdown	Shelter 62008

DATE	POS	WKS	ARTIST–RECORD TITLE	LABEL & NO.
12/8/79+	**10**	13	2. **Don't Do Me Like That**	Backstreet 41138
2/9/80	**15**	10	3. Refugee	Backstreet 41169
5/16/81	**19**	7	4. The Waiting #1 Mainstream Rock hit (6 weeks)	Backstreet 51100
8/1/81	**3**	15	5. **Stop Draggin' My Heart Around** **STEVIE NICKS (with Tom Petty and The Heartbreakers)**	Modern 7336
12/4/82+	**20**	11	6. You Got Lucky #1 Mainstream Rock hit (3 weeks)	Backstreet 52144
3/12/83	**21**	7	7. Change Of Heart	Backstreet 52181
4/6/85	**13**	9	8. Don't Come Around Here No More Sales #8 / Airplay #21	MCA 52496
3/1/86	**37**	2	9. Needles And Pins [L] **TOM PETTY and the HEARTBREAKERS with STEVIE NICKS** recorded at the Wiltern Theater in Los Angeles	MCA 52772
5/23/87	**18**	6	10. Jammin' Me Sales #16 / Airplay #23 #1 Mainstream Rock hit (4 weeks); co-written by Bob Dylan	MCA 53065
5/27/89	**12**	9	11. I Won't Back Down Sales #8 / Airplay #19 #1 Mainstream Rock hit (5 weeks); George Harrison (backing vocal, guitar)	MCA 53369
8/26/89	**23**	7	12. Runnin' Down A Dream Sales #11 / Airplay #31 #1 Mainstream Rock hit (1 week)	MCA 53682
12/2/89+	**7**	12	13. **Free Fallin'** Sales #3 / Airplay #9 **TOM PETTY** (above 3) #1 Mainstream Rock hit (1 week)	MCA 53748
8/3/91	**28**	5	14. Learning To Fly Airplay #63 #1 Mainstream Rock hit (6 weeks)	MCA 54124
2/26/94	**14**	10	15. Mary Jane's Last Dance Sales #15 / Airplay #31 #1 Mainstream Rock hit (2 weeks)	MCA 54732
12/17/94+	**13**	17	16. You Don't Know How It Feels Sales #12 / Airplay #19 **TOM PETTY** #1 Mainstream Rock hit (1 week)	Warner 18030
			PHAIR, Liz	
			Born on 4/17/67 in New Haven, Connecticut. Rock singer/songwriter.	
11/29/03	**32**	6	1. Why Can't I? Airplay #34 from the album *Liz Phair* on Capitol 83928	album cut
			PHARRELL	
			Born Pharrell Williams on 4/5/73 in Virginia Beach, Virginia. Male rapper/producer. Member of prolific production trio The Neptunes (recorded as N*E*R*D).	
3/1/03	**6**	17	1. **Beautiful** Airplay #6 / Sales #14 **SNOOP DOGG featuring Pharrell, Uncle Charlie Wilson**	Priority 77887
7/26/03	**5**	16	2. **Frontin'** Airplay #5 / Sales #7 **PHARRELL Featuring Jay-Z** #1 R&B hit (6 weeks)	Star Trak 58647
			PHIFE DAWG — see TRIBE CALLED QUEST	
			PHILLIPS, Esther	
			Born Esther Mae Jones on 12/23/35 in Galveston, Texas. Died of liver failure on 8/7/84 (age 48). R&B singer. Recorded with Johnny Otis as "Little Esther."	
11/17/62	**8**	10	1. **Release Me** #1 R&B hit (3 weeks); #5 Country hit for Jimmy Heap in 1954	Lenox 5555

DATE	POS	WKS	ARTIST–RECORD TITLE	LABEL & NO.
9/20/75	**20**	9	2. What A Diff'rence A Day Makes *#5 hit for the Dorsey Brothers Orchestra in 1934*	Kudu 925
			PHILLIPS, John — see MAMAS AND THE PAPAS, The	
			PHILLIPS, Phil, With The Twilights	
			Born John Phillip Baptiste on 3/14/31 in Lake Charles, Louisiana. R&B singer.	Mercury 71465
7/20/59	**2** (2)	14	● 1. **Sea Of Love** *#1 R&B hit (1 week); first released on Khoury's 711 in 1959*	
			PHOTOGLO, Jim	
			Born in Los Angeles, California. Pop singer/songwriter.	
5/31/80	**31**	4	1. We Were Meant To Be Lovers **PHOTOGLO**	20th Century 2446
5/30/81	**25**	7	2. Fool In Love With You	20th Century 2487
			PICKETT, Bobby "Boris," And The Crypt-Kickers	
			Born on 2/11/38 in Somerville, Massachusetts. Novelty singer. The Crypt- Kickers: Leon Russell, Johnny MacCrae, Rickie Page and Gary Paxton.	
9/15/62	**1** (2)	12	● 1. **Monster Mash** [N]	Garpax 44167
12/22/62	**30**	4	2. Monsters' Holiday [X-N]	Garpax 44171
6/30/73	**10**	12	● 3. **Monster Mash** [N-R] *same version as #1 above*	Parrot 348
			PICKETT, Wilson	
			Born on 3/18/41 in Prattville, Alabama. R&B singer/songwriter. Nicknamed the "Wicked Pickett." Member of The Falcons from 1961-63. Inducted into the Rock and Roll Hall of Fame in 1991.	
8/14/65	**21**	6	1. In The Midnight Hour *#1 R&B hit (1 week)*	Atlantic 2289
3/5/66	**13**	8	2. 634-5789 (Soulsville, U.S.A.) *#1 R&B hit (7 weeks)*	Atlantic 2320
8/13/66	**6**	8	3. **Land Of 1000 Dances** *#1 R&B hit (1 week)*	Atlantic 2348
12/10/66	**23**	6	4. Mustang Sally *#15 R&B hit for Sir Mack Rice in 1965*	Atlantic 2365
2/25/67	**29**	3	5. Everybody Needs Somebody To Love	Atlantic 2381
4/22/67	**32**	2	6. I Found A Love - Part 1	Atlantic 2394
8/26/67	**8**	9	7. **Funky Broadway** *#1 R&B hit (1 week)*	Atlantic 2430
11/11/67	**22**	5	8. Stag-O-Lee *adapted from the traditional folk song "Stack-O-Lee"*	Atlantic 2448
5/11/68	**15**	6	9. She's Lookin' Good	Atlantic 2504
7/6/68	**24**	4	10. I'm A Midnight Mover *written by Bobby Womack*	Atlantic 2528
1/4/69	**23**	6	11. Hey Jude *Duane Allman (guitar solo)*	Atlantic 2591
5/23/70	**25**	9	12. Sugar Sugar	Atlantic 2722
10/24/70	**14**	9	13. Engine Number 9	Atlantic 2765
2/6/71	**17**	8	● 14. Don't Let The Green Grass Fool You	Atlantic 2781

DATE	POS	WKS	ARTIST–RECORD TITLE	LABEL & NO.
5/15/71	**13**	9	● 15. **Don't Knock My Love - Pt. 1** #1 R&B hit (1 week)	Atlantic 2797
1/15/72	**24**	8	16. Fire And Water	Atlantic 2852
			PIERCE, Webb	
			Born on 8/8/21 in West Monroe, Louisiana. Died of heart failure on 2/24/91 (age 69). Country singer/songwriter/guitarist. Appeared in the movies *Buffalo Guns*, *Music City USA* and *Road To Nashville*.	
8/31/59	**24**	7	1. **I Ain't Never** written by Mel Tillis	Decca 30923
			PILOT	
			Pop-rock trio from Edinburgh, Scotland: David Paton (vocals, guitar), Bill Lyall (keyboards) and Stuart Tosh (drums). Lyall died of AIDS in December 1989 (age 36).	
5/10/75	**5**	12	● 1. **Magic** produced by Alan Parsons	EMI 3992
			PINETTE, Rick — see OAK	
			P!NK	
			Born Alecia Moore on 9/8/79 in Doylestown, Pennsylvania; raised in Philadelphia, Pennsylvania. Female pop-dance singer/songwriter.	
3/4/00	**7**	23	● 1. **There You Go** Sales #2 / Airplay #6 Kandi (backing vocal)	LaFace 24456
9/2/00	**4**	23	2. **Most Girls** Airplay #3 / Sales #15	LaFace 24490
2/10/01	**33**	4	3. You Make Me Sick Airplay #31	LaFace 24533

4/21/01	**1** (5)	17	4. **Lady Marmalade** Airplay #1 (6)
			      CHRISTINA AGUILERA, LIL' KIM, MYA and P!NK
			      co-produced by Missy "Misdemeanor" Elliott; from the movie *Moulin Rouge* starring Nicole Kidman and Ewan McGregor
				Interscope 497066

11/10/01	**4**	21	5. **Get The Party Started** Airplay #4	Arista 15074
3/23/02	**8**	18	6. **Don't Let Me Get Me** Airplay #8 / Sales #29	Arista 15133
7/20/02	**8**	17	7. **Just Like A Pill** Airplay #8 / Sales #32	Arista 15186
11/30/02+	**20**	13	● 8. Family Portrait Airplay #21 / Sales #30	Arista 51158
			PINK FLOYD	
			Progressive-rock group formed in England: David Gilmour (vocals, guitar), Roger Waters (vocals, bass), Rick Wright (keyboards) and Nick Mason (drums). Group inducted into the Rock and Roll Hall of Fame in 1996. Group name taken from Georgia bluesmen Pink Anderson and Floyd Council.	
6/23/73	**13**	9	1. Money	Harvest 3609
2/9/80	**1** (4)	19	▲ 2. **Another Brick In The Wall (Part II)**	Columbia 11187
			PINK LADY	
			Female disco duo from Japan: Mie Nemoto and Kei Masuda. Starred in the 1979 TV variety show *Pink Lady & Jeff*.	
7/21/79	**37**	3	1. Kiss In The Dark	Elektra/Curb 46040
			PIPKINS, The	
			Vocal duo formed in England: Roger Greenaway and Tony Burrows (low voice). Worked together in studio group White Plains.	
6/6/70	**9**	10	1. **Gimme Dat Ding** **[N]** featured in the British children's TV show *Oliver & The Overlord*	Capitol 2819

DATE	POS	WKS	ARTIST–RECORD TITLE	LABEL & NO.
			PIPS — see KNIGHT, Gladys	
			PITNEY, Gene	
			Born on 2/17/41 in Hartford, Connecticut; raised in Rockville, Connecticut. Pop singer/songwriter. Inducted into the Rock and Roll Hall of Fame in 2002.	
2/27/61	39	1	1. (I Wanna) Love My Life Away	Musicor 1002
12/18/61+	13	10	2. Town Without Pity	Musicor 1009
			title song from the movie starring Kirk Douglas	
5/19/62	4	8	3. **(The Man Who Shot) Liberty Valance**	Musicor 1020
			recorded for but not included in the movie starring John Wayne and Jimmy Stewart	
9/29/62	2 (1)	11	4. **Only Love Can Break A Heart**	Musicor 1022
			#1 Adult Contemporary hit (2 weeks)	
1/5/63	12	8	5. Half Heaven - Half Heartache	Musicor 1026
4/13/63	12	7	6. Mecca	Musicor 1028
8/3/63	21	6	7. True Love Never Runs Smooth	Musicor 1032
11/16/63	17	6	8. Twenty Four Hours From Tulsa	Musicor 1034
8/29/64	7	10	9. **It Hurts To Be In Love**	Musicor 1040
11/7/64	9	9	10. **I'm Gonna Be Strong**	Musicor 1045
3/20/65	31	4	11. I Must Be Seeing Things	Musicor 1070
5/22/65	13	7	12. Last Chance To Turn Around	Musicor 1093
8/21/65	28	4	13. Looking Through The Eyes Of Love	Musicor 1103
12/18/65	37	2	14. Princess In Rags	Musicor 1130
5/14/66	25	5	15. Backstage	Musicor 1171
6/15/68	16	8	16. She's A Heartbreaker	Musicor 1306
			PIXIES THREE, The	
			Female vocal trio from Hanover, Pennsylvania: Midge Bollinger, Debbie Swisher and Kaye McColl.	
10/5/63	40	1	1. Birthday Party	Mercury 72130
			PLANET SOUL	
			Dance duo from Miami, Florida: producer George Costa and singer Nadine Renee.	
11/18/95+	26	18	● 1. Set U Free Sales #25 / Airplay #25	Strictly Rhythm 12362
			PLANT, Robert	
			Born on 8/20/48 in West Bromwich, West Midlands, England. Lead singer of Led Zeppelin and The Honeydrippers.	
9/3/83	20	9	1. Big Log	Es Paranza 99844
12/24/83+	39	5	2. In The Mood	Es Paranza 99820
6/15/85	36	4	3. Little By Little	Es Paranza 99644
			#1 Mainstream Rock hit (2 weeks)	
6/4/88	25	7	4. Tall Cool One Sales #18 / Airplay #27	Es Paranza 99348
			#1 Mainstream Rock hit (4 weeks); Jimmy Page (guitar)	
			PLASTIC ONO BAND — see LENNON, John	
			PLATT, Eddie, And His Orchestra	
			Born Eddie Platakis on 12/8/21 in Cleveland, Ohio; raised in Rossford, Ohio. Saxophonist/bandleader.	
3/10/58	20	4	1. Tequila Jockey #20 / Best Seller #35 / Top 100 #35 **[I]**	ABC-Paramount 9899

Robert Palmer created one of the 1980s' most striking videos with his model-heavy images for "Addicted To Love." The concept worked so well, Robert returned to it for his next two videos, which were both #2 hits.

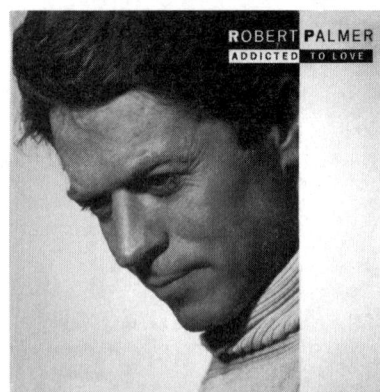

Sean Paul had a busy year in 2002, appearing on singles by Jim Crow, Shaggy, and Busta Rhymes. However, that exposure paid off in 2003, when "Get Busy" topped the Hot 100, followed by his duet with Beyoncé, "Baby Boy."

Paul & Paula were not the given names of Ray Hildebrand and Jill Jackson, but they did seem much catchier for a song titled "Hey Paula." The duo used studio outtakes from their #1 hit to create its follow-up, "Young Lovers."

Peaches & Herb broke up in 1970, but a fresh Peach teamed with the original Herb in 1976. That "reunited" duo came back with their two biggest hits, "Shake Your Groove Thing" and the #1 hit "Reunited."

Peter And Gordon discovered it was a small world when the man dating Peter's sister, Paul McCartney, offered them a #1 hit. Fortunately, the duo didn't live in "A World Without Love."

Peter, Paul & Mary scored hits with songs written by Bob Dylan and Gordon Lightfoot, but achieved their greatest chart flight with a John Denver–penned tune, the #1 hit, "Leaving On A Jet Plane."

The Platters served up a doo-wop classic with their #1 hit "The Great Pretender." Although they never pretended to be actors, the group did appear in the films *Rock Around The Clock* and *The Girl Can't Help It.*

Poison risked damage to their rock star credibility by releasing an acoustic ballad. "Every Rose Has Its Thorn" proved anything but toxic, justifying the band's faith in the song by going all the way to #1.

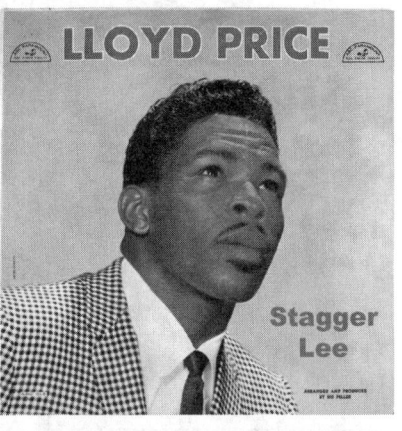

The Police spent eight weeks at #1 with their biggest hit, "Every Breath You Take." The 1983 Grammy-winning Song of the Year was revived in 1997 as the backing track for Puff Daddy's #1 hit "I'll Be Missing You."

Perez Prado And His Orchestra hit the top of the Best Sellers in Stores, Most Played in Juke Boxes, and Most Played by Jockeys charts with his colorful instrumental "Cherry Pink And Apple Blossom White." Though his hits stopped in 1962, his song "Mambo No. 5" was revived in 1999 as a Top 10 hit by Lou Bega.

Billy Preston teamed with The Beatles on their hit "Get Back" and released singles for their label in the early 1970s, but by the time of his first #1 hit, "Will It Go Round In Circles," he had left the Fab Four for A&M Records.

Lloyd Price topped the pop and R&B charts with his adaptation of the folk song "Stack-O-Lee." In the years that followed, acts like Wilson Pickett and Tommy Roe adapted Price's hit, called "Stagger Lee," into their own Top 40 singles.

Maxi Priest earned his first #1 hit on the Hot 100 with the song "Close To You." The reggae singer came close to having it become his first #1 hit on the R&B chart as well, but it stalled at #2.

Prince has been known as a musical innovator. When he took a chance by leaving out the bass line in a track for his movie *Purple Rain*, he was rewarded with his first chart-topper. "When Doves Cry" spent five weeks at #1.

Puff Daddy wasn't exaggerating when he stated in his #1 hit "Can't Nobody Hold Me Down." The rapper scored three chart-toppers in 1997 alone, and continued earning Top 10 hits into the 21st century as P. Diddy.

DATE	POS	WKS	ARTIST–RECORD TITLE	LABEL & NO.
			PLATTERS, The	
			R&B vocal group from Los Angeles, California: Tony Williams, David Lynch, Paul Robi, Herb Reed and Zola Taylor. Sonny Turner replaced Williams in 1961. Sandra Dawn and Nate Nelson (of The Flamingos) replaced Taylor and Robi in 1965. Lynch died of cancer on 1/2/81 (age 61). Nelson died of a heart attack on 6/1/84 (age 52). Robi died of cancer on 2/1/89 (age 57). Williams died of emphysema on 8/14/92 (age 64). Group inducted into the Rock and Roll Hall of Fame in 1990.	
10/1/55	**5**	20	● 1. **Only You (And You Alone)** Juke Box #5 / Best Seller #5 / Top 100 #5 / Jockey #5 #1 R&B hit (7 weeks)	Mercury 70633
12/24/55+	**1 (2)**	19	● 2. **The Great Pretender** Top 100 #1 (2) / Jockey #1 (2) / Juke Box #1 (1) / Best Seller #2 #1 R&B hit (11 weeks)	Mercury 70753
3/31/56	**4**	16	3. **(You've Got) The Magic Touch** Juke Box #4 / Top 100 #4 / Jockey #5 / Best Seller #5	Mercury 70819
7/7/56	**1 (5)**	20	● 4. **My Prayer /** Top 100 #1 (5) / Jockey #1 (3) / Best Seller #1 (2) / Juke Box #1 (1) #1 R&B hit (2 weeks); #3 hit for the Ink Spots in 1939	
8/11/56	**39**	1	5. Heaven On Earth Top 100 #39 / Best Seller: flip / Juke Box: flip	Mercury 70893
10/6/56	**11**	12	6. You'll Never Never Know / Juke Box #11 / Top 100 #14 / Best Seller #15 / Jockey #18	
10/6/56	**13**	9	7. It Isn't Right Best Seller #13 / Juke Box #13 / Top 100 #23	Mercury 70948
1/12/57	**20**	6	8. On My Word Of Honor / Juke Box #20 / Best Seller #23 / Top 100 #27	
1/26/57	**20**	2	9. One In A Million Best Seller #20 / Top 100 #31	Mercury 71011
3/23/57	**11**	11	10. I'm Sorry / Juke Box #11 / Best Seller #14 / Top 100 #19	
4/13/57	**16**	9	11. He's Mine Best Seller #16 / Juke Box #18 / Top 100 #23 / Jockey #24	Mercury 71032
6/10/57	**24**	7	12. My Dream / Best Seller #24 / Top 100 #26	
7/15/57		2	13. I Wanna Best Seller: flip	Mercury 71093
4/7/58	**1 (1)**	14	● 14. **Twilight Time** Best Seller #1 (1) / Top 100 #1 (1) / Jockey #1 (1) #1 R&B hit (3 weeks); #8 hit for The Three Suns in 1944	Mercury 71289
12/1/58+	**1 (3)**	16	● 15. **Smoke Gets In Your Eyes** #1 hit for Paul Whiteman's Orchestra in 1934 (from the 1933 musical *Roberta* starring Bob Hope)	Mercury 71383
4/6/59	**12**	11	16. Enchanted	Mercury 71427
2/15/60	**8**	11	17. **Harbor Lights** #1 hit for Sammy Kaye in 1950	Mercury 71563
8/22/60	**36**	1	18. Red Sails In The Sunset #1 hit for both Bing Crosby and Guy Lombardo in 1935	Mercury 71656
10/24/60	**21**	8	19. To Each His Own #1 hit for Eddy Howard in 1946	Mercury 71697
1/30/61	**30**	2	20. If I Didn't Care #2 hit for the Ink Spots in 1939	Mercury 71749
8/21/61	**25**	4	21. I'll Never Smile Again #1 hit for Tommy Dorsey in 1940; David Carroll (orch., above 5)	Mercury 71847
6/4/66	**31**	5	22. I Love You 1000 Times	Musicor 1166
3/25/67	**14**	7	23. With This Ring	Musicor 1229
			PLAYA	
			R&B vocal trio from Louisville, Kentucky: Ben Bush, John Peacock and Stephen Garrett.	
6/6/98	**38**	4	1. Cheers 2 U Sales #20	Def Jam 568214

DATE	POS	WKS	ARTIST–RECORD TITLE	LABEL & NO.
			PLAYER	
			Pop-rock group formed in Los Angeles, California: Peter Beckett (vocals, guitar), John Crowley (vocals, guitar), Wayne Cooke (keyboards), Ronn Moss (bass) and John Friesen (drums). Moss played "Ridge Forrester" on the TV soap *The Bold & The Beautiful*.	
11/19/77+	**1** (3)	16	● 1. **Baby Come Back**	RSO 879
4/1/78	**10**	12	2. **This Time I'm In It For Love**	RSO 890
10/21/78	**27**	3	3. Prisoner Of Your Love	RSO 908
			PLAYMATES, The	
			Pop vocal trio from Waterbury, Connecticut: Donny Conn, Morey Carr and Chic Hetti.	
1/27/58	**19**	7	1. Jo-Ann Best Seller #19 / Top 100 #20	Roulette 4037
6/9/58	**22**	2	2. Don't Go Home Jockey #22 / Top 100 #36 / Best Seller #38	Roulette 4072
11/10/58	**4**	12	● 3. **Beep Beep** **[N]**	Roulette 4115
7/27/59	**15**	9	4. What Is Love?	Roulette 4160
11/21/60	**37**	2	5. Wait For Me	Roulette 4276
			PM DAWN	
			Black dance-rap duo from Jersey City, New Jersey: brothers Attrell "Prince Be" and Jarrett "DJ Minutemix" Cordes.	
10/26/91	**1** (1)	18	● 1. **Set Adrift On Memory Bliss** Sales #1 (3) / Airplay #2	Gee Street 866094
			samples "True" by Spandau Ballet	
2/8/92	**28**	6	2. Paper Doll Airplay #20 / Sales #46	Gee Street 866374
9/26/92	**3**	24	● 3. **I'd Die Without You** Airplay #1 (2) / Sales #5	Gee Street/LaFace 24034
			from the movie *Boomerang* starring Eddie Murphy	
3/27/93	**6**	19	4. **Looking Through Patient Eyes** Airplay #4 / Sales #20	Gee Street 862024
			Cathy Dennis (backing vocal); samples "Father Figure" by George Michael	
			POCO	
			Country-rock group formed in California by Rusty Young and Buffalo Springfield members Richie Furay and Jim Messina. Changing personnel included future Eagles members Randy Meisner and Timothy B. Schmit. 1979 lineup: Rusty Young, Paul Cotton, Charlie Harrison, Kim Bullard and Steve Chapman. Disbanded in late 1984. In 1989, Young, Furay, Messina, Meisner and George Grantham reunited as Poco.	
2/10/79	**17**	9	1. Crazy Love	ABC 12439
			#1 Adult Contemporary hit (7 weeks)	
6/16/79	**20**	7	2. Heart Of The Night	MCA 41023
9/30/89	**18**	8	3. Call It Love Sales #16 / Airplay #21	RCA 9038
1/20/90	**39**	1	4. Nothin' To Hide Sales #32	RCA 9131
			co-written and produced by Richard Marx	
			P.O.D.	
			Christian hard-rock group from San Diego, California: Sonny (vocals), Marcos (guitar), Traa (bass) and Wuv (drums). P.O.D.: Payable On Death.	
3/16/02	**28**	7	1. Youth Of The Nation Airplay #27	album cut
			#1 Modern Rock hit (2 weeks); from the album *Satellite* on Atlantic 83475	

DATE	POS	WKS	ARTIST–RECORD TITLE	LABEL & NO.
			POINT BLANK	
			Rock group from Texas: Bubba Keith (vocals), Rusty Burns and Kim Davis (guitars), Mike Hamilton (keyboards), Bill Randolph (bass) and Buzzy Gruen (drums). Randolph died of a heart attack on 6/19/2001 (age 50).	
8/29/81	39	2	1. Nicole	MCA 51132
			POINTER, Bonnie	
			Born on 7/11/50 in Oakland, California. Member of the Pointer Sisters from 1971-78.	
7/28/79	11	15	1. Heaven Must Have Sent You	Motown 1459
2/16/80	40	2	2. I Can't Help Myself (Sugar Pie, Honey Bunch)	Motown 1478
			POINTER SISTERS	
			R&B vocal group from Oakland, California: sisters Ruth (born on 3/19/46), Anita (born on 1/23/48), June (born on 11/30/54) and Bonnie Pointer. Sang in nostalgic 1940s style from 1973-77. Appeared as the "Wilson Sisters" in the 1976 movie *Car Wash*. Bonnie went solo in 1978, group continued as a trio in a more contemporary style.	
9/8/73	11	12	1. Yes We Can Can #46 R&B hit for Lee Dorsey in 1970	Blue Thumb 229
11/9/74	13	8	2. Fairytale	ABC/Blue Thumb 254
8/23/75	20	8	3. How Long (Betcha' Got A Chick On The Side) #1 R&B hit (2 weeks)	ABC/Blue Thumb 265
12/16/78+	2 (2)	16	● 4. **Fire** written by Bruce Springsteen	Planet 45901
4/14/79	30	4	5. Happiness	Planet 45902
8/30/80	3	17	● 6. **He's So Shy**	Planet 47916
6/27/81	2 (3)	16	● 7. **Slow Hand**	Planet 47929
2/13/82	13	10	8. Should I Do It	Planet 47960
7/24/82	16	8	9. American Music	Planet 13254
10/30/82	30	6	10. I'm So Excited also see #13 below	Planet 13327
2/11/84	5	14	11. **Automatic**	Planet 13730
5/12/84	3	15	12. **Jump (For My Love)**	Planet 13780
9/8/84	9	18	13. **I'm So Excited** Sales #7 / Airplay #12 **[R]** slightly different mix than #10 above	Planet 13857
12/22/84+	6	14	14. **Neutron Dance** Sales #5 / Airplay #5 from the movie *Beverly Hills Cop* starring Eddie Murphy	Planet 13951
7/27/85	11	13	15. Dare Me Sales #8 / Airplay #13	RCA 14126
12/6/86	33	3	16. Goldmine Sales #33 / Airplay #34	RCA 5062
			POISON	
			Hard-rock group formed in Harrisburg, Pennsylvania: Bret Michaels (vocals), C.C. DeVille (guitar), Bobby Dall (bass) and Rikki Rockett (drums).	
4/11/87	9	9	1. **Talk Dirty To Me** Sales #6 / Airplay #11	Capitol 5686
10/17/87	13	9	2. I Won't Forget You Sales #12 / Airplay #12	Enigma 44038
5/21/88	6	11	3. **Nothin' But A Good Time** Sales #3 / Airplay #11	Enigma 44145
8/27/88	12	9	4. Fallen Angel Sales #10 / Airplay #15	Enigma 44191
11/12/88	1 (3)	14	● 5. **Every Rose Has Its Thorn** Sales #1 (3) / Airplay #1 (3)	Enigma 44203
3/4/89	10	10	6. Your Mama Don't Dance Sales #9 / Airplay #11	Enigma 44293
7/14/90	3	14	● 7. **Unskinny Bop** Sales #3 / Airplay #3	Enigma 44584

DATE	POS	WKS	ARTIST–RECORD TITLE	LABEL & NO.
10/20/90	**4**	15	● 8. **Something To Believe In** Sales #4 / Airplay #5	Enigma 44617
3/23/91	**38**	1	9. Ride The Wind Sales #38 / Airplay #39	Enigma 44616
6/29/91	**35**	2	10. Life Goes On Sales #47 / Airplay #73	Capitol 44705
			POLICE, The	
			Pop-rock trio formed in England: Gordon "Sting" Sumner (vocals, bass), Andy Summers (guitar) and Stewart Copeland (drums). Sting went on to a highly successful solo career. Group inducted into the Rock and Roll Hall of Fame in 2003.	
4/7/79	**32**	5	1. Roxanne	A&M 2096
11/22/80+	**10**	13	2. **De Do Do Do, De Da Da Da**	A&M 2275
2/21/81	**10**	13	3. **Don't Stand So Close To Me**	A&M 2301
10/10/81	**3**	15	4. **Every Little Thing She Does Is Magic** #1 Mainstream Rock hit (2 weeks)	A&M 2371
1/30/82	**11**	10	5. Spirits In The Material World	A&M 2390
6/4/83	**1 (8)**	20	● 6. **Every Breath You Take** #1 Mainstream Rock hit (9 weeks)	A&M 2542
8/27/83	**3**	13	7. **King Of Pain** #1 Mainstream Rock hit (5 weeks)	A&M 2569
11/19/83	**16**	9	8. Synchronicity II	A&M 2571
1/21/84	**8**	10	9. **Wrapped Around Your Finger**	A&M 2614
			PONI-TAILS	
			Pop female vocal trio from Lyndhurst, Ohio: Toni Cistone, Patti McCabe and LaVerne Novak. McCabe died of cancer on 1/17/89.	
7/28/58	**7**	12	1. **Born Too Late** Hot 100 #7 / Best Seller #11	ABC-Paramount 9934
			POP, Iggy	
			Born James Jewel Osterberg on 4/21/47 in Muskegon, Michigan. Punk-rock pioneer. Leader of The Stooges from 1969-74. Acted in the movies *Cry Baby*, *Hardware* and *The Crow: City Of Angels*. Adopted nickname "Iggy" from his first band, The Iguanas.	
1/26/91	**28**	3	1. Candy Sales #23 / Airplay #38 Kate Pierson (of The B-52's, female vocal)	Virgin 98900
			POPPY FAMILY (Featuring Susan Jacks)	
			Pop group from Canada: Susan Jacks (vocals), her husband Terry Jacks (guitar), Craig MacCaw (guitar) and Satwan Singh (percussion). Group and marriage broke up in 1973; Susan and Terry began solo careers.	
4/25/70	**2 (2)**	13	● 1. **Which Way You Goin' Billy?**	London 129
9/19/70	**29**	6	2. That's Where I Went Wrong	London 139
			PORTRAIT	
			Male R&B vocal group: Eric Kirkland and Michael Saulsberry (from Los Angeles, California), Irving Washington (from Providence, Rhode Island) and Phillip Johnson (from Tulsa, Oklahoma).	
12/19/92+	**11**	18	1. Here We Go Again! Airplay #8 / Sales #17	Capitol 44865

DATE	POS	WKS	ARTIST–RECORD TITLE	LABEL & NO.
			POSEY, Sandy	
			Born on 6/18/44 in Jasper, Alabama; raised in West Memphis, Arkansas. Pop singer.	
8/6/66	12	12	1. Born A Woman	MGM 13501
12/10/66	12	8	2. Single Girl	MGM 13612
4/8/67	31	2	3. What A Woman In Love Won't Do	MGM 13702
7/1/67	12	8	4. I Take It Back	MGM 13744
			POSITIVE K	
			Born Darryl Gibson in the Bronx, New York. Male rapper.	
2/6/93	14	14	● 1. I Got A Man Sales #5 / Airplay #19	Island 864305
			samples "Rescue Me" by A Taste Of Honey	
			POST, Mike	
			Born on 9/29/44 in Los Angeles, California. Composer/producer.	
6/21/75	10	10	1. **The Rockford Files** **[I]**	MGM 14772
			theme from the TV series starring James Garner	
10/3/81	10	10	2. **The Theme From Hill Street Blues** **[I]**	Elektra 47186
			MIKE POST featuring Larry Carlton	
			theme from the TV series starring Daniel J. Travanti	
4/3/82	25	7	3. **(Theme From) Magnum P.I.** **[I]**	Elektra 47400
			theme from the TV series starring Tom Selleck	
			POURCEL('S), Franck, French Fiddles	
			Born on 1/1/15 in Marseilles, France. String orchestra leader/violinist.	
4/27/59	9	11	1. **Only You** **[I]**	Capitol 4165
			POWELL, Jane	
			Born Suzanne Burce on 4/1/29 in Portland, Oregon. Pop singer/actress. Appeared in several movies.	
10/6/56	15	9	1. True Love Best Seller #15 / Top 100 #24	Verve 2018
			Buddy Bregman (orch.); Cole Porter song from the movie *High Society* starring Bing Crosby and Frank Sinatra	
			POWELL, Jesse	
			Born in Gary, Indiana. R&B singer/songwriter.	
2/20/99	10	14	1. **You** Sales #8 / Airplay #17	Silas/MCA 55500
			POWERS, Joey	
			Born in 1939 in Canonsburg, Pennsylvania. Pop singer.	
12/7/63+	10	9	1. **Midnight Mary**	Amy 892
			POWER STATION, The	
			All-star rock group: Robert Palmer (vocals), Andy Taylor (guitar), John Taylor (bass) and Tony Thompson (drums). The Taylors were members of Duran Duran. Thompson was a member of Chic. Palmer died of a heart attack on 9/26/2003 (age 54). Thompson died of cancer on 11/12/2003 (age 48).	
3/30/85	6	12	1. **Some Like It Hot** Sales #6 / Airplay #8	Capitol 5444
6/22/85	9	10	2. **Get It On** Sales #8 / Airplay #10	Capitol 5479
10/5/85	34	3	3. Communication	Capitol 5511

DATE	POS	WKS	ARTIST–RECORD TITLE	LABEL & NO.
			POZO-SECO SINGERS	
			Folk-rock trio from Texas: Don Williams, Susan Taylor and Lofton Kline. Williams later became a major country star.	
10/8/66	32	6	1. I Can Make It With You	Columbia 43784
1/14/67	32	4	2. Look What You've Done	Columbia 43927
			PRADO, Perez, And His Orchestra	
			Born Damaso Perez Prado on 12/11/16 in Mantanzas, Cuba. Died of a stroke on 9/14/89 (age 72). Bandleader/organist. Known as "The King of The Mambo." Appeared in the movie *Underwater!*	
3/5/55	1 (10)	26	● 1. **Cherry Pink And Apple Blossom White** Best Seller #1 (10) / Juke Box #1 (8) / Jockey #1 (6) **[I]** Billy Regis (trumpet solo); from the movie *Underwater!* starring Jane Russell; French song written in 1950	RCA Victor 5965
6/23/58	1 (1)	17	● 2. **Patricia** Top 100 #1 (1) / Jockey #1 (1) / Best Seller #2 **[I]** #1 R&B hit (2 weeks)	RCA Victor 7245
			PRAS — see MICHEL, Pras	
			PRATT & McCLAIN	
			Pop vocal duo: Truett Pratt (from San Antonio, Texas) and Jerry McClain (from Pasadena, California).	
4/24/76	5	10	1. **Happy Days** theme from the TV series starring Ron Howard and Henry Winkler	Reprise 1351
			PRELUDE	
			Folk trio formed in England: husband-and-wife Irene (vocals) and Brian (vocals, guitar) Hume, with Ian Vardy (guitar).	
11/2/74	22	5	1. After The Goldrush written by Neil Young in 1970	Island 002
			PREMIERS, The	
			Latin-rock group from San Gabriel, California: George Delgado (vocals), Larry Perez (guitar), Phil Ruiz and Joe Urzua (horns), Frank Zuniga (bass) and Johnny Perez (drums).	
7/4/64	19	6	1. Farmer John	Warner 5443
			PRESIDENTS, The	
			R&B vocal trio from Washington DC: Archie Powell, Bill Shorter and Tony Boyd.	
11/14/70	11	9	1. 5-10-15-20 (25-30 Years Of Love)	Sussex 207
			PRESIDENTS OF THE UNITED STATES OF AMERICA, The	
			Rock trio from Seattle, Washington: Chris Ballew (vocals), Dave Dederer (guitar) and Jason Finn (drums).	
9/16/95	21 ^	14	1. Lump #1 Modern Rock hit (1 week); from the album *The Presidents Of The United States Of America* on Columbia 67291	album cut
3/16/96	29	6	2. Peaches Sales #22 / Airplay #37	Columbia 78254

DATE	POS	WKS	ARTIST–RECORD TITLE	LABEL & NO.

PRESLEY, Elvis

Born on 1/8/35 in Tupelo, Mississippi. Died of heart failure on 8/16/77 (age 42). Known as "The King of Rock & Roll." Moved to Memphis in 1948. First recorded for Sun in 1954. His backing group included The Jordanaires (vocals), Scotty Moore (guitar), Bill Black (bass) and D.J. Fontana (drums). Starred in 31 feature movies (beginning with *Love Me Tender* in 1956). In U.S. Army from 3/24/58 to 3/5/60. Married Priscilla Beaulieu on 5/1/67; divorced on 10/11/73. Priscilla pursued acting in the 1980s beginning with a role on TV's *Dallas*. Their only child, Lisa Marie, (born on 2/1/68) married Michael Jackson on 5/26/94; divorced in 1996. Elvis's last "live" performance was in Indianapolis on 6/26/77. Won Grammy's Lifetime Achievement Award in 1971. Inducted into the Rock and Roll Hall of Fame in 1986.

DATE	POS	WKS	ARTIST–RECORD TITLE	LABEL & NO.
3/10/56	**1** (8)	22	▲² 1. **Heartbreak Hotel** / Best Seller #1 (8) / Juke Box #1 (8) / Top 100 #1 (7) / Jockey #1 (3) #1 Country hit (17 weeks)	
3/17/56	**19**	10	2. I Was The One Jockey #19 / Top 100 #23 / Best Seller: flip / Juke Box: flip	RCA Victor 47-6420
4/28/56	**20**	5	● 3. Blue Suede Shoes Best Seller #20 / Top 100 #24 / Jockey #24 **[EP]** from the EP *Elvis Presley*	RCA Victor EPA-747
6/2/56	**1** (1)	19	▲ 4. **I Want You, I Need You, I Love You** / Best Seller #1 (1) / Top 100 #3 / Juke Box #3 / Jockey #6 #1 Country hit (2 weeks)	
6/9/56	**31**	3	5. My Baby Left Me Top 100 #31 / Best Seller: flip / Juke Box: flip first recorded by Arthur "Big Boy" Crudup in 1950	RCA Victor 47-6540
8/4/56	**1** (11)	23	▲⁴ 6. **Don't Be Cruel** / Best Seller #1 (11) / Juke Box #1 (11) / Jockey #1 (8) / Top 100 #1 (7) #1 R&B hit (6 weeks) / #1 Country hit (10 weeks)	
8/4/56	**1** (11)	23	7. **Hound Dog** Best Seller #1 (11) / Juke Box #1 (11) / Top 100 #2 / Jockey #4 #1 R&B hit (6 weeks) / #1 Country hit (10 weeks); #1 R&B hit for Big Mama Thornton in 1953	RCA Victor 47-6604
10/20/56	**1** (5)	19	▲³ 8. **Love Me Tender** / Best Seller #1 (5) / Jockey #1 (5) / Top 100 #1 (4) / Juke Box #1 (1) title song from Presley's first movie; adapted from the 1861 tune "Aura Lee"	
11/10/56	**20**	4	9. Anyway You Want Me (That's How I Will Be) Jockey #20 / Top 100 #27 / Best Seller: flip / Juke Box: flip	RCA Victor 47-6643
11/24/56+	**2** (2)	14	10. **Love Me** / Jockey #2 / Top 100 #6 / Best Seller #7 / Juke Box #8 **[EP]**	
12/29/56	**19**	4	11. When My Blue Moon Turns To Gold Again Jockey #19 / Top 100 #27 **[EP]** first recorded by Wiley & Gene in 1941; above 2 from the E.P. *Elvis*	RCA Victor EPA-992
1/5/57	**24**	3	12. Poor Boy Jockey #24 / Top 100 #35 **[EP]** from the Presley movie and the EP *Love Me Tender*	RCA Victor EPA-4006
1/26/57	**1** (3)	14	▲ 13. **Too Much** / Best Seller #1 (3) / Juke Box #1 (1) / Top 100 #2 / Jockey #2	
2/9/57	**21**	4	14. Playing For Keeps Jockey #21 / Top 100 #34 / Best Seller: flip / Juke Box: flip	RCA Victor 47-6800
4/6/57	**1** (9)	22	▲² 15. **All Shook Up** Juke Box #1 (9) / Best Seller #1 (8) / Top 100 #1 (8) / Jockey #1 (7) #1 R&B hit (4 weeks) / #1 Country hit (1 week)	RCA Victor 47-6870
4/29/57	**25**	1	16. (There'll Be) Peace In The Valley (For Me) Best Seller #25 / Top 100 #39 **[EP]** from the EP *Peace In The Valley*; #5 Country hit for Red Foley in 1951	RCA Victor EPA-4054

DATE	POS	WKS	ARTIST–RECORD TITLE	LABEL & NO.
6/24/57	**1** (7)	18	▲² 17. **(Let Me Be Your) Teddy Bear /** Best Seller #1 (7) / Top 100 #1 (7) / Jockey #1 (3) #1 R&B hit (1 week) / #1 Country hit (1 week)	
7/8/57	**20**	13	18. Loving You Jockey #20 / Top 100 #28 / Best Seller: flip above 2 from the Presley movie *Loving You*	RCA Victor 47-7000
10/14/57	**1** (7)	19	▲² 19. **Jailhouse Rock /** Best Seller #1 (7) / Top 100 #1 (6) / Jockey #1 (2) #1 R&B hit (5 weeks) / #1 Country hit (1 week)	
10/21/57	**18**	6	20. Treat Me Nice Jockey #18 / Top 100 #27 / Best Seller: flip above 2 from the Presley movie *Jailhouse Rock*	RCA Victor 47-7035
1/27/58	**1** (5)	16	▲ 21. **Don't /** Best Seller #1 (5) / Top 100 #1 (1) / Jockey #1 (1)	
2/3/58	**8**	7	22. **I Beg Of You** Top 100 #8 / Jockey #11 / Best Seller: flip	RCA Victor 47-7150
4/21/58	**2** (1)	13	▲ 23. **Wear My Ring Around Your Neck /** Best Seller #2 / Top 100 #3 / Jockey #3 #1 R&B hit (3 weeks)	
5/5/58	**15**	2	24. Doncha' Think It's Time Jockey #15 / Top 100 #21 / Best Seller: flip	RCA Victor 47-7240
6/30/58	**1** (2)	14	▲ 25. **Hard Headed Woman /** Best Seller #1 (2) / Jockey #1 (1) / Top 100 #2	
7/14/58	**25**	4	26. Don't Ask Me Why Jockey #25 / Top 100 #28 / Best Seller: flip above 2 from the Presley movie *King Creole*	RCA Victor 47-7280
11/10/58	**4**	14	▲ 27. **One Night /** #11 R&B hit for Smiley Lewis in 1956	
11/10/58	**8**	12	28. **I Got Stung**	RCA Victor 47-7410
3/30/59	**2** (1)	11	▲ 29. **(Now and Then There's) A Fool Such As I /** #4 Country hit for Hank Snow in 1953	
3/30/59	**4**	10	30. **I Need Your Love Tonight**	RCA Victor 47-7506
7/13/59	**1** (2)	10	● 31. **A Big Hunk O' Love /**	
7/13/59	**12**	10	32. My Wish Came True	RCA Victor 47-7600
4/11/60	**1** (4)	13	▲ 33. **Stuck On You /**	
4/25/60	**17**	7	34. Fame And Fortune	RCA Victor 47-7740
7/25/60	**1** (5)	16	▲ 35. **It's Now Or Never /** adapted from the Italian song "O Sole Mio" of 1899	
8/1/60	**32**	2	36. A Mess Of Blues	RCA Victor 47-7777
11/14/60	**1** (6)	14	▲² 37. **Are You Lonesome To-night? /** #4 hit for Vaughn Deleath in 1927	
11/28/60	**20**	8	38. I Gotta Know	RCA Victor 47-7810
2/20/61	**1** (2)	11	▲ 39. **Surrender /** adapted from the Italian song "Torna A Surriento"	
3/13/61	**32**	2	40. Lonely Man from the Presley movie *Wild In The Country*	RCA Victor 47-7850
4/24/61	**14**	5	41. Flaming Star **[EP]** title song from the movie starring Presley; from the "Compact 33 Double" EP *Elvis By Request*	RCA Victor LPC-128
5/22/61	**5**	7	● 42. **I Feel So Bad /** #8 R&B hit for Chuck Willis in 1954	
6/19/61	**26**	2	43. Wild In The Country title song from the movie starring Presley	RCA Victor 47-7880
9/4/61	**4**	7	● 44. **(Marie's the Name) His Latest Flame /**	
8/28/61	**5**	10	45. **Little Sister**	RCA Victor 47-7908
12/18/61+	**2** (1)	12	▲ 46. **Can't Help Falling In Love /** #1 Adult Contemporary hit (6 weeks); inspired by the French melody "Plasir d'Amour"	

DATE	POS	WKS	ARTIST–RECORD TITLE	LABEL & NO.
12/18/61+	**23**	5	47. Rock-A-Hula Baby ("Twist" Special)	RCA Victor 47-7968
			above 2 from the Presley movie Blue Hawaii	
3/24/62	**1 (2)**	11	▲ **48. Good Luck Charm /**	
4/7/62	**31**	5	49. Anything That's Part Of You	RCA Victor 47-7992
5/19/62	**15**	7	▲ 50. Follow That Dream **[EP]**	RCA Victor EPA-4368
			title song from the Presley movie and EP	
8/11/62	**5**	9	● **51. She's Not You**	RCA Victor 47-8041
10/6/62	**30**	4	52. King Of The Whole Wide World **[EP]**	RCA Victor EPA-4371
			from the Presley movie and EP Kid Galahad	
10/27/62	**2 (5)**	14	▲ **53. Return To Sender**	RCA Victor 47-8100
			from the Presley movie Girls! Girls! Girls!	
2/23/63	**11**	7	● 54. One Broken Heart For Sale	RCA Victor 47-8134
			from the Presley movie It Happened At The World's Fair	
7/13/63	**3**	8	● 55. (You're the) Devil In Disguise	RCA Victor 47-8188
11/2/63	**8**	7	● **56. Bossa Nova Baby /**	
			from the Presley movie Fun In Acapulco	
11/9/63	**32**	3	57. Witchcraft	RCA Victor 47-8243
			#5 R&B hit for The Spiders in 1956	
3/7/64	**12**	7	● 58. Kissin' Cousins /	
			title song from the Presley movie	
3/14/64	**29**	4	59. It Hurts Me	RCA Victor 47-8307
5/23/64	**34**	2	60. Kiss Me Quick	RCA Victor 447-0639
			recorded on 6/25/61; issued on RCA's "Gold Standard Series"	
5/30/64	**21**	5	● 61. What'd I Say /	
5/30/64	**29**	4	62. Viva Las Vegas	RCA Victor 47-8360
			above 2 from the Presley movie Viva Las Vegas	
8/8/64	**16**	6	63. Such A Night	RCA Victor 47-8400
			recorded on 4/4/60	
10/31/64	**12**	8	● 64. Ask Me /	
			adapted from the Italian song "Io" written by Domenico Modugno	
10/24/64	**16**	8	65. Ain't That Loving You Baby	RCA Victor 47-8440
			recorded on 6/10/58	
3/13/65	**21**	6	66. Do The Clam	RCA Victor 47-8500
			from the Presley movie Girl Happy	
5/8/65	**3**	11	▲ **67. Crying In The Chapel**	RCA Victor 447-0643
			#1 Adult Contemporary hit (7 weeks); recorded on 10/31/60; issued on RCA's "Gold Standard Series"	
7/3/65	**11**	6	68. (Such An) Easy Question	RCA Victor 47-8585
			#1 Adult Contemporary hit (2 weeks); recorded on 3/18/62; from the Presley movie Tickle Me	
9/18/65	**11**	7	● 69. I'm Yours	RCA Victor 47-8657
			#1 Adult Contemporary hit (3 weeks); recorded on 6/26/61	
12/4/65	**14**	6	● 70. Puppet On A String	RCA Victor 447-0650
			from the Presley movie Girl Happy; issued on RCA's "Gold Standard Series"	
1/22/66	**33**	3	● 71. Tell Me Why	RCA Victor 47-8740
			recorded on 1/12/57	
4/9/66	**25**	5	● 72. Frankie And Johnny	RCA Victor 47-8780
			title song from the Presley movie	
7/9/66	**19**	5	73. Love Letters	RCA Victor 47-8870
			#11 hit for Dick Haymes in 1945	
11/5/66	**40**	2	74. Spinout	RCA Victor 47-8941
			title song from the Presley movie	
2/18/67	**33**	4	75. Indescribably Blue	RCA Victor 47-9056

DATE	POS	WKS	ARTIST–RECORD TITLE	LABEL & NO.
11/4/67	38	2	76. Big Boss Man	RCA Victor 47-9341
4/20/68	28	4	77. U.S. Male	RCA Victor 47-9465
			written and originally recorded by Jerry Reed; vocal group on nearly all of above titles: The Jordanaires	
12/14/68+	12	11	● 78. If I Can Dream	RCA Victor 47-9670
4/12/69	35	2	79. Memories	RCA Victor 47-9731
			from the NBC-TV special Elvis	
5/17/69	3	11	▲ 80. **In The Ghetto**	RCA Victor 47-9741
			written by Mac Davis	
8/2/69	35	4	● 81. Clean Up Your Own Back Yard	RCA Victor 47-9747
			from the Presley movie The Trouble With Girls	
9/20/69	1 (1)	13	▲ 82. **Suspicious Minds**	RCA Victor 47-9764
12/13/69+	6	11	▲ 83. **Don't Cry Daddy** /	RCA Victor 47-9768
			written by Mac Davis	
12/13/69+		11	84. Rubberneckin'	
			from Presley's last feature movie Change Of Habit	
2/21/70	16	8	● 85. Kentucky Rain	RCA Victor 47-9791
			written by Eddie Rabbitt	
5/23/70	9	11	● 86. **The Wonder Of You** / [L]	
			#1 Adult Contemporary hit (1 week)	
5/23/70		11	87. Mama Liked The Roses	RCA Victor 47-9835
8/22/70	32	3	● 88. I've Lost You /	
8/22/70		3	89. The Next Step Is Love	RCA Victor 47-9873
11/7/70	11	8	● 90. You Don't Have To Say You Love Me /	
			#1 Adult Contemporary hit (1 week)	
11/7/70		8	91. Patch It Up	RCA Victor 47-9916
			written by Eddie Rabbitt	
1/2/71	21	8	● 92. I Really Don't Want To Know /	
			#11 hit for Les Paul & Mary Ford in 1954	
1/2/71		8	93. There Goes My Everything	RCA Victor 47-9960
3/27/71	33	4	94. Where Did They Go, Lord /	
3/27/71		4	95. Rags To Riches	RCA Victor 47-9980
			#1 hit for Tony Bennett in 1953	
8/14/71	36	2	96. I'm Leavin'	RCA Victor 47-9998
3/11/72	40	1	97. Until It's Time For You To Go	RCA Victor 74-0619
			written by Buffy Sainte-Marie	
9/9/72	2 (1)	12	▲ 98. **Burning Love**	RCA Victor 74-0769
12/23/72+	20	8	● 99. Separate Ways	RCA Victor 74-0815
			featured in the movie Elvis on Tour	
5/5/73	17	7	100. Steamroller Blues / [L]	
			written by James Taylor in 1970; from the TV special Aloha From Hawaii Via Satellite	
5/5/73		7	101. Fool	RCA Victor 74-0910
3/23/74	39	2	102. I've Got A Thing About You Baby /	
			written by Tony Joe White	
3/23/74		2	103. Take Good Care Of Her	RCA Victor APBO-0196
6/29/74	17	7	104. If You Talk In Your Sleep	RCA Victor APBO-0280
11/9/74	14	9	105. Promised Land	RCA Victor PB-10074
			written by Chuck Berry	
2/15/75	20	6	106. My Boy	RCA Victor PB-10191
			#1 Adult Contemporary hit (1 week)	
6/7/75	35	3	107. T-R-O-U-B-L-E	RCA Victor PB-10278

DATE	POS	WKS	ARTIST–RECORD TITLE	LABEL & NO.
5/1/76	**28**	5	108. Hurt / *#8 R&B hit for Roy Hamilton in 1955*	
5/1/76		5	109. For The Heart	RCA Victor PB-10601
2/5/77	**31**	5	110. Moody Blue / *#1 Country hit (1 week)*	
2/5/77		5	111. She Thinks I Still Care *written by Dickey Lee; #1 Country hit for George Jones in 1962*	RCA PB-10857
7/16/77	**18**	12	▲ 112. Way Down *#1 Country hit (1 week); Presley's last chart hit while still alive*	RCA PB-10998
12/3/77	**22**	7	● 113. My Way **[L]** *from the CBS-TV special Elvis In Concert; co-written in 1969 by Paul Anka; based on the French standard "Comme d'Habitude"*	RCA PB-11165
2/28/81	**28**	5	114. Guitar Man **[R]** *#1 Country hit (1 week); Jerry Reed (guitar); remix of Presley's #43 hit from 1968*	RCA PB-12158

PRESSHA

Born David Jones in Atlanta, Georgia. Male R&B singer.

DATE	POS	WKS	ARTIST–RECORD TITLE	LABEL & NO.
9/12/98	**27**	10	1. Splackavellie *Sales #15*	Tony Mercedes 24302

PRESTON, Billy

Born on 9/9/46 in Houston, Texas; raised in Los Angeles, California. R&B singer/keyboardist. Prolific session musician. Regular on TV's *Shindig*. Appeared in the 1978 movie *Sgt. Pepper's Lonely Hearts Club Band*.

DATE	POS	WKS	ARTIST–RECORD TITLE	LABEL & NO.
5/13/72	**2 (1)**	14	● 1. **Outa-Space** **[I]** *#1 R&B hit (1 week)*	A&M 1320
5/19/73	**1 (2)**	14	● 2. **Will It Go Round In Circles**	A&M 1411
10/13/73	**4**	13	● 3. **Space Race** **[I]** *#1 R&B hit (1 week)*	A&M 1463
8/3/74	**1 (1)**	14	● 4. **Nothing From Nothing**	A&M 1544
1/4/75	**22**	6	5. Struttin' **[I]**	A&M 1644
3/1/80	**4**	15	6. **With You I'm Born Again** **BILLY PRESTON & SYREETA** *from the movie Fast Break starring Gabe Kaplan*	Motown 1477

PRESTON, Johnny

Born John Preston Courville on 8/18/39 in Port Arthur, Texas. Rock and roll singer. Discovered by the Big Bopper.

DATE	POS	WKS	ARTIST–RECORD TITLE	LABEL & NO.
12/21/59+	**1 (3)**	14	● 1. **Running Bear** *Indian sounds by the Big Bopper and George Jones; written and backing vocal by the Big Bopper*	Mercury 71474
4/4/60	**7**	12	2. **Cradle Of Love**	Mercury 71598
7/25/60	**14**	7	3. Feel So Fine	Mercury 71651

PRETENDERS, The

Pop-rock group formed in England: Chrissie Hynde (vocals, guitar; born on 9/7/51 in Akron, Ohio; see #5 below), James Honeyman-Scott (guitar), Pete Farndon (bass) and Martin Chambers (drums). Honeyman-Scott died of a drug overdose on 6/16/82 (age 24); replaced by Robbie McIntosh. Fardon died of a drug overdose on 4/14/83 (age 30); replaced by Malcolm Foster. Hynde was married to Jim Kerr of Simple Minds from 1984-90.

DATE	POS	WKS	ARTIST–RECORD TITLE	LABEL & NO.
4/12/80	**14**	12	1. **Brass In Pocket (I'm Special)**	Sire 49181
1/29/83	**5**	14	2. **Back On The Chain Gang** *from the movie The King Of Comedy starring Robert DeNiro and Jerry Lewis*	Sire 29840

DATE	POS	WKS	ARTIST–RECORD TITLE	LABEL & NO.
1/7/84	**19**	9	3. Middle Of The Road	Sire 29444
4/7/84	**28**	6	4. Show Me	Sire 29317
9/7/85	**28**	4	5. I Got You Babe Sales #24	A&M 2758
			UB40 WITH CHRISSIE HYNDE	
11/1/86	**10**	12	6. **Don't Get Me Wrong** Airplay #7 / Sales #11	Sire 28630
			#1 Mainstream Rock hit (3 weeks)	
9/24/94	**16**	23	7. I'll Stand By You Airplay #11 / Sales #39	Sire 18160
			PRETTY POISON	
			Dance group from Philadelphia, Pennsylvania: Jade Starling (vocals), Whey Cooler (keyboards), Louie Franco (guitar) and Bobby Corea (drums).	
10/31/87	**8**	14	● 1. **Catch Me (I'm Falling)** Sales #8 / Airplay #9	Virgin 99416
			from the movie *Hiding Out* starring Jon Cryer	
5/7/88	**36**	4	2. Nightime Airplay #33 / Sales #35	Virgin 99350
			PRICE, Kelly	
			Born on 4/4/73 in Queens, New York. Female R&B singer/songwriter.	
7/18/98	**12**	15	● 1. Friend of Mine Sales #7 / Airplay #74	Island 572330
			#1 R&B hit (5 weeks); samples "Summer Breeze" by Seals & Crofts	
2/6/99	**2 (3)**	21	▲ 2. **Heartbreak Hotel** Sales #2 / Airplay #5	Arista 13619
			WHITNEY HOUSTON (Feat. Faith Evans & Kelly Price)	
			#1 R&B hit (7 weeks)	
			PRICE, Lloyd	
			Born on 3/9/33 in Kenner, Louisiana. R&B singer/songwriter/pianist. Formed record labels Double-L (1963) and Turntable (1969). Inducted into the Rock and Roll Hall of Fame in 1998.	
4/6/57	**29**	6	1. Just Because Top 100 #29	ABC-Paramount 9792
1/5/59	**1 (4)**	15	● 2. **Stagger Lee**	ABC-Paramount 9972
			#1 R&B hit (4 weeks); adapted from the traditional folk song "Stack-O-Lee"	
3/30/59	**23**	4	3. Where Were You (On Our Wedding Day)?	ABC-Paramount 9997
5/11/59	**2 (3)**	14	● 4. **Personality**	ABC-Paramount 10018
			#1 R&B hit (4 weeks)	
8/17/59	**3**	12	5. **I'm Gonna Get Married**	ABC-Paramount 10032
			#1 R&B hit (3 weeks); Don Costa (orch., above 4)	
11/23/59	**20**	9	6. Come Into My Heart	ABC-Paramount 10062
2/15/60	**14**	9	7. Lady Luck	ABC-Paramount 10075
5/30/60	**40**	1	8. No If's - No And's	ABC-Paramount 10102
7/18/60	**19**	7	9. Question	ABC-Paramount 10123
10/26/63	**21**	6	10. Misty	Double-L 722
			first recorded by Erroll Garner in 1954	
			PRICE, Ray	
			Born on 1/12/26 in Perryville, Texas; raised in Dallas, Texas. Country singer. Known as "The Cherokee Cowboy."	
11/7/70+	**11**	14	1. For The Good Times	Columbia 45178
			#1 Country hit (1 week); written by Kris Kristofferson	

DATE	POS	WKS	ARTIST–RECORD TITLE	LABEL & NO.
			PRIDE, Charley	
			Born on 3/18/38 in Sledge, Mississippi. Black country singer.	
12/18/71+	**21**	11	● 1. Kiss An Angel Good Mornin'	RCA Victor 0550
			#1 Country hit (5 weeks)	
			PRIEST, Maxi	
			Born Max Elliott on 6/10/60 in London, England (of Jamaican parents). Dancehall reggae singer.	
12/10/88+	**25**	7	1. Wild World Sales #24 / Airplay #24	Virgin 99269
8/11/90	**1** (1)	17	● 2. **Close To You** Sales #1 (1) / Airplay #3	Charisma 98951
10/5/91	**6**	16	3. **Set The Night To Music** Airplay #23 / Sales #25	Atlantic 87607
			ROBERTA FLACK with Maxi Priest	
12/7/91	**37**	1	4. Housecall (Your Body Can't Lie To Me)	Epic 73928
			Sales #32 / Airplay #39	
			SHABBA RANKS (Featuring Maxi Priest)	
7/20/96	**20**	10	5. That Girl Sales #16 / Airplay #41	Virgin 38550
			MAXI PRIEST FEATURING SHAGGY	
			samples "Green Onions" by Booker T. & The MG's	
			PRIMA, Louis, And Keely Smith	
			Prima was born on 12/7/11 in New Orleans, Louisiana. Died on 8/24/78 (age 66). Jazz trumpeter/singer/bandleader. Smith was born on 3/9/32 in Norfolk, Virginia. Female singer. They were married from 1952-61.	
11/24/58	**18**	7	1. That Old Black Magic	Capitol 4063
			Sam Butera and The Witnesses (backing combo); performed by Prima & Smith in the movie *Senior Prom*; #1 hit for Glenn Miller in 1943	
12/12/60+	**15**	8	2. Wonderland By Night [I]	Dot 16151
			LOUIS PRIMA	
			PRIMITIVE RADIO GODS	
			Group is actually solo alternative-rock artist Chris O'Connor. Touring group includes Luke McAuliffe (guitar), Jeff Sparks (bass) and Tim Lauteiro (drums).	
6/15/96	**10** ᴬ	19	1. **Standing Outside A Broken Phone Booth With Money In My Hand**	album cut
			#1 Modern Rock hit (6 weeks); samples "How Blue Can You Get" by B.B. King; from the album *Rocket* on Ergo/Columbia 67600	
			PRINCE	
			Born Prince Roger Nelson on 6/7/58 in Minneapolis, Minnesota. R&B singer/songwriter/multi-instrumentalist. Starred in the movies *Purple Rain*, *Under The Cherry Moon*, *Sign 'O' The Times* and *Graffiti Bridge*. Founded the Paisley Park record label. The Revolution: Wendy Melvoin (guitar), Lisa Coleman (keyboards), Matt Fink (keyboards), Eric Leeds (sax), Brownmark (bass) and Bobby Z (drums). Melvoin and Coleman formed duo Wendy & Lisa in 1987. The New Power Generation: Rosie Gaines (vocals), Levi Seacer (guitar), Tommy Barbarella (keyboards), Sonny T. (bass) and Michael Bland (drums). Prince changed his name on 6/7/93 to a combination male/female symbol [⚥]. By 1994, referred to as "The Artist Formerly Known As Prince" or "The Artist." Announced in May 2000 that he would once again be known as "Prince." Inducted into the Rock and Roll Hall of Fame in 2004.	
12/8/79+	**11**	12	● 1. I Wanna Be Your Lover	Warner 49050
			#1 R&B hit (2 weeks)	
3/19/83	**6**	15	2. **Little Red Corvette**	Warner 29746
6/18/83	**12**	10	3. **1999**	Warner 29896
			also see #32 below	

DATE	POS	WKS	ARTIST–RECORD TITLE	LABEL & NO.
9/17/83	8	11	4. **Delirious**	Warner 29503
6/9/84	1 (5)	16	▲ 5. **When Doves Cry** #1 R&B hit (8 weeks)	Warner 29286

PRINCE AND THE REVOLUTION:

DATE	POS	WKS	ARTIST–RECORD TITLE	LABEL & NO.
8/11/84	1 (2)	14	● 6. **Let's Go Crazy** Sales #4 / Airplay #5 #1 R&B hit (1 week)	Warner 29216
10/6/84	2 (2)	11	● 7. **Purple Rain** Sales #2 / Airplay #2	Warner 29174
12/22/84+	8	10	8. **I Would Die 4 U** Airplay #8 / Sales #14	Warner 29121
3/2/85	25	6	9. Take Me With U Airplay #20	Warner 29079
			Apollonia (female vocal); above 5 form the movie *Purple Rain* starring Prince	
5/18/85	2 (1)	14	10. **Raspberry Beret** Airplay #1 (1) / Sales #2	Paisley Park 28972
8/3/85	7	10	11. **Pop Life** Airplay #7 / Sales #11	Paisley Park 28998
3/8/86	1 (2)	13	● 12. **Kiss** Airplay #1 (2) / Sales #1 (1) #1 R&B hit (4 weeks)	Paisley Park 28751
6/14/86	23	6	13. Mountains Sales #21 / Airplay #23	Paisley Park 28711
			above 2 from the movie *Under The Cherry Moon* starring Prince	

PRINCE:

DATE	POS	WKS	ARTIST–RECORD TITLE	LABEL & NO.
3/14/87	3	11	14. **Sign 'O' The Times** Sales #3 / Airplay #5 #1 R&B hit (3 weeks)	Paisley Park 28399
8/29/87	2 (1)	13	15. **U Got The Look** Sales #2 / Airplay #3 Sheena Easton (backing vocal)	Paisley Park 28289
12/5/87+	10	12	16. **I Could Never Take The Place Of Your Man** Sales #9 / Airplay #10	Paisley Park 28288
5/14/88	8	9	17. **Alphabet St.** Sales #7 / Airplay #11	Paisley Park 27900
7/1/89	1 (1)	11	▲ 18. **Batdance** Sales #1 (3) / Airplay #2 #1 R&B hit (1 week)	Warner 22924
9/2/89	18	7	● 19. **Partyman** Sales #14 / Airplay #19	Warner 22814
12/2/89	36	3	20. The Arms Of Orion Airplay #35 / Sales #37 **PRINCE with Sheena Easton** above 3 from the movie *Batman* starring Michael Keaton	Warner 22757
8/11/90	6	9	● 21. **Thieves In The Temple** Airplay #5 / Sales #6 #1 R&B hit (1 week); from the movie *Graffiti Bridge* starring Prince	Paisley Park 19751

PRINCE AND THE NEW POWER GENERATION:

DATE	POS	WKS	ARTIST–RECORD TITLE	LABEL & NO.
9/28/91	21	5	● 22. Gett Off Sales #8 / Airplay #56	Paisley Park 19225
10/5/91	1 (2)	16	● 23. **Cream** Airplay #5 / Sales #10	Paisley Park 19175
12/21/91+	3	17	24. **Diamonds And Pearls** Airplay #2 / Sales #10 #1 R&B hit (1 week)	Paisley Park 19083
4/18/92	23	7	25. Money Don't Matter 2 Night Airplay #24 / Sales #69	Paisley Park 19020
10/24/92	36	1	26. My Name Is Prince Sales #22 / Airplay #37	Paisley Park 18707
12/19/92+	7	19	● 27. **7** Airplay #12 / Sales #13 samples "Tramp" by Lowell Fulsom	Paisley Park 18824
3/12/94	3	22	● 28. **The Most Beautiful Girl In The World** Airplay #3 / Sales #5	NPG/Bellmark 72514
			♀	
8/27/94	31	7	29. Letitgo Sales #32 / Airplay #36 **PRINCE**	Warner 18074
9/30/95	12	5	30. I Hate U Sales #6 / Airplay #46 ♀ **with The New Power Generation**	NPG/Warner 17811

DATE	POS	WKS	ARTIST–RECORD TITLE	LABEL & NO.
11/30/96	31 A	5	31. Betcha By Golly Wow! ♀ *from the album Emancipation on NPG 54982*	album cut
1/16/99	40	1	32. 1999　　　　　　Airplay #33 / Sales #61 **[R]** **PRINCE** *same version as #3 above*	Warner 21881

PRISM

Rock group from Canada: Henry Small (vocals), Lindsay Mitchell and Tom Lavin (guitars), John Hall (keyboards), Allen Harlow (bass) and Rocket Norton (drums).

3/13/82	39	2	1. Don't Let Him Know *#1 Mainstream Rock hit (1 week); co-written by Bryan Adams*	Capitol 5082

PROBY, P.J.

Born James Marcus Smith on 11/6/38 in Houston, Texas. Rock and roll singer/songwriter.

2/25/67	23	5	1. Niki Hoeky	Liberty 55936

PROCLAIMERS, The

Pop-rock duo from Edinburgh, Scotland: identical twin brothers Craig and Charlie Reid (born on 3/5/62).

6/26/93	3	16	● 1. **I'm Gonna Be (500 Miles)**　　Sales #4 / Airplay #11 *featured in the movie Benny & Joon starring Johnny Depp; produced by Pete Wingfield; #21 Modern Rock hit in 1989*	Chrysalis 24846

PROCOL HARUM

Pop-rock group formed in England: Gary Brooker (vocals, piano), Keith Reid (lyrics), Ray Royer (guitar), Matthew Fisher (organ), Dave Knights (bass) and Bobby Harrison (drums). Numerous personnel changes. Robin Trower was lead guitarist from 1968-71.

7/1/67	5	10	1. **A Whiter Shade Of Pale** *melody based on the Bach cantata Sleepers Awake*	Deram 7507
11/11/67	34	2	2. Homburg	A&M 885
6/24/72	16	8	3. Conquistador　　　　　　　　　**[L]** *featuring the Edmonton Symphony Orchestra*	A&M 1347

PRODIGY

Techno-rave-dance group from England: Maxim Reality and Keith Flint (vocals), Liam Howlett (instruments) and Leeroy Thornhill (dancer).

3/1/97	30	5	● 1. Firestarter　　　　　　　　Sales #20 *samples "SOS" by The Breeders and "Close (To The Edit)" by The Art Of Noise*	Maverick 17387

PRODUCT G&B, The — see SANTANA

PROFYLE

Male R&B vocal group from Shreveport, Louisiana: Baby Boy, Face, Hershey and L Jai.

9/23/00	14	10	1. Liar　　　　　　　Sales #4 / Airplay #37 *#1 R&B hit (1 week)*	Motown 158262

DATE	POS	WKS	ARTIST–RECORD TITLE	LABEL & NO.
			PRUETT, Jeanne	
6/23/73	28	5	Born Norma Jean Bowman on 1/30/37 in Pell City, Alabama. Country singer/songwriter. 1. Satin Sheets #1 Country hit (3 weeks)	MCA 40015
			PRYMARY COLORZ	
9/28/02	4 S	7	Interracial Contemporary Christian vocal group: Marcus Dilley, Jonathan Thomas, Raj Nichols and Josh Royals. 1. **If You Only Knew**	Big 3 838277
			PSEUDO ECHO	
6/6/87	6	10	Pop-rock-dance group formed in Melbourne, Australia: Brian Canham (vocals, guitar), James Leigh (keyboards), Pierre Gigliotti (bass) and Vince Leigh (drums). 1. **Funky Town** Sales #6 / Airplay #8	RCA 5217
			PSYCHEDELIC FURS	
5/2/87	26	5	Techno-rock group formed in England: brothers Richard (vocals) and Tim (bass) Butler, John Ashton (guitar), and Philip Calvert (drums). 1. Heartbreak Beat Sales #23 / Airplay #28	Columbia 06420
			PUBLIC ANNOUNCEMENT	
2/28/98 1/6/01	5 39	20 2	R&B vocal group from Chicago, Illinois: Earl Robinson, Felony Davis, Euclid Gray and Glen Wright. Former backing group for R. Kelly. ▲ 1. **Body Bumpin' Yippie-Yi-Yo** Sales #3 / Airplay #45 2. Mamacita Sales #4	A&M 582444 RCA 60342
			PUBLIC ENEMY	
6/9/90 7/30/94	34 S 33	3 5	Highly influential rap trio from Long Island, New York: Carlton Ridenhour ("Chuck D"), William Drayton ("Flavor Flav") and Norman Rogers ("Terminator X"). 1. 911 Is A Joke 2. Give It Up Sales #14 / Airplay #70 samples "Opus De Soul" by Albert King, Steve Cropper & Pop Staples	Def Jam 73309 Def Jam 853316
			PUCKETT, Gary, And The Union Gap	
			Born on 10/17/42 in Hibbing, Minnesota; raised in Yakima, Washington. Soft-rock singer/guitarist. Formed The Union Gap in San Diego, California: Gary Withem (keyboards), Dwight Bement (sax), Kerry Chater (bass) and Paul Wheatbread (drums). Bement and Wheatbread later joined Flash Cadillac & The Continental Kids.	
12/2/67+ 3/16/68	4 2 (3)	15 13	**THE UNION GAP FEATURING GARY PUCKETT:** ● 1. **Woman, Woman** ● 2. **Young Girl**	Columbia 44297 Columbia 44450
6/22/68 9/28/68	2 (2) 7	11 10	**GARY PUCKETT AND THE UNION GAP:** ● 3. **Lady Willpower** ● 4. **Over You**	Columbia 44547 Columbia 44644

DATE	POS	WKS	ARTIST–RECORD TITLE	LABEL & NO.
3/22/69	**15**	8	5. Don't Give In To Him	Columbia 44788
9/6/69	**9**	9	6. **This Girl Is A Woman Now**	Columbia 44967

PUDDLE OF MUDD

Hard-rock group formed in Los Angeles, California: Wes Scantlin (vocals, guitar), Paul Phillips (guitar), Doug Ardito (bass) and Greg Upchurch (drums).

DATE	POS	WKS	ARTIST–RECORD TITLE	LABEL & NO.
2/2/02	**5**	30	1. **Blurry** Airplay #5 #1 Mainstream Rock hit (10 weeks) / #1 Modern Rock hit (9 weeks)	album cut
11/2/02	**13**	19	2. **She Hates Me** Airplay #13 #1 Mainstream Rock hit (1 week); above 2 from the album *Come Clean* on Flawless 493074	album cut

PUFF DADDY

Born Sean Combs on 11/4/69 in Harlem, New York. Rapper/songwriter/producer/entrepreneur. Founder of Bad Boy Entertainment in 1993. Changed performing name to P. Diddy in 2001. Played "Lawrence Musgrove" in the movie *Monster's Ball*. The most successful hip-hop artist of all-time.

DATE	POS	WKS	ARTIST–RECORD TITLE	LABEL & NO.
11/30/96+	**18**	13	● 1. **No Time** Sales #7 **LIL' KIM Featuring Puff Daddy** samples "Take Me Just As I Am" by Lyn Collins	Undeas/Big Beat 98044
1/25/97	**1 (6)**	26	▲² 2. **Can't Nobody Hold Me Down** Sales #1 (7) / Airplay #25 **PUFF DADDY Featuring Mase** #1 R&B hit (6 weeks); samples "The Message" by Grandmaster Flash and "Break My Stride" by Matthew Wilder	Bad Boy 79083
6/14/97	**1 (11)**	29	▲³ 3. **I'll Be Missing You** Sales #1 (9) / Airplay #4 **PUFF DADDY & FAITH EVANS (Featuring 112)** #1 R&B hit (8 weeks); "tribute to The Notorious B.I.G."; samples "Every Breath You Take" by The Police	Bad Boy 79097
7/26/97	**19**	10	● 4. **Someone** Sales #10 **SWV (Featuring Puff Daddy)** samples "Ten Crack Commandments" and "The World Is Filled" by The Notorious B.I.G.	RCA 64926
8/2/97	**1 (2)**	28	▲ 5. **Mo Money Mo Problems** Sales #1 (4) / Airplay #12 **THE NOTORIOUS B.I.G. Featuring Puff Daddy & Mase** Kelly Price (female vocal); samples "I'm Coming Out" by Diana Ross	Bad Boy 79100
12/6/97+	**2 (2)**	6	▲ 6. **It's All About The Benjamins /** Sales #2 / Airplay #62 **PUFF DADDY & THE FAMILY Feat. The Notorious B.I.G., Lil' Kim, The Lox, Dave Grohl, Perfect, FuzzBubble & Rob Zombie** samples "I Did It For Love" by Love Unlimited Orchestra	
1/17/98	**4**	12	▲ 7. **Been Around The World** Sales #1 (2) / Airplay #58 **PUFF DADDY & THE FAMILY Featuring The Notorious B.I.G. & Mase** samples "Let's Dance" by David Bowie and "All Around The World" by Lisa Stansfield	Bad Boy 79130
3/28/98	**19**	13	● 8. **Victory** Sales #11 **PUFF DADDY & THE FAMILY Featuring The Notorious B.I.G. & Busta Rhymes** samples "Alone In The Ring" (from the movie *Rocky*) by Bill Conti	Bad Boy 79155
6/27/98	**4**	15	▲ 9. **Come With Me** Sales #2 **PUFF DADDY featuring Jimmy Page** melody is from Led Zeppelin's "Kashmir"; from the movie *Godzilla* starring Matthew Broderick	Epic 78954
7/25/98	**8**	16	● 10. **Lookin' At Me** Sales #5 / Airplay #69 **MA$E Featuring Puff Daddy**	Bad Boy 79176

DATE	POS	WKS	ARTIST–RECORD TITLE	LABEL & NO.
3/20/99	**9**	8	11. **All Night Long** Sales #9 / Airplay #29 **FAITH EVANS (feat. Puff Daddy)** samples "I Hear Music In The Streets" by Unlimited Touch	Bad Boy 79203
10/23/99	**2 (3)**	10	● 12. **Satisfy You** Sales #1 (3) / Airplay #13 **PUFF DADDY (Featuring R. KELLY)** #1 R&B hit (2 weeks); samples "Why You Treat Me So Bad" by Club Nouveau	Bad Boy 79283
9/1/01	**33**	3	13. Bad Boy For Life Airplay #30 / Sales #49 **P. DIDDY, BLACK ROB & MARK CURRY**	Bad Boy 79400
12/8/01	**28**	5	14. Son Of A Gun (I Betcha Think This Song Is About You) Airplay #26 **JANET Featuring Missy Elliott and P. Diddy with Carly Simon** samples "You're So Vain" by Carly Simon	Virgin 46171
3/30/02	**11**	14	15. Pass The Courvoisier Part II Airplay #10 / Sales #14 **BUSTA RHYMES featuring P. Diddy & Pharrell**	J Records 21154
4/6/02	**2 (4)**	19	16. **I Need A Girl (Part One)** Airplay #2 / Sales #23 **P. DIDDY Featuring Usher & Loon**	Bad Boy 79436
6/15/02	**4**	22	17. **I Need A Girl (Part Two)** Airplay #4 / Sales #17 **P. DIDDY AND GINUWINE Featuring Loon, Mario Winans & Tammy Ruggeri**	Bad Boy 79441
9/14/02	**20**	8	18. Trade It All (Part 2) Airplay #13 **FABOLOUS featuring P. DIDDY & JAGGED EDGE** from the movie *Barbershop* starring Ice Cube (soundtrack on Epic 86575)	album cut
12/14/02+	**1 (1)**	19	19. **Bump, Bump, Bump** Airplay #1 (2) / Sales #24 **B2K & P. DIDDY** produced and co-written by R. Kelly	Epic 79842
1/4/03	**33**	4	20. Do That... Sales #22 / Airplay #33 **BABY (AKA DA #1 STUNNA) Featuring P. Diddy**	Cash Money 060079
7/12/03	**1 (4)**	27	21. **Shake Ya Tailfeather** Airplay #1 (4) **NELLY/P. DIDDY/MURPHY LEE** from the movie *Bad Boys II* starring Will Smith and Martin Lawrence (soundtrack on Bad Boy 000716)	album cut
			PUPPIES, The Rap duo from Miami, Florida: brother-and-sister Calvin and Tamara Mills.	
8/13/94	**40**	1	1. Funky Y-2-C Sales #22	Chaos/Columbia 77461
			PURE PRAIRIE LEAGUE Country-rock group formed in Cincinnati, Ohio: Craig Fuller (vocals, guitar), George Powell and Larry Goshorn (guitars), Michael Connor (keyboards), Mike Reilly (bass) and Billy Hinds (drums). By 1979, Vince Gill had replaced Fuller. Gill went on to a highly successful country career.	
4/12/75	**27**	3	1. Amie	RCA Victor 10184
5/24/80	**10**	11	2. **Let Me Love You Tonight** #1 Adult Contemporary hit (3 weeks)	Casablanca 2266
10/4/80	**34**	4	3. I'm Almost Ready	Casablanca 2294
5/23/81	**28**	7	4. Still Right Here In My Heart	Casablanca 2332
			PURIFY, James & Bobby R&B vocal duo: cousins James Purify (born on 5/12/44 in Pensacola, Florida) and Robert Lee Dickey (born on 9/2/39 in Tallahassee, Florida).	
10/22/66	**6**	10	1. **I'm Your Puppet**	Bell 648
2/25/67	**38**	1	2. Wish You Didn't Have To Go	Bell 660

DATE	POS	WKS	ARTIST–RECORD TITLE	LABEL & NO.
5/13/67	25	5	3. Shake A Tail Feather	Bell 669
10/7/67	23	5	4. Let Love Come Between Us	Bell 685

PURSELL, Bill

Born in Oakland, California; raised in Tulare, California. Session pianist.

2/16/63	9	10	1. **Our Winter Love** **[I]**	Columbia 42619

PYRAMIDS, The

Surf group from Long Beach, California: Skip Mercer and Willie Glover (guitars), Tom Pittman (sax), Steve Leonard (bass) and Ron McMullen (drums). Performed with shaved heads. Appeared in the movie *Bikini Beach*.

2/22/64	18	6	1. Penetration **[I]**	Best 13002

Q

Q

Pop group from Beaver Falls, Pennsylvania: Don Garvin (guitar), Robert Peckman (bass), Bill Thomas (keyboards) and Bill Vogel (drums). All share vocals.

4/9/77	23	7	1. Dancin' Man	Epic/Sweet City 50335

QB FINEST

All-star rap group: Nas, Capone, Mobb Deep, Tragedy, MC Shan, Marley Marl, Nature, Cormega and Millennium Thug. QB: Queens Bridge.

3/31/01	26	9	1. Oochie Wally Sales #13 / Airplay #19 **QB FINEST Featuring NAS And Bravehearts** Shelene Thomas (female vocal)	Columbia 79586

Q-TIP

Born Jonathan Davis on 11/20/70 in Queens, New York. Male rapper. Member of A Tribe Called Quest.

9/13/97	36 A	3	1. Got 'Til It's Gone **JANET Featuring Q-Tip and Joni Mitchell** samples "Big Yellow Taxi" by Joni Mitchell	album cut
9/18/99	26	9	2. Vivrant Thing Airplay #16 / Sales #67	Violator 562170
11/27/99+	▲ 3.	5	3. Hot Boyz Sales #2 / Airplay #24 **MISSY "MISDEMEANOR" ELLIOTT [featuring NAS, EVE & Q-TIP]** #1 R&B hit (6 weeks); Lil' Mo (vocal ad libs)	The Gold Mind 64029

QUAD CITY DJ'S

Dance trio formed in Florida: female singer Lana LeFleur, with producers Nathaniel "C.C. Lemonhead" Orange and Johnny "Jay-Ski" McGowan. Orange and McGowan also produced for 95 South and 69 Boyz.

6/1/96	3	29	▲ 1. **C'Mon N' Ride It (The Train)** Sales #4 / Airplay #6 samples "Theme From Together Brothers" by Love Unlimited Orchestra	Big Beat 98083
1/11/97	37	1	2. Space Jam Sales #26 title song from the movie starring Michael Jordan	Warner Sunset 87018

DATE	POS	WKS	ARTIST–RECORD TITLE	LABEL & NO.
			QUAKER CITY BOYS	
1/26/59	39	1	String band from Philadelphia, Pennsylvania. Led by Tommy Reilly. 　　1.　Teasin'	Swan 4023
			QUARTERFLASH	
			Pop-rock group from Portland, Oregon: husband-and-wife Marv (guitar) and Rindy (vocals, saxophone) Ross, with Jack Charles (guitar), Rick DiGiallonardo (keyboards), Rich Gooch (bass) and Brian David Willis (drums). Group originally known as Seafood Mama.	
11/7/81+	3	19	● 　1.　**Harden My Heart** 　　　　#1 Mainstream Rock hit (3 weeks)	Geffen 49824
3/13/82	16	7	2.　Find Another Fool	Geffen 50006
7/2/83	14	11	3.　Take Me To Heart	Geffen 29603
			QUATRO, Suzi	
			Born on 6/3/50 in Detroit, Michigan. Rock singer/songwriter/guitarist. Portrayed "Leather Tuscadero" on TV's *Happy Days* in 1977. Her older sister Patti was a member of Fanny.	
2/24/79	4	15	● 　1.　**Stumblin' In** 　　　　**SUZI QUATRO AND CHRIS NORMAN**	RSO 917
			QUEEN	
			Rock group formed in England: Freddie Mercury (vocals), Brian May (guitar), John Deacon (bass) and Roger Taylor (drums). Mercury died of AIDS on 11/24/91 (age 45). Group inducted into the Rock and Roll Hall of Fame in 2001.	
3/29/75	12	10	1.　Killer Queen	Elektra 45226
2/7/76	9	17	● 　2.　**Bohemian Rhapsody** 　　　　also see #13 below	Elektra 45297
6/12/76	16	11	3.　You're My Best Friend	Elektra 45318
12/4/76+	13	12	4.　Somebody To Love 　　　　also see #14 below	Elektra 45362
11/26/77+	4	17	▲ 　5.　**We Will Rock You/We Are The Champions** 　　　　"We Will Rock You" did not chart; however, it received extensive airplay as both sides were segued together on the album *News Of The World*	Elektra 45441
12/9/78+	24	6	6.　Bicycle Race /	
12/9/78+		6	7.　　Fat Bottomed Girls	Elektra 45541
1/12/80	1 (4)	17	● 　8.　**Crazy Little Thing Called Love**	Elektra 46579
8/30/80	1 (3)	21	▲ 　9.　**Another One Bites The Dust**	Elektra 47031
12/5/81+	29	8	10.　Under Pressure 　　　　**QUEEN & DAVID BOWIE**	Elektra 47235
5/15/82	11	8	11.　Body Language	Elektra 47452
3/3/84	16	8	12.　Radio Ga-Ga	Capitol 5317
4/4/92	2 (1)	13	13.　**Bohemian Rhapsody**　　Sales #2 / Airplay #9 **[R]** 　　　　featured in the movie *Wayne's World* starring Mike Myers and Dana Carvey; same version as #2 above	Hollywood 64794
5/22/93	30	4	14.　Somebody To Love　　Airplay #25 / Sales #72 **[L-R]** 　　　　**GEORGE MICHAEL And QUEEN** 　　　　recorded at Wembley Stadium for the Freddie Mercury Tribute Concert	Hollywood 64647

DATE	POS	WKS	ARTIST–RECORD TITLE	LABEL & NO.
12/18/93+	**23**	11	**QUEEN LATIFAH** Born Dana Owens on 3/18/70 in Newark, New Jersey. Female rapper/actress. Appeared in several movies and TV shows. Latifah is Arabic for delicate and sensitive. 1. U.N.I.T.Y. Sales #16 / Airplay #24 samples "Message From The Inner City" by The Crusaders	Motown 2225
2/14/98	**28**	6	**QUEEN PEN** Born Lynise Walters in Harlem, New York. Female rapper. 1. All My Love Sales #23 / Airplay #51 **QUEEN PEN Featuring Eric Williams of BLACKstreet** samples "Never Too Much" by Luther Vandross	Lil' Man 97023
4/13/91	**9**	11	**QUEENSRŸCHE** Hard-rock group from Bellevue, Washington: Geoff Tate (vocals), Chris DeGarmo and Michael Wilton (guitars), Eddie Jackson (bass), and Scott Rockenfield (drums). 1. **Silent Lucidity** Sales #4 / Airplay #15 #1 Mainstream Rock hit (1 week)	EMI 50345
9/17/66 12/10/66	**1** (1) **22**	12 6	**? (QUESTION MARK) & THE MYSTERIANS** Garage-rock band formed in Saginaw, Michigan: Rudy "?" Martinez (vocals), Bobby Balderrama (guitar), Frank Rodriguez (organ), Frank Lugo (bass) and Eddie Serrato (drums). All were born in Texas to Mexican parents. ● 1. **96 Tears** 2. I Need Somebody **? & THE MYSTERIANS**	Cameo 428 Cameo 441
10/15/83 1/28/84	**5** **31**	14 4	**QUIET RIOT** Hard-rock group formed in Los Angeles, California: Kevin DuBrow (vocals), Carlos Cavazo (guitar), Rudy Sarzo (bass) and Frankie Banali (drums). Sarzo later joined Whitesnake. ● 1. **Cum On Feel The Noize** 2. Bang Your Head (Metal Health)	Pasha 04005 Pasha 04267
9/8/58	**18**	6	**QUIN-TONES, The** Black doo-wop group from York, Pennsylvania: Roberta Haymon, Phyllis Carr, Carolyn Holmes, Kenny Sexton, Jeannie Crist and Ronnie Scott. 1. Down The Aisle Of Love Best Seller #18 / Hot 100 #20	Hunt 321
			R	
3/3/79 7/14/79	**30** **13**	4 10	**RABBITT, Eddie** Born on 11/27/41 in Brooklyn, New York; raised in East Orange, New Jersey. Died of cancer on 5/7/98 (age 56). Country singer/songwriter/guitarist. 1. Every Which Way But Loose #1 Country hit (3 weeks); title song from the movie starring Clint Eastwood 2. Suspicions #1 Country hit (1 week)	Elektra 45554 Elektra 46053

DATE	POS	WKS	ARTIST–RECORD TITLE	LABEL & NO.
7/26/80	5	15	● 3. **Drivin' My Life Away** *#1 Country hit (1 week); from the movie* Roadie *starring Meat Loaf*	Elektra 46656
12/6/80+	1 (2)	18	● 4. **I Love A Rainy Night** *#1 Country hit (1 week) / #1 Adult Contemporary hit (3 weeks)*	Elektra 47066
8/8/81	5	15	5. **Step By Step** *#1 Country hit (1 week)*	Elektra 47174
12/5/81+	15	10	6. Someone Could Lose A Heart Tonight *#1 Country hit (1 week)*	Elektra 47239
5/22/82	35	4	7. I Don't Know Where To Start	Elektra 47435
11/13/82+	7	21	8. **You And I** **EDDIE RABBITT with CRYSTAL GAYLE** *#1 Country hit (1 week)*	Elektra 69936
			RADIOHEAD Alternative-rock group from Oxford, England: Thom Yorke (vocals), brothers Jon (guitar) and Colin (bass) Greenwood, Ed O'Brien (guitar), and Phil Selway (drums).	
8/7/93	34	5	1. Creep Sales #23	Capitol 44932
			RAEKWON Born Corey Woods on 1/12/70 in Staten Island, New York. Male rapper. Member of Wu-Tang Clan. Also recorded as Chef Raekwon.	
10/28/95	37	2	1. Ice Cream Sales #19 / Airplay #74 Ghostface Killah, Method Man and Cappachino (guest rappers)	Loud/RCA 64426
			RAFFERTY, Gerry Born on 4/16/47 in Paisley, Scotland. Adult Contemporary singer/songwriter/guitarist. Co-leader of Stealers Wheel.	
5/13/78	2 (6)	15	● 1. **Baker Street** Raphael Ravenscroft (sax solo)	United Artists 1192
8/26/78	12	10	2. **Right Down The Line** *#1 Adult Contemporary hit (4 weeks)*	United Artists 1233
1/6/79	28	6	3. Home And Dry	United Artists 1266
6/16/79	17	7	4. Days Gone Down (Still Got The Light In Your Eyes)	United Artists 1298
9/8/79	21	8	5. Get It Right Next Time	United Artists 1316
			RAIDERS — see REVERE, Paul	
			RAINBOW Hard-rock group formed in England: Joe Lynn Turner (vocals), Ritchie Blackmore (guitar), Dave Rosenthal (keyboards), Roger Glover (bass) and Bobby Rondinelli (drums). Both Blackmore and Glover were members of Deep Purple.	
6/19/82	40	1	1. Stone Cold *#1 Mainstream Rock hit (1 week)*	Mercury 76146
			RAINDROPS, The Prolific songwriting team of Ellie Greenwich (born on 10/23/40) and husband Jeff Barry (born on 4/3/38). Divorced in 1965, but continued to work together.	
8/31/63	17	7	1. The Kind Of Boy You Can't Forget	Jubilee 5455

DATE	POS	WKS	ARTIST–RECORD TITLE	LABEL & NO.
			RAINWATER, Marvin	
			Born Marvin Percy on 7/2/25 in Wichita, Kansas. Country singer/songwriter/guitarist.	
6/10/57	**18**	12	● 1. Gonna Find Me A Bluebird	MGM 12412
			Juke Box #18 / Best Seller #19 / Top 100 #22	
			RAITT, Bonnie	
			Born on 11/8/49 in Burbank, California. Blues-rock singer/guitarist. Daughter of Broadway actor/singer John Raitt. Married to actor Michael O'Keefe from 1991-99. Inducted into the Rock and Roll Hall of Fame in 2000.	
8/17/91	**5**	15	1. **Something To Talk About** Sales #14 / Airplay #19	Capitol 44724
1/18/92	**18**	10	2. **I Can't Make You Love Me** Sales #23 / Airplay #25	Capitol 44729
5/23/92	**34**	4	3. Not The Only One Airplay #35	Capitol 44764
4/9/94	**19**	10	4. Love Sneakin' Up On You Airplay #14	Capitol 58125
3/4/95	**33**	6	5. You Got It Airplay #36 / Sales #42	Arista 12795
			from the movie *Boys On The Side* starring Whoopi Goldberg	
			RAMBEAU, Eddie	
			Born Edward Flurie on 6/30/43 in Hazleton, Pennsylvania. Pop singer/songwriter.	
6/5/65	**35**	2	1. Concrete And Clay	DynoVoice 204
			RAM JAM	
			Rock group formed in Long Island, New York: Myke Scavone (vocals), Bill Bartlett (guitar), Howie Blauvelt (bass) and Peter Charles (drums). Bartlett was a member of The Lemon Pipers. Blauvelt died of a heart attack on 10/25/93 (age 44).	
7/23/77	**18**	8	1. Black Betty	Epic 50357
			written by legendary black folksinger Hudie Ledbetter (Leadbelly); a remix hit #13 on the Dance charts in 1990	
			RAMPAGE	
			Born in Brooklyn, New York. Male rapper. Childhood friend of Busta Rhymes. Member of the Flipmode Squad.	
8/9/97	**34**	5	1. Take It To The Streets Sales #21	Violator 64171
			RAMPAGE Featuring Billy Lawrence	
			samples "I Hear Music In The Streets" by Unlimited Touch	
			RAMRODS	
			Instrumental rock and roll group from Connecticut: Vincent Bell Lee (lead guitar), his cousin Eugene Moore (guitar), Richard Lane (sax) and his sister Claire Lane (drums).	
2/20/61	**30**	1	1. (Ghost) Riders In The Sky [I]	Amy 813
			#1 hit for Vaughn Monroe in 1949	
			RAN-DELLS, The	
			Rock and roll trio from Villas, New Jersey: brothers Steve and Robert Rappaport, with cousin John Spirt.	
8/31/63	**16**	8	1. Martian Hop [N]	Chairman 4403

DATE	POS	WKS	ARTIST–RECORD TITLE	LABEL & NO.
			RANDOLPH, Boots	
			Born Homer Randolph on 6/3/27 in Paducah, Kentucky. Session saxophonist.	
3/30/63	35	3	1. Yakety Sax [I]	Monument 804
			RANDY & THE RAINBOWS	
			White doo-wop group from Queens, New York: brothers Dominick "Randy" and Frank Safuto, brothers Mike and Sal Zero, and Ken Arcipowski.	
7/27/63	10	10	1. **Denise**	Rust 5059
			RANKS, Shabba	
			Born Rawlston Gordon on 1/17/66 in Sturgetown, Jamaica. Male reggae singer.	
12/7/91	37	1	1. Housecall (Your Body Can't Lie To Me) Sales #32 / Airplay #39	Epic 73928
			SHABBA RANKS (Featuring Maxi Priest)	
8/1/92	40	1	2. Mr. Loverman Sales #23 / Airplay #55	Epic 74257
			Chevelle Franklin (female vocal); from the movie *Deep Cover* starring Larry Fishburne	
1/2/93	33	2	● 3. Slow And Sexy Sales #14 / Airplay #63	Epic 74741
			SHABBA RANKS (featuring Johnny Gill)	
			RAPPIN' 4-TAY	
			Born Anthony Forté in 1969 in San Francisco. Male rapper.	
11/12/94	36	9	1. Playaz Club Sales #26 / Airplay #49	Chrysalis/EMI 58267
4/29/95	39	2	2. I'll Be Around Sales #26 / Airplay #63	Chrysalis/EMI 58331
			RAPPIN' 4-TAY Featuring The Spinners	
			Rappin' 4-Tay raps new verse over the Spinners' 1972 hit, with its original music and chorus	
			RARE EARTH	
			Rock group from Detroit, Michigan: Pete Rivera (vocals, drums), Rod Richards (guitar), Kenny James (keyboards), Gil Bridges (sax), Ed Guzman (percussion) and John Persh (bass). In 1971, Ray Monette replaced Richards and Mark Olson replaced James. Mike Urso replaced Persh in 1972. Persh died of a staph virus in January 1981 (age 38). Olson died of alcohol-related complications in 1982. Guzman died on 7/29/93 (age 49). One of the first white acts signed to a Motown label.	
4/4/70	4	17	● 1. **Get Ready**	Rare Earth 5012
8/22/70	7	11	2. **(I Know) I'm Losing You**	Rare Earth 5017
1/2/71	17	8	3. Born To Wander	Rare Earth 5021
8/7/71	7	10	4. **I Just Want To Celebrate**	Rare Earth 5031
12/18/71+	19	7	5. Hey Big Brother	Rare Earth 5038
6/17/78	39	2	6. Warm Ride	Prodigal 0640
			written by the Bee Gees	
			RASCAL FLATTS	
			Country vocal trio formed in Columbus, Ohio: Jay DeMarcus, Gary LeVox and Joe Don Rooney.	
8/12/00	38	0	1. Prayin' For Daylight Airplay #33 / Sales #42	Lyric Street 164039
11/9/02	23	10	2. These Days Airplay #22	album cut
			#1 Country hit (3 weeks)	

DATE	POS	WKS	ARTIST–RECORD TITLE	LABEL & NO.
6/7/03	30	3	3. Love You Out Loud Airplay #28	album cut
11/22/03	34	3	4. I Melt Airplay #33	album cut
			above 3 from the album Melt *on Lyric Street 165031*	

RASCALS, The

"Blue-eyed soul" pop-rock group formed in New York: Felix Cavaliere (vocals, organ; see #14 below), Gene Cornish (vocals, guitar), Eddie Brigati (vocals, bass) and Dino Danelli (drums). All except Danelli had been in Joey Dee's Starliters. Group inducted into the Rock and Roll Hall of Fame in 1997.

THE YOUNG RASCALS:

DATE	POS	WKS	ARTIST–RECORD TITLE	LABEL & NO.
3/26/66	**1** (1)	12	1. **Good Lovin'**	Atlantic 2321
7/9/66	**20**	4	2. You Better Run	Atlantic 2338
2/25/67	**16**	9	3. I've Been Lonely Too Long	Atlantic 2377
5/6/67	**1** (4)	11	● 4. **Groovin'**	Atlantic 2401
7/22/67	**10**	8	5. **A Girl Like You**	Atlantic 2424
9/23/67	**4**	9	6. **How Can I Be Sure**	Atlantic 2438
12/23/67+	**20**	5	7. It's Wonderful	Atlantic 2463

THE RASCALS:

DATE	POS	WKS	ARTIST–RECORD TITLE	LABEL & NO.
4/20/68	**3**	11	● 8. **A Beautiful Morning**	Atlantic 2493
7/27/68	**1** (5)	13	● 9. **People Got To Be Free**	Atlantic 2537
12/14/68+	**24**	6	10. A Ray Of Hope	Atlantic 2584
3/1/69	**39**	2	11. Heaven	Atlantic 2599
6/7/69	**27**	5	12. See	Atlantic 2634
9/20/69	**26**	5	13. Carry Me Back	Atlantic 2664
4/12/80	**36**	3	14. Only A Lonely Heart Sees **FELIX CAVALIERE**	Epic 50829

RASPBERRIES

Pop-rock group formed in Mentor, Ohio: Eric Carmen (vocals, guitar), Wally Bryson (guitar), David Smalley (bass) and Jim Bonfanti (drums). Scott McCarl and Michael McBride replaced Smalley and Bonfanti in 1974. Carmen went solo in 1975.

DATE	POS	WKS	ARTIST–RECORD TITLE	LABEL & NO.
8/19/72	**5**	11	● 1. **Go All The Way**	Capitol 3348
12/9/72+	**16**	9	2. I Wanna Be With You	Capitol 3473
5/12/73	**35**	7	3. Let's Pretend	Capitol 3546
10/12/74	**18**	6	4. Overnight Sensation (Hit Record)	Capitol 3946

RATT

Hard-rock group formed in Los Angeles, California: Stephen Pearcy (vocals), Warren DeMartini and Robbin Crosby (guitars), Juan Croucier (bass) and Bobby Blotzer (drums). Crosby died of AIDS on 6/6/2002 (age 42).

DATE	POS	WKS	ARTIST–RECORD TITLE	LABEL & NO.
7/14/84	**12**	10	1. Round And Round	Atlantic 89693
8/17/85	**40**	1	2. Lay It Down	Atlantic 89546

RAWLS, Lou

Born on 12/1/35 in Chicago, Illinois. R&B-Adult Contemporary singer known for his very deep voice. Hosted own TV variety show in 1969.

DATE	POS	WKS	ARTIST–RECORD TITLE	LABEL & NO.
10/15/66	**13**	8	1. Love Is A Hurtin' Thing *#1 R&B hit (1 week)*	Capitol 5709

DATE	POS	WKS	ARTIST—RECORD TITLE	LABEL & NO.
5/6/67	29	4	2. Dead End Street Monologue/Dead End Street the first 1:27 of this tune is a monologue by Rawls	Capitol 5869
8/30/69	18	8	3. Your Good Thing (Is About To End)	Capitol 2550
10/16/71	17	11	4. A Natural Man	MGM 14262
7/10/76	2 (2)	13	● 5. **You'll Never Find Another Love Like Mine** #1 R&B hit (2 weeks) / #1 Adult Contemporary hit (1 week)	Philadelphia I. 3592
2/25/78	24	8	6. Lady Love	Philadelphia I. 3634
			RAY, Diane	
			Born on 9/1/42 in Gastonia, North Carolina. Pop singer.	
9/7/63	31	3	1. Please Don't Talk To The Lifeguard first recorded by Andrea Carroll in 1961	Mercury 72117
			RAY, James	
			Born James Ray Raymond in 1941 in Washington DC. R&B singer.	
12/25/61+	22	7	1. If You Gotta Make A Fool Of Somebody Hutch Davie (orch.)	Caprice 110
			RAY, Jimmy	
			Born on 10/3/75 in Walthamstow, East London, England. Pop-rock singer.	
2/21/98	13	10	● 1. Are You Jimmy Ray? Sales #10 / Airplay #29	Epic 78816
			RAY, Johnnie	
			Born on 1/10/27 in Dallas, Oregon. Died of liver failure on 2/25/90 (age 63). Pop singer best known for his pleading voice.	
9/8/56	2 (1)	23	● 1. **Just Walking In The Rain** Top 100 #2 / Juke Box #2 / Jockey #3 / Best Seller #3 first recorded by The Prisonaires in 1953	Columbia 40729
1/19/57	10	10	2. **You Don't Owe Me A Thing /** Best Seller #10 / Top 100 #10 / Jockey #10 / Juke Box #12 written by Marty Robbins	
2/2/57	36	2	3. Look Homeward, Angel Top 100 #36 / Best Seller: flip	Columbia 40803
5/6/57	12	5	4. Yes Tonight, Josephine Jockey #12 / Top 100 #18 Ray Conniff (orch. and chorus, all of above)	Columbia 40893
			RAYBON BROS.	
			Country vocal duo from Greenville, Alabama: brothers Tim and Marty Raybon.	
6/21/97	22	8	● 1. Butterfly Kisses Sales #11	MCA 72016
			RAYBURN, Margie	
			Born in 1924 in Madera, California. Died of a heart attack on 6/14/2000 (age 76). Member of The Sunnysiders. Married Norman Milkin of The Sunnysiders.	
11/11/57	9	13	1. **I'm Available** Jockey #9 / Best Seller #15 / Top 100 #16	Liberty 55102
			RAYDIO — see PARKER, Ray Jr.	

DATE	POS	WKS	ARTIST—RECORD TITLE	LABEL & NO.
			RAYE, Collin	
			Born on 8/22/59 in DeQueen, Arkansas. Country singer.	
12/12/98	37	3	1. Someone You Used To Know Airplay #35 / Sales #62	Epic 79011
5/15/99	37	4	2. Anyone Else Airplay #29	album cut
			from the album *The Walls Came Down* on Epic 68876	
			RAY, GOODMAN & BROWN — see MOMENTS, The	
			RAY J	
			Born Willie Ray Norwood on 1/17/81 in McComb, Mississippi; raised in California. Male rapper. Brother of Brandy. Acted on TV's *The Sinbad Show* and in the movie *Steel*.	
3/15/97	25	8	1. Let It Go Sales #15	EastWest 64206
			from the movie *Set It Off* starring Jada Pinkett and Queen Latifah	
6/30/01	30	5	2. Wait A Minute Airplay #27 / Sales #55	Atlantic 85066
			RAY-J Featuring Lil' Kim	
			RAYNE, Tha' — see JAHEIM	
			RAYS, The	
			Black doo-wop group formed in Harlem, New York: Harold Miller, Walter Ford, David Jones and Harry James.	
10/21/57	3	17	● 1. **Silhouettes /** Top 100 #3 / Best Seller #4 / Jockey #5	
1/20/58		4	2. Daddy Cool Best Seller: flip	Cameo 117
			RAYVON — see SHAGGY	
			REA, Chris	
			Born on 3/4/51 in Middlesborough, Cleveland, England. Soft-rock singer/songwriter/guitarist.	
7/29/78	12	10	1. Fool (If You Think It's Over)	United Artists 1198
			#1 Adult Contemporary hit (3 weeks)	
			READY FOR THE WORLD	
			R&B-funk-dance group from Flint, Michigan: Melvin Riley (vocals), Gordon Strozier (guitar), Greg Potts (keyboards), Willie Triplett (percussion), John Eaton (bass) and Gerald Valentine (drums).	
8/24/85	1 (1)	13	1. **Oh Sheila** Sales #1 (1) / Airplay #3	MCA 52636
			#1 R&B hit (2 weeks)	
1/25/86	21	6	2. Digital Display Sales #14	MCA 52734
12/27/86+	9	12	3. **Love You Down** Sales #9 / Airplay #12	MCA 52947
			#1 R&B hit (2 weeks)	
			REAL LIFE	
			Pop-rock group from Melbourne, Australia: David Sterry (vocals, guitar), Richard Zatorski (keyboards), Allan Johnson (bass) and Danny Simcic (drums).	
1/14/84	29	6	1. Send Me An Angel	Curb/MCA 52287
			also see #3 below	
5/5/84	40	1	2. Catch Me I'm Falling	Curb/MCA 52362
6/10/89	26	8	3. Send Me An Angel '89 Airplay #22 / Sales #28 **[R]**	Curb/MCA 10531
			new recording of #1 above	

DATE	POS	WKS	ARTIST–RECORD TITLE	LABEL & NO.
			REAL McCOY	
			Techno-dance trio: German rapper/songwriter Olaf "O-Jay" Jeglitza with American singers Vanessa Mason and Lisa Cork.	
9/17/94	3	40	▲ 1. **Another Night** Sales #2 / Airplay #2	Arista 12724
3/11/95	3	17	● 2. **Run Away** Airplay #4 / Sales #6	Arista 12808
6/24/95	19	13	3. Come And Get Your Love Sales #21 / Airplay #29	Arista 12834
3/29/97	27	8	4. One More Time Airplay #25 / Sales #29	Arista 13328
			REBELS, The	
			Rock and roll instrumental group from Lackawanna, New York: twin brothers Jimmy (guitar) and Mickey (sax) Kipper, Paul Balon (guitar) and Tom Gorman (drums). Balon died of heart failure on 12/17/2003 (age 61).	
1/26/63	8	12	1. **Wild Weekend** [I]	Swan 4125
			REDBONE	
			Native American "swamp-rock" group formed in Los Angeles, California: brothers Lolly (vocals, guitar) and Pat (vocals, bass) Vegas, Anthony Bellamy (guitar) and Peter De Poe (drums).	
1/8/72	21	7	1. The Witch Queen Of New Orleans	Epic 10749
2/9/74	5	18	● 2. **Come And Get Your Love**	Epic 11035
			REDDING, Gene	
			Born in 1945 in Anderson, Indiana. R&B singer. No relation to Otis Redding.	
7/6/74	24	5	1. This Heart	Haven 7000
			REDDING, Otis	
			Born on 9/9/41 in Dawson, Georgia. Died in a plane crash on 12/10/67 (age 26) in Madison, Wisconsin. Plane crash also killed four members of the Bar-Kays. R&B singer/songwriter/producer/pianist. Own record label, Jotis.Inducted into the Rock and Roll Hall of Fame in 1989. Won Grammy's Lifetime Achievement Award in 1999.	
6/19/65	21	6	1. I've Been Loving You Too Long (To Stop Now)	Volt 126
10/23/65	35	3	2. Respect	Volt 128
4/2/66	31	3	3. Satisfaction	Volt 132
10/29/66	29	4	4. Fa-Fa-Fa-Fa-Fa (Sad Song)	Volt 138
12/31/66+	25	6	5. Try A Little Tenderness #6 hit for Ted Lewis in 1933	Volt 141
6/3/67	26	4	6. Tramp **OTIS & CARLA**	Stax 216
9/23/67	30	2	7. Knock On Wood **OTIS & CARLA**	Stax 228
2/10/68	1 (4)	14	● 8. **(Sittin' On) The Dock Of The Bay** #1 R&B hit (3 weeks); recorded on 11/22/67	Volt 157
5/11/68	25	5	9. The Happy Song (Dum-Dum)	Volt 163
7/27/68	36	1	10. Amen	Atco 6592
12/14/68+	21	5	11. Papa's Got A Brand New Bag [L] recorded at the Whisky A Go-Go	Atco 6636

DATE	POS	WKS	ARTIST–RECORD TITLE	LABEL & NO.

REDDY, Helen

Born on 10/25/41 in Melbourne, Australia. Adult Contemporary singer. Acted in the movies *Airport 1975*, *Pete's Dragon* and *Sgt. Pepper's Lonely Hearts Club Band*.

DATE	POS	WKS	ARTIST–RECORD TITLE	LABEL & NO.
5/8/71	**13**	9	1. I Don't Know How To Love Him *from the rock opera Jesus Christ Superstar*	Capitol 3027
10/14/72	**1 (1)**	14	● 2. **I Am Woman** *from the movie Stand Up And Be Counted starring Stella Stevens*	Capitol 3350
3/10/73	**12**	10	3. Peaceful	Capitol 3527
7/28/73	**1 (1)**	14	● 4. **Delta Dawn** #1 Adult Contemporary hit (2 weeks)	Capitol 3645
11/17/73	**3**	13	● 5. **Leave Me Alone (Ruby Red Dress)** #1 Adult Contemporary hit (4 weeks)	Capitol 3768
3/30/74	**15**	9	6. Keep On Singing #1 Adult Contemporary hit (2 weeks)	Capitol 3845
7/20/74	**9**	12	7. **You And Me Against The World** #1 Adult Contemporary hit (1 week)	Capitol 3897
11/2/74	**1 (1)**	13	● 8. **Angie Baby** #1 Adult Contemporary hit (1 week)	Capitol 3972
3/1/75	**22**	5	9. Emotion #1 Adult Contemporary hit (1 week)	Capitol 4021
7/26/75	**35**	2	10. Bluebird *written by Leon Russell*	Capitol 4108
8/30/75	**8**	9	11. **Ain't No Way To Treat A Lady** #1 Adult Contemporary hit (1 week)	Capitol 4128
12/27/75+	**19**	9	12. Somewhere In The Night	Capitol 4192
8/21/76	**29**	5	13. I Can't Hear You No More / #1 Adult Contemporary hit (1 week)	Capitol 4312
8/28/76		4	14. Music Is My Life	
6/11/77	**18**	12	15. You're My World	Capitol 4418

REDEYE

Rock group formed in Los Angeles, California: Douglas "Red" Mark (vocals), Dave Hodgkins (guitar), Bill Kirkham (bass) and Bob Bereman (drums). Mark was a member of The Sunshine Company.

DATE	POS	WKS	ARTIST–RECORD TITLE	LABEL & NO.
12/26/70+	**27**	7	1. Games	Pentagram 204

RED HOT CHILI PEPPERS

Rock group formed in Los Angeles, California: Anthony Kiedis (vocals), John Frusciante (guitar), Michael "Flea" Balzary (bass) and Chad Smith (drums). Frusciante left in May 1992; replaced by Zander Schloss, then by Arik Marshall, then by Jesse Tobias and finally by Dave Navarro (of Jane's Addiction) in September 1993. Frusciante returned in 1998, replacing Navarro. Kiedis appeared in the movie *Point Break*. Flea and Kiedis appeared in the movie *The Chase*. Navarro married actress Carmen Electra on 11/22/2003.

DATE	POS	WKS	ARTIST–RECORD TITLE		LABEL & NO.
4/18/92	**2 (1)**	23	● 1. **Under The Bridge**	Sales #2 / Airplay #3	Warner 18978
9/11/93	**22**	11	2. Soul To Squeeze	Sales #10 / Airplay #43	Warner 18401
			#1 Modern Rock hit (5 weeks); from the movie *Coneheads* starring Dan Aykroyd and Jane Curtin		
10/7/95	**27** ᴬ	14	3. My Friends		album cut
			#1 Mainstream Rock hit (4 weeks) / #1 Modern Rock hit (4 weeks); from the album *One Hot Minute* on Warner 45733		
1/11/97	**40** ᴬ	1	4. Love Rollercoaster		album cut
			from the animated movie *Beavis And Butt-Head Do America* (soundtrack on Geffen 25002)		

DATE	POS	WKS	ARTIST–RECORD TITLE	LABEL & NO.
7/31/99	9	20	5. **Scar Tissue** Airplay #8 / Sales #13 #1 Mainstream Rock hit (10 weeks) / #1 Modern Rock hit (16 weeks)	Warner 16913
3/25/00	14	15	6. Otherside Sales #9 / Airplay #21 #1 Modern Rock hit (13 weeks)	Warner 16875
7/27/02	34	6	7. By The Way Airplay #33 / Sales #74 #1 Mainstream Rock hit (7 weeks) / #1 Modern Rock hit (14 weeks)	Warner 38574
			REDMAN	
			Born Reggie Noble on 4/17/70 in Newark, New Jersey. Male rapper.	
9/2/95	13	8	● 1. **How High** Sales #7 / Airplay #64 **REDMAN/METHOD MAN** samples "I Am Woman" by The Cover Girls; from the rap concert movie *The Show!*	Def Jam 579924
10/10/98	3	17	● 2. **How Deep Is Your Love** Sales #1 (2) / Airplay #16 **DRU HILL Featuring REDMAN** #1 R&B hit (3 weeks)	Island 572424
12/7/02	36	2	3. React Sales #7 / Airplay #34 **ERICK SERMON Featuring Redman**	J Records 21221
			REDNEX	
			Euro-dance group from Sweden. Core members: Goran Danielsson, Annika Ljungberg, Cool James and Pat Reiniz (vocals), Bosse Nilsson (fiddle), General Custer (banjo) and Animal (drums).	
4/1/95	25	11	● 1. Cotton Eye Joe Sales #8 / Airplay #75 techno-dance version of traditional bluegrass song	Battery 46501
			REED, Dan, Network	
			Funk-rock group from Portland, Oregon: Dan Reed (vocals), Brion James (guitar), Blake Sakomoto (keyboards), Melvin Brannon (bass) and Daniel Pred (drums).	
4/30/88	38	2	1. Ritual Sales #27	Mercury 870183
			REED, Jerry	
			Born Jerry Reed Hubbard on 3/20/37 in Atlanta, Georgia. Country singer/songwriter/guitarist/actor. Acted in several movies. Regular on TV's *Concrete Cowboys*.	
1/9/71	8	14	● 1. **Amos Moses** [N]	RCA Victor 9904
5/29/71	9	9	2. **When You're Hot, You're Hot** [N] #1 Country hit (5 weeks)	RCA Victor 9976
			REED, Jimmy	
			Born Mathis James Reed on 9/6/25 in Dunleith, Mississippi. Died from an epileptic seizure on 8/29/76 (age 50). Blues singer/guitarist. Inducted into the Rock and Roll Hall of Fame in 1991.	
11/4/57	32	3	1. Honest I Do Top 100 #32 / Best Seller #36	Vee-Jay 253
2/29/60	37	2	2. Baby What You Want Me To Do	Vee-Jay 333
			REED, Lou	
			Born on 3/2/42 in Freeport, Long Island, New York. Lead singer/songwriter of the New York seminal rock band Velvet Underground. Appeared in the movie *One Trick Pony*.	
3/31/73	16	8	1. Walk On The Wild Side produced by David Bowie and Mick Ronson	RCA Victor 0887

DATE	POS	WKS	ARTIST–RECORD TITLE	LABEL & NO.
			REESE, Della	
			Born Delloreese Patricia Early on 7/6/31 in Detroit. R&B singer/actress. Appeared in several movies and TV shows.	
9/9/57	**12**	13	1. And That Reminds Me	Jubilee 5292
			Jockey #12 / Best Seller #23 / Top 100 #29	
			Honey Dreamers (backing vocals); Billy Rock (orch.)	
10/5/59	**2** (1)	15	2. **Don't You Know**	RCA Victor 7591
			#1 R&B hit (2 weeks)	
12/28/59+	**16**	8	3. Not One Minute More	RCA Victor 7644
			Glenn Osser (orch., above 2)	
			REEVES, Jim	
			Born on 8/20/23 in Panola County, Texas. Died in a plane crash on 7/31/64 (age 40) in Nashville, Tennessee. Country singer. Appeared in the 1963 movie *Kimberley Jim*.	
5/6/57	**11**	14	1. Four Walls Jockey #11 / Top 100 #12 / Juke Box #13 / Best Seller #14	RCA Victor 6874
			#1 Country hit (8 weeks)	
1/11/60	**2** (3)	20	● 2. **He'll Have To Go**	RCA Victor 7643
			#1 Country hit (14 weeks)	
7/11/60	**37**	1	3. I'm Gettin' Better	RCA Victor 7756
11/28/60	**31**	4	4. Am I Losing You	RCA Victor 7800
			REEVES, Martha — see MARTHA & THE VANDELLAS	
			REFLECTIONS, The	
			Rock and roll vocal group from Detroit, Michigan: Tony Micale, Danny Bennie, Phil Castrodale, Johnny Dean and Ray Steinberg.	
5/2/64	**6**	9	1. (Just Like) Romeo & Juliet	Golden World 9
			RE-FLEX	
			Techno-rock/dance group formed in London, England: Baxter (vocals, guitar), Paul Fishman (keyboards), Nigel Ross-Scott (bass) and Roland Kerridge (drums).	
2/18/84	**24**	5	1. The Politics Of Dancing	Capitol 5301
			REGENTS, The	
			Italian-American doo-wop group from the Bronx, New York: Guy Villari, Sal Cuomo, Chuck Fassert, Don Jacobucci and Tony "Hot Rod" Gravagna.	
5/22/61	**13**	7	1. Barbara-Ann	Gee 1065
			first released on Cousins 1002 in 1961	
7/31/61	**28**	4	2. Runaround	Gee 1071
			REGINA	
			Born Regina Richards in Brooklyn, New York. Female dance singer.	
7/19/86	**10**	12	1. **Baby Love** Sales #10 / Airplay #11	Atlantic 89417
			REID, Clarence	
			Born on 2/14/45 in Cochran, Georgia. R&B singer/songwriter. Also recorded X-rated party albums as Blowfly.	
9/13/69	**40**	2	1. Nobody But You Babe	Alston 4574
			answer to "It's Your Thing" by The Isley Brothers	

DATE	POS	WKS	ARTIST–RECORD TITLE	LABEL & NO.
			R.E.M.	
			Alternative-rock group formed in Athens, Georgia: Michael Stipe (vocals), Peter Buck (guitar), Mike Mills (bass) and Bill Berry (drums). Developed huge following with college audiences in the early 1980s as one of the first alternative-rock bands. Berry retired from the group in 1997.	
10/17/87	9	10	1. **The One I Love**　　　　Sales #5 / Airplay #13	I.R.S. 53171
2/25/89	6	11	2. **Stand**　　　　Sales #4 / Airplay #5	Warner 27688
			#1 Mainstream Rock hit (1 week) / #1 Modern Rock hit (2 weeks); became the theme for TV's *Get A Life* starring Chris Elliott	
4/20/91	4	14	● 3. **Losing My Religion**　　　　Sales #5 / Airplay #8	Warner 19392
			#1 Mainstream Rock hit (3 weeks) / #1 Modern Rock hit (8 weeks)	
8/10/91	10	11	4. **Shiny Happy People**　　　　Airplay #25 / Sales #38	Warner 19242
			Kate Pierson of The B-52's (backing vocals)	
11/28/92	28	8	5. Drive　　　　Sales #32 / Airplay #34	Warner 18729
			#1 Modern Rock hit (5 weeks)	
3/13/93	30	6	6. Man On The Moon　　　　Airplay #26 / Sales #56	Warner 18642
			tribute to the late comedian Andy Kaufman	
10/16/93	29	7	7. Everybody Hurts　　　　Sales #34 / Airplay #38	Warner 18638
10/1/94	21	18	8. What's The Frequency, Kenneth?　　　　Airplay #14 / Sales #31	Warner 18050
			#1 Modern Rock hit (5 weeks)	
1/21/95	19	7	9. Bang And Blame　　　　Airplay #17 / Sales #52	Warner 17994
			#1 Modern Rock hit (3 weeks)	
			REMBRANDTS, The	
			Pop-rock duo from Los Angeles, California: Danny Wilde and Phil Solem.	
3/16/91	14	9	1. Just The Way It Is, Baby　　　　Airplay #15 / Sales #18	Atco 98874
9/30/95	17	10	2. I'll Be There For You (Theme from "Friends") /	
			Airplay #1 (8) / Sales #35	
			#1 Adult Contemporary hit (7 weeks); theme from TV series *Friends*	
9/30/95		10	3.　This House Is Not A Home　　　　Sales: flip	EastWest 64384
			RENAY, Diane	
			Born Renee Diane Kushner in Philadelphia.	
2/15/64	6	8	1. **Navy Blue**	20th Century 456
			#1 Adult Contemporary hit (1 week)	
4/25/64	29	4	2. Kiss Me Sailor	20th Century 477
			RENE & RENE	
			Vocal duo from Laredo, Texas: Rene Ornelas (born 8/26/36) and Rene Herrera (born 10/2/35).	
12/14/68+	14	9	1. Lo Mucho Que Te Quiero (The More I Love You)	White Whale 287
			RENO, Mike — see LOVERBOY	
			REO SPEEDWAGON	
			Rock group from Champaign, Illinois: Kevin Cronin (vocals), Gary Richrath (guitar), Neal Doughty (keyboards), Bruce Hall (bass) and Alan Gratzer (drums). Group appeared in the movie *FM*.	
12/27/80+	1 (1)	20	▲ 1. **Keep On Loving You**	Epic 50953
3/28/81	5	15	● 2. **Take It On The Run**	Epic 01054
7/4/81	24	6	3. Don't Let Him Go	Epic 02127
8/29/81	20	7	4. In Your Letter	Epic 02457

DATE	POS	WKS	ARTIST–RECORD TITLE		LABEL & NO.
6/19/82	7	13	5. **Keep The Fire Burnin'**		Epic 02967
10/2/82	26	6	6. Sweet Time		Epic 03175
11/17/84	29	5	7. I Do'wanna Know	Airplay #27	Epic 04659
1/26/85	1 (3)	14	● 8. **Can't Fight This Feeling**	Airplay #1 (3) / Sales #1 (2)	Epic 04713
4/20/85	19	9	9. One Lonely Night	Airplay #19 / Sales #21	Epic 04848
8/17/85	34	3	10. Live Every Moment		Epic 05412
2/28/87	16	7	11. That Ain't Love	Sales #16 / Airplay #17	Epic 06656
9/19/87	19	8	12. In My Dreams	Airplay #17 / Sales #18	Epic 07255
7/30/88	20	9	13. Here With Me	Airplay #19 / Sales #23	Epic 07901

RESTLESS HEART

Country group formed in Nashville, Tennessee: Larry Stewart (vocals, guitar, keyboards), Dave Innis (guitar, keyboards), Greg Jennings (guitar), Paul Gregg (bass) and John Dittrich (drums).

DATE	POS	WKS	ARTIST–RECORD TITLE		LABEL & NO.
5/30/87	33	5	1. I'll Still Be Loving You	Sales #29 / Airplay #40	RCA 5065
			#1 Country hit (1 week)		
12/5/92+	11	13	2. When She Cries	Airplay #12 / Sales #22	RCA 62412

REUNION

Pop group formed in New York: Joey Levine (vocals), Marc Bellack, Paul DiFranco and Norman Dolph. Levine was lead singer of the Ohio Express.

DATE	POS	WKS	ARTIST–RECORD TITLE		LABEL & NO.
9/28/74	8	10	1. **Life Is A Rock (But The Radio Rolled Me)** [N]		RCA Victor 10056

REVELS, The

Black vocal group from Philadelphia, Pennsylvania: John Kelly, John Grant, Henry Colclough, John Jones and Bill Jackson.

DATE	POS	WKS	ARTIST–RECORD TITLE		LABEL & NO.
11/23/59	35	2	1. Midnight Stroll		Norgolde 103
			Harold Karr (orch.)		

REVERE, Paul, And The Raiders

Born on 1/7/38 in Harvard, Nebraska. Rock and roll keyboardist. The Raiders had numerous personnel changes through the years. Core members: Mark Lindsay (vocals), Freddy Weller (guitar), Keith Allison (bass) and Michael Smith (drums). On daily ABC-TV show *Where The Action Is* in 1965. Own TV show *Happening* in 1968. Weller went on to a prolific country music career. Smith died on 3/6/2001 (age 58).

DATE	POS	WKS	ARTIST–RECORD TITLE		LABEL & NO.
4/17/61	38	1	1. Like, Long Hair [I]		Gardena 116
			based on Rachmaninoff's "Prelude In C-Sharp Minor"		

PAUL REVERE AND THE RAIDERS FEATURING MARK LINDSAY:

DATE	POS	WKS	ARTIST–RECORD TITLE		LABEL & NO.
12/25/65+	11	11	2. Just Like Me		Columbia 43461
3/26/66	4	12	3. **Kicks**		Columbia 43556
7/9/66	6	7	4. **Hungry**		Columbia 43678
10/15/66	20	5	5. The Great Airplane Strike		Columbia 43810
12/17/66+	4	10	6. **Good Thing**		Columbia 43907
3/4/67	22	6	7. Ups And Downs		Columbia 44018
5/6/67	5	8	8. **Him Or Me - What's It Gonna Be?**		Columbia 44094
			PAUL REVERE AND THE RAIDERS (above 2)		
9/2/67	17	5	9. I Had A Dream		Columbia 44227
2/24/68	19	6	10. Too Much Talk		Columbia 44444

DATE	POS	WKS	ARTIST–RECORD TITLE	LABEL & NO.
7/13/68	**27**	6	11. Don't Take It So Hard	Columbia 44553
3/8/69	**18**	9	12. Mr. Sun, Mr. Moon	Columbia 44744
6/14/69	**20**	8	● 13. Let Me	Columbia 44854
5/29/71	**1** (1)	15	▲ 14. **Indian Reservation (The Lament Of The Cherokee Reservation Indian)**	Columbia 45332
10/2/71	**23**	6	15. Birds Of A Feather **RAIDERS** (above 2)	Columbia 45453

REYNOLDS, Debbie

Born Mary Reynolds on 4/1/32 in El Paso, Texas. Actress/singer. Starred in several movies. Married to Eddie Fisher from 1955-59. Mother of actress Carrie Fisher.

DATE	POS	WKS	ARTIST–RECORD TITLE	LABEL & NO.
7/22/57	**1** (5)	23	● 1. **Tammy** Top 100 #1 (5) / Jockey #1 (5) / Best Seller #1 (3) Joseph Gershenson (orch.); from the movie soundtrack *Tammy And The Bachelor* starring Reynolds	Coral 61851
1/20/58	**20**	1	2. A Very Special Love Jockey #20 / Top 100 #83 George Cates (orch.)	Coral 61897
2/22/60	**25**	8	3. Am I That Easy To Forget Billy Vaughn (orch.); #9 Country hit for Carl Belew in 1959	Dot 15985

REYNOLDS, Jody

Born on 12/3/38 in Denver, Colorado; raised in Oklahoma. Male rockabilly singer/guitarist.

DATE	POS	WKS	ARTIST–RECORD TITLE	LABEL & NO.
5/26/58	**5**	14	1. **Endless Sleep** Top 100 #5 / Best Seller #5 / Jockey #7 Al Casey (guitar)	Demon 1507

REYNOLDS, Lawrence

Born in Mobile, Alabama. White folk-pop-country singer.

DATE	POS	WKS	ARTIST–RECORD TITLE	LABEL & NO.
10/11/69	**28**	6	1. Jesus Is A Soul Man	Warner 7322

RHYTHM HERITAGE

Studio group assembled by producers Steve Barri and Michael Omartian. Vocals by Oren and Luther Waters.

DATE	POS	WKS	ARTIST–RECORD TITLE	LABEL & NO.
1/10/76	**1** (1)	12	● 1. **Theme From S.W.A.T.** **[I]** from the TV series *S.W.A.T.* starring Steve Forrest	ABC 12135
5/8/76	**20**	8	2. Baretta's Theme ("Keep Your Eye On The Sparrow") from the TV series *Baretta* starring Robert Blake	ABC 12177

RHYTHM SYNDICATE

R&B group from Connecticut: Evan Rogers (vocals), Carl Sturken (guitar), John Nevin (keyboards), Rob Mingrino (bass) and Kevin Cloud (drums).

DATE	POS	WKS	ARTIST–RECORD TITLE	LABEL & NO.
6/15/91	**2** (2)	13	1. **P.A.S.S.I.O.N** Airplay #5 / Sales #19	Impact 54046
9/28/91	**13**	8	2. Hey Donna Airplay #29 **RYTHM SYNDICATE** (above 2)	Impact 54208

RICH, Charlie

Born on 12/14/32 in Colt, Arkansas. Died of a blood clot on 7/25/95 (age 62). Country singer/songwriter/pianist. Known as "The Silver Fox."

DATE	POS	WKS	ARTIST–RECORD TITLE	LABEL & NO.
5/2/60	**22**	9	1. Lonely Weekends The Gene Lowery Chorus (backing vocals)	Phillips 3552
9/25/65	**21**	7	2. Mohair Sam	Smash 1993

DATE	POS	WKS	ARTIST–RECORD TITLE	LABEL & NO.
6/9/73	**15**	12	▲ 3. Behind Closed Doors #1 Country hit (2 weeks)	Epic 10950
10/27/73	**1** (2)	17	● 4. **The Most Beautiful Girl** #1 Country hit (3 weeks) / #1 Adult Contemporary hit (3 weeks)	Epic 11040
2/23/74	**18**	8	5. There Won't Be Anymore #1 Country hit (2 weeks); recorded in 1965	RCA Victor 0195
3/9/74	**11**	9	6. A Very Special Love Song #1 Country hit (3 weeks) / #1 Adult Contemporary hit (2 weeks)	Epic 11091
8/24/74	**24**	7	7. I Love My Friend #1 Country hit (1 week) / #1 Adult Contemporary hit (1 week)	Epic 20006
6/28/75	**19**	6	8. Every Time You Touch Me (I Get High) #1 Adult Contemporary hit (1 week)	Epic 50103
			RICH, Tony, Project Born Anthony Jeffries on 11/19/71 in Detroit, Michigan. R&B singer/songwriter/keyboardist.	
1/13/96	**2** (2)	38	▲ 1. **Nobody Knows**　　　Sales #3 / Airplay #4	LaFace 24115
			RICHARD, Cliff Born Harry Rodger Webb on 10/14/40 in Lucknow, India (British parents); raised in England. Pop singer/guitarist/actor. Appeared in the movies *Expresso Bongo*, *The Young Ones*, *Summer Holiday* and *Wonderful Life*. Knighted by Queen Elizabeth II in 1995.	
11/2/59	**30**	4	1. Living Doll **CLIFF RICHARD and The Drifters** from the movie *Serious Charge* starring Anthony Quayle	ABC-Paramount 10042
1/18/64	**25**	7	2. It's All In The Game	Epic 9633
8/14/76	**6**	12	● 3. **Devil Woman**	Rocket 40574
11/17/79+	**7**	14	4. **We Don't Talk Anymore**	EMI America 8025
4/5/80	**34**	3	5. Carrie	EMI America 8035
9/27/80	**10**	13	6. **Dreaming**	EMI America 8057
11/22/80+	**20**	11	7. Suddenly **OLIVIA NEWTON-JOHN AND CLIFF RICHARD** from the movie *Xanadu* starring Newton-John	MCA 51007
1/24/81	**17**	11	8. A Little In Love	EMI America 8068
2/6/82	**23**	8	9. Daddy's Home　　　**[L]**	EMI America 8103
			RICHIE, Lionel Born on 6/20/49 in Tuskegee, Alabama. R&B-Adult Contemporary singer/songwriter/pianist. Former lead singer of the Commodores. Appeared in the movie *Thank God It's Friday*.	
7/18/81	**1** (9)	19	▲ 1. **Endless Love** **DIANA ROSS & LIONEL RICHIE** #1 R&B hit (7 weeks) / #1 Adult Contemporary hit (3 weeks); title song from the movie starring Brooke Shields	Motown 1519
10/23/82	**1** (2)	13	● 2. **Truly** #1 Adult Contemporary hit (4 weeks)	Motown 1644
1/22/83	**4**	16	3. **You Are** #1 Adult Contemporary hit (6 weeks)	Motown 1657
4/16/83	**5**	12	4. **My Love** #1 Adult Contemporary hit (4 weeks)	Motown 1677
10/1/83	**1** (4)	17	● 5. **All Night Long (All Night)** #1 R&B hit (7 weeks) / #1 Adult Contemporary hit (4 weeks)	Motown 1698

DATE	POS	WKS	ARTIST–RECORD TITLE	LABEL & NO.
12/3/83+	**7**	14	6. **Running With The Night**	Motown 1710
3/10/84	**1** (2)	17	● 7. **Hello**	Motown 1722
			#1 R&B hit (3 weeks) / #1 Adult Contemporary hit (6 weeks)	
7/7/84	**3**	14	8. **Stuck On You**	Motown 1746
			#1 Adult Contemporary hit (5 weeks)	
10/13/84	**8**	13	9. **Penny Lover** Airplay #5 / Sales #13	Motown 1762
			#1 Adult Contemporary hit (4 weeks)	
11/9/85	**1** (4)	16	● 10. **Say You, Say Me** Airplay #1 (5) / Sales #1 (3)	Motown 1819
			#1 R&B hit (2 weeks) / #1 Adult Contemporary hit (5 weeks); from the movie *White Nights* starring Mikhail Baryshnikov	
7/19/86	**2** (2)	14	11. **Dancing On The Ceiling** Airplay #1 (1) / Sales #3	Motown 1843
10/18/86	**9**	10	12. **Love Will Conquer All** Sales #8 / Airplay #8	Motown 1866
			#1 Adult Contemporary hit (2 weeks)	
1/10/87	**7**	10	13. **Ballerina Girl** Sales #5 / Airplay #8	Motown 1873
			#1 Adult Contemporary hit (4 weeks)	
4/18/87	**20**	7	14. Se La Sales #17 / Airplay #23	Motown 1883
5/23/92	**21**	9	15. Do It To Me Sales #23 / Airplay #31	Motown 2160
			#1 R&B hit (1 week)	
5/4/96	**39**	1	16. Don't Wanna Lose You Sales #26 / Airplay #59	Mercury 852857

RIDDLE, Nelson, and His Orchestra

Born on 6/1/21 in Oradell, New Jersey. Died on 10/6/85 (age 64). Trombonist/prolific arranger/conductor.

DATE	POS	WKS	ARTIST–RECORD TITLE	LABEL & NO.
12/31/55+	**1** (4)	24	● 1. **Lisbon Antigua** Best Seller #1 (4) / Jockey #1 (2) / Top 100 #2 / Juke Box #2 **[I]**	Capitol 3287
3/31/56	**20**	4	2. Port Au Prince Jockey #20 / Top 100 #32 **[I]**	Capitol 3374
8/4/56	**39**	2	3. Theme From "The Proud Ones" Top 100 #39 **[I]**	Capitol 3472
			title song from the movie *The Proud Ones* starring Robert Ryan	
8/4/62	**30**	3	4. Route 66 Theme **[I]**	Capitol 4741
			from the TV series starring George Maharis and Martin Milner	

RIFF

R&B vocal group from Paterson, New Jersey: Ken Kelly, Steven Capers, Anthony Fuller, Dwayne Jones and Michael Best.

DATE	POS	WKS	ARTIST–RECORD TITLE	LABEL & NO.
4/27/91	**25**	6	1. My Heart Is Failing Me Sales #24 / Airplay #29	SBK 07342

RIGHTEOUS BROTHERS, The

"Blue-eyed soul" vocal duo: Bill Medley (born on 9/19/40 in Santa Ana, California) and Bobby Hatfield (born on 8/10/40 in Beaver Dam, Wisconsin; died on 11/5/2003, age 63). Inducted into the Rock and Roll Hall of Fame in 2003.

DATE	POS	WKS	ARTIST–RECORD TITLE	LABEL & NO.
12/26/64+	**1** (2)	13	1. **You've Lost That Lovin' Feelin'**	Philles 124
4/17/65	**9**	10	2. **Just Once In My Life**	Philles 127
7/31/65	**4**	22	3. **Unchained Melody**	Philles 129
			also see #11 & 12 below	
12/11/65+	**5**	8	4. **Ebb Tide**	Philles 130
			#2 hit for Frank Chacksfield in 1953; all of above produced by Phil Spector	
3/19/66	**1** (3)	11	● 5. **(You're My) Soul And Inspiration**	Verve 10383
6/18/66	**18**	5	6. He	Verve 10406
8/27/66	**30**	3	7. Go Ahead And Cry	Verve 10430
6/15/74	**3**	10	8. **Rock And Roll Heaven**	Haven 7002

DATE	POS	WKS	ARTIST–RECORD TITLE	LABEL & NO.
10/5/74	**20**	4	9. Give It To The People	Haven 7004
12/7/74	**32**	3	10. Dream On	Haven 7006
9/8/90	**13**	11	11. Unchained Melody Airplay #3 **[R]** #1 Adult Contemporary hit (2 weeks); featured in the movie *Ghost* starring Patrick Swayze and Demi Moore	Verve Forecast 871882
10/13/90	**19**	12	▲ 12. Unchained Melody Sales #4 **[R]** newly recorded 1990 version	Curb 76842
			RIGHT SAID FRED (R*S*F) Pop-dance-novelty trio from England: brothers Richard (vocals) and Fred (guitar) Fairbrass, with Rob Manzoli (guitar).	
1/18/92	**1** (3)	17	▲ 1. **I'm Too Sexy** Sales #1 (7) / Airplay #8	Charisma 98671
			RILEY, Cheryl Pepsii Born in Brooklyn, New York. R&B singer.	
12/10/88	**32**	5	1. Thanks For My Child Sales #31 / Airplay #31 #1 R&B hit (1 week)	Columbia 07996
			RILEY, Jeannie C. Born Jeanne Carolyn Stephenson on 10/19/45 in Anson, Texas. Country singer.	
8/31/68	**1** (1)	12	● 1. **Harper Valley P.T.A.** #1 Country hit (3 weeks); written by Tom T. Hall	Plantation 3
			RIMES, LeAnn Born Margaret LeAnn Rimes on 8/28/82 in Jackson, Mississippi; raised in Garland, Texas. Country singer. Married actor Dean Sheremet on 2/23/2002. Won the 1996 Best New Artist Grammy Award.	
6/29/96	**26**	6	● 1. Blue Sales #11	Curb 76959
7/5/97	**2** (4)	61	▲³ 2. **How Do I Live** Sales #2 / Airplay #3 #1 Adult Contemporary hit (11 weeks); from the movie *Con Air* starring Nicolas Cage	Curb 73022
9/20/97	**34**	5	● 3. You Light Up My Life Sales #20	Curb 73027
4/25/98	**18**	21	● 4. Looking Through Your Eyes Sales #13 / Airplay #70 from the animated movie *Quest For Camelot*	Curb 73055
3/13/99	**29**	4	● 5. Written In The Stars Sales #13 **ELTON JOHN & LEANN RIMES** from Elton John and Tim Rice's musical interpretation of the stage show *Aida*	Rocket/Curb 566918
12/4/99+	**23**	10	6. Big Deal Sales #18 / Airplay #39	Curb 73086
8/5/00	**11**	14	7. I Need You Sales #3 / Airplay #23 from the TV movie *Jesus* starring Jeremy Sisto	Curb/Capitol 58863
2/2/02	**11**	14	● 8. Can't Fight The Moonlight Sales #4 / Airplay #15 theme from the movie *Coyote Ugly* starring Piper Perabo	Curb 73116
			RINKY-DINKS, The — see DARIN, Bobby	
			RIOS, Miguel Born on 6/7/44 in Granada, Spain. Adult Contemporary singer.	
6/20/70	**14**	8	1. A Song Of Joy (Himno A La Alegria) #1 Adult Contemporary hit (2 weeks)	A&M 1193

DATE	POS	WKS	ARTIST–RECORD TITLE	LABEL & NO.
			RIP CHORDS, The	
			Rock and roll group formed in California: Terry Melcher, Bruce Johnston, Phil Stewart, Richard Rotkin, Arnie Marcus and Ernie Bringas. Melcher is the son of Doris Day. Johnston went on to join The Beach Boys.	
1/4/64	4	11	1. **Hey Little Cobra**	Columbia 42921
5/23/64	28	5	2. Three Window Coupe	Columbia 43035
			RIPERTON, Minnie	
			Born on 11/8/47 in Chicago, Illinois. Died of cancer on 7/12/79 (age 31). R&B singer. Her daughter Maya Rudolph is a cast member of TV's *Saturday Night Live*.	
2/15/75	1 (1)	13	● 1. **Lovin' You**	Epic 50057
			RITCHIE FAMILY, The	
			Female disco trio from Philadelphia, Pennsylvania: Cheryl Jackson, Cassandra Wooten and Gwen Oliver. Named for producer Ritchie Rome.	
9/6/75	11	12	1. Brazil [I]	20th Century 2218
			#2 hit for Xavier Cugat in 1943	
10/2/76	17	11	2. The Best Disco In Town	Marlin 3306
			RITENOUR, Lee	
			Born on 1/11/52 in Los Angeles, California. Guitarist/composer/arranger. Nicknamed "Captain Fingers."	
5/23/81	15	9	1. Is It You	Elektra 47124
			Eric Tagg (vocal)	
			RITTER, Tex	
			Born Maurice Ritter on 1/12/05 in Murvaul, Texas. Died of a heart attack on 1/2/74 (age 68). Country singer/guitarist/actor. Starred in numerous western movies. Father of actor John Ritter (died 9/11/03, age 54).	
7/7/56	28	6	1. The Wayward Wind Top 100 #28	Capitol 3430
			Harry Geller (orch.)	
8/14/61	20	4	2. I Dreamed Of A Hill-Billy Heaven [S]	Capitol 4567
			Ralph Carmichael (orch.); #10 Country hit for Eddie Dean in 1955	
			RIVERS, Johnny	
			Born John Ramistella on 11/7/42 in Brooklyn, New York; raised in Baton Rouge, Louisiana. Rock and roll singer/songwriter/guitarist. Started own Soul City record label in 1966.	
6/13/64	2 (2)	10	1. **Memphis** [L]	Imperial 66032
			first recorded by Chuck Berry in 1959	
8/22/64	12	7	2. Maybelline [L]	Imperial 66056
			above 2 written by Chuck Berry	
11/14/64	9	9	3. **Mountain Of Love**	Imperial 66075
2/27/65	20	4	4. Midnight Special [L]	Imperial 66087
			first recorded by Leadbelly in 1941	
6/19/65	7	8	5. **Seventh Son** [L]	Imperial 66112
			first recorded by Willie Mabon in 1955	
10/30/65	26	4	6. Where Have All The Flowers Gone	Imperial 66133
1/15/66	35	3	7. Under Your Spell Again	Imperial 66144
			#4 Country hit for Buck Owens in 1959	

DATE	POS	WKS	ARTIST–RECORD TITLE	LABEL & NO.
3/26/66	3	10	8. **Secret Agent Man** theme from the TV series *Secret Agent* starring Patrick McGoohan	Imperial 66159
6/25/66	19	6	9. **(I Washed My Hands In) Muddy Water** **[L]** #8 Country hit for Stonewall Jackson in 1965; all live recordings above recorded at the Whiskey A Go-Go in Los Angeles	Imperial 66175
10/8/66	1 (1)	12	10. **Poor Side Of Town**	Imperial 66205
2/18/67	3	8	11. **Baby I Need Your Lovin'**	Imperial 66227
6/17/67	10	6	12. **The Tracks Of My Tears**	Imperial 66244
12/2/67+	14	8	13. Summer Rain	Imperial 66267
11/11/72+	6	14	● 14. **Rockin' Pneumonia - Boogie Woogie Flu**	United Artists 50960
5/5/73	38	2	15. Blue Suede Shoes	United Artists 198
8/9/75	22	5	16. Help Me Rhonda Brian Wilson of The Beach Boys (backing vocal)	Soul City/Epic 50121
7/30/77	10	15	● 17. **Swayin' To The Music (Slow Dancin')**	Big Tree 16094
			RIVIERAS, The	
			Teen rock and roll band from South Bend, Indiana: Marty Fortson (vocals), Jim Boal and Willie Gout (guitars), Otto Nuss (organ), Doug Gean (bass) and Paul Dennert (drums).	
2/1/64	5	9	1. **California Sun**	Riviera 1401
			ROACHFORD	
			R&B-rock group formed in England: Andrew Roachford (vocals, keyboards), Hawi Gondwe (guitar), Derrick Taylor (bass) and Chris Taylor (drums).	
5/27/89	25	5	1. Cuddly Toy (Feel For Me) Sales #25 / Airplay #26	Epic 68549
			ROAD APPLES, The	
			Pop group from Boston, Massachusetts. Led by singer/guitarist David Finnerty.	
12/27/75+	35	4	1. Let's Live Together	Polydor 14285
			ROB BASE & D.J. E-Z ROCK	
			Rap duo from Harlem, New York: Robert "Rob Base" Ginyard and Rodney "D.J. E-Z Rock" Bryce.	
10/15/88	36	3	▲ 1. It Takes Two Sales #23 samples "Think (About It)" by Lyn Collins	Profile 5186
			ROBBINS, Marty	
			Born Martin Robinson on 9/26/25 in Glendale, Arizona. Died of a heart attack on 12/8/82 (age 57). Country singer/songwriter/guitarist. Appeared in the movies *Road To Nashville* and *Guns Of A Stranger*.	
11/24/56	17	7	1. Singing The Blues Juke Box #17 / Top 100 #26 #1 Country hit (13 weeks)	Columbia 21545
4/27/57	2 (1)	21	● 2. **A White Sport Coat (And A Pink Carnation)** Best Seller #2 / Top 100 #3 / Jockey #4 / Juke Box #4 #1 Country hit (5 weeks)	Columbia 40864
12/9/57+	15	9	3. The Story Of My Life Jockey #15 / Top 100 #30 / Best Seller #31 #1 Country hit (4 weeks)	Columbia 41013
5/5/58	26	5	4. Just Married Best Seller #26 / Top 100 #35 #1 Country hit (2 weeks)	Columbia 41143
8/25/58	27	5	5. She Was Only Seventeen (He Was One Year More) Hot 100 #27	Columbia 41208

DATE	POS	WKS	ARTIST–RECORD TITLE	LABEL & NO.
3/16/59	38	3	6. The Hanging Tree title song from the movie starring Gary Cooper; Ray Conniff (orch., above 5)	Columbia 41325
11/30/59+	1 (2)	16	7. **El Paso** #1 Country hit (7 weeks); also issued with a special promotional red and white sleeve	Columbia 41511
4/11/60	26	4	8. Big Iron	Columbia 41589
8/1/60	31	3	9. Is There Any Chance	Columbia 41686
12/5/60	34	5	10. Ballad Of The Alamo from the movie *The Alamo* starring John Wayne	Columbia 41809
2/13/61	3	12	11. **Don't Worry** #1 Country hit (10 weeks)	Columbia 41922
8/18/62	16	7	12. Devil Woman #1 Country hit (8 weeks)	Columbia 42486
12/8/62	18	5	13. Ruby Ann #1 Country hit (1 week)	Columbia 42614
			ROBERT & JOHNNY R&B vocal duo from the Bronx, New York: Robert Carr and Johnny Mitchell. Carr died on 5/18/93.	
3/3/58	32	6	1. We Belong Together Best Seller #32 / Top 100 #33	Old Town 1047
			ROBERTS, Austin	
			Born on 9/19/45 in Newport News, Virginia. Pop singer/songwriter.	
11/11/72	12	10	1. Something's Wrong With Me	Chelsea 0101
8/30/75	9	9	2. **Rocky**	Private Stock 45,020
			ROBERTS, Kane	
			Born in Boston, Massachusetts. Rock singer/guitarist.	
6/22/91	38	2	1. Does Anybody Really Fall In Love Anymore?	DGC 19009
			ROBERTSON, Don	
			Born on 12/5/22 in Peking, China; raised in Chicago, Illinois. Pianist/songwriter.	
5/5/56	6	14	1. **The Happy Whistler** Jockey #6 / Best Seller #9 / Top 100 #9 / Juke Box #12 **[I]**	Capitol 3391
			ROBIC, Ivo	
			Born on 1/29/26 in Bjelovar, Yugoslavia. Died of cancer on 3/10/2000 (age 74). Male singer. Pronounced: eevo robish.	
8/31/59	13	11	1. Morgen **[F]** **IVO ROBIC and The Song-Masters** German song also known as "One More Sunrise"; "Morgen": Tomorrow	Laurie 3033
			ROBIN S	
			Born Robin Stone in Queens, New York. Female dance singer.	
5/1/93	5	22	● 1. **Show Me Love** Airplay #3 / Sales #10	Big Beat 10118
			ROBINSON, Dawn — see EN VOGUE	

Queen scored their second #1 hit in 1980 with "Another One Bites The Dust." Although it appeared their career bit the dust in the mid-1980s, they enjoyed a huge comeback in 1992 thanks to a reissue of "Bohemian Rhapsody."

Eddie Rabbitt achieved 17 #1 hits on the Country charts, but only one on the Hot 100. Fans loved "I Love A Rainy Night," as it not only topped the pop and Country charts, but the Adult Contemporary chart as well.

The Young Rascals covered a song by the Olympics, "Good Lovin'," and took it all the way to #1. Twenty years later, Bruce Willis covered the song for a memorable Shakespearean-themed episode of the TV show *Moonlighting*.

REO Speedwagon perfected the power ballad with their first #1 hit, "Keep On Loving You." Four years later, they found themselves at #1 again with another power ballad, "Can't Fight This Feeling."

Lionel Richie can truly be called a master songwriter. Every year for nine straight years, from 1978 to 1986, he wrote a #1 song on the pop chart. One of those hits, 1982's "Truly," became Lionel's second solo chart-topper.

The Righteous Brothers were not related, but were rather the duo of Bill Medley and the late Bobby Hatfield. Their second #1 hit, "(You're My) Soul And Inspiration," had an inspired B-side, titled "B Side Blues."

Jeannie C. Riley reached #1 on the Pop and Country charts with "Harper Valley P.T.A." The song not only won a Country Music Association Award for Single of the Year, but also served as the inspiration for a 1980s TV series starring Barbara Eden.

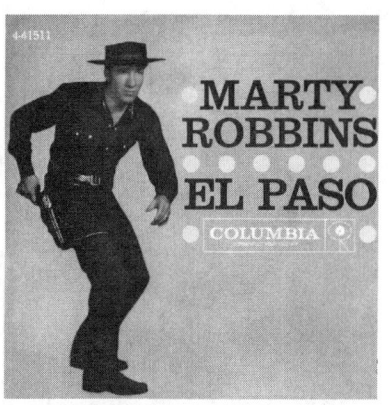

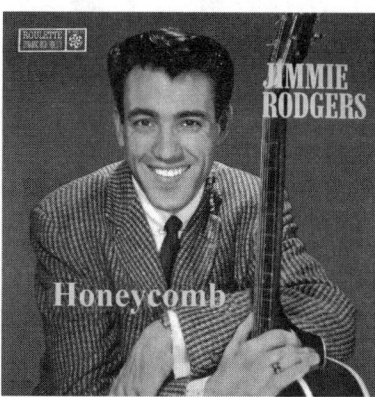

Marty Robbins wrote "El Paso" because of his interest in the Old West. His musical cowboy tale not only reached #1 on the pop and Country charts, but also earned a Grammy for Best Country & Western Performance.

Jimmie Rodgers discovered the song "Honeycomb" while serving at a Nashville Air Force base. After reworking the song in his own style, Rodgers had a #1 hit, the first of five Top 10 hits.

Tommy Roe co-wrote his second #1 hit, "Dizzy," with Freddy Weller of Paul Revere And The Raiders while taking part in *Dick Clark's Caravan Of Stars* traveling show. The song sold a dizzying 2 million copies.

Kenny Rogers hit #1 on the pop, Adult Contemporary, and Country charts with the Lionel Richie–written hit "Lady," and he even managed a #42 spot on the R&B chart. Lionel Richie recorded his own version for his album *Time*.

Diana Ross always had a chic sense of style, and in 1980 she gave her music the "Chic" treatment as well. Bernard Edwards and Nile Rodgers of the dance band Chic co-wrote her fifth #1 solo hit, "Upside Down."

Roxette may not have been as well-known as fellow Swedish exports ABBA and Ace of Base, but they had more #1 hits than both those acts combined. "Listen To Your Heart" was the second of four chart-toppers.

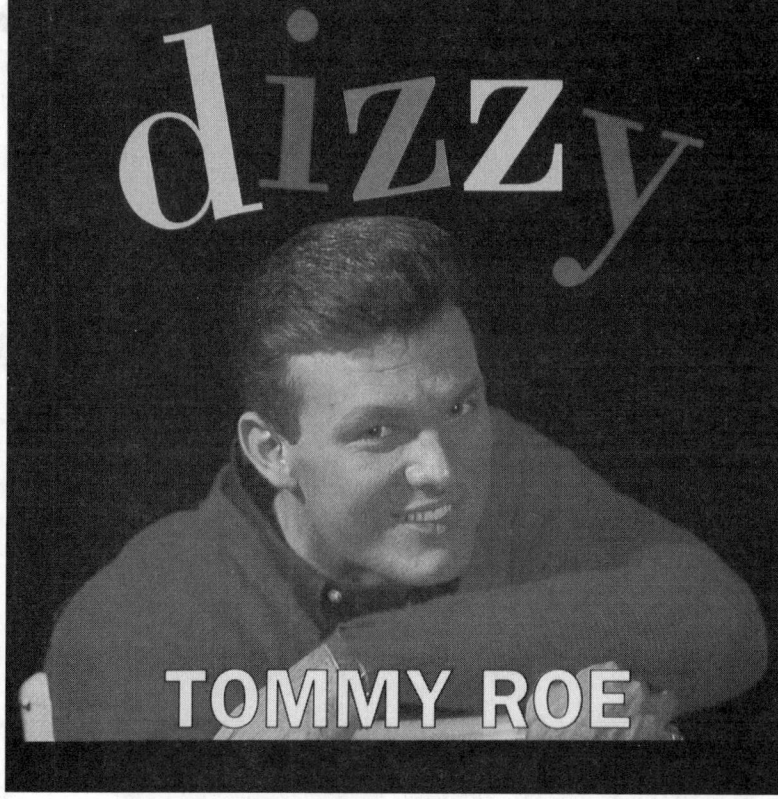

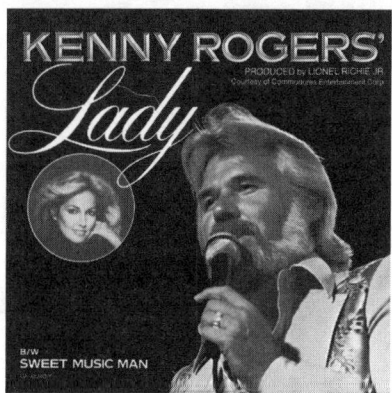

DATE	POS	WKS	ARTIST–RECORD TITLE	LABEL & NO.
			ROBINSON, Floyd	
			Born in 1937 in Nashville, Tennessee. Rock and roll singer/songwriter/ guitarist.	
8/3/59	**20**	12	1. Makin' Love	RCA Victor 7529
			produced by Chet Atkins	
			ROBINSON, Smokey	
			Born William Robinson on 2/19/40 in Detroit, Michigan. R&B singer/prolific songwriter. Lead singer of The Miracles. Formerly married to Claudette Rogers (also with The Miracles). Vice President of Motown Records (1985-88). Inducted into the Rock and Roll Hall of Fame in 1987. Won Grammy's Lifetime Achievement Award in 1999.	
1/19/74	**27**	6	1. Baby Come Close	Tamla 54239
5/31/75	**26**	6	2. Baby That's Backatcha	Tamla 54258
			#1 R&B hit (1 week)	
10/18/75	**36**	3	3. The Agony And The Ecstasy	Tamla 54261
11/17/79+	**4**	17	4. **Cruisin'**	Tamla 54306
5/3/80	**31**	4	5. Let Me Be The Clock	Tamla 54311
3/21/81	**2 (3)**	16	● 6. **Being With You**	Tamla 54321
			#1 R&B hit (5 weeks)	
2/27/82	**33**	5	7. Tell Me Tomorrow - Part I	Tamla 1601
5/9/87	**8**	12	8. **Just To See Her** Sales #8 / Airplay #8	Motown 1877
			#1 Adult Contemporary hit (1 week)	
8/15/87	**10**	11	9. **One Heartbeat** Airplay #10 / Sales #11	Motown 1897
			ROBINSON, Vicki Sue	
			Born on 5/31/54 in Philadelphia, Pennsylvania. Died of cancer on 4/27/2000 (age 45). Disco singer. Appeared in the original Broadway productions of *Hair* and *Jesus Christ Superstar*.	
6/19/76	**10**	13	● 1. **Turn The Beat Around**	RCA Victor 10562
			ROBYN	
			Born Robyn Carlsson on 6/12/79 in Stockholm, Sweden. Female dance singer.	
5/31/97	**7**	26	● 1. **Do You Know (What It Takes)** Sales #13 / Airplay #13	RCA 64865
11/15/97	**7**	21	● 2. **Show Me Love** Airplay #9 / Sales #11	RCA 64970
3/28/98	**32** A	7	3. Do You Really Want Me (Show Respect)	album cut
			from the album *Robyn Is Here* on RCA 67477	
			ROCHELL AND THE CANDLES	
			R&B vocal group from Los Angeles, California: Johnny Wyatt, Rochell Henderson, Melvin Sasso and T.C. Henderson. Wyatt died in December 1983 (age 45).	
3/27/61	**26**	4	1. Once Upon A Time	Swingin' 623
			ROCHELL AND THE CANDLES with Johnny Wyatt	
			ROCK-A-TEENS	
			Rock and roll teen group from Richmond, Virginia: Vic Mizell (leader), Bobby "Boo" Walker, Bill Cook, Paul Evans, Eddie Robertson and Bill Smith.	
10/12/59	**16**	9	1. Woo-Hoo [I]	Roulette 4192

DATE	POS	WKS	ARTIST–RECORD TITLE	LABEL & NO.
			### ROCKETS	
			Rock group from Detroit, Michigan: David Gilbert (vocals), Jim McCarty and Dennis Robbins (guitars), Don Backus (keyboards), Bob Haralson (bass) and John Badanjek (drums). McCarty and Badanjek were with Mitch Ryder's Detroit Wheels. Gilbert died of cancer on 8/1/2001 (age 49).	
8/11/79	30	6	1. Oh Well	RSO 935
			### ROCKWELL	
			Born Kennedy Gordy on 3/15/64 in Detroit, Michigan. R&B singer/songwriter. Son of Motown chairman Berry Gordy.	
2/11/84	2 (3)	14	● 1. **Somebody's Watching Me**	Motown 1702
			#1 R&B hit (5 weeks); Michael Jackson (backing vocal)	
6/23/84	35	2	2. Obscene Phone Caller	Motown 1731
			### ROCKY FELLERS, The	
			Rock and roll family group from Manila, Philippines: Pop Feller and his four sons (Eddie, Albert, Tony and Junior Feller).	
4/27/63	16	8	1. Killer Joe	Scepter 1246
			### RODGERS, Eileen	
			Born in 1933 in Pittsburgh, Pennsylvania. Adult Contemporary singer.	
9/8/56	18	10	1. Miracle Of Love Jockey #18 / Top 100 #19 / Best Seller #23	Columbia 40708
9/29/58	26	4	2. Treasure Of Your Love Hot 100 #26	Columbia 41214
			Ray Conniff (orch., above 2)	
			### RODGERS, Jimmie	
			Born on 9/18/33 in Camas, Washington. Pop-folk singer/guitarist. Hosted own TV variety series in 1959. Career hampered following mysterious assault on the San Diego Freeway on 12/1/67, which left him with a fractured skull. Returned to performing a year later. Starred in movies *The Little Shepherd Of Kingdom Come* and *Back Door To Hell*. Not to be confused with the country music pioneer of the same name.	
8/19/57	1 (4)	23	● 1. **Honeycomb** Jockey #1 (4) / Best Seller #1 (2) / Top 100 #1 (2)	Roulette 4015
			#1 R&B hit (2 weeks); first recorded by Georgie Shaw in 1954	
11/18/57	3	14	● 2. **Kisses Sweeter Than Wine**	Roulette 4031
			Jockey #3 / Top 100 #7 / Best Seller #8	
			#19 hit for The Weavers in 1951	
2/24/58	7	9	● 3. **Oh-Oh, I'm Falling In Love Again**	Roulette 4045
			Jockey #7 / Top 100 #22 / Best Seller #23	
5/19/58	3	15	● 4. **Secretly /** Jockey #3 / Best Seller #3 / Top 100 #4	Roulette 4070
5/26/58	16	1	5. Make Me A Miracle Jockey #16 / Top 100 #54 / Best Seller: flip	
8/11/58	10	10	6. **Are You Really Mine** Hot 100 #10 / Best Seller #10	Roulette 4090
12/1/58	11	10	7. Bimbombey	Roulette 4116
3/30/59	36	3	8. I'm Never Gonna Tell	Roulette 4129
			Hugo Peretti (of Hugo & Luigi; orch., all of above)	
6/15/59	32	4	9. Ring-A-Ling-A-Lario /	
7/6/59	40	1	10. Wonderful You	Roulette 4158
10/12/59	32	3	11. Tucumcari	Roulette 4191
2/1/60	24	5	12. T.L.C. Tender Love And Care	Roulette 4218
			Joe Reisman (orch., above 4)	
6/18/66	37	2	13. It's Over	Dot 16861
10/14/67	31	4	14. Child Of Clay	A&M 871

DATE	POS	WKS	ARTIST–RECORD TITLE	LABEL & NO.
			ROE, Tommy	
			Born on 5/9/42 in Atlanta, Georgia. Pop-rock and roll singer/songwriter/guitarist.	
8/11/62	**1 (2)**	11	● 1. **Sheila**	ABC-Paramount 10329
11/3/62	**35**	2	2. Susie Darlin'	ABC-Paramount 10362
10/26/63	**3**	11	3. **Everybody**	ABC-Paramount 10478
2/8/64	**36**	4	4. Come On	ABC-Paramount 10515
7/2/66	**8**	10	● 5. **Sweet Pea**	ABC 10762
10/1/66	**6**	11	6. **Hooray For Hazel**	ABC 10852
1/28/67	**23**	5	7. It's Now Winters Day	ABC 10888
2/15/69	**1 (4)**	13	● 8. **Dizzy**	ABC 11164
5/17/69	**29**	3	9. Heather Honey	ABC 11211
12/6/69+	**8**	11	● 10. **Jam Up Jelly Tight**	ABC 11247
9/25/71	**25**	7	11. Stagger Lee	ABC 11307
			ROGER	
			Born Roger Troutman on 11/29/51 in Hamilton, Ohio. Shot to death by his brother Larry in a murder-suicide on 4/25/99 (age 47). R&B singer/songwriter/guitarist. Leader of the family funk group Zapp.	
12/12/87+	**3**	13	1. **I Want To Be Your Man** Sales #3 / Airplay #5	Reprise 28229
			#1 R&B hit (1 week)	
6/22/96	**6**	21	2. **California Love** Sales #3 / Airplay #19	Death Row 854652
			2 PAC (featuring Dr. Dre and Roger Troutman) samples "So Ruff So Tuff" by Roger and "Woman To Woman" by Joe Cocker	
			ROGERS, Julie	
			Born Julie Rolls on 4/6/43 in London, England. Adult Contemporary singer.	
12/5/64+	**10**	9	1. **The Wedding**	Mercury 72332
			#1 Adult Contemporary hit (3 weeks); Argentinian hit "La Novia" introduced in the U.S. in 1961 by Anita Bryant on Columbia 42148	
			ROGERS, Kenny/First Edition	
			Born on 8/21/38 in Houston, Texas. Country singer/songwriter/guitarist/actor. Member of the Kirby Stone Four and The New Christy Minstrels in the mid-1960s. Formed The First Edition in 1967. Went solo in 1973. Starred in the theatrical movie *Six Pack* and several TV movies. Married to actress Marianne Gordon from 1977-93. Later started the Kenny Rogers Roasters restaurant chain.	
			THE FIRST EDITION:	
2/24/68	**5**	8	1. **Just Dropped In (To See What Condition My Condition Was In)**	Reprise 0655
2/8/69	**19**	8	2. But You Know I Love You	Reprise 0799
			KENNY ROGERS AND THE FIRST EDITION:	
7/5/69	**6**	9	3. **Ruby, Don't Take Your Love To Town**	Reprise 0829
			written by Mel Tillis	
10/25/69	**26**	6	4. Ruben James	Reprise 0854
3/14/70	**11**	12	5. Something's Burning	Reprise 0888
			written by Mac Davis	

DATE	POS	WKS	ARTIST–RECORD TITLE	LABEL & NO.
7/25/70	17	8	6. Tell It All Brother	Reprise 0923
11/14/70	33	5	7. Heed The Call	Reprise 0953
			KENNY ROGERS:	
4/23/77	5	13	● 8. **Lucille** #1 Country hit (2 weeks)	United Artists 929
9/10/77	28	4	9. Daytime Friends #1 Country hit (1 week)	United Artists 1027
7/15/78	32	3	10. Love Or Something Like It #1 Country hit (1 week)	United Artists 1210
12/23/78+	16	13	11. The Gambler #1 Country hit (3 weeks)	United Artists 1250
5/12/79	5	13	● 12. **She Believes In Me** #1 Country hit (2 weeks) / #1 Adult Contemporary hit (2 weeks)	United Artists 1273
9/22/79	7	12	13. **You Decorated My Life** #1 Country hit (2 weeks)	United Artists 1315
12/1/79+	3	15	● 14. **Coward Of The County** #1 Country hit (3 weeks)	United Artists 1327
4/12/80	4	14	15. **Don't Fall In Love With A Dreamer** **KENNY ROGERS with Kim Carnes**	United Artists 1345
6/28/80	14	8	16. Love The World Away from the movie *Urban Cowboy* starring John Travolta	United Artists 1359
10/4/80	1 (6)	19	● 17. **Lady** #1 Country hit (1 week) / #1 Adult Contemporary hit (4 weeks); written by Lionel Richie	Liberty 1380
4/25/81	14	12	18. What Are We Doin' In Love **DOTTIE WEST (with Kenny Rogers)** #1 Country hit (1 week)	Liberty 1404
6/13/81	3	14	19. **I Don't Need You** #1 Country hit (2 weeks) / #1 Adult Contemporary hit (6 weeks)	Liberty 1415
9/12/81	14	10	20. Share Your Love With Me #1 Adult Contemporary hit (2 weeks); Gladys Knight & The Pips and Lionel Richie (backing vocals)	Liberty 1430
1/16/82	13	11	21. Through The Years #1 Adult Contemporary hit (2 weeks); above 5 (except #18) produced by Lionel Richie	Liberty 1444
7/24/82	13	10	22. Love Will Turn You Around #1 Country hit (1 week) / #1 Adult Contemporary hit (2 weeks); from the movie *Six Pack* starring Rogers	Liberty 1471
1/29/83	6	15	23. **We've Got Tonight** **KENNY ROGERS and SHEENA EASTON** #1 Country hit (1 week)	Liberty 1492
5/28/83	37	3	24. All My Life	Liberty 1495
9/10/83	1 (2)	18	▲ 25. **Islands In The Stream** **KENNY ROGERS with Dolly Parton** #1 Country hit (2 weeks) / #1 Adult Contemporary hit (4 weeks)	RCA 13615
2/4/84	23	6	26. This Woman above 2 feature writing and production work by the Bee Gees	RCA 13710
10/13/84	15	9	27. What About Me? Airplay #14 / Sales #16 **KENNY ROGERS with KIM CARNES and JAMES INGRAM** #1 Adult Contemporary hit (2 weeks)	RCA 13899
5/6/00	40	2	28. Buy Me A Rose Airplay #34 **KENNY ROGERS With Alison Krauss & Billy Dean** #1 Country hit (1 week); from the album *She Rides Wild Horses* on DreamCatcher 004	album cut

DATE	POS	WKS	ARTIST–RECORD TITLE	LABEL & NO.
			ROGERS, Shorty — see BROWN, Boots	
			ROGERS, Timmie "Oh Yeah!"	
			Born on 7/4/15 in Detroit, Michigan. Black vaudeville and nightclub comedian.	
11/4/57	**36**	4	1. Back To School Again Top 100 #36 / Best Seller #37 Bernie Lowe (orch.)	Cameo 116
			ROLLING STONES, The	
			Blues-influenced rock group formed in London, England: Mick Jagger (vocals), Keith Richards (lead guitar), Brian Jones (guitar), Bill Wyman (bass) and Charlie Watts (drums). Group took name from a Muddy Waters song. Promoted as the bad boys in contrast to The Beatles. Jones drowned on 7/3/69 (age 27); replaced by Mick Taylor. Ron Wood replaced Taylor in 1975. Movie *Gimme Shelter* is a documentary of group's performance at the 1969 Altamont concert. Won Grammy's Lifetime Achievement Award in 1986. Inducted into the Rock and Roll Hall of Fame in 1989. Wyman left group in late 1992. Considered by many as the world's all-time greatest rock and roll band.	
8/1/64	**24**	5	1. Tell Me (You're Coming Back)	London 9682
8/22/64	**26**	6	2. It's All Over Now	London 9687
11/7/64	**6**	9	3. **Time Is On My Side** first recorded by Irma Thomas earlier in 1964	London 9708
1/30/65	**19**	5	4. Heart Of Stone	London 9725
4/10/65	**9**	8	5. **The Last Time**	London 9741
6/19/65	**1 (4)**	12	● 6. **(I Can't Get No) Satisfaction**	London 9766
10/16/65	**1 (2)**	11	7. **Get Off Of My Cloud**	London 9792
1/8/66	**6**	6	8. **As Tears Go By**	London 9808
3/5/66	**2 (3)**	9	9. **19th Nervous Breakdown**	London 9823
5/21/66	**1 (2)**	10	10. **Paint It, Black**	London 901
7/16/66	**8**	8	11. **Mothers Little Helper /**	
8/6/66	**24**	4	12. Lady Jane	London 902
10/8/66	**9**	6	13. **Have You Seen Your Mother, Baby,** **Standing In The Shadow?**	London 903
2/4/67	**1 (1)**	9	● 14. **Ruby Tuesday**	London 904
9/23/67	**14**	6	15. Dandelion	London 905
1/13/68	**25**	4	16. She's A Rainbow	London 906
6/15/68	**3**	11	17. **Jumpin' Jack Flash**	London 908
7/26/69	**1 (4)**	14	● 18. **Honky Tonk Women**	London 910
5/1/71	**1 (2)**	12	19. **Brown Sugar**	Rolling Stones 19100
7/3/71	**28**	5	20. Wild Horses	Rolling Stones 19101
5/6/72	**7**	9	21. **Tumbling Dice**	Rolling Stones 19103
7/29/72	**22**	4	22. Happy	Rolling Stones 19104
9/22/73	**1 (1)**	13	● 23. **Angie**	Rolling Stones 19105
2/2/74	**15**	6	24. Doo Doo Doo Doo Doo (Heartbreaker)	Rolling Stones 19109
8/17/74	**16**	7	25. It's Only Rock 'N Roll (But I Like It)	Rolling Stones 19301
11/16/74	**17**	7	26. Ain't Too Proud To Beg	Rolling Stones 19302
5/8/76	**10**	7	27. **Fool To Cry**	Rolling Stones 19304
6/10/78	**1 (1)**	16	● 28. **Miss You**	Rolling Stones 19307
9/23/78	**8**	9	29. **Beast Of Burden**	Rolling Stones 19309
1/13/79	**31**	4	30. Shattered	Rolling Stones 19310
7/5/80	**3**	14	31. **Emotional Rescue**	Rolling Stones 20001

DATE	POS	WKS	ARTIST–RECORD TITLE	LABEL & NO.
10/18/80	26	5	32. She's So Cold	Rolling Stones 21001
8/29/81	2 (3)	19	33. **Start Me Up**	Rolling Stones 21003
			#1 Mainstream Rock hit (13 weeks)	
12/12/81+	13	12	34. Waiting On A Friend	Rolling Stones 21004
4/10/82	20	6	35. Hang Fire	Rolling Stones 21300
7/3/82	25	5	36. Going To A Go-Go [L]	Rolling Stones 21301
11/19/83	9	10	37. **Undercover Of The Night**	Rolling Stones 99813
3/22/86	5	10	38. **Harlem Shuffle** Sales #5 / Airplay #7	Rolling Stones 05802
6/14/86	28	4	39. One Hit (To The Body) Sales #23 / Airplay #36	Rolling Stones 05906
9/9/89	5	9	40. **Mixed Emotions** Sales #4 / Airplay #11	Rolling Stones 69008
			#1 Mainstream Rock hit (5 weeks)	
11/25/89	23	8	41. Rock And A Hard Place Sales #19 / Airplay #23	Rolling Stones 73057
			#1 Mainstream Rock hit (5 weeks)	
			ROMANTICS, The	
			Pop-rock group from Detroit, Michigan: Wally Palmar (vocals, guitar), Coz Canler (guitar), Mike Skill (bass) and Jimmy Marinos (drums).	
12/3/83+	3	15	1. **Talking In Your Sleep**	Nemperor 04135
3/31/84	37	3	2. One In A Million	Nemperor 04373
			ROME	
			Born Jerome Woods on 3/5/70 in Benton Harbor, Michigan. Male R&B singer.	
4/5/97	6	21	▲ 1. **I Belong To You (Every Time I See Your Face)** Sales #3 / Airplay #26	RCA 64759
8/16/97	31	8	2. Do You Like This Sales #19	RCA 64874
			ROMEO VOID	
			Pop-rock-dance group from San Francisco, California: Debora Iyall (vocals), Peter Woods (guitar), Ben Bossi (sax), Frank Zincavage (bass) and Aaron Smith (drums).	
10/20/84	35	2	1. A Girl In Trouble (Is A Temporary Thing)	Columbia 04534
			RONALD AND RUBY	
			Teen pop vocal duo from New Jersey: Lee "Ronald" Morris and Beverly "Ruby" Ross.	
3/24/58	20	3	1. Lollipop Jockey #20 / Top 100 #39 / Best Seller #40	RCA Victor 7174
			RONDO, Don	
			Born in Springfield, Massachusetts. Adult Contemporary baritone singer.	
11/3/56	11	12	1. Two Different Worlds Jockey #11 / Top 100 #19 / Best Seller #23 Dave Terry (orch.)	Jubilee 5256
7/29/57	7	15	2. **White Silver Sands** Jockey #7 / Best Seller #9 / Top 100 #10 Billy Rock (orch.)	Jubilee 5288
			RONETTES, The	
			R&B-rock and roll "girl group" from New York: sisters Veronica "Ronnie Spector" Bennett and Estelle Bennett Vann, with cousin Nedra Talley Ross. Veronica was married to Phil Spector from 1968-74.	
9/14/63	2 (3)	10	1. **Be My Baby**	Philles 116

DATE	POS	WKS	ARTIST–RECORD TITLE	LABEL & NO.
1/11/64	24	6	2. Baby, I Love You	Philles 118
5/16/64	39	1	3. (The Best Part Of) Breakin' Up	Philles 120
7/18/64	34	4	4. Do I Love You?	Philles 121
11/21/64	23	7	5. Walking In The Rain	Philles 123
			all of above produced by Phil Spector	

RONNIE and THE HI-LITES

Doo-wop group from Jersey City, New Jersey: Ronnie Goodson (lead singer; 12 years old in 1962), Sonny Caldwell, John Whitney, Stanley Brown and Kenny Overby. Goodson died of a brain tumor on 11/4/80 (age 31).

DATE	POS	WKS	ARTIST–RECORD TITLE	LABEL & NO.
4/21/62	16	8	1. I Wish That We Were Married	Joy 260

RONNY & THE DAYTONAS

Rock and roll band formed in Tulsa, Oklahoma: Ronny Dayton (vocals), Jimmy Johnson (guitar), Van Evans (bass) and Lynn Williams (drums).

DATE	POS	WKS	ARTIST–RECORD TITLE	LABEL & NO.
8/22/64	4	10	1. G.T.O.	Mala 481
1/8/66	27	5	2. Sandy	Mala 513
			above 2 produced by Bill Justis	

RONSTADT, Linda

Born on 7/15/46 in Tucson, Arizona. Pop-rock-country singer. Formed the Stone Poneys with Bobby Kimmel (guitar) and Ken Edwards (keyboards). Went solo in 1968. In 1971 formed backing band with Glenn Frey, Don Henley, Randy Meisner and Bernie Leadon (later became the Eagles). Appeared in the 1978 movie *FM*. Acted in the Broadway and movie versions of *The Pirates Of Penzance*.

DATE	POS	WKS	ARTIST–RECORD TITLE	LABEL & NO.
12/9/67+	13	13	1. Different Drum	Capitol 2004
			STONE PONEYS Featuring Linda Ronstadt	
			written by Michael Nesmith	
9/12/70	25	7	2. Long Long Time	Capitol 2846
1/4/75	1 (1)	10	3. **You're No Good**	Capitol 3990
			Andrew Gold (guitar solo)	
4/26/75	2 (2)	13	4. **When Will I Be Loved**	Capitol 4050
			#1 Country hit (1 week)	
10/4/75	5	10	5. **Heat Wave**	Asylum 45282
1/24/76	25	6	6. Tracks Of My Tears	Asylum 45295
9/4/76	11	11	7. That'll Be The Day	Asylum 45340
10/8/77	3	16	▲ 8. **Blue Bayou**	Asylum 45431
10/29/77	5	12	9. **It's So Easy**	Asylum 45438
			first recorded by Buddy Holly in 1958	
2/25/78	31	3	10. Poor Poor Pitiful Me	Asylum 45462
			written by Warren Zevon	
5/20/78	32	3	11. Tumbling Dice	Asylum 45479
9/9/78	16	8	12. Back In The U.S.A.	Asylum 45519
11/18/78+	7	13	13. **Ooh Baby Baby**	Asylum 45546
			David Sanborn (sax solo)	
2/9/80	10	12	14. **How Do I Make You**	Asylum 46602
4/19/80	8	11	15. **Hurt So Bad**	Asylum 46624
7/19/80	31	4	16. I Can't Let Go	Asylum 46654
10/23/82	29	5	17. Get Closer	Asylum 69948
1/29/83	37	3	18. I Knew You When	Asylum 69853

DATE	POS	WKS	ARTIST–RECORD TITLE	LABEL & NO.
1/24/87	2 (1)	12	● 19. **Somewhere Out There** Sales #1 (2) / Airplay #7 **LINDA RONSTADT AND JAMES INGRAM** from the animated movie *An American Tail*	MCA 52973
10/28/89	2 (2)	16	● 20. **Don't Know Much** Sales #1 (2) / Airplay #4 #1 Adult Contemporary hit (5 weeks)	Elektra 69261
2/24/90	11	9	21. All My Life Sales #10 / Airplay #14 **LINDA RONSTADT (featuring Aaron Neville)** (above 2) #1 Adult Contemporary hit (3 weeks)	Elektra 64987
			ROOFTOP SINGERS, The	
			Folk trio from New York: Erik Darling, Willard Svanoe and Lynne Taylor. Darling was a member of The Tarriers. Taylor died in 1982.	
1/12/63	1 (2)	11	● 1. **Walk Right In** #1 Adult Contemporary hit (5 weeks); first recorded by Gus Cannon's Jug Stompers in 1929	Vanguard 35017
4/20/63	20	5	2. Tom Cat	Vanguard 35019
			ROOTS, The	
			Hip-hop group from Philadelphia, Pennsylvania: Tariq Trotter, Ahmir-Khalib Thompson, Malik Abdul-Basit and Leonard Hubbard.	
2/8/97	34	5	1. What They Do Sales #17	DGC 19407
4/3/99	39	2	2. You Got Me Airplay #24 **THE ROOTS featuring Erykah Badu** co-written and backing vocals by Jill Scott	MCA 55539
			ROSE, David, and His Orchestra	
			Born on 6/15/10 in London, England; raised in Chicago, Illinois. Died of heart failure on 8/23/90 (age 80). Conductor/composer/arranger. Married to Martha Raye (1938-41) and Judy Garland (1941-43).	
6/2/62	1 (1)	13	● 1. **The Stripper** [I] #1 Adult Contemporary hit (2 weeks)	MGM 13064
			ROSE GARDEN, The	
			Pop group formed in Parkersburg, West Virginia: Diana Di Rose (vocals), John Noreen and James Groshong (guitars), William Fleming (bass, piano) and Bruce Boudin (drums).	
12/9/67	17	7	1. Next Plane To London	Atco 6510
			ROSE ROYCE	
			R&B-dance group from Los Angeles, California: Gwen Dickey (vocals), Kenji Brown (guitar), Victor Nix (keyboards), Ken Copeland, Fred Dunn and Mike Moore (horns), Terral Santiel (percussion), Lequient Jobe (bass) and Henry Garner (drums).	
12/11/76+	1 (1)	14	▲ 1. **Car Wash** #1 R&B hit (2 weeks)	MCA 40615
3/19/77	10	10	2. **I Wanna Get Next To You** above 2 from the movie *Car Wash* starring Richard Pryor and Franklin Ajaye	MCA 40662
10/22/77	39	2	3. Do Your Dance - Part 1	Whitfield 8440
1/13/79	32	4	4. Love Don't Live Here Anymore	Whitfield 8712

DATE	POS	WKS	ARTIST–RECORD TITLE	LABEL & NO.
			ROSIE And The Originals	
			Pop group from San Diego, California: Rosalie Hamlin (vocals), David Ponci and Noah Tafolla (guitars), Tony Gomez (sax) and Carl Von Goodat (drums).	
12/12/60+	5	12	1. **Angel Baby**	Highland 1011
			ROSS, Diana	
			Born Diane Ernestine Ross on 3/26/44 in Detroit, Michigan. R&B singer/actress. Lead singer of The Supremes from 1961-69. Starred in the movies *Lady Sings The Blues*, *Mahogany* and *The Wiz*. Own Broadway show *An Evening With Diana Ross* in 1976. Married to Norwegian shipping magnate Arne Naess from 1986-2000.	
5/2/70	20	8	1. Reach Out And Touch (Somebody's Hand)	Motown 1165
8/15/70	1 (3)	13	2. **Ain't No Mountain High Enough**	Motown 1169
			#1 R&B hit (1 week)	
1/9/71	16	8	3. Remember Me	Motown 1176
5/15/71	29	5	4. Reach Out I'll Be There	Motown 1184
9/11/71	38	3	5. Surrender	Motown 1188
3/3/73	34	4	6. Good Morning Heartache	Motown 1211
			first recorded by Billie Holiday in 1946; from the movie *Lady Sings The Blues* starring Ross	
7/7/73	1 (1)	16	7. **Touch Me In The Morning**	Motown 1239
			#1 Adult Contemporary hit (1 week)	
10/13/73	12	10	8. You're A Special Part Of Me	Motown 1280
			DIANA ROSS & MARVIN GAYE	
1/26/74	14	8	9. Last Time I Saw Him	Motown 1278
			#1 Adult Contemporary hit (3 weeks)	
3/30/74	19	10	10. My Mistake (Was To Love You)	Motown 1269
			DIANA ROSS & MARVIN GAYE	
11/22/75+	1 (1)	13	11. **Theme From Mahogany (Do You Know Where You're Going To)**	Motown 1377
			#1 Adult Contemporary hit (1 week); from the movie *Mahogany* starring Ross	
4/24/76	1 (2)	13	12. **Love Hangover**	Motown 1392
			#1 R&B hit (1 week)	
8/21/76	25	8	13. One Love In My Lifetime	Motown 1398
12/3/77+	27	7	14. Gettin' Ready For Love	Motown 1427
8/18/79	19	9	15. The Boss	Motown 1462
8/9/80	1 (4)	17	● 16. **Upside Down**	Motown 1494
			#1 R&B hit (4 weeks)	
10/4/80	5	14	17. **I'm Coming Out**	Motown 1491
11/15/80+	9	15	18. **It's My Turn**	Motown 1496
			title song from the movie starring Jill Clayburgh and Michael Douglas	
7/18/81	1 (9)	19	▲ 19. **Endless Love**	Motown 1519
			DIANA ROSS & LIONEL RICHIE	
			#1 R&B hit (7 weeks) / #1 Adult Contemporary hit (3 weeks); title song from the movie starring Brooke Shields	
10/24/81	7	14	20. **Why Do Fools Fall In Love**	RCA 12349
1/30/82	8	10	21. **Mirror, Mirror**	RCA 13021
10/16/82	10	10	22. **Muscles**	RCA 13348
			written and produced by Michael Jackson	
3/19/83	40	2	23. So Close	RCA 13424
7/23/83	31	3	24. Pieces Of Ice	RCA 13549

DATE	POS	WKS	ARTIST–RECORD TITLE	LABEL & NO.
8/4/84	19	8	25. All Of You **JULIO IGLESIAS & DIANA ROSS**	Columbia 04507
9/22/84	19	8	26. Swept Away Sales #17 / Airplay #18 written and produced by Daryl Hall	RCA 13864
3/9/85	10	9	27. **Missing You** Sales #5 / Airplay #13 #1 R&B hit (3 weeks); dedicated to Marvin Gaye; written and produced by Lionel Richie	RCA 13966
			ROSS, Jack	
			Born in Los Angeles, California. Died on 12/16/82 (age 66). Comedian.	
4/7/62	16	6	1. Cinderella **[C-L]**	Dot 16333
			ROSS, Jackie	
			Born on 1/30/46 in St. Louis, Missouri; raised in Chicago, Illinois. Female R&B singer.	
8/15/64	11	8	1. Selfish One	Chess 1903
			ROSS, Spencer	
			Born Robert Mersey in Manhattan, New York. Conductor/arranger.	
1/18/60	13	10	1. Tracy's Theme **[I]** Jimmy Abato (sax); from the 12/7/59 TV drama special *Philadelphia Story*	Columbia 41532
			ROTH, David Lee	
			Born on 10/10/55 in Bloomington, Indiana. Lead singer of Van Halen from 1973-1985.	
1/26/85	3	11	1. **California Girls** Airplay #3 / Sales #4 Carl Wilson (backing vocal)	Warner 29102
4/20/85	12	10	2. Just A Gigolo/I Ain't Got Nobody Airplay #11 / Sales #16 "Just A Gigolo" was a #1 hit for Ted Lewis in 1931/"I Ain't Got Nobody" was a #34 hit for Marion Harris in 1921; this medley arrangement first recorded by Louis Prima in 1956	Warner 29040
7/26/86	16	8	3. Yankee Rose Sales #15 / Airplay #22	Warner 28656
1/30/88	6	11	4. **Just Like Paradise** Sales #4 / Airplay #8 #1 Mainstream Rock hit (4 weeks)	Warner 28119
			ROUTERS, The	
			Rock and roll instrumental group formed in Los Angeles, California: Mike Gordon, Al Kait, Bill Moody and Lynn Frazier.	
11/24/62	19	7	1. Let's Go (pony) **[I]**	Warner 5283
			ROVER BOYS, The	
			White vocal group formed in Toronto, Ontario, Canada: Bill Albert, Doug Wells, Larry Amato and Al Osten.	
5/19/56	16	7	1. Graduation Day Jockey #16 / Best Seller #19 / Top 100 #20 **THE ROVER BOYS featuring Billy Albert** Don Costa (orch.)	ABC-Paramount 9700
			ROVERS, The — see IRISH ROVERS	

DATE	POS	WKS	ARTIST–RECORD TITLE	LABEL & NO.
			ROWLAND, Kelly	
			Born on 2/11/81 in Atlanta, Georgia. Female R&B singer. Member of Destiny's Child. Played "Kia" in the movie *Freddy Vs. Jason*.	
7/20/02	**1** (10)	27	1. **Dilemma** Airplay #1 (12) / Sales #17 **NELLY Featuring Kelly Rowland** #1 R&B hit (9 weeks); samples "Love, Need And Want You" by Patti LaBelle	Fo' Reel 019509
11/9/02	**27**	8	2. Stole Airplay #27	Columbia 79820
			ROXETTE	
			Pop-rock duo from Sweden: Marie Fredriksson (born on 5/30/58) and Per Gessle (born on 6/12/59).	
2/25/89	**1** (1)	13	● 1. **The Look** Airplay #1 (2) / Sales #2	EMI 50190
6/24/89	**14**	9	2. Dressed For Success Sales #12 / Airplay #18	EMI 50204
9/9/89	**1** (1)	14	3. **Listen To Your Heart** Airplay #1 (1) / Sales #3	EMI 50223
1/6/90	**2** (2)	14	4. **Dangerous** Sales #2 / Airplay #3	EMI 50233
4/21/90	**1** (2)	17	● 5. **It Must Have Been Love** Airplay #1 (3) / Sales #2 from the movie *Pretty Woman* starring Richard Gere and Julia Roberts	EMI 50283
3/16/91	**1** (1)	14	6. **Joyride** Sales #1 (1) / Airplay #2	EMI 50342
6/29/91	**2** (1)	13	7. **Fading Like A Flower (Every Time You Leave)** Airplay #11 / Sales #23	EMI 50355
11/23/91+	**32**	8	8. Spending My Time Airplay #32 / Sales #49	EMI 50366
3/28/92	**36**	4	9. Church Of Your Heart Airplay #34	EMI 50380
			ROXY MUSIC	
			Art-rock group from England: Bryan Ferry (vocals, keyboards), Phil Manzanera (guitar), Andy MacKay (horns) and Paul Thompson (drums).	
2/21/76	**30**	5	1. Love Is The Drug	Atco 7042
			ROYAL, Billy Joe	
			Born on 4/3/42 in Valdosta, Georgia; raised in Marietta, Georgia. Country-rock singer/guitarist.	
7/31/65	**9**	8	1. **Down In The Boondocks**	Columbia 43305
10/9/65	**14**	8	2. I Knew You When	Columbia 43390
1/15/66	**38**	1	3. I've Got To Be Somebody above 3 written and produced by Joe South	Columbia 43465
11/1/69	**15**	10	4. Cherry Hill Park	Columbia 44902
			ROYAL GUARDSMEN, The	
			Novelty-pop group from Ocala, Florida: Barry Winslow (vocals, guitar), Chris Nunley (vocals), Tom Richards (guitar), Bill Balough (bass) and Billy Taylor (organ). "Snoopy" songs inspired by Snoopy the Beagle in the "Peanuts" comic strip.	
12/17/66	**2** (4)	11	● 1. **Snoopy Vs. The Red Baron** **[N]**	Laurie 3366
3/11/67	**15**	5	2. The Return Of The Red Baron **[N]**	Laurie 3379
1/4/69	**35**	5	3. Baby Let's Wait	Laurie 3461

DATE	POS	WKS	ARTIST–RECORD TITLE	LABEL & NO.
11/28/81+	**10**	12	**ROYAL PHILHARMONIC ORCHESTRA** Orchestra based in London, England. Conducted by Louis Clark. Founded in 1946 by Sir Thomas Beecham. 1. **Hooked On Classics** [I] **LOUIS CLARK CONDUCTING THE ROYAL PHILHARMONIC ORCHESTRA** Tchaikovsky Piano Concerto No. 1/Flight of the Bumble Bee/Mozart Symphony No. 40 in G Minor/Rhapsody In Blue/Karelia Suite/The Marriage of Figaro/Romeo & Juliet/Trumpet Voluntary/Hallelujah Chorus/Grieg Piano Concerto in A Minor/March of the Toreadors/1812 Overture	RCA 12304
5/27/72	**11**	8	**ROYAL SCOTS DRAGOON GUARDS** The military band of Scotland's armored regiment. Led by bagpipe soloist Major Tony Crease. 1. Amazing Grace [I] **THE PIPES AND DRUMS AND THE MILITARY BAND OF THE ROYAL SCOTS DRAGOON GUARDS** Rev. John Newton wrote the words in 1779; William Walker composed the melody in 1844	RCA Victor 0709
2/3/58 11/16/59	**3** **26**	12 6	**ROYAL TEENS** Rock and roll group from Fort Lee, New Jersey: Bob Gaudio, Bill Crandall, Billy Dalton and Tom Austin. Gaudio later joined The 4 Seasons. 1. **Short Shorts** Top 100 #3 / Best Seller #4 / Jockey #6 2. Believe Me	ABC-Paramount 9882 Capitol 4261
11/10/58	**17**	10	**ROYALTONES, The** Rock and roll instrumental band from Dearborn, Michigan: David Sanderson (guitar), George Katsakis (sax), brothers Mike (piano) and Greg (drums) Popoff and Kenny Anderson (bass). Sanderson died of a heart attack on 6/25/94 (age 59). 1. Poor Boy [I]	Jubilee 5338
7/25/92	**37**	4	**ROZALLA** Born Rozalla Miller on 3/18/64 in Ndola, Zambia. Female dance singer. 1. Everybody's Free (To Feel Good) Airplay #26 / Sales #50	Epic 74388
			R*S*F — see RIGHT SAID FRED	
2/15/92	**26**	8	**RTZ** Rock group formed in Boston, Massachusetts: Brad Delp (vocals), Barry Goudreau (guitar), Brian Maes (keyboards), Tim Archibald (bass) and David Stefanelli (drums). Delp and Goudreau were members of Boston. RTZ: Return To Zero. 1. Until Your Love Comes Back Around Airplay #30 / Sales #71	Giant 19051
8/31/74	**37**	2	**RUBETTES, The** Pop-rock group from London, England: Alan Wilkins (vocals), Tony Thorpe (guitar), Peter Arnisson and Bill Herd (keyboards), Mickey Clarke (bass), and John Richardson (drums). 1. Sugar Baby Love	Polydor 15089

DATE	POS	WKS	ARTIST–RECORD TITLE	LABEL & NO.
			RUBICON	
			Pop-rock group from San Francisco, California: Greg Eckler (vocals, drums), Brad Gillis (guitar), Jerry Martini, Max Haskett and Dennis Marcellino (horns), Jim Pugh (keyboards), and Jack Blades (bass). Martini was a member of Sly & The Family Stone. Gillis and Blades later formed Night Ranger.	
4/8/78	28	3	1. I'm Gonna Take Care Of Everything	20th Century 2362
			RUBY AND THE ROMANTICS	
			R&B vocal group from Akron, Ohio: Ruby Nash Curtis (born on 11/12/39), Leroy Fann, Ed Roberts, George Lee and Ronald Mosley. Fann died in November 1973 (age 37). Roberts died of cancer on 8/10/93 (age 57).	
2/23/63	**1** (1)	10	1. **Our Day Will Come** #1 R&B hit (2 weeks)	Kapp 501
6/15/63	16	6	2. My Summer Love	Kapp 525
8/31/63	27	5	3. Hey There Lonely Boy	Kapp 544
			RUDE BOYS	
			R&B vocal group from Cleveland, Ohio: brothers Ed Banks and J. Little, with Larry Marcus and Melvin Sephus.	
3/30/91	16	12	1. **Written All Over Your Face** Sales #11 / Airplay #22 #1 R&B hit (1 week)	Atlantic 87805
			RUFF ENDZ	
			R&B vocal duo from Baltimore, Maryland: David Chance and Dante Jordan.	
7/8/00	5	25	1. **No More** Sales #3 / Airplay #12 #1 R&B hit (1 week)	Epic 79400
			RUFFIN, David	
			Born on 1/18/41 in Meridian, Mississippi. Died of a drug overdose on 6/1/91 (age 50). R&B singer. Brother of Jimmy Ruffin. Co-lead singer of The Temptations from 1963-68.	
2/22/69	9	9	1. **My Whole World Ended (The Moment You Left Me)**	Motown 1140
11/29/75+	9	11	2. **Walk Away From Love** #1 R&B hit (1 week)	Motown 1376
9/15/85	20	7	3. A Nite At The Apollo Live! The Way You Do The Things You Do/My Girl Sales #21 / Airplay #23 **[L]** **DARYL HALL JOHN OATES with David Ruffin & Eddie Kendrick** recorded at the reopening of New York's Apollo Theatre	RCA 14178
			RUFFIN, Jimmy	
			Born on 5/7/39 in Collinsville, Mississippi. R&B singer. Brother of David Ruffin.	
9/10/66	7	14	1. **What Becomes Of The Brokenhearted**	Soul 35022
12/24/66+	17	8	2. I've Passed This Way Before	Soul 35027
4/8/67	29	3	3. Gonna Give Her All The Love I've Got	Soul 35032
3/22/80	10	9	4. **Hold On To My Love** co-written and produced by Robin Gibb	RSO 1021
			RUFUS — see KHAN, Chaka	

DATE	POS	WKS	ARTIST–RECORD TITLE	LABEL & NO.
			RUGBYS, The	
			Rock group from Nashville, Tennessee: Steve McNicol (vocals, guitar), Ed Vernon (keyboards), Mike Mornei (bass) and Glenn Howerton (drums).	
9/27/69	24	6	1. You, I	Amazon 1
			RUNDGREN, Todd	
			Born on 6/22/48 in Upper Darby, Pennsylvania. Pop-rock singer/songwriter/multi-instrumentalist. Leader of Utopia.	
12/26/70+	20	9	1. We Gotta Get You A Woman **RUNT**	Ampex 31001
5/6/72	16	9	2. I Saw The Light	Bearsville 0003
11/10/73	5	12	3. **Hello It's Me**	Bearsville 0009
6/26/76	34	3	4. Good Vibrations	Bearsville 0309
7/8/78	29	5	5. Can We Still Be Friends	Bearsville 0324
			RUN-D.M.C.	
			Highly influential rap trio from Queens, New York: rappers Joseph Simmons (Run) and Darryl McDaniels (DMC) with DJ Jason Mizell (Jam Master Jay). Group appeared in the movies *Krush Groove* and *Tougher Than Leather*. Jam Master Jay was shot to death on 10/30/2002 (age 37).	
8/16/86	4	10	● 1. **Walk This Way** Sales #2 / Airplay #7 with Aerosmith's Steve Tyler (vocals) and Joe Perry (guitar)	Profile 5112
11/29/86	29	7	2. You Be Illin' Sales #26 / Airplay #36	Profile 5119
4/3/93	21	10	● 3. Down With The King Sales #7 / Airplay #46 samples "Where Do I Go" by the cast of *Hair*	Profile 5391
			RUNT — see RUNDGREN, Todd	
			RUSH	
			Hard-rock trio formed in Toronto, Ontario, Canada: Geddy Lee (vocals, bass), Alex Lifeson (guitar) and Neil Peart (drums).	
10/9/82	21	6	1. New World Man #1 Mainstream Rock hit (2 weeks)	Mercury 76179
			RUSH, Jennifer	
			Born Heidi Stern on 9/29/60 in Queens, New York. Pop singer/songwriter.	
7/4/87	36	3	1. Flames Of Paradise Sales #32 / Airplay #34 **JENNIFER RUSH (with Elton John)**	Epic 07119
			RUSH, Merrillee, & The Turnabouts	
			Born in Seattle, Washington. Female pop singer. The Turnabouts: Carl Wilson (guitar), Neil Rush (sax), Terry Craig (bass) and Pete Sack (drums).	
6/1/68	7	12	1. **Angel Of The Morning**	Bell 705
			RUSHEN, Patrice	
			Born on 9/30/54 in Los Angeles, California. R&B singer/songwriter/pianist.	
6/5/82	23	7	1. Forget Me Nots	Elektra 47427

DATE	POS	WKS	ARTIST—RECORD TITLE	LABEL & NO.
			RUSSELL, Bobby	
			Born on 4/19/41 in Nashville, Tennessee. Died of a heart attack on 11/19/92 (age 51). Singer/songwriter. Married to Vicki Lawrence from 1972-74.	
11/23/68	36	2	1. 1432 Franklin Pike Circle Hero	Elf 90,020
8/28/71	28	7	2. Saturday Morning Confusion [N]	United Artists 50788
			RUSSELL, Brenda	
			Born Brenda Gordon in Brooklyn, New York. R&B singer/songwriter/pianist.	
10/13/79	30	6	1. So Good, So Right	Horizon 123
4/2/88	6	13	2. **Piano In The Dark** Sales #6 / Airplay #11	A&M 3003
			Joe Esposito (of Brooklyn Dreams, backing vocal)	
			RUSSELL, Leon	
			Born Claude Russell Bridges on 4/2/42 in Lawton, Oklahoma. Rock singer/songwriter/multi-instrumentalist. Prolific session musician.	
9/23/72	11	7	1. Tight Rope	Shelter 7325
9/13/75	14	10	2. Lady Blue	Shelter 40378
			RYAN, Charlie, and the Timberline Riders	
			Born on 12/19/15 in Graceville, Minnesota; raised in Montana. Country singer/songwriter.	
8/8/60	33	4	1. Hot Rod Lincoln [N-S]	4 Star 1733
			#29 hit for Tiny Hill in 1951 (as "Hot Rod Race")	
			RYDELL, Bobby	
			Born Robert Ridarelli on 4/26/42 in Philadelphia, Pennsylvania. Teen pop idol. Appeared in the movies *Bye Bye Birdie* and *That Lady From Peking*.	
8/10/59	11	9	1. Kissin' Time	Cameo 167
			Georgie Young And The Rockin' Bocs (backing group)	
10/26/59	6	14	2. **We Got Love**	Cameo 169
2/8/60	2 (1)	13	● 3. **Wild One /**	
2/22/60	19	10	4. Little Bitty Girl	Cameo 171
5/16/60	5	8	5. **Swingin' School /**	
			from the movie *Because They're Young* starring James Darren and Tuesday Weld	
5/16/60	18	8	6. Ding-A-Ling	Cameo 175
8/1/60	4	11	7. **Volare**	Cameo 179
11/14/60	14	10	8. Sway	Cameo 182
			#15 hit for Dean Martin in 1954	
2/6/61	11	8	9. Good Time Baby	Cameo 186
5/8/61	21	5	10. That Old Black Magic	Cameo 190
			#1 hit for Glenn Miller in 1943 (from the movie *Star-Spangled Rhythm* starring Bing Crosby)	
7/10/61	25	5	11. The Fish	Cameo 192
11/6/61	21	6	12. I Wanna Thank You	Cameo 201
12/25/61	21	3	13. Jingle Bell Rock [X]	Cameo 205
			BOBBY RYDELL CHUBBY CHECKER	
3/10/62	18	7	14. (I've Got) Bonnie	Cameo 209
6/23/62	14	7	15. I'll Never Dance Again	Cameo 217
10/27/62	10	8	16. **The Cha-Cha-Cha**	Cameo 228

DATE	POS	WKS	ARTIST–RECORD TITLE	LABEL & NO.
2/23/63	23	6	17. Butterfly Baby	Cameo 242
6/1/63	17	5	18. Wildwood Days	Cameo 252
12/7/63+	4	12	19. **Forget Him**	Cameo 280

RYDER, Mitch, And The Detroit Wheels

Born William Levise on 2/26/45 in Detroit, Michigan. White rock and roll/R&B singer. The Detroit Wheels: Jim McCarty and Joe Cubert (guitars), Earl Elliott (bass) and John Badanjek (drums). McCarty and Badanjek later joined the Rockets.

DATE	POS	WKS	ARTIST–RECORD TITLE	LABEL & NO.
1/8/66	10	8	1. **Jenny Take A Ride!** medley: Little Richard's "Jenny, Jenny" and Chuck Willis's "C.C. Rider"	New Voice 806
3/26/66	17	6	2. Little Latin Lupe Lu	New Voice 808
10/22/66	4	14	3. **Devil With A Blue Dress On &** **Good Golly Miss Molly**	New Voice 817
2/18/67	6	9	4. **Sock It To Me-Baby!**	New Voice 820
5/13/67	24	4	5. Too Many Fish In The Sea & Three Little Fishes "Three Little Fishes" was a #1 hit for Kay Kyser in 1939	New Voice 822
9/30/67	30	4	6. What Now My Love **MITCH RYDER**	DynoVoice 901

RYTHM SYNDICATE — see RHYTHM SYNDICATE

S

SAADIQ, Raphael

Born Raphael Wiggins on 5/14/66 in Oakland, California. R&B singer. Member of Tony! Toni! Tone!

DATE	POS	WKS	ARTIST–RECORD TITLE	LABEL & NO.

4/8/95	19	12	1. Ask Of You Sales #10 / Airplay #30
			    RAPHAEL SAADIQ (of Tony! Toni! Toné!)
			    contains the melody of "Sukiyaki"; from the movie *Higher Learning* starring Laurence Fishburne
				550 Music/Epic 77862

SACARIO — see MARTINEZ, Angie

SADE

Born Helen Folasade Adu on 1/16/59 in Ibadan, Nigeria, Africa (of Nigerian/English parents); raised in London, England. Jazz-styled R&B singer/fashion designer/model. Appeared in the 1986 movie *Absolute Beginners*. Won the 1985 Best New Artist Grammy Award.

DATE	POS	WKS	ARTIST–RECORD TITLE	LABEL & NO.
3/30/85	5	13	1. **Smooth Operator** Airplay #4 / Sales #6 #1 Adult Contemporary hit (2 weeks)	Portrait 04807
12/28/85+	5	13	2. **The Sweetest Taboo** Sales #6 / Airplay #6 #1 Adult Contemporary hit (1 week)	Portrait 05713
4/19/86	20	7	3. Never As Good As The First Time Sales #20 / Airplay #20	Portrait 05846
6/11/88	16	8	4. Paradise Sales #15 / Airplay #21 #1 R&B hit (1 week)	Epic 07904
1/23/93	28	4	5. No Ordinary Love Sales #32 / Airplay #33 from the movie *Indecent Proposal* starring Robert Redford and Demi Moore	Epic 74734

DATE	POS	WKS	ARTIST–RECORD TITLE	LABEL & NO.
			SADLER, SSgt Barry (U.S. Army Special Forces)	
			Born on 11/1/40 in Carlsbad, New Mexico. Died of heart failure on 11/5/89 (age 49). Staff Sergeant of U.S. Army Special Forces (Green Berets). Served in Vietnam.	
2/19/66	**1** (5)	11	● 1. **The Ballad Of The Green Berets** #1 Adult Contemporary hit (5 weeks)	RCA Victor 8739
5/14/66	**28**	4	2. The "A" Team Sid Bass (orch., above 2)	RCA Victor 8804
			SAFARIS	
			White vocal group from Los Angeles, California: Jim Stephens, Richard Clasky, Sheldon Briar and Marvin Rosenberg. Briar died on 12/24/99 (age 57).	
7/11/60	**6**	11	1. **Image Of A Girl** with The Phantom's Band	Eldo 101
			SA-FIRE	
			Born Wilma Cosme in the Bronx, New York. Latin American dance singer.	
3/18/89	**12**	12	1. Thinking Of You Airplay #9 / Sales #14	Cutting 872502
			SAGA	
			Rock group formed in Toronto, Ontario, Canada: Michael Sadler (vocals), brothers Ian (guitar) and Jim (bass) Crichton, Jim Gilmour (keyboards), and Steve Negus (drums).	
1/29/83	**26**	8	1. On The Loose	Portrait 03359
			SAGER, Carole Bayer	
			Born on 3/8/46 in Manhattan, New York. Pop singer/prolific songwriter. Married to Burt Bacharach from 1982-91.	
6/13/81	**30**	7	1. Stronger Than Before	Boardwalk 02054
			SAIGON KICK	
			Hard-rock group formed in Miami, Florida: Matt Kramer (vocals), Jason Bieler (guitar), Tom DeFile (bass) and Phil Varone (drums).	
10/17/92	**12**	15	● 1. Love Is On The Way Sales #12 / Airplay #20	Third Stone 98530
			SAILCAT	
			Pop duo from Alabama: Court Pickett (vocals) and John Wyker (vocals, guitar).	
7/15/72	**12**	10	1. Motorcycle Mama	Elektra 45782
			SAINTE-MARIE, Buffy	
			Born on 2/20/41 in Saskatchewan, Canada. Folk singer/songwriter.	
4/29/72	**38**	2	1. Mister Can't You See	Vanguard 35151
			ST. PETERS, Crispian	
			Born Peter Smith on 4/5/44 in Swanley, Kent, England. Pop singer/guitarist.	
7/9/66	**4**	8	1. **The Pied Piper**	Jamie 1320
7/22/67	**36**	2	2. You Were On My Mind	Jamie 1310

DATE	POS	WKS	ARTIST–RECORD TITLE	LABEL & NO.
			SAKAMOTO, Kyu	
			Born on 11/10/41 in Kawasaki, Japan. Died in a plane crash on 8/12/85 (age 43). Male singer.	
5/25/63	**1** (3)	12	● 1. **Sukiyaki** [F] #1 Adult Contemporary hit (5 weeks)	Capitol 4945
			SALSOUL ORCHESTRA, The	
			Disco orchestra conducted by producer/arranger Vincent Montana. Vocalists included Phyllis Rhodes, Ronni Tyson, Carl Helm, Philip Hurt and Jocelyn Brown.	
2/14/76	**18**	9	1. Tangerine [I] #1 hit for Jimmy Dorsey in 1942	Salsoul 2004
10/30/76	**30**	5	2. Nice 'N' Naasty	Salsoul 2011
			SALT-N-PEPA	
			Female hip-hop trio from Queens, New York: Cheryl "Salt" James, Sandra "Pepa" Denton and Dee Dee "Spinderella" Roper. Appeared in the movie *Who's The Man?*. Pepa was married to Treach (of Naughty By Nature) from 1999-2001.	
12/26/87+	**19**	13	▲ 1. Push It Sales #18 / Airplay #21	Next Plateau 315
4/21/90	**26**	8	▲ 2. Expression Sales #17	Next Plateau 329
5/11/91	**21**	14	● 3. Do You Want Me Sales #8 / Airplay #10 Herby "Hurby Luv Bug" Azor (male vocal)	Next Plateau 331
10/12/91	**13**	13	● 4. Let's Talk About Sex Sales #9 / Airplay #17	Next Plateau 333
10/23/93	**4**	23	● 5. **Shoop** Sales #2 / Airplay #2 samples "I'm Blue" by The Sweet Inspirations and "Super Sporm" by Captain Sky	Next Plateau 857314
1/29/94	**3**	24	▲ 6. **Whatta Man** Sales #2 / Airplay #4 **SALT 'N' PEPA with En Vogue** samples "What A Man" by Linda Lyndell	Next Plateau 857390
10/15/94	**32**	5	7. None Of Your Business Sales #19 / Airplay #74	Next Plateau 857776
10/28/95	**38**	3	8. Ain't Nuthin' But A She Thing Sales #17 samples "What Becomes Of The Brokenhearted" by Jimmy Ruffin	London 850346
			SALVO, Sammy	
			Born on 1/20/39 in Birmingham, Alabama. Pop singer.	
3/3/58	**23**	1	1. Oh Julie Jockey #23 / Top 100 #78	RCA Victor 7097
			SAM & DAVE	
			R&B vocal duo: Sam Moore (born on 10/12/35 in Miami, Florida) and Dave Prater (born on 5/9/37 in Ocilla, Georgia). Prater was killed in a car crash on 4/9/88 (age 50). Duo inducted into the Rock and Roll Hall of Fame in 1992.	
6/4/66	**21**	7	● 1. Hold On! I'm A Comin' #1 R&B hit (1 week)	Stax 189
9/30/67	**2** (3)	11	● 2. **Soul Man** #1 R&B hit (7 weeks)	Stax 231
2/17/68	**9**	9	3. **I Thank You**	Stax 242
			SAMI JO	
			Born Sami Jo Cole in Batesville, Arkansas. Female country singer.	
3/23/74	**21**	7	1. Tell Me A Lie	MGM South 7029

DATE	POS	WKS	ARTIST–RECORD TITLE	LABEL & NO.
			SAMMIE	
			Born Sammie Bush on 3/1/87 in Boynton Beach, Florida. Pre-teen male R&B singer.	
2/26/00	24	9	● 1. I Like It Sales #4	Freeworld 58776
			SAM THE SHAM AND THE PHARAOHS	
			Born Domingo Samudio on 3/6/39 in Dallas, Texas. Leader of rock and roll group The Pharaohs: Ray Stinnet (guitar), Butch Gibson (sax), David Martin (bass) and Jerry Patterson (drums). Martin died of a heart attack on 8/2/87 (age 50).	
5/1/65	2 (2)	14	● 1. **Wooly Bully**	MGM 13322
8/21/65	26	4	2. Ju Ju Hand	MGM 13364
11/13/65	33	3	3. Ring Dang Doo	MGM 13397
7/2/66	2 (2)	11	● 4. **Lil' Red Riding Hood**	MGM 13506
10/15/66	22	5	5. The Hair On My Chinny Chin Chin	MGM 13581
1/21/67	27	4	6. How Do You Catch A Girl	MGM 13649
			SANDERS, Felicia	
			Born in Manhattan, New York; raised in California. Died on 2/7/75. Adult Contemporary singer.	
5/28/55	29	3	1. Blue Star (The "Medic" Theme) Best Seller #29 Norman Leyden (orch.); theme from the TV series starring Richard Boone	Columbia 40508
			SANDLER, Adam	
			Born on 9/9/66 in Brooklyn, New York. Actor/comedian. Cast member of TV's "Saturday Night Live" (1990-95). Starred in several movies.	
12/30/95	10 A	2	1. **The Chanukah Song** [X-C-L]	album cut
1/3/98 -	25 A	2	2. The Chanukah Song [X-C-L-R] above 2 are the same version from the album *What The Hell Happened To Me?* on Warner 46151	album cut
			SANDPEBBLES, The	
			R&B vocal trio: Calvin White, Andrea Bolden and Lonzine Wright.	
1/6/68	22	6	1. Love Power	Calla 141
			SANDPIPERS, The	
			Adult Contemporary vocal trio from Los Angeles, California: Jim Brady, Michael Piano and Richard Shoff.	
8/13/66	9	9	1. **Guantanamera** [F]	A&M 806
11/12/66	30	4	2. Louie, Louie [F]	A&M 819
5/2/70	17	8	3. Come Saturday Morning from the movie *The Sterile Cuckoo* starring Liza Minnelli	A&M 1185
			SANDS, Jodie	
			Born in Philadelphia, Pennsylvania. Teen pop singer.	
6/10/57	15	9	1. With All My Heart Jockey #15 / Top 100 #20 / Best Seller #21 Peter DeAngelis (orch.)	Chancellor 1003

DATE	POS	WKS	ARTIST—RECORD TITLE	LABEL & NO.
			SANDS, Tommy	
			Born on 8/27/37 in Chicago, Illinois. Teen idol/pop-rock and roll singer/actor. Mother was a vocalist with Art Kassel's band. Married to Nancy Sinatra from 1960-65. In the movies *Sing Boy Sing, Mardi Gras, Babes In Toyland* and *The Longest Day*.	
2/23/57	2 (2)	12	● 1. **Teen-Age Crush**	Capitol 3639
			Best Seller #2 / Top 100 #3 / Jockey #4 / Juke Box #7 introduced by Sands on the 1/30/57 Kraft TV production of *The Singin' Idol*	
5/27/57	16	8	2. Goin' Steady / Jockey #16 / Best Seller #18 / Top 100 #19	
			#2 Country hit for Faron Young in 1953	
6/24/57		2	3. Ring My Phone Best Seller: flip	Capitol 3723
			from the Kraft NBC-TV show *Flesh And Blood*	
2/24/58	24	2	4. Sing Boy Sing Jockey #24 / Best Seller #46 / Top 100 #46	Capitol 3867
			title song from the movie starring Sands; Bob Bain (orch., all of above)	
			SANFORD/TOWNSEND BAND, The	
			Pop-rock duo from Los Angeles, California: Ed Sanford and John Townsend.	
7/16/77	9	12	1. **Smoke From A Distant Fire**	Warner 8370
			SANG, Samantha	
			Born Cheryl Gray on 8/5/53 in Melbourne, Australia. Pop singer.	
1/7/78	3	17	▲ 1. **Emotion**	Private Stock 45,178
			Barry Gibb (backing vocal); written by Barry and Robin Gibb	
			SAN REMO GOLDEN STRINGS	
			R&B instrumental studio band formed in Detroit, Michigan.	
10/9/65	27	5	1. Hungry For Love [I]	Ric-Tic 104
			SANTA ESMERALDA	
			Spanish-flavored disco studio project produced by Nicolas Skorsky and Jean-Manuel de Scarano. Featured vocalist Leroy Gomez.	
12/10/77+	15	12	1. Don't Let Me Be Misunderstood	Casablanca 902
			SANTA ESMERALDA Starring Leroy Gomez	
			SANTAMARIA, Mongo	
			Born Ramon Santamaria on 4/7/22 in Havana, Cuba. Died of a stroke on 2/1/2003 (age 80). Conga player.	
4/13/63	10	6	1. **Watermelon Man** [I]	Battle 45909
			written by Herbie Hancock	
3/8/69	32	2	2. Cloud Nine [I]	Columbia 44740
			SANTANA	
			Born Carlos Santana on 7/20/47 in Autlan de Navarro, Mexico. Latin-rock guitarist. Formed his group in San Francisco, California. Various members over the years include Alex Ligertwood (vocals), Gregg Rolie (keyboards, vocals), Neal Schon (guitar), David Brown (bass) and Michael Shrieve (drums). Rolie and Schon later joined Journey. Inducted into the Rock and Roll Hall of Fame in 1998.	
2/7/70	9	11	1. **Evil Ways**	Columbia 45069
11/21/70+	4	12	2. **Black Magic Woman**	Columbia 45270
			first recorded by Fleetwood Mac in 1968	

DATE	POS	WKS	ARTIST–RECORD TITLE	LABEL & NO.
3/6/71	**13**	8	3. Oye Como Va **[F]**	Columbia 45330
10/30/71	**12**	8	4. Everybody's Everything	Columbia 45472
3/11/72	**36**	4	5. No One To Depend On	Columbia 45552
11/19/77	**27**	5	6. She's Not There	Columbia 10616
2/17/79	**32**	3	7. Stormy	Columbia 10873
1/19/80	**35**	3	8. You Know That I Love You	Columbia 11144
5/16/81	**17**	11	9. Winning	Columbia 01050
8/28/82	**15**	10	10. Hold On	Columbia 03160
8/21/99	**1** (12)	50	▲ 11. **Smooth** Airplay #1 (5) / Sales #1 (2) **SANTANA Feat. Rob Thomas** 1999 Grammy winner: Record of the Year	Arista 13718
2/12/00	**1** (10)	24	▲ 12. **Maria Maria** Sales #1 (5) / Airplay #1 (1) **SANTANA Featuring The Product G&B** #1 R&B hit (3 weeks); "45" issued for above 2 on Arista 13773	Arista 13773
10/12/02	**5**	33	13. **The Game Of Love** Airplay #5 / Sales #19 **SANTANA featuring Michelle Branch** #1 Adult Contemporary hit (4 weeks)	Arista 15203
8/30/03	**8**	29	14. **Why Don't You & I** Airplay #8 **SANTANA Featuring Alex Band or Chad Kroeger** the Chad Kroeger (of Nickelback) version is from Santana's album *Shaman* on Arista 14737; the Alex Band (of The Calling) version is available as a promo single only (Arista 53233)	album cut
			SANTIAGO, Lina	
			Born on 9/5/78 in Los Angeles, California. Female dance singer.	
3/30/96	**35**	3	1. Feels So Good (Show Me Your Love) Airplay #28 / Sales #38	Universal 56004
			SANTO & JOHNNY	
			Guitar duo from Brooklyn, New York: brothers Santo (born on 10/24/37) and Johnny (born on 4/30/41) Farina.	
8/17/59	**1** (2)	13	● 1. **Sleep Walk** **[I]**	Canadian American 103
12/14/59	**23**	7	2. Tear Drop **[I]**	Canadian American 107
			SANTOS, Larry	
			Born on 6/2/41 in Oneonta, New York. Pop singer/songwriter.	
4/3/76	**36**	2	1. We Can't Hide It Anymore	Casablanca 844
			SAPPHIRES, The	
			R&B vocal trio from Philadelphia, Pennsylvania: Carol Jackson, George Garner and Joe Livingston.	
2/22/64	**25**	5	1. Who Do You Love	Swan 4162
			SAVAGE, Chantay	
			Born on 7/16/67 in Chicago, Illinois. Female dance singer/songwriter.	
3/16/96	**24**	9	● 1. I Will Survive Sales #14	RCA 64492
			SAVAGE GARDEN	
			Adult Alternative-pop duo from Brisbane, Queensland, Australia: Darren Hayes (born on 5/8/72) and Daniel Jones (born on 7/22/73).	
3/1/97	**4**	26	● 1. **I Want You** Airplay #3 / Sales #8	Columbia 78503

DATE	POS	WKS	ARTIST–RECORD TITLE	LABEL & NO.
8/30/97	37	1	2. To The Moon And Back Sales #40 / Airplay #48	Columbia 78576
12/6/97+	1 (2)	52	3. **Truly Madly Deeply** Airplay #1 (5) / Sales #5 #1 Adult Contemporary hit (11 weeks)	Columbia 78723
7/25/98	24	10	4. To The Moon And Back Airplay #26 **[R]**	Columbia 78576
3/20/99	19	6	5. The Animal Song Sales #15 / Airplay #48 from the movie *The Other Sister* starring Juliette Lewis	Hollywood 79112
11/13/99+	1 (4)	28	● 6. **I Knew I Loved You** Airplay #1 (6) / Sales #1 (2) #1 Adult Contemporary hit (17 weeks)	Columbia 79236
4/29/00	24	9	7. Crash And Burn Airplay #26 from the album *Affirmation* on Columbia 63711	album cut

SAYER, Leo

Born Gerard Sayer on 5/21/48 in Shoreham, Sussex, England. Pop singer/songwriter.

DATE	POS	WKS	ARTIST–RECORD TITLE	LABEL & NO.
3/22/75	9	9	1. **Long Tall Glasses (I Can Dance)**	Warner 8043
11/6/76+	1 (1)	17	● 2. **You Make Me Feel Like Dancing**	Warner 8283
3/26/77	1 (1)	14	● 3. **When I Need You** #1 Adult Contemporary hit (1 week)	Warner 8332
7/23/77	17	10	4. How Much Love	Warner 8319
11/5/77	38	2	5. Thunder In My Heart	Warner 8465
1/28/78	36	2	6. Easy To Love	Warner 8502
10/18/80	2 (5)	15	● 7. **More Than I Can Say** #1 Adult Contemporary hit (3 weeks)	Warner 49565
2/14/81	23	6	8. Living In A Fantasy	Warner 49657

SCAGGS, Boz

Born William Scaggs on 6/8/44 in Canton, Ohio; raised in Dallas, Texas. Eclectic singer/songwriter. Later became based in San Francisco, California.

DATE	POS	WKS	ARTIST–RECORD TITLE	LABEL & NO.
5/22/76	38	3	1. It's Over	Columbia 10319
8/7/76	3	15	● 2. **Lowdown**	Columbia 10367
3/19/77	11	12	3. Lido Shuffle	Columbia 10491
4/19/80	15	9	4. Breakdown Dead Ahead	Columbia 11241
7/12/80	17	9	5. JoJo Ray Parker Jr. (guitar, above 2)	Columbia 11281
9/6/80	14	10	6. Look What You've Done To Me Glenn Frey, Don Henley and Timothy B. Schmit (backing vocals); from the movie *Urban Cowboy* starring John Travolta	Columbia 11349
12/27/80+	14	9	7. Miss Sun Lisa Dal Bello (backing vocal)	Columbia 11406
6/11/88	35	4	8. Heart Of Mine Airplay #33 / Sales #34	Columbia 07780

SCANDAL/PATTY SMYTH

Rock group formed in New York: Patty Smyth (vocals; born on 6/26/57), Zack Smith and Keith Mack (guitars), Ivan Elias (bass) and Thommy Price (drums). Smyth married pro tennis player John McEnroe in 1997.

DATE	POS	WKS	ARTIST–RECORD TITLE	LABEL & NO.
7/21/84	7	15	1. **The Warrior** Sales #19 / Airplay #26 **SCANDAL FEATURING PATTY SMYTH** #1 Mainstream Rock hit (2 weeks)	Columbia 04424
8/29/92	2 (6)	20	● 2. **Sometimes Love Just Ain't Enough** Sales #3 / Airplay #3 **PATTY SMYTH with Don Henley** #1 Adult Contemporary hit (4 weeks)	MCA 54403
2/13/93	33	4	3. No Mistakes Airplay #33 **PATTY SMYTH**	MCA 54554

DATE	POS	WKS	ARTIST–RECORD TITLE	LABEL & NO.
6/13/81	2 (2)	18	**SCARBURY, Joey** Born on 6/7/55 in Ontario, California. Adult Contemporary singer. ● 1. **Theme From "Greatest American Hero"** **(Believe It or Not)** from the *Greatest American Hero* TV series starring William Katt	Elektra 47147
12/31/94+ 6/21/97	37 12	3 9	**SCARFACE** Born Brad Jordan on 11/9/69 in Houston, Texas. Male rapper. Member of The Geto Boys. 1. I Never Seen A Man Cry (aka I Seen A Man Die) Sales #19 ● 2. Smile Sales #4 / Airplay #62 **SCARFACE Featuring 2 Pac & Johnny P**	Rap-A-Lot 38461 Rap-A-Lot 38581
3/12/88	20	8	**SCARLETT & BLACK** Electro-pop duo from England: Robin Hild and Sue West. 1. You Don't Know Sales #19 / Airplay #21	Virgin 99405
11/12/83	14	10	**SCHILLING, Peter** Born on 1/28/56 in Stuttgart, Germany. Pop singer/songwriter. 1. Major Tom (Coming Home) inspired by David Bowie's 1973 hit "Space Oddity"	Elektra 69811
10/24/87	25	5	**SCHMIT, Timothy B.** Born on 10/30/47 in Sacramento, California. Singer/songwriter/bassist. Member of Poco and the Eagles. 1. Boys Night Out Sales #21 / Airplay #30	MCA 53137
6/27/81	14	11	**SCHNEIDER, John** Born on 4/8/60 in Mount Kisco, New York. Country singer/actor. Played "Bo Duke" on TV's *The Dukes Of Hazzard*. 1. It's Now Or Never	Scotti Brothers 02105
4/9/55	14	6	**SCHUMANN, Walter, The Voices of** Born on 10/8/13 in Brooklyn, New York. Died on 8/21/58 (age 44). Leader of own choral group. Composer of the theme for TV's *Dragnet*. 1. The Ballad Of Davy Crockett Jockey #14 / Best Seller #29 from the ABC-TV *Disneyland* series which featured 3 "Davy Crockett" segments (Dec. 1954 - Feb. 1955)	RCA Victor 6041
1/16/82	28	7	**SCHWARTZ, Eddie** Born in 1949 in Toronto, Ontario, Canada. Pop-rock singer/songwriter. 1. All Our Tomorrows	Atco 7342
3/31/01	10	12	**S CLUB 7** Teen multi-racial pop vocal group formed in England: Tina Barrett, Paul Cattermole, Jon Lee, Bradley McIntosh, Jo O'Meara, Hannah Spearritt and Rachel Stevens. Group starred in its own TV series on the Fox Family Channel. 1. **Never Had A Dream Come True** Sales #2 / Airplay #21	A&M 7074

DATE	POS	WKS	ARTIST–RECORD TITLE	LABEL & NO.
			SCORPIONS	
			Hard-rock group from Germany: Klaus Meine (vocals), Rudolf Schenker and Matthias Jabs (guitars), Francis Buchholz (bass) and Herman Rarebell (drums).	
4/28/84	25	7	1. Rock You Like A Hurricane	Mercury 818440
6/29/91	4	16	● 2. **Wind Of Change** Sales #5 / Airplay #9	Mercury 868180
			SCOTT, Bobby	
			Born on 1/29/37 in Mount Pleasant, New York. Died of cancer on 11/5/90 (age 53). White pop-jazz singer/pianist.	
1/21/56	13	10	1. Chain Gang	ABC-Paramount 9658
			Jockey #13 / Juke Box #13 / Top 100 #15 / Best Seller #17 Don Costa (orch.)	
			SCOTT, Freddie	
			Born on 4/24/33 in Providence, Rhode Island. R&B singer/songwriter.	
8/10/63	10	9	1. **Hey, Girl**	Colpix 692
2/18/67	39	2	2. Are You Lonely For Me	Shout 207
			#1 R&B hit (4 weeks)	
			SCOTT, Jack	
			Born Jack Scafone on 1/28/36 in Windsor, Ontario, Canada. Rock and roll-ballad singer/songwriter/guitarist.	
7/7/58	3	16	● 1. **My True Love /** Hot 100 #3 / Best Seller #7 / Jockey #13	
6/16/58	11	18	2. Leroy Best Seller #11 / Top 100 #25	Carlton 462
10/20/58	28	4	3. With Your Love Hot 100 #28	Carlton 483
12/28/58+	8	13	4. **Goodbye Baby**	Carlton 493
8/3/59	35	4	5. The Way I Walk	Carlton 514
1/18/60	5	13	● 6. **What In The World's Come Over You**	Top Rank 2028
5/9/60	3	12	7. **Burning Bridges /**	
5/30/60	34	2	8. Oh, Little One	Top Rank 2041
9/5/60	38	2	9. It Only Happened Yesterday	Top Rank 2055
			The Chantones (backing vocals, all of above)	
			SCOTT, Linda	
			Born Linda Joy Sampson on 6/1/45 in Queens, New York. Pop singer. Co-host of TV's *Where The Action Is*.	
4/3/61	3	10	1. **I've Told Every Little Star**	Canadian American 123
			#10 hit for Jack Denny in 1933 (from the Broadway musical *Music In The Air* starring Walter Slezak)	
7/24/61	9	10	2. **Don't Bet Money Honey**	Canadian American 127
11/27/61	12	8	3. I Don't Know Why	Canadian American 129
			#2 hit for Wayne King in 1931	
			SCOTT, Peggy, & Jo Jo Benson	
			R&B vocal duo. Scott was born Peggy Stoutmeyer on 6/25/48 in Opp, Alabama. Benson was born in 1940 in Columbia, Ohio.	
7/6/68	31	7	1. Lover's Holiday	SSS International 736
11/30/68	27	4	2. Pickin' Wild Mountain Berries	SSS International 748
2/15/69	37	3	3. Soulshake	SSS International 761

DATE	POS	WKS	ARTIST–RECORD TITLE	LABEL & NO.
			SCRITTI POLITTI	
			Pop-dance trio formed in England: Green Gartside (vocals), David Gamson (keyboards) and Fred Maher (drums).	
10/26/85	**11**	13	1. Perfect Way Airplay #10 / Sales #11	Warner 28949
			SEA, Johnny	
			Born John Seay on 7/15/40 in Gulfport, Mississippi. Country singer/songwriter/guitarist.	
6/25/66	**35**	2	1. Day For Decision **[S]** featuring a chorus singing the patriotic song "America"	Warner 5820
			SEAL	
			Born Sealhenry Samuel on 2/19/63 in Paddington, England (of Nigerian/Brazilian parents). Male singer/songwriter.	
7/13/91	**7**	13	1. **Crazy** Sales #17 / Airplay #19	ZTT/Sire 19298
7/9/94	**21**	14	2. Prayer For The Dying Airplay #16 / Sales #56	ZTT/Sire 18138
7/8/95	**1** (1)	32	● 3. **Kiss From A Rose** Airplay #1 (10) / Sales #5 #1 Adult Contemporary hit (12 weeks); from the movie *Batman Forever* starring Val Kilmer; 1995 Grammy winner: Record of the Year	ZTT/Sire 17896
2/17/96	**33**	7	4. Don't Cry Airplay #17	ZTT/Warner 17708
12/21/96+	**10**	9	5. **Fly Like An Eagle** Airplay #12 / Sales #13 from the movie *Space Jam* starring Michael Jordan	Warner Sunset 87046
			SEALS & CROFTS	
			Pop duo: Jim Seals (born on 10/17/41 in Sidney, Texas) and Dash Crofts (born on 8/14/40 in Cisco, Texas). With The Champs from 1958-65. Jim is the brother of "England" Dan Seals and the cousin of country singers Troy Seals, Brady Seals (of Little Texas) and Johnny Duncan.	
10/21/72	**6**	11	1. **Summer Breeze**	Warner 7606
2/17/73	**20**	9	2. Hummingbird	Warner 7671
6/16/73	**6**	12	3. **Diamond Girl**	Warner 7708
10/13/73	**21**	8	4. We May Never Pass This Way (Again)	Warner 7740
5/17/75	**18**	8	5. I'll Play For You	Warner 8075
6/5/76	**6**	15	6. **Get Closer** **SEALS & CROFTS (Featuring Carolyn Willis)**	Warner 8190
10/22/77	**28**	5	7. My Fair Share love theme from the movie *One on One* starring Robby Benson	Warner 8405
5/27/78	**18**	7	8. You're The Love	Warner 8551
			SEARCHERS, The	
			Rock and roll band from Liverpool, England: Mike Pender and John McNally (vocals, guitars), Tony Jackson (vocals, bass) and Chris Curtis (drums). Jackson died of liver failure on 8/18/2003 (age 63).	
3/21/64	**13**	8	1. Needles And Pins	Kapp 577
6/20/64	**16**	8	2. Don't Throw Your Love Away	Kapp 593
9/12/64	**34**	3	3. Some Day We're Gonna Love Again	Kapp 609
11/14/64	**35**	2	4. When You Walk In The Room	Kapp 618
12/19/64+	**3**	11	5. **Love Potion Number Nine**	Kapp 27
2/20/65	**29**	3	6. What Have They Done To The Rain	Kapp 644
4/10/65	**21**	4	7. Bumble Bee	Kapp 49

DATE	POS	WKS	ARTIST–RECORD TITLE	LABEL & NO.
			SEBASTIAN, John	
			Born on 3/17/44 in Brooklyn, New York. Pop-rock singer/songwriter/ guitarist. Formed The Lovin' Spoonful in 1965.	
4/10/76	**1** (1)	11	● 1. **Welcome Back** #1 Adult Contemporary hit (2 weeks); theme from the TV series *Welcome Back Kotter* starring Gabe Kaplan	Reprise 1349
			SECADA, Jon	
			Born Juan Secada on 10/4/63 in Havana, Cuba; raised in Hialeah, Florida. Singer/songwriter.	
5/23/92	**5**	30	● 1. **Just Another Day** Airplay #3 / Sales #8 Gloria Estefan (backing vocal)	SBK 07383
10/24/92	**13**	21	2. Do You Believe In Us Airplay #12 / Sales #29	SBK 50408
3/6/93	**18**	17	3. Angel Airplay #10 / Sales #33	SBK 50406
7/17/93	**27**	8	4. I'm Free Airplay #15	SBK 50434
5/14/94	**10**	27	5. **If You Go** Airplay #6 / Sales #15	SBK 58156
1/21/95	**29**	6	6. Mental Picture Airplay #28	SBK 58272
			SECRETS, The	
			White "girl group" from Cleveland, Ohio: Karen Gray, Jackie Allen, Carole Raymont and Pat Miller.	
12/7/63	**18**	6	1. The Boy Next Door	Philips 40146
			SEDAKA, Neil	
			Born on 3/13/39 in Brooklyn, New York. Pop singer/songwriter/pianist. Prolific songwriting partnership with Howard Greenfield.	
12/28/58+	**14**	9	1. The Diary	RCA Victor 7408
10/26/59	**9**	13	2. **Oh! Carol** written for singer/songwriter Carole King	RCA Victor 7595
4/18/60	**9**	9	3. **Stairway To Heaven**	RCA Victor 7709
8/29/60	**17**	9	4. You Mean Everything To Me /	
10/3/60	**28**	3	5. Run Samson Run	RCA Victor 7781
12/31/60+	**4**	12	6. **Calendar Girl**	RCA Victor 7829
5/8/61	**11**	7	7. Little Devil	RCA Victor 7874
11/27/61+	**6**	11	8. **Happy Birthday, Sweet Sixteen**	RCA Victor 7957
7/7/62	**1** (2)	12	9. **Breaking Up Is Hard To Do** also see #18 below	RCA Victor 8046
10/20/62	**5**	9	10. **Next Door To An Angel**	RCA Victor 8086
2/16/63	**17**	7	11. Alice In Wonderland	RCA Victor 8137
5/18/63	**26**	5	12. Let's Go Steady Again	RCA Victor 8169
12/7/63	**33**	4	13. Bad Girl	RCA Victor 8254
11/16/74+	**1** (1)	15	14. **Laughter In The Rain** #1 Adult Contemporary hit (2 weeks)	Rocket 40313
4/26/75	**22**	5	15. The Immigrant #1 Adult Contemporary hit (1 week); dedicated to John Lennon (because of his immigration difficulties)	Rocket 40370
8/2/75	**27**	4	16. That's When The Music Takes Me	Rocket 40426
9/20/75	**1** (3)	12	● 17. **Bad Blood** Elton John (backing vocal)	Rocket 40460
12/27/75+	**8**	11	18. **Breaking Up Is Hard To Do** **[R]** #1 Adult Contemporary hit (1 week); slow version of #9 above	Rocket 40500

DATE	POS	WKS	ARTIST—RECORD TITLE	LABEL & NO.
5/1/76	**16**	7	19. Love In The Shadows	Rocket 40543
7/24/76	**36**	2	20. Steppin' Out	Rocket 40582
			Elton John (backing vocal)	
5/10/80	**19**	10	21. Should've Never Let You Go	Elektra 46615
			NEIL SEDAKA and DARA SEDAKA	
			SEDUCTION	
			Female dance trio from New York: Idalis Leon, April Harris and Michelle Visage.	
9/2/89	**23**	8	1. You're My One And Only (True Love) Sales #21 / Airplay #24	Vendetta 1433
			Martha Wash (lead vocal)	
12/9/89+	**2** (2)	14	● 2. **Two To Make It Right** Sales #2 / Airplay #2	Vendetta 1464
			samples "Kiss" by The Art Of Noise Featuring Tom Jones	
3/17/90	**13**	10	3. Heartbeat Sales #12 / Airplay #15	Vendetta 1473
7/7/90	**11**	10	4. Could This Be Love Airplay #7 / Sales #15	Vendetta 1509
			SEEDS, The	
			Garage-rock band from Los Angeles, California: Richard "Sky Saxon" Marsh (vocals, bass), Jan Savage (guitar), Daryl Hooper (keyboards) and Rick Aldridge (drums).	
2/11/67	**36**	3	1. Pushin' Too Hard	GNP Crescendo 372
			SEEKERS, The	
			Pop-folk group formed in Australia: Judith Durham (vocals), Keith Potger and Bruce Woodley (guitars), and Athol Guy (bass). Potger formed The New Seekers in 1970.	
4/10/65	**4**	10	1. **I'll Never Find Another You**	Capitol 5383
6/26/65	**19**	6	2. A World Of Our Own	Capitol 5430
12/31/66+	**2** (2)	12	● 3. **Georgy Girl**	Capitol 5756
			title song from the movie starring Lynn Redgrave and James Mason	
			SEGER, Bob	
			Born on 5/6/45 in Dearborn, Michigan; raised in Detroit, Michigan. Rock singer/songwriter/guitarist. Formed own backing group, The Silver Bullet Band, in 1976: Alto Reed (horns), Robyn Robbins (keyboards), Drew Abbott (guitar), Chris Campbell (bass) and Charlie Martin (drums). Various personnel changes since then. Inducted into the Rock and Roll Hall of Fame in 2004.	
1/25/69	**17**	9	1. Ramblin' Gamblin' Man	Capitol 2297
			BOB SEGER SYSTEM	
1/15/77	**4**	13	2. **Night Moves**	Capitol 4369
5/14/77	**24**	4	3. Mainstreet	Capitol 4422
			BOB SEGER & THE SILVER BULLET BAND:	
6/3/78	**4**	11	4. **Still The Same**	Capitol 4581
8/19/78	**12**	10	5. Hollywood Nights	Capitol 4618
11/25/78+	**13**	11	6. We've Got Tonite	Capitol 4653
5/5/79	**28**	5	7. Old Time Rock & Roll	Capitol 4702
			BOB SEGER:	
3/1/80	**6**	12	8. **Fire Lake**	Capitol 4836
			Glenn Frey, Don Henley and Timothy B. Schmit (backing vocals)	
5/10/80	**5**	11	9. **Against The Wind**	Capitol 4863

DATE	POS	WKS	ARTIST–RECORD TITLE	LABEL & NO.
8/16/80	**14**	9	10. You'll Accomp'ny Me	Capitol 4904
9/26/81	**5**	12	11. **Tryin' To Live My Life Without You** [L] recorded on 10/6/80 at the Boston Garden	Capitol 5042
			BOB SEGER & THE SILVER BULLET BAND:	
12/18/82+	**2 (4)**	19	12. **Shame On The Moon** #1 Adult Contemporary hit (2 weeks); Glenn Frey (backing vocal); written by Rodney Crowell	Capitol 5187
3/26/83	**12**	9	13. Even Now	Capitol 5213
6/11/83	**27**	6	14. Roll Me Away	Capitol 5235
12/1/84+	**17**	8	15. Understanding Sales #16 / Airplay #19 from the movie *Teachers* starring Nick Nolte and JoBeth Williams	Capitol 5413
3/29/86	**13**	9	16. American Storm Sales #9 / Airplay #18	Capitol 5532
5/31/86	**12**	9	17. Like A Rock Sales #9 / Airplay #19 #1 Mainstream Rock hit (2 weeks)	Capitol 5592
5/30/87	**1 (1)**	14	18. **Shakedown** Sales #1 (2) / Airplay #1 (1) **BOB SEGER** #1 Mainstream Rock hit (4 weeks); from the movie *Beverly Hills Cop II* starring Eddie Murphy	MCA 53094
9/14/91	**24**	5	19. The Real Love Sales #54 / Airplay #62 **BOB SEGER & THE SILVER BULLET BAND** Patty Smyth and J.D. Souther (backing vocals)	Capitol 44743
			SELENA	
			Born Selena Quintanilla on 4/16/71 in Corpus Christi, Texas. Shot to death by Yolanda Saldivar (founder of Selena's fan club) on 3/31/95 (age 23). Latin singer. Jennifer Lopez starred in the 1997 biographical movie *Selena*.	
7/15/95	**8** A	21	1. **I Could Fall In Love** from the album *Dreaming Of You* on EMI Latin 34123	album cut
10/28/95	**22**	13	2. Dreaming Of You Sales #16 / Airplay #25	EMI Latin 58490
			SELLARS, Marilyn	
			Born on 12/31/50 in Northfield, Minnesota. Country singer.	
9/28/74	**37**	2	1. One Day At A Time	Mega 1205
			SEMBELLO, Michael	
			Born on 4/17/54 in Philadelphia, Pennsylvania. Pop-rock singer/guitarist. Prolific studio musician.	
7/2/83	**1 (2)**	16	1. **Maniac** from the movie *Flashdance* starring Jennifer Beals	Casablanca 812516
10/29/83	**34**	2	2. Automatic Man	Warner 29485
			SEMISONIC	
			Rock trio from Minneapolis, Minnesota: Dan Wilson (vocals, guitar), John Munson (bass) and Jacob Slichter (drums).	
5/16/98	**11** A	29	1. Closing Time #1 Modern Rock hit (5 weeks); from the album *Feeling Strangely Fine* on MCA 11733	album cut
			SENATOR BOBBY	
			Senator Bobby is comedian Bill Minkin doing an impression of Senator Robert Kennedy.	
1/21/67	**20**	4	1. Wild Thing [C]	Parkway 127

DATE	POS	WKS	ARTIST–RECORD TITLE	LABEL & NO.
			SENSATIONS, The	
			R&B vocal group from Philadelphia, Pennsylvania: Yvonne Mills Baker, Sam Armstrong, Alphonso Howell and Richard Curtain. Howell died on 5/7/98 (age 61).	
2/10/62	4	12	1. **Let Me In**	Argo 5405
			SERENDIPITY SINGERS, The	
			Pop-folk group formed in Denver, Colorado: Jon Arbenz, Mike Brovsky, Diane Decker, Brooks Hatch, John Madden, Bryan Sennett, Tom Tiemann, Lynn Weintraub and Bob Young.	
3/21/64	6	11	1. **Don't Let The Rain Come Down (Crooked Little Man)**	Philips 40175
6/13/64	30	5	2. Beans In My Ears **[N]**	Philips 40198
			SERMON, Erick	
			Born on 11/25/68 in Bayshore, New York. Male rapper. One-half of EPMD duo with Parrish Smith.	
6/16/01	22	10	1. Music Airplay #17 / Sales #31	NY.LA 497578
			ERICK SERMON featuring MARVIN GAYE	
			samples "Turn On Some Music" by Marvin Gaye; from the movie *What's The Worst That Could Happen?* starring Martin Lawrence	
12/7/02	36	2	2. React Sales #7 / Airplay #34	J Records 21221
			ERICK SERMON Featuring Redman	
			SETZER, Brian, Orchestra	
			Born on 4/10/60 in Long Island, New York. Lead singer/guitarist of the Stray Cats. Played Eddie Cochran in the 1987 movie *La Bamba*. Formed own 16-piece swing orchestra in 1994.	
9/12/98	23 ᴬ	11	1. Jump Jive An' Wail Hot 100 #94 (3 wks)	album cut
			from the album *The Dirty Boogie* on Interscope 90183; written and first recorded by Louis Prima in 1956	
			SEVEN MARY THREE	
			Rock group from Virginia: Jason Ross (vocals), Jason Pollock (guitar), Casey Daniel (bass) and Giti Khalsa (drums).	
2/24/96	39	3	1. Cumbersome Sales #33 / Airplay #45	Mammoth 98111
			#1 Mainstream Rock hit (4 weeks)	
			702	
			Female R&B vocal trio from Las Vegas, Nevada: Kameelah Williams and sisters Irish and Lemisha Grinstead. Group named after the Las Vegas area code.	
2/18/95	15	14	● 1. This Lil' Game We Play Sales #7 / Airplay #25	Biv 10 0252
			SUBWAY featuring 702	
12/7/96	32	6	● 2. Steelo Sales #20	Biv 10 0530
			Missy Elliott (rap); samples "Voices In My Head" by The Police	
2/15/97	10	17	● 3. **Get It Together** Sales #4 / Airplay #46	Biv 10/Motown 0612
8/23/97	35	4	4. All I Want Sales #21	Biv 10/Motown 0676
			samples "It's Great To Be Here" by The Jackson 5; from the movie *Good Burger* starring Kenan Thompson and Kel Mitchell	
5/15/99	4	38	● 5. **Where My Girls At?** Sales #2 / Airplay #3	Motown 860891

DATE	POS	WKS	ARTIST–RECORD TITLE	LABEL & NO.
			SEVILLE, David/THE CHIPMUNKS	
			Born Ross Bagdasarian on 1/27/19 in Fresno, California. Died on 1/16/72 (age 52). Novelty singer/songwriter. Creator of The Chipmunks, cartoon characters Seville named Alvin, Simon and Theodore after Liberty label executives Alvin Bennett, Simon Waronker and Theodore Keep. The Chipmunks starred in own prime-time animated TV show in the early 1960s and a Saturday morning cartoon series in the mid-1980s. His son, Ross Jr., resurrected the act in 1980.	
			THE MUSIC OF DAVID SEVILLE:	
4/14/58	**1** (3)	18	● 1. **Witch Doctor** Top 100 #1 (3) / Best Seller #1 (2) / Jockey #2 **[N]** #1 R&B hit (1 week)	Liberty 55132
7/14/58	**34**	2	2. The Bird On My Head Best Seller #34 / Top 100 #36 **[N]**	Liberty 55140
			DAVID SEVILLE AND THE CHIPMUNKS:	
12/8/58	**1** (4)	11	● 3. **The Chipmunk Song** **[X-N]**	Liberty 55168
2/23/59	**3**	9	● 4. **Alvin's Harmonica** **[N]**	Liberty 55179
7/13/59	**16**	6	5. Ragtime Cowboy Joe **[N]** #1 hit for Bob Roberts in 1912	Liberty 55200
3/7/60	**33**	2	6. Alvin's Orchestra **[N]**	Liberty 55233
12/26/60	**21**	1	7. Rudolph The Red Nosed Reindeer **[X-N]**	Liberty 55289
1/6/62 -	**39**	1	8. The Chipmunk Song (Christmas Don't Be Late)**[X-N-R]**	Liberty 55250
3/31/62	**40**	1	9. The Alvin Twist **[N]**	Liberty 55424
12/29/62	**40**	1	10. The Chipmunk Song (Christmas Don't Be Late)**[X-N-R]**	Liberty 55250
			SEXTON, Charlie	
			Born on 8/11/68 in San Antonio, Texas. Rock singer/guitarist.	
2/8/86	**17**	10	1. Beat's So Lonely Sales #9 / Airplay #30	MCA 52715
			SEYMOUR, Phil	
			Born on 5/15/52 in Tulsa, Oklahoma. Died of cancer on 8/17/93 (age 41). Pop-rock singer/drummer/bassist. Former member of the Dwight Twilley Band.	
2/21/81	**22**	7	1. Precious To Me	Boardwalk 5703
			SHADES OF BLUE	
			"Blue-eyed soul" vocal group from Detroit, Michigan: Linda Kerr, Robert Kerr, Ernest Dernai and Nick Marinelli.	
5/28/66	**12**	8	1. Oh How Happy	Impact 1007
			SHADOWS OF KNIGHT, The	
			Garage-rock group from Chicago, Illinois: Jim Sohns (vocals), Joe Kelley and Jerry McGeorge (guitars), Warren Rogers (bass) and Tom Schiffour (drums).	
4/16/66	**10**	8	1. **Gloria**	Dunwich 116
7/2/66	**39**	1	2. Oh Yeah	Dunwich 122
			SHAGGY	
			Born Orville Richard Burrell on 10/22/68 in Kingston, Jamaica. Reggae singer.	
6/17/95	**3**	23	▲ 1. **Boombastic /** Sales #1 (2) / Airplay #27 #1 R&B hit (1 week); samples "Baby Let Me Kiss You" by King Floyd	

DATE	POS	WKS	ARTIST–RECORD TITLE	LABEL & NO.
7/29/95		17	2. Summer Time Sales: flip **SHAGGY (featuring Rayvon)** #3 hit for Mungo Jerry in 1970 as "In The Summertime"	Virgin 38482
7/20/96	**20**	10	3. That Girl Sales #16 / Airplay #41 **MAXI PRIEST FEATURING SHAGGY** samples "Green Onions" by Booker T. & The MG's	Virgin 38550
11/11/00+	**1 (2)**	23	4. **It Wasn't Me** Airplay #1 (5) / Sales #2 **SHAGGY (Featuring Ricardo "RikRok" Ducent)**	MCA 155782
1/20/01	**1 (1)**	23	5. **Angel** Airplay #1 (5) / Sales #10 **SHAGGY Featuring Rayvon** samples "The Joker" by Steve Miller and "Angel Of The Morning" by Merrilee Rush	MCA 155811
			SHAI R&B vocal group formed in Washington DC: Garfield Bright, Marc Gay, Carl Martin and Darnell Van Rensalier. Pronounced: shy.	
10/24/92	**2 (8)**	24	▲ 1. **If I Ever Fall In Love** Sales #2 / Airplay #2	Gasoline Alley 54518
2/13/93	**10**	20	● 2. **Comforter** Airplay #8 / Sales #15	Gasoline Alley 54596
7/3/93	**10**	20	3. **Baby I'm Yours** Airplay #5 / Sales #24	Gasoline Alley 54574
7/2/94	**34**	6	4. The Place Where You Belong Sales #25 / Airplay #52 from the movie *Beverly Hills Cop III* starring Eddie Murphy	MCA 54807
			SHAKESPEAR'S SISTER Female vocal duo: Siobhan Fahey and Marcella Detroit. Fahey was a member of Bananarama. Married David A. Stewart (of Eurythmics). Detroit was born Marcy Levy in Detroit.	
7/25/92	**4**	14	● 1. **Stay** Sales #4 / Airplay #17	London 869730
			SHAKIRA Born Shakira Isabel Mebarak Ripoll on 2/9/77 in Barranquilla, Colombia. Female Latin-pop singer.	
11/24/01	**6**	19	1. **Whenever, Wherever** Airplay #6	album cut
4/6/02	**9**	13	2. **Underneath Your Clothes** Airplay #9 above 2 from the album *Laundry Service* on Epic 63900	album cut
			SHALAMAR R&B-dance vocal trio formed in Los Angeles, California: Jody Watley, Jeffrey Daniels and Howard Hewett. "Uptown Festival" was recorded by anonymous session singers prior to formation of actual group.	
4/16/77	**25**	8	1. Uptown Festival (Part 1) Going To A Go-Go/I Can't Help Myself (Sugar Pie, Honey Bunch)/Uptight (Everything's Alright)/Stop! In The Name Of Love/It's The Same Old Song	Soul Train 10885
2/2/80	**8**	13	● 2. **The Second Time Around** #1 R&B hit (1 week)	Solar 11709
8/6/83	**22**	10	3. Dead Giveaway	Solar 69819
4/14/84	**17**	10	4. Dancing In The Sheets from the movie *Footloose* starring Kevin Bacon and Lori Singer	Columbia 04372
			SHAMEN, The Techno-rave dance group from Aberdeen, Scotland: brothers Derek and Keith McKenzie, Richard West, Colin Angus, Will Sinnott and Peter Stephenson. Sinnott drowned on 5/23/90 (age 31).	
2/22/92	**38**	2	1. Move Any Mountain (Progen 91) Airplay #36 / Sales #41	Epic 74044

DATE	POS	WKS	ARTIST–RECORD TITLE	LABEL & NO.
			SHANA	
			Born Shana Petrone on 5/8/72 in Parkridge, Illinois; raised in Ft. Lauderdale, Florida. Female dance singer.	
1/13/90	40	1	1. I Want You Sales #35 / Airplay #40	Vision 4511
			SHANGRI-LAS, The	
			"Girl group" formed in Queens, New York. Consisted of two sets of sisters: Mary and Betty Weiss, and twins Mary Ann and Marge Ganser. Mary Ann died of encephalitis in 1971. Marge died of cancer on 7/28/96 (age 48).	
9/5/64	5	9	1. **Remember (Walkin' in the Sand)**	Red Bird 10-008
10/24/64	1 (1)	10	2. **Leader Of The Pack**	Red Bird 10-014
1/16/65	18	5	3. **Give Him A Great Big Kiss**	Red Bird 10-018
6/19/65	29	4	4. Give Us Your Blessings	Red Bird 10-030
11/20/65	6	8	5. **I Can Never Go Home Anymore**	Red Bird 10-043
2/26/66	33	2	6. Long Live Our Love	Red Bird 10-048
			SHANICE	
			Born Shanice Wilson on 5/14/73 in Pittsburgh, Pennsylvania; raised in Los Angeles, California. Female R&B singer.	
12/14/91+	2 (3)	21	1. **I Love Your Smile** Airplay #1 (5) / Sales #6 #1 R&B hit (4 weeks)	Motown 2093
5/16/92	31	5	2. Silent Prayer Airplay #29 / Sales #33 **SHANICE featuring Johnny Gill**	Motown 2165
11/14/92+	4	20	3. **Saving Forever For You** Airplay #4 / Sales #6 from the album *Beverly Hills 90210 (The Soundtrack)*	Giant 18719
4/3/99	12	6	4. When I Close My Eyes Sales #9 / Airplay #59	LaFace 24365
			SHANNON	
			Born Brenda Shannon Greene on 5/12/57 in Washington DC. Female dance singer.	
1/7/84	8	12	● 1. **Let The Music Play**	Mirage 99810
			SHANNON, Del	
			Born Charles Westover on 12/30/34 in Coopersville, Michigan. Died of a self-inflicted gunshot wound on 2/8/90 (age 55). Pop singer/songwriter. Inducted into the Rock and Roll Hall of Fame in 1999.	
3/27/61	1 (4)	12	● 1. **Runaway** electric organ (musitron) solo by co-writer Max Crook	Big Top 3067
6/19/61	5	11	2. **Hats Off To Larry**	Big Top 3075
10/9/61	28	5	3. So Long Baby	Big Top 3083
1/6/62	38	2	4. Hey! Little Girl	Big Top 3091
1/26/63	12	7	5. Little Town Flirt	Big Top 3131
7/25/64	22	7	6. Handy Man	Amy 905
12/19/64+	9	10	7. **Keep Searchin' (We'll Follow The Sun)**	Amy 915
3/13/65	30	4	8. Stranger In Town	Amy 919
1/23/82	33	4	9. Sea Of Love produced by Tom Petty	Network 47951

DATE	POS	WKS	ARTIST–RECORD TITLE	LABEL & NO.
			SHARP, Dee Dee	
			Born Dione LaRue on 9/9/45 in Philadelphia, Pennsylvania. R&B singer. Married record producer Kenny Gamble in 1967.	
3/10/62	3	12	1. **Slow Twistin'** **CHUBBY CHECKER (with Dee Dee Sharp)**	Parkway 835
3/17/62	2 (2)	15	● 2. **Mashed Potato Time** #1 R&B hit (4 weeks)	Cameo 212
6/23/62	9	9	3. **Gravy (For My Mashed Potatoes)**	Cameo 219
11/10/62	5	9	4. **Ride!**	Cameo 230
3/9/63	10	9	5. **Do The Bird**	Cameo 244
11/2/63	33	5	6. **Wild!**	Cameo 274
			SHAW, Georgie	
			Born in 1930 in Philadelphia, Pennsylvania. Male Adult Contemporary singer.	
11/12/55	23	6	1. **No Arms Can Ever Hold You** **(Like These Arms Of Mine)** Top 100 #23 / Best Seller #25	Decca 29679
2/11/56	39	1	2. **Go On With The Wedding** Top 100 #39 **KITTY KALLEN and GEORGIE SHAW** Jack Pleis (orch., above 2)	Decca 29776
			SHAW, Tommy	
			Born on 9/11/53 in Montgomery, Alabama. Lead guitarist of Styx from 1976-84. Joined Damn Yankees in 1990.	
11/3/84	33	3	1. **Girls With Guns**	A&M 2676
			SHEIK, Duncan	
			Born on 11/18/69 in Montclair, New Jersey; raised in Hilton Head, South Carolina. Alternative pop-rock singer/songwriter/guitarist.	
2/1/97	16	42	1. **Barely Breathing** Airplay #7 / Sales #56	Atlantic 87027
			SHEILA E.	
			Born Sheila Escovedo on 12/12/59 in San Francisco, California. R&B singer/percussionist. Member of The Blackout Allstars. Her brother Peto was in Con Funk Shun.	
7/21/84	7	16	1. **The Glamorous Life** Sales #7 / Airplay #14	Warner 29285
12/8/84	34	5	2. **The Belle Of St. Mark** Airplay #26 / Sales #30	Warner 29180
12/28/85+	11	12	3. **A Love Bizarre** Airplay #10 / Sales #12 Prince (backing vocal); from the movie *Krush Groove* starring Sheila E.	Paisley Park 28890
			SHELLS, The	
			R&B vocal group from Brooklyn, New York: Nate Bouknight, Gus Geter, Bob Nurse, Shade Alston and Dan Small.	
12/31/60+	21	5	1. **Baby Oh Baby**	Johnson 104
			SHELTON, Blake	
			Born on 6/18/76 in Ada, Oklahoma. Country singer/guitarist.	
7/28/01	18	10	1. **Austin** Sales #7 / Airplay #22 #1 Country hit (5 weeks)	Giant 16767

DATE	POS	WKS	ARTIST–RECORD TITLE	LABEL & NO.
1/25/03	**28**	7	2. The Baby <div align="right">Airplay #27</div> #1 Country hit (3 weeks); from the album *The Dreamer* on Warner 48237	album cut
			SHE MOVES	
			Trio of female singers/dancers: Carla, Danielle and Diana. Met while performing as dancers at New York Knicks basketball games.	
11/22/97	**32**	10	1. Breaking All The Rules <div align="right">Sales #29 / Airplay #38</div>	Geffen 19415
			SHEP AND THE LIMELITES	
			R&B vocal trio from Queens, New York: James "Shep" Sheppard (formerly with The Heartbeats), with Clarence Bassett and Charles Baskerville. Sheppard was shot to death on 1/24/70 (age 34).	
4/10/61	**2** (1)	11	1. **Daddy's Home** sequel to "A Thousand Miles Away" by The Heartbeats	Hull 740
			SHEPARD, Vonda	
			Born on 7/7/63 in Manhattan, New York; raised in Los Angeles, California. Singer/songwriter/keyboardist. Had a recurring role as a singer on TV's *Ally McBeal*.	
7/25/87	**6**	13	1. **Can't We Try** <div align="right">Sales #4 / Airplay #9</div> **DAN HILL (with Vonda Sheppard)**	Columbia 07050
5/2/98	**16** ᴬ	11	2. Searchin' My Soul theme from TV's *Ally McBeal* starring Calista Flockhart (soundtrack on 550 Music/Epic 69365)	album cut
			SHEPHERD SISTERS	
			Family rock and roll vocal group from Middletown, Ohio: sisters Martha, Mary Lou, Gayle and Judy Shepherd.	
11/4/57	**18**	7	1. Alone (Why Must I Be Alone) <div align="right">Best Seller #18 / Top 100 #20 / Jockey #22</div>	Lance 125
			SHEPPARD, T.G.	
			Born William Browder on 7/20/44 in Humbolt, Tennessee. Country singer.	
5/16/81	**37**	2	1. I Loved 'Em Every One #1 Country hit (1 week)	Warner/Curb 49690
			SHERIDAN, Tony — see BEATLES, The	
			SHERIFF	
			Pop-rock group from Toronto, Ontario, Canada: Freddy Curci (vocals), Steve DeMarchi (guitar), Arnold Lanni (keyboards), Wolf Hassel (bass) and Rob Elliott (drums). Curci and DeMarchi later joined Alias.	
12/17/88+	**1** (1)	13	● 1. **When I'm With You** <div align="right">Sales #1 (1) / Airplay #1 (1) **[R]**</div> #1 Adult Contemporary hit (1 week); originally charted at #61 in 1983	Capitol 44302

Santo & Johnny recorded the final instrumental of the 1950s, their #1 hit "Sleep Walk." Unfortunately, the brothers couldn't make any future hits rise and shine on the charts; the #23 "Tear Drop" was their last Top 40 hit.

Seal lost the 1991 Grammy Award for Best New Artist to Marc Cohn, but he proved to be a late bloomer. The 1995 chart-topping "Kiss From A Rose," from the *Batman Forever* soundtrack, won Grammy Awards for Record of the Year and Song of the Year.

Neil Sedaka had the last laugh on those who felt his career was over when his comeback hit, "Laughter In The Rain," released on Elton John's Rocket label, became his first #1 single in over a decade.

Michael Sembello envisioned the song "Maniac" as being appropriate for a horror movie, but when it appeared on the soundtrack to the dance classic *Flashdance,* Sembello scared up his only chart-topper.

Shaggy collaborated with chart-topping artists like Maxi Priest and Janet Jackson on minor hits, but his first #1 single, "It Wasn't Me," was a pairing with a relative unknown, Ricardo "RikRok" Ducent.

The Shangri-Las reached #1 with "Leader Of The Pack" in November, 1964. The following week, a parody of the song, "Leader Of The Laundromat" by The Detergents, entered the Hot 100.

Del Shannon wrote "Runaway" with Max Crook while working as a carpet salesman, and the song became a runaway hit. Not only did it reach #1, but it served as the theme song to the 1980s TV series *Crime Story.*

The Shirelles recorded "Will You Love Me Tomorrow" as a favor for their producer's songwriting friends, Gerry Goffin and Carole King. However, they were the ones done a favor, as the song climbed to #1.

Carly Simon auctioned off the identity of the person referred to in her #1 hit, "You're So Vain," in a 2003 charity auction. The winner, TV producer Dick Ebersol, was sworn never to reveal the name to the public.

Sir Mix-A-Lot received only late-night airplay after his video for "Baby Got Back" was deemed too suggestive, but his ode to ballooning backsides nonetheless gave the Seattle rapper a #1 pop hit.

Sisqó rose to fame with "Thong Song," but probably felt incomplete when it missed the top spot. Thankfully, the Dru Hill singer's follow-up, "Incomplete," with "Thong Song" as the B-side, did the trick and rose to #1.

Percy Sledge scored his only #1 pop hit with "When A Man Loves A Woman." Although Percy's performance didn't earn him a Grammy Award, Michael Bolton's 1991 remake of the song won for Best Pop Male Vocalist.

Sly and the Family Stone earned their first #1 hit with "Everyday People." Everyday people loved the song, as it would later be a Top 40 hit for Joan Jett, and provide the chorus for Arrested Development's "People Everyday."

Snow blanketed the pop airways in 1993 with the rap-reggae mixture "Informer," a #1 hit he wrote in prison after being framed for murder. The Canadian dancehall artist's career soon underwent a thaw, managing only one more hit.

DATE	POS	WKS	ARTIST–RECORD TITLE	LABEL & NO.
			SHERMAN, Allan	
			Born Allan Copelon on 11/30/24 in Chicago, Illinois. Died on 11/21/73 (age 48). Novelty singer/songwriter. Creator/producer of TV's *I've Got A Secret*.	
8/10/63	**2** (3)	8	1. **Hello Mudduh, Hello Fadduh!** **(A Letter From Camp)** [C-L] Lou Busch (orch.); melody adopted from Ponchielli's *Dance Of The Hours*	Warner 5378
5/8/65	**40**	1	2. Crazy Downtown [C-L] parody of Petula Clark's "Downtown"	Warner 5614
			SHERMAN, Bobby	
			Born on 7/22/43 in Santa Monica, California. Teen idol singer/actor. Regular on TV's *Shindig*. Played "Jeremy Bolt" on TV's *Here Come The Brides*.	
9/6/69	**3**	11	● 1. **Little Woman**	Metromedia 121
12/6/69+	**9**	9	● 2. **La La La (If I Had You)**	Metromedia 150
2/28/70	**9**	11	● 3. **Easy Come, Easy Go**	Metromedia 177
6/6/70	**24**	5	4. Hey, Mister Sun	Metromedia 188
8/15/70	**5**	13	● 5. **Julie, Do Ya Love Me**	Metromedia 194
2/27/71	**16**	7	6. Cried Like A Baby	Metromedia 206
5/15/71	**29**	5	7. The Drum	Metromedia 217
			SHERRYS, The	
			R&B "girl group" from Philadelphia, Pennsylvania: sisters Dinell and Delphine Cook, with Charlotte Butler and Delores Wylie.	
11/10/62	**35**	2	1. Pop Pop Pop - Pie	Guyden 2068
			SHIELDS, The	
			R&B vocal group formed in Los Angeles, California: Frankie Ervin, Jesse Belvin, Johnny "Guitar" Watson, Mel Williams and Buster Williams.	
9/15/58	**12**	9	1. You Cheated Best Seller #12 / Hot 100 #15	Dot 15805
			SHIRELLES, The	
			R&B-pop "girl group" from Passaic, New Jersey: Shirley Owens Alston, Beverly Lee, Doris Kenner and Addie "Micki" Harris. Harris died on 6/10/82 (age 42). Kenner died of cancer on 2/4/2000 (age 58). Group inducted into the Rock and Roll Hall of Fame in 1996.	
10/17/60	**39**	3	1. Tonights The Night	Scepter 1208
12/12/60+	**1** (2)	15	2. **Will You Love Me Tomorrow**	Scepter 1211
2/6/61	**3**	14	3. **Dedicated To The One I Love** [R] originally charted at #83 in 1959	Scepter 1203
5/1/61	**4**	8	4. **Mama Said**	Scepter 1217
10/23/61	**21**	5	5. Big John	Scepter 1223
1/6/62	**8**	11	6. **Baby It's You**	Scepter 1227
3/31/62	**1** (3)	13	● 7. **Soldier Boy**	Scepter 1228
7/7/62	**22**	6	8. Welcome Home Baby	Scepter 1234
10/6/62	**36**	3	9. Stop The Music	Scepter 1237
12/15/62+	**19**	9	10. Everybody Loves A Lover	Scepter 1243
4/20/63	**4**	9	11. **Foolish Little Girl**	Scepter 1248
7/13/63	**26**	4	12. Don't Say Goodnight And Mean Goodbye	Scepter 1255

DATE	POS	WKS	ARTIST–RECORD TITLE	LABEL & NO.
			SHIRLEY, Don, Trio	
10/9/61	40	1	Born on 1/27/27 in Kingston, Jamaica. Black pianist/organist. 1. Water Boy [I]	Cadence 1392
			SHIRLEY (AND COMPANY)	
2/22/75	12	8	Disco group: Shirley Goodman (female vocals), Jesus Alvarez (male vocals), Walter Morris (guitar), Bernadette Randle (keyboards), Seldon Powell (sax), Jonathan Williams (bass) and Clarence Oliver (drums). Goodman was half of Shirley & Lee duo. 1. Shame, Shame, Shame #1 R&B hit (1 week); written and produced by Sylvia Robinson (Mickey & Sylvia)	Vibration 532
			SHIRLEY & LEE	
9/8/56	20	9	R&B duo from New Orleans, Louisiana: Shirley Goodman (born on 6/19/36) and Leonard Lee (born on 6/29/36; died on 10/23/76, age 40). Also see Shirley (And Company). 1. Let The Good Times Roll Best Seller #20 / Top 100 #27 #1 R&B hit (3 weeks)	Aladdin 3325
1/5/57	38	1	2. I Feel Good Top 100 #38	Aladdin 3338
			SHOCKING BLUE, The	
12/20/69+	1 (1)	13	Rock group from The Hague, Netherlands: Mariska Veres (vocals), Robbie Leeuwen (guitar), Klassje Wal (bass) and Cor Beek (drums). Beek died on 4/2/98 (age 49). ● 1. **Venus**	Colossus 108
			SHONDELL, Troy	
9/25/61	6	12	Born Gary Schelton on 5/14/39 in Fort Wayne, Indiana. Pop-country singer/songwriter. 1. **This Time**	Liberty 55353
			SHORE, Dinah	
5/21/55	12	3	Born Frances Rose Shore on 3/1/17 in Winchester, Tennessee. Died of cancer on 2/24/94 (age 76). Pop singer. Hosted own TV variety shows (1951-63) and morning TV talk show (1970-80). Married to actor George Montgomery from 1943-62. 1. Whatever Lola Wants (Lola Gets) Jockey #12 / Best Seller #28 from the Broadway musical Damn Yankees starring Gwen Verdon	RCA Victor 6077
12/10/55	20	1	2. Love And Marriage Jockey #20 / Top 100 #42 from the TV production Our Town starring Frank Sinatra	RCA Victor 6266
2/23/57	19	10	3. Chantez-Chantez (Shan-Tay, "Sing") Jockey #19 / Top 100 #27	RCA Victor 6792
9/9/57	15	7	4. Fascination Jockey #15 / Top 100 #98 from the movie Love In The Afternoon starring Gary Cooper and Audrey Hepburn	RCA Victor 6980
12/2/57	24	1	5. I'll Never Say "Never Again" Again Jockey #24 #4 hit for Ozzie Nelson in 1935; Harry Zimmerman (orch., all of above)	RCA Victor 7056
			SIGLER, Bunny	
7/22/67	22	7	Born Walter Sigler on 3/27/41 in Philadelphia. R&B singer/songwriter. 1. Let The Good Times Roll & Feel So Good	Parkway 153

DATE	POS	WKS	ARTIST–RECORD TITLE	LABEL & NO.
			SILHOUETTES, The	
			R&B vocal group from Philadelphia, Pennsylvania: William Horton, Richard Lewis, Earl Beal and Raymond Edwards. Horton died on 1/23/95 (age 65). Edwards died of cancer on 3/4/97 (age 74). Beal died on 3/22/2001 (age 76).	
1/20/58	**1** (2)	13	● 1. **Get A Job** Top 100 #1 (2) / Best Seller #2 / Jockey #3	Ember 1029
			#1 R&B hit (6 weeks)	
			SILK	
			R&B vocal group from Atlanta, Georgia: Tim Cameron, Jim Gates, John Rasboro, Gary Jenkins and Gary Glenn.	
2/27/93	**1** (2)	22	▲ 1. **Freak Me** Airplay #1 (3) / Sales #1 (2)	Keia/Elektra 64654
			#1 R&B hit (8 weeks)	
7/10/93	**26**	6	2. Girl U For Me / Sales #30 / Airplay #38	
7/10/93		6	3. Lose Control Airplay #48	Keia/Elektra 64643
			above 3 co-written and co-produced by Keith Sweat	
3/13/99	**13**	15	● 4. If You (Lovin' Me) Sales #7 / Airplay #42	Elektra 64072
			SILKIE, The	
			Folk group formed in Hull, England: Silvia Tatler (vocals), Ivor Aylesbury and Mike Ramsden (guitars), and Kevin Cunningham (bass).	
11/6/65	**10**	7	1. **You've Got To Hide Your Love Away**	Fontana 1525
			The Beatles contributed musical accompaniment and production assistance; song is from The Beatles' movie *Help!*	
			SILKK THE SHOCKER	
			Born Zyshonne Miller on 2/22/80 in New Orleans, Louisiana. Male rapper. Brother of Master P and C-Murder. Member of the group Tru.	
9/6/97	**25**	13	● 1. I Miss My Homies Sales #15	No Limit 53290
			MASTER P Featuring Pimp C, The Shocker, Mo B. Dick, O'Dell, Sons of Funk and Mercedes	
2/7/98	**16**	25	▲ 2. Make Em' Say Uhh! Sales #9	No Limit 53302
			MASTER P Featuring Fiend, Silkk (The Shocker), Mia X and Mystikal	
3/28/98	**2** (2)	17	▲ 3. Let's Ride Sales #1 (1) / Airplay #55	Def Jam 568475
			MONTELL JORDAN Featuring Master P & Silkk "The Shocker"	
			#1 R&B hit (3 weeks)	
8/22/98	**27**	7	4. Goodbye To My Homies Sales #17	No Limit 53326
			MASTER P Featuring Silkk the Shocker, Sons of Funk and Mo B. Dick	
			samples "It's So Hard To Say Goodbye To Yesterday" by Boyz II Men	
9/12/98	**34**	10	5. Movin' On Airplay #38	University 95032
			MYA featuring Silkk the Shocker	
3/6/99	**18**	8	6. It Ain't My Fault 2 Sales #8	No Limit 53470
			SILKK THE SHOCKER And Mystikal	
			SILVER	
			Pop-rock group formed in Los Angeles, California: John Batdorf (vocals, guitar), Greg Collier (guitar), Brent Mydland (keyboards), Tom Leadon (bass) and Harry Stinson (drums). Mydland later joined the Grateful Dead; died of a drug overdose on 7/26/90 (age 37).	
8/7/76	**16**	12	1. Wham Bam	Arista 0189

DATE	POS	WKS	ARTIST–RECORD TITLE	LABEL & NO.
			SILVERCHAIR	
			Rock trio from Newcastle, Australia: Daniel Johns (vocals, guitar), Chris Joannou (bass) and Ben Gillies (drums). Johns married Natalie Imbruglia on 12/31/2003.	
8/12/95	28 ᴬ	11	1. Tomorrow	album cut
			#1 Mainstream Rock hit (3 weeks) / #1 Modern Rock hit (3 weeks); from the album *Frogstomp* on Epic 67247	
			SILVER CONDOR	
			Rock group from New York: Joe Cerisano (vocals), Earl Slick (guitar), John Corey (keyboards), Jay Davis (bass) and Claude Pepper (drums).	
8/29/81	32	4	1. You Could Take My Heart Away	Columbia 02268
			SILVER CONVENTION	
			Disco studio group from Germany. Vocals by Penny McLean, Ramona Wolf and Linda Thompson.	
10/25/75	1 (3)	13	● 1. **Fly, Robin, Fly** [I]	Midland Int'l. 10339
			#1 R&B hit (1 week)	
4/17/76	2 (3)	15	● 2. **Get Up And Boogie (That's Right)**	Midland Int'l. 10571
			SILVETTI	
			Born Bebu Silvetti in 1944 in Argentina. Died of cancer on 7/5/2003 (age 59). Disco producer.	
3/19/77	39	3	1. Spring Rain [I]	Salsoul 2014
			SIMEONE, Harry, Chorale	
			Born on 5/9/11 in Newark, New Jersey. Conductor/arranger.	
12/28/58	13	6	● 1. The Little Drummer Boy [X]	20th Fox 121
12/28/59	15	3	2. The Little Drummer Boy [X-R]	20th Fox 121
12/19/60	24	3	3. The Little Drummer Boy [X-R]	20th Fox 121
12/25/61	22	2	4. The Little Drummer Boy [X-R]	20th Fox 121
12/15/62	28	3	5. The Little Drummer Boy [X-R]	20th Fox 45-121
			SIMMONS, Gene	
			Born in 1933 in Tupelo, Mississippi. Nicknamed "Jumpin' Gene." Not to be confused with the leader of Kiss.	
8/29/64	11	8	1. Haunted House [N]	Hi 2076
			SIMMONS, Patrick—see DOOBIE BROTHERS, The	
			SIMON, Carly	
			Born on 6/25/45 in Manhattan, New York. Pop singer/songwriter/pianist. Father co-founded Simon & Schuster publishing. Folk duo with sister Lucy (The Simon Sisters) in the mid-1960s. Won the 1971 Best New Artist Grammy Award. Married to James Taylor from 1972-83.	
6/5/71	10	10	1. **That's The Way I've Always Heard It Should Be**	Elektra 45724
1/1/72	13	10	2. Anticipation	Elektra 45759
12/16/72+	1 (3)	14	● 3. **You're So Vain**	Elektra 45824
			#1 Adult Contemporary hit (2 weeks); Mick Jagger (backing vocal)	
4/21/73	17	9	4. The Right Thing To Do	Elektra 45843
2/16/74	5	13	● 5. **Mockingbird**	Elektra 45880

DATE	POS	WKS	ARTIST–RECORD TITLE	LABEL & NO.
6/1/74	**14**	6	6. Haven't Got Time For The Pain	Elektra 45887
5/24/75	**21**	5	7. Attitude Dancing	Elektra 45246
			Carole King (backing vocal)	
8/27/77	**2** (3)	15	● 8. **Nobody Does It Better**	Elektra 45413
			#1 Adult Contemporary hit (7 weeks); from the James Bond movie *The Spy Who Loved Me* starring Roger Moore	
5/6/78	**6**	11	9. **You Belong To Me**	Elektra 45477
			James Taylor (backing vocal)	
9/23/78	**36**	3	10. Devoted To You	Elektra 45506
			CARLY SIMON and JAMES TAYLOR	
8/23/80	**11**	13	● 11. Jesse	Warner 49518
12/6/86+	**18**	9	12. Coming Around Again Sales #15 / Airplay #30	Arista 9525
			from the movie *Heartburn* starring Meryl Streep and Jack Nicholson	
12/8/01	**28**	5	13. Son Of A Gun (I Betcha Think This Song Is About You) Airplay #26	Virgin 46171
			JANET Featuring Missy Elliott and P. Diddy with Carly Simon	
			samples "You're So Vain" by Simon	

SIMON, Joe

Born on 9/2/43 in Simmesport, Louisiana. R&B singer/songwriter.

DATE	POS	WKS	ARTIST–RECORD TITLE	LABEL & NO.
6/8/68	**25**	7	1. (You Keep Me) Hangin' On	Sound Stage 7 2608
3/29/69	**13**	11	● 2. The Chokin' Kind	Sound Stage 7 2628
			#1 R&B hit (3 weeks)	
2/6/71	**40**	3	3. Your Time To Cry	Spring 108
12/11/71+	**11**	11	● 4. Drowning In The Sea Of Love	Spring 120
8/19/72	**11**	8	● 5. Power Of Love	Spring 128
			#1 R&B hit (2 weeks)	
4/14/73	**37**	2	6. Step By Step	Spring 133
8/25/73	**18**	8	7. Theme From Cleopatra Jones	Spring 138
			JOE SIMON featuring The Mainstreeters	
			title song from the movie starring Tamara Dobson	
5/10/75	**8**	11	8. **Get Down, Get Down (Get On The Floor)**	Spring 156
			#1 R&B hit (2 weeks)	

SIMON, Paul

Born on 10/13/41 in Newark, New Jersey; raised in Queens, New York. Singer/songwriter/guitarist. Met Art Garfunkel in high school, recorded together as Tom & Jerry in 1957. Worked as Jerry Landis, Tico And The Triumphs, Paul Kane, Harrison Gregory and True Taylor in the early 1960s. To England from 1963-64. Returned to the U.S. and recorded first album with Garfunkel in 1964. Went solo in 1971. Married to actress/author Carrie Fisher from 1983-85. Married singer Edie Brickell on 5/30/92. In the movies *Annie Hall* and *One-Trick Pony*. Inducted into the Rock and Roll Hall of Fame in 2001.

DATE	POS	WKS	ARTIST–RECORD TITLE	LABEL & NO.
2/19/72	**4**	11	1. **Mother And Child Reunion**	Columbia 45547
4/22/72	**22**	8	2. Me And Julio Down By The Schoolyard	Columbia 45585
6/2/73	**2** (2)	11	3. **Kodachrome**	Columbia 45859
8/18/73	**2** (1)	14	● 4. **Loves Me Like A Rock**	Columbia 45907
			PAUL SIMON (with The Dixie Hummingbirds)	
			#1 Adult Contemporary hit (2 weeks)	
1/5/74	**35**	3	5. American Tune	Columbia 45900
9/6/75	**23**	6	6. Gone At Last	Columbia 10197
			PAUL SIMON/PHOEBE SNOW and The Jessy Dixon Singers	

DATE	POS	WKS	ARTIST–RECORD TITLE	LABEL & NO.
1/3/76	**1** (3)	13	● 7. **50 Ways To Leave Your Lover** #1 Adult Contemporary hit (2 weeks); Patti Austin, Phoebe Snow and Valerie Simpson (backing vocals)	Columbia 10270
5/29/76	**40**	2	8. Still Crazy After All These Years	Columbia 10332
11/5/77+	**5**	14	● 9. **Slip Slidin' Away** Oak Ridge Boys (backing vocals)	Columbia 10630
2/11/78	**17**	7	10. (What A) Wonderful World **ART GARFUNKEL with JAMES TAYLOR & PAUL SIMON** #1 Adult Contemporary hit (5 weeks)	Columbia 10676
8/16/80	**6**	12	11. **Late In The Evening**	Warner 49511
11/22/80	**40**	2	12. One-Trick Pony above 2 from the movie *One-Trick Pony* starring Simon	Warner 49601
4/25/87	**23**	7	13. You Can Call Me Al Airplay #20 / Sales #27	Warner 28667

SIMON & GARFUNKEL

Folk-rock duo from New York: Paul Simon and Art Garfunkel. Recorded as Tom & Jerry in 1957. Duo split in 1964; Simon was working solo in England; Garfunkel was in graduate school. They re-formed in 1965 and stayed together until 1971. Reunited in 1981 and 2003 for national tours. Inducted into the Rock and Roll Hall of Fame in 1990.

DATE	POS	WKS	ARTIST–RECORD TITLE	LABEL & NO.
12/4/65+	**1** (2)	12	● 1. **The Sounds Of Silence**	Columbia 43396
2/26/66	**5**	10	2. **Homeward Bound**	Columbia 43511
5/14/66	**3**	10	3. **I Am A Rock**	Columbia 43617
8/27/66	**25**	4	4. The Dangling Conversation	Columbia 43728
11/19/66	**13**	6	5. A Hazy Shade Of Winter	Columbia 43873
4/1/67	**16**	7	6. At The Zoo	Columbia 44046
8/12/67	**23**	5	7. Fakin' It	Columbia 44232
3/16/68	**11**	9	8. Scarborough Fair (/Canticle) a medieval folk ballad first published in 1673; song also known as "Parsley, Sage, Rosemary And Thyme"	Columbia 44465
5/4/68	**1** (3)	12	● 9. **Mrs. Robinson** 1968 Grammy winner: Record of the Year; above 2 from the movie *The Graduate* starring Dustin Hoffman and Anne Bancroft (soundtrack versions of "Mrs. Robinson" are different)	Columbia 44511
4/19/69	**7**	9	10. **The Boxer**	Columbia 44785
2/14/70	**1** (6)	13	● 11. **Bridge Over Troubled Water** #1 Adult Contemporary hit (6 weeks); Larry Knechtel (piano); 1970 Grammy winner: Record of the Year	Columbia 45079
4/18/70	**4**	12	● 12. **Cecilia**	Columbia 45133
9/26/70	**18**	8	13. El Condor Pasa	Columbia 45237
11/1/75	**9**	9	14. **My Little Town** #1 Adult Contemporary hit (2 weeks)	Columbia 10230
5/1/82	**27**	6	15. Wake Up Little Susie **[L]** recorded on 9/19/81 in New York's Central Park	Warner 50053

SIMONE, Nina

Born Eunice Waymon on 2/21/33 in Tryon, South Carolina. Died of cancer on 4/21/2003 (age 70). Jazz-styled singer.

DATE	POS	WKS	ARTIST–RECORD TITLE	LABEL & NO.
8/24/59	**18**	11	1. I Loves You, Porgy from folk opera *Porgy And Bess*	Bethlehem 11021

DATE	POS	WKS	ARTIST–RECORD TITLE	LABEL & NO.
			SIMPLE MINDS	
			Pop-rock group formed in Glasgow, Scotland: Jim Kerr (vocals), Charles Burchill (guitar, keyboards), Michael MacNeil (keyboards), John Giblin (bass) and Mel Gaynor (drums). MacNeil and Giblin left in 1989. Kerr was married to Chrissie Hynde of The Pretenders from 1984-90.	
3/23/85	1 (1)	14	1. **Don't You (Forget About Me)** Sales #1 (2) / Airplay #1 (1) #1 Mainstream Rock hit (3 weeks); from the movie *The Breakfast Club* starring Molly Ringwald and Emilio Estevez	A&M 2703
10/26/85	3	16	2. **Alive & Kicking** Airplay #3 / Sales #5	A&M 2783
2/8/86	14	9	3. **Sanctify Yourself** Airplay #14 / Sales #16	A&M 2810
5/3/86	28	6	4. **All The Things She Said** Airplay #26 / Sales #27	A&M 2828
6/29/91	40	1	5. See The Lights Airplay #72 #1 Modern Rock hit (2 weeks)	A&M 1553
			SIMPLE PLAN	
			Punk-rock group from Montreal, Quebec, Canada: Pierre Bouvier (vocals), Jeff Stinco (guitar), Seb Lefebvre (guitar), David Desrosiers (bass) and Chuck Comeau (drums).	
12/6/03	24	11	1. Perfect Airplay #25 from the album *No Pads, No Helmets...Just Balls* on Lava 83534	album cut
			SIMPLY RED	
			Born Mick Hucknall on 6/8/60 in Denton, Manchester, England. "Blue-eyed soul" singer. Nicknamed "Red" because of his red hair. His backing group included Fritz McIntyre and Tim Kellett (keyboards), Sylvan Richardson (guitar), Tony Bowers (bass) and Chris Joyce (drums).	
5/10/86	1 (1)	14	1. **Holding Back The Years** Sales #1 (1) / Airplay #3	Elektra 69564
8/30/86	28	6	2. **Money$ Too Tight (To Mention)** Airplay #27 / Sales #29	Elektra 69528
4/18/87	27	6	3. The Right Thing Sales #26 / Airplay #26	Elektra 69487
5/27/89	1 (1)	15	● 4. **If You Don't Know Me By Now** Sales #1 (1) / Airplay #1 (1) #1 Adult Contemporary hit (6 weeks)	Elektra 69297
11/2/91	23	4	5. Something Got Me Started Airplay #43	EastWest 98711
			SIMPSON, Jessica	
			Born on 7/10/80 in Waco, Texas; raised in Richardson, Texas. Pop-dance singer. Began career singing on the Christian Youth Conference circuit, which included Kirk Franklin and CeCe Winans. Married Nick Lachey (of 98°) on 10/26/2002 (they appear as themselves in the MTV reality series *Newlyweds*).	
10/23/99	3	17	▲ 1. **I Wanna Love You Forever** Sales #1 (6) / Airplay #20	Columbia 79262
7/22/00	21	9	2. I Think I'm In Love With You Airplay #17 samples "Jack And Diane" by John Mellencamp	Columbia 79467
6/9/01	15	13	3. Irresistible Airplay #13	Columbia 79578
			SIMPSONS, The	
			The voices of the Fox network's animated TV series. Nancy Cartwright is Bart; Dan Castellaneta is Homer; Julie Kavner is Marge; Yeardley Smith is Lisa; and the show's creator Matt Groening is Maggie.	
12/15/90+	11 ^A	9	1. Do The Bartman **[N]** from the album *The Simpsons Sing The Blues* on Geffen 24308	album cut
			SIMS, Kym	
			Born on 12/28/66 in Chicago, Illinois. Dance singer/songwriter.	
2/1/92	38	1	1. Too Blind To See It Airplay #22	Atco 98667

DATE	POS	WKS	ARTIST–RECORD TITLE	LABEL & NO.
			SINATRA, Frank	
			Born on 12/12/15 in Hoboken, New Jersey. Died of a heart attack on 5/14/98 (age 82). With Harry James from 1939-40; with Tommy Dorsey, 1940-42. Went solo in late 1942. Starred in several movies. Won an Oscar for the movie *From Here To Eternity* in 1953. Own TV show in 1957. Own Reprise record company In 1961, sold to Warner Bros. in 1963. Won Grammy's Lifetime Achievement Award in 1965. Married to actress Ava Gardner from 1951-57. Married to actress Mia Farrow from 1966-68. Father of Nancy Sinatra. Regarded by many as the greatest popular singer of the 20th century.	
1/22/55	19	4	1. Melody Of Love Jockey #19 **FRANK SINATRA and RAY ANTHONY And His Orchestra**	Capitol 3018
5/7/55	1 (2)	21	2. **Learnin' The Blues** Jockey #1 (2) / Juke Box #2 / Best Seller #2	Capitol 3102
9/24/55	13	5	3. Same Old Saturday Night Jockey #13 / Top 100 #65	Capitol 3218
11/5/55	5	15	4. **Love And Marriage** Top 100 #5 / Jockey #5 / Best Seller #6 / Juke Box #7 introduced by Sinatra on TV's *Producer's Showcase* production of *Our Town* (9/19/55); Sinatra's version later used as the theme for the TV series *Married With Children*	Capitol 3260
12/17/55+	7	9	5. **(Love Is) The Tender Trap** Jockey #7 / Top 100 #23 / Best Seller #24 from the movie *The Tender Trap* starring Sinatra	Capitol 3290
3/24/56	21	3	6. Flowers Mean Forgiveness Jockey #21 / Top 100 #35	Capitol 3350
6/2/56	13	6	7. (How Little It Matters) How Little We Know Jockey #13 / Top 100 #30	Capitol 3423
11/3/56+	3	17	8. **Hey! Jealous Lover** Jockey #3 / Top 100 #6 / Juke Box #7 / Best Seller #8	Capitol 3552
2/9/57	15	6	9. Can I Steal A Little Love Jockey #15 / Top 100 #20 from the movie *Rock Pretty Baby* starring Sal Mineo	Capitol 3608
7/22/57	25	1	10. You're Cheatin' Yourself (If You're Cheatin' On Me) Jockey #25	Capitol 3744
10/28/57+	2 (1)	17	11. **All The Way** Jockey #2 / Best Seller #15 / Top 100 #15 from the movie *The Joker Is Wild* starring Sinatra	Capitol 3793
1/20/58	6	14	12. **Witchcraft** Jockey #6 / Best Seller #20 / Top 100 #20	Capitol 3859
5/12/58	22	1	13. How Are Ya' Fixed For Love? Jockey #22 / Top 100 #97 **FRANK SINATRA and KEELY SMITH**	Capitol 3952
9/7/59	30	1	14. High Hopes **FRANK SINATRA "and a bunch of kids"** from the movie *A Hole In The Head* starring Sinatra	Capitol 4214
11/16/59	38	3	15. Talk To Me	Capitol 4284
11/28/60	25	2	16. Ol' Mac Donald adaptation of a children's song originating in the early 1700s	Capitol 4466
1/20/62	34	3	17. Pocketful Of Miracles title song from the movie starring Bette Davis	Reprise 20,040
10/10/64	27	6	18. Softly, As I Leave You	Reprise 0301
1/30/65	32	3	19. Somewhere In Your Heart	Reprise 0332
1/15/66	28	4	20. It Was A Very Good Year #1 Adult Contemporary hit (1 week)	Reprise 0429
5/28/66	1 (1)	11	● 21. **Strangers In The Night** #1 Adult Contemporary hit (7 weeks); from the movie *A Man Could Get Killed* starring James Garner; 1966 Grammy winner: Record of the Year	Reprise 0470
9/17/66	25	5	22. Summer Wind #1 Adult Contemporary hit (1 week)	Reprise 0509
12/3/66	4	9	23. **That's Life** #1 Adult Contemporary hit (3 weeks)	Reprise 0531

DATE	POS	WKS	ARTIST–RECORD TITLE	LABEL & NO.
3/25/67	**1** (4)	11	● 24. **Somethin' Stupid** **NANCY SINATRA & FRANK SINATRA** #1 Adult Contemporary hit (9 weeks)	Reprise 0561
8/26/67	30	4	25. The World We Knew (Over And Over) #1 Adult Contemporary hit (5 weeks)	Reprise 0610
11/16/68	23	5	26. Cycles	Reprise 0764
4/12/69	27	6	27. My Way French song ("Comme d'Habitude") with English lyrics by Paul Anka	Reprise 0817
5/31/80	32	6	28. Theme From New York, New York introduced in the movie musical *New York, New York* by Liza Minnelli (her version "Bubbled Under" at #104 in 1977)	Reprise 49233

SINATRA, Nancy

Born on 6/8/40 in Jersey City, New Jersey; raised in Los Angeles, California. Daughter of Frank Sinatra. Married to Tommy Sands from 1960-65. Appeared in the movies *For Those Who Think Young, Get Yourself A College Girl, The Oscar* and *Speedway*.

DATE	POS	WKS	ARTIST–RECORD TITLE	LABEL & NO.
2/5/66	**1** (1)	12	● 1. **These Boots Are Made For Walkin'**	Reprise 0432
4/30/66	7	7	2. **How Does That Grab You, Darlin'?**	Reprise 0461
7/30/66	36	2	3. Friday's Child	Reprise 0491
12/10/66	5	9	● 4. **Sugar Town** #1 Adult Contemporary hit (2 weeks)	Reprise 0527
3/25/67	**1** (4)	11	● 5. **Somethin' Stupid** **NANCY SINATRA & FRANK SINATRA** #1 Adult Contemporary hit (9 weeks)	Reprise 0561
4/8/67	15	5	6. Love Eyes	Reprise 0559
7/8/67	14	7	7. Jackson **NANCY SINATRA & LEE HAZLEWOOD**	Reprise 0595
10/7/67	24	4	8. Lightning's Girl	Reprise 0620
11/4/67	20	4	9. Lady Bird **NANCY SINATRA & LEE HAZLEWOOD**	Reprise 0629
1/27/68	26	5	10. Some Velvet Morning **NANCY SINATRA & LEE HAZLEWOOD**	Reprise 0651

SINCLAIR, Gordon

Born on 6/3/1900 in Toronto, Ontario, Canada. Died on 5/17/84 (age 83). Broadcaster/author.

DATE	POS	WKS	ARTIST–RECORD TITLE	LABEL & NO.
1/26/74	24	4	1. The Americans (A Canadian's Opinion) **[S]** originally broadcast as an editorial on CFRB-Toronto on 6/5/73	Avco 4628

SINGING DOGS, The

Actual recordings of dogs barking, produced by Don Charles in Copenhagen. The dogs: Dolly, Pearl, Caesar and King.

DATE	POS	WKS	ARTIST–RECORD TITLE	LABEL & NO.
12/17/55	22	1	1. Oh! Susanna Best Seller #22 / Top 100 #37 **[N]**	RCA Victor 6344

SINGING NUN, The

Born Jeanine Deckers on 10/17/33 in Fichermont, Belgium. Committed suicide on 3/31/85 (age 51). Actual nun; assumed the name Sister Luc-Gabrielle. Recorded under the name Soeur Sourire ("Sister Smile").

DATE	POS	WKS	ARTIST–RECORD TITLE	LABEL & NO.
11/16/63	**1** (4)	12	1. **Dominique** **[F]** #1 Adult Contemporary hit (4 weeks)	Philips 40152

DATE	POS	WKS	ARTIST–RECORD TITLE	LABEL & NO.
			SIOUXSIE AND THE BANSHEES	
			Avant-punk group formed by singer Siouxsie Sioux (Susan Dallion) and bassist Steve Severin (Steve Havoc). Fluctuating personnel around group's nucleus: Sioux, Severin and Peter "Budgie" Clark (drums). Husband-and-wife, Sioux and Budgie, also recorded as The Creatures.	
9/21/91	23	6	1. Kiss Them For Me Airplay #50 / Sales #58 #1 Modern Rock hit (5 weeks)	Geffen 19031
			SIR DOUGLAS QUINTET	
			Rock group formed in Houston, Texas: Doug Sahm (vocals, guitar), Augie Myers (organ), Frank Morin (horns), Harvey Regan (bass) and John Perez (drums). Sahm died of heart failure on 11/18/99 (age 58).	
4/17/65	13	9	1. She's About A Mover	Tribe 8308
3/5/66	31	5	2. The Rains Came	Tribe 8314
3/15/69	27	6	3. Mendocino	Smash 2191
			SIR MIX-A-LOT	
			Born Anthony Ray on 8/12/63 in Seattle, Washington. Male rapper. Appeared as the host of the anthology TV series *The Watcher*.	
5/2/92	1 (5)	24	▲² 1. **Baby Got Back** Sales #1 (9) / Airplay #16	Def American 18947
			SISQÓ	
			Born Mark Andrews on 11/9/78 in Baltimore, Maryland. R&B singer/songwriter. Member of Dru Hill. Appeared as "Dr. Rupert Brooks" in the 2002 movie *Snow Dogs*.	
4/11/98	6	14	● 1. It's All About Me Sales #5 / Airplay #50 **MYA With Special Guest SISQO** samples "Moments In Love" by The Art Of Noise	University 97024
1/22/00	40	1	2. Got To Get It Airplay #33 **SISQÓ (featuring Make It Hot)**	Dragon 562455
2/12/00	3	24	3. **Thong Song** Airplay #1 (7) / Sales #67 samples "Livin' La Vida Loca" by Ricky Martin; from the movie *Nutty Professor II: The Klumps* starring Eddie Murphy and Janet Jackson	Def Soul 562599
8/5/00	1 (2)	19	▲ 4. **Incomplete** Sales #1 (4) / Airplay #15 #1 R&B hit (5 weeks); Shae Jones (backing vocal)	Def Soul 562854
			SISTER HAZEL	
			Pop-rock group formed in Gainesville, Florida: Ken Block (vocals), Ryan Newell and Andrew Copeland (guitars), Jeff Beres (bass) and Mark Trojanowski (drums).	
7/12/97	11	33	1. All For You Airplay #7 / Sales #31	Universal 56135
			SISTER SLEDGE	
			Dance vocal group from Philadelphia, Pennsylvania: sisters Debra, Joni, Kim and Kathy Sledge.	
3/10/79	9	13	1. **He's The Greatest Dancer** #1 R&B hit (1 week)	Cotillion 44245
5/12/79	2 (2)	11	● 2. **We Are Family** #1 R&B hit (1 week)	Cotillion 44251
3/6/82	23	6	3. My Guy	Cotillion 47000
			SISTERS WITH VOICES — see SWV	

DATE	POS	WKS	ARTIST–RECORD TITLE	LABEL & NO.
			SIXPENCE NONE THE RICHER	
			Pop group from Austin, Texas: Leigh Nash (vocals), Matt Slocum and Sean Kelly (guitars), Justin Cary (bass) and Dale Baker (drums).	
2/27/99	**2** (1)	28	● 1. **Kiss Me** Airplay #2 / Sales #5	Squint 79101
			from the movie She's All That starring Freddie Prinze, Jr.	
10/2/99	**32**	7	2. There She Goes Airplay #23	album cut
			from the album Sixpence None The Richer on Squint 7032	
			SIX TEENS, The	
			Black teen R&B vocal group from Los Angeles, California: Trudy Williams, Ken Sinclair, Ed Wells, Richard Owens, Darryl Lewis, Beverly Pecot and Louise Williams. Wells died on 2/20/2001 (age 63). Sinclair died of cancer on 3/16/2003 (age 63).	
9/1/56	**25**	1	1. A Casual Look Best Seller #25 / Top 100 #48	Flip 315
			69 BOYZ	
			Bass-rap group from Jacksonville, Florida. Led by rappers Albert Bryant and Mike Phillips. Produced by Nathaniel "C.C. Lemonhead" Orange and Johnny "Jay-Ski" McGowan (they also produced 95 South and formed Quad City DJ's).	
8/6/94+	**8**	31	▲ 1. **Tootsee Roll** Sales #3 / Airplay #38	Down Low 6911
			produced by 95 South	
8/1/98	**31**	4	2. Woof Woof Sales #20	Atlantic 84123
			from the movie Dr. Dolittle starring Eddie Murphy	
			SKEE-LO	
			Born Anthony Roundtree on 3/5/75 in Riverside, California. Male rapper.	
7/29/95	**13**	13	● 1. I Wish Sales #7 / Airplay #58	Sunshine 78032
			SKID ROW	
			Hard-rock group formed in New Jersey: Sebastian Bach (vocals), Dave Sabo and Scott Hill (guitars), Rachel Bolan (bass) and Rob Affuso (drums).	
7/29/89	**4**	13	● 1. **18 And Life** Sales #4 / Airplay #6	Atlantic 88883
12/9/89+	**6**	13	2. **I Remember You** Sales #3 / Airplay #13	Atlantic 88886
			SKIP & FLIP	
			Duo of Gary "Flip" Paxton and Clyde "Skip" Battin. Paxton formed the Hollywood Argyles and later started own Garpax record label. Battin died of Alzheimer's disease on 7/6/2003 (age 69).	
7/27/59	**11**	9	1. It Was I	Brent 7002
4/25/60	**11**	10	2. Cherry Pie	Brent 7010
			first recorded by Marvin & Johnny in 1954	
			SKYLARK	
			Pop group from Vancouver, British Columbia, Canada: Donny Gerrard and Bonnie Jean Cook (vocals), with David Foster (keyboards) and Duris Maxwell (drums). Foster was later a prolific producer/songwriter.	
3/31/73	**9**	14	1. **Wildflower**	Capitol 3511

DATE	POS	WKS	ARTIST–RECORD TITLE	LABEL & NO.
			SKYLINERS, The	
			White doo-wop group from Pittsburgh, Pennsylvania: Jimmy Beaumont, Janet Vogel, Wally Lester and Joe VerScharen, with Jackie Taylor (guitar). Vogel committed suicide on 2/21/80.	
3/23/59	12	10	1. Since I Don't Have You	Calico 103
6/15/59	26	7	2. This I Swear	Calico 106
6/20/60	24	6	3. Pennies From Heaven	Calico 117
			#1 hit for Bing Crosby in 1936	
			SKYY	
			R&B-pop-dance group from Brooklyn, New York: sisters Denise, Delores and Bonnie Dunning (vocals), Solomon Roberts (vocals, guitar), Anibal Sierra (guitar), Larry Greenberg (keyboards), Gerald LaBon (bass) and Tommy McConnell (drums).	
2/20/82	26	4	1. Call Me	Salsoul 2152
			#1 R&B hit (2 weeks)	
			SLADE	
			Hard-rock group formed in Wolverhampton, England: Noddy Holder (vocals), David Hill (guitar), Jim Lea (bass, keyboards) and Don Powell (drums).	
5/5/84	20	8	1. Run Runaway	CBS Associated 04398
			#1 Mainstream Rock hit (2 weeks)	
8/11/84	37	3	2. My Oh My	CBS Associated 04528
			SLAUGHTER	
			Hard-rock group formed in Las Vegas, Nevada: Mark Slaughter (vocals), Tim Kelly (guitar), Dana Strum (bass) and Blas Elias (drums). Kelly died in a car crash on 2/5/98 (age 35).	
6/2/90	27	6	1. Up All Night Sales #15	Chrysalis 23486
9/22/90	19	8	2. Fly To The Angels Sales #9 / Airplay #35	Chrysalis 23527
2/16/91	39	1	3. Spend My Life Sales #27	Chrysalis 23605
			SLAVE	
			R&B-funk band from Dayton, Ohio: Mike Williamson (vocals), Dan Webster (guitar), Steve Washington and Floyd Miller (horns), Mark Hicks (keyboards), Mark Adams (bass) and Roger Parker (drums).	
7/23/77	32	6	1. Slide [I]	Cotillion 44218
			#1 R&B hit (1 week)	
			SLEDGE, Percy	
			Born on 11/25/40 in Leighton, Alabama. R&B singer.	
4/30/66	1 (2)	10	● 1. **When A Man Loves A Woman**	Atlantic 2326
			#1 R&B hit (4 weeks)	
8/6/66	17	6	2. Warm And Tender Love	Atlantic 2342
11/19/66	20	7	3. It Tears Me Up	Atlantic 2358
7/22/67	40	1	4. Love Me Tender	Atlantic 2414
			adapted from the 1861 tune "Aura Lee"	
4/6/68	11	11	5. Take Time To Know Her	Atlantic 2490

DATE	POS	WKS	ARTIST–RECORD TITLE	LABEL & NO.
			SLICK RICK	
			Born Ricky Walters on 1/14/65 in South Wimbledon, London, England (to Jamaican parents). Male rapper. Moved to New York City in 1979.	
8/10/91	40 S	1	1. I Shouldn't Have Done It	Def Jam 73739
7/6/96	28	9	2. I Like Sales #14	Def Jam/RAL 575046
			MONTELL JORDAN FEATURING SLICK RICK	
			samples "I Get Lifted" by KC & The Sunshine Band; from the movie *The Nutty Professor* starring Eddie Murphy	
			SLY & THE FAMILY STONE	
			Interracial "psychedelic soul" group from San Francsico, California: Sylvester "Sly Stone" Stewart (lead singer, keyboards; born on 3/15/44 in Dallas, Texas), Sly's brother Freddie Stone (guitar), Cynthia Robinson (trumpet), Jerry Martini (sax), Sly's sister Rosie Stone (piano, vocals), Sly's cousin Larry Graham (bass) and Gregg Errico (drums). Graham formed Graham Central Station in 1973. Martini later joined Rubicon. Group inducted into the Rock and Roll Hall of Fame in 1993.	
3/2/68	8	12	1. **Dance To The Music**	Epic 10256
1/4/69	1 (4)	14	● 2. **Everyday People**	Epic 10407
			#1 R&B hit (2 weeks)	
4/26/69	22	6	3. Stand!	Epic 10450
8/30/69	2 (2)	13	4. **Hot Fun In The Summertime**	Epic 10497
1/10/70	1 (2)	12	● 5. **Thank You (Falettinme Be Mice Elf Agin) /**	
			#1 R&B hit (5 weeks)	
1/10/70		12	6. Everybody Is A Star	Epic 10555
6/20/70	38	3	7. I Want To Take You Higher [R]	Epic 10450
			originally charted at #60 in 1969	
11/13/71	1 (3)	13	● 8. **Family Affair**	Epic 10805
			#1 R&B hit (5 weeks)	
2/26/72	23	6	9. Runnin' Away	Epic 10829
7/14/73	12	13	● 10. If You Want Me To Stay	Epic 11017
8/17/74	32	3	11. Time For Livin'	Epic 11140
			all of above written and produced by Sly Stone	
			SLY FOX	
			Biracial pop-dance duo: Gary "Mudbone" Cooper and Michael Camacho.	
2/15/86	7	14	1. **Let's Go All The Way** Sales #6 / Airplay #7	Capitol 5552
			originally released on Capitol 5463	
			SMALL, Millie	
			Born Millicent Small on 10/6/46 in Jamaica. Reggae-ska singer. Nicknamed "The Blue Beat Girl."	
6/6/64	2 (1)	9	1. **My Boy Lollipop**	Smash 1893
9/5/64	40	2	2. Sweet William	Smash 1920
			SMALL FACES	
			Rock group formed in England: Steve Marriott (vocals, guitar), Ian McLagan (organ), Ronnie Lane (bass) and Kenney Jones (drums). In 1968, Marriott formed Humble Pie. In 1969, remaining members formed Faces with former Jeff Beck Group members Rod Stewart (vocals) and Ron Wood (bass). Wood joined the Rolling Stones in 1976. Jones joined the Who in 1978. Marriott died in a fire on 4/20/91 (age 44). Lane died of multiple sclerosis on 6/4/97 (age 51).	
1/13/68	16	8	1. Itchycoo Park	Immediate 501
			SMALL FACES	

DATE	POS	WKS	ARTIST–RECORD TITLE	LABEL & NO.
11/27/71	**24**	6	2. (I Know) I'm Losing You **ROD STEWART With Faces**	Mercury 73244
1/15/72	**17**	8	3. Stay With Me **FACES**	Warner 7545

SMASHING PUMPKINS, The

Rock group formed in Chicago, Illinois: Billy Corgan (vocals, guitar), James Iha (guitar), D'Arcy Wretzky (bass) and Jimmy Chamberlin (drums). Touring keyboardist Jonathan Melvoin, brother of Wendy Melvoin (of Prince's Revolution), died of a heroin overdose on 7/12/96 (age 34).

DATE	POS	WKS	ARTIST–RECORD TITLE	LABEL & NO.
11/19/94	**30** ᴬ	4	1. Landslide first recorded by Fleetwood Mac in 1975; from the album *Pisces Isacariot* on Virgin 39834	album cut
11/11/95+	**22**	12	● 2. Bullet With Butterfly Wings Sales #20 / Airplay #26	Virgin 38522
2/10/96	**12**	19	● 3. 1979 Airplay #9 / Sales #24 #1 Mainstream Rock hit (2 weeks) / #1 Modern Rock hit (1 week)	Virgin 38534
7/13/96	**36**	6	4. Tonight, Tonight Airplay #33 / Sales #44	Virgin 38547
2/1/97	**39**	2	5. Thirty-Three Airplay #42 / Sales #51	Virgin 38574

SMASH MOUTH

Pop-rock group from San Jose, California: Steve Harwell (vocals), Greg Camp (guitar), Paul DeLisle (bass) and Kevin Coleman (drums).

DATE	POS	WKS	ARTIST–RECORD TITLE	LABEL & NO.
9/6/97+	**2** (1)ᴬ	49	1. **Walkin' On The Sun** #1 Modern Rock hit (5 weeks); from the album *Fush Yu Mang* on Interscope 90142	album cut
7/18/98	**27** ᴬ	7	2. Can't Get Enough Of You Baby from the movie *Can't Hardly Wait* starring Jennifer Love Hewitt (soundtrack on Elektra 62201)	album cut
6/5/99	**4**	27	3. **All Star** Airplay #1 (5) from the movie *Mystery Men* starring Ben Stiller	album cut
11/27/99+	**11**	20	4. Then The Morning Comes Airplay #8 above 2 from the album *Astro Lounge* on Interscope 90316	album cut
8/18/01	**25**	6	5. I'm A Believer Airplay #24 from the animated movie *Shrek* (soundtrack on DreamWorks 450305)	album cut

SMILEZ & SOUTHSTAR

Male rap duo from Orlando, Florida: Rodney "Smilez" Bailey and Robert "Southstar" Campman.

DATE	POS	WKS	ARTIST–RECORD TITLE	LABEL & NO.
2/8/03	**28**	6	1. Tell Me (What's Goin' On) Airplay #29 samples "Stop, Look, Listen (To Your Heart)" by The Stylistics; from the album *Crash The Party* on Artist Direct 01030	album cut

SMITH

Pop-rock group from Los Angeles, California: Gayle McCormick (vocals), Rick Cliburn and Alan Parker (guitars), Larry Moss (keyboards), Jerry Carter (bass) and Robert Evans (drums).

DATE	POS	WKS	ARTIST–RECORD TITLE	LABEL & NO.
10/4/69	**5**	11	1. **Baby It's You**	Dunhill/ABC 4206

SMITH, Frankie

Born in Philadelphia, Pennsylvania. R&B singer/songwriter/producer.

DATE	POS	WKS	ARTIST–RECORD TITLE	LABEL & NO.
7/11/81	**30**	7	● 1. Double Dutch Bus **[N]** #1 R&B hit (4 weeks)	WMOT 5356

DATE	POS	WKS	ARTIST–RECORD TITLE	LABEL & NO.
			SMITH, Huey (Piano), And The Clowns	
			Born on 1/26/34 in New Orleans, Louisiana. The Clowns featured lead singer Bobby Marchan.	
3/31/58	9	9	1. **Don't You Just Know It** Top 100 #9 / Best Seller #13	Ace 545
			SMITH, Hurricane	
			Born Norman Smith on 2/22/23 in London, England. Pop singer/producer.	
12/23/72+	3	12	1. **Oh, Babe, What Would You Say?**	Capitol 3383
			SMITH, Jimmy	
			Born on 12/8/25 in Norristown, Pennsylvania. Jazz organist.	
6/9/62	21	7	1. Walk On The Wild Side (Part 1) [I] **JIMMY SMITH AND THE BIG BAND** title song from the movie starring Laurence Harvey and Jane Fonda	Verve 10255
			SMITH, Keely — see PRIMA, Louis / SINATRA, Frank	
			SMITH, Michael W.	
			Born Michael Whitaker Smith on 10/7/57 in Kenova, West Virginia. Contemporary Christian singer/songwriter/keyboardist.	
6/8/91	6	11	1. **Place In This World** Airplay #17 / Sales #21 co-written by Amy Grant	Reunion 19019
10/31/92	27	5	2. I Will Be Here For You Airplay #36 / Sales #37 #1 Adult Contemporary hit (2 weeks)	Reunion/Geffen 19139
			SMITH, O.C.	
			Born Ocie Lee Smith on 6/21/36 in Mansfield, Louisiana; raised in Los Angeles, California. Died on 11/23/2001 (age 65). Male R&B singer.	
4/20/68	40	2	1. The Son Of Hickory Holler's Tramp	Columbia 44425
9/21/68	2 (1)	12	● 2. **Little Green Apples**	Columbia 44616
9/20/69	34	2	3. Daddy's Little Man	Columbia 44948
			SMITH, Patti, Group	
			Born on 12/31/46 in Chicago, Illinois; raised in New Jersey. Punk-rock singer. Her group: Lenny Kaye (guitar), Richard Sohl (keyboards), Ivan Kral (bass) and J.D. Daughtery (drums). Sohl died on 6/3/90 (age 37). Not to be confused with Patty Smyth of Scandal.	
5/13/78	13	9	1. Because The Night written by Smith and Bruce Springsteen	Arista 0318
			SMITH, Ray	
			Born on 10/31/34 in Melber, Kentucky. Committed suicide on 11/29/79 (age 45). Rockabilly singer/guitarist.	
2/1/60	22	8	1. Rockin' Little Angel melody adapted from the 1844 tune "Buffalo Gals"	Judd 1016
			SMITH, Rex	
			Born on 9/19/56 in Jacksonville, Florida. Actor/singer. Acted in several movies and Broadway shows. Brother of Michael Lee Smith of Starz.	
5/12/79	10	10	● 1. **You Take My Breath Away** introduced by Smith on 3/25/79 in the TV movie Sooner Or Later	Columbia 10908

DATE	POS	WKS	ARTIST–RECORD TITLE	LABEL & NO.
8/8/81	**32**	4	2. Everlasting Love **REX SMITH/RACHEL SWEET**	Columbia 02169
			SMITH, Sammi	
			Born Jewel Fay Smith on 8/5/43 in Orange, California; raised in Oklahoma. Female country singer.	Mega 0015
2/20/71	**8**	11	● 1. **Help Me Make It Through The Night** #1 Country hit (3 weeks); written by Kris Kristofferson	
			SMITH, Somethin', & The Redheads	
			Adult Contemporary (1930s-styled) trio from Los Angeles, California: Smith (vocals, guitar), Saul Striks (piano) and Major Short (violin).	
4/2/55	**7**	23	1. **It's A Sin To Tell A Lie** Best Seller #7/ Juke Box #8 / Jockey #9 #1 hit for Fats Waller in 1936	Epic 9093
7/14/56	**27**	3	2. In A Shanty In Old Shanty Town Top 100 #27 #1 hit for Ted Lewis in 1932	Epic 9168
			SMITH, Verdelle	
			Born on 8/28/30 in St. Petersburg, Florida. Black female singer.	
8/13/66	**38**	2	1. Tar And Cement	Capitol 5632
			SMITH, Whistling Jack	
			Studio session production featuring the Mike Sammes Singers. Billy Moeller (born on 2/2/46 in Liverpool, England) was later hired to tour as Whistling Jack Smith. Not to be confused with the 1920s singer "Whispering" Jack Smith.	
5/13/67	**20**	5	1. I Was Kaiser Bill's Batman **[I]**	Deram 85005
			SMITH, Will	
			Born on 9/25/68 in Philadelphia, Pennsylvania. Rapper/actor. One-half of D.J. Jazzy Jeff & The Fresh Prince (1986-93). Starred on TV's *Fresh Prince of Bel Air* and in such movies as *Bad Boys, Independence Day, Men In Black* and *Enemy Of The State*. Married actress Jada Pinkett on 12/31/97.	
7/5/97	**1** (4)ᴬ	22	1. **Men In Black** samples "Forget Me Nots" by Patrice Rushen; from the movie *Men In Black* starring Smith and Tommy Lee Jones (soundtrack on Columbia 68169)	album cut
2/28/98	**1** (3)	28	● 2. **Gettin' Jiggy Wit It** Sales #1 (2) / Airplay #8 samples "He's The Greatest Dancer" by Sister Sledge, "Sang And Dance" by The Bar-Kays and "Love Rap" by Spoonie Gee	Columbia 78804
10/10/98	**20**	8	3. Just The Two Of Us Airplay #6 / Sales #30	Columbia 79038
12/12/98+	**17**	18	4. Miami Airplay #8 samples "And The Beat Goes On" by The Whispers	album cut
5/22/99	**1** (1)	14	● 5. **Wild Wild West** Sales #1 (1) / Airplay #2 **WILL SMITH featuring Dru Hill and Kool Mo Dee** samples "Wild, Wild West" by Kool Moe Dee and "I Wish" by Stevie Wonder; title song from the movie starring Smith and Kevin Kline	Overbrook 79157
11/20/99	**25**	4	6. Will 2K Airplay #20 **WILL SMITH (Featuring K-Ci)** samples "Rock The Casbah" by The Clash	Columbia 79287

DATE	POS	WKS	ARTIST–RECORD TITLE	LABEL & NO.
			SMITHEREENS, The	
			Power-pop group formed in Carteret, New Jersey: Pat DiNizio (vocals, guitar), Jim Babjak (guitar), Mike Mesaros (bass) and Dennis Diken (drums).	
3/10/90	38	2	1. A Girl Like You Sales #34 / Airplay #40	Enigma/Capitol 44480
3/14/92	37	5	2. Too Much Passion Airplay #36	Capitol 44784
			SMOKIE	
			Pop-rock group from Bradford, Yorkshire, England: Chris Norman (vocals), Alan Silson (guitar), Terry Utley (bass) and Pete Spencer (drums).	
1/22/77	25	8	1. Living Next Door To Alice	RSO 860
			SMOOTH — see IMMATURE	
			SMYTH, Patty — see SCANDAL	
			SNAP!	
			Techno-dance duo formed in Pittsburgh, Pennsylvania: Turbo B (rap) and his cousin Jackie Harris (vocals). By 1992 Turbo B replaced by Niki Harris; Jackie Harris replaced by Pennye Ford.	
6/2/90	2 (1)	16	▲ 1. **The Power** Sales #1 (3) / Airplay #11	Arista 2013
10/13/90	35	2	● 2. Ooops Up Sales #25	Arista 2060
			samples "I Don't Believe You Want To Get Up And Dance (Oops, Up Side Your Head)" by The Gap Band	
9/19/92+	5	30	● 3. **Rhythm Is A Dancer** Airplay #4 / Sales #5	Arista 12437
			SNEAKER	
			Pop-rock group formed in Los Angeles, California: Mitch Crane (vocals, guitar), Michael Carey Schneider (vocals, keyboards), Tim Torrance (guitar), Jim King (keyboards), Michael Cottage (bass) and Mike Hughes (drums).	
12/19/81+	34	6	1. More Than Just The Two Of Us	Handshake 02557
			SNIFF 'N' THE TEARS	
			Rock group formed in London, England: Paul Roberts (vocals), Loz Netto and Mick Dyche (guitars), Alan Fealdman (keyboards), Chris Birkin (bass) and Luigi Salvoni (drums).	
8/18/79	15	9	1. Driver's Seat	Atlantic 3604
			SNOOP DOGG	
			Born Calvin Broadus on 10/20/71 in Long Beach, California. Male rapper/ actor. Has appeared in several movies and TV shows.	
			SNOOP DOGGY DOGG:	
2/13/93	2 (1)	24	▲ 1. **Nuthin' But A "G" Thang** Sales #1 (1) / Airplay #10	Death Row 53819
			#1 R&B hit (2 weeks); samples "I Want'a Do Something Freaky To You" by Leon Haywood	
6/5/93	8	14	● 2. **Dre Day** Sales #4 / Airplay #17	Death Row 53827
			DR. DRE (featuring Snoop Doggy Dogg) (above 2)	
12/4/93+	8	10	● 3. **What's My Name?** Sales #6 / Airplay #17	Death Row 98340
2/19/94	8	15	● 4. **Gin & Juice** Sales #5 / Airplay #22	Death Row 98318
			samples "Watching You" by Slave	
11/23/96	33	7	5. Never Leave Me Alone Sales #23	Death Row 97012
			NATE DOGG featuring Snoop Doggy Dogg	
			Val Young (female vocal); samples "Where Is The Love" by Roberta Flack & Donny Hathaway	

DATE	POS	WKS	ARTIST–RECORD TITLE	LABEL & NO.
			SNOOP DOGG:	
9/5/98	**19**	10	6. Still A G Thang Sales #12	No Limit 53450
10/24/98	**12**	6	● 7. Come And Get With Me Sales #4	Elektra 64080
			KEITH SWEAT Featuring Snoop Dogg	
6/24/00	**28**	2	8. Crybaby Sales #2	Columbia 79348
			MARIAH CAREY Featuring Snoop Dogg	
			samples "Piece Of My Love" by Guy	
7/8/00	**23**	8	9. The Next Episode Airplay #16 / Sales #62	Aftermath 497333
			DR. DRE Featuring Snoop Dogg	
			Kurupt (backing vocal)	
3/1/03	**6**	17	10. **Beautiful** Airplay #6 / Sales #14	Priority 77887
			SNOOP DOGG featuring Pharrell, Uncle Charlie Wilson	
10/4/03	**3**	18	11. **Holidae In** Airplay #3 / Sales #42	Disturb. Tha P. 52816
			CHINGY featuring Ludacris & Snoop Dogg	
			SNOW	
			Born Darrin O'Brien on 10/30/69 in Toronto, Ontario, Canada. White male reggae singer.	
2/6/93	**1 (7)**	19	▲ 1. **Informer** Sales #1 (6) / Airplay #4	EastWest 98471
6/5/93	**19**	9	2. Girl, I've Been Hurt Airplay #16 / Sales #22	EastWest 98438
			SNOW, Phoebe	
			Born Phoebe Laub on 7/17/52 in New York; raised in New Jersey. Pop-folk singer/guitarist/songwriter.	
2/8/75	**5**	11	1. **Poetry Man**	Shelter 40353
			#1 Adult Contemporary hit (1 week)	
9/6/75	**23**	6	2. Gone At Last	Columbia 10197
			PAUL SIMON/PHOEBE SNOW and The Jessy Dixon Singers	
			SOFT CELL	
			Techno-pop duo from London, England: Marc Almond (vocals) and David Ball (synthesizer).	
5/22/82	**8**	15	1. **Tainted Love**	Sire 49855
			first recorded by Gloria Jones in 1964	
			SOHO	
			Interracial dance trio formed in London, England: identical twin sisters Jackie and Pauline Cuff (vocals), with Timothy Brinkhurst (guitar).	
10/20/90	**14**	9	● 1. Hippychick Sales #8 / Airplay #22	Atco 98908
			samples "How Soon Is Now" by The Smiths	
			SOLÉ	
			Born on 7/17/73 in Kansas City, Missouri. Female rapper.	
4/24/99	**5**	12	● 1. **Who Dat** Sales #2 / Airplay #47	Tony Mercedes 53469
			JT MONEY Featuring Solé	
12/11/99	**21**	5	● 2. 4,5,6 Sales #7	DreamWorks 59029
			SOLÉ Featuring J.T. Money and Kandi	

DATE	POS	WKS	ARTIST–RECORD TITLE	LABEL & NO.
			SOMETHIN' FOR THE PEOPLE	
			R&B vocal trio from Oakland, California: Jeff "Fuzzy" Young, Curtis "Sauce" Wilson and Rochad "Cat Daddy" Holiday.	
9/13/97	**4**	23	● 1. **My Love Is The Shhh!** Sales #5 / Airplay #17 **SOMETHIN' FOR the PEOPLE featuring Trina & Tamara**	Warner 17327
			SOMMERS, Joanie	
			Born on 2/24/41 in Buffalo, New York. Pop singer. Appeared in the movies *Everything's Ducky* and *The Lively Set*.	
6/16/62	**7**	11	1. **Johnny Get Angry**	Warner 5275
			SON BY FOUR	
			Latin vocal group from Puerto Rico: brothers Javier and George Montes, with cousin Pedro Quiles and friend Angel Lopez.	
7/15/00	**26**	12	1. **Purest Of Pain (A Puro Dolor)** Sales #11 / Airplay #35 sung in English and Spanish	Sony Discos 83942
			SONIQUE	
			Born in England. Black female dance-pop singer. Half of the duo S-Express.	
2/5/00	**8**	21	1. **It Feels So Good** Sales #9 / Airplay #9	Caffeine 156247
			SONNY & CHER	
			Husband-and-wife duo: Sonny Bono (born on 2/16/35 in Detroit, Michigan) and Cher (born on 5/20/46). Began career as session singers for Phil Spector. First recorded as Caesar & Cleo for Vault in 1963. Married from 1969-75. In the movies *Good Times* (1967) and *Chastity* (1969). Own CBS-TV variety series from 1971-74, 1976-77. Sonny was mayor of Palm Springs, California, from 1988-92; elected to Congress in 1994. Sonny died in a skiing accident on 1/5/98 (age 62).	
7/31/65	**1** (3)	10	● 1. **I Got You Babe**	Atco 6359
9/4/65	**10**	8	2. **Laugh At Me** **SONNY**	Atco 6369
9/11/65	**8**	9	3. **Baby Don't Go**	Reprise 0392
9/25/65	**20**	4	4. Just You	Atco 6345
10/23/65	**15**	6	5. But You're Mine	Atco 6381
2/12/66	**14**	6	6. What Now My Love	Atco 6395
10/15/66	**21**	4	7. Little Man	Atco 6440
1/28/67	**6**	8	8. **The Beat Goes On**	Atco 6461
11/13/71	**7**	11	9. **All I Ever Need Is You** #1 Adult Contemporary hit (5 weeks)	Kapp 2151
3/11/72	**8**	11	10. **A Cowboys Work Is Never Done**	Kapp 2163
8/5/72	**32**	5	11. When You Say Love adapted from a Budweiser jingle	Kapp 2176
			SONS OF FUNK — see MASTER P	
			SOPWITH "CAMEL," The	
			Pop group from San Francisco, California: Peter Kraemer (vocals, sax), Terry MacNeil and William Sievers (guitars), Martin Beard (bass) and Norman Mayell (drums). Named after a type of airplane used in World War I.	
1/28/67	**26**	4	1. Hello Hello	Kama Sutra 217

DATE	POS	WKS	ARTIST–RECORD TITLE	LABEL & NO.
			S.O.S. BAND, The	
			Funk-R&B-disco group from Atlanta, Georgia: Mary Davis (vocals, keyboards), Bruno Speight (guitar), Willie Killebrew (sax), Bill Ellis (flute), Jason Bryant (keyboards), John Simpson (bass) and James Earl Jones III (drums).	
6/28/80	3	14	▲ 1. **Take Your Time (Do It Right) Part 1** #1 R&B hit (5 weeks)	Tabu 5522
			SOUL, David	
			Born David Solberg on 8/28/43 in Chicago, Illinois. Actor/singer. Portrayed "Joshua Bolt" on TV's *Here Come The Brides* and "Ken Hutchinson" on TV's *Starsky & Hutch*.	
2/19/77	1 (1)	13	● 1. **Don't Give Up On Us** #1 Adult Contemporary hit (1 week)	Private Stock 45,129
			SOUL, Jimmy	
			Born James McCleese on 8/24/42 in Weldon, North Carolina. Died of a heart attack on 6/25/88 (age 45). R&B/calypso-styled singer.	
5/5/62	22	8	1. **Twistin' Matilda (and the channel)** twist version of the calypso song "Matilda" (popularized by Harry Belafonte)	S.P.Q.R. 3300
4/20/63	1 (2)	11	2. **If You Wanna Be Happy** #1 R&B hit (1 week); based on the calypso song "Ugly Woman"	S.P.Q.R. 3305
			SOUL ASYLUM	
			Rock group from Minneapolis, Minnesota: Dave Pirner (vocals, guitar), Dan Murphy (guitar), Karl Mueller (bass) and Grant Young (drums). Pirner appeared in the movie *Reality Bites*. Sterling Campbell replaced Young in early 1995.	
7/10/93	5	19	● 1. **Runaway Train** Sales #5 / Airplay #9	Columbia 74966
7/1/95	20	8	2. **Misery** Airplay #16 / Sales #30 #1 Modern Rock hit (3 weeks)	Columbia 77959
			SOUL CHILDREN, The	
			R&B vocal group from Memphis, Tennessee: Anita Louis, Shelbra Bennett, John Colbert and Norman West.	
3/23/74	36	2	1. **I'll Be The Other Woman**	Stax 0182
			SOULDECISION	
			White male vocal trio from Vancouver, British Columbia, Canada: David Bowman, Ken Lewko and Trevor Guthrie.	
8/19/00	22	16	1. **Faded** Sales #10 / Airplay #32 **SOULDECISION (Featuring Thrust)**	MCA 156606
			SOUL FOR REAL	
			R&B vocal group from Long Island, New York: brothers Chris, Andre, Brian and Jason Dalyrimple.	
1/28/95	2 (4)	21	● 1. **Candy Rain** Sales #1 (3) / Airplay #11 #1 R&B hit (3 weeks)	Uptown/MCA 54906
5/13/95	17	24	● 2. **Every Little Thing I Do** Sales #12 / Airplay #20 samples "Outstanding" by The Gap Band	Uptown/MCA 55032

DATE	POS	WKS	ARTIST–RECORD TITLE	LABEL & NO.
			SOUL SURVIVORS	
			Garage-rock band from Philadelphia, Pennsylvania: vocals by Kenny Jeremiah and brothers Charles and Richard Ingui, with Edward Leonetti (guitar), Paul Venturini (organ) and Joey Forgione (drums).	
9/23/67	4	12	1. **Expressway (To Your Heart)**	Crimson 1010
1/20/68	33	3	2. Explosion (In Your Soul)	Crimson 1012
			S.O.U.L. S.Y.S.T.E.M., The	
			Dance group assembled by Robert Clivilles and David Cole (C & C Music Factory). Featuring lead singer Michelle Visage (of Seduction).	
1/23/93	34	2	1. It's Gonna Be A Lovely Day Airplay #21 / Sales #43 **THE S.O.U.L. S.Y.S.T.E.M. Introducing Michelle Visage**	Arista 12486
			SOUL II SOUL	
			R&B-dance group from London, England, led by the duo of Beresford Romeo and Nellee Hooper. Features female vocalists Caron Wheeler, Do'Reen Waddell and Rose Windross, with musical backing by the Reggae Philharmonic Orchestra. Waddell died after being struck by a car on 3/1/2002 (age 36).	
7/29/89	11	10	▲ 1. Keep On Movin' Sales #8 / Airplay #12 #1 R&B hit (2 weeks)	Virgin 99205
10/14/89	4	18	▲ 2. **Back To Life** Sales #3 / Airplay #5 #1 R&B hit (1 week)	Virgin 99171
			SOUNDGARDEN	
			Hard-rock group formed in Seattle, Washington: Chris Cornell (vocals), Kim Thayil (guitar), Ben Shepherd (bass) and Matt Cameron (drums).	
7/23/94	24 A	11	1. Black Hole Sun #1 Mainstream Rock hit (7 weeks); from the album *Superunknown* on A&M 0198	album cut
6/1/96	37 A	2	2. Pretty Noose	album cut
9/28/96	40 A	1	3. Burden In My Hand #1 Mainstream Rock hit (5 weeks); above 2 from the album *Down On The Upside* on A&M 0526	album cut
			SOUNDS OF SUNSHINE	
			Adult Contemporary vocal trio from Los Angeles, California: brothers Walt, Warner and George Wilder.	
7/24/71	39	2	1. Love Means (You Never Have To Say You're Sorry) song title taken from a line of dialogue in the 1970 movie *Love Story* starring Ali MacGraw and Ryan O'Neal	Ranwood 896
			SOUNDS ORCHESTRAL	
			Orchestral pop studio trio from England: John Pearson (piano), Tony Reeves (bass) and Ken Clare (drums).	
4/10/65	10	11	1. **Cast Your Fate To The Wind** [I] #1 Adult Contemporary hit (3 weeks)	Parkway 942
			SOUP DRAGONS, The	
			Rock-dance fusion band from Glasgow, Scotland: Sean Dickson (vocals), Jim McCulloch (guitar), Sushil Dade (bass) and Paul Quinn (drums).	
9/19/92	35	4	1. Divine Thing Sales #39 / Airplay #41	Big Life 865764

DATE	POS	WKS	ARTIST–RECORD TITLE	LABEL & NO.
			SOUTH, Joe	
			Born Joe Souter on 2/28/40 in Atlanta, Georgia. Pop-country singer/songwriter/guitarist.	
2/1/69	12	9	1. Games People Play	Capitol 2248
1/17/70	12	9	2. Walk A Mile In My Shoes **JOE SOUTH and The Believers**	Capitol 2704
			SOUTHER, J.D.	
			Born John David Souther on 11/2/45 in Detroit, Michigan; raised in Amarillo, Texas. Pop-rock singer/songwriter/guitarist. Teamed with Chris Hillman and Richie Furay as The Souther, Hillman, Furay Band in 1974.	
9/21/74	27	4	1. Fallin' In Love **THE SOUTHER, HILLMAN, FURAY BAND**	Asylum 45201
10/20/79	7	13	2. **You're Only Lonely** #1 Adult Contemporary hit (5 weeks)	Columbia 11079
3/14/81	11	10	3. Her Town Too **JAMES TAYLOR AND J.D. SOUTHER**	Columbia 60514
			SOVINE, Red	
			Born Woodrow Wilson Sovine on 7/17/18 in Charleston, West Virginia. Died of a heart attack on 4/4/80 (age 61). Country singer/songwriter/guitarist.	
8/28/76	40	1	● 1. Teddy Bear [S] #1 Country hit (3 weeks)	Starday 142
			SPACEHOG	
			Rock group from Leeds, England: Royston Langdon (vocals, bass), Richard Steel and Antony Langdon (guitars), and Jonny Cragg (drums). Langdon married actress Liv Tyler on 3/25/2003.	
4/13/96	32	4	1. In The Meantime Airplay #25 / Sales #44 #1 Mainstream Rock hit (4 weeks)	Sire 64303
			SPANDAU BALLET	
			Pop group formed in London, England: Tony Hadley (vocals), brothers Gary (guitar) and Martin (bass) Kemp, Steve Norman (sax), and John Keeble (drums). The Kemps starred in the 1990 movie *The Krays*. Gary Kemp married actress Sadie Frost.	
8/27/83	4	13	1. **True** #1 Adult Contemporary hit (1 week)	Chrysalis 42720
12/17/83+	29	6	2. Gold	Chrysalis 42743
9/1/84	34	4	3. Only When You Leave	Chrysalis 42792
			SPANKY AND OUR GANG	
			Folk-pop group formed in Chicago, Illinois: Elaine "Spanky" McFarlane (born on 6/19/42 in Peoria, Illinois), Malcolm Hale, Kenny Hodges, Lefty Baker, Nigel Pickering and John Seiter. Spanky became the new lead singer of The Mamas & The Papas in the early 1980s. Named after the "Little Rascals" series. Hale died of liver failure on 10/31/68 (age 27). Baker died of liver failure on 8/11/71 (age 29).	
6/3/67	9	5	1. **Sunday Will Never Be The Same**	Mercury 72679
9/16/67	31	3	2. Making Every Minute Count	Mercury 72714
10/28/67	14	9	3. Lazy Day	Mercury 72732
2/3/68	30	4	4. Sunday Mornin'	Mercury 72765
5/18/68	17	7	5. Like To Get To Know You	Mercury 72795

DATE	POS	WKS	ARTIST–RECORD TITLE	LABEL & NO.
			SPARKLE	
			Born in Harlem, New York. Female R&B singer.	
5/30/98	32 ^A	7	1. Be Careful	album cut
			SPARKLE featuring R. Kelly	
			#1 R&B Airplay hit (6 weeks); from the album *Sparkle* on Rock Land 90149	
			SPARXXX, Bubba	
			Born Warren Mathis on 3/6/77 in LaGrange, Georgia. White rapper.	
9/22/01	15	10	1. Ugly Airplay #13 / Sales #34	Beat Club 497602
			samples "Get Ur Freak On" by Missy "Misdemeanor" Elliott	
			SPEARS, Britney	
			Born on 12/2/81 in Kentwood, Louisiana. Teen pop singer/actress. Regular on TV's *The Mickey Mouse Club* (1992-93). Played "Lucy" in the movie *Crossroads*.	
11/21/98+	1 (2)	29	▲ 1. **...Baby One More Time** Sales #1 (4) / Airplay #8	Jive 42545
6/12/99	21	12	2. Sometimes Airplay #14	album cut
			from the album *...Baby One More Time* on Jive 41651	
10/2/99	10	12	3. **(You Drive Me) Crazy** Airplay #6	Jive 42606
			from the movie *Drive Me Crazy* starring Melissa Joan Hart	
2/26/00	14	6	▲ 4. From The Bottom Of My Broken Heart	Jive 42653
			Sales #1 (1) / Airplay #53	
4/29/00	9	14	5. **Oops!...I Did It Again** Airplay #8	Jive 42700
8/26/00	23	6	6. Lucky Airplay #18	Jive 42742
12/30/00+	11	8	● 7. Stronger Sales #1 (1) / Airplay #53	Jive 42861
11/24/01	27	3	8. I'm A Slave 4 U Airplay #30 / Sales #73	Jive 42967
11/8/03	35	4	9. Me Against The Music Sales #3 / Airplay #38	Jive 58215
			BRITNEY SPEARS featuring Madonna	
			SPENCE, Judson	
			Born on 4/29/65 in Pascagoula, Mississippi. Pop-rock singer/songwriter/ multi-instrumentalist.	
11/26/88	32	4	1. Yeah, Yeah, Yeah Airplay #29 / Sales #34	Atlantic 88999
			SPENCER, Tracie	
			Born on 7/12/76 in Waterloo, Iowa. R&B singer.	
11/19/88	38	3	1. Symptoms Of True Love Airplay #39	Capitol 44140
1/26/91	3	14	2. **This House** Sales #4 / Airplay #8	Capitol 44652
8/14/99	18	7	3. It's All About You (Not About Me) Sales #6 / Airplay #68	Capitol 58777
			SPICE GIRLS	
			Female vocal group from England: Victoria Adams (Posh Spice), Melanie Brown (Scary Spice), Emma Bunton (Baby Spice), Melanie Chisholm (Sporty Spice) and Geri Halliwell (Ginger Spice). Group starred in the movie *Spiceworld*. Halliwell left group in May 1998.	
1/25/97	1 (4)	22	▲ 1. **Wannabe** Sales #1 (4) / Airplay #6	Virgin 38579
5/24/97	3	18	● 2. **Say You'll Be There** Sales #4 / Airplay #6	Virgin 38592
8/16/97	4	18	● 3. **2 Become 1** Airplay #5 / Sales #8	Virgin 38604
11/8/97	18	15	● 4. Spice Up Your Life Sales #11 / Airplay #72	Virgin 38620
			from the movie *Spiceworld* starring Spice Girls	

DATE	POS	WKS	ARTIST–RECORD TITLE	LABEL & NO.
2/14/98	**9**	9	5. **Too Much** Sales #11 / Airplay #36	Virgin 38630
6/20/98	**16**	11	6. Stop Sales #11 / Airplay #70	Virgin 38641
12/26/98	**11**	4	● 7. Goodbye Sales #4	Virgin 38652
			SPIDER	
			Rock group formed in New York: Amanda Blue (vocals), Keith Lentin (guitar), Holly Knight (keyboards), Jim Lowell (bass) and Anton Fig (drums). Knight later joined Device. Fig joined house band of TV's *Late Night With David Letterman*.	
6/7/80	**39**	2	1. New Romance (It's A Mystery)	Dreamland 100
			SPIN DOCTORS	
			Rock group formed in New York: Christopher Barron (vocals), Eric Schenkman (guitar), Mark White (bass) and Aaron Comess (drums).	
11/14/92	**17**	12	1. Little Miss Can't Be Wrong Sales #23 / Airplay #24	Epic Associated 74473
2/20/93	**7**	22	2. **Two Princes** Airplay #6 / Sales #14	Epic Associated 74804
			SPINNERS	
			R&B vocal group formed in Detroit, Michigan: Henry Fambrough, Bobby Smith, Billy Henderson, Pervis Jackson and George Dixon. Chico Edwards replaced Dixon in 1964. G.C. Cameron replaced Edwards in 1968. Philippe Wynne replaced Cameron in early 1972. John Edwards replaced Wynne in 1977. Wynne died on 7/14/84 (age 43).	
7/17/61	**27**	5	1. That's What Girls Are Made For *Harvey Fuqua (of The Moonglows; lead vocal)*	Tri-Phi 1001
8/14/65	**35**	2	2. I'll Always Love You	Motown 1078
8/22/70	**14**	10	3. It's A Shame *written and produced by Stevie Wonder*	V.I.P. 25057
10/7/72	**3**	11	● 4. **I'll Be Around** #1 R&B hit (5 weeks)	Atlantic 2904
1/20/73	**4**	12	● 5. **Could It Be I'm Falling In Love** #1 R&B hit (1 week)	Atlantic 2927
5/19/73	**11**	11	● 6. One Of A Kind (Love Affair) #1 R&B hit (4 weeks)	Atlantic 2962
9/8/73	**29**	3	7. Ghetto Child	Atlantic 2973
2/23/74	**20**	8	8. Mighty Love - Pt. 1 #1 R&B hit (2 weeks)	Atlantic 3006
6/8/74	**18**	6	9. I'm Coming Home	Atlantic 3027
8/3/74	**1** (1)	15	● 10. **Then Came You** **DIONNE WARWICKE AND SPINNERS**	Atlantic 3202
10/26/74	**15**	5	11. Love Don't Love Nobody - Pt. I	Atlantic 3206
4/5/75	**37**	2	12. Living A Little, Laughing A Little	Atlantic 3252
8/30/75	**5**	13	● 13. "They Just Can't Stop It" the (Games People Play) #1 R&B hit (1 week)	Atlantic 3284
1/24/76	**36**	3	14. Love Or Leave	Atlantic 3309
10/2/76	**2** (3)	17	● 15. **The Rubberband Man** #1 R&B hit (1 week)	Atlantic 3355
1/26/80	**2** (2)	16	● 16. **Working My Way Back To You/Forgive Me, Girl**	Atlantic 3637
5/24/80	**4**	14	17. **Cupid/I've Loved You For A Long Time**	Atlantic 3664
4/29/95	**39**	2	18. I'll Be Around Sales #26 / Airplay #63 **[R]** **RAPPIN' 4-TAY Featuring The Spinners** Rappin' 4-Tay raps new verse over the Spinners hit (#3 in 1972) with its original music and chorus	Chrysalis/EMI 58331

DATE	POS	WKS	ARTIST–RECORD TITLE	LABEL & NO.
			SPIRAL STARECASE	
			Pop-rock group from Sacramento, California: Pat Upton (vocals, guitar), Harvey Kaplan (organ), Dick Lopes (sax), Bobby Raymond (bass) and Vinny Parello (drums). Kaplan is the father of Brenda K. Starr.	
5/3/69	12	11	1. More Today Than Yesterday	Columbia 44741
			SPIRIT	
			Rock group from Los Angeles, California: Jay Ferguson (vocals), Randy California (guitar), John Locke (keyboards), Mark Andes (bass) and Ed Cassidy (drums). Ferguson and Andes later formed Jo Jo Gunne. Andes later joined Firefall and Heart. California drowned in Hawaii on 1/2/97 (age 45).	
3/8/69	25	5	1. I Got A Line On You	Ode 115
			SPOKESMEN, The	
			Pop-folk trio: Johnny Madara, David White and Roy Gilmore. White was with Danny & The Juniors.	
10/9/65	36	3	1. The Dawn Of Correction answer song to "Eve Of Destruction" by Barry McGuire	Decca 31844
			SPORTY THIEVZ	
			Rap trio from Brooklyn, New York: Marlon Brando, King Kirk and Big Dubez. Brando died in a car crash on 5/11/2001 (age 22).	
6/26/99	12	6	● 1. No Pigeons Sales #3 / Airplay #40 a parody of "No Scrubs" by TLC	Roc-A-Blok 79190
			SPRINGFIELD, Dusty	
			Born Mary O'Brien on 4/16/39 in London, England. Died of cancer on 3/2/99 (age 59). Pop singer. Member of The Springfields (see #1 below) with her brother Tom Springfield and Tim Feild. Inducted into the Rock and Roll Hall of Fame in 1999.	
9/1/62	20	6	1. Silver Threads And Golden Needles **THE SPRINGFIELDS**	Philips 40038
2/15/64	12	7	2. I Only Want To Be With You	Philips 40162
5/2/64	38	2	3. Stay Awhile	Philips 40180
7/11/64	6	10	4. **Wishin' And Hopin'**	Philips 40207
6/4/66	4	10	5. **You Don't Have To Say You Love Me**	Philips 40371
10/1/66	20	5	6. All I See Is You	Philips 40396
4/22/67	40	2	7. I'll Try Anything	Philips 40439
10/14/67	22	5	8. The Look Of Love from the James Bond movie spoof *Casino Royale* starring David Niven and Peter Sellers	Philips 40465
12/14/68+	10	10	9. **Son-Of-A Preacher Man**	Atlantic 2580
5/24/69	31	4	10. The Windmills Of Your Mind from the movie *The Thomas Crown Affair* starring Steve McQueen	Atlantic 2623
11/29/69	24	9	11. A Brand New Me	Atlantic 2685
12/26/87+	2 (2)	13	12. **What Have I Done To Deserve This?** Sales #1(1)/Airplay #4 **PET SHOP BOYS (and Dusty Springfield)**	EMI-Manhattan 50107
			SPRINGFIELD, Rick	
			Born Richard Springthorpe on 8/23/49 in Sydney, Australia. Pop-rock singer/songwriter/guitarist/actor. Portrayed "Noah Drake" on the TV soap opera *General Hospital*. Starred in the movie *Hard To Hold*.	
9/2/72	14	9	1. Speak To The Sky	Capitol 3340

DATE	POS	WKS	ARTIST–RECORD TITLE	LABEL & NO.
5/9/81	**1** (2)	22	● 2. **Jessie's Girl**	RCA 12201
9/12/81	**8**	12	3. **I've Done Everything For You**	RCA 12166
			written by Sammy Hagar	
12/26/81+	**20**	10	4. Love Is Alright Tonite	RCA 13008
3/13/82	**2** (4)	16	5. **Don't Talk To Strangers**	RCA 13070
6/19/82	**21**	9	6. What Kind Of Fool Am I	RCA 13245
10/9/82	**32**	5	7. I Get Excited	RCA 13303
4/23/83	**9**	13	8. **Affair Of The Heart**	RCA 13497
7/23/83	**18**	11	9. Human Touch	RCA 13576
11/12/83	**23**	6	10. Souls	RCA 13650
3/17/84	**5**	12	11. **Love Somebody**	RCA 13738
6/9/84	**26**	6	12. Don't Walk Away	RCA 13813
9/8/84	**20**	9	13. Bop 'Til You Drop *Airplay #16 / Sales #28*	RCA 13861
			above 3 from the movie Hard To Hold starring Springfield	
12/15/84+	**27**	6	14. Bruce *Sales #27 / Airplay #27* **[N]**	Mercury 880405
			recorded in 1978; an autobiographical song about Springfield being mistaken for Bruce Springsteen	
4/20/85	**26**	6	15. Celebrate Youth *Sales #24 / Airplay #26*	RCA 14047
7/13/85	**22**	8	16. State Of The Heart *Sales #20 / Airplay #23*	RCA 14120
3/5/88	**22**	6	17. Rock Of Life *Sales #20 / Airplay #21*	RCA 6853

SPRINGFIELDS, The — see SPRINGFIELD, Dusty

SPRINGSTEEN, Bruce

Born on 9/23/49 in Freehold, New Jersey. Rock and roll singer/ songwriter/guitarist. Nicknamed "The Boss." His E-Street Band: Steve Van Zant (guitar), Clarence Clemons (sax), Roy Bittan (keyboards), Gary Tallent (bass) and Max Weinberg (drums). Married to model/actress Julianne Phillips from 1985-89. Married backing singer Patti Scialfa on 6/8/91. Inducted into the Rock and Roll Hall of Fame in 1999.

DATE	POS	WKS	ARTIST–RECORD TITLE	LABEL & NO.
10/11/75	**23**	5	1. Born To Run	Columbia 10209
7/15/78	**33**	2	2. Prove It All Night	Columbia 10763
11/8/80	**5**	14	3. **Hungry Heart**	Columbia 11391
			Mark Volman and Howard Kaylan of The Turtles (backing vocals)	
2/21/81	**20**	6	4. Fade Away	Columbia 11431
5/26/84	**2** (4)	15	▲ 5. **Dancing In The Dark**	Columbia 04463
			#1 Mainstream Rock hit (6 weeks)	
8/18/84	**7**	13	● 6. **Cover Me** *Airplay #7 / Sales #9*	Columbia 04561
11/24/84+	**9**	11	● 7. **Born In The U.S.A.** *Sales #9 / Airplay #11*	Columbia 04680
3/2/85	**6**	12	8. **I'm On Fire** *Airplay #5 / Sales #7*	Columbia 04772
6/8/85	**5**	13	9. **Glory Days** *Airplay #4 / Sales #7*	Columbia 04924
9/14/85	**9**	9	10. **I'm Goin' Down** *Sales #8 / Airplay #9*	Columbia 05603
12/21/85+	**6**	9	● 11. **My Hometown** *Sales #5 / Airplay #7*	Columbia 05728
			#1 Adult Contemporary hit (1 week)	
11/29/86	**8**	9	12. **War** *Sales #8 / Airplay #12* **[L]**	Columbia 06432
			BRUCE SPRINGSTEEN & THE E STREET BAND	
			recorded on 9/30/85 at the LA Coliseum	
10/3/87	**5**	11	13. **Brilliant Disguise** *Sales #5 / Airplay #5*	Columbia 07595
			#1 Mainstream Rock hit (1 week)	
12/19/87+	**9**	11	14. **Tunnel Of Love** *Sales #6 / Airplay #15*	Columbia 07663
			#1 Mainstream Rock hit (4 weeks)	
3/19/88	**13**	8	15. One Step Up *Sales #11 / Airplay #18*	Columbia 07726

DATE	POS	WKS	ARTIST–RECORD TITLE	LABEL & NO.
3/21/92	**16**	9	16. Human Touch / Airplay #14 / Sales #27 #1 Mainstream Rock hit (3 weeks)	
3/21/92		9	17. Better Days	Columbia 74273
3/5/94	**9**	15	● 18. **Streets Of Philadelphia** Airplay #7 / Sales #10 from the movie *Philadelphia* starring Tom Hanks and Denzel Washington	Columbia 77384
4/5/97	**19**	13	19. Secret Garden Airplay #15 / Sales #26 **[R]** originally hit #63 in 1995; reissued due to inclusion in the movie *Jerry Maguire* starring Tom Cruise	Columbia 77847
			SPYRO GYRA	
			Jazz-pop group formed in Buffalo, New York. Led by saxophonist Jay Beckenstein.	
7/28/79	**24**	8	1. Morning Dance **[I]** #1 Adult Contemporary hit (1 week)	Infinity 50,011
			SQUEEZE	
			New wave pop-rock group formed in London, England. Led by vocalists/ guitarists Chris Difford and Glenn Tilbrook.	
10/17/87	**15**	10	1. Hourglass Sales #16 / Airplay #16	A&M 2967
1/23/88	**32**	5	2. 853-5937 Sales #30 / Airplay #33	A&M 2994
			SQUIER, Billy	
			Born on 5/12/50 in Wellesley Hills, Massachusetts. Hard-rock singer/ songwriter/guitarist.	
6/20/81	**17**	11	1. The Stroke	Capitol 5005
10/17/81	**35**	3	2. In The Dark	Capitol 5040
11/27/82	**32**	6	3. Everybody Wants You #1 Mainstream Rock hit (6 weeks)	Capitol 5163
7/14/84	**15**	12	4. Rock Me Tonite #1 Mainstream Rock hit (2 weeks)	Capitol 5370
			STACEY Q	
			Born Stacey Swain on 11/30/58 in Los Angeles, California. Female dance singer.	
8/16/86	**3**	13	1. **Two Of Hearts** Sales #1 (1) / Airplay #7	Atlantic 89381
2/21/87	**35**	4	2. We Connect Sales #29	Atlantic 89331
			STAFFORD, Jim	
			Born on 1/16/44 in Eloise, Florida. Pop-novelty singer/songwriter/guitarist. Hosted own summer variety TV show in 1975 and *Those Amazing Animals* from 1980-81. Married to Bobbie Gentry from 1978-79.	
7/14/73	**39**	1	1. Swamp Witch	MGM 14496
12/29/73+	**3**	15	● 2. **Spiders & Snakes**	MGM 14648
5/4/74	**12**	9	3. My Girl Bill **[N]**	MGM 14718
7/20/74	**7**	11	4. **Wildwood Weed** **[N]**	MGM 14737
1/18/75	**24**	5	5. Your Bulldog Drinks Champagne **[N]**	MGM 14775
9/27/75	**37**	2	6. I Got Stoned And I Missed It **[N]**	MGM 14819

DATE	POS	WKS	ARTIST–RECORD TITLE	LABEL & NO.
			STAFFORD, Jo	
			Born on 11/12/17 in Coalinga, California. Female pop singer. Member of The Pied Pipers from 1940-43. Married orchestra leader Paul Weston. Hosted own TV musical series from 1954-55.	
11/20/54+	15	6	1. Teach Me Tonight Jockey #15 / Juke Box #16 / Best Seller #23	Columbia 40351
10/15/55	13	7	2. Suddenly There's A Valley	Columbia 40559
			Jockey #13 / Top 100 #16 / Juke Box #18 / Best Seller #21	
			Norman Luboff Choir (backing vocals)	
12/3/55+	14	14	3. It's Almost Tomorrow	Columbia 40595
			Juke Box #14 / Top 100 #19 / Jockey #20 / Best Seller #25	
12/22/56	38	1	4. On London Bridge Top 100 #38	Columbia 40782
			Paul Weston (orch., all of above)	
			STAFFORD, Terry	
			Born on 11/22/41 in Hollis, Oklahoma; raised in Amarillo, Texas. Died on 3/17/96 (age 54). Male pop-rock and roll singer/songwriter. Appeared in the movie *Wild Wheels*.	
3/21/64	3	10	1. **Suspicion**	Crusader 101
			first recorded by Elvis Presley in 1962	
6/6/64	25	6	2. I'll Touch A Star	Crusader 105
			STAIND	
			Alternative-metal rock group from Boston, Massachusetts: Aaron Lewis (vocals), Mike Mushok (guitar), Johnny April (bass) and Jon Wysocki (drums).	
6/16/01	5	34	1. **It's Been Awhile** Airplay #5	album cut
			#1 Mainstream Rock hit (20 weeks) / #1 Modern Rock hit (16 weeks); from the album *Break The Cycle* on Flip/Elektra 62626	
9/27/03	24	18	2. So Far Away Airplay #22	album cut
			#1 Mainstream Rock hit (14 weeks) / #1 Modern Rock hit (7 weeks); from the album *14 Shades Of Grey* on Flip 62882	
			STALLION	
			Pop-rock group from Denver, Colorado: Buddy Stephens (vocals), Danny O'Neil (guitar), Wally Damrick (keyboards), Jorg Gonzalez (bass) and Larry Thompson (drums).	
4/23/77	37	2	1. Old Fashioned Boy (You're The One)	Casablanca 877
			STALLONE, Frank	
			Born on 7/30/50 in Philadelphia, Pennsylvania. Singer/songwriter/actor. Brother of actor Sylvester Stallone.	
8/20/83	10	10	1. **Far From Over**	RSO 815023
			from the movie *Staying Alive* starring John Travolta	
			STAMPEDERS	
			Pop-rock trio from Calgary, Alberta, Canada: Rick Dodson (guitar), Ronnie King (bass) and Kim Berly (drums). All share vocals.	
9/11/71	8	10	1. **Sweet City Woman**	Bell 45,120
4/3/76	40	2	2. Hit The Road Jack **[N]**	Quality 501
			featuring a telephone conversation with Wolfman Jack	

DATE	POS	WKS	ARTIST–RECORD TITLE	LABEL & NO.
			STAMPLEY, Joe	
			Born on 6/6/43 in Springhill, Louisiana. Country singer/songwriter/pianist.	
3/3/73	37	3	1. Soul Song #1 Country hit (1 week)	Dot 17442
			STANDELLS, The	
			Early punk-rock group from Los Angeles, California: Dick Dodd (vocals, drums), Larry Tamblyn and Tony Valentino (guitars) and Gary Lane (bass). Dodd was an original Mouseketeer on TV's *The Mickey Mouse Club*. Tamblyn is the brother of actor Russ Tamblyn.	
6/11/66	11	9	1. Dirty Water	Tower 185
			STANLEY, Michael, Band	
			Born Michael Stanley Gee on 3/25/48 in Cleveland, Ohio. Rock singer/guitarist. His band: Kevin Raleigh (vocals, keyboards), Bob Pelander (keyboards), Gary Markshay (guitar), Rick Bell (sax), Mike Gismondi (bass) and Tom Dobeck (drums). Dan Powers replaced Markshay in 1982.	
1/10/81	33	5	1. He Can't Love You Clarence Clemons (sax solo)	EMI America 8063
11/12/83	39	1	2. My Town	EMI America 8178
			STANSFIELD, Lisa	
			Born on 4/11/66 in Rochdale, Manchester, England. Dance singer/songwriter.	
2/24/90	3	14	▲ 1. **All Around The World** Sales #1 (1) / Airplay #3 #1 R&B hit (2 weeks)	Arista 9928
6/16/90	14	8	2. You Can't Deny It Sales #11 / Airplay #18 #1 R&B hit (1 week)	Arista 2024
9/8/90	21	7	3. This Is The Right Time Airplay #20 / Sales #24	Arista 2049
11/23/91+	27	9	4. Change Airplay #24 / Sales #40	Arista 12362
			STAPLE SINGERS, The	
			R&B family group from Winoma, Mississippi: Roebuck "Pop" Staples (guitar), with his daughters Mavis, Cleotha and Yvonne Staples (vocals). Pop Staples died on 12/19/2000 (age 84). Group inducted into the Rock and Roll Hall of Fame in 1999.	
3/20/71	27	5	1. Heavy Makes You Happy (Sha-Na-Boom Boom)	Stax 0083
11/13/71	12	10	▲ 2. Respect Yourself	Stax 0104
4/15/72	1 (1)	14	3. **I'll Take You There** #1 R&B hit (4 weeks)	Stax 0125
8/26/72	38	3	4. This World	Stax 0137
4/14/73	33	3	5. Oh La De Da	Stax 0156
11/10/73	9	11	● 6. **If You're Ready (Come Go With Me)** #1 R&B hit (3 weeks)	Stax 0179
3/23/74	23	7	7. Touch A Hand, Make A Friend	Stax 0196
11/1/75	1 (1)	12	● 8. **Let's Do It Again** #1 R&B hit (2 weeks); written and produced by Curtis Mayfield; title song from the movie starring Sidney Poitier and Bill Cosby	Curtom 0109
			STAPLETON, Cyril, And His Orchestra	
			Born on 12/31/14 in Nottingham, England. Died on 2/25/74 (age 59). Orchestra leader.	
9/29/56	25	2	1. The Italian Theme Top 100 #25 **[I]**	London 1672

DATE	POS	WKS	ARTIST–RECORD TITLE	LABEL & NO.
1/19/59	**13**	10	2. The Children's Marching Song (Nick Nack Taddy Whack) based on the traditional nursery song "This Old Man"; featuring the children from the movie *The Inn Of The Sixth Happiness* starring Ingrid Bergman	London 1851
			STARBUCK	
			Pop-rock group from Atlanta, Georgia: Bruce Blackman (vocals, keyboards), Bo Wagner (marimbas), Sloan Hayes (keyboards), Tom Strain and Ron Norris (guitars), Jim Cobb (bass) and Dave Snavely (drums). Strain, Norris and Snavely left after "Moonlight Feels Alright," replaced by Darryl Kutz (guitar), Dave Shaver (keyboards) and Ken Crysler (drums).	
5/29/76	**3**	14	1. **Moonlight Feels Right**	Private Stock 45,039
5/21/77	**38**	2	2. Everybody Be Dancin'	Private Stock 45,144
			STARCHER, Buddy	
			Born Oby Edgar Starcher on 3/16/06 in Ripley, West Virginia. Died on 11/2/2001 (age 95). Country singer/songwriter/DJ.	
5/14/66	**39**	1	1. History Repeats Itself **[S]** an accounting of "coincidental" parallels between the careers and deaths of Presidents Lincoln and Kennedy	Boone 1038
			STARGARD	
			Disco trio: Rochelle Runnells, Debra Anderson and Janice Williams. Appeared as "The Diamonds" in the movie *Sgt. Pepper's Lonely Hearts Club Band*.	
3/4/78	**21**	7	1. Theme Song From "Which Way Is Up" #1 R&B hit (2 weeks); from the movie *Which Way Is Up* starring Richard Pryor	MCA 40825
			STARLAND VOCAL BAND	
			Pop group formed in Washington DC: Bill and wife Taffy Danoff, John Carroll and future wife Margot Chapman. Bill and Taffy had fronted the folk group Fat City (backed John Denver on "Take Me Home, Country Roads"). Group hosted own summer TV variety series in 1977. Won the 1976 Best New Artist Grammy Award.	
6/5/76	**1** (2)	14	● 1. **Afternoon Delight**	Windsong 10588
			STARLETS, The	
			Female R&B vocal group from Chicago, Illinois: Dynetta Boone, Jane Hall, Maxine Edwards, Mickey McKinney, Jeanette Miles and Bernice Williams. While under contract to PAM Records, The Starlets recorded "I Sold My Heart To The Junkman" on the Newtown label. Newtown credited one of its artists, The Blue-Belles (Patti LaBelle's group), on the label.	
6/12/61	**38**	2	1. Better Tell Him No	PAM 1003
5/12/62	**15**	7	2. I Sold My Heart To The Junkman **THE BLUE-BELLES**	Newtown 5000
			STARPOINT	
			Dance group from Maryland: brothers Ernesto, George, Orlando and Greg Phillips, with Renee Diggs and Kayode Adeyemo.	
11/16/85	**25**	9	1. Object Of My Desire Sales #19 / Airplay #30	Elektra 69621

DATE	POS	WKS	ARTIST–RECORD TITLE	LABEL & NO.
			STARR, Brenda K.	
			Born Brenda Kaplan on 10/15/66 in Manhattan, New York. R&B-dance singer/actress. Daughter of Harvey Kaplan (of Spiral Starecase).	
5/7/88	**13**	12	1. I Still Believe Sales #10 / Airplay #14	MCA 53288
9/3/88	**24**	7	2. What You See Is What You Get Sales #16 / Airplay #26	MCA 53367
			STARR, Edwin	
			Born Charles Hatcher on 1/21/42 in Nashville, Tennessee; raised in Cleveland, Ohio. Died of a heart attack on 4/2/2003 (age 61). R&B singer/songwriter.	
9/4/65	**21**	6	1. Agent Double-O-Soul	Ric-Tic 103
3/22/69	**6**	9	2. **Twenty-Five Miles**	Gordy 7083
7/25/70	**1** (3)	13	3. **War**	Gordy 7101
1/2/71	**26**	4	4. Stop The War Now	Gordy 7104
			STARR, Kay	
			Born Katherine Starks on 7/21/22 in Dougherty, Oklahoma; raised in Dallas, Texas and Memphis, Tennessee. Pop singer. Appeared in the movies *Make Believe Ballroom* and *When You're Smiling*.	
8/6/55	**17**	1	1. Good And Lonesome Juke Box #17 Hal Mooney (orch. and chorus)	RCA Victor 6146
1/7/56	**1** (6)	20	● 2. **Rock And Roll Waltz** Juke Box #1 (6) / Top 100 #1 (4) / Best Seller #1 (1) / Jockey #1 (1) Hugo Winterhalter (orch. and chorus)	RCA Victor 6359
6/30/56	**40**	1	3. Second Fiddle Top 100 #40 Joe Reisman (orch. and chorus)	RCA Victor 6541
9/16/57	**9**	10	4. **My Heart Reminds Me** Jockey #9 / Top 100 #53 Pete King (orch.)	RCA Victor 6981
			STARR, Randy	
			Born Warren Nadel on 7/2/30 in Brooklyn, New York. Pop singer/songwriter/guitarist.	
5/6/57	**32**	2	1. After School Top 100 #32 "Bugs" Bower (orch.)	Dale 100
			STARR, Ringo	
			Born Richard Starkey on 7/7/40 in Liverpool, England. Drummer with Rory Storm and the Hurricanes before joining The Beatles in 1962. First solo album in 1970. Acted in several movies. Played "Mr. Conductor" on PBS-TV's *Shining Time Station* from 1989-91. Married actress Barbara Bach on 4/27/81. Continues to tour with an ever-revolving lineup of top musicians ("The All-Star Band").	
5/8/71	**4**	11	● 1. **It Don't Come Easy** Badfinger (harmony vocals)	Apple 1831
4/15/72	**9**	7	2. **Back Off Boogaloo** above 2 produced by George Harrison	Apple 1849
10/20/73	**1** (1)	12	● 3. **Photograph** George Harrison (harmony vocal, 12-string guitar)	Apple 1865
12/29/73+	**1** (1)	12	● 4. **You're Sixteen** Nilsson (backing vocal); Paul McCartney (kazoo)	Apple 1870
3/23/74	**5**	11	5. **Oh My My** Martha Reeves and Merry Clayton (backing vocals); Billy Preston (keyboards); Tom Scott (sax)	Apple 1872

DATE	POS	WKS	ARTIST–RECORD TITLE	LABEL & NO.
11/30/74+	6	10	6. **Only You** #1 Adult Contemporary hit (1 week)	Apple 1876
2/22/75	3	10	7. **No No Song /** Nilsson (backing vocal); written by Hoyt Axton	Apple 1880
2/22/75		10	8. Snookeroo written by Elton John (also on piano and backing vocal)	
7/5/75	31	3	9. It's All Down To Goodnight Vienna / written by John Lennon (also on piano)	Apple 1882
7/5/75		3	10. Oo-Wee Dr. John (piano)	
10/16/76	26	6	11. A Dose Of Rock 'N' Roll Melissa Manchester (backing vocal); Peter Frampton (guitar)	Atlantic 3361
12/5/81	38	2	12. Wrack My Brain written and produced by George Harrison (also on guitar and backing vocal)	Boardwalk 130
			STARSHIP — see JEFFERSON STARSHIP	
			STARS on 45 Studio group assembled in Holland by producer Jaap Eggermont.	
5/2/81	1 (1)	14	● 1. **Medley** Intro "Venus"/Sugar Sugar/No Reply/I'll Be Back/Drive My Car/Do You Want To Know A Secret/We Can Work It Out/I Should Have Known Better/Nowhere Man/You're Going To Lose That Girl/Stars on 45	Radio 3810
4/17/82	28	5	2. Stars on 45 III **STARS ON (A Tribute To Stevie Wonder)** Uptight Everything's All Right/My Cherie Amour/Yester Me, Yester You/Master Blaster/You Are The Sunshine Of My Life/Isn't She Lovely/Stars On Jingle/Sir Duke/I Wish/I Was Made To Love Her/Superstition/Fingertips	Radio 4019
			STARZ Hard-rock group formed in New York: Michael Lee Smith (vocals), Rich Ranno and Brendan Harkin (guitars), Pete Sweval (bass) and Joe Dube (drums). Smith is the brother of Rex Smith.	
4/30/77	33	2	1. Cherry Baby	Capitol 4399
			STATLER BROTHERS, The Country vocal group from Staunton, Virginia: brothers Harold and Don Reid, with Lew DeWitt and Phil Balsley. DeWitt died of Crohn's disease on 8/15/90 (age 52).	
12/11/65+	4	9	1. **Flowers On The Wall**	Columbia 43315
			STATON, Candi Born Canzata Staton on 5/13/40 in Hanceville, Alabama. R&B singer. Formerly married to Clarence Carter.	
10/3/70	24	9	1. Stand By Your Man	Fame 1472
6/26/76	20	11	2. Young Hearts Run Free #1 R&B hit (1 week)	Warner 8181

DATE	POS	WKS	ARTIST–RECORD TITLE	LABEL & NO.
			STATUS QUO, The	
			Psychedelic-rock group from London, England: Francis Michael Rossi (vocals, guitar), Rick Parfitt (guitar), Roy Lynes (organ), Alan Lancaster (bass) and John Coghlan (drums).	
6/29/68	**12**	11	1. Pictures Of Matchstick Men	Cadet Concept 7001
			STEALERS WHEEL	
			Pop-rock duo from Scotland: Gerry Rafferty (vocals, guitar) and Joe Egan (vocals, keyboards).	
3/31/73	**6**	13	1. **Stuck In The Middle With You**	A&M 1416
3/9/74	**29**	3	2. Star	A&M 1483
			STEAM	
			Group from Bridgeport, Connecticut. "Na Na Hey Hey Kiss Him Goodbye" was recorded by the trio of Gary DeCarlo, Paul Leka and Dale Frashuer, and released as by Steam. After the song became a hit, Leka assembled an actual Steam group: Bill Steer (vocals), Jay Babins and Tom Zuke (guitars), Hank Schorz (keyboards), Mike Daniels (bass) and Ray Corries (drums).	
11/8/69	**1** (2)	13	● 1. **Na Na Hey Hey Kiss Him Goodbye**	Fontana 1667
			STEEL BREEZE	
			Pop-rock group from Sacramento, California: Ric Jacobs (vocals), Ken Goorabian and Waylin Carpenter (guitars), Rod Toner (keyboards), Vinnie Pantleoni (bass) and Barry Lowenthal (drums).	
9/18/82	**16**	11	1. You Don't Want Me Anymore	RCA 13283
2/19/83	**30**	6	2. Dreamin' Is Easy	RCA 13427
			STEELHEART	
			Hard-rock group from Norwalk, Connecticut: Michael Matijevic (vocals), Chris Risola and Frank Dicostanzo (guitars), Jimmy Ward (bass) and John Fowler (drums).	
6/1/91	**23**	9	1. I'll Never Let You Go (Angel Eyes) Sales #11 / Airplay #71	MCA 53801
			STEELY DAN	
			Jazz-rock group formed in Los Angeles, California, by Donald Fagen (vocals, keyboards) and Walter Becker (bass, vocals). Group, primarily known as a studio unit, featured Fagen and Becker with various studio musicians. Inducted into the Rock and Roll Hall of Fame in 2001.	
12/30/72+	**6**	11	1. **Do It Again**	ABC 11338
4/7/73	**11**	11	2. Reeling In The Years	ABC 11352
6/8/74	**4**	11	3. **Rikki Don't Lose That Number**	ABC 11439
6/21/75	**37**	2	4. Black Friday	ABC 12101
1/7/78	**11**	11	5. Peg	ABC 12320
			Michael McDonald (backing vocal)	
5/6/78	**19**	8	6. Deacon Blues	ABC 12355
7/1/78	**22**	5	7. FM (No Static At All)	MCA 40894
			Timothy B. Schmit (backing vocals); from the movie *FM* starring Michael Brandon	
9/23/78	**26**	5	8. Josie	ABC 12404
12/13/80+	**10**	13	9. **Hey Nineteen**	MCA 51036
3/28/81	**22**	7	10. Time Out Of Mind	MCA 51082
			Mark Knopfler of Dire Straits (guitar solo)	

DATE	POS	WKS	ARTIST–RECORD TITLE	LABEL & NO.
			STEIN, Lou	
			Born on 4/22/22 in Philadelphia, Pennsylvania. Died on 12/10/2002 (age 80). Session pianist.	
3/30/57	**31**	3	1. Almost Paradise Top 100 #31 **[I]** Bill Fontaine (orch.)	RKO Unique 385
			STEINER, Tommy Shane	
			Born in 1973 in Austin, Texas. Country singer/songwriter.	
5/4/02	**39**	3	1. What If She's An Angel Airplay #36	album cut
			STEINMAN, Jim	
			Born on 11/1/47 in Brooklyn, New York. Songwriter/pianist/producer. Produced songs for Meat Loaf, Air Supply and Bonnie Tyler.	
7/18/81	**32**	6	1. Rock And Roll Dreams Come Through Rory Dodd (vocal)	Cleveland I./Epic 02111
			STEPHENSON, Van	
			Born on 11/4/53 in Hamilton, Ohio. Died of cancer on 4/8/2001 (age 47). Pop-country singer/songwriter.	
5/12/84	**22**	10	1. Modern Day Delilah	MCA 52376
			STEPPENWOLF	
			Hard-rock group formed in Los Angeles, California: Joachim "John Kay" Krauledat (vocals, guitar; born on 4/12/44), Michael Monarch (guitar; born on 7/5/50), John "Goldy McJohn" Goadsby (keyboards; born on 5/2/45) and Jerry "Edmonton" McCrohan (drums; born on 10/24/46). All but Monarch were members of Canadian group Sparrow. Many personnel changes except for Kay. Group named after a 1927 Herman Hesse novel. Edmonton died in a car crash on 11/28/93 (age 47).	
7/20/68	**2** (3)	12	● 1. **Born To Be Wild**	Dunhill/ABC 4138
10/26/68	**3**	13	● 2. **Magic Carpet Ride**	Dunhill/ABC 4161
3/15/69	**10**	8	3. **Rock Me**	Dunhill/ABC 4182
9/6/69	**31**	5	4. Move Over	Dunhill/ABC 4205
2/7/70	**39**	1	5. Monster	Dunhill/ABC 4221
5/9/70	**35**	3	6. Hey Lawdy Mama	Dunhill/ABC 4234
10/5/74	**29**	3	7. Straight Shootin' Woman	Mums 6031
			STEREO MC'S	
			Dance trio from London, England: Rob Birch, Nick Hallam and Owen Rossiter.	
7/20/91	**39**	1	1. Elevate My Mind Sales #35 / Airplay #41	4th & B'way 447519
4/24/93	**20**	11	2. Connected Airplay #24 / Sales #29 samples "Let Me (Let Me Be Your Lover)" by Jimmy "Bo" Horne	Gee Street 864744
			STEREOS, The	
			R&B vocal group from Steubenville, Ohio: Bruce Robinson, Nathaniel Hicks, Sam Profit, George Otis and Ronnie Collins.	
10/16/61	**29**	3	1. I Really Love You	Cub 9095
			STEVE & EYDIE — see LAWRENCE, Steve/ GORME, Eydie	

DATE	POS	WKS	ARTIST–RECORD TITLE	LABEL & NO.
			STEVENS, April — see TEMPO, Nino	
			STEVENS, Cat	
			Born Steven Georgiou on 7/21/47 in London, England. Pop-folk singer/songwriter/guitarist. Converted to Muslim religion in 1979; took name Yusuf Islam.	
3/6/71	**11**	10	1. Wild World	A&M 1231
7/10/71	**30**	7	2. Moon Shadow	A&M 1265
10/9/71	**7**	10	3. **Peace Train**	A&M 1291
			#1 Adult Contemporary hit (3 weeks)	
4/22/72	**6**	11	4. **Morning Has Broken**	A&M 1335
			#1 Adult Contemporary hit (1 week)	
12/2/72+	**16**	9	5. Sitting	A&M 1396
8/4/73	**31**	5	6. The Hurt	A&M 1418
4/20/74	**10**	11	7. **Oh Very Young**	A&M 1503
8/24/74	**6**	9	8. **Another Saturday Night**	A&M 1602
1/11/75	**26**	4	9. Ready	A&M 1645
8/16/75	**33**	4	10. Two Fine People	A&M 1700
7/23/77	**33**	3	11. (Remember The Days Of The) Old Schoolyard	A&M 1948
			STEVENS, Connie	
			Born Concetta Ingolia on 8/8/38 in Brooklyn, New York. Pop singer/actress. Played "Cricket Blake" on TV's *Hawaiian Eye* from 1959-63. Appeared in the several movies. Married to Eddie Fisher from 1967-69.	
4/27/59	**4**	11	● 1. **Kookie, Kookie (Lend Me Your Comb)** [N] **EDWARD BYRNES And CONNIE STEVENS**	Warner 5047
3/14/60	**3**	17	2. **Sixteen Reasons** Don Ralke (orch., above 2)	Warner 5137
			STEVENS, Dodie	
			Born Geraldine Pasquale on 2/17/46 in Chicago, Illinois; raised in Temple City, California. Female pop singer.	
3/9/59	**3**	14	● 1. **Pink Shoe Laces** Bobby Hammack (orch.)	Crystalette 724
			STEVENS, Ray	
			Born Harold Ray Ragsdale on 1/24/39 in Clarksdale, Georgia. Country-novelty singer/songwriter. Hosted own TV variety show in 1970. Also recorded as Henhouse Five Plus Too.	
9/18/61	**35**	1	1. Jeremiah Peabody's Poly Unsaturated Quick Dissolving Fast Acting Pleasant Tasting Green And Purple Pills [N]	Mercury 71843
7/14/62	**5**	9	2. **Ahab, The Arab** [N]	Mercury 71966
6/29/63	**17**	6	3. Harry The Hairy Ape [N]	Mercury 72125
8/31/68	**28**	3	4. Mr. Businessman	Monument 1083
4/26/69	**8**	10	● 5. **Gitarzan** [N]	Monument 1131
7/26/69	**27**	4	6. Along Came Jones [N]	Monument 1150
4/18/70	**1** (2)	13	● 7. **Everything Is Beautiful**	Barnaby 2011
			#1 Adult Contemporary hit (3 weeks); intro features the children's hymn "Jesus Loves The Little Children"	
4/27/74	**1** (3)	12	● 8. **The Streak** [N]	Barnaby 600
5/24/75	**14**	10	9. Misty	Barnaby 614

DATE	POS	WKS	ARTIST–RECORD TITLE	LABEL & NO.
2/5/77	40	1	10. In The Mood **[N]** **HENHOUSE FIVE PLUS TOO** a chicken-clucking version of Glenn Miller's 1940 #1 hit	Warner 8301
			STEVENSON, B.W.	
8/25/73	9	12	Born Louis Stevenson on 10/5/49 in Dallas, Texas. Died of heart failure on 4/28/88 (age 38). Soft-rock singer/guitarist. 1. **My Maria** #1 Adult Contemporary hit (1 week); Larry Carlton (guitar)	RCA Victor 0030
			STEVIE B	
4/8/89	32	5	Born Steven Hill in Miami, Florida. Dance-pop singer/multi-instrumentalist. 1. I Wanna Be The One Sales #26 / Airplay #37	LMR 74003
7/29/89	37	2	2. In My Eyes Sales #34	LMR 74004
3/10/90	29	5	3. Love Me For Life Sales #29 / Airplay #30	LMR 84006
7/28/90	15	8	4. Love & Emotion Airplay #14 / Sales #16	LMR/RCA 2645
10/27/90	1 (4)	16	● 5. **Because I Love You (The Postman Song)** Airplay #1 (5) / Sales #1 (1) #1 Adult Contemporary hit (2 weeks)	LMR/RCA 2724
2/23/91	12	9	6. I'll Be By Your Side Airplay #11 / Sales #13	LMR/RCA 2758
4/1/95	29	12	7. Dream About You / Airplay #24 / Sales #45	
4/1/95		12	8. Funky Melody Sales: flip	Emporia/Thump 2205
			STEVIE V — see ADVENTURES OF	
			STEWART, Al	
1/22/77	8	10	Born on 9/5/45 in Glasgow, Scotland. Pop singer/songwriter/guitarist. 1. **Year Of The Cat** written about British comedian Tony Hancock	Janus 266
10/21/78	7	13	2. **Time Passages** #1 Adult Contemporary hit (10 weeks)	Arista 0362
2/17/79	29	4	3. Song On The Radio above 3 produced by Alan Parsons	Arista 0389
9/27/80	24	6	4. Midnight Rocks	Arista 0552
			STEWART, Amii	
2/24/79	1 (1)	14	Born in 1956 in Washington DC. Disco singer/dancer/actress. In the Broadway musical *Bubbling Brown Sugar*. ▲ 1. **Knock On Wood**	Ariola America 7736
			STEWART, Billy	
5/1/65	26	4	Born on 3/24/37 in Washington DC. Died in a car crash on 1/17/70 (age 32). R&B singer/keyboardist. Nicknamed "Fat Boy." 1. I Do Love You	Chess 1922
7/10/65	24	5	2. Sitting In The Park	Chess 1932
8/6/66	10	7	3. **Summertime** from the folk opera *Porgy And Bess*; #12 hit for Billie Holiday in 1936	Chess 1966
11/5/66	29	5	4. Secret Love #1 hit for Doris Day in 1954	Chess 1978

DATE	POS	WKS	ARTIST–RECORD TITLE	LABEL & NO.
			STEWART, David A.	
			Born on 9/9/52 in Sunderland, England. One-half of the Eurythmics. Married Siobhan Fahey (of Bananarama and Shakespear's Sister) on 8/1/87. Candy Dulfer is a female saxophonist from Amsterdam.	
6/8/91	11	9	1. Lily Was Here Airplay #26 / Sales #55 **[I]** **DAVID A. STEWART Introducing Candy Dulfer** from the Dutch movie *Lily Was Here* starring Marion Van Thijn	Arista 2187
			STEWART, Jermaine	
			Born on 9/7/57 in Columbus, Ohio. Died of cancer on 3/17/97 (age 39). R&B-dance singer.	
6/28/86	5	13	1. **We Don't Have To Take Our Clothes Off** Sales #4 / Airplay #5	Arista 9424
4/16/88	27	5	2. Say It Again Airplay #24 / Sales #26	Arista 9636
			STEWART, John	
			Born on 9/5/39 in San Diego, California. Folk-pop singer/songwriter. Member of The Kingston Trio from 1961-67. Brother of Mike Stewart (drummer for We Five).	
6/2/79	5	13	1. **Gold**	RSO 931
9/29/79	28	5	2. Midnight Wind Stevie Nicks (backing vocal, above 2); Lindsey Buckingham (guitar, above 2)	RSO 1000
1/26/80	34	4	3. Lost Her In The Sun	RSO 1016
			STEWART, Rod	
			Born on 1/10/45 in Highgate, London, England. Pop-rock singer/songwriter. Member of the Jeff Beck Group from 1967-69. Member of Faces from 1969-75. Won Grammy's Living Legends Award in 1989. Married to actress Alana Hamilton from 1979-84. Married to supermodel Rachel Hunter from 1990-2003. Inducted into the Rock and Roll Hall of Fame in 1994.	
8/28/71	1 (5)	15	● 1. **Maggie May** Ron Wood (guitar); Pete Sears (of Jefferson Starship; piano)	Mercury 73224
11/27/71	24	6	2. (I Know) I'm Losing You **ROD STEWART With Faces**	Mercury 73244
9/16/72	13	7	3. You Wear It Well	Mercury 73330
12/16/72	40	1	4. Angel written by Jimi Hendrix	Mercury 73344
10/23/76	1 (8)	17	● 5. **Tonight's The Night (Gonna Be Alright)** French whispers by Rod's then-love, Swedish actress Britt Ekland	Warner 8262
2/26/77	21	9	6. The First Cut Is The Deepest written by Cat Stevens	Warner 8321
7/2/77	30	4	7. The Killing Of Georgie (Part I And II)	Warner 8396
11/26/77+	4	15	● 8. **You're In My Heart (The Final Acclaim)**	Warner 8475
3/11/78	28	4	9. Hot Legs	Warner 8535
5/27/78	22	6	10. I Was Only Joking	Warner 8568
12/23/78+	1 (4)	18	▲ 11. **Da Ya Think I'm Sexy?**	Warner 8724
5/12/79	22	6	12. Ain't Love A Bitch	Warner 8810
11/29/80+	5	17	13. **Passion**	Warner 49617
10/31/81	5	15	14. **Young Turks**	Warner 49843
2/13/82	20	8	15. Tonight I'm Yours (Don't Hurt Me)	Warner 49886
6/11/83	14	9	16. Baby Jane	Warner 29608

DATE	POS	WKS	ARTIST–RECORD TITLE	LABEL & NO.
10/1/83	35	3	17. What Am I Gonna Do (I'm So In Love With You)	Warner 29564
6/2/84	6	13	18. **Infatuation**	Warner 29256
			Jeff Beck (guitar solo)	
9/15/84	10	10	19. **Some Guys Have All The Luck** Airplay #8 / Sales #19	Warner 29215
6/14/86	6	12	20. **Love Touch** Airplay #4 / Sales #7	Warner 28668
			theme from the movie *Legal Eagles* starring Robert Redford and Debra Winger	
6/4/88	12	9	21. Lost In You Sales #9 / Airplay #17	Warner 27927
9/10/88	12	10	22. Forever Young Sales #13 / Airplay #13	Warner 27796
			Andy Taylor (guitar solo, above 2)	
1/28/89	4	13	23. **My Heart Can't Tell You No** Airplay #3 / Sales #5	Warner 27729
6/10/89	11	10	24. Crazy About Her Sales #10 / Airplay #13	Warner 27657
12/2/89+	3	14	25. **Downtown Train** Airplay #2 / Sales #3	Warner 22685
			#1 Adult Contemporary hit (1 week) / #1 Mainstream Rock hit (2 weeks)	
4/7/90	10	10	26. **This Old Heart Of Mine (1989 Version)** Airplay #7 / Sales #15 **[R]**	Warner 19983
			ROD STEWART (with Ronald Isley)	
			#1 Adult Contemporary hit (5 weeks); solo version by Stewart charted at #83 in 1976	
3/23/91	5	14	27. **Rhythm Of My Heart** Airplay #3 / Sales #9	Warner 19366
7/27/91	10	11	28. **The Motown Song** Airplay #24 / Sales #36	Warner 19322
			ROD STEWART (with The Temptations)	
11/16/91+	20	14	29. Broken Arrow Airplay #19 / Sales #35	Warner 19274
			written by Robbie Robertson (The Band)	
5/15/93	5	17	● 30. **Have I Told You Lately** Sales #6 / Airplay #7 **[L-R]**	Warner 18511
			#1 Adult Contemporary hit (5 weeks)	
9/11/93	19	12	31. Reason To Believe Airplay #12 / Sales #67 **[L-R]**	Warner 18427
			ROD STEWART (with Ronnie Wood)	
			studio version charted at #62 in 1971	
12/4/93+	1 (3)	20	▲ 32. **All For Love** Sales #1 (5) / Airplay #3	A&M 0476
			BRYAN ADAMS ROD STEWART STING	
			from the movie *The Three Musketeers* starring Kiefer Sutherland and Charlie Sheen	
2/12/94	36	3	33. Having A Party Airplay #31 **[L]**	Warner 18424
			ROD STEWART With Ronnie Wood	
8/1/98	39	1	34. Ooh La La Airplay #45	Warner 17195
			first recorded by Rod Stewart & Faces in 1973	

STEWART, Sandy

Born Sandra Galitz on 7/10/37 in Philadelphia, Pennsylvania. Pop singer. Regular on the Eddie Fisher and Perry Como variety TV shows.

DATE	POS	WKS	ARTIST–RECORD TITLE	LABEL & NO.
1/12/63	20	5	1. My Coloring Book	Colpix 669
			Don Costa (orch.)	

STEWART, Sandy — see NICKS, Stevie

STIGERS, Curtis

Born on 10/18/65 in Boise, Idaho. Pop-jazz singer/saxophonist.

DATE	POS	WKS	ARTIST–RECORD TITLE	LABEL & NO.
10/5/91	9	11	1. **I Wonder Why** Airplay #28 / Sales #62	Arista 12331

Britney Spears struck gold with her debut hit, the chart-topping "Baby One More Time." Britney would be in the spotlight time and time again, from sharing a kiss with Madonna to sharing a Vegas wedding with longtime friend Jason Alexander.

The Spice Girls were the first group to have their first four singles all reach #1 in Great Britain. Although not quite that popular in America, the #1 status reached by "Wannabe" showed they were more than just pop star wannabes.

The Staple Singers earned their first #1 hit with the uplifting "I'll Take You There." They would not reach the top spot again until three years later, with their appropriately named hit "Let's Do It Again."

Steam didn't even exist at the time their hit, "Na Na Hey Hey Kiss Him Goodbye," climbed the charts. Written for a record's B-side and released under a pseudonym, the laugh was on the songwriters when the song went to #1.

Ray Stevens was best known as the novelty singer behind such funny hits as "Gitarzan" and "The Streak," but he also had a chance to successfully show his serious side and beautiful voice with the #1 hit, "Everything Is Beautiful."

Rod Stewart endured some controversy with his hit "Tonight's The Night (Gonna Be Alright)," as it told the story of a young girl's seduction. Although some radio stations banned it, fans nonetheless pushed the track to #1.

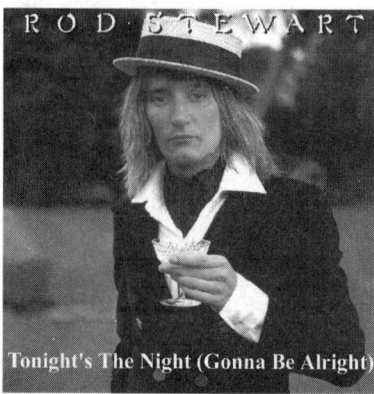

Barbra Streisand, an accomplished actress and singer, often had her biggest musical hits come from her movies. Her first #1, "The Way We Were," was the title song from the movie starring herself and Robert Redford.

Styx were a well-known rock band who had a total of 16 Top 40 hits, but their only #1 hit came courtesy of the ballad "Babe," a song singer Dennis DeYoung wrote for his wife.

Sugar Ray not only earned a chart-topping Airplay hit with their debut single "Fly," but lead singer Mark McGrath also proved himself pretty "fly" at trivia, when he became a regular participant on VH1's *Rock & Roll Jeopardy.*

Donna Summer integrated her cover of Richard Harris' #2 hit "MacArthur Park" into a disco medley called the "MacArthur Park Suite." The medley not only included the chart-topping title song, but also its follow-up Top 10 hit, "Heaven Knows."

Surface scored their first #1 hit with a song appropriately titled "The First Time." Although its follow-up was titled "Never Gonna Let You Down," it must have been a disappointment when it became their last Top 40 hit.

Survivor earned five Top 10 hits in the 1980s, including the #1 *Rocky III* smash, "Eye Of The Tiger." Unfortunately, they could not survive the changing musical trends, and have been non-existent in the Top 40 since 1986.

Sweet Sensation had their wish for a #1 hit come true when, after six dance-able tracks, they released the chart-topping ballad "If Wishes Came True." Their career, however, soon soured, and it would be their last Top 40 hit.

SWV reached #1 with the hit "Weak," but 1993 was a strong year for the R&B trio. They also reached the Top 10 with "I'm So Into You" and a medley of their hit "Right Here" combined with Michael Jackson's "Human Nature."

DATE	POS	WKS	ARTIST–RECORD TITLE	LABEL & NO.
			STILLS, Stephen	
			Born on 1/3/45 in Dallas, Texas. Singer/songwriter/guitarist. Member of Buffalo Springfield and Crosby, Stills & Nash.	
12/19/70+	**14**	10	1. Love The One You're With	Atlantic 2778
			Rita Coolidge, David Crosby, Graham Nash and John Sebastian (backing vocals)	
3/27/71	37	2	2. Sit Yourself Down	Atlantic 2790
			Rita Coolidge, David Crosby, Mama Cass, Graham Nash and John Sebastian (backing vocals)	
			STING	
			Born Gordon Sumner on 10/2/51 in Wallsend, England. Pop singer/songwriter/bassist. Lead singer of The Police. Acted in several movies. Married actress/producer Trudie Styler on 8/20/92. Nicknamed "Sting" because of a yellow and black jersey he liked to wear. Recipient of *Billboard's* Century Award in 2003.	
6/15/85	**3**	14	1. **If You Love Somebody Set Them Free** Sales #3 / Airplay #3	A&M 2738
			#1 Mainstream Rock hit (3 weeks)	
9/7/85	**8**	11	2. **Fortress Around Your Heart** Sales #7 / Airplay #7	A&M 2767
			#1 Mainstream Rock hit (2 weeks)	
11/23/85	17	9	3. Love Is The Seventh Wave Airplay #17 / Sales #19	A&M 2787
2/1/86	16	8	4. Russians Airplay #15 / Sales #17	A&M 2799
10/24/87	**7**	12	5. **We'll Be Together** Sales #6 / Airplay #8	A&M 2983
2/6/88	15	8	6. Be Still My Beating Heart Sales #14 / Airplay #15	A&M 2992
2/2/91	**5**	9	7. **All This Time** Sales #8 / Airplay #9	A&M 1541
			#1 Mainstream Rock hit (7 weeks) / #1 Modern Rock hit (2 weeks)	
3/20/93	17	11	8. If I Ever Lose My Faith In You Airplay #14 / Sales #67	A&M 0111
7/17/93	23	8	9. Fields Of Gold Airplay #12 / Sales #66	A&M 0258
12/4/93+	**1** (3)	20	▲ 10. **All For Love** Sales #1 (5) / Airplay #3	A&M 0476
			BRYAN ADAMS ROD STEWART STING	
			from the movie *The Three Musketeers* starring Kiefer Sutherland and Charlie Sheen	
12/17/94	38	1	11. When We Dance Airplay #40 / Sales #49	A&M 0846
7/1/00	17	15	12. Desert Rose Sales #17 / Airplay #17	A&M 497321
			STING Featuring Cheb Mami	
			STITES, Gary	
			Born on 7/23/40 in Denver, Colorado. Pop singer/songwriter/guitarist.	
5/18/59	24	5	1. Lonely For You	Carlton 508
			STOLOFF, Morris	
			Born on 8/1/1898 in Philadelphia, Pennsylvania. Died on 4/16/80 (age 81). Composer/conductor/violinist. Became musical director for Columbia Pictures in 1936.	
4/21/56	**1** (3)	22	● 1. **Moonglow and Theme From "Picnic"**	Decca 29888
			Jockey #1 (3) / Best Seller #2 / Top 100 #2 / Juke Box #4 **[I]**	
			MORRIS STOLOFF Conducting The Columbia Pictures Orchestra	
			from the movie *Picnic* starring William Holden and Kim Novak	
			STONE, Cliffie, And His Orchestra	
			Born Clifford Snyder on 3/1/17 in Burbank, California. Died of a heart attack on 1/16/98 (age 80). Country bandleader/songwriter.	
8/13/55	14	4	1. The Popcorn Song Juke Box #14 / Best Seller #25 **[N]**	Capitol 3131
			Bob Roubian (vocal)	

DATE	POS	WKS	ARTIST—RECORD TITLE	LABEL & NO.
			STONE, Kirby, Four	
			Born on 4/27/18 in Manhattan, New York. Died in July 1981 (age 63). His vocal group included Eddie Hall, Larry Foster and Mike Gardner.	
7/28/58	25	1	1. Baubles, Bangles And Beads Jockey #25 / Hot 100 #50 Jimmy Carroll (orch.); from the musical *Kismet* starring Alfred Drake; introduced by Peggy Lee in 1953	Columbia 41183
			STONEBOLT	
			Pop group from Vancouver, British Columbia, Canada: David Willis (vocals), Ray Roper (guitar), John Webster (keyboards), Dan Atchison (bass) and Brian Lousley (drums).	
9/30/78	29	5	1. I Will Still Love You	Parachute 512
			STONE PONEYS — see RONSTADT, Linda	
			STONE TEMPLE PILOTS	
			Hard-rock group formed in San Diego, California: Scott Weiland (vocals), brothers Dean (guitar) and Robert (bass) DeLeo, and Eric Kretz (drums).	
8/14/93	39 ᴬ	4	1. Plush	album cut
8/13/94	38 ᴬ	2	2. Vasoline #1 Mainstream Rock hit (2 weeks)	album cut
10/1/94	18 ᴬ	24	3. Interstate Love Song #1 Mainstream Rock hit (15 weeks); above 3 from the album *Purple* on Atlantic 82607	album cut
3/23/96	28 ᴬ	8	4. Big Bang Baby #1 Mainstream Rock hit (1 week)	album cut
7/20/96	36 ᴬ	5	5. Trippin' On A Hole In A Paper Heart #1 Mainstream Rock hit (4 weeks); above 2 from the album *Tiny Music...Songs From The Vatican Gift Shop* on Atlantic 82871	album cut
			STOOKEY, Paul — see PETER, PAUL & MARY	
			STORIES	
			Rock group from Brooklyn, New York: Ian Lloyd (vocals, bass), Steve Love (guitar), Michael Brown (keyboards) and Bryan Madey (drums). Brown was a member of Left Banke.	
7/14/73	1 (2)	15	● 1. **Brother Louie**	Kama Sutra 577
			STORM, The	
			Rock group formed in San Francisco, California: Kevin Chalfant (vocals), Gregg Rolie (vocals, keyboards), Josh Ramos (guitar), Ross Valory (bass) and Steve Smith (drums). Rolie was in Santana. Rolie, Valory and Smith were members of Journey.	
1/4/92	26	6	1. I've Got A Lot To Learn About Love Airplay #26	Interscope 98726
			STORM, Billy	
			Born on 6/29/38 in Dayton, Ohio. Lead singer of The Valiants.	
5/18/59	28	6	1. I've Come Of Age Frank DeVol (orch.); melody is from "Tchaikowsky's 5th Symphony (2nd movement)"	Columbia 41356

DATE	POS	WKS	ARTIST–RECORD TITLE	LABEL & NO.
			STORM, Gale	
			Born Josephine Cottle on 4/5/22 in Bloomington, Texas. Pop singer/actress. Starred in several movie musicals. Star of TV's *My Little Margie* (1952-55) and *The Gale Storm Show* (1956-62).	
10/22/55	2 (3)	17	● 1. **I Hear You Knocking** Juke Box #2 / Top 100 #2 / Best Seller #3 / Jockey #4 #2 R&B hit for Smiley Lewis in 1955	Dot 15412
12/24/55+	6	12	2. **Teen Age Prayer** / Jockey #6 / Juke Box #6 / Top 100 #9 / Best Seller #13	
12/31/55+	5	9	3. **Memories Are Made Of This** Jockey #5 / Top 100 #16 / Best Seller: flip / Juke Box: flip	Dot 15436
3/3/56	9	14	4. **Why Do Fools Fall In Love** Jockey #9 / Juke Box #14 / Best Seller #15 / Top 100 #15	Dot 15448
5/5/56	6	14	5. **Ivory Tower** Jockey #6 / Juke Box #6 / Top 100 #10 / Best Seller #15	Dot 15458
4/29/57	4	18	6. **Dark Moon** Juke Box #4 / Top 100 #5 / Best Seller #6 / Jockey #6 Billy Vaughn (orch., all of above)	Dot 15558
			STRAIT, George	
			Born on 5/18/52 in Poteet, Texas; raised in Pearsall, Texas. Country singer. Starred in the movie *Pure Country*.	
2/27/99	38	5	1. Meanwhile Sales #29 / Airplay #32	MCA 72084
5/22/99	27	11	2. Write This Down Airplay #18 #1 Country hit (4 weeks); from the album *Always Never The Same* on MCA 70050	album cut
3/25/00	31	8	3. The Best Day Airplay #24 #1 Country hit (3 weeks); from the album *Latest Greatest Straitest Hits* on MCA 170100	album cut
10/28/00	40	1	4. Go On Airplay #33 from the album *George Strait* on MCA 170143	album cut
12/15/01	34	7	5. Run Airplay #31	album cut
5/25/02	27	8	6. Living And Living Well Airplay #26 #1 Country hit (2 weeks)	album cut
11/16/02	23	12	7. She'll Leave You With A Smile Airplay #20 #1 Country hit (2 weeks); above 3 from the album *The Road Less Traveled* on MCA 170220	album cut
12/13/03	38	2	8. Cowboys Like Us Airplay #37 from the album *Honytonkville* on MCA Nashville 000114	album cut
			STRANGELOVES, The	
			Writers/producers Bob Feldman, Jerry Goldstein and Richard Gottehrer.	
7/10/65	11	8	1. I Want Candy	Bang 501
10/23/65	39	1	2. Cara-Lin	Bang 508
2/5/66	30	4	3. Night Time	Bang 514
			STRAWBERRY ALARM CLOCK	
			Psychedelic-rock group formed in Los Angeles, California: Greg Munford (vocals), Ed King and Lee Freeman (guitars), Mark Weitz (keyboards), Gary Lovetro (bass) and Randy Seol (drums). King later joined Lynyrd Skynyrd.	
10/14/67	1 (1)	14	● 1. **Incense And Peppermints**	Uni 55018
1/27/68	23	6	2. Tomorrow	Uni 55046

DATE	POS	WKS	ARTIST–RECORD TITLE	LABEL & NO.
			STRAY CATS	
			Rockabilly trio from Long Island, New York: Brian Setzer (vocals, guitar), Lee Rocker (bass) and Slim Jim Phantom (drums). Setzer portrayed Eddie Cochran in the movie *La Bamba*. Phantom married actress Britt Ekland. Setzer formed own "jump" orchestra in 1998.	
10/23/82	9	13	1. **Rock This Town**	EMI America 8132
1/8/83	3	14	2. **Stray Cat Strut**	EMI America 8122
8/20/83	5	12	3. **(She's) Sexy + 17**	EMI America 8168
12/3/83	35	3	4. I Won't Stand In Your Way	EMI America 8185
			STREET PEOPLE	
			Studio group featuring Rupert Holmes.	
2/21/70	36	5	1. Jennifer Tomkins	Musicor 1365
			STREISAND, Barbra	
			Born on 4/24/42 in Brooklyn, New York. Singer/actress. Starred in several movies and Broadway shows. Married to actor Elliott Gould from 1963-71. Married actor James Brolin on 7/2/98. Won Grammy's Lifetime Achievement Award in 1995.	
5/23/64	5	12	1. **People** #1 Adult Contemporary hit (3 weeks); from the Broadway musical *Funny Girl* starring Streisand	Columbia 42965
1/22/66	32	3	2. Second Hand Rose #3 hit in 1922 for Fanny Brice (the subject of *Funny Girl*)	Columbia 43469
12/12/70+	6	12	3. **Stoney End**	Columbia 45236
8/28/71	40	1	4. Where You Lead also see #5 below for medley version	Columbia 45414
8/12/72	37	4	5. Sweet Inspiration/Where You Lead [L]	Columbia 45626
12/22/73+	1 (3)	17	▲ 6. **The Way We Were** #1 Adult Contemporary hit (2 weeks); title song from the movie starring Streisand and Robert Redford	Columbia 45944
1/8/77	1 (3)	18	▲ 7. **Love Theme From "A Star Is Born" (Evergreen)** #1 Adult Contemporary hit (6 weeks); from the movie *A Star Is Born* starring Streisand and Kris Kristofferson	Columbia 10450
5/28/77	4	14	8. **My Heart Belongs To Me** #1 Adult Contemporary hit (4 weeks)	Columbia 10555
7/1/78	25	5	9. Songbird #1 Adult Contemporary hit (2 weeks)	Columbia 10756
8/26/78	21	6	10. Love Theme From "Eyes Of Laura Mars" (Prisoner) from the movie *Eyes Of Laura Mars* starring Faye Dunaway	Columbia 10777
11/4/78	1 (2)	15	▲ 11. **You Don't Bring Me Flowers** **BARBRA & NEIL**	Columbia 10840
7/7/79	3	13	● 12. **The Main Event/Fight** from the movie *The Main Event* starring Streisand and Ryan O'Neal	Columbia 11008
10/27/79	1 (2)	13	▲ 13. **No More Tears (Enough Is Enough)** **BARBRA STREISAND/DONNA SUMMER**	Columbia 11125
2/23/80	37	3	14. Kiss Me In The Rain	Columbia 11179
9/13/80	1 (3)	19	▲ 15. **Woman In Love** #1 Adult Contemporary hit (5 weeks)	Columbia 11364
11/15/80+	3	15	● 16. **Guilty** **BARBRA STREISAND & BARRY GIBB**	Columbia 11390
2/14/81	10	10	17. **What Kind Of Fool** **BARBRA STREISAND & BARRY GIBB** #1 Adult Contemporary hit (4 weeks); above 3 written and produced by Barry Gibb (Bee Gees)	Columbia 11430

DATE	POS	WKS	ARTIST–RECORD TITLE	LABEL & NO.
11/28/81+	11	11	18. Comin' In And Out Of Your Life	Columbia 02621
12/10/83	40	2	19. The Way He Makes Me Feel #1 Adult Contemporary hit (2 weeks); from the movie *Yentl* starring Streisand	Columbia 04177
11/12/88	25	5	20. Till I Loved You Sales #22 / Airplay #32 **BARBRA STREISAND AND DON JOHNSON** love theme from the Broadway musical *Goya*	Columbia 08062
11/23/96	8	15	● 21. **I Finally Found Someone** Sales #7 / Airplay #20 **BARBRA STREISAND and BRYAN ADAMS** from the movie *The Mirror Has Two Faces* starring Streisand	Columbia 78480
			STRING-A-LONGS, The Guitar rock and roll instrumental group from Plainview, Texas: Keith McCormack, Richard Stephens, Jim Torres (guitars), Aubrey DeCordova (bass) and Don Allen (drums).	
1/23/61	3	13	1. **Wheels** [I]	Warwick 603
4/17/61	35	2	2. Brass Buttons [I]	Warwick 625
			STRONG, Barrett Born on 2/5/41 in Mississippi. R&B singer/songwriter.	
3/21/60	23	8	1. Money (That's what I want)	Anna 1111
			STRUNK, Jud Born Justin Strunk on 6/11/36 in Jamestown, New York; raised in Farmington, Maine. Killed in a plane crash on 10/15/81 (age 45). Singer/songwriter. Regular on TV's *Laugh In*.	
3/24/73	14	10	1. Daisy A Day Mike Curb Congregation (backing vocals)	MGM 14463
			STRYPER Christian hard-rock group from Los Angeles, California: brothers Michael (vocals) and Robert (drums) Sweet, with Oz Fox (guitar) and Tim Gaines (bass).	
12/26/87+	23	8	1. Honestly Sales #22 / Airplay #23	Enigma 75009
			STUDDARD, Ruben Born on 7/14/78 in Birmingham, Alabama. Black male vocalist. Winner on the second season of TV's *American Idol* in 2003.	
6/28/03	2 (2)	5	● 1. **Flying Without Wings** Sales #2 the *Hot 100 Sales* chart also showed the B-side ("Superstar")	J Records 51786
			STYLE COUNCIL, The Techno-pop duo from England: Paul Weller (vocals) and Mick Talbot (keyboards).	
5/12/84	29	6	1. My Ever Changing Moods	Geffen 29359
			STYLES Born David Styles on 4/4/72 in Yonkers, New York. Male rapper. Former member of The Lox.	
8/24/02	22	9	1. Good Times Airplay #21 samples "I Get High (On Your Memory)" by Freda Payne; from the album *A Gangster And A Gentleman* on Ruff Ryders 493339	album cut

DATE	POS	WKS	ARTIST–RECORD TITLE	LABEL & NO.
10/19/02	3	18	2. **Jenny From The Block** Airplay #3 / Sales #16 **JENNIFER LOPEZ Featuring Jadakiss & Styles** samples "South Bronx" by Boogie Down Productions and "Hijack" by Herbie Mann	Epic 79825
			STYLISTICS, The	
			R&B vocal group from Philadelphia, Pennsylvania: Russell Thompkins Jr., Airrion Love, James Smith, James Dunn and Herb Murrell.	
7/17/71	39	1	1. Stop, Look, Listen (To Your Heart)	Avco Embassy 4572
11/27/71+	9	13	● 2. **You Are Everything**	Avco 4581
3/11/72	3	14	● 3. **Betcha By Golly, Wow** **THE STYLISTICS featuring RUSSELL THOMPKINS, JR.**	Avco 4591
7/1/72	25	6	4. People Make The World Go Round	Avco 4595
11/11/72	10	8	● 5. **I'm Stone In Love With You**	Avco 4603
3/3/73	5	9	● 6. **Break Up To Make Up**	Avco 4611
6/9/73	23	5	7. You'll Never Get To Heaven (If You Break My Heart)	Avco 4618
11/17/73	14	11	8. Rockin' Roll Baby	Avco 4625
4/13/74	2 (2)	14	● 9. **You Make Me Feel Brand New**	Avco 4634
8/17/74	18	7	10. Let's Put It All Together	Avco 4640
			STYX	
			Pop-rock group from Chicago, Illinois: Dennis DeYoung (vocals, keyboards), John Curulewski and James Young (guitars), and twin brothers Chuck (bass) and John (drums) Panozzo. Tommy Shaw replaced Curulewski in 1976. Disbanded in 1984. Reunited in 1990 with Glen Burtnick replacing Shaw, who joined Damn Yankees. John Panozzo died on 7/16/96 (age 47). In Greek mythology, Styx is a river in Hades.	
1/18/75	6	11	1. **Lady**	Wooden Nickel 10102
3/27/76	27	5	2. Lorelei	A&M 1786
12/18/76	36	3	3. Mademoiselle	A&M 1877
10/29/77+	8	15	4. **Come Sail Away**	A&M 1977
4/1/78	29	4	5. Fooling Yourself (The Angry Young Man)	A&M 2007
10/21/78	21	7	6. Blue Collar Man (Long Nights)	A&M 2087
4/7/79	16	13	7. Renegade	A&M 2110
10/20/79	1 (2)	14	● 8. **Babe**	A&M 2188
1/19/80	26	5	9. Why Me	A&M 2206
1/24/81	3	15	10. **The Best Of Times**	A&M 2300
3/28/81	9	13	11. **Too Much Time On My Hands**	A&M 2323
2/12/83	3	16	● 12. **Mr. Roboto**	A&M 2525
4/30/83	6	13	13. **Don't Let It End**	A&M 2543
6/2/84	40	2	14. Music Time	A&M 2625
1/26/91	3	12	15. **Show Me The Way** Sales #5 / Airplay #6	A&M 1536
5/18/91	25	6	16. Love At First Sight Airplay #25	A&M 1548
			SUAVE'	
			Born on 2/22/66 in Los Angeles, California. R&B singer. Son of Waymond Anderson (of GQ).	
4/23/88	20	7	1. My Girl Sales #16 / Airplay #25	Capitol 44124

DATE	POS	WKS	ARTIST–RECORD TITLE	LABEL & NO.
			SUBLIME	
			Ska-rock trio from Long Beach, California: Brad Nowell (vocals, guitar), Eric Wilson (bass) and Bud Gaugh (drums). Nowell died of a drug overdose on 5/25/96 (age 28).	
10/19/96	**29** A	14	1. What I Got	album cut
			#1 Modern Rock hit (3 weeks); from the album *Sublime* on Gasoline Alley 11413	
			SUBWAY	
			Black teen vocal group from Chicago, Illinois: Eric McNeal, Roy Jones, Keith Thomas and Trerail Puckett.	
2/18/95	**15**	14	● 1. This Lil' Game We Play Sales #7 / Airplay #25	Biv 10 0252
			SUBWAY featuring 702	
			SUGARHILL GANG	
			Rap trio from Harlem, New York: Michael "Wonder Mike" Wright, Guy "Master Gee" O'Brien and Henry "Big Bank Hank" Jackson.	
1/5/80	**36**	2	1. Rapper's Delight	Sugar Hill 542
			samples "Good Times" by Chic	
			SUGARLOAF	
			Rock group from Denver, Colorado: Jerry Corbetta (vocals, keyboards), Bob Webber (guitar), Bob Raymond (bass) and Bob MacVittie (drums). Myron Pollock replaced MacVittie in 1974.	
9/19/70	**3**	12	1. **Green-Eyed Lady**	Liberty 56183
2/1/75	**9**	11	2. **Don't Call Us, We'll Call You**	Claridge 402
			features brief snippet of The Beatles' "I Feel Fine"	
			SUGAR RAY	
			Rock group from Los Angeles, California: Mark McGrath (vocals), Craig Bullock (DJ), Rodney Sheppard (guitar), Murphy Karges (bass) and Stan Frazier (drums).	
8/9/97	**1 (6)**A	50	1. **Fly**	album cut
			SUGAR RAY Featuring Super Cat	
			#1 Modern Rock hit (8 weeks); from the album *Floored* on Lava/Atlantic 83006	
1/30/99	**3**	27	● 2. **Every Morning** Airplay #2 / Sales #4	Lava/Atlantic 84462
			#1 Modern Rock hit (6 weeks)	
7/17/99	**7**	29	3. **Someday** Airplay #4 / Sales #30	Lava/Atlantic 84536
2/5/00	**29**	7	4. **Falls Apart (Run Away)** Airplay #26	album cut
			from the album *14:59* on Lava/Atlantic 83151	
6/23/01	**13**	18	5. When It's Over Airplay #12	album cut
			from the album *Sugar Ray* on Lava/Atlantic 83414	
			SUMMER, Donna	
			Born LaDonna Andrea Gaines on 12/31/48 in Boston, Massachusetts. R&B singer/songwriter. Dubbed "The Queen of Disco." Acted in European productions of *Hair, Godspell, The Me Nobody Knows* and *Porgy And Bess.* Married Bruce Sudano (of Alive & Kicking and Brooklyn Dreams) on 7/16/80.	
12/20/75+	**2 (2)**	14	● 1. **Love To Love You Baby**	Oasis 401
9/3/77	**6**	14	● 2. **I Feel Love**	Casablanca 884
1/28/78	**37**	3	3. I Love You	Casablanca 907

DATE	POS	WKS	ARTIST–RECORD TITLE	LABEL & NO.
6/3/78	3	14	● 4. **Last Dance** from the movie *Thank God It's Friday* starring Jeff Goldblum and Debra Winger	Casablanca 926
9/30/78	1 (3)	15	● 5. **MacArthur Park**	Casablanca 939
1/20/79	4	14	● 6. **Heaven Knows** **DONNA SUMMER with Brooklyn Dreams**	Casablanca 959
4/28/79	1 (3)	17	▲ 7. **Hot Stuff**	Casablanca 978
6/9/79	1 (5)	15	▲ 8. **Bad Girls** #1 R&B hit (1 week)	Casablanca 988
9/15/79	2 (2)	14	● 9. **Dim All The Lights**	Casablanca 2201
10/27/79	1 (2)	13	▲ 10. **No More Tears (Enough Is Enough)** **BARBRA STREISAND/DONNA SUMMER**	Columbia 11125
1/26/80	5	12	● 11. **On The Radio**	Casablanca 2236
9/27/80	3	13	● 12. **The Wanderer**	Geffen 49563
10/11/80	36	3	13. Walk Away	Casablanca 2300
1/10/81	33	3	14. Cold Love	Geffen 49634
3/28/81	40	2	15. Who Do You Think You're Foolin'	Geffen 49664
7/17/82	10	11	16. **Love Is In Control (Finger On The Trigger)**	Geffen 29982
2/5/83	33	6	17. The Woman In Me	Geffen 29805
6/18/83	3	17	18. **She Works Hard For The Money** #1 R&B hit (3 weeks)	Mercury 812370
9/1/84	21	8	19. There Goes My Baby Airplay #27	Geffen 29291
5/20/89	7	10	● 20. **This Time I Know It's For Real** Sales #4 / Airplay #8	Atlantic 88899
			SUMMER, Henry Lee	
			Born on 7/5/55 in Brazil, Indiana. Rock singer/songwriter/guitarist.	
4/2/88	20	7	1. I Wish I Had A Girl Sales #17 / Airplay #24 #1 Mainstream Rock hit (1 week)	CBS Associated 07720
7/1/89	18	8	2. Hey Baby Airplay #15 / Sales #18	CBS Associated 68891
			SUNNY & THE SUNGLOWS	
			Latin group from San Antonio, Texas: Sunny Ozuna, with brothers Jesse, Oscar and Ray Villanueva, Tony Tostado, Gilbert Fernandez and Alfred Luna.	
9/28/63	11	9	1. Talk To Me	Tear Drop 3014
			SUNNYSIDERS, The	
			Vocal group formed in New York: Freddy Morgan (banjo), Norman Milkin, Jad Paul and Margie Rayburn. Morgan and Paul were members of Spike Jones & The City Slickers from 1947-58. Morgan died in 1970 (age 60). Rayburn died of a heart attack on 6/14/2000 (age 76).	
5/21/55	12	10	1. Hey, Mr. Banjo Juke Box #12 / Jockey #19 / Best Seller #20	Kapp 113
			SUNSCREEM	
			Techno-pop group from Essex, England: Lucia Holm (vocals), Darren Woodford (guitar), Paul Carnell (keyboards), Rob Fricker (bass) and Sean Wright (drums).	
4/10/93	36	5	1. Love U More Airplay #28	Columbia 74769

DATE	POS	WKS	ARTIST–RECORD TITLE	LABEL & NO.
			SUNSHINE COMPANY, The	
			Pop group formed in Los Angeles, California: Mary Nance (vocals), Doug "Red" Mark and Maury Manseau (guitars), Larry Sims (bass) and Merle Brigante (drums). Mark later formed Redeye.	
11/18/67	36	3	1. Back On The Street Again	Imperial 66260
			SUPERCAT — see SUGAR RAY	
			SUPERTRAMP	
			Rock group formed in England: Roger Hodgson (vocals, guitar), Rick Davies (vocals, keyboards), John Helliwell (sax), Dougie Thomson (bass) and Bob Siebenberg (drums). Thomson is the brother of Ali Thomson. Hodgson left in 1983.	
5/17/75	35	2	1. Bloody Well Right	A&M 1660
7/2/77	15	11	2. Give A Little Bit	A&M 1938
4/28/79	6	13	3. **The Logical Song**	A&M 2128
8/4/79	15	8	4. Goodbye Stranger	A&M 2162
11/3/79	10	11	5. **Take The Long Way Home**	A&M 2193
10/4/80	15	8	6. Dreamer [L]	A&M 2269
10/30/82	11	11	7. It's Raining Again	A&M 2502
2/26/83	31	5	8. My Kind Of Lady	A&M 2517
6/8/85	28	7	9. Cannonball Sales #25	A&M 2731
			SUPREMES, The	
			R&B vocal trio from Detroit, Michigan: Diana Ross, Mary Wilson and Florence Ballard. Cindy Birdsong (of Patti LaBelle's Blue Belles) replaced Ballard in 1967. Jean Terrell replaced Ross after "Someday We'll Be Together." Lynda Laurence replaced Birdsong in 1972. Terrell and Laurence left in 1973. Mary Wilson re-formed group with Scherrie Payne (sister of Freda Payne) and Cindy Birdsong. Birdsong left again in 1976; replaced by Susaye Greene. Ballard died of heart failure on 2/22/76 (age 32). Group inducted into the Rock and Roll Hall of Fame in 1988.	
12/28/63+	23	7	1. When The Lovelight Starts Shining Through His Eyes	Motown 1051
7/18/64	1 (2)	13	2. **Where Did Our Love Go**	Motown 1060
10/10/64	1 (4)	12	● 3. **Baby Love**	Motown 1066
11/21/64	1 (2)	13	4. **Come See About Me**	Motown 1068
3/6/65	1 (2)	10	● 5. **Stop! In The Name Of Love**	Motown 1074
5/8/65	1 (1)	10	6. **Back In My Arms Again** #1 R&B hit (1 week)	Motown 1075
8/14/65	11	7	7. Nothing But Heartaches	Motown 1080
10/30/65	1 (2)	10	8. **I Hear A Symphony**	Motown 1083
1/29/66	5	8	9. **My World Is Empty Without You**	Motown 1089
5/7/66	9	7	10. **Love Is Like An Itching In My Heart**	Motown 1094
8/20/66	1 (2)	11	11. **You Can't Hurry Love** #1 R&B hit (2 weeks)	Motown 1097
11/5/66	1 (2)	10	12. **You Keep Me Hangin' On** #1 R&B hit (4 weeks)	Motown 1101
2/4/67	1 (1)	10	13. **Love Is Here And Now You're Gone** #1 R&B hit (2 weeks)	Motown 1103
4/15/67	1 (1)	10	14. **The Happening** title song from the movie starring Anthony Quinn	Motown 1107

DATE	POS	WKS	ARTIST–RECORD TITLE	LABEL & NO.
			DIANA ROSS AND THE SUPREMES:	
8/19/67	**2** (2)	10	15. **Reflections**	Motown 1111
11/25/67	**9**	6	16. **In And Out Of Love**	Motown 1116
4/6/68	**28**	5	17. Forever Came Today	Motown 1122
7/6/68	**30**	3	18. Some Things You Never Get Used To	Motown 1126
10/26/68	**1** (2)	15	19. **Love Child**	Motown 1135
12/14/68+	**2** (2)	12	▲ 20. **I'm Gonna Make You Love Me**	Motown 1137
			DIANA ROSS AND THE SUPREMES & THE TEMPTATIONS	
2/1/69	**10**	7	21. **I'm Livin' In Shame**	Motown 1139
3/22/69	**25**	6	22. I'll Try Something New	Motown 1142
			DIANA ROSS AND THE SUPREMES & THE TEMPTATIONS	
4/26/69	**27**	5	23. The Composer	Motown 1146
6/14/69	**31**	4	24. No Matter What Sign You Are	Motown 1148
11/15/69	**1** (1)	15	▲ 25. **Someday We'll Be Together**	Motown 1156
			#1 R&B hit (4 weeks)	
3/14/70	**10**	10	26. **Up The Ladder To The Roof**	Motown 1162
8/1/70	**21**	8	27. Everybody's Got The Right To Love	Motown 1167
11/21/70	**7**	12	28. **Stoned Love**	Motown 1172
			#1 R&B hit (1 week)	
12/12/70+	**14**	8	29. River Deep - Mountain High	Motown 1173
			THE SUPREMES & FOUR TOPS	
5/22/71	**16**	8	30. Nathan Jones	Motown 1182
1/29/72	**16**	9	31. Floy Joy	Motown 1195
6/3/72	**37**	3	32. Automatically Sunshine	Motown 1200
8/7/76	**40**	1	33. I'm Gonna Let My Heart Do The Walking	Motown 1391
			SURFACE	
			R&B trio from New Jersey: Bernard Jackson (vocals, bass), David Townsend (guitar, keyboards) and Dave Conley (drums, sax). Townsend is the son of Ed Townsend.	
6/20/87	**20**	8	1. Happy Airplay #19 / Sales #21	Columbia 06611
7/29/89	**5**	11	● 2. **Shower Me With Your Love** Sales #5 / Airplay #6	Columbia 68746
			#1 R&B hit (1 week)	
11/24/90+	**1** (2)	18	● 3. **The First Time** Airplay #1 (2) / Sales #2	Columbia 73502
			#1 R&B hit (1 week) / #1 Adult Contemporary hit (2 weeks)	
6/1/91	**17**	8	4. Never Gonna Let You Down Airplay #28 / Sales #47	Columbia 73643
			SURFARIS, The	
			Teen rock and roll-surf band from Glendora, California: Ron Wilson (drums), Jim Fuller and Bob Berryhill (guitars), Pat Connolly (bass) and Jim Pash (sax, clarinet). Wilson died of an aneurysm in May 1989.	
7/6/63	**2** (1)	10	1. **Wipe Out** **[I]**	Dot 16479
8/27/66	**16**	10	2. Wipe Out **[I-R]**	Dot 144
			above 2 are the same version	
			SURVIVOR	
			Rock group formed in Chicago, Illinois: Dave Bickler (vocals), Frankie Sullivan (guitar), Jim Peterik (keyboards), Stephan Ellis (bass) and Marc Droubay (drums). Peterik was lead singer for Ides Of March. Jimi Jamison replaced Bickler in 1983.	
11/21/81	**33**	4	1. Poor Man's Son	Scotti Brothers 02560

DATE	POS	WKS	ARTIST–RECORD TITLE	LABEL & NO.
6/26/82	1 (6)	18	▲² 2. **Eye Of The Tiger** #1 Mainstream Rock hit (5 weeks); from the movie *Rocky III* starring Sylvester Stallone	Scotti Brothers 02912
10/16/82	17	7	3. American Heartbeat	Scotti Brothers 03213
10/20/84	13	13	4. I Can't Hold Back Airplay #11 / Sales #15 #1 Mainstream Rock hit (3 weeks)	Scotti Brothers 04603
2/9/85	8	11	5. **High On You** Airplay #8 / Sales #13	Scotti Brothers 04685
5/11/85	4	14	6. **The Search Is Over** Airplay #4 / Sales #6 #1 Adult Contemporary hit (4 weeks)	Scotti Brothers 04871
11/23/85+	2 (2)	16	7. **Burning Heart** Sales #1 (1) / Airplay #2 from the movie *Rocky IV* starring Sylvester Stallone	Scotti Brothers 05663
11/15/86+	9	13	8. **Is This Love** Sales #8 / Airplay #8	Scotti Brothers 06381
			SWAN, Billy	
			Born on 5/12/42 in Cape Girardeau, Missouri. Pop-country singer/songwriter/keyboardist.	
10/26/74	1 (2)	12	● 1. **I Can Help** #1 Country hit (2 weeks)	Monument 8621
			SWANN, Bettye	
			Born Betty Champion on 10/24/44 in Shreveport, Louisiana. R&B singer.	
7/1/67	21	7	1. Make Me Yours #1 R&B hit (2 weeks)	Money 126
4/19/69	38	2	2. Don't Touch Me	Capitol 2382
			SWAYZE, Patrick	
			Born on 8/18/52 in Houston, Texas. Starred in several movies.	
1/16/88	3	13	1. **She's Like The Wind** Sales #2 / Airplay #2 **PATRICK SWAYZE (featuring Wendy Fraser)** #1 Adult Contemporary hit (2 weeks); from the movie *Dirty Dancing* starring Swayze and Jennifer Grey	RCA 5363
			SWEAT, Keith	
			Born on 7/22/61 in Harlem, New York. R&B singer/songwriter/producer.	
2/6/88	5	13	● 1. **I Want Her** Sales #5 / Airplay #5 #1 R&B hit (3 weeks)	Vintertainment 69431
6/30/90	14	12	● 2. Make You Sweat Sales #10 / Airplay #14 #1 R&B hit (1 week)	Vintertainment 64961
12/22/90+	7	12	3. **I'll Give All My Love To You** Sales #4 / Airplay #12 #1 R&B hit (1 week)	Vintertainment 64915
1/4/92	17	10	4. Keep It Comin' Airplay #15 / Sales #45 #1 R&B hit (2 weeks)	Elektra 64812
6/22/96	2 (1)	35	▲ 5. **Twisted** Sales #2 / Airplay #7 #1 R&B hit (3 weeks)	Elektra 64282
10/5/96	3	31	▲ 6. **Nobody** Sales #3 / Airplay #10 **KEITH SWEAT featuring Athena Cage** #1 R&B hit (3 weeks); Kut Klose (backing vocals, above 2)	Elektra 64245
2/14/98	31	3	7. Am I Dreaming Sales #16 **OL SKOOL [Featuring Keith Sweat and Xscape]**	Universal 56163
10/24/98	12	6	● 8. Come And Get With Me Sales #4 **KEITH SWEAT Featuring Snoop Dogg**	Elektra 64080
3/13/99	16	6	9. I'm Not Ready Sales #5	Elektra 64062

DATE	POS	WKS	ARTIST–RECORD TITLE	LABEL & NO.
			SWEATHOG	
			Rock group: Lenny Goldsmith (vocals, keyboards), Bob Morris (guitar), Dave Johnson (bass) and Barry Frost (drums).	
12/11/71	33	4	1. Hallelujah	Columbia 45492
			SWEET	
			Rock and roll band formed in England: Brian Connolly (vocals), Andy Scott (guitar, keyboards), Steve Priest (bass) and Mick Tucker (drums). Connolly died of kidney failure on 2/10/97 (age 52). Tucker died of leukemia on 2/14/2002 (age 53).	
3/17/73	3	15	● 1. **Little Willy**	Bell 45,251
8/2/75	5	14	2. **Ballroom Blitz**	Capitol 4055
11/22/75+	5	11	● 3. **Fox On The Run**	Capitol 4157
3/6/76	20	7	4. Action	Capitol 4220
4/15/78	8	14	5. **Love Is Like Oxygen**	Capitol 4549
			SWEET, Rachel — see SMITH, Rex	
			SWEET INSPIRATIONS, The	
			R&B vocal group: Cissy Houston (mother of Whitney Houston), Estelle Brown, Sylvia Shemwell and Myrna Smith.	
3/30/68	18	10	1. Sweet Inspiration	Atlantic 2476
			SWEET SENSATION	
			R&B group from Manchester, England: Marcel King (lead vocals), St. Clair Palmer, Vincent James and Junior Daye (backing vocals), Garry Shaughnessy (guitar), Leroy Smith (keyboards), Barry Johnson (bass) and Roy Flowers (drums).	
2/15/75	14	8	1. Sad Sweet Dreamer	Pye 71002
			SWEET SENSATION	
			Female dance trio from the Bronx, New York: Betty LeBron, and sisters Margie and Mari Fernandez. Sheila Bega replaced Mari in 1989.	
3/25/89	14	8	1. Sincerely Yours Sales #9 / Airplay #21	Atco 99246
			featuring a short rap break by Romeo J.D.	
7/15/89	23	7	2. Hooked On You Sales #16 / Airplay #25 **[R]**	Atco 99210
			remix of their #64 hit from 1987	
3/31/90	13	10	3. Love Child Airplay #13 / Sales #16	Atco 98983
7/7/90	1 (1)	13	4. **If Wishes Came True** Airplay #2 / Sales #5	Atco 98953
			SWINGING BLUE JEANS, The	
			Rock and roll group from Liverpool, England: Ray Ennis (vocals, guitar), Ralph Ellis (guitar), Les Braid (bass) and Norman Kuhlke (drums).	
3/28/64	24	5	1. Hippy Hippy Shake	Imperial 66021
			SWINGIN' MEDALLIONS	
			Rock and roll group from Greenwood, South Carolina: John McElrath (vocals), Jimbo Dores (guitar), Brent Fortson (organ), Carroll Bledsoe, Charlie Webber and Steve Caldwell (horns), Jim Perkins (bass) and Joe Morris (drums). Caldwell died of cancer on 1/28/2002 (age 54). Webber died of cancer on 1/17/2003 (age 57).	
6/4/66	17	6	1. Double Shot (Of My Baby's Love)	Smash 2033

DATE	POS	WKS	ARTIST–RECORD TITLE	LABEL & NO.
			SWING OUT SISTER	
			Pop-dance trio formed in England: Corinne Drewery (vocals), Andy Connell (keyboards) and Martin Jackson (drums).	
9/26/87	6	11	1. **Breakout** Sales #4 / Airplay #5	Mercury 888016
			#1 Adult Contemporary hit (2 weeks)	
2/20/88	31	3	2. Twilight World Sales #23	Mercury 888484
			SWITCH	
			Funk group from Mansfield, Ohio: Phillip Ingram (vocals) brothers Bobby (keyboards) and Tommy (bass) DeBarge, Greg Williams and Ed Fluellen (horns), and Jody Sims (drums). The DeBarges are brothers to the family group DeBarge. Bobby DeBarge died of AIDS on 8/16/95 (age 36).	
12/2/78	36	3	1. There'll Never Be	Gordy 7159
			SWV (Sisters With Voices)	
			Female R&B vocal trio from Brooklyn, New York: Cheryl "Coko" Gamble, Tamara "Taj" Johnson and Leanne "Lelee" Lyons.	
3/6/93	6	21	● 1. **I'm So Into You** Sales #5 / Airplay #6	RCA 62451
5/8/93	1 (2)	22	▲ 2. **Weak** Sales #2 / Airplay #2	RCA 62521
			#1 R&B hit (2 weeks)	
7/31/93	2 (3)	19	● 3. **Right Here/Human Nature /** Sales #4 / Airplay #5 **[R]**	
			#1 R&B hit (7 weeks); new mix of "Right Here" (#92 in 1993) with excerpts from Michael Jackson's "Human Nature"	
7/31/93		19	4. Downtown Airplay #36	RCA 62614
4/23/94	18	15	5. Anything Airplay #16 / Sales #19	RCA 62834
			samples "Get Up And Dance"; from the movie *Above The Rim* starring 2 Pac and Duane Martin	
4/20/96	5	16	● 6. **You're The One** Sales #2 / Airplay #15	RCA 64516
			#1 R&B hit (1 week)	
8/24/96	22	10	7. Use Your Heart Sales #15	RCA 64607
7/26/97	19	10	● 8. Someone Sales #10	RCA 64926
			SWV (Featuring Puff Daddy)	
			samples "Ten Crack Commandments" and "The World Is Filled" by The Notorious B.I.G.	
3/28/98	25	5	9. Rain Sales #16 / Airplay #56	RCA 65402
			SYBIL	
			Born Sybil Lynch in Paterson, New Jersey. R&B singer/songwriter.	
11/4/89	20	9	● 1. **Don't Make Me Over** Sales #23 / Airplay #24	Next Plateau 325
			SYLK-E. FYNE	
			Born in Los Angeles, California. Female rapper.	
3/14/98	6	13	● 1. **Romeo And Juliet** Sales #4 / Airplay #42	RCA 64973
			SYLK-E. FYNE Featuring Chill	
			samples "You Don't Have To Cry" by René & Angela	
			SYLVERS, The	
			R&B family vocal group from Memphis, Tennessee: Olympia-Ann, Leon, Charmaine, James, Edmund, Ricky, Angelia, Pat, John and Foster (see #1 below) Sylvers. Edmund died of lung cancer on 3/11/2004 (age 47).	
6/30/73	22	8	1. Misdemeanor	MGM 14580
			FOSTER SYLVERS	

DATE	POS	WKS	ARTIST–RECORD TITLE	LABEL & NO.
3/13/76	**1** (1)	15	● 2. **Boogie Fever** #1 R&B hit (1 week)	Capitol 4179
11/13/76+	**5**	17	● 3. **Hot Line**	Capitol 4336
5/21/77	**17**	10	4. High School Dance	Capitol 4405
			SYLVESTER	
			Born Sylvester James on 9/6/47 in Los Angeles, California. Died of AIDS on 12/16/88 (age 41). Male disco singer.	
9/30/78	**19**	10	1. Dance (Disco Heat)	Fantasy 827
2/17/79	**36**	3	2. You Make Me Feel (Mighty Real)	Fantasy 846
5/5/79	**40**	2	3. I (Who Have Nothing)	Fantasy 855
			SYLVIA	
			Born Sylvia Vanderpool on 5/29/36 in Harlem, New York. R&B-disco singer/songwriter/producer. Half of Mickey & Sylvia duo.	
4/21/73	**3**	13	● 1. **Pillow Talk** #1 R&B hit (2 weeks)	Vibration 521
			SYLVIA	
			Born Sylvia Kirby on 12/9/56 in Kokomo, Indiana. Country singer/songwriter.	
10/9/82	**15**	9	● 1. Nobody #1 Country hit (1 week)	RCA 13223
			SYMS, Sylvia	
			Born on 12/2/17 in Brooklyn, New York. Died of a heart attack on 5/10/92 (age 74). Singer/actress. Appeared in several movie musicals.	
6/16/56	**20**	2	1. I Could Have Danced All Night Jockey #20 / Top 100 #35 from the Broadway musical *My Fair Lady* starring Julie Andrews and Rex Harrison	Decca 29903
9/1/56	**21**	3	2. English Muffins And Irish Stew Jockey #21 / Top 100 #51 Jack Pleis (orch., above 2)	Decca 29969
			SYNCH	
			Pop-rock group from Wilkes-Barre, Pennsylvania: Jimmy Harnen (vocals), brothers Bill (keyboards) and Rich (drums) Kossuth, Jon Lorance (guitar), Chuck Yarmey (keyboards) and Mike Warner (bass).	
4/22/89	**10**	11	1. **Where Are You Now?** Sales #9 / Airplay #12 **[R]** **JIMMY HARNEN W/SYNCH** originally charted at #77 in 1986	WTG 68625
			SYNDICATE OF SOUND	
			Garage-rock band from San Jose, California: Don Baskin (vocals), Jim Sawyers and John Sharkey (guitars), Bob Gonzalez (bass) and John Duckworth (drums).	
6/25/66	**8**	6	1. **Little Girl**	Bell 640
			SYREETA — see PRESTON, Billy	
			SYSTEM, The	
			Techno-funk-dance duo from New York: Mic Murphy (vocals, guitar) and David Frank (synthesizer).	
5/16/87	**4**	13	1. **Don't Disturb This Groove** Sales #4 / Airplay #4 #1 R&B hit (1 week)	Atlantic 89320

DATE	POS	WKS	ARTIST–RECORD TITLE	LABEL & NO.

T

TACO

Born Taco Ockerse in 1955 in Jakarta, Indonesia (to Dutch parents). Techno-pop singer.

7/23/83	4	14	● 1. **Puttin' On The Ritz** written in 1929 by Irving Berlin; #1 hit for Harry Richman in 1930	RCA 13574

TAG TEAM

Hip-hop duo from Atlanta, Georgia: Cecil Glenn and Steve Gibson.

6/12/93	2 (7)	41	▲⁴ 1. **Whoomp! (There It Is)** Sales #1 (16) / Airplay #9 #1 R&B hit (1 week); samples Kano's "I'm Ready"	Life 79500

TAKE THAT

"Boy band" from England: Gary Barlow, Howard Donald, Jason Orange, Mark Owen and Robbie Williams.

9/2/95	7	25	1. **Back For Good** Sales #9 / Airplay #12	Arista 12848

TALKING HEADS

New-wave/rock group formed in New York: David Byrne (vocals, guitar), Jerry Harrison (keyboards, guitar), Tina Weymouth (bass) and Chris Frantz (drums). Husband-and-wife Weymouth and Frantz (married on 6/18/77) also formed Tom Tom Club (see #2 below). Group inducted into the Rock and Roll Hall of Fame in 2002.

12/23/78+	26	9	1. Take Me To The River	Sire 1032
4/10/82	31	4	2. Genius Of Love **TOM TOM CLUB** lyrics mention funk masters Bootsy Collins, Hamilton Bohannon, Kurtis Blow and James Brown	Sire 49882
9/3/83	9	11	3. **Burning Down The House**	Sire 29565
11/8/86	25	7	4. Wild Wild Life Sales #23 / Airplay #25	Sire 28629

TALK TALK

Techno-rock/dance trio from England: Mark Hollis (vocals), Paul Webb (bass) and Lee Harris (drums).

4/21/84	31	6	1. It's My Life	EMI America 8195

TA MARA & THE SEEN

Dance group from Minneapolis, Minnesota: Margaret "Ta Mara" Cox (vocals), Oliver Leiber (guitar), Gina Fellicetta (keyboards), Keith Woodson (bass) and Jamie Chez (drums). Leiber is the son of songwriter Jerry Leiber (of Leiber & Stoller).

11/30/85+	24	10	1. Everybody Dance Airplay #22 / Sales #26	A&M 2768

TAMIA

Born Tamia Washington on 5/9/75 in Windsor, Ontario, Canada. Female R&B singer.

9/14/96	25	10	1. Missing You Sales #15 **BRANDY, TAMIA, GLADYS KNIGHT & CHAKA KHAN** from the movie *Set It Off* starring Jada Pinkett and Queen Latifah	EastWest 64262

DATE	POS	WKS	ARTIST–RECORD TITLE	LABEL & NO.
5/2/98	37	4	2. Imagination Sales #33 / Airplay #66 Jermaine Dupri (rap); samples "I Want You Back" by The Jackson 5	Qwest 17253
8/22/98	30	15	3. So Into You Sales #20 Mario Winans (backing vocal); samples "Say Yeah" by The Commodores	Qwest 17194
8/7/99	21	15	● 4. Spend My Life With You Sales #11 / Airplay #34 **ERIC BENÉT featuring Tamia** #1 R&B hit (2 weeks)	Warner 16958
2/17/01	10	13	5. **Stranger In My House** Sales #4 / Airplay #29	Elektra 67151
6/21/03	4	24	6. **Into You** Airplay #4 / Sales #71 **FABOLOUS Featuring Ashanti or Tamia** the version with Ashanti is from his album *Street Dreams* on Desert Storm 62791; the version with Tamia is available as a promo single only	Desert Storm 67452

TAMI SHOW

Pop group formed in Chicago, Illinois: sisters Cathy and Claire Massey (vocals), Tommy Gawenda (guitar), George McCrae (keyboards), Mark Jiaras (bass) and Ken Harck (drums). The *T.A.M.I. Show* is a 1964 movie of a superstar concert in Santa Monica, California.

DATE	POS	WKS	ARTIST–RECORD TITLE	LABEL & NO.
9/7/91	28	5	1. The Truth	RCA 2694

TAMS, The

R&B "beach music" group from Atlanta, Georgia: brothers Charles and Joseph Pope, with Robert Smith, Floyd Ashton and Horace Key. Joseph Pope died on 3/16/96 (age 63).

DATE	POS	WKS	ARTIST–RECORD TITLE	LABEL & NO.
1/18/64	9	9	1. **What Kind Of Fool (Do You Think I Am)**	ABC-Paramount 10502

TANEGA, Norma

Born on 1/30/39 in Vallejo, California. White pop-folk singer/songwriter/pianist/guitarist.

DATE	POS	WKS	ARTIST–RECORD TITLE	LABEL & NO.
3/19/66	22	6	1. Walkin' My Cat Named Dog	New Voice 807

TANK

Born Durrell Babbs in Milwaukee, Wisconsin. Male R&B singer/songwriter.

DATE	POS	WKS	ARTIST–RECORD TITLE	LABEL & NO.
5/12/01	38	1	1. Maybe I Deserve Airplay #31 from the album *Force Of Nature* on Blackground 50404	album cut

TARRIERS, The

Folk trio formed in New York: Erik Darling, Bob Carey and Alan Arkin. Darling later formed The Rooftop Singers. Arkin went on to act in several movies.

DATE	POS	WKS	ARTIST–RECORD TITLE	LABEL & NO.
10/13/56	9	15	1. **Cindy, Oh Cindy** Juke Box #9 / Best Seller #12 / Top 100 #12 / Jockey #12 **VINCE MARTIN With The Tarriers**	Glory 247
12/22/56+	4	16	2. **The Banana Boat Song** Juke Box #4 / Best Seller #5 / Top 100 #6 / Jockey #6	Glory 249

TASTE OF HONEY, A

Disco group from Los Angeles, California: Janice Johnson (vocals, guitar), Hazel Payne (vocals, bass), Perry Kibble (keyboards) and Donald Johnson (drums). Re-formed in 1980 as a duo: Janice Johnson and Payne. Won the 1978 Best New Artist Grammy Award. Kibble died of heart failure in February 1999 (age 49).

DATE	POS	WKS	ARTIST–RECORD TITLE	LABEL & NO.
7/22/78	1 (3)	17	▲ 1. **Boogie Oogie Oogie** #1 R&B hit (1 week)	Capitol 4565

DATE	POS	WKS	ARTIST–RECORD TITLE	LABEL & NO.
4/11/81	3	16	● 2. **Sukiyaki** #1 R&B hit (1 week) / #1 Adult Contemporary hit (2 weeks)	Capitol 4953
			t.A.T.u.	
			Female teen dance-rock duo from Moscow, Russia: Julia Volkova and Lena Katina.	
2/8/03	20	9	1. All The Things She Said Sales #3 / Airplay #21	Interscope 019354
			TAVARES	
			Family R&B vocal group from New Bedford, Massachusetts: brothers Ralph, Antone, Feliciano, Arthur, and Perry Tavares. Feliciano was married to actress/singer Lola Falana.	
11/3/73	35	3	1. Check It Out	Capitol 3674
5/17/75	25	5	2. Remember What I Told You To Forget /	
5/17/75		1	3. My Ship	Capitol 4010
8/23/75	10	13	4. **It Only Takes A Minute** #1 R&B hit (1 week)	Capitol 4111
7/10/76	15	11	● 5. Heaven Must Be Missing An Angel (Part 1)	Capitol 4270
12/11/76	34	2	6. Don't Take Away The Music	Capitol 4348
4/23/77	22	7	7. Whodunit #1 R&B hit (1 week)	Capitol 4398
4/15/78	32	4	8. More Than A Woman from the movie *Saturday Night Fever* starring John Travolta; written by the Bee Gees	Capitol 4500
11/20/82	33	9	9. A Penny For Your Thoughts written and co-produced by Kenny Nolan	RCA 13292
			TAYLOR, Andy see DURAN DURAN	
			TAYLOR, Bobby, & The Vancouvers	
			Interracial R&B group formed in Vancouver, British Columbia, Canada: Bobby Taylor (vocals), Tommy Chong and Edward Patterson (guitars), Robbie King (keyboards), Wes Henderson (bass) and Ted Lewis (drums). Chong later one-half of Cheech & Chong. King died of cancer on 9/17/2003 (age 56).	
5/18/68	29	5	1. Does Your Mama Know About Me	Gordy 7069
			TAYLOR, James	
			Born on 3/12/48 in Boston, Massachusetts. Soft-rock singer/songwriter/guitarist. Married to Carly Simon from 1972-83. Appeared in the movie *Two Lane Blacktop*. Brother of Livingston Taylor. Inducted into the Rock and Roll Hall of Fame in 2000.	
9/26/70	3	14	1. **Fire And Rain**	Warner 7423
3/20/71	37	1	2. Country Road	Warner 7460
6/19/71	1 (1)	12	● 3. **You've Got A Friend** #1 Adult Contemporary hit (1 week)	Warner 7498
10/16/71	31	5	4. Long Ago And Far Away Joni Mitchell (backing vocal, above 2); Carole King (piano: #1, 2 & 4)	Warner 7521
12/16/72+	14	9	5. Don't Let Me Be Lonely Tonight	Warner 7655
2/16/74	5	13	● 6. **Mockingbird** **CARLY SIMON & JAMES TAYLOR**	Elektra 45880
7/19/75	5	10	7. **How Sweet It Is (To Be Loved By You)** #1 Adult Contemporary hit (1 week); David Sanborn (sax)	Warner 8109

DATE	POS	WKS	ARTIST–RECORD TITLE	LABEL & NO.
8/7/76	22	8	8. Shower The People #1 Adult Contemporary hit (1 week); Carly Simon (harmony vocal, above 2)	Warner 8222
7/9/77	4	13	9. **Handy Man** #1 Adult Contemporary hit (1 week)	Columbia 10557
11/5/77	20	9	10. Your Smiling Face	Columbia 10602
2/11/78	17	7	11. (What A) Wonderful World **ART GARFUNKEL with JAMES TAYLOR & PAUL SIMON** #1 Adult Contemporary hit (5 weeks)	Columbia 10676
9/23/78	36	3	12. Devoted To You **CARLY SIMON and JAMES TAYLOR**	Elektra 45506
6/30/79	28	5	13. Up On The Roof	Columbia 11005
3/14/81	11	10	14. Her Town Too **JAMES TAYLOR AND J.D. SOUTHER**	Columbia 60514
			TAYLOR, John — see DURAN DURAN	
			TAYLOR, Johnnie	
			Born on 5/5/38 in Crawfordsville, Arkansas. Died of a heart attack on 5/31/2000 (age 62). Soul singer. Known as the "Soul Philosopher."	
11/2/68	5	13	● 1. **Who's Making Love** #1 R&B hit (3 weeks)	Stax 0009
1/25/69	20	8	2. Take Care Of Your Homework	Stax 0023
5/31/69	36	5	3. Testify (I Wonna)	Stax 0033
7/18/70	37	2	4. Steal Away	Stax 0068
11/14/70	39	2	5. I Am Somebody Part II	Stax 0078
2/13/71	28	5	6. Jody's Got Your Girl And Gone #1 R&B hit (2 weeks)	Stax 0085
7/14/73	11	12	● 7. I Believe In You (You Believe In Me) #1 R&B hit (2 weeks)	Stax 0161
10/27/73	15	8	8. Cheaper To Keep Her	Stax 0176
3/16/74	34	2	9. We're Getting Careless With Our Love	Stax 0193
3/6/76	1 (4)	13	▲ 10. **Disco Lady** #1 R&B hit (6 weeks); first single certified platinum by R.I.A.A.	Columbia 10281
6/26/76	33	3	11. Somebody's Gettin' It	Columbia 10334
			TAYLOR, Little Johnny	
			Born Johnny Merrett on 2/11/43 in Gregory, Arkansas; raised in Memphis, Tennessee and Los Angeles, California. Died of diabetes on 5/17/2002 (age 59). Blues singer/songwriter/harmonica player.	
9/14/63	19	8	1. Part Time Love #1 R&B hit (1 week)	Galaxy 722
			TAYLOR, Livingston	
			Born on 11/21/50 in Boston, Massachusetts. Singer/songwriter/guitarist. Younger brother of James Taylor.	
12/16/78+	30	5	1. I Will Be In Love With You	Epic 50604
9/13/80	38	2	2. First Time Love	Epic 50894
			TAYLOR, R. Dean	
			Born in 1939 in Toronto, Ontario, Canada. Pop singer/songwriter.	
9/19/70	5	13	1. **Indiana Wants Me** first pressings featured sirens on the intro	Rare Earth 5013

DATE	POS	WKS	ARTIST–RECORD TITLE	LABEL & NO.
			T-BONES, The	
			Instrumental studio group: Danny Hamilton (guitar), Joe Frank Carollo (bass) and Tommy Reynolds (drums). Later recorded as Hamilton, Joe Frank & Reynolds.	
12/25/65+	3	11	1. **No Matter What Shape (Your Stomach's In)** [I] melody taken from an Alka Seltzer jingle	Liberty 55836
			T-BOZ — see DA BRAT / TLC	
			TCHAIKOVSKY, Bram — see BRAM TCHAIKOVSKY	
			TEARS FOR FEARS	
			Synth-pop duo from England: Roland Orzabal (vocals, guitar, keyboards) and Curt Smith (vocals, bass). Smith left in 1992.	
4/13/85	1 (2)	14	1. **Everybody Wants To Rule The World** Sales #1 (2) / Airplay #1 (2)	Mercury 880659
6/29/85	1 (3)	13	● 2. **Shout** Airplay #1 (3) / Sales #1 (2)	Mercury 880294
9/21/85	3	12	3. **Head Over Heels** Airplay #2 / Sales #4	Mercury 880899
5/3/86	27	6	4. Mothers Talk Sales #26 / Airplay #28	Mercury 884638
9/9/89	2 (1)	12	5. **Sowing The Seeds Of Love** Sales #1 (2) / Airplay #4 #1 Modern Rock hit (1 week)	Fontana 874710
1/27/90	36	2	6. Woman In Chains Sales #25 Oleta Adams (female vocal); Phil Collins (drums)	Fontana 876248
8/21/93	25	9	7. Break It Down Again Airplay #18 / Sales #61 #1 Modern Rock hit (3 weeks)	Mercury 862330
			TECHNIQUES	
			White pop vocal group from Georgia: Jim Tinney, Jim Moore, Jim Falin and Buddy Funk.	
11/25/57	29	2	1. Hey! Little Girl Best Seller #29 / Top 100 #33	Roulette 4030
			TECHNOTRONIC	
			Techno-dance studio group created by Belgian DJ/producer Thomas DeQuincey (born Jo Bogaert) and female rapper Ya Kid K (of Hi Tek 3). Non-vocalist Felly, a model from Zaire, fronted the group for videos.	
11/11/89+	2 (2)	16	▲ 1. **Pump Up The Jam** Sales #1 (4) / Airplay #6 **TECHNOTRONIC Featuring FELLY**	SBK 07311
2/17/90	7	12	● 2. **Get Up! (Before The Night Is Over)** Sales #5 / Airplay #11	SBK 07315
7/4/92	6	18	3. **Move This** Airplay #5 / Sales #10 **TECHNOTRONIC featuring YA KID K** featured in a 1992 Revlon TV commercial	SBK/EMI 50400
			TEDDY BEARS, The	
			White doo-wop trio from Los Angeles, California: Phil Spector, Carol Connors and Marshall Leib. Spector became a well-known writer and producer; owner of Philles Records. He was inducted into the Rock and Roll Hall of Fame in 1989. Leib died of a heart attack on 3/15/2002 (age 63).	
10/13/58	1 (3)	18	● 1. **To Know Him, Is To Love Him** Hot 100 #1 (0) Sandy Nelson (drums)	Dore 503

DATE	POS	WKS	ARTIST–RECORD TITLE	LABEL & NO.
			TEEGARDEN & VAN WINKLE	
			Rock and roll duo from Tulsa, Oklahoma: David Teegarden (drums) and Skip "Van Winkle" Knape (keyboards). Teegarden was a member of Bob Seger's Silver Bullet Band from 1978-81.	
10/17/70	**22**	5	1. God, Love And Rock & Roll	Westbound 170
			TEENAGERS, The — see LYMON, Frankie	
			TEEN QUEENS, The	
			R&B teen doo-wop duo from Los Angeles, California: sisters Betty and Rosie Collins. Sisters of Aaron Collins of The Cadets/The Jacks.	
3/10/56	**14**	8	1. Eddie My Love Best Seller #14 / Juke Box #16 / Top 100 #22	RPM 453
			TEE SET, The	
			Pop group from Delft, Netherlands: Peter Tetteroo (vocals), Hans Van Eijck (organ), Dill Bennink (guitar), Franklin Madjid (bass) and Joop Blom (drums). Tetteroo died of cancer on 9/5/2002.	
2/7/70	**5**	10	1. **Ma Belle Amie**	Colossus 107
			TEMPO, Nino, & April Stevens	
			Brother-and-sister duo from Niagara Falls, New York: Nino Tempo (born on 1/6/35) and April Stevens (born on 4/29/36).	
10/5/63	**1** (1)	12	1. **Deep Purple** #1 hit for Larry Clinton & His Orchestra in 1939	Atco 6273
12/28/63+	**11**	7	2. Whispering #1 hit for Paul Whiteman & His Orchestra in 1920	Atco 6281
3/14/64	**32**	3	3. Stardust #1 hit for Isham Jones & His Orchestra in 1931	Atco 6286
10/1/66	**26**	5	4. All Strung Out	White Whale 236
			TEMPOS, The	
			Pop vocal group from Pittsburgh, Pennsylvania: Mike Lazo, Gene Schachter, Jim Drake and Tom Minoto.	
8/10/59	**23**	6	1. See You In September Billy Mure (orch.)	Climax 102
			TEMPTATIONS, The	
			White doo-wop group from Flushing, New York: Neil Stevens, Larry Curtis, Artie Sands and Artie Marin.	
5/9/60	**29**	3	1. Barbara	Goldisc 3001
			TEMPTATIONS, The	
			R&B vocal group from Detroit, Michigan: Eddie Kendricks, David Ruffin, Paul Williams, Melvin Franklin and Otis Williams. Dennis Edwards (of The Contours) replaced Ruffin in 1968. Ricky Owens and Richard Street replaced Kendricks and Paul Williams in 1971. Damon Harris replaced Owens in early 1972. Paul Williams died of a self-inflicted gunshot on 8/17/73 (age 34). Ruffin died of a drug overdose on 6/1/91 (age 50). Kendricks died of cancer on 10/5/92 (age 52). Franklin died of heart failure on 2/23/95 (age 52). Group inducted into the Rock and Roll Hall of Fame in 1989.	
3/21/64	**11**	8	1. The Way You Do The Things You Do	Gordy 7028
7/4/64	**33**	4	2. I'll Be In Trouble	Gordy 7032
9/26/64	**26**	6	3. Girl (Why You Wanna Make Me Blue)	Gordy 7035

DATE	POS	WKS	ARTIST–RECORD TITLE	LABEL & NO.
1/30/65	**1** (1)	11	▲ 4. **My Girl** #1 R&B hit (6 weeks)	Gordy 7038
4/17/65	18	7	5. It's Growing	Gordy 7040
8/7/65	17	7	6. Since I Lost My Baby	Gordy 7043
11/6/65	13	6	7. My Baby	Gordy 7047
3/26/66	29	3	8. Get Ready #1 R&B hit (1 week)	Gordy 7049
6/11/66	13	10	● 9. Ain't Too Proud To Beg #1 R&B hit (8 weeks)	Gordy 7054
9/3/66	3	9	● 10. **Beauty Is Only Skin Deep** #1 R&B hit (5 weeks)	Gordy 7055
12/3/66	8	8	● 11. **(I Know) I'm Losing You** #1 R&B hit (2 weeks)	Gordy 7057
5/13/67	8	8	12. **All I Need**	Gordy 7061
8/12/67	6	9	● 13. **You're My Everything**	Gordy 7063
10/21/67	14	8	14. (Loneliness Made Me Realize) It's You That I Need	Gordy 7065
1/27/68	4	11	● 15. **I Wish It Would Rain** #1 R&B hit (3 weeks)	Gordy 7068
5/18/68	13	8	● 16. I Could Never Love Another (After Loving You) #1 R&B hit (1 week)	Gordy 7072
8/17/68	26	5	17. Please Return Your Love To Me	Gordy 7074
11/23/68+	6	11	● 18. **Cloud Nine**	Gordy 7081
12/14/68+	**2** (2)	12	▲ 19. **I'm Gonna Make You Love Me** **DIANA ROSS AND THE SUPREMES & THE TEMPTATIONS**	Motown 1137
2/22/69	6	11	● 20. **Run Away Child, Running Wild** #1 R&B hit (2 weeks)	Gordy 7084
3/22/69	25	6	21. I'll Try Something New **DIANA ROSS AND THE SUPREMES & THE TEMPTATIONS**	Motown 1142
5/31/69	20	6	22. Don't Let The Joneses Get You Down	Gordy 7086
8/30/69	**1** (2)	15	▲ 23. **I Can't Get Next To You** #1 R&B hit (5 weeks)	Gordy 7093
1/24/70	7	10	● 24. **Psychedelic Shack**	Gordy 7096
6/6/70	3	13	▲ 25. **Ball Of Confusion (That's What The World Is Today)**	Gordy 7099
10/17/70	33	4	26. Ungena Za Ulimwengu (Unite The World)	Gordy 7102
2/20/71	**1** (2)	13	▲ 27. **Just My Imagination (Running Away With Me)** #1 R&B hit (3 weeks)	Gordy 7105
11/20/71	18	8	● 28. Superstar (Remember How You Got Where You Are)	Gordy 7111
3/18/72	30	4	29. Take A Look Around	Gordy 7115
10/28/72	**1** (1)	12	▲ 30. **Papa Was A Rollin' Stone**	Gordy 7121
3/10/73	7	11	● 31. **Masterpiece** #1 R&B hit (2 weeks)	Gordy 7126
7/7/73	40	2	32. The Plastic Man	Gordy 7129
9/8/73	35	4	33. Hey Girl (I Like Your Style)	Gordy 7131
1/12/74	27	4	34. Let Your Hair Down #1 R&B hit (1 week)	Gordy 7133
2/1/75	40	1	35. Happy People #1 R&B hit (1 week); co-written by Lionel Richie	Gordy 7138
4/19/75	26	9	36. Shakey Ground #1 R&B hit (1 week)	Gordy 7142
8/23/75	37	2	37. Glasshouse	Gordy 7144
7/27/91	10	11	38. **The Motown Song**　　　Airplay #24 / Sales #36 **ROD STEWART (with The Temptations)**	Warner 19322

DATE	POS	WKS	ARTIST–RECORD TITLE	LABEL & NO.
			10cc	
			Art-rock group formed in Manchester, England: Eric Stewart (vocals, guitar), Lol Creme (guitar, keyboards), Graham Gouldman (bass) and Kevin Godley (drums). Stewart and Gouldman were members of The Mindbenders. All had been in Hotlegs. Paul Burgess (drums) replaced Godley and Creme in 1976.	
6/14/75	**2** (3)	11	1. **I'm Not In Love**	Mercury 73678
1/29/77	**5**	14	● 2. **The Things We Do For Love**	Mercury 73875
6/25/77	**40**	1	3. People In Love	Mercury 73917
			10,000 MANIACS	
			Alternative-rock group formed in Jamestown, New York: Natalie Merchant (vocals), Robert Buck (guitar), Dennis Drew (keyboards), Steven Gustafson (bass) and Jerome Augustyniak (drums). Mary Ramsey replaced Merchant in 1994. Buck died of liver failure on 12/19/2000 (age 42).	
11/27/93+	**11**	24	1. Because The Night Airplay #8 / Sales #29 **[L]**	Elektra 64595
8/2/97	**25**	7	2. More Than This Airplay #29 / Sales #40	Geffen 19411
			#102 hit for Roxy Music in 1983	
			TEN YEARS AFTER	
			Blues-rock group formed in Nottingham, England: Alvin Lee (vocals, guitar), Chick Churchill (keyboards), Leo Lyons (bass) and Ric Lee (drums).	
11/20/71	**40**	2	1. I'd Love To Change The World	Columbia 45457
			TEPPER, Robert	
			Born in Bayonne, New Jersey. Rock singer/songwriter.	
3/1/86	**22**	7	1. No Easy Way Out Airplay #19 / Sales #23	Scotti Brothers 05750
			from the movie *Rocky IV* starring Sylvester Stallone	
			TERRELL, Tammi	
			Born Thomasina Montgomery on 4/29/45 in Philadelphia, Pennsylvania. Died of a brain tumor on 3/16/70 (age 24). R&B singer.	
			MARVIN GAYE & TAMMI TERRELL:	
6/3/67	**19**	9	1. Ain't No Mountain High Enough	Tamla 54149
9/30/67	**5**	10	2. **Your Precious Love**	Tamla 54156
12/16/67+	**10**	9	3. **If I Could Build My Whole World Around You**	Tamla 54161
4/27/68	**8**	11	4. **Ain't Nothing Like The Real Thing**	Tamla 54163
			#1 R&B hit (1 week)	
8/10/68	**7**	10	5. **You're All I Need To Get By**	Tamla 54169
			#1 R&B hit (5 weeks)	
10/19/68	**24**	6	6. Keep On Lovin' Me Honey	Tamla 54173
2/15/69	**30**	4	7. Good Lovin' Ain't Easy To Come By	Tamla 54179
			Valerie Simpson actually sang female part due to Terrell's poor health	
			TERRY, Tony	
			Born on 3/12/64 in Pinehurst, North Carolina; raised in Washington DC. R&B-funk singer/songwriter.	
9/28/91	**14**	10	1. With You Airplay #16 / Sales #27	Epic 73713

DATE	POS	WKS	ARTIST–RECORD TITLE	LABEL & NO.
			TESLA	
			Hard-rock group formed in Sacramento, California: Jeff Keith (vocals), Frank Hannon and Tommy Skeoch (guitars), Brian Wheat (bass) and Troy Luccetta (drums). Band named after the inventor of the alternating current generator, Nikola Tesla.	
11/11/89+	10	16	● 1. **Love Song** Sales #4 / Airplay #18	Geffen 22856
2/9/91	8	13	2. **Signs** Sales #4 / Airplay #15 **[L]**	Geffen 19653
			recorded on 7/2/90 at the Trocadero in Philadelphia	
			TEX, Joe	
			Born Joseph Arrington Jr. on 8/8/33 in Rogers, Texas. Died of a heart attack on 8/13/82 (age 49). R&B singer/songwriter.	
1/2/65	5	8	1. **Hold What You've Got**	Dial 4001
10/16/65	23	5	2. **I Want To (Do Everything For You)**	Dial 4016
			#1 R&B hit (3 weeks)	
1/1/66	29	4	3. A Sweet Woman Like You	Dial 4022
			#1 R&B hit (1 week)	
6/18/66	39	1	4. S.Y.S.L.J.F.M. (The Letter Song)	Dial 4028
			S.Y.S.L.J.F.M.: "Save Your Sweet Love Just For Me"	
4/8/67	35	3	5. Show Me	Dial 4055
11/25/67	10	10	● 6. **Skinny Legs And All** **[L]**	Dial 4063
3/2/68	33	3	7. Men Are Gettin' Scarce	Dial 4069
2/26/72	2 (2)	16	● 8. **I Gotcha**	Dial 1010
			#1 R&B hit (1 week); all of above written by Joe Tex	
4/23/77	12	10	● 9. Ain't Gonna Bump No More (With No Big Fat Woman)	Epic 50313
			all of above produced by Buddy Killen	
			TG4	
			Female R&B vocal group formed in Orlando, Florida: Ambee, Ashley, Davida and Keisha. TG4: Tom Girl 4.	
11/2/02	5 ˢ	19	1. **Virginity**	T.U.G./A&M 497811
			THALIA	
			Born Ariadna Thalia Sodi Miranda on 8/26/72 in Mexico City, Mexico. Female Latin singer. Married record executive Tommy Mottola (former husband of Mariah Carey) on 12/2/2000.	
7/12/03	22	10	1. I Want You Airplay #23	Virgin 47305
			THALIA featuring Fat Joe	
			samples "A Little Bit Of Love" by Brenda Russell	
			THEM	
			Rock group from Belfast, Northern Ireland: Van Morrison (vocals), brothers Jackie (piano) and Pat (drums) McAuley, Billy Harrison (guitar), Alan Henderson (bass) and Pete Bardens (keyboards).	
6/26/65	24	6	1. Here Comes The Night	Parrot 9749
12/4/65	33	2	2. Mystic Eyes	Parrot 9796
			THINK	
			Studio group assembled by producers Lou Stallman and Bobby Susser.	
1/1/72	23	5	1. Once You Understand	Laurie 3583
			featuring dialogue between a teenager and his parents	

DATE	POS	WKS	ARTIST–RECORD TITLE	LABEL & NO.
			THIN LIZZY	
			Rock group formed in Dublin, Ireland: Phil Lynott (vocals, bass), Brian Robertson and Scott Gorham (guitars), and Brian Downey (drums). Lynott died on 1/4/86 (age 34).	
6/5/76	12	9	1. The Boys Are Back In Town	Mercury 73786
			3RD BASS	
			White rap duo from Queens, New York: Pete Nash and Michael Berrin. Supported by black DJ Richard Lawson.	
8/10/91	29	6	● 1. Pop Goes The Weasel Sales #10 / Airplay #48 samples "Sledgehammer" by Peter Gabriel, "You Haven't Done Nothin'" by Stevie Wonder and "Eminence Front" by The Who	Def Jam 73728
			THIRD EYE BLIND	
			Rock group from San Francisco, California: Stephan Jenkins (vocals), Kevin Cadogan (guitar), Arion Salazar (bass) and Brad Hargreaves (drums).	
7/5/97	4	38	● 1. **Semi-Charmed Life** Airplay #1 (3) / Sales #11 #1 Modern Rock hit (8 weeks)	Elektra 64173
12/6/97+	9	40	2. **How's It Going To Be** Airplay #11 / Sales #20	Elektra 64130
12/5/98+	5	19	3. **Jumper** Airplay #5 / Sales #15	Elektra 64058
1/29/00	14	19	4. Never Let You Go Airplay #11 from the album *Blue* on Elektra 62415	album cut
			38 SPECIAL	
			Southern-rock group formed in Jacksonville, Florida: Donnie Van Zant (vocals), Don Barnes and Jeff Carlisi (guitars), Larry Junstrom (bass), and Steve Brookins and Jack Grondin (drums). Danny Chauncey (guitar) and Max Carl (keyboards) replaced Barnes and Brookins in 1988. Van Zant is the brother of Lynyrd Skynyrd's Ronnie Van Zant.	
4/18/81	27	6	1. Hold On Loosely	A&M 2316
5/22/82	10	12	2. **Caught Up In You** #1 Mainstream Rock hit (1 week)	A&M 2412
10/2/82	38	2	3. You Keep Runnin' Away	A&M 2431
12/3/83+	19	9	4. If I'd Been The One #1 Mainstream Rock hit (4 weeks)	A&M 2594
2/18/84	20	8	5. Back Where You Belong	A&M 2615
10/27/84	25	5	6. Teacher Teacher Sales #25 / Airplay #27 from the movie *Teachers* starring Nick Nolte and JoBeth Williams	Capitol 5405
5/24/86	14	9	7. Like No Other Night Airplay #11 / Sales #17	A&M 2831
3/11/89	6	14	8. **Second Chance** Airplay #5 / Sales #9 **THIRTY EIGHT SPECIAL** #1 Adult Contemporary hit (2 weeks)	A&M 1273
8/31/91	33	4	9. The Sound Of Your Voice Airplay #59	Charisma 98773
			THOMAS, B.J.	
			Born Billy Joe Thomas on 8/7/42 in Hugo, Oklahoma; raised in Rosenberg, Texas. Pop-country singer.	
3/12/66	8	10	1. **I'm So Lonesome I Could Cry** **B.J. THOMAS AND THE TRIUMPHS** written by Hank Williams	Scepter 12129
6/4/66	22	5	2. Mama	Scepter 12139
7/23/66	34	4	3. Billy And Sue **B.J. THOMAS AND THE TRIUMPHS**	Hickory 1395

DATE	POS	WKS	ARTIST–RECORD TITLE	LABEL & NO.
8/3/68	**28**	7	4. The Eyes Of A New York Woman	Scepter 12219
12/14/68+	**5**	12	● 5. **Hooked On A Feeling**	Scepter 12230
11/22/69+	**1 (4)**	19	● 6. **Raindrops Keep Fallin' On My Head**	Scepter 12265
			#1 Adult Contemporary hit (7 weeks); from the movie *Butch Cassidy And The Sundance Kid* starring Paul Newman and Robert Redford	
4/11/70	**26**	6	7. Everybody's Out Of Town	Scepter 12277
7/11/70	**9**	10	8. **I Just Can't Help Believing**	Scepter 12283
			#1 Adult Contemporary hit (1 week)	
1/9/71	**38**	3	9. Most Of All	Scepter 12299
3/13/71	**16**	9	10. No Love At All	Scepter 12307
8/14/71	**34**	3	11. Mighty Clouds Of Joy	Scepter 12320
2/26/72	**15**	9	12. Rock And Roll Lullaby	Scepter 12344
			#1 Adult Contemporary hit (1 week); Duane Eddy (guitar); The Blossoms and Dave Somerville (of the Diamonds; backing vocals)	
3/1/75	**1 (1)**	14	● 13. **(Hey Won't You Play) Another Somebody Done Somebody Wrong Song**	ABC 12054
			#1 Country hit (1 week) / #1 Adult Contemporary hit (1 week)	
8/6/77	**17**	10	14. Don't Worry Baby	MCA 40735
			THOMAS, Carl	
			Born in Chicago, Illinois. R&B singer/songwriter.	
4/15/00	**20**	13	1. I Wish Airplay #16	Bad Boy 79321
			#1 R&B hit (6 weeks)	
			THOMAS, Carla	
			Born on 12/21/42 in Memphis, Tennessee. R&B singer. Daughter of Rufus Thomas.	
2/20/61	**10**	10	1. **Gee Whiz (Look At His Eyes)**	Atlantic 2086
9/24/66	**14**	10	● 2. **B-A-B-Y**	Stax 195
6/3/67	**26**	4	3. Tramp	Stax 216
			OTIS & CARLA	
9/23/67	**30**	2	4. Knock On Wood	Stax 228
			OTIS & CARLA	
			THOMAS, Ian	
			Born in Hamilton, Ontario, Canada. Pop singer/songwriter. Brother of comedian Dave Thomas ("Doug McKenzie").	
12/29/73+	**34**	3	1. Painted Ladies	Janus 224
			THOMAS, Irma	
			Born Irma Lee on 2/18/41 in Ponchatoula, Louisiana. R&B singer. Nicknamed "The Soul Queen of New Orleans."	
4/25/64	**17**	7	1. Wish Someone Would Care	Imperial 66013
			THOMAS, Rufus	
			Born on 3/26/17 in Cayce, Mississippi; raised in Memphis, Tennessee. Died on 12/15/2001 (age 84). R&B singer/songwriter. Father of Carla Thomas.	
11/2/63	**10**	9	● 1. **Walking The Dog**	Stax 140
2/28/70	**28**	8	2. Do The Funky Chicken	Stax 0059
1/23/71	**25**	8	3. (Do The) Push And Pull Part I	Stax 0079
			#1 R&B hit (2 weeks)	
9/18/71	**31**	4	4. The Breakdown (Part I)	Stax 0098

DATE	POS	WKS	ARTIST–RECORD TITLE	LABEL & NO.
			THOMAS, Timmy	
			Born on 11/13/44 in Evansville, Indiana. R&B singer/songwriter/ keyboardist.	
12/23/72+	3	11	1. **Why Can't We Live Together** #1 R&B hit (2 weeks)	Glades 1703
			THOMPSON, Chris — see NIGHT	
			THOMPSON, Kay	
			Born on 11/9/13 in St. Louis, Missouri. Died on 7/2/98 (age 84). Wrote *Eloise* series of children's books. Appeared in the 1957 movie *Funny Face*.	
3/17/56	39	2	1. Eloise Top 100 #39 **[N]** Archie Bleyer (orch.)	Cadence CCS 3
			THOMPSON, Sue	
			Born Eva Sue McKee on 7/19/26 in Nevada, Missouri; raised in San Jose, California. Pop-country singer.	
9/25/61	5	11	1. **Sad Movies (Make Me Cry)** #1 Adult Contemporary hit (1 week)	Hickory 1153
1/13/62	3	11	2. **Norman**	Hickory 1159
7/21/62	31	5	3. Have A Good Time	Hickory 1174
10/20/62	17	6	4. James (Hold The Ladder Steady)	Hickory 1183
2/6/65	23	4	5. Paper Tiger all of above (except #3) written by John D. Loudermilk	Hickory 1284
			THOMPSON TWINS	
			Synth-rock/dance trio from England: Tom Bailey (vocals, synthesizer), Alannah Currie (xylophone, percussion) and Joe Leeway (congas, synthesizer). Leeway left in 1986.	
3/12/83	30	5	1. Lies	Arista 1024
2/25/84	3	15	2. **Hold Me Now**	Arista 9164
6/9/84	11	9	3. Doctor! Doctor!	Arista 9209
10/5/85	6	14	4. **Lay Your Hands On Me** Airplay #5 / Sales #7	Arista 9396
1/25/86	8	11	5. **King For A Day** Airplay #7 / Sales #8	Arista 9450
4/25/87	31	5	6. Get That Love Sales #27 / Airplay #30	Arista 9577
10/28/89	28	4	7. Sugar Daddy Airplay #27 / Sales #31	Warner 22819
			THOMSON, Ali	
			Born in Glasgow, Scotland. Pop singer/songwriter. Younger brother of Supertramp's Dougie Thomson.	
7/12/80	15	9	1. Take A Little Rhythm	A&M 2243
			THOMSON, Cyndi	
			Born on 10/19/76 in Tifton, Georgia. Country singer/songwriter.	
8/18/01	26	8	1. What I Really Meant To Say Sales #12 / Airplay #23 #1 Country hit (3 weeks)	Capitol 58987

DATE	POS	WKS	ARTIST–RECORD TITLE	LABEL & NO.
			THREE CHUCKLES, The	
			White vocal trio from Brooklyn, New York: Teddy Randazzo (accordion), Tom Romano (guitar) and Russ Gilberto (bass). Appeared in the movies *Rock Rock Rock* and *The Girl Can't Help It*. Randazzo died of a heart attack on 11/21/2003 (age 66).	
11/13/54	20	8	1. Runaround Best Seller #20	"X" 0066
			THREE DEGREES, The	
			Female R&B vocal trio from Philadelphia, Pennsylvania: Fayette Pinkney, Sheila Ferguson and Valerie Holiday.	
7/25/70	29	4	1. Maybe	Roulette 7079
3/16/74	1 (2)	14	● 2. **TSOP (The Sound Of Philadelphia)** [I] **MFSB featuring The Three Degrees** #1 R&B hit (1 week) / #1 Adult Contemporary hit (2 weeks); theme from the TV show "Soul Train"	Philadelphia I. 3540
10/19/74	2 (1)	13	▲ 3. **When Will I See You Again** #1 Adult Contemporary hit (1 week)	Philadelphia I. 3550
			THREE DOG NIGHT	
			Pop-rock group formed in Los Angeles, California. Headed by the three lead singers: Danny Hutton (born on 9/10/42), Cory Wells (born on 2/5/42) and Chuck Negron (born on 6/8/42). Backing band included Mike Allsup (guitar), Jimmy Greenspoon (keyboards), Joe Schermie (bass) and Floyd Sneed (drums).	
3/29/69	29	4	1. Try A Little Tenderness #6 hit for Ted Lewis in 1933	Dunhill/ABC 4177
5/31/69	5	12	● 2. **One** written by Nilsson	Dunhill/ABC 4191
8/16/69	4	12	3. **Easy To Be Hard** from the off-Broadway rock musical *Hair* starring Steve Curry	Dunhill/ABC 4203
11/8/69	10	12	4. **Eli's Coming** written by Laura Nyro	Dunhill/ABC 4215
3/7/70	15	8	5. Celebrate	Dunhill/ABC 4229
6/6/70	1 (2)	13	● 6. **Mama Told Me (Not To Come)** written by Randy Newman	Dunhill/ABC 4239
9/12/70	15	8	7. Out In The Country	Dunhill/ABC 4250
12/5/70+	19	9	8. One Man Band	Dunhill/ABC 4262
3/27/71	1 (6)	15	● 9. **Joy To The World** written by Hoyt Axton	Dunhill/ABC 4272
7/17/71	7	11	10. **Liar** written by Russ Ballard	Dunhill/ABC 4282
11/20/71	4	10	● 11. **An Old Fashioned Love Song** #1 Adult Contemporary hit (1 week)	Dunhill/ABC 4294
1/8/72	5	10	12. **Never Been To Spain** written by Hoyt Axton	Dunhill/ABC 4299
4/1/72	12	8	13. The Family Of Man	Dunhill/ABC 4306
8/26/72	1 (1)	9	● 14. **Black & White** #1 Adult Contemporary hit (1 week)	Dunhill/ABC 4317
12/9/72+	19	9	15. Pieces Of April	Dunhill/ABC 4331
6/2/73	3	13	● 16. **Shambala**	Dunhill/ABC 4352
11/17/73	17	6	17. Let Me Serenade You	Dunhill/ABC 4370
4/13/74	4	12	● 18. **The Show Must Go On** first recorded by Leo Sayer in 1973	Dunhill/ABC 4382

DATE	POS	WKS	ARTIST–RECORD TITLE	LABEL & NO.
7/13/74	**16**	8	19. Sure As I'm Sittin' Here	Dunhill/ABC 15001
11/2/74	**33**	3	20. Play Something Sweet (Brickyard Blues)	Dunhill/ABC 15013
8/9/75	**32**	3	21. Til The World Ends	ABC 12114

3 DOORS DOWN

Rock group from Escatawpa, Mississippi: Brad Arnold (vocals), Matt Roberts (guitar), Todd Harrell (bass) and Chris Henderson (drums).

DATE	POS	WKS	ARTIST–RECORD TITLE	LABEL & NO.
7/15/00	**3**	36	1. **Kryptonite** Airplay #1 (6) #1 Mainstream Rock hit (9 weeks) / #1 Modern Rock hit (11 weeks)	album cut
9/22/01	**24**	12	2. Be Like That Airplay #25 from the movie *American Pie 2* starring Jason Biggs; above 2 from the album *The Better Life* on Republic 153920	album cut
12/28/02+	**4**	37	3. **When I'm Gone** Airplay #5 #1 Mainstream Rock hit (17 weeks)	album cut
9/20/03	**5**	36↑	4. **Here Without You** Airplay #5 above 2 from the album *Away From The Sun* on Republic 066165	album cut

311

Rock-funk group from Omaha, Nebraska: Nicholas Hexum and Doug Martinez (vocals), Tim Mahoney (guitar), P-Nut (bass) and Chad Sexton (drums). 311 is the police code for indecent exposure. Pronounced: three eleven.

DATE	POS	WKS	ARTIST–RECORD TITLE	LABEL & NO.
9/14/96	**37** ᴬ	6	1. Down #1 Modern Rock hit (4 weeks)	album cut
12/28/96+	**36** ᴬ	7	2. All Mixed Up above 2 from the album *311* on Capricorn 42041	album cut

3LW

Female R&B vocal trio from New Jersey: Naturi Naughton, Kiely Williams and Adrienne Bailon. 3LW: 3 Little Women.

DATE	POS	WKS	ARTIST–RECORD TITLE	LABEL & NO.
1/20/01	**23**	14	1. No More (Baby I'ma Do Right) Sales #20 / Airplay #21	Epic 79505

3T

R&B teen vocal trio: brothers Taryll, T.J. and Taj Jackson. Sons of Tito Jackson (The Jacksons).

DATE	POS	WKS	ARTIST–RECORD TITLE	LABEL & NO.
10/28/95+	**15**	29	● 1. Anything Sales #9 / Airplay #22	MJJ Music 77913

THUNDER, Johnny

Born Gil Hamilton on 8/15/41 in Leesburg, Florida. R&B singer.

DATE	POS	WKS	ARTIST–RECORD TITLE	LABEL & NO.
1/5/63	**4**	9	1. **Loop De Loop**	Diamond 129

THUNDERCLAP NEWMAN

Rock trio formed in England: Andy Newman (keyboards), John "Speedy" Keene (vocals, drums) and Jimmy McCulloch (guitars). McCulloch was a member of Paul McCartney's Wings from 1975-77; died of heart failure on 9/27/79 (age 26). Keene died on 3/21/2002 (age 56).

DATE	POS	WKS	ARTIST–RECORD TITLE	LABEL & NO.
10/25/69	**37**	2	1. Something In The Air from the movie *The Magic Christian* starring Peter Sellers and Ringo Starr	Track 2656

T.I. — see BONE CRUSHER

DATE	POS	WKS	ARTIST–RECORD TITLE	LABEL & NO.
			TIERRA	
			Latin group formed in Los Angeles, California: brothers Steve (trombone, timbales) and Rudy (guitar) Salas, Joey Guerra (keyboards), Bobby Navarrete (reeds), Andre Baeza (congas), Steve Falomir (bass) and Phil Madayag (drums). The Salas brothers and Baeza were formerly with El Chicano.	
12/13/80+	**18**	15	1. Together	Boardwalk 5702
			TIFFANY	
			Born Tiffany Darwish on 10/2/71 in Norwalk, California. Teen pop singer.	
9/26/87	**1** (2)	13	1. **I Think We're Alone Now** Sales #1 (2) / Airplay #1 (2)	MCA 53167
12/12/87+	**1** (2)	14	2. **Could've Been** Airplay #1 (3) / Sales #1 (2)	MCA 53231
			#1 Adult Contemporary hit (1 week)	
3/12/88	**7**	9	3. **I Saw Him Standing There** Sales #2 / Airplay #8	MCA 53285
12/3/88+	**6**	14	4. **All This Time** Sales #7 / Airplay #9	MCA 53371
4/1/89	**35**	1	5. Radio Romance Sales #26	MCA 53623
			TIJUANA BRASS, The — see ALPERT, Herb	
			TILLOTSON, Johnny	
			Born on 4/20/39 in Jacksonville, Florida; raised in Palatka, Florida. Teen idol pop singer/songwriter. Appeared in the movie *Just For Fun*.	
10/24/60	**2** (1)	12	1. **Poetry In Motion**	Cadence 1384
2/6/61	**25**	5	2. Jimmy's Girl	Cadence 1391
8/28/61	**7**	8	3. **Without You**	Cadence 1404
1/20/62	**35**	1	4. Dreamy Eyes **[R]**	Cadence 1409
			originally charted at #63 in 1958	
5/19/62	**3**	12	5. **It Keeps Right On A-Hurtin'**	Cadence 1418
8/25/62	**17**	6	6. Send Me The Pillow You Dream On	Cadence 1424
11/17/62	**24**	5	7. I Can't Help It (If I'm Still In Love With You)	Cadence 1432
			#2 Country hit for Hank Williams in 1951	
3/23/63	**24**	6	8. Out Of My Mind	Cadence 1434
8/24/63	**18**	7	9. You Can Never Stop Me Loving You	Cadence 1437
11/30/63+	**7**	10	10. **Talk Back Trembling Lips**	MGM 13181
			#1 Country hit for Ernest Ashworth in 1963	
3/14/64	**37**	2	11. Worried Guy	MGM 13193
6/6/64	**36**	2	12. I Rise, I Fall	MGM 13232
11/28/64	**31**	6	13. She Understands Me	MGM 13284
			song charted in 1966 by Bobby Vinton as "Dum-De-Da"	
10/2/65	**35**	2	14. Heartaches By The Number	MGM 13376
			#2 Country hit for Ray Price in 1959	
			'TIL TUESDAY	
			Pop-rock group formed in Boston, Massachusetts: Aimee Mann (vocals, bass), Robert Holmes (guitar), Joey Pesce (keyboards) and Michael Hausman (drums).	
5/18/85	**8**	13	1. **Voices Carry** Airplay #7 / Sales #9	Epic 04795
11/1/86	**26**	5	2. What About Love Sales #24 / Airplay #30	Epic 06289

DATE	POS	WKS	ARTIST–RECORD TITLE	LABEL & NO.
			TIMBALAND AND MAGOO	
			Rap duo from Norfolk, Virginia: Timothy "Timbaland" Mosley and Melvin "Magoo" Barcliff.	

8/9/97	**12**	15	● 1. Up Jumps Da Boogie Sales #7
			    MAGOO and TIMBALAND
			    Aaliyah and Missy Elliott (guest vocals)
				Blackground 98018

3/7/98	**37** A	6	2. Luv 2 Luv U from the album *Welcome To Our World* on Blackground 92772	album cut
5/2/98	**37**	3	3. Clock Strikes Sales #27 samples the theme from TV's *Knight Rider* starring David Hasselhoff	Blackground 97995
			TIMBERLAKE, Justin	
			Born on 1/31/81 in Memphis, Tennessee. Member of *NSYNC. Regular on TV's *The Mickey Mouse Club* (1992-93).	
9/21/02	**11**	14	1. Like I Love You Airplay #11 / Sales #20	Jive 40054
12/28/02+	**3**	17	2. **Cry Me A River** Sales #2 / Airplay #3	Jive 40073
3/29/03	**5**	19	3. **Rock Your Body** Airplay #6	album cut
8/30/03	**27**	6	4. Señorita Airplay #29 Pharrell (additional vocals); above 2 from the album *Justified* on Jive 41823	album cut
			TIMBUK 3	
			Husband-and-wife alternative pop-rock duo from Austin, Texas: Patrick and Barbara MacDonald.	
11/22/86	**19**	9	1. The Future's So Bright, I Gotta Wear Shades Sales #14 / Airplay #24	I.R.S. 52940
			TIME, The	
			R&B-funk-dance group from Minneapolis, Minnesota: Morris Day (vocals; see #3 below), Jerome Benton (dancer), Jesse Johnson (guitar), Jimmy "Jam" Harris, Monte Moir and Paul Peterson (keyboards), Terry Lewis (bass), and Jellybean Johnson (drums). Group featured in the movie *Purple Rain*. Lewis and Harris became highly successful songwriting/production team. Lewis married Karyn White.	
1/5/85	**20**	10	1. Jungle Love Airplay #14 / Sales #23	Warner 29181
4/13/85	**36**	2	2. The Bird Airplay #28 above 2 from the movie *Purple Rain* starring Prince and Apollonia Kotero	Warner 29094

3/26/88	**23**	6	3. Fishnet Sales #15 / Airplay #24
			    MORRIS DAY
			    #1 R&B hit (2 weeks)
				Warner 28201

7/14/90	**9**	11	● 4. **Jerk-Out** Sales #9 / Airplay #9 #1 R&B hit (1 week)	Paisley Park 19750
			TIMES TWO	
			White male electro-pop duo from Pt. Reyes, California: Shanti Jones and John Dollar.	
4/23/88	**21**	8	1. Strange But True Airplay #20 / Sales #21	Reprise 27998
			TIMEX SOCIAL CLUB	
			R&B-funk-dance trio from Berkeley, California: Michael Marshall, Marcus Thompson and Alex Hill.	
7/12/86	**8**	12	1. **Rumors** Airplay #6 / Sales #8 #1 R&B hit (2 weeks)	Jay 7001

DATE	POS	WKS	ARTIST–RECORD TITLE	LABEL & NO.
			TIMMY -T-	
			Born Timmy Torres on 9/21/67 in Fresno, California. Dance-pop singer/songwriter.	
5/5/90	**40**	1	1. Time After Time Sales #30	Jam City 5003
1/19/91	**1** (1)	16	▲ 2. **One More Try** Sales #1 (5) / Airplay #2	Quality 15114
			TIN TIN	
			Pop duo from Australia: Steve Kipner (keyboards) and Steve Groves (guitar).	
5/8/71	**20**	6	1. Toast And Marmalade For Tea	Atco 6794
			TINY TIM	
			Born Herbert Khaury on 4/12/30 in Brooklyn, New York. Died of heart failure on 11/30/96 (age 66). Novelty singer/ukulele player. Shot to national attention with appearances on TV's *Rowan & Martin's Laugh-In*. Married "Miss Vicki" on Johnny Carson's *Tonight Show* on 12/18/69; divorced in 1977.	
6/8/68	**17**	6	1. Tip-Toe Thru' The Tulips With Me **[N]** #1 hit for Nick Lucas in 1929 (from the movie musical *Gold Diggers Of Broadway*)	Reprise 0679
			TIPPIN, Aaron	
			Born on 7/3/58 in Pensacola, Florida; raised in Traveler's Rest, South Carolina. Country singer/songwriter.	
10/27/01	**20**	14	1. Where The Stars And Stripes And The Eagle Fly Sales #3 / Airplay #33	Lyric Street 64059
			TLC	
			Female R&B vocal trio from Atlanta, Georgia: Tionne "T-Boz" Watkins (see #9 below), Lisa "Left Eye" Lopes and Rozonda "Chilli" Thomas. Founded and managed by Pebbles. T-Boz married Mack 10 on 8/19/2000. Left Eye died in a car crash on 4/25/2002 (age 30).	
3/21/92	**6**	17	▲ 1. **Ain't 2 Proud 2 Beg** Sales #3 / Airplay #9 samples "Escape-ism" by James Brown, "Jungle Boogie" by Kool & The Gang, "School Boy Crush" by AWB, "Fly, Robin, Fly" by Silver Convention and "Take Me To The Mardi Gras" by Bob James	LaFace 24008
6/27/92	**2** (6)	24	▲ 2. **Baby-Baby-Baby** Airplay #1 (2) / Sales #3 #1 R&B hit (2 weeks)	LaFace 24028
10/3/92	**7**	21	● 3. **What About Your Friends** Sales #6 / Airplay #7	LaFace 24025
2/27/93	**30**	5	4. Hat 2 Da Back Sales #24 / Airplay #29 samples "Big Ole Butt" by L.L. Cool J and "What Makes You Happy" by KC & The Sunshine Band	LaFace 24043
11/19/94+	**1** (4)	29	▲ 5. **Creep** Sales #1 (5) / Airplay #3 #1 R&B hit (9 weeks); samples "Hey Young World" by Slick Rick	LaFace 24082
3/4/95	**2** (3)	19	● 6. **Red Light Special** Sales #2 / Airplay #4	LaFace 24097
6/10/95	**1** (7)	28	▲ 7. **Waterfalls** Sales #1 (3) / Airplay #2	LaFace 24107
11/18/95	**5**	16	● 8. **Diggin' On You** Sales #5 / Airplay #10	LaFace 24119
8/31/96	**40**	1	9. Touch Myself Sales #24 **T-BOZ** samples "My Mike Sounds Nice" by Salt-N-Pepa; from the movie *Fled* starring Laurence Fishburne	Rowdy 35080
2/27/99	**1** (4)	25	● 10. **No Scrubs** Airplay #1 (13) / Sales #1 (4) #1 R&B hit (5 weeks)	LaFace 24385
8/21/99	**1** (3)	24	● 11. **Unpretty** Sales #2 / Airplay #2	LaFace 24424
11/9/02	**28**	5	12. Girl Talk Airplay #31 / Sales #63	Arista 15171

DATE	POS	WKS	ARTIST–RECORD TITLE	LABEL & NO.
			TOADIES	
			Rock group from Fort Worth, Texas: Todd Lewis (vocals, guitar), Darrel Herbert (guitar), Lisa Umbarger (bass) and Mark Reznicek (drums).	album cut
11/18/95	40 ᴬ	1	1. Possum Kingdom	
			from the album *Rubberneck* on Interscope 92402	
			TOAD THE WET SPROCKET	
			Alternative-rock group from Santa Barbara, California: Glen Phillips (vocals), Todd Nichols (guitar), Dean Dinning (bass) and Randy Guss (drums). Name taken from a Monty Python skit.	
7/25/92	15	18	1. All I Want Airplay #8 / Sales #28	Columbia 74355
12/19/92+	18	11	2. Walk On The Ocean Airplay #21 / Sales #57	Columbia 74706
7/16/94	33	4	3. Fall Down Airplay #31	Columbia 77474
			#1 Modern Rock hit (6 weeks)	
11/11/95	23 ᴬ	13	4. Good Intentions	album cut
			from the TV soundtrack album *Friends* on Reprise 46008	
			TOBY BEAU	
			Pop group from Texas: Balde Silva (vocals, harmonica), Danny McKenna (guitar), Ron Rose (banjo), Steve Zipper (bass) and Rob Young (drums).	RCA 11250
7/1/78	13	12	1. My Angel Baby	
			#1 Adult Contemporary hit (1 week)	
			TODD, Art And Dotty	
			Pop vocal duo from Elizabeth, New Jersey. Art Todd was born on 3/11/20. Doris "Dotty" Todd was born on 6/22/13; died on 12/12/2000 (age 87). Married in 1941.	
4/21/58	6	11	1. **Chanson D'Amour (Song Of Love)**	Era 1064
			Jockey #6 / Best Seller #13 / Top 100 #13	
			TODD, Nick	
			Born Nicholas Boone on 6/1/35 in Jacksonville, Florida. Pop singer. Younger brother of Pat Boone.	
2/10/58	21	2	1. At The Hop Jockey #21 / Top 100 #70	Dot 15675
			Billy Vaughn (orch.)	
			TOKENS, The	
			White vocal group formed in Brooklyn, New York: brothers Phil and Mitch Margo, Hank Medress, and Jay Siegel. Formed own B.T. Puppy record label in 1964. The Margos and Siegel recorded as Cross Country in 1973 (see #5 below).	
4/24/61	15	6	1. Tonight I Fell In Love	Warwick 615
11/27/61	1 (3)	13	● 2. **The Lion Sleeps Tonight**	RCA Victor 7954
			#14 hit for The Weavers in 1952 (as "Wimoweh")	
4/9/66	30	5	3. I Hear Trumpets Blow	B.T. Puppy 518
5/20/67	36	2	4. Portrait Of My Love	Warner 5900
9/22/73	30	4	5. In The Midnight Hour	Atco 6934
			CROSS COUNTRY	

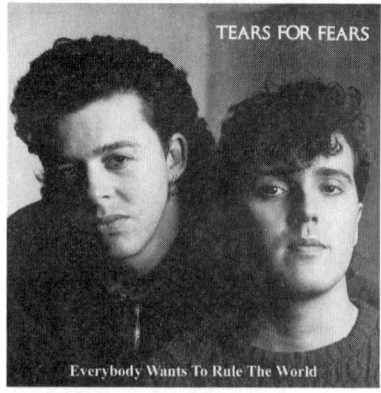

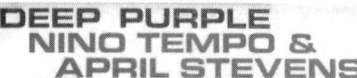

Johnnie Taylor may not have recorded a disco hit with his deceptively titled "Disco Lady," but that didn't mean fans didn't like it. The song became a #1 hit and the first record certified platinum by the RIAA.

Tears For Fears definitely ruled the pop charts in 1985. Three songs from their *Songs From The Big Chair* album reached the Top 10, including the #1 hit "Everybody Wants To Rule The World."

The Teddy Bears had only one Top 40 hit, "To Know Him, Is To Love Him," but one of the group's members, songwriter Phil Spector, would go on to write other classics like "Be My Baby," "Chapel Of Love," and "Da Doo Ron Ron."

Nino Tempo & April Stevens reached #1 with "Deep Purple." According to legend, the hard-rock band Deep Purple took their name from the song, because it was a favorite of the grandmother of one of the group's members.

B.J. Thomas scored the triple crown with "(Hey Won't You Play) Another Somebody Done Somebody Wrong Song." This long-titled song went to #1 on the Hot 100, as well as the Country and Adult Contemporary charts.

Tiffany rose to #1 with a cover of Tommy James's hit "I Think We're Alone Now." She was replaced at the top by another Tommy James cover song, Billy Idol's live version of "Mony Mony."

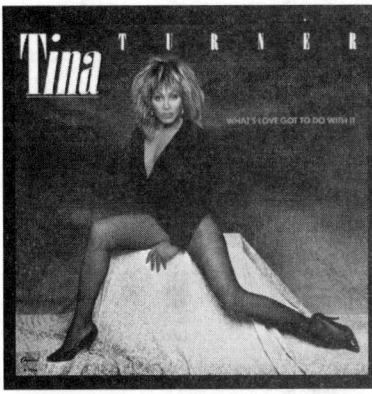

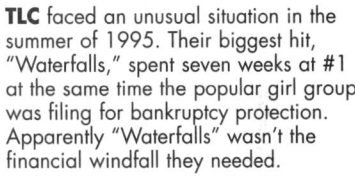

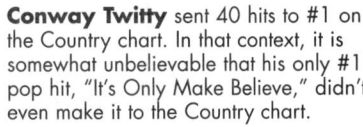

TLC faced an unusual situation in the summer of 1995. Their biggest hit, "Waterfalls," spent seven weeks at #1 at the same time the popular girl group was filing for bankruptcy protection. Apparently "Waterfalls" wasn't the financial windfall they needed.

Tina Turner didn't initially care for her eventual #1 hit "What's Love Got To Do With It," but grew to appreciate its songwriters. Terry Britten and Graham Lyle went on to write her biggest hits, like "Typical Male" and "We Don't Need Another Hero (Thunderdome)."

The Turtles may have had a #1 hit with "Happy Together," but things were not so happy within the group. Differences eventually broke the group apart in 1970, and two members went on to join Frank Zappa's group, Mothers Of Invention.

Conway Twitty sent 40 hits to #1 on the Country chart. In that context, it is somewhat unbelievable that his only #1 pop hit, "It's Only Make Believe," didn't even make it to the Country chart.

2Pac teamed with Jodeci members K-Ci & JoJo for his first #1 hit, "How Do U Want It," shortly before Shakur's shooting death in 1996. K-Ci & JoJo would have a #1 hit of their own two years later with "All My Life."

Bonnie Tyler turned to songwriter Jim Steinman to give her music a rock sound. Their collaboration, "Total Eclipse Of The Heart," spent four weeks at #1. Steinman also wrote her next Top 40 hit, "Holding Out For A Hero."

Usher failed to reach the Top 40 with any hits from his debut album, but that slow start didn't deter him. His second album, *My Way*, ushered in a new era, spinning off the #1 hit "Nice And Slow."

DATE	POS	WKS	ARTIST—RECORD TITLE	LABEL & NO.
			TOMMY TUTONE	
			Rock group formed in San Francisco, California: Tommy Heath (vocals), Jim Keller (guitar), Jon Lyons (bass) and Victor Carberry (drums).	
6/21/80	38	2	1. Angel Say No	Columbia 11278
3/13/82	4	16	● 2. **867-5309/Jenny**	Columbia 02646
			#1 Mainstream Rock hit (3 weeks)	
			TOM TOM CLUB — see TALKING HEADS	
			TONE LOC	
			Born Anthony Smith on 3/3/66 in Los Angeles, California. Male rapper/ actor. Appeared in several movies.	
12/24/88+	2 (1)	14	▲² 1. **Wild Thing** Sales #1 (2) / Airplay #3	Delicious Vinyl 102
			samples "Jamie's Cryin'" by Van Halen	
3/18/89	3	11	▲ 2. **Funky Cold Medina** Sales #2 / Airplay #5	Delicious Vinyl 104
			samples "All Right Now" by Free, "(Not Just) Knee Deep" by Funkadelic and "Christine Sixteen" by Kiss	
			TONEY, Oscar Jr.	
			Born on 5/26/39 in Selma, Alabama; raised in Columbus, Georgia. R&B singer.	
6/17/67	23	5	1. For Your Precious Love	Bell 672
			TONIC	
			Rock group from Los Angeles, California: Emerson Hart (vocals, guitar), Jeff Russo (guitar), Dan Rothchild (bass) and Kevin Shepard (drums).	
6/28/97	11 ᴬ	49	1. If You Could Only See	album cut
			#1 Mainstream Rock hit (5 weeks); from the album *Lemon Parade* on Polydor 531042	
			TONY AND JOE	
			Rock and roll vocal duo: Tony Savonne and Joe Saraceno.	
8/4/58	33	1	1. The Freeze Hot 100 #33 / Best Seller #39	Era 1075
			TONY! TONI! TONÉ!	
			R&B-funk trio from Oakland, California: brothers Raphael Saadiq (vocals, bass, keyboards) and Dwayne Wiggins (vocals, guitar), with cousin Tim Riley (drums). Trio appeared in the movie *House Party 2*.	
9/22/90	9	17	● 1. **Feels Good** Sales #5 / Airplay #15	Wing 877436
			#1 R&B hit (2 weeks)	
2/2/91	34	4	2. It Never Rains (In Southern California) Sales #19	Wing 879068
			#1 R&B hit (2 weeks)	
			TONY TONI TONE:	
6/26/93	7	17	● 3. **If I Had No Loot** Sales #7 / Airplay #9	Wing 859056
			samples "The 'P' Is Free" by KRS-1, "The Wrong Nigga To Fuck Wit" by Ice Cube and "Knock On Wood" by Eddie Floyd	
10/9/93	10	14	● 4. **Anniversary** Sales #8 / Airplay #11	Wing 859566
2/5/94	31	6	5. (Lay Your Head On My) Pillow Sales #28 / Airplay #28	Wing 858260
1/4/97	30 ᴬ	12	6. Let's Get Down	album cut
			from the album *House Of Music* on Mercury 534250	
5/17/97	22	8	7. Thinking Of You Sales #15	Mercury 574382

DATE	POS	WKS	ARTIST—RECORD TITLE	LABEL & NO.
			TOO $HORT — see E-40	
			TORME, Mel	
			Born Melvin Howard on 9/13/25 in Chicago, Illinois. Died of a stroke on 6/5/99 (age 73). Jazz singer/songwriter/pianist/drummer/actor. Wrote "The Christmas Song." Frequently appeared as himself on TV's *Night Court*. Nicknamed "The Velvet Fog." Won Grammy's Lifetime Achievement Award in 1999.	
12/15/62	**36**	3	1. Comin' Home Baby	Atlantic 2165
			Claus Ogermann (orch.)	
			TORNADOES, The	
			Surf-rock instrumental group formed in England: Alan Caddy (lead guitar), George Bellamy (rhythm guitar), Roger Jackson (keyboards), Heinz Burt (bass) and Clem Cattini (drums). Burt died of muscular dystrophy on 4/7/2000 (age 57).	
11/17/62	**1** (3)	13	1. Telstar [I]	London 9561
			TOROK, Mitchell	
			Born on 10/28/29 in Houston, Texas. Pop-country singer/songwriter/guitarist.	
4/29/57	**25**	3	1. Pledge Of Love Best Seller #25 / Top 100 #26	Decca 30230
8/31/59	**27**	6	2. Caribbean	Guyden 2018
			alternate recording of Torok's #1 Country hit in 1953 on Abbott 140	
			TOTAL	
			Female R&B vocal trio from Harlem, New York: JaKima Raynor, Keisha Spivey and Pam Long.	
4/22/95	**13**	14	● 1. Can't You See Sales #9 / Airplay #28	Tommy Boy 7676
			TOTAL featuring The Notorious B.I.G.	
			samples "The Payback" by James Brown; from the movie *New Jersey Drive* starring Sharron Corley	
1/6/96	**22**	14	● 2. No One Else Sales #10 / Airplay #51	Bad Boy 79042
			Da Brat (rap); samples "South Bronx" by KRS-One	
5/18/96	**12**	19	● 3. Kissin' You Sales #7 / Airplay #43	Bad Boy 79056
9/6/97	**16**	22	● 4. What About Us Sales #11 / Airplay #47	LaFace 24272
			from the movie *Soul Food* starring Vanessa Williams	
1/31/98	**6**	20	● 5. **What You Want** Sales #6 / Airplay #26	Bad Boy 79141
			MASE (FEATURING TOTAL)	
			samples "Right On For The Darkness" by Curtis Mayfield	
11/7/98+	**7**	16	● 6. **Trippin'** Sales #6 / Airplay #49	Bad Boy 79185
			TOTAL (Feat. Missy Elliott)	
			TOTO	
			Pop-rock group formed in Los Angeles, California: Bobby Kimball (vocals), Steve Lukather (guitar), David Paich and Steve Porcaro (keyboards), David Hungate (bass) and Jeff Porcaro (drums). Prominent session musicians. Steve and Jeff's brother, Mike Porcaro, replaced Hungate in 1983. Fergie Frederiksen replaced Kimball in early 1984. Joseph Williams (son of conductor John Williams) replaced Frederiksen in early 1986. Jeff Porcaro died of a heart attack on 8/5/92 (age 38).	
11/11/78+	**5**	14	● 1. **Hold The Line**	Columbia 10830
2/9/80	**26**	8	2. 99	Columbia 11173
5/8/82	**2** (5)	18	● 3. **Rosanna**	Columbia 02811

DATE	POS	WKS	ARTIST–RECORD TITLE	LABEL & NO.
9/11/82	**30**	5	4. Make Believe	Columbia 03143
11/20/82+	**1** (1)	16	● 5. **Africa**	Columbia 03335
3/26/83	**10**	12	6. **I Won't Hold You Back**	Columbia 03597
			#1 Adult Contemporary hit (3 weeks)	
11/24/84	**30**	6	7. Stranger In Town Airplay #22	Columbia 04672
9/27/86	**11**	12	8. I'll Be Over You Sales #10 / Airplay #11	Columbia 06280
			#1 Adult Contemporary hit (2 weeks)	
2/7/87	**38**	2	9. Without Your Love Airplay #32	Columbia 06570
3/26/88	**22**	8	10. Pamela Sales #17 / Airplay #20	Columbia 07715

TOWER OF POWER

Interracial funk group from Oakland, California: Lenny Williams (vocals), Willie Fulton (guitar), Greg Adams, Mic Gillette, Steve Kupka, Emilio Castillo, Lenny Pickett (horns), Chester Thompson (keyboards), Francis Prestia (bass) and David Garibaldi (drums).

DATE	POS	WKS	ARTIST–RECORD TITLE	LABEL & NO.
8/26/72	**29**	5	1. You're Still A Young Man	Warner 7612
6/16/73	**17**	11	2. So Very Hard To Go	Warner 7687
8/24/74	**26**	4	3. Don't Change Horses (In The Middle Of A Stream)	Warner 7828

TOWNSELL, Lidell, & M.T.F.

Born in Chicago, Illinois. Black dance DJ/mixer. M.T.F. (More Than Friends): singer Martell and rapper Silk E.

DATE	POS	WKS	ARTIST–RECORD TITLE	LABEL & NO.
3/28/92	**26**	12	1. Nu Nu Airplay #20 / Sales #25	Mercury 866780

TOWNSEND, Ed

Born on 4/16/29 in Fayetteville, Tennessee. Died of heart failure on 8/13/2003 (age 74). R&B singer/songwriter.

DATE	POS	WKS	ARTIST–RECORD TITLE	LABEL & NO.
4/28/58	**13**	13	1. For Your Love Jockey #13 / Best Seller #15 / Top 100 #15	Capitol 3926
			Gerald Wilson (orch.)	

TOWNSHEND, Pete

Born on 5/19/45 in London, England. Rock singer/songwriter/guitarist. Member of The Who. Currently plagued by a significant hearing loss.

DATE	POS	WKS	ARTIST–RECORD TITLE	LABEL & NO.
7/5/80	**9**	12	1. **Let My Love Open The Door**	Atco 7217
12/21/85+	**26**	7	2. Face The Face Sales #24 / Airplay #27	Atco 99590

TOYA

Born LeToya Luckett on 3/11/81 in Houston, Texas. R&B singer. Former member of Destiny's Child.

DATE	POS	WKS	ARTIST–RECORD TITLE	LABEL & NO.
6/30/01	**16**	17	1. I Do!! Sales #2 / Airplay #20	Arista 13972
9/7/02	**3**	20	2. **Hey Ma** Airplay #3 / Sales #21	Roc-A-Fella 063958
			CAM'RON (feat. Juelz Santana, Freekey Zekey and Toya)	

TOYS, The

Black female vocal trio from Queens, New York: Barbara Harris, June Montiero and Barbara Parritt.

DATE	POS	WKS	ARTIST–RECORD TITLE	LABEL & NO.
10/2/65	**2** (3)	11	● 1. **A Lover's Concerto**	DynoVoice 209
			adapted from Bach's *Minuet From The Anna Magdalena Notebook*	
1/1/66	**18**	6	2. Attack	DynoVoice 214

DATE	POS	WKS	ARTIST–RECORD TITLE	LABEL & NO.
			T'PAU	
			Pop-rock-dance group from Shrewsbury, England: Carol Decker (vocals), Dean Howard and Ronnie Rogers (guitars), Mick Chetwood (keyboards), Paul Jackson (bass) and Tim Burgess (drums). Band named after a Vulcan Princess in an episode of the TV series *Star Trek*.	
6/6/87	4	16	1. **Heart And Soul** Airplay #3 / Sales #5	Virgin 99466
			TQ	
			Born Terrance Quaites in Mobile, Alabama; raised in Los Angeles, California. R&B singer/songwriter.	
10/3/98	12	11	● 1. Westside Sales #5 / Airplay #69 samples "The Breaks" by Kurtis Blow and "In All My Wildest Dreams" by Joe Sample	ClockWork 79022
			TRADE WINDS, The/THE INNOCENCE	
			Pop singing/songwriting/production duo from New York: Pete Anders and Vinnie Poncia.	
2/27/65	32	4	1. New York's A Lonely Town **THE TRADE WINDS**	Red Bird 020
1/7/67	34	3	2. There's Got To Be A Word! **THE INNOCENCE**	Kama Sutra 214
			TRAIN	
			Rock group from San Francisco, California: Patrick Monahan (vocals), Rob Hotchkiss and Jimmy Stafford (guitars), Charlie Colin (bass) and Scott Underwood (drums).	
11/20/99+	20	17	1. Meet Virginia Airplay #17 from the album *Train* on Aware/Columbia 38052	album cut
4/28/01	5	38	2. **Drops Of Jupiter (Tell Me)** Airplay #2 from the album *Drops Of Jupiter* on Aware/Columbia 69888	album cut
7/26/03	19	18	3. Calling All Angels Airplay #19 #1 Adult Contemporary hit (3 weeks); from the album *My Private Nation* on Columbia 86593	album cut
			TRAMMPS, The	
			Disco vocal group from Philadelphia, Pennsylvania: Jimmy Ellis, Earl Young, Harold Wade, Stanley Wade and Robert Upchurch.	
2/21/76	35	4	1. Hold Back The Night	Buddah 507
6/5/76	27	5	2. That's Where The Happy People Go	Atlantic 3306
3/25/78	11	13	3. Disco Inferno **[R]** originally hit #53 in 1977; from the movie *Saturday Night Fever* starring John Travolta	Atlantic 3389
			TRAPT	
			Rock group from Los Gatos, California: Chris Brown (vocals, guitar), Simon Ormandy (guitar), Peter Charell (bass) and Aaron Montgomery (drums).	
10/11/03	16	17	1. Headstrong Airplay #17 #1 Mainstream Rock hit (1 week) / #1 Modern Rock hit (5 weeks); from the album *Trapt* on Warner 48296	album cut

DATE	POS	WKS	ARTIST–RECORD TITLE	LABEL & NO.
			TRASHMEN, The	
			Garage-rock group from Minneapolis, Minnesota: Tony Andreason, Dal Winslow and Bob Reed (guitars), with Steve Wahrer (drums). Wahrer died of throat cancer on 1/21/89 (age 47).	
12/28/63+	4	10	1. **Surfin' Bird**	Garrett 4002
2/29/64	30	4	2. Bird Dance Beat	Garrett 4003
			TRAVIS, Randy	
			Born Randy Traywick on 5/4/59 in Marshville, North Carolina. Country singer/songwriter/guitarist/actor. Acted in several movies and TV shows.	
5/17/03	31	5	1. Three Wooden Crosses Airplay #28 #1 Country hit (1 week); from the album *Rise And Shine* on Warner 886236	album cut
			TRAVIS & BOB	
			Pop-country duo from Jackson, Alabama: Travis Pritchett and Bob Weaver.	
4/6/59	8	9	1. **Tell Him No**	Sandy 1017
			TRAVOLTA, John	
			Born on 2/18/54 in Englewood, New Jersey. Actor/singer. Played "Vinnie Barbarino" on the TV series *Welcome Back Kotter*. Starred in several movies. Married actress Kelly Preston on 9/5/91.	
6/12/76	10	10	1. **Let Her In**	Midland Int'l. 10623
11/27/76	38	2	2. Whenever I'm Away From You	Midland Int'l. 10780
3/19/77	34	3	3. All Strung Out On You	Midland Int'l. 10907
4/8/78	1 (1)	16	▲ 4. **You're The One That I Want** **JOHN TRAVOLTA AND OLIVIA NEWTON-JOHN**	RSO 891
8/19/78	5	12	● 5. **Summer Nights** **JOHN TRAVOLTA, OLIVIA NEWTON-JOHN & CAST** above 2 from the movie *Grease* starring Travolta and Newton-John	RSO 906
11/30/96	25 ᴬ	10	6. The Grease Megamix **JOHN TRAVOLTA & OLIVIA NEWTON-JOHN** medley: Greased Lightnin'/You're The One That I Want/Summer Nights; from the various artists album *Pure Disco* on Polydor 535877	album cut
			TREMELOES, The	
			Pop-rock group from England: Len "Chip" Hawkes (vocals, bass), Alan Blakely and Ricky West (guitars), and Dave Munden (drums). Hawkes is the father of Chesney Hawkes. Blakely died of cancer on 6/10/96 (age 54).	
5/6/67	13	8	1. Here Comes My Baby written by Cat Stevens	Epic 10139
7/15/67	11	10	2. Silence Is Golden first recorded by The 4 Seasons in 1964	Epic 10184
10/21/67	36	4	3. Even The Bad Times Are Good	Epic 10233
			TRESVANT, Ralph	
			Born on 5/16/68 in Roxbury, Massachusetts. R&B singer. Member of New Edition.	
11/17/90+	4	16	● 1. **Sensitivity** Sales #3 / Airplay #3 #1 R&B hit (1 week)	MCA 53932
4/6/91	34	3	2. Stone Cold Gentleman Sales #32 / Airplay #34 Bobby Brown (guest rapper)	MCA 54043

DATE	POS	WKS	ARTIST–RECORD TITLE	LABEL & NO.
5/30/92	**10**	18	3. **The Best Things In Life Are Free** Airplay #5 / Sales #16 **LUTHER VANDROSS and JANET JACKSON with BBD and** **Ralph Tresvant** #1 R&B hit (1 week)	Perspective 0010
			T. REX	
			Glam-rock band from England: Marc Bolan (vocals, guitar; born Marc Feld on 7/30/47), Mickey Finn (guitar; born on 6/3/47), Steve Currie (bass) and Bill Legend (drums). Bolan died in a car crash on 9/16/77 (age 30). Finn died of liver failure on 1/11/2003 (age 55).	
1/29/72	**10**	11	1. **Bang A Gong (Get It On)**	Reprise 1032
			TRICK DADDY	
			Born Maurice Young in Miami, Florida. Male rapper/producer.	
8/25/01	**17**	10	1. I'm A Thug Airplay #16 samples "Cheatin' Is" by Millie Jackson	Slip n Slide 85141
			TRINA & TAMARA — see SOMETHIN' **FOR THE PEOPLE**	
			TRIPLETS, The	
			Triplet sisters Diana, Sylvia and Vicky Villegas. Born on 4/18/65 in Mexico (American mother and Mexican father).	
4/6/91	**14**	10	1. You Don't Have To Go Home Tonight Airplay #12 / Sales #13	Mercury 878864
			TRITT, Travis	
			Born James Travis Tritt on 2/9/63 in Marietta, Georgia. Country singer/songwriter/guitarist.	
10/21/00	**27**	10	1. Best Of Intentions Sales #19 / Airplay #24 #1 Country hit (1 week)	Columbia 79404
4/14/01	**33**	9	2. It's A Great Day To Be Alive Airplay #27	album cut
11/17/01	**39**	1	3. Love Of A Woman Airplay #34 above 2 from the album *Down The Road I Go* on Columbia 62165	album cut
			TRIUMPH	
			Hard-rock trio formed in Toronto, Ontario, Canada: Rik Emmett (vocals, guitar), Mike Levine (keyboards, bass) and Gil Moore (drums).	
8/25/79	**38**	2	1. Hold On	RCA 11569
10/18/86	**27**	5	2. Somebody's Out There Sales #20 / Airplay #40	MCA 52898
			TRIUMPHS, The — see THOMAS, B.J.	
			TROCCOLI, Kathy	
			Born on 6/24/58 in Brooklyn, New York. Christian singer/songwriter.	
3/7/92	**14**	14	1. Everything Changes Airplay #7 / Sales #50	Reunion 19118
			TROGGS, The	
			Rock group from Andover, England: Reg Presley (vocals), Chris Britton (guitar), Pete Staples (bass) and Ronnie Bullis (drums). Bullis died on 11/13/92 (age 51).	
7/9/66	**1** (2)	9	1. **Wild Thing** /	

DATE	POS	WKS	ARTIST–RECORD TITLE	LABEL & NO.
9/3/66	29	2	2. With A Girl Like You	Atco 6415
3/23/68	7	12	3. **Love Is All Around**	Fontana 1607

TROY, Doris

Born Doris Higginsen on 1/6/37 in Harlem, New York. Died of emphysema on 2/16/2004 (age 67). R&B singer/songwriter.

DATE	POS	WKS	ARTIST–RECORD TITLE	LABEL & NO.
7/6/63	10	8	1. **Just One Look**	Atlantic 2188

TRUE, Andrea, Connection

Born on 5/29/52 in Nashville, Tennessee. White female disco singer/actress. Appeared in several X-rated movies in the 1970s.

DATE	POS	WKS	ARTIST–RECORD TITLE	LABEL & NO.
4/24/76	4	16	● 1. **More, More, More (Pt. 1)**	Buddah 515
3/26/77	27	5	2. N.Y., You Got Me Dancing	Buddah 564

TRUTH HURTS

Born Shari Watson in Los Angeles, California. Female hip-hop singer.

DATE	POS	WKS	ARTIST–RECORD TITLE	LABEL & NO.
5/4/02	9	16	1. **Addictive** Airplay #8 / Sales #23	Aftermath 497710

TUBES, The

Pop-rock group from San Francisco, California: Fee Waybill (vocals), Bill Spooner and Roger Steen (guitars), Michael Cotton and Vince Welnick (keyboards), Rick Anderson (bass) and Prairie Prince (drums).

DATE	POS	WKS	ARTIST–RECORD TITLE	LABEL & NO.
8/1/81	35	3	1. Don't Want To Wait Anymore	Capitol 5007
5/7/83	10	12	2. **She's A Beauty** #1 Mainstream Rock hit (5 weeks)	Capitol 5217

TUCKER, Tanya

Born on 10/10/58 in Seminole, Texas; raised in Wilcox, Arizona. Country singer.

DATE	POS	WKS	ARTIST–RECORD TITLE	LABEL & NO.
6/7/75	37	2	1. Lizzie And The Rainman #1 Country hit (1 week)	MCA 40402

TUCKER, Tommy

Born Robert Higginbotham on 3/5/39 in Springfield, Ohio. Died of poisoning on 1/22/82 (age 42). R&B singer/pianist.

DATE	POS	WKS	ARTIST–RECORD TITLE	LABEL & NO.
2/29/64	11	8	1. Hi-Heel Sneakers	Checker 1067

TUNE WEAVERS, The

R&B vocal group from Boston, Massachusetts: Margo Sylvia, her husband John Sylvia, Gilbert Lopez and Charlotte Davis. Margo Sylvia died of a heart attack on 10/25/91 (age 55).

DATE	POS	WKS	ARTIST–RECORD TITLE	LABEL & NO.
9/23/57	5	14	1. **Happy, Happy Birthday Baby** Top 100 #5 / Best Seller #8 / Jockey #12 Frank Paul (orch.)	Checker 872

TURBANS, The

R&B vocal group from Philadelphia, Pennsylvania: Al Banks, Matthew Platt, Charles Williams and Andrew Jones. Banks died in 1980 (age 43).

DATE	POS	WKS	ARTIST–RECORD TITLE	LABEL & NO.
1/14/56	33	1	1. When You Dance Top 100 #33	Herald 458

DATE	POS	WKS	ARTIST–RECORD TITLE	LABEL & NO.
			TURNER, Ike & Tina	
			Husband-and-wife R&B duo: guitarist Ike Turner (born on 11/5/31 in Clarksdale, Mississippi) and singer Tina Turner (born on 11/26/38 in Brownsville, Tennessee). Married from 1958-76. Duo inducted into the Rock and Roll Hall of Fame in 1991.	
10/3/60	27	6	1. A Fool In Love	Sue 730
9/4/61	14	5	2. It's Gonna Work Out Fine	Sue 749
			Mickey & Sylvia (backing vocals)	
1/13/62	38	2	3. Poor Fool	Sue 753
8/8/70	34	6	4. I Want To Take You Higher	Liberty 56177
			IKE & TINA TURNER & THE IKETTES	
2/13/71	4	11	● 5. **Proud Mary**	Liberty 56216
10/27/73	22	6	6. Nutbush City Limits	United Artists 298
			TURNER, Jesse Lee	
			Born in Bowling, Texas. Male rockabilly singer.	
1/26/59	20	6	1. The Little Space Girl **[N]**	Carlton 496
			TURNER, Sammy	
			Born Samuel Black on 6/2/32 in Paterson, New Jersey. Black ballad singer.	
7/6/59	3	14	1. **Lavender-Blue**	Big Top 3016
			#4 hit for Sammy Kaye in 1949	
11/16/59	19	7	2. Always	Big Top 3029
			#1 hit for Vincent Lopez in 1926	
			TURNER, Spyder	
			Born Dwight Turner in 1947 in Beckley, West Virginia. R&B singer.	
1/14/67	12	8	1. Stand By Me **[N]**	MGM 13617
			vocal impressions of Jackie Wilson, David Ruffin, Billy Stewart, Smokey Robinson and Chuck Jackson	
			TURNER, Tina	
			Born Anna Mae Bullock on 11/26/38 in Brownsville, Tennessee. R&B singer/actress. Half of Ike & Tina Turner duo. Married to Ike from 1958-76. Acted in the movies *Tommy* and *Mad Max-Beyond Thunderdome*. Her autobiography, *What's Love Got To Do With It*, was made into a movie in 1993.	
2/18/84	26	7	1. Let's Stay Together	Capitol 5322
6/23/84	1 (3)	18	● 2. **What's Love Got To Do With It** Sales #18	Capitol 5354
			1984 Grammy winner: Record of the Year	
10/6/84	5	13	3. **Better Be Good To Me** Airplay #5 / Sales #6	Capitol 5387
1/26/85	7	12	4. **Private Dancer** Sales #7 / Airplay #10	Capitol 5433
			Jeff Beck (guitar); written by Mark Knopfler (of Dire Straits)	
5/18/85	37	3	5. Show Some Respect	Capitol 5461
7/20/85	2 (1)	12	6. **We Don't Need Another Hero (Thunderdome)**	Capitol 5491
			Sales #3 / Airplay #3	
10/12/85	15	10	7. One Of The Living Sales #13 / Airplay #14	Capitol 5518
			above 2 from the movie *Mad Max-Beyond Thunderdome* starring Mel Gibson and Turner	
12/7/85+	15	9	8. It's Only Love Airplay #14 / Sales #16	A&M 2791
			BRYAN ADAMS/TINA TURNER	
9/6/86	2 (3)	12	9. **Typical Male** Sales #1 (2) / Airplay #2	Capitol 5615

DATE	POS	WKS	ARTIST–RECORD TITLE		LABEL & NO.
12/20/86+	30	5	10. Two People	Sales #27 / Airplay #32	Capitol 5644
3/7/87	13	7	11. What You Get Is What You See	Sales #12 / Airplay #16	Capitol 5668
9/23/89	15	8	12. The Best	Sales #12 / Airplay #20	Capitol 44442
			Edgar Winter (sax solo)		
1/6/90	39	1	13. Steamy Windows	Sales #32	Capitol 44473
			written by Tony Joe White; above 2 produced by Dan Hartman		
7/3/93	9	17	14. **I Don't Wanna Fight**	Airplay #3 / Sales #28	Virgin 12652
			#1 Adult Contemporary hit (7 weeks); from Tina's autobiographical movie *What's Love Got To Do With It* starring Angela Bassett and Laurence Fishburne		

TURTLES, The

Pop-rock group formed in Los Angeles, California: Mark Volman and Howard Kaylan (vocals), Jim Tucker (guitar), Al Nichol (keyboards), Chuck Portz (bass) and Don Murray (drums). Volman and Kaylan (under the names Flo and Eddie) later joined Frank Zappa's group. Murray died on 3/22/96 (age 50).

DATE	POS	WKS	ARTIST–RECORD TITLE	LABEL & NO.
8/21/65	8	8	1. **It Ain't Me Babe**	White Whale 222
			written by Bob Dylan	
11/20/65	29	4	2. Let Me Be	White Whale 224
2/19/66	20	9	3. You Baby	White Whale 227
3/4/67	1 (3)	12	● 4. **Happy Together**	White Whale 244
5/27/67	3	8	5. **She'd Rather Be With Me**	White Whale 249
8/26/67	12	7	6. You Know What I Mean	White Whale 254
12/2/67	14	7	7. She's My Girl	White Whale 260
10/12/68	6	9	8. **Elenore**	White Whale 276
1/25/69	6	9	9. **You Showed Me**	White Whale 292

TUXEDO JUNCTION

Female disco group: Jamie Edlin, Marilyn Jackson, Sue Allen and Marti McCall.

DATE	POS	WKS	ARTIST–RECORD TITLE	LABEL & NO.
7/1/78	32	2	1. Chattanooga Choo Choo	Butterfly 1205
			#1 hit for Glenn Miller in 1941 (from the movie *Sun Valley Serenade* starring Sonja Henie)	

TWAIN, Shania

Born Eileen Regina Edwards on 8/28/65 in Windsor, Ontario, Canada; raised in Timmins, Ontario, Canada. Country singer/songwriter. Married record producer Robert John "Mutt" Lange on 12/28/93.

DATE	POS	WKS	ARTIST–RECORD TITLE		LABEL & NO.
7/8/95	31	7	● 1. Any Man Of Mine	Sales #13	Mercury 856448
			#1 Country hit (2 weeks)		
10/18/97	25	7	● 2. Love Gets Me Every Time	Sales #12	Mercury 568062
			#1 Country hit (5 weeks)		
1/10/98	40	1	3. Don't Be Stupid (You Know I Love You)	Sales #24	Mercury 568242
2/21/98	2 (9)	41	▲ 4. **You're Still The One**	Sales #2 / Airplay #2	Mercury 568452
			#1 Country hit (1 week) / #1 Adult Contemporary hit (8 weeks)		
12/5/98	4	12	5. **From This Moment On**	Sales #5 / Airplay #15	Mercury 566450
			#1 Adult Contemporary hit (1 week)		
5/1/99	7	16	6. **That Don't Impress Me Much**	Airplay #5 / Sales #11	Mercury 172118
5/29/99	23	10	7. **Man! I Feel Like A Woman!**	Airplay #18	album cut
			from the album *Come On Over* on Mercury 536003		
11/9/02	34	5	8. I'm Gonna Getcha Good!	Airplay #31	album cut
7/5/03	20	16	9. Forever And For Always	Airplay #17	album cut
			#1 Adult Contemporary hit (6 weeks); above 2 from the album *Up!* on Mercury 170314		

DATE	POS	WKS	ARTIST–RECORD TITLE	LABEL & NO.
			TWEET	
			Born Charlene Keys on 3/4/71 in Rochester, New York. Female R&B singer/songwriter.	
2/16/02	**7**	15	1. **Oops (Oh My)** Airplay #5 / Sales #15 #1 R&B hit (3 weeks)	Goldmind 67280
6/22/02	**31**	6	2. Call Me Sales #22 / Airplay #31	Goldmind 67312
			12 GAUGE	
			Born Isiah Pinkney in Augusta, Georgia. Male hardcore rapper.	
3/26/94	**28**	9	● 1. Dunkie Butt (Please Please Please) Sales #10	Danzalot 75373
			20 FINGERS featuring GILLETTE	
			Duo of Chicago-based dance producers Charles Babie and Manfred Mohr, with female rapper Sandra Gillette.	
11/12/94+	**14**	18	● 1. Short Dick Man Sales #4 / Airplay #55 **[N]**	SOS/Zoo 14194
			TWILLEY, Dwight	
			Born on 6/6/51 in Tulsa, Oklahoma. Rock singer/songwriter/pianist. Formed the Dwight Twilley Band with Phil Seymour (bass, drums) in 1974.	
6/21/75	**16**	8	1. I'm On Fire **DWIGHT TWILLEY BAND**	Shelter 40380
3/3/84	**16**	10	2. Girls	EMI America 8196
			TWISTA	
			Born Carl Mitchell in Chicago, Illinois. Male rapper.	
9/7/96	**22**	13	● 1. Po Pimp Sales #10 **DO OR DIE featuring Twista**	Rap-A-Lot 38559
12/20/03+	**1** (1)	19	2. **Slow Jamz** Airplay #1 (2) / Sales #17 **TWISTA Featuring Kanye West & Jamie Foxx** #1 R&B hit (1 week); samples "A House Is Not A Home" by Luther Vandross	Atlantic 88288
			TWISTED SISTER	
			Hard-rock group from Long Island, New York: Dee Snider (vocals), Jay French and Eddie Ojeda (guitars), Mark Mendosa (bass), and A.J. Pero (drums).	
8/18/84	**21**	7	1. We're Not Gonna Take It	Atlantic 89641
			TWITTY, Conway	
			Born Harold Jenkins on 9/1/33 in Friars Point, Mississippi; raised in Helena, Arkansas. Died of an abdominal aneurysm on 6/5/93 (age 59). Legendary country singer. Appeared in the movies *Sexpot Goes To College* and *College Confidential*. Switched from pop to country music in 1965.	
9/29/58	**1** (2)	17	● 1. **It's Only Make Believe** Hot 100 #1 (0) / Best Seller #30	MGM 12677
2/16/59	**28**	7	2. The Story Of My Love	MGM 12748
8/24/59	**29**	3	3. Mona Lisa #1 hit for Nat "King" Cole in 1950	MGM 12804
10/12/59	**10**	13	4. **Danny Boy**	MGM 12826
1/18/60	**6**	10	● 5. **Lonely Blue Boy**	MGM 12857
4/25/60	**26**	5	6. What Am I Living For	MGM 12886
7/11/60	**35**	5	7. Is A Blue Bird Blue	MGM 12911

DATE	POS	WKS	ARTIST–RECORD TITLE	LABEL & NO.
1/16/61	22	5	8. C'est Si Bon (It's So Good) #21 hit for Danny Kaye in 1950	MGM 12969
9/15/73	22	7	9. You've Never Been This Far Before #1 Country hit (3 weeks)	MCA 40094
			2 IN A ROOM Dance duo from Washington Heights, New York: rapper Rafael Vargas and remixer Roger Pauletta.	
11/10/90	15	12	● 1. Wiggle It Sales #7 / Airplay #24	Cutting 98887
			2 LIVE CREW/LUKE Rap group from Miami, Florida: Luther "Luke" Campbell, David Hobbs, Chris Wong Won and Mark Ross. Luke went solo in 1996.	
10/21/89	26	9	● 1. Me So Horny Sales #18 **THE 2 LIVE CREW** samples "Firecracker" by Mass Production	Skyywalker 130
8/4/90	20	7	● 2. Banned In The U.S.A. Sales #8 **LUKE Featuring 2 LIVE CREW** samples "Born In The U.S.A." by Bruce Springsteen	Luke 98915
5/2/98	26	11	● 3. Raise The Roof Sales #14 **LUKE Featuring No Good But So Good** samples "Theme From King Kong" by John Barry	Luke/Island 572250
			2PAC Born Tupac Shakur on 6/16/71 in Brooklyn, New York; raised in Oakland, California. Died on 9/13/96 (age 25) of wounds suffered on 9/7/96 in a shooting in Las Vegas, Nevada. Gangsta rapper/actor. Member of Digital Underground in 1991. Appeared in several movies.	
8/21/93	11	15	● 1. I Get Around Sales #5 / Airplay #24 samples "Computer Love" by Zapp	Interscope 98372
11/13/93+	12	14	● 2. Keep Ya Head Up Sales #8 / Airplay #15 samples "O-o-h Child" by The Five Stairsteps and "Be Alright" by Roger	Interscope 98345
3/11/95	9	17	▲ 3. **Dear Mama /** Sales #3 / Airplay #39 samples "In My Wildest Dreams" by Joe Sample and "Sadie" by The Spinners	
6/3/95		5	4. Old School samples "We Share" by the Soul Searchers and "Dedication" by Brand Nubian	Interscope 98273
6/22/96	1 (2)	21	▲² 5. **How Do U Want It /** Sales #1 (4) / Airplay #68 **2 PAC (featuring KC and JoJo)** #1 R&B hit (3 weeks); samples "Body Heat" by Quincy Jones	
6/22/96	6	21	6. **California Love** Sales #3 / Airplay #19 **2 PAC (featuring Dr. Dre and Roger Troutman)** samples "So Ruff So Tuff" by Roger and "Woman To Woman" by Joe Cocker	Death Row 854652
6/21/97	12	9	● 7. Smile Sales #4 / Airplay #62 **SCARFACE Featuring 2 Pac & Johnny P**	Rap-A-Lot 38581
3/21/98	21	8	● 8. Do For Love Sales #10 / Airplay #66 **2PAC Featuring Eric Williams of BLACKstreet** samples "What You Won't Do For Love" by Bobby Caldwell	Amaru/Jive 42516
12/26/98+	32	5	9. Changes Airplay #21 samples "The Way It Is" by Bruce Hornsby And The Range; from the album *Greatest Hits* on Amaru/Jive 90301	album cut
12/14/02	19	11	10. Thugz Mansion Airplay #18 from the album *Better Dayz* on Amaru 497070	album cut

DATE	POS	WKS	ARTIST–RECORD TITLE	LABEL & NO.
11/15/03	**19**	11	11. Runnin (Dying To Live) Airplay #17 / Sales #24 **[R]** **TUPAC Featuring The Notorious B.I.G.** new mix (produced by Eminem) of their #81 hit in 1997	Amaru 001670
			2 UNLIMITED	
			Techno-house dance duo from Amsterdam, Netherlands: Ray Slijngard (born on 6/28/71) and Anita Doth (born on 12/25/71).	
4/1/95	**38**	2	1. Get Ready For This Airplay #33 **[R]** originally charted at #76 in 1992	Radikal/Critique 15535
			TYCOON	
			Pop-rock group from New York: Norman Mershon (vocals), Jon Gordon (guitar), Mark Rivera (sax), Michael Fonfara (keyboards), Mark Kreider (bass) and Richard Steinberg (drums).	
4/28/79	**26**	5	1. Such A Woman	Arista 0398
			TYLER, Bonnie	
			Born Gaynor Hopkins on 6/8/53 in Swansea, Wales. Pop-rock singer. Known for her raspy vocals.	
4/22/78	**3**	15	● 1. **It's A Heartache** Mike Gibbins of Badfinger (drums)	RCA 11249
8/13/83	**1 (4)**	18	▲ 2. **Total Eclipse Of The Heart** Rory Dodd (male vocal)	Columbia 03906
4/7/84	**34**	4	3. Holding Out For A Hero from the movie *Footloose* starring Kevin Bacon and Lori Singer	Columbia 04370
			TYMES, The	
			R&B vocal group from Philadelphia, Pennsylvania: George Williams, George Hilliard, Donald Banks, Albert Berry and Norman Burnett. Female singers Terri Gonzalez and Melanie Moore replaced Hilliard and Berry in 1973.	
6/22/63	**1 (1)**	12	1. **So Much In Love**	Parkway 871
8/31/63	**7**	8	2. **Wonderful! Wonderful!**	Parkway 884
1/4/64	**19**	6	3. Somewhere	Parkway 891
12/28/68	**39**	1	4. People from the movie *Funny Girl* starring Barbra Streisand	Columbia 44630
9/7/74	**12**	8	5. You Little Trustmaker	RCA Victor 10022
			TYRESE	
			Born Tyrese Gibson on 12/30/78 in Watts, California. Male R&B singer/songwriter/actor. Starred in the movies *Baby Boy* and *2 Fast 2 Furious*.	
9/19/98	**36**	3	1. Nobody Else Sales #22	RCA 65538
2/20/99	**12**	19	2. Sweet Lady Airplay #8 from the album *Tyrese* on RCA 66901	album cut
7/22/00	**26**	7	3. What'Chu Like Airplay #19 **DA BRAT Featuring Tyrese**	So So Def 79330
2/8/03	**7**	20	4. **How You Gonna Act Like That** Airplay #6 / Sales #61	J Records 52518

DATE	POS	WKS	ARTIST–RECORD TITLE	LABEL & NO.
			<div align="center">**U**</div>	
			UB40	
			Reggae group formed in Birmingham, England: brothers Ali (vocals) and Robin (guitar) Campbell, Terence "Astro" Wilson (vocals), Norman Hassan (percussion), Michael Virtue (keyboards), Brian Travers (sax), Earl Falconer (bass) and James Brown (drums). Name taken from British unemployment form.	
3/17/84	**34**	4	1. Red Red Wine 　　also see #3 below	A&M 2600
9/7/85	**28**	4	2. I Got You Babe　　　　　　　　　Sales #24 **UB40 WITH CHRISSIE HYNDE**	A&M 2758
9/3/88	**1** (1)	12	● 3. **Red Red Wine**　　　Sales #1 (2) / Airplay #1 (1)　**[R]** 　　longer version than #1 above (includes rap by Astro)	A&M 1244
10/27/90	**6**	15	● 4. **The Way You Do The Things You Do** 　　　　　　　　　　　Sales #5 / Airplay #10	Virgin 98978
5/18/91	**7**	12	5. **Here I Am (Come And Take Me)**　Airplay #9 / Sales #23	Virgin 99141
6/5/93	**1** (7)	23	▲ 6. **Can't Help Falling In Love**　Airplay #1 (4) / Sales #2 　　from the movie *Sliver* starring Sharon Stone and William Baldwin	Virgin 12653
			UGK — see JAY-Z	
			UGLY KID JOE	
			Rock group from Isla Vista, California: Whitfield Crane (vocals), Klaus Eichstadt and Dave Fortman (guitars), Cordell Crockett (bass), and Mark Davis (drums).	
4/25/92	**9**	11	1. **Everything About You.**　　　Sales #5 / Airplay #37 　　from the movie *Wayne's World* starring Mike Myers and Dana Carvey (not on the soundtrack album)	Mercury 866632
3/6/93	**6**	13	● 2. **Cats In The Cradle**　　　　Sales #4 / Airplay #27	Stardog 864888
			U-KREW, The	
			Rap group from Portland, Oregon: Kevin Morse, Larry Bell, Lavell Alexander, James McClendon and Hakim Muhammad.	
3/24/90	**24**	7	1. If U Were Mine　　　　　　Sales #17 / Airplay #31	Enigma 75051
			ULLMAN, Tracey	
			Born on 12/30/59 in Buckinghamshire, England. Actress/singer/comedienne. Hosted own TV show from 1987-90. Acted in several movies.	
3/17/84	**8**	11	1. **They Don't Know**	MCA/Stiff 52347
			UNCLE KRACKER	
			Born Matthew Shafer on 6/6/74 in Mount Clemens, Michigan. White pop-rock singer/DJ. Member of Kid Rock's posse.	
4/7/01	**5**	27	1. **Follow Me**　　　　　　　　　Airplay #5 　　from the album *Double Wide* on Lava 83279	album cut
5/3/03	**9**	28	2. **Drift Away**　　　　　　　Airplay #9　**[R]** **UNCLE KRACKER (Featuring Dobie Gray)** 　　#1 Adult Contemporary hit (28 weeks); from the album *No Stranger To Shame* on Lava 83542	album cut

DATE	POS	WKS	ARTIST–RECORD TITLE	LABEL & NO.
			UNCLE SAM	
			Born Sam Turner in Detroit, Michigan. R&B singer.	
12/6/97+	6	22	▲ 1. **I Don't Ever Want To See You Again** Sales #4 / Airplay #27 Michael McCary of Boyz II Men (monologue); Nathan Morris of Boyz II Men (backing vocal; producer)	Stonecreek 78689
			UNDERGROUND SUNSHINE	
			Rock group from Montello, Wisconsin: brothers Egbert (vocals, bass) and Frank (drums) Kohl, with John Dahlberg (guitar) and Jane Little (keyboards).	
8/23/69	26	5	1. Birthday first recorded by The Beatles in 1968	Intrepid 75002
			UNDISPUTED TRUTH, The	
			R&B vocal trio from Detroit, Michigan: Joe Harris, Billie Calvin and Brenda Evans.	
7/31/71	3	13	1. **Smiling Faces Sometimes**	Gordy 7108
			UNIFICS, The	
			R&B vocal group from Washington DC: Al Johnson, Hal Worthington, Michael Ward and Greg Cook. Worthington was shot to death on 2/20/90 (age 42).	
10/19/68	25	5	1. Court Of Love	Kapp 935
1/18/69	36	4	2. The Beginning Of My End	Kapp 957
			UNION GAP, The — see PUCKETT, Gary	
			UNIT FOUR plus TWO	
			Pop-rock group from Hertfordshire, England: Peter Moules (vocals), David Meikle and Howard Lubin (guitars), Thomas Moeller (keyboards), Rod Garwood (bass) and Hugh Halliday (drums).	
5/29/65	28	4	1. Concrete And Clay	London 9751
			UNV	
			R&B vocal group from Detroit, Michigan: brothers John and Shawn Powe, with John Clay and Demetrius Peete. UNV: Universal Nubian Voices.	
7/10/93	29	7	1. Something's Goin' On Sales #17 / Airplay #36	Maverick/Sire 18564
			UPCHURCH, Philip, Combo	
			Born on 7/19/41 in Chicago, Illinois. R&B guitarist.	
6/26/61	29	3	1. You Can't Sit Down Part 2 [I]	Boyd 3398
			URBAN, Keith	
			Born on 10/26/67 in Whangarei, New Zealand; raised in Caboolture, Queensland, Australia. Country singer.	
2/24/01	37	3	1. But For The Grace Of God Airplay #31 #1 Country hit (1 week)	album cut
8/25/01	35	4	2. Where The Blacktop Ends Airplay #30 above 2 from the album Keith Urban on Capitol 97591	album cut
9/21/02	23	14	3. Somebody Like You Airplay #22 #1 Country hit (6 weeks)	album cut
5/24/03	38	2	4. Raining On Sunday Airplay #36	album cut

DATE	POS	WKS	ARTIST–RECORD TITLE	LABEL & NO.
10/25/03	**30**	6	5. Who Wouldn't Wanna Be Me Airplay #27 #1 Country hit (1 week); above 3 from the album *Golden Road* on Capitol 32936	album cut

URBAN DANCE SQUAD

Rap-dance group from Amsterdam, Netherlands: Patrick Remington, Magic Stick, DNA, Silly Sil and Tres Manos.

DATE	POS	WKS	ARTIST–RECORD TITLE	LABEL & NO.
2/2/91	**21**	7	1. Deeper Shade Of Soul Sales #8	Arista 2026

URIAH HEEP

Hard-rock group from England: David Byron (vocals), Mick Box (guitar), Ken Hensley (keyboards), Gary Thain (bass) and Keith Baker (drums). Thain died of a drug overdose on 3/19/76 (age 27). Byron died on 2/28/85 (age 38).

DATE	POS	WKS	ARTIST–RECORD TITLE	LABEL & NO.
9/16/72	**39**	3	1. Easy Livin	Mercury 73307

USA FOR AFRICA

USA: United Support of Artists. Collection of top artists to help starving people in Africa. Soloists in order: Lionel Richie, Stevie Wonder, Paul Simon, Kenny Rogers, James Ingram, Tina Turner, Billy Joel, Michael Jackson, Diana Ross, Dionne Warwick, Willie Nelson, Al Jarreau, Bruce Springsteen, Kenny Loggins, Steve Perry, Daryl Hall, Huey Lewis, Cyndi Lauper, Kim Carnes, Bob Dylan and Ray Charles.

DATE	POS	WKS	ARTIST–RECORD TITLE	LABEL & NO.
3/23/85	**1** (4)	12	▲⁴ 1. **We Are The World** Sales #1 (5) / Airplay #1 (4) #1 R&B hit (2 weeks) / #1 Adult Contemporary hit (2 weeks)	Columbia 04839

USHER

Born Usher Raymond on 10/14/78 in Chattanooga, Tennessee. Male R&B singer/actor. Appeared in several movies and TV shows.

DATE	POS	WKS	ARTIST–RECORD TITLE	LABEL & NO.
8/23/97	**2** (7)	40	▲ 1. **You Make Me Wanna...** Sales #2 / Airplay #4 #1 R&B hit (11 weeks)	LaFace 24265
1/24/98	**1** (2)	22	▲ 2. **Nice & Slow** Sales #1 (4) / Airplay #15 #1 R&B hit (8 weeks); Jagged Edge (backing vocals)	LaFace 24290
6/20/98	**2** (3)	24	▲ 3. **My Way** Sales #1 (3) / Airplay #29	LaFace 24323
6/23/01	**1** (4)	22	4. **U Remind Me** Sales #1 (3) / Airplay #3 #1 R&B hit (4 weeks)	Arista 13992
10/13/01	**1** (6)	29	5. **U Got It Bad** Airplay #1 (10) #1 R&B hit (7 weeks)	Arista 15036
3/2/02	**3**	22	6. **U Don't Have To Call** Airplay #3 / Sales #10	Arista 15134
4/6/02	**2** (4)	19	7. **I Need A Girl (Part One)** Airplay #2 / Sales #23 **P. DIDDY Featuring Usher & Loon**	Bad Boy 79436

US3

Jazz-rap collaboration by British producers Mel Simpson (keyboards) and Geoff Wilkinson (samples). Samples of recordings on the Blue Note jazz record label serve as the backdrop for new rap solos and jazz playing by some of Britain's top players. Pronounced: us three.

DATE	POS	WKS	ARTIST–RECORD TITLE	LABEL & NO.
1/22/94	**9**	18	● 1. **Cantaloop** Sales #6 / Airplay #20 Rahsaan (rap); samples "Cantaloupe Island" by Herbie Hancock	Blue Note 44945

UTOPIA

Pop-rock group: Todd Rundgren (vocals, guitar), Roger Powell (keyboards), Kasim Sulton (bass) and John Wilcox (drums).

DATE	POS	WKS	ARTIST–RECORD TITLE	LABEL & NO.
3/29/80	**27**	5	1. Set Me Free	Bearsville 49180

DATE	POS	WKS	ARTIST–RECORD TITLE	LABEL & NO.
			U2	
			Rock group formed in Dublin, Ireland: Paul "Bono" Hewson (vocals), Dave "The Edge" Evans (guitar), Adam Clayton (bass) and Larry Mullen Jr. (drums). Released concert tour documentary movie *Rattle And Hum* in 1988.	
12/1/84	33	5	1. Pride (In The Name Of Love) a tribute to Rev. Martin Luther King	Island 99704
4/4/87	**1 (3)**	13	2. **With Or Without You**　　Airplay #1 (3) / Sales #1 (1) #1 Mainstream Rock hit (5 weeks)	Island 99469
6/20/87	**1 (2)**	13	3. **I Still Haven't Found What I'm Looking For** Airplay #1 (1) / Sales #2	Island 99430
10/3/87	13	9	4. Where The Streets Have No Name　Sales #11 / Airplay #16	Island 99408
10/8/88	3	13	● 5. **Desire**　　　　　　　Sales #1 (1) / Airplay #5 #1 Mainstream Rock hit (5 weeks) / #1 Modern Rock hit (5 weeks)	Island 99250
1/14/89	14	8	6. Angel Of Harlem　　　　Sales #11 / Airplay #14 #1 Mainstream Rock hit (6 weeks); a tribute to Billie Holiday; above 2 from the U2 concert tour movie *Rattle And Hum*	Island 99254
12/14/91+	9	15	7. **Mysterious Ways**　　　Airplay #11 / Sales #16 #1 Mainstream Rock hit (12 weeks) / #1 Modern Rock hit (9 weeks)	Island 866188
3/28/92	10	14	8. **One**　　　　　　　　Airplay #7 / Sales #17 #1 Mainstream Rock hit (2 weeks) / #1 Modern Rock hit (1 week)	Island 866533
8/8/92	32	6	9. Even Better Than The Real Thing　Airplay #43 / Sales #55 #1 Mainstream Rock hit (3 weeks)	Island 866977
12/5/92	35	5	10. Who's Gonna Ride Your Wild Horses Sales #42 / Airplay #42	Island 864521
6/24/95	16	10	11. Hold Me, Thrill Me, Kiss Me, Kill Me Airplay #15 / Sales #19 #1 Mainstream Rock hit (1 week) / #1 Modern Rock hit (4 weeks); from the movie *Batman Forever* starring Val Kilmer	Island 87131
6/1/96	7	10	● 12. **Theme From Mission: Impossible** Sales #4 / Airplay #10　**[I]** **ADAM CLAYTON & LARRY MULLEN** samples the original #41 hit by Lalo Schifrin from 1968; from the movie *Mission: Impossible* starring Tom Cruise	Mother/Island 576670
2/22/97	10	4	● 13. **Discothéque**　　　　Sales #9 / Airplay #22 #1 Modern Rock hit (4 weeks); samples "Fane" by Freeform	Island 854774
4/26/97	26	8	14. Staring At The Sun　　　Airplay #16 / Sales #36 #1 Modern Rock hit (3 weeks)	Island 854972
12/2/00+	21	15	15. Beautiful Day　　　　　Airplay #19 2000 Grammy winner: Record of the Year	Island 562972

V

DATE	POS	WKS	ARTIST–RECORD TITLE	LABEL & NO.
			VALE, Jerry	
			Born Genaro Vitaliano on 7/8/32 in the Bronx, New York. Adult Contemporary ballad singer.	
3/24/56	30	5	1. Innamorata (Sweetheart)　　　　Top 100 #30 from the movie *Artists & Models* starring Dean Martin and Jerry Lewis	Columbia 40634
7/28/56	14	17	2. You Don't Know Me Best Seller #14 / Top 100 #14 / Juke Box #14 / Jockey #15 Percy Faith (orch., above 2)	Columbia 40710
1/23/65	24	4	3. Have You Looked Into Your Heart #1 Adult Contemporary hit (1 week)	Columbia 43181

DATE	POS	WKS	ARTIST–RECORD TITLE	LABEL & NO.
			VALENS, Ritchie	
			Born Richard Valenzuela on 5/13/41 in Pacoima, California. Killed in the plane crash that also took the lives of Buddy Holly and the Big Bopper on 2/3/59 (age 17). Latin-rock singer/songwriter/guitarist. Appeared in the movie *Go Johnny Go*. The 1987 movie *La Bamba* was based on his life. Inducted into the Rock and Roll Hall of Fame in 2001.	
12/15/58+	**2** (2)	18	● 1. **Donna** /	
1/19/59	22	8	2. La Bamba [F]	Del-Fi 4110
			VALENTE, Caterina	
			Born on 1/14/31 in Paris, France (Italian parents). Singer/dancer/actress.	
4/9/55	8	14	1. **The Breeze And I (Andalucia)** Jockey #8 / Best Seller #13	Decca 29467
			Werner Müller (orch.); #1 hit for Jimmy Dorsey in 1940	
			VALENTI, John	
			Born John LaVigni in Chicago, Illinois. "Blue-eyed soul" singer/songwriter/drummer.	
10/30/76	37	2	1. Anything You Want	Ariola America 7625
			VALENTINO, Mark	
			Born Anthony Busillo on 3/12/42 in Philadelphia, Pennsylvania. Rock and roll singer.	
12/8/62	27	3	1. The Push And Kick	Swan 4121
			Frank Slay (orch.)	
			VALINO, Joe	
			Born Joseph Paolino on 3/9/29 in South Philadelphia, Pennsylvania. Died of a heart attack on 12/26/96 (age 67). Big band-styled singer.	
10/27/56	12	14	1. Garden Of Eden	Vik 0226
			Top 100 #12 / Jockey #12 / Best Seller #13 / Juke Box #13	
			George Siravo (orch.)	
			VALJEAN	
			Born Valjean Johns on 11/19/34 in Shattuck, Oklahoma. Male pianist.	
6/16/62	28	4	1. Theme From Ben Casey [I]	Carlton 573
			VALLI, Frankie	
			Born Francis Castelluccio on 5/3/37 in Newark, New Jersey. Lead singer of The 4 Seasons.	
2/12/66	39	1	1. (You're Gonna) Hurt Yourself	Smash 2015
6/3/67	**2** (1)	14	● 2. **Can't Take My Eyes Off You**	Philips 40446
9/16/67	18	5	3. I Make A Fool Of Myself	Philips 40484
1/20/68	29	4	4. To Give (The Reason I Live)	Philips 40510
1/18/75	**1** (1)	14	● 5. **My Eyes Adored You**	Private Stock 45,003
6/14/75	6	9	6. **Swearin' To God**	Private Stock 45,021
11/8/75	11	8	7. Our Day Will Come	Private Stock 45,043
5/8/76	36	2	8. Fallen Angel	Private Stock 45,074
6/17/78	**1** (2)	15	▲ 9. **Grease**	RSO 897
			title song from the movie starring John Travolta and Olivia Newton-John; written and produced by Barry Gibb	

DATE	POS	WKS	ARTIST–RECORD TITLE	LABEL & NO.
			VALLI, June	
			Born on 6/30/30 in the Bronx, New York. Died on 3/12/93 (age 62). Pop singer. Voice for "Chiquita Banana" commercials.	
5/14/55	**29**	1	1. Unchained Melody Best Seller #29	RCA Victor 6078
			Hugo Winterhalter (orch.); from the movie *Unchained* starring football great Elroy "Crazylegs" Hirsch	
4/18/60	**29**	4	2. Apple Green	Mercury 71588
			Belford Hendricks (orch.)	
			VANDENBERG	
			Born Adrian Vandenberg on 1/31/54 in Holland. Hard-rock guitarist. His group: Bert Heerink (vocals), Dick Kemper (bass) and Jos Zoomer (drums). Vandenberg later joined Whitesnake.	
3/12/83	**39**	2	1. Burning Heart	Atco 99947
			VANDROSS, Luther	
			Born on 4/20/51 in the Bronx, New York. R&B singer/songwriter. Prolific session singer. Appeared in the movie *The Meteor Man*. His older sister Patricia was a member of The Crests.	
11/14/81	**33**	4	1. Never Too Much	Epic 02409
			#1 R&B hit (2 weeks)	
10/29/83	**27**	5	2. How Many Times Can We Say Goodbye	Arista 9073
			DIONNE WARWICK AND LUTHER VANDROSS	
4/27/85	**29**	6	3. 'Til My Baby Comes Home Sales #26	Epic 04760
			Billy Preston (organ solo)	
12/27/86+	**15**	11	4. Stop To Love Sales #14 / Airplay #14	Epic 06523
			#1 R&B hit (2 weeks)	
3/4/89	**30**	4	5. She Won't Talk To Me Airplay #33 / Sales #35	Epic 08513
2/10/90	**6**	15	● 6. **Here And Now** Sales #6 / Airplay #7	Epic 73029
			#1 R&B hit (2 weeks)	
5/11/91	**4**	12	7. **Power Of Love/Love Power** Airplay #14 / Sales #22	Epic 73778
			#1 R&B hit (2 weeks); Cissy Houston, Darlene Love, Lisa Fischer and others (backing vocals)	
9/14/91	**9**	11	8. **Don't Want To Be A Fool** Airplay #21	Epic 73879
5/30/92	**10**	18	9. **The Best Things In Life Are Free** Airplay #5 / Sales #16	Perspective 0010
			LUTHER VANDROSS and JANET JACKSON with BBD and Ralph Tresvant	
			#1 R&B hit (1 week); from the movie *Mo' Money* starring Damon Wayans	
9/10/94	**2 (1)**	13	● 10. **Endless Love** Sales #2 / Airplay #5	Columbia 77629
			LUTHER VANDROSS & MARIAH CAREY	
7/21/01	**26**	4	11. Take You Out Sales #5 / Airplay #75	J Records 21084
8/16/03	**38**	4	12. Dance With My Father Sales #24 / Airplay #35	J Records 57595
			VAN DYKE, Leroy	
			Born on 10/4/29 in Spring Fork, Missouri. Country singer.	
12/8/56+	**19**	7	1. Auctioneer Juke Box #19 / Best Seller #21 / Top 100 #29	Dot 15503
			Andy Nelson (guitar)	
11/20/61	**5**	12	2. **Walk On By**	Mercury 71834
			#1 Country hit (19 weeks)	
3/31/62	**35**	2	3. If A Woman Answers (Hang Up The Phone)	Mercury 71926
			The Merry Melody Singers (backing vocals, above 2)	

DATE	POS	WKS	ARTIST–RECORD TITLE	LABEL & NO.
			VANGELIS	
			Born Evangelos Papathanassiou on 3/29/43 in Valos, Greece. Keyboardist/songwriter.	
2/20/82	**1** (1)	15	1. **Chariots Of Fire - Titles** [I] #1 Adult Contemporary hit (5 weeks); from the Academy Award-winning movie *Chariots Of Fire* starring Ian Charleson and Ben Cross; first pressings issued only as "Titles"	Polydor 2189
			VAN HALEN	
			Hard-rock group formed in Pasadena, California: David Lee Roth (vocals), Eddie Van Halen (guitar), Michael Anthony (bass) and Alex Van Halen (drums). The Van Halen brothers were born in Nijmegen, Netherlands; moved to Pasadena in 1968. Sammy Hagar replaced Roth as lead singer in 1985. Eddie married actress Valerie Bertinelli on 4/11/81.	
3/11/78	**36**	3	1. You Really Got Me	Warner 8515
5/26/79	**15**	9	2. Dance The Night Away	Warner 8823
3/13/82	**12**	9	3. (Oh) Pretty Woman #1 Mainstream Rock hit (2 weeks)	Warner 50003
6/26/82	**38**	3	4. Dancing In The Street	Warner 29986
1/21/84	**1** (5)	15	● 5. **Jump** #1 Mainstream Rock hit (8 weeks)	Warner 29384
4/21/84	**13**	10	6. I'll Wait	Warner 29307
6/30/84	**13**	10	7. Panama	Warner 29250
3/29/86	**3**	11	8. **Why Can't This Be Love** Airplay #2 / Sales #7 #1 Mainstream Rock hit (3 weeks)	Warner 28740
6/14/86	**22**	7	9. Dreams Airplay #18 / Sales #25	Warner 28702
8/30/86	**22**	9	10. Love Walks In Airplay #15 / Sales #24	Warner 28626
6/18/88	**34**	2	11. Black And Blue Sales #29 #1 Mainstream Rock hit (3 weeks)	Warner 27891
7/23/88	**5**	12	12. **When It's Love** Airplay #4 / Sales #7 #1 Mainstream Rock hit (1 week)	Warner 27827
11/5/88	**13**	10	13. Finish What Ya Started Sales #14 / Airplay #16	Warner 27746
3/11/89	**35**	3	14. Feels So Good Airplay #35	Warner 27565
11/2/91	**27**	5	15. Top Of The World Airplay #49 #1 Mainstream Rock hit (4 weeks)	Warner 19151
4/15/95	**30**	9	16. Can't Stop Lovin' You Airplay #32 / Sales #44	Warner 17909
			VANILLA FUDGE	
			Psychedelic-rock group formed in New York: Mark Stein (vocals, keyboards), Vinnie Martell (guitar), Tim Bogert (bass) and Carmine Appice (drums).	
8/3/68	**6**	9	1. **You Keep Me Hangin' On** [R] originally charted at #67 in 1967	Atco 6590
10/26/68	**38**	4	2. Take Me For A Little While #114 hit for Evie Sands in 1965	Atco 6616
			VANILLA ICE	
			Born Robert Van Winkle on 10/31/68 in Miami Lakes, Florida. White rapper. Starred in the movie *Cool As Ice*.	
9/22/90	**1** (1)	15	▲ 1. **Ice Ice Baby** Sales #1 (4) / Airplay #1 (2) samples "Under Pressure" by Queen & David Bowie	SBK 07335
12/15/90+	**4**	12	● 2. **Play That Funky Music** Sales #2 / Airplay #11	SBK 07339

DATE	POS	WKS	ARTIST–RECORD TITLE	LABEL & NO.
			VANITY FARE	
			Pop group from England: Trevor Brice (vocals), Tony Goulden (guitar), Barry Landeman (piano), Tony Jarrett (bass) and Dick Allix (drums).	
12/20/69+	12	9	1. Early In The Morning	Page One 21,027
5/16/70	5	14	● 2. **Hitchin' A Ride**	Page One 21,029
			VANNELLI, Gino	
			Born on 6/16/52 in Montreal, Quebec, Canada. Pop singer/songwriter.	
10/26/74	22	5	1. People Gotta Move	A&M 1614
10/14/78	4	13	2. **I Just Wanna Stop**	A&M 2072
4/4/81	6	14	3. **Living Inside Myself**	Arista 0588
			VANWARMER, Randy	
			Born Randall Van Wormer on 3/30/55 in Indian Hills, Colorado. Died of leukemia on 1/12/2004 (age 48). Pop singer/songwriter/guitarist.	
4/21/79	4	14	● 1. **Just When I Needed You Most** #1 Adult Contemporary hit (2 weeks)	Bearsville 0334
			VAPORS, The	
			Pub-rock group from Guildford, Surrey, England: David Fenton (vocals), Ed Bazalgette (guitar), Steve Smith (bass) and Howard Smith (drums).	
11/15/80	36	3	1. Turning Japanese	United Artists 1364
			VASSAR, Phil	
			Born on 5/28/65 in Lynchburg, Virginia. Country singer/songwriter.	
11/18/00	35	3	1. Just Another Day In Paradise Airplay #26 #1 Country hit (1 week)	album cut
4/27/02	37	2	2. That's When I Love You Airplay #36 above 2 from the album *Phil Vassar* on Arista 18891	album cut
			VAUGHAN, Frankie	
			Born Frank Abelson on 2/3/28 in Liverpool, England. Died of heart failure on 9/17/99 (age 71). Popular entertainer in England. In movie *Let's Make Love* (1960). In London cast of *42nd Street* in 1985.	
7/28/58	22	1	1. Judy Jockey #22 / Hot 100 #100 Mark Jeffrey (orch.)	Epic 9273
			VAUGHAN, Sarah	
			Born on 3/27/24 in Newark, New Jersey. Died of cancer on 4/3/90 (age 66). Jazz singer. Nicknamed "The Divine One." Won Grammy's Lifetime Achievement Award in 1989.	
11/27/54+	6	15	1. **Make Yourself Comfortable** Jockey #6 / Best Seller #8 / Juke Box #8	Mercury 70469
2/26/55	12	9	2. How Important Can It Be? Jockey #12 / Best Seller #18 / Juke Box #20	Mercury 70534
4/23/55	6	11	3. **Whatever Lola Wants** Jockey #6 / Juke Box #9 / Best Seller #12 from the Broadway musical *Damn Yankees* starring Gwen Verdon	Mercury 70595
7/16/55	14	1	4. Experience Unnecessary Jockey #14	Mercury 70646
12/3/55	11	7	5. C'est La Vie Jockey #11 / Top 100 #22	Mercury 70727
3/3/56	13	7	6. Mr. Wonderful Jockey #13 / Top 100 #38 from the Broadway musical starring Sammy Davis Jr.	Mercury 70777

DATE	POS	WKS	ARTIST–RECORD TITLE	LABEL & NO.
7/21/56	19	7	7. Fabulous Character Jockey #19 / Top 100 #27 Hugo Peretti (of Hugo & Luigi; orch., all of above)	Mercury 70885
1/12/57	19	5	8. The Banana Boat Song Jockey #19 / Top 100 #31 David Carroll (orch.)	Mercury 71020
8/17/59	7	11	● 9. **Broken-Hearted Melody**	Mercury 71477

VAUGHN, Billy, and His Orchestra

Born Richard Vaughn on 4/12/19 in Glasgow, Kentucky. Died of cancer on 9/26/91 (age 72). Orchestra leader. Member of The Hilltoppers vocal group.

DATE	POS	WKS	ARTIST–RECORD TITLE	LABEL & NO.
12/11/54+	2 (1)	27	● 1. **Melody Of Love** Best Seller #2 / Jockey #2 / Juke Box #3 **[I]**	Dot 15247
9/24/55	5	15	2. **The Shifting Whispering Sands (Parts 1 & 2)** Jockey #5 / Best Seller #5 / Top 100 #5 / Juke Box #10 **[S]** Ken Nordine (narration)	Dot 15409
2/25/56	37	2	3. A Theme From (The Three Penny Opera) "Moritat" Top 100 #37 **[I]** written in 1928; also known as "Mack The Knife"	Dot 15444
9/8/56	18	6	4. When The White Lilacs Bloom Again Juke Box #18 / Jockey #21 / Top 100 #22 **[I]**	Dot 15491
12/16/57	10	7	5. **Raunchy /** Jockey #10 / Best Seller #25 / Top 100 #33 **[I]**	
1/13/58	5	21	● 6. **Sail Along Silvery Moon** Best Seller #5 / Top 100 #5 / Jockey #6 **[I]** #4 hit for Bing Crosby in 1937	Dot 15661
4/14/58	30	4	7. Tumbling Tumbleweeds Best Seller #30 / Top 100 #35 **[I]** #13 hit for the Sons of The Pioneers in 1934	Dot 15710
8/25/58	20	8	8. La Paloma Best Seller #20 / Hot 100 #26 **[I]**	Dot 15795
2/2/59	37	1	9. Blue Hawaii **[I]** #5 hit for Bing Crosby in 1937 (from the movie *Waikiki Wedding* starring Crosby)	Dot 15879
7/18/60	19	7	10. Look For A Star **[I]** from the movie *Circus Of Horrors* starring Donald Pleasence	Dot 16106
3/6/61	28	3	11. Wheels **[I]**	Dot 16174
8/11/62	13	8	12. A Swingin' Safari **[I]** written by Bert Kaempfert	Dot 16374

VEE, Bobby

Born Robert Velline on 4/30/43 in Fargo, North Dakota. Pop singer. Appeared in the movies *Swingin' Along, It's Trad Dad, Play It Cool, C'mon Let's Live A Little* and *Just For Fun*.

DATE	POS	WKS	ARTIST–RECORD TITLE	LABEL & NO.
9/5/60	6	13	1. **Devil Or Angel** #3 R&B hit for The Clovers in 1956	Liberty 55270
12/12/60+	6	11	2. **Rubber Ball**	Liberty 55287
2/27/61	33	3	3. Stayin' In	Liberty 55296
8/21/61	1 (3)	11	● 4. **Take Good Care Of My Baby**	Liberty 55354
11/20/61	2 (1)	13	5. **Run To Him**	Liberty 55388
3/17/62	15	6	6. Please Don't Ask About Barbara	Liberty 55419
6/9/62	15	6	7. Sharing You	Liberty 55451
9/15/62	20	6	8. Punish Her	Liberty 55479
12/22/62+	3	11	9. **The Night Has A Thousand Eyes**	Liberty 55521
4/13/63	13	7	10. Charms	Liberty 55530
7/20/63	34	2	11. Be True To Yourself	Liberty 55581
8/12/67	3	13	● 12. **Come Back When You Grow Up**	Liberty 55964

DATE	POS	WKS	ARTIST–RECORD TITLE	LABEL & NO.
12/16/67	37	2	13. Beautiful People **BOBBY VEE And The Strangers** (above 2)	Liberty 56009
5/18/68	35	4	14. My Girl/Hey Girl	Liberty 56033
			VEGA, Suzanne	
			Born on 7/11/59 in Sacramento, California. Folk-pop singer/songwriter/ guitarist. Married record producer Mitchell Froom on 3/17/95.	
7/4/87	3	12	1. **Luka** Sales #2 / Airplay #3	A&M 2937
11/3/90	5	14	● 2. **Tom's Diner** Sales #2 / Airplay #9 **D.N.A. Featuring SUZANNE VEGA**	A&M 1529
			VELVETS, The	
			R&B doo-wop group from Odessa, Texas: Virgil Johnson, Will Soloman, Mark Prince, Clarence Rigby and Bob Thursby. Rigby died in a car crash in 1978.	
6/26/61	26	4	1. Tonight (Could Be The Night)	Monument 441
			VENGABOYS	
			Dance group assembled by Spanish producers Danski and DJ Delmundo: Kim, Robin, Deniece and Roy. Pronounced: bengaboys.	
3/27/99	26	9	1. We Like To Party! Sales #17 / Airplay #47	Groovilicious 071
			VENTURES, The	
			Instrumental group from Seattle, Washington: guitarists Nokie Edwards, Bob Bogle and Don Wilson, with drummer Howie Johnson. Mel Taylor replaced Johnson in 1961. Johnson died in January 1988 (age 50). Taylor died on 8/11/96 (age 62).	
7/25/60	2 (1)	14	1. **Walk — Don't Run** [I] also see #4 below	Dolton 25
11/14/60	15	10	2. Perfidia [I] #3 hit for Xavier Cugat in 1941	Dolton 28
2/13/61	29	5	3. Ram-Bunk-Shush [I] #10 R&B hit for Bill Doggett in 1957	Dolton 32
8/1/64	8	7	4. **Walk-Don't Run '64** [I-R] new version of #1 above	Dolton 96
11/21/64	35	3	5. Slaughter On Tenth Avenue [I] #19 hit for Lennie Hayton in 1949	Dolton 300
4/12/69	4	9	6. **Hawaii Five-O** [I] theme from the TV series starring Jack Lord	Liberty 56068
			VENUS, Vik	
			Born Jack Spector on 9/15/28 in Brooklyn, New York. Died of a heart attack on 3/8/94 (age 65). Popular New York radio personality.	
7/26/69	38	3	1. Moonflight [N] **VIK VENUS Alias: Your Main Moon Man** a Dickie Goodman-type recording of "bubblegum" hits	Buddah 118
			VERA, Billy	
			Born William McCord on 5/28/44 in Riverside, California; raised in Westchester County, New York. Pop singer/songwriter. Acted in the movies *Buckaroo Banzai* and *The Doors*.	
3/23/68	36	1	1. Country Girl - City Man **BILLY VERA & JUDY CLAY**	Atlantic 2480

DATE	POS	WKS	ARTIST–RECORD TITLE	LABEL & NO.
6/6/81	39	2	2. I Can Take Care Of Myself [L] **BILLY & THE BEATERS**	Alfa 7002
12/6/86+	1 (2)	15	● 3. **At This Moment** Sales #1 (2) / Airplay #1 (1) [L-R] **BILLY VERA & THE BEATERS** #1 Adult Contemporary hit (1 week); re-charted due to play on the TV series *Family Ties* starring Michael J. Fox	Rhino 74403
			VERNE, Larry	
			Born Larry Vern Erickson on 2/8/36 in Minneapolis, Minnesota. Novelty singer.	
9/5/60	1 (1)	10	1. **Mr. Custer** [N]	Era 3024
			VERTICAL HORIZON	
			Rock group from Boston, Massachusetts: Matt Scannell (vocals), Keith Kane (guitar), Sean Hurley (bass) and Ed Toth (drums).	
2/19/00	1 (1)	34	1. **Everything You Want** Sales #2 / Airplay #2	RCA 65981
9/23/00	23	13	2. You're A God Airplay #17 from the album *Everything You Want* on RCA 67818	album cut
			VERVE, The	
			Rock group from Wigan, England: Richard Ashcroft (vocals), Nick McCabe (guitar), Simon Jones (bass) and Peter Salisbury (drums).	
3/28/98	12	8	1. Bitter Sweet Symphony Airplay #15 / Sales #17 popularized in a Nike commercial; samples "The Last Time" by The Andrew Loog Oldham Orchestra	Hut/Virgin 38634
			VERVE PIPE, The	
			Rock group from East Lansing, Michigan: brothers Brian (vocals) and Brad (bass) Vander Ark, A.J. Dunning (guitar), Doug Corella (keyboards) and Donny Brown (drums).	
4/19/97	5	29	● 1. **The Freshmen** Sales #8 / Airplay #8 #1 Modern Rock hit (3 weeks)	RCA 64734
			VIBRATIONS, The	
			R&B vocal group from Los Angeles, California: James Johnson, Carlton Fisher, Richard Owens, Dave Govan and Don Bradley. Also recorded as The Jayhawks and The Marathons.	
7/28/56	18	2	1. Stranded In The Jungle Best Seller #18 / Top 100 #29 [N] **THE JAYHAWKS**	Flash 109
3/13/61	25	4	2. The Watusi	Checker 969
5/22/61	20	7	3. Peanut Butter **THE MARATHONS**	Arvee 5027
4/25/64	26	5	4. My Girl Sloopy	Atlantic 2221
			VILLAGE PEOPLE	
			Disco vocal group from New York: Victor Willis (policeman), Randy Jones (cowboy), David Hodo (construction worker), Felipe Rose (indian), Glenn Hughes (leather man) and Alexander Briley (army man). Group appeared in the movie *Can't Stop The Music*. Hughes died of cancer on 3/4/2001 (age 50).	
7/29/78	25	6	● 1. Macho Man	Casablanca 922
11/11/78+	2 (3)	20	▲ 2. **Y.M.C.A.**	Casablanca 945
3/31/79	3	13	● 3. **In The Navy**	Casablanca 973

DATE	POS	WKS	ARTIST–RECORD TITLE	LABEL & NO.
			VILLAGE STOMPERS, The	
			Dixieland-styled band from Greenwich Village, New York: Dick Brady, Ralph Casale, Don Coates, Frank Hubbell, Mitchell May, Joe Muranyi, Al McManus and Lenny Pogan.	
10/5/63	**2** (1)	12	1. **Washington Square** [I] #1 Adult Contemporary hit (3 weeks)	Epic 9617
			VINCENT, Gene, and His Blue Caps	
			Born Vincent Eugene Craddock on 2/11/35 in Norfolk, Virginia. Died of a bleeding ulcer on 10/12/71 (age 36). Rock singer/songwriter/guitarist. Formed the Blue Caps in Norfolk in 1956. Appeared in the movies *The Girl Can't Help It* and *Hot Rod Gang*. Injured in car crash that killed Eddie Cochran in 1960. Inducted into the Rock and Roll Hall of Fame in 1998.	
6/23/56	7	15	1. **Be-Bop-A-Lula** Best Seller #7 / Top 100 #9 / Juke Box #10 / Jockey #11	Capitol 3450
9/16/57	13	12	2. Lotta Lovin' / Best Seller #13 / Top 100 #14 / Jockey #18	
9/23/57		7	3. Wear My Ring Best Seller: flip	Capitol 3763
1/13/58	23	1	4. Dance To The Bop Jockey #23 / Top 100 #43 / Best Seller #44	Capitol 3839
			VINTON, Bobby	
			Born Stanley Robert Vinton on 4/16/35 in Canonsburg, Pennsylvania. Pop singer. Nicknamed "The Polish Prince." Hosted own musical variety TV series from 1975-78.	
6/16/62	**1** (4)	13	● 1. **Roses Are Red (My Love)** #1 Adult Contemporary hit (4 weeks)	Epic 9509
9/15/62	12	7	2. Rain Rain Go Away	Epic 9532
9/22/62	38	2	3. I Love You The Way You Are	Diamond 121
1/5/63	33	3	4. Trouble Is My Middle Name /	
1/12/63	38	2	5. Let's Kiss And Make Up	Epic 9561
3/30/63	21	6	6. Over The Mountain (Across The Sea)	Epic 9577
6/1/63	3	10	7. **Blue On Blue**	Epic 9593
8/24/63	**1** (3)	12	8. **Blue Velvet** #1 Adult Contemporary hit (8 weeks); #16 hit for Tony Bennett in 1951	Epic 9614
12/7/63+	**1** (4)	12	9. **There! I've Said It Again** #1 Adult Contemporary hit (5 weeks); #1 hit for Vaughn Monroe in 1945	Epic 9638
3/7/64	9	8	10. **My Heart Belongs To Only You**	Epic 9662
5/30/64	13	6	11. Tell Me Why #2 hit for The Four Aces in 1952	Epic 9687
8/22/64	17	6	12. Clinging Vine	Epic 9705
11/7/64	**1** (1)	14	13. **Mr. Lonely**	Epic 9730
3/20/65	17	5	14. Long Lonely Nights	Epic 9768
5/22/65	22	6	15. L-O-N-E-L-Y	Epic 9791
10/16/65	38	1	16. What Color (Is A Man)	Epic 9846
12/25/65+	23	6	17. Satin Pillows	Epic 9869
5/28/66	40	1	18. Dum-De-Da song charted in 1964 by Johnny Tillotson as "She Understands Me"	Epic 10014
12/17/66+	11	8	19. Coming Home Soldier	Epic 10090
10/14/67	6	11	20. **Please Love Me Forever**	Epic 10228
1/27/68	24	4	21. Just As Much As Ever	Epic 10266
4/13/68	33	6	22. Take Good Care Of My Baby	Epic 10305

DATE	POS	WKS	ARTIST–RECORD TITLE	LABEL & NO.
8/3/68	23	5	23. Halfway To Paradise	Epic 10350
11/16/68	9	12	● 24. **I Love How You Love Me**	Epic 10397
5/3/69	34	2	25. To Know You Is To Love You	Epic 10461
7/12/69	34	2	26. The Days Of Sand And Shovels	Epic 10485
3/18/72	24	8	27. Every Day Of My Life	Epic 10822
7/8/72	19	10	28. Sealed With A Kiss	Epic 10861
10/12/74	3	11	● 29. **My Melody Of Love**	ABC 12022
			#1 Adult Contemporary hit (1 week)	
4/19/75	33	2	30. Beer Barrel Polka /	
			#1 hit for Will Glahe in 1939	
4/19/75		2	31. Dick And Jane	ABC 12056

VIRTUES, The

Rock and roll instrumental band from Philadelphia, Pennsylvania: Frank "Virtue" Virtuoso (bass), Jimmy Bruno (guitar), John Renner (sax) and Joe Vespe (drums).

DATE	POS	WKS	ARTIST–RECORD TITLE	LABEL & NO.
3/23/59	5	12	1. **Guitar Boogie Shuffle** [I]	Hunt 324

VISAGE, Michelle — see S.O.U.L. S.Y.S.T.E.M.

VISCOUNTS, The

Rock and roll instrumental group from New Jersey: Harry Haller (tenor sax), brothers Bobby (guitar) and Joe (bass) Spievak, Larry Vecchio (organ) and Clark Smith (drums).

DATE	POS	WKS	ARTIST–RECORD TITLE	LABEL & NO.
1/1/66	39	1	1. Harlem Nocturne [I-R]	Amy 940
			originally charted at #52 in 1959	

VITAMIN C

Born Colleen Fitzpatrick on 7/20/72 in Old Bridge, New Jersey. Former lead singer of Eve's Plum. Portrayed "Amber Von Tussle" in the 1988 movie *Hairspray*. Named for her orange hair.

DATE	POS	WKS	ARTIST–RECORD TITLE	LABEL & NO.
8/21/99	18	5	● 1. Smile Sales #7	Elektra 64041
			VITAMIN C [featuring Lady Saw]	
5/20/00	38	4	2. Graduation (Friends Forever) Airplay #39	album cut
			from the album *Vitamin C* on Elektra 62406	

VIXEN

Female hard-rock group formed in Los Angeles, California: Janet Gardner (vocals, guitar), Jan Kuehnemund (guitar), Share Pedersen (bass) and Roxy Petrucci (drums).

DATE	POS	WKS	ARTIST–RECORD TITLE	LABEL & NO.
10/29/88	26	5	1. Edge Of A Broken Heart Sales #21 / Airplay #31	EMI-Manhattan 50141
			written, produced and arranged by Richard Marx	
2/25/89	22	6	2. Cryin' Sales #16 / Airplay #30	EMI-Manhattan 50167

VOGUES, The

Pop-Adult Contemporary vocal group formed in Turtle Creek, Pennsylvania: Bill Burkette, Hugh Geyer, Chuck Blasko and Don Miller.

DATE	POS	WKS	ARTIST–RECORD TITLE	LABEL & NO.
10/9/65	4	9	1. **You're The One**	Co & Ce 229
12/11/65+	4	12	2. **Five O'Clock World**	Co & Ce 232
			later used as the theme for TV's *The Drew Carey Show*	
3/19/66	21	6	3. Magic Town	Co & Ce 234
6/25/66	29	4	4. The Land Of Milk And Honey	Co & Ce 238

DATE	POS	WKS	ARTIST–RECORD TITLE	LABEL & NO.
7/13/68	7	11	● 5. **Turn Around, Look At Me**	Reprise 0686
9/21/68	7	8	● 6. **My Special Angel**	Reprise 0766
			#1 Adult Contemporary hit (2 weeks)	
12/7/68	27	4	7. Till	Reprise 0788
3/29/69	34	2	8. No, Not Much	Reprise 0803
			VOICES OF THEORY	
			Male Latino R&B vocal group from Philadelphia, Pennsylvania: James Cartagena, Mechi Cebollero, David Cordoba, Hector Ramos and Eric Serrano.	
5/23/98	10	22	● 1. **Say It** Sales #11 / Airplay #37	H.O.L.A. 341032
10/31/98	36	3	2. Wherever You Go Sales #18	H.O.L.A. 341075
			VOICES THAT CARE	
			All-star group to benefit Persian Gulf War troops and their families. Soloists in order: Ralph Tresvant, Randy Travis, Celine Dion, Peter Cetera, Bobby Brown, Brenda Russell, Luther Vandross, Garth Brooks, Kathy Mattea, Nelson, Michael Bolton, Little Richard, Pointer Sisters, Will Smith and Mark Knopfler.	
3/30/91	11	11	● 1. Voices That Care Sales #4 / Airplay #19	Giant 19350
			VOLUME'S, The	
			R&B doo-wop group from Detroit, Michigan: Ed Union, Elijah Davis, Larry Wright, Joe Truvillion and Ernest Newson.	
6/2/62	22	6	1. I Love You	Chex 1002
			VOUDOURIS, Roger	
			Born on 12/29/54 in Sacramento, California. Died on 8/3/2003 (age 48). Pop singer/songwriter/guitarist.	
4/28/79	21	10	1. Get Used To It	Warner 8762
			VOXPOPPERS, The	
			Pop-rock and roll group from Brooklyn, New York, featuring brothers Freddie, Sal and Harry Tamburo.	
5/5/58	18	1	1. Wishing For Your Love	Mercury 71282
			Jockey #18 / Best Seller #41 / Top 100 #44	

W

DATE	POS	WKS	ARTIST–RECORD TITLE	LABEL & NO.
			WADE, Adam	
			Born on 3/17/37 in Pittsburgh, Pennsylvania. Black ballad singer.	
3/27/61	7	10	1. **Take Good Care Of Her**	Coed 546
5/29/61	5	9	2. **The Writing On The Wall**	Coed 550
8/7/61	10	7	3. **As If I Didn't Know**	Coed 553
			WADSWORTH MANSION	
			Pop-rock group formed in Los Angeles, California: brothers Steve (vocals) and Mike (drums) Jablecki, Wayne Gagnon (guitar), and John Poole (bass).	
2/13/71	7	7	1. **Sweet Mary**	Sussex 209

DATE	POS	WKS	ARTIST–RECORD TITLE	LABEL & NO.
			WAGNER, Jack	
			Born on 10/3/59 in Washington, Missouri. Actor/singer. Portrayed "Frisco Jones" on the TV soap opera *General Hospital* (1983-87).	
11/24/84+	2 (2)	12	1. **All I Need** Sales #2 / Airplay #2	Qwest 29238
			#1 Adult Contemporary hit (2 weeks)	
			WAIKIKIS, The	
			Hawaiian music-styled instrumental group from Belgium.	
1/9/65	33	3	1. Hawaii Tattoo [I]	Kapp 30
			WAILERS, The	
			Teen rock and roll instrumental group from Tacoma, Washington: John Greek and Rich Dangel (guitars), Mark Marush (sax), Kent Morrill (piano) and Mike Burk (drums).	
6/1/59	36	2	1. Tall Cool One [I]	Golden Crest 518
5/30/64	38	1	2. Tall Cool One [I-R]	Golden Crest 518
			WAINWRIGHT, Loudon III	
			Born on 9/5/46 in Chapel Hill, North Carolina. Folk singer/songwriter/guitarist.	
2/24/73	16	9	1. Dead Skunk [N]	Columbia 45726
			WAITE, John	
			Born on 7/4/55 in Lancaster, Lancashire, England. Lead singer of The Babys and Bad English.	
7/21/84	1 (1)	16	1. **Missing You** Sales #8 / Airplay #17	EMI America 8212
			#1 Mainstream Rock hit (2 weeks)	
11/10/84	37	4	2. Tears	EMI America 8238
8/31/85	25	6	3. Every Step Of The Way Sales #21 / Airplay #24	EMI America 8282
			WAKELIN, Johnny, & The Kinshasa Band	
			Born in Brighton, Sussex, England. White reggae-styled singer/songwriter.	
8/16/75	21	6	1. Black Superman - "Muhammad Ali" [N]	Pye 71012
			WALKER, Chris	
			Born in Houston, Texas. Male R&B singer/jazz bassist.	
4/18/92	29	6	1. Take Time Airplay #28	Pendulum 64813
			Shazzy (female rapper)	
			WALKER, Clay	
			Born Ernest Clayton Walker on 8/19/69 in Beaumont, Texas. Country singer/songwriter/guitarist.	
12/26/98	39	1	1. You're Beginning To Get To Me Airplay #31	Giant 17158
6/10/00	40	1	2. The Chain Of Love Airplay #34	album cut
			from the album *Live, Laugh, Love* on Giant 24717	

DATE	POS	WKS	ARTIST–RECORD TITLE	LABEL & NO.
			WALKER, Jr., & The All Stars	
			Born Autry DeWalt Walker on 6/14/31 in Blythesville, Arkansas. Died of cancer on 11/23/95 (age 64). R&B singer/saxophonist. The All Stars: Willie Woods (guitar), Vic Thomas (keyboards) and James Graves (drums). Woods died on 5/27/97 (age 60).	
3/6/65	**4**	10	1. **Shotgun** #1 R&B hit (4 weeks)	Soul 35008
7/3/65	**36**	2	2. Do The Boomerang	Soul 35012
8/21/65	**29**	5	3. Shake And Fingerpop	Soul 35013
5/21/66	**20**	6	4. (I'm A) Road Runner	Soul 35015
9/3/66	**18**	5	5. How Sweet It Is (To Be Loved By You)	Soul 35024
3/11/67	**31**	4	6. Pucker Up Buttercup	Soul 35030
12/23/67+	**24**	6	7. Come See About Me	Soul 35041
9/14/68	**31**	6	8. Hip City - Pt. 2	Soul 35048
6/21/69	**4**	11	9. **What Does It Take (To Win Your Love)** #1 R&B hit (2 weeks)	Soul 35062
11/22/69	**16**	9	10. These Eyes	Soul 35067
2/28/70	**21**	9	11. Gotta Hold On To This Feeling	Soul 35070
8/1/70	**32**	4	12. Do You See My Love (For You Growing)	Soul 35073
			WALKER BROS., The	
			"Blue-eyed soul" trio from Los Angeles, California: Scott Engel, Gary Leeds and John Maus.	
11/13/65	**16**	6	1. Make It Easy On Yourself	Smash 2009
4/30/66	**13**	7	2. The Sun Ain't Gonna Shine (Anymore)	Smash 2032
			WALLACE, Jerry	
			Born on 12/15/28 in Guilford, Missouri; raised in Glendale, Arizona. Pop-country singer/guitarist.	
9/15/58	**11**	9	1. How The Time Flies Hot 100 #11 / Best Seller #33	Challenge 59013
9/7/59	**8**	15	● 2. **Primrose Lane** **JERRY WALLACE With the Jewels**	Challenge 59047
2/1/60	**36**	2	3. Little Coco Palm	Challenge 59060
1/9/61	**26**	4	4. There She Goes #3 Country hit for Carl Smith in 1955	Challenge 59098
12/22/62+	**24**	7	5. Shutters And Boards	Challenge 9171
8/22/64	**19**	7	6. In The Misty Moonlight	Challenge 59246
9/30/72	**38**	2	7. If You Leave Me Tonight I'll Cry #1 Country hit (2 weeks); from TV's *Rod Serling's Night Gallery: The Tune In Dan's Cafe*	Decca 32989
			WALLFLOWERS, The	
			Rock group formed in Los Angeles, California: Jakob Dylan (vocals), Michael Ward (guitar), Rami Jaffe (keyboards), Greg Richling (bass) and Mario Calire (drums). Dylan is the son of Bob Dylan.	
10/5/96	**33** A	7	1. 6th Avenue Heartache	album cut
2/8/97	**2** (5)A	59	2. **One Headlight** #1 Mainstream Rock hit (5 weeks) / #1 Modern Rock hit (5 weeks)	album cut
7/19/97	**23** A	13	3. The Difference above 3 from the album *Bringing Down The Horse* on Interscope 90055	album cut

DATE	POS	WKS	ARTIST–RECORD TITLE	LABEL & NO.
5/16/98	27 A	7	4. Heroes *written and first recorded by David Bowie in 1977; from the movie* Godzilla *starring Matthew Broderick (soundtrack on Epic 69338)*	album cut
			WALSH, Joe	
			Born on 11/20/47 in Wichita, Kansas. Rock singer/songwriter/guitarist. Member of The James Gang and the Eagles.	
9/22/73	23	7	1. Rocky Mountain Way	Dunhill/ABC 4361
7/1/78	12	9	2. Life's Been Good	Asylum 45493
6/14/80	19	8	3. All Night Long *from the movie* Urban Cowboy *starring John Travolta*	Full Moon 46639
6/27/81	34	4	4. A Life Of Illusion *#1 Mainstream Rock hit (1 week)*	Asylum 47144
			WALTERS, Jamie — see HEIGHTS, The	
			WAMMACK, Travis	
			Born in 1946 in Walnut, Mississippi; raised in Memphis, Tennessee. Prolific session guitarist.	
8/9/75	38	2	1. (Shu-Doo-Pa-Poo-Poop) Love Being Your Fool	Capricorn 0239
			WANDERLEY, Walter	
			Born on 5/12/32 in Recife, Brazil. Died of cancer on 9/4/86 (age 54). Samba organist.	
10/1/66	26	4	1. Summer Samba (So Nice) **[I]**	Verve 10421
			WANG CHUNG	
			Pop-rock trio from London, England: Jack Hues (vocals, guitar, keyboards), Nick Feldman (bass, keyboards) and Darren Costin (drums). Costin left in 1985.	
3/10/84	38	3	1. Don't Let Go	Geffen 29377
5/26/84	16	10	2. Dance Hall Days	Geffen 29310
10/25/86	2 (2)	15	3. **Everybody Have Fun Tonight** Sales #2 / Airplay #2	Geffen 28562
2/14/87	9	11	4. **Let's Go!** Airplay #6 / Sales #10	Geffen 28531
7/25/87	36	2	5. Hypnotize Me Airplay #33 *from the movie* Innerspace *starring Dennis Quaid and Martin Short*	Geffen 28359
			WAR	
			Latin funk-rock band from Long Beach, California: Howard Scott (guitar), Lee Oskar (harmonica), Lonnie Jordan (keyboards), Charles Miller (sax), Thomas Allen (percussion), Morris Dickerson (bass) and Harold Brown (drums). All share vocals. Eric Burdon's backup band until 1971. Miller was shot to death June 1980 (age 41). Allen died of an aneurysm on 8/30/88 (age 57).	
7/11/70	3	13	● 1. **Spill The Wine** **ERIC BURDON AND WAR**	MGM 14118
9/25/71	35	2	2. All Day Music	United Artists 50815
4/1/72	16	10	● 3. Slippin' Into Darkness	United Artists 50867
12/30/72+	7	9	● 4. **The World Is A Ghetto**	United Artists 50975
3/24/73	2 (2)	12	● 5. **The Cisco Kid**	United Artists 163
8/4/73	8	10	6. **Gypsy Man**	United Artists 281
12/8/73+	15	10	7. Me And Baby Brother	United Artists 350
7/13/74	33	2	8. Ballero **[I-L]**	United Artists 432

DATE	POS	WKS	ARTIST–RECORD TITLE	LABEL & NO.
6/14/75	6	13	● 9. **Why Can't We Be Friends?**	United Artists 629
10/11/75	7	11	10. **Low Rider**	United Artists 706
			#1 R&B hit (1 week)	
7/31/76	7	12	● 11. **Summer**	United Artists 834
			#1 Adult Contemporary hit (1 week)	
2/11/78	39	2	12. Galaxy	MCA 40820
			WARD, Anita	
			Born on 12/20/56 in Memphis, Tennessee. Disco singer.	
5/26/79	1 (2)	15	1. **Ring My Bell**	Juana 3422
			#1 R&B hit (5 weeks)	
			WARD, Billy, And His Dominoes	
			Born on 9/19/21 in Los Angeles, California. Died on 2/16/2002 (age 80). R&B pianist. His vocal group: Charlie White (tenor), Joe Lamont (baritone) and Bill Brown (bass). Signed by King/Federal in 1950. Lead singers, at various times: Clyde McPhatter (1950-53), Jackie Wilson (1953-57) and Eugene Mumford.	
9/15/56	13	6	1. St. Therese Of The Roses Jockey #13 / Best Seller #20 / Top 100 #27	Decca 29933
			Jack Pleis (orch.)	
7/15/57	12	17	● 2. Star Dust Jockey #12 / Top 100 #13 / Best Seller #14	Liberty 55071
			#1 hit for Isham Jones in 1931	
10/7/57	20	8	3. Deep Purple Best Seller #20 / Top 100 #22	Liberty 55099
			#1 hit for Larry Clinton in 1939; Vic Schoen (orch., above 2)	
			WARD, Dale	
			Male pop-country singer.	
2/1/64	25	5	1. Letter From Sherry	Dot 16520
			Robin Ward (female vocal; not related to Dale Ward)	
			WARD, Joe	
			Born in 1947 in Brooklyn, New York. Member of NBC-TV's *Juvenile Jury* from 1952-55.	
12/24/55	20	3	1. Nuttin For Xmas Juke Box #20 / Best Seller #22 / Top 100 #22 **[X-N]**	King 45-4854
			Dave Terry (orch.)	
			WARD, Robin	
			Born Jacqueline McDonnell in Hawaii. Female pop singer.	
11/16/63	14	7	1. Wonderful Summer	Dot 16530
			Perry Botkin, Jr. (orch.)	
			WARINER, Steve	
			Born Steve Noel Wariner on 12/25/54 in Noblesville, Indiana. Country singer/songwriter/bassist.	
5/22/99	30	5	1. Two Teardrops Airplay #21	album cut
			from the album *Two Teardrops* on Capitol 96139	

DATE	POS	WKS	ARTIST–RECORD TITLE	LABEL & NO.
			WARNES, Jennifer	
			Born on 3/3/47 in Seattle, Washington; raised in Orange County, California. Adult Contemporary singer/actress.	
2/26/77	6	14	1. **Right Time Of The Night**	Arista 0223
			#1 Adult Contemporary hit (1 week)	
9/22/79	19	8	2. I Know A Heartache When I See One	Arista 0430
10/2/82	1 (3)	15	▲ 3. **Up Where We Belong**	Island 99996
			JOE COCKER and JENNIFER WARNES	
			love theme from the movie *An Officer And A Gentleman* starring Richard Gere and Debra Winger	
10/10/87	1 (1)	15	● 4. **(I've Had) The Time Of My Life** Airplay #1 (2) / Sales #1 (1)	RCA 5224
			BILL MEDLEY AND JENNIFER WARNES	
			#1 Adult Contemporary hit (4 weeks); love theme from the movie *Dirty Dancing* starring Patrick Swayze and Jennifer Grey	
			WARRANT	
			Male hard-rock group from Los Angeles, California: Jani Lane (vocals), Erik Turner and Joey Allen (guitars), Jerry Dixon (bass) and Steven Sweet (drums).	
6/10/89	27	6	1. Down Boys Airplay #26 / Sales #28	Columbia 68606
8/5/89	2 (2)	14	● 2. **Heaven** Sales #1 (1) / Airplay #2	Columbia 68985
2/3/90	20	9	3. Sometimes She Cries Airplay #15 / Sales #23	Columbia 73095
9/29/90	10	9	4. **Cherry Pie** Sales #6 / Airplay #18	Columbia 73510
1/5/91	10	11	5. **I Saw Red** Airplay #11 / Sales #12	Columbia 73597
			WARREN G	
			Born Warren Griffin on 11/10/71 in Long Beach, California. Male rapper.	
5/7/94	2 (3)	18	▲ 1. **Regulate** Sales #1 (2) / Airplay #15	Death Row 98280
			WARREN G. & NATE DOGG	
			samples "I Keep Forgettin'" by Michael McDonald; from the movie *Above The Rim* starring 2 Pac and Duane Martin	
7/30/94	9	14	● 2. **This DJ** Sales #5 / Airplay #20	Violator/RAL 853236
9/28/96	32	4	3. What's Love Got To Do With It Sales #15	Interscope 97008
			WARREN G featuring Adina Howard	
			from the movie *Supercop* starring Jackie Chan	
3/22/97	20	10	● 4. I Shot The Sheriff Sales #9	Def Jam 573564
			samples "Love's Gonna Get Cha" by Boogie Down Productions; written by Bob Marley	
6/28/97	35	5	5. Smokin' Me Out Sales #21	Def Jam 571024
			WARREN G Featuring Ronald Isley	
			contains an interpolation of "Coolin' Me Out" by The Isley Brothers	
7/18/98	18	9	6. Nobody Does It Better Sales #10	Breakaway 4000
			NATE DOGG featuring WARREN G	
			samples "Let's Get Closer" by Atlantic Starr	
10/2/99	23	9	● 7. I Want It All Sales #7	G-Funk 73721
			WARREN G Featuring Mack 10	
			samples "I Like It" by DeBarge	
			WARWICK, Dionne	
			Born Marie Dionne Warwick on 12/12/40 in East Orange, New Jersey. Black Adult Contemporary singer. Niece of Cissy Houston (of Sweet Inspirations) and cousin of Whitney Houston. Added an "e" to her last name for a time in the 1970s. Co-hosted TV's *Solid Gold* from 1980-81 and 1985-86.	
1/5/63	21	7	1. Don't Make Me Over	Scepter 1239
1/4/64	8	9	2. **Anyone Who Had A Heart**	Scepter 1262

DATE	POS	WKS	ARTIST–RECORD TITLE	LABEL & NO.
5/9/64	6	11	3. **Walk On By**	Scepter 1274
9/19/64	34	3	4. You'll Never Get To Heaven (If You Break My Heart)	Scepter 1282
11/7/64	20	6	5. Reach Out For Me	Scepter 1285
1/22/66	39	1	6. Are You There (With Another Girl)	Scepter 12122
4/23/66	8	8	7. **Message To Michael**	Scepter 12133
7/16/66	22	5	8. Trains And Boats And Planes	Scepter 12153
10/22/66	26	5	9. I Just Don't Know What To Do With Myself	Scepter 12167
5/27/67	15	9	10. Alfie title song from the movie starring Michael Caine	Scepter 12187
8/26/67	32	3	11. The Windows Of The World	Scepter 12196
2/3/68	2 (4)	11	● 12. **(Theme From) Valley Of The Dolls** / from the movie *Valley Of The Dolls* starring Sharon Tate and Patty Duke	
11/4/67	4	10	13. **I Say A Little Prayer**	Scepter 12203
4/27/68	10	9	14. **Do You Know The Way To San José**	Scepter 12216
9/21/68	33	4	15. Who Is Gonna Love Me?	Scepter 12226
11/23/68	19	6	16. Promises, Promises from the Broadway musical starring Jerry Orbach	Scepter 12231
2/8/69	7	11	17. **This Girl's In Love With You**	Scepter 12241
6/7/69	37	3	18. The April Fools title song from the movie starring Jack Lemmon	Scepter 12249
10/11/69	16	7	19. You've Lost That Lovin' Feeling	Scepter 12262
1/3/70	6	10	20. **I'll Never Fall In Love Again** #1 Adult Contemporary hit (3 weeks); from the Broadway musical *Promises, Promises* starring Jerry Orbach	Scepter 12273
5/9/70	32	3	21. Let Me Go To Him	Scepter 12276
10/31/70	37	2	22. Make It Easy On Yourself [L]	Scepter 12294
8/3/74	1 (1)	15	● 23. **Then Came You** **DIONNE WARWICKE AND SPINNERS**	Atlantic 3202
7/28/79	5	17	● 24. **I'll Never Love This Way Again**	Arista 0419
12/15/79+	15	11	25. Deja Vu #1 Adult Contemporary hit (1 week); above 2 produced by Barry Manilow (backing vocals by Manilow and Ron Dante)	Arista 0459
9/6/80	23	6	26. No Night So Long #1 Adult Contemporary hit (3 weeks)	Arista 0527
5/29/82	38	3	27. Friends In Love **DIONNE WARWICK AND JOHNNY MATHIS**	Arista 0673
11/6/82+	10	13	28. **Heartbreaker** #1 Adult Contemporary hit (1 week); Barry Gibb (backing vocal)	Arista 1015
10/29/83	27	5	29. How Many Times Can We Say Goodbye **DIONNE WARWICK AND LUTHER VANDROSS**	Arista 9073
11/23/85+	1 (4)	17	● 30. **That's What Friends Are For** Sales #1 (5) / Airplay #1 (3) **DIONNE & FRIENDS: Elton John, Gladys Knight and** **Stevie Wonder** #1 R&B hit (3 weeks) / #1 Adult Contemporary hit (2 weeks); first recorded by Rod Stewart in 1982	Arista 9422
7/25/87	12	9	31. Love Power Sales #7 / Airplay #14 **DIONNE WARWICK & JEFFREY OSBORNE** #1 Adult Contemporary hit (1 week)	Arista 9567

DATE	POS	WKS	ARTIST–RECORD TITLE	LABEL & NO.
			WASHINGTON, Baby	
			Born Justine Washington on 11/13/40 in Bamberg, South Carolina; raised in Harlem, New York. R&B singer/pianist.	
6/1/63	40	1	1. That's How Heartaches Are Made	Sue 783
			WASHINGTON, Dinah	
			Born Ruth Lee Jones on 8/29/24 in Tuscaloosa, Alabama. Died of an alcohol/pill overdose on 12/14/63 (age 39). R&B singer. Inducted into the Rock and Roll Hall of Fame in 1993 as an early influence.	
6/22/59	8	14	1. **What A Diff'rence A Day Makes** #5 hit for the Dorsey Brothers in 1934	Mercury 71435
10/26/59	17	8	2. Unforgettable #12 hit for Nat King Cole in 1952	Mercury 71508
2/8/60	5	12	● 3. **Baby (You've Got What It Takes)** **DINAH WASHINGTON & BROOK BENTON** #1 R&B hit (10 weeks)	Mercury 71565
6/6/60	7	10	4. **A Rockin' Good Way (To Mess Around And Fall In Love)** **DINAH WASHINGTON & BROOK BENTON** #1 R&B hit (4 weeks); first recorded by The Spaniels in 1958	Mercury 71629
7/18/60	24	6	5. This Bitter Earth #1 R&B hit (1 week)	Mercury 71635
11/7/60	30	2	6. Love Walked In #1 hit for Sammy Kaye's Orchestra in 1938	Mercury 71696
11/6/61	23	6	7. September In The Rain #1 hit for Guy Lombardo in 1937	Mercury 71876
6/23/62	36	3	8. Where Are You #5 hit for Mildred Bailey in 1937	Roulette 4424
			WASHINGTON, Grover Jr.	
			Born on 12/12/43 in Buffalo, New York. Died on 12/17/99 (age 56). Jazz-R&B saxophonist.	
3/7/81	2 (3)	16	1. **Just The Two Of Us** **GROVER WASHINGTON, JR. (with Bill Withers)**	Elektra 47103
			WASHINGTON, Keith	
			Born in Detroit, Michigan. R&B singer/songwriter.	
7/13/91	40	1	1. Kissing You Sales #41 / Airplay #75 #1 R&B hit (1 week)	Qwest 19414
			WAS (NOT WAS)	
			Interracial pop-dance-R&B group from Detroit, Michigan. Fronted by composer/bassist Don Fagenson ("Don Was") and lyricist/flutist David Weiss ("David Was"). Includes vocalists Sweet Pea Atkinson and Sir Harry Bowens. Group appeared in the movie *The Freshman*.	
11/5/88	16	10	1. Spy In The House Of Love Sales #9 / Airplay #26	Chrysalis 43266
2/18/89	7	9	2. **Walk The Dinosaur** Sales #5 / Airplay #10	Chrysalis 43331
			WATERFRONT	
			Male pop-rock duo from Cardiff, Wales: Chris Duffy (vocals) and Phil Cillia (guitar).	
5/6/89	10	10	1. **Cry** Sales #8 / Airplay #10	Polydor 871110

DATE	POS	WKS	ARTIST–RECORD TITLE	LABEL & NO.
			WATERS, Crystal	
			Born in 1964 in Philadelphia, Pennsylvania. Black dance singer/songwriter.	
6/1/91	8	9	● 1. **Gypsy Woman (She's Homeless)** Sales #8 / Airplay #16	Mercury 868208
7/9/94	11	34	● 2. **100% Pure Love** Airplay #9 / Sales #13	Mercury 858485
4/5/97	40	1	3. **Say...If You Feel Alright** Sales #42 / Airplay #52	Mercury 578943
			samples "September" by Earth, Wind & Fire	
			WATLEY, Jody	
			Born on 1/30/59 in Chicago, Illinois. Female R&B singer. Member of Shalamar (1977-84). Won the 1987 Best New Artist Grammy Award.	
3/21/87	2 (4)	14	1. **Looking For A New Love** Sales #1 (3) / Airplay #2	MCA 52956
			#1 R&B hit (3 weeks)	
10/24/87	6	14	2. **Don't You Want Me** Sales #5 / Airplay #6	MCA 53162
2/27/88	10	10	3. **Some Kind Of Lover** Airplay #9 / Sales #10	MCA 53235
4/1/89	2 (2)	12	● 4. **Real Love** Sales #1 (2) / Airplay #3	MCA 53484
			#1 R&B hit (1 week)	
7/8/89	9	11	5. **Friends** Sales #5 / Airplay #14	MCA 53660
			JODY WATLEY (With Eric B. & Rakim)	
11/18/89+	4	14	6. **Everything** Airplay #5 / Sales #7	MCA 53714
3/21/92	19	11	7. **I'm The One You Need** Airplay #14	MCA 54276
10/26/96	6	14	▲ 8. **This Is For The Lover In You** Sales #3 / Airplay #37	Epic 78443
			BABYFACE Featuring LL Cool J, Howard Hewett, Jody Watley and Jeffrey Daniels	
			#17 R&B hit for Shalamar in 1981	
			WATTS 103rd STREET RHYTHM BAND — **see WRIGHT, Charles**	
			WA WA NEE	
			Pop group from Australia: brothers Paul (vocals, keyboards) and Mark (bass) Gray, with Steve Williams (guitar) and Chris Sweeney (drums).	
10/31/87	35	3	1. **Sugar Free** Airplay #31 / Sales #34	Epic 07283
			WAYLON & WILLIE — see JENNINGS, Waylon / NELSON, Willie	
			WAYNE, Jimmy	
			Born on 10/23/72 in Bessemer City, North Carolina; raised in Gastonia, North Carolina. Country singer/songwriter.	
6/14/03	32	6	1. **Stay Gone** Sales #12 / Airplay #33	DreamWorks 000345
			WAYNE, Thomas	
			Born Thomas Wayne Perkins on 7/22/40 in Battsville, Mississippi. Died in a car accident on 8/15/71 (age 31). Brother of guitarist Luther Perkins of Johnny Cash's band.	
2/16/59	5	13	1. **Tragedy** **THOMAS WAYNE With The DeLons**	Fernwood 109
			WEATHERLY, Jim	
			Born on 3/17/43 in Pontotoc, Mississippi. Pop-country singer/songwriter.	
10/12/74	11	8	1. **The Need To Be**	Buddah 420

DATE	POS	WKS	ARTIST–RECORD TITLE	LABEL & NO.
			WEBER, Joan	
			Born on 12/12/35 in Paulsboro, New Jersey. Died on 5/13/81 (age 45). Pop singer.	
12/4/54+	**1** (4)	16	● 1. **Let Me Go Lover**	Columbia 40366
			Jockey #1 (4) / Juke Box #1 (4) / Best Seller #1 (2) Jimmy Carroll (orch.); written in 1953 as "Let Me Go Devil" and first recorded by Georgie Shaw; Weber's version was an overnight sensation after being featured 6 times on the 11/15/54 *Studio One* CBS-TV production	
			WEDNESDAY	
			Pop group from Oshawa, Ontario, Canada: Mike O'Neil (vocals), Paul Andrew-Smith, John Dufek and Randy Begg.	
2/16/74	34	4	1. Last Kiss	Sussex 507
			WEEZER	
			Rock group from Los Angeles, California: Rivers Cuomo (vocals, guitar), Brian Bell (guitar), Matt Sharp (bass) and Patrick Wilson (drums).	
12/17/94+	18 ᴬ	13	1. Buddy Holly	album cut
			from the album *Weezer* on DGC 24629	
			WE FIVE	
			Pop group from San Francisco, California: Beverly Bivens (vocals), Bob Jones and Jerry Burgan (guitars), Pete Fullerton (bass), and Mike Stewart (drums). Stewart (brother of John Stewart) died on 11/13/2002 (age 57).	
8/7/65	3	13	1. **You Were On My Mind**	A&M 770
			#1 Adult Contemporary hit (5 weeks)	
12/25/65	31	2	2. Let's Get Together	A&M 784
			WEISBERG, Tim — see FOGELBERG, Dan	
			WEISSBERG, Eric, & Steve Mandell	
			Prominent session musicians. Weissberg was a member of The Tarriers.	
2/3/73	**2** (4)	11	● 1. **Dueling Banjos** [I]	Warner 7659
			#1 Adult Contemporary hit (2 weeks); from the movie *Deliverance* starring Burt Reynolds	
			WELCH, Bob	
			Born on 7/31/46 in Los Angeles, California. Pop-rock singer/guitarist. Member of Fleetwood Mac (1971-74).	
11/19/77+	8	11	1. **Sentimental Lady**	Capitol 4479
			Christine McVie and Lindsey Buckingham (backing vocals)	
2/25/78	14	10	2. Ebony Eyes	Capitol 4543
7/1/78	31	3	3. Hot Love, Cold World	Capitol 4588
3/17/79	19	8	4. Precious Love	Capitol 4685
			WELCH, Lenny	
			Born on 5/15/38 in Asbury Park, New Jersey. Black Adult Contemporary singer.	
11/23/63	4	12	1. **Since I Fell For You**	Cadence 1439
			#3 R&B hit for Annie Laurie & Paul Gayten in 1947	

DATE	POS	WKS	ARTIST–RECORD TITLE	LABEL & NO.
4/11/64	**25**	5	2. Ebb Tide	Cadence 1422
			featured in the movie *Sweet Bird Of Youth* starring Paul Newman; #2 hit for Frank Chacksfield's Orchestra in 1953	
2/14/70	**34**	4	3. Breaking Up Is Hard To Do	Common. United 3004
			Charlie Calello (orch.)	

WELK, Lawrence

Born on 3/11/03 in Strasburg, North Dakota. Died of pneumonia on 5/17/92 (age 89). Accordion player/polka bandleader since the mid-1920s. Band's style labeled as "champagne music." Hosted own TV musical variety show from 1955-82.

DATE	POS	WKS	ARTIST–RECORD TITLE	LABEL & NO.
3/3/56	**17**	2	1. Moritat (A Theme From "The Threepenny Opera") Juke Box #17 / Top 100 #31 **[I]** **LAWRENCE WELK And His Sparkling Sextet**	Coral 61574
4/7/56	**17**	2	2. The Poor People Of Paris Juke Box #17 / Top 100 #45 **[I]**	Coral 61592
8/11/56	**32**	3	3. Weary Blues Top 100 #32 **THE McGUIRE SISTERS and LAWRENCE WELK And His Champagne Music** traditional tune first recorded in 1923 by The New Orleans Rhythm Kings	Coral 61670
9/29/56	**15**	10	4. Tonight You Belong To Me Top 100 #15 / Best Seller #16 / Jockey #16 / Juke Box #17 **LAWRENCE WELK And His Sparkling Strings (with The Lennon Sisters and The Sparklers)** #1 hit for Gene Austin in 1927	Coral 61701
12/5/60	**21**	3	5. Last Date **[I]**	Dot 16145
12/31/60+	**1 (2)**	13	● 6. Calcutta **[I]** written in Germany in 1958; above 2 feature Frank Scott (on piano and harpsichord, respectively)	Dot 16161

WELLS, Mary

Born on 5/13/43 in Detroit, Michigan. Died of cancer on 7/26/92 (age 49). R&B singer.

DATE	POS	WKS	ARTIST–RECORD TITLE	LABEL & NO.
8/21/61	**33**	3	1. I Don't Want To Take A Chance	Motown 1011
5/5/62	**8**	10	2. **The One Who Really Loves You**	Motown 1024
8/25/62	**9**	9	3. **You Beat Me To The Punch** #1 R&B hit (1 week)	Motown 1032
12/15/62+	**7**	10	4. **Two Lovers** #1 R&B hit (4 weeks)	Motown 1035
3/9/63	**15**	6	5. Laughing Boy	Motown 1039
7/6/63	**40**	1	6. Your Old Stand By	Motown 1042
10/12/63	**22**	7	7. You Lost The Sweetest Boy /	
1/25/64	**29**	6	8. What's Easy For Two Is So Hard For One	Motown 1048
4/11/64	**1 (2)**	13	9. **My Guy**	Motown 1056
6/13/64	**17**	6	10. What's The Matter With You Baby /	
5/23/64	**19**	6	11. Once Upon A Time **MARVIN GAYE & MARY WELLS** (above 2)	Motown 1057
1/30/65	**34**	2	12. Use Your Head	20th Century 555

WESLEY, Fred — see JB's

Frankie Valli rose to fame as part of The 4 Seasons, who scored four #1 hits during the 1960s. In 1978, he reached #1 for the second time as a solo artist, singing "Grease," the title song from the popular 1950s-themed movie starring John Travolta and Olivia Newton-John.

Billy Vera & The Beaters had more than one moment to enjoy their biggest hit, "At This Moment." The song first charted in 1981, and then went to #1 six years later after being featured on the TV series *Family Ties*.

Larry Verne was working in a photo studio when he was approached about singing his eventual #1 hit, "Mr. Custer." Sadly, the novelty song would be Verne's last stand on the Top 40—his follow-up, "Mister Livingston," stalled at #75.

Vertical Horizon wanted their first hit, "Everything You Want," to reach #1, but it took some time to achieve. The Boston group's hit spent nearly half a year on the Hot 100 before finally cracking the top spot.

Bobby Vinton earned his first #1 hit in 1962 with the song "Roses Are Red (My Love)." Another track from the same album, "Mr. Lonely," also topped the charts...over two years later!

Dionne Warwick called upon some notable friends, namely Elton John, Gladys Knight, and Stevie Wonder, to help record "That's What Friends Are For." As a friendly gesture, the chart-topping song's proceeds were donated to AIDS research.

Joan Weber was only a teenager when she topped the charts with "Let Me Go Lover," orchestrated by Jimmy Carroll. Sadly, she was abandoned by her fans, as she never had another Top 40 hit.

Mary Wells earned her first #1 hit with 1964's "My Guy," written by Smokey Robinson. Smokey also wrote The Temptations' first #1 hit, "My Girl," which peaked less than a year later.

Karyn White turned her romance with former Time member Terry Lewis into chart gold. White and Lewis's partner, Jimmy Jam, helped write and produce the singer's first #1 hit, "Romantic."

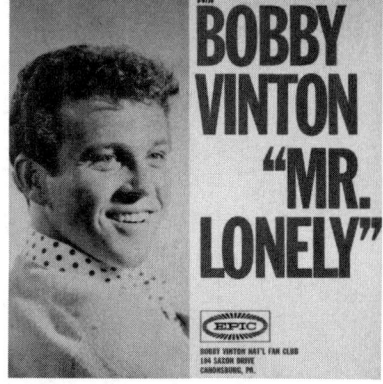

Whitesnake sang "Like a drifter I was born to walk alone" in their 1987 #1 hit, "Here I Go Again." That line definitely applied to lead singer David Coverdale, as no other original member of the band was still around at that time.

Wild Cherry may not have had a fruitful chart career, but they did have one bumper crop when "Play That Funky Music" went all the way to #1. Fifteen years later, rapper Vanilla Ice would use the song as the basis for his own Top 10 hit.

Vanessa Williams balanced her time between acting in movies like *Soul Food* and *Eraser*, creating pop music hits, and being a wife to NBA star Rick Fox. Rick might agree with the title of her #1 hit, "Save The Best For Last."

Wilson Phillips scored their third #1 hit in four tries with "You're In Love." Chynna Phillips of the trio was obviously in love when she married actor William Baldwin in 1995.

Steve Winwood rolled through bands like Blind Faith, the Spencer Davis Group, and Traffic before establishing a solo career in the 1980s. The biggest of his 10 Top 40 hits was the #1 smash "Roll With It."

Stevie Wonder earned two 1973 Grammy Awards for his #1 hit "Superstition": Best R&B Song and Best R&B Male Vocalist. Maybe it was magic, but between 1973 and 1976 three of his albums won the Grammy Award for Album of the Year.

Paul Young covered "Everytime You Go Away" from the Hall & Oates album *Voices* and scored a #1 hit. As a result, Daryl Hall received a 1985 Grammy Award nomination for Song of the Year.

DATE	POS	WKS	ARTIST–RECORD TITLE	LABEL & NO.
4/25/81	**14**	12	**WEST, Dottie** Born Dorothy Marsh on 10/11/32 in McMinnville, Tennessee. Died in a car crash on 9/4/91 (age 58). Country singer. 　1. What Are We Doin' In Love 　　**DOTTIE WEST (with Kenny Rogers)** 　　#1 Country hit (1 week)	Liberty 1404
12/20/03+	**1** (1)	19	**WEST, Kanye** Born in 1977 in Chicago, Illinois. Male rapper/songwriter/producer. 　1. **Slow Jamz**　　　　　　　Airplay #1 (2) / Sales #17 　　**TWISTA Featuring Kanye West & Jamie Foxx** 　　#1 R&B hit (1 week); samples "A House Is Not A Home" by Luther Vandross	Atlantic 88288
12/27/03+	**15**	15	2. Through The Wire　　　　　Airplay #13 / Sales #29 　　samples "Through The Fire" by Chaka Khan	Roc-A-Fella 001441
8/11/90	**35**	3	**WEST COAST RAP ALL-STARS, The** Rap benefit for inner city youth: Above The Law, Body & Soul, Def Jef, Digital Underground, Eazy-E, Ice-T, J.J. Fad, King Tee, M.C. Hammer, Michel'le, N.W.A., Oaktown's 3-5-7, Tone Loc and Young MC ●　1. We're All In The Same Gang　　　Sales #17 　　produced by Dr. Dre	Warner 19819
5/27/00	**20**	11	**WESTLIFE** "Boy band" from Dublin, Ireland: Nicky Byrne, Shane Filan, Kian Egan, Mark Feehily and Bryan McFadden. ●　1. Swear It Again　　　　　　Sales #2	Arista 13816
			WESTON, Kim — see GAYE, Marvin	
10/5/96	**21**	11	**WESTSIDE CONNECTION** All-star rap trio from Los Angeles, California: Ice Cube, Mack 10 and WC. 　1. Bow Down　　　　　　　　Sales #9	Lench Mob 53227
4/19/97	**40**	2	2. Gangstas Make The World Go Round　　Sales #28 　　samples "People Make The World Go Round" by The Stylistics	Lench Mob 53264
7/6/74	**10**	11	**WET WILLIE** Southern-rock group from Mobile, Alabama: brothers Jimmy Hall (vocals; see #4 below) and Jack Hall (bass), Rick Hirsch (guitar), John Anthony (keyboards) and Lewis Ross (drums). Michael Duke (keyboards, vocals) joined in late 1975. 　1. **Keep On Smilin'**	Capricorn 0043
1/28/78	**30**	4	2. Street Corner Serenade	Epic 50478
6/30/79	**29**	5	3. Weekend	Epic 50714
11/1/80	**27**	4	4. I'm Happy That Love Has Found You 　　**JIMMY HALL**	Epic 50931
			WHAM! — see MICHAEL, George	
10/22/88	**11**	13	**WHEN IN ROME** Electro-dance trio from England: Clive Farrington and Andrew Mann (vocals), with Michael Floreale (keyboards). 　1. The Promise　　　　　Sales #9 / Airplay #12	Virgin 99323

DATE	POS	WKS	ARTIST–RECORD TITLE	LABEL & NO.
			WHISPERS, The	
			R&B-dance vocal group from Los Angeles, California: twin brothers Walter and Wallace Scott, with Leaveil Degree, Marcus Hutson and Nicholas Caldwell.	
3/15/80	19	8	● 1. **And The Beat Goes On** #1 R&B hit (5 weeks)	Solar 11894
5/24/80	28	4	2. Lady	Solar 11928
3/28/81	28	5	3. It's A Love Thing	Solar 12154
7/11/87	7	12	4. **Rock Steady** Airplay #5 / Sales #8 #1 R&B hit (1 week)	Solar 70006
			WHISTLE	
			R&B vocal group from Brooklyn, New York: Kerry Hodge, Brian Faust, Rick Bennett and Tarek Stevens.	
5/19/90	35	4	1. Always And Forever Sales #31 / Airplay #34	Select 2014
			WHITCOMB, Ian	
			Born on 7/10/41 in Woking, Surrey, England. Pop singer/songwriter.	
6/19/65	8	8	1. **You Turn Me On (Turn On Song)** **IAN WHITCOMB And Bluesville**	Tower 134
			WHITE, Barry	
			Born on 9/12/44 in Galveston, Texas; raised in Los Angeles, California. Died of kidney failure on 7/4/2003 (age 58). Smooth soul singer/songwriter/keyboardist. Formed Love Unlimited, which included future wife Glodean James. Leader of 40-piece Love Unlimited Orchestra.	
5/5/73	3	12	● 1. **I'm Gonna Love You Just A Little More Baby** #1 R&B hit (2 weeks)	20th Century 2018
9/1/73	32	6	2. I've Got So Much To Give	20th Century 2042
11/17/73+	7	15	● 3. **Never, Never Gonna Give Ya Up**	20th Century 2058
8/10/74	1 (1)	9	● 4. **Can't Get Enough Of Your Love, Babe** #1 R&B hit (3 weeks)	20th Century 2120
11/16/74+	2 (2)	12	● 5. **You're The First, The Last, My Everything** #1 R&B hit (1 week)	20th Century 2133
3/22/75	8	7	6. **What Am I Gonna Do With You** #1 R&B hit (1 week)	20th Century 2177
6/21/75	40	2	7. I'll Do For You Anything You Want Me To	20th Century 2208
1/24/76	32	4	8. Let The Music Play	20th Century 2265
10/1/77	4	12	● 9. **It's Ecstasy When You Lay Down Next To Me** #1 R&B hit (5 weeks)	20th Century 2350
5/27/78	24	5	10. Oh What A Night For Dancing	20th Century 2365
4/7/90	31	4	● 11. The Secret Garden (Sweet Seduction Suite) Sales #20 **QUINCY JONES/Al B. Sure!/James Ingram/El DeBarge/Barry White** #1 R&B hit (1 week)	Qwest 19992
11/5/94	18	15	● 12. Practice What You Preach Sales #9 #1 R&B hit (3 weeks)	A&M 0778
			WHITE, Karyn	
			Born on 10/14/65 in Los Angeles, California. R&B-dance singer. Married to producer Terry Lewis (of The Time).	
2/7/87	27	5	1. Facts Of Love Airplay #27 / Sales #29 **JEFF LORBER Featuring Karyn White**	Warner 28588

DATE	POS	WKS	ARTIST–RECORD TITLE		LABEL & NO.
11/26/88+	7	14	● 2. **The Way You Love Me** #1 R&B hit (1 week)	Sales #6 / Airplay #7	Warner 27773
2/25/89	8	10	● 3. **Superwoman** #1 R&B hit (3 weeks)	Airplay #9 / Sales #10	Warner 27783
7/1/89	6	12	4. **Secret Rendezvous**	Sales #6 / Airplay #8	Warner 27863
8/24/91	1 (1)	19	5. **Romantic** #1 R&B hit (1 week)	Airplay #2 / Sales #26	Warner 19319
12/21/91+	12	13	6. The Way I Feel About You	Airplay #7 / Sales #68	Warner 19088
			WHITE, Tony Joe		
			Born on 7/23/43 in Goodwill, Louisiana. Bayou-rock singer/songwriter.		
7/26/69	8	8	1. **Polk Salad Annie** produced by Billy Swan		Monument 1104
			WHITE LION		
			Rock group formed in Brooklyn, New York: Mike Tramp (vocals), Vito Bratta (guitar), James Lomenzo (bass) and Greg D'Angelo (drums).		
4/9/88	8	11	1. **Wait**	Sales #7 / Airplay #7	Atlantic 89126
12/17/88+	3	12	2. **When The Children Cry**	Sales #3 / Airplay #3	Atlantic 89015
			WHITE PLAINS		
			Studio group from England. Featuring Tony Burrows (vocals), who was also with The Brotherhood Of Man, Edison Lighthouse, First Class and The Pipkins.		
5/23/70	13	10	1. My Baby Loves Lovin'		Deram 85058
			WHITESNAKE		
			Hard-rock group formed in England: David Coverdale (vocals), John Sykes (guitar), Neil Murray (bass) and Aynsley Dunbar (drums). Coverdale was a member of Deep Purple. Dunbar was a member of Jefferson Starship. Numerous personnel changes. 1989 lineup: Coverdale (vocals), Steve Vai and Adrian Vandenberg (guitars), Rudy Sarzo (bass) and Tommy Aldridge (drums). Sarzo was a member of Quiet Riot. Coverdale was married to actress Tawny Kitaen from 1989-92.		
8/8/87	1 (1)	14	1. **Here I Go Again**	Sales #1 (1) / Airplay #1 (1)	Geffen 28339
11/7/87	2 (1)	13	2. **Is This Love**	Sales #2 / Airplay #2	Geffen 28233
12/16/89	37	3	3. Fool For Your Loving new version of their #53 hit from 1980	Sales #36 / Airplay #39 **[R]**	Geffen 22715
2/17/90	28	6	4. The Deeper The Love	Airplay #25 / Sales #27	Geffen 19951
			WHITE TOWN		
			Born Jyoti Mishra on 7/30/66 in Rourkela, India; raised in England. Male synth-pop singer/multi-instrumentalist.		
4/5/97	23	15	1. Your Woman	Airplay #15 / Sales #36	Chrysalis/EMI 58638
			WHITFIELD, David		
			Born on 2/2/26 in Hull, Yorkshire, England. Classical-styled tenor.		
8/14/54	10	18	● 1. **Cara Mia** **DAVID WHITFIELD with MANTOVANI His Orchestra and Chorus**	Best Seller #10 / Jockey #17	London 1486
1/1/55 -	19	2	2. Santo Natale (Merry Christmas) Stanley Black (orch.)	Jockey #19 / Best Seller #27 **[X]**	London 45-1508

DATE	POS	WKS	ARTIST–RECORD TITLE	LABEL & NO.
			WHITING, Margaret	
			Born on 7/22/24 in Detroit, Michigan; raised in Hollywood, California. Pop singer.	
12/8/56	**20**	5	1. The Money Tree Jockey #20 / Top 100 #49 Billy May (orch.)	Capitol 3586
11/19/66	**26**	5	2. The Wheel Of Hurt #1 Adult Contemporary hit (4 weeks); Arnold Goland (orch.)	London 101
			WHITTAKER, Roger	
			Born on 3/22/36 in Nairobi, Kenya, Africa (of British parents). Adult Contemporary singer.	
5/10/75	**19**	9	1. The Last Farewell #1 Adult Contemporary hit (1 week); recorded in 1971	RCA Victor 50030
			WHO, The	
			Rock group formed in London, England: Roger Daltrey (vocals), Pete Townshend (guitar, vocals), John Entwistle (bass) and Keith Moon (drums). Group starred in the movies *Tommy*, *Quadrophenia* and *The Kids Are Alright*. Moon died of a drug overdose on 9/7/78 (age 31); replaced by Kenney Jones (formerly with Small Faces). Eleven fans trampled to death at group's concert in Cincinnati on 12/3/79. Entwistle died of a heart attack on 6/27/2002 (age 57). Group inducted into the Rock and Roll Hall of Fame in 1990. Won Grammy's Lifetime Achievement Award in 2001.	
5/20/67	**24**	4	1. Happy Jack	Decca 32114
10/28/67	**9**	9	2. **I Can See For Miles**	Decca 32206
5/4/68	**40**	2	3. Call Me Lightning	Decca 32288
8/31/68	**25**	6	4. Magic Bus	Decca 32362
5/3/69	**19**	5	5. Pinball Wizard	Decca 32465
8/23/69	**37**	2	6. I'm Free	Decca 32519
8/1/70	**27**	6	7. Summertime Blues [L]	Decca 32708
10/17/70	**12**	9	8. See Me, Feel Me #5, 6 & 8: from the group's 1969 rock opera album *Tommy*	Decca 32729
8/7/71	**15**	10	9. Won't Get Fooled Again written for the aborted movie project *Lifehouse*	Decca 32846
12/4/71	**34**	5	10. Behind Blue Eyes	Decca 32888
8/5/72	**17**	8	11. Join Together	Decca 32983
1/13/73	**39**	2	12. The Relay	Track 33041
1/3/76	**16**	10	13. Squeeze Box	MCA 40475
9/16/78	**14**	9	14. Who Are You song later used as the theme for TV's *CSI: Crime Scene Investigation*	MCA 40948
4/4/81	**18**	10	15. You Better You Bet #1 Mainstream Rock hit (5 weeks)	Warner 49698
10/9/82	**28**	6	16. Athena all of above (except #7) written by Pete Townshend	Warner 29905
			WIEDLIN, Jane	
			Born on 5/20/58 in Oconomowoc, Wisconsin; raised in California. Rhythm guitarist of the Go-Go's.	
6/11/88	**9**	10	1. **Rush Hour** Sales #8 / Airplay #13	EMI-Manhattan 50118

DATE	POS	WKS	ARTIST—RECORD TITLE	LABEL & NO.
			WILCOX, Harlow, and the Oakies	
			Born on 1/28/43 in Norman, Oklahoma. Session guitarist.	
11/22/69	30	6	1. Groovy Grubworm [I]	Plantation 28
			WILD CHERRY	
			White funk group from Steubenville, Ohio: Robert Parissi (vocals, guitar), Bryan Bassett (guitar), Mark Avsec (keyboards), Allen Wentz (bass) and Ron Beitle (drums).	
7/31/76	1 (3)	18	▲ 1. **Play That Funky Music** #1 R&B hit (2 weeks)	Epic 50225
			WILDE, Kim	
			Born Kim Smith on 11/18/60 in Chiswick, London, England. Pop-rock-dance singer. Daughter of singer Marty Wilde.	
7/17/82	25	8	1. Kids In America	EMI America 8110
4/18/87	1 (1)	13	2. **You Keep Me Hangin' On** Sales #1 (2) / Airplay #1 (1)	MCA 53024
			WILDER, Matthew	
			Born on 1/24/53 in Manhattan, New York. White singer/songwriter/keyboardist.	
11/26/83+	5	14	1. **Break My Stride**	Private I 04113
3/24/84	33	4	2. The Kid's American	Private I 04363
			WILLIAMS, Andy	
			Born Howard Andrew Williams on 12/3/28 in Wall Lake, Iowa. Pop singer. Hosted own TV variety show from 1962-71. Appeared in the movie *I'd Rather Be Rich*. Formerly married to singer/actress Claudine Longet.	
8/18/56	7	17	1. **Canadian Sunset** Jockey #7 / Top 100 #8 / Juke Box #9 / Best Seller #10	Cadence 1297
12/22/56	33	3	2. Baby Doll Top 100 #33 title song from the movie starring Carroll Baker	Cadence 1303
3/2/57	1 (3)	14	3. **Butterfly** Top 100 #1 (3) / Jockey #1 (2) / Juke Box #2 / Best Seller #4	Cadence 1308
6/3/57	8	14	4. **I Like Your Kind Of Love** Jockey #8 / Top 100 #9 / Best Seller #10 / Juke Box #19 Peggy Powers (female vocal)	Cadence 1323
10/14/57	17	3	5. Lips Of Wine Jockey #17 / Top 100 #39	Cadence 1336
2/24/58	3	14	6. **Are You Sincere** Jockey #3 / Top 100 #10 / Best Seller #11	Cadence 1340
9/22/58	17	6	7. Promise Me, Love Hot 100 #17	Cadence 1351
1/12/59	11	15	8. The Hawaiian Wedding Song (Ke Kali Nei Au)	Cadence 1358
9/28/59	5	11	9. **Lonely Street**	Cadence 1370
12/28/59+	7	9	10. **The Village Of St. Bernadette**	Cadence 1374
6/5/61	37	2	11. The Bilbao Song new Johnny Mercer lyrics added to song from the 1929 German musical *Happy End*; Archie Bleyer (orch., all of above)	Cadence 1398
7/14/62	38	1	12. Stranger On The Shore	Columbia 42451
11/3/62	39	1	13. Don't You Believe It	Columbia 42523
3/23/63	2 (4)	12	14. **Can't Get Used To Losing You** / #1 Adult Contemporary hit (4 weeks)	
4/13/63	26	7	15. Days Of Wine And Roses title song from the movie starring Jack Lemmon and Lee Remick	Columbia 42674

DATE	POS	WKS	ARTIST–RECORD TITLE	LABEL & NO.
7/6/63	**13**	8	16. Hopeless	Columbia 42784
1/25/64	**13**	8	17. A Fool Never Learns	Columbia 42950
5/16/64	**34**	4	18. Wrong For Each Other	Columbia 43015
10/3/64	**28**	5	19. On The Street Where You Live from the movie *My Fair Lady* starring Audrey Hepburn and Rex Harrison	Columbia 43128
12/19/64+	**24**	7	20. Dear Heart title song from the movie starring Glenn Ford and Angela Lansbury	Columbia 43180
4/24/65	**36**	3	21. ......And Roses And Roses	Columbia 43257
10/16/65	**40**	1	22. Ain't It True	Columbia 43358
4/22/67	**34**	3	23. Music To Watch Girls By tune used in a Diet Pepsi commercial	Columbia 44065
11/30/68	**33**	4	24. Battle Hymn Of The Republic **ANDY WILLIAMS with the St. Charles Borromeo Choir** recorded at St. Patrick's Cathedral on 6/8/68 as a eulogy to Senator Robert F. Kennedy	Columbia 44650
5/3/69	**22**	7	25. Happy Heart #1 Adult Contemporary hit (2 weeks)	Columbia 44818
2/27/71	**9**	10	26. **(Where Do I Begin) Love Story** #1 Adult Contemporary hit (4 weeks); theme song from the movie *Love Story* starring Ryan O'Neal and Ali McGraw	Columbia 45317
5/20/72	**34**	4	27. Love Theme From "The Godfather" (Speak Softly Love)	Columbia 45579
			WILLIAMS, Billy	
			Born on 12/28/10 in Waco, Texas. Died on 10/17/72 (age 61). Lead singer of The Charioteers from 1930-50.	
6/17/57	**3**	18	● 1. **I'm Gonna Sit Right Down And Write Myself A Letter /** Jockey #3 / Top 100 #6 / Best Seller #7 #5 hit for Fats Waller in 1935	
8/26/57		5	2. Date With The Blues Best Seller: flip	Coral 61830
2/16/59	**39**	3	3. Nola #3 hit for Vincent Lopez in 1922; Dick Jacobs (orch., above 3)	Coral 62069
			WILLIAMS, Danny	
			Born on 1/7/42 in Port Elizabeth, South Africa. Black ballad singer.	
4/4/64	**9**	10	1. **White On White** Don Costa (orch.)	United Artists 685
			WILLIAMS, Deniece	
			Born Deniece Chandler on 6/3/51 in Gary, Indiana. R&B singer/songwriter.	
3/5/77	**25**	7	1. Free	Columbia 10429
4/22/78	**1** (1)	11	● 2. **Too Much, Too Little, Too Late** **JOHNNY MATHIS/DENIECE WILLIAMS** #1 R&B hit (4 weeks) / #1 Adult Contemporary hit (1 week)	Columbia 10693
5/1/82	**10**	9	3. **It's Gonna Take A Miracle** #1 R&B hit (2 weeks)	ARC 02812
4/14/84	**1** (2)	14	▲ 4. **Let's Hear It For The Boy** #1 R&B hit (3 weeks); from the movie *Footloose* starring Kevin Bacon and Lori Singer	Columbia 04417

DATE	POS	WKS	ARTIST–RECORD TITLE	LABEL & NO.
			WILLIAMS, Don	
			Born on 5/27/39 in Floydada, Texas. Country singer/songwriter/guitarist. Member of the Pozo-Seco Singers.	
11/15/80	24	9	1. I Believe In You #1 Country hit (2 weeks)	MCA 41304
			WILLIAMS, Eric — see QUEEN PEN / 2PAC	
			WILLIAMS, John	
			Born on 2/8/32 in Flushing, Long Island, New York. Composer/conductor. Conducted the Boston Pops Orchestra from 1980-93. His son, Joseph, joined Toto in 1986.	
9/13/75	32	4	1. Main Title (Theme From "Jaws") **[I]**	MCA 40439
8/13/77	10	7	2. **Star Wars (Main Title)** **[I]** performed by The London Symphony Orchestra	20th Century 2345
1/21/78	13	8	3. Theme From "Close Encounters Of The Third Kind"**[I]** all of above from soundtracks composed by Williams	Arista 0300
			WILLIAMS, Larry	
			Born on 5/10/35 in New Orleans, Louisiana. Committed suicide on 1/2/80 (age 44). R&B-rock and roll singer/songwriter/pianist.	
7/8/57	5	17	1. **Short Fat Fannie /** Best Seller #5 / Top 100 #6 / Jockey #15 #1 R&B hit (1 week)	
8/12/57		5	2. High School Dance Best Seller: flip **LARRY WILLIAMS And His Band** (above 2)	Specialty 608
11/11/57	14	14	3. Bony Moronie Best Seller #14 / Top 100 #18	Specialty 615
			WILLIAMS, Mason	
			Born on 8/24/38 in Abilene, Texas. Folk guitarist. Comedy writer for *The Smothers Brothers Comedy Hour* (1967-69).	
7/13/68	2 (2)	11	1. **Classical Gas** **[I]** #1 Adult Contemporary hit (3 weeks)	Warner 7190
			WILLIAMS, Maurice, & The Zodiacs	
			Born on 4/26/38 in Lancaster, South Carolina. R&B singer. The Zodiacs: Wiley Bennett, Henry Gaston, Charles Thomas, Albert Hill and Willie Morrow.	
10/10/60	1 (1)	14	1. **Stay**	Herald 552
			WILLIAMS, Otis — see CHARMS	
			WILLIAMS, Roger	
			Born Louis Weertz on 10/1/24 in Omaha, Nebraska. Pianist.	
8/20/55	1 (4)	26	● 1. **Autumn Leaves** Best Seller #1 (4) / Top 100 #2 / Juke Box #2 / Jockey #3 **[I]** from the 1947 French song "Les Feuilles Mortes"	Kapp 116
1/14/56	38	1	2. Wanting You Top 100 #38 **[I]** from the 1928 musical *The New Moon* starring Evelyn Herbert	Kapp 127
3/24/56	37	1	3. La Mer (Beyond The Sea) Top 100 #37 **[I]** #26 hit for Benny Goodman in 1948	Kapp 138
3/16/57	15	10	4. Almost Paradise Jockey #15 / Best Seller #22 / Top 100 #26 **[I]**	Kapp 175
11/11/57	22	7	● 5. Till Jockey #22 / Top 100 #27 / Best Seller #28 Marty Gold (orch., above 2)	Kapp 197

DATE	POS	WKS	ARTIST–RECORD TITLE	LABEL & NO.
9/8/58	**10**	11	6. **Near You**　　　　　Hot 100 #10 / Best Seller #16　**[I]** Hal Kanner (orch.); #1 hit (17 weeks) for Francis Craig in 1947	Kapp 233
10/15/66	**7**	14	7. **Born Free** #1 Adult Contemporary hit (6 weeks); title song from the movie starring Virginia McKenna	Kapp 767

WILLIAMS, Vanessa

Born on 3/18/63 in Tarrytown, New York. R&B singer/actress. In 1983, became the first black woman to win the Miss America pageant; relinquished crown after *Penthouse* magazine scandal. Acted in several movies and Broadway shows. Married NBA player Rick Fox on 9/26/99.

DATE	POS	WKS	ARTIST–RECORD TITLE	LABEL & NO.
2/11/89	**8**	11	1. **Dreamin'**　　　　　Sales #8 / Airplay #10 #1 R&B hit (2 weeks)	Wing 871078
9/21/91	**18**	11	2. Running Back To You　　　Airplay #17 / Sales #33 #1 R&B hit (2 weeks)	Wing 867518
2/15/92	**1** (5)	23	● 3. **Save The Best For Last**　Airplay #1 (8) / Sales #2 #1 R&B hit (3 weeks) / #1 Adult Contemporary hit (3 weeks)	Wing 865136
6/13/92	**26**	9	4. Just For Tonight　　　Airplay #27 / Sales #48	Wing 865888
3/6/93	**3**	20	5. **Love Is**　　　　　Airplay #2 / Sales #13 **VANESSA WILLIAMS and BRIAN McKNIGHT** #1 Adult Contemporary hit (3 weeks); from the album *Beverly Hills,* *90210 - The Soundtrack*	Giant 18630
12/10/94+	**18**	16	6. The Sweetest Days　　　Sales #21 / Airplay #21	Wing 851110
7/8/95	**4**	19	● 7. **Colors Of The Wind**　Sales #4 / Airplay #11 from the Disney animated movie *Pocahontas*	Hollywood 64001

WILLIE D — see GETO BOYS, The

WILLIS, Bruce

Born Walter Bruce Willis on 3/19/55 in Idar-Oberstein, West Germany; raised in Penns Grove, New Jersey. Leading movie actor. Starred on TV's *Moonlighting* and several movies. Married to actress Demi Moore from 1987-2000.

DATE	POS	WKS	ARTIST–RECORD TITLE	LABEL & NO.
1/31/87	**5**	10	1. **Respect Yourself**　　　Sales #5 / Airplay #6	Motown 1876

WILLIS, Chuck

Born on 1/31/28 in Atlanta, Georgia. Died of a perforated ulcer on 4/10/58 (age 30). R&B singer/songwriter.

DATE	POS	WKS	ARTIST–RECORD TITLE	LABEL & NO.
5/13/57	**12**	8	1. C. C. Rider　　　　Top 100 #12 / Best Seller #13 #1 R&B hit (2 weeks); inspired the "Stroll" dance craze; #14 hit for Ma Rainey in 1925 (as "See See Rider Blues")	Atlantic 1130
3/10/58	**33**	3	2. Betty And Dupree　　Best Seller #33 / Top 100 #33 Jesse Stone (orch., above 2)	Atlantic 1168
5/12/58	**9**	17	● 3. **What Am I Living For** /Jockey #9 / Best Seller #15 / Top 100 #15 #1 R&B hit (1 week)	
5/26/58	**24**	2	4.　Hang Up My Rock And Roll Shoes 　　　　　　　Top 100 #24 / Best Seller: flip Reggie Obrecht (orch., above 2)	Atlantic 1179

WILLS, Mark

Born Daryl Mark Williams on 8/8/73 in Cleveland, Tennessee; raised in Blue Ridge, Georgia. Country singer.

DATE	POS	WKS	ARTIST–RECORD TITLE	LABEL & NO.
5/1/99	**34**	3	1. Wish You Were Here　　　Airplay #22 #1 Country hit (1 week); from the album *Wish You Were Here* on Mercury 536317	album cut

DATE	POS	WKS	ARTIST–RECORD TITLE	LABEL & NO.
2/12/00	**36**	4	2. Back At One Airplay #27 *from the album Permanently on Mercury 546296*	album cut
12/21/02+	**23**	14	3. 19 Somethin' Airplay #20 #1 Country hit (6 weeks); from the album *Greatest Hits* on Mercury 170313	album cut

WILL TO POWER

Pop-dance trio from Florida: Bob Rosenberg, Dr. J. and Maria Mendez. Rosenberg is the son of singer Gloria Mann. By 1990, reduced to a duo of Rosenberg and Elin Michaels. Group name taken from the work of 19th-century German philosopher Friedrich Nietzsche.

DATE	POS	WKS	ARTIST–RECORD TITLE	LABEL & NO.
10/15/88	**1** (1)	15	● 1. **Baby, I Love Your Way/Freebird Medley (Free Baby)** Sales #1 (1) / Airplay #1 (1)	Epic 08034
12/8/90+	**7**	12	2. **I'm Not In Love** Airplay #4 / Sales #7	Epic 73636

WILSON, Al

Born on 6/19/39 in Meridian, Mississippi. R&B singer/drummer.

DATE	POS	WKS	ARTIST–RECORD TITLE	LABEL & NO.
9/21/68	**27**	5	1. The Snake *produced by Johnny Rivers (owned Soul City Records)*	Soul City 767
11/24/73+	**1** (1)	16	● 2. **Show And Tell**	Rocky Road 30073
11/9/74	**30**	3	3. La La Peace Song	Rocky Road 30200
5/1/76	**29**	4	4. I've Got A Feeling (We'll Be Seeing Each Other Again)	Playboy 6062

WILSON, Ann — see HEART

WILSON, Brian — see BEACH BOYS, The

WILSON, Charlie — see SNOOP DOGG

WILSON, Danny — see DANNY WILSON

WILSON, J. Frank, and The Cavaliers

Born on 12/11/41 in Lufkin, Texas. Died on 10/4/91 (age 49). The Cavaliers: Sid Holmes (guitar), Lewis Elliott (bass) and Ray Smith (drums).

DATE	POS	WKS	ARTIST–RECORD TITLE	LABEL & NO.
9/26/64	**2** (1)	12	1. **Last Kiss**	Josie 923

WILSON, Jackie

Born on 6/9/34 in Detroit, Michigan. Died on 1/21/84 (age 49). Sang with local gospel groups; became an amateur boxer. Worked as a solo singer until 1953, then joined Billy Ward And His Dominoes as Clyde McPhatter's replacement. Solo since 1957. Godfather of Jody Watley. Cousin of Hubert Johnson of The Contours. Wilson collapsed after suffering a stroke on stage at the Latin Casino in Cherry Hill, New Jersey on 9/29/75; spent the rest of his life in nursing homes. Inducted into the Rock and Roll Hall of Fame in 1987.

DATE	POS	WKS	ARTIST–RECORD TITLE	LABEL & NO.
4/21/58	**22**	10	1. To Be Loved Top 100 #22 / Best Seller #23	Brunswick 55052
12/8/58+	**7**	16	2. **Lonely Teardrops** #1 R&B hit (7 weeks)	Brunswick 55105
4/13/59	**13**	9	3. That's Why (I Love You So)	Brunswick 55121
7/6/59	**20**	6	4. I'll Be Satisfied	Brunswick 55136
10/12/59	**37**	1	5. You Better Know It #1 R&B hit (1 week); from the movie *Go Johnny Go* starring Wilson and Alan Freed	Brunswick 55149
1/4/60	**34**	3	6. Talk That Talk	Brunswick 55165

DATE	POS	WKS	ARTIST–RECORD TITLE	LABEL & NO.
4/11/60	4	12	● 7. **Night /** based on Saint-Saens' *Samson & Delilah* aria "My Heart At Thy Sweet Voice"	
4/25/60	15	9	8. Doggin' Around #1 R&B hit (3 weeks)	Brunswick 55166
8/1/60	12	9	9. (You Were Made For) All My Love /	
8/1/60	15	8	10. A Woman, A Lover, A Friend #1 R&B hit (4 weeks)	Brunswick 55167
10/24/60	8	12	11. **Alone At Last /** based on Tchaikovsky's "Piano Concerto in B Flat"	
11/28/60	32	2	12. Am I The Man	Brunswick 55170
1/16/61	9	6	13. **My Empty Arms** based on "Vesti La Giubba" from the opera *I Pagliacci*	Brunswick 55201
3/27/61	20	5	14. Please Tell Me Why /	
3/27/61	40	1	15. Your One And Only Love	Brunswick 55208
6/26/61	19	5	16. I'm Comin' On Back To You	Brunswick 55216
9/11/61	37	2	17. Years From Now	Brunswick 55219
2/3/62	34	4	18. The Greatest Hurt Bob Mersey (orch.)	Brunswick 55221
3/23/63	5	9	19. **Baby Workout** #1 R&B hit (3 weeks)	Brunswick 55239
8/10/63	33	1	20. Shake! Shake! Shake!	Brunswick 55246
11/19/66	11	8	21. Whispers (Gettin' Louder)	Brunswick 55300
9/2/67	6	9	22. **(Your Love Keeps Lifting Me) Higher And Higher** #1 R&B hit (1 week)	Brunswick 55336
12/16/67	32	2	23. Since You Showed Me How To Be Happy	Brunswick 55354
8/31/68	34	2	24. I Get The Sweetest Feeling	Brunswick 55381
			WILSON, Meri	
			Born on 6/15/49 in Japan (father was a U.S. Air Force officer); raised in Marietta, Georgia. Died in a car crash on 12/28/2002 (age 53). Was the director of elementary education for Georgia.	
7/2/77	18	10	● 1. Telephone Man **[N]**	GRT 127
			WILSON, Nancy	
			Born on 2/20/37 in Chillicothe; raised in Columbus, Ohio. Jazz stylist with Rusty Bryant's Carolyn Club Band in Columbus. First recorded for Dot in 1956. Moved to New York City in 1959.	
7/18/64	11	7	1. (You Don't Know) How Glad I Am	Capitol 5198
6/15/68	29	9	2. Face It Girl, It's Over	Capitol 2136
			WILSON PHILLIPS	
			Pop-Adult Contemporary vocal trio formed in Los Angeles, California: sisters Carnie and Wendy Wilson, with Chynna Phillips. Carnie and Wendy's father is Brian Wilson (The Beach Boys). Chynna, the daughter of Michelle and John Phillips (The Mamas & The Papas), acted in the movie *Caddyshack II*. Carnie became host of own TV talk show in 1995.	
4/7/90	1 (1)	18	● 1. **Hold On** Sales #2 / Airplay #2 #1 Adult Contemporary hit (1 week)	SBK 07322
7/21/90	1 (2)	15	● 2. **Release Me** Airplay #1 (3) / Sales #3 #1 Adult Contemporary hit (1 week)	SBK 07327
10/27/90	4	15	3. **Impulsive** Airplay #2 / Sales #8 Joe Walsh (rhythm & slide guitar)	SBK 07337

DATE	POS	WKS	ARTIST–RECORD TITLE	LABEL & NO.
2/23/91	**1** (1)	14	4. **You're In Love** Airplay #1 (1) / Sales #2 #1 Adult Contemporary hit (4 weeks)	SBK 07343
6/15/91	**12**	9	5. The Dream Is Still Alive Airplay #29	SBK 07356
5/23/92	**20**	8	6. You Won't See Me Cry Sales #22 / Airplay #27	SBK 07385
9/12/92	**30**	3	7. Give It Up Airplay #40 / Sales #42	SBK 50398

WILTON PLACE STREET BAND

Studio disco group assembled in Los Angeles, California, by producer Trevor Lawrence (who resided on Wilton Place in L.A.).

3/12/77	**24**	7	1. Disco Lucy (I Love Lucy Theme) **[I]** discofied theme from the TV series *I Love Lucy* starring Lucille Ball	Island 078

WINANS, CeCe — see HOUSTON, Whitney

WINANS, Mario — see PUFF DADDY

WINCHESTER, Jesse

Born on 5/17/44 in Shreveport, Louisiana. Pop singer/songwriter/guitarist.

5/30/81	**32**	5	1. Say What	Bearsville 49711

WIND — see ORLANDO, Tony

WINDING, Kai

Born on 5/18/22 in Aarhus, Denmark. Died on 5/6/83 (age 60). Jazz trombonist. Moved to U.S. in 1934. With Benny Goodman and Stan Kenton in the mid-1940s.

7/27/63	**8**	9	1. **More** **[I]** theme from the Italian documentary movie *Mondo Cane*	Verve 10295

WING AND A PRAYER FIFE AND DRUM CORPS., The

Disco studio group assembled by producer Harold Wheeler. Vocals by Linda November, Vivian Cherry, Arlene Martell and Helen Miles.

12/20/75+	**14**	12	1. Baby Face #1 hit for Jan Garber in 1926; #1 hit for Art Mooney in 1948	Wing & A Prayer 103

WINGER

Hard-rock group formed in New York: Kip Winger (vocals, bass), Reb Beach (guitar), Paul Taylor (keyboards; left in 1992) and Rod Morgenstein (drums). Kip was a member of Alice Cooper's band.

4/8/89	**26**	6	1. Seventeen Sales #24 / Airplay #28	Atlantic 88958
7/8/89	**19**	9	2. Headed For A Heartbreak Airplay #18 / Sales #20	Atlantic 88922
11/17/90+	**12**	12	3. Miles Away Sales #8 / Airplay #14	Atlantic 87824

WINGFIELD, Pete

Born on 5/7/48 in Kiphook, Hampshire, England. Pop singer/keyboardist/producer.

10/25/75	**15**	8	1. Eighteen With A Bullet hit #18 with a bullet on the 11/22/75 *Billboard* "Hot 100" chart	Island 026

WINGS — see McCARTNEY, Paul

DATE	POS	WKS	ARTIST–RECORD TITLE	LABEL & NO.
			WINSTONS, The	
			R&B group from Washington DC: Richard Spencer (vocals), Ray Maritano (sax), Quincy Mattison (guitar), Phil Tolotta (organ), Sonny Peckrol (bass) and G.C. Coleman (drums).	
6/14/69	**7**	10	● 1. **Color Him Father**	Metromedia 117
			WINTER, Edgar, Group	
			Born on 12/28/46 in Beaumont, Texas. Rock singer/keyboardist/ saxophonist. Younger brother of rock guitarist Johnny Winter. Group included Dan Hartman (1972-76), Ronnie Montrose (1972-74) and Rick Derringer (1974-76).	
4/21/73	**1 (1)**	14	● 1. **Frankenstein** **[I]**	Epic 10967
			Ronnie Montrose (lead guitar)	
9/8/73	**14**	9	2. Free Ride	Epic 11024
8/10/74	**33**	2	3. River's Risin'	Epic 11143
			EDGAR WINTER	
			above 3 produced by Rick Derringer	
			WINTERHALTER, Hugo, and his Orchestra	
			Born on 8/15/09 in Wilkes-Barre, Pennsylvania. Died of cancer on 9/17/73 (age 64). Conductor/arranger for RCA Records from 1950-63.	
12/18/54+	**25**	5	1. Song Of The Barefoot Contessa Best Seller #25	RCA Victor 5888
			from the movie *The Barefoot Contessa* starring Humphrey Bogart and Ava Gardner	
7/28/56	**2 (2)**	23	● 2. **Canadian Sunset**	RCA Victor 6537
			Jockey #2 / Top 100 #2 / Best Seller #3 / Juke Box #3 **[I]**	
			HUGO WINTERHALTER and his Orchestra with EDDIE HEYWOOD	
			WINWOOD, Steve	
			Born on 5/12/48 in Birmingham, England. Rock singer/keyboardist/ guitarist. Lead singer of Spencer Davis Group, Blind Faith and Traffic.	
2/28/81	**7**	12	1. **While You See A Chance**	Island 49656
7/5/86	**1 (1)**	14	2. **Higher Love** Airplay #1 (2) / Sales #2	Island 28710
			#1 Mainstream Rock hit (4 weeks); Chaka Khan (backing vocal); 1986 Grammy winner: Record of the Year	
10/25/86	**20**	7	3. Freedom Overspill Airplay #19 / Sales #21	Island 28595
			Joe Walsh (slide guitar)	
3/14/87	**8**	12	4. **The Finer Things** Airplay #4 / Sales #9	Island 28498
			#1 Adult Contemporary hit (3 weeks)	
7/4/87	**13**	10	5. Back In The High Life Again Airplay #10 / Sales #16	Island 28472
			#1 Adult Contemporary hit (3 weeks); James Taylor (backing vocal)	
11/7/87	**9**	12	6. **Valerie** Airplay #7 / Sales #14 **[R]**	Island 28231
			remixed version of his #70 hit in 1982	
6/18/88	**1 (4)**	14	7. **Roll With It** Airplay #1 (4) / Sales #1 (1)	Virgin 99326
			#1 Adult Contemporary hit (2 weeks) / #1 Mainstream Rock hit (4 weeks)	
9/10/88	**6**	11	8. **Don't You Know What The Night Can Do?** Airplay #6 / Sales #8	Virgin 99290
			#1 Mainstream Rock hit (2 weeks); tune used in a Michelob TV commercial	
12/10/88+	**11**	11	9. Holding On Airplay #10 / Sales #13	Virgin 99261
			#1 Adult Contemporary hit (2 weeks)	
11/17/90	**18**	9	10. One And Only Man Airplay #16 / Sales #21	Virgin 98892
			#1 Mainstream Rock hit (2 weeks)	

DATE	POS	WKS	ARTIST–RECORD TITLE	LABEL & NO.
			WISEGUYS, The	
			Techno-rock duo from England: Regal and Touché.	album cut
8/18/01	31	6	1. Start The Commotion Airplay #32	
			samples "Wild Child" by The Ventures; from the album *The Antidote* on Mammoth 810015	
			WITHERS, Bill	
			Born on 7/4/38 in Slab Fork, West Virginia. R&B singer/guitarist/composer. Married to actress Denise Nicholas.	
8/14/71	3	12	● 1. **Ain't No Sunshine**	Sussex 219
			produced by Booker T. Jones	
5/27/72	1 (3)	14	● 2. **Lean On Me**	Sussex 235
			#1 R&B hit (1 week)	
9/9/72	2 (2)	10	● 3. **Use Me**	Sussex 241
3/3/73	31	5	4. Kissing My Love	Sussex 250
1/21/78	30	4	5. Lovely Day	Columbia 10627
			all of above written by Withers	
3/7/81	2 (3)	16	6. **Just The Two Of Us**	Elektra 47103
			GROVER WASHINGTON, JR. (with Bill Withers)	
			WOLF, Peter	
			Born Peter Blankfield on 3/7/46 in the Bronx, New York. Lead singer of the J. Geils Band until 1983. Married to actress Faye Dunaway from 1974-79. Not to be confused with the producer of the same name.	
7/28/84	12	10	1. Lights Out	EMI America 8208
11/17/84	36	2	2. I Need You Tonight	EMI America 8241
3/21/87	15	9	3. Come As You Are Sales #13 / Airplay #15	EMI America 8350
			#1 Mainstream Rock hit (1 week)	
			WOLFMAN JACK — see FLASH CADILLAC / GUESS WHO / STAMPEDERS	
			WOMACK, Bobby	
			Born on 3/4/44 in Cleveland, Ohio. R&B singer/songwriter/guitarist. Nicknamed "The Preacher."	
1/8/72	27	7	1. That's The Way I Feel About Cha	United Artists 50847
			(The Preacher) BOBBY WOMACK (& Peace)	
1/13/73	31	6	● 2. Harry Hippie	United Artists 50946
			BOBBY WOMACK & Peace	
8/11/73	29	6	3. Nobody Wants You When You're Down And Out	United Artists 255
3/9/74	10	11	● 4. **Lookin' For A Love**	United Artists 375
			#1 R&B hit (3 weeks)	
			WOMACK, Lee Ann	
			Born on 8/19/66 in Jacksonville, Texas. Country singer.	
4/24/99	38	2	1. I'll Think Of A Reason Later Airplay #22	album cut
			from the album *Some Things I Know* on Decca 70040	
7/1/00+	14	32	▲ 2. I Hope You Dance Sales #6 / Airplay #14	MCA 172185
			#1 Country hit (5 weeks) / #1 Adult Contemporary hit (11 weeks); Sons Of The Desert (backing vocals)	

DATE	POS	WKS	ARTIST–RECORD TITLE	LABEL & NO.
			WONDER, Stevie	
			Born Steveland Morris on 5/13/50 in Saginaw, Michigan. Singer/ songwriter/multi-instrumentalist/producer. Blind since birth. Signed to Motown in 1960, did backup work. First recorded in 1962, named "Little Stevie Wonder" by Berry Gordy, Jr. Married to Syreeta Wright from 1970-72. Near-fatal auto accident on 8/16/73. In the movies *Bikini Beach* and *Muscle Beach Party*. Inducted into the Rock and Roll Hall of Fame in 1989. Won Grammy's Lifetime Achievement Award in 1996.	
7/6/63	**1** (3)	12	1. **Fingertips - Pt 2** [L] #1 R&B hit (6 weeks)	Tamla 54080
10/19/63	**33**	4	2. Workout Stevie, Workout **LITTLE STEVIE WONDER** (above 2)	Tamla 54086
7/11/64	**29**	4	3. Hey Harmonica Man	Tamla 54096
1/22/66	**3**	9	4. **Uptight (Everything's Alright)** #1 R&B hit (5 weeks)	Tamla 54124
5/7/66	**20**	4	5. Nothing's Too Good For My Baby	Tamla 54130
7/30/66	**9**	8	6. **Blowin In The Wind** #1 R&B hit (1 week); written by Bob Dylan	Tamla 54136
11/26/66	**9**	8	7. **A Place In The Sun**	Tamla 54139
4/1/67	**32**	3	8. Travlin' Man	Tamla 54147
6/24/67	**2** (2)	12	9. **I Was Made To Love Her** #1 R&B hit (4 weeks)	Tamla 54151
10/21/67	**12**	5	10. I'm Wondering	Tamla 54157
4/27/68	**9**	9	11. **Shoo-Be-Doo-Be-Doo-Da-Day** #1 R&B hit (1 week)	Tamla 54165
8/17/68	**35**	3	12. You Met Your Match	Tamla 54168
11/9/68	**2** (2)	13	13. **For Once In My Life**	Tamla 54174
6/21/69	**4**	11	14. **My Cherie Amour /**	
3/22/69	**39**	1	15. I Don't Know Why	Tamla 54180
11/1/69	**7**	12	16. **Yester-Me, Yester-You, Yesterday**	Tamla 54188
2/21/70	**26**	5	17. Never Had A Dream Come True	Tamla 54191
7/4/70	**3**	13	18. **Signed, Sealed, Delivered I'm Yours** #1 R&B hit (6 weeks)	Tamla 54196
10/31/70	**9**	8	19. **Heaven Help Us All**	Tamla 54200
3/27/71	**13**	9	20. We Can Work It Out	Tamla 54202
9/4/71	**8**	11	21. **If You Really Love Me**	Tamla 54208
6/24/72	**33**	5	22. Superwoman (Where Were You When I Needed You)	Tamla 54216
12/9/72+	**1** (1)	13	23. **Superstition** #1 R&B hit (3 weeks)	Tamla 54226
3/31/73	**1** (1)	13	24. **You Are The Sunshine Of My Life** #1 Adult Contemporary hit (2 weeks); Jim Gilstrap and Gloria Barley (first verse soloists)	Tamla 54232
9/1/73	**4**	12	25. **Higher Ground** #1 R&B hit (1 week)	Tamla 54235
11/24/73+	**8**	14	26. **Living For The City** #1 R&B hit (2 weeks)	Tamla 54242
4/27/74	**16**	9	27. Don't You Worry 'Bout A Thing	Tamla 54245
8/17/74	**1** (1)	14	28. **You Haven't Done Nothin** #1 R&B hit (2 weeks); The Jackson 5 (doo-doo-wop vocals)	Tamla 54252
11/30/74+	**3**	14	29. **Boogie On Reggae Woman** #1 R&B hit (2 weeks)	Tamla 54254
12/4/76+	**1** (1)	15	30. **I Wish** #1 R&B hit (5 weeks)	Tamla 54274

DATE	POS	WKS	ARTIST–RECORD TITLE	LABEL & NO.
4/16/77	**1** (3)	13	31. **Sir Duke** #1 R&B hit (1 week); a tribute to Duke Ellington	Tamla 54281
9/17/77	**32**	4	32. Another Star	Tamla 54286
12/3/77+	**36**	5	33. As	Tamla 54291
11/10/79	**4**	14	34. **Send One Your Love** #1 Adult Contemporary hit (4 weeks)	Tamla 54303
10/4/80	**5**	16	35. **Master Blaster (Jammin')** #1 R&B hit (7 weeks); inspired by Bob Marley's classic reggae tune "Jamming"	Tamla 54317
1/17/81	**11**	11	36. I Ain't Gonna Stand For It	Tamla 54320
1/30/82	**4**	13	37. **That Girl** #1 R&B hit (9 weeks)	Tamla 1602
4/10/82	**1** (7)	15	● 38. **Ebony And Ivory** **PAUL McCARTNEY (with Stevie Wonder)** #1 Adult Contemporary hit (5 weeks)	Columbia 02860
6/19/82	**13**	9	39. Do I Do	Tamla 1612
9/1/84	**1** (3)	15	● 40. **I Just Called To Say I Love You** Sales #1 (3) / Airplay #1 (3) #1 R&B hit (3 weeks) / #1 Adult Contemporary hit (3 weeks)	Motown 1745
12/15/84+	**17**	10	41. Love Light In Flight Airplay #15 / Sales #19 above 2 from the movie *The Woman In Red* starring Gene Wilder and Kelly LeBrock	Motown 1769
9/14/85	**1** (1)	14	42. **Part-Time Lover** Airplay #1 (3) / Sales #2 #1 R&B hit (6 weeks) / #1 Adult Contemporary hit (3 weeks); Luther Vandross (backing vocal)	Tamla 1808
11/23/85+	**1** (4)	17	● 43. **That's What Friends Are For** Sales #1 (5) / Airplay #1 (3) **DIONNE & FRIENDS: Elton John, Gladys Knight and Stevie Wonder** #1 R&B hit (3 weeks) / #1 Adult Contemporary hit (2 weeks); first recorded by Rod Stewart in 1982	Arista 9422
12/14/85+	**10**	11	44. **Go Home** Sales #11 / Airplay #11 #1 Adult Contemporary hit (1 week)	Tamla 1817
3/22/86	**24**	6	45. Overjoyed Sales #18 / Airplay #26 #1 Adult Contemporary hit (2 weeks)	Tamla 1832
11/7/87	**19**	7	46. Skeletons Sales #11 / Airplay #32 #1 R&B hit (2 weeks)	Motown 1907

WONDER, Wayne

Born VonWayne Charles in Jamaica. Reggae singer.

DATE	POS	WKS	ARTIST–RECORD TITLE	LABEL & NO.
3/15/03	**11**	21	1. No Letting Go Airplay #11 / Sales #49	VP/Atlantic 88254

WONDER WHO? — see 4 SEASONS

WOOD, Brenton

Born Alfred Smith on 7/26/41 in Shreveport, Louisiana; raised in San Pedro, California. R&B singer/songwriter/pianist.

DATE	POS	WKS	ARTIST–RECORD TITLE	LABEL & NO.
6/24/67	**34**	1	1. The Oogum Boogum Song	Double Shot 111
9/9/67	**9**	10	2. **Gimme Little Sign**	Double Shot 116
12/16/67	**34**	3	3. Baby You Got It	Double Shot 121

WOOD, Lauren

Born in Pittsburgh, Pennsylvania. Pop singer/songwriter/keyboardist.

DATE	POS	WKS	ARTIST–RECORD TITLE	LABEL & NO.
10/27/79	**24**	6	1. Please Don't Leave Michael McDonald (harmony vocal)	Warner 49043

DATE	POS	WKS	ARTIST–RECORD TITLE	LABEL & NO.
			WOODS, Stevie	
			Born in Columbus, Ohio. Male R&B singer/songwriter. Son of jazz great Rusty Bryant.	
11/14/81	**25**	10	1. Steal The Night	Cotillion 46016
3/20/82	**38**	3	2. Just Can't Win 'Em All	Cotillion 46030
			WOOLEY, Sheb	
			Born Shelby Wooley on 4/10/21 in Erick, Oklahoma. Died of leukemia on 9/16/2003 (age 82). Country singer/songwriter/actor. Played "Pete Nolan" on the TV series *Rawhide*. Appeared in several movies. Also made comical recordings under pseudonym Ben Colder.	
6/2/58	**1** (6)	14	● 1. **The Purple People Eater** Best Seller #1 (6) / Top 100 #1 (6) / Jockey #1 (4) **[N]**	MGM 12651
			WORLD PARTY	
			Group is actually rock singer/keyboardist Karl Wallinger (born on 10/19/57 in Prestatyn, Wales). Wallinger was also a member of The Waterboys.	
4/4/87	**27**	5	1. Ship Of Fools (Save Me From Tomorrow) Sales #20 / Airplay #37	Chrysalis 43052
			WORLEY, Darryl	
			Born on 10/31/64 in Pyburn, Tennessee; raised in Savannah, Tennessee. Country singer/songwriter/guitarist.	
8/17/02	**28**	7	1. I Miss My Friend Airplay #25 #1 Country hit (1 week); from the album *I Miss My Friend* on DreamWorks 50351	album cut
3/22/03	**22**	10	2. Have You Forgotten? Airplay #21 #1 Country hit (7 weeks); from the album *Have You Forgotten* on DreamWorks 000064	album cut
			WRAY, Link, & His Ray Men	
			Born on 5/2/35 in Dunn, North Carolina. Rock and roll guitarist.	
5/12/58	**16**	10	1. Rumble Best Seller #16 / Top 100 #16 **[I]**	Cadence 1347
3/16/59	**23**	3	2. Raw-Hide **[I]** **LINK WRAY AND THE WRAYMEN**	Epic 9300
			WRECKX-N-EFFECT	
			Male rap duo: Aqil Davidson and Markell Riley. Member Brandon Mitchell (died of a gunshot wound in 1990). Riley is the brother of Guy member/prolific producer Teddy Riley. First recorded for Motown in 1989.	
10/24/92	**2** (3)	23	▲² 1. **Rump Shaker** Sales #1 (3) / Airplay #8 samples "Back To The Hotel" by N2Deep	MCA 54388
			WRIGHT, Betty	
			Born on 12/21/53 in Miami, Florida. R&B singer.	
9/7/68	**33**	2	1. Girls Can't Do What The Guys Do	Alston 4569
12/11/71+	**6**	12	● 2. **Clean Up Woman**	Alston 4601
5/6/78	**8**	14	3. **Dance With Me** **PETER BROWN with Betty Wright**	Drive 6269

DATE	POS	WKS	ARTIST–RECORD TITLE	LABEL & NO.
			WRIGHT, Charles, And The Watts 103rd Street Rhythm Band	
			Born in 1942 in Clarksdale, Mississippi. R&B singer/songwriter/pianist/ guitarist/producer. Leader of an eight-man, R&B-funk band from the Watts section of Los Angeles, California. Evolved from the Soul Runners. Big break came through assistance by comedian Bill Cosby.	
3/22/69	**11**	10	1. Do Your Thing **THE WATTS 103RD STREET RHYTHM BAND**	Warner 7250
5/30/70	**16**	10	2. Love Land	Warner 7365
9/12/70	**12**	10	3. Express Yourself	Warner 7417
			WRIGHT, Chely	
			Born on 10/25/70 in Kansas City, Missouri. Female country singer/guitarist.	
8/21/99	**36**	4	1. Single White Female Airplay #25 / Sales #38 #1 Country hit (1 week)	MCA 72092
			WRIGHT, Dale	
			Born Harlan Dale Riffe on 2/4/38 in Middletown, Ohio. Rock and roll singer/songwriter. Worked as a DJ in the Midwest.	
2/24/58	**38**	2	1. She's Neat Best Seller #38 / Top 100 #39 **DALE WRIGHT with the Rock-Its**	Fraternity 792
			WRIGHT, Gary	
			Born on 4/26/43 in Creskill, New Jersey. Pop-rock singer/songwriter/ keyboardist. Appeared in *Captain Video* TV series at age seven. In the Broadway play *Fanny*. Co-leader of the rock group Spooky Tooth.	
1/31/76	**2** (3)	14	● 1. **Dream Weaver**	Warner 8167
5/15/76	**2** (2)	18	2. **Love Is Alive**	Warner 8143
8/1/81	**16**	10	3. Really Wanna Know You	Warner 49769
			WRIGHT, Priscilla	
			Born in 1941 in London, Ontario, Canada. Teen pop singer.	
6/25/55	**16**	9	1. The Man In The Raincoat Jockey #16 / Best Seller #18 / Juke Box #20 **PRISCILLA WRIGHT With Don Wright and The Septette**	Unique 303
			WYATT, Keke	
			Born Ketara Wyatt in Indianapolis, Indiana. Female R&B singer.	
12/2/00	**26**	10	1. My First Love Airplay #21 **AVANT Featuring Ketara Wyatt** from Avant's album *My Thoughts* on Magic Johnson 112069	album cut
2/16/02	**27**	7	2. Nothing In This World Airplay #25 **KEKE WYATT featuring Avant** from Wyatt's album *Soul Sista* on MCA 112609	album cut
			WYNETTE, Tammy	
			Born Virginia Wynette Pugh on 5/5/42 in Itawamba County, Mississippi. Died of a blood clot on 4/6/98 (age 55). With 20 #1 country hits from 1967-76, dubbed "The First Lady of Country Music." Discovered by producer Billy Sherrill. Married to country star George Jones from 1969-75.	
12/28/68+	**19**	9	1. Stand By Your Man #1 Country hit (3 weeks)	Epic 10398
2/15/92	**11**	12	2. Justified & Ancient Sales #10 / Airplay #12 **THE KLF (Featuring Tammy Wynette)**	Arista 12401

DATE	POS	WKS	ARTIST–RECORD TITLE	LABEL & NO.
			X	
			XSCAPE	
			Female R&B vocal group formed in Atlanta, Georgia: sisters LaTocha and Tamika Scott, with Kandi Burruss and Tameka Cottle.	
10/2/93	**2** (1)	17	▲ 1. **Just Kickin' It** Sales #1 (1) / Airplay #5 #1 R&B hit (4 weeks)	So So Def 77119
1/8/94	**8**	14	● 2. **Understanding** Sales #7 / Airplay #15 #1 R&B hit (2 weeks)	So So Def 77335
7/15/95	**32**	6	● 3. Feels So Good Sales #15	So So Def 77921
10/14/95	**8**	14	● 4. **Who Can I Run To?** Sales #5 / Airplay #29 #1 R&B hit (1 week); originally recorded by The Jones Girls in 1979	So So Def 78056
4/27/96	**10**	11	● 5. **Keep On, Keepin' On** Sales #4 / Airplay #42 **MC LYTE Featuring Xscape** samples "Liberian Girl" by Michael Jackson; from the movie *Sunset Park* starring Rhea Perlman	Flavor Unit 64302
2/14/98	**31**	3	6. Am I Dreaming Sales #16 **OL SKOOL [Featuring Keith Sweat and Xscape]**	Universal 56163
5/2/98	**7**	13	● 7. **The Arms Of The One Who Loves You** Sales #5 / Airplay #63	So So Def 78788
10/24/98	**9**	6	8. **My Little Secret** Sales #3 / Airplay #55 Jagged Edge (backing vocals)	So So Def 79036
2/19/00	**34**	3	9. One Night Stand Sales #9 / Airplay #75 **J-SHIN Featuring LaTocha Scott Of Xscape**	Slip n Slide 84489
8/26/00	**20**	12	10. Bounce With Me Sales #7 / Airplay #29 **LIL BOW WOW (featuring Xscape)** #1 R&B hit (1 week); from the movie *Big Momma's House* starring Martin Lawrence	So So Def 79476
			Y	
			YA KID K — see TECHNOTRONIC	
			YANKOVIC, "Weird Al"	
			Born on 10/23/59 in Lynwood, California. Novelty singer/accordionist. Specializes in song parodies. Starred in the movie *UHF*.	
3/17/84	**12**	7	● 1. Eat It [N] Rick Derringer (guitar); parody of "Beat It" by Michael Jackson	Rock 'n' Roll 04374
5/9/92	**35**	2	2. Smells Like Nirvana Sales #12 [N] parody of "Smells Like Teen Spirit" by Nirvana	Scotti Brothers 75314
			YARBROUGH, Glenn	
			Born on 1/12/30 in Milwaukee, Wisconsin. Folk singer. Lead singer of The Limeliters (1959-63).	
4/17/65	**12**	9	1. Baby The Rain Must Fall title song from the movie starring Lee Remick and Steve McQueen	RCA Victor 8498

DATE	POS	WKS	ARTIST–RECORD TITLE	LABEL & NO.
			YARBROUGH & PEOPLES	
			Male/female R&B-funk duo from Dallas, Texas. Cavin Yarbrough and Alisa Peoples. Discovered by The Gap Band.	
3/14/81	**19**	7	● 1. Don't Stop The Music #1 R&B hit (5 weeks)	Mercury 76085
			YARDBIRDS, The	
			Rock group formed in Surrey, England: Keith Relf (vocals, harmonica; electrocuted on 5/14/76, age 33), Anthony "Top" Topham and Chris Dreja (guitars), Paul "Sam" Samwell-Smith (bass, keyboards) and Jim McCarty (drums). Formed as the Metropolitan Blues Quartet at Kingston Art School. Topham replaced by Eric Clapton in 1963. Clapton replaced by Jeff Beck in 1965. Samwell-Smith left in 1966; Dreja switched to bass and Jimmy Page (guitar) was added. Beck left in December 1966. Group disbanded in July 1968. Page formed the New Yardbirds in October 1968, which evolved into Led Zeppelin. Relf and McCarty formed Renaissance in 1969. Relf later in Armageddon, 1975; McCarty in Illusion, 1977. The Yardbirds were inducted into the Rock and Roll Hall of Fame in 1992.	
6/5/65	**6**	9	1. **For Your Love**	Epic 9790
8/21/65	**9**	8	2. **Heart Full Of Soul** above 2 written by Graham Gouldman (10cc)	Epic 9823
11/20/65	**17**	7	3. I'm A Man first recorded by Bo Diddley in 1955	Epic 9857
4/9/66	**11**	8	4. Shapes Of Things	Epic 10006
7/16/66	**13**	7	5. Over Under Sideways Down	Epic 10035
12/24/66	**30**	4	6. Happenings Ten Years Time Ago	Epic 10094
			YEARWOOD, Trisha	
			Born Patricia Lynn Yearwood on 9/19/64 in Monticello, Georgia. Country singer/songwriter.	
7/12/97	**23**	5	1. How Do I Live Sales #10 from the movie Con Air starring Nicolas Cage	MCA 72015
			YELLOW BALLOON, The	
			Pop group formed in Los Angeles, California: Alex Valdez (vocals), Paul Canella (guitar), Frosty Green (keyboards), Don Braught (bass) and Don Grady (drums). Grady played "Robbie Douglas" on TV's My Three Sons.	
4/29/67	**25**	5	1. Yellow Balloon	Canterbury 508
			YES	
			Progressive-rock group formed in London, England: Jon Anderson (vocals), Peter Banks (guitar), Tony Kaye (keyboards), Chris Squire (bass) and Bill Bruford (drums). Banks, who went on to form Flash and After The Fire, replaced by Steve Howe in 1971. Kaye (joined Badfinger in 1978) replaced by Rick Wakeman in 1971. Bruford left to join King Crimson; replaced by Alan White in late 1972. Wakeman replaced by Patrick Moraz in 1974; re-joined in 1976 when Moraz left. Wakeman and Anderson left in 1980; replaced by The Buggles' Trevor Horn (guitar) and Geoff Downes (keyboards). Group disbanded in 1980. Howe and Downes joined Asia. Re-formed in 1983 with Anderson, Kaye, Squire, White and South African guitarist Trevor Rabin. Anderson left group in 1988. Anderson, Bruford, Wakeman and Howe formed self-named group in early 1989. Yes reunited in 1991 with Anderson, Bruford, Wakeman, Howe, Kaye, Squire, White and Rabin. Bruford, Wakeman and Howe had left group by 1994.	
12/4/71	**40**	2	1. Your Move	Atlantic 2819
3/4/72	**13**	10	2. Roundabout	Atlantic 2854

DATE	POS	WKS	ARTIST–RECORD TITLE	LABEL & NO.
11/19/83+	**1** (2)	17	3. **Owner Of A Lonely Heart** #1 Mainstream Rock hit (4 weeks)	Atco 99817
3/24/84	**24**	7	4. Leave It	Atco 99787
10/31/87	**30**	6	5. Love Will Find A Way　　　　Sales #27 / Airplay #30 #1 Mainstream Rock hit (3 weeks)	Atco 99449
2/6/88	**40**	1	6. Rhythm Of Love　　　　　　　　　　Sales #40	Atco 99419
			YING YANG TWINS	
			Rap duo from Atlanta, Georgia: D'Angelo Holmes and Eric Jackson. They are not related.	
6/28/03	**2** (1)	36	1. **Get Low**　　　　　　　Airplay #2 / Sales #21 **LIL JON & THE EAST SIDE BOYZ Featuring Ying Yang Twins**	BME 2377
12/27/03+	**9**	19	2. **Salt Shaker**　　　　　　Airplay #8 / Sales #14 **YING YANG TWINS Feat. LIL JON & The EAST SIDE BOYZ**	Collipark 2485
			YOST, Dennis — see CLASSICS IV	
			YOUNG, Barry	
			Adult Contemporary singer.	
12/4/65+	**13**	7	1. One Has My Name (The Other Has My Heart) Ernie Freeman (arranger; similar to his Dean Martin arrangements); #1 Country hit for Jimmy Wakely in 1948	Dot 16756
			YOUNG, Faron	
			Born on 2/25/32 in Shreveport, Louisiana. Died of a self-inflicted gunshot wound on 12/10/96 (age 64). Country singer/guitarist. In movies *The Young Sheriff*, *Daniel Boone* and *Hidden Guns*. Founder and one-time publisher of the *Music City News* magazine in Nashville.	
5/1/61	**12**	11	1. Hello Walls #1 Country hit (9 weeks); written by Willie Nelson	Capitol 4533
			YOUNG, John Paul	
			Born on 6/21/50 in Glasgow, Scotland; raised in Sydney, Australia. Pop singer/songwriter/pianist.	
8/5/78	**7**	15	1. **Love Is In The Air** #1 Adult Contemporary hit (2 weeks)	Scotti Brothers 402
			YOUNG, Kathy, with The Innocents	
			Born on 10/21/45 in Santa Ana, California. Teen pop singer. The Innocents were a vocal trio: James West, Al Candelaria and Darron Stankey.	
9/19/60	**28**	3	1. Honest I Do **THE INNOCENTS**	Indigo 105
10/31/60	**3**	15	2. **A Thousand Stars** first recorded by The Rivileers in 1954	Indigo 108
1/9/61	**28**	3	3. Gee Whiz **THE INNOCENTS**	Indigo 111
3/6/61	**30**	6	4. Happy Birthday Blues	Indigo 115

DATE	POS	WKS	ARTIST–RECORD TITLE	LABEL & NO.
			YOUNG, Neil	
			Born on 11/12/45 in Toronto, Ontario, Canada. Rock singer/songwriter/guitarist. Member of Buffalo Springfield and Crosby, Stills, Nash & Young. Appeared in the 1987 movie *Made In Heaven*. Inducted into the Rock and Roll Hall of Fame in 1995.	
12/5/70	33	3	1. Only Love Can Break Your Heart	Reprise 0958
2/12/72	**1** (1)	13	● 2. **Heart Of Gold**	Reprise 1065
			Linda Ronstadt and James Taylor (backing vocals)	
5/20/72	31	4	3. Old Man	Reprise 1084
			YOUNG, Paul	
			Born on 1/17/56 in Bedfordshire, England. Pop-rock singer/songwriter/guitarist.	
3/3/84	22	8	1. Come Back And Stay	Columbia 04313
6/1/85	**1** (1)	15	● 2. **Everytime You Go Away** Sales #1 (2) / Airplay #1 (1)	Columbia 04867
			#1 Adult Contemporary hit (2 weeks); written by Daryl Hall (from the Hall & Oates 1980 album *Voices*)	
9/21/85	13	9	3. I'm Gonna Tear Your Playhouse Down Sales #13 / Airplay #13	Columbia 05577
8/18/90	8	11	4. **Oh Girl** Airplay #6 / Sales #14	Columbia 73377
			#1 Adult Contemporary hit (3 weeks)	
2/22/92	22	6	5. What Becomes Of The Brokenhearted Airplay #26 / Sales #39	MCA 54331
			#1 Adult Contemporary hit (2 weeks); from the movie *Fried Green Tomatoes* starring Kathy Bates	
			YOUNG, Victor, And His Singing Strings	
			Born on 8/8/1900 in Chicago, Illinois. Died on 11/11/56 (age 56). Conductor/composer/violinist.	
7/8/57	13	9	1. (Main Theme) Around The World Jockey #13 / Best Seller #20 / Top 100 #26 **[I]**	Decca 30262
			from the movie *Around The World In 80 Days* starring David Niven	
			YOUNGBLOODS, The	
			Folk-rock group formed in Boston, Massachusetts: Jesse Colin Young (vocals, bass), Lowell "Banana" Levinger and Jerry Corbitt (guitars), and Joe Bauer (drums; died in 1982).	
8/2/69	5	12	● 1. **Get Together** **[R]**	RCA Victor 9752
			re-popularized as the theme for the National Conference of Christians & Jews; originally charted at #62 in 1967	
			YOUNGBLOODZ	
			Rap duo from Atlanta, Georgia: "Sean Paul" Joseph and Jeffrey "J-Bo" Grigsby.	
9/6/03	4	25	1. **Damn!** Airplay #4 / Sales #40	So So Def 52215
			YOUNGBLOODZ Featuring Lil' Jon	
			YOUNG GUNZ	
			Male rap duo: Chris and Neef.	
9/6/03	14	11	1. Can't Stop, Won't Stop Airplay #13	album cut
			samples "Overweight Lovers In The House" by Heavy D and "Super Rappin'" by Grandmaster Flash; from the various artists album *The Chain Gang Vol. II* on Roc-A-Fella 000971	

DATE	POS	WKS	ARTIST—RECORD TITLE	LABEL & NO.
			YOUNG-HOLT UNLIMITED	
			Soul-jazz instrumental group from Chicago, Illinois: Eldee Young (bass), Isaac "Red" Holt (drums; both of the Ramsey Lewis Trio) and Don Walker (piano). Walker left by 1968.	
1/21/67	40	2	1. Wack Wack **[I]** **THE YOUNG HOLT TRIO**	Brunswick 55305
12/7/68+	3	12	● 2. **Soulful Strut** **[I]** instrumental track used for Barbara Acklin's 1969 hit "Am I The Same Girl"	Brunswick 55391
			YOUNG M.C.	
			Born Marvin Young on 5/10/67 in London, England; raised in Queens, New York. Rapper. Co-writer of Tone Loc's "Wild Thing" and "Funky Cold Medina." Graduated with economics degree from University of Southern California.	
8/26/89	7	20	▲ 1. **Bust A Move** Sales #2 / Airplay #14	Delicious Vinyl 105
1/6/90	33	3	2. Principal's Office Sales #21	Delicious Vinyl 99137
			YOUNG RASCALS — see RASCALS	
			YO-YO	
			Born Yolanda Whitaker on 8/4/71 in Los Angeles, California. Female rapper.	
6/29/91	36	3	1. You Can't Play With My Yo-Yo Sales #17 **YO-YO Featuring Ice Cube**	EastWest 98831
			YURO, Timi	
			Born Rosemarie Timotea Aurro on 8/4/40 in Chicago, Illinois; raised in Los Angeles, California. Died on 3/30/2004 (age 63). White female soul singer.	
7/31/61	4	10	1. **Hurt** #8 R&B hit for Roy Hamilton in 1955	Liberty 55343
8/11/62	12	6	2. What's A Matter Baby (Is It Hurting You)	Liberty 55469
8/10/63	24	7	3. Make The World Go Away #2 Country hit for Ray Price in 1963	Liberty 55587
			# Z	
			ZACHARIAS, Helmut, And His Magic Violins	
			Born on 1/27/20 in Germany. Died of lung failure on 2/28/2002 (age 82). Violinist.	
9/8/56	12	7	1. When The White Lilacs Bloom Again Jockey #12 / Top 100 #16 / Best Seller #19 / Juke Box #19 **[I]**	Decca 30039
			ZACHERLE, John, "The Cool Ghoul"	
			Born on 9/26/18 in Philadelphia, Pennsylvania. Hosted horror movies on WCAU-TV in Philadelphia during the late 1950s.	
3/10/58	6	7	1. **Dinner With Drac Part 1** Top 100 #6 / Best Seller #8 **[N]** The Applejacks (instrumental backing)	Cameo 130

DATE	POS	WKS	ARTIST–RECORD TITLE	LABEL & NO.
			ZADORA, Pia	
			Born Pia Schipani on 5/4/56 in Hoboken, New Jersey. Singer/actress. Appeared in several movies.	
2/12/83	**36**	3	1. The Clapping Song	Elektra/Curb 69889
			ZAGER, Michael, Band	
			Born on 1/3/43 in Passaic, New Jersey. Disco keyboardist/producer. Member of Ten Wheel Drive from 1968-73.	
4/29/78	**36**	4	1. Let's All Chant **[I]**	Private Stock 45,184
			ZAGER & EVANS	
			Pop-folk duo from Lincoln, Nebraska: Denny Zager and Rick Evans (both sing and play guitar).	
6/28/69	**1** (6)	12	● 1. **In The Year 2525 (Exordium & Terminus)** #1 Adult Contemporary hit (2 weeks)	RCA Victor 0174
			ZAHND, Ricky, & The Blue Jeaners	
			Born on 7/22/46 in Manhattan, New York. Lawyer since 1972. From 1979-86, was vice president of the New York Knicks basketball team and the New York Rangers hockey team.	
12/24/55	**21**	2	1. (I'm Gettin') Nuttin' For Christmas Best Seller #21 / Top 100 #40 **[X-N]** Tony Mottola (orch.)	Columbia 4-40576
			ZANDER, Robin — see HEART	
			ZAPPA, Frank	
			Born Francis Vincent Zappa Jr. on 12/21/40 in Baltimore, Maryland (of Sicilian parentage). Died of prostate cancer on 12/4/93 (age 52). Rock music's leading satirist. Singer/songwriter/guitarist/activist. Formed The Mothers Of Invention in 1965. In the movies *200 Motels* and *Baby Snakes*. Father of Dweezil and Moon Unit Zappa. Inducted into the Rock and Roll Hall of Fame in 1995. Won Grammy's Lifetime Achievement Award in 1997.	

9/4/82	**32**	3	1. Valley Girl **[N]**
			    featuring Frank's daughter, Moon Unit Zappa; inspired the 1983
			    movie of the same title starring Nicolas Cage
				Barking Pumpkin 02972

			ZEVON, Warren	
			Born on 1/24/47 in Chicago, Illinois. Died of cancer on 9/7/2003 (age 56). Rock singer/songwriter/pianist. Parents were Russian immigrants. Recorded with female vocalist Tule Livingston as the duo Lyme & Cybelle in 1966. Worked as the keyboardist/bandleader for The Everly Brothers, shortly before their breakup. Wrote Linda Ronstadt's "Poor Poor Pitiful Me." Recorded with three R.E.M. members as the Hindu Love Gods in 1990.	

4/22/78	**21**	6	1. Werewolves Of London
			    Fleetwood Mac's Mick Fleetwood (drums) and John McVie (bass
			    guitar); produced by Jackson Browne
				Asylum 45472

			ZHANÉ	
			Female R&B-dance vocal duo from Philadelphia, Pennsylvania: Reneé Neufville and Jean Norris. Pronounced: jah-nay.	
9/18/93	**6**	20	● 1. **Hey Mr. D.J.** Airplay #5 / Sales #6 samples "Looking Up To You" by Michael Wycoff	Flavor Unit 77177
1/29/94	**17**	14	2. Groove Thang Sales #18 / Airplay #20	Motown 2228

DATE	POS	WKS	ARTIST–RECORD TITLE	LABEL & NO.
7/30/94	40	1	3. Sending My Love *Sales #36 / Airplay #67*	Motown 2242
12/10/94	28	5	4. Shame *Airplay #31 / Sales #37* from the movie *A Low Down Dirty Shame* starring Keenan Ivory Wayans	Hollywood 42269
3/22/97	39	2	5. Request Line *Sales #30 / Airplay #66* samples "It Seems To Hang On" by Ashford & Simpson	Illtown/Motown 0614
7/17/99	10	10	● 6. **Jamboree** *Sales #4 / Airplay #58* **NAUGHTY BY NATURE (Feat. Zhané)** samples "I'm Always Dancin' To The Music" by Benny Golson	Arista 13712
			ZODIACS, The — see WILLIAMS, Maurice	
			ZOMBIES, The	
			Rock group from Hertfordshire, England: Rod Argent (keyboards), Colin Blunstone (vocals), Paul Atkinson (guitar), Chris White (bass) and Hugh Grundy (drums). Disbanded in late 1967. Rod formed Argent in 1969. Atkinson died of liver failure on 4/1/2004 (age 58).	
11/7/64	2 (1)	12	1. **She's Not There**	Parrot 9695
1/30/65	6	8	2. **Tell Her No**	Parrot 9723
2/22/69	3	11	● 3. **Time Of The Season** recorded in 1967	Date 1628
			ZZ TOP	
			Boogie-rock trio formed in Houston, Texas: Billy Gibbons (vocals, guitar), Dusty Hill (vocals, bass) and Frank Beard (drums). Gibbons had been lead guitarist in Moving Sidewalks, a Houston psychedelic-rock band. Hill and Beard had played in American Blues, based in Dallas. Group appeared in the movie *Back To The Future III*. Inducted into the Rock and Roll Hall of Fame in 2004.	
8/16/75	20	4	1. Tush	London 220
3/1/80	34	3	2. I Thank You	Warner 49163
5/7/83	37	3	3. Gimme All Your Lovin	Warner 29693
6/2/84	8	12	4. **Legs**	Warner 29272
10/26/85	8	13	5. **Sleeping Bag** *Airplay #7 / Sales #10* #1 Mainstream Rock hit (2 weeks)	Warner 28884
2/8/86	21	7	6. Stages *Airplay #16 / Sales #27* #1 Mainstream Rock hit (2 weeks)	Warner 28810
4/19/86	22	7	7. Rough Boy *Airplay #17 / Sales #25*	Warner 28733
8/30/86	35	3	8. Velcro Fly *Airplay #30*	Warner 28650

THE SONGS

Lists, alphabetically, all titles in the artist section. The artist's name is listed next to each title along with the highest position attained and year of peak popularity. Some titles show the letter "F" as a position, indicating the title was listed as a flip side and did not chart on its own. Titles which hit the Top 40 of the Airplay and Sales charts but did not hit the Hot 100 are denoted by the letters "A" (Airplay chart) and "S" (Sales chart), following their peak positions.

A song with more than one charted version is listed once, with the artists' names listed below the title in chronological order. Many songs that have the same title, but are different tunes, are listed separately, with the most popular title listed first. This will make it easy to determine which songs are the same composition, the number of charted versions of a particular song, and which of these are the most popular.

Cross references have been used throughout to aid in finding a title. Please keep the following in mind when searching for titles:

- Titles such a "I.O.U." and "SOS" will be found at the beginning of their respective letters; however, titles such as "T-R-O-U-B-L-E" and "R-O-C-K," which are spellings of words, are listed under their regular spellings.

- Two-word titles that have the *exact* same spelling as one-word titles are listed together alphabetically. ("Dream Lover" is listed directly before "Dreamlover.")

- Titles that are identical except for an apostrophized word in one of the titles are shown together. ("Lovin' You" appears immediately above "Loving You.")

POS/YR	RECORD TITLE. . .ARTIST

A

28/66	"A" Team...SSgt Barry Sadler
1/70	ABC...Jackson 5
27/01	AM To PM...Christina Milian
35/97	ATLiens...OutKast
35/00	Aaron's Party (Come Get It)...Aaron Carter
26/82	Abacab...Genesis
16/64	Abigail Beecher...Freddy Cannon
15/63	Abilene...George Hamilton IV
22A/94	About A Girl...Nirvana
31/60	About This Thing Called Love...Fabian
32/74	Abra-Ca-Dabra...DeFranco Family
1/82	Abracadabra...Steve Miller Band
	Abraham, Martin And John
4/68	Dion
33/69	Miracles
35/69	Moms Mabley
8/71	Tom Clay (medley)
26/71	Absolutely Right...Five Man Electrical Band
6/00	Absolutely (Story Of A Girl)...Ninedays
4/92	Achy Breaky Heart...Billy Ray Cyrus
18/90	Across The River...Bruce Hornsby
32/03	Act A Fool...Ludacris
13/65	Action...Freddy Cannon
20/76	Action...Sweet
7/92	Addams Groove...Hammer
1/86	Addicted To Love...Robert Palmer
9/02	Addictive...Truth Hurts
3/98	Adia...Sarah McLachlan
	Admiral Halsey ..see: Uncle Albert
8/84	Adult Education...Daryl Hall - John Oates
9/83	Affair Of The Heart...Rick Springfield
16/57	Affair To Remember (Our Love Affair)...Vic Damone
1/83	Africa...Toto
6/89	After All...Cher & Peter Cetera
18/70	After Midnight...Eric Clapton
32/57	After School...Randy Starr
23/83	After The Fall...Journey
32/82	After The Glitter Fades...Stevie Nicks
22/74	After The Goldrush...Prelude
10/56	After The Lights Go Down Low...Al Hibbler
2/79	After The Love Has Gone...Earth, Wind & Fire
8/77	After The Lovin'...Engelbert Humperdinck
6/91	After The Rain...Nelson
1/76	Afternoon Delight...Starland Vocal Band
1/93	Again...Janet Jackson
4/01	Again...Lenny Kravitz
36/92	Again Tonight...John Mellencamp
1/84	Against All Odds (Take A Look At Me Now)...Phil Collins
5/80	Against The Wind...Bob Seger
21/65	Agent Double-O-Soul...Edwin Starr
36/75	Agony And The Ecstasy...Smokey Robinson
29/81	Ah! Leah!...Donnie Iris
5/62	Ahab, The Arab...Ray Stevens

POS/YR	RECORD TITLE. . .ARTIST
28/81	Ai No Corrida...Quincy Jones
17/81	Ain't Even Done With The Night...John Cougar
12/77	Ain't Gonna Bump No More (With No Big Fat Woman)...Joe Tex
39/66	Ain't Gonna Lie...Keith
20/57	Ain't Got No Home...Clarence "Frog Man" Henry
30A/94	Ain't Got Nothing If You Ain't Got Love...Michael Bolton
24/70	Ain't It Funky Now...James Brown
1/02	Ain't It Funny...Jennifer Lopez
40/65	Ain't It True...Andy Williams
22/79	Ain't Love A Bitch...Rod Stewart
	Ain't No Mountain High Enough
19/67	Marvin Gaye & Tammi Terrell
1/70	Diana Ross
13/79	Ain't No Stoppin' Us Now...McFadden & Whitehead
3/71	Ain't No Sunshine...Bill Withers
16/68	Ain't No Way...Aretha Franklin
8/75	Ain't No Way To Treat A Lady...Helen Reddy
4/73	Ain't No Woman (Like The One I've Got)...Four Tops
22/83	Ain't Nobody...Rufus & Chaka Khan
F/96	Ain't Nobody...Monica
25/01	Ain't Nothing 'Bout You...Brooks & Dunn
	Ain't Nothing Like The Real Thing
8/68	Marvin Gaye & Tammi Terrell
21/77	Donny & Marie Osmond
20/64	Ain't Nothing You Can Do...Bobby Bland
38/95	Ain't Nuthin' But A She Thing...Salt-N-Pepa
19/64	Ain't She Sweet...Beatles
	Ain't That A Shame
1/55	Pat Boone
10/55	Fats Domino
22/63	4 Seasons
35/79	Cheap Trick
33/61	Ain't That Just Like A Woman...Fats Domino
16/64	Ain't That Loving You Baby...Elvis Presley
8/65	Ain't That Peculiar...Marvin Gaye
6/92	Ain't 2 Proud 2 Beg...TLC
	Ain't Too Proud To Beg
13/66	Temptations
17/74	Rolling Stones
21/72	Ain't Understanding Mellow...Jerry Butler & Brenda Lee Eager
3/03	Air Force Ones...Nelly
6/74	Air That I Breathe...Hollies
31/70	Airport Love Theme...Vincent Bell
	Al Di La'
6/62	Emilio Pericoli
29/64	Ray Charles Singers
14/55	Alabama Jubilee...Ferko String Band
	(Aladdin's Theme) ..see: Whole New World
	Alamo ..see: Ballad Of The
29/71	Albert Flasher...Guess Who

POS/YR	RECORD TITLE. . . ARTIST
	Alley-Oop
1/60	Hollywood Argyles
15/60	Danté & the Evergreens
24A/94	**Allison Road**...Gin Blossoms
16/99	**Almost Doesn't Count**...Brandy
32/59	**Almost Grown**...Chuck Berry
32/78	**Almost Like Being In Love**...Michael Johnson
25/84	**Almost Over You**...Sheena Easton
	Almost Paradise
15/57	Roger Williams
31/57	Lou Stein
7/84	**Almost Paradise...Love Theme From Footloose**...Mike Reno & Ann Wilson
24/66	**Almost Persuaded**...David Houston
28/78	**Almost Summer**...Celebration
1/87	**Alone**...Heart
28/97	**Alone**...Bee Gees
1/72	**Alone Again (Naturally)**...Gilbert O'Sullivan
8/60	**Alone At Last**...Jackie Wilson
	Alone (Why Must I Be Alone)
18/57	Shepherd Sisters
28/64	Four Seasons
	Along Came Jones
9/59	Coasters
27/69	Ray Stevens
14/85	**Along Comes A Woman**...Chicago
7/66	**Along Comes Mary**...Association
8/88	**Alphabet St.**...Prince
32/74	**Already Gone**...Eagles
4/90	**Alright**...Janet Jackson
19/93	**Alright**...Kris Kross
	(also see: All Right)
2/73	**Also Sprach Zarathustra (2001)**...Deodato
40/62	**Alvin Twist**...David Seville/The Chipmunks
3/59	**Alvin's Harmonica**...David Seville/The Chipmunks
33/60	**Alvin's Orchestra**...David Seville/The Chipmunks
1/87	**Always**...Atlantic Starr
4/94	**Always**...Bon Jovi
19/59	**Always**...Sammy Turner
20/94	**Always**...Erasure
	Always And Forever
18/78	Heatwave
35/90	Whistle
1/96	**Always Be My Baby**...Mariah Carey
20/94	**Always In My Heart**...Tevin Campbell
	Always On My Mind
5/82	Willie Nelson
4/88	Pet Shop Boys
1/02	**Always On Time**...Ja Rule
	Always Something There To Remind Me ..see: (There's)
30/92	**Always The Last To Know**...Del Amitri
18/68	**Always Together**...Dells
33/64	**Always Together**...Al Martino
31/98	**Am I Dreaming**...Ol' Skool
31/60	**Am I Losing You**...Jim Reeves

POS/YR	RECORD TITLE. . . ARTIST
	Am I That Easy To Forget
25/60	Debbie Reynolds
18/68	Engelbert Humperdinck
32/60	**Am I The Man**...Jackie Wilson
1/86	**Amanda**...Boston
1/00	**Amazed**...Lonestar
24/94	**Amazing**...Aerosmith
	Amazing Grace
15/71	Judy Collins
11/72	Royal Scots Dragoon Guards
37/68	**Ame Caline (Soul Coaxing)**...Raymond Lefevre
	Amen
7/65	Impressions
36/68	Otis Redding
8/81	**America**...Neil Diamond
27/72	**American City Suite**...Cashman & West
13/80	**American Dream**...Dirt Band
17/82	**American Heartbeat**...Survivor
37/03	**American Life**...Madonna
16/82	**American Music**...Pointer Sisters
	American Pie
1/72	Don McLean
29/00	Madonna
13/86	**American Storm**...Bob Seger
26/72	**American Trilogy**...Mickey Newbury
35/74	**American Tune**...Paul Simon
1/70	**American Woman**...Guess Who
	Americans
4/74	Byron MacGregor
24/74	Gordon Sinclair
27/75	**Amie**...Pure Prairie League
7/59	**Among My Souvenirs**...Connie Francis
18/61	**Amor**...Ben E. King
	(Amos & Andy Song) ..see: Like A Sunday In Salem
8/71	**Amos Moses**...Jerry Reed
38/55	**Amukiriki (The Lord Willing)**...Les Paul & Mary Ford
37/57	**Anastasia**...Pat Boone
22/67	**And Get Away**...Esquires
22/82	**And I Am Telling You I'm Not Going**...Jennifer Holliday
12/64	**And I Love Her**...Beatles
29/73	**And I Love You So**...Perry Como
F/94	**And On And On**...Janet Jackson
21/94	**And Our Feelings**...Babyface
36/65	**And Roses And Roses**...Andy Williams
37/90	**And So It Goes**...Billy Joel
	And That Reminds Me
9/57	Kay Starr
12/57	Della Reese
19/80	**And The Beat Goes On**...Whispers
21/85	**And We Danced**...Hooters
2/69	**And When I Die**...Blood, Sweat & Tears
1/01	**Angel**...Shaggy
3/88	**Angel**...Aerosmith
4/99	**Angel**...Sarah McLachlan
5/85	**Angel**...Madonna

POS/YR	RECORD TITLE. . . ARTIST
18/93	**Angel**...Jon Secada
20/73	**Angel**...Aretha Franklin
20/03	**Angel**...Amanda Perez
40/72	**Angel**...Rod Stewart
	Angel Baby
5/61	Rosie & The Originals
29/92	Angelica
30/58	**Angel Baby**...Dean Martin
5/89	**Angel Eyes**...Jeff Healey Band
	(also see: I'll Never Let You Go)
40/82	**Angel In Blue**...J. Geils Band
6/77	**Angel In Your Arms**...Hot
14/89	**Angel Of Harlem**...U2
1/99	**Angel Of Mine**...Monica
	Angel Of The Morning
7/68	Merrilee Rush
4/81	Juice Newton
22/61	**Angel On My Shoulder**...Shelby Flint
38/80	**Angel Say No**...Tommy Tutone
33/58	**Angel Smile**...Nat "King" Cole
30/89	**Angel Song**...Great White
27/60	**Angela Jones**...Johnny Ferguson
4/89	**Angelia**...Richard Marx
11/56	**Angels In The Sky**...Crew Cuts
22/59	**Angels Listened In**...Crests
1/73	**Angie**...Rolling Stones
	(also see: Different Worlds)
1/74	**Angie Baby**...Helen Reddy
38/01	**Angry All The Time**...Tim McGraw
	(Angry Young Man) ..see: Fooling Yourself
19/87	**Animal**...Def Leppard
19/99	**Animal Song**...Savage Garden
1/74	**Annie's Song**...John Denver
10/93	**Anniversary**...Tony Toni Tone
1/80	**Another Brick In The Wall**...Pink Floyd
5/71	**Another Day**...Paul McCartney
1/89	**Another Day In Paradise**...Phil Collins
27/00	**Another Dumb Blonde**...Hoku
13/88	**Another Lover**...Giant Steps
3/94	**Another Night**...Real McCoy
22/86	**Another Night**...Aretha Franklin
1/80	**Another One Bites The Dust**...Queen
32/74	**Another Park, Another Sunday**...Doobie Brothers
11/88	**Another Part Of Me**...Michael Jackson
32/76	**Another Rainy Day In New York City**...Chicago
7/93	**Another Sad Love Song**...Toni Braxton
	Another Saturday Night
10/63	Sam Cooke
6/74	Cat Stevens
22/60	**Another Sleepless Night**...Jimmy Clanton
	Another Somebody Done Somebody Wrong Song ..see: (Hey Won't You Play)
32/77	**Another Star**...Stevie Wonder
20/58	**Another Time, Another Place**...Patti Page
32/80	**Answering Machine**...Rupert Holmes
	(Anthony's Song) ..see: Movin' Out

POS/YR	RECORD TITLE. . . ARTIST
13/72	**Anticipation**...Carly Simon
21A/95	**Ants Marching**...Dave Matthews Band
	Any Day Now
23/62	Chuck Jackson
14/82	Ronnie Milsap
31/95	**Any Man Of Mine**...Shania Twain
	Any Other Way ..see: (If There Was)
2/94	**Any Time, Any Place**...Janet Jackson
14/65	**Any Way You Want It**...Dave Clark Five
23/80	**Any Way You Want It**...Journey
31/61	**Anybody But Me**...Brenda Lee
31/60	**Anymore**...Teresa Brewer
37/99	**Anyone Else**...Collin Raye
8/64	**Anyone Who Had A Heart**...Dionne Warwick
15/96	**Anything**...3T
18/94	**Anything**...SWV
28/02	**Anything**...Jaheim
1/88	**Anything For You**...Gloria Estefan
29/90	**Anything I Want**...Kevin Paige
26/91	**Anything Is Possible**...Debbie Gibson
31/62	**Anything That's Part Of You**...Elvis Presley
37/76	**Anything You Want**...John Valenti
6A/98	**Anytime**...Brian McKnight
33/76	**Anytime (I'll Be There)**...Paul Anka
12/94	**Anytime You Need A Friend**...Mariah Carey
20/56	**Anyway You Want Me (That's How I Will Be)**...Elvis Presley
15/99	**Anywhere**...112
2/61	**Apache**...Jorgen Ingmann
	Apartment ..see: Theme From The
24/56	**Ape Call**...Nervous Norvus
	Apple Blossom Time ..see: (I'll Be With You In)
29/60	**Apple Green**...June Valli
32/65	**Apple Of My Eye**...Roy Head
6/67	**Apples, Peaches, Pumpkin Pie**...Jay & The Techniques
37/69	**April Fools**...Dionne Warwick
28/56	**April In Paris**...Count Basie
1/57	**April Love**...Pat Boone
1/69	**Aquarius/Let The Sunshine In (The Flesh Failures)**...5th Dimension
29/98	**Are U Still Down**...Jon B.
15/84	**Are We Ourselves?**...Fixx
39/69	**Are You Happy**...Jerry Butler
16/03	**Are You Happy Now?**...Michelle Branch
13/98	**Are You Jimmy Ray?**...Jimmy Ray
39/67	**Are You Lonely For Me**...Freddy Scott
	Are You Lonesome To-night?
1/60	Elvis Presley
14/74	Donny Osmond
15/73	**Are You Man Enough**...Four Tops
14/70	**Are You Ready?**...Pacific Gas & Electric
10/58	**Are You Really Mine**...Jimmie Rodgers
11/56	**Are You Satisfied?**...Rusty Draper
3/58	**Are You Sincere**...Andy Williams
4A/98	**Are You That Somebody?**...Aaliyah
39/66	**Are You There (With Another Girl)**...Dionne Warwick

POS/YR	RECORD TITLE. . .ARTIST
24/01	**Area Codes**...Ludacris
26/77	**Ariel**...Dean Friedman
10/70	**Arizona**...Mark Lindsay
3/89	**Armageddon It**...Def Leppard
28/73	**Armed And Extremely Dangerous**...First Choice
36/89	**Arms Of Orion**...Prince with Sheena Easton
7/98	**Arms Of The One Who Loves You**...Xscape
9/91	**Around The Way Girl**...LL Cool J
	Around The World In 80 Days
12/57	Mantovani
13/57	Victor Young
25/57	Bing Crosby
28/01	**Around The World (La La La La La)**...ATC
29/79	**Arrow Through Me**...Wings
1/81	**Arthur's Theme (Best That You Can Do)**...Christopher Cross
20/60	**Artificial Flowers**...Bobby Darin
36/78	**As**...Stevie Wonder
6/95	**As I Lay Me Down**...Sophie B. Hawkins
10/61	**As If I Didn't Know**...Adam Wade
4A/98	**As Long As You Love Me**...Backstreet Boys
	As Tears Go By
22/65	Marianne Faithfull
6/66	Rolling Stones
31/70	**As The Years Go By**...Mashmakhan
12/64	**As Usual**...Brenda Lee
23/87	**As We Lay**...Shirley Murdock
36/96	**Ascension (Don't Ever Wonder)**...Maxwell
37/80	**Ashes By Now**...Rodney Crowell
8/61	**Asia Minor**...Kokomo
12/64	**Ask Me**...Elvis Presley
18/56	**Ask Me**...Nat "King" Cole
40/71	**Ask Me No Questions**...B.B. King
27/72	**Ask Me What You Want**...Millie Jackson
19/95	**Ask Of You**...Raphael Saadiq
24/65	**Ask The Lonely**...Four Tops
19/61	**Astronaut, The**...Jose Jimenez
30/77	**At Midnight (My Love Will Lift You Up)**...Rufus, Feat. Chaka Khan
	At My Front Door
7/55	Pat Boone
17/55	El Dorados
3/75	**At Seventeen**...Janis Ian
	(At The Copa) ..see: Copacabana
	At The Hop
1/58	Danny & The Juniors
21/58	Nick Todd
18/66	**At The Scene**...Dave Clark Five
16/67	**At The Zoo**...Simon & Garfunkel
1/87	**At This Moment**...Billy Vera & The Beaters
6/94	**At Your Best (You Are Love)**...Aaliyah
28/82	**Athena**...Who
27/81	**Atlanta Lady (Something About Your Love)**...Marty Balin
7/69	**Atlantis**...Donovan
39/80	**Atomic**...Blondie
18/66	**Attack**...Toys

POS/YR	RECORD TITLE. . .ARTIST
21/75	**Attitude Dancing**...Carly Simon
15/73	**Aubrey**...Bread
19/57	**Auctioneer**...Leroy Van Dyke
	Auld Lang Syne
7/00	Kenny G (The Millenium Mix)
2s/03	Kenny G (Freedom Mix)
	(also see: I Understand)
18/01	**Austin**...Blake Shelton
15/84	**Authority Song**...John Cougar Mellencamp
25/75	**Autobahn**...Kraftwerk
5/84	**Automatic**...Pointer Sisters
34/83	**Automatic Man**...Michael Sembello
37/72	**Automatically Sunshine**...Supremes
	Autumn Leaves
1/55	Roger Williams
35/55	Steve Allen/George Cates
19/68	**Autumn Of My Life**...Bobby Goldsboro
18/56	**Autumn Waltz**...Tony Bennett
35/97	**Avenues**...Refugee Camp All-Stars
3/85	**Axel F**...Harold Faltermeyer

B

POS/YR	RECORD TITLE. . .ARTIST
26/90	**B.B.D. (I Thought It Was Me)?**...Bell Biv DeVoe
1/79	**Babe**...Styx
4/95	**Baby**...Brandy
14/66	**B-A-B-Y**...Carla Thomas
15/02	**Baby**...Ashanti
28/03	**Baby, The**...Blake Shelton
1/91	**Baby Baby**...Amy Grant
2/92	**Baby-Baby-Baby**...TLC
8/69	**Baby, Baby Don't Cry**...Miracles
12/61	**Baby Blue**...Echoes
14/72	**Baby Blue**...Badfinger
1/03	**Baby Boy**...Beyoncé
1/78	**Baby Come Back**...Player
32/68	**Baby, Come Back**...Equals
27/74	**Baby Come Close**...Smokey Robinson
1/83	**Baby, Come To Me**...Patti Austin (with James Ingram)
33/56	**Baby Doll**...Andy Williams
1/89	**Baby Don't Forget My Number**...Milli Vanilli
1/72	**Baby Don't Get Hooked On Me**...Mac Davis
8/65	**Baby Don't Go**...Sonny & Cher
39/64	**Baby, Don't You Cry (The New Swingova Rhythm)**...Ray Charles
	Baby Don't You Do It
27/64	Marvin Gaye
34/72	Band
30/63	**Baby Don't You Weep**...Garnet Mimms
14/76	**Baby Face**...Wing & Prayer Fife & Drum Corps
1/92	**Baby Got Back**...Sir Mix-A-Lot
11/78	**Baby Hold On**...Eddie Money
35/70	**Baby Hold On**...Grass Roots
37/92	**Baby Hold On To Me**...Gerald Levert (with Eddie Levert)
26/84	**Baby I Lied**...Deborah Allen

4/67	Baby I Love You...Aretha Franklin
	Baby, I Love You
24/64	Ronettes
9/69	Andy Kim
	Baby, I Love Your Way
12/76	Peter Frampton
1/88	Will To Power (medley)
6/94	Big Mountain
	Baby I Need Your Loving
11/64	Four Tops
3/67	Johnny Rivers
3/71	Baby I'm - A Want You...Bread
25/79	Baby I'm Burnin'...Dolly Parton
14/69	Baby, I'm For Real...Originals
10/93	Baby I'm Yours...Shai
11/65	Baby, I'm Yours...Barbara Lewis
16/90	Baby, It's Tonight...Jude Cole
	Baby It's You
8/62	Shirelles
5/69	Smith
14/83	Baby Jane...Rod Stewart
29/71	Baby Let Me Kiss You...King Floyd
24/72	Baby Let Me Take You (In My Arms)...Detroit Emeralds
35/69	Baby Let's Wait...Royal Guardsmen
1/64	Baby Love...Supremes
10/86	Baby Love...Regina
25/82	Baby Makes Her Blue Jeans Talk...Dr. Hook
11/68	Baby, Now That I've Found You...Foundations
21/61	Baby Oh Baby...Shells
1/99	Baby One More Time...Britney Spears
16/66	Baby Scratch My Back...Slim Harpo
6/61	Baby Sittin' Boogie...Buzz Clifford
23/70	Baby Take Me In Your Arms...Jefferson
10/59	Baby Talk...Jan & Dean
38/80	Baby Talks Dirty...Knack
26/75	Baby That's Backatcha...Smokey Robinson
12/65	Baby The Rain Must Fall...Glenn Yarbrough
4/77	Baby, What A Big Surprise...Chicago
37/60	Baby What You Want Me To Do...Jimmy Reed
5/63	Baby Workout...Jackie Wilson
34/67	Baby You Got It...Brenton Wood
34/67	Baby You're A Rich Man...Beatles
5/60	Baby (You've Got What It Takes)...Dinah Washington & Brook Benton
26/61	Baby's First Christmas...Connie Francis
5/94	Back & Forth...Aaliyah
	Back At One
2/99	Brian McKnight
36/00	Mark Wills
7/95	Back For Good...Take That
13/00	Back Here...BBMak
5/74	Back Home Again...John Denver
37/81	Back In Black...AC/DC
	Back In Love Again ..see: (Every Time I Turn Around)
1/65	Back In My Arms Again...Supremes
26/94	Back In The Day...Ahmad

13/87	Back In The High Life Again...Steve Winwood
38/77	Back In The Saddle...Aerosmith
	Back In The U.S.A.
37/59	Chuck Berry
16/78	Linda Ronstadt
9/72	Back Off Boogaloo...Ringo Starr
34/89	Back On Holiday...Robbie Nevil
33/80	Back On My Feet Again...Babys
5/83	Back On The Chain Gang...Pretenders
36/67	Back On The Street Again...Sunshine Company
3/72	Back Stabbers...O'Jays
19/99	Back That Azz Up...Juvenile
24/99	Back 2 Good...Matchbox 20
4/89	Back To Life...Soul II Soul
36/57	Back To School Again...Timmie Rogers
14/93	Back To The Hotel...N2Deep
28/77	Back Together Again...Daryl Hall & John Oates
40/73	Back When My Hair Was Short...Gunhill Road
20/84	Back Where You Belong...38 Special
10/69	Backfield In Motion...Mel & Tim
25/66	Backstage...Gene Pitney
37/97	Backyard Boogie...Mack 10
1/87	Bad...Michael Jackson
1/73	Bad, Bad Leroy Brown...Jim Croce
1/75	Bad Blood...Neil Sedaka
8/86	Bad Boy...Miami Sound Machine
35/83	Bad Boy...Ray Parker Jr.
36/57	Bad Boy...Jive Bombers
33/01	Bad Boy For Life...P. Diddy, Black Rob & Mark Curry
8/93	Bad Boys...Inner Circle
14/79	Bad Case Of Loving You (Doctor, Doctor)...Robert Palmer
33/63	Bad Girl...Neil Sedaka
36/93	Bad Girl...Madonna
1/79	Bad Girls...Donna Summer
15/75	Bad Luck...Harold Melvin
37/60	Bad Man Blunder...Kingston Trio
1/88	Bad Medicine...Bon Jovi
2/69	Bad Moon Rising...Creedence Clearwater Revival
25/90	Bad Of The Heart...George LaMond
4/75	Bad Time...Grand Funk
9/64	Bad To Me...Billy J. Kramer
6/00	Bag Lady...Erykah Badu
1/99	Bailamos...Enrique Iglesias
2/78	Baker Street...Gerry Rafferty
3/70	Ball Of Confusion (That's What The World Is Today)...Temptations
19/69	Ball Of Fire...Tommy James
14/58	Ballad Of A Teenage Queen...Johnny Cash
7/68	Ballad Of Bonnie And Clyde...Georgie Fame
	Ballad Of Davy Crockett
1/55	Bill Hayes
5/55	"Tennessee" Ernie Ford
5/55	Fess Parker
14/55	Walter Schumann

POS/YR	RECORD TITLE. . .ARTIST
3/98	**Because Of You**...98°
27/88	**Because Of You**...Cover Girls
	Because The Night
13/78	Patti Smith Group
11/94	10,000 Maniacs
4/60	**Because They're Young**...Duane Eddy
1/96	**Because You Loved Me**...Celine Dion
10/93	**Bed Of Roses**...Bon Jovi
17/88	**Beds Are Burning**...Midnight Oil
17/62	**Beechwood 4-5789**...Marvelettes
4/98	**Been Around The World**...Puff Daddy & The Family
24/58	**Been So Long**...Pastels
24/73	**Been To Canaan**...Carole King
4/58	**Beep Beep**...Playmates
33/75	**Beer Barrel Polka**...Bobby Vinton
22/03	**Beer For My Horses**...Toby Keith w/Willie Nelson
17/65	**Before And After**...Chad & Jeremy
7/95	**Before I Let You Go**...BLACKstreet
23/78	**Before My Heart Finds Out**...Gene Cotton
1/75	**Before The Next Teardrop Falls**...Freddy Fender
7/95	**Before You Walk Out Of My Life**...Monica
29/67	**Beg, Borrow And Steal**...Ohio Express
16/67	**Beggin'**...4 Seasons
36/69	**Beginning Of My End**...Unifics
7/71	**Beginnings**...Chicago
34/71	**Behind Blue Eyes**...Who
15/73	**Behind Closed Doors**...Charlie Rich
2/81	**Being With You**...Smokey Robinson
1/99	**Believe**...Cher
13/95	**Believe**...Elton John
28/73	**Believe In Humanity**...Carole King
26/59	**Believe Me**...Royal Teens
4/58	**Believe What You Say**...Ricky Nelson
28/69	**Bella Linda**...Grassroots
34/84	**Belle Of St. Mark**...Sheila E.
12/70	**Bells, The**...Originals
13/58	**Belonging To Someone**...Patti Page
1/72	**Ben**...Michael Jackson
	Ben Casey ..see: Theme From
5/68	**Bend Me, Shape Me**...American Breed
1/74	**Bennie And The Jets**...Elton John
1/00	**Bent**...Matchbox Twenty
4/67	**Bernadette**...Four Tops
14/57	**Bernardine**...Pat Boone
16/75	**Bertha Butt Boogie**...Jimmy Castor Bunch
15/89	**Best, The**...Tina Turner
31/00	**Best Day**...George Strait
17/76	**Best Disco In Town**...Ritchie Family
34/95	**Best Friend**...Brandy
32/68	**Best Of Both Worlds**...Lulu
27/00	**Best Of Intentions**...Travis Tritt
1/77	**Best Of My Love**...Emotions
1/75	**Best Of My Love**...Eagles
3/81	**Best Of Times**...Styx

POS/YR	RECORD TITLE. . .ARTIST
39/64	**(Best Part Of) Breakin' Up**...Ronettes
3/74	**Best Thing That Ever Happened To Me**...Gladys Knight
10/92	**Best Things In Life Are Free**...Luther Vandross & Janet Jackson
	Betcha By Golly, Wow
3/72	Stylistics
31A/96	Prince
	(Betcha Got A Chick On The Side) ..see: How Long
36/87	**Betcha Say That**...Gloria Estefan
7/76	**Beth**...Kiss
1/81	**Bette Davis Eyes**...Kim Carnes
5/84	**Better Be Good To Me**...Tina Turner
F/92	**Better Days**...Bruce Springsteen
25/99	**Better Days (and the bottom drops out)**...Citizen King
18/91	**Better Love**...Londonbeat
12/80	**Better Love Next Time**...Dr. Hook
13A/95	**Better Man**...Pearl Jam
27/00	**Better Off Alone**...Alice Deejay
38/61	**Better Tell Him No**...Starlets
36/93	**Better Than You**...Lisa Keith
33/58	**Betty And Dupree**...Chuck Willis
37/58	**Betty Lou Got A New Pair Of Shoes**...Bobby Freeman
11/00	**Between Me And You**...Ja Rule
33/03	**Beware Of The Boys (Mundian To Bach Ke)**...Pan'jabi MC
40/61	**Bewildered**...James Brown
	Beyond The Sea
37/56	Roger Williams
6/60	Bobby Darin
	Bible Tells Me So
7/55	Don Cornell
22/55	Nick Noble
24/79	**Bicycle Race**...Queen
1/61	**Big Bad John**...Jimmy Dean
28A/96	**Big Bang Baby**...Stone Temple Pilots
26/58	**Big Beat**...Fats Domino
38/58	**Big Bopper's Wedding**...Big Bopper
38/67	**Big Boss Man**...Elvis Presley
23/73	**Big City Miss Ruth Ann**...Gallery
19/61	**Big Cold Wind**...Pat Boone
18/97	**Big Daddy**...Heavy D
23/00	**Big Deal**...LeAnn Rimes
21/82	**Big Fun**...Kool & The Gang
1/62	**Big Girls Don't Cry**...4 Seasons
1/59	**Big Hunk O' Love**...Elvis Presley
3/59	**Big Hurt**...Miss Toni Fisher
26/60	**Big Iron**...Marty Robbins
21/61	**Big John**...Shirelles
20/83	**Big Log**...Robert Plant
5/87	**Big Love**...Fleetwood Mac
3/58	**Big Man**...Four Preps
20/64	**Big Man In Town**...4 Seasons
13A/96	**Big Me**...Foo Fighters
18/00	**Big Pimpin'**...Jay-Z

POS/YR	RECORD TITLE. . .ARTIST
6/95	**Big Poppa**...Notorious B.I.G.
F/58	**Big River**...Johnny Cash
14/79	**Big Shot**...Billy Joel
28/03	**Big Star**...Kenny Chesney
8/87	**Big Time**...Peter Gabriel
	Big Yellow Taxi
29/70	Neighborhood
24/75	Joni Mitchell (live)
33/03	**Bigger Than My Body**...John Mayer
3/80	**Biggest Part Of Me**...Ambrosia
37/61	**Bilbao Song**...Andy Williams
	Bill Bailey ..see: Won't You Come Home
1/83	**Billie Jean**...Michael Jackson
1/99	**Bills, Bills, Bills**...Destiny's Child
7/58	**Billy**...Kathy Linden
34/66	**Billy And Sue**...B.J. Thomas
1/74	**Billy, Don't Be A Hero**...Bo Donaldson
	Billy Jack ..see: One Tin Soldier
11/58	**Bimbombey**...Jimmie Rodgers
36/85	**Bird, The**...Time
	(also see: Do The)
30/64	**Bird Dance Beat**...Trashmen
1/58	**Bird Dog**...Everly Brothers
34/58	**Bird On My Head**...David Seville
12/63	**Birdland**...Chubby Checker
3/65	**Birds And The Bees**...Jewel Akens
23/71	**Birds Of A Feather**...Raiders
17/55	**Birth Of The Boogie**...Bill Haley
26/69	**Birthday**...Underground Sunshine
40/63	**Birthday Party**...Pixies Three
36/89	**Birthday Suit**...Johnny Kemp
2/97	**Bitch**...Meredith Brooks
4/74	**Bitch Is Back**...Elton John
28/77	**Bite Your Lip (Get up and dance!)**...Elton John
4/64	**Bits And Pieces**...Dave Clark Five
36/73	**Bitter Bad**...Melanie
12/98	**Bitter Sweet Symphony**...Verve
15/01	**Bizounce**...Olivia
34/88	**Black And Blue**...Van Halen
1/72	**Black & White**...Three Dog Night
16/99	**Black Balloon**...Goo Goo Dolls
18/77	**Black Betty**...Ram Jam
1/90	**Black Cat**...Janet Jackson
	Black Denim Trousers
6/55	Cheers
38/55	Vaughn Monroe
15/72	**Black Dog**...Led Zeppelin
F/71	**Black-Eyed Blues**...Joe Cocker
37/75	**Black Friday**...Steely Dan
24A/94	**Black Hole Sun**...Soundgarden
4/66	**Black Is Black**...Los Bravos
4/71	**Black Magic Woman**...Santana
1/91	**Black Or White**...Michael Jackson
13/69	**Black Pearl**...Sonny Charles & The Checkmates, Ltd.
17/57	**Black Slacks**...Joe Bennett
21/75	**Black Superman - "Muhammad Ali"**...Johnny Wakelin

POS/YR	RECORD TITLE. . .ARTIST
1/90	**Black Velvet**...Alannah Myles
1/75	**Black Water**...Doobie Brothers
7/63	**Blame It On The Bossa Nova**...Eydie Gorme
1/89	**Blame It On The Rain**...Milli Vanilli
1/90	**Blaze Of Glory**...Jon Bon Jovi
39/64	**Bless Our Love**...Gene Chandler
15/61	**Bless You**...Tony Orlando
31/02	**Blessed**...Martina McBride
34/95	**Blessed**...Elton John
34/81	**Blessed Are The Believers**...Anne Murray
	(Blind Man In The Bleachers) ..see: Last Game Of The Season
1/77	**Blinded By The Light**...Manfred Mann's Earth Band
36/99	**Bling Bling**...B.G.
33/58	**Blob, The**...Five Blobs
35/75	**Bloody Well Right**...Supertramp
2/55	**Blossom Fell**...Nat "King" Cole
16/79	**Blow Away**...George Harrison
	Blowin' In The Wind
2/63	Peter, Paul & Mary
9/66	Stevie Wonder
35/03	**Blowin' Me Up (With Her Love)**...JC Chasez
21/70	**Blowing Away**...5th Dimension
6/91	**Blowing Kisses In The Wind**...Paula Abdul
26/96	**Blue**...LeAnn Rimes
9/60	**Blue Angel**...Roy Orbison
35/67	**Blue Autumn**...Bobby Goldsboro
	Blue Bayou
29/63	Roy Orbison
3/77	Linda Ronstadt
20/58	**Blue Blue Day**...Don Gibson
21/78	**Blue Collar Man (Long Nights)**...Styx
6/00	**Blue (Da Ba Dee)**...Eiffel 65
12/82	**Blue Eyes**...Elton John
21/75	**Blue Eyes Crying In The Rain**...Willie Nelson
37/59	**Blue Hawaii**...Billy Vaughn
8/84	**Blue Jean**...David Bowie
5/57	**Blue Monday**...Fats Domino
23/71	**Blue Money**...Van Morrison
1/61	**Blue Moon**...Marcels
15/79	**Blue Morning, Blue Day**...Foreigner
3/63	**Blue On Blue**...Bobby Vinton
	Blue Star
29/55	Felicia Sanders
F/55	Les Baxter
	Blue Suede Shoes
2/56	Carl Perkins
20/56	Elvis Presley
38/73	Johnny Rivers
16/60	**Blue Tango**...Bill Black's Combo
1/63	**Blue Velvet**...Bobby Vinton
24/64	**Blue Winter**...Connie Francis
	Blueberry Hill
29/56	Louis Armstrong & Gordon Jenkins
2/57	Fats Domino
35/75	**Bluebird**...Helen Reddy
12/78	**Bluer Than Blue**...Michael Johnson

POS/YR	RECORD TITLE. . . ARTIST
5/73	**Break Up To Make Up**...Stylistics
26/02	**Break Ya Neck**...Busta Rhymes
35/68	**Break Your Promise**...Delfonics
8/84	**Breakdance**...Irene Cara
31/71	**Breakdown, The**...Rufus Thomas
40/78	**Breakdown**...Tom Petty
15/80	**Breakdown Dead Ahead**...Boz Scaggs
5/96	**Breakfast At Tiffany's**...Deep Blue Something
22/81	**Breaking Away**...Balance
7/61	**Breakin' In A Brand New Broken Heart**...Connie Francis
6/92	**Breakin' My Heart (Pretty Brown Eyes)**...Mint Condition
9/84	**Breakin'...There's No Stopping Us**...Ollie & Jerry
	Breakin' Up ..see: (Best Part Of)
31/66	**Breakin' Up Is Breakin' My Heart**...Roy Orbison
32/97	**Breaking All The Rules**...She Moves
	Breaking Up Is Hard To Do
1/62	Neil Sedaka
34/70	Lenny Welch
28/72	Partridge Family
8/76	Neil Sedaka (new version)
18/83	**Breaking Us In Two**...Joe Jackson
15/81	**Breakup Song (They Don't Write 'Em)**...Greg Kihn Band
2/00	**Breathe**...Faith Hill
36/03	**Breathe**...Michelle Branch
3/94	**Breathe Again**...Toni Braxton
7/58	**Breathless**...Jerry Lee Lewis
34/01	**Breathless**...Corrs
8/55	**Breeze And I (Andalucia)**...Caterina Valente
19A/98	**Brick**...Ben Folds Five
5/77	**Brick House**...Commodores
	Bridge Over Troubled Water
1/70	Simon & Garfunkel
6/71	Aretha Franklin
23/03	**Bright Lights**...Matchbox Twenty
5/87	**Brilliant Disguise**...Bruce Springsteen
5/00	**Bring It All To Me**...Blaque (Feat. *NSYNC)
	Bring It On Home To Me
13/62	Sam Cooke
32/65	Animals
17/68	Eddie Floyd
29/67	**Bring It Up**...James Brown
5/03	**Bring Me To Life**...Evanescence
36/02	**Bring On The Rain**...Jo Dee Messina with Tim McGraw
12/71	**Bring The Boys Home**...Freda Payne
2/61	**Bristol Stomp**...Dovells
27/62	**Bristol Twistin' Annie**...Dovells
24/00	**Broadway**...Goo Goo Dolls
20/92	**Broken Arrow**...Rod Stewart
9/95	**Brokenhearted**...Brandy
12/79	**Broken Hearted Me**...Anne Murray
7/59	**Broken-Hearted Melody**...Sarah Vaughan
1/85	**Broken Wings**...Mr. Mister

POS/YR	RECORD TITLE. . . ARTIST
27/03	**Brokenheartsville**...Joe Nichols
1/73	**Brother Louie**...Stories
22/69	**Brother Love's Travelling Salvation Show**...Neil Diamond
32/70	**Brother Rapp**...James Brown
10/67	**Brown Eyed Girl**...Van Morrison
1/71	**Brown Sugar**...Rolling Stones
27/95	**Brown Sugar**...D'Angelo
27/85	**Bruce**...Rick Springfield
18A/95	**Buddy Holly**...Weezer
3/89	**Buffalo Stance**...Neneh Cherry
33/99	**Bug A Boo**...Destiny's Child
3/69	**Build Me Up Buttercup**...Foundations
13/97	**Building A Mystery**...Sarah McLachlan
24/60	**Bulldog**...Fireballs
22/96	**Bullet With Butterfly Wings**...Smashing Pumpkins
21/65	**Bumble Bee**...Searchers
21/61	**Bumble Boogie**...B. Bumble & The Stingers
1/03	**Bump, Bump, Bump**...B2K & P. Diddy
1/94	**Bump N' Grind**...R. Kelly
12/75	**Bungle In The Jungle**...Jethro Tull
40A/96	**Burden In My Hand**...Soundgarden
9/56	**Burn That Candle**...Bill Haley
40/81	**Burnin' For You**...Blue Öyster Cult
3/60	**Burning Bridges**...Jack Scott
34/71	**Burning Bridges**...Mike Curb Congregation
9/83	**Burning Down The House**...Talking Heads
2/86	**Burning Heart**...Survivor
39/83	**Burning Heart**...Vandenberg
2/72	**Burning Love**...Elvis Presley
5/66	**Bus Stop**...Hollies
17/56	**Bus Stop Song (A Paper Of Pins)**...Four Lads
7/89	**Bust A Move**...Young MC
25/63	**Bust Out**...Busters
4/63	**Busted**...Ray Charles
34/79	**Bustin' Loose**...Chuck Brown
36A/96	**But Anyway**...Blues Traveler
37/01	**But For The Grace Of God**...Keith Urban
4/61	**But I Do**...Clarence Henry
22/66	**But It's Alright**...J.J. Jackson
19/69	**But You Know I Love You**...First Edition
15/65	**But You're Mine**...Sonny & Cher
16/97	**Butta Love**...Next
29/75	**Butter Boy**...Fanny
14/02	**Butterflies**...Michael Jackson
	Butterfly
1/57	Charlie Gracie
1/57	Andy Williams
1/01	**Butterfly**...Crazy Town
16A/97	**Butterfly**...Mariah Carey
23/63	**Butterfly Baby**...Bobby Rydell
	Butterfly Kisses
10A/97	Bob Carlisle
22/97	Raybon Bros.
40/00	**Buy Me A Rose**...Kenny Rogers
11/58	**Buzz-Buzz-Buzz**...Hollywood Flames

POS/YR	RECORD TITLE. . . ARTIST
	By The Time I Get To Phoenix
26/67	Glen Campbell
37/69	Isaac Hayes
25/93	**By The Time This Night Is Over**...Kenny G
	with Peabo Bryson
34/02	**By The Way**...Red Hot Chili Peppers
12/65	**Bye, Bye, Baby (Baby, Goodbye)**...4 Seasons
4/00	**Bye Bye Bye**...*NSYNC
2/57	**Bye Bye Love**...Everly Brothers

C

POS/YR	RECORD TITLE. . . ARTIST
12/97	**C U When U Get There**...Coolio
	C.C. Rider
12/57	Chuck Willis
34/63	LaVern Baker
10/66	Animals
	(also see: Jenny Take A Ride)
2/87	**C'est La Vie**...Robbie Nevil
9/99	**C'est La Vie**...B*Witched
11/55	**C'est La Vie**...Sarah Vaughan
22/61	**C'est Si Bon (It's So Good)**...Conway Twitty
	C'mon ..see: Come On
22/57	**Ca, C'est L'amour**...Tony Bennett
23/68	**Cab Driver**...Mills Brothers
22/62	**Cajun Queen**...Jimmy Dean
1/61	**Calcutta**...Lawrence Welk
4/61	**Calendar Girl**...Neil Sedaka
4/66	**California Dreamin'**...Mama's & The Papa's
	California Girls
3/65	Beach Boys
3/85	David Lee Roth
6/96	**California Love**...2Pac
16/67	**California Nights**...Lesley Gore
25/69	**California Soul**...5th Dimension
5/64	**California Sun**...Rivieras
18/89	**Call It Love**...Poco
1/80	**Call Me**...Blondie
13/70	**Call Me**...Aretha Franklin
21/58	**Call Me**...Johnny Mathis
22/66	**Call Me**...Chris Montez
26/82	**Call Me**...Skyy
31/02	**Call Me**...Tweet
35/97	**Call Me**...Le Click
10/73	**Call Me (Come Back Home)**...Al Green
40/68	**Call Me Lightning**...Who
19/62	**Call Me Mr. In-Between**...Burl Ives
6/74	**Call On Me**...Chicago
22/63	**Call On Me**...Bobby Bland
15/85	**Call To The Heart**...Giuffria
21/00	**Callin' Me**...Lil' Zane
19/03	**Calling All Angels**...Train
18/86	**Calling America**...Electric Light Orchestra
16/77	**Calling Dr. Love**...Kiss
32/77	**Calling Occupants Of Interplanetary Craft**...Carpenters
2/75	**Calypso**...John Denver

POS/YR	RECORD TITLE. . . ARTIST
5/69	**Can I Change My Mind**...Tyrone Davis
19/99	**Can I Get A......**Jay-Z
	Can I Get A Witness
22/63	Marvin Gaye
39/71	Lee Michaels
15/57	**Can I Steal A Little Love**...Frank Sinatra
27/95	**Can I Touch You...There?**...Michael Bolton
31/74	**Can This Be Real**...Natural Four
	(Can We Rock?) ..see: What's Up Doc?
29/78	**Can We Still Be Friends**...Todd Rundgren
9/94	**Can We Talk**...Tevin Campbell
4/94	**Can You Feel The Love Tonight**...Elton John
16/56	**Can You Find It In Your Heart**...Tony Bennett
38/78	**Can You Fool**...Glen Campbell
1/64	**Can't Buy Me Love**...Beatles
36/95	**Can't Cry Anymore**...Sheryl Crow
25/01	**Can't Deny It**...Fabolous
11/02	**Can't Fight The Moonlight**...LeAnn Rimes
1/85	**Can't Fight This Feeling**...REO Speedwagon
5/74	**Can't Get Enough**...Bad Company
27A/98	**Can't Get Enough Of You Baby**...Smash Mouth
	Can't Get Enough Of Your Love, Babe
1/74	Barry White
20/93	Taylor Dayne
9/75	**Can't Get It Out Of My Head**...Electric Light Orchestra
2/63	**Can't Get Used To Losing You**...Andy Williams
7/02	**Can't Get You Out Of My Head**...Kylie Minogue
	Can't Help Falling In Love
2/62	Elvis Presley
24/87	Corey Hart
1/93	UB40
39/76	**Can't Hide Love**...Earth, Wind & Fire
12/03	**Can't Hold Us Down**...Christina Aguilera
2/92	**Can't Let Go**...Mariah Carey
4/03	**Can't Let You Go**...Fabolous
1/90	**(Can't Live Without Your) Love And Affection**...Nelson
1/97	**Can't Nobody Hold Me Down**...Puff Daddy
29/83	**Can't Shake Loose**...Agnetha Fältskog
3/78	**Can't Smile Without You**...Barry Manilow
6/88	**Can't Stay Away From You**...Gloria Estefan
6/90	**Can't Stop**...After 7
13/77	**Can't Stop Dancin'**...Captain & Tennille
12/90	**Can't Stop Fallin' Into Love**...Cheap Trick
30/95	**Can't Stop Lovin' You**...Van Halen
25/70	**Can't Stop Loving You**...Tom Jones
2/91	**Can't Stop This Thing We Started**...Bryan Adams
14/03	**Can't Stop, Won't Stop**...Young Gunz
	Can't Take My Eyes Off You
2/67	Frankie Valli
7/68	Lettermen (medley)
35A/98	Lauryn Hill
6/87	**Can't We Try**...Dan Hill (with Vonda Sheppard)
2/65	**Can't You Hear My Heartbeat**...Herman's Hermits

POS/YR	RECORD TITLE. . .ARTIST
13/95	**Can't You See**...Total
4/64	**Can't You See That She's Mine**...Dave Clark Five
20/87	**Can'tcha Say (You Believe In Me)/Still In Love**...Boston
	Canadian Sunset
2/56	Hugo Winterhalter/Eddie Heywood
7/56	Andy Williams
3/70	**Candida**...Dawn
	Candle In The Wind
6/88	Elton John
1/97	Elton John (1997)
	(Candles In The Rain) ..see: Lay Down
21/87	**Candy**...Cameo
28/91	**Candy**...Iggy Pop
3/63	**Candy Girl**...Four Seasons
1/72	**Candy Man**...Sammy Davis, Jr.
25/61	**Candy Man**...Roy Orbison
2/95	**Candy Rain**...Soul For Real
15/58	**Cannonball**...Duane Eddy
28/85	**Cannonball**...Supertramp
9/94	**Cantaloop**...US3
16/86	**Captain Of Her Heart**...Double
1/77	**Car Wash**...Rose Royce
39/65	**Cara-Lin**...Strangeloves
	Cara Mia
10/54	David Whitfield with Mantovani
4/65	Jay & The Americans
18/02	**Caramel**...City High
10/74	**Carefree Highway**...Gordon Lightfoot
1/85	**Careless Whisper**...Wham!
27/59	**Caribbean**...Mitchell Torok
1/84	**Caribbean Queen (No More Love On The Run)**...Billy Ocean
10/95	**Carnival**...Natalie Merchant
18/58	**Carol**...Chuck Berry
21/75	**Carolina In The Pines**...Michael Murphey
32/66	**Caroline, No**...Brian Wilson
29/68	**Carpet Man**...5th Dimension
3/87	**Carrie**...Europe
34/80	**Carrie**...Cliff Richard
9/67	**Carrie-Anne**...Hollies
26/69	**Carry Me Back**...Rascals
11/77	**Carry On Wayward Son**...Kansas
9/80	**Cars**...Gary Numan
5/87	**Casanova**...Levert
2/00	**Case Of The Ex (Whatcha Gonna Do)**...Mya
27/67	**Casino Royale**...Herb Alpert
	Cast Your Fate To The Wind
22/63	Vince Guaraldi Trio
10/65	Sounds Orchestral
	Castles In The Air
F/72	Don McLean
36/81	Don McLean
25/56	**Casual Look**...Six Teens
26/67	**Cat In The Window (The Bird In The Sky)**...Petula Clark
30/77	**Cat Scratch Fever**...Ted Nugent

POS/YR	RECORD TITLE. . .ARTIST
	Cat's In The Cradle
1/74	Harry Chapin
6/93	Ugly Kid Joe
1/58	**Catch A Falling Star**...Perry Como
8/87	**Catch Me (I'm Falling)**...Pretty Poison
40/84	**Catch Me I'm Falling**...Real Life
23/65	**Catch The Wind**...Donovan
4/65	**Catch Us If You Can**...Dave Clark Five
23/62	**Caterina**...Perry Como
1/60	**Cathy's Clown**...Everly Brothers
	Cats In The Cradle ..see: Cat's
37/87	**Caught Up In The Rapture**...Anita Baker
10/82	**Caught Up In You**...38 Special
2/87	**Causing A Commotion**...Madonna
	(Cave Man) ..see: Troglodyte
4/70	**Cecilia**...Simon & Garfunkel
15/70	**Celebrate**...Three Dog Night
26/85	**Celebrate Youth**...Rick Springfield
1/81	**Celebration**...Kool & The Gang
31/03	**Celebrity**...Brad Paisley
39/95	**Cell Therapy**...Goodie Mob.
1/82	**Centerfold**...J. Geils Band
24/84	**Centipede**...Rebbie Jackson
14/58	**Certain Smile**...Johnny Mathis
23/58	**Cerveza**...Boots Brown
10/62	**Cha-Cha-Cha**...Bobby Rydell
34/58	**Cha-Hua-Hua**...Pets
2/60	**Chain Gang**...Sam Cooke
13/56	**Chain Gang**...Bobby Scott
2/68	**Chain Of Fools**...Aretha Franklin
40/00	**Chain Of Love**...Clay Walker
32/68	**Chained**...Marvin Gaye
17/62	**Chains**...Cookies
38/96	**Chains**...Tina Arena
10/56	**Chains Of Love**...Pat Boone
12/88	**Chains Of Love**...Erasure
20A/96	**Champagne Supernova**...Oasis
1/57	**Chances Are**...Johnny Mathis
27/92	**Change**...Lisa Stansfield
10/03	**Change Clothes**...Jay-Z
31/65	**Change Is Gonna Come**...Sam Cooke
3/87	**Change Of Heart**...Cyndi Lauper
19/78	**Change Of Heart**...Eric Carmen
21/83	**Change Of Heart**...Tom Petty
5/96	**Change The World**...Eric Clapton
19A/97	**Change Would Do You Good**...Sheryl Crow
32/99	**Changes**...2Pac
37/77	**Changes In Latitudes, Changes In Attitudes**...Jimmy Buffett
	Chanson D'Amour (Song Of Love)
6/58	Art & Dotty Todd
12/58	Fontane Sisters
10/99	**Chanté's Got A Man**...Chanté Moore
19/57	**Chantez-Chantez**...Dinah Shore
6/58	**Chantilly Lace**...Big Bopper

POS/YR	RECORD TITLE. . .ARTIST
	Chanukah Song
10A/95	Adam Sandler
25A/97	Adam Sandler
	Chapel In The Moonlight
32/65	Bachelors
25/67	Dean Martin
1/64	**Chapel Of Love**...Dixie Cups
	Charade
36/64	Sammy Kaye
36/64	Henry Mancini
1/82	**Chariots Of Fire - Titles**...Vangelis
40/71	**Charity Ball**...Fanny
2/59	**Charlie Brown**...Coasters
13/63	**Charms**...Bobby Vee
33/79	**Chase**...Giorgio Moroder
39/91	**Chasin' The Wind**...Chicago
	Chattanooga Choo Choo
36/62	Floyd Cramer
32/78	Tuxedo Junction
34/60	**Chattanooga Shoe Shine Boy**...Freddy Cannon
15/73	**Cheaper To Keep Her**...Johnnie Taylor
12/66	**Cheater, The**...Bob Kuban
14/88	**Check It Out**...John Cougar Mellencamp
35/73	**Check It Out**...Tavares
28/70	**Check Out Your Mind**...Impressions
20/93	**Check Yo Self**...Ice Cube
12/55	**Chee Chee-oo Chee (Sang the Little Bird)**...Perry Como & Jaye P. Morgan
38/98	**Cheers 2 U**...Playa
32/78	**Cheeseburger In Paradise**...Jimmy Buffett
	Cherchez La Femme ..see: Whispering
	Cherish
1/66	Association
9/71	David Cassidy
2/85	**Cherish**...Kool & The Gang
2/89	**Cherish**...Madonna
33/77	**Cherry Baby**...Starz
8/88	**Cherry Bomb**...John Cougar Mellencamp
	Cherry, Cherry
6/66	Neil Diamond
31/73	Neil Diamond (Live)
15/69	**Cherry Hill Park**...Billy Joe Royal
10/90	**Cherry Pie**...Warrant
11/60	**Cherry Pie**...Skip & Flip
	Cherry Pink And Apple Blossom White
1/55	Perez Prado
14/55	Alan Dale
5/75	**Chevy Van**...Sammy Johns
15/68	**Chewy Chewy**...Ohio Express
35/71	**Chicago**...Graham Nash
9/71	**Chick-A-Boom (Don't Ya Jes' Love It)**...Daddy Dewdrop
31/67	**Child Of Clay**...Jimmie Rodgers
F/95	**Childhood**...Michael Jackson
21/96	**Children**...Robert Miles
13/90	**Children Of The Night**...Richard Marx
	Children's Marching Song
13/59	Cyril Stapleton
16/59	Mitch Miller

POS/YR	RECORD TITLE. . .ARTIST
38/60	**China Doll**...Ames Brothers
10/83	**China Girl**...David Bowie
15/73	**China Grove**...Doobie Brothers
10/62	**Chip Chip**...Gene McDaniels
	Chipmunk Song
1/58	David Seville/The Chipmunks
39/61	David Seville/The Chipmunks
40/62	David Seville/The Chipmunks
29/80	**Chiquitita**...Abba
20/71	**Chirpy Chirpy Cheep Cheep**...Mac & Katie Kissoon
34/81	**Chloe**...Elton John
21/69	**Choice Of Colors**...Impressions
13/69	**Chokin' Kind**...Joe Simon
26/68	**Choo Choo Train**...Box Tops
23/94	**Choose**...Color Me Badd
F/55	**Chop Chop Boom**...Crew-Cuts
25/77	**Christine Sixteen**...Kiss
18/99	**Christmas Song (Chestnuts Roasting On An Open Fire)**...Christina Aguilera
4/79	**Chuck E.'s In Love**...Rickie Lee Jones
9/64	**Chug-A-Lug**...Roger Miller
14/56	**Church Bells May Ring**...Diamonds
10/83	**Church Of The Poison Mind**...Culture Club
36/92	**Church Of Your Heart**...Roxette
24/59	**Ciao, Ciao Bambina (Chiow, Chiow, Bambeena)**...Jacky Noguez
	Cinco Robles (Five Oaks)
22/57	Russell Arms
35/57	Les Paul & Mary Ford
16/62	**Cinderella**...Jack Ross
34/77	**Cinderella**...Firefall
	Cindy, Oh Cindy
9/56	Vince Martin/The Tarriers
10/56	Eddie Fisher
8/62	**Cindy's Birthday**...Johnny Crawford
11/69	**Cinnamon**...Derek
25/63	**Cinnamon Cinder (It's A Very Nice Dance)**...Pastel Six
7/88	**Circle In The Sand**...Belinda Carlisle
33/78	**Circle Is Small (I Can See It In Your Eyes)**...Gordon Lightfoot
18/94	**Circle Of Life**...Elton John
38/82	**Circles**...Atlantic Starr
2/73	**Cisco Kid**...War
23/69	**Cissy Strut**...Meters
18/85	**C-I-T-Y**...John Cafferty
19/56	**City Of Angels**...Highlights
18/72	**City Of New Orleans**...Arlo Guthrie
2/72	**Clair**...Gilbert O'Sullivan
	Clam ..see: Do The
6/74	**Clap For The Wolfman**...Guess Who
	Clapping Song (Clap Pat Clap Slap)
8/65	Shirley Ellis
36/83	Pia Zadora
38/59	**Class, The**...Chubby Checker
2/68	**Classical Gas**...Mason Williams
30/58	**Claudette**...Everly Brothers

POS/YR	RECORD TITLE. . .ARTIST
30/59	**Come To Me**...Marv Johnson
25/94	**Come To My Window**...Melissa Etheridge
37/67	**Come To The Sunshine**...Harpers Bizarre
	Come Together
1/69	Beatles
23/78	Aerosmith
7/93	**Come Undone**...Duran Duran
4/98	**Come With Me**...Puff Daddy
30/95	**Comedown**...Bush
10/93	**Comforter**...Shai
20/89	**Coming Home**...Cinderella
36/62	**Comin' Home Baby**...Mel Torme
11/82	**Comin' In And Out Of Your Life**...Barbra Streisand
11/66	**Coming On Strong**...Brenda Lee
18/87	**Coming Around Again**...Carly Simon
11/67	**Coming Home Soldier**...Bobby Vinton
1/91	**Coming Out Of The Dark**...Gloria Estefan
1/80	**Coming Up**...Paul McCartney
30/69	**Commotion**...Creedence Clearwater Revival
34/85	**Communication**...Power Station
32/94	**Completely**...Michael Bolton
2/02	**Complicated**...Avril Lavigne
27/69	**Composer, The**...Supremes
	Concrete And Clay
28/65	Unit Four plus Two
35/65	Eddie Rambeau
17/56	**Confidential**...Sonny Knight
37/79	**Confusion**...Electric Light Orchestra
10/86	**Conga**...Miami Sound Machine
20/93	**Connected**...Stereo MC's
16/72	**Conquistador**...Procol Harum
11/62	**Conscience**...James Darren
38/92	**Constant Craving**...k.d. lang
16/95	**Constantly**...Immature
19/01	**Contagious**...Isley Brothers
33/61	**Continental Walk**...Hank Ballard **(also see: Do The New)**
5/87	**Control**...Janet Jackson
8/72	**Convention '72**...Delegates
1/76	**Convoy**...C.W. McCall
32/73	**Cook With Honey**...Judy Collins
29/71	**Cool Aid**...Paul Humphrey
10/80	**Cool Change**...Little River Band
4/85	**Cool It Now**...New Edition
7/66	**Cool Jerk**...Capitols
13/81	**Cool Love**...Pablo Cruise
11/82	**Cool Night**...Paul Davis
12/57	**Cool Shake**...Del Vikings
8/78	**Copacabana (At The Copa)**...Barry Manilow
37/73	**Corazón**...Carole King
9/61	**Corinna, Corinna**...Ray Peterson
18/72	**Corner Of The Sky**...Jackson 5
15/64	**Cotton Candy**...Al Hirt
25/95	**Cotton Eye Joe**...Rednex
13/62	**Cotton Fields**...Highwaymen
33/80	**Could I Have This Dance**...Anne Murray

POS/YR	RECORD TITLE. . .ARTIST
26/01	**Could It Be**...Jaheim
37/72	**Could It Be Forever**...David Cassidy
4/73	**Could It Be I'm Falling In Love**...Spinners
6/75	**Could It Be Magic**...Barry Manilow
11/90	**Could This Be Love**...Seduction
23/57	**Could This Be Magic**...Dubs
1/88	**Could've Been**...Tiffany
3/77	**Couldn't Get It Right**...Climax Blues Band
35/61	**Count Every Star**...Donnie & The Dreamers
2/65	**Count Me In**...Gary Lewis
8/78	**Count On Me**...Jefferson Starship
8/96	**Count On Me**...Whitney Houston & CeCe Winans
5/55	**Count Your Blessings (Instead of Sheep)**...Eddie Fisher
15/96	**Counting Blue Cars**...Dishwalla
25/60	**Country Boy**...Fats Domino
11/76	**Country Boy (You Got Your Feet In L.A.)**...Glen Campbell
36/68	**Country Girl - City Man**...Billy Vera & Judy Clay
37/71	**Country Road**...James Taylor
11/91	**Couple Days Off**...Huey Lewis
25/68	**Court Of Love**...Unifics
25/02	**Courtesy Of The Red, White And Blue (The Angry American)**...Toby Keith
31/64	**Cousin Of Mine**...Sam Cooke
2/89	**Cover Girl**...New Kids On The Block
7/84	**Cover Me**...Bruce Springsteen
31/89	**Cover Of Love**...Michael Damian
6/73	**Cover Of "Rolling Stone"**...Dr. Hook
3/80	**Coward Of The County**...Kenny Rogers
33/02	**Cowboy In Me**...Tim McGraw
27/00	**Cowboy Take Me Away**...Dixie Chicks
38/03	**Cowboys Like Us**...George Strait
6/68	**Cowboys To Girls**...Intruders
8/72	**Cowboys Work Is Never Done**...Sonny & Chér
19/77	**Crackerbox Palace**...George Harrison
1/70	**Cracklin' Rosie**...Neil Diamond
2/90	**Cradle Of Love**...Billy Idol
7/60	**Cradle Of Love**...Johnny Preston
24/00	**Crash And Burn**...Savage Garden
19A/97	**Crash Into Me**...Dave Matthews Band
7/91	**Crazy**...Seal
9/61	**Crazy**...Patsy Cline
11/01	**Crazy**...K-Ci & JoJo
14/88	**Crazy**...Icehouse
17/94	**Crazy**...Aerosmith
29/90	**Crazy**...Boys
F/58	**Crazy**...Hollywood Flames **(also see: You Drive Me)**
11/89	**Crazy About Her**...Rod Stewart
36/60	**Crazy Arms**...Bob Beckham
	Crazy Downtown ..see: Downtown
40/58	**Crazy Eyes For You**...Bobby Hamilton
15/01	**Crazy For This Girl**...Evan & Jaron
1/85	**Crazy For You**...Madonna

POS/YR	RECORD TITLE. . . ARTIST
14/72	**Crazy Horses**...Osmonds
1/03	**Crazy In Love**...Beyoncé
15/85	**Crazy In The Night (Barking At Airplanes)**...Kim Carnes
	Crazy Little Mama ..see: At My Front Door
1/80	**Crazy Little Thing Called Love**...Queen
15/58	**Crazy Love**...Paul Anka
17/79	**Crazy Love**...Poco
29/79	**Crazy Love**...Allman Brothers Band
22/72	**Crazy Mama**...J.J. Cale
35/76	**Crazy On You**...Heart
2/55	**Crazy Otto (medley)**...Johnny Maddox
1/91	**Cream**...Prince
1/95	**Creep**...TLC
34/93	**Creep**...Radiohead
5/67	**Creeque Alley**...Mamas & The Papas
16/71	**Cried Like A Baby**...Bobby Sherman
21/97	**Criminal**...Fiona Apple
	Crimson And Clover
1/69	Tommy James
7/82	Joan Jett
16/55	**Croce Di Oro (Cross Of Gold)**...Patti Page
1/73	**Crocodile Rock**...Elton John
	(Crooked Little Man) ..see: Don't Let The Rain Come Down
7/87	**Cross My Broken Heart**...Jets
	Cross Of Gold ..see: Croce Di Oro
19/63	**Cross Fire!**...Orlons
23/59	**Crossfire**...Johnny & The Hurricanes
1/96	**Crossroads, Tha**...Bone thugs-n-harmony
28/69	**Crossroads**...Cream
26/62	**Crowd, The**...Roy Orbison
	Cruel Summer
9/84	Bananarama
10/98	Ace Of Base
12/79	**Cruel To Be Kind**...Nick Lowe
4/80	**Cruisin'**...Smokey Robinson
29/90	**Cruising For Bruising**...Basia
9/83	**Crumblin' Down**...John Cougar Mellencamp
F/72	**Crunchy Granola Suite**...Neil Diamond
3/98	**Crush**...Jennifer Paige
3/86	**Crush On You**...Jets
10/89	**Cry**...Waterfront
16/85	**Cry**...Godley & Creme
18/66	**Cry**...Ronnie Dove
33/02	**Cry**...Faith Hill
4/63	**Cry Baby**...Garnet Mimms
18/56	**Cry Baby**...Bonnie Sisters
28/00	**Crybaby**...Mariah Carey
38/62	**Cry Baby Cry**...Angels
7/91	**Cry For Help**...Rick Astley
15/94	**Cry For You**...Jodeci
2/68	**Cry Like A Baby**...Box Tops
3/03	**Cry Me A River**...Justin Timberlake
	Cry Me A River
9/55	Julie London
11/70	Joe Cocker
23/63	**Cry To Me**...Betty Harris

POS/YR	RECORD TITLE. . . ARTIST
12/93	**Cryin'**...Aerosmith
22/89	**Cryin'**...Vixen
	Crying
2/61	Roy Orbison
25/66	Jay & The Americans
5/81	Don McLean
15/93	**Crying Game**...Boy George
3/65	**Crying In The Chapel**...Elvis Presley
6/62	**Crying In The Rain**...Everly Brothers
6/66	**Crying Time**...Ray Charles
2/69	**Crystal Blue Persuasion**...Tommy James
25/89	**Cuddly Toy (Feel For Me)**...Roachford
13/89	**Cult Of Personality**...Living Colour
5/83	**Cum On Feel The Noize**...Quiet Riot
39/96	**Cumbersome**...Seven Mary Three
	Cupid
17/61	Sam Cooke
39/70	Johnny Nash
22/76	Tony Orlando & Dawn
4/80	Spinners (medley)
13/97	**Cupid**...112
	Curious Mind ..see: Um, Um, Um, Um, Um, Um
15/84	**Curly Shuffle**...Jump 'N The Saddle
10/75	**Cut The Cake**...AWB
15/83	**Cuts Like A Knife**...Bryan Adams
23/68	**Cycles**...Frank Sinatra

D

POS/YR	RECORD TITLE. . . ARTIST
19/68	**D. W. Washburn**...Monkees
20/73	**D'yer Mak'er**...Led Zeppelin
36/71	**D.O.A.**...Bloodrock
35/88	**Da'Butt**...E.U.
15/97	**Da' Dip**...Freak Nasty
	Da Doo Ron Ron
3/63	Crystals
1/77	Shaun Cassidy
1/79	**Da Ya Think I'm Sexy?**...Rod Stewart
F/57	**Daddy Cool**...Rays
19/73	**Daddy Could Swear, I Declare**...Gladys Knight
4/72	**Daddy Don't You Walk So Fast**...Wayne Newton
	Daddy-O
11/55	Fontane Sisters
14/55	Bonnie Lou
	Daddy's Home
2/61	Shep & The Limelites
9/73	Jermaine Jackson
23/82	Cliff Richard
34/69	**Daddy's Little Man**...O.C. Smith
14/73	**Daisy A Day**...Jud Strunk
20/75	**Daisy Jane**...America
15/64	**Daisy Petal Pickin'**...Jimmy Gilmer/Fireballs
4/03	**Damn!**...Youngbloodz
5/92	**Damn I Wish I Was Your Lover**...Sophie B. Hawkins
27/79	**Damned If I Do**...Alan Parsons Project

POS/YR	RECORD TITLE. . .ARTIST
38/78	**Dance Across The Floor**...Jimmy "Bo" Horne
8/64	**Dance, Dance, Dance**...Beach Boys
6/78	**Dance, Dance, Dance (Yowsah, Yowsah, Yowsah)**...Chic
19/78	**Dance (Disco Heat)**...Sylvester
31/58	**Dance Everyone Dance**...Betty Madigan
16/84	**Dance Hall Days**...Wang Chung
30/88	**Dance Little Sister**...Terence Trent D'Arby
10/61	**Dance On Little Girl**...Paul Anka
19/58	**Dance Only With Me**...Perry Como
24/61	**(Dance The) Mess Around**...Chubby Checker
15/79	**Dance The Night Away**...Van Halen
23/58	**Dance To The Bop**...Gene Vincent
8/68	**Dance To The Music**...Sly & The Family Stone
36/00	**Dance Tonight**...Lucy Pearl
39/76	**Dance Wit Me**...Rufus Feat. Chaka Khan
6/75	**Dance With Me**...Orleans
8/78	**Dance With Me**...Peter Brown with Betty Wright
8/01	**Dance With Me**...Debelah Morgan
15/59	**Dance With Me**...Drifters
39/01	**Dance With Me**...112
1/55	**Dance With Me Henry (Wallflower)**...Georgia Gibbs
38/03	**Dance With My Father**...Luther Vandross
12/62	**(Dance With The) Guitar Man**...Duane Eddy
19/00	**Dancin'**...Guy
28/75	**Dancin' Fool**...Guess Who
23/77	**Dancin' Man**...Q
12/62	**Dancin' Party**...Chubby Checker
18/79	**Dancin' Shoes**...Nigel Olsson
2/84	**Dancing In The Dark**...Bruce Springsteen
13/73	**Dancing In The Moonlight**...King Harvest
17/84	**Dancing In The Sheets**...Shalamar
	Dancing In The Street
2/64	Martha & The Vandellas
38/82	Van Halen
7/85	Mick Jagger/David Bowie
2/74	**Dancing Machine**...Jackson 5
2/86	**Dancing On The Ceiling**...Lionel Richie
1/77	**Dancing Queen**...Abba
14/67	**Dandelion**...Rolling Stones
5/66	**Dandy**...Herman's Hermits
7/64	**Dang Me**...Roger Miller
14/01	**Danger (Been So Long)**...Mystikal
12/55	**Danger! Heartbreak Ahead**...Jaye P. Morgan
2/86	**Danger Zone**...Kenny Loggins
2/90	**Dangerous**...Roxette
9/98	**Dangerous**...Busta Rhymes
25/66	**Dangling Conversation**...Simon & Garfunkel
	Dangling On A String ..see: (You've Got Me)
2/73	**Daniel**...Elton John
13/63	**Danke Schoen**...Wayne Newton
10/59	**Danny Boy**...Conway Twitty
7/73	**Danny's Song**...Anne Murray
11/85	**Dare Me**...Pointer Sisters
32/90	**Dare To Fall In Love**...Brent Bourgeois

POS/YR	RECORD TITLE. . .ARTIST
15/75	**Dark Horse**...George Harrison
1/74	**Dark Lady**...Chér
	Dark Moon
4/57	Gale Storm
6/57	Bonnie Guitar
19/68	**Darlin'**...Beach Boys
15/67	**Darling Be Home Soon**...Lovin' Spoonful
7/55	**Darling Je Vous Aime Beaucoup**...Nat "King" Cole
F/57	**Date With The Blues**...Billy Williams
13/70	**Daughter Of Darkness**...Tom Jones
	Davy Crockett ..see: Ballad Of
3/64	**Dawn (Go Away)**...Four Seasons
36/65	**Dawn Of Correction**...Spokesmen
4/72	**Day After Day**...Badfinger
13/72	**Day By Day**...Godspell
18/86	**Day By Day**...Hooters
5/72	**Day Dreaming**...Aretha Franklin
35/66	**Day For Decision**...Johnny Sea
23/72	**Day I Found Myself**...Honey Cone
21/87	**Day-In Day-Out**...David Bowie
21/69	**Day Is Done**...Peter, Paul & Mary
	Day-O ..see: Banana Boat
	Day The Rains Came
21/58	Jane Morgan
30/58	Raymond Lefevre
17/99	**Day The World Went Away**...Nine Inch Nails
5/66	**Day Tripper**...Beatles
23/77	**Daybreak**...Barry Manilow
39/74	**Daybreak**...Nilsson
2/66	**Daydream**...Lovin' Spoonful
	Daydream Believer
1/67	Monkees
12/80	Anne Murray
6/98	**Daydreamin'**...Tatyana Ali
14/02	**Days Go By**...Dirty Vegas
17/79	**Days Gone Down (Still Got The Light In Your Eyes)**...Gerry Rafferty
39A/96	**Days Of Our Livez**...Bone Thugs-N-Harmony
34/69	**Days Of Sand And Shovels**...Bobby Vinton
	Days Of Wine And Roses
26/63	Andy Williams
33/63	Henry Mancini
28/77	**Daytime Friends**...Kenny Rogers
3/77	**Dazz**...Brick
12/93	**Dazzey Duks**...Duice
10/81	**De Do Do Do, De Da Da Da**...Police
19/78	**Deacon Blues**...Steely Dan
29/67	**Dead End Street**...Lou Rawls
22/83	**Dead Giveaway**...Shalamar
8/64	**Dead Man's Curve**...Jan & Dean
16/73	**Dead Skunk**...Loudon Wainwright III
30/90	**Deadbeat Club**...B-52's
	Dear Heart
24/65	Andy Williams
30/65	Jack Jones
24/62	**Dear Ivan**...Jimmy Dean
9/62	**Dear Lady Twist**...Gary (U.S.) Bonds

POS/YR	RECORD TITLE. . .ARTIST
13/62	**Dear Lonely Hearts**...Nat King Cole
9/95	**Dear Mama**...2Pac
11/62	**Dear One**...Larry Finnegan
20/95	**December**...Collective Soul
	December, 1963 (Oh, What a Night)
1/76	Four Seasons
14/94	Four Seasons (remix)
7/59	**Deck Of Cards**...Wink Martindale
7/58	**DeDe Dinah**...Frankie Avalon
31/93	**Dedicated**...R. Kelly
36/66	**Dedicated Follower Of Fashion**...Kinks
	Dedicated To The One I Love
3/61	Shirelles
2/67	Mamas & The Papas
F/71	**Deep Blue**...George Harrison
22/80	**Deep Inside My Heart**...Randy Meisner
	Deep Purple
20/57	Billy Ward
1/63	Nino Tempo & April Stevens
14/76	Donny & Marie Osmond
7/93	**Deeper And Deeper**...Madonna
24/70	**Deeper & Deeper**...Freda Payne
21/91	**Deeper Shade Of Soul**...Urban Dance Squad
11/79	**Deeper Than The Night**...Olivia Newton-John
28/90	**Deeper The Love**...Whitesnake
15/80	**Deja Vu**...Dionne Warwick
9/98	**Deja Vu (Uptown Baby)**...Lord Tariq & Peter Gunz
22/60	**Delaware**...Perry Como
40/58	**Delicious!**...Jim Backus
15/68	**Delilah**...Tom Jones
	Delilah Jones ..see: Man With The Golden Arm
8/83	**Delirious**...Prince
1/73	**Delta Dawn**...Helen Reddy
10/63	**Denise**...Randy & The Rainbows
25/79	**Dependin' On You**...Doobie Brothers
5/83	**Der Kommissar**...After The Fire
15/62	**Desafinado**...Stan Getz/Charlie Byrd
10/84	**Desert Moon**...Dennis DeYoung
33/63	**Desert Pete**...Kingston Trio
17/00	**Desert Rose**...Sting
8/71	**Desiderata**...Les Crane
3/88	**Desire**...U2
4/80	**Desire**...Andy Gibb
16/78	**Desirée**...Neil Diamond
	Detroit City
16/63	Bobby Bare
27/67	Tom Jones
	Devil In Disguise ..see: (You're the)
2/88	**Devil Inside**...INXS
6/60	**Devil Or Angel**...Bobby Vee
3/79	**Devil Went Down To Georgia**...Charlie Daniels Band
4/66	**Devil With A Blue Dress On**...Mitch Ryder (medley)
6/76	**Devil Woman**...Cliff Richard
16/62	**Devil Woman**...Marty Robbins

POS/YR	RECORD TITLE. . .ARTIST
36/77	**Devil's Gun**...C.J. & Co.
	Devoted To You
10/58	Everly Brothers
36/78	Carly Simon & James Taylor
33/74	**Devotion**...Earth, Wind & Fire
13/89	**Dial My Heart**...Boys
24/72	**Dialogue**...Chicago
6/73	**Diamond Girl**...Seals & Crofts
5/87	**Diamonds**...Herb Alpert (with Janet Jackson)
3/92	**Diamonds And Pearls**...Prince
18/60	**Diamonds And Pearls**...Paradons
35/75	**Diamonds And Rust**...Joan Baez
1/57	**Diana**...Paul Anka
10/64	**Diane**...Bachelors
14/59	**Diary, The**...Neil Sedaka
15/72	**Diary**...Bread
F/75	**Dick And Jane**...Bobby Vinton
9/82	**Did It In A Minute**...Daryl Hall & John Oates
38/03	**Did My Time**...Korn
29/76	**Did You Boogie (With Your Baby)**...Flash Cadillac & The Continental Kids
2/66	**Did You Ever Have To Make Up Your Mind?**...Lovin' Spoonful
27/99	**Did You Ever Think**...R. Kelly
32/69	**Did You See Her Eyes**...Illusion
	Didn't I (Blow Your Mind This Time)
10/70	Delfonics
8/89	New Kids On The Block
1/87	**Didn't We Almost Have It All**...Whitney Houston
8/02	**Die Another Day**...Madonna
	Died In Your Arms ..see: (I Just)
23A/97	**Difference, The**...Wallflowers
4/01	**Differences**...Ginuwine
7/86	**Different Corner**...George Michael
13/68	**Different Drum**...Linda Ronstadt
18/79	**Different Worlds**...Maureen McGovern
31/01	**Dig In**...Lenny Kravitz
5/95	**Diggin' On You**...TLC
14/86	**Digging Your Scene**...Blow Monkeys
21/86	**Digital Display**...Ready For The World
1/02	**Dilemma**...Nelly
2/79	**Dim All The Lights**...Donna Summer
11/55	**Dim, Dim The Lights (I Want Some Atmosphere)**...Bill Haley
18/60	**Ding-A-Ling**...Bobby Rydell
	(also see: My Ding-A-Ling)
25/58	**Ding Dong**...McGuire Sisters
36/75	**Ding Dong; Ding Dong**...George Harrison
11/67	**Ding Dong! The Witch Is Dead**...Fifth Estate
6/58	**Dinner With Drac**...John Zacherle
25/90	**Dirty Cash (Money Talks)**...Adventures Of Stevie V
36/90	**Dirty Deeds**...Joan Jett
1/88	**Dirty Diana**...Michael Jackson
3/83	**Dirty Laundry**...Don Henley
11/66	**Dirty Water**...Standells
12/79	**Dirty White Boy**...Foreigner

POS/YR	RECORD TITLE. . . ARTIST
36/67	**Dis-Advantages Of You**...Brass Ring
8/91	**Disappear**...INXS
1/76	**Disco Duck**...Rick Dees
11/78	**Disco Inferno**...Trammps
1/76	**Disco Lady**...Johnnie Taylor
24/77	**Disco Lucy (I Love Lucy Theme)**...Wilton Place Street Band
12/79	**Disco Nights (Rock-Freak)**...GQ
28/75	**Disco Queen**...Hot Chocolate
	(Disco 'Round) ..see: I Love The Nightlife
10/97	**Discothéque**...U2
29/02	**Disease**...Matchbox Twenty
35A/96	**Distance, The**...Cake
28/74	**Distant Lover**...Marvin Gaye
30/66	**Distant Shores**...Chad & Jeremy
10/93	**Ditty**...Paperboy
35/92	**Divine Thing**...Soup Dragons
	Dixie ..see: Theme From
30/55	**Dixie Danny**...Laurie Sisters
1/69	**Dizzy**...Tommy Roe
	Do ..also see: Doo
2/91	**Do Anything**...Natural Selection
21/98	**Do For Love**...2Pac
13/82	**Do I Do**...Stevie Wonder
11/92	**Do I Have To Say The Words?**...Bryan Adams
34/64	**Do I Love You?**...Ronettes
36/70	**Do It**...Neil Diamond
6/73	**Do It Again**...Steely Dan
20/68	**Do It Again**...Beach Boys
18/67	**Do It Again A Little Bit Slower**...Jon & Robin & The In Crowd
11/75	**Do It Any Way You Wanna**...People's Choice
13/74	**Do It Baby**...Miracles
29/85	**Do It For Love**...Sheena Easton
19/79	**Do It Or Die**...Atlanta Rhythm Section
2/74	**Do It ('Til You're Satisfied)**...B.T. Express
21/92	**Do It To Me**...Lionel Richie
3/90	**Do Me!**...Bell Biv DeVoe
27/62	**Do-Re-Mi**...Lee Dorsey
23/80	**Do Right**...Paul Davis
38/68	**Do Something To Me**...Tommy James
33/03	**Do That**......Baby
1/80	**Do That To Me One More Time**...Captain & Tennille
11A/91	**Do The Bartman**...Simpsons
10/63	**Do The Bird**...Dee Dee Sharp
36/65	**Do The Boomerang**...Jr. Walker
21/65	**Do The Clam**...Elvis Presley
18/65	**Do The Freddie**...Freddie & The Dreamers **(also see: Let's Do The Freddie)**
28/70	**Do The Funky Chicken**...Rufus Thomas
37/62	**(Do The New) Continental**...Dovells
25/71	**(Do The) Push And Pull**...Rufus Thomas
13/84	**Do They Know It's Christmas?**...Band Aid
31/65	**Do-Wacka-Do**...Roger Miller
1/64	**Do Wah Diddy Diddy**...Manfred Mann
13/85	**Do What You Do**...Jermaine Jackson

POS/YR	RECORD TITLE. . . ARTIST
37/70	**Do What You Wanna Do**...Five Flights Up
39/76	**Do What You Want, Be What You Are**...Daryl Hall & John Oates
24/77	**Do Ya**...Electric Light Orchestra
	Do Ya Think I'm Sexy? ..see: Da Ya
18/77	**Do Ya Wanna Get Funky With Me**...Peter Brown
7/82	**Do You Believe In Love**...Huey Lewis
	Do You Believe In Magic
9/65	Lovin' Spoonful
31/78	Shaun Cassidy
13/92	**Do You Believe In Us**...Jon Secada
10/76	**Do You Feel Like We Do**...Peter Frampton
10/68	**Do You Know The Way To San José**...Dionne Warwick
6/71	**Do You Know What I Mean**...Lee Michaels
7/97	**Do You Know (What It Takes)**...Robyn
	Do You Know Where You're Going To ..see: Theme From Mahogany
31/97	**Do You Like This**...Rome
	Do You Love Me
3/62	Contours
11/64	Dave Clark Five
11/88	Contours
30/80	**Do You Love What You Feel**...Rufus & Chaka
32A/98	**Do You Really Want Me (Show Respect)**...Robyn
2/83	**Do You Really Want To Hurt Me**...Culture Club
4/90	**Do You Remember?**...Phil Collins
32/70	**Do You See My Love (For You Growing)**...Jr. Walker
18/95	**Do You Sleep?**...Lisa Loeb
40/94	**Do You Wanna Get Funky**...C+C Music Factory
5/77	**Do You Wanna Make Love**...Peter McCann
20/82	**Do You Wanna Touch Me (Oh Yeah)**...Joan Jett
37/85	**Do You Want Crying**...Katrina & The Waves
21/91	**Do You Want Me**...Salt-N-Pepa
	Do You Want To Dance
5/58	Bobby Freeman
12/65	Beach Boys
17/73	Bette Midler
2/64	**Do You Want To Know A Secret**...Beatles
39/77	**Do Your Dance**...Rose Royce
11/69	**Do Your Thing**...Watts 103rd Street Rhythm Band
30/72	**Do Your Thing**...Isaac Hayes
	Dock Of The Bay ..see: (Sittin' On)
9/89	**Doctor, The**...Doobie Brothers
11/84	**Doctor! Doctor!**...Thompson Twins **(also see: Bad Case Of Loving You)**
6/89	**Dr. Feelgood**...Mötley Crüe
28/83	**Dr. Heckyll & Mr. Jive**...Men At Work
	Doctor Kildare ..see: Theme From
8/72	**Doctor My Eyes**...Jackson Browne
	Doctor Tarr ..see: (System Of)
	Dr. Zhivago ..see: Somewhere My Love
11/75	**Doctor's Orders**...Carol Douglas
38/69	**Does Anybody Know I'm Here**...Dells

POS/YR	RECORD TITLE. . .ARTIST
38/91	**Does Anybody Really Fall In Love Anymore?**...Kane Roberts
7/71	**Does Anybody Really Know What Time It Is?**...Chicago
36/83	**Does It Make You Remember**...Kim Carnes
34/91	**Does She Love That Man?**...Breathe
5/61	**Does Your Chewing Gum Lose It's Flavor (On The Bedpost Over Night)**...Lonnie Donegan
29/68	**Does Your Mama Know About Me**...Bobby Taylor
19/79	**Does Your Mother Know**...Abba
F/55	**Doesn't Anybody Love Me?**...McGuire Sisters
1/00	**Doesn't Really Matter**...Janet Jackson
6/71	**Doesn't Somebody Want To Be Wanted**...Partridge Family
34/79	**Dog & Butterfly**...Heart
30/55	**Dogface Soldier**...Russ Morgan
15/60	**Doggin' Around**...Jackie Wilson
32/69	**Doggone Right**...Miracles
9/96	**Doin It**...LL Cool J
6/87	**Doing It All For My Baby**...Huey Lewis
22/73	**Doing It To Death**...JB's
31/60	**Doll House**...Donnie Brooks
13/55	**Domani (Tomorrow)**...Julius LaRosa
1/63	**Dominique**...Singing Nun
9/71	**Domino**...Van Morrison
18/88	**Domino Dancing**...Pet Shop Boys
14/87	**Dominoes**...Robbie Nevil
1/58	**Don't**...Elvis Presley
15/84	**Don't Answer Me**...Alan Parsons Project
19/80	**Don't Ask Me Why**...Billy Joel
25/58	**Don't Ask Me Why**...Elvis Presley
40/89	**Don't Ask Me Why**...Eurythmics
26/63	**Don't Be Afraid, Little Darlin'**...Steve Lawrence
	Don't Be Angry
14/55	Crew-Cuts
25/55	Nappy Brown
	Don't Be Cruel
1/56	Elvis Presley
11/60	Bill Black's Combo
4/88	Cheap Trick
8/88	**Don't Be Cruel**...Bobby Brown
40/98	**Don't Be Stupid (You Know I Love You)**...Shania Twain
9/61	**Don't Bet Money Honey**...Linda Scott
20/61	**Don't Blame Me**...Everly Brothers
37/67	**Don't Blame The Children**...Sammy Davis, Jr.
1/62	**Don't Break The Heart That Loves You**...Connie Francis
4/79	**Don't Bring Me Down**...Electric Light Orchestra
12/66	**Don't Bring Me Down**...Animals
9/75	**Don't Call Us, We'll Call You**...Sugarloaf/Jerry Corbetta
	Don't Cha ..also see: Don't You / Doncha'
17/02	**dontchange**...Musiq

POS/YR	RECORD TITLE. . .ARTIST
26/74	**Don't Change Horses (In The Middle Of A Stream)**...Tower Of Power
36/71	**Don't Change On Me**...Ray Charles
11/89	**Don't Close Your Eyes**...Kix
13/85	**Don't Come Around Here No More**...Tom Petty
21/60	**Don't Come Knockin'**...Fats Domino
35/73	**Don't Cross The River**...America
10/83	**Don't Cry**...Asia
10/91	**Don't Cry**...Guns N' Roses
33/96	**Don't Cry**...Seal
39/61	**Don't Cry, Baby**...Etta James
6/70	**Don't Cry Daddy**...Elvis Presley
8/97	**Don't Cry For Me Argentina**...Madonna
10/79	**Don't Cry Out Loud**...Melissa Manchester
4/87	**Don't Disturb This Groove**...System
	Don't Do It ..see: Baby Don't You Do It
10/80	**Don't Do Me Like That**...Tom Petty
2/87	**Don't Dream It's Over**...Crowded House
23/72	**Don't Ever Be Lonely (A Poor Little Fool Like Me)**...Cornelius Brothers & Sister Rose
40/79	**Don't Ever Wanna Lose Ya**...New England
8/73	**Don't Expect Me To Be Your Friend**...Lobo
4/80	**Don't Fall In Love With A Dreamer**...Kenny Rogers with Kim Carnes
12/76	**(Don't Fear) The Reaper**...Blue Öyster Cult
17/82	**Don't Fight It**...Kenny Loggins/Steve Perry
1/57	**Don't Forbid Me**...Pat Boone
19/65	**Don't Forget I Still Love You**...Bobbi Martin
2/86	**Don't Forget Me (When I'm Gone)**...Glass Tiger
29/83	**Don't Forget To Dance**...Kinks
10/86	**Don't Get Me Wrong**...Pretenders
15/69	**Don't Give In To Him**...Gary Puckett
26/81	**Don't Give It Up**...Robbie Patton
37/68	**Don't Give Up**...Petula Clark
1/77	**Don't Give Up On Us**...David Soul
35A/97	**Don't Go Away**...Oasis
19/90	**Don't Go Away Mad (Just Go Away)**...Mötley Crüe
1/76	**Don't Go Breaking My Heart**...Elton John & Kiki Dee
22/58	**Don't Go Home**...Playmates
17/62	**Don't Go Near The Indians**...Rex Allen
18/67	**Don't Go Out Into The Rain (You're Going To Melt)**...Herman's Hermits
	Don't Go To Strangers
38/56	Vaughn Monroe
36/60	Etta Jones
4/62	**Don't Hang Up**...Orlons
26/01	**Don't Happen Twice**...Kenny Chesney
21/79	**Don't Hold Back**...Chanson
2/77	**Don't It Make My Brown Eyes Blue**...Crystal Gayle
8/65	**Don't Just Stand There**...Patty Duke
13/71	**Don't Knock My Love**...Wilson Pickett
2/89	**Don't Know Much**...Linda Ronstadt/Aaron Neville

POS/YR	RECORD TITLE. . .ARTIST
12/88	**Don't Know What You Got (Till It's Gone)**...Cinderella
30/03	**Don't Know Why**...Norah Jones
12A/97	**Don't Leave Me**...BLACKstreet
	Don't Leave Me This Way
1/77	Thelma Houston
40/87	Communards
	Don't Let Go
13/58	Roy Hamilton
18/80	Isaac Hayes
38/84	**Don't Let Go**...Wang Chung
2/97	**Don't Let Go (Love)**...En Vogue
24/81	**Don't Let Him Go**...REO Speedwagon
39/82	**Don't Let Him Know**...Prism
6/83	**Don't Let It End**...Styx
14/73	**Don't Let Me Be Lonely Tonight**...James Taylor
	Don't Let Me Be Misunderstood
15/65	Animals
15/78	Santa Esmeralda
35/69	**Don't Let Me Down**...Beatles with Billy Preston
8/02	**Don't Let Me Get Me**...P!nk
17/71	**Don't Let The Green Grass Fool You**...Wilson Pickett
20/69	**Don't Let The Joneses Get You Down**...Temptations
6/64	**Don't Let The Rain Come Down (Crooked Little Man)**...Serendipity Singers
39/67	**Don't Let The Rain Fall Down On Me**...Critters
4/64	**Don't Let The Sun Catch You Crying**...Gerry & The Pacemakers
	Don't Let The Sun Go Down On Me
2/74	Elton John
1/92	George Michael/Elton John
4/78	**Don't Look Back**...Boston
11/89	**Don't Look Back**...Fine Young Cannibals
39/87	**Don't Look Down - The Sequel**...Go West
4/85	**Don't Lose My Number**...Phil Collins
	Don't Make Me Over
21/63	Dionne Warwick
20/89	Sybil
15/87	**Don't Make Me Wait For Love**...Kenny G
3/87	**Don't Mean Nothing**...Richard Marx
33/65	**Don't Mess Up A Good Thing**...Fontella Bass & Bobby McClure
7/66	**Don't Mess With Bill**...Marvelettes
8/02	**Don't Mess With My Man**...Nivea
37/87	**Don't Need A Gun**...Billy Idol
34/83	**Don't Pay The Ferryman**...Chris DeBurgh
40/59	**Don't Pity Me**...Dion & The Belmonts
	Don't Play That Song
11/62	Ben E. King
11/70	Aretha Franklin
	Don't Pull Your Love
4/71	Hamilton, Joe Frank & Reynolds
27/76	Glen Campbell (medley)
2/89	**Don't Rush Me**...Taylor Dayne
26/63	**Don't Say Goodnight And Mean Goodbye**...Shirelles

POS/YR	RECORD TITLE. . .ARTIST
39/80	**Don't Say Goodnight (It's Time For Love)**...Isley Brothers
7/63	**Don't Say Nothin' Bad (About My Baby)**...Cookies
15/72	**Don't Say You Don't Remember**...Beverly Bremers
21/00	**Don't Say You Love Me**...M2M
20/63	**Don't Set Me Free**...Ray Charles
9/88	**Don't Shed A Tear**...Paul Carrack
18/89	**Don't Shut Me Out**...Kevin Paige
5/67	**Don't Sleep In The Subway**...Petula Clark
1A/96	**Don't Speak**...No Doubt
10/81	**Don't Stand So Close To Me**...Police
F/55	**Don't Stay Away Too Long**...Eddie Fisher
3/77	**Don't Stop**...Fleetwood Mac
9/81	**Don't Stop Believin'**...Journey
33/76	**Don't Stop Believin'**...Olivia Newton-John
19/81	**Don't Stop The Music**...Yarbrough & Peoples
1/79	**Don't Stop 'Til You Get Enough**...Michael Jackson
34/76	**Don't Take Away The Music**...Tavares
2/95	**Don't Take It Personal (just one of dem days)**...Monica
27/68	**Don't Take It So Hard**...Paul Revere & The Raiders
17/94	**Don't Take The Girl**...Tim McGraw
32/59	**Don't Take Your Guns To Town**...Johnny Cash
37/75	**Don't Take Your Love**...Manhattans
2/82	**Don't Talk To Strangers**...Rick Springfield
4/01	**Don't Tell Me**...Madonna
27/75	**Don't Tell Me Goodnight**...Lobo
10/89	**Don't Tell Me Lies**...Breathe
40/83	**Don't Tell Me You Love Me**...Night Ranger
24/00	**Don't Think I'm Not**...Kandi
	Don't Think Twice, It's All Right
9/63	Peter, Paul & Mary
12/65	Wonder Who?
22/60	**Don't Throw Away All Those Teardrops**...Frankie Avalon
	Don't Throw It All Away ..see: (Our Love)
16/64	**Don't Throw Your Love Away**...Searchers
38/69	**Don't Touch Me**...Bettye Swann
19/91	**Don't Treat Me Bad**...Firehouse
4/94	**Don't Turn Around**...Ace Of Base
4/93	**Don't Walk Away**...Jade
26/84	**Don't Walk Away**...Rick Springfield
21/97	**Don't Wanna Be A Player**...Joe
2/90	**Don't Wanna Fall In Love**...Jane Child
1/89	**Don't Wanna Lose You**...Gloria Estefan
39/96	**Don't Wanna Lose You**...Lionel Richie
19/03	**Don't Wanna Try**...Frankie J.
9/91	**Don't Want To Be A Fool**...Luther Vandross
21/78	**Don't Want To Live Without It**...Pablo Cruise
35/81	**Don't Want To Wait Anymore**...Tubes
3/61	**Don't Worry**...Marty Robbins
	Don't Worry Baby
24/64	Beach Boys
17/77	B.J. Thomas

POS/YR	RECORD TITLE. . . ARTIST
1/88	**Don't Worry Be Happy**...Bobby McFerrin
29/71	**(Don't Worry) If There's A Hell Below We're All Going To Go**...Curtis Mayfield
	Don't Ya Wanna Play This Game No More **..see: (Sartorial Eloquence)**
	Don't You ..also see: Doncha'
39/62	**Don't You Believe It**...Andy Williams
6/67	**Don't You Care**...Buckinghams
1/85	**Don't You (Forget About Me)**...Simple Minds
30/02	**Don't You Forget It**...Glenn Lewis
	(also see: I Love You)
25/83	**Don't You Get So Mad**...Jeffrey Osborne
9/58	**Don't You Just Know It**...Huey (Piano) Smith
2/59	**Don't You Know**...Della Reese
6/88	**Don't You Know What The Night Can Do?**...Steve Winwood
1/82	**Don't You Want Me**...Human League
6/87	**Don't You Want Me**...Jody Watley
16/74	**Don't You Worry 'Bout A Thing**...Stevie Wonder
	(Don't You Worry 'Bout Me) ..see: Opus 17
33/79	**Don't You Write Her Off**...McGuinn, Clark & Hillman
15/58	**Doncha' Think It's Time**...Elvis Presley
2/59	**Donna**...Ritchie Valens
6/63	**Donna The Prima Donna**...Dion
15/74	**Doo Doo Doo Doo Doo (Heartbreaker)**...Rolling Stones
1/98	**Doo Wop (That Thing)**...Lauryn Hill
	Door Is Still Open To My Heart
F/55	Don Cornell
6/64	Dean Martin
35/74	**Doraville**...Atlanta Rhythm Section
26/76	**Dose Of Rock 'N' Roll**...Ringo Starr
39/58	**Dottie**...Danny & The Juniors
22/71	**Double Barrel**...Dave & Ansil Collins
30/81	**Double Dutch Bus**...Frankie Smith
14/71	**Double Lovin'**...Osmonds
17/66	**Double Shot (Of My Baby's Love)**...Swingin' Medallions
2/78	**Double Vision**...Foreigner
37A/96	**Down**...311
21/02	**Down A** Chick**...Ja Rule
33/68	**Down At Lulu's**...Ohio Express
9/63	**(Down At) Papa Joe's**...Dixiebelles
27/89	**Down Boys**...Warrant
4/72	**Down By The Lazy River**...Osmonds
13/60	**Down By The Station**...Four Preps
6/02	**Down 4 U**...Inc.
9/65	**Down In The Boondocks**...Billy Joe Royal
4/96	**Down Low (Nobody Has To Know)**...R. Kelly
3/69	**Down On The Corner**...Creedence Clearwater Revival
18/58	**Down The Aisle Of Love**...Quin-Tones
37/63	**Down The Aisle (Wedding Song)**...Patti LaBelle
1/83	**Down Under**...Men At Work
21/93	**Down With The King**...Run-D.M.C.

POS/YR	RECORD TITLE. . . ARTIST
	Downtown
1/65	Petula Clark
40/65	Allan Sherman (Crazy Downtown)
37/89	**Downtown**...One 2 Many
F/93	**Downtown**...SWV
31/88	**Downtown Life**...Daryl Hall/John Oates
3/90	**Downtown Train**...Rod Stewart
	Dr. ..see: Doctor
10/64	**Drag City**...Jan & Dean
4/71	**Draggin' The Line**...Tommy James
28/81	**Draw Of The Cards**...Kim Carnes
8/93	**Dre Day**...Dr. Dre
19/58	**Dream**...Betty Johnson
12/68	**Dream A Little Dream Of Me**...Mama Cass
29/95	**Dream About You**...Stevie B
	Dream Baby (How Long Must I Dream)
4/62	Roy Orbison
31/71	Glen Campbell
37/84	**Dream (Hold On To Your Dream)**...Irene Cara
12/91	**Dream Is Still Alive**...Wilson Phillips
2/59	**Dream Lover**...Bobby Darin
1/93	**Dreamlover**...Mariah Carey
	Dream Merchant
38/67	Jerry Butler
36/75	New Birth
6/76	**Dream On**...Aerosmith
32/74	**Dream On**...Righteous Brothers
25/65	**Dream On Little Dreamer**...Perry Como
26/79	**Dream Police**...Cheap Trick
2/76	**Dream Weaver**...Gary Wright
	Dreamboat ..see: (He's My)
15/80	**Dreamer**...Supertramp
8/89	**Dreamin'**...Vanessa Williams
11/60	**Dreamin'**...Johnny Burnette
10/80	**Dreaming**...Cliff Richard
16/88	**Dreaming**...Orchestral Manoeuvres In The Dark
27/79	**Dreaming**...Blondie
30/83	**Dreamin' Is Easy**...Steel Breeze
22/95	**Dreaming Of You**...Selena
1/77	**Dreams**...Fleetwood Mac
22/86	**Dreams**...Van Halen
26/94	**Dreams**...Gabrielle
32/68	**Dreams Of The Everyday Housewife**...Glen Campbell
5/86	**Dreamtime**...Daryl Hall
35/62	**Dreamy Eyes**...Johnny Tillotson
21/73	**Dreidel**...Don McLean
5/85	**Dress You Up**...Madonna
14/89	**Dressed For Success**...Roxette
	Drift Away
5/73	Dobie Gray
9/03	Uncle Kracker
6/63	**Drip Drop**...Dion
3/84	**Drive**...Cars
9/01	**Drive**...Incubus
28/92	**Drive**...R.E.M.
28/02	**Drive (For Daddy Gene)**...Alan Jackson
15/79	**Driver's Seat**...Sniff 'n' the Tears

POS/YR	RECORD TITLE. . . ARTIST
8/75	**Emma**...Hot Chocolate
	Emotion
3/78	Samantha Sang
10/01	Destiny's Child
22/75	**Emotion**...Helen Reddy
15/86	**Emotion In Motion**...Ric Ocasek
3/80	**Emotional Rescue**...Rolling Stones
39/03	**Emotional Rollercoaster**...Vivian Green
1/91	**Emotions**...Mariah Carey
7/61	**Emotions**...Brenda Lee
18/80	**Empire Strikes Back (medley)**...Meco
13/57	**Empty Arms**...Teresa Brewer
13/82	**Empty Garden (Hey Hey Johnny)**...Elton John
12/59	**Enchanted**...Platters
12/58	**Enchanted Island**...Four Lads
	Enchanted Sea
15/59	Islanders
28/59	Martin Denny
7/58	**End, The**...Earl Grant
	End Of Our Road
15/68	Gladys Knight
40/70	Marvin Gaye
8/89	**End Of The Innocence**...Don Henley
1/92	**End of the Road**...Boyz II Men
2/63	**End Of The World**...Skeeter Davis
	Endless Love
1/81	Diana Ross & Lionel Richie
2/94	Luther Vandross & Mariah Carey
21/87	**Endless Nights**...Eddie Money
5/58	**Endless Sleep**...Jody Reynolds
2/88	**Endless Summer Nights**...Richard Marx
12/59	**Endlessly**...Brook Benton
33/74	**Energy Crisis '74**...Dickie Goodman
7/65	**Engine Engine #9**...Roger Miller
14/70	**Engine Number 9**...Wilson Pickett
8/65	**England Swings**...Roger Miller
21/56	**English Muffins And Irish Stew**...Sylvia Syms
8/90	**Enjoy The Silence**...Depeche Mode
6/77	**Enjoy Yourself**...Jacksons
	(Enough Is Enough) ..see: No More Tears
16/91	**Enter Sandman**...Metallica
3/74	**Entertainer, The**...Marvin Hamlisch/"The Sting"
31/65	**Entertainer, The**...Tony Clarke
34/75	**Entertainer, The**...Billy Joel
9/90	**Epic**...Faith No More
19/67	**Epistle To Dippy**...Donovan
9/74	**Eres Tu (Touch The Wind)**...Mocedades
3/92	**Erotica**...Madonna
1/90	**Escapade**...Janet Jackson
12/02	**Escape**...Enrique Iglesias
1/79	**Escape (The Pina Colada Song)**...Rupert Holmes
35/71	**Escape-ism**...James Brown
19/62	**Eso Beso (That Kiss!)**...Paul Anka
1/89	**Eternal Flame**...Bangles
1/65	**Eve Of Destruction**...Barry McGuire
	(also see: Dawn Of Correction / Day For Decision)

POS/YR	RECORD TITLE. . . ARTIST
32/92	**Even Better Than The Real Thing**...U2
33/80	**Even It Up**...Heart
12/83	**Even Now**...Bob Seger
19/78	**Even Now**...Barry Manilow
36/67	**Even The Bad Times Are Good**...Tremeloes
5/82	**Even The Nights Are Better**...Air Supply
	Evergreen ..see: Love Theme From A Star Is Born
5/78	**Everlasting Love**...Andy Gibb
	Everlasting Love
13/67	Robert Knight
6/74	Carl Carlton
32/81	Rex Smith/Rachel Sweet
27/95	Gloria Estefan
12/89	**Everlasting Love**...Howard Jones
16/61	**Everlovin'**...Rick Nelson
6/61	**Every Beat Of My Heart**...Pips
1/83	**Every Breath You Take**...Police
	Every Day ..also see: Everyday
	Every Day Of My Life
37/56	McGuire Sisters
24/72	Bobby Vinton
20/95	**Every Day Of The Week**...Jade
2/91	**Every Heartbeat**...Amy Grant
16/78	**Every Kinda People**...Robert Palmer
13/64	**Every Little Bit Hurts**...Brenda Holloway
14/87	**Every Little Kiss**...Bruce Hornsby
3/89	**Every Little Step**...Bobby Brown
17/95	**Every Little Thing I Do**...Soul For Real
3/81	**Every Little Thing She Does Is Magic**...Police
3/99	**Every Morning**...Sugar Ray
39/58	**Every Night (I Pray)**...Chantels
	Every 1's A Winner ..see: Everyone's
1/88	**Every Rose Has Its Thorn**...Poison
25/85	**Every Step Of The Way**...John Waite
30/63	**Every Step Of The Way**...Johnny Mathis
	Every Time ..also see: Everytime
6/97	**Every Time I Close My Eyes**...Babyface
13/79	**Every Time I Think Of You**...Babys
4/77	**(Every Time I Turn Around) Back In Love Again**...L.T.D.
19/75	**Every Time You Touch Me (I Get High)**...Charlie Rich
30/79	**Every Which Way But Loose**...Eddie Rabbitt
5/81	**Every Woman In The World**...Air Supply
3/63	**Everybody**...Tommy Roe
4/98	**Everybody (Backstreet's Back)**...Backstreet Boys
38/77	**Everybody Be Dancin'**...Starbuck
24/86	**Everybody Dance**...Ta Mara & The Seen
38/78	**Everybody Dance**...Chic
8/90	**Everybody Everybody**...Black Box
2/86	**Everybody Have Fun Tonight**...Wang Chung
29/93	**Everybody Hurts**...R.E.M.
F/70	**Everybody Is A Star**...Sly & The Family Stone
15/64	**Everybody Knows (I Still Love You)**...Dave Clark Five
31/59	**Everybody Likes To Cha Cha Cha**...Sam Cooke

POS/YR	RECORD TITLE. . . ARTIST
4/65	Everybody Loves A Clown...Gary Lewis
	Everybody Loves A Lover
6/58	Doris Day
19/63	Shirelles
6/62	Everybody Loves Me But You...Brenda Lee
1/64	Everybody Loves Somebody...Dean Martin
32/78	Everybody Needs Love...Stephen Bishop
39/67	Everybody Needs Love...Gladys Knight
29/67	Everybody Needs Somebody To Love...Wilson Pickett
	Everybody Plays The Fool
3/72	Main Ingredient
8/91	Aaron Neville
1/85	Everybody Wants To Rule The World...Tears For Fears
32/82	Everybody Wants You...Billy Squier
12/71	Everybody's Everything...Santana
37/92	Everybody's Free (To Feel Good)...Rozalla
20/55	Everybody's Got A Home But Me...Eddie Fisher
21/70	Everybody's Got The Right To Love...Supremes
18/80	Everybody's Got To Learn Sometime...Korgis
26/70	Everybody's Out Of Town...B.J. Thomas
1/60	Everybody's Somebody's Fool...Connie Francis
6/69	Everybody's Talkin'...Nilsson
24/94	Everyday...Phil Collins
36/83	Everyday I Write The Book...Elvis Costello
11/97	Everyday Is A Winding Road...Sheryl Crow
	Everyday People
1/69	Sly & The Family Stone
37/83	Joan Jett
	(also see: People Everyday)
19/69	Everyday With You Girl...Classics IV
6/79	Every 1's A Winner...Hot Chocolate
17/65	Everyone's Gone To The Moon...Jonathan King
4/90	Everything...Jody Watley
24/97	Everything...Mary J. Blige
9/92	Everything About You....Ugly Kid Joe
14/92	Everything Changes...Kathy Troccoli
14A/96	Everything Falls Apart...Dog's Eye View
1/91	(Everything I Do) I Do It For You...Bryan Adams
5/72	Everything I Own...Bread
30/86	Everything In My Heart...Corey Hart
1/70	Everything Is Beautiful...Ray Stevens
35/99	Everything Is Everything...Lauryn Hill
F/96	Everything Remains Raw...Busta Rhymes
1/85	Everything She Wants...Wham!
10/68	Everything That Touches You...Association
1/00	Everything You Want...Vertical Horizon
3/88	Everything Your Heart Desires...Daryl Hall John Oates
40A/95	Everything Zen...Bush
16/64	Everything's Alright...Newbeats
37/93	Everything's Gonna Be Alright...Father MC
38/70	Everything's Tuesday...Chairman Of The Board
1/85	Everytime You Go Away...Paul Young

POS/YR	RECORD TITLE. . . ARTIST
12/01	Everywhere...Michelle Branch
14/88	Everywhere...Fleetwood Mac
9/70	Evil Ways...Santana
10/76	Evil Woman...Electric Light Orchestra
19/70	Evil Woman Don't Play Your Games With Me...Crow
21/99	Ex-Factor...Lauryn Hill
8/03	Excuse Me Miss...Jay-Z
1/95	Exhale (Shoop Shoop)...Whitney Houston
	Exodus
2/61	Ferrante & Teicher
31/61	Mantovani
36/61	Eddie Harris
	Exorcist, Theme From ..see: Tubular Bells
14/55	Experience Unnecessary...Sarah Vaughan
33/68	Explosion (In Your Soul)...Soul Survivors
4/75	Express...B.T. Express
2/89	Express Yourself...Madonna
12/70	Express Yourself...Charles Wright
26/90	Expression...Salt-N-Pepa
4/67	Expressway (To Your Heart)...Soul Survivors
3/82	Eye In The Sky...Alan Parsons Project
1/82	Eye Of The Tiger...Survivor
28/68	Eyes Of A New York Woman...B.J. Thomas
	Eyes Of Laura Mars ..see: Love Theme From
4/84	Eyes Without A Face...Billy Idol

F

POS/YR	RECORD TITLE. . . ARTIST
22/78	FM (No Static At All)...Steely Dan
37/94	Fa All Y'all...Da Brat
29/66	Fa-Fa-Fa-Fa-Fa (Sad Song)...Otis Redding
16/57	Fabulous...Charlie Gracie
28/03	Fabulous...Jaheim
19/56	Fabulous Character...Sarah Vaughan
29/68	Face It Girl, It's Over...Nancy Wilson
26/86	Face The Face...Pete Townshend
27/87	Facts Of Love...Jeff Lorber Feat. Karyn White
20/81	Fade Away...Bruce Springsteen
22/00	Faded...SoulDecision
10/99	Faded Pictures...Case & Joe
2/91	Fading Like A Flower (Every Time You Leave)...Roxette
28/90	Fairweather Friend...Johnny Gill
13/74	Fairytale...Pointer Sisters
1/87	Faith...George Michael
14/93	Faithful...Go West
12/83	Faithfully...Journey
25/87	Fake...Alexander O'Neal
35/83	Fake Friends...Joan Jett
23/67	Fakin' It...Simon & Garfunkel
33/94	Fall Down...Toad The Wet Sprocket
17/83	Fall In Love With Me...Earth, Wind & Fire
34/03	Fall Into Me...Emerson Drive
12/88	Fallen Angel...Poison
36/76	Fallen Angel...Frankie Valli

	Fallen Star
20/57	Nick Noble
23/57	Jimmy Newman
1/01	**Fallin'**...Alicia Keys
30/58	**Fallin'**...Connie Francis
13/78	**Falling**...LeBlanc & Carr
22/63	**Falling**...Roy Orbison
	Fallin' In Love
1/75	Hamilton, Joe Frank & Reynolds
35A/96	La Bouche
27/74	**Fallin' In Love**...Souther, Hillman, Furay Band
18/96	**Falling**...Montell Jordan
35/97	**Falling In Love (Is Hard On The Knees)**...Aerosmith
25/87	**Falling In Love (Uh-Oh)**...Miami Sound Machine
29/00	**Falls Apart (Run Away)**...Sugar Ray
1/75	**Fame**...David Bowie
4/80	**Fame**...Irene Cara
17/60	**Fame And Fortune**...Elvis Presley
1/71	**Family Affair**...Sly & The Family Stone
1/01	**Family Affair**...Mary J. Blige
6/83	**Family Man**...Daryl Hall & John Oates
12/72	**Family Of Man**...Three Dog Night
20/03	**Family Portrait**...P!nk
31/70	**Fancy**...Bobbie Gentry
39/77	**Fancy Dancer**...Commodores
38/60	**Fannie Mae**...Buster Brown
12/76	**Fanny (Be Tender With My Love)**...Bee Gees
3/94	**Fantastic Voyage**...Coolio
1/95	**Fantasy**...Mariah Carey
23/82	**Fantasy**...Aldo Nova
32/78	**Fantasy**...Earth, Wind & Fire
18/94	**Far Behind**...Candlebox
10/83	**Far From Over**...Frank Stallone
38/84	**Farewell My Summer Love**...Michael Jackson
19/64	**Farmer John**...Premiers
21/87	**Fascinated**...Company B
	Fascination
7/57	Jane Morgan
15/57	Dinah Shore
17/57	Dick Jacobs
	(also see: Keep Feeling)
6/88	**Fast Car**...Tracy Chapman
8/96	**Fastlove**...George Michael
F/79	**Fat Bottomed Girls**...Queen
18/98	**Father**...LL Cool J
1/88	**Father Figure**...George Michael
34/86	**Feel It Again**...Honeymoon Suite
28/02	**Feel It Boy**...Beenie Man
1/74	**Feel Like Makin' Love**...Roberta Flack
10/75	**Feel Like Makin' Love**...Bad Company
17/95	**Feel Me Flow**...Naughty By Nature
	Feel So Fine
14/60	Johnny Preston
22/67	Bunny Sigler (medley)
5/97	**Feel So Good**...Mase
	Feelin' Groovy ..see: 59th Street Bridge

36/01	**Feelin' On Yo Booty**...R. Kelly
10/73	**Feelin' Stronger Every Day**...Chicago
33/72	**Feeling Alright**...Joe Cocker
6/75	**Feelings**...Morris Albert
9/90	**Feels Good**...Tony! Toni! Toné!
4/77	**Feels Like The First Time**...Foreigner
4/78	**Feels So Good**...Chuck Mangione
32/95	**Feels So Good**...Xscape
35/89	**Feels So Good**...Van Halen
35/96	**Feels So Good (Show Me Your Love)**...Lina Santiago
20/81	**Feels So Right**...Alabama
25/94	**Feenin'**...Jodeci
32/61	**Fell In Love On Monday**...Fats Domino
13/76	**Fernando**...Abba
6/65	**Ferry Cross The Mersey**...Gerry & The Pacemakers
	Fever
24/56	Little Willie John
8/58	Peggy Lee
7/65	McCoys
23/78	**Ffun**...Con Funk Shun
39/58	**Fibbin'**...Patti Page
23/93	**Fields Of Gold**...Sting
6/01	**Fiesta Remix**...R. Kelly
27/99	**15 Minutes**...Marc Nelson
1/76	**Fifth Of Beethoven**...Walter Murphy
13/67	**59th Street Bridge Song (Feelin' Groovy)**...Harpers Bizarre
1/76	**50 Ways To Leave Your Lover**...Paul Simon
	Fight ..see: Main Event
	Fight For Your Right (To Party!) ..see: (You Gotta)
4/75	**Fight The Power**...Isley Brothers
20/03	**Fighter**...Christina Aguilera
15/01	**Fill Me In**...Craig David
	(Final Acclaim) ..see: You're In My Heart
8/87	**Final Countdown**...Europe
5/92	**Finally**...Ce Ce Peniston
17/74	**Finally Got Myself Together (I'm A Changed Man)**...Impressions
29/85	**Find A Way**...Amy Grant
16/82	**Find Another Fool**...Quarterflash
27/61	**Find Another Girl**...Jerry Butler
29/81	**Find Your Way Back**...Jefferson Starship
22/84	**Fine Fine Day**...Tony Carey
8/87	**Finer Things**...Steve Winwood
7/60	**Finger Poppin' Time**...Hank Ballard
1/63	**Fingertips**...Little Stevie Wonder
13/88	**Finish What Ya Started**...Van Halen
35/79	**Fins**...Jimmy Buffett
1/75	**Fire**...Ohio Players
2/68	**Fire**...Arthur Brown
2/79	**Fire**...Pointer Sisters
17/81	**Fire And Ice**...Pat Benatar
3/70	**Fire And Rain**...James Taylor
24/72	**Fire And Water**...Wilson Pickett
28/74	**Fire, Baby I'm On Fire**...Andy Kim

POS/YR	RECORD TITLE. . . ARTIST
23/58	**For My Good Fortune**...Pat Boone
2/68	**For Once In My Life**...Stevie Wonder
	For Sentimental Reasons ..see: (I Love You)
11/71	**For The Good Times**...Ray Price
F/76	**For The Heart**...Elvis Presley
13/70	**For The Love Of Him**...Bobbi Martin
9/74	**For The Love Of Money**...O'Jays
22/75	**For The Love Of You**...Isley Brothers
32/86	**For Tonight**...Nancy Martinez
7/67	**For What It's Worth**...Buffalo Springfield
6/64	**For You**...Rick Nelson
21/91	**For You**...Outfield
33/97	**For You**...Kenny Lattimore
F/70	**For You Blue**...Beatles
4/97	**For You I Will**...Monica
4/81	**For Your Eyes Only**...Sheena Easton
6/65	**For Your Love**...Yardbirds
	For Your Love
13/58	Ed Townsend
20/67	Peaches & Herb
	For Your Precious Love
11/58	Jerry Butler & The Impressions
26/64	Garnet Mimms
23/67	Oscar Toney, Jr.
8/90	**Forever**...Kiss
	Forever
9/60	Little Dippers
25/64	Pete Drake
37/03	**4 Ever**...Lil' Mo
40/85	**Forever**...Kenny Loggins
9A/96	**Forever**...Mariah Carey
	(also see: I'll Be Loving You)
20/03	**Forever And For Always**...Shania Twain
28/68	**Forever Came Today**...Supremes
35/56	**Forever Darling**...Ames Brothers
20/79	**Forever In Blue Jeans**...Neil Diamond
18/93	**Forever In Love**...Kenny G
19/86	**(Forever) Live And Die**...Orchestral Manoeuvres In The Dark
15/92	**Forever Love**...Color Me Badd
26/85	**Forever Man**...Eric Clapton
28/80	**Forever Mine**...O'Jays
25/91	**Forever My Lady**...Jodeci
12/88	**Forever Young**...Rod Stewart
1/89	**Forever Your Girl**...Paula Abdul
4/64	**Forget Him**...Bobby Rydell
12/58	**Forget Me Not**...Kalin Twins
23/82	**Forget Me Nots**...Patrice Rushen
2/80	**Forgive Me Girl (medley)**...Spinners
13/55	**Forgive My Heart**...Nat "King" Cole
25/00	**Forgot About Dre**...Dr. Dre
8/85	**Fortress Around Your Heart**...Sting
4/99	**Fortunate**...Maxwell
14/69	**Fortunate Son**...Creedence Clearwater Revival
9/59	**Forty Miles Of Bad Road**...Duane Eddy
36/79	**Found A Cure**...Ashford & Simpson
25/94	**Found Out About You**...Gin Blossoms
21/99	**4,5,6**...Solé

POS/YR	RECORD TITLE. . . ARTIST
19/85	**Four In The Morning (I Can't Take Any More)**...Night Ranger
1/97	**4 Seasons Of Loneliness**...Boyz II Men
	Four Walls
11/57	Jim Reeves
15/57	Jim Lowe
36/68	**1432 Franklin Pike Circle Hero**...Bobby Russell
5/76	**Fox On The Run**...Sweet
1/73	**Frankenstein**...Edgar Winter Group
9/59	**Frankie**...Connie Francis
	Frankie And Johnny
20/61	Brook Benton
14/63	Sam Cooke
25/66	Elvis Presley
36/57	**Fraulein**...Bobby Helms
	Freak ..also see: Freek
2/95	**Freak Like Me**...Adina Howard
1/93	**Freak Me**...Silk
4/72	**Freddie's Dead**...Curtis Mayfield
20/71	**Free**...Chicago
23/56	**Free**...Tommy Leonetti
25/77	**Free**...Deniece Williams
6/96	**Free As A Bird**...Beatles
	Free Bird
19/75	Lynyrd Skynyrd
38/77	Lynyrd Skynyrd (Live)
1/88	Will To Power (medley)
7/90	**Free Fallin'**...Tom Petty
22/74	**Free Man In Paris**...Joni Mitchell
14/73	**Free Ride**...Edgar Winter Group
F/74	**Free Wheelin'**...Bachman-Turner Overdrive
8/92	**Free Your Mind**...En Vogue
3/85	**Freedom**...Wham!
8/90	**Freedom**...George Michael
20/86	**Freedom Overspill**...Steve Winwood
14/95	**Freek 'n You**...Jodeci
3/85	**Freeway Of Love**...Aretha Franklin
33/58	**Freeze, The**...Tony & Joe
4/82	**Freeze-Frame**...J. Geils Band
	Freight Train
6/57	Rusty Draper
40/57	Chas. McDevitt
9/85	**Fresh**...Kool & The Gang
5/97	**Freshmen, The**...Verve Pipe
18/92	**Friday I'm In Love**...Cure
	(Friday Night) ..see: Livin' It Up
16/67	**Friday On My Mind**...Easybeats
36/66	**Friday's Child**...Nancy Sinatra
12/98	**Friend of Mine**...Kelly Price
5/56	**Friendly Persuasion (Thee I Love)**...Pat Boone
9/89	**Friends**...Jody Watley (w/Eric B. & Rakim)
34/71	**Friends**...Elton John
40/73	**Friends**...Bette Midler
2/86	**Friends And Lovers**...Gloria Loring & Carl Anderson
38/82	**Friends In Love**...Dionne Warwick & Johnny Mathis
17/69	**Friendship Train**...Gladys Knight

POS/YR	RECORD TITLE. . .ARTIST
1/65	**Get Off Of My Cloud**...Rolling Stones
18/72	**Get On The Good Foot**...James Brown
11/67	**Get On Up**...Esquires
22/96	**Get On Up**...Jodeci
11/89	**Get On Your Feet**...Gloria Estefan
	Get Out ..see G.H.E.T.T.O.U.T.
1/88	**Get Outta My Dreams, Get Into My Car**...Billy Ocean
31/94	**Get Over It**...Eagles
8/01	**Get Over Yourself**...Eden's Crush
	Get Ready
29/66	Temptations
4/70	Rare Earth
38/95	**Get Ready For This**...2 Unlimited
31/87	**Get That Love**...Thompson Twins
30/76	**Get The Funk Out Ma Face**...Brothers Johnson
4/01	**Get The Party Started**...P!nk
	Get Together
31/65	We Five
5/69	Youngbloods
2/76	**Get Up And Boogie (That's Right)**...Silver Convention
	(Get up and dance!) ..see: Bite Your Lip
7/90	**Get Up! (Before The Night Is Over)**...Technotronic
34/71	**Get Up, Get Into It, Get Involved**...James Brown
	Get Up I Feel Like Being A Sex Machine ..see: Sex Machine
7/01	**Get Ur Freak On**...Missy Elliott
21/79	**Get Used To It**...Roger Voudouris
26/85	**Getcha Back**...Beach Boys
21/91	**Gett Off**...Prince
1/98	**Gettin' Jiggy Wit It**...Will Smith
27/78	**Gettin' Ready For Love**...Diana Ross
18/67	**Gettin' Together**...Tommy James
38/90	**Getting Away With It**...Electronic
20/79	**Getting Closer**...Wings
7/94	**Getto Jam**...Domino
29/73	**Ghetto Child**...Spinners
15/99	**Ghetto Cowboy**...Mo Thugs Family & Bone Thugs N Harmony
16/97	**Ghetto Love**...Da Brat
15/98	**Ghetto Supastar (That Is What You Are)**...Pras Michel
8/97	**G.H.E.T.T.O.U.T.**...Changing Faces
	(Ghost) Riders In The Sky
30/61	Ramrods
31/81	Outlaws
22/56	**Ghost Town**...Don Cherry
33/88	**Ghost Town**...Cheap Trick
1/84	**Ghostbusters**...Ray Parker Jr.
24/04	**Gigolo**...Nick Cannon
37/83	**Gimme All Your Lovin**...ZZ Top
9/70	**Gimme Dat Ding**...Pipkins
12/69	**Gimme Gimme Good Lovin'**...Crazy Elephant
9/67	**Gimme Little Sign**...Brenton Wood

POS/YR	RECORD TITLE. . .ARTIST
	Gimme Some Lovin'
7/67	Spencer Davis Group
18/80	Blues Brothers
7/02	**Gimme The Light**...Sean Paul
8/94	**Gin & Juice**...Snoop Doggy Dogg
6/62	**Gina**...Johnny Mathis
9/58	**Ginger Bread**...Frankie Avalon
38/61	**Ginnie Bell**...Paul Dino
21/62	**Ginny Come Lately**...Brian Hyland
17/86	**Girl Can't Help It**...Journey
30/65	**Girl Come Running**...4 Seasons
5/64	**Girl From Ipanema**...Stan Getz/Astrud Gilberto
39/67	**Girl I Knew Somewhere**...Monkees
27/90	**Girl I Used To Know**...Brother Beyond
1/89	**Girl I'm Gonna Miss You**...Milli Vanilli
19/93	**Girl, I've Been Hurt**...Snow
21/66	**Girl In Love**...Outsiders
35/84	**Girl In Trouble (Is A Temporary Thing)**...Romeo Void
2/83	**Girl Is Mine**...Michael Jackson/Paul McCartney
10/67	**Girl Like You**...Young Rascals
32/95	**Girl Like You**...Edwyn Collins
38/90	**Girl Like You**...Smithereens
19/61	**Girl Of My Best Friend**...Ral Donner
37/79	**Girl Of My Dreams**...Bram Tchaikovsky
28/66	**Girl On A Swing**...Gerry & The Pacemakers
10/99	**Girl On TV**...LFO
28/02	**Girl Talk**...TLC
5/68	**Girl Watcher**...O'Kaysions
26/64	**Girl (Why You Wanna Make Me Blue)**...Temptations
13/57	**Girl With The Golden Braids**...Perry Como
26/93	**Girl U For Me**...Silk
2/89	**Girl You Know It's True**...Milli Vanilli
10/67	**Girl, You'll Be A Woman Soon**...Neil Diamond
5/88	**Girlfriend**...Pebbles
5/02	**Girlfriend**...*NSYNC
30/03	**Girlfriend**...B2K
16/84	**Girls**...Dwight Twilley
34/85	**Girls Are More Fun**...Ray Parker Jr.
34/80	**Girls Can Get It**...Dr. Hook
33/68	**Girls Can't Do What The Guys Do**...Betty Wright
12/87	**Girls, Girls, Girls**...Mötley Crüe
17/01	**Girls, Girls, Girls**...Jay-Z
14/62	**(Girls, Girls, Girls) Made To Love**...Eddie Hodges
33/64	**Girls Grow Up Faster Than Boys**...Cookies
39/67	**Girls In Love**...Gary Lewis
2/84	**Girls Just Want To Have Fun**...Cyndi Lauper
6/90	**Girls Nite Out**...Tyler Collins
33/78	**Girls' School**...Wings
33/84	**Girls With Guns**...Tommy Shaw
8/69	**Gitarzan**...Ray Stevens
15/77	**Give A Little Bit**...Supertramp
18/65	**Give Him A Great Big Kiss**...Shangri-Las

POS/YR	RECORD TITLE. . . ARTIST
21/72	**Give Ireland Back To The Irish**...Wings
18/80	**Give It All You Got**...Chuck Mangione
30/73	**Give It To Me**...J. Geils Band
40/81	**Give It To Me Baby**...Rick James
20/74	**Give It To The People**...Righteous Brothers
10/99	**Give It To You**...Jordan Knight
26/95	**Give It 2 You**...Da Brat
18/84	**Give It Up**...KC
30/92	**Give It Up**...Wilson Phillips
33/94	**Give It Up**...Public Enemy
15/69	**Give It Up Or Turnit A Loose**...James Brown
15/93	**Give It Up, Turn It Loose**...En Vogue
38/76	**Give It Up (Turn It Loose)**...Tyrone Davis
40/75	**Give It What You Got**...B.T. Express
	Give Me ..also see: Gimme
3/70	**Give Me Just A Little More Time**...Chairmen Of The Board
2/00	**Give Me Just One Night (Una Noche)**...98°
1/73	**Give Me Love - (Give Me Peace On Earth)**...George Harrison
3/96	**Give Me One Reason**...Tracy Chapman
4/80	**Give Me The Night**...George Benson
31/73	**Give Me Your Love**...Barbara Mason
	Give More Power To The People ..see: (For God's Sake)
14/69	**Give Peace A Chance**...Plastic Ono Band
23/87	**Give To Live**...Sammy Hagar
29/92	**Give U My Heart**...Babyface
30/56	**Give Us This Day**...Joni James
29/65	**Give Us Your Blessings**...Shangri-Las
34/73	**Give Your Baby A Standing Ovation**...Dells
21/98	**Given To Fly**...Pearl Jam
	Giving Him Something He Can Feel ..see: Something He Can Feel
8/81	**Giving It Up For Your Love**...Delbert McClinton
38/64	**Giving Up**...Gladys Knight
38/89	**Giving Up On Love**...Rick Astley
4/90	**Giving You The Benefit**...Pebbles
3/88	**Giving You The Best That I Got**...Anita Baker
6/64	**Glad All Over**...Dave Clark Five
19/55	**Glad Rag Doll**...Crazy Otto
26/67	**Glad To Be Unhappy**...Mamas & The Papas
7/84	**Glamorous Life**...Sheila E.
31/89	**Glamour Boys**...Living Colour
37/75	**Glasshouse**...Temptations
8/56	**Glendora**...Perry Como
2/82	**Gloria**...Laura Branigan
10/66	**Gloria**...Shadows Of Knight
25/77	**Gloria**...Enchantment
34/72	**Glory Bound**...Grass Roots
5/85	**Glory Days**...Bruce Springsteen
1/86	**Glory Of Love**...Peter Cetera
28/96	**Glycerine**...Bush
30/66	**Go Ahead And Cry**...Righteous Brothers
5/72	**Go All The Way**...Raspberries

POS/YR	RECORD TITLE. . . ARTIST
	Go Away Little Girl
1/63	Steve Lawrence
12/66	Happenings
1/71	Donny Osmond
36/70	**Go Back**...Crabby Appleton
28A/98	**Go Deep**...Janet Jackson
32/71	**Go Down Gamblin'**...Blood, Sweat & Tears
10/86	**Go Home**...Stevie Wonder
23/84	**Go Insane**...Lindsey Buckingham
5/60	**Go, Jimmy, Go**...Jimmy Clanton
10/65	**Go Now!**...Moody Blues
40/00	**Go On**...George Strait
	Go On With The Wedding
11/56	Patti Page
39/56	Kitty Kallen & Georgie Shaw
24/97	**Go The Distance**...Michael Bolton
16/67	**Go Where You Wanna Go**...5th Dimension
10/77	**Go Your Own Way**...Fleetwood Mac
36/59	**God Bless America**...Connie Francis
	God Bless The USA
30s/91	Lee Greenwood
16/01	Lee Greenwood
4/03	American Idol Finalists
18/61	**God, Country And My Baby**...Johnny Burnette
22/70	**God, Love And Rock & Roll**...Teegarden & Van Winkle
	(God Must Have Spent) A Little More Time On You
8/99	*NSYNC
29/99	Alabama (featuring *NSYNC)
39/66	**God Only Knows**...Beach Boys
	Godfather ..see: Love Theme From
17/82	**Goin' Down**...Greg Guidry
36/73	**Goin' Home**...Osmonds
	Goin' Out Of My Head
6/64	Little Anthony & The Imperials
7/68	Lettermen (medley)
16/57	**Goin' Steady**...Tommy Sands
26/98	**Going Back To Cali**...Notorious B.I.G.
31/88	**Going Back To Cali**...LL Cool J
35/64	**Going Going Gone**...Brook Benton
15/69	**Going In Circles**...Friends Of Distinction
	Going To A Go-Go
11/66	Miracles
25/82	Rolling Stones
11/69	**Going Up The Country**...Canned Heat
5/79	**Gold**...John Stewart
29/84	**Gold**...Spandau Ballet
10/76	**Golden Years**...David Bowie
8/65	**Goldfinger**...Shirley Bassey
33/86	**Goldmine**...Pointer Sisters
	Gone
4/57	Ferlin Husky
24/72	Joey Heatherton
11/01	**Gone**...*NSYNC
23/75	**Gone At Last**...Paul Simon/Phoebe Snow
31/64	**Gone, Gone, Gone**...Everly Brothers
7/98	**Gone Till November**...Wyclef Jean

POS/YR	RECORD TITLE. . . ARTIST
23/77	**Gone Too Far**...England Dan & John Ford Coley
	(Gong-Gong Song) ..see: I'm Blue
18/57	**Gonna Find Me A Bluebird**...Marvin Rainwater
	Gonna Fly Now (Theme From 'Rocky')
1/77	Bill Conti
28/77	Maynard Ferguson
11/56	**Gonna Get Along Without Ya Now**...Patience & Prudence
29/67	**Gonna Give Her All The Love I've Got**...Jimmy Ruffin
1/91	**Gonna Make You Sweat (Everybody Dance Now)**...C & C Music Factory
36/69	**Goo Goo Barabajagal (Love Is Hot)**...Donovan/Jeff Beck Group
30/95	**Good**...Better Than Ezra
17/55	**Good And Lonesome**...Kay Starr
7/92	**Good Enough**...Bobby Brown
	Good Foot ..see: Get On The
8/92	**Good For Me**...Amy Grant
39/79	**Good Friend**...Mary MacGregor
11/79	**Good Girls Don't**...Knack
	Good Golly, Miss Molly
10/58	Little Richard
4/66	Mitch Ryder (medley)
25/76	**Good Hearted Woman**...Waylon Jennings & Willie Nelson
23A/95	**Good Intentions**...Toad The Wet Sprocket
18/63	**Good Life**...Tony Bennett
1/66	**Good Lovin'**...Young Rascals
30/69	**Good Lovin' Ain't Easy To Come By**...Marvin Gaye & Tammi Terrell
36/75	**Good Lovin' Gone Bad**...Bad Company
1/62	**Good Luck Charm**...Elvis Presley
29/02	**Good Morning Beautiful**...Steve Holy
34/73	**Good Morning Heartache**...Diana Ross
3/69	**Good Morning Starshine**...Oliver
11/64	**Good News**...Sam Cooke
	(Good Ol' Boys) ..see: Theme From The Dukes Of Hazzard
21/69	**Good Old Rock 'N Roll (medley)**...Cat Mother & the All Night News Boys
11A/98	**Good Riddance (Time Of Your Life)**...Green Day
22/02	**Good Stuff**...Kenny Chesney
28/92	**Good Stuff**...the B-52's
2/68	**Good, The Bad And The Ugly**...Hugo Montenegro
1/89	**Good Thing**...Fine Young Cannibals
4/67	**Good Thing**...Paul Revere & The Raiders
11/61	**Good Time Baby**...Bobby Rydell
9/72	**Good Time Charlie's Got The Blues**...Danny O'Keefe
1/79	**Good Times**...Chic
11/64	**Good Times**...Sam Cooke
22/02	**Good Times**...Styles
3/60	**Good Timin'**...Jimmy Jones
40/79	**Good Timin'**...Beach Boys

POS/YR	RECORD TITLE. . .ARTIST
	Good Vibrations
1/66	Beach Boys
34/76	Todd Rundgren
1/91	**Good Vibrations**...Marky Mark & The Funky Bunch
11/98	**Goodbye**...Spice Girls
13/69	**Goodbye**...Mary Hopkin
17/86	**Goodbye**...Night Ranger
8/59	**Goodbye Baby**...Jack Scott
33/64	**Goodbye Baby (Baby Goodbye)**...Solomon Burke
3/61	**Goodbye Cruel World**...James Darren
19/00	**Goodbye Earl**...Dixie Chicks
15/78	**Goodbye Girl**...David Gates
33/86	**Goodbye Is Forever**...Arcadia
11/59	**Goodbye Jimmy, Goodbye**...Kathy Linden
31/68	**Goodbye My Love**...James Brown
15/79	**Goodbye Stranger**...Supertramp
7/72	**Goodbye To Love**...Carpenters
27/98	**Goodbye To My Homies**...Master P
21/02	**Goodbye To You**...Michelle Branch
2/73	**Goodbye Yellow Brick Road**...Elton John
21/65	**Goodnight**...Roy Orbison
	Goodnight My Love
32/57	McGuire Sisters
32/63	Fleetwoods
27/69	Paul Anka
5/79	**Goodnight Tonight**...Wings
20/57	**Goody Goody**...Frankie Lymon
37/68	**Goody Goody Gumdrops**...1910 Fruitgum Co.
12/83	**Goody Two Shoes**...Adam Ant
10/85	**Goonies 'R' Good Enough**...Cyndi Lauper
8/03	**Gossip Folks**...Missy Elliott
24/60	**Got A Girl**...Four Preps
10/84	**Got A Hold On Me**...Christine McVie
40/91	**Got A Love For You**...Jomanda
39/58	**Got A Match?**...Daddy-O's
20/94	**Got Me Waiting**...Heavy D & The Boyz
1/88	**Got My Mind Set On You**...George Harrison
36A/97	**Got 'Til It's Gone**...Janet Jackson
12/79	**Got To Be Real**...Cheryl Lynn
4/71	**Got To Be There**...Michael Jackson
40/00	**Got To Get It**...Sisqó
	Got To Get You Into My Life
7/76	Beatles
9/78	Earth, Wind & Fire
22/65	**Got To Get You Off My Mind**...Solomon Burke
1/77	**Got To Give It Up**...Marvin Gaye
33/99	**Got Your Money**...Ol' Dirty Bastard
9/97	**Gotham City**...R. Kelly
34/02	**Gots Ta Be**...B2K
23/98	**Gotta Be**...Jagged Edge
10/02	**Gotta Get Thru This**...Daniel Bedingfield
21/70	**Gotta Hold On To This Feeling**...Jr. Walker
26/99	**Gotta Man**...Eve
24/79	**Gotta Serve Somebody**...Bob Dylan
4/00	**Gotta Tell You**...Samantha Mumba
4/59	**Gotta Travel On**...Billy Grammer

POS/YR	RECORD TITLE. . .ARTIST
1/66	**Hanky Panky**...Tommy James
10/90	**Hanky Panky**...Madonna
	Happening, The
1/67	Supremes
32/67	Herb Alpert
30/66	**Happenings Ten Years Time Ago**...Yardbirds
11/72	**Happiest Girl In The Whole U.S.A.**....Donna Fargo
15/99	**Happily Ever After**...Case
30/79	**Happiness**...Pointer Sisters
35/74	**Happiness Is Just Around The Bend**...Main Ingredient
	Happiness Street
20/56	Georgia Gibbs
38/56	Tony Bennett
8/02	**Happy**...Ashanti
20/87	**Happy**...Surface
22/72	**Happy**...Rolling Stones
16/78	**Happy Anniversary**...Little River Band
30/61	**Happy Birthday Blues**...Kathy Young
6/62	**Happy Birthday, Sweet Sixteen**...Neil Sedaka
5/76	**Happy Days**...Pratt & McClain
10/60	**Happy-Go-Lucky-Me**...Paul Evans
5/57	**Happy, Happy Birthday Baby**...Tune Weavers
22/69	**Happy Heart**...Andy Williams
24/67	**Happy Jack**...Who
19/76	**Happy Music**...Blackbyrds
1/59	**Happy Organ**...Dave 'Baby' Cortez
40/75	**Happy People**...Temptations
34/59	**Happy Reindeer**...Dancer, Prancer & Nervous
25/68	**Happy Song (Dum-Dum)**...Otis Redding
27/66	**Happy Summer Days**...Ronnie Dove
1/67	**Happy Together**...Turtles
6/56	**Happy Whistler**...Don Robertson
8/60	**Harbor Lights**...Platters
	Hard Day's Night
1/64	Beatles
29/66	Ramsey Lewis Trio
3/84	**Hard Habit To Break**...Chicago
1/58	**Hard Headed Woman**...Elvis Presley
15/99	**Hard Knock Life (Ghetto Anthem)**...Jay-Z
15/77	**Hard Luck Woman**...Kiss
30/77	**Hard Rock Cafe**...Carole King
4/55	**Hard To Get**...Gisele MacKenzie
26/91	**Hard To Handle**...Black Crowes
7/81	**Hard To Say**...Dan Fogelberg
	Hard To Say I'm Sorry
1/82	Chicago
8/97	Az Yet
3/82	**Harden My Heart**...Quarterflash
18/03	**Harder To Breathe**...Maroon5
5/99	**Hardest Thing**...98°
39/66	**Harlem Nocturne**...Viscounts
5/86	**Harlem Shuffle**...Rolling Stones
1/68	**Harper Valley P.T.A.**....Jeannie C. Riley
31/73	**Harry Hippie**...Bobby Womack
17/63	**Harry The Hairy Ape**...Ray Stevens
13/75	**Harry Truman**...Chicago

POS/YR	RECORD TITLE. . .ARTIST
30/93	**Hat 2 Da Back**...TLC
5/61	**Hats Off To Larry**...Del Shannon
11/64	**Haunted House**...Gene Simmons
	Hava Nagila ..see: Dance Everyone Dance
31/62	**Have A Good Time**...Sue Thompson
5/64	**Have I The Right?**...Honeycombs
5/93	**Have I Told You Lately**...Rod Stewart (Live)
29/57	**Have I Told You Lately That I Love You?**...Ricky Nelson
1/99	**Have You Ever?**...Brandy
12/92	**Have You Ever Needed Someone So Bad**...Def Leppard
1/95	**Have You Ever Really Loved A Woman?**...Bryan Adams
8/71	**Have You Ever Seen The Rain**...Creedence Clearwater Revival
22/03	**Have You Forgotten?**...Darryl Worley
18/63	**Have You Heard**...Duprees
24/65	**Have You Looked Into Your Heart**...Jerry Vale
1/75	**Have You Never Been Mellow**...Olivia Newton-John
	Have You Seen Her
3/71	Chi-Lites
4/90	M.C. Hammer
	(Have You Seen My Wife Mr. Jones) ..see: New York Mining Disaster 1941
9/66	**Have You Seen Your Mother, Baby, Standing In The Shadow?**...Rolling Stones
14/74	**Haven't Got Time For The Pain**...Carly Simon
26/79	**Haven't Stopped Dancing Yet**...Gonzalez
	Having A Party
17/62	Sam Cooke
36/94	Rod Stewart (with Ronnie Wood)
	Having My Baby ..see: (You're)
4/69	**Hawaii Five-O**...Ventures
33/65	**Hawaii Tattoo**...Waikikis
11/59	**Hawaiian Wedding Song (Ke Kali Nei Au)**...Andy Williams
18/96	**Hay**...Crucial Conflict
9/92	**Hazard**...Richard Marx
	Hazy Shade Of Winter
13/66	Simon & Garfunkel
2/88	Bangles
	He
4/55	Al Hibbler
10/55	McGuire Sisters
18/66	Righteous Brothers
	He Ain't Heavy, He's My Brother
7/70	Hollies
20/70	Neil Diamond
F/76	Olivia Newton-John
15/00	**He Can't Love U**...Jagged Edge
33/81	**He Can't Love You**...Michael Stanley Band
30/99	**He Didn't Have To Be**...Brad Paisley
	He Don't Love You (Like I Love You)
7/60	Jerry Butler
1/75	Tony Orlando & Dawn
34/62	**He Knows I Love Him Too Much**...Paris Sisters

POS/YR	RECORD TITLE. . .ARTIST
2/00	**He Loves U Not**...Dream
2/00	**He Wasn't Man Enough**...Toni Braxton
	He Will Break Your Heart ..see: He Don't Love You
	He'll Have To Go (Stay)
2/60	Jim Reeves
4/60	Jeanne Black
25/86	**He'll Never Love You (Like I Do)**...Freddie Jackson
36/76	**He's A Friend**...Eddie Kendricks
30/81	**He's A Liar**...Bee Gees
1/62	**He's A Rebel**...Crystals
1/58	**He's Got The Whole World (In His Hands)**...Laurie London
7/95	**He's Mine**...MoKenStef
16/57	**He's Mine**...Platters
14/61	**(He's My) Dreamboat**...Connie Francis
1/63	**He's So Fine**...Chiffons
3/80	**He's So Shy**...Pointer Sisters
11/63	**He's Sure The Boy I Love**...Crystals
30/61	**(He's) The Great Impostor**...Fleetwoods
9/79	**He's The Greatest Dancer**...Sister Sledge
14/79	**Head Games**...Foreigner
3A/96	**Head Over Feet**...Alanis Morissette
3/85	**Head Over Heels**...Tears For Fears
11/84	**Head Over Heels**...Go-Go's
35/97	**Head Over Heels**...Allure
1/87	**Head To Toe**...Lisa Lisa & Cult Jam
35/80	**Headed For A Fall**...Firefall
19/89	**Headed For A Heartbreak**...Winger
16/03	**Headstrong**...Trapt
27/93	**Heal The World**...Michael Jackson
13/89	**Healing Hands**...Elton John
18/01	**Heard It All Before**...Sunshine Anderson
14/77	**Heard It In A Love Song**...Marshall Tucker Band
	Heart
6/55	Eddie Fisher
13/55	Four Aces
4/87	**Heart And Soul**...T'Pau
8/83	**Heart And Soul**...Huey Lewis
	Heart And Soul
18/61	Cleftones
25/61	Jan & Dean
3/82	**Heart Attack**...Olivia Newton-John
9/65	**Heart Full Of Soul**...Yardbirds
21/80	**Heart Hotels**...Dan Fogelberg
15/62	**Heart In Hand**...Brenda Lee
24/81	**Heart Like A Wheel**...Steve Miller Band
32/90	**Heart Like A Wheel**...Human League
1/79	**Heart Of Glass**...Blondie
1/72	**Heart Of Gold**...Neil Young
35/88	**Heart Of Mine**...Boz Scaggs
6/84	**Heart Of Rock & Roll**...Huey Lewis
12/90	**Heart Of Stone**...Taylor Dayne
19/65	**Heart Of Stone**...Rolling Stones
20/90	**Heart Of Stone**...Cher
21/90	**Heart Of The Matter**...Don Henley

POS/YR	RECORD TITLE. . .ARTIST
20/79	**Heart Of The Night**...Poco
25/83	**Heart Of The Night**...Juice Newton
15/83	**Heart To Heart**...Kenny Loggins
1/79	**Heartache Tonight**...Eagles
7/61	**Heartaches**...Marcels
	Heartaches By The Number
1/59	Guy Mitchell
35/65	Johnny Tillotson
5/86	**Heartbeat**...Don Johnson
13/90	**Heartbeat**...Seduction
3/73	**Heartbeat - It's A Lovebeat**...DeFranco Family
26/87	**Heartbreak Beat**...Psychedelic Furs
1/56	**Heartbreak Hotel**...Elvis Presley
2/99	**Heartbreak Hotel**...Whitney Houston
22/81	**Heartbreak Hotel**...Jacksons
38/60	**Heartbreak (It's Hurtin' Me)**...Little Willie John
39/74	**Heartbreak Kid**...Bo Donaldson
1/99	**Heartbreaker**...Mariah Carey
10/83	**Heartbreaker**...Dionne Warwick
23/80	**Heartbreaker**...Pat Benatar
37/78	**Heartbreaker**...Dolly Parton
	(also see: Doo Doo Doo Doo Doo)
24/78	**Heartless**...Heart
5/82	**Heartlight**...Neil Diamond
8/81	**Hearts**...Marty Balin
28/92	**Hearts Don't Think (They Feel)!**...Natural Selection
	Hearts Of Stone
1/55	Fontane Sisters
15/55	Charms
20/61	Bill Black's Combo
37/73	Blue Ridge Rangers
19/81	**Hearts On Fire**...Randy Meisner
26/87	**Hearts On Fire**...Bryan Adams
2/85	**Heat Is On**...Glenn Frey
4/82	**Heat Of The Moment**...Asia
19/91	**Heat Of The Moment**...After 7
6/87	**Heat Of The Night**...Bryan Adams
	Heat Wave
4/63	Martha & The Vandellas
5/75	Linda Ronstadt
29/69	**Heather Honey**...Tommy Roe
	Heaven
1/85	Bryan Adams
8/02	DJ Sammy & Yanou
2/89	**Heaven**...Warrant
27/98	**Heaven**...Nu Flavor
39/69	**Heaven**...Rascals
5/89	**Heaven Help Me**...Deon Estus (with George Michael)
9/70	**Heaven Help Us All**...Stevie Wonder
12/86	**Heaven In Your Eyes**...Loverboy
1/87	**Heaven Is A Place On Earth**...Belinda Carlisle
4/79	**Heaven Knows**...Donna Summer with Brooklyn Dreams
24/69	**Heaven Knows**...Grass Roots
15/76	**Heaven Must Be Missing An Angel**...Tavares
11/79	**Heaven Must Have Sent You**...Bonnie Pointer

POS/YR	RECORD TITLE. . .ARTIST
39/56	**Heaven On Earth**...Platters
6/77	**Heaven On The 7th Floor**...Paul Nicholas
27/98	**Heaven's What I Feel**...Gloria Estefan
40/59	**Heavenly Lover**...Teresa Brewer
27/71	**Heavy Makes You Happy (Sha-Na-Boom Boom)**...Staple Singers
33/70	**Heed The Call**...Kenny Rogers & The First Edition
10/74	**Helen Wheels**...Paul McCartney
17/03	**Hell Yeah**...Ginuwine
13/02	**Hella Good**...No Doubt
1/84	**Hello**...Lionel Richie
6/81	**Hello Again**...Neil Diamond
20/84	**Hello Again**...Cars
1/64	**Hello, Dolly!**...Louis Armstrong
1/67	**Hello Goodbye**...Beatles
26/63	**Hello Heartache, Goodbye Love**...Little Peggy March
26/67	**Hello Hello**...Sopwith "Camel"
35/73	**Hello Hurray**...Alice Cooper
1/68	**Hello, I Love You**...Doors
5/73	**Hello It's Me**...Todd Rundgren
9/61	**Hello Mary Lou**...Ricky Nelson
2/63	**Hello Mudduh, Hello Fadduh! (A Letter From Camp)**...Allan Sherman
24/76	**Hello Old Friend**...Eric Clapton
	Hello Stranger
3/63	Barbara Lewis
15/77	Yvonne Elliman
12/61	**Hello Walls**...Faron Young
23/60	**Hello Young Lovers**...Paul Anka
1/65	**Help!**...Beatles
14/77	**Help Is On Its Way**...Little River Band
7/74	**Help Me**...Joni Mitchell
	Help Me Girl
29/66	Animals
37/66	Outsiders
	Help Me Make It Through The Night
8/71	Sammi Smith
33/72	Gladys Knight
	Help Me, Rhonda
1/65	Beach Boys
22/75	Johnny Rivers
29/03	**Help Pour Out The Rain (Lacey's Song)**...Buddy Jewell
35/68	**Help Yourself**...Tom Jones
30/01	**Hemorrhage (In My Hands)**...Fuel
6/62	**Her Royal Majesty**...James Darren
11/81	**Her Town Too**...James Taylor & J.D. Souther
6/90	**Here And Now**...Luther Vandross
8/68	**Here Comes The Judge**...Shorty Long
19/68	**Here Comes The Judge**...Pigmeat Markham
23/77	**Here Come Those Tears Again**...Jackson Browne
13/67	**Here Comes My Baby**...Tremeloes
14/59	**Here Comes Summer**...Jerry Keller
15/71	**Here Comes That Rainy Day Feeling Again**...Fortunes

POS/YR	RECORD TITLE. . .ARTIST
1/94	**Here Comes The Hotstepper**...Ini Kamoze
24/65	**Here Comes The Night**...Them
4/84	**Here Comes The Rain Again**...Eurythmics
16/71	**Here Comes The Sun**...Richie Havens
	Here I Am (Come And Take Me)
10/73	Al Green
7/91	UB40
5/81	**Here I Am (Just When I Thought I Was Over You)**...Air Supply
1/87	**Here I Go Again**...Whitesnake
37/69	**Here I Go Again**...Miracles
18/02	**Here Is Gone**...Goo Goo Dolls
27/65	**Here It Comes Again**...Fortunes
6/90	**Here We Are**...Gloria Estefan
3/91	**Here We Go**...C + C Music Factory
11/93	**Here We Go Again!**...Portrait
15/67	**Here We Go Again**...Ray Charles
20/88	**Here With Me**...REO Speedwagon
5/03	**Here Without You**...3 Doors Down
3/78	**Here You Come Again**...Dolly Parton
30/01	**Here's To The Night**...Eve 6
1/93	**Hero**...Mariah Carey
3/01	**Hero**...Enrique Iglesias
3/02	**Hero**...Chad Kroeger
27A/98	**Heroes**...Wallflowers
12/67	**Heroes And Villains**...Beach Boys
1/62	**Hey! Baby**...Bruce Channel
5/02	**Hey Baby**...No Doubt
18/89	**Hey Baby**...Henry Lee Summer
12/67	**Hey Baby (They're Playing Our Song)**...Buckinghams
19/72	**Hey Big Brother**...Rare Earth
23/64	**Hey, Bobba Needle**...Chubby Checker
7/78	**Hey Deanie**...Shaun Cassidy
13/91	**Hey Donna**...Rythm Syndicate
	Hey, Girl
10/63	Freddie Scott
35/68	Bobby Vee (medley)
9/72	Donny Osmond
35/73	**Hey Girl (I Like Your Style)**...Temptations
29/64	**Hey Harmonica Man**...Stevie Wonder
3/57	**Hey! Jealous Lover**...Frank Sinatra
25/93	**Hey Jealousy**...Gin Blossoms
32/64	**Hey Jean, Hey Dean**...Dean & Jean
31/66	**Hey Joe**...Leaves
	Hey Jude
1/68	Beatles
23/69	Wilson Pickett
36/89	**Hey Ladies**...Beastie Boys
35/70	**Hey Lawdy Mama**...Steppenwolf
33/99	**Hey Leonardo (she likes me for me)**...Blessid Union Of Souls
31/67	**Hey, Leroy, Your Mama's Callin' You**...Jimmy Castor
20/62	**Hey, Let's Twist**...Joey Dee
4/64	**Hey Little Cobra**...Rip Chords
13/63	**Hey Little Girl**...Major Lance
20/59	**Hey Little Girl**...Dee Clark

POS/YR	RECORD TITLE. . .ARTIST
29/57	**Hey! Little Girl**...Techniques
38/62	**Hey! Little Girl**...Del Shannon
3/95	**Hey Lover**...LL Cool J
3/02	**Hey Ma**...Cam'ron
12/55	**Hey, Mr. Banjo**...Sunnysiders
6/93	**Hey Mr. D.J.**....Zhané
24/70	**Hey, Mister Sun**...Bobby Sherman
10/81	**Hey Nineteen**...Steely Dan
1/63	**Hey Paula**...Paul & Paula
1/54	**Hey There**...Rosemary Clooney
	Hey There Lonely Girl (Boy)
27/63	Ruby & The Romantics
2/70	Eddie Holman
31/80	Robert John
F/71	**Hey Tonight**...Creedence Clearwater Revival
16/68	**Hey, Western Union Man**...Jerry Butler
1/75	**(Hey Won't You Play) Another Somebody Done Somebody Wrong Song**...B.J. Thomas
1/03	**Hey Ya!**...OutKast
21/75	**Hey You**...Bachman-Turner Overdrive
14/70	**Hi-De-Ho**...Blood, Sweat & Tears
	Hi-Heel Sneakers
11/64	Tommy Tucker
25/68	José Feliciano
10/73	**Hi, Hi, Hi**...Wings
33/62	**Hide & Go Seek**...Bunker Hill
29/61	**Hide Away**...Freddy King
21/58	**Hideaway**...Four Esquires
20/62	**Hide 'Nor Hair**...Ray Charles
3/91	**High Enough**...Damn Yankees
	High-Heel ..see: Hi-Heel
30/59	**High Hopes**...Frank Sinatra
8/85	**High On You**...Survivor
21/58	**High School Confidential**...Jerry Lee Lewis
17/77	**High School Dance**...Sylvers
F/57	**High School Dance**...Larry Williams
28/59	**High School U.S.A. (Area)**...Tommy Facenda
37/58	**High Sign**...Diamonds
22/71	**High Time We Went**...Joe Cocker
7/00	**Higher**...Creed
	Higher & Higher ..see: (Your Love Keeps Lifting Me)
4/73	**Higher Ground**...Stevie Wonder
1/86	**Higher Love**...Steve Winwood
37/74	**Higher Plane**...Kool & The Gang
26/79	**Highway Song**...Blackfoot
14/75	**Hijack**...Herbie Mann
	Hill Street Blues ..see: Theme From
6/80	**Him**...Rupert Holmes
5/67	**Him Or Me - What's It Gonna Be?**...Paul Revere & The Raiders
31/68	**Hip City**...Jr. Walker
8/93	**Hip Hop Hooray**...Naughty By Nature
37/67	**Hip Hug-Her**...Booker T. & The M.G.'s
3/86	**Hip To Be Square**...Huey Lewis
24/64	**Hippy Hippy Shake**...Swinging Blue Jeans
14/90	**Hippychick**...Soho

POS/YR	RECORD TITLE. . .ARTIST
	His Latest Flame ..see: (Marie's the Name)
39/66	**History Repeats Itself**...Buddy Starcher
2/01	**Hit 'Em Up Style (Oops!)**...Blu Cantrell
3/96	**Hit Me Off**...New Edition
9/80	**Hit Me With Your Best Shot**...Pat Benatar
	(Hit Record) ..see: Overnight Sensation
	Hit The Road Jack
1/61	Ray Charles
40/76	Stampeders
30/63	**Hitch Hike**...Marvin Gaye
34/68	**Hitch It To The Horse**...Fantastic Johnny C
	(Hitchhiker, The) ..see: Popeye
5/70	**Hitchin' A Ride**...Vanity Fare
9/73	**Hocus Pocus**...Focus
35/76	**Hold Back The Night**...Trammps
14/72	**Hold Her Tight**...Osmonds
4/82	**Hold Me**...Fleetwood Mac
35/99	**Hold Me**...Brian McKnight
3/84	**Hold Me Now**...Thompson Twins
8/65	**Hold Me, Thrill Me, Kiss Me**...Mel Carter
16/95	**Hold Me, Thrill Me, Kiss Me, Kill Me**...U2
5/68	**Hold Me Tight**...Johnny Nash
40/83	**Hold Me 'Til The Mornin' Comes**...Paul Anka
2/54	**Hold My Hand**...Don Cornell
10/95	**Hold My Hand**...Hootie & The Blowfish
1/90	**Hold On**...Wilson Phillips
2/90	**Hold On**...En Vogue
15/82	**Hold On**...Santana
16/95	**Hold On**...Jamie Walters
18/79	**Hold On**...Ian Gomm
38/79	**Hold On**...Triumph
40/80	**Hold On**...Kansas
21/66	**Hold On! I'm A Comin'**...Sam & Dave
27/81	**Hold On Loosely**....38 Special
12/92	**Hold On My Heart**...Genesis
10/81	**Hold On Tight**...ELO
33/99	**Hold On To Me**...John Michael Montgomery
10/80	**Hold On To My Love**...Jimmy Ruffin
1/88	**Hold On To The Nights**...Richard Marx
5/79	**Hold The Line**...Toto
5/65	**Hold What You've Got**...Joe Tex
3/91	**Hold You Tight**...Tara Kemp
5/72	**Hold Your Head Up**...Argent
37/82	**Holdin' On**...Tané Cain
11/89	**Holding On**...Steve Winwood
17/75	**Holdin' On To Yesterday**...Ambrosia
1/86	**Holding Back The Years**...Simply Red
34/84	**Holding Out For A Hero**...Bonnie Tyler
4/91	**Hole Hearted**...Extreme
3/03	**Holidae In**...Chingy
16/67	**Holiday**...Bee Gees
16/84	**Holiday**...Madonna
29/87	**Holiday**...Other Ones
35/99	**Holla Holla**...Ja Rule
6/69	**Holly Holy**...Neil Diamond

POS/YR	RECORD TITLE. . .ARTIST
	Hollywood
32/77	Rufus, Feat. Chaka Khan
4s/03	Madonna
12/78	**Hollywood Nights**...Bob Seger
6/74	**Hollywood Swinging**...Kool & The Gang
23/66	**Holy Cow**...Lee Dorsey
34/67	**Homburg**...Procol Harum
28/79	**Home And Dry**...Gerry Rafferty
25/65	**Home Of The Brave**...Jody Miller
37/92	**Home Sweet Home '91**...Mötley Crüe ('91)
5/66	**Homeward Bound**...Simon & Garfunkel
28/60	**Honest I Do**...Innocents
32/57	**Honest I Do**...Jimmy Reed
23/88	**Honestly**...Stryper
24/79	**Honesty**...Billy Joel
1/68	**Honey**...Bobby Goldsboro
1/97	**Honey**...Mariah Carey
6/55	**Honey-Babe**...Art Mooney
11/67	**Honey Chile**...Martha & The Vandellas
19/70	**Honey Come Back**...Glen Campbell
27/74	**Honey, Honey**...Abba
39/92	**Honey Love**...R. Kelly
F/57	**Honey Rock**...Barney Kessel
1/57	**Honeycomb**...Jimmie Rodgers
19/87	**Honeythief, The**...Hipsway
8/72	**Honky Cat**...Elton John
2/56	**Honky Tonk**...Bill Doggett (Parts 1 & 2)
1/69	**Honky Tonk Women**...Rolling Stones
11/63	**Honolulu Lulu**...Jan & Dean
34A/98	**Hooch**...Everything
23/61	**Hoochi Coochi Coo**...Hank Ballard
23/96	**Hook**...Blues Traveler
	Hooked On A Feeling
5/69	B.J. Thomas
1/74	Blue Swede
10/82	**Hooked On Classics**...Royal Philharmonic Orchestra
31/82	**Hooked On Swing (medley)**...Larry Elgart
23/89	**Hooked On You**...Sweet Sensation
6/66	**Hooray For Hazel**...Tommy Roe
38/63	**Hootenanny**...Glencoves
36/82	**Hope You Love Me Like You Say You Do**...Huey Lewis
13/63	**Hopeless**...Andy Williams
28/93	**Hopelessly**...Rick Astley
3/78	**Hopelessly Devoted To You**...Olivia Newton-John
2/68	**Horse, The**...Cliff Nobles & Co.
1/72	**Horse With No Name**...America
3/78	**Hot Blooded**...Foreigner
5/00	**Hot Boyz**...Missy "Misdemeanor" Elliott
1/78	**Hot Child In The City**...Nick Gilder
1/56	**Hot Diggity (Dog Ziggity Boom)**...Perry Como
2/69	**Hot Fun In The Summertime**...Sly & The Family Stone
11/83	**Hot Girls In Love**...Loverboy
1/02	**Hot In Herre**...Nelly
23/82	**Hot In The City**...Billy Idol

POS/YR	RECORD TITLE. . .ARTIST
28/78	**Hot Legs**...Rod Stewart
5/77	**Hot Line**...Sylvers
31/78	**Hot Love, Cold World**...Bob Welch
21/79	**Hot Number**...Foxy
15/71	**Hot Pants**...James Brown
11/63	**Hot Pastrami**...Dartells
36/63	**Hot Pastrami With Mashed Potatoes**...Joey Dee
15/80	**Hot Rod Hearts**...Robbie Dupree
	Hot Rod Lincoln
26/60	Johnny Bond
33/60	Charlie Ryan
9/72	Commander Cody
7/00	**(Hot S**t) Country Grammar**...Nelly
14/69	**Hot Smoke & Sasafrass**...Bubble Puppy
1/79	**Hot Stuff**...Donna Summer
18/79	**Hot Summer Nights**...Night
1/77	**Hotel California**...Eagles
3/63	**Hotel Happiness**...Brook Benton
1/56	**Hound Dog**...Elvis Presley
9/59	**Hound Dog Man**...Fabian
15/87	**Hourglass**...Squeeze
9/55	**House Of Blue Lights**...Chuck Miller
37/95	**House Of Love**...Amy Grant with Vince Gill
28/90	**House Of Pain**...Faster Pussycat
	House Of The Rising Sun
1/64	Animals
7/70	Frijid Pink
6/68	**House That Jack Built**...Aretha Franklin
16/56	**House With Love In It**...Four Lads
37/91	**Housecall (Your Body Can't Lie To Me)**...Shabba Ranks
21/65	**Houston**...Dean Martin
33/60	**How About That**...Dee Clark
38/92	**How About That**...Bad Company
	How Am I Supposed To Live Without You
12/83	Laura Branigan
1/90	Michael Bolton
22/58	**How Are Ya' Fixed For Love?**...Frank Sinatra & Keely Smith
4A/97	**How Bizarre**...OMC
12/81	**How 'Bout Us**...Champaign
	How Can I Be Sure
4/67	Young Rascals
25/72	David Cassidy
11/91	**How Can I Ease The Pain**...Lisa Fischer
3/88	**How Can I Fall?**...Breathe
22/73	**How Can I Tell Her**...Lobo
3/90	**How Can We Be Lovers**...Michael Bolton
1/71	**How Can You Mend A Broken Heart**...Bee Gees
1/77	**How Deep Is Your Love**...Bee Gees
3/98	**How Deep Is Your Love**...Dru Hill
	How Do I Live
2/97	LeAnn Rimes
23/97	Trisha Yearwood
10/80	**How Do I Make You**...Linda Ronstadt
22/80	**How Do I Survive**...Amy Holland
1/96	**How Do U Want It**...2Pac

POS/YR	RECORD TITLE. . . ARTIST
8/95	I Believe...Blessid Union Of Souls
31/03	I Believe...Diamond Rio
33/64	I Believe...Bachelors
33/82	I Believe...Chilliwack
2/96	I Believe I Can Fly...R. Kelly
22/72	I Believe In Music...Gallery
24/80	I Believe In You...Don Williams
4/97	I Believe In You And Me...Whitney Houston
11/73	I Believe In You (You Believe In Me)...Johnnie Taylor
15/75	(I Believe) There's Nothing Stronger Than Our Love...Paul Anka/Odia Coates
27/77	I Believe You...Dorothy Moore
27/75	I Belong To You...Love Unlimited
28/95	I Belong To You...Toni Braxton
6/97	I Belong To You (Every Time I See Your Face)...Rome
35/02	I Breathe In, I Breathe Out...Chris Cagle
12/03	I Can...Nas
	I Can Dance ..see: Long Tall Glasses
14/98	I Can Do That...Montell Jordan
6/84	I Can Dream About You...Dan Hartman
24/69	I Can Hear Music...Beach Boys
1/74	I Can Help...Billy Swan
28/97	I Can Love You...Mary J. Blige
5/95	I Can Love You Like That...All-4-One
32/66	I Can Make It With You...Pozo-Seco Singers
6/65	I Can Never Go Home Anymore...Shangri-Las
	I Can See Clearly Now
1/72	Johnny Nash
18/94	Jimmy Cliff
9/67	I Can See For Miles...Who
	(I Can See It In Your Eyes) ..see: Circle Is Small
22/69	I Can Sing A Rainbow (medley)...Dells
39/81	I Can Take Care Of Myself...Billy & The Beaters
22/68	I Can Take Or Leave Your Loving...Herman's Hermits
35/73	I Can Understand It...New Birth
7/92	I Can't Dance...Genesis
26/84	I Can't Drive 55...Sammy Hagar
1/69	I Can't Get Next To You...Temptations
	(I Can't Get No) Satisfaction
1/65	Rolling Stones
31/66	Otis Redding
1/82	I Can't Go For That (No Can Do)...Daryl Hall & John Oates
34/66	I Can't Grow Peaches On A Cherry Tree...Just Us
29/76	I Can't Hear You No More...Helen Reddy
12/80	I Can't Help It...Andy Gibb & Olivia Newton-John
24/62	I Can't Help It (If I'm Still In Love With You)...Johnny Tillotson
	I Can't Help Myself
1/65	Four Tops
22/72	Donnie Elbert
40/80	Bonnie Pointer

POS/YR	RECORD TITLE. . . ARTIST
39/60	(I Can't Help You) I'm Falling Too...Skeeter Davis
	(also see: Please Help Me, I'm Falling)
13/84	I Can't Hold Back...Survivor
31/80	I Can't Let Go...Linda Ronstadt
22/56	I Can't Love You Enough...LaVern Baker
18/92	I Can't Make You Love Me...Bonnie Raitt
28/69	I Can't See Myself Leaving You...Aretha Franklin
5/96	I Can't Sleep Baby (If I)...R. Kelly
10/81	I Can't Stand It...Eric Clapton
14/79	I Can't Stand It No More...Peter Frampton
28/68	I Can't Stand Myself (When You Touch Me)...James Brown
	I Can't Stand The Rain
38/73	Ann Peebles
18/78	Eruption
7/63	I Can't Stay Mad At You...Skeeter Davis
9/68	I Can't Stop Dancing...Archie Bell
1/62	I Can't Stop Loving You...Ray Charles
35/64	I Can't Stop Talking About You...Steve & Eydie
8/80	I Can't Tell You Why...Eagles
37/68	I Can't Turn You Loose...Chambers Brothers
3/86	I Can't Wait...Nu Shooz
16/86	I Can't Wait...Stevie Nicks
8/91	I Can't Wait Another Minute...Hi-Five
16/02	I Care 4 U...Aaliyah
23/97	I Care 'Bout You...Milestone
32/66	I Chose To Sing The Blues...Ray Charles
8A/95	I Could Fall In Love...Selena
20/56	I Could Have Danced All Night...Sylvia Syms
13/68	I Could Never Love Another (After Loving You)...Temptations
18/81	I Could Never Miss You (More Than I Do)...Lulu
10/88	I Could Never Take The Place Of Your Man...Prince
	I Could Not Ask For More
37/99	Edwin McCain
35/01	Sara Evans
9/66	I Couldn't Live Without Your Love...Petula Clark
32/83	I Couldn't Say No...Robert Ellis Orrall w/Carlene Carter
17/61	I Count The Tears...Drifters
6/59	I Cried A Tear...LaVern Baker
40/01	I Cry...Ja Rule
	I Didn't Get To Sleep At All ..see: (Last Night)
35/72	I Didn't Know I Loved You (Till I Saw You Rock And Roll)...Gary Glitter
2/86	I Didn't Mean To Turn You On...Robert Palmer
23/90	I Didn't Want To Need You...Heart
9/67	I Dig Rock And Roll Music...Peter, Paul & Mary
16/01	I Do!!...Toya
17/98	I Do...Lisa Loeb

POS/YR	RECORD TITLE. . . ARTIST
	I Do
37/65	Marvelows
24/83	J. Geils Band
13/99	**I Do (Cherish You)**...98°
15/76	**I Do, I Do, I Do, I Do, I Do**...Abba
	I Do It For You ..see: (Everything I Do)
	I Do Love You
26/65	Billy Stewart
20/79	GQ
37/60	**(I Do The) Shimmy Shimmy**...Bobby Freeman
29/84	**I Do'wanna Know**...REO Speedwagon
23/86	**I Do What I Do...(Theme for 9 1/2 Weeks)**...John Taylor Jonathan Elias
20/87	**I Do You**...Jets
18/71	**I Don't Blame You At All**...Miracles
39/83	**I Don't Care Anymore**...Phil Collins
6/98	**I Don't Ever Want To See You Again**...Uncle Sam
1/90	**I Don't Have The Heart**...James Ingram
35/02	**I Don't Have To Be Me ('Til Monday)**...Steve Azar
23/91	**I Don't Know Anybody Else**...Black Box
	I Don't Know How To Love Him
13/71	Helen Reddy
28/71	Yvonne Elliman
23/79	**I Don't Know If It's Right**...Evelyn "Champagne" King
35/82	**I Don't Know Where To Start**...Eddie Rabbitt
12/61	**I Don't Know Why**...Linda Scott
39/69	**I Don't Know Why**...Stevie Wonder **(also see: But I Do)**
8/75	**I Don't Like To Sleep Alone**...Paul Anka/Odia Coates
38/87	**I Don't Mind At All**...Bourgeois Tagg
3/81	**I Don't Need You**...Kenny Rogers
5s/02	**I Don't Really Know**...Brandy Moss-Scott
35/00	**I Don't Wanna**...Aaliyah **(also see: I Don't Want To)**
37/64	**I Don't Wanna Be A Loser**...Lesley Gore
1/91	**I Don't Wanna Cry**...Mariah Carey
9/93	**I Don't Wanna Fight**...Tina Turner
2/88	**I Don't Wanna Go On With You Like That**...Elton John
3/88	**I Don't Wanna Live Without Your Love**...Chicago
35/65	**I Don't Wanna Lose You Baby**...Chad & Jeremy
20/69	**I Don't Want Nobody To Give Me Nothing**...James Brown
19/97	**I Don't Want To**...Toni Braxton **(also see: I Don't Wanna)**
31/88	**I Don't Want To Be A Hero**...Johnny Hates Jazz
22/64	**I Don't Want To Be Hurt Anymore**...Nat King Cole
	I Don't Want To Be Right ..see: (If Loving You Is Wrong)
36/61	**I Don't Want To Cry**...Chuck Jackson
17/71	**I Don't Want To Do Wrong**...Gladys Knight
5/88	**I Don't Want To Live Without You**...Foreigner

POS/YR	RECORD TITLE. . . ARTIST
	I Don't Want To Miss A Thing
1/98	Aerosmith
17/99	Mark Chesnutt
34/64	**I Don't Want To See Tomorrow**...Nat King Cole
16/64	**I Don't Want To See You Again**...Peter & Gordon
39/65	**I Don't Want To Spoil The Party**...Beatles
33/61	**I Don't Want To Take A Chance**...Mary Wells
11/98	**I Don't Want To Wait**...Paula Cole
36/80	**I Don't Want To Walk Without You**...Barry Manilow
4/88	**I Don't Want Your Love**...Duran Duran
9/57	**I Dreamed**...Betty Johnson
20/61	**I Dreamed Of A Hill-Billy Heaven**...Tex Ritter
6/89	**I Drove All Night**...Cyndi Lauper
12/61	**I Fall To Pieces**...Patsy Cline
21/74	**I Feel A Song (In My Heart)**...Gladys Knight
1/64	**I Feel Fine**...Beatles
3/84	**I Feel For You**...Chaka Khan
38/57	**I Feel Good**...Shirley & Lee
F/76	**I Feel Like A Bullet (In The Gun Of Robert Ford)**...Elton John
6/77	**I Feel Love**...Donna Summer
5/61	**I Feel So Bad**...Elvis Presley
	I Feel The Earth Move
F/71	Carole King
25/89	Martika
37/93	**I Feel You**...Depeche Mode
8/96	**I Finally Found Someone**...Barbra Streisand & Bryan Adams
9/66	**I Fought The Law**...Bobby Fuller Four
30/65	**I Found A Girl**...Jan & Dean
32/67	**I Found A Love**...Wilson Pickett
31/82	**I Found Somebody**...Glenn Frey
10/88	**I Found Someone**...Cher
F/70	**I Found That Girl**...Jackson 5
1/64	**I Get Around**...Beach Boys
11/93	**I Get Around**...2Pac
32/82	**I Get Excited**...Rick Springfield
37/75	**I Get Lifted**...George McCrae
3/98	**I Get Lonely**...Janet Jackson
34/68	**I Get The Sweetest Feeling**...Jackie Wilson
2/88	**I Get Weak**...Belinda Carlisle
13A/96	**I Go Blind**...Hootie & The Blowfish
7/78	**I Go Crazy**...Paul Davis
6/90	**I Go To Extremes**...Billy Joel
9/65	**I Go To Pieces**...Peter & Gordon
10/58	**I Got A Feeling**...Ricky Nelson
25/69	**I Got A Line On You**...Spirit
14/93	**I Got A Man**...Positive K
10/73	**I Got A Name**...Jim Croce
27/93	**I Got A Thang 4 Ya!**...Lo-Key?
24/59	**I Got A Wife**...Mark IV
20/62	**I Got A Woman**...Jimmy McGriff
27/73	**I Got Ants In My Pants**...James Brown
8/95	**I Got 5 On It**...Luniz
7/95	**I Got Id**...Pearl Jam

POS/YR	RECORD TITLE. . . ARTIST
20/79	**I Got My Mind Made Up (You Can Get It Girl)**...Instant Funk
3/67	**I Got Rhythm**...Happenings
37/75	**I Got Stoned And I Missed It**...Jim Stafford
8/58	**I Got Stung**...Elvis Presley
6/68	**I Got The Feelin'**...James Brown
16/66	**I Got The Feelin' (Oh No No)**...Neil Diamond
16/98	**I Got The Hook Up!**...Master P
28/63	**I Got What I Wanted**...Brook Benton
	I Got You Babe
1/65	Sonny & Cher
28/85	UB40 With Chrissie Hynde
3/65	**I Got You (I Feel Good)**...James Brown
2/72	**I Gotcha**...Joe Tex
35/64	**I Gotta Dance To Keep From Crying**...Miracles
20/60	**I Gotta Know**...Elvis Presley
4/84	**I Guess That's Why They Call It The Blues**...Elton John
34/69	**I Guess The Lord Must Be In New York City**...Nilsson
17/67	**I Had A Dream**...Paul Revere & The Raiders
11/67	**I Had Too Much To Dream (Last Night)**...Electric Prunes
8/88	**I Hate Myself For Loving You**...Joan Jett
12/95	**I Hate U**...Prince
36/64	**I Have A Boyfriend**...Chiffons
4/93	**I Have Nothing**...Whitney Houston
1/65	**I Hear A Symphony**...Supremes
30/66	**I Hear Trumpets Blow**...Tokens
	I Hear You Knocking
2/55	Gale Storm
4/71	Dave Edmunds
4/87	**I Heard A Rumour**...Bananarama
	I Heard It Through The Grapevine
2/67	Gladys Knight
1/68	Marvin Gaye
1/74	**I Honestly Love You**...Olivia Newton-John
14/01	**I Hope You Dance**...Lee Ann Womack
1/84	**I Just Called To Say I Love You**...Stevie Wonder
9/70	**I Just Can't Help Believing**...B.J. Thomas
1/87	**I Just Can't Stop Loving You**...Michael Jackson
1/87	**(I Just) Died In Your Arms**...Cutting Crew
17/57	**I Just Don't Know**...Four Lads
26/66	**I Just Don't Know What To Do With Myself**...Dionne Warwick
17/61	**I Just Don't Understand**...Ann-Margret
12/79	**I Just Fall In Love Again**...Anne Murray
27/03	**I Just Wanna Be Mad**...Terri Clark
11/00	**I Just Wanna Love U (Give It 2 Me)**...Jay-Z
4/78	**I Just Wanna Stop**...Gino Vannelli
1/77	**I Just Want To Be Your Everything**...Andy Gibb
7/71	**I Just Want To Celebrate**...Rare Earth
33/77	**I Just Want To Make Love To You**...Foghat (Live)
4/82	**I Keep Forgettin' (Every Time You're Near)**...Michael McDonald

POS/YR	RECORD TITLE. . . ARTIST
35/02	**I Keep Looking**...Sara Evans
	I Kissed You ..see: ('Til)
1/00	**I Knew I Loved You**...Savage Garden
1/87	**I Knew You Were Waiting (For Me)**...Aretha Franklin & George Michael
	I Knew You When
14/65	Billy Joe Royal
F/72	Donny Osmond
37/83	Linda Ronstadt
4/95	**I Know**...Dionne Farris
19/79	**I Know A Heartache When I See One**...Jennifer Warnes
3/65	**I Know A Place**...Petula Clark
35/93	**(I Know I Got) Skillz**...Shaquille O'Neal
	(I Know) I'm Losing You
8/66	Temptations
7/70	Rare Earth
24/71	Rod Stewart With Faces
13/83	**I Know There's Something Going On**...Frida
9/87	**I Know What I Like**...Huey Lewis
3/03	**I Know What You Want**...Busta Rhymes & Mariah Carey
36/98	**I Know Where It's At**...All Saints
3/62	**I Know (You Don't Love Me No More)**...Barbara George
30/88	**I Know You're Out There Somewhere**...Moody Blues
27/00	**I Learned From The Best**...Whitney Houston
19/62	**I Left My Heart In San Francisco**...Tony Bennett
28/96	**I Like**...Montell Jordan
34/95	**I Like**...Kut Klose
3/77	**I Like Dreamin'**...Kenny Nolan
7/89	**I Like It**...Dino
17/64	**I Like It**...Gerry & The Pacemakers
24/00	**I Like It**...Sammie
25/97	**I Like It**...Blackout Allstars
31/83	**I Like It**...DeBarge
25/95	**I Like It, I Love It**...Tim McGraw
	I Like It Like That
2/61	Chris Kenner
7/65	Dave Clark Five
27/64	**I Like It Like That**...Miracles
25/67	**I Like The Way**...Tommy James
1/91	**I Like The Way (The Kissing Game)**...Hi-Five
37/77	**I Like To Do It**...KC & The Sunshine Band
28/74	**I Like To Live The Love**...B.B. King
8/57	**I Like Your Kind Of Love**...Andy Williams
38/71	**I Likes To Do It**...People's Choice
31/89	**I Live By The Groove**...Paul Carrack
13/88	**I Live For Your Love**...Natalie Cole
26/95	**I Live My Life For You**...Firehouse
34/00	**I Lost It**...Kenny Chesney
12/74	**I Love**...Tom T. Hall
1/81	**I Love A Rainy Night**...Eddie Rabbitt
	I Love How You Love Me
5/61	Paris Sisters
9/68	Bobby Vinton

POS/YR	RECORD TITLE. . .ARTIST
	I Love Lucy ..see: Disco Lucy
F/97	**I Love Me Some Him**...Toni Braxton
5/76	**I Love Music**...O'Jays
21/57	**I Love My Baby (My Baby Loves Me)**...Jill Corey
24/74	**I Love My Friend**...Charlie Rich
1/82	**I Love Rock 'N Roll**...Joan Jett
5/78	**I Love The Nightlife (Disco 'Round)**...Alicia Bridges
9/60	**I Love The Way You Love**...Marv Johnson
26/03	**I Love This Bar**...Toby Keith
12/81	**I Love You**...Climax Blues Band
14/68	**I Love You**...People
14/02	**I Love You**...Faith Evans
22/62	**I Love You**...Volume's
24/99	**I Love You**...Martina McBride
37/78	**I Love You**...Donna Summer
2/96	**I Love You Always Forever**...Donna Lewis
3/63	**I Love You Because**...Al Martino
39/63	**(I Love You) Don't You Forget It**...Perry Como
30/66	**I Love You Drops**...Vic Dana
21/71	**I Love You For All Seasons**...Fuzz
17/58	**(I Love You) For Sentimental Reasons**...Sam Cooke
40/60	**I Love You In The Same Old Way**...Paul Anka
28/55	**I Love You Madly**...Four Coins
9/64	**I Love You More And More Every Day**...Al Martino
31/66	**I Love You 1000 Times**...Platters
26/93	**I Love You Period**....Dan Baird
38/62	**I Love You The Way You Are**...Bobby Vinton
2/92	**I Love Your Smile**...Shanice
37/81	**I Loved 'Em Every One**...T.G. Sheppard
18/59	**I Loves You, Porgy**...Nina Simone
10/81	**I Made It Through The Rain**...Barry Manilow
18/67	**I Make A Fool Of Myself**...Frankie Valli
34/03	**I Melt**...Rascal Flatts
37/68	**I Met Her In Church**...Box Tops
28/02	**I Miss My Friend**...Darryl Worley
25/97	**I Miss My Homies**...Master P
5/85	**I Miss You**...Klymaxx
14/94	**I Miss You**...Aaron Hall
22/95	**I Miss You**...NIIU
	I Miss You So
34/57	Chris Connor
33/59	Paul Anka
34/65	Little Anthony & The Imperials
19/81	**I Missed Again**...Phil Collins
31/65	**I Must Be Seeing Things**...Gene Pitney
2/02	**I Need A Girl (Part One)**...P. Diddy
4/02	**I Need A Girl (Part Two)**...P. Diddy & Ginuwine
28/79	**I Need A Lover**...John Cougar
14/87	**I Need Love**...LL Cool J
22/66	**I Need Somebody**...? (Question Mark) & The Mysterians
25/76	**I Need To Be In Love**...Carpenters
3/99	**I Need To Know**...Marc Anthony

POS/YR	RECORD TITLE. . .ARTIST
9/72	**I Need You**...America
11/00	**I Need You**...LeAnn Rimes
37/82	**I Need You**...Paul Carrack
1/54	**I Need You Now**...Eddie Fisher
36/84	**I Need You Tonight**...Peter Wolf
4/59	**I Need Your Love Tonight**...Elvis Presley
37/81	**I Need Your Lovin'**...Teena Marie
20/62	**I Need Your Loving**...Don Gardner & Dee Dee Ford
12/77	**I Never Cry**...Alice Cooper
9/67	**I Never Loved A Man (The Way I Love You)**...Aretha Franklin
37/95	**I Never Seen A Man Cry (aka I Seen A Man Die)**...Scarface
	I Only Have Eyes For You
11/59	Flamingos
18/75	Art Garfunkel
22/56	**I Only Know I Love You**...Four Aces
	I Only Want To Be With You
12/64	Dusty Springfield
12/76	Bay City Rollers
31/89	Samantha Fox
25/71	**I Play And Sing**...Dawn
19/80	**I Pledge My Love**...Peaches & Herb
9/82	**I Ran (So Far Away)**...Flock Of Seagulls
39/82	**I Really Don't Need No Light**...Jeffrey Osborne
	I Really Don't Want To Know
18/60	Tommy Edwards
22/66	Ronnie Dove
21/71	Elvis Presley
29/61	**I Really Love You**...Stereos
8/89	**I Remember Holding You**...Boys Club
5/62	**I Remember You**...Frank Ifield
6/90	**I Remember You**...Skid Row
36/64	**I Rise, I Fall**...Johnny Tillotson
5/66	**I Saw Her Again**...Mamas & The Papas
	I Saw Her (Him) Standing There
14/64	Beatles
7/88	Tiffany
14/63	**I Saw Linda Yesterday**...Dickey Lee
10/91	**I Saw Red**...Warrant
16/72	**I Saw The Light**...Todd Rundgren
	I Say A Little Prayer
4/67	Dionne Warwick
10/68	Aretha Franklin
38/97	Diana King
4/67	**I Second That Emotion**...Miracles
26/66	**I See The Light**...Five Americans
38/74	**I Shall Sing**...Art Garfunkel
	I Shot The Sheriff
1/74	Eric Clapton
20/97	Warren G
25/03	**I Should Be**......Dru Hill
35/02	**I Should Be Sleeping**...Emerson Drive
28/88	**I Should Be So Lucky**...Kylie Minogue
40s/91	**I Shouldn't Have Done It**...Slick Rick
15/62	**I Sold My Heart To The Junkman**...Blue-Belles
6/69	**I Started A Joke**...Bee Gees

POS/YR	RECORD TITLE. . .ARTIST
19/56	**I Was The One**...Elvis Presley
19/66	**(I Washed My Hands In) Muddy Water**...Johnny Rivers
	I (Who Have Nothing)
29/63	Ben E. King
14/70	Tom Jones
40/79	Sylvester
10/65	**I Will**...Dean Martin
1/92	**I Will Always Love You**...Whitney Houston
22/68	**I Will Always Think About You**...New Colony Six
27/92	**I Will Be Here For You**...Michael W. Smith
30/79	**I Will Be In Love With You**...Livingston Taylor
34/87	**I Will Be There**...Glass Tiger
33A/98	**I Will Buy You A New Life**...Everclear
9/97	**I Will Come To You**...Hanson
1/63	**I Will Follow Him**...Little Peggy March
32/99	**I Will Get There**...Boyz II Men
32/00	**I Will Love Again**...Lara Fabian
14/99	**I Will Remember You**...Sarah McLachlan (Live)
20/92	**I Will Remember You**...Amy Grant
29/78	**I Will Still Love You**...Stonebolt
	I Will Survive
1/79	Gloria Gaynor
24/96	Chantay Savage
18A/98	**I Will Wait**...Hootie & The Blowfish
1/77	**I Wish**...Stevie Wonder
13/95	**I Wish**...Skee-Lo
14/01	**I Wish**...R. Kelly
20/00	**I Wish**...Carl Thomas
20/88	**I Wish I Had A Girl**...Henry Lee Summer
32/63	**I Wish I Were A Princess**...Little Peggy March
4/68	**I Wish It Would Rain**...Temptations
3/90	**I Wish It Would Rain Down**...Phil Collins
16/62	**I Wish That We Were Married**...Ronnie & The Hi-Lites
28/92	**I Wish The Phone Would Ring**...Exposé
28/64	**I Wish You Love**...Gloria Lynne
13/71	**I Woke Up In Love This Morning**...Partridge Family
12/89	**I Won't Back Down**...Tom Petty
13/87	**I Won't Forget You**...Poison
10/83	**I Won't Hold You Back**...Toto
11/74	**I Won't Last A Day Without You**...Carpenters
35/83	**I Won't Stand In Your Way**...Stray Cats
25/63	**I Wonder**...Brenda Lee
F/57	**I Wonder If I Care As Much**...Everly Brothers
34/85	**I Wonder If I Take You Home**...Lisa-Lisa & Cult Jam
8/68	**I Wonder What She's Doing Tonite**...Tommy Boyce & Bobby Hart
21/63	**I Wonder What She's Doing Tonight**...Barry & The Tamerlanes
9/91	**I Wonder Why**...Curtis Stigers
22/58	**I Wonder Why**...Dion & The Belmonts
8/85	**I Would Die 4 U**...Prince
20/82	**I Wouldn't Have Missed It For The World**...Ronnie Milsap

POS/YR	RECORD TITLE. . .ARTIST
22/56	**I Wouldn't Know Where To Begin**...Eddy Arnold
36/77	**I Wouldn't Want To Be Like You**...Alan Parsons
1/76	**I Write The Songs**...Barry Manilow
3/92	**I'd Die Without You**...PM Dawn
1/93	**I'd Do Anything For Love (But I Won't Do That)**...Meat Loaf
28/94	**I'd Give Anything**...Gerald Levert
13/95	**I'd Lie For You (And That's The Truth)**...Meat Loaf
	I'd Like To Teach The World To Sing (In Perfect Harmony)
7/72	New Seekers
13/72	Hillside Singers
40/71	**I'd Love To Change The World**...Ten Years After
2/72	**I'd Love You To Want Me**...Lobo
38/80	**I'd Rather Leave While I'm In Love**...Rita Coolidge
2/76	**I'd Really Love To See You Tonight**...England Dan & John Ford Coley
18/87	**I'd Still Say Yes**...Klymaxx
15/69	**I'd Wait A Million Years**...Grass Roots
36/73	**I'll Always Love My Mama**...Intruders
3/88	**I'll Always Love You**...Taylor Dayne
35/65	**I'll Always Love You**...Spinners
5/98	**I'll Be**...Edwin McCain
7/97	**I'll Be**...Foxy Brown
14/87	**I'll Be Alright Without You**...Journey
	I'll Be Around
3/72	Spinners
39/95	Rappin' 4-Tay
12/91	**I'll Be By Your Side**...Stevie B
8/65	**I'll Be Doggone**...Marvin Gaye
	I'll Be Good To You
3/76	Brothers Johnson
18/90	Quincy Jones
4/56	**I'll Be Home**...Pat Boone
33/64	**I'll Be In Trouble**...Temptations
1/89	**I'll Be Loving You (Forever)**...New Kids On The Block
1/97	**I'll Be Missing You**...Puff Daddy & Faith Evans
11/86	**I'll Be Over You**...Toto
20/59	**I'll Be Satisfied**...Jackie Wilson
36/74	**I'll Be The Other Woman**...Soul Children
	I'll Be There
1/70	Jackson 5
1/92	Mariah Carey
8/91	**I'll Be There**...Escape Club
12/61	**I'll Be There**...Damita Jo
14/65	**I'll Be There**...Gerry & The Pacemakers **(also see: Stand By Me)**
1/89	**I'll Be There For You**...Bon Jovi
3/95	**I'll Be There For You (medley)**...Method Man
17/95	**I'll Be There For You (Theme from "Friends")**...Rembrandts
31/59	**(I'll Be With You In) Apple Blossom Time**...Tab Hunter

POS/YR	RECORD TITLE. . . ARTIST
3/59	I'm Gonna Get Married...Lloyd Price
34/02	I'm Gonna Getcha Good!...Shania Twain
12/61	I'm Gonna Knock On Your Door...Eddie Hodges
40/76	I'm Gonna Let My Heart Do The Walking...Supremes
3/73	I'm Gonna Love You Just A Little More Baby...Barry White
	I'm Gonna Make You Love Me
26/68	Madeline Bell
2/69	Supremes & Temptations
10/69	I'm Gonna Make You Mine...Lou Christie
29/02	I'm Gonna Miss Her (The Fishin' Song)...Brad Paisley
3/57	I'm Gonna Sit Right Down And Write Myself A Letter...Billy Williams
28/78	I'm Gonna Take Care Of Everything...Rubicon
13/85	I'm Gonna Tear Your Playhouse Down...Paul Young
27/80	I'm Happy That Love Has Found You...Jimmy Hall
1/65	I'm Henry VIII, I Am...Herman's Hermits
27/61	I'm Hurtin'...Roy Orbison
19/74	I'm In Love...Aretha Franklin
40/81	I'm In Love...Evelyn King
	I'm In Love Again
3/56	Fats Domino
38/56	Fontane Sisters
32/94	I'm In The Mood...Ce Ce Peniston
38/61	I'm In The Mood For Love...Chimes
2/77	I'm In You...Peter Frampton
	I'm Into Something Good
13/64	Herman's Hermits
38/64	Earl-Jean
12/73	I'm Just A Singer (In A Rock And Roll Band)...Moody Blues
27/01	I'm Just Talkin' About Tonight...Toby Keith
33/61	I'm Learning About Love...Brenda Lee
36/71	I'm Leavin'...Elvis Presley
	I'm Leaving It Up To You
1/63	Dale & Grace
4/74	Donny & Marie Osmond
9/01	I'm Like A Bird...Nelly Furtado
10/69	I'm Livin' In Shame...Supremes
	I'm Losing You ..see: (I Know)
40/59	I'm Movin' On...Ray Charles
37/73	I'm Never Gonna Be Alone Anymore... Cornelius Brothers & Sister Rose
36/59	I'm Never Gonna Tell...Jimmie Rodgers
27/60	I'm Not Afraid...Ricky Nelson
40/97	I'm Not Giving You Up...Gloria Estefan
14/78	I'm Not Gonna Let It Bother Me Tonight...Atlanta Rhythm Section
	I'm Not In Love
2/75	10cc
7/91	Will To Power
4/75	I'm Not Lisa...Jessi Colter
34/70	I'm Not My Brothers Keeper...Flaming Ember
16/99	I'm Not Ready...Keith Sweat
32/86	I'm Not The One...Cars

POS/YR	RECORD TITLE. . . ARTIST
20/67	(I'm Not Your) Steppin' Stone...Monkees
6/85	I'm On Fire...Bruce Springsteen
16/75	I'm On Fire...Dwight Twilley Band
26/75	I'm On Fire...5000 Volts
15/64	I'm On The Outside (Looking In)...Little Anthony & The Imperials
9/94	I'm Ready...Tevin Campbell
16/59	I'm Ready...Fats Domino
9/66	I'm Ready For Love...Martha & The Vandellas
1/01	I'm Real...Jennifer Lopez
	I'm So Excited
30/82	Pointer Sisters
9/84	Pointer Sisters
6/93	I'm So Into You...SWV
8/66	I'm So Lonesome I Could Cry...B.J. Thomas
14/64	I'm So Proud...Impressions
1/60	I'm Sorry...Brenda Lee
1/75	I'm Sorry...John Denver
11/57	I'm Sorry...Platters
36/58	I'm Sorry I Made You Cry...Connie Francis
14/57	I'm Stickin' With You...Jimmy Bowen
3/72	I'm Still In Love With You...Al Green
7/97	I'm Still In Love With You...New Edition
31/88	I'm Still Searching...Glass Tiger
12/83	I'm Still Standing...Elton John
10/72	I'm Stone In Love With You...Stylistics
1/65	I'm Telling You Now...Freddie & The Dreamers
15/89	I'm That Type Of Guy...LL Cool J
38/62	(I'm The Girl On) Wolverton Mountain...Jo Ann Campbell
	I'm The One Who Loves You ..see: (Remember Me)
19/92	I'm The One You Need...Jody Watley (also see: Come 'Round Here)
8/95	I'm The Only One...Melissa Etheridge
1/92	I'm Too Sexy...R*S*F (Right Said Fred)
27/57	I'm Waiting Just For You...Pat Boone
	I'm Walkin'
4/57	Fats Domino
4/57	Ricky Nelson
4/03	I'm With You...Avril Lavigne
12/67	I'm Wondering...Stevie Wonder
1/98	I'm Your Angel...R. Kelly & Celine Dion
1/90	I'm Your Baby Tonight...Whitney Houston
1/77	I'm Your Boogie Man...KC & The Sunshine Band
3/86	I'm Your Man...Wham!
6/66	I'm Your Puppet...James & Bobby Purify
11/65	I'm Yours...Elvis Presley
33/59	I've Been Around...Fats Domino
35/69	I've Been Hurt...Bill Deal
9/87	I've Been In Love Before...Cutting Crew
27/72	I've Been Lonely For So Long...Frederick Knight
16/67	I've Been Lonely Too Long...Young Rascals
21/65	I've Been Loving You Too Long (To Stop Now)...Otis Redding
9/74	(I've Been) Searchin' So Long...Chicago

POS/YR	RECORD TITLE. . .ARTIST
1/91	I've Been Thinking About You...Londonbeat
34/75	I've Been This Way Before...Neil Diamond
28/59	I've Come Of Age...Billy Storm
8/81	I've Done Everything For You...Rick Springfield
5/71	I've Found Someone Of My Own...Free Movement
29/76	I've Got A Feeling (We'll Be Seeing Each Other Again)...Al Wilson
26/92	I've Got A Lot To Learn About Love...Storm
18/83	I've Got A Rock N' Roll Heart...Eric Clapton
39/74	I've Got A Thing About You Baby...Elvis Presley
25/65	I've Got A Tiger By The Tail...Buck Owens
	I've Got A Woman ..see: I Got A Woman
18/62	(I've Got) Bonnie...Bobby Rydell
5/77	I've Got Love On My Mind...Natalie Cole
33/64	I've Got Sand In My Shoes...Drifters
32/73	I've Got So Much To Give...Barry White
12/74	I've Got The Music In Me...Kiki Dee Band
38/66	I've Got To Be Somebody...Billy Joe Royal
4/74	I've Got To Use My Imagination...Gladys Knight
9/66	I've Got You Under My Skin...4 Seasons
11/69	I've Gotta Be Me...Sammy Davis, Jr.
8/68	I've Gotta Get A Message To You...Bee Gees
25/78	I've Had Enough...Wings
6/59	I've Had It...Bell Notes
1/87	(I've Had) The Time Of My Life...Bill Medley & Jennifer Warnes
32/70	I've Lost You...Elvis Presley
4/80	I've Loved You For A Long Time (medley)...Spinners
3/82	I've Never Been To Me...Charlene
40/68	I've Never Found A Girl (To Love Me Like You Do)...Eddie Floyd
17/67	I've Passed This Way Before...Jimmy Ruffin
3/61	I've Told Every Little Star...Linda Scott
37/95	Ice Cream...Chef Raekwon
1/90	Ice Ice Baby...Vanilla Ice
9/91	Iesha...Another Bad Creation
4/71	If...Bread
4/93	If...Janet Jackson
32/62	If A Man Answers...Bobby Darin
35/62	If A Woman Answers (Hang Up The Phone)...Leroy Van Dyke
14/83	If Anyone Falls...Stevie Nicks
7/58	If Dreams Came True...Pat Boone
24/78	If Ever I See You Again...Roberta Flack
10/84	If Ever You're In My Arms Again...Peabo Bryson
12/69	If I Can Dream...Elvis Presley
1/78	If I Can't Have You...Yvonne Elliman
10/68	If I Could Build My Whole World Around You...Marvin Gaye & Tammi Terrell
15/02	If I Could Go!...Angie Martinez
10/72	If I Could Reach You...5th Dimension

POS/YR	RECORD TITLE. . .ARTIST
27/97	If I Could Teach The World...Bone Thugs-N-Harmony
12/99	If I Could Turn Back The Hands Of Time...R. Kelly
3/89	If I Could Turn Back Time...Cher
	If I Didn't Care
22/59	Connie Francis
30/61	Platters
2/92	If I Ever Fall In Love...Shai
17/93	If I Ever Lose My Faith In You...Sting
39/75	If I Ever Lose This Heaven...AWB
38/01	If I Fall You're Going Down With Me...Dixie Chicks
	If I Give My Heart To You
3/54	Doris Day
34/59	Kitty Kallen
31/60	If I Had A Girl...Rod Lauren
	If I Had A Hammer
10/62	Peter, Paul & Mary
3/63	Trini Lopez
36/82	If I Had My Wish Tonight...David Lasley
7/93	If I Had No Loot...Tony Toni Tone
23/65	If I Loved You...Chad & Jeremy
8/55	If I May...Nat "King" Cole/Four Knights
34/65	If I Ruled The World...Tony Bennett
39/79	If I Said You Have A Beautiful Body Would You Hold It Against Me...Bellamy Brothers
16/95	If I Wanted To...Melissa Etheridge
	If I Were A Carpenter
8/66	Bobby Darin
20/68	Four Tops
36/70	Johnny Cash & June Carter
9/71	If I Were Your Woman...Gladys Knight
19/84	If I'd Been The One...38 Special
7/88	If It Isn't Love...New Edition
10/97	If It Makes You Happy...Sheryl Crow
	(If Loving You Is Wrong) I Don't Want To Be Right
3/72	Luther Ingram
31/79	Barbara Mandrell
39/01	If My Heart Had Wings...Faith Hill
23/63	If My Pillow Could Talk...Connie Francis
25/71	If Not For You...Olivia Newton-John
29/86	If She Knew What She Wants...Bangles
17/87	If She Would Have Been Faithful......Chicago
28/82	If The Love Fits Wear It...Leslie Pearl
35/91	(If There Was) Any Other Way...Celine Dion
	If There's A Hell Below ..see: (Don't Worry)
6/84	If This Is It...Huey Lewis
24/90	If U Were Mine...U-Krew
28/73	If We Make It Through December...Merle Haggard
1/90	If Wishes Came True...Sweet Sensation
	If You ..also see: If U
4/92	If You Asked Me To...Celine Dion
11/68	If You Can Want...Miracles
11A/97	If You Could Only See...Tonic

POS/YR	RECORD TITLE. . . ARTIST
10/75	**It Only Takes A Minute**...Tavares
40/68	**It Should Have Been Me**...Gladys Knight
29/62	**It Started All Over Again**...Brenda Lee
27/73	**It Sure Took A Long, Long Time**...Lobo
14/67	**It Takes Two**...Marvin Gaye & Kim Weston
36/88	**It Takes Two**...Rob Base & D.J. E-Z Rock
20/66	**It Tears Me Up**...Percy Sledge
15/93	**It Was A Good Day**...Ice Cube
28/66	**It Was A Very Good Year**...Frank Sinatra
16/77	**It Was Almost Like A Song**...Ronnie Milsap
11/59	**It Was I**...Skip & Flip
1/01	**It Wasn't Me**...Shaggy
10/88	**It Would Take A Strong Strong Man**...Rick Astley
37/77	**It's A Crazy World**...Mac McAnally
33/01	**It's A Great Day To Be Alive**...Travis Tritt
3/78	**It's A Heartache**...Bonnie Tyler
20/78	**It's A Laugh**...Daryl Hall & John Oates
28/76	**It's A Long Way There**...Little River Band
28/81	**It's A Love Thing**...Whispers
8/66	**It's A Man's Man's Man's World**...James Brown
12/75	**It's A Miracle**...Barry Manilow
13/84	**It's A Miracle**...Culture Club
6/83	**It's A Mistake**...Men At Work
32/70	**It's A New Day**...James Brown
14/70	**It's A Shame**...Spinners
26/91	**It's A Shame (My Sister)**...Monie Love
9/87	**It's A Sin**...Pet Shop Boys
7/55	**It's A Sin To Tell A Lie**...Somethin' Smith & The Redheads
6/98	**It's All About Me**...Mya With Sisqo
2/98	**It's All About The Benjamins**...Puff Daddy & The Family
18/99	**It's All About You (Not About Me)**...Tracie Spencer
2/96	**It's All Coming Back To Me Now**...Celine Dion
31/75	**It's All Down To Goodnight Vienna**...Ringo Starr
	It's All In The Game
1/58	Tommy Edwards
25/64	Cliff Richard
24/70	Four Tops
26/64	**It's All Over Now**...Rolling Stones
	It's All Right
4/63	Impressions
37A/93	Huey Lewis
29/96	**It's All The Way Live (Now)**...Coolio
	It's Almost Tomorrow
20/55	David Carroll
20/55	Snooky Lanson
7/56	Dream Weavers
14/56	Jo Stafford
31/65	**It's Alright**...Adam Faith
20/58	**(It's Been A Long Time) Pretty Baby**...Gino & Gina
5/01	**It's Been Awhile**...Staind
4/77	**It's Ecstasy When You Lay Down Next To Me**...Barry White
17/03	**It's Five O'Clock Somewhere**...Alan Jackson & Jimmy Buffett

POS/YR	RECORD TITLE. . . ARTIST
30/69	**It's Getting Better**...Mama Cass
12/72	**It's Going To Take Some Time**...Carpenters
34/93	**It's Gonna Be A Lovely Day**...S.O.U.L. S.Y.S.T.E.M.
	(also see: Lovely Day)
23/65	**It's Gonna Be Alright**...Gerry & The Pacemakers
1/00	**It's Gonna Be Me**...*NSYNC
10/82	**It's Gonna Take A Miracle**...Deniece Williams
14/61	**It's Gonna Work Out Fine**...Ike & Tina Turner
18/65	**It's Growing**...Temptations
10/71	**It's Impossible**...Perry Como
	(It's In His Kiss) ..see: Shoop Shoop Song
38/83	**It's Inevitable**...Charlie
3/59	**It's Just A Matter Of Time**...Brook Benton
3/89	**(It's Just) The Way That You Love Me**...Paula Abdul
9/59	**It's Late**...Ricky Nelson
	It's My Life
31/84	Talk Talk
10/04	No Doubt
23/66	**It's My Life**...Animals
33/00	**It's My Life**...Bon Jovi
1/63	**It's My Party**...Lesley Gore
9/81	**It's My Turn**...Diana Ross
7/89	**It's No Crime**...Babyface
38/97	**It's No Good**...Depeche Mode
37/89	**It's No Secret**...Kylie Minogue
12/89	**It's Not Enough**...Starship
5/57	**It's Not For Me To Say**...Johnny Mathis
9/87	**It's Not Over ('Til It's Over)**...Starship
4/99	**It's Not Right But It's Okay**...Whitney Houston
10/65	**It's Not Unusual**...Tom Jones
	It's Now Or Never
1/60	Elvis Presley
14/81	John Schneider
23/67	**It's Now Winters Day**...Tommy Roe
29/76	**It's O.K.**...Beach Boys
20/72	**It's One Of Those Nights (Yes Love)**...Partridge Family
15/86	**It's Only Love**...Bryan Adams/Tina Turner
31/66	**It's Only Love**...Tommy James
	It's Only Make Believe
1/58	Conway Twitty
10/70	Glen Campbell
16/74	**It's Only Rock 'N Roll (But I Like It)**...Rolling Stones
9/64	**It's Over**...Roy Orbison
37/66	**It's Over**...Jimmie Rodgers
38/76	**It's Over**...Boz Scaggs
6/01	**It's Over Now**...One Twelve
11/82	**It's Raining Again**...Supertramp
21/77	**It's Sad To Belong**...England Dan & John Ford Coley
5/77	**It's So Easy**...Linda Ronstadt
2/91	**It's So Hard To Say Goodbye To Yesterday**...Boyz II Men

POS/YR	RECORD TITLE. . . ARTIST
1/80	It's Still Rock And Roll To Me...Billy Joel
	It's The Same Old Song
5/65	Four Tops
35/78	KC & The Sunshine Band
4/59	It's Time To Cry...Paul Anka
1/71	It's Too Late...Carole King
23/66	It's Too Late...Bobby Goldsboro
4/58	It's Too Soon To Know...Pat Boone
6/63	It's Up To You...Rick Nelson
20/68	It's Wonderful...Young Rascals
6/57	It's You I Love...Fats Domino
33/78	It's You That I Need...Enchantment
7/97	It's Your Love...Tim McGraw with Faith Hill
2/69	It's Your Thing...Isley Brothers
25/56	Italian Theme...Cyril Stapleton
25/58	Itchy Twitchy Feeling...Bobby Hendricks
16/68	Itchycoo Park...Small Faces
1/60	Itsy Bitsy Teenie Weenie Yellow Polkadot Bikini...Brian Hyland
	Ivory Tower
2/56	Cathy Carr
6/56	Gale Storm
11/56	Charms
18/57	Ivy Rose...Perry Como
8/01	Izzo (H.O.V.A.)...Jay-Z

J

POS/YR	RECORD TITLE. . . ARTIST
22A/95	J.A.R. (Jason Andrew Relva)...Green Day
1/82	Jack & Diane...John Cougar
8/78	Jack And Jill...Raydio
3/75	Jackie Blue...Ozark Mountain Daredevils
14/67	Jackson...Nancy Sinatra & Lee Hazlewood
1/87	Jacob's Ladder...Huey Lewis
7/01	Jaded...Aerosmith
1/57	Jailhouse Rock...Elvis Presley
26/92	Jam...Michael Jackson
29/62	Jam, The...Bobby Gregg
32/87	Jam Tonight...Freddie Jackson
8/70	Jam Up Jelly Tight...Tommy Roe
14/57	Jamaica Farewell...Harry Belafonte
	Jambalaya (On The Bayou)
30/62	Fats Domino
16/73	Blue Ridge Rangers
10/99	Jamboree...Naughty By Nature
17/62	James (Hold The Ladder Steady)...Sue Thompson
14/85	Jamie...Ray Parker Jr.
30/62	Jamie...Eddie Holland
18/87	Jammin' Me...Tom Petty
14/80	Jane...Jefferson Starship
4/90	Janie's Got A Gun...Aerosmith
	Jar ..see: J.A.R.
4/64	Java...Al Hirt
	Jaws ..see: Theme From / Mr. Jaws
	Jayne ..see: Ballad of

POS/YR	RECORD TITLE. . . ARTIST
2/74	Jazzman...Carole King
20/69	Jealous Kind Of Fella...Garland Green
	Jealous Lover ..see: Theme From The Apartment
19/60	Jealous Of You...Connie Francis
23/96	Jealousy...Natalie Merchant
2/69	Jean...Oliver
17/77	Jeans On...David Dundas
8/58	Jennie Lee...Jan & Arnie
40/68	Jennifer Eccles...Hollies
26/68	Jennifer Juniper...Donovan
36/70	Jennifer Tomkins...Street People
	Jenny ..see: 867-5309
3/02	Jenny From The Block...Jennifer Lopez
10/57	Jenny, Jenny...Little Richard
10/66	Jenny Take A Ride!...Mitch Ryder
2/83	Jeopardy...Greg Kihn Band
35/61	Jeremiah Peabody's Poly Unsaturated Pills...Ray Stevens
7/65	Jerk, The...Larks
9/90	Jerk-Out...Time
11/80	Jesse...Carly Simon
30/73	Jesse...Roberta Flack
26/94	Jessie...Joshua Kadison
1/81	Jessie's Girl...Rick Springfield
	Jesus Christ Superstar ..see: Superstar
23/92	Jesus He Knows Me...Genesis
28/69	Jesus Is A Soul Man...Lawrence Reynolds
35/73	Jesus Is Just Alright...Doobie Brothers
7/96	Jesus To A Child...George Michael
7/74	Jet...Paul McCartney
8/77	Jet Airliner...Steve Miller Band
28/99	Jigga My Nigga...Jay-Z
	Jim Dandy
17/57	LaVerne Baker
25/74	Black Oak Arkansas
28/87	Jimmy Lee...Aretha Franklin
33/73	Jimmy Loves Mary-Anne...Looking Glass
10/67	Jimmy Mack...Martha & The Vandellas
25/61	Jimmy's Girl...Johnny Tillotson
	Jingle Bell Rock
6/57	Bobby Helms
35/58	Bobby Helms
36/60	Bobby Helms
21/61	Bobby Rydell/Chubby Checker
10/70	Jingle Jangle...Archies
1/75	Jive Talkin'...Bee Gees
19/58	Jo-Ann...Playmates
17/80	JoJo...Boz Scaggs
2/84	Joanna...Kool & The Gang
21/70	Joanne...Michael Nesmith
31/97	Jock Jam...ESPN Presents
28/71	Jody's Got Your Girl And Gone...Johnnie Taylor
19/90	Joey...Concrete Blonde
	John And Yoko ..see: Ballad Of
1/62	Johnny Angel...Shelley Fabares
8/58	Johnny B. Goode...Chuck Berry

Last Kiss
2/64	J. Frank Wilson
34/74	Wednesday
2/99	Pearl Jam

36/89	**Last Mile**...Cinderella
3/61	**Last Night**...Mar-Keys
9/96	**Last Night**...Az Yet
8/72	**(Last Night) I Didn't Get To Sleep At All**...5th Dimension
3/73	**Last Song**...Edward Bear
23/92	**Last Song**...Elton John
9/65	**Last Time**...Rolling Stones
40/84	**Last Time I Made Love**...Joyce Kennedy & Jeffrey Osborne
14/74	**Last Time I Saw Him**...Diana Ross
1/66	**Last Train To Clarksville**...Monkees
39/80	**Last Train To London**...Electric Light Orchestra
25/67	**Last Waltz**...Engelbert Humperdinck
40/66	**Last Word In Lonesome Is Me**...Eddy Arnold
21/89	**Last Worthless Evening**...Don Henley
27/57	**Lasting Love**...Sal Mineo
6/80	**Late In The Evening**...Paul Simon
1/98	**Lately**...Divine
4/93	**Lately**...Jodeci
10/65	**Laugh At Me**...Sonny
15/65	**Laugh, Laugh**...Beau Brummels
10/69	**Laughing**...Guess Who
15/63	**Laughing Boy**...Mary Wells
1/75	**Laughter In The Rain**...Neil Sedaka
14/65	**Laurie (Strange Things Happen)**...Dickey Lee
3/59	**Lavender-Blue**...Sammy Turner
	LaVerne & Shirley Theme ..see: **Making Our Dreams Come True**
13/83	**Lawyers In Love**...Jackson Browne
11/70	**Lay A Little Lovin' On Me**...Robin McNamara
6/70	**Lay Down (Candles In The Rain)**...Melanie/Edwin Hawkins Singers
3/78	**Lay Down Sally**...Eric Clapton
16/56	**Lay Down Your Arms**...Chordettes
40/85	**Lay It Down**...Ratt
7/69	**Lay Lady Lay**...Bob Dylan
6/85	**Lay Your Hands On Me**...Thompson Twins
7/89	**Lay Your Hands On Me**...Bon Jovi
31/94	**(Lay Your Head On My) Pillow**...Tony Toni Tone

Layla
10/72	Derek & The Dominos
12/92	Eric Clapton (Live)

14/67	**Lazy Day**...Spanky & Our Gang
40/64	**Lazy Elsie Molly**...Chubby Checker
12/58	**Lazy Mary (Luna Mezzo Mare)**...Lou Monte
14/61	**Lazy River**...Bobby Darin
21/58	**Lazy Summer Night**...Four Preps
1/78	**Le Freak**...Chic
5/79	**Lead Me On**...Maxine Nightingale
9/82	**Leader Of The Band**...Dan Fogelberg
19/65	**Leader Of The Laundromat**...Detergents
1/64	**Leader Of The Pack**...Shangri-Las
25/62	**Léah**...Roy Orbison

Lean On Me
1/72	Bill Withers
1/87	Club Nouveau

9/66	**Leaning On The Lamp Post**...Herman's Hermits
19/00	**Learn To Fly**...Foo Fighters
1/55	**Learnin' The Blues**...Frank Sinatra
28/91	**Learning To Fly**...Tom Petty
6/82	**Leather And Lace**...Stevie Nicks (with Don Henley)
11/89	**Leave A Light On**...Belinda Carlisle
27/84	**Leave A Tender Moment Alone**...Billy Joel
24/84	**Leave It**...Yes
3/73	**Leave Me Alone (Ruby Red Dress)**...Helen Reddy
21/73	**Leaving Me**...Independents
1/69	**Leaving On A Jet Plane**...Peter, Paul & Mary
9/58	**Left Right Out Of Your Heart**...Patti Page
36/97	**Legend Of A Cowgirl**...Imani Coppola
	(Legend Of Billy Jack) ..see: **One Tin Soldier**
31/80	**Legend Of Wooley Swamp**...Charlie Daniels Band
8/84	**Legs**...ZZ Top

Lemon Tree
35/62	Peter, Paul & Mary
20/65	Trini Lopez

11/58	**Leroy**...Jack Scott
31/68	**Les Bicyclettes De Belsize**...Engelbert Humperdinck
34/68	**Lesson, The**...Vikki Carr
28/99	**Lesson In Leavin'**...Jo Dee Messina
12/87	**Lessons In Love**...Level 42
40/00	**Lessons Learned**...Tracy Lawrence

Let A Man Come In And Do The Popcorn
21/69	James Brown (Part One)
40/70	James Brown (Part Two)

36/69	**Let A Woman Be A Woman - Let A Man Be A Man**...Dyke & The Blazers
3/76	**Let 'Em In**...Wings
34/89	**Let Go**...Sharon Bryant
9/95	**Let Her Cry**...Hootie & The Blowfish
10/76	**Let Her In**...John Travolta
39/85	**Let Him Go**...Animotion
1/70	**Let It Be**...Beatles

Let It Be Me
7/60	Everly Brothers
5/64	Betty Everett & Jerry Butler
36/69	Glen Campbell & Bobbie Gentry
40/82	Willie Nelson

F/96	**Let It Flow**...Toni Braxton
25/97	**Let It Go**...Ray J
	(also see: Letitgo)
12/67	**Let It Out (Let It All Hang Out)**...Hombres
23/74	**Let It Ride**...Bachman-Turner Overdrive
30/76	**Let It Shine**...Olivia Newton-John
32/93	**Let It Snow**...Boyz II Men
5/82	**Let It Whip**...Dazz Band
23/67	**Let Love Come Between Us**...James & Bobby Purify

POS/YR	RECORD TITLE. . .ARTIST
20/69	**Let Me**...Paul Revere & The Raiders
29/65	**Let Me Be**...Turtles
31/80	**Let Me Be The Clock**...Smokey Robinson
7/87	**Let Me Be The One**...Exposé
29/95	**Let Me Be The One**...Blessid Union Of Souls
6/74	**Let Me Be There**...Olivia Newton-John
21/80	**Let Me Be Your Angel**...Stacy Lattisaw
1/57	**(Let Me Be Your) Teddy Bear**...Elvis Presley
20/61	**Let Me Belong To You**...Brian Hyland
2/01	**Let Me Blow Ya Mind**...Eve
30/97	**Let Me Clear My Throat**...DJ Kool
38/82	**Let Me Go**...Ray Parker Jr.
35/80	**Let Me Go, Love**...Nicolette Larson
	Let Me Go, Lover!
8/54	Patti Page
1/55	Joan Weber
6/55	Teresa Brewer with The Lancers
17/55	Sunny Gale
32/70	**Let Me Go To Him**...Dionne Warwick
4/62	**Let Me In**...Sensations
36/73	**Let Me In**...Osmonds
33/98	**Let Me Let Go**...Faith Hill
10/80	**Let Me Love You Tonight**...Pure Prairie League
34/93	**Let Me Ride**...Dr. Dre
17/73	**Let Me Serenade You**...Three Dog Night
18/82	**Let Me Tickle Your Fancy**...Jermaine Jackson
9/80	**Let My Love Open The Door**...Pete Townshend
37/91	**Let The Beat Hit 'Em**...Lisa Lisa & Cult Jam
16/58	**Let The Bells Keep Ringing**...Paul Anka
	Let The Four Winds Blow
29/57	Roy Brown
15/61	Fats Domino
	Let The Good Times Roll
20/56	Shirley & Lee
22/67	Bunny Sigler (medley)
7/60	**Let The Little Girl Dance**...Billy Bland
8/84	**Let The Music Play**...Shannon
32/76	**Let The Music Play**...Barry White
	Let The Sunshine In ..see: Aquarius
	Let Them ..also see: Let 'Em
7/61	**Let There Be Drums**...Sandy Nelson
27/74	**Let Your Hair Down**...Temptations
1/76	**Let Your Love Flow**...Bellamy Brothers
28/71	**Let Your Love Go**...Bread
36/78	**Let's All Chant**...Michael Zager Band
1/83	**Let's Dance**...David Bowie
4/62	**Let's Dance**...Chris Montez
1/75	**Let's Do It Again**...Staple Singers
40/65	**Let's Do The Freddie**...Chubby Checker **(also see: Do The Freddie)**
21/67	**Let's Fall In Love**...Peaches & Herb
14/03	**Let's Get Down**...Bow Wow
30A/97	**Let's Get Down**...Tony Toni Toné
1/73	**Let's Get It On**...Marvin Gaye
11/00	**Let's Get Married**...Jagged Edge
32/74	**Let's Get Married**...Al Green
15/92	**Let's Get Rocked**...Def Leppard

POS/YR	RECORD TITLE. . .ARTIST
9/80	**Let's Get Serious**...Jermaine Jackson
8/61	**Let's Get Together**...Hayley Mills **(also see: Get Together)**
9/87	**Let's Go!**...Wang Chung
14/79	**Let's Go**...Cars
19/62	**Let's Go (pony)**...Routers
39/61	**Let's Go Again**...Hank Ballard
7/86	**Let's Go All The Way**...Sly Fox
1/84	**Let's Go Crazy**...Prince
30/83	**Let's Go Dancin' (Ooh La, La, La)**...Kool & The Gang
31/66	**Let's Go Get Stoned**...Ray Charles
6/60	**Let's Go, Let's Go, Let's Go**...Hank Ballard
26/63	**Let's Go Steady Again**...Neil Sedaka
3/81	**Let's Groove**...Earth, Wind & Fire
	Let's Hang On!
3/65	4 Seasons
32/82	Barry Manilow
37/60	**Let's Have A Party**...Wanda Jackson
1/84	**Let's Hear It For The Boy**...Deniece Williams
38/63	**Let's Kiss And Make Up**...Bobby Vinton
20/63	**Let's Limbo Some More**...Chubby Checker
8/67	**Let's Live For Today**...Grass Roots
35/76	**Let's Live Together**...Road Apples
11/65	**Let's Lock The Door**...Jay & The Americans
24/96	**Let's Make A Night To Remember**...Bryan Adams
35/73	**Let's Pretend**...Raspberries
18/74	**Let's Put It All Together**...Stylistics
2/98	**Let's Ride**...Montell Jordan
20/66	**Let's Start All Over Again**...Ronnie Dove
	Let's Stay Together
1/72	Al Green
26/84	Tina Turner
31/74	**Let's Straighten It Out**...Latimore
13/91	**Let's Talk About Sex**...Salt-N-Pepa
7/60	**Let's Think About Living**...Bob Luman
20/63	**Let's Turkey Trot**...Little Eva
8/61	**Let's Twist Again**...Chubby Checker
2/87	**Let's Wait Awhile**...Janet Jackson
39/87	**Let's Work**...Mick Jagger
	Let's Work Together
26/70	Canned Heat
32/70	Wilbert Harrison
31/94	**Letitgo**...Prince
	Letter, The
1/67	Box Tops
20/69	Arbors
7/70	Joe Cocker with Leon Russell
25/64	**Letter From Sherry**...Dale Ward
19/62	**Letter Full Of Tears**...Gladys Knight
	Letter Song ..see: S.Y.S.L.J.F.M.
25/58	**Letter To An Angel**...Jimmy Clanton
33/73	**Letter To Myself**...Chi-Lites
39/75	**Letting Go**...Wings
24/72	**Levon**...Elton John
7/71	**Liar**...Three Dog Night
14/00	**Liar**...Profyle

POS/YR	RECORD TITLE. . .ARTIST
12/65	**Liar, Liar**...Castaways
	Liberty Valance ..see: **(Man Who Shot)**
32/89	**Licence To Chill**...Billy Ocean
14/68	**Licking Stick - Licking Stick**...James Brown
11/77	**Lido Shuffle**...Boz Scaggs
13/62	**Lie To Me**...Brook Benton
16/57	**Liechtensteiner Polka**...Will Glahé
18/91	**Lies**....EMF
20/66	**Lies**...Knickerbockers
27/87	**Lies**...Jonathan Butler
30/83	**Lies**...Thompson Twins
38/90	**Lies**...En Vogue
35/91	**Life Goes On**...Poison
7/86	**Life In A Northern Town**...Dream Academy
19/85	**Life In One Day**...Howard Jones
11/77	**Life In The Fast Lane**...Eagles
6/92	**Life Is A Highway**...Tom Cochrane
8/74	**Life Is A Rock (But The Radio Rolled Me)**...Reunion
34/81	**Life Of Illusion**...Joe Walsh
12/78	**Life's Been Good**...Joe Walsh
20/03	**Lifestyles Of The Rich And Famous**...Good Charlotte
22/01	**Lifetime**...Maxwell
32/92	**Lift Me Up**...Howard Jones
	Light My Fire
1/67	Doors
3/68	Jose Feliciano
33/87	**Light Of Day**...Barbusters (Joan Jett)
1/66	**Lightnin' Strikes**...Lou Christie
12A/95	**Lightning Crashes**...Live
24/67	**Lightning's Girl**...Nancy Sinatra
14/02	**Lights, Camera, Action!**...Mr. Cheeks
12/84	**Lights Out**...Peter Wolf
11/67	**(Lights Went Out In) Massachusetts**...Bee Gees
27/66	**Like A Baby**...Len Barry
1/89	**Like A Prayer**...Madonna
12/86	**Like A Rock**...Bob Seger
2/65	**Like A Rolling Stone**...Bob Dylan
36/76	**Like A Sad Song**...John Denver
31/03	**Like A Stone**...Audioslave
40/78	**Like A Sunday In Salem (The Amos & Andy Song)**...Gene Cotton
1/84	**Like A Virgin**...Madonna
24/67	**Like An Old Time Movie**...Scott McKenzie
13/03	**Like Glue**...Sean Paul
11/02	**Like I Love You**...Justin Timberlake
38/61	**Like, Long Hair**...Paul Revere & The Raiders
14/86	**Like No Other Night**...38 Special
22/60	**Like Strangers**...Everly Brothers
F/95	**Like This And Like That**...Monica
17/68	**Like To Get To Know You**...Spanky & Our Gang
11/91	**Lily Was Here**...David A. Stewart & Candy Dulfer
	Limbo Rock
2/62	Chubby Checker
40/62	Champs

POS/YR	RECORD TITLE. . .ARTIST
28/63	**Linda**...Jan & Dean
	Ling, Ting, Tong
28/54	Five Keys
26/55	Charms
8/94	**Linger**...Cranberries
	Lion Sleeps Tonight
1/61	Tokens
3/72	Robert John
17/57	**Lips Of Wine**...Andy Williams
15/56	**Lipstick And Candy And Rubbersole Shoes**...Julius LaRosa
5/59	**Lipstick On Your Collar**...Connie Francis
10/01	**Liquid Dreams**...O-Town
	Lisbon Antigua
1/56	Nelson Riddle
19/56	Mitch Miller
3/66	**Listen People**...Herman's Hermits
11/72	**Listen To The Music**...Doobie Brothers
1/75	**Listen To What The Man Said**...Wings
1/89	**Listen To Your Heart**...Roxette
16/68	**Little Arrows**...Leapy Lee
21/63	**Little Band Of Gold**...James Gilreath
2/67	**Little Bit Me, A Little Bit You**...Monkees
11/76	**Little Bit More**...Dr. Hook
16/65	**Little Bit Of Heaven**...Ronnie Dove
38/86	**Little Bit Of Love (Is All It Takes)**...New Edition
	Little Bit Of Soap
12/61	Jarmels
34/79	Nigel Olsson
2/67	**Little Bit O' Soul**...Music Explosion
19/60	**Little Bitty Girl**...Bobby Rydell
	Little Bitty Pretty One
6/57	Thurston Harris
25/62	Clyde McPhatter
13/72	Jackson 5
9/62	**Little Bitty Tear**...Burl Ives
29/62	**Little Black Book**...Jimmy Dean
17/58	**Little Blue Man**...Betty Johnson
17/61	**Little Boy Sad**...Johnny Burnette
36/85	**Little By Little**...Robert Plant
7/64	**Little Children**...Billy J. Kramer
36/60	**Little Coco Palm**...Jerry Wallace
2/57	**Little Darlin'**...Diamonds
15/63	**Little Deuce Coupe**...Beach Boys
11/61	**Little Devil**...Neil Sedaka
8/62	**Little Diane**...Dion
30/59	**Little Dipper**...Robert Maxwell (Mickey Mozart Quintet)
	Little Drummer Boy
13/58	Harry Simeone Chorale
15/59	Harry Simeone Chorale
24/60	Harry Simeone Chorale
22/61	Harry Simeone Chorale
28/62	Harry Simeone Chorale
23/61	**Little Egypt (Ying-Yang)**...Coasters
8/66	**Little Girl**...Syndicate Of Sound
35/00	**Little Girl**...John Michael Montgomery
20/66	**Little Girl I Once Knew**...Beach Boys

POS/YR	RECORD TITLE. . . ARTIST
	Little Green Apples
2/68	O.C. Smith
39/68	Roger Miller
21/70	**Little Green Bag**...George Baker Selection
9/64	**Little Honda**...Hondells
17/81	**Little In Love**...Cliff Richard
29/89	**Little Jackie Wants To Be A Star**...Lisa Lisa & Cult Jam
3/80	**Little Jeannie**...Elton John
17/66	**Little Latin Lupe Lu**...Mitch Ryder
19/89	**Little Liar**...Joan Jett
4/87	**Little Lies**...Fleetwood Mac
37/90	**Little Love**...Corey Hart
33/56	**Little Love Can Go A Long, Long Way**...Dream Weavers
21/66	**Little Man**...Sonny & Chér
39/99	**Little Man**...Alan Jackson
17/92	**Little Miss Can't Be Wrong**...Spin Doctors
3/79	**Little More Love**...Olivia Newton-John
3/64	**Little Old Lady (From Pasadena)**...Jan & Dean
38/67	**Little Old Wine Drinker, Me**...Dean Martin
4/67	**Little Ole Man (Uptight-Everything's Alright)**...Bill Cosby
6/83	**Little Red Corvette**...Prince
23/62	**Little Red Rented Rowboat**...Joe Dowell
2/66	**Lil' Red Riding Hood**...Sam The Sham & The Pharoahs
11/63	**Little Red Rooster**...Sam Cooke
14/89	**Little Respect**...Erasure
32/57	**Little Sandy Sleighfoot**...Jimmy Dean
5/61	**Little Sister**...Elvis Presley
20/59	**Little Space Girl**...Jesse Lee Turner
1/58	**Little Star**...Elegants
13/65	**Little Things**...Bobby Goldsboro
35/60	**Little Things Mean A Lot**...Joni James
20/83	**Little Too Late**...Pat Benatar
12/63	**Little Town Flirt**...Del Shannon
25/57	**Little White Lies**...Betty Johnson
3/73	**Little Willy**...Sweet
3/69	**Little Woman**...Bobby Sherman
F/72	**Little Woman Love**...Wings
	Live And Die ..see: (Forever)
4/92	**Live And Learn**...Joe Public
	Live And Let Die
2/73	Wings
33/92	Guns N' Roses
34/85	**Live Every Moment**...REO Speedwagon
22/91	**Live For Loving You**...Gloria Estefan
39A/95	**Live Forever**...Oasis
32/86	**Live Is Life**...Opus
40/88	**Live My Life**...Boy George
1/86	**Live To Tell**...Madonna
20/76	**Livin' For The Weekend**...O'Jays
19/74	**Livin' For You**...Al Green
31/84	**Livin' In Desperate Times**...Olivia Newton-John
40/77	**Livin' In The Life**...Isley Brothers
6/01	**Livin' It Up**...Ja Rule
15/79	**Livin' It Up (Friday Night)**...Bell & James
1/99	**Livin' La Vida Loca**...Ricky Martin
1/87	**Livin' On A Prayer**...Bon Jovi
18/93	**Livin' On The Edge**...Aerosmith
13/77	**Livin' Thing**...Electric Light Orchestra
22/63	**Living A Lie**...Al Martino
37/75	**Living A Little, Laughing A Little**...Spinners
27/02	**Living And Living Well**...George Strait
30/59	**Living Doll**...Cliff Richard
8/74	**Living For The City**...Stevie Wonder
17/87	**Living In A Box**...Living In A Box
23/81	**Living In A Fantasy**...Leo Sayer
22/72	**Living In A House Divided**...Chér
4/86	**Living In America**...James Brown
20/94	**Living In Danger**...Ace Of Base
9/89	**Living In Sin**...Bon Jovi
11/73	**Living In The Past**...Jethro Tull
6/81	**Living Inside Myself**...Gino Vannelli
25/77	**Living Next Door To Alice**...Smokie
32/73	**Living Together, Growing Together**...5th Dimension
1/89	**Living Years**...Mike & The Mechanics
37/75	**Lizzie And The Rainman**...Tanya Tucker
14/69	**Lo Mucho Que Te Quiero**...Rene & Rene
F/78	**Load-Out, The**...Jackson Browne
	Loco-Motion, The
1/62	Little Eva
1/74	Grand Funk
3/88	Kylie Minogue
	Loddy Lo
12/63	Chubby Checker
17/64	Chubby Checker
6/79	**Logical Song**...Supertramp
9/70	**Lola**...Kinks
	Lollipop
2/58	Chordettes
20/58	Ronald & Ruby
23/98	**Lollipop (Candyman)**...Aqua
39/78	**London Town**...Wings
14/67	**(Loneliness Made Me Realize) It's You That I Need**...Temptations
22/65	**L-O-N-E-L-Y**...Bobby Vinton
6/60	**Lonely Blue Boy**...Conway Twitty
	Lonely Boy
1/59	Paul Anka
F/72	Donny Osmond
7/77	**Lonely Boy**...Andrew Gold
6/62	**Lonely Bull (El Solo Torro)**...Herb Alpert
3/71	**Lonely Days**...Bee Gees
24/59	**Lonely For You**...Gary Stites
26/58	**Lonely Island**...Sam Cooke
32/61	**Lonely Man**...Elvis Presley
3/76	**Lonely Night (Angel Face)**...Captain & Tennille
6/85	**Lonely Ol' Night**...John Cougar Mellencamp
23/59	**Lonely One**...Duane Eddy
5/75	**Lonely People**...America
5/59	**Lonely Street**...Andy Williams
39/63	**Lonely Surfer**...Jack Nitzsche

POS/YR	RECORD TITLE. . . ARTIST
7/59	**Lonely Teardrops**...Jackie Wilson
12/60	**Lonely Teenager**...Dion
22/60	**Lonely Weekends**...Charlie Rich
6/79	**Lonesome Loser**...Little River Band
7/58	**Lonesome Town**...Ricky Nelson
31/71	**Long Ago And Far Away**...James Taylor
1/70	**Long And Winding Road**...Beatles
F/70	**Long As I Can See The Light**...Creedence Clearwater Revival
2/72	**Long Cool Woman (In A Black Dress)**...Hollies
26/72	**Long Dark Road**...Hollies
6A/97	**Long December**...Counting Crows
39/02	**Long Goodbye**...Brooks & Dunn
38/72	**Long Haired Lover From Liverpool**...Little Jimmy Osmond
33/66	**Long Live Our Love**...Shangri-Las
17/65	**Long Lonely Nights**...Bobby Vinton
20/70	**Long Lonesome Highway**...Michael Parks
25/70	**Long Long Time**...Linda Ronstadt
20/78	**Long, Long Way From Home**...Foreigner
	(Long Nights) ..see: Blue Collar Man
F/95	**Long Road**...Pearl Jam
8/80	**Long Run**...Eagles
9/75	**Long Tall Glasses (I Can Dance)**...Leo Sayer
	Long Tall Sally
6/56	Little Richard
8/56	Pat Boone
22/77	**Long Time**...Boston
7/02	**Long Time Gone**...Dixie Chicks
8/73	**Long Train Runnin'**...Doobie Brothers
36A/94	**Long View**...Green Day
2/80	**Longer**...Dan Fogelberg
14/84	**Longest Time**...Billy Joel
6/55	**Longest Walk**...Jaye P. Morgan
5/74	**Longfellow Serenade**...Neil Diamond
1/89	**Look, The**...Roxette
39/75	**Look At Me (I'm In Love)**...Moments
1/88	**Look Away**...Chicago
	Look For A Star
16/60	Garry Miles
19/60	Billy Vaughn
26/60	Garry Mills
29/60	Deane Hawley
36/57	**Look Homeward, Angel**...Johnnie Ray
14/61	**Look In My Eyes**...Chantels
11/75	**Look In My Eyes Pretty Woman**...Tony Orlando & Dawn
4/97	**Look Into My Eyes**...BONE thugs-n-harmony
	Look Of Love
22/67	Dusty Springfield
4/68	Sergio Mendes
18/83	**Look Of Love**...ABC
27/65	**Look Of Love**...Lesley Gore
35/88	**Look Out Any Window**...Bruce Hornsby
32/66	**Look Through Any Window**...Hollies
24/66	**Look Through My Window**...Mamas & The Papas

POS/YR	RECORD TITLE. . . ARTIST
14/70	**Look What They've Done To My Song Ma**...New Seekers
4/72	**Look What You Done For Me**...Al Green
32/67	**Look What You've Done**...Pozo Seco Singers
14/80	**Look What You've Done To Me**...Boz Scaggs
8/98	**Lookin' At Me**...Mase
5/58	**Looking Back**...Nat "King" Cole
	Lookin' For A Love
39/72	J. Geils Band
10/74	Bobby Womack
5/80	**Lookin' For Love**...Johnny Lee
2/70	**Lookin' Out My Back Door**...Creedence Clearwater Revival
16/72	**Lookin' Through The Windows**...Jackson 5
2/87	**Looking For A New Love**...Jody Watley
39/83	**Looking For A Stranger**...Pat Benatar
29/76	**Looking For Space**...John Denver
6/93	**Looking Through Patient Eyes**...PM Dawn
	Looking Through The Eyes Of Love
28/65	Gene Pitney
39/73	Partridge Family
18/98	**Looking Through Your Eyes**...LeAnn Rimes
1/77	**Looks Like We Made It**...Barry Manilow
4/63	**Loop De Loop**...Johnny Thunder
4/74	**Lord's Prayer**...Sister Janet Mead
27/76	**Lorelei**...Styx
F/93	**Lose Control**...Silk
1/02	**Lose Yourself**...Eminem
10/94	**Loser**...Beck
4/91	**Losing My Religion**...R.E.M.
6/63	**Losing You**...Brenda Lee
34/80	**Lost Her In The Sun**...John Stewart
1/87	**Lost In Emotion**...Lisa Lisa & Cult Jam
3/80	**Lost In Love**...Air Supply
35/85	**Lost In Love**...New Edition
5/99	**Lost In You**...Garth Brooks As Chris Gaines
12/88	**Lost In You**...Rod Stewart
1/89	**Lost In Your Eyes**...Debbie Gibson
35/61	**Lost Love**...H.B. Barnum
9/77	**Lost Without Your Love**...Bread
8/79	**Lotta Love**...Nicolette Larson
13/57	**Lotta Lovin'**...Gene Vincent
	Louie Louie
2/63	Kingsmen
30/66	Sandpipers
3/96	**Loungin**...LL Cool J
24/01	**Love**...Musiq Soulchild
	(also see: Luv)
F/57	**Love Affair**...Sal Mineo
	Love And Affection ..see: (Can't Live Without Your)
15/90	**Love & Emotion**...Stevie B
	Love And Marriage
5/55	Frank Sinatra
20/55	Dinah Shore
17/91	**Love And Understanding**...Cher
22/03	**Love @ 1st Sight**...Mary J. Blige
23/02	**Love At First Sight**...Kylie Minogue

POS/YR	RECORD TITLE. . . ARTIST
25/91	**Love At First Sight**...Styx
	Love Ballad
20/76	L.T.D.
18/79	George Benson
	Love Being Your Fool ..see: (Shu-Doo-Pa-Poo-Poop)
1/88	**Love Bites**...Def Leppard
11/86	**Love Bizarre**...Sheila E.
25/67	**Love Bug Leave My Heart Alone**...Martha & The Vandellas
10/62	**Love Came To Me**...Dion
2/69	**Love (Can Make You Happy)**...Mercy
36/93	**Love Can Move Mountains**...Celine Dion
23/88	**Love Changes (Everything)**...Climie Fisher
	Love Child
1/68	Supremes
13/90	Sweet Sensation
17/82	**Love Come Down**...Evelyn King
3/01	**Love Don't Cost A Thing**...Jennifer Lopez
32/79	**Love Don't Live Here Anymore**...Rose Royce
15/74	**Love Don't Love Nobody**...Spinners
36/93	**Love Don't Love You**...En Vogue
15/67	**Love Eyes**...Nancy Sinatra
30/76	**Love Fire**...Jigsaw
25/97	**Love Gets Me Every Time**...Shania Twain
5/70	**Love Grows (Where My Rosemary Goes)**...Edison Lighthouse
1/76	**Love Hangover**...Diana Ross
11/71	**Love Her Madly**...Doors
8/76	**Love Hurts**...Nazareth
7/73	**Love I Lost**...Harold Melvin
20/67	**Love I Saw In You Was Just A Mirage**...Miracles
5/89	**Love In An Elevator**...Aerosmith
36/77	**Love In 'C' Minor**...Cerrone
22/83	**Love In Store**...Fleetwood Mac
15/82	**Love In The First Degree**...Alabama
16/76	**Love In The Shadows**...Neil Sedaka
24/89	**Love In Your Eyes**...Eddie Money
3/93	**Love Is**...Vanessa Williams & Brian McKnight
36/90	**Love Is**...Alannah Myles
5/83	**Love Is A Battlefield**...Pat Benatar
10/57	**Love Is A Golden Ring**...Frankie Laine
13/66	**Love Is A Hurtin' Thing**...Lou Rawls
	Love Is A Many-Splendored Thing
1/55	Four Aces
26/55	Don Cornell
23/83	**Love Is A Stranger**...Eurythmics
4/91	**Love Is A Wonderful Thing**...Michael Bolton
2/76	**Love Is Alive**...Gary Wright
7/68	**Love Is All Around**...Troggs
15/58	**Love Is All We Need**...Tommy Edwards
20/82	**Love Is Alright Tonite**...Rick Springfield
34/00	**Love Is Blind**...Eve
	Love Is Blue
1/68	Paul Mauriat
22/69	Dells (medley)
16/86	**Love Is Forever**...Billy Ocean

POS/YR	RECORD TITLE. . . ARTIST
1/67	**Love Is Here And Now You're Gone**...Supremes
10/82	**Love Is In Control (Finger On The Trigger)**...Donna Summer
7/78	**Love Is In The Air**...John Paul Young
26/68	**(Love Is Like A) Baseball Game**...Intruders
37/82	**Love Is Like A Rock**...Donnie Iris
9/66	**Love Is Like An Itching In My Heart**...Supremes
8/78	**Love Is Like Oxygen**...Sweet
12/92	**Love Is On The Way**...Saigon Kick
	Love Is Strange
11/57	Mickey & Sylvia
13/67	Peaches & Herb
10/79	**Love Is The Answer**...England Dan & John Ford Coley
30/76	**Love Is The Drug**...Roxy Music
17/85	**Love Is The Seventh Wave**...Sting
7/56	**(Love Is) The Tender Trap**...Frank Sinatra
1/78	**(Love Is) Thicker Than Water**...Andy Gibb
16/73	**Love Jones**...Brighter Side Of Darkness **(also see: Basketball Jones)**
16/70	**Love Land**...Charles Wright
	Love Letters
5/62	Ketty Lester
19/66	Elvis Presley
1/57	**Love Letters In The Sand**...Pat Boone
17/85	**Love Light In Flight**...Stevie Wonder
7/98	**Love Like This**...Faith Evans
13/75	**L-O-V-E (Love)**...Al Green
	Love, Love, Love
30/56	Clovers
30/56	Diamonds
1/76	**Love Machine**...Miracles
15/68	**Love Makes A Woman**...Barbara Acklin
11/66	**Love Makes The World Go Round**...Deon Jackson
26/63	**Love (Makes the World Go 'Round)**...Paul Anka
33/58	**Love Makes The World Go 'Round**...Perry Como
13/91	**Love Makes Things Happen**...Pebbles
2/57	**Love Me**...Elvis Presley
14/76	**Love Me**...Yvonne Elliman
17/98	**Love Me**...112
26/92	**Love Me All Up**...Stacy Earl
1/64	**Love Me Do**...Beatles
10/74	**Love Me For A Reason**...Osmonds
29/90	**Love Me For Life**...Stevie B
	Love Me Forever
24/57	Eydie Gorme
25/57	Four Esquires
	Love Me Or Leave Me
12/55	Sammy Davis, Jr.
19/55	Lena Horne
	Love Me Tender
1/56	Elvis Presley
21/62	Richard Chamberlain
40/67	Percy Sledge

POS/YR	RECORD TITLE. . . ARTIST
11/57	**Love Me To Pieces**...Jill Corey
22/82	**Love Me Tomorrow**...Chicago
13/69	**Love Me Tonight**...Tom Jones
25/68	**Love Me Two Times**...Doors
12/62	**Love Me Warm And Tender**...Paul Anka
	Love Me With All Your Heart
3/64	Ray Charles Singers
38/66	Bachelors
39/71	**Love Means (You Never Have To Say You're Sorry)**...Sounds Of Sunshine
	Love My Life Away ..see: (I Wanna)
5/91	**Love Of A Lifetime**...Firehouse
39/01	**Love Of A Woman**...Travis Tritt
40/58	**Love Of My Life**...Everly Brothers
9/03	**Love Of My Life (An Ode To Hip Hop)**...Erykah Badu
21/63	**Love Of My Man**...Theola Kilgore
40/91	**Love On A Rooftop**...Desmond Child
	Love On A Two-Way Street
3/70	Moments
26/81	Stacy Lattisaw
2/81	**Love On The Rocks**...Neil Diamond
36/76	**Love Or Leave**...Spinners
	Love Or Let Me Be Lonely
6/70	Friends Of Distinction
40/82	Paul Davis
32/78	**Love Or Something Like It**...Kenny Rogers
13/88	**Love Overboard**...Gladys Knight
34/79	**Love Pains**...Yvonne Elliman
36/86	**Love Parade**...Dream Academy
37/82	**Love Plus One**...Haircut One Hundred
	Love Potion Number Nine
23/59	Clovers
3/65	Searchers
	Love Power
22/68	Sandpebbles
4/91	Luther Vandross (medley)
12/87	**Love Power**...Dionne Warwick & Jeffrey Osborne
22/76	**Love Really Hurts Without You**...Billy Ocean
	Love Rollercoaster
1/76	Ohio Players
40A/97	Red Hot Chili Peppers
3/89	**Love Shack**...B-52's
31/63	**Love She Can Count On**...Miracles
33/93	**Love Shoulda Brought You Home**...Toni Braxton
19/94	**Love Sneakin' Up On You**...Bonnie Raitt
40/63	**Love So Fine**...Chiffons
3/76	**Love So Right**...Bee Gees
5/84	**Love Somebody**...Rick Springfield
2/89	**Love Song**...Cure
10/90	**Love Song**...Tesla
12/74	**Love Song**...Anne Murray
38/80	**Love Stinks**...J. Geils Band
	Love Story ..see: Theme From
1/90	**Love Takes Time**...Mariah Carey
11/79	**Love Takes Time**...Orleans

POS/YR	RECORD TITLE. . . ARTIST
	Love The One You're With
14/71	Stephen Stills
18/71	Isley Brothers
14/80	**Love The World Away**...Kenny Rogers
1/77	**Love Theme From A Star Is Born (Evergreen)**...Barbra Streisand
21/78	**Love Theme From Eyes Of Laura Mars (Prisoner)**...Barbra Streisand
37/61	**(Love Theme From) One Eyed Jacks**...Ferrante & Teicher
	Love Theme From One On One ..see: My Fair Share
1/69	**Love Theme From Romeo & Juliet**...Henry Mancini
15/85	**Love Theme From St. Elmo's Fire**...David Foster
34/72	**Love Theme From The Godfather**...Andy Williams
10/91	**Love...Thy Will Be Done**...Martika
2/76	**Love To Love You Baby**...Donna Summer
6/86	**Love Touch**...Rod Stewart
1/73	**Love Train**...O'Jays
31/96	**Love U 4 Life**...Jodeci
36/93	**Love U More**...Sunscreem
30/60	**Love Walked In**...Dinah Washington
22/86	**Love Walks In**...Van Halen
30/71	**Love We Had (Stays On My Mind)**...Dells
9/86	**Love Will Conquer All**...Lionel Richie
6/78	**Love Will Find A Way**...Pablo Cruise
30/87	**Love Will Find A Way**...Yes
40/69	**Love Will Find A Way**...Jackie DeShannon
22A/95	**Love Will Keep Us Alive**...Eagles
1/75	**Love Will Keep Us Together**...Captain & Tennille
1/90	**Love Will Lead You Back**...Taylor Dayne
1/91	**Love Will Never Do (Without You)**...Janet Jackson
9/88	**Love Will Save The Day**...Whitney Houston
30/84	**Love Will Show Us How**...Christine McVie
13/82	**Love Will Turn You Around**...Kenny Rogers
5/75	**Love Won't Let Me Wait**...Major Harris
	Love You ..also see: Love U / Luv U
	Love You Down
9/87	Ready For The World
25/98	Inoj
1/79	**Love You Inside Out**...Bee Gees
24/81	**Love You Like I Never Loved Before**...John O'Banion
26/58	**Love You Most Of All**...Sam Cooke
30/03	**Love You Out Loud**...Rascal Flatts
1/70	**Love You Save**...Jackson 5
7/60	**Love You So**...Ron Holden
10/86	**Love Zone**...Billy Ocean
7/82	**Love's Been A Little Bit Hard On Me**...Juice Newton
20/77	**Love's Grown Deep**...Kenny Nolan
19/71	**Love's Lines, Angles And Rhymes**...5th Dimension

POS/YR	RECORD TITLE. . .ARTIST
26/66	**Love's Made A Fool Of You**...Bobby Fuller Four
1/74	**Love's Theme**...Love Unlimited Orchestra
2A/97	**Lovefool**...Cardigans
30/78	**Lovely Day**...Bill Withers
12/80	**Lovely One**...Jacksons
20/56	**Lovely One**...Four Voices
2/89	**Lover In Me**...Sheena Easton
7/62	**Lover Please**...Clyde McPhatter
2/65	**Lover's Concerto**...Toys
31/68	**Lover's Holiday**...Peggy Scott & Jo Jo Benson
40/80	**Lover's Holiday**...Change
31/61	**Lover's Island**...Blue Jays
6/59	**Lover's Question**...Clyde McPhatter
2/85	**Loverboy**...Billy Ocean
2/01	**Loverboy**...Mariah Carey
4/85	**Lovergirl**...Teena Marie
36/62	**Lovers By Night, Strangers By Day**...Fleetwoods
3/62	**Lovers Who Wander**...Dion
2/73	**Loves Me Like A Rock**...Paul Simon
25/61	**Lovey Dovey**...Buddy Knox
9/85	**Lovin' Every Minute Of It**...Loverboy
16/79	**Lovin', Touchin', Squeezin'**...Journey
26/71	**Loving Her Was Easier (Than Anything I'll Ever Do Again)**...Kris Kristofferson
1/75	**Lovin' You**...Minnie Riperton
32/67	**Lovin' You**...Bobby Darin
20/57	**Loving You**...Elvis Presley
29/72	**Loving You Just Crossed My Mind**...Sam Neely
3/76	**Lowdown**...Boz Scaggs
35/71	**Lowdown**...Chicago
7/75	**Low Rider**...War
	Lt. Calley ..see: Battle Hymn Of
29/94	**Lucas With The Lid Off**...Lucas
5/77	**Lucille**...Kenny Rogers
	Lucille
21/57	Little Richard
21/60	Everly Brothers
25/77	**Luckenbach, Texas**...Waylon Jennings
23/00	**Lucky**...Britney Spears
30/85	**Lucky**...Greg Kihn
25/60	**Lucky Devil**...Carl Dobkins, Jr.
38/85	**Lucky In Love**...Mick Jagger
14/59	**Lucky Ladybug**...Billy & Lillie
25/57	**Lucky Lips**...Ruth Brown
30/96	**Lucky Love**...Ace Of Base
18/94	**Lucky One**...Amy Grant
20/84	**Lucky One**...Laura Branigan
4/84	**Lucky Star**...Madonna
29/70	**Lucretia Mac Evil**...Blood, Sweat & Tears
1/75	**Lucy In The Sky With Diamonds**...Elton John
3/87	**Luka**...Suzanne Vega
7/99	**Lullaby**...Shawn Mullins
16/56	**Lullaby Of Birdland**...Blue Stars
23/61	**Lullaby Of Love**...Frank Gari

POS/YR	RECORD TITLE. . .ARTIST
21A/95	**Lump**...Presidents Of The United States Of America
37A/98	**Luv 2 Luv U**...Timbaland & Magoo
4/02	**Luv U Better**...LL Cool J
2/75	**Lyin' Eyes**...Eagles
27/90	**Lyin' To Myself**...David Cassidy

M

POS/YR	RECORD TITLE. . .ARTIST
1/97	**MMMBop**...Hanson
15/59	**M.T.A.**...Kingston Trio
5/70	**Ma Belle Amie**...Tee Set
	MacArthur Park
2/68	Richard Harris
38/71	Four Tops
1/78	Donna Summer
	Macarena
1/96	Los Del Rio (bayside boys mix)
23/96	Los Del Rio (non stop)
22/74	**Machine Gun**...Commodores
25/78	**Macho Man**...Village People
	Mack The Knife
8/56	Dick Hyman
11/56	Richard Hayman & Jan August
17/56	Lawrence Welk
20/56	Louis Armstrong
37/56	Billy Vaughn
1/59	Bobby Darin
27/60	Ella Fitzgerald
3/86	**Mad About You**...Belinda Carlisle
	Made To Love ..see: (Girls, Girls, Girls)
32/03	**Made You Look**...Nas
36/76	**Mademoiselle**...Styx
23/60	**Madison, The**...Al Brown
30/60	**Madison Time**...Ray Bryant Combo
1/71	**Maggie May**...Rod Stewart
1/80	**Magic**...Olivia Newton-John
5/75	**Magic**...Pilot
12/84	**Magic**...Cars
25/68	**Magic Bus**...Who
3/68	**Magic Carpet Ride**...Steppenwolf
9/76	**Magic Man**...Heart
4/58	**Magic Moments**...Perry Como
2/03	**Magic Stick**...Lil' Kim
	Magic Touch ..see: (You've Got)
21/66	**Magic Town**...Vogues
39/77	**Magical Mystery Tour**...Ambrosia
8/78	**Magnet And Steel**...Walter Egan
35/61	**Magnificent Seven**...Al Caiola
	Magnum P.I. ..see: Theme From
	Mahogany ..see: Theme From
3/79	**Main Event/Fight**...Barbra Streisand
	Main Theme From Exodus ..see: Exodus
	Main Title And Molly-O ..see: Man With The Golden Arm
24/77	**Mainstreet**...Bob Seger
36/61	**Majestic, The**...Dion

POS/YR	RECORD TITLE. . . ARTIST
14/83	**Major Tom (Coming Home)**...Peter Schilling
25/80	**Make A Little Magic**...Dirt Band
5/82	**Make A Move On Me**...Olivia Newton-John
28/69	**Make Believe**...Wind
30/82	**Make Believe**...Toto
16/98	**Make Em' Say Uhh!**...Master P
	Make It Easy On Yourself
20/62	Jerry Butler
16/65	Walker Bros.
37/70	Dionne Warwick
22/71	**Make It Funky**...James Brown
5/92	**Make It Happen**...Mariah Carey
5/98	**Make It Hot**...Nicole
4/88	**Make It Real**...Jets
1/70	**Make It With You**...Bread
36/92	**Make Love Like A Man**...Def Leppard
29/83	**Make Love Stay**...Dan Fogelberg
16/58	**Make Me A Miracle**...Jimmie Rodgers
28/66	**Make Me Belong To You**...Barbara Lewis
3/88	**Make Me Lose Control**...Eric Carmen
9/70	**Make Me Smile**...Chicago
27/72	**Make Me The Woman That You Go Home To**...Gladys Knight
11/65	**Make Me Your Baby**...Barbara Lewis
21/67	**Make Me Yours**...Bettye Swann
	Make The World Go Away
24/63	Timi Yuro
6/65	Eddy Arnold
14/90	**Make You Sweat**...Keith Sweat
36/69	**Make Your Own Kind Of Music**...Mama Cass Elliot
	Make Yourself Comfortable
6/55	Sarah Vaughan
26/55	Andy Griffith
30/55	Peggy King
27/02	**Makin' Good Love**...Avant
5/79	**Makin' It**...David Naughton
20/59	**Makin' Love**...Floyd Robinson
13/82	**Making Love**...Roberta Flack
31/67	**Making Every Minute Count**...Spanky & Our Gang
35/87	**Making Love In The Rain**...Herb Alpert
2/83	**Making Love Out Of Nothing At All**...Air Supply
35/67	**Making Memories**...Frankie Laine
25/76	**Making Our Dreams Come True**...Cyndi Grecco
8/60	**Mama**...Connie Francis
22/66	**Mama**...B.J. Thomas **(also see: Mamma)**
9/79	**Mama Can't Buy You Love**...Elton John
14/63	**Mama Didn't Lie**...Jan Bradley
11/56	**Mama From The Train**...Patti Page
28/92	**Mama, I'm Coming Home**...Ozzy Osbourne
F/70	**Mama Liked The Roses**...Elvis Presley
11/57	**Mama Look At Bubu**...Harry Belafonte
4/61	**Mama Said**...Shirelles
17/91	**Mama Said Knock You Out**...LL Cool J

POS/YR	RECORD TITLE. . . ARTIST
	Mama Sang A Song
32/62	Stan Kenton
38/62	Walter Brennan
34/56	**Mama, Teach Me To Dance**...Eydie Gorme
1/70	**Mama Told Me (Not To Come)**...Three Dog Night
30/82	**Mama Used To Say**...Junior
2/71	**Mama's Pearl**...Jackson 5
39/01	**Mamacita**...Public Announcement
9/54	**Mambo Italiano**...Rosemary Clooney
3/99	**Mambo No. 5 (A Little Bit Of...)**...Lou Bega
18/55	**Mambo Rock**...Bill Haley
19/66	**Mame**...Herb Alpert
32/76	**Mamma Mia**...Abba
16/55	**Man Chases A Girl**...Eddie Fisher
23/99	**Man! I Feel Like A Woman!**...Shania Twain
31/79	**Man I'll Never Be**...Boston
1/88	**Man In The Mirror**...Michael Jackson
	Man In The Raincoat
14/55	Marion Marlowe
16/55	Priscilla Wright
40/82	**Man On The Corner**...Genesis
30/93	**Man On The Moon**...R.E.M.
14/82	**Man On Your Mind**...Little River Band
15/86	**Man Size Love**...Klymaxx
25/03	**Man To Man**...Gary Allan
4/62	**(Man Who Shot) Liberty Valance**...Gene Pitney
39A/95	**Man Who Sold The World**...Nirvana
	Man With The Golden Arm (Main Title/Molly-O/Delilah Jones)
14/56	Richard Maltby
16/56	Elmer Bernstein
22/56	Dick Jacobs
37/56	McGuire Sisters
19/68	**Man Without Love (Quando M'innamoro)**...Engelbert Humperdinck
4/87	**Mandolin Rain**...Bruce Hornsby
1/75	**Mandy**...Barry Manilow
1/82	**Maneater**...Daryl Hall & John Oates
10/57	**Mangos**...Rosemary Clooney
10/59	**Manhattan Spiritual**...Reg Owen
1/83	**Maniac**...Michael Sembello
2/86	**Manic Monday**...Bangles
7/60	**Many Tears Ago**...Connie Francis
20/58	**March From The River Kwai and Colonel Bogey**...Mitch Miller
8/77	**Margaritaville**...Jimmy Buffett
6/63	**Maria Elena**...Los Indios Tabajaras
1/00	**Maria Maria**...Santana Feat. The Product G&B
	Marianne
3/57	Hilltoppers
4/57	Terry Gilkyson & The Easy Riders
15/65	**Marie**...Bachelors
4/61	**(Marie's the Name) His Latest Flame**...Elvis Presley
31/59	**Marina**...Rocco Granata
36/63	**Marlena**...Four Seasons
28/69	**Marrakesh Express**...Crosby, Stills & Nash

POS/YR	RECORD TITLE. . . ARTIST
40/79	**Married Men**...Bette Midler
16/63	**Martian Hop**...Ran-Dells
39/62	**Mary Ann Regrets**...Burl Ives
28/72	**Mary Had A Little Lamb**...Wings
27/67	**Mary In The Morning**...Al Martino
14/94	**Mary Jane's Last Dance**...Tom Petty
26/59	**Mary Lou**...Ronnie Hawkins
12/56	**Mary's Boy Child**...Harry Belafonte
39/62	**Mary's Little Lamb**...James Darren
23/87	**Mary's Prayer**...Danny Wilson
2/62	**Mashed Potato Time**...Dee Dee Sharp
	Massachusetts ..see: (Lights Went Out In)
5/80	**Master Blaster (Jammin')**...Stevie Wonder
18/68	**Master Jack**...Four Jacks & A Jill
33/73	**Master Of Eyes**...Aretha Franklin
3/92	**Masterpiece**...Atlantic Starr
7/73	**Masterpiece**...Temptations
20/64	**Matador, The**...Major Lance
17/64	**Matchbox**...Beatles
2/85	**Material Girl**...Madonna
10/86	**Matter Of Trust**...Billy Joel
39/69	**May I**...Bill Deal
15/65	**May The Bird Of Paradise Fly Up Your Nose**..."Little" Jimmy Dickens
11/59	**May You Always**...McGuire Sisters
	Maybe
15/58	Chantels
29/70	Three Degrees
17/58	**Maybe Baby**...Crickets
38/01	**Maybe I Deserve**...Tank
14/64	**Maybe I Know**...Lesley Gore
22/79	**Maybe I'm A Fool**...Eddie Money
10/77	**Maybe I'm Amazed**...Wings
20/71	**Maybe Tomorrow**...Jackson 5
	Maybellene
5/55	Chuck Berry
12/64	Johnny Rivers
35A/98	**Me**...Paula Cole
35/03	**Me Against The Music**...Britney Spears
15/74	**Me And Baby Brother**...War
	Me And Bobby McGee
1/71	Janis Joplin
40/72	Jerry Lee Lewis
22/72	**Me And Julio Down By The Schoolyard**...Paul Simon
1/72	**Me And Mrs. Jones**...Billy Paul
34/71	**Me And My Arrow**...Nilsson
5/71	**Me And You And A Dog Named Boo**...Lobo
4/04	**Me, Myself And I**...Beyoncé
34/89	**Me Myself And I**...De La Soul
26/89	**Me So Horny**...2 Live Crew
40/81	**Me (Without You)**...Andy Gibb
5/63	**Mean Woman Blues**...Roy Orbison
38/99	**Meanwhile**...George Strait
12/63	**Mecca**...Gene Pitney
	"Medic" Theme ..see: Blue Star
22/69	**Medicine Man**...Buchanan Brothers
1/81	**Medley**...Stars On 45

POS/YR	RECORD TITLE. . . ARTIST
11/87	**Meet Me Half Way**...Kenny Loggins
33/94	**(Meet) The Flintstones**...B-52's
20/00	**Meet Virginia**...Train
2/66	**Mellow Yellow**...Donovan
5/57	**Melodie D'Amour (Melody of Love)**...Ames Brothers
	Melody Of Love
2/55	Billy Vaughn
3/55	Four Aces
8/55	David Carroll
19/55	Frank Sinatra & Ray Anthony
30/55	Leo Diamond
35/69	**Memories**...Elvis Presley
	Memories Are Made Of This
1/56	Dean Martin
5/56	Gale Storm
	Memories Of You
22/55	Four Coins
20/56	Benny Goodman/Rosemary Clooney
39/83	**Memory**...Barry Manilow
28/97	**Memory Remains**...Metallica
	Memphis
5/63	Lonnie Mack
2/64	Johnny Rivers
33/67	**Memphis Soul Stew**...King Curtis
	Men ..see: Theme From The
33/68	**Men Are Gettin' Scarce**...Joe Tex
1A/97	**Men In Black**...Will Smith
6/66	**Men In My Little Girl's Life**...Mike Douglas
27/69	**Mendocino**...Sir Douglas Quintet
29/95	**Mental Picture**...Jon Secada
14/90	**Mentirosa**...Mellow Man Ace
2/88	**Mercedes Boy**...Pebbles
30/69	**Mercy**...Ohio Express
35/64	**Mercy, Mercy**...Don Covay
	Mercy Mercy Me (The Ecology)
4/71	Marvin Gaye
16/91	Robert Palmer (medley)
	Mercy, Mercy, Mercy
5/67	Buckinghams
11/67	"Cannonball" Adderley
2/03	**Mesmerize**...Ja Rule
32/60	**Mess Of Blues**...Elvis Presley
8/66	**Message To Michael**...Dionne Warwick
5/85	**Method Of Modern Love**...Daryl Hall/John Oates
16/58	**Mexican Hat Rock**...Applejacks
7/61	**Mexico**...Bob Moore
17/99	**Miami**...Will Smith
1/85	**Miami Vice Theme**...Jan Hammer
1/61	**Michael**...Highwaymen
18/66	**Michelle**...David & Jonathan
1/82	**Mickey**...Toni Basil
8/63	**Mickey's Monkey**...Miracles
5/02	**Middle, The**...Jimmy Eat World
19/84	**Middle Of The Road**...Pretenders
6/74	**Midnight At The Oasis**...Maria Muldaur
5/87	**Midnight Blue**...Lou Gramm

POS/YR	RECORD TITLE. . .ARTIST
6/75	**Midnight Blue**...Melissa Manchester
5/68	**Midnight Confessions**...Grass Roots
10/70	**Midnight Cowboy**...Ferrante & Teicher
	Midnight Hour ..see: In The
2/62	**Midnight In Moscow**...Kenny Ball
10/64	**Midnight Mary**...Joey Powers
	Midnight Rider
27/72	Joe Cocker
19/74	Gregg Allman
24/80	**Midnight Rocks**...Al Stewart
	Midnight Special
16/60	Paul Evans
20/65	Johnny Rivers
35/59	**Midnight Stroll**...Revels
1/73	**Midnight Train To Georgia**...Gladys Knight
28/79	**Midnight Wind**...John Stewart
34/71	**Mighty Clouds Of Joy**...B.J. Thomas
38/59	**Mighty Good**...Ricky Nelson
20/74	**Mighty Love**...Spinners
29/74	**Mighty Mighty**...Earth, Wind & Fire
10/68	**Mighty Quinn (Quinn The Eskimo)**...Manfred Mann
12/91	**Miles Away**...Winger
3/03	**Milkshake**...Kelis
33/64	**Miller's Cave**...Bobby Bare
	Million To One
5/60	Jimmy Charles
23/73	Donny Osmond
	Millionaire ..see: (How To Be A)
26/69	**Mind, Body and Soul**...Flaming Ember
18/73	**Mind Games**...John Lennon
23/92	**Mind Playing Tricks On Me**...Geto Boys
38/69	**Minotaur, The**...Dick Hyman
14/79	**Minute By Minute**...Doobie Brothers
9/91	**Miracle**...Whitney Houston
12/90	**Miracle**...Jon Bon Jovi
18/56	**Miracle Of Love**...Eileen Rodgers
3/75	**Miracles**...Jefferson Starship
40/83	**Miracles**...Stacy Lattisaw
10/67	**Mirage**...Tommy James
30/83	**Mirror Man**...Human League
8/82	**Mirror, Mirror**...Diana Ross
22/73	**Misdemeanor**...Foster Sylvers
20/95	**Misery**...Soul Asylum
38/95	**Mishale**...Andru Donalds
10/85	**Misled**...Kool & The Gang
23/94	**Misled**...Celine Dion
9/03	**Miss Independent**...Kelly Clarkson
5/84	**Miss Me Blind**...Culture Club
14/81	**Miss Sun**...Boz Scaggs
1/78	**Miss You**...Rolling Stones
3/03	**Miss You**...Aaliyah
39/94	**Miss You In A Heartbeat**...Def Leppard
7/89	**Miss You Like Crazy**...Natalie Cole
1/89	**Miss You Much**...Janet Jackson
29/88	**Missed Opportunity**...Daryl Hall/John Oates
2/96	**Missing**...Everything But The Girl

POS/YR	RECORD TITLE. . .ARTIST
1/84	**Missing You**...John Waite
4/01	**Missing You**...Case
10/85	**Missing You**...Diana Ross
23/82	**Missing You**...Dan Fogelberg
25/96	**Missing You**...Brandy, Tamia, Gladys Knight & Chaka Khan
29/61	**Missing You**...Ray Peterson
12/92	**Missing You Now**...Michael Bolton Feat. Kenny G
7/60	**Mission Bell**...Donnie Brooks
14/86	**Missionary Man**...Eurythmics
32/70	**Mississippi**...John Phillips
21/70	**Mississippi Queen**...Mountain
33/85	**Mistake No. 3**...Culture Club
	Mister ..see: Mr.
	Misty
12/59	Johnny Mathis
21/63	Lloyd Price
14/75	Ray Stevens
3/76	**Misty Blue**...Dorothy Moore
14/80	**Misunderstanding**...Genesis
5/89	**Mixed Emotions**...Rolling Stones
37/64	**Mixed-Up, Shook-Up, Girl**...Patty & The Emblems
4/94	**Mmm Mmm Mmm Mmm**...Crash Test Dummies
1/97	**Mo Money Mo Problems**...Notorious B.I.G.
5s/03	**mOBSCENE**...Marilyn Manson
32/58	**Mocking Bird, The**...Four Lads
	Mockingbird
7/63	Inez Foxx (with Charlie Foxx)
5/74	Carly Simon & James Taylor
20/61	**Model Girl**...Johnny Mastro
22/84	**Modern Day Delilah**...Van Stephenson
18/81	**Modern Girl**...Sheena Easton
14/83	**Modern Love**...David Bowie
10/86	**Modern Woman**...Billy Joel
21/65	**Mohair Sam**...Charlie Rich
	Molly-O ..see: Man With The Golden Arm
1/02	**Moment Like This**...Kelly Clarkson
2/55	**Moments To Remember**...Four Lads
	Mona Lisa
25/59	Carl Mann
29/59	Conway Twitty
1/66	**Monday, Monday**...Mama's & The Papa's
13/73	**Money**...Pink Floyd
27/85	**Money Changes Everything**...Cyndi Lauper
23/92	**Money Don't Matter 2 Night**...Prince
1/85	**Money For Nothing**...Dire Straits
9/76	**Money Honey**...Bay City Rollers
17/98	**Money, Power & Respect**...Lox
23/91	**Moneytalks**...AC/DC
	(also see: Dirty Cash)
	Money (That's what I want)
23/60	Barrett Strong
16/64	Kingsmen
20/56	**Money Tree**...Margaret Whiting
28/86	**Money$ Too Tight (To Mention)**...Simply Red

POS/YR	RECORD TITLE. . .ARTIST
1/88	**Monkey**...George Michael
8/63	**Monkey Time**...Major Lance
39/70	**Monster**...Steppenwolf
	Monster Mash
1/62	Bobby "Boris" Pickett
10/73	Bobby "Boris" Pickett
30/62	**Monsters' Holiday**...Bobby "Boris" Pickett
8/70	**Montego Bay**...Bobby Bloom
15/68	**Monterey**...Animals
	Mony Mony
3/68	Tommy James
1/87	Billy Idol
31/77	**Moody Blue**...Elvis Presley
1/61	**Moody River**...Pat Boone
24/69	**Moody Woman**...Jerry Butler
	Moon River
11/61	Jerry Butler
11/61	Henry Mancini
30/71	**Moon Shadow**...Cat Stevens
28/58	**Moon Talk**...Perry Como
38/69	**Moonflight**...Vik Venus
	Moonglow and Theme From "Picnic"
1/56	Morris Stoloff
4/56	George Cates
13/56	McGuire Sisters (Picnic)
3/76	**Moonlight Feels Right**...Starbuck
3/57	**Moonlight Gambler**...Frankie Laine
	Moonlight Swim
24/57	Tony Perkins
37/57	Nick Noble
23/87	**Moonlighting (Theme)**...Al Jarreau
4/56	**More**...Perry Como
8/63	**More**...Kai Winding
17/93	**More And More**...Captain Hollywood Project
	(More I Love You) ..see: Lo Mucho Que Te Quiero
16/66	**More I See You**...Chris Montez
	More Love
23/67	Miracles
10/80	Kim Carnes
17/61	**More Money For You And Me**...Four Preps
4/76	**More, More, More**...Andrea True Connection
5/76	**More Than A Feeling**...Boston
25/02	**More Than A Woman**...Aaliyah
32/78	**More Than A Woman**...Tavares
14/91	**More Than Ever**...Nelson
2/80	**More Than I Can Say**...Leo Sayer
34/82	**More Than Just The Two Of Us**...Sneaker
27/01	**More Than That**...Backstreet Boys
25/97	**More Than This**...10,000 Maniacs
1/91	**More Than Words**...Extreme
2/90	**More Than Words Can Say**...Alias
18/89	**More Than You Know**...Martika
12/69	**More Today Than Yesterday**...Spiral Starecase
13/59	**Morgen**...Ivo Robic
	Moritat ..see: Mack The Knife
21/83	**Mornin'**...Al Jarreau
14/75	**Mornin' Beautiful**...Tony Orlando & Dawn

POS/YR	RECORD TITLE. . .ARTIST
1/73	**Morning After**...Maureen McGovern
24/79	**Morning Dance**...Spyro Gyra
17/69	**Morning Girl**...Neon Philharmonic
6/72	**Morning Has Broken**...Cat Stevens
	Morning Side Of The Mountain
27/59	Tommy Edwards
8/75	Donny & Marie Osmond
1/81	**Morning Train (Nine To Five)**...Sheena Easton
1/73	**Most Beautiful Girl**...Charlie Rich
3/94	**Most Beautiful Girl In The World**...Prince
4/00	**Most Girls**...P!nk
14/55	**Most Of All**...Don Cornell
38/71	**Most Of All**...B.J. Thomas
27/62	**Most People Get Married**...Patti Page
31/56	**Mostly Martha**...Crew Cuts
4/72	**Mother And Child Reunion**...Paul Simon
37/71	**Mother Freedom**...Bread
1/61	**Mother-In-Law**...Ernie K-Doe
32A/96	**Mother Mother**...Tracy Bonham
11/69	**Mother Popcorn**...James Brown
8/66	**Mothers Little Helper**...Rolling Stones
27/86	**Mothers Talk**...Tears For Fears
12/72	**Motorcycle Mama**...Sailcat
36/87	**Motortown**...Kane Gang
10/91	**Motown Song**...Rod Stewart (w/The Temptations)
3/91	**Motownphilly**...Boyz II Men
	Mountain Of Love
21/60	Harold Dorman
9/64	Johnny Rivers
2/61	**Mountain's High**...Dick & DeeDee
23/86	**Mountains**...Prince
4/96	**Mouth**...Merril Bainbridge
38/92	**Move Any Mountain (Progen 91)**...Shamen
12/86	**Move Away**...Culture Club
10/02	**Move B***h**...Ludacris
5s/02	**Move It Like This**...Baha Men
31/69	**Move Over**...Steppenwolf
6/92	**Move This**...Technotronic
	Move Two Mountains ..see: (You've Got To)
14/76	**Movin'**...Brass Construction
19/75	**Movin' On**...Bad Company
34/98	**Movin' On**...Mya
17/78	**Movin' Out (Anthony's Song)**...Billy Joel
34/94	**Moving On Up**...M People
16/63	**Mr. Bass Man**...Johnny Cymbal
2/71	**Mr. Big Stuff**...Jean Knight
1/59	**Mr. Blue**...Fleetwoods
35/78	**Mr. Blue Sky**...Electric Light Orchestra
9/71	**Mr. Bojangles**...Nitty Gritty Dirt Band
28/68	**Mr. Businessman**...Ray Stevens
38/72	**Mister Can't You See**...Buffy Sainte-Marie
1/60	**Mr. Custer**...Larry Verne
17/66	**Mr. Dieingly Sad**...Critters
	Mr. Dream Merchant ..see: Dream Merchant
4/75	**Mr. Jaws**...Dickie Goodman
5A/94	**Mr. Jones**...Counting Crows

POS/YR	RECORD TITLE. . .ARTIST
6/57	**Mr. Lee**...Bobbettes
1/64	**Mr. Lonely**...Bobby Vinton
40/92	**Mr. Loverman**...Shabba Ranks
21/60	**Mr. Lucky**...Henry Mancini
3/83	**Mr. Roboto**...Styx
	Mister Sandman
1/54	Chordettes
5/55	Four Aces
37/81	Emmylou Harris
36/66	**Mr. Spaceman**...Byrds
18/69	**Mr. Sun, Mr. Moon**...Paul Revere & The Raiders
1/65	**Mr. Tambourine Man**...Byrds
12/85	**Mr. Telephone Man**...New Edition
17/94	**Mr. Vain**...Culture Beat
6/93	**Mr. Wendal**...Arrested Development
	Mr. Wonderful
13/56	Sarah Vaughan
14/56	Peggy Lee
18/56	Teddi King
1/65	**Mrs. Brown You've Got A Lovely Daughter**...Herman's Hermits
	Mrs. Robinson
1/68	Simon & Garfunkel
37/69	Booker T. & The M.G.'s
1/01	**Ms. Jackson**...OutKast
	Muddy Water ..see: (I Washed My Hands In)
	Muhammad Ali ..see: Black Superman
5/60	**Mule Skinner Blues**...Fendermen
30/62	**Multiplication**...Bobby Darin
18/98	**Mummers' Dance**...Loreena McKennitt
39/59	**Mummy, The**...Bob McFadden & Dor
39/82	**Murphy's Law**...Cheri
10/82	**Muscles**...Diana Ross
39/67	**Museum**...Herman's Hermits
1/00	**Music**...Madonna
22/01	**Music**...Erick Sermon
3/79	**Music Box Dancer**...Frank Mills
F/76	**Music Is My Life**...Helen Reddy
2/99	**Music Of My Heart**...*NSYNC & Gloria Estefan
40/84	**Music Time**...Styx
	Music To Watch Girls By
15/67	Bob Crewe Generation
34/67	Andy Williams
4/76	**Muskrat Love**...Captain & Tennille
12/75	**Must Of Got Lost**...J. Geils Band
8/66	**Must To Avoid**...Herman's Hermits
23/66	**Mustang Sally**...Wilson Pickett
21/56	**Mutual Admiration Society**...Teresa Brewer
1/98	**My All**...Mariah Carey
13/78	**My Angel Baby**...Toby Beau
3/01	**My Baby**...Lil' Romeo
13/65	**My Baby**...Temptations
10/97	**MyBabyDaddy**...B-Rock & The Bizz
	(My Baby Don't Love Me) ..see: No More
31/56	**My Baby Left Me**...Elvis Presley
13/70	**My Baby Loves Lovin'**...White Plains

POS/YR	RECORD TITLE. . .ARTIST
22/66	**My Baby Loves Me**...Martha & The Vandellas
17/68	**My Baby Must Be A Magician**...Marvelettes
	(My Baby Shot Me Down) ..see: Bang Bang
30/67	**My Back Pages**...Byrds
29/00	**My Best Friend**...Tim McGraw
35/78	**My Best Friend's Girl**...Cars
19/56	**My Blue Heaven**...Fats Domino
4/97	**My Body**...LSG
11/55	**My Bonnie Lassie**...Ames Brothers
26/64	**My Bonnie (My Bonnie Lies Over The Ocean)**...Beatles/Tony Sheridan
	(also see: Bonnie Came Back)
31/96	**My Boo**...Ghost Town DJ's
21/62	**My Boomerang Won't Come Back**...Charlie Drake
20/75	**My Boy**...Elvis Presley
	My Boy - Flat Top
16/55	Dorothy Collins
39/55	Boyd Bennett
2/64	**My Boy Lollipop**...Millie Small
1/63	**My Boyfriend's Back**...Angels
25/89	**My Brave Face**...Paul McCartney
12/58	**My Bucket's Got A Hole In It**...Ricky Nelson
4/69	**My Cherie Amour**...Stevie Wonder
	My Coloring Book
18/63	Kitty Kallen
20/63	Sandy Stewart
8/67	**My Cup Runneth Over**...Ed Ames
6/63	**My Dad**...Paul Petersen
34/60	**My Dearest Darling**...Etta James
1/72	**My Ding-A-Ling**...Chuck Berry
	(also see: Ding-A-Ling)
24/57	**My Dream**...Platters
9/61	**My Empty Arms**...Jackie Wilson
29/84	**My Ever Changing Moods**...Style Council
34/01	**My Everything**...98°
1/75	**My Eyes Adored You**...Frankie Valli
28/77	**My Fair Share**...Seals & Crofts
16A/98	**My Father's Eyes**...Eric Clapton
39/99	**My Favorite Girl**...Dave Hollister
9A/98	**My Favorite Mistake**...Sheryl Crow
26/00	**My First Love**...Avant
28/99	**My First Night With You**...Mya
27A/95	**My Friends**...Red Hot Chili Peppers
23/03	**My Front Porch Looking In**...Lonestar
	My Girl
1/65	Temptations
35/68	Bobby Vee (medley)
20/85	Daryl Hall/John Oates (medley)
20/88	Suave'
25/82	**My Girl**...Donnie Iris
12/74	**My Girl Bill**...Jim Stafford
22/81	**My Girl (Gone, Gone, Gone)**...Chilliwack
14/65	**My Girl Has Gone**...Miracles
	My Girl Josephine
14/60	Fats Domino
29/67	Jerry Jaye
	My Girl Sloopy ..see: Hang On Sloopy

My Guy
1/64	Mary Wells
23/82	Sister Sledge

2/59	**My Happiness**...Connie Francis
4/77	**My Heart Belongs To Me**...Barbra Streisand
9/64	**My Heart Belongs To Only You**...Bobby Vinton
28/91	**My Heart Belongs To You**...Russ Irwin
4/89	**My Heart Can't Tell You No**...Rod Stewart
38/64	**My Heart Cries For You**...Ray Charles
1/60	**My Heart Has A Mind Of Its Own**...Connie Francis
3/59	**My Heart Is An Open Book**...Carl Dobkins, Jr.
25/91	**My Heart Is Failing Me**...Riff
	My Heart Reminds Me ..see: And That Reminds Me
	My Heart Sings ..see: (All Of A Sudden)
38/89	**My Heart Skips A Beat**...Cover Girls
1/98	**My Heart Will Go On (Love Theme From 'Titanic')**...Celine Dion
13/66	**My Heart's Symphony**...Gary Lewis
8/60	**My Home Town**...Paul Anka
6/86	**My Hometown**...Bruce Springsteen
18/61	**My Kind Of Girl**...Matt Monro
31/83	**My Kind Of Lady**...Supertramp
30/90	**My Kinda Girl**...Babyface

My Last Date (With You)
26/61	Skeeter Davis
38/61	Joni James
	(also see: Last Date)

3/79	**My Life**...Billy Joel
26/02	**My List**...Toby Keith
22/56	**My Little Angel**...Four Lads
9/98	**My Little Secret**...Xscape
9/75	**My Little Town**...Simon & Garfunkel
1/66	**My Love**...Petula Clark
1/73	**My Love**...Paul McCartney
5/83	**My Love**...Lionel Richie
16/65	**My Love, Forgive Me**...Robert Goulet
21/90	**My Love Is A Fire**...Donny Osmond
28/95	**My Love Is For Real**...Paula Abdul
13/03	**My Love Is Like...WO**...Mya
4/97	**My Love Is The Shhh!**...Somethin' For The People
4/00	**My Love Is Your Love**...Whitney Houston
2/92	**My Lovin' (You're Never Gonna Get It)**...En Vogue
13/67	**My Mammy**...Happenings
9/73	**My Maria**...B.W. Stevenson
26/59	**My Melancholy Baby**...Tommy Edwards
3/74	**My Melody Of Love**...Bobby Vinton
19/74	**My Mistake (Was To Love You)**...Diana Ross & Marvin Gaye
39/81	**My Mother's Eyes**...Bette Midler
16/73	**My Music**...Loggins & Messina
10/90	**My, My, My**...Johnny Gill
36/99	**My Name Is**...Eminem
20/91	**My Name Is Not Susan**...Whitney Houston
36/92	**My Name Is Prince**...Prince

27/00	**My Next Thirty Years**...Tim McGraw
37/84	**My Oh My**...Slade

My One Sin
24/55	Nat "King" Cole
28/57	Four Coins

My Own True Love
33/59	Jimmy Clanton
13/62	Duprees

21/57	**My Personal Possession**...Nat "King" Cole/Four Knights
14/69	**My Pledge Of Love**...Joe Jeffrey Group
1/56	**My Prayer**...Platters
1/89	**My Prerogative**...Bobby Brown
4/02	**My Sacrifice**...Creed
1/79	**My Sharona**...Knack
F/75	**My Ship**...Tavares
30/91	**My Side Of The Bed**...Susanna Hoffs
	(My Sister) ..see: It's A Shame
31/69	**My Song**...Aretha Franklin

My Special Angel
7/57	Bobby Helms
7/68	Vogues

16/63	**My Summer Love**...Ruby & The Romantics

My Sweet Lady
17/74	Cliff DeYoung
32/77	John Denver

1/70	**My Sweet Lord**...George Harrison
29/74	**My Thang**...James Brown
39/83	**My Town**...Michael Stanley Band
40/02	**My Town**...Montgomery Gentry
32/65	**My Town, My Guy And Me**...Lesley Gore
31/56	**My Treasure**...Hilltoppers
22/63	**My True Confession**...Brook Benton
3/58	**My True Love**...Jack Scott
3/61	**My True Story**...Jive Five
2/98	**My Way**...Usher

My Way
27/69	Frank Sinatra
22/77	Elvis Presley

9/69	**My Whole World Ended (The Moment You Left Me)**...David Ruffin
24/63	**My Whole World Is Falling Down**...Brenda Lee
12/59	**My Wish Came True**...Elvis Presley
16/72	**My World**...Bee Gees
5/66	**My World Is Empty Without You**...Supremes
9/92	**Mysterious Ways**...U2
24/85	**Mystery Lady**...Billy Ocean
33/65	**Mystic Eyes**...Them

N

Na Na Hey Hey Kiss Him Goodbye
1/69	Steam
12/87	Nylons

8/76	**Nadia's Theme (The Young And The Restless)**...Barry DeVorzon & Perry Botkin, Jr.

POS/YR	RECORD TITLE. . .ARTIST
23/64	**Nadine (Is It You?)**...Chuck Berry
25/61	**"Nag"**...Halos
36/97	**Naked Eye**...Luscious Jackson
5/96	**Name**...Goo Goo Dolls
3/65	**Name Game**...Shirley Ellis
12/78	**Name Of The Game**...Abba
8/67	**Nashville Cats**...Lovin' Spoonful
3/86	**Nasty**...Janet Jackson
16/71	**Nathan Jones**...Supremes
21/78	**Native New Yorker**...Odyssey
38/60	**Natural Born Lover**...Fats Domino
10/73	**Natural High**...Bloodstone
17/71	**Natural Man**...Lou Rawls
29/96	**Natural One**...Folk Implosion
8/67	**Natural Woman**...Aretha Franklin
40/68	**Naturally Stoned**...Avant-Garde
40/61	**Nature Boy**...Bobby Darin
3/88	**Naughty Girls (Need Love Too)**...Samantha Fox
	Naughty Lady Of Shady Lane
3/54	Ames Brothers
17/55	Archie Bleyer
23/85	**Naughty Naughty**...John Parr
6/64	**Navy Blue**...Diane Renay
22/70	**Neanderthal Man**...Hotlegs
10/58	**Near You**...Roger Williams
40/58	**Nee Nee Na Na Na Na Nu Nu**...Dicky Doo & The Don'ts
11/74	**Need To Be**...Jim Weatherly
31/64	**Need To Belong**...Jerry Butler
25/58	**Need You**...Donnie Owens
1/88	**Need You Tonight**...INXS
	Needles And Pins
13/64	Searchers
37/86	Tom Petty with Stevie Nicks
2/73	**Neither One Of Us (Wants To Be The First To Say Goodbye)**...Gladys Knight
	Nel Blu Dipinto Di Blu ..see: Volare
24/67	**Neon Rainbow**...Box Tops
6/85	**Neutron Dance**...Pointer Sisters
4/85	**Never**...Heart
21/93	**Never A Time**...Genesis
20/86	**Never As Good As The First Time**...Sade
6/59	**Never Be Anyone Else But You**...Ricky Nelson
15/80	**Never Be The Same**...Christopher Cross
28/82	**Never Been In Love**...Randy Meisner
5/72	**Never Been To Spain**...Three Dog Night
	Never Can Say Goodbye
2/71	Jackson 5
22/71	Isaac Hayes
9/75	Gloria Gaynor
13/71	**Never Ending Song Of Love**...Delaney & Bonnie
17/85	**Never Ending Story**...Limahl
4/98	**Never Ever**...All Saints
F/94	**Never Forget You**...Mariah Carey
20/68	**Never Give You Up**...Jerry Butler
11/76	**Never Gonna Fall In Love Again**...Eric Carmen

POS/YR	RECORD TITLE. . .ARTIST
1/88	**Never Gonna Give You Up**...Rick Astley
17/91	**Never Gonna Let You Down**...Surface
4/83	**Never Gonna Let You Go**...Sergio Mendes
17/99	**Never Gonna Let You Go**...Faith Evans
10/01	**Never Had A Dream Come True**...S Club 7
26/70	**Never Had A Dream Come True**...Stevie Wonder
15/94	**Never Keeping Secrets**...Babyface
28/88	**Never Knew Love Like This**...Alexander O'Neal/Cherrelle
6/80	**Never Knew Love Like This Before**...Stephanie Mills
33/96	**Never Leave Me Alone**...Nate Dogg
3/03	**Never Leave You - Uh Oooh, Uh Oooh!**...Lumidee
29/75	**Never Let Her Go**...David Gates
27/87	**Never Let Me Down**...David Bowie
14/00	**Never Let You Go**...Third Eye Blind
5/94	**Never Lie**...Immature
7/97	**Never Make A Promise**...Dru Hill
	Never My Love
2/67	Association
12/71	5th Dimension
7/74	Blue Swede
7/74	**Never, Never Gonna Give Ya Up**...Barry White
	Never On Sunday
19/60	Don Costa
13/61	Chordettes
28A/87	**Never Say Goodbye**...Bon Jovi
26/03	**Never Scared**...Bone Crusher
30/93	**Never Should've Let You Go**...Hi-Five
3/85	**Never Surrender**...Corey Hart
7/88	**Never Tear Us Apart**...INXS
33/81	**Never Too Much**...Luther Vandross
22/56	**Never Turn Back**...Al Hibbler
	New ..also see: Nu
27/95	**New Age Girl**...Deadeye Dick
17/85	**New Attitude**...Patti LaBelle
22/02	**New Day Has Come**...Celine Dion
37/64	**New Girl In School**...Jan & Dean
1/77	**New Kid In Town**...Eagles
	New Lovers ..see: (Welcome)
36/63	**New Mexican Rose**...Four Seasons
10/84	**New Moon On Monday**...Duran Duran
6/60	**New Orleans**...U.S. Bonds
39/80	**New Romance (It's A Mystery)**...Spider
3/88	**New Sensation**...INXS
27/84	**New Song**...Howard Jones
21/82	**New World Man**...Rush
13/79	**New York Groove**...Ace Frehley
14/67	**New York Mining Disaster 1941**...Bee Gees
	New York, New York ..see: Theme From
27/77	**New York, You Got Me Dancing**...Andrea True Connection
32/65	**New York's A Lonely Town**...Trade Winds
5/62	**Next Door To An Angel**...Neil Sedaka
23/00	**Next Episode**...Dr. Dre
17/67	**Next Plane To London**...Rose Garden

POS/YR	RECORD TITLE. . . ARTIST
F/70	**Next Step Is Love**...Elvis Presley
1/86	**Next Time I Fall**...Peter Cetera w/Amy Grant
1/98	**Nice & Slow**...Usher
37/82	**Nice Girls**...Eye To Eye
30/76	**Nice 'N' Naasty**...Salsoul Orchestra
4/72	**Nice To Be With You**...Gallery
29/90	**Nicety**...Michel'le
35/72	**Nickel Song**...Melanie
39/81	**Nicole**...Point Blank
4/60	**Night**...Jackie Wilson
	(also see: Nite)
1/74	**Night Chicago Died**...Paper Lace
1/78	**Night Fever**...Bee Gees
3/63	**Night Has A Thousand Eyes**...Bobby Vee
34/85	**Night Is Still Young**...Billy Joel
11/56	**Night Lights**...Nat "King" Cole
4/77	**Night Moves**...Bob Seger
28/86	**Night Moves**...Marilyn Martin
6/81	**Night Owls**...Little River Band
3/85	**Nightshift**...Commodores
1/73	**Night The Lights Went Out In Georgia**...Vicki Lawrence
3/71	**Night They Drove Old Dixie Down**...Joan Baez
30/66	**Night Time**...Strangeloves
36/88	**Nightime**...Pretty Poison
38/99	**Night To Remember**...Joe Diffie
35/62	**Night Train**...James Brown
33/84	**Nightbird**...Stevie Nicks/Sandy Stewart
9/75	**Nightingale**...Carole King
15/88	**Nightmare On My Street**...DJ Jazzy Jeff & The Fresh Prince
10/76	**Nights Are Forever Without You**...England Dan & John Ford Coley
2/72	**Nights In White Satin**...Moody Blues
24/91	**Nights Like This**...After 7
7/75	**Nights On Broadway**...Bee Gees
23/67	**Niki Hoeky**...P.J. Proby
7/86	**Nikita**...Elton John
38/00	**911**...Wyclef Jean
34s/90	**911 Is A Joke**...Public Enemy
1/81	**9 To 5**...Dolly Parton
15/85	**19**...Paul Hardcastle
33/71	**1900 Yesterday**...Liz Damon's Orient Express
	****1999****
12/83	Prince
40/99	Prince
12/96	**1979**...Smashing Pumpkins
23/03	**19 Somethin'**...Mark Wills
2/66	**19th Nervous Breakdown**...Rolling Stones
7/67	**98.6**...Keith
26/80	**99**...Toto
2/84	**99 Luftballons**...Nena
11/57	**Ninety-Nine Ways**...Tab Hunter
23/56	**Ninety Nine Years (Dead Or Alive)**...Guy Mitchell
1/66	**96 Tears**...? (Question Mark) & The Mysterians
7/88	**Nite And Day**...Al B. Sure!

POS/YR	RECORD TITLE. . . ARTIST
	Nitty Gritty
8/64	Shirley Ellis
19/69	Gladys Knight
	No Arms Can Ever Hold You
23/55	Georgie Shaw
26/55	Pat Boone
27/65	Bachelors
39/74	**No Charge**...Melba Montgomery
23/58	**No Chemise, Please**...Gerry Granahan
1/96	**No Diggity**...BLACKstreet
22/86	**No Easy Way Out**...Robert Tepper
	No Gettin' Over Me ..see: (There's)
40/60	**No If's - No And's**...Lloyd Price
11/03	**No Letting Go**...Wayne Wonder
34/85	**No Lookin' Back**...Michael McDonald
16/71	**No Love At All**...B.J. Thomas
21/58	**No Love (But Your Love)**...Johnny Mathis
8/70	**No Matter What**...Badfinger
3/66	**No Matter What Shape (Your Stomach's In)**...T-Bones
31/69	**No Matter What Sign You Are**...Supremes
35/67	**No Milk Today**...Herman's Hermits
33/93	**No Mistakes**...Patty Smyth
5/00	**No More**...Ruff Endz
	No More
6/55	DeJohn Sisters
17/55	McGuire Sisters
23/01	**No More (Baby I'ma Do Right)**...3LW
15/02	**No More Drama**...Mary J. Blige
23/95	**No More "I Love You's"**...Annie Lennox
7/90	**No More Lies**...Michel'le
6/84	**No More Lonely Nights**...Paul McCartney
25/73	**No More Mr. Nice Guy**...Alice Cooper
17/89	**No More Rhyme**...Debbie Gibson
1/79	**No More Tears (Enough Is Enough)**...Barbra Streisand/Donna Summer
23/84	**No More Words**...Berlin
13/90	**No Myth**...Michael Penn
23/80	**No Night So Long**...Dionne Warwick
3/98	**No, No, No**...Destiny's Child
3/75	**No No Song**...Ringo Starr
	No, Not Much!
2/56	Four Lads
34/69	Vogues
	No One
34/61	Connie Francis
21/63	Ray Charles
22/96	**No One Else**...Total
4/86	**No One Is To Blame**...Howard Jones
19/58	**No One Knows**...Dion & The Belmonts
36/72	**No One To Depend On**...Santana
28/93	**No Ordinary Love**...Sade
	No Other Arms ..also see: No Arms Can Ever Hold You
27/59	**No Other Arms, No Other Lips**...Chordettes
10/64	**No Particular Place To Go**...Chuck Berry
12/99	**No Pigeons**...Sporty Thievz
37/99	**No Place That Far**...Sara Evans

POS/YR	RECORD TITLE. . . ARTIST
20/93	**No Rain**...Blind Melon
29/81	**No Reply At All**...Genesis
1/99	**No Scrubs**...TLC
28/03	**No Shoes, No Shirt, No Problems**...Kenny Chesney
12/92	**No Son Of Mine**...Genesis
13/02	**No Such Thing**...John Mayer
F/70	**No Sugar Tonight**...Guess Who
	No Sunshine..see: Ain't No Sunshine
14/79	**No Tell Lover**...Chicago
5/70	**No Time**...Guess Who
18/97	**No Time**...Lil' Kim
33/83	**No Time For Talk**...Christopher Cross
23/84	**No Way Out**...Jefferson Starship
38A/96	**No Woman, No Cry**...Fugees
3/96	**Nobody**...Keith Sweat
15/82	**Nobody**...Sylvia
8/68	**Nobody But Me**...Human Beinz
21/59	**Nobody But You**...Dee Clark
40/69	**Nobody But You Babe**...Clarence Reid
2/77	**Nobody Does It Better**...Carly Simon
18/98	**Nobody Does It Better**...Nate Dogg
36/98	**Nobody Else**...Tyrese
12/64	**Nobody I Know**...Peter & Gordon
2/96	**Nobody Knows**...Tony Rich Project
30/60	**Nobody Loves Me Like You**...Flamingos
18/82	**Nobody Said It Was Easy**...Le Roux
5/84	**Nobody Told Me**...John Lennon
13/01	**Nobody Wants To Be Lonely**...Ricky Martin w/Christina Aguilera
29/73	**Nobody Wants You When You're Down And Out**...Bobby Womack
21/81	**Nobody Wins**...Elton John
8/88	**Nobody's Fool**...Kenny Loggins
13/87	**Nobody's Fool**...Cinderella
2/98	**Nobody's Supposed To Be Here**...Deborah Cox
39/59	**Nola**...Billy Williams
32/94	**None Of Your Business**...Salt-N-Pepa
3/62	**Norman**...Sue Thompson
4/60	**North To Alaska**...Johnny Horton
36/02	**Not A Day Goes By**...Lonestar
34/85	**Not Enough Love In The World**...Don Henley
28/92	**Not Enough Time**...INXS
2/96	**Not Gon' Cry**...Mary J. Blige
26/88	**Not Just Another Girl**...Ivan Neville
12/63	**Not Me**...Orlons
16/60	**Not One Minute More**...Della Reese
25/65	**Not The Lovin' Kind**...Dino, Desi & Billy
34/92	**Not The Only One**...Bonnie Raitt
6/97	**Not Tonight**...Lil' Kim
10/02	**Nothin'**...N.O.R.E.
	(also see: Nuthin' / Nuttin')
10/86	**Nothin' At All**...Heart
6/88	**Nothin' But A Good Time**...Poison
38/97	**Nothin' But The Cavi Hit**...Mack 10 & Dogg Pound
19/93	**Nothin' My Love Can't Fix**...Joey Lawrence

POS/YR	RECORD TITLE. . . ARTIST
39/90	**Nothin' To Hide**...Poco
	Nothin' Yet ..see: (We Ain't Got)
29/92	**Nothing Broken But My Heart**...Celine Dion
34/69	**Nothing But A Heartache**...Flirtations
11/65	**Nothing But Heartaches**...Supremes
12/62	**Nothing Can Change This Love**...Sam Cooke
18/65	**Nothing Can Stop Me**...Gene Chandler
1/90	**Nothing Compares 2 U**...Sinéad O'Connor
34/92	**Nothing Else Matters**...Metallica
1s/03	**Nothing Fails**...Madonna
	Nothing For Xmas ..see: Nuttin'
1/74	**Nothing From Nothing**...Billy Preston
27/02	**Nothing In This World**...Keke Wyatt
12/87	**Nothing's Gonna Change My Love For You**...Glenn Medeiros
1/87	**Nothing's Gonna Stop Us Now**...Starship
20/66	**Nothing's Too Good For My Baby**...Stevie Wonder
21/90	**Notice Me**...Nikki
2/87	**Notorious**...Duran Duran
38/87	**Notorious**...Loverboy
3/92	**November Rain**...Guns N' Roses
39A/96	**Novocaine For The Soul**...Eels
25/58	**Now And For Always**...George Hamilton IV
7/94	**Now and Forever**...Richard Marx
	(Now And Then There's) A ..see: Fool Such As I
11/91	**Now That We Found Love**...Heavy D & The Boyz
3/66	**Nowhere Man**...Beatles
40/96	**Nowhere To Go**...Melissa Etheridge
8/65	**Nowhere To Run**...Martha & The Vandellas
26/92	**Nu Nu**...Lidell Townsell & M.T.F.
11/04	**Numb**...Linkin Park
9/75	**#9 Dream**...John Lennon
22/01	**#1**...Nelly
29A/97	**#1 Crush**...Garbage
22/73	**Nutbush City Limits**...Ike & Tina Turner
2/93	**Nuthin' But A "G" Thang**...Dr. Dre
23/62	**Nutrocker**...B. Bumble & The Stingers
40/94	**Nuttin' But Love**...Heavy D & The Boyz
	Nuttin' For Xmas
6/55	Art Mooney/Barry Gordon
20/55	Joe Ward
21/55	Ricky Zahnd
36/55	Fontane Sisters

O

POS/YR	RECORD TITLE. . . ARTIST
10/60	**O Dio Mio**...Annette
4/02	**'03 Bonnie & Clyde**...Jay-Z
6/91	**O.P.P.**...Naughty By Nature
25/85	**Object Of My Desire**...Starpoint
38/94	**Objects In The Rear View Mirror May Appear Closer Than They Are**...Meat Loaf
35/84	**Obscene Phone Caller**...Rockwell

POS/YR	RECORD TITLE. . . ARTIST
6/85	**Obsession**...Animotion
	Ode To Billie Joe
1/67	Bobbie Gentry
28/67	Kingpins
39A/95	**Ode To My Family**...Cranberries
10/80	**Off The Wall**...Michael Jackson
	Oh ..also see: O
3/73	**Oh, Babe, What Would You Say?**...Hurricane Smith
23/64	**Oh Baby Don't You Weep**...James Brown
4/02	**Oh Boy**...Cam'ron
10/58	**Oh, Boy!**...Crickets
9/59	**Oh! Carol**...Neil Sedaka
15/78	**Oh! Darling**...Robin Gibb
20/90	**Oh Father**...Madonna
	Oh Girl
1/72	Chi-Lites
8/90	Paul Young
39/85	**Oh Girl**...Boy Meets Girl
	Oh Happy Day
4/69	Edwin Hawkins' Singers
40/70	Glen Campbell
12/66	**Oh How Happy**...Shades Of Blue
	Oh Julie
5/58	Crescendos
23/58	Sammy Salvo
38/82	**Oh Julie**...Barry Manilow
33/73	**Oh La De Da**...Staple Singers
34/60	**Oh, Little One**...Jack Scott
7/58	**Oh Lonesome Me**...Don Gibson
22/70	**Oh Me Oh My (I'm A Fool For You Baby)**...Lulu
5/74	**Oh My My**...Ringo Starr
4/81	**Oh No**...Commodores
24/65	**Oh No Not My Baby**...Maxine Brown
7/58	**Oh-Oh, I'm Falling In Love Again**...Jimmie Rodgers
29/86	**Oh, People**...Patti LaBelle
	Oh, Pretty Woman
1/64	Roy Orbison
12/82	Van Halen
1/85	**Oh Sheila**...Ready For The World
3/84	**Oh Sherrie**...Steve Perry
22/55	**Oh! Susanna**...Singing Dogs
10/74	**Oh Very Young**...Cat Stevens
30/79	**Oh Well**...Rockets
10/69	**Oh, What A Night**...Dells
	(also see: December, 1963)
24/78	**Oh What A Night For Dancing**...Barry White
F/71	**Oh Woman Oh Why**...Paul McCartney
39/66	**Oh Yeah**...Shadows Of Knight
14/70	**Ohio**...Crosby, Stills, Nash & Young
3/57	**Old Cape Cod**...Patti Page
5/75	**Old Days**...Chicago
20/80	**Old-Fashion Love**...Commodores
37/77	**Old Fashioned Boy (You're The One)**...Stallion
4/71	**Old Fashioned Love Song**...Three Dog Night
5/60	**Old Lamplighter**...Browns

POS/YR	RECORD TITLE. . . ARTIST
25/60	**Ol' Mac Donald**...Frank Sinatra
31/72	**Old Man**...Neil Young
13/96	**Old Man & Me (When I Get To Heaven)**...Hootie & The Blowfish
10/85	**Old Man Down The Road**...John Fogerty
34/56	**Old Philosopher**...Eddie Lawrence
5/62	**Old Rivers**...Walter Brennan
F/95	**Old School**...2Pac
	Old Schoolyard ..see: (Remember The Days Of The)
15/81	**Old Songs**...Barry Manilow
28/79	**Old Time Rock & Roll**...Bob Seger
25/61	**Ole Buttermilk Sky**...Bill Black's Combo
11/67	**On A Carousel**...Hollies
39/92	**On A Sunday Afternoon**...Lighter Shade Of Brown
5/74	**On And On**...Gladys Knight
11/77	**On And On**...Stephen Bishop
12/97	**On&On**...Erykah Badu
1/94	**On Bended Knee**...Boyz II Men
	On Broadway
9/63	Drifters
7/78	George Benson
38/56	**On London Bridge**...Jo Stafford
1/86	**On My Own**...Patti LaBelle & Michael McDonald
39/97	**On My Own**...Peach Union
20/57	**On My Word Of Honor**...Platters
2/89	**On Our Own**...Bobby Brown
7/84	**On The Dark Side**...John Cafferty
26/83	**On The Loose**...Saga
5/80	**On The Radio**...Donna Summer
4/61	**On The Rebound**...Floyd Cramer
16/68	**On The Road Again**...Canned Heat
20/80	**On The Road Again**...Willie Nelson
38/78	**On The Shelf**...Donny & Marie Osmond
	On The Street Where You Live
4/56	Vic Damone
18/56	Eddie Fisher
28/64	Andy Williams
27/82	**On The Way To The Sky**...Neil Diamond
27/91	**On The Way Up**...Elisa Fiorillo
29/82	**On The Wings Of Love**...Jeffrey Osborne
14/63	**On Top Of Spaghetti**...Tom Glazer
5/89	**Once Bitten Twice Shy**...Great White
11/61	**Once In Awhile**...Chimes
19/64	**Once Upon A Time**...Marvin Gaye & Mary Wells
26/61	**Once Upon A Time**...Rochell & The Candles
10/75	**Once You Get Started**...Rufus Feat. Chaka Khan
23/72	**Once You Understand**...Think
5/69	**One**...Three Dog Night
7/89	**One**...Bee Gees
9/92	**One, The**...Elton John
10/92	**One**...U2
30/00	**One, The**...Backstreet Boys
35/89	**One**...Metallica
37/02	**One, The**...Gary Allan
10/91	**One And Only**...Chesney Hawkes

POS/YR	RECORD TITLE. . . ARTIST
18/90	**One And Only Man**...Steve Winwood
1/71	**One Bad Apple**...Osmonds
11/63	**One Broken Heart For Sale**...Elvis Presley
37/74	**One Day At A Time**...Marilyn Sellars
34/65	**One Dyin' And A Buryin'**...Roger Miller
	One Eyed Jacks ..see: Love Theme From
	One Fine Day
5/63	Chiffons
12/80	Carole King
24/71	**One Fine Morning**...Lighthouse
38/87	**One For The Mockingbird**...Cutting Crew
28/88	**One Good Reason**...Paul Carrack
4/88	**One Good Woman**...Peter Cetera
13/66	**One Has My Name (The Other Has My Heart)**...Barry Young
2A/97	**One Headlight**...Wallflowers
10/87	**One Heartbeat**...Smokey Robinson
11/74	**One Hell Of A Woman**...Mac Davis
28/86	**One Hit (To The Body)**...Rolling Stones
11/94	**100% Pure Love**...Crystal Waters
14/82	**One Hundred Ways**...Quincy Jones/James Ingram
9/97	**One I Gave My Heart To**...Aaliyah
9/87	**One I Love**...R.E.M.
20/57	**One In A Million**...Platters
37/84	**One In A Million**...Romantics
25A/97	**One In A Million**...Aaliyah
9/80	**One In A Million You**...Larry Graham
14/65	**One Kiss For Old Times' Sake**...Ronnie Dove
6/02	**One Last Breath**...Creed
13/93	**One Last Cry**...Brian McKnight
35/79	**One Last Kiss**...J. Geils Band
2/70	**One Less Bell To Answer**...5th Dimension
37/73	**One Less Set Of Footsteps**...Jim Croce
19/85	**One Lonely Night**...REO Speedwagon
25/76	**One Love In My Lifetime**...Diana Ross
19/71	**One Man Band**...Three Dog Night
28/73	**One Man Band (Plays All Alone)**...Ronnie Dyson
7/75	**One Man Woman/One Woman Man**...Paul Anka/Odia Coates
8/61	**One Mint Julep**...Ray Charles
15/01	**One Minute Man**...Missy Elliott
5/88	**One Moment In Time**...Whitney Houston
15/72	**One Monkey Don't Stop No Show**...Honey Cone
2/95	**One More Chance/Stay With Me**...Notorious B.I.G.
29/01	**One More Day**...Diamond Rio
29/66	**One More Heartache**...Marvin Gaye
1/85	**One More Night**...Phil Collins
	One More Sunrise ..see: Morgen
27/97	**One More Time**...Real McCoy
32/65	**One More Time**...Ray Charles Singers
	One More Try
1/88	George Michael
29/99	Divine
1/91	**One More Try**...Timmy -T-

POS/YR	RECORD TITLE. . . ARTIST
	One Nation Under A Groove
28/78	Funkadelic
23/94	Ice Cube (Bop Gun)
4/58	**One Night**...Elvis Presley
3/85	**One Night In Bangkok**...Murray Head
13/85	**One Night Love Affair**...Bryan Adams
34/00	**One Night Stand**...J-Shin
11/73	**One Of A Kind (Love Affair)**...Spinners
15/85	**One Of The Living**...Tina Turner
1/75	**One Of These Nights**...Eagles
4/96	**One Of Us**...Joan Osborne
31/60	**One Of Us (Will Weep Tonight)**...Patti Page
7/83	**One On One**...Daryl Hall & John Oates
	One On One, Love Theme From ..see: My Fair Share
29/76	**One Piece At A Time**...Johnny Cash
24/81	**One Step Closer**...Doobie Brothers
22/86	**One Step Closer To You**...Gavin Christopher
13/88	**One Step Up**...Bruce Springsteen
	One Summer Night
7/58	Danleers
22/61	Diamonds
1/95	**One Sweet Day**...Mariah Carey & Boyz II Men
1/81	**One That You Love**...Air Supply
30/83	**One Thing**...INXS
4/83	**One Thing Leads To Another**...Fixx
	One Tin Soldier (The Legend Of Billy Jack)
34/70	Original Caste
26/71	Coven
10/71	**One Toke Over The Line**...Brewer & Shipley
9/61	**One Track Mind**...Bobby Lewis
40/80	**One-Trick Pony**...Paul Simon
2/65	**1-2-3**...Len Barry
3/88	**1-2-3**...Gloria Estefan
5/68	**1, 2, 3, Red Light**...1910 Fruitgum Co.
5/96	**1,2,3,4 (Sumpin' New)**...Coolio
38/00	**One Voice**...Billy Gilman
24/79	**One Way Or Another**...Blondie
1/98	**One Week**...Barenaked Ladies
8/62	**One Who Really Loves You**...Mary Wells
22/93	**One Woman**...Jade
15/82	**One You Love**...Glenn Frey
36/80	**Only A Lonely Heart Sees**...Felix Cavaliere
19/00	**Only God Knows Why**...Kid Rock
25/63	**Only In America**...Jay & The Americans
33/01	**Only In America**...Brooks & Dunn
4/87	**Only In My Dreams**...Debbie Gibson
2/62	**Only Love Can Break A Heart**...Gene Pitney
33/70	**Only Love Can Break Your Heart**...Neil Young
28/76	**Only Love Is Real**...Carole King
33/57	**Only One Love**...George Hamilton IV
	Only Sixteen
28/59	Sam Cooke
6/76	Dr. Hook
24/78	**Only The Good Die Young**...Billy Joel
2/60	**Only The Lonely**...Roy Orbison
9/82	**Only The Lonely**...Motels
4/69	**Only The Strong Survive**...Jerry Butler

P

10/64	**P.S. I Love You**...Beatles
8/62	**P.T. 109**...Jimmy Dean
10/83	**P.Y.T. (Pretty Young Thing)**...Michael Jackson
9/82	**Pac-Man Fever**...Buckner & Garcia
13/58	**Padre**...Toni Arden
1/66	**Paint It, Black**...Rolling Stones
	Paint Me A Picture ..see: (You Don't Have To)
34/74	**Painted Ladies**...Ian Thomas
15/63	**Painted, Tainted Rose**...Al Martino
	Paladin ..see: Ballad Of
3/62	**Palisades Park**...Freddy Cannon
26/76	**Paloma Blanca**...George Baker Selection
22/88	**Pamela**...Toto
13/84	**Panama**...Van Halen
35/66	**Pandora's Golden Heebie Jeebies**...Association
1/86	**Papa Don't Preach**...Madonna
31/74	**Papa Don't Take No Mess**...James Brown
	Papa Joe's ..see: (Down At)
4/54	**Papa Loves Mambo**...Perry Como
1/72	**Papa Was A Rollin' Stone**...Temptations
	Papa's Got A Brand New Bag
8/65	James Brown
21/69	Otis Redding
34/67	**Paper Cup**...5th Dimension
28/92	**Paper Doll**...PM Dawn
9/87	**Paper In Fire**...John Cougar Mellencamp
	Paper Roses
5/60	Anita Bryant
5/73	Marie Osmond
23/65	**Paper Tiger**...Sue Thompson
1/66	**Paperback Writer**...Beatles
32/82	**Paperlate**...Genesis
16/88	**Paradise**...Sade
36/03	**Paradise**...LL Cool J
39/78	**Paradise By The Dashboard Light**...Meat Loaf
5/89	**Paradise City**...Guns N' Roses
34/86	**Paranoimia**...Art Of Noise with Max Headroom
12/88	**Parents Just Don't Understand**...D.J. Jazzy Jeff & The Fresh Prince
38/58	**Part Of Me**...Jimmy Clanton
31/75	**Part Of The Plan**...Dan Fogelberg
19/63	**Part Time Love**...Little Johnny Taylor
22/75	**Part Time Love**...Gladys Knight
22/78	**Part-Time Love**...Elton John
1/85	**Part-Time Lover**...Stevie Wonder
2/85	**Party All The Time**...Eddie Murphy
29/98	**Party Continues**...JD & Da Brat
	Party Doll
1/57	Buddy Knox
5/57	Steve Lawrence
5/62	**Party Lights**...Claudine Clark
27/00	**Party Up (Up In Here)**...DMX
34/81	**Party's Over (Hopelessly In Love)**...Journey
18/89	**Partyman**...Prince

27/03	**Pass That Dutch**...Missy Elliott
11/02	**Pass The Courvoisier**...Busta Rhymes
10/83	**Pass The Dutchie**...Musical Youth
2/91	**P.A.S.S.I.O.N**...Rythm Syndicate
5/81	**Passion**...Rod Stewart
12/67	**Pata Pata**...Miriam Makeba
F/70	**Patch It Up**...Elvis Presley
4/70	**Patches**...Clarence Carter
6/62	**Patches**...Dickey Lee
4/89	**Patience**...Guns N' Roses
1/58	**Patricia**...Perez Prado
26/74	**Payback, The**...James Brown
13/71	**Pay To The Piper**...Chairmen Of The Board
28/67	**Pay You Back With Interest**...Hollies
39/68	**Paying The Cost To Be The Boss**...B.B. King
11/90	**Peace In Our Time**...Eddie Money
	Peace In The Valley ..see: (There'll Be)
38/77	**Peace Of Mind**...Boston
31/75	**Peace Pipe**...B.T. Express
7/71	**Peace Train**...Cat Stevens
32/70	**Peace Will Come (According To Plan)**...Melanie
12/73	**Peaceful**...Helen Reddy
22/73	**Peaceful Easy Feeling**...Eagles
29/96	**Peaches**...Presidents Of The United States Of America
4/01	**Peaches & Cream**...One Twelve
36/65	**Peaches "N" Cream**...Ikettes
20/61	**Peanut Butter**...Marathons
22/57	**Peanuts**...Little Joe & The Thrillers
28/59	**Peek-A-Boo**...Cadillacs
11/78	**Peg**...Steely Dan
3/57	**Peggy Sue**...Buddy Holly
18/64	**Penetration**...Pyramids
24/60	**Pennies From Heaven**...Skyliners
33/82	**Penny For Your Thoughts**...Tavares
1/67	**Penny Lane**...Beatles
8/84	**Penny Lover**...Lionel Richie
	People
5/64	Barbra Streisand
39/68	Tymes
13/85	**People Are People**...Depeche Mode
35/91	**People Are Still Having Sex**...LaTour
12/67	**People Are Strange**...Doors
8/92	**People Everyday**...Arrested Development
14/65	**People Get Ready**...Impressions
1/68	**People Got To Be Free**...Rascals
22/74	**People Gotta Move**...Gino Vannelli
40/77	**People In Love**...10cc
25/72	**People Make The World Go Round**...Stylistics
23/79	**People Of The South Wind**...Kansas
12/64	**People Say**...Dixie Cups
18/61	**"Pepe"**...Duane Eddy
5/63	**Pepino The Italian Mouse**...Lou Monte
26A/96	**Pepper**...Butthole Surfers
14/56	**Pepper-Hot Baby**...Jaye P. Morgan
1/62	**Peppermint Twist**...Joey Dee

POS/YR	RECORD TITLE. . . ARTIST
10/62	**Percolator (Twist)**...Billy Joe & The Checkmates
24/03	**Perfect**...Simple Plan
11/85	**Perfect Way**...Scritti Politti
3/88	**Perfect World**...Huey Lewis
15/60	**Perfidia**...Ventures
28/90	**Personal Jesus**...Depeche Mode
2/59	**Personality**...Lloyd Price
19/82	**Personally**...Karla Bonoff
	Peter Gunn
8/59	Ray Anthony
27/60	Duane Eddy
5/59	**Petite Fleur**...Chris Barber's Jazz Band
16/56	**Petticoats Of Portugal**...Dick Jacobs
1/75	**Philadelphia Freedom**...Elton John Band
26/58	**Philadelphia U.S.A.**...Nu Tornados
32/66	**Phoenix Love Theme (Senza Fine)**...Brass Ring
1/73	**Photograph**...Ringo Starr
12/83	**Photograph**...Def Leppard
1/81	**Physical**...Olivia Newton-John
6/88	**Piano In The Dark**...Brenda Russell
25/74	**Piano Man**...Billy Joel
1/75	**Pick Up The Pieces**...AWB
27/68	**Pickin' Wild Mountain Berries**...Peggy Scott & Jo Jo Benson
	Picnic ..see: Moonglow
4/03	**Picture**...Kid Rock
12/68	**Pictures Of Matchstick Men**...Status Quo
7/91	**Piece Of My Heart**...Tara Kemp
12/68	**Piece Of My Heart**...Big Brother & The Holding Company
19/73	**Pieces Of April**...Three Dog Night
31/83	**Pieces Of Ice**...Diana Ross
4/66	**Pied Piper**...Crispian St. Peters
	Pillow ..see: (Lay Your Head On My)
3/73	**Pillow Talk**...Sylvia
13/80	**Pilot Of The Airwaves**...Charlie Dore
3/03	**P.I.M.P.**...50 Cent
	(Pina Colada Song) ..see: Escape
	Pinball Wizard
19/69	Who
29/73	New Seekers (medley)
15/00	**Pinch Me**...Barenaked Ladies
11/60	**Pineapple Princess**...Annette
27/98	**Pink**...Aerosmith
5/88	**Pink Cadillac**...Natalie Cole
8/84	**Pink Houses**...John Cougar Mellencamp
31/64	**Pink Panther Theme**...Henry Mancini
3/59	**Pink Shoe Laces**...Dodie Stevens
	Piove ..see: Ciao, Ciao Bambina
4/63	**Pipeline**...Chantay's
9/66	**Place In The Sun**...Stevie Wonder
6/91	**Place In This World**...Michael W. Smith
34/94	**Place Where You Belong**...Shai
38/59	**Plain Jane**...Bobby Darin
19/55	**Plantation Boogie**...Lenny Dee
40/73	**Plastic Man**...Temptations
18/01	**Play**...Jennifer Lopez

POS/YR	RECORD TITLE. . . ARTIST
11/72	**Play Me**...Neil Diamond
6/55	**Play Me Hearts And Flowers (I Wanna Cry)**...Johnny Desmond
33/74	**Play Something Sweet (Brickyard Blues)**...Three Dog Night
	Play That Funky Music
1/76	Wild Cherry
4/91	Vanilla Ice
17/82	**Play The Game Tonight**...Kansas
36/94	**Playaz Club**...Rappin' 4-Tay
7/62	**Playboy**...Marvelettes
17/68	**Playboy**...Gene & Debbe
13/95	**Player's Anthem**...Junior M.A.F.I.A.
37/94	**Player's Ball**...OutKast
10/91	**Playground**...Another Bad Creation
2/73	**Playground In My Mind**...Clint Holmes
21/57	**Playing For Keeps**...Elvis Presley
F/55	**Playmates**...Fontane Sisters
3/67	**Pleasant Valley Sunday**...Monkees
18/78	**Please Come Home For Christmas**...Eagles
5/74	**Please Come To Boston**...Dave Loggins
15/62	**Please Don't Ask About Barbara**...Bobby Vee
	Please Don't Go
1/80	KC & The Sunshine Band
6/92	K.W.S.
21/97	**Please Don't Go**...No Mercy
36/96	**Please Don't Go**...Immature
39/61	**Please Don't Go**...Ral Donner
10/88	**Please Don't Go Girl**...New Kids On The Block
24/79	**Please Don't Leave**...Lauren Wood
31/63	**Please Don't Talk To The Lifeguard**...Diane Ray
7/93	**Please Forgive Me**...Bryan Adams
8/60	**Please Help Me, I'm Falling**...Hank Locklin **(also see: I Can't Help You)**
	Please Love Me Forever
12/61	Cathy Jean & The Roommates
6/67	Bobby Vinton
3/75	**Please Mr. Please**...Olivia Newton-John
	Please Mr. Postman
1/61	Marvelettes
1/75	Carpenters
11/59	**Please Mr. Sun**...Tommy Edwards
3/64	**Please Please Me**...Beatles
	(Please Please Please) ..see: Dunkie Butt
10/99	**Please Remember Me**...Tim McGraw
26/68	**Please Return Your Love To Me**...Temptations
14/61	**Please Stay**...Drifters
20/61	**Please Tell Me Why**...Jackie Wilson
28/66	**Please Tell Me Why**...Dave Clark Five
14/87	**Pleasure Principle**...Janet Jackson
	Pledge Of Love
12/57	Ken Copeland
25/57	Mitchell Torok
	Pledging My Love
17/55	Johnny Ace
17/55	Teresa Brewer
39A/93	**Plush**...Stone Temple Pilots

POS/YR	RECORD TITLE. . .ARTIST
21/02	**Po' Folks**...Nappy Roots
22/96	**Po Pimp**...Do Or Die
34/62	**Pocketful Of Miracles**...Frank Sinatra
2/60	**Poetry In Motion**...Johnny Tillotson
5/75	**Poetry Man**...Phoebe Snow
37/70	**Point It Out**...Miracles
28/78	**Point Of Know Return**...Kansas
5/87	**Point Of No Return**...Exposé
21/62	**Point Of No Return**...Gene McDaniels
28/86	**Point Of No Return**...Nu Shooz
3/90	**Poison**...Bell Biv DeVoe
7/89	**Poison**...Alice Cooper
25/83	**Poison Arrow**...ABC
7/59	**Poison Ivy**...Coasters
15/90	**Policy Of Truth**...Depeche Mode
24/84	**Politics Of Dancing**...Re-Flex
8/69	**Polk Salad Annie**...Tony Joe White
	Pomp & Circumstance ..see: Graduation Song
6/96	**Pony**...Ginuwine
1/61	**Pony Time**...Chubby Checker
	Poor ..also see: Po
17/58	**Poor Boy**...Royaltones
24/57	**Poor Boy**...Elvis Presley
38/62	**Poor Fool**...Ike & Tina Turner
22/59	**Poor Jenny**...Everly Brothers
1/58	**Poor Little Fool**...Ricky Nelson
27/63	**Poor Little Rich Girl**...Steve Lawrence
14/57	**Poor Man's Roses (Or A Rich Man's Gold)**...Patti Page
33/81	**Poor Man's Son**...Survivor
	Poor People Of Paris
1/56	Les Baxter
17/56	Lawrence Welk
19/56	Russ Morgan
31/78	**Poor Poor Pitiful Me**...Linda Ronstadt
1/66	**Poor Side Of Town**...Johnny Rivers
19/01	**Pop**...*NSYNC
35/82	**Pop Goes The Movies**...Meco
29/91	**Pop Goes The Weasel**...3rd Bass
20/88	**Pop Goes The World**...Men Without Hats
7/85	**Pop Life**...Prince
1/79	**Pop Muzik**...M
35/62	**Pop Pop Pop - Pie**...Sherrys
15/89	**Pop Singer**...John Cougar Mellencamp
24/72	**Pop That Thang**...Isley Brothers
9/72	**Popcorn, The**...Hot Butter
30/69	**Popcorn, The**...James Brown
14/55	**Popcorn Song**...Cliffie Stone
10/62	**Popeye (The Hitchhiker)**...Chubby Checker
21/66	**Popsicle**...Jan & Dean
3/64	**Popsicles And Icicles**...Murmaids
20/56	**Port Au Prince**...Nelson Riddle
	Portrait Of My Love
9/61	Steve Lawrence
36/67	Tokens
19/56	**Portuguese Washerwomen**...Joe "Fingers" Carr
	Poseidon Adventure ..see: Morning After

POS/YR	RECORD TITLE. . .ARTIST
7/65	**Positively 4th Street**...Bob Dylan
21/90	**Possession**...Bad English
30/85	**Possession Obsession**...Daryl Hall/John Oates
40A/95	**Possum Kingdom**...Toadies
2/88	**Pour Some Sugar On Me**...Def Leppard
2/90	**Power, The**...Snap!
24/78	**Power Of Gold**...Dan Fogelberg/Tim Weisberg
11/98	**Power Of Good-Bye**...Madonna
1/85	**Power Of Love**...Huey Lewis
4/91	**Power Of Love (medley)**...Luther Vandross
11/72	**Power Of Love**...Joe Simon
	Power Of Love
26/88	Laura Branigan
1/94	Celine Dion
11/71	**Power To The People**...John Lennon
35/91	**Power Windows**...Billy Falcon
18/94	**Practice What You Preach**...Barry White
36/99	**Praise You**...Fatboy Slim
2/90	**Pray**...M.C. Hammer
21/94	**Prayer For The Dying**...Seal
38/00	**Prayin' For Daylight**...Rascal Flatts
1/90	**Praying For Time**...George Michael
3/72	**Precious And Few**...Climax
19/79	**Precious Love**...Bob Welch
30/71	**Precious, Precious**...Jackie Moore
22/81	**Precious To Me**...Phil Seymour
21/86	**Press**...Paul McCartney
20/82	**Pressure**...Billy Joel
	Pretty Baby ..see: (It's Been A Long Time)
15/67	**Pretty Ballerina**...Left Banke
9/60	**Pretty Blue Eyes**...Steve Lawrence
	(Pretty Brown Eyes) ..see: Breakin' My Heart
29/66	**Pretty Flamingo**...Manfred Mann
25/95	**Pretty Girl**...Jon B.
39/79	**Pretty Girls**...Melissa Manchester
36/59	**Pretty Girls Everywhere**...Eugene Church
7/61	**Pretty Little Angel Eyes**...Curtis Lee
25/65	**Pretty Little Baby**...Marvin Gaye
37A/96	**Pretty Noose**...Soundgarden
15/63	**Pretty Paper**...Roy Orbison
	Pretty Woman ..see: Oh, Pretty Woman
5/90	**Price Of Love**...Bad English
10/63	**Pride And Joy**...Marvin Gaye
33/84	**Pride (In The Name Of Love)**...U2
34/84	**Prime Time**...Alan Parsons Project
8/59	**Primrose Lane**...Jerry Wallace
30/61	**Princess**...Frank Gari
37/65	**Princess In Rags**...Gene Pitney
33/90	**Principal's Office**...Young M.C.
20/56	**Priscilla**...Eddie Cooley
30/89	**Prisoner, The**...Howard Jones
	(also see: Love Theme From Eyes Of Laura Mars)
18/63	**Prisoner Of Love**...James Brown
27/78	**Prisoner Of Your Love**...Player
7/85	**Private Dancer**...Tina Turner
1/81	**Private Eyes**...Daryl Hall & John Oates

POS/YR	RECORD TITLE. . . ARTIST
2/58	**Problems**...Everly Brothers
9/01	**Promise**...Jagged Edge
11/88	**Promise, The**...When In Rome
40/88	**Promise Me**...Cover Girls
17/58	**Promise Me, Love**...Andy Williams
1/91	**Promise Of A New Day**...Paula Abdul
14/74	**Promised Land**...Elvis Presley
9/79	**Promises**...Eric Clapton
38/81	**Promises In The Dark**...Pat Benatar
11/83	**Promises, Promises**...Naked Eyes
19/68	**Promises, Promises**...Dionne Warwick
29/63	**Proud**...Johnny Crawford
	Proud Mary
2/69	Creedence Clearwater Revival
4/71	Ike & Tina Turner
22/75	**Proud One**...Osmonds
	Proud Ones ..see: Theme From
33/78	**Prove It All Night**...Bruce Springsteen
7/88	**Prove Your Love**...Taylor Dayne
7/70	**Psychedelic Shack**...Temptations
5/66	**Psychotic Reaction**...Count Five
31/67	**Pucker Up Buttercup**...Jr. Walker
2/63	**Puff (The Magic Dragon)**...Peter, Paul & Mary
38/03	**Pump It Up**...Joe Budden
2/90	**Pump Up The Jam**...Technotronic
13/88	**Pump Up The Volume**...M/A/R/R/S
26/94	**Pumps And A Bump**...Hammer
20/62	**Punish Her**...Bobby Vee
	Puppet Man
24/70	5th Dimension
26/71	Tom Jones
14/65	**Puppet On A String**...Elvis Presley
	Puppy Love
2/60	Paul Anka
3/72	Donny Osmond
38/64	**Puppy Love**...Barbara Lewis
31/90	**Pure**...Lightning Seeds
26/00	**Purest Of Pain (A Puro Dolor)**...Son By Four
19/01	**Purple Hills**...D-12
1/58	**Purple People Eater**...Sheb Wooley
2/84	**Purple Rain**...Prince
5A/97	**Push**...Matchbox 20
27/62	**Push And Kick**...Mark Valentino
	Push And Pull ..see: (Do The)
19/88	**Push It**...Salt-N-Pepa
36/67	**Pushin' Too Hard**...Seeds
26/99	**Pushin' Weight**...Ice Cube
25/63	**Pushover**...Etta James
17/58	**Pussy Cat**...Ames Brothers
8/58	**Put A Light In The Window**...Four Lads
	Put A Little Love In Your Heart
4/69	Jackie DeShannon
9/89	Annie Lennox & Al Green
32/58	**Put A Ring On My Finger**...Les Paul & Mary Ford
40/83	**Put It In A Magazine**...Sonny Charles
8/01	**Put It On Me**...Ja Rule
20/03	**Put That Woman First**...Jaheim

POS/YR	RECORD TITLE. . . ARTIST
2/71	**Put Your Hand In The Hand**...Ocean
10/74	**Put Your Hands Together**...O'Jays
37A/97	**Put Your Hands Where My Eyes Could See**...Busta Rhymes
2/59	**Put Your Head On My Shoulder**...Paul Anka
27/89	**Put Your Mouth On Me**...Eddie Murphy
4/83	**Puttin' On The Ritz**...Taco

Q

POS/YR	RECORD TITLE. . . ARTIST
38/93	**Quality Time**...Hi-Five
1/61	**Quarter To Three**...U.S. Bonds
2/56	**Que Sera, Sera (Whatever Will Be, Will Be)**...Doris Day
2/81	**Queen Of Hearts**...Juice Newton
40/76	**Queen Of My Soul**...Average White Band
34/83	**Queen Of The Broken Hearts**...Loverboy
9/58	**Queen Of The Hop**...Bobby Darin
12/65	**Queen Of The House**...Jody Miller
	(also see: King Of The Road)
36A/94	**Queen Of The Night**...Whitney Houston
39/57	**Queen Of The Senior Prom**...Mills Brothers
13/69	**Quentin's Theme**...Charles Randolph Grean Sounde
19/60	**Question**...Lloyd Price
21/70	**Question**...Moody Blues
37/68	**Question Of Temperature**...Balloon Farm
24/71	**Questions 67 And 68**...Chicago
25/68	**Quick Joey Small (Run Joey Run)**...Kasenetz-Katz Singing Orchestral Circus
8/64	**Quicksand**...Martha & The Vandellas
4/59	**Quiet Village**...Martin Denny
2/97	**Quit Playing Games (With My Heart)**...Backstreet Boys
27/61	**Quite A Party**...Fireballs

R

POS/YR	RECORD TITLE. . . ARTIST
15/65	**Race Is On**...Jack Jones
13/74	**Radar Love**...Golden Earring
16/84	**Radio Ga-Ga**...Queen
35/89	**Radio Romance**...Tiffany
28/85	**Radioactive**...Firm
1/64	**Rag Doll**...4 Seasons
17/88	**Rag Doll**...Aerosmith
F/71	**Rags To Riches**...Elvis Presley
16/59	**Ragtime Cowboy Joe**...David Seville/The Chipmunks
9/86	**Rain, The**...Oran "Juice" Jones
14/93	**Rain**...Madonna
23/66	**Rain**...Beatles
25/98	**Rain**...SWV
19/71	**Rain Dance**...Guess Who
7/03	**Rain On Me**...Ashanti
10/66	**Rain On The Roof**...Lovin' Spoonful

POS/YR	RECORD TITLE. . . ARTIST
24/63	**Remember Then**...Earls
5/64	**Remember (Walkin' in the Sand)**...Shangri-Las
25/75	**Remember What I Told You To Forget**...Tavares
6/57	**Remember You're Mine**...Pat Boone
3/78	**Reminiscing**...Little River Band
26/75	**Rendezvous**...Hudson Brothers
33/96	**Renee**...Lost Boyz
16/79	**Renegade**...Styx
39/76	**Renegade**...Michael Murphey
39/97	**Request Line**...Zhané
4/65	**Rescue Me**...Fontella Bass
9/91	**Rescue Me**...Madonna
	Respect
35/65	Otis Redding
1/67	Aretha Franklin
	Respect Yourself
12/71	Staple Singers
5/87	Bruce Willis
15/66	**Respectable**...Outsiders
35/92	**Restless Heart**...Peter Cetera
	Resurrection Shuffle
38/71	Tom Jones
40/71	Ashton, Gardner & Dyke
2/97	**Return Of The Mack**...Mark Morrison
15/67	**Return Of The Red Baron**...Royal Guardsmen
4/94	**Return To Innocence**...Enigma
4/58	**Return To Me**...Dean Martin
2/62	**Return To Sender**...Elvis Presley
	Reuben ..see: Ruben
1/79	**Reunited**...Peaches & Herb
25/59	**Reveille Rock**...Johnny & The Hurricanes
15/62	**Revenge**...Brook Benton
8/63	**Reverend Mr. Black**...Kingston Trio
12/68	**Revolution**...Beatles
16/66	**Rhapsody In The Rain**...Lou Christie
11/76	**Rhiannon (Will You Ever Win)**...Fleetwood Mac
1/75	**Rhinestone Cowboy**...Glen Campbell
24/64	**Rhythm**...Major Lance
32/00	**Rhythm Divine**...Enrique Iglesias
5/93	**Rhythm Is A Dancer**...Snap!
5/87	**Rhythm Is Gonna Get You**...Gloria Estefan
F/55	**Rhythm 'N' Blues (Mama's Got The Rhythm - Papa's Got The Blues)**...McGuire Sisters
2/90	**Rhythm Nation**...Janet Jackson
40/88	**Rhythm Of Love**...Yes
5/91	**Rhythm Of My Heart**...Rod Stewart
3/85	**Rhythm Of The Night**...DeBarge
11/95	**Rhythm Of The Night**...Corona
3/63	**Rhythm Of The Rain**...Cascades
1/77	**Rich Girl**...Daryl Hall & John Oates
7/91	**Rico Suave**...Gerardo
5/62	**Ride!**...Dee Dee Sharp
25/65	**Ride Away**...Roy Orbison
4/70	**Ride Captain Ride**...Blues Image
23/75	**Ride 'Em Cowboy**...Paul Davis
2/80	**Ride Like The Wind**...Christopher Cross
37/67	**Ride, Ride, Ride**...Brenda Lee

POS/YR	RECORD TITLE. . . ARTIST
16/64	**Ride The Wild Surf**...Jan & Dean
38/91	**Ride The Wind**...Poison
3/01	**Ride Wit Me**...Nelly
28/65	**Ride Your Pony**...Lee Dorsey
	Riders In The Sky ..see: (Ghost)
14/71	**Riders On The Storm**...Doors
36/01	**Riding With Private Malone**...David Ball
2/76	**Right Back Where We Started From**...Maxine Nightingale
29/84	**Right By Your Side**...Eurythmics
12/78	**Right Down The Line**...Gerry Rafferty
2/93	**Right Here**...SWV (Human Nature)
2/91	**Right Here, Right Now**...Jesus Jones
1/89	**Right Here Waiting**...Richard Marx
14/93	**Right Kind Of Love**...Jeremy Jordan
23/71	**Right On The Tip Of My Tongue**...Brenda & The Tabulations
7/87	**Right On Track**...Breakfast Club
	Right Or Wrong
29/61	Wanda Jackson
14/64	Ronnie Dove
9/73	**Right Place Wrong Time**...Dr. John
27/87	**Right Thing**...Simply Red
17/73	**Right Thing To Do**...Carly Simon
2/03	**Right Thurr**...Chingy
6/77	**Right Time Of The Night**...Jennifer Warnes
4/74	**Rikki Don't Lose That Number**...Steely Dan
32/59	**Ring-A-Ling-A-Lario**...Jimmie Rodgers
33/65	**Ring Dang Doo**...Sam The Sham & The Pharoahs
	Ring My Bell
1/79	Anita Ward
20/91	D.J. Jazzy Jeff & The Fresh Prince
F/57	**Ring My Phone**...Tommy Sands
17/63	**Ring Of Fire**...Johnny Cash
31/72	**Ring The Living Bell**...Melanie
1/64	**Ringo**...Lorne Greene
17/71	**Rings**...Cymarron
10/62	**Rinky Dink**...Baby Cortez
14/83	**Rio**...Duran Duran
	Rip It Up
17/56	Little Richard
25/56	Bill Haley
36/64	**Rip Van Winkle**...Devotions
1/79	**Rise**...Herb Alpert
38/88	**Ritual**...Dan Reed Network
14/71	**River Deep - Mountain High**...Supremes & Four Tops
31/69	**River Is Wide**...Grassroots
	River Kwai March ..see: March From
3/93	**River Of Dreams**...Billy Joel
33/74	**River's Risin'**...Edgar Winter
30/78	**Rivers Of Babylon**...Boney M
	Road Runner ..see: (I'm A)
3/90	**Roam**...B-52's
25/59	**Robbin' The Cradle**...Tony Bellus
16/56	**R-O-C-K**...Bill Haley
23/55	**Rock-A-Beatin' Boogie**...Bill Haley
10/57	**Rock-A-Billy**...Guy Mitchell

POS/YR	RECORD TITLE. . .ARTIST
	Rock-A-Bye Your Baby With A Dixie Melody
10/56	Jerry Lewis
37/61	Aretha Franklin
23/62	**Rock-A-Hula Baby ("Twist" Special)**...Elvis Presley
23/89	**Rock And A Hard Place**...Rolling Stones
	Rock And Roll ..also see: Rock 'N' Roll / Rockin' Roll
7/72	**Rock And Roll**...Gary Glitter
12/76	**Rock And Roll All Nite**...Kiss (Live)
	Rock And Roll Dreams Come Through
32/81	Jim Steinman
13/94	Meat Loaf
20/85	**Rock And Roll Girls**...John Fogerty
3/74	**Rock And Roll Heaven**...Righteous Brothers
23/74	**Rock And Roll, Hoochie Koo**...Rick Derringer
19/58	**Rock And Roll Is Here To Stay**...Danny & The Juniors
28/76	**Rock And Roll Love Letter**...Bay City Rollers
15/72	**Rock And Roll Lullaby**...B.J. Thomas
	Rock And Roll Music
8/57	Chuck Berry
5/76	Beach Boys
1/56	**Rock And Roll Waltz**...Kay Starr
	Rock Around The Clock
1/55	Bill Haley
39/74	Bill Haley
2/86	**R.O.C.K. In The U.S.A. (A Salute To 60's Rock)**...John Cougar Mellencamp
8/56	**Rock Island Line**...Lonnie Donegan
13/55	**Rock Love**...Fontane Sisters
10/69	**Rock Me**...Steppenwolf
1/86	**Rock Me Amadeus**...Falco
34/64	**Rock Me Baby**...B.B. King
38/72	**Rock Me Baby**...David Cassidy
1/74	**Rock Me Gently**...Andy Kim
18/85	**Rock Me Tonight (For Old Times Sake)**...Freddie Jackson
15/84	**Rock Me Tonite**...Billy Squier
	Rock 'N' Roll ..also see: Rock And Roll / Rockin' Roll
13/79	**Rock 'N' Roll Fantasy**...Bad Company
30/78	**Rock 'N' Roll Fantasy**...Kinks
15/75	**Rock N' Roll (I Gave You The Best Years Of My Life)**...Mac Davis
19/83	**Rock 'N' Roll Is King**...ELO
29/72	**Rock 'N Roll Soul**...Grand Funk Railroad
16/83	**Rock Of Ages**...Def Leppard
22/88	**Rock Of Life**...Rick Springfield
	Rock On
5/74	David Essex
1/89	Michael Damian
36/56	**Rock Right**...Georgia Gibbs
7/87	**Rock Steady**...Whispers
9/71	**Rock Steady**...Aretha Franklin
1/74	**Rock The Boat**...Hues Corporation
14/01	**Rock The Boat**...Aaliyah
8/83	**Rock The Casbah**...Clash

POS/YR	RECORD TITLE. . .ARTIST
30/87	**Rock The Night**...Europe
9/82	**Rock This Town**...Stray Cats
2/03	**Rock Wit U (Awww Baby)**...Ashanti
7/89	**Rock Wit'cha**...Bobby Brown
1/80	**Rock With You**...Michael Jackson
25/84	**Rock You Like A Hurricane**...Scorpions
1/74	**Rock Your Baby**...George McCrae
5/03	**Rock Your Body**...Justin Timberlake
17/57	**Rock Your Little Baby To Sleep**...Buddy Knox
38/59	**Rocka-Conga**...Applejacks
12/89	**Rocket**...Def Leppard
6/72	**Rocket Man**...Elton John
39/78	**Rocket Ride**...Kiss
6/88	**Rocket 2 U**...Jets
10/75	**Rockford Files**...Mike Post
27/75	**Rockin' All Over The World**...John Fogerty
14/60	**Rockin' Around The Christmas Tree**...Brenda Lee
25/85	**Rockin' At Midnight**...Honeydrippers
9/75	**Rockin' Chair**...Gwen McCrae
7/60	**Rockin' Good Way (To Mess Around And Fall In Love)**...Dinah Washington & Brook Benton
22/60	**Rockin' Little Angel**...Ray Smith
1/76	**Rockin' Me**...Steve Miller
6/73	**Rockin' Pneumonia And The Boogie Woogie Flu**...Johnny Rivers
	Rockin' Robin
2/58	Bobby Day
2/72	Michael Jackson
	Rockin' Roll ..also see: Rock And Roll / Rock 'N' Roll
14/73	**Rockin' Roll Baby**...Stylistics
18/74	**Rockin' Soul**...Hues Corporation
9/75	**Rocky**...Austin Roberts
9/73	**Rocky Mountain High**...John Denver
23/73	**Rocky Mountain Way**...Joe Walsh
	Rocky, Theme From ..see: Gonna Fly Now
30/79	**Rolene**...Moon Martin
27/83	**Roll Me Away**...Bob Seger
14/75	**Roll On Down The Highway**...Bachman-Turner Overdrive
29/56	**Roll Over Beethoven**...Chuck Berry
10/95	**Roll To Me**...del Amitri
1/88	**Roll With It**...Steve Winwood
34/79	**Roller**...April Wine
13/55	**Rollin' Stone**...Fontane Sisters
17/02	**Rollout (My Business)**...Ludacris
26/84	**Romancing The Stone**...Eddy Grant
1/91	**Romantic**...Karyn White
6/90	**Romeo**...Dino
6/98	**Romeo And Juliet**...Sylk-E. Fyne
27/92	**Romeo & Juliet**...Stacy Earl
	(also see: Just Like / Love Theme)
11/80	**Romeo's Tune**...Steve Forbert
3/89	**Roni**...Bobby Brown
6/64	**Ronnie**...4 Seasons
17/90	**Room At The Top**...Adam Ant

POS/YR	RECORD TITLE. . .ARTIST
9/89	**Room To Move**...Animotion
16/89	**Rooms On Fire**...Stevie Nicks
2/82	**Rosanna**...Toto
3/80	**Rose, The**...Bette Midler
6/56	**Rose And A Baby Ruth**...George Hamilton IV
3/71	**Rose Garden**...Lynn Anderson
	(also see: I Beg Your Pardon)
26/98	**Rose Is Still A Rose**...Aretha Franklin
	Roses And Roses ..see: And Roses
1/62	**Roses Are Red (My Love)**...Bobby Vinton
24/57	**Rosie Lee**...Mello-Tones
30/80	**Rotation**...Herb Alpert
22/86	**Rough Boy**...ZZ Top
	Rough Neck ..see: RuffNeck
1/57	**Round And Round**...Perry Como
12/84	**Round And Round**...Ratt
12/91	**Round And Round**...Tevin Campbell
21/65	**Round Every Corner**...Petula Clark
31A/94	**Round Here**...Counting Crows
13/72	**Roundabout**...Yes
30/62	**Route 66 Theme**...Nelson Riddle
37/82	**Route 101**...Herb Alpert
32/79	**Roxanne**...Police
16/74	**Rub It In**...Billy "Crash" Craddock
3/90	**Rub You The Right Way**...Johnny Gill
6/61	**Rubber Ball**...Bobby Vee
37/79	**Rubber Biscuit**...Blues Brothers
16/70	**Rubber Duckie**...Ernie (Jim Henson)
2/76	**Rubberband Man**...Spinners
F/70	**Rubberneckin'**...Elvis Presley
26/69	**Ruben James**...Kenny Rogers & The First Edition
28/60	**Ruby**...Ray Charles
18/62	**Ruby Ann**...Marty Robbins
	Ruby Baby
2/63	Dion
33/75	Billy "Crash" Craddock
6/69	**Ruby, Don't Take Your Love To Town**...Kenny Rogers & The First Edition
30/60	**Ruby Duby Du**...Tobin Mathews & Co.
	(Ruby Red Dress) ..see: Leave Me Alone
1/67	**Ruby Tuesday**...Rolling Stones
21/60	**Rudolph The Red Nosed Reindeer**...David Seville/The Chipmunks
34/56	**Rudy's Rock**...Bill Haley
35/93	**RuffNeck**...MC Lyte
16/58	**Rumble**...Link Wray
28/86	**Rumbleseat**...John Cougar Mellencamp
8/86	**Rumors**...Timex Social Club
12/62	**Rumors**...Johnny Crawford
2/92	**Rump Shaker**...Wreckx-N-Effect
34/01	**Run**...George Strait
	Run Away .. also see: Runaway
6/69	**Run Away Child, Running Wild**...Temptations
12/65	**Run, Baby Run (Back Into My Arms)**...Newbeats
33/78	**Run For Home**...Lindisfarne

POS/YR	RECORD TITLE. . .ARTIST
18/82	**Run For The Roses**...Dan Fogelberg
4/75	**Run Joey Run**...David Geddes
36/60	**Run Red Run**...Coasters
25/66	**Run, Run, Look And See**...Brian Hyland
27/72	**Run Run Run**...Jo Jo Gunne
20/84	**Run Runaway**...Slade
28/60	**Run Samson Run**...Neil Sedaka
F/70	**Run Through The Jungle**...Creedence Clearwater Revival
2/61	**Run To Him**...Bobby Vee
16/72	**Run To Me**...Bee Gees
6/85	**Run To You**...Bryan Adams
31/93	**Run To You**...Whitney Houston
8/95	**Run-Around**...Blues Traveler
	Runaround
20/54	Three Chuckles
23/60	Fleetwoods
28/61	**Runaround**...Regents
	Runaround Sue
1/61	Dion
13/78	Leif Garrett
3/95	**Run Away**...Real McCoy
1/61	**Runaway**...Del Shannon
3/95	**Runaway**...Janet Jackson
12/78	**Runaway**...Jefferson Starship
39/84	**Runaway**...Bon Jovi
5/93	**Runaway Train**...Soul Asylum
22/84	**Runner**...Manfred Mann's Earth Band
23/72	**Runnin' Away**...Sly & The Family Stone
23/89	**Runnin' Down A Dream**...Tom Petty
19/03	**Runnin (Dying To Live)**...Tupac
18/91	**Running Back To You**...Vanessa Williams
1/60	**Running Bear**...Johnny Preston
11/78	**Running On Empty**...Jackson Browne
1/61	**Running Scared**...Roy Orbison
30/85	**Running Up That Hill**...Kate Bush
7/84	**Running With The Night**...Lionel Richie
39/72	**Runway, The**...Grass Roots
32/91	**Rush**...Big Audio Dynamite II
9/88	**Rush Hour**...Jane Wiedlin
1/91	**Rush, Rush**...Paula Abdul
16/86	**Russians**...Sting
33/65	**Rusty Bells**...Brenda Lee

S

POS/YR	RECORD TITLE. . .ARTIST
15/75	**S.O.S.**...Abba
39/66	**S.Y.S.L.J.F.M. (The Letter Song)**...Joe Tex
20/61	**Sacred**...Castells
13/89	**Sacred Emotion**...Donny Osmond
18/90	**Sacrifice**...Elton John
1/79	**Sad Eyes**...Robert John
29/60	**Sad Mood**...Sam Cooke
5/61	**Sad Movies (Make Me Cry)**...Sue Thompson
27/65	**Sad, Sad Girl**...Barbara Mason
5/84	**Sad Songs (Say So Much)**...Elton John

POS/YR	RECORD TITLE. . .ARTIST
31/88	Sayin' Sorry (Don't Make It Right)...Denise Lopez
9/99	Scar Tissue...Red Hot Chili Peppers
	Scarborough Fair
11/68	Simon & Garfunkel
16/68	Sergio Mendes
13/59	Scarlet Ribbons (For Her Hair)...Browns
33/75	School Boy Crush...AWB
3/57	School Day...Chuck Berry
28/61	School Is In...Gary (U.S.) Bonds
5/61	School Is Out...Gary (U.S.) Bonds
7/72	School's Out...Alice Cooper
6/72	Scorpio...Dennis Coffey
5/95	Scream...Michael Jackson & Janet Jackson
20/87	Se La...Lionel Richie
	Se Si Bon ..see: Whispering
14/59	Sea Cruise...Frankie Ford
21/61	Sea Of Heartbreak...Don Gibson
	Sea Of Love
2/59	Phil Phillips
33/82	Del Shannon
3/85	Honeydrippers
	Sealed With A Kiss
3/62	Brian Hyland
19/68	Gary Lewis
19/72	Bobby Vinton
4/85	Search Is Over...Survivor
3/57	Searchin'...Coasters
16A/98	Searchin' My Soul...Vonda Shepard
	Searchin' So Long ..see: (I've Been)
27/66	Searching For My Love...Bobby Moore & The Rhythm Aces
1/88	Seasons Change...Exposé
1/74	Seasons In The Sun...Terry Jacks
38/69	Seattle...Perry Como
34/74	Second Avenue...Garfunkel
6/89	Second Chance...Thirty Eight Special
40/56	Second Fiddle...Kay Starr
7/62	Second Hand Love...Connie Francis
32/66	Second Hand Rose...Barbra Streisand
39/85	Second Nature...Dan Hartman
28/98	Second Round K.O....Canibus
8/80	Second Time Around...Shalamar
3/94	Secret...Madonna
18/58	Secret, The...Gordon MacRae
3/66	Secret Agent Man...Johnny Rivers
19/97	Secret Garden...Bruce Springsteen
31/90	Secret Garden (Sweet Seduction Suite)...Quincy Jones/Al B. Sure!/James Ingram/El DeBarge/Barry White
	Secret Love
29/66	Billy Stewart
20/75	Freddy Fender
3/86	Secret Lovers...Atlantic Starr
6/89	Secret Rendezvous...Karyn White
19/86	Secret Separation...Fixx
3/58	Secretly...Jimmie Rodgers
35/68	Security...Etta James

POS/YR	RECORD TITLE. . .ARTIST
28/80	Seduction, The...James Last Band
27/69	See...Rascals
	See Me, Feel Me
12/70	Who
29/73	New Seekers (medley)
25/56	See Saw...Moonglows
14/68	See Saw...Aretha Franklin
	See See ..see: C.C.
9/64	See The Funny Little Clown...Bobby Goldsboro
40/91	See The Lights...Simple Minds
	See You ..also see: C U
	See You In September
23/59	Tempos
3/66	Happenings
6/56	See You Later, Alligator...Bill Haley
4/84	Self Control...Laura Branigan
11/64	Selfish One...Jackie Ross
4/97	Semi-Charmed Life...Third Eye Blind
6/57	Send For Me...Nat "King" Cole
23/83	Send Her My Love...Journey
	Send In The Clowns
36/75	Judy Collins
19/77	Judy Collins
	Send Me An Angel
29/84	Real Life
26/89	Real Life ('89)
13/63	Send Me Some Lovin'...Sam Cooke
	Send Me The Pillow You Dream On
17/62	Johnny Tillotson
22/65	Dean Martin
4/79	Send One Your Love...Stevie Wonder
5/90	Sending All My Love...Linear
40/94	Sending My Love...Zhané
27/03	Señorita...Justin Timberlake
4/91	Sensitivity...Ralph Tresvant
27/95	Sentimental...Deborah Cox
8/78	Sentimental Lady...Bob Welch
8/85	Sentimental Street...Night Ranger
	(Senza Fine) ..see: Phoenix Love Theme
1/85	Separate Lives...Phil Collins & Marilyn Martin
20/73	Separate Ways...Elvis Presley
8/83	Separate Ways (Worlds Apart)...Journey
23/00	Separated...Avant
8/79	September...Earth, Wind & Fire
23/61	September In The Rain...Dinah Washington
17/80	September Morn'...Neil Diamond
23/80	Sequel...Harry Chapin
21/87	Serious...Donna Allen
13/78	Serpentine Fire...Earth, Wind & Fire
1/91	Set Adrift On Memory Bliss...PM Dawn
23/65	Set Me Free...Kinks
27/80	Set Me Free...Utopia
6/91	Set The Night To Music...Roberta Flack with Maxi Priest
26/96	Set U Free...Planet Soul
7/93	7...Prince
33/66	7 And 7 Is...Love
21/81	Seven Bridges Road...Eagles

POS/YR	RECORD TITLE. . . ARTIST
27/62	**Seven Day Weekend**...Gary (US) Bonds
10/02	**7 Days**...Craig David
	Seven Days
17/56	Dorothy Collins
18/56	Crew Cuts
30/58	**"7-11" (Mambo No. 5)**...Gone All Stars
9/59	**(Seven Little Girls) Sitting In The Back Seat**...Paul Evans
14/67	**7 Rooms Of Gloom**...Four Tops
19/87	**Seven Wonders**...Fleetwood Mac
22/81	**Seven Year Ache**...Rosanne Cash
7/65	**Seventh Son**...Johnny Rivers
	Seventeen
3/55	Fontane Sisters
5/55	Boyd Bennett
18/55	Rusty Draper
26/89	**Seventeen**...Winger
36/84	**17**...Rick James
F/94	**70's Love Groove**...Janet Jackson
8/98	**Sex and Candy**...Marcy Playground
28/86	**Sex As A Weapon**...Pat Benatar
15/70	**Sex Machine**...James Brown
20/93	**Sex Me**...R. Kelly
3/83	**Sexual Healing**...Marvin Gaye
	Sexy + 17 ..see: (She's)
5/80	**Sexy Eyes**...Dr. Hook
20/84	**Sexy Girl**...Glenn Frey
17/74	**Sexy Mama**...Moments
12/65	**Sha La La**...Manfred Mann
7/74	**Sha-La-La (Make Me Happy)**...Al Green
28/00	**Shackles (Praise You)**...Mary Mary
1/78	**Shadow Dancing**...Andy Gibb
25/79	**Shadows In The Moonlight**...Anne Murray
13/82	**Shadows Of The Night**...Pat Benatar
19/62	**Shadrack**...Brook Benton
	Shaft ..see: Theme From
38/64	**Shaggy Dog**...Mickey Lee Lane
7/65	**Shake**...Sam Cooke
25/67	**Shake A Tail Feather**...James & Bobby Purify
29/65	**Shake And Fingerpop**...Jr. Walker
28/89	**Shake For The Sheik**...Escape Club
13/79	**Shake It**...Ian Matthews
4/82	**Shake It Up**...Cars
18/66	**Shake Me, Wake Me (When It's Over)**...Four Tops
	Shake, Rattle And Roll
7/54	Bill Haley
31/67	Arthur Conley
33/63	**Shake! Shake! Shake!**...Jackie Wilson
1/76	**(Shake, Shake, Shake) Shake Your Booty**...KC & The Sunshine Band
13/00	**Shake Ya Ass**...Mystikal
1/03	**Shake Ya Tailfeather**...Nelly/P. Diddy/Murphy Lee
1/87	**Shake You Down**...Gregory Abbott
7/79	**Shake Your Body (Down To The Ground)**...Jacksons
22/00	**Shake Your Bon-Bon**...Ricky Martin

POS/YR	RECORD TITLE. . . ARTIST
5/79	**Shake Your Groove Thing**...Peaches & Herb
4/87	**Shake Your Love**...Debbie Gibson
23/77	**Shake Your Rump To The Funk**...Bar-Kays
1/87	**Shakedown**...Bob Seger
31/79	**Shakedown Cruise**...Jay Ferguson
26/75	**Shakey Ground**...Temptations
22/65	**Shakin' All Over**...Guess Who?
3/73	**Shambala**...Three Dog Night
	Shame
9/78	Evelyn "Champagne" King
28/94	Zhané
21/85	**Shame**...Motels
23/62	**Shame On Me**...Bobby Bare
2/83	**Shame On The Moon**...Bob Seger
29/68	**Shame, Shame**...Magic Lanterns
12/75	**Shame, Shame, Shame**...Shirley (& Company)
31/82	**Shanghai Breezes**...John Denver
	Shangri-La
11/57	Four Coins
15/64	Robert Maxwell
27/64	Vic Dana
6/76	**Shannon**...Henry Gross
9/00	**Shape Of My Heart**...Backstreet Boys
22/68	**Shape Of Things To Come**...Max Frost
11/66	**Shapes Of Things**...Yardbirds
10/70	**Share The Land**...Guess Who
	Share Your Love With Me
13/69	Aretha Franklin
14/81	Kenny Rogers
6/79	**Sharing The Night Together**...Dr. Hook
15/62	**Sharing You**...Bobby Vee
31/79	**Shattered**...Rolling Stones
2/88	**Shattered Dreams**...Johnny Hates Jazz
30/75	**Shaving Cream**...Benny Bell
23/70	**She**...Tommy James
1/90	**She Ain't Worth It**...Glenn Medeiros & Bobby Brown
12/00	**She Bangs**...Ricky Martin
5/79	**She Believes In Me**...Kenny Rogers
33/70	**She Belongs To Me**...Rick Nelson
5/83	**She Blinded Me With Science**...Thomas Dolby
3/84	**She Bop**...Cyndi Lauper
30/70	**She Came In Through The Bathroom Window**...Joe Cocker
19/62	**She Can't Find Her Keys**...Paul Petersen
	She Comes To Me ..see: (When She Needs Good Lovin')
37/01	**She Couldn't Change Me**...Montgomery Gentry
5/62	**She Cried**...Jay & The Americans
23/77	**She Did It**...Eric Carmen
1/89	**She Drives Me Crazy**...Fine Young Cannibals
13/02	**She Hates Me**...Puddle Of Mudd
27/67	**She Is Still A Mystery**...Lovin' Spoonful
1/64	**She Loves You**...Beatles
18/59	**She Say (Oom Dooby Doom)**...Diamonds
30/91	**She Talks To Angels**...Black Crowes
F/77	**She Thinks I Still Care**...Elvis Presley

POS/YR	RECORD TITLE. . . ARTIST
38/75	**(Shu-Doo-Pa-Poo-Poop) Love Being Your Fool**...Travis Wammack
32/61	**Shu Rah**...Fats Domino
23/63	**Shut Down**...Beach Boys
24/63	**Shutters And Boards**...Jerry Wallace
13/95	**Shy Guy**...Diana King
22/58	**Sick And Tired**...Fats Domino
18/03	**Sick Of Being Lonely**...Field Mob
8/74	**Sideshow**...Blue Magic
25/64	**Sidewalk Surfin'**...Jan & Dean
18/86	**Sidewalk Talk**...Jellybean
1/94	**Sign, The**...Ace Of Base
32/84	**Sign Of Fire**...Fixx
3/87	**Sign 'O' The Times**...Prince
11/66	**Sign Of The Times**...Petula Clark
4/88	**Sign Your Name**...Terence Trent D'Arby
	Signed, Sealed, Delivered I'm Yours
3/70	Stevie Wonder
18/77	Peter Frampton
	Signs
3/71	Five Man Electrical Band
8/91	Tesla
11/67	**Silence Is Golden**...Tremeloes
9/91	**Silent Lucidity**...Queensrÿche
31/92	**Silent Prayer**...Shanice
6/86	**Silent Running (On Dangerous Ground)**...Mike + The Mechanics
13/89	**Silhouette**...Kenny G
	Silhouettes
3/57	Rays
10/57	Diamonds
5/65	Herman's Hermits
1/76	**Silly Love Songs**...Wings
25/70	**Silver Bird**...Mark Lindsay
20/55	**Silver Dollar**...Teresa Brewer
38/76	**Silver Star**...Four Seasons
20/62	**Silver Threads And Golden Needles**...Springfields
4/68	**Simon Says**...1910 Fruitgum Co.
38/00	**Simple Kind Of Life**...No Doubt
30/93	**Simple Life**...Elton John
2/88	**Simply Irresistible**...Robert Palmer
	Since I Don't Have You
12/59	Skyliners
23/81	Don McLean
4/63	**Since I Fell For You**...Lenny Welch
17/65	**Since I Lost My Baby**...Temptations
	Since I Met You Baby
12/56	Ivory Joe Hunter
34/57	Mindy Carson
32/67	**Since You Showed Me How To Be Happy**...Jackie Wilson
31/87	**Since You've Been Gone**...Outfield
38/59	**Since You've Been Gone**...Clyde McPhatter (also see: Sweet Sweet Baby)
	Sincerely
1/55	McGuire Sisters
20/55	Moonglow's
14/89	**Sincerely Yours**...Sweet Sensation

POS/YR	RECORD TITLE. . . ARTIST
3/73	**Sing**...Carpenters
5/76	**Sing A Song**...Earth, Wind & Fire
24/58	**Sing Boy Sing**...Tommy Sands
14/03	**Sing For The Moment**...Eminem
	Singing The Blues
1/56	Guy Mitchell
17/56	Marty Robbins
12/66	**Single Girl**...Sandy Posey
36/99	**Single White Female**...Chely Wright
3/60	**Sink The Bismarck**...Johnny Horton
1/77	**Sir Duke**...Stevie Wonder
	Sissy ..see: Cissy
5/84	**Sister Christian**...Night Ranger
1/75	**Sister Golden Hair**...America
24/74	**Sister Mary Elephant (Shudd-Up!)**...Cheech & Chong
18/85	**Sisters Are Doin' It For Themselves**...Eurythmics & Aretha Franklin
36/67	**Sit Down, I Think I Love You**...Mojo Men
37/71	**Sit Yourself Down**...Stephen Stills
	Sittin' In The Balcony
18/57	Eddie Cochran
38/57	Johnny Dee
19/90	**Sittin' In The Lap Of Luxury**...Louie Louie
	(Sittin' On) The Dock Of The Bay
1/68	Otis Redding
11/88	Michael Bolton
30/96	**Sittin' On Top Of The World**...Da Brat
2/96	**Sittin' Up In My Room**...Brandy
16/73	**Sitting**...Cat Stevens
27/83	**Sitting At The Wheel**...Moody Blues
24/65	**Sitting In The Park**...Billy Stewart
32/63	**Six Days On The Road**...Dave Dudley
40/93	**Six Feet Deep**...Geto Boys
28/59	**Six Nights A Week**...Crests
18/67	**Six O'Clock**...Lovin' Spoonful
13/66	**634-5789 (Soulsville, U.S.A.)**...Wilson Pickett
2/59	**16 Candles**...Crests
3/60	**Sixteen Reasons**...Connie Stevens
	Sixteen Tons
1/55	"Tennessee" Ernie Ford
17/55	Johnny Desmond
33A/96	**6th Avenue Heartache**...Wallflowers
6/82	**'65 Love Affair**...Paul Davis
10/02	**Sk8er Boi**...Avril Lavigne
19/87	**Skeletons**...Stevie Wonder
	Skillz ..see: (I Know I Got)
13/74	**Skin Tight**...Ohio Players
39/87	**Skin Trade**...Duran Duran
10/67	**Skinny Legs And All**...Joe Tex
22/58	**Skinny Minnie**...Bill Haley
25/68	**Skip A Rope**...Henson Cargill
3/75	**Sky High**...Jigsaw
14/68	**Sky Pilot**...Animals
4/93	**Slam**...Onyx
35/64	**Slaughter On Tenth Avenue**...Ventures
1/86	**Sledgehammer**...Peter Gabriel

POS/YR	RECORD TITLE. . . ARTIST
13/60	**Sleep**...Little Willie John
1/59	**Sleep Walk**...Santo & Johnny
8/85	**Sleeping Bag**...ZZ Top
	Sleeping Beauty ..see: To A
32/93	**Sleeping Satellite**...Tasmin Archer
8/99	**Slide**...Goo Goo Dolls
32/77	**Slide**...Slave
6/68	**Slip Away**...Clarence Carter
5/78	**Slip Slidin' Away**...Paul Simon
19/75	**Slippery When Wet**...Commodores
33/56	**Slippin' And Slidin'**...Little Richard
39/83	**Slipping Away**...Dave Edmunds
16/72	**Slippin' Into Darkness**...War
3/66	**Sloop John B**...Beach Boys
33/93	**Slow And Sexy**...Shabba Ranks
20/77	**Slow Dancin' Don't Turn Me On**...Addrisi Bros.
10/77	**Slow Dancin' (Swayin' To The Music)**...Johnny Rivers
25/64	**Slow Down**...Beatles
34/77	**Slowdown**...John Miles
2/81	**Slow Hand**...Pointer Sisters
1/04	**Slow Jamz**...Twista
18/92	**Slow Motion**...Color Me Badd
20/76	**Slow Ride**...Foghat
3/62	**Slow Twistin'**...Chubby Checker (with Dee Dee Sharp)
	Slow Walk
17/56	Sil Austin
26/57	Bill Doggett
30/70	**Sly, Slick, And The Wicked**...Lost Generation
F/71	**Smackwater Jack**...Carole King
29/72	**Small Beginnings**...Flash
21/62	**Small Sad Sam**...Phil McLean
6/85	**Small Town**...John Cougar Mellencamp
20/59	**Small World**...Johnny Mathis
25/88	**Small World**...Huey Lewis
35/92	**Smells Like Nirvana**..."Weird Al" Yankovic
6/92	**Smells Like Teen Spirit**...Nirvana
12/97	**Smile**...Scarface
18/99	**Smile**...Vitamin C
39/00	**Smile**...Lonestar
5/69	**Smile A Little Smile For Me**...Flying Machine
34/83	**Smile Has Left Your Eyes**...Asia
21/55	**Smiles**...Crazy Otto
3/71	**Smiling Faces Sometimes**...Undisputed Truth
9/77	**Smoke From A Distant Fire**...Sanford/Townsend Band
	Smoke Gets In Your Eyes
1/59	Platters
27/73	Blue Haze
4/73	**Smoke On The Water**...Deep Purple
17/60	**Smokie**...Bill Black's Combo
	Smokin' In The Boy's Room
3/74	Brownsville Station
16/85	Mötley Crüe
35/97	**Smokin' Me Out**...Warren G
22/87	**Smoking Gun**...Robert Cray Band

POS/YR	RECORD TITLE. . . ARTIST
24/81	**Smoky Mountain Rain**...Ronnie Milsap
12/62	**Smoky Places**...Corsairs
1/99	**Smooth**...Santana Feat. Rob Thomas
	Smooth Criminal
7/89	Michael Jackson
23/01	Alien Ant Farm
5/85	**Smooth Operator**...Sade
12/85	**Smuggler's Blues**...Glenn Frey
16/03	**Snake**...R. Kelly
27/68	**Snake, The**...Al Wilson
8/62	**Snap Your Fingers**...Joe Henderson
31/69	**Snatching It Back**...Clarence Carter
F/75	**Snookeroo**...Ringo Starr
2/66	**Snoopy Vs. The Red Baron**...Royal Guardsmen **(also see: Return Of The Red Baron)**
8/70	**Snowbird**...Anne Murray
3/89	**So Alive**...Love & Rockets
31/93	**So Alone**...Men At Large
16/99	**So Anxious**...Ginuwine
23/84	**So Bad**...Paul McCartney
11/90	**So Close**...Daryl Hall/John Oates
38/59	**So Close**...Brook Benton
40/83	**So Close**...Diana Ross
1/88	**So Emotional**...Whitney Houston
14/71	**So Far Away**...Carole King
19/86	**So Far Away**...Dire Straits
24/03	**So Far Away**...Staind
11/59	**So Fine**...Fiestas
30/01	**So Fresh, So Clean**...OutKast
10/03	**So Gone**...Monica
30/79	**So Good, So Right**...Brenda Russell
36/69	**So Good Together**...Andy Kim
39/69	**So I Can Love You**...Emotions
26/85	**So In Love**...Orchestral Manoeuvres In The Dark
25/01	**So In Love With Two**...Mikaila
7/77	**So In To You**...Atlanta Rhythm Section
30/98	**So Into You**...Tamia
28/61	**So Long Baby**...Del Shannon
6/59	**So Many Ways**...Brook Benton
	So Much In Love
1/63	Tymes
5/94	All-4-One
2/57	**So Rare**...Jimmy Dorsey
7/60	**So Sad (To Watch Good Love Go Bad)**...Everly Brothers
21/62	**So This Is Love**...Castells
17/73	**So Very Hard To Go**...Tower Of Power
30/83	**So Wrong**...Patrick Simmons
21/74	**So You Are A Star**...Hudson Brothers
29/67	**So You Want To Be A Rock 'N' Roll Star**...Byrds
31/77	**So You Win Again**...Hot Chocolate
17/02	**Soak Up The Sun**...Sheryl Crow
14/67	**Society's Child (Baby I've Been Thinking)**...Janis Ian
12/97	**Sock It 2 Me**...Missy "Misdemeanor" Elliott
6/67	**Sock It To Me-Baby!**...Mitch Ryder
35/57	**Soft**...Bill Doggett

POS/YR	RECORD TITLE. . . ARTIST
	Soft Summer Breeze
11/56	Eddie Heywood
34/56	Diamonds
27/64	**Softly, As I Leave You**...Frank Sinatra
F/55	**Softly, Softly**...Jaye P. Morgan
29/72	**Softly Whispering I Love You**...English Congregation
1/62	**Soldier Boy**...Shirelles
2/89	**Soldier Of Love**...Donny Osmond
12/85	**Solid**...Ashford & Simpson
7/83	**Solitaire**...Laura Branigan
17/75	**Solitaire**...Carpenters
21/70	**Solitary Man**...Neil Diamond
34/64	**Some Day We're Gonna Love Again**...Searchers
36/81	**Some Days Are Diamonds (Some Days Are Stone)**...John Denver
13/65	**Some Enchanted Evening**...Jay & The Americans
	Some Guys Have All The Luck
39/73	Persuaders
10/84	Rod Stewart
37/59	**Some Kind-A Earthquake**...Duane Eddy
26/83	**Some Kind Of Friend**...Barry Manilow
10/88	**Some Kind Of Lover**...Jody Watley
3/75	**Some Kind Of Wonderful**...Grand Funk
32/61	**Some Kind Of Wonderful**...Drifters
6/85	**Some Like It Hot**...Power Station
18/85	**Some Things Are Better Left Unsaid**...Daryl Hall/John Oates
30/68	**Some Things You Never Get Used To**...Supremes
26/68	**Some Velvet Morning**...Nancy Sinatra & Lee Hazlewood
11/85	**Somebody**...Bryan Adams
23/02	**Somebody Like You**...Keith Urban
5/67	**Somebody To Love**...Jefferson Airplane
	Somebody To Love
13/77	Queen
30/93	George Michael & Queen
22/58	**Somebody Touched Me**...Buddy Knox
18/56	**Somebody Up There Likes Me**...Perry Como
7/82	**Somebody's Baby**...Jackson Browne
8/70	**Somebody's Been Sleeping**...100 Proof Aged in Soul
33/76	**Somebody's Gettin' It**...Johnnie Taylor
13/81	**Somebody's Knockin'**...Terri Gibbs
27/86	**Somebody's Out There**...Triumph
2/84	**Somebody's Watching Me**...Rockwell
32/71	**Somebody's Watching You**...Little Sister
1/91	**Someday**...Mariah Carey
7/87	**Someday**...Glass Tiger
7/99	**Someday**...Sugar Ray
7/04	**Someday**...Nickelback
30/96	**Someday**...All-4-One
	(also see: Some Day)
25/72	**Someday Never Comes**...Creedence Clearwater Revival
36/82	**Someday, Someway**...Marshall Crenshaw
1/69	**Someday We'll Be Together**...Supremes
19/97	**Someone**...SWV
35/59	**Someone**...Johnny Mathis
15/82	**Someone Could Lose A Heart Tonight**...Eddie Rabbitt
4/75	**Someone Saved My Life Tonight**...Elton John
21/80	**Someone That I Used To Love**...Natalie Cole
3/01	**Someone To Call My Lover**...Janet Jackson
19/92	**Someone To Hold**...Trey Lorenz
10/95	**Someone To Love**...Jon B.
13/55	**Someone You Love**...Nat "King" Cole
37/98	**Someone You Used To Know**...Collin Raye
37/77	**Somethin' 'Bout 'Cha**...Latimore
21/95	**Somethin' 4 Da Honeyz**...Montell Jordan
1/67	**Somethin' Stupid**...Nancy Sinatra & Frank Sinatra
3/69	**Something**...Beatles
35/03	**Something**...Lasgo
F/97	**Something About The Way You Look Tonight**...Elton John
7/86	**Something About You**...Level 42
19/65	**Something About You**...Four Tops
13/75	**Something Better To Do**...Olivia Newton-John
23/91	**Something Got Me Started**...Simply Red
4/90	**Something Happened On The Way To Heaven**...Phil Collins
	Something He Can Feel
28/76	Aretha Franklin
6/92	En Vogue
32A/93	**Something In Common**...Bobby Brown & Whitney Houston
31/91	**Something In My Heart**...Michel'le
37/69	**Something In The Air**...Thunderclap Newman
38/93	**Something In Your Eyes**...Bell Biv DeVoe
28/99	**Something Like That**...Tim McGraw
29/87	**Something Real (Inside Me/Inside You)**...Mr. Mister
7/87	**Something So Strong**...Crowded House
4/90	**Something To Believe In**...Poison
5/91	**Something To Talk About**...Bonnie Raitt
11/70	**Something's Burning**...Kenny Rogers & The First Edition
29/93	**Something's Goin' On**...U.N.V.
37/62	**Something's Got A Hold On Me**...Etta James
	Something's Gotta Give
5/55	McGuire Sisters
9/55	Sammy Davis, Jr.
12/72	**Something's Wrong With Me**...Austin Roberts
21/99	**Sometimes**...Britney Spears
31/77	**Sometimes**...Facts Of Life
36/80	**Sometimes A Fantasy**...Billy Joel
2/92	**Sometimes Love Just Ain't Enough**...Patty Smyth with Don Henley
20/90	**Sometimes She Cries**...Warrant
3/78	**Sometimes When We Touch**...Dan Hill
19/64	**Somewhere**...Tymes
26/66	**Somewhere**...Len Barry
21/82	**Somewhere Down The Road**...Barry Manilow

POS/YR	RECORD TITLE. . . ARTIST
32/03	**Somewhere I Belong**...Linkin Park
	Somewhere In The Night
19/76	Helen Reddy
9/79	Barry Manilow
32/65	**Somewhere In Your Heart**...Frank Sinatra
9/66	**Somewhere, My Love**...Ray Conniff
2/87	**Somewhere Out There**...Linda Ronstadt & James Ingram
32/66	**Somewhere There's A Someone**...Dean Martin
28/01	**Son Of A Gun (I Betcha Think This Song Is About You)**...Janet Jackson
10/69	**Son Of A Preacher Man**...Dusty Springfield
40/68	**Son Of Hickory Holler's Tramp**...O.C. Smith
28/74	**Son Of Sagittarius**...Eddie Kendricks
8/56	**Song For A Summer Night**...Mitch Miller
7/98	**Song For Mama**...Boyz II Men
14/70	**Song Of Joy (Himno A La Alegria)**...Miguel Rios (also see: Joy)
F/57	**(Song Of) Raintree County**...Nat "King" Cole
25/55	**Song Of The Barefoot Contessa**...Hugo Winterhalter
11/55	**Song Of The Dreamer**...Eddie Fisher
29/79	**Song On The Radio**...Al Stewart
1/72	**Song Sung Blue**...Neil Diamond
4/87	**Songbird**...Kenny G
25/78	**Songbird**...Barbra Streisand
30/70	**Soolaimón (African Trilogy II)**...Neil Diamond
21/96	**Soon As I Get Home**...Faith Evans
9/71	**Sooner Or Later**...Grass Roots
34/69	**Sophisticated Cissy**...Meters
25/76	**Sophisticated Lady (She's A Different Lady)**...Natalie Cole
2/59	**Sorry (I Ran All the Way Home)**...Impalas
6/76	**Sorry Seems To Be The Hardest Word**...Elton John
	Soul And Inspiration ..see: (You're My)
27/87	**Soul City**...Partland Brothers
	(Soul Coaxing) ..see: Ame Caline
18/69	**Soul Deep**...Box Tops
17/67	**Soul Finger**...Bar-Kays
20/85	**Soul Kiss**...Olivia Newton-John
17/68	**Soul-Limbo**...Booker T. & The M.G.'s
35/73	**Soul Makossa**...Manu Dibango
	Soul Man
2/67	Sam & Dave
14/79	Blues Brothers
29/71	**Soul Power**...James Brown
17/89	**Soul Provider**...Michael Bolton
23/68	**Soul Serenade**...Willie Mitchell
37/73	**Soul Song**...Joe Stampley
22/93	**Soul To Squeeze**...Red Hot Chili Peppers
17/62	**Soul Twist**...King Curtis
3/69	**Soulful Strut**...Young-Holt Unlimited
23/83	**Souls**...Rick Springfield
37/69	**Soulshake**...Peggy Scott & Jo Jo Benson
	(Soulsville, U.S.A.) ..see: 634-5789
36/67	**Sound Of Love**...Five Americans
33/91	**Sound Of Your Voice**...38 Special

POS/YR	RECORD TITLE. . . ARTIST
1/66	**Sounds Of Silence**...Simon & Garfunkel
14/01	**South Side**...Moby
3/63	**South Street**...Orlons
29/75	**South's Gonna Do It**...Charlie Daniels Band
18/82	**Southern Cross**...Crosby, Stills & Nash
23/01	**Southern Hospitality**...Ludacris
1/77	**Southern Nights**...Glen Campbell
15/64	**Southtown, U.S.A.**...Dixiebelles
2/89	**Sowing The Seeds Of Love**...Tears For Fears
30/83	**Space Age Love Song**...Flock Of Seagulls
22/01	**Space Between**...Dave Matthews Band
37/97	**Space Jam**...Quad City DJ's
15/73	**Space Oddity**...David Bowie
4/73	**Space Race**...Billy Preston
23/72	**Spaceman**...Nilsson
40/85	**Spanish Eddie**...Laura Branigan
15/66	**Spanish Eyes**...Al Martino
27/66	**Spanish Flea**...Herb Alpert
	Spanish Harlem
10/61	Ben E. King
2/71	Aretha Franklin
31/62	**Spanish Lace**...Gene McDaniels
	(Speak Softly Love) ..see: Love Theme From The Godfather
14/72	**Speak To The Sky**...Rick Springfield
38/69	**Special Delivery**...1910 Fruitgum Co.
5/80	**Special Lady**...Ray, Goodman, & Brown
26/68	**Special Occasion**...Miracles
17/56	**Speedoo**...Cadillacs
6/62	**Speedy Gonzales**...Pat Boone
39/91	**Spend My Life**...Slaughter
21/99	**Spend My Life With You**...Eric Benét
32/92	**Spending My Time**...Roxette
40/83	**Spice Of Life**...Manhattan Transfer
18/97	**Spice Up Your Life**...Spice Girls
3/74	**Spiders & Snakes**...Jim Stafford
18A/96	**Spiderwebs**...No Doubt
7/86	**Spies Like Us**...Paul McCartney
3/70	**Spill The Wine**...Eric Burdon & War
2/69	**Spinning Wheel**...Blood, Sweat & Tears
40/66	**Spinout**...Elvis Presley
23/70	**Spirit In The Dark**...Aretha Franklin
40/77	**Spirit In The Night**...Manfred Mann's Earth Band
3/70	**Spirit In The Sky**...Norman Greenbaum
35/75	**Spirit Of The Boogie**...Kool & The Gang
11/82	**Spirits In The Material World**...Police
27/98	**Splackavellie**...Pressha
3/58	**Splish Splash**...Bobby Darin
	Spooky
3/68	Classics IV
17/79	Atlanta Rhythm Section
32A/88	**Spotlight**...Madonna
39/77	**Spring Rain**...Silvetti
37/76	**Springtime Mama**...Henry Gross
16/88	**Spy In The House Of Love**...Was (Not Was)
16/76	**Squeeze Box**...Who

POS/YR	RECORD TITLE. . . ARTIST
19/98	**Still A G Thang**...Snoop Dogg
40/76	**Still Crazy After All These Years**...Paul Simon
11/02	**Still Fly**...Big Tymers
	Still In Love ..see: Can'tcha Say (You Believe In Me)
22/82	**Still In Saigon**...Charlie Daniels Band
24/98	**Still Not A Player**...Big Punisher
28/81	**Still Right Here In My Heart**...Pure Prairie League
5/76	**Still The One**...Orleans
4/78	**Still The Same**...Bob Seger
19/82	**Still They Ride**...Journey
11/70	**Still Water (Love)**...Four Tops
33/02	**Stingy**...Ginuwine
12/73	**Stir It Up**...Johnny Nash
27/02	**Stole**...Kelly Rowland
7/80	**Stomp!**...Brothers Johnson
36/78	**Stone Blue**...Foghat
40/82	**Stone Cold**...Rainbow
34/91	**Stone Cold Gentleman**...Ralph Tresvant
10/87	**Stone Love**...Kool & The Gang
7/70	**Stoned Love**...Supremes
30/73	**Stoned Out Of My Mind**...Chi-Lites
3/68	**Stoned Soul Picnic**...5th Dimension
14/71	**Stones**...Neil Diamond
6/71	**Stoney End**...Barbra Streisand
2/58	**Stood Up**...Ricky Nelson
16/98	**Stop**...Spice Girls
9/74	**Stop And Smell The Roses**...Mac Davis
8/64	**Stop And Think It Over**...Dale & Grace
3/81	**Stop Draggin' My Heart Around**...Stevie Nicks (with Tom Petty)
	Stop! In The Name Of Love
1/65	Supremes
29/83	Hollies
39/71	**Stop, Look, Listen (To Your Heart)**...Stylistics
7/66	**Stop Stop Stop**...Hollies
36/62	**Stop The Music**...Shirelles
26/71	**Stop The War Now**...Edwin Starr
34/62	**Stop The Wedding**...Etta James
15/87	**Stop To Love**...Luther Vandross
	Stormy
5/68	Classics IV
32/79	Santana
23/71	**Story In Your Eyes**...Moody Blues
15/58	**Story Of My Life**...Marty Robbins
16/61	**Story Of My Love**...Paul Anka
28/59	**Story Of My Love**...Conway Twitty
16/55	**Story Untold**...Crew-Cuts
10/83	**Straight From The Heart**...Bryan Adams
39/81	**Straight From The Heart**...Allman Brothers Band
36/68	**Straight Life**...Bobby Goldsboro
15/78	**Straight On**...Heart
29/74	**Straight Shootin' Woman**...Steppenwolf
1/89	**Straight Up**...Paula Abdul
13/90	**Stranded**...Heart

POS/YR	RECORD TITLE. . . ARTIST
	Stranded In The Jungle
15/56	Cadets
18/56	Jayhawks
39/56	Gadabouts
21/88	**Strange But True**...Times Two
14/76	**Strange Magic**...Electric Light Orchestra
11/78	**Strange Way**...Firefall
10/01	**Stranger In My House**...Tamia
23/83	**Stranger In My House**...Ronnie Milsap
30/65	**Stranger In Town**...Del Shannon
30/84	**Stranger In Town**...Toto
	Stranger On The Shore
1/62	Mr. Acker Bilk
38/62	Andy Williams
1/66	**Strangers In The Night**...Frank Sinatra
8/67	**Strawberry Fields Forever**...Beatles
5/77	**Strawberry Letter 23**...Brothers Johnson
39/68	**Strawberry Shortcake**...Jay & The Techniques
3/83	**Stray Cat Strut**...Stray Cats
1/74	**Streak, The**...Ray Stevens
30/78	**Street Corner Serenade**...Wet Willie
22/97	**Street Dreams**...Nas
36/79	**Street Life**...Crusaders
12/91	**Street Of Dreams**...Nia Peeples
27/76	**Street Singin'**...Lady Flash
9/94	**Streets Of Philadelphia**...Bruce Springsteen
8/91	**Strike It Up**...Black Box
	String Along
39/60	Fabian
25/63	Rick Nelson
1/62	**Stripper, The**...David Rose
17/81	**Stroke, The**...Billy Squier
3/94	**Stroke You Up**...Changing Faces
4/58	**Stroll, The**...Diamonds
5/95	**Strong Enough**...Sheryl Crow
11/01	**Stronger**...Britney Spears
30/81	**Stronger Than Before**...Carole Bayer Sager
40/84	**Strung Out**...Steve Perry
7/84	**Strut**...Sheena Easton
22/75	**Struttin'**...Billy Preston
6/73	**Stuck In The Middle With You**...Stealers Wheel
1/60	**Stuck On You**...Elvis Presley
3/84	**Stuck On You**...Lionel Richie
1/86	**Stuck With You**...Huey Lewis
21/78	**Stuff Like That**...Quincy Jones
4/79	**Stumblin' In**...Suzi Quatro & Chris Norman
13/03	**Stunt 101**...G-Unit
14/58	**Stupid Cupid**...Connie Francis
24/96	**Stupid Girl**...Garbage
1/01	**Stutter**...Joe
18/72	**Suavecito**...Malo
39/65	**Subterranean Homesick Blues**...Bob Dylan
16/64	**Such A Night**...Elvis Presley
26/79	**Such A Woman**...Tycoon
11/65	**(Such An) Easy Question**...Elvis Presley
4/85	**Suddenly**...Billy Ocean
20/81	**Suddenly**...Olivia Newton-John & Cliff Richard

POS/YR	RECORD TITLE. . . ARTIST
9/83	**Suddenly Last Summer**...Motels
	Suddenly There's A Valley
9/55	Gogi Grant
13/55	Jo Stafford
20/55	Julius LaRosa
7/03	**Suga Suga**...Baby Bash
37/74	**Sugar Baby Love**...Rubettes
10/72	**Sugar Daddy**...Jackson 5
28/89	**Sugar Daddy**...Thompson Twins
36/84	**Sugar Don't Bite**...Sam Harris
32/65	**Sugar Dumpling**...Sam Cooke
35/87	**Sugar Free**...Wa Wa Nee
25/95	**Sugar Hill**...AZ
30/64	**Sugar Lips**...Al Hirt
5/58	**Sugar Moon**...Pat Boone
22/69	**Sugar On Sunday**...Clique
1/63	**Sugar Shack**...Jimmy Gilmer/Fireballs
	Sugar, Sugar
1/69	Archies
25/70	Wilson Pickett
	(also see: Suga Suga)
5/66	**Sugar Town**...Nancy Sinatra
9/85	**Sugar Walls**...Sheena Easton
1/58	**Sugartime**...McGuire Sisters
9/90	**Suicide Blonde**...INXS
21/69	**Suite: Judy Blue Eyes**...Crosby, Stills & Nash
	Sukiyaki
1/63	Kyu Sakamoto
3/81	Taste Of Honey
8/95	4 P.M. (For Positive Music)
4/79	**Sultans Of Swing**...Dire Straits
7/76	**Summer**...War
6/72	**Summer Breeze**...Seals & Crofts
3/99	**Summer Girls**...LFO
1/66	**Summer In The City**...Lovin' Spoonful
F/75	**Summer Madness**...Kool & The Gang
	Summer Night ..see: Song For A
5/78	**Summer Nights**...John Travolta & Olivia Newton-John
24/65	**Summer Nights**...Marianne Faithfull
	Summer Of '42 ..see: Theme From
5/85	**Summer Of '69**...Bryan Adams
	Summer Place ..see: Theme From A
14/68	**Summer Rain**...Johnny Rivers
30/90	**Summer Rain**...Belinda Carlisle
26/66	**Summer Samba (So Nice)**...Walter Wanderley
33/71	**Summer Sand**...Dawn
30/60	**Summer Set**...Monty Kelly
7/64	**Summer Song**...Chad & Jeremy
21/73	**Summer (The First Time)**...Bobby Goldsboro
	Summer Time ..see: In The Summertime
25/66	**Summer Wind**...Frank Sinatra
11/60	**Summer's Gone**...Paul Anka
4/91	**Summertime**...D.J. Jazzy Jeff & The Fresh Prince
10/66	**Summertime**...Billy Stewart

POS/YR	RECORD TITLE. . . ARTIST
	Summertime Blues
8/58	Eddie Cochran
14/68	Blue Cheer
27/70	Who
F/58	**Summertime Lies**...Four Preps
	Summertime, Summertime
26/58	Jamies
38/62	Jamies
13/66	**Sun Ain't Gonna Shine (Anymore)**...Walker Bros.
20/86	**Sun Always Shines On T.V.**...A-Ha
38/85	**Sun City**...Artists United Against Apartheid
18/65	**Sunday And Me**...Jay & The Americans
31/67	**Sunday For Tea**...Peter & Gordon
	Sunday Mornin'
30/68	Spanky & Our Gang
35/69	Oliver
9/67	**Sunday Will Never Be The Same**...Spanky & Our Gang
1/74	**Sundown**...Gordon Lightfoot
39/77	**Sunflower**...Glen Campbell
7/84	**Sunglasses At Night**...Corey Hart
2/66	**Sunny**...Bobby Hebb
14/66	**Sunny Afternoon**...Kinks
7/97	**Sunny Came Home**...Shawn Colvin
34/72	**Sunny Days**...Lighthouse
34/76	**Sunrise**...Eric Carmen
22/85	**Sunset Grill**...Don Henley
4/72	**Sunshine**...Jonathan Edwards
23/89	**Sunshine**...Dino
20/67	**Sunshine Girl**...Parade
13/65	**Sunshine, Lollipops And Rainbows**...Lesley Gore
5/68	**Sunshine Of Your Love**...Cream
1/74	**Sunshine On My Shoulders**...John Denver
1/66	**Sunshine Superman**...Donovan
13/70	**Super Bad**...James Brown
31/73	**Super Fly Meets Shaft**...John & Ernest
16/81	**Super Freak**...Rick James
36/98	**SuperThug (What What)**...Noreaga
8/73	**Superfly**...Curtis Mayfield
	(also see: Freddie's Dead)
15/03	**Superman**...Eminem
26/79	**Superman**...Herbie Mann
14/01	**Superman (It's Not Easy)**...Five For Fighting
5/75	**Supernatural Thing**...Ben E. King
30/88	**Supersonic**...J.J. Fad
2/71	**Superstar**...Carpenters
35/76	**Superstar**...Paul Davis
14/71	**Superstar - Jesus Christ Superstar**...Murray Head
18/71	**Superstar (Remember How You Got Where You Are)**...Temptations
1/73	**Superstition**...Stevie Wonder
31/88	**Superstitious**...Europe
8/89	**Superwoman**...Karyn White
11/01	**Superwoman**...Lil' Mo

POS/YR	RECORD TITLE. . . ARTIST
33/72	**Superwoman (Where Were You When I Needed You)**...Stevie Wonder
16/74	**Sure As I'm Sittin' Here**...Three Dog Night
9/66	**Sure Gonna Miss Her**...Gary Lewis
1/63	**Surf City**...Jan & Dean
7/63	**Surfer Girl**...Beach Boys
31/62	**Surfer's Stomp**...Mar-Kets
4/64	**Surfin' Bird**...Trashmen
14/62	**Surfin' Safari**...Beach Boys
	Surfin' U.S.A.
3/63	Beach Boys
36/74	Beach Boys
20/77	Leif Garrett
1/61	**Surrender**...Elvis Presley
38/71	**Surrender**...Diana Ross
6/89	**Surrender To Me**...Ann Wilson & Robin Zander
2/01	**Survivor**...Destiny's Child
11/68	**Susan**...Buckinghams
	Susie Darlin'
5/58	Robin Luke
35/62	Tommy Roe
3/64	**Suspicion**...Terry Stafford
13/79	**Suspicions**...Eddie Rabbitt
1/69	**Suspicious Minds**...Elvis Presley
1/85	**Sussudio**...Phil Collins
17/86	**Suzanne**...Journey
	Suzie-Q
27/57	Dale Hawkins
11/68	Creedence Clearwater Revival
27A/96	**Swallowed**...Bush
39/73	**Swamp Witch**...Jim Stafford
F/55	**Swanee**...Jaye P. Morgan
34/57	**Swanee River Rock (Talkin' 'Bout That River)**...Ray Charles
	S.W.A.T. ..see: Theme From
14/60	**Sway**...Bobby Rydell
	(Swayin' To The Music) ..see: Slow Dancin'
20/00	**Swear It Again**...Westlife
6/75	**Swearin' To God**...Frankie Valli
16/93	**Sweat (A La La La La Long)**...Inner Circle
	Sweet And Gentle
10/55	Alan Dale
12/55	Georgia Gibbs
7/71	**Sweet And Innocent**...Donny Osmond
19/81	**Sweet Baby**...Stanley Clarke/George Duke
13/68	**Sweet Blindness**...5th Dimension
4/69	**Sweet Caroline (Good Times Never Seemed So Good)**...Neil Diamond
7/69	**Sweet Cherry Wine**...Tommy James
1/88	**Sweet Child O' Mine**...Guns N' Roses
8/71	**Sweet City Woman**...Stampeders
28/69	**Sweet Cream Ladies, Forward March**...Box Tops
5/82	**Sweet Dreams**...Air Supply
13/96	**Sweet Dreams**...La Bouche
15/66	**Sweet Dreams**...Tommy McLain
1/83	**Sweet Dreams (Are Made of This)**...Eurythmics
36/75	**Sweet Emotion**...Aerosmith

POS/YR	RECORD TITLE. . . ARTIST
7/86	**Sweet Freedom**...Michael McDonald
6/71	**Sweet Hitch-Hiker**...Creedence Clearwater Revival
8/74	**Sweet Home Alabama**...Lynyrd Skynyrd
	Sweet Inspiration
18/68	Sweet Inspirations
37/72	Barbra Streisand (medley)
12/99	**Sweet Lady**...Tyrese
17/78	**Sweet Life**...Paul Davis
2/58	**Sweet Little Sixteen**...Chuck Berry
5/76	**Sweet Love**...Commodores
8/86	**Sweet Love**...Anita Baker
36/79	**Sweet Lui-Louise**...Ironhorse
7/71	**Sweet Mary**...Wadsworth Mansion
40/75	**Sweet Maxine**...Doobie Brothers
4/60	**Sweet Nothin's**...Brenda Lee
7/56	**Sweet Old Fashioned Girl**...Teresa Brewer
8/66	**Sweet Pea**...Tommy Roe
27/94	**Sweet Potatoe Pie**...Domino
9/72	**Sweet Seasons**...Carole King
20/87	**Sweet Sixteen**...Billy Idol
2/67	**Sweet Soul Music**...Arthur Conley
33/75	**Sweet Sticky Thing**...Ohio Players
13/75	**Sweet Surrender**...John Denver
15/72	**Sweet Surrender**...Bread
28/98	**Sweet Surrender**...Sarah McLachlan
5/68	**(Sweet Sweet Baby) Since You've Been Gone**...Aretha Franklin
10/66	**Sweet Talkin' Guy**...Chiffons
17/78	**Sweet Talkin' Woman**...Electric Light Orchestra
	Sweet Thing
5/76	Rufus Feat. Chaka Khan
28/93	Mary J. Blige
26/82	**Sweet Time**...REO Speedwagon
33/73	**Sweet Understanding Love**...Four Tops
40/64	**Sweet William**...Millie Small
29/66	**Sweet Woman Like You**...Joe Tex
9/59	**Sweeter Than You**...Ricky Nelson
18/95	**Sweetest Days**...Vanessa Williams
5/86	**Sweetest Taboo**...Sade
7/82	**Sweetest Thing (I've Ever Known)**...Juice Newton
32/67	**Sweetest Thing This Side Of Heaven**...Chris Bartley
10/81	**Sweetheart**...Franke & The Knockouts
16/61	**Sweets For My Sweet**...Drifters
19/84	**Swept Away**...Diana Ross
6/98	**Swing My Way**...K.P. & Envyi
11/90	**Swing The Mood (medley)**...Jive Bunny & the Mastermixers
39/60	**Swingin' On A Rainbow**...Frankie Avalon
13/62	**Swingin' Safari**...Billy Vaughn
5/60	**Swingin' School**...Bobby Rydell
23/58	**Swingin' Shepherd Blues**...Moe Koffman Quartette
38/63	**Swinging On A Star**...Big Dee Irwin/Little Eva
17/77	**Swingtown**...Steve Miller Band
26/61	**Switch-A-Roo**...Hank Ballard

POS/YR	RECORD TITLE. . . ARTIST
5/72	**Sylvia's Mother**...Dr. Hook
38/88	**Symptoms Of True Love**...Tracie Spencer
16/83	**Synchronicity II**...Police
37/76	**(System Of) Doctor Tarr And Professor Fether**...Alan Parsons Project

T

POS/YR	RECORD TITLE. . . ARTIST
30/92	**T.L.C.**...Linear
24/60	**T.L.C. Tender Love And Care**...Jimmie Rodgers
1/74	**TSOP (The Sound Of Philadelphia)**...MFSB feat. The Three Degrees
23/60	**Ta Ta**...Clyde McPhatter
8/82	**Tainted Love**...Soft Cell
1/95	**Take A Bow**...Madonna
3/78	**Take A Chance On Me**...Abba
2/69	**Take A Letter Maria**...R.B. Greaves
15/80	**Take A Little Rhythm**...Ali Thomson
30/72	**Take A Look Around**...Temptations
16/59	**Take A Message To Mary**...Everly Brothers
12/00	**Take A Picture**...Filter
20/69	**Take Care Of Your Homework**...Johnnie Taylor
25/61	**Take Five**...Dave Brubeck Quartet
	Take Good Care Of Her
7/61	Adam Wade
F/74	Elvis Presley
	Take Good Care Of My Baby
1/61	Bobby Vee
33/68	Bobby Vinton
10/82	**Take It Away**...Paul McCartney
12/72	**Take It Easy**...Eagles
24/86	**Take It Easy**...Andy Taylor
10/82	**Take It Easy On Me**...Little River Band
33/76	**Take It Like A Man**...Bachman-Turner Overdrive
5/81	**Take It On The Run**...REO Speedwagon
4/76	**Take It To The Limit**...Eagles
34/97	**Take It To The Streets**...Rampage
16/65	**Take Me Back**...Little Anthony & The Imperials
18/82	**Take Me Down**...Alabama
38/68	**Take Me For A Little While**...Vanilla Fudge
7/86	**Take Me Home**...Phil Collins
8/79	**Take Me Home**...Cher
2/71	**Take Me Home, Country Roads**...John Denver
4/86	**Take Me Home Tonight**...Eddie Money
11/75	**Take Me In Your Arms (Rock Me)**...Doobie Brothers
14/99	**Take Me There**...BLACKstreet & Mya
14/83	**Take Me To Heart**...Quarterflash
26/79	**Take Me To The River**...Talking Heads
25/85	**Take Me With U**...Prince
1/86	**Take My Breath Away**...Berlin
17/81	**Take My Heart (You Can Have It If You Want It)**...Kool & The Gang
16/82	**Take Off**...Bob & Doug McKenzie
1/85	**Take On Me**...A-Ha

POS/YR	RECORD TITLE. . . ARTIST
10/79	**Take The Long Way Home**...Supertramp
11/76	**Take The Money And Run**...Steve Miller
8/63	**Take These Chains From My Heart**...Ray Charles
20/92	**Take This Heart**...Richard Marx
29/92	**Take Time**...Chris Walker
11/68	**Take Time To Know Her**...Percy Sledge
26/01	**Take You Out**...Luther Vandross
3/80	**Take Your Time (Do It Right)**...S.O.S. Band
32/86	**Taken In**...Mike + The Mechanics
21A/97	**Takes A Little Time**...Amy Grant
12/74	**Takin' Care Of Business**...Bachman-Turner Overdrive
13/76	**Takin' It To The Streets**...Doobie Brothers
11/99	**Taking Everything**...Gerald Levert
7/64	**Talk Back Trembling Lips**...Johnny Tillotson
9/87	**Talk Dirty To Me**...Poison
19/89	**Talk It Over**...Grayson Hugh
15/67	**Talk Talk**...Music Machine
34/60	**Talk That Talk**...Jackie Wilson
4/86	**Talk To Me**...Stevie Nicks
21/87	**Talk To Me**...Chico DeBarge
38/59	**Talk To Me**...Frank Sinatra
	Talk To Me, Talk To Me
20/58	Little Willie John
11/63	Sunny & The Sunglows
15/57	**Talkin' To The Blues**...Jim Lowe
12/64	**Talking About My Baby**...Impressions
3/84	**Talking In Your Sleep**...Romantics
18/78	**Talking In Your Sleep**...Crystal Gayle
27/72	**Talking Loud And Saying Nothing**...James Brown
25/88	**Tall Cool One**...Robert Plant
	Tall Cool One
36/59	Wailers
38/64	Wailers
	Tall Oak Tree ..see: (There Was A)
7/59	**Tall Paul**...Annette
6/59	**Tallahassee Lassie**...Freddy Cannon
	Tammy
1/57	Debbie Reynolds
5/57	Ames Brothers
18/76	**Tangerine**...Salsoul Orchestra
31/75	**Tangled Up In Blue**...Bob Dylan
34/68	**Tapioca Tundra**...Monkees
38/66	**Tar And Cement**...Verdelle Smith
13/86	**Tarzan Boy**...Baltimora
7/65	**Taste Of Honey**...Herb Alpert
18/72	**Taurus**...Dennis Coffey
24/72	**Taxi**...Harry Chapin
7/58	**Tea For Two**...Tommy Dorsey (Cha Cha)
	Teach Me Tonight
2/55	DeCastro Sisters
15/55	Jo Stafford
25/62	George Maharis
16/70	**Teach Your Children**...Crosby, Stills, Nash & Young
21/58	**Teacher, Teacher**...Johnny Mathis

POS/YR	RECORD TITLE. . .ARTIST
25/84	**Teacher Teacher**...38 Special
31/61	**Tear, A**...Gene McDaniels
23/59	**Tear Drop**...Santo & Johnny
20/57	**Tear Drops**...Lee Andrews
5/56	**Tear Fell**...Teresa Brewer
15/76	**Tear The Roof Off The Sucker (Give Up The Funk)**...Parliament
15A/98	**Tearin' Up My Heart**...*NSYNC
37/84	**Tears**...John Waite
20/64	**Tears And Roses**...Al Martino
2/92	**Tears In Heaven**...Eric Clapton
1/70	**Tears Of A Clown**...Miracles
4/58	**Tears On My Pillow**...Little Anthony & The Imperials
39/59	**Teasin'**...Quaker City Boys
17/60	**Teddy**...Connie Francis
40/76	**Teddy Bear**...Red Sovine
	(also see: Let Me Be Your)
32/73	**Teddy Bear Song**...Barbara Fairchild
	Teen Age ..also see: Teenage
2/57	**Teen-Age Crush**...Tommy Sands
5/62	**Teen Age Idol**...Rick Nelson
	Teen Age Prayer
6/56	Gale Storm
19/56	Gloria Mann
1/60	**Teen Angel**...Mark Dinning
4/59	**Teen Beat**...Sandy Nelson
29/59	**Teen Commandments**...Paul Anka-Geo. Hamilton IV-Johnny Nash
	Teenage Queen ..see: Ballad Of
5/59	**Teenager In Love**...Dion & The Belmonts
2/57	**Teenager's Romance**...Ricky Nelson
9/83	**Telefone (Long Distance Love Affair)**...Sheena Easton
7/77	**Telephone Line**...Electric Light Orchestra
18/77	**Telephone Man**...Meri Wilson
39/01	**Tell Her**...Lonestar
1/83	**Tell Her About It**...Billy Joel
	Tell Her No
6/65	Zombies
27/83	Juice Newton
40/73	**Tell Her She's Lovely**...El Chicano
4/63	**Tell Him**...Exciters
8/59	**Tell Him No**...Travis & Bob
17/70	**Tell It All Brother**...Kenny Rogers & The First Edition
	Tell It Like It Is
2/67	Aaron Neville
8/81	Heart
33/64	**Tell It On The Mountain**...Peter, Paul & Mary
7/88	**Tell It To My Heart**...Taylor Dayne
10/67	**Tell It To The Rain**...4 Seasons
7/60	**Tell Laura I Love Her**...Ray Peterson
23/68	**Tell Mama**...Etta James
5/95	**Tell Me**...Groove Theory
18/96	**Tell Me**...Dru Hill
22/62	**Tell Me**...Dick & DeeDee
21/74	**Tell Me A Lie**...Sami Jo

POS/YR	RECORD TITLE. . .ARTIST
2/99	**Tell Me It's Real**...K-Ci & JoJo
31/90	**Tell Me Something**...Indecent Obsession
3/74	**Tell Me Something Good**...Rufus
37/67	**Tell Me To My Face**...Keith
33/82	**Tell Me Tomorrow**...Smokey Robinson
6/92	**Tell Me What You Want Me To Do**...Tevin Campbell
28/03	**Tell Me (What's Goin' On)**...Smilez & Southstar
31/95	**Tell Me When**...Human League
9/90	**Tell Me Why**...Exposé
13/64	**Tell Me Why**...Bobby Vinton
18/61	**Tell Me Why**...Belmonts
33/66	**Tell Me Why**...Elvis Presley
24/64	**Tell Me (You're Coming Back)**...Rolling Stones
1/62	**Telstar**...Tornadoes
39/70	**Temma Harbour**...Mary Hopkin
39/91	**Temple Of Love**...Harriet
6/91	**Temptation**...Corina
27/61	**Temptation**...Everly Brothers
15/71	**Temptation Eyes**...Grass Roots
	Ten Commandments ..see: Teen Commandments
22/58	**Ten Commandments Of Love**...Harvey & The Moonglows
38/84	**10-9-8**...Face To Face
26/02	**Ten Rounds With José Cuervo**...Tracy Byrd
25/83	**Tender Is The Night**...Jackson Browne
10/86	**Tender Love**...Force M.D.'s
	Tender, Love and Care ..see: T.L.C.
14/90	**Tender Lover**...Babyface
	Tender Trap ..see: (Love Is)
31/85	**Tender Years**...John Cafferty
31/61	**Tenderly**...Bert Kaempfert
27/85	**Tenderness**...General Public
6/92	**Tennessee**...Arrested Development
23/70	**Tennessee Bird Walk**...Jack Blanchard & Misty Morgan
35/64	**Tennessee Waltz**...Sam Cooke
	Tequila
1/58	Champs
20/58	Eddie Platt
	Testify ..see: (I Wanna)
1/00	**Thank God I Found You**...Mariah Carey With Joe & 98°
1/75	**Thank God I'm A Country Boy**...John Denver
22/78	**Thank God It's Friday**...Love & Kisses
2A/98	**Thank U**...Alanis Morissette
3/01	**Thankyou**...Dido
21/95	**Thank You**...Boyz II Men
1/70	**Thank You (Falettinme Be Mice Elf Agin)**...Sly & The Family Stone
25/78	**Thank You For Being A Friend**...Andrew Gold
35/64	**Thank You Girl**...Beatles
16/59	**Thank You Pretty Baby**...Brook Benton
32/88	**Thanks For My Child**...Cheryl Pepsii Riley
37/74	**Thanks For Saving My Life**...Billy Paul
16/87	**That Ain't Love**...REO Speedwagon

POS/YR	RECORD TITLE. . .ARTIST
7/99	**That Don't Impress Me Much**...Shania Twain
4/82	**That Girl**...Stevie Wonder
20/96	**That Girl**...Maxi Priest
22/80	**That Girl Could Sing**...Jackson Browne
	(That Kiss!) ..see: Eso Beso
6/73	**That Lady**...Isley Brothers
20/64	**That Lucky Old Sun**...Ray Charles
	That Old Black Magic
13/55	Sammy Davis, Jr.
18/58	Louis Prima & Keely Smith
21/61	Bobby Rydell
21/81	**That Old Song**...Ray Parker Jr.
28/62	**That Stranger Used To Be My Girl**...Trade Martin
12/63	**That Sunday, That Summer**...Nat King Cole
5s/02	**That Was Then**...Roy Jones Jr.
20/86	**That Was Then, This Is Now**...Monkees
12/85	**That Was Yesterday**...Foreigner
29/03	**That'd Be Alright**...Alan Jackson
	That'll Be The Day
1/57	Crickets
11/76	Linda Ronstadt
6/84	**That's All!**...Genesis
17/56	**That's All...**"Tennessee" Ernie Ford
3/55	**That's All I Want From You**...Jaye P. Morgan
16/56	**That's All There Is To That**...Nat "King" Cole/Four Knights
6/60	**That's All You Gotta Do**...Brenda Lee
40/63	**That's How Heartaches Are Made**...Baby Washington
39/58	**That's How Much I Love You**...Pat Boone
31/61	**That's It - I Quit - I'm Movin' On**...Sam Cooke
4/66	**That's Life**...Frank Sinatra
28/83	**That's Love**...Jim Capaldi
9/62	**That's Old Fashioned (That's The Way Love Should Be)**...Everly Brothers
3/77	**That's Rock 'N' Roll**...Shaun Cassidy
16/89	**That's The Way**...Katrina & The Waves
25/00	**That's The Way**...Jo Dee Messina
12/64	**That's The Way Boys Are**...Lesley Gore
27/72	**That's The Way I Feel About Cha**...Bobby Womack
1/75	**That's The Way (I Like It)**...KC & The Sunshine Band
10/71	**That's The Way I've Always Heard It Should Be**...Carly Simon
6/00	**That's The Way It Is**...Celine Dion
1/93	**That's The Way Love Goes**...Janet Jackson
7/69	**That's The Way Love Is**...Marvin Gaye
33/63	**That's The Way Love Is**...Bobby Bland
12/75	**That's The Way Of The World**...Earth, Wind & Fire
1/86	**That's What Friends Are For**...Dionne Warwick
27/61	**That's What Girls Are Made For**...Spinners
18/93	**That's What Love Can Do**...Boy Krazy
19/87	**That's What Love Is All About**...Michael Bolton
7/91	**That's What Love Is For**...Amy Grant

POS/YR	RECORD TITLE. . .ARTIST
35/64	**That's What Love Is Made Of**...Miracles
37/02	**That's When I Love You**...Phil Vassar
27/75	**That's When The Music Takes Me**...Neil Sedaka
29/70	**That's Where I Went Wrong**...Poppy Family
27/76	**That's Where The Happy People Go**...Trammps
13/59	**That's Why (I Love You So)**...Jackie Wilson
35/60	**Theme For Young Lovers**...Percy Faith
	Theme From A Summer Place
1/60	Percy Faith
16/65	Lettermen
28/62	**Theme From Ben Casey**...Valjean
18/73	**Theme From Cleopatra Jones**...Joe Simon
	Theme From Close Encounters
13/78	John Williams
25/78	Meco
39/61	**Theme From Dixie**...Duane Eddy
10/62	**Theme From Dr. Kildare (Three Stars Will Shine Tonight)**...Richard Chamberlain
	Theme From Exorcist ..see: Tubular Bells
2/81	**Theme From Greatest American Hero (Believe It Or Not)**...Joey Scarbury
10/81	**Theme From Hill Street Blues**...Mike Post
32/75	**Theme From Jaws (Main Title)**...John Williams
	Theme From Love Story
9/71	Andy Williams (Where Do I Begin)
13/71	Henry Mancini
31/71	Francis Lai
25/82	**(Theme From) Magnum P.I.**...Mike Post
1/76	**Theme From Mahogany (Do You Know Where You're Going To)**...Diana Ross
7/96	**Theme From Mission: Impossible**...Adam Clayton & Larry Mullen
	Theme from Moonlighting ..see: Moonlighting
32/80	**Theme From New York, New York**...Frank Sinatra
	Theme From Picnic ..see: Moonglow
	Theme From Pink Panther ..see: Pink Panther Theme
	Theme From Rocky ..see: Gonna Fly Now
1/71	**Theme From Shaft**...Isaac Hayes
21/71	**Theme From Summer Of '42**...Peter Nero
	Theme From Superfly ..see: Freddie's Dead
1/76	**Theme From S.W.A.T.**...Rhythm Heritage
10/60	**Theme From The Apartment**...Ferrante & Teicher
21/80	**Theme From The Dukes Of Hazzard (Good Ol' Boys)**...Waylon Jennings
	Theme From The Man With The Golden Arm ..see: Man With The Golden Arm
38/72	**Theme From The Men**...Isaac Hayes
39/56	**Theme From The Proud Ones**...Nelson Riddle
	Theme From The Three Penny Opera ..see: Mack The Knife
27/60	**Theme From The Unforgiven (The Need For Love)**...Don Costa
2/68	**Theme From Valley Of The Dolls**...Dionne Warwick

POS/YR	RECORD TITLE. . .ARTIST
21/78	**Theme From Which Way Is Up**...Stargard
35/78	**Themes From The Wizard Of Oz**...Meco
1/74	**Then Came You**...Dionne Warwicke & Spinners
6/63	**Then He Kissed Me**...Crystals
11/00	**Then The Morning Comes**...Smash Mouth
	Then You Can Tell Me Goodbye
6/67	Casinos
27/76	Glen Campbell (medley)
34/75	**There Goes Another Love Song**...Outlaws
	There Goes My Baby
2/59	Drifters
21/84	Donna Summer
	There Goes My Everything
20/67	Engelbert Humperdinck
F/71	Elvis Presley
19/58	**There Goes My Heart**...Joni James
29/03	**There Goes My Life**...Kenny Chesney
1/64	**There! I've Said It Again**...Bobby Vinton
20/68	**There Is**...Dells
11/67	**There Is A Mountain**...Donovan
	(There Is Love) ..see: Wedding Song
40/01	**There Is No Arizona**...Jamie O'Neal
32/73	**There It Is**...Tyrone Davis
33/59	**There Must Be A Way**...Joni James
22/85	**There Must Be An Angel (Playing With My Heart)**...Eurythmics
26/61	**There She Goes**...Jerry Wallace
31/01	**There She Goes**...Babyface
32/99	**There She Goes**...Sixpence None The Richer
23/60	**(There Was A) Tall Oak Tree**...Dorsey Burnette
36/68	**There Was A Time**...James Brown
31/92	**There Will Never Be Another Tonight**...Bryan Adams
33/66	**There Will Never Be Another You**...Chris Montez
18/74	**There Won't Be Anymore**...Charlie Rich
7/00	**There You Go**...P!nk
10/01	**There You'll Be**...Faith Hill
25/57	**(There'll Be) Peace In The Valley (For Me)**...Elvis Presley
1/86	**There'll Be Sad Songs (To Make You Cry)**...Billy Ocean
26/69	**There'll Come A Time**...Betty Everett
36/78	**There'll Never Be**...Switch
14/57	**There's A Gold Mine In The Sky**...Pat Boone
	There's A Kind Of Hush (All Over The World)
4/67	Herman's Hermits
12/76	Carpenters
3/61	**There's A Moon Out Tonight**...Capris
	(There's) Always Something There To Remind Me
27/70	R.B. Greaves
8/83	Naked Eyes
21/69	**There's Gonna Be A Showdown**...Archie Bell
34/67	**There's Got To Be A Word!**...Innocence
30/03	**(there's gotta be) More To Life**...Stacie Orrico
5/81	**(There's) No Gettin' Over Me**...Ronnie Milsap

POS/YR	RECORD TITLE. . .ARTIST
20/62	**There's No Other (Like My Baby)**...Crystals
8/54	**(There's No Place Like) Home For The Holidays**...Perry Como
	There's Nothing Stronger Than Our Love ..see: (I Believe)
10/58	**There's Only One Of You**...Four Lads
31/60	**There's Something On Your Mind**...Bobby Marchan
12/88	**There's The Girl**...Heart
36/98	**There's Your Trouble**...Dixie Chicks
21/99	**These Are The Times**...Dru Hill
1/66	**These Boots Are Made For Walkin'**...Nancy Sinatra
23/02	**These Days**...Rascal Flatts
1/86	**These Dreams**...Heart
	These Eyes
6/69	Guess Who?
16/69	Jr. Walker
30/96	**They Don't Care About Us**...Michael Jackson
7/98	**They Don't Know**...Jon B
8/84	**They Don't Know**...Tracey Ullman
5/75	**They Just Can't Stop It the (Games People Play)**...Spinners
35/97	**They Like It Slow**...H-Town
1/70	**(They Long To Be) Close To You**...Carpenters
25/92	**They Want EFX**...DAS EFX
3/66	**They're Coming To Take Me Away, Ha-Haaa!**...Napoleon XIV
	Thicker Than Water ..see: (Love Is)
6/90	**Thieves In The Temple**...Prince
	Thin Line Between Love & Hate
15/71	Persuaders
37/96	H-Town
3/62	**Things**...Bobby Darin
5/85	**Things Can Only Get Better**...Howard Jones
23/67	**Things I Should Have Said**...Grass Roots
16/69	**Things I'd Like To Say**...New Colony Six
4/91	**Things That Make You Go Hmmmm......** C + C Music Factory
5/77	**Things We Do For Love**...10 CC
29/97	**Things'll Never Change**...E-40
7/68	**Think**...Aretha Franklin
25/64	**Think**...Brenda Lee
28/90	**Think**...Information Society
33/60	**Think**...James Brown
20/80	**Think About Me**...Fleetwood Mac
30/66	**Think I'll Go Somewhere And Cry Myself To Sleep**...Al Martino
16/82	**Think I'm In Love**...Eddie Money
27/58	**Think It Over**...Crickets
34/78	**Think It Over**...Cheryl Ladd
9/84	**Think Of Laura**...Christopher Cross
11/61	**Think Twice**...Brook Benton
16/92	**Thinkin' Back**...Color Me Badd
12/98	**Thinkin' Bout It**...Gerald Levert
40/94	**Thinkin' Problem**...David Ball
12/89	**Thinking Of You**...Sa-Fire
18/73	**Thinking Of You**...Loggins & Messina

POS/YR	RECORD TITLE. . .ARTIST
22/97	**Thinking Of You**...Tony Toni Toné
14/75	**Third Rate Romance**...Amazing Rhythm Aces
23/80	**Third Time Lucky (First Time I Was A Fool)**...Foghat
39/97	**Thirty-Three**...Smashing Pumpkins
37/98	**32 Flavors**...Alana Davis
14/95	**This Ain't A Love Song**...Bon Jovi
24/60	**This Bitter Earth**...Dinah Washington
10/86	**This Could Be The Night**...Loverboy
1/65	**This Diamond Ring**...Gary Lewis
9/94	**This DJ**...Warren G
12/66	**This Door Swings Both Ways**...Herman's Hermits
12/59	**This Friendly World**...Fabian
9/69	**This Girl Is A Woman Now**...Gary Puckett
	This Guy's [Girl's] In Love With You
1/68	Herb Alpert
7/69	Dionne Warwick
24/74	**This Heart**...Gene Redding
3/91	**This House**...Tracie Spencer
F/95	**This House Is Not A Home**...Rembrandts
5/00	**This I Promise You**...*NSYNC
26/59	**This I Swear**...Skyliners
35A/95	**This Is A Call**...Foo Fighters
6/96	**This Is For The Lover In You**...Babyface
1/95	**This Is How We Do It**...Montell Jordan
11/80	**This Is It**...Kenny Loggins
35/78	**This Is Love**...Paul Anka
39/01	**This Is Me**...Dream
25/69	**This Is My Country**...Impressions
5s/03	**This Is My Party**...Fabolous
3/67	**This Is My Song**...Petula Clark
32/85	**This Is Not America**...David Bowie/Pat Metheny Group
1/03	**This Is The Night**...Clay Aiken
21/90	**This Is The Right Time**...Lisa Stansfield
18/87	**This Is The Time**...Billy Joel
39/77	**This Is The Way That I Feel**...Marie Osmond
24/97	**This Is Your Night**...Amber
7/98	**This Kiss**...Faith Hill
15/95	**This Lil' Game We Play**...Subway
32/65	**This Little Bird**...Marianne Faithfull
11/81	**This Little Girl**...Gary U.S. Bonds
21/63	**This Little Girl**...Dion
26/58	**This Little Girl Of Mine**...Everly Brothers
24/58	**This Little Girl's Gone Rockin'**...Ruth Brown
	This Magic Moment
16/60	Drifters
6/69	Jay & The Americans
33/82	**This Man Is Mine**...Heart
10/76	**This Masquerade**...George Benson
19/79	**This Night Won't Last Forever**...Michael Johnson
	This Old Heart Of Mine
12/66	Isley Brothers
10/90	Rod Stewart (with Ronald Isley)

POS/YR	RECORD TITLE. . .ARTIST
	This Ole House
1/54	Rosemary Clooney
26/54	Stuart Hamblen
7/89	**This One's For The Children**...New Kids On The Block
39/03	**This One's For The Girls**...Martina McBride
29/76	**This One's For You**...Barry Manilow
20/59	**This Should Go On Forever**...Rod Bernard
25/77	**This Song**...George Harrison
6/61	**This Time**...Troy Shondell
24/83	**This Time**...Bryan Adams
27/80	**This Time**...John Cougar
20/00	**This Time Around**...Hanson
7/89	**This Time I Know It's For Real**...Donna Summer
10/78	**This Time I'm In It For Love**...Player
1/92	**This Used To Be My Playground**...Madonna
6/75	**This Will Be**...Natalie Cole
23/84	**This Woman**...Kenny Rogers
38/72	**This World**...Staple Singers
13/03	**Thoia Thoing**...R. Kelly
3/00	**Thong Song**...Sisqó
6/63	**Those Lazy-Hazy-Crazy Days Of Summer**...Nat King Cole
9/61	**Those Oldies But Goodies (Remind Me Of You)**...Little Caesar & The Romans
2/68	**Those Were The Days**...Mary Hopkin
13/65	**Thou Shalt Not Steal**...Dick & DeeDee
13/92	**Thought I'd Died And Gone To Heaven**...Bryan Adams
5/02	**Thousand Miles**...Vanessa Carlton
3/60	**Thousand Stars**...Kathy Young
3A/98	**3 AM**...Matchbox 20
5/91	**3 A.M. Eternal**...KLF
	Three Bells
1/59	Browns
23/59	Dick Flood
35/61	**Three Hearts In A Tangle**...Roy Drusky
24/67	**Three Little Fishes (medley)**...Mitch Ryder
17/93	**Three Little Pigs**...Green Jell?
15/60	**Three Nights A Week**...Fats Domino
33/65	**Three O'Clock In The Morning**...Bert Kaempfert
	Three Penny Opera ..see: Mack The Knife
36/74	**Three Ring Circus**...Blue Magic
11/59	**Three Stars**...Tommy Dee with Carol Kay
	(Three Stars Will Shine Tonight) ..see: Theme From Dr. Kildare
1/78	**Three Times A Lady**...Commodores
19/80	**Three Times In Love**...Tommy James
28/64	**Three Window Coupe**...Rip Chords
31/03	**Three Wooden Crosses**...Randy Travis
15/70	**Thrill Is Gone**...B.B. King
4/84	**Thriller**...Michael Jackson
16/89	**Through The Storm**...Aretha Franklin & Elton John
15/04	**Through The Wire**...Kanye West
13/82	**Through The Years**...Kenny Rogers

POS/YR	RECORD TITLE. . .ARTIST
4/86	**Throwing It All Away**...Genesis
22/94	**thuggish-ruggish-Bone**...Bone Thugs-N-Harmony
19/02	**Thugz Mansion**...2Pac
17/72	**Thunder And Lightning**...Chi Coltrane
38/77	**Thunder In My Heart**...Leo Sayer
9/78	**Thunder Island**...Jay Ferguson
25/66	**Thunderball**...Tom Jones
14/90	**Tic-Tac-Toe**...Kyper
1/65	**Ticket To Ride**...Beatles
1/81	**Tide Is High**...Blondie
1/73	**Tie A Yellow Ribbon Round The Ole Oak Tree**...Dawn Feat. Tony Orlando
3/63	**Tie Me Kangaroo Down, Sport**...Rolf Harris
38/83	**Tied Up**...Olivia Newton-John
37/60	**Ties That Bind**...Brook Benton
3/59	**Tiger**...Fabian
11/72	**Tight Rope**...Leon Russell
1/68	**Tighten Up**...Archie Bell
7/70	**Tighter, Tighter**...Alive & Kicking
12/59	**Tijuana Jail**...Kingston Trio
38/66	**Tijuana Taxi**...Herb Alpert
11/96	**Til I Hear It From You**...Gin Blossoms
4/59	**('Til) I Kissed You**...Everly Brothers
29/85	**'Til My Baby Comes Home**...Luther Vandross
32/75	**Til The World Ends**...Three Dog Night
31/95	**'Til You Do Me Right**...After 7
	Till
22/57	Roger Williams
14/62	Angels
27/68	Vogues
26/62	**Till Death Do Us Part**...Bob Braun
25/88	**Till I Loved You**...Barbra Streisand & Don Johnson
20/63	**Till Then**...Classics
30/59	**Till There Was You**...Anita Bryant
14/96	**Time**...Hootie & The Blowfish
15/81	**Time**...Alan Parsons Project
	Time After Time
1/84	Cyndi Lauper
6/98	Inoj
40/90	**Time After Time**...Timmy -T-
36/66	**Time After Time**...Chris Montez
23/93	**Time And Chance**...Color Me Badd
30/60	**Time And The River**...Nat King Cole
26/88	**Time And Tide**...Basia
2/83	**Time (Clock Of The Heart)**...Culture Club
32/90	**Time For Letting Go**...Jude Cole
32/74	**Time For Livin'**...Sly & The Family Stone
39/68	**Time For Livin'**...Association
	(Time For Us) ..see: Love Theme From Romeo & Juliet
11/68	**Time Has Come Today**...Chambers Brothers
1/73	**Time In A Bottle**...Jim Croce
6/64	**Time Is On My Side**...Rolling Stones
6/69	**Time Is Tight**...Booker T. & The M.G.'s
15/81	**Time Is Time**...Andy Gibb
7/91	**Time, Love And Tenderness**...Michael Bolton

POS/YR	RECORD TITLE. . .ARTIST
	Time Of My Life ..see: (I've Had)
3/69	**Time Of The Season**...Zombies
22/81	**Time Out Of Mind**...Steely Dan
7/78	**Time Passages**...Al Stewart
33/73	**Time To Get Down**...O'Jays
	Time To Love-A Time To Cry ..see: Petite Fleur
18/84	**Time Will Reveal**...DeBarge
5/66	**Time Won't Let Me**...Outsiders
7/76	**Times Of Your Life**...Paul Anka
17/71	**Timothy**...Buoys
4/74	**Tin Man**...America
5/55	**Tina Marie**...Perry Como
17/68	**Tip-Toe Thru' The Tulips With Me**...Tiny Tim
11/71	**Tired Of Being Alone**...Al Green
8/80	**Tired Of Toein' The Line**...Rocky Burnette
6/65	**Tired Of Waiting For You**...Kinks
	To ..also see: Too / Two
26/62	**To A Sleeping Beauty**...Jimmy Dean
5/84	**To All The Girls I've Loved Before**...Julio Iglesias & Willie Nelson
6/86	**To Be A Lover**...Billy Idol
22/58	**To Be Loved**...Jackie Wilson
1/92	**To Be With You**...Mr. Big
21/60	**To Each His Own**...Platters
29/68	**To Give (The Reason I Live)**...Frankie Valli
	To Know You [Him] Is To Love You [Him]
1/58	Teddy Bears
24/65	Peter & Gordon
34/69	Bobby Vinton
38/73	**To Know You Is To Love You**...B.B. King
	To Love Somebody
17/67	Bee Gees
11/92	Michael Bolton
11A/98	**To Love You More**...Celine Dion
1/67	**To Sir With Love**...Lulu
35/69	**To Susan On The West Coast Waiting**...Donovan
25/57	**To The Aisle**...Five Satins
17/75	**To The Door Of The Sun (Alle Porte Del Sole)**...Al Martino
25/56	**To The Ends Of The Earth**...Nat "King" Cole
	To The Moon And Back
37/97	Savage Garden
24/98	Savage Garden
27/56	**To You, My Love**...Nick Noble
20/71	**Toast And Marmalade For Tea**...Tin Tin
14/64	**Tobacco Road**...Nashville Teens
17/64	**Today**...New Christy Minstrels
39/63	**(Today I Met) The Boy I'm Gonna Marry**...Darlene Love
23/76	**Today's The Day**...America
6/61	**Together**...Connie Francis
18/81	**Together**...Tierra
1/98	**Together Again**...Janet Jackson
19/66	**Together Again**...Ray Charles
1/88	**Together Forever**...Rick Astley
35/91	**Together Forever**...Lisette Melendez
37/72	**Together Let's Find Love**...5th Dimension

POS/YR	RECORD TITLE. . . ARTIST
26/60	**Togetherness**...Frankie Avalon
20/63	**Tom Cat**...Rooftop Singers
1/58	**Tom Dooley**...Kingston Trio
5/90	**Tom's Diner**...D.N.A. Feat. Suzanne Vega
29/59	**Tomboy**...Perry Como
23/68	**Tomorrow**...Strawberry Alarm Clock
28A/95	**Tomorrow**...Silverchair
26/86	**Tomorrow Doesn't Matter Tonight**...Starship
39/88	**Tomorrow People**...Ziggy Marley
7/90	**Tonight**...New Kids On The Block
8/61	**Tonight**...Ferrante & Teicher
13/84	**Tonight**...Kool & The Gang
26/61	**Tonight (Could Be The Night)**...Velvets
16/83	**Tonight, I Celebrate My Love**...Peabo Bryson/Roberta Flack
15/61	**Tonight I Fell In Love**...Tokens
20/82	**Tonight I'm Yours (Don't Hurt Me)**...Rod Stewart
13/61	**Tonight My Love, Tonight**...Paul Anka
7/86	**Tonight She Comes**...Cars
36/96	**Tonight, Tonight**...Smashing Pumpkins
3/87	**Tonight, Tonight, Tonight**...Genesis
	Tonight You Belong To Me
4/56	Patience & Prudence
15/56	Lawrence Welk/Lennon Sisters
28/65	**Tonight's The Night**...Solomon Burke
39/60	**Tonight's The Night**...Shirelles
1/76	**Tonight's The Night (Gonna Be Alright)**...Rod Stewart
12/96	**Tonite's Tha Night**...Kris Kross
38/92	**Too Blind To See It**...Kym Sims
4/69	**Too Busy Thinking About My Baby**...Marvin Gaye
1/98	**Too Close**...Next
39/56	**Too Close For Comfort**...Eydie Gorme
10/92	**Too Funky**...George Michael
33/97	**Too Gone, Too Long**...En Vogue
	Too Hot
5/80	Kool & The Gang
24/96	Coolio
24/78	**Too Hot Ta Trot**...Commodores
5/85	**Too Late For Goodbyes**...Julian Lennon
12/90	**Too Late To Say Goodbye**...Richard Marx
2/72	**Too Late To Turn Back Now**...Cornelius Brothers & Sister Rose
5/92	**2 Legit 2 Quit**...Hammer
	Too Many Fish In The Sea
25/65	Marvelettes
24/67	Mitch Ryder (medley)
13/65	**Too Many Rivers**...Brenda Lee
8/91	**Too Many Walls**...Cathy Dennis
1/57	**Too Much**...Elvis Presley
9/98	**Too Much**...Spice Girls
39A/96	**Too Much**...Dave Matthews Band
1/79	**Too Much Heaven**...Bee Gees
35/67	**Too Much Of Nothing**...Peter, Paul & Mary
37/92	**Too Much Passion**...Smithereens
19/68	**Too Much Talk**...Paul Revere & The Raiders

POS/YR	RECORD TITLE. . . ARTIST
30/60	**Too Much Tequila**...Champs
9/81	**Too Much Time On My Hands**...Styx
1/78	**Too Much, Too Little, Too Late**...Johnny Mathis/Deniece Williams
5/83	**Too Shy**...Kajagoogoo
40/81	**Too Tight**...Con Funk Shun
13/69	**Too Weak To Fight**...Clarence Carter
13/72	**Too Young**...Donny Osmond
21/56	**Too Young To Go Steady**...Nat "King" Cole
30/78	**Took The Last Train**...David Gates
8/95	**Tootsee Roll**...69 Boyz
1/73	**Top Of The World**...Carpenters
27/91	**Top Of The World**...Van Halen
27/58	**Topsy I**...Cozy Cole
3/58	**Topsy II**...Cozy Cole
	Torero
18/58	Renato Carosone
21/58	Julius LaRosa
1A/98	**Torn**...Natalie Imbruglia
1/77	**Torn Between Two Lovers**...Mary MacGregor
39/59	**Torquay**...Fireballs
17/84	**Torture**...Jacksons
20/62	**Torture**...Kris Jensen
1/61	**Tossin' And Turnin'**...Bobby Lewis
	Total Eclipse Of The Heart
1/83	Bonnie Tyler
2/95	Nicki French
23/74	**Touch A Hand, Make A Friend**...Staple Singers
37/80	**Touch And Go**...Cars
9/98	**Touch It**...Monifah
3/69	**Touch Me**...Doors
19/74	**Touch Me**...Fancy
2/91	**Touch Me (All Night Long)**...Cathy Dennis
4/87	**Touch Me (I Want Your Body)**...Samantha Fox
1/73	**Touch Me In The Morning**...Diana Ross
14/96	**Touch Me Tease Me**...Case
16/81	**Touch Me When We're Dancing**...Carpenters
40/96	**Touch Myself**...T-Boz
9/87	**Touch Of Grey**...Grateful Dead
	Touch The Wind ..see: Eres Tu
	Tough ..also see: Tuff
22/85	**Tough All Over**...John Cafferty
32/03	**Tough Little Boys**...Gary Allan
5/61	**Tower Of Strength**...Gene McDaniels
13/62	**Town Without Pity**...Gene Pitney
1/89	**Toy Soldiers**...Martika
24/56	**Tra La La**...Georgia Gibbs
35/64	**Tra La La La Suzy**...Dean & Jean
2/69	**Traces**...Classics IV
	Tracks Of My Tears
16/65	Miracles
10/67	Johnny Rivers
25/76	Linda Ronstadt
9/69	**Tracy**...Cuff Links
13/60	**Tracy's Theme**...Spencer Ross
20/02	**Trade It All**...Fabolous
1/79	**Tragedy**...Bee Gees

	Tragedy
5/59	Thomas Wayne
10/61	Fleetwoods
39/85	**Tragedy**...John Hunter
23/80	**Train In Vain (Stand By Me)**...Clash
36/60	**Train Of Love**...Annette
27/74	**Train Of Thought**...Chér
38/79	**Train, Train**...Blackfoot
22/66	**Trains And Boats And Planes**...Dionne Warwick
26/67	**Tramp**...Otis Redding & Carla Thomas
38/75	**Trampled Under Foot**...Led Zeppelin
8/56	**Transfusion**...Nervous Norvus
35/61	**Transistor Sister**...Freddy Cannon
13/71	**Trapped By A Thing Called Love**...Denise LaSalle
2/70	**Travelin' Band**...Creedence Clearwater Revival
1/61	**Travelin' Man**...Ricky Nelson
25/03	**Travelin' Soldier**...Dixie Chicks
32/67	**Travlin' Man**...Stevie Wonder
16/56	**Treasure Of Love**...Clyde McPhatter
26/58	**Treasure Of Your Love**...Eileen Rodgers
3/71	**Treat Her Like A Lady**...Cornelius Brothers & Sister Rose
2/65	**Treat Her Right**...Roy Head
18/57	**Treat Me Nice**...Elvis Presley
18/81	**Treat Me Right**...Pat Benatar
18/94	**Tremor Christ**...Pearl Jam
35/96	**Tres Delinquentes**...Delinquent Habits
29/61	**Triangle**...Janie Grant
25/57	**Tricky**...Ralph Marterie
7/99	**Trippin'**...Total
36A/96	**Trippin' On A Hole In A Paper Heart**...Stone Temple Pilots
6/72	**Troglodyte (Cave Man)**...Jimmy Castor Bunch
9/82	**Trouble**...Lindsey Buckingham
35/75	**T-R-O-U-B-L-E**...Elvis Presley
35/88	**Trouble**...Nia Peeples
20/60	**Trouble In Paradise**...Crests
33/63	**Trouble Is My Middle Name**...Bobby Vinton
7/73	**Trouble Man**...Marvin Gaye
4/83	**True**...Spandau Ballet
3/86	**True Blue**...Madonna
40/90	**True Blue Love**...Lou Gramm
1/86	**True Colors**...Cyndi Lauper
32/87	**True Faith**...New Order
35/69	**True Grit**...Glen Campbell
	True Love
3/56	Bing Crosby & Grace Kelly
15/56	Jane Powell
13/88	**True Love**...Glenn Frey
21/63	**True Love Never Runs Smooth**...Gene Pitney
	True Love, True Love ..see: **(If You Cry)**
14/65	**True Love Ways**...Peter & Gordon
1/82	**Truly**...Lionel Richie
1/98	**Truly Madly Deeply**...Savage Garden
30/61	**Trust In Me**...Etta James
28/91	**Truth, The**...TAMI Show

23/69	**Try A Little Kindness**...Glen Campbell
	Try A Little Tenderness
25/67	Otis Redding
29/69	Three Dog Night
1/00	**Try Again**...Aaliyah
23/83	**Try Again**...Champaign
15/64	**Try It Baby**...Marvin Gaye
33/58	**Try The Impossible**...Lee Andrews
11/75	**Try To Remember (medley)**...Gladys Knight
12/66	**Try Too Hard**...Dave Clark Five
10/76	**Tryin' To Get The Feeling Again**...Barry Manilow
5/81	**Tryin' To Live My Life Without You**...Bob Seger
10/77	**Tryin' To Love Two**...William Bell
15/74	**Trying To Hold On To My Woman**...Lamont Dozier
40/70	**Trying To Make A Fool Of Me**...Delfonics
6/97	**Tubthumping**...Chumbawamba
7/74	**Tubular Bells**...Mike Oldfield
38/96	**Tucker's Town**...Hootie & The Blowfish
32/59	**Tucumcari**...Jimmie Rodgers
24/68	**Tuesday Afternoon (Forever Afternoon)**...Moody Blues
17/62	**Tuff**...Ace Cannon
10/86	**Tuff Enuff**...Fabulous Thunderbirds
30/80	**Tulsa Time**...Eric Clapton
	Tumbling Dice
7/72	Rolling Stones
32/78	Linda Ronstadt
30/58	**Tumbling Tumbleweeds**...Billy Vaughn
9/88	**Tunnel Of Love**...Bruce Springsteen
27/64	**Turn Around**...Dick & DeeDee
7/68	**Turn Around, Look At Me**...Vogues
3/70	**Turn Back The Hands Of Time**...Tyrone Davis
16/66	**Turn-Down Day**...Cyrkle
10/98	**Turn It Up [Remix]/Fire It Up**...Busta Rhymes
9/59	**Turn Me Loose**...Fabian
35/81	**Turn Me Loose**...Loverboy
2s/03	**Turn Me On**...Norah Jones
5/01	**Turn Off The Light**...Nelly Furtado
28/62	**Turn On Your Love Light**...Bobby Bland
	Turn The Beat Around
10/76	Vicki Sue Robinson
13/94	Gloria Estefan
13/78	**Turn To Stone**...Electric Light Orchestra
32/84	**Turn To You**...Go-Go's
1/65	**Turn! Turn! Turn!**...Byrds
29/85	**Turn Up The Radio**...Autograph
5/82	**Turn Your Love Around**...George Benson
36/80	**Turning Japanese**...Vapors
13/90	**Turtle Power!**...Partners In Kryme
36/58	**Turvy II**...Cozy Cole
20/75	**Tush**...ZZ Top
8/79	**Tusk**...Fleetwood Mac
	Tutti' Frutti
12/56	Pat Boone
17/56	Little Richard

POS/YR	RECORD TITLE. . .ARTIST
	Tweedlee Dee
2/55	Georgia Gibbs
14/55	LaVern Baker
	Twelfth Of Never
9/57	Johnny Mathis
8/73	Donny Osmond
20/67	**Twelve Thirty (Young Girls Are Coming To The Canyon)**...Mamas & The Papas
6/69	**Twenty-Five Miles**...Edwin Starr
4/70	**25 Or 6 To 4**...Chicago
17/63	**Twenty Four Hours From Tulsa**...Gene Pitney
10/99	**24/7**...Kevon Edmonds
15/63	**Twenty Miles**...Chubby Checker
1/03	**21 Questions**...50 Cent
31/64	**20-75**...Willie Mitchell
2/58	**26 Miles (Santa Catalina)**...Four Preps
38/81	**Twilight**...ELO
1/58	**Twilight Time**...Platters
31/88	**Twilight World**...Swing Out Sister
10/83	**Twilight Zone**...Golden Earring
30/80	**Twilight Zone/Twilight Tone**...Manhattan Transfer
14/65	**Twine Time**...Alvin Cash
39/66	**Twinkle Toes**...Roy Orbison
	Twist, The
1/60	Chubby Checker
28/60	Hank Ballard
1/62	Chubby Checker
16/88	Fat Boys/Chubby Checker (Yo, Twist!)
	(also see: Percolator)
	Twist And Shout
17/62	Isley Brothers
2/64	Beatles
23/86	Beatles
26/62	**Twist-Her**...Bill Black's Combo
25/63	**Twist It Up**...Chubby Checker
5/84	**Twist Of Fate**...Olivia Newton-John
	("Twist" Special) ..see: Rock-A-Hula Baby
9/62	**Twist, Twist Senora**...Gary (U.S.) Bonds
2/96	**Twisted**...Keith Sweat
22/62	**Twistin' Matilda (and the channel)**...Jimmy Soul
34/62	**Twistin' Postman**...Marvelettes
9/62	**Twistin' The Night Away**...Sam Cooke
27/60	**Twistin' U.S.A.**...Danny & The Juniors
	Twistin' White Silver Sands ..see: White Silver Sands
17/59	**Twixt Twelve And Twenty**...Pat Boone
4/97	**2 Become 1**...Spice Girls
11/56	**Two Different Worlds**...Don Rondo
16/71	**Two Divided By Love**...Grass Roots
19/78	**Two Doors Down**...Dolly Parton
6/63	**Two Faces Have I**...Lou Christie
33/75	**Two Fine People**...Cat Stevens
1/89	**Two Hearts**...Phil Collins
16/55	**Two Hearts**...Pat Boone
40/81	**Two Hearts**...Stephanie Mills/Teddy Pendergrass

POS/YR	RECORD TITLE. . .ARTIST
F/55	**Two Hound Dogs**...Bill Haley
38/83	**Two Less Lonely People In The World**...Air Supply
31/68	**Two Little Kids**...Peaches & Herb
18/55	**Two Lost Souls**...Perry Como & Jaye P. Morgan
7/63	**Two Lovers**...Mary Wells
10/88	**Two Occasions**...Deele
3/86	**Two Of Hearts**...Stacey Q
11/78	**Two Out Of Three Ain't Bad**...Meat Loaf
30/87	**Two People**...Tina Turner
30/80	**Two Places At The Same Time**...Ray Parker Jr.
7/93	**Two Princes**...Spin Doctors
38/84	**Two Sides Of Love**...Sammy Hagar
12/93	**Two Steps Behind**...Def Leppard
30/99	**Two Teardrops**...Steve Wariner
	2001 Space Odyssey ..see: Also Sprach Zarathustra
22/78	**Two Tickets To Paradise**...Eddie Money
32/63	**Two Tickets To Paradise**...Brook Benton
2/90	**Two To Make It Right**...Seduction
28/02	**Two Wrongs**...Wyclef Jean
2/86	**Typical Male**...Tina Turner

U

POS/YR	RECORD TITLE. . .ARTIST
	U ..also see: You
8/90	**U Can't Touch This**...M.C. Hammer
3/02	**U Don't Have To Call**...Usher
1/01	**U Got It Bad**...Usher
2/87	**U Got The Look**...Prince
7/99	**U Know What's Up**...Donell Jones
1/01	**U Remind Me**...Usher
33/94	**U Send Me Swingin'**...Mint Condition
28/94	**U Will Know**...BMU (Black Men United)
28/68	**U.S. Male**...Elvis Presley
15/01	**Ugly**...Bubba Sparxxx
37/02	**Uh Huh**...B2K
14/59	**Uh! Oh!**...Nutty Squirrels (Part 2)
16/92	**Uhh Ahh**...Boyz II Men
5/64	**Um, Um, Um, Um, Um, Um**...Major Lance
1/91	**Unbelievable**...EMF
36/99	**Unbelievable**...Diamond Rio
F/94	**Unbelievable**...Notorious B.I.G.
1/96	**Un-Break My Heart**...Toni Braxton
26/02	**Unbroken**...Tim McGraw
9/62	**Unchain My Heart**...Ray Charles
	Unchained Melody
1/55	Les Baxter
3/55	Al Hibbler
6/55	Roy Hamilton
29/55	June Valli
4/65	Righteous Brothers
13/90	Righteous Brothers
19/90	Righteous Brothers (new version)
1/71	**Uncle Albert/Admiral Halsey**...Paul & Linda McCartney
29/82	**Under Pressure**...Queen & David Bowie

POS/YR	RECORD TITLE. . . ARTIST
4/64	**Under The Boardwalk**...Drifters
2/92	**Under The Bridge**...Red Hot Chili Peppers
24/88	**Under The Milky Way**...Church
35/66	**Under Your Spell Again**...Johnny Rivers
1/77	**Undercover Angel**...Alan O'Day
9/83	**Undercover Of The Night**...Rolling Stones
3/02	**Underneath It All**...No Doubt
9/02	**Underneath Your Clothes**...Shakira
35/64	**Understand Your Man**...Johnny Cash
8/94	**Understanding**...Xscape
17/85	**Understanding**...Bob Seger
22/69	**Undun**...Guess Who
9/73	**Uneasy Rider**...Charlie Daniels
	Unforgettable
17/59	Dinah Washington
14/91	Natalie Cole with Nat "King" Cole
35/92	**Unforgiven, The**...Metallica
	(also see: Theme From)
33/70	**Ungena Za Ulimwengu (Unite The World)**...Temptations
7/68	**Unicorn, The**...Irish Rovers
4A/98	**Uninvited**...Alanis Morissette
24/76	**Union Man**...Cate Bros.
3/83	**Union Of The Snake**...Duran Duran
13/70	**United We Stand**...Brotherhood Of Man
23/94	**U.N.I.T.Y.**...Queen Latifah
39/68	**Unknown Soldier**...Doors
1/99	**Unpretty**...TLC
3/90	**Unskinny Bop**...Poison
21A/94	**Until I Fall Away**...Gin Blossoms
10/96	**Until It Sleeps**...Metallica
40/72	**Until It's Time For You To Go**...Elvis Presley
3/74	**Until You Come Back To Me (That's What I'm Gonna Do)**...Aretha Franklin
26/92	**Until Your Love Comes Back Around**...RTZ
25/00	**Untitled (How Does It Feel)**...D'Angelo
5/03	**Unwell**...Matchbox Twenty
	Up A Lazy River ..see: Lazy River
27/90	**Up All Night**...Slaughter
4/70	**Up Around The Bend**...Creedence Clearwater Revival
16/75	**Up In A Puff Of Smoke**...Polly Brown
12/97	**Up Jumps Da Boogie**...Magoo & Timbaland
25/70	**Up On Cripple Creek**...Band
	Up On The Roof
5/63	Drifters
28/79	James Taylor
10/70	**Up The Ladder To The Roof**...Supremes
13/62	**Uptown**...Crystals
7/67	**Up-Up And Away**...5th Dimension
1/82	**Up Where We Belong**...Joe Cocker & Jennifer Warnes
22/67	**Ups And Downs**...Paul Revere & The Raiders
1/80	**Upside Down**...Diana Ross
3/66	**Uptight (Everything's Alright)**...Stevie Wonder **(also see: Little Ole Man)**
25/77	**Uptown Festival (Motown Medley)**...Shalamar
3/83	**Uptown Girl**...Billy Joel

POS/YR	RECORD TITLE. . . ARTIST
4/81	**Urgent**...Foreigner
2/72	**Use Me**...Bill Withers
4/78	**Use Ta Be My Girl**...O'Jays
34/65	**Use Your Head**...Mary Wells
22/96	**Use Your Heart**...SWV
27/61	**Utopia**...Frank Gari

V

POS/YR	RECORD TITLE. . . ARTIST
8/82	**Vacation**...Go-Go's
9/62	**Vacation**...Connie Francis
9/87	**Valerie**...Steve Winwood
3/68	**Valleri**...Monkees
32/82	**Valley Girl**...Frank Zappa
8/57	**Valley Of Tears**...Fats Domino
	Valley Of The Dolls ..see: Theme From
5/88	**Valley Road**...Bruce Hornsby
9/85	**Valotte**...Julian Lennon
38A/94	**Vasoline**...Stone Temple Pilots
2/70	**Vehicle**...Ides Of March
35/86	**Velcro Fly**...ZZ Top
8/72	**Ventura Highway**...America
1/59	**Venus**...Frankie Avalon
	Venus
1/70	Shocking Blue
1/86	Bananarama
12/75	**Venus And Mars Rock Show**...Wings
7/62	**Venus In Blue Jeans**...Jimmy Clanton
19/89	**Veronica**...Elvis Costello
23/58	**Very Precious Love**...Ames Brothers
31/93	**Very Special**...Big Daddy Kane
	Very Special Love
20/58	Debbie Reynolds
23/58	Johnny Nash
11/74	**Very Special Love Song**...Charlie Rich
26/64	**Very Thought Of You**...Rick Nelson
16/92	**Vibeology**...Paula Abdul
31/79	**Victim Of Love**...Elton John
32/87	**Victim Of Love**...Bryan Adams
10/87	**Victory**...Kool & The Gang
19/98	**Victory**...Puff Daddy & The Family
40/79	**Video Killed The Radio Star**...Buggles
18/86	**Vienna Calling**...Falco
1/85	**View To A Kill**...Duran Duran
22/62	**Village Of Love**...Nathaniel Mayer
7/60	**Village Of St. Bernadette**...Andy Williams
12/72	**Vincent**...Don McLean
5s/02	**Virginity**...TG4
1/90	**Vision Of Love**...Mariah Carey
29/64	**Viva Las Vegas**...Elvis Presley
28/70	**Viva Tirado**...El Chicano
26/99	**Vivrant Thing**...Q-Tip
1/90	**Vogue**...Madonna
15/81	**Voice, The**...Moody Blues
33/04	**Voice Within**...Christina Aguilera
32/80	**Voices**...Cheap Trick

POS/YR	RECORD TITLE. . .ARTIST
8/85	**Voices Carry**...'Til Tuesday
25/89	**Voices Of Babylon**...Outfield
11/91	**Voices That Care**...Voices That Care
	Volare (Nel Blu Dipinto Di Blu)
1/58	Domenico Modugno
12/58	Dean Martin
4/60	Bobby Rydell
33/75	Al Martino
27/65	**Voodoo Woman**...Bobby Goldsboro
29/85	**Vox Humana**...Kenny Loggins
29/82	**Voyeur**...Kim Carnes

W

POS/YR	RECORD TITLE. . .ARTIST
36/74	**WOLD**...Harry Chapin
40/67	**Wack Wack**...Young Holt Trio
	Wade In The Water
19/66	Ramsey Lewis
37/67	Herb Alpert
2/62	**Wah Watusi**...Orlons
	(also see: El Watusi / Watusi)
8/88	**Wait**...White Lion
30/01	**Wait A Minute**...Ray-J
37/61	**Wait A Minute**...Coasters
23/57	**Wait And See**...Fats Domino
18/80	**Wait For Me**...Daryl Hall & John Oates
37/60	**Wait For Me**...Playmates
26/63	**Wait Til' My Bobby Gets Home**...Darlene Love
18/58	**Waitin' In School**...Ricky Nelson
19/81	**Waiting, The**...Tom Petty
2/81	**Waiting For A Girl Like You**...Foreigner
5/88	**Waiting For A Star To Fall**...Boy Meets Girl
13/91	**Waiting For Love**...Alias
27/91	**Waiting For That Day**...George Michael
8/99	**Waiting For Tonight**...Jennifer Lopez
13/82	**Waiting On A Friend**...Rolling Stones
1/84	**Wake Me Up Before You Go-Go**...Wham!
	Wake The Town And Tell The People
5/55	Les Baxter
13/55	Mindy Carson
12/76	**Wake Up Everybody**...Harold Melvin
	Wake Up Little Susie
1/57	Everly Brothers
27/82	Simon & Garfunkel
39/85	**Wake Up (Next To You)**...Graham Parker
7/58	**Walk, The**...Jimmy McCracklin
12/70	**Walk A Mile In My Shoes**...Joe South
23/65	**Walk Away**...Matt Monro
36/80	**Walk Away**...Donna Summer
9/76	**Walk Away From Love**...David Ruffin
	Walk Away Renee
5/66	Left Banke
14/68	Four Tops
	Walk Don't Run
2/60	Ventures
8/64	Ventures ('64)
10/56	**Walk Hand In Hand**...Tony Martin

POS/YR	RECORD TITLE. . .ARTIST
12/65	**Walk In The Black Forest**...Horst Jankowski
1/63	**Walk Like A Man**...4 Seasons
19/74	**Walk Like A Man**...Grand Funk
1/86	**Walk Like An Egyptian**...Bangles
7/86	**Walk Of Life**...Dire Straits
5/61	**Walk On By**...Leroy Van Dyke
	Walk On By
6/64	Dionne Warwick
30/69	Isaac Hayes
18/93	**Walk On The Ocean**...Toad The Wet Sprocket
16/73	**Walk On The Wild Side**...Lou Reed
21/62	**Walk On The Wild Side**...Jimmy Smith
	(also see: Wildside)
9/88	**Walk On Water**...Eddie Money
17/72	**Walk On Water**...Neil Diamond
7/61	**Walk Right Back**...Everly Brothers
1/63	**Walk Right In**...Rooftop Singers
7/89	**Walk The Dinosaur**...Was (Not Was)
	Walk This Way
10/77	Aerosmith
4/86	Run-D.M.C.
28/91	**Walk Through Fire**...Bad Company
6/03	**Walked Outta Heaven**...Jagged Edge
12/57	**Walkin' After Midnight**...Patsy Cline
	Walkin' In The Rain
23/64	Ronettes
19/70	Jay & The Americans
14/72	**Walkin' In The Rain With The One I Love**...Love Unlimited
	Walkin' In The Sand ..see: Remember
37/67	**Walkin' In The Sunshine**...Roger Miller
12/63	**Walkin' Miracle**...Essex
22/66	**Walkin' My Cat Named Dog**...Norma Tanega
2A/98	**Walkin' On The Sun**...Smash Mouth
26/63	**Walking Proud**...Steve Lawrence
29/58	**Walking Along**...Diamonds
9/89	**Walking Away**...Information Society
11/87	**Walking Down Your Street**...Bangles
13/91	**Walking In Memphis**...Marc Cohn
6/75	**Walking In Rhythm**...Blackbyrds
18/84	**Walking On A Thin Line**...Huey Lewis
14/92	**Walking On Broken Glass**...Annie Lennox
9/85	**Walking On Sunshine**...Katrina & The Waves
10/63	**Walking The Dog**...Rufus Thomas
	Walking The Floor ..see: I'm Walking
6/60	**Walking To New Orleans**...Fats Domino
32/80	**Walks Like A Lady**...Journey
2/62	**Wanderer, The**...Dion
3/80	**Wanderer, The**...Donna Summer
13/03	**Wanksta**...50 Cent
5/83	**Wanna Be Startin' Somethin'**...Michael Jackson
1/97	**Wannabe**...Spice Girls
28/93	**Wannagirl**...Jeremy Jordan
1/71	**Want Ads**...Honey Cone
7/87	**Wanted Dead Or Alive**...Bon Jovi
38/56	**Wanting You**...Roger Williams

POS/YR	RECORD TITLE. . . ARTIST
	War
1/70	Edwin Starr
8/86	Bruce Springsteen
17/84	**War Song**...Culture Club
17/66	**Warm And Tender Love**...Percy Sledge
13/92	**Warm It Up**...Kris Kross
39/78	**Warm Ride**...Rare Earth
25/62	**Warmed Over Kisses (Left Over Love)**...Brian Hyland
F/95	**Warning**...Notorious B.I.G.
7/84	**Warrior, The**...Scandal
24/90	**Was It Nothing At All**...Michael Damian
2/63	**Washington Square**...Village Stompers
37/81	**Wasn't That A Party**...Rovers
8/75	**Wasted Days And Wasted Nights**...Freddy Fender
9/82	**Wasted On The Way**...Crosby, Stills & Nash
13/02	**Wasting My Time**...Default
17/03	**Wat Da Hook Gon Be**...Murphy Lee
32/97	**Watch Me Do My Thing**...Immature
40/79	**Watch Out For Lucy**...Eric Clapton
30/67	**Watch The Flowers Grow**...4 Seasons
11/71	**Watching Scotty Grow**...Bobby Goldsboro
10/81	**Watching The Wheels**...John Lennon
40/61	**Water Boy**...Don Shirley Trio
2/95	**Water Runs Dry**...Boyz II Men
1/95	**Waterfalls**...TLC
4/59	**Waterloo**...Stonewall Jackson
6/74	**Waterloo**...Abba
10/63	**Watermelon Man**...Mongo Santamaria Band
25/61	**Watusi, The**...Vibrations
	(also see: El Watusi / Wah Watusi)
39/03	**Wave On Wave**...Pat Green
5A/98	**Way, The**...Fastball
18/77	**Way Down**...Elvis Presley
3/60	**Way Down Yonder In New Orleans**...Freddie Cannon
40/83	**Way He Makes Me Feel**...Barbra Streisand
12/92	**Way I Feel About You**...Karyn White
24/78	**Way I Feel Tonight**...Bay City Rollers
35/59	**Way I Walk**...Jack Scott
4/75	**Way I Want To Touch You**...Captain & Tennille
1/86	**Way It Is**...Bruce Hornsby
7/72	**Way Of Love**...Chér
20/94	**Way She Loves Me**...Richard Marx
	Way That You Love Me ..see: (It's Just)
	Way We Were
1/74	Barbra Streisand
11/75	Gladys Knight (medley)
	Way You Do The Things You Do
11/64	Temptations
20/78	Rita Coolidge
20/85	Daryl Hall John Oates/David Ruffin/Eddie Kendrick (medley)
6/90	UB40
13/61	**Way You Look Tonight**...Lettermen
6/01	**Way You Love Me**...Faith Hill
7/89	**Way You Love Me**...Karyn White

POS/YR	RECORD TITLE. . . ARTIST
1/88	**Way You Make Me Feel**...Michael Jackson
1/04	**Way You Move**...OutKast
24/58	**Ways Of A Woman In Love**...Johnny Cash
	Wayward Wind
1/56	Gogi Grant
28/56	Tex Ritter
5/67	**(We Ain't Got) Nothin' Yet**...Blues Magoos
	(We All Shine On) ..see: Instant Karma
14/88	**We All Sleep Alone**...Cher
2/79	**We Are Family**...Sister Sledge
4/78	**We Are The Champions (medley)**...Queen
1/85	**We Are The World**...USA for Africa
25/84	**We Are The Young**...Dan Hartman
5/85	**We Belong**...Pat Benatar
32/58	**We Belong Together**...Robert & Johnny
1/85	**We Built This City**...Starship
21/68	**We Can Fly**...Cowsills
	We Can Work It Out
1/66	Beatles
13/71	Stevie Wonder
8/99	**We Can't Be Friends**...Deborah Cox with R.L.
8/90	**We Can't Go Wrong**...Cover Girls
36/76	**We Can't Hide It Anymore**...Larry Santos
35/87	**We Connect**...Stacey Q
29/00	**We Danced**...Brad Paisley
1/89	**We Didn't Start The Fire**...Billy Joel
5/86	**We Don't Have To Take Our Clothes Off**...Jermaine Stewart
2/85	**We Don't Need Another Hero (Thunderdome)**...Tina Turner
7/80	**We Don't Talk Anymore**...Cliff Richard
20/92	**We Got A Love Thang**...Ce Ce Peniston
37/96	**We Got It**...Immature
6/59	**We Got Love**...Bobby Rydell
35/69	**We Got More Soul**...Dyke & The Blazers
2/82	**We Got The Beat**...Go-Go's
13/65	**We Gotta Get Out Of This Place**...Animals
20/71	**We Gotta Get You A Woman**...Runt
12/77	**We Just Disagree**...Dave Mason
26/99	**We Like To Party!**...Vengaboys
27/80	**We Live For Love**...Pat Benatar
39/64	**We Love You Beatles**...Carefrees
21/73	**We May Never Pass This Way (Again)**...Seals & Crofts
15/02	**We Thuggin**...Fat Joe
22/83	**We Two**...Little River Band
16/91	**We Want The Funk**...Gerardo
31/80	**We Were Meant To Be Lovers**...Photoglo
4/78	**We Will Rock You (medley)**...Queen
7/87	**We'll Be Together**...Sting
9/78	**We'll Never Have To Say Goodbye Again**...England Dan & John Ford Coley
4/64	**We'll Sing In The Sunshine**...Gale Garnett
14/68	**We're A Winner**...Impressions
7/77	**We're All Alone**...Rita Coolidge
35/90	**We're All In The Same Gang**...West Coast Rap All-Stars
1/73	**We're An American Band**...Grand Funk

POS/YR	RECORD TITLE. . .ARTIST
23/01	**What It Feels Like For A Girl**...Madonna
9/90	**What It Takes**...Aerosmith
13/99	**What It's Like**...Everlast
10/81	**What Kind Of Fool**...Barbra Streisand & Barry Gibb
17/62	**What Kind Of Fool Am I**...Sammy Davis Jr.
21/82	**What Kind Of Fool Am I**...Rick Springfield
	What Kind Of Fool Do You Think I Am
9/64	Tams
23/69	Bill Deal
18/62	**What Kind Of Love Is This**...Joey Dee
5/90	**What Kind Of Man Would I Be?**...Chicago
17/96	**What Kind Of Man Would I Be**...Mint Condition
40/65	**What Now**...Gene Chandler
	What Now My Love
14/66	Sonny & Cher
24/66	Herb Alpert
30/67	Mitch Ryder
	What The World Needs Now Is Love
7/65	Jackie DeShannon
8/71	Tom Clay (medley)
4s/03	American Idol Finalists
34/97	**What They Do**...Roots
22/03	**What Was I Thinkin'**...Dierks Bentley
9/63	**What Will Mary Say**...Johnny Mathis
8/01	**What Would You Do?**...City High
22A/95	**What Would You Say**...Dave Matthews Band
29/99	**What Ya Want**...Eve & Nokio
	What You ..also see: What Cha / Whatcha / What'Chu
8/89	**What You Don't Know**...Exposé
13/87	**What You Get Is What You See**...Tina Turner
5/86	**What You Need**...INXS
24/88	**What You See Is What You Get**...Brenda K. Starr
6/98	**What You Want**...Mase
9/79	**What You Won't Do For Love**...Bobby Caldwell
26/00	**What'Chu Like**...Da Brat
	What'd I Say
6/59	Ray Charles
30/61	Jerry Lee Lewis
24/62	Bobby Darin
21/64	Elvis Presley
	What's ..also see: Wot's
12/62	**What's A Matter Baby**...Timi Yuro
29/64	**What's Easy For Two Is So Hard For One**...Mary Wells
19/82	**What's Forever For**...Michael Murphey
	What's Going On
2/71	Marvin Gaye
12/87	Cyndi Lauper
27/01	Artists Against AIDS
3/99	**What's It Gonna Be?!**...Busta Rhymes
	What's Love Got To Do With It
1/84	Tina Turner
32/96	Warren G
2/02	**What's Luv?**...Fat Joe
8/94	**What's My Name?**...Snoop Doggy Dog

POS/YR	RECORD TITLE. . .ARTIST
3/65	**What's New Pussycat?**...Tom Jones
21/97	**What's On Tonight**...Montell Jordan
3/88	**What's On Your Mind (Pure Energy)**...Information Society
35/62	**What's So Good About Good-by**...Miracles
21/94	**What's The Frequency, Kenneth?**...R.E.M.
17/64	**What's The Matter With You Baby**...Marvin Gaye & Mary Wells
20/69	**What's The Use Of Breaking Up**...Jerry Butler
14/93	**What's Up**...4 Non Blondes
39/93	**What's Up Doc? (Can We Rock?)**... Fu-Schnickens w/Shaquille O'Neal
21/00	**What's Your Fantasy**...Ludacris
7/62	**What's Your Name**...Don & Juan
13/78	**What's Your Name**...Lynyrd Skynyrd
	Whatcha ..also see: What Cha / What You / What'Chu
23/98	**Whatcha Gone Do?**...Link
6/77	**Whatcha Gonna Do**...Pablo Cruise
9/71	**Whatcha See Is Whatcha Get**...Dramatics
16/97	**Whatever**...En Vogue
1/74	**Whatever Gets You Thru The Night**...John Lennon
	Whatever Lola Wants
6/55	Sarah Vaughan
12/55	Dinah Shore
	(Whatever Will Be, Will Be) ..see: Que Sera, Sera
38/74	**Whatever You Got, I Want**...Jackson 5
37/99	**Whatever You Say**...Martina McBride
3/94	**Whatta Man**...Salt 'N' Pepa with En Vogue
26/66	**Wheel Of Hurt**...Margaret Whiting
	Wheels
3/61	String-A-Longs
28/61	Billy Vaughn
5/58	**When**...Kalin Twins
	When A Man Loves A Woman
1/66	Percy Sledge
35/80	Bette Midler
1/91	Michael Bolton
22/99	**When A Woman's Fed Up**...R. Kelly
27/82	**When All Is Said And Done**...Abba
4/94	**When Can I See You**...Babyface
1/84	**When Doves Cry**...Prince
30/82	**When He Shines**...Sheena Easton
12/99	**When I Close My Eyes**...Shanice
6A/95	**When I Come Around**...Green Day
18/69	**When I Die**...Motherlode
	When I Fall In Love
7/62	Lettermen
23/93	Celine Dion & Clive Griffin
	(When I Get To Heaven) ..see: Old Man & Me
9/64	**When I Grow Up (To Be A Man)**...Beach Boys
8/92	**When I Look Into Your Eyes**...Firehouse
10/89	**When I Looked At Him**...Exposé
1/77	**When I Need You**...Leo Sayer

POS/YR	RECORD TITLE. . .ARTIST
31/99	**When I Said I Do**...Clint Black (w/Lisa Hartman Black)
29/57	**When I See You**...Fats Domino
1/89	**When I See You Smile**...Bad English
35/01	**When I Think About Angels**...Jamie O'Neal
1/86	**When I Think Of You**...Janet Jackson
20/80	**When I Wanted You**...Barry Manilow
15/67	**When I Was Young**...Animals
7/90	**When I'm Back On My Feet Again**...Michael Bolton
4/03	**When I'm Gone**...3 Doors Down
25/65	**When I'm Gone**...Brenda Holloway
1/89	**When I'm With You**...Sheriff
5/88	**When It's Love**...Van Halen
13/01	**When It's Over**...Sugar Ray
26/82	**When It's Over**...Loverboy
18/66	**When Liking Turns To Loving**...Ronnie Dove
19/56	**When My Blue Moon Turns To Gold Again**...Elvis Presley
14/56	**When My Dreamboat Comes Home**...Fats Domino
28/62	**When My Little Girl Is Smiling**...Drifters
11/93	**When She Cries**...Restless Heart
37/66	**(When She Needs Good Lovin') She Comes To Me**...Chicago Loop
11/81	**When She Was My Girl**...Four Tops
5/87	**When Smokey Sings**...ABC
10/62	**When The Boy In Your Arms (Is The Boy In Your Heart)**...Connie Francis
19/58	**When The Boys Talk About The Girls**...Valerie Carr
3/89	**When The Children Cry**...White Lion
2/86	**When The Going Gets Tough, The Tough Get Going**...Billy Ocean
14/86	**When The Heart Rules The Mind**...GTR
19/02	**When The Last Time**...Clipse
37/83	**When The Lights Go Out**...Naked Eyes
10/98	**When The Lights Go Out**...Five
23/64	**When The Lovelight Starts Shining Through His Eyes**...Supremes
11/90	**When The Night Comes**...Joe Cocker
18/56	**When The Saints Go Marching In**...Bill Haley
	When The White Lilacs Bloom Again
12/56	Helmut Zacharias
18/56	Billy Vaughn
38/94	**When We Dance**...Sting
10/61	**When We Get Married**...Dreamlovers
36/88	**When We Kiss**...Bardeux
23/88	**When We Was Fab**...George Harrison
	When Will I Be Loved
8/60	Everly Brothers
2/75	Linda Ronstadt
2/74	**When Will I See You Again**...Three Degrees
15/99	**When You Believe**...Whitney Houston & Mariah Carey
14/84	**When You Close Your Eyes**...Night Ranger
33/56	**When You Dance**...Turbans
12/96	**When You Love A Woman**...Journey

POS/YR	RECORD TITLE. . .ARTIST
32/72	**When You Say Love**...Sonny & Chér
35/64	**When You Walk In The Room**...Searchers
30/60	**When You Wish Upon A Star**...Dion & The Belmonts
22/97	**When You're Gone**...Cranberries
9/71	**When You're Hot, You're Hot**...Jerry Reed
6/79	**When You're In Love With A Beautiful Woman**...Dr. Hook
23/67	**When You're Young And In Love**...Marvelettes
35/85	**When Your Heart Is Weak**...Cock Robin
39/64	**Whenever He Holds You**...Bobby Goldsboro
5/78	**Whenever I Call You "Friend"**...Kenny Loggins
38/76	**Whenever I'm Away From You**...John Travolta
6/01	**Whenever, Wherever**...Shakira
32/60	**Where Are You**...Frankie Avalon
36/62	**Where Are You**...Dinah Washington
39/02	**Where Are You Going**...Dave Matthews Band
10/89	**Where Are You Now?**...Jimmy Harnen w/Synch
30A/93	**Where Are You Now**...Janet Jackson
	Where Did Our Love Go
1/64	Supremes
15/71	Donnie Elbert
33/71	**Where Did They Go, Lord**...Elvis Presley
1/88	**Where Do Broken Hearts Go**...Whitney Houston
	(Where Do I Begin) ..see: Theme From Love Story
38/86	**Where Do The Children Go**...Hooters
5/96	**Where Do You Go**...No Mercy
25/65	**Where Do You Go**...Cher
4/91	**Where Does My Heart Beat Now**...Celine Dion
8/97	**Where Have All The Cowboys Gone?**...Paula Cole
	Where Have All The Flowers Gone
21/62	Kingston Trio
26/65	Johnny Rivers
34/01	**Where I Come From**...Alan Jackson
29/00	**Where I Wanna Be**...Donell Jones
5/72	**Where Is The Love**...Roberta Flack & Donny Hathaway
8/03	**Where Is The Love?**...Black Eyed Peas
4/99	**Where My Girls At?**...702
3/60	**Where Or When**...Dion & The Belmonts
28/73	**Where Peaceful Waters Flow**...Gladys Knight
	Where The Action Is ..see: Action
35/01	**Where The Blacktop Ends**...Keith Urban
4/61	**Where The Boys Are**...Connie Francis
3/01	**Where The Party At**...Jagged Edge
20/01	**Where The Stars And Stripes And The Eagle Fly**...Aaron Tippin
13/87	**Where The Streets Have No Name**...U2
23/59	**Where Were You (On Our Wedding Day)?**...Lloyd Price
28/66	**Where Were You When I Needed You**...Grass Roots

POS/YR	RECORD TITLE. . . ARTIST
23/79	**Where Were You When I Was Falling In Love**...Lobo
28/02	**Where Were You (When The World Stopped Turning)**...Alan Jackson
21/67	**Where Will The Words Come From**...Gary Lewis
20/92	**Where You Goin' Now**...Damn Yankees
	Where You Lead
40/71	Barbra Streisand
37/72	Barbra Streisand (medley)
27A/97	**Where's The Love**...Hanson
26/69	**Where's The Playground Susie**...Glen Campbell
36/98	**Wherever You Go**...Voices Of Theory
5/02	**Wherever You Will Go**...Calling
	Which Way Is Up ..see: Theme From
2/70	**Which Way You Goin' Billy?**...Poppy Family
7/81	**While You See A Chance**...Steve Winwood
6/90	**Whip Appeal**...Babyface
14/80	**Whip It**...Devo
28/83	**Whirly Girl**...Oxo
37/84	**Whisper To A Scream (Birds Fly)**...Icicle Works
	Whispering
11/64	Nino Tempo & April Stevens
27/77	Dr. Buzzard's Original "Savannah" Band (medley)
9/57	**Whispering Bells**...Dell-Vikings
11/66	**Whispers (Gettin' Louder)**...Jackie Wilson
	White Christmas
13/54	Bing Crosby
7/55	Bing Crosby
34/57	Bing Crosby
26/60	Bing Crosby
12/61	Bing Crosby
38/62	Bing Crosby
18/04	**White Flag**...Dido
26/84	**White Horse**...Laid Back
19/76	**White Knight**...Cledus Maggard
28/72	**White Lies, Blue Eyes**...Bullet
9/64	**White On White**...Danny Williams
8/67	**White Rabbit**...Jefferson Airplane
6/68	**White Room**...Cream
	White Silver Sands
7/57	Don Rondo
18/57	Owen Bradley Quintet
22/57	Dave Gardner
9/60	Bill Black's Combo
2/57	**White Sport Coat (And A Pink Carnation)**...Marty Robbins
36/83	**White Wedding**...Billy Idol
5/67	**Whiter Shade Of Pale**...Procol Harum
21/66	**Who Am I**...Petula Clark
40/98	**Who Am I "Sim Simma"**...Beenie Man
14/78	**Who Are You**...Who
8/95	**Who Can I Run To?**...Xscape
33/64	**Who Can I Turn To**...Tony Bennett
1/82	**Who Can It Be Now?**...Men At Work
5/99	**Who Dat**...JT Money
17/96	**Who Do U Love**...Deborah Cox

POS/YR	RECORD TITLE. . . ARTIST
15/89	**Who Do You Give Your Love To?**...Michael Morales
25/64	**Who Do You Love**...Sapphires
15/74	**Who Do You Think You Are**...Bo Donaldson
40/81	**Who Do You Think You're Foolin'**...Donna Summer
16/87	**Who Found Who**...Jellybean/Elisa Fiorillo
28/01	**Who I Am**...Jessica Andrews
33/68	**Who Is Gonna Love Me?**...Dionne Warwick
14/93	**Who Is It**...Michael Jackson
40/00	**Who Let The Dogs Out**...Baha Men
3/75	**Who Loves You**...Four Seasons
9/57	**Who Needs You**...Four Lads
7/61	**Who Put The Bomp (In The Bomp, Bomp, Bomp)**...Barry Mann
16/84	**Who Wears These Shoes?**...Elton John
19/68	**Who Will Answer?**...Ed Ames
11/96	**Who Will Save Your Soul**...Jewel
7/87	**Who Will You Run To**...Heart
30/03	**Who Wouldn't Wanna Be Me**...Keith Urban
31/96	**Who You Are**...Pearl Jam
18/76	**Who'd She Coo?**...Ohio Players
29/80	**Who'll Be The Fool Tonight**...Larsen-Feiten Band
34/65	**Who'll Be The Next In Line**...Kinks
F/70	**Who'll Stop The Rain**...Creedence Clearwater Revival
4/81	**Who's Crying Now**...Journey
35/92	**Who's Gonna Ride Your Wild Horses**...U2
6/85	**Who's Holding Donna Now**...DeBarge
27/73	**Who's In The Strawberry Patch With Sally**...Tony Orlando & Dawn
3/86	**Who's Johnny**...El DeBarge
	Who's Making Love
5/68	Johnnie Taylor
39/81	Blues Brothers
	Who's Sorry Now
4/58	Connie Francis
40/75	Marie Osmond
1/87	**Who's That Girl**...Madonna
21/84	**Who's That Girl?**...Eurythmics
40/70	**Who's Your Baby?**...Archies
22/02	**Who's Your Daddy?**...Toby Keith
7/85	**Who's Zoomin' Who**...Aretha Franklin
22/77	**Whodunit**...Tavares
3/57	**Whole Lot Of Shakin' Going On**...Jerry Lee Lewis
4/70	**Whole Lotta Love**...Led Zeppelin
6/59	**Whole Lotta Loving**...Fats Domino
1/93	**Whole New World (Aladdin's Theme)**...Peabo Bryson & Regina Belle
9/90	**Whole Wide World**...A'me Lorain
19/02	**Whole World**...OutKast
2/93	**Whoomp! (There It Is)**...Tag Team
11/93	**Whoot, There It Is**...95 South
	Why
1/59	Frankie Avalon
13/72	Donny Osmond

POS/YR	RECORD TITLE. . . ARTIST
34/92	**Why**...Annie Lennox
5/57	**Why Baby Why**...Pat Boone
32/03	**Why Can't I?**...Liz Phair
33/85	**Why Can't I Have You**...Cars
	Why Can't I Touch You ..see: (If You Let Me Make Love To You Then)
3/86	**Why Can't This Be Love**...Van Halen
6/75	**Why Can't We Be Friends?**...War
3/73	**Why Can't We Live Together**...Timmy Thomas
	Why Do Fools Fall In Love
6/56	Frankie Lymon
9/56	Gale Storm
12/56	Diamonds
7/81	Diana Ross
38/63	**Why Do Lovers Break Each Other's Heart?**...Bob B. Soxx & The Blue Jeans
26/96	**Why Does It Hurt So Bad**...Whitney Houston
10/58	**Why Don't They Understand**...George Hamilton IV
23/02	**Why Don't We Fall In Love**...Amerie
8/03	**Why Don't You & I**...Santana Feat. Alex Band or Chad Kroeger
37/63	**Why Don't You Believe Me**...Duprees
9/96	**Why I Love You So Much**...Monica
13/83	**Why Me?**...Irene Cara
16/73	**Why Me**...Kris Kristofferson
26/80	**Why Me**...Styx
18/80	**Why Not Me**...Fred Knoblock
39/87	**Why You Treat Me So Bad**...Club Nouveau
3/69	**Wichita Lineman**...Glen Campbell
6/91	**Wicked Game**...Chris Isaak
7/00	**Wifey**...Next
15/90	**Wiggle It**...2 In A Room
22/63	**Wiggle Wobble**...Les Cooper
33/63	**Wild!**...Dee Dee Sharp
2/84	**Wild Boys**...Duran Duran
29/56	**Wild Cherry**...Don Cherry
31/67	**Wild Honey**...Beach Boys
28/71	**Wild Horses**...Rolling Stones
26/61	**Wild In The Country**...Elvis Presley
22/57	**Wild Is The Wind**...Johnny Mathis
	Wild Night
28/71	Van Morrison
3/94	John Mellencamp Me'Shell Ndegéocello
2/60	**Wild One**...Bobby Rydell
34/65	**Wild One**...Martha & The Vandellas
	Wild Thing
1/66	Troggs
20/67	Senator Bobby
14/74	Fancy
2/89	**Wild Thing**...Tone Loc
8/63	**Wild Weekend**...Rebels
25/86	**Wild Wild Life**...Talking Heads
1/88	**Wild, Wild West**...Escape Club
1/99	**Wild Wild West**...Will Smith
34/90	**Wild Women Do**...Natalie Cole

POS/YR	RECORD TITLE. . . ARTIST
	Wild World
11/71	Cat Stevens
25/89	Maxi Priest
27/93	Mr. Big
3/75	**Wildfire**...Michael Murphey
9/73	**Wildflower**...Skylark
10/91	**Wildside**...Marky Mark & The Funky Bunch
17/63	**Wildwood Days**...Bobby Rydell
7/74	**Wildwood Weed**...Jim Stafford
1/73	**Will It Go Round In Circles**...Billy Preston
25/99	**Will 2K**...Will Smith
32/69	**Will You Be Staying After Sunday**...Peppermint Rainbow
7/93	**Will You Be There**...Michael Jackson
39/94	**Will You Be There (In The Morning)**...Heart
	Will You Love Me Tomorrow
1/61	Shirelles
24/68	4 Seasons
39/78	Dave Mason
19/92	**Will You Marry Me?**...Paula Abdul
3/87	**Will You Still Love Me?**...Chicago
	Willie And The Hand Jive
9/58	Johnny Otis Show
26/74	Eric Clapton
26/94	**Willing To Forgive**...Aretha Franklin
15/65	**Willow Weep For Me**...Chad & Jeremy
22/58	**Win Your Love For Me**...Sam Cooke
1/66	**Winchester Cathedral**...New Vaudeville Band
1/89	**Wind Beneath My Wings**...Bette Midler
4/91	**Wind Of Change**...Scorpions
31/69	**Windmills Of Your Mind**...Dusty Springfield
32/67	**Windows Of The World**...Dionne Warwick
38/83	**Winds Of Change**...Jefferson Starship
1/67	**Windy**...Association
12/61	**Wings Of A Dove**...Ferlin Husky
8/81	**Winner Takes It All**...Abba
21/76	**Winners And Losers**...Hamilton, Joe Frank & Reynolds
17/81	**Winning**...Santana
16/70	**Winter World Of Love**...Engelbert Humperdinck
	Wipe Out
2/63	Surfaris
16/66	Surfaris
12/87	Fat Boys (with The Beach Boys)
35/57	**Wisdom Of A Fool**...Five Keys
17/64	**Wish Someone Would Care**...Irma Thomas
38/67	**Wish You Didn't Have To Go**...James & Bobby Purify
34/99	**Wish You Were Here**...Mark Wills
6/64	**Wishin' And Hopin'**...Dusty Springfield
18/58	**Wishing For Your Love**...Voxpoppers
25A/98	**Wishing I Was There**...Natalie Imbruglia
26/83	**Wishing (If I Had A Photograph Of You)**...Flock Of Seagulls
9/92	**Wishing On A Star**...Cover Girls
1/88	**Wishing Well**...Terence Trent D'Arby
11/74	**Wishing You Were Here**...Chicago

POS/YR	RECORD TITLE. . .ARTIST
1/58	**Witch Doctor**...David Seville
21/72	**Witch Queen Of New Orleans**...Redbone
6/58	**Witchcraft**...Frank Sinatra
32/63	**Witchcraft**...Elvis Presley
9/72	**Witchy Woman**...Eagles
29/66	**With A Girl Like You**...Troggs
1/78	**With A Little Luck**...Wings
15/57	**With All My Heart**...Jodie Sands
1/00	**With Arms Wide Open**...Creed
5/89	**With Every Beat Of My Heart**...Taylor Dayne
39/59	**With Open Arms**...Jane Morgan
1/87	**With Or Without You**...U2
35/69	**With Pen In Hand**...Vikki Carr
21/59	**With The Wind And The Rain In Your Hair**...Pat Boone
27/65	**With These Hands**...Tom Jones
14/67	**With This Ring**...Platters
14/91	**With You**...Tony Terry
4/80	**With You I'm Born Again**...Billy Preston & Syreeta
30/57	**With You On My Mind**...Nat "King" Cole
12/76	**With Your Love**...Jefferson Starship
28/58	**With Your Love**...Jack Scott
	Without Love (There Is Nothing)
19/57	Clyde McPhatter
29/63	Ray Charles
5/70	Tom Jones
2/02	**Without Me**...Eminem
	Without You
1/72	Nilsson
3/94	Mariah Carey
7/61	**Without You**...Johnny Tillotson
8/90	**Without You**...Mötley Crüe
31/00	**Without You**...Dixie Chicks
24/82	**Without You (Not Another Lonely Night)**...Franke & The Knockouts
20/80	**Without Your Love**...Roger Daltrey
38/87	**Without Your Love**...Toto
14/64	**Wives And Lovers**...Jack Jones
	Wizard Of Oz ..see: Themes From The
17/00	**Wobble Wobble**...504 Boyz
40/75	**Wolf Creek Pass**...C.W. McCall
6/62	**Wolverton Mountain**...Claude King (also see: I'm The Girl On)
2/81	**Woman**...John Lennon
14/66	**Woman**...Peter & Gordon
15/60	**Woman, A Lover, A Friend**...Jackie Wilson
36/90	**Woman In Chains**...Tears For Fears
1/80	**Woman In Love**...Barbra Streisand
	Woman In Love
14/55	Four Aces
19/55	Frankie Laine
33/83	**Woman In Me**...Donna Summer
24/83	**Woman In You**...Bee Gees
4/81	**Woman Needs Love (Just Like You Do)**...Ray Parker Jr.
22/74	**Woman To Woman**...Shirley Brown
4/68	**Woman, Woman**...Gary Puckett

POS/YR	RECORD TITLE. . .ARTIST
29/65	**Woman's Got Soul**...Impressions
7/02	**Woman's Worth**...Alicia Keys
36/71	**Women's Love Rights**...Laura Lee
15/71	**Won't Get Fooled Again**...Who
19/60	**Won't You Come Home Bill Bailey**...Bobby Darin
20/96	**Wonder**...Natalie Merchant
11/61	**Wonder Like You**...Rick Nelson
	Wonder Of You
25/59	Ray Peterson
9/70	Elvis Presley
11/00	**Wonderful**...Everclear
39/95	**Wonderful**...Adam Ant
22/62	**Wonderful Dream**...Majors
14/63	**Wonderful Summer**...Robin Ward
4/58	**Wonderful Time Up There**...Pat Boone
16/78	**Wonderful Tonight**...Eric Clapton
	Wonderful! Wonderful!
14/57	Johnny Mathis
7/63	Tymes
	(also see: Wun'erful, Wun'erful!)
	Wonderful World
12/60	Sam Cooke
4/65	Herman's Hermits
17/78	Art Garfunkel w/James Taylor & Paul Simon
	(also see: What A)
25/70	**Wonderful World, Beautiful People**...Jimmy Cliff
40/59	**Wonderful You**...Jimmie Rodgers
12/57	**Wondering**...Patti Page
21/80	**Wondering Where The Lions Are**...Bruce Cockburn
25/80	**Wonderland**...Commodores
	Wonderland By Night
1/61	Bert Kaempfert
15/61	Louis Prima
18/61	Anita Bryant
8/96	**Wonderwall**...Oasis
8/96	**Woo-Hah!! Got You All In Check**...Busta Rhymes
16/59	**Woo-Hoo**...Rock-A-Teens
	Woo Woo Song ..see: You Should Be Mine
1/61	**Wooden Heart**...Joe Dowell
	Woodstock
11/70	Crosby, Stills, Nash & Young
23/71	Matthews' Southern Comfort
31/98	**Woof Woof**...69 Boyz
2/65	**Wooly Bully**...Sam The Sham & the Pharaohs
19/88	**Word In Spanish**...Elton John
37A/91	**Word To The Mutha!**...Bell Biv DeVoe
6/86	**Word Up**...Cameo
11/67	**Words**...Monkees
15/68	**Words**...Bee Gees
5/86	**Words Get In The Way**...Miami Sound Machine
5/67	**Words Of Love**...Mamas & The Papas
13/57	**Words Of Love**...Diamonds
35/02	**Work In Progress**...Alan Jackson

POS/YR	RECORD TITLE. . .ARTIST
2/02	**Work It**...Missy Elliott
18/66	**Work Song**...Herb Alpert
32/74	**Workin' At The Car Wash Blues**...Jim Croce
33/62	**Workin' For The Man**...Roy Orbison
20/69	**Workin' On A Groovy Thing**...5th Dimension
29/82	**Working For The Weekend**...Loverboy
8/66	**Working In The Coal Mine**...Lee Dorsey
	Working My Way Back To You
9/66	4 Seasons
2/80	Spinners (medley)
33/63	**Workout Stevie, Workout**...Little Stevie Wonder
37/69	**World**...James Brown
19/96	**World I Know**...Collective Soul
7/73	**World Is A Ghetto**...War
19/65	**World Of Our Own**...Seekers
21/58	**World Outside**...Four Coins
30/67	**World We Knew (Over And Over)**...Frank Sinatra
1/64	**World Without Love**...Peter & Gordon
34/02	**World's Greatest**...R. Kelly
37/64	**Worried Guy**...Johnny Tillotson
20/59	**Worried Man**...Kingston Trio
3/69	**Worst That Could Happen**...Brooklyn Bridge
10/87	**Wot's It To Ya**...Robbie Nevil
5/85	**Would I Lie To You?**...Eurythmics
13/92	**Would I Lie To You?**...Charles & Eddie
8/66	**Wouldn't It Be Nice**...Beach Boys
38/81	**Wrack My Brain**...Ringo Starr
20/85	**Wrap Her Up**...Elton John
35/02	**Wrapped Around**...Brad Paisley
8/84	**Wrapped Around Your Finger**...Police
2/76	**Wreck Of The Edmund Fitzgerald**...Gordon Lightfoot
	Wringle Wrangle
12/57	Fess Parker
33/57	Bill Hayes
27/99	**Write This Down**...George Strait
5/61	**Writing On The Wall**...Adam Wade
16/91	**Written All Over Your Face**...Rude Boys
29/99	**Written In The Stars**...Elton John & LeAnn Rimes
36/99	**Wrong Again**...Martina McBride
34/64	**Wrong For Each Other**...Andy Williams
32/57	**Wun'erful, Wun'erful!**...Stan Freberg

X

POS/YR	RECORD TITLE. . .ARTIST
8/80	**Xanadu**...Olivia Newton-John/Electric Light Orchestra

Y

POS/YR	RECORD TITLE. . .ARTIST
2/79	**Y.M.C.A.**....Village People
7/61	**Ya Ya**...Lee Dorsey
19/84	**Yah Mo B There**...James Ingram (with Michael McDonald)
35/63	**Yakety Sax**...Boots Randolph
1/58	**Yakety Yak**...Coasters
16/86	**Yankee Rose**...David Lee Roth
32/88	**Yeah, Yeah, Yeah**...Judson Spence
8/77	**Year Of The Cat**...Al Stewart
35/80	**Years**...Wayne Newton
37/61	**Years From Now**...Jackie Wilson
21/65	**Yeh, Yeh**...Georgie Fame
25/67	**Yellow Balloon**...Yellow Balloon
4/61	**Yellow Bird**...Arthur Lyman Group
23/70	**Yellow River**...Christie
	Yellow Rose Of Texas
1/55	Mitch Miller
3/55	Johnny Desmond
16/55	Stan Freberg
2/66	**Yellow Submarine**...Beatles
30/59	**"Yep!"**...Duane Eddy
22/00	**Yes!**...Chad Brock
	Yes, I'm Ready
5/65	Barbara Mason
2/80	Teri DeSario with K.C.
34/60	**Yes Sir, That's My Baby**...Ricky Nelson
12/57	**Yes Tonight, Josephine**...Johnnie Ray
11/73	**Yes We Can Can**...Pointer Sisters
31/68	**Yester Love**...Miracles
7/69	**Yester-Me, Yester-You, Yesterday**...Stevie Wonder
	Yesterday
1/65	Beatles
25/67	Ray Charles
2/73	**Yesterday Once More**...Carpenters
19/69	**Yesterday, When I Was Young**...Roy Clark
21/64	**Yesterday's Gone**...Chad & Jeremy
11/82	**Yesterday's Songs**...Neil Diamond
3/71	**Yo-Yo**...Osmonds
8/60	**Yogi**...Ivy Three
	You ..also see: U
10/99	**You**...Jesse Powell
20/75	**You**...George Harrison
21/58	**You**...Aquatones
25/78	**You**...Rita Coolidge
32/96	**You**...Monifah
34/68	**You**...Marvin Gaye
1/74	**You Ain't Seen Nothing Yet**...Bachman-Turner Overdrive
12/61	**You Always Hurt The One You Love**...Clarence Henry
7/83	**You And I**...Eddie Rabbitt with Crystal Gayle
13/78	**You And I**...Rick James
9/77	**You And Me**...Alice Cooper
F/70	**You And Me**...Aretha Franklin

POS/YR	RECORD TITLE. . .ARTIST
9/74	**You And Me Against The World**...Helen Reddy
4/83	**You Are**...Lionel Richie
9/72	**You Are Everything**...Stylistics
26/62	**You Are Mine**...Frankie Avalon
7/58	**You Are My Destiny**...Paul Anka
12/85	**You Are My Lady**...Freddie Jackson
6/55	**You Are My Love**...Joni James
27/76	**You Are My Starship**...Norman Connors
7/62	**You Are My Sunshine**...Ray Charles
1/95	**You Are Not Alone**...Michael Jackson
5/75	**You Are So Beautiful**...Joe Cocker
17/87	**You Are The Girl**...Cars
25/61	**You Are The Only One**...Ricky Nelson
1/73	**You Are The Sunshine Of My Life**...Stevie Wonder
9/76	**You Are The Woman**...Firefall
20/66	**You Baby**...Turtles
29/86	**You Be Illin'**...Run-D.M.C.
9/62	**You Beat Me To The Punch**...Mary Wells
6/78	**You Belong To Me**...Carly Simon
7/62	**You Belong To Me**...Duprees
2/85	**You Belong To The City**...Glenn Frey
37/59	**You Better Know It**...Jackie Wilson
24/62	**You Better Move On**...Arthur Alexander
20/66	**You Better Run**...Young Rascals
9/67	**You Better Sit Down Kids**...Chér
29/94	**You Better Wait**...Steve Perry
18/81	**You Better You Bet**...Who
26/97	**You Bring Me Up**...K-Ci & JoJo
23/87	**You Can Call Me Al**...Paul Simon
6/61	**You Can Depend On Me**...Brenda Lee
35/00	**You Can Do It**...Ice Cube
37/79	**You Can Do It**...Dobie Gray
8/82	**You Can Do Magic**...America
	You Can Have Her
12/61	Roy Hamilton
34/74	Sam Neely
36/58	**You Can Make It If You Try**...Gene Allison
18/63	**You Can Never Stop Me Loving You**...Johnny Tillotson
9/79	**You Can't Change That**...Raydio
14/90	**You Can't Deny It**...Lisa Stansfield
15/84	**You Can't Get What You Want (Till You Know What You Want)**...Joe Jackson
38/03	**You Can't Hide Beautiful**...Aaron Lines
	You Can't Hurry Love
1/66	Supremes
10/83	Phil Collins
36/91	**You Can't Play With My Yo-Yo**...Yo-Yo
40/66	**You Can't Roller Skate In A Buffalo Herd**...Roger Miller
20/56	**You Can't Run Away From It**...Four Aces
	You Can't Sit Down
29/61	Philip Upchurch Combo
3/63	Dovells
12/77	**You Can't Turn Me Off (In The Middle Of Turning Me On)**...High Inergy

POS/YR	RECORD TITLE. . .ARTIST
12/58	**You Cheated**...Shields
29/91	**You Could Be Mine**...Guns N' Roses
32/72	**You Could Have Been A Lady**...April Wine
15/82	**You Could Have Been With Me**...Sheena Easton
32/81	**You Could Take My Heart Away**...Silver Condor
7/79	**You Decorated My Life**...Kenny Rogers
10/66	**You Didn't Have To Be So Nice**...Lovin' Spoonful
1/78	**You Don't Bring Me Flowers**...Barbra Streisand & Neil Diamond
3/63	**You Don't Have To Be A Baby To Cry**...Caravelles
1/77	**You Don't Have To Be A Star**...Marilyn McCoo & Billy Davis, Jr.
14/91	**You Don't Have To Go Home Tonight**...Triplets
32/97	**You Don't Have To Hurt No More**...Mint Condition
15/66	**(You Don't Have To) Paint Me A Picture**...Gary Lewis
	You Don't Have To Say You Love Me
4/66	Dusty Springfield
11/70	Elvis Presley
20/88	**You Don't Know**...Scarlett & Black
11/64	**(You Don't Know) How Glad I Am**...Nancy Wilson
13/95	**You Don't Know How It Feels**...Tom Petty
	You Don't Know Me
14/56	Jerry Vale
2/62	Ray Charles
3/04	**You Don't Know My Name**...Alicia Keys
4/61	**You Don't Know What You've Got (Until You Lose It)**...Ral Donner
8/72	**You Don't Mess Around With Jim**...Jim Croce
10/57	**You Don't Owe Me A Thing**...Johnnie Ray
2/64	**You Don't Own Me**...Lesley Gore
16/82	**You Don't Want Me Anymore**...Steel Breeze
10/99	**(You Drive Me) Crazy**...Britney Spears
31/82	**You Dropped A Bomb On Me**...Gap Band
24/69	**You Gave Me A Mountain**...Frankie Laine
36/99	**You Get What You Give**...New Radicals
38/01	**You Gets No Love**...Faith Evans
3/85	**You Give Good Love**...Whitney Houston
1/86	**You Give Love A Bad Name**...Bon Jovi
38/79	**You Gonna Make Me Love Somebody Else**...Jones Girls
	You Got It
9/89	Roy Orbison
33/95	Bonnie Raitt
3/87	**You Got It All**...Jets
3/89	**You Got It (The Right Stuff)**...New Kids On The Block
20/83	**You Got Lucky**...Tom Petty
39/99	**You Got Me**...Roots
11/74	**You Got The Love**...Rufus feat. Chaka Khan
18/67	**You Got To Me**...Neil Diamond

POS/YR	RECORD TITLE. . . ARTIST
	You Got What It Takes
10/60	Marv Johnson
7/67	Dave Clark Five
40/69	**You Got Yours And I'll Get Mine**...Delfonics
5/95	**You Gotta Be**...Des'ree
7/87	**(You Gotta) Fight For Your Right (To Party!)**...Beastie Boys
34/99	**You Had Me From Hello**...Kenny Chesney
1/74	**You Haven't Done Nothin**...Stevie Wonder
24/69	**You, I**...Rugbys
	You Keep Me Hangin' On
1/66	Supremes
6/68	Vanilla Fudge
1/87	Kim Wilde
25/68	**(You Keep Me) Hangin' On**...Joe Simon
38/82	**You Keep Runnin' Away**...38 Special
19/67	**You Keep Running Away**...Four Tops
30/94	**You Know How We Do It**...Ice Cube
17/86	**You Know I Love You...Don't You?**...Howard Jones
35/80	**You Know That I Love You**...Santana
12/67	**You Know What I Mean**...Turtles
6/96	**You Learn**...Alanis Morissette
32/92	**You Lied To Me**...Cathy Dennis
	You Light Up My Life
1/77	Debby Boone
34/97	LeAnn Rimes
12/74	**You Little Trustmaker**...Tymes
22/63	**You Lost The Sweetest Boy**...Mary Wells
10/77	**You Made Me Believe In Magic**...Bay City Rollers
9/77	**You Make Loving Fun**...Fleetwood Mac
2/74	**You Make Me Feel Brand New**...Stylistics
1/77	**You Make Me Feel Like Dancing**...Leo Sayer
36/79	**You Make Me Feel (Mighty Real)**...Sylvester
33/01	**You Make Me Sick**...P!nk
2/97	**You Make Me Wanna......**Usher
5/81	**You Make My Dreams**...Daryl Hall & John Oates
7/80	**You May Be Right**...Billy Joel
17/60	**You Mean Everything To Me**...Neil Sedaka
7/94	**You Mean The World To Me**...Toni Braxton
35/68	**You Met Your Match**...Stevie Wonder
7/84	**You Might Think**...Cars
15/64	**You Must Believe Me**...Impressions
	You Must Have Been A Beautiful Baby
5/61	Bobby Darin
35/67	Dave Clark Five
18/96	**You Must Love Me**...Madonna
40/79	**You Need A Woman Tonight**...Captain & Tennille
11/58	**You Need Hands**...Eydie Gorme
25/70	**You Need Love Like I Do (Don't You)**...Gladys Knight
1/78	**You Needed Me**...Anne Murray
14/64	**You Never Can Tell**...Chuck Berry
10/78	**You Never Done It Like That**...Captain & Tennille

POS/YR	RECORD TITLE. . . ARTIST
3/72	**You Ought To Be With Me**...Al Green
	You Oughta Know
13A/95	Alanis Morissette
F/96	Alanis Morissette (Live)
	You Really Got A Hold On Me ..see: You've Really
	You Really Got Me
7/64	Kinks
36/78	Van Halen
27/65	**You Really Know How To Hurt A Guy**...Jan & Dean
29/92	**You Remind Me**...Mary J. Blige
4/95	**You Remind Me Of Something**...R. Kelly
10/01	**You Rock My World**...Michael Jackson
2/00	**You Sang To Me**...Marc Anthony
37/81	**You Saved My Soul**...Burton Cummings
	You Send Me
1/57	Sam Cooke
8/57	Teresa Brewer
3/76	**You Sexy Thing**...Hot Chocolate
35/80	**You Shook Me All Night Long**...AC/DC
1/76	**You Should Be Dancing**...Bee Gees
17/97	**You Should Be Mine (Don't Waste Your Time)**...Brian McKnight
13/86	**You Should Be Mine (The Woo Woo Song)**...Jeffrey Osborne
39/64	**You Should Have Seen The Way He Looked At Me**...Dixie Cups
5/82	**You Should Hear How She Talks About You**...Melissa Manchester
F/57	**You Shouldn't Do That**...Sal Mineo
32/01	**You Shouldn't Kiss Me Like This**...Toby Keith
6/69	**You Showed Me**...Turtles
11/85	**You Spin Me Round (Like A Record)**...Dead Or Alive
10/79	**You Take My Breath Away**...Rex Smith
3/60	**You Talk Too Much**...Joe Jones
38/65	**You Tell Me Why**...Beau Brummels
38/92	**You Think You Know Her**...Cause & Effect
40/79	**You Thrill Me**...Exile
39/79	**You Took The Words Right Out Of My Mouth**...Meat Loaf
8/65	**You Turn Me On**...Ian Whitcomb
25/73	**You Turn Me On, I'm A Radio**...Joni Mitchell
24/95	**You Used To Love Me**...Faith Evans
36/72	**You Want It, You Got It**...Detroit Emeralds
8/94	**You Want This**...Janet Jackson
13/72	**You Wear It Well**...Rod Stewart
12/60	**(You Were Made For) All My Love**...Jackie Wilson
21/65	**You Were Made For Me**...Freddie & The Dreamers
27/58	**You Were Made For Me**...Sam Cooke
2/97	**You Were Meant For Me**...Jewel
21/59	**You Were Mine**...Fireflies
34/99	**You Were Mine**...Dixie Chicks
	You Were On My Mind
3/65	We Five
36/67	Crispian St. Peters

POS/YR	RECORD TITLE. . .ARTIST
30/65	You Were Only Fooling (While I Was Falling In Love)...Vic Damone
22/62	You Win Again...Fats Domino
28/99	You Won't Ever Be Lonely...Andy Griggs
8/74	You Won't See Me...Anne Murray
20/92	You Won't See Me Cry...Wilson Phillips
22/65	You'd Better Come Home...Petula Clark
14/80	You'll Accomp'ny Me...Bob Seger
21/99	You'll Be In My Heart...Phil Collins
	You'll Lose A Good Thing
8/62	Barbara Lynn
32/76	Freddy Fender
2/76	You'll Never Find Another Love Like Mine...Lou Rawls
	You'll Never Get To Heaven (If You Break My Heart)
34/64	Dionne Warwick
23/73	Stylistics
11/56	You'll Never Never Know...Platters
34/64	You'll Never Walk Alone...Patti LaBelle
6/95	You'll See...Madonna
	You're ..also see: Your
18/86	You're A Friend Of Mine...Clarence Clemons & Jackson Browne
23/00	You're A God...Vertical Horizon
36/78	You're A Part Of Me...Gene Cotton with Kim Carnes
12/73	You're A Special Part Of Me...Diana Ross & Marvin Gaye
15/64	You're A Wonderful One...Marvin Gaye
	You're All I Need To Get By
7/68	Marvin Gaye & Tammi Terrell
19/71	Aretha Franklin
34/75	Tony Orlando & Dawn
3/95	Method Man (medley)
28/91	You're Amazing...Robert Palmer
39/98	You're Beginning To Get To Me...Clay Walker
25/57	You're Cheatin' Yourself (If You're Cheatin' On Me)...Frank Sinatra
35/83	You're Driving Me Out Of My Mind...Little River Band
40/98	You're Easy On The Eyes...Terri Clark
39/66	(You're Gonna) Hurt Yourself...Frankie Valli
34/59	You're Gonna Miss Me...Connie Francis
1/74	(You're) Having My Baby...Paul Anka/Odia Coates
1/91	You're In Love...Wilson Phillips
4/78	You're In My Heart (The Final Acclaim)...Rod Stewart
1/96	You're Makin' Me High...Toni Braxton
16/76	You're My Best Friend...Queen
6/67	You're My Everything...Temptations
27/81	You're My Girl...Franke & The Knockouts (also see: Say)
14/57	You're My One And Only Love...Ricky Nelson
23/89	You're My One And Only (True Love)...Seduction

POS/YR	RECORD TITLE. . .ARTIST
	(You're My) Soul And Inspiration
1/66	Righteous Brothers
38/78	Donny & Marie Osmond
	You're My World
26/64	Cilla Black
18/77	Helen Reddy
	(You're Never Gonna Get It) ..see: My Lovin'
1/75	You're No Good...Linda Ronstadt
25/65	You're Nobody Till Somebody Loves You...Dean Martin
10/89	You're Not Alone...Chicago
9/85	You're Only Human (Second Wind)...Billy Joel
7/79	You're Only Lonely...J.D. Souther
	You're Sixteen
8/60	Johnny Burnette
1/74	Ringo Starr
17/59	You're So Fine...Falcons
1/73	You're So Vain...Carly Simon
29/72	You're Still A Young Man...Tower Of Power
2/98	You're Still The One...Shania Twain
34/80	You're Supposed To Keep Your Love For Me...Jermaine Jackson
3/63	(You're the) Devil In Disguise...Elvis Presley
2/75	You're The First, The Last, My Everything...Barry White
3/85	You're The Inspiration...Chicago
18/78	You're The Love...Seals & Crofts
F/58	You're The Nearest Thing To Heaven...Johnny Cash
4/65	You're The One...Vogues
5/96	You're The One...SWV
22/70	You're The One...Little Sister
1/78	You're The One That I Want...John Travolta & Olivia Newton-John
	You're The Only Woman (You & I)
13/80	Ambrosia
36/90	Brat Pack
11/61	You're The Reason...Bobby Edwards
3/63	You're The Reason I'm Living...Bobby Darin
33/66	You've Been Cheatin'...Impressions
36/65	You've Been In Love Too Long...Martha & The Vandellas
	(You've Got) ..see: Personality
	You've Got A Friend
1/71	James Taylor
29/71	Roberta Flack & Donny Hathaway
38/70	(You've Got Me) Dangling On A String...Chairmen Of The Board
33/77	You've Got Me Runnin'...Gene Cotton
4/56	(You've Got) The Magic Touch...Platters
28/71	You've Got To Crawl (Before You Walk)...8th Day
10/65	You've Got To Hide Your Love Away...Silkie
20/60	(You've Got To) Move Two Mountains...Marv Johnson
	(You've Got What It Takes) ..see: Baby
7/65	You've Got Your Troubles...Fortunes

POS/YR	RECORD TITLE. . .ARTIST
	You've Lost That Lovin' Feelin'
1/65	Righteous Brothers
16/69	Dionne Warwick
12/80	Daryl Hall & John Oates
	You've Made Me So Very Happy
39/67	Brenda Holloway
2/69	Blood, Sweat & Tears
22/73	**You've Never Been This Far Before**...Conway Twitty
8/63	**You've Really Got A Hold On Me**...Miracles
35/02	**Young**...Kenny Chesney
25/55	**Young Abe Lincoln**...Don Cornell
28/75	**Young Americans**...David Bowie
17/63	**Young And In Love**...Dick & DeeDee
	Young And The Restless ..see: Nadia's Theme
23/58	**Young And Warm And Wonderful**...Tony Bennett
	Young Blood
8/57	Coasters
20/76	Bad Company
40/79	**Young Blood**...Rickie Lee Jones
12/60	**Young Emotions**...Ricky Nelson
2/68	**Young Girl**...Gary Puckett
20/76	**Young Hearts Run Free**...Candi Staton
	Young Love
1/57	Tab Hunter
1/57	Sonny James
17/57	Crew-Cuts
25/73	Donny Osmond
38/82	**Young Love**...Air Supply
6/63	**Young Lovers**...Paul & Paula
	(also see: Theme For)
5/81	**Young Turks**...Rod Stewart
5/62	**Young World**...Rick Nelson
33/02	**Young'n (Holla Back)**...Fabolous
	Your ..also see: You're
17/90	**Your Baby Never Looked Good In Blue**...Exposé
18/03	**Your Body Is A Wonderland**...John Mayer
13/94	**Your Body's Callin'**...R. Kelly
24/75	**Your Bulldog Drinks Champagne**...Jim Stafford
29/62	**Your Cheating Heart**...Ray Charles
34/61	**Your Friends**...Dee Clark
18/69	**Your Good Thing (Is About To End)**...Lou Rawls
33/82	**Your Imagination**...Daryl Hall & John Oates

POS/YR	RECORD TITLE. . .ARTIST
6/86	**Your Love**...Outfield
15/77	**Your Love**...Marilyn McCoo & Billy Davis Jr.
38/75	**Your Love**...Graham Central Station
13/83	**Your Love Is Driving Me Crazy**...Sammy Hagar
	(Your Love Keeps Lifting Me) Higher And Higher
6/67	Jackie Wilson
2/77	Rita Coolidge
24/61	**Your Ma Said You Cried In Your Sleep Last Night**...Kenny Dino
	Your Mama Don't Dance
4/73	Loggins & Messina
10/89	Poison
40/71	**Your Move**...Yes
14/62	**Your Nose Is Gonna Grow**...Johnny Crawford
40/63	**Your Old Stand By**...Mary Wells
40/61	**Your One And Only Love**...Jackie Wilson
28/63	**Your Other Love**...Connie Francis
5/67	**Your Precious Love**...Marvin Gaye & Tammi Terrell
	(also see: For Your Precious Love)
20/77	**Your Smiling Face**...James Taylor
8/71	**Your Song**...Elton John
40/71	**Your Time To Cry**...Joe Simon
33/67	**Your Unchanging Love**...Marvin Gaye
32/63	**Your Used To Be**...Brenda Lee
20/57	**Your Wild Heart**...Joy Layne
9/86	**Your Wildest Dreams**...Moody Blues
23/97	**Your Woman**...White Town
28/02	**Youth Of The Nation**...P.O.D.
	(Yowsah, Yowsah, Yowsah) ..see: Dance, Dance, Dance
4/68	**Yummy Yummy Yummy**...Ohio Express

Z

POS/YR	RECORD TITLE. . .ARTIST
8/63	**Zip-A-Dee Doo-Dah**...Bob B. Soxx & The Blue Jeans
36/67	**Zip Code**...Five Americans
16/57	**Zip Zip**...Diamonds
22A/94	**Zombie**...Cranberries
11/66	**Zorba The Greek**...Herb Alpert
17/58	**Zorro**...Chordettes

THE RECORD HOLDERS

TOP ARTIST AND RECORD ACHIEVEMENTS

TOP 100 HITS OF THE ROCK ERA

The rankings on the following two pages begin with America's first #1 rock and roll hit "(We're Gonna) Rock Around The Clock" in the summer of 1955 and run through the year 2003. There are two rankings (of 50 titles each) because *Billboard* changed its chart methodology on 11/30/91 by using Broadcast Data Systems and SoundScan, resulting in songs having much longer runs at #1 than ever before. ("Cherry Pink And Apple Blossom White" and "Sincerely" debuted prior to "Rock Around The Clock" and therefore are not included in any of the following rankings.)

PK YR	WKS CHR	WKS T40	WKS T10	WKS @ #1	TITLE...ARTIST
					1955–1989
56	28	23	21	11	1. Don't Be Cruel / Hound Dog...Elvis Presley
56	26	22	17	10	2. Singing The Blues...Guy Mitchell
81	26	21	15	10	3. Physical...Olivia Newton-John
77	25	21	14	10	4. You Light Up My Life...Debby Boone
59	26	22	16	9	5. Mack The Knife...Bobby Darin
57	30	22	15	9	6. All Shook Up...Elvis Presley
81	26	20	14	9	7. Bette Davis Eyes...Kim Carnes
68	19	19	14	9	8. Hey Jude...The Beatles
81	27	19	13	9	9. Endless Love...Diana Ross & Lionel Richie
60	21	17	12	9	10. The Theme From "A Summer Place"...Percy Faith
55	24	24	19	8	11. Rock Around The Clock...Bill Haley & His Comets
56	28	22	16	8	12. The Wayward Wind...Gogi Grant
55	22	19	16	8	13. Sixteen Tons..."Tennessee" Ernie Ford
56	27	22	15	8	14. Heartbreak Hotel...Elvis Presley
83	22	20	13	8	15. Every Breath You Take...The Police
78	20	18	13	8	16. Night Fever...Bee Gees
76	23	17	11	8	17. Tonight's The Night (Gonna Be Alright)...Rod Stewart
57	34	24	17	7	18. Love Letters In The Sand...Pat Boone
57	27	19	15	7	19. Jailhouse Rock...Elvis Presley
57	25	18	14	7	20. (Let Me Be Your) Teddy Bear...Elvis Presley
78	25	19	12	7	21. Shadow Dancing...Andy Gibb
58	21	18	12	7	22. At The Hop...Danny & The Juniors
61	23	17	12	7	23. Tossin' And Turnin'...Bobby Lewis
82	20	16	12	7	24. I Love Rock 'N Roll...Joan Jett & The Blackhearts
82	19	15	12	7	25. Ebony And Ivory...Paul McCartney & Stevie Wonder
64	15	14	12	7	26. I Want To Hold Your Hand...The Beatles
66	15	13	12	7	27. I'm A Believer...The Monkees
83	24	17	11	7	28. Billie Jean...Michael Jackson
68	15	15	11	7	29. I Heard It Through The Grapevine...Marvin Gaye
55	21	21	17	6	30. Love Is A Many-Splendored Thing...Four Aces
56	25	20	16	6	31. Rock And Roll Waltz...Kay Starr
56	24	20	16	6	32. The Poor People Of Paris...Les Baxter
55	19	19	16	6	33. The Yellow Rose Of Texas...Mitch Miller
78	25	19	15	6	34. Le Freak...Chic

PK YR	WKS CHR	WKS T40	WKS T10	WKS @ #1	TITLE...ARTIST
56	24	19	15	6	35. Memories Are Made Of This...Dean Martin
82	25	18	15	6	36. Eye Of The Tiger...Survivor
83	25	20	14	6	37. Flashdance...What A Feeling...Irene Cara
57	26	19	14	6	38. April Love...Pat Boone
80	25	19	13	6	39. Lady...Kenny Rogers
83	22	18	13	6	40. Say Say Say...Paul McCartney & Michael Jackson
59	21	18	13	6	41. The Battle Of New Orleans...Johnny Horton
57	21	17	13	6	42. Young Love...Tab Hunter
82	25	20	12	6	43. Centerfold...The J. Geils Band
80	25	19	12	6	44. Call Me...Blondie
58	22	19	12	6	45. It's All In The Game...Tommy Edwards
79	22	16	12	6	46. My Sharona...The Knack
69	17	16	11	6	47. Aquarius/Let The Sunshine In...The 5th Dimension
72	18	15	11	6	48. The First Time Ever I Saw Your Face...Roberta Flack
72	18	15	11	6	49. Alone Again (Naturally)...Gilbert O'Sullivan
71	17	15	11	6	50. Joy To The World...Three Dog Night

1990–2003

PK YR	WKS CHR	WKS T40	WKS T10	WKS @ #1	TITLE...ARTIST
98	47	45	29	18[A]	1. Iris...Goo Goo Dolls
96	63	52	28	16[A]	2. Don't Speak...No Doubt
95	27	26	19	16	3. One Sweet Day...Mariah Carey & Boyz II Men
96	60	37	23	14	4. Macarena...Los Del Rio
94	33	31	22	14	5. I'll Make Love To You...Boyz II Men
97	42	28	17	14	6. Candle In The Wind 1997 / Something About The Way You Look Tonight...Elton John
92	26	24	16	14	7. I Will Always Love You...Whitney Houston
92	32	28	19	13	8. End Of The Road...Boyz II Men
98	27	27	18	13	9. The Boy Is Mine...Brandy & Monica
99	58	50	30	12	10. Smooth...Santana Featuring Rob Thomas
02	23	21	16	12	11. Lose Yourself...Eminem
98	44	43	32	11[A]	12. Torn...Natalie Imbruglia
96	42	37	25	11	13. Un-Break My Heart...Toni Braxton
94	30	26	18	11	14. I Swear...All-4-One
97	33	29	17	11	15. I'll Be Missing You...Puff Daddy & Faith Evans & 112
00	28	25	17	11	16. Independent Women...Destiny's Child
02	29	27	19	10	17. Dilemma...Nelly Featuring Kelly Rowland
00	26	24	18	10	18. Maria Maria...Santana Featuring The Product G&B
02	32	26	17	10	19. Foolish...Ashanti
03	32+	28	17	9	20. Hey Ya!...OutKast
03	30	26	17	9	21. In Da Club...50 Cent
03	29	26	15	9	22. Baby Boy...Beyoncé (Featuring Sean Paul)
03	27	24	16	8	23. Crazy In Love...Beyoncé (Featuring Jay-Z)
95	25	23	16	8	24. Fantasy...Mariah Carey

PK YR	WKS CHR	WKS T40	WKS T10	WKS @ #1	TITLE...ARTIST
93	29	26	14	8	25. Dreamlover...Mariah Carey
93	23	20	14	8	26. That's The Way Love Goes...Janet Jackson
92	21	18	13	8	27. Jump...Kris Kross
96	20	16	12	8	28. Tha Crossroads...Bone Thugs-N-Harmony
95	34	28	18	7	29. Waterfalls...TLC
02	26	25	18	7	30. Hot In Herre...Nelly
95	30	27	15	7	31. Take A Bow...Madonna
93	29	23	15	7	32. Can't Help Falling In Love...UB40
95	29	24	14	7	33. This Is How We Do It...Montell Jordan
01	22	20	14	7	34. All For You...Janet Jackson
93	25	19	13	7	35. Informer...Snow
91	22	17	10	7	36. (Everything I Do) I Do It For You...Bryan Adams
91	20	15	10	7	37. Black Or White...Michael Jackson
97	59	50	25	6ᴬ	38. Fly...Sugar Ray
94	41	33	21	6	39. The Sign...Ace Of Base
01	32	29	20	6	40. U Got It Bad...Usher
01	41	36	19	6	41. Family Affair...Mary J. Blige
96	33	30	19	6	42. Because You Loved Me...Celine Dion
01	34	29	19	6	43. Fallin'...Alicia Keys
94	27	25	17	6	44. On Bended Knee...Boyz II Men
97	28	26	16	6	45. Can't Nobody Hold Me Down...Puff Daddy & Mase
02	27	23	15	6	46. Ain't It Funny...Jennifer Lopez featuring Ja Rule
98	18	15	10	6	47. I'm Your Angel...R. Kelly & Celine Dion
98	53	49	23	5	48. Too Close...Next
01	31	29	19	5	49. I'm Real...Jennifer Lopez featuring Ja Rule
98	23	23	16	5	50. The First Night...Monica

ᴬ Indicates that the total weeks at #1 is from *Billboard*'s Hot 100 Airplay chart
(prior to *Billboard* allowing Airplay-only hits to make the main Hot 100 chart)

+ still charted as of the 5/22/04 cut-off date

PK YR: Year record reached its peak position

WKS CHR: Total weeks charted in the Top 100

WKS T40: Total weeks charted in the Top 40

WKS T10: Total weeks charted in the Top 10

WKS @ #1: Total weeks record held the #1 position

Records are ranked according to the number of weeks they held the #1 position (WKS @ #1).
Ties are broken in this order:

1. Total weeks in the Top 10
2. Total weeks in the Top 40
3. Total weeks charted in the Top 100

TOP 25 #1 HITS BY DECADE

PK YR	WKS CHR	WKS T40	WKS T10	WKS @ #1	TITLE...ARTIST
					1955-1959
56	28	23	21	11	1. Don't Be Cruel / Hound Dog...Elvis Presley
56	26	22	17	10	2. Singing The Blues...Guy Mitchell
59	26	22	16	9	3. Mack The Knife...Bobby Darin
57	30	22	15	9	4. All Shook Up...Elvis Presley
55	24	24	19	8	5. Rock Around The Clock...Bill Haley & His Comets
56	28	22	16	8	6. The Wayward Wind...Gogi Grant
55	22	19	16	8	7. Sixteen Tons..."Tennessee" Ernie Ford
56	27	22	15	8	8. Heartbreak Hotel...Elvis Presley
57	34	24	17	7	9. Love Letters In The Sand...Pat Boone
57	27	19	15	7	10. Jailhouse Rock...Elvis Presley
57	25	18	14	7	11. (Let Me Be Your) Teddy Bear...Elvis Presley
58	21	18	12	7	12. At The Hop...Danny & The Juniors
55	21	21	17	6	13. Love Is A Many-Splendored Thing...Four Aces
56	25	20	16	6	14. Rock And Roll Waltz...Kay Starr
56	24	20	16	6	15. The Poor People Of Paris...Les Baxter
55	19	19	16	6	16. The Yellow Rose Of Texas...Mitch Miller
56	24	19	15	6	17. Memories Are Made Of This...Dean Martin
57	26	19	14	6	18. April Love...Pat Boone
59	21	18	13	6	19. The Battle Of New Orleans...Johnny Horton
57	21	17	13	6	20. Young Love...Tab Hunter
58	22	19	12	6	21. It's All In The Game...Tommy Edwards
58	14	14	10	6	22. The Purple People Eater...Sheb Wooley
57	31	23	16	5	23. Tammy...Debbie Reynolds
55	29	29	16	5	24. The Ballad Of Davy Crockett...Bill Hayes
56	23	19	15	5	25. Love Me Tender...Elvis Presley
					1960-1969
68	19	19	14	9	1. Hey Jude...The Beatles
60	21	17	12	9	2. The Theme From "A Summer Place"...Percy Faith
61	23	17	12	7	3. Tossin' And Turnin'...Bobby Lewis
64	15	14	12	7	4. I Want To Hold Your Hand...The Beatles
66	15	13	12	7	5. I'm A Believer...The Monkees
68	15	15	11	7	6. I Heard It Through The Grapevine...Marvin Gaye
69	17	16	11	6	7. Aquarius/Let The Sunshine In...The 5th Dimension
60	16	14	11	6	8. Are You Lonesome To-night?...Elvis Presley
69	13	12	9	6	9. In The Year 2525...Zager & Evans
60	20	16	11	5	10. It's Now Or Never...Elvis Presley
62	18	14	11	5	11. I Can't Stop Loving You...Ray Charles
68	18	15	10	5	12. Love Is Blue...Paul Mauriat
62	16	14	10	5	13. Big Girls Don't Cry...The 4 Seasons
61	16	13	10	5	14. Big Bad John...Jimmy Dean
63	15	13	10	5	15. Sugar Shack...Jimmy Gilmer & The Fireballs

PK YR	WKS CHR	WKS T40	WKS T10	WKS @ #1	TITLE...ARTIST
68	15	13	10	5	16. Honey...Bobby Goldsboro
67	17	15	9	5	17. To Sir With Love...Lulu
60	17	13	9	5	18. Cathy's Clown...The Everly Brothers
68	14	13	9	5	19. People Got To Be Free...The Rascals
69	12	12	9	5	20. Get Back...The Beatles
66	13	11	9	5	21. The Ballad Of The Green Berets...SSgt Barry Sadler
62	14	12	7	5	22. Sherry...The 4 Seasons
64	10	9	6	5	23. Can't Buy Me Love...The Beatles
69	22	18	12	4	24. Sugar, Sugar...The Archies
68	16	14	11	4	25. (Sittin' On) The Dock Of The Bay...Otis Redding
					1970-1979
77	25	21	14	10	1. You Light Up My Life...Debby Boone
78	20	18	13	8	2. Night Fever...Bee Gees
76	23	17	11	8	3. Tonight's The Night (Gonna Be Alright)...Rod Stewart
78	25	19	12	7	4. Shadow Dancing...Andy Gibb
78	25	19	15	6	5. Le Freak...Chic
79	22	16	12	6	6. My Sharona...The Knack
72	18	15	11	6	7. The First Time Ever I Saw Your Face...Roberta Flack
72	18	15	11	6	8. Alone Again (Naturally)...Gilbert O'Sullivan
71	17	15	11	6	9. Joy To The World...Three Dog Night
70	14	13	10	6	10. Bridge Over Troubled Water...Simon & Garfunkel
77	23	17	12	5	11. Best Of My Love...Emotions
70	16	16	11	5	12. I'll Be There...The Jackson 5
76	19	15	11	5	13. Silly Love Songs...Paul McCartney & Wings
71	17	15	11	5	14. Maggie May...Rod Stewart
79	20	15	10	5	15. Bad Girls...Donna Summer
71	17	15	10	5	16. It's Too Late...Carole King
73	16	13	9	5	17. Killing Me Softly With His Song...Roberta Flack
71	15	12	9	5	18. One Bad Apple...The Osmonds
77	31	23	16	4	19. I Just Want To Be Your Everything...Andy Gibb
78	27	22	13	4	20. Stayin' Alive...Bee Gees
70	22	19	13	4	21. Raindrops Keep Fallin' On My Head...B.J. Thomas
79	21	18	12	4	22. Da Ya Think I'm Sexy?...Rod Stewart
78	23	17	12	4	23. Kiss You All Over...Exile
73	23	17	11	4	24. Tie A Yellow Ribbon Round The Ole Oak Tree...Dawn featuring Tony Orlando
72	19	17	11	4	25. American Pie - Parts I & II...Don McLean
					1980-1989
81	26	21	15	10	1. Physical...Olivia Newton-John
81	26	20	14	9	2. Bette Davis Eyes...Kim Carnes
81	27	19	13	9	3. Endless Love...Diana Ross & Lionel Richie
83	22	20	13	8	4. Every Breath You Take...The Police
82	20	16	12	7	5. I Love Rock 'N Roll...Joan Jett & The Blackhearts

PK YR	WKS CHR	WKS T40	WKS T10	WKS @ #1	TITLE...ARTIST
82	19	15	12	7	6. Ebony And Ivory...Paul McCartney & Stevie Wonder
83	24	17	11	7	7. Billie Jean...Michael Jackson
82	25	18	15	6	8. Eye Of The Tiger...Survivor
83	25	20	14	6	9. Flashdance...What A Feeling...Irene Cara
80	25	19	13	6	10. Lady...Kenny Rogers
83	22	18	13	6	11. Say Say Say...Paul McCartney & Michael Jackson
82	25	20	12	6	12. Centerfold...The J. Geils Band
80	25	19	12	6	13. Call Me...Blondie
84	19	14	9	6	14. Like A Virgin...Madonna
80	22	19	14	5	15. (Just Like) Starting Over...John Lennon
84	21	16	11	5	16. When Doves Cry...Prince
84	21	15	10	5	17. Jump...Van Halen
80	29	17	14	4	18. Upside Down...Diana Ross
83	24	17	13	4	19. All Night Long (All Night)...Lionel Richie
82	23	17	13	4	20. Maneater...Daryl Hall & John Oates
80	25	19	12	4	21. Another Brick In The Wall...Pink Floyd
80	22	17	12	4	22. Crazy Little Thing Called Love...Queen
83	29	18	11	4	23. Total Eclipse Of The Heart...Bonnie Tyler
83	25	19	10	4	24. Down Under...Men At Work
86	23	17	10	4	25. That's What Friends Are For...Dionne & Friends

				1990-1999	
98	47	45	29	18A	1. Iris...Goo Goo Dolls
96	63	52	28	16A	2. Don't Speak...No Doubt
95	27	26	19	16	3. One Sweet Day...Mariah Carey & Boyz II Men
96	60	37	23	14	4. Macarena...Los Del Rio
94	33	31	22	14	5. I'll Make Love To You...Boyz II Men
97	42	28	17	14	6. Candle In The Wind 1997 / Something About The Way You Look Tonight...Elton John
92	26	24	16	14	7. I Will Always Love You...Whitney Houston
92	32	28	19	13	8. End of the Road...Boyz II Men
98	27	27	18	13	9. The Boy Is Mine...Brandy & Monica
99	58	50	30	12	10. Smooth...Santana Featuring Rob Thomas
98	44	43	32	11A	11. Torn...Natalie Imbruglia
96	42	37	25	11	12. Un-Break My Heart...Toni Braxton
94	30	26	18	11	13. I Swear...All-4-One
97	33	29	17	11	14. I'll Be Missing You...Puff Daddy & Faith Evans & 112
95	25	23	16	8	15. Fantasy...Mariah Carey
93	29	26	14	8	16. Dreamlover...Mariah Carey
93	23	20	14	8	17. That's The Way Love Goes...Janet Jackson
92	21	18	13	8	18. Jump...Kris Kross
96	20	16	12	8	19. Tha Crossroads...Bone Thugs-N-Harmony
95	34	28	18	7	20. Waterfalls...TLC
95	30	27	15	7	21. Take A Bow...Madonna
93	29	23	15	7	22. Can't Help Falling In Love...UB40
95	29	24	14	7	23. This Is How We Do It...Montell Jordan
93	25	19	13	7	24. Informer...Snow
91	22	17	10	7	25. (Everything I Do) I Do It For You...Bryan Adams

PK YR	WKS CHR	WKS T40	WKS T10	WKS @ #1	TITLE...ARTIST
					2000-2003
02	23	21	16	12	1. Lose Yourself...Eminem
00	28	25	17	11	2. Independent Women...Destiny's Child
02	29	27	19	10	3. Dilemma...Nelly Featuring Kelly Rowland
00	26	24	18	10	4. Maria Maria...Santana Featuring The Product G&B
02	32	26	17	10	5. Foolish...Ashanti
03	32+	28	17	9	6. Hey Ya!...OutKast
03	30	26	17	9	7. In Da Club...50 Cent
03	29	26	15	9	8. Baby Boy...Beyoncé (Featuring Sean Paul)
03	27	24	16	8	9. Crazy In Love...Beyoncé (Featuring Jay-Z)
02	26	25	18	7	10. Hot In Herre...Nelly
01	22	20	14	7	11. All For You...Janet Jackson
01	32	29	20	6	12. U Got It Bad...Usher
01	41	36	19	6	13. Family Affair...Mary J. Blige
01	34	29	19	6	14. Fallin'...Alicia Keys
02	27	23	15	6	15. Ain't It Funny...Jennifer Lopez featuring Ja Rule
01	31	29	19	5	16. I'm Real...Jennifer Lopez featuring Ja Rule
01	20	17	12	5	17. Lady Marmalade...Christina Aguilera, Lil' Kim, Mya & P!nk
01	49	40	23	4	18. How You Remind Me...Nickelback
00	33	28	17	4	19. I Knew I Loved You...Savage Garden
01	24	22	16	4	20. U Remind Me...Usher
01	26	23	14	4	21. Stutter...Joe (featuring Mystikal)
03	23	20	13	4	22. 21 Questions...50 Cent Featuring Nate Dogg
03	30	27	12	4	23. Shake Ya Tailfeather...Nelly/P. Diddy/Murphy Lee
00	24	22	12	4	24. Music...Madonna
03	21	20	12	4	25. All I Have...Jennifer Lopez Featuring LL Cool J

TOP 100 ARTISTS 1955-2003

ARTIST	POINTS	ARTIST	POINTS
1. ELVIS PRESLEY ●	8,067	31. PAUL ANKA	2,227
2. THE BEATLES ●●	4,696	32. FATS DOMINO	2,214
3. ELTON JOHN	4,473	33. DIANA ROSS	2,079
▲ 4. MADONNA	4,333	34. RAY CHARLES	2,034
5. STEVIE WONDER	3,707	▲ 35. PUFF DADDY	2,007
6. MICHAEL JACKSON	3,455	36. KENNY ROGERS/FIRST EDITION	2,002
▲ 7. JANET JACKSON	3,448	37. DIONNE WARWICK	1,994
8. MARIAH CAREY	3,349	38. THE EVERLY BROTHERS	1,976
9. THE ROLLING STONES ●	3,138	39. BOBBY VINTON	1,971
10. PAUL McCARTNEY/WINGS	2,983	40. PERRY COMO ●	1,964
11. WHITNEY HOUSTON	2,926	▲ 41. R. KELLY	1,961
12. BEE GEES ●	2,854	42. BRENDA LEE	1,908
13. ARETHA FRANKLIN	2,845	43. GLADYS KNIGHT/THE PIPS	1,861
14. PAT BOONE	2,842	44. PHIL COLLINS	1,849
15. MARVIN GAYE ●	2,796	45. FRANK SINATRA ●	1,838
16. THE SUPREMES ●	2,745	46. THE JACKSON 5	1,823
17. ROD STEWART	2,574	47. BRYAN ADAMS	1,810
18. THE TEMPTATIONS ●●●●	2,558	48. BOYZ II MEN	1,806
19. CHICAGO ●	2,545	49. SAM COOKE ●	1,757
20. THE BEACH BOYS ●●	2,479	50. THE MIRACLES ●	1,755
21. PRINCE	2,479	51. DONNA SUMMER	1,718
22. RICKY NELSON ●	2,476	52. CARPENTERS ●	1,702
23. NEIL DIAMOND	2,432	53. NAT "KING" COLE ●	1,680
24. JAMES BROWN	2,371	54. BARRY MANILOW	1,679
25. THE 4 SEASONS ●	2,325	55. BARBRA STREISAND	1,675
26. DARYL HALL & JOHN OATES	2,301	56. ANDY WILLIAMS	1,653
27. CONNIE FRANCIS	2,295	57. CHER	1,652
28. BILLY JOEL	2,293	58. JOHN COUGAR MELLENCAMP	1,621
29. OLIVIA NEWTON-JOHN	2,267	59. THE PLATTERS ●●●●	1,608
30. GEORGE MICHAEL/WHAM!	2,237	60. CHUBBY CHECKER	1,605

SYMBOLS
▲ = Hot Artist (at least five Top 40 hits from 2000 through 2003)
● = Deceased (solo artist or key member of a group)

ARTIST	POINTS		ARTIST	POINTS
61. THREE DOG NIGHT	1,595		81. BOB SEGER	1,341
62. FOUR TOPS ●	1,562		82. HERMAN'S HERMITS ●	1,315
63. LIONEL RICHIE	1,555		83. FOREIGNER	1,298
64. BOBBY DARIN ●	1,550		▲ 84. JAY-Z	1,295
65. CELINE DION	1,531		85. JOHNNY MATHIS	1,291
66. ROY ORBISON ●	1,527		86. TLC ●	1,289
67. HEART	1,526		87. BRUCE SPRINGSTEEN	1,279
68. BROOK BENTON ●	1,519		88. FLEETWOOD MAC	1,272
69. LINDA RONSTADT	1,496		89. SPINNERS ●	1,258
70. KOOL & THE GANG ●	1,491		90. JEFFERSON AIRPLANE/STARSHIP ●●	1,257
71. BON JOVI	1,478		91. SIMON & GARFUNKEL	1,257
72. NEIL SEDAKA	1,456		92. SANTANA	1,251
73. DION/DION & THE BELMONTS	1,449		93. COMMODORES	1,250
74. GLORIA ESTEFAN/			94. MICHAEL BOLTON	1,248
MIAMI SOUND MACHINE	1,443		95. GLEN CAMPBELL	1,242
75. AEROSMITH	1,420		96. ELECTRIC LIGHT ORCHESTRA	1,231
76. DURAN DURAN	1,402		97. TONY ORLANDO/DAWN	1,231
77. THE 5TH DIMENSION ●	1,400		98. BOBBY RYDELL	1,220
78. EAGLES	1,391		99. RICHARD MARX	1,216
79. HUEY LEWIS & THE NEWS	1,365		100. ERIC CLAPTON	1,208
80. JACKIE WILSON ●	1,361			

POINT SYSTEM

Points are awarded according to the following formula:

1. Each artist's charted singles are given points based on their highest charted position:

    #1 = 100 points for its first week at #1,
      plus 10 points for each additional week at #1
    #2 = 90 points for its first week at #2,
      plus 5 points for each additional week at #2
    #3 = 80 points for its first week at #3,
      plus 3 points for each additional week at #3
    #4-5 = 70 points
    #6-10 = 60 points
    #11-15 = 55 points
    #16-20 = 50 points
    #21-30 = 45 points
    #31-40 = 40 points

2. Points awarded for Hot 100 Airplay hits:

    #1 = 85 points for its first week at #1,
      plus 5 points for each additional week at #1
    #2 = 75 points for its first week at #2,
      plus 3 points for each additional week at #2
    #3 = 65 points for its first week at #3,
      plus 2 points for each additional week at #3
    #4-5 = 55 points
    #6-10 = 45 points
    #11-15 = 40 points
    #16-20 = 35 points
    #21-30 = 30 points
    #31-40 = 25 points

3. Points awarded for Hot 100 Sales hits:

    #1 = 40 points for its first week at #1,
      plus 5 points for each additional week at #1
    #2 = 40 points for its first week at #2,
      plus 3 points for each additional week at #2
    #3 = 40 points for its first week at #3,
      plus 2 points for each additional week at #3
    #4-5 = 40 points

4. Total weeks charted in the Top 40 are added in. In the case of a tie, the artist listed first is determined by the following tie-breaker rules:

1) Most charted singles
2) Most Top 40 singles
3) Most Top 10 singles

When two or more artists combine for a hit single, such as Barbra Streisand and Bryan Adams, the full point value is given to each artist. Duos, such as Simon & Garfunkel, are considered regular recording teams, and their points are not shared by either artist individually.

TOP 25 ARTISTS BY DECADE

ARTIST	POINTS		ARTIST	POINTS		ARTIST	POINTS
1955-1959			**1960-1969**			**1970-1979**	
1. ELVIS PRESLEY	3,324		1. THE BEATLES	4,135		1. ELTON JOHN	2,021
2. PAT BOONE	2,462		2. ELVIS PRESLEY	3,455		2. PAUL McCARTNEY	2,020
3. PERRY COMO	1,603		3. THE SUPREMES	2,286		3. BEE GEES	1,898
4. FATS DOMINO	1,389		4. THE 4 SEASONS	1,978		4. CARPENTERS	1,644
5. RICKY NELSON	1,373		5. BRENDA LEE	1,908		5. THE JACKSON 5	1,551
6. THE PLATTERS	1,240		6. THE BEACH BOYS	1,908		6. CHICAGO	1,480
7. NAT "KING" COLE	1,168		7. RAY CHARLES	1,737		7. STEVIE WONDER	1,467
8. THE EVERLY BROTHERS	1,049		8. MARVIN GAYE	1,736		8. THREE DOG NIGHT	1,310
9. FRANK SINATRA	1,028		9. BOBBY VINTON	1,720		9. OLIVIA NEWTON-JOHN	1,265
10. THE McGUIRE SISTERS	989		10. CONNIE FRANCIS	1,590		10. NEIL DIAMOND	1,257
11. BILL HALEY & HIS COMETS	930		11. THE TEMPTATIONS	1,589		11. ELVIS PRESLEY	1,238
12. THE FOUR LADS	906		12. CHUBBY CHECKER	1,505		12. BARRY MANILOW	1,151
13. JOHNNY MATHIS	899		13. THE ROLLING STONES	1,494		13. EAGLES	1,104
14. THE DIAMONDS	871		14. ROY ORBISON	1,456		14. JOHN DENVER	1,091
15. PAUL ANKA	815		15. THE MIRACLES	1,346		15. DIANA ROSS	1,090
16. PATTI PAGE	796		16. JAMES BROWN	1,341		16. TONY ORLANDO & DAWN	1,078
17. JIMMIE RODGERS	780		17. HERMAN'S HERMITS	1,315		17. DONNA SUMMER	1,066
18. TERESA BREWER	729		18. DION	1,212		18. GLADYS KNIGHT & THE PIPS	1,050
19. CONNIE FRANCIS	705		19. SAM COOKE	1,206		19. HELEN REDDY	1,038
20. THE FONTANE SISTERS	704		20. ARETHA FRANKLIN	1,163		20. ROD STEWART	983
21. FRANKIE AVALON	684		21. DAVE CLARK FIVE	1,150		21. ARETHA FRANKLIN	969
22. ANDY WILLIAMS	682		22. DIONNE WARWICK	1,143		22. BARBRA STREISAND	967
23. CHUCK BERRY	626		23. STEVIE WONDER	1,131		23. EARTH, WIND & FIRE	953
24. BILLY VAUGHN	606		24. BROOK BENTON	1,106		24. JAMES BROWN	949
25. GEORGIA GIBBS	602		25. BOBBY RYDELL	1,082		25. SPINNERS	929

ARTIST	POINTS		ARTIST	POINTS		ARTIST	POINTS
1980-1989			**1990-1999**			**2000-2003**	
1. MICHAEL JACKSON	1,944		1. MARIAH CAREY	2,984		1. NELLY	1,193
2. MADONNA	1,893		2. JANET JACKSON	2,158		2. ASHANTI	1,095
3. DARYL HALL & JOHN OATES	1,801		3. MADONNA	1,839		3. JA RULE	1,058
4. PRINCE	1,679		4. BOYZ II MEN	1,806		4. JAY-Z	907
5. GEORGE MICHAEL	1,631		5. WHITNEY HOUSTON	1,614		5. JENNIFER LOPEZ	886
6. LIONEL RICHIE	1,460		6. CELINE DION	1,395		6. LUDACRIS	867
7. BILLY JOEL	1,447		7. R. KELLY	1,310		7. CHRISTINA AGUILERA	849
8. ELTON JOHN	1,436		8. PUFF DADDY	1,251		8. DESTINY'S CHILD	822
9. PHIL COLLINS	1,379		9. TLC	1,239		9. PUFF DADDY	756
10. JOHN COUGAR MELLENCAMP	1,270		10. MICHAEL BOLTON	1,066		10. EMINEM	710
11. HUEY LEWIS & THE NEWS	1,222		11. ELTON JOHN	1,016		11. P!NK	686
12. DURAN DURAN	1,222		12. MONICA	992		12. R. KELLY	651
13. KOOL & THE GANG	1,195		13. BRYAN ADAMS	988		13. 50 CENT	647
14. KENNY ROGERS	1,141		14. TONI BRAXTON	982		14. *NSYNC	627
15. STEVIE WONDER	1,109		15. THE NOTORIOUS B.I.G.	922		15. MADONNA	601
16. WHITNEY HOUSTON	1,104		16. BRANDY	913		16. MISSY "MISDEMEANOR" ELLIOTT	573
17. RICK SPRINGFIELD	1,067		17. EN VOGUE	880		17. USHER	557
18. JOURNEY	1,051		18. MICHAEL JACKSON	850		18. JAGGED EDGE	554
19. DIANA ROSS	989		19. MASE	829		19. AALIYAH	537
20. BRUCE SPRINGSTEEN	981		20. PRINCE	800		20. JANET JACKSON	519
21. PAUL McCARTNEY	963		21. ROD STEWART	762		21. FABOLOUS	511
22. OLIVIA NEWTON-JOHN	962		22. COLOR ME BADD	731		22. TIM McGRAW	496
23. AIR SUPPLY	946		23. AEROSMITH	707		23. EVE	495
24. CHICAGO	941		24. BABYFACE	701		24. SEAN PAUL	494
25. BILLY OCEAN	940		25. SWV (Sisters With Voices)	667		25. TOBY KEITH	470

TOP 40 ARTIST ACHIEVEMENTS

ARTIST	TOTAL	ARTIST	TOTAL
MOST CHART HITS*		**MOST TOP 10 HITS**	
1. ELVIS PRESLEY	114	1. ELVIS PRESLEY	38
2. ELTON JOHN	59	2. MADONNA	35
3. THE BEATLES	52	3. THE BEATLES	34
4. MADONNA	49	4. JANET JACKSON	29
5. STEVIE WONDER	46	5. STEVIE WONDER	28
6. ARETHA FRANKLIN	45	6. MICHAEL JACKSON	28
7. JAMES BROWN	44	7. ELTON JOHN	27
8. THE ROLLING STONES	41	8. MARIAH CAREY	23
9. MARVIN GAYE	41	9. THE ROLLING STONES	23
10. MICHAEL JACKSON	38	10. WHITNEY HOUSTON	23
11. PAT BOONE	38	11. PAUL McCARTNEY	22
12. THE TEMPTATIONS	38	12. GEORGE MICHAEL	21
13. NEIL DIAMOND	38	13. THE SUPREMES	20
14. JANET JACKSON	37	14. CHICAGO	20
15. PAUL McCARTNEY	37	15. PRINCE	19
16. FATS DOMINO	37	16. RICKY NELSON	19
17. THE BEACH BOYS	36	17. PAT BOONE	18
18. RICKY NELSON	36	18. MARVIN GAYE	18
19. BEE GEES	35	19. BEE GEES	17
20. CHICAGO	35	20. ARETHA FRANKLIN	17
21. CONNIE FRANCIS	35	21. ROD STEWART	16
22. ROD STEWART	34	22. THE TEMPTATIONS	16
23. THE SUPREMES	33	23. DARYL HALL & JOHN OATES	16
24. BILLY JOEL	33	24. CONNIE FRANCIS	16
25. PAUL ANKA	33	25. THE BEACH BOYS	15
26. RAY CHARLES	33	26. THE 4 SEASONS	15
27. WHITNEY HOUSTON	32	27. OLIVIA NEWTON-JOHN	15
28. PRINCE	32	28. THE EVERLY BROTHERS	15

ARTIST	TOTAL	ARTIST	TOTAL
MOST #1 HITS		**MOST WEEKS AT THE #1 POSITION**	
1. THE BEATLES	20	1. ELVIS PRESLEY	80
2. ELVIS PRESLEY	18	2. MARIAH CAREY	61
3. MARIAH CAREY	15	3. THE BEATLES	59
4. MICHAEL JACKSON	13	4. BOYZ II MEN	50
5. MADONNA	12	5. MICHAEL JACKSON	37
6. THE SUPREMES	12	6. ELTON JOHN	34
7. WHITNEY HOUSTON	11	7. JANET JACKSON	33
8. STEVIE WONDER	10	8. MADONNA	32
9. JANET JACKSON	10	9. WHITNEY HOUSTON	31
10. GEORGE MICHAEL	10	10. PAUL McCARTNEY	30
11. ELTON JOHN	9	11. BEE GEES	27
12. PAUL McCARTNEY	9	12. STEVIE WONDER	25
13. BEE GEES	9	13. PUFF DADDY	24
14. THE ROLLING STONES	8	14. GEORGE MICHAEL	23
15. PHIL COLLINS	7	15. THE SUPREMES	22
16. PAT BOONE	6	16. SANTANA	22
17. DARYL HALL & JOHN OATES	6	17. MONICA	22
18. DIANA ROSS	6	18. PAT BOONE	21
19. PAULA ABDUL	6	19. LIONEL RICHIE	21
20. PRINCE	5	20. NELLY	21
21. THE 4 SEASONS	5	21. ROD STEWART	20
22. OLIVIA NEWTON-JOHN	5	22. DIANA ROSS	20
23. PUFF DADDY	5	23. JENNIFER LOPEZ	20
24. BOYZ II MEN	5	24. THE 4 SEASONS	18
25. BARBRA STREISAND	5	25. OLIVIA NEWTON-JOHN	18
26. LIONEL RICHIE	5	26. CELINE DION	18
27. BON JOVI	5	27. TLC	18
28. EAGLES	5	28. GOO GOO DOLLS	18
29. KC & THE SUNSHINE BAND	5		

*Only "Most Chart Hits" includes songs that peaked exclusively in the Top 5 on *Billboard*'s Hot 100 Sales chart after *Billboard* introduced a new methodology to the Hot 100 on 12/5/98. Ties are broken according to rank in the "Top 100 Artists" section.

#1 SINGLES LISTED CHRONOLOGICALLY
1955-2003

For the years 1955 through 1958 (when *Billboard* published more than one weekly pop chart) special columns are used to show the weeks each #1 record spent on each of the various pop charts. The #1 hits of the Hot 100 are shown exclusively from October 20, 1958, through December 27, 2003.

The date shown is the earliest date that a record hit #1 on any of the pop charts. The weeks column (next to date) lists the total weeks at #1, from whichever chart it achieved its highest total. This total is not a combined total from the various pop charts.

Because of the multiple charts used in our research from 1955-1958, some dates are duplicated, as certain #1 hits may have peaked on the same week on different charts. *Billboard* also showed ties at #1 on some of these charts; therefore, the total weeks for each year may calculate out to more than 52.

Lines are drawn in on the charts column to show when any of the four pop charts were not published.

See "Researching the Charts" (page 8) for more details about researching the four pop charts.

DATE: Date title first hit the #1 position
WKS: Total weeks title held the #1 position
↕ Indicates title hit #1, dropped down, then returned to the #1 spot

* Consensus #1 record—hit #1 on all Pop charts published (1955–58)
A Indicates a record peaked at #1 on the Hot 100 Airplay chart prior to *Billboard* including Airplay hits on the Hot 100 on 12/5/98

CHARTS COLUMN:
BS Best Sellers
JY Jockey
JB Juke Box
TP Top 100
HT Hot 100

971 records hit the #1 position on *Billboard*'s pop charts from 1955 through 2003. "The Twist," which hit #1 in 1960 and again in 1962, is counted twice. There have been 901 #1 records since the Hot 100 chart began in 1958.

Billboard has not published an issue for the last week of the year since 1976. For the years 1976 through 1991, *Billboard* considered the charts listed in the last published issue of the year to be "frozen," and all chart positions remained the same for the unpublished week. This frozen chart data is included in our tabulations. Since 1992, *Billboard* has *compiled* a pop chart for the last week of the year, even though an issue is *not published*. This chart is available only through *Billboard*'s Web site or by mail. Our tabulations include this unpublished chart data.

DATE	WKS	RECORD TITLE	ARTIST	CHARTS			
		1955					
				BS	JY	JB	TP
1/01	4	* 1. Let Me Go Lover	Joan Weber	2	4↕	4	—
2/05	3	2. Hearts Of Stone	The Fontane Sisters	1	—	3	—
2/12	10	* 3. Sincerely	The McGuire Sisters	6	10	7	—
3/26	5	* 4. The Ballad Of Davy Crockett	Bill Hayes	5	3	3	—
4/30	10	* 5. Cherry Pink And Apple Blossom White	Perez "Prez" Prado	10	6↕	8	—
5/14	3	6. Dance With Me Henry (Wallflower)	Georgia Gibbs	—	—	3	—
5/14	2 ↕	7. Unchained Melody	Les Baxter	—	2↕	—	—
7/09	8	* 8. (We're Gonna) Rock Around The Clock	Bill Haley & His Comets	8	6↕	7	—
7/09	2 ↕	9. Learnin' The Blues	Frank Sinatra	—	2↕	—	—
9/03	6	* 10. The Yellow Rose Of Texas	Mitch Miller	6↕	6	6	—
9/17	2	11. Ain't That A Shame	Pat Boone	—	—	2	—
10/08	6	* 12. Love Is A Many-Splendored Thing	Four Aces	2↕	6	3	3
10/29	4	13. Autumn Leaves	Roger Williams	4	—	—	—
		11/12/55: BILLBOARD'S "TOP 100" CHART DEBUTS.					
11/26	8	* 14. Sixteen Tons	"Tennessee" Ernie Ford	7	6	8	6

DATE	WKS	RECORD TITLE	ARTIST	CHARTS			
				BS	JY	JB	TP
		1956					
1/07	6	* 1. Memories Are Made Of This	Dean Martin	5	6	4	5
2/18	6	* 2. Rock And Roll Waltz	Kay Starr	1	1	6	4
2/18	2	3. The Great Pretender	The Platters	—	2	1	2
2/25	4	4. Lisbon Antigua	Nelson Riddle	4	2↕	—	—
3/17	6	* 5. The Poor People Of Paris	Les Baxter	4	6↕	3	6
4/21	8	* 6. Heartbreak Hotel	Elvis Presley	8	3	8	7
5/05	1	7. Hot Diggity (Dog Ziggity Boom)	Perry Como	—	1	—	—
6/02	3	8. Moonglow And Theme From "Picnic"	Morris Stoloff	—	3	—	—
6/16	8	* 9. The Wayward Wind	Gogi Grant	6	8	4	7
7/28	4	10. I Almost Lost My Mind	Pat Boone	—	—	4	2
7/28	1	11. I Want You, I Need You, I Love You	Elvis Presley	1	—	—	—
8/04	5	* 12. My Prayer	The Platters	2	3	1	5
8/18	11	* 13. Don't Be Cruel/					
		14. Hound Dog	Elvis Presley	11	8	11	7
11/03	5	* 15. Love Me Tender	Elvis Presley	5	5	1	4↕
11/03	3	16. The Green Door	Jim Lowe	—	—	3	3
12/08	10	* 17. Singing The Blues	Guy Mitchell	9	9	10	9
		1957					
2/09	3	1. Too Much	Elvis Presley	3	—	1	—
2/09	1	2. Don't Forbid Me	Pat Boone	—	—	1	1
2/09	1	3. Young Love	Sonny James	—	1	—	—
2/16	6	* 4. Young Love	Tab Hunter	4	6	5↕	6
3/30	3	5. Butterfly	Andy Williams	—	2	—	3
3/30	1	6. Party Doll	Buddy Knox & The Rhythm Orchids	1	—	—	—
4/06	2	7. Round And Round	Perry Como	1	2	—	1
4/13	9	8. All Shook Up	Elvis Presley	8	7	9	8
4/13	2	* 9. Butterfly	Charlie Gracie	—	—	2	—
6/03	7	* 10. Love Letters In The Sand	Pat Boone	5	7	—	5
		6/17/57: BILLBOARD TERMINATES "JUKE BOX" CHART.					
7/08	7	* 11. (Let Me Be Your) Teddy Bear	Elvis Presley	7	3		7
8/19	5	* 12. Tammy	Debbie Reynolds	3↕	5		5
9/09	1	13. Diana	Paul Anka	1	—		—
9/23	4	* 14. Honeycomb	Jimmie Rodgers	2	4		2
9/23	1	15. That'll Be The Day	The Crickets	1	—		—
10/14	4	* 16. Wake Up Little Susie	The Everly Brothers	1	4		2
10/21	7↕	* 17. Jailhouse Rock	Elvis Presley	7↕	2		6
10/21	1	18. Chances Are	Johnny Mathis	—	1		—
12/02	3	* 19. You Send Me	Sam Cooke	2	1		3
12/16	6	* 20. April Love	Pat Boone	2	6		1
		1958					
1/06	7	* 1. At The Hop	Danny & The Juniors	5	3		7
2/10	5	* 2. Don't	Elvis Presley	5	1		1
2/17	4	3. Sugartime	The McGuire Sisters	—	4		—
2/24	2	4. Get A Job	The Silhouettes	—	—		2

DATE	WKS		RECORD TITLE	ARTIST	BS	JY	JB	TP
3/17	5	* 5.	Tequila	The Champs	5	2		5
3/24	1	6.	Catch A Falling Star	Perry Como	—	1		—
4/14	4	7.	He's Got The Whole World (In His Hands)	Laurie London	—	4		—
4/21	1	* 8.	Twilight Time	The Platters	1	1		1
4/28	3	9.	Witch Doctor	David Seville	2	—		3
5/12	5	* 10.	All I Have To Do Is Dream	The Everly Brothers	4	5		3
6/09	6	* 11.	The Purple People Eater	Sheb Wooley	6	4		6
7/21	2	12.	Hard Headed Woman	Elvis Presley	2	1		—
7/21	1	13.	Yakety Yak	The Coasters	—	—		1

7/28/58: BILLBOARD LAST "JOCKEYS" AND "TOP 100" CHARTS.

DATE	WKS		RECORD TITLE	ARTIST	BS	JY	TP	HT
7/28	1	14.	Patricia	Perez Prado	—	1	1	

8/4/58: BILLBOARD'S "HOT 100" CHART DEBUTS.

DATE	WKS		RECORD TITLE	ARTIST	BS	JY	TP	HT
8/04	2	* 15.	Poor Little Fool	Ricky Nelson	2		2	
8/18	5↕	* 16.	Nel Blu Dipinto Di Blu (Volare)	Domenico Modugno	5↕		5↕	
8/25	1	17.	Little Star	The Elegants	—		1	
8/25	1	18.	Bird Dog	The Everly Brothers	1		—	
9/29	6	* 19.	It's All In The Game	Tommy Edwards	3		6	

10/13/58: BILLBOARD LAST "BEST SELLERS" CHART;
"HOT 100" CHART USED EXCLUSIVELY FROM HERE ON.

DATE	WKS		RECORD TITLE	ARTIST	BS	JY	TP	HT
11/10	2↕	20.	It's Only Make Believe	Conway Twitty				2↕
11/17	1	21.	Tom Dooley	The Kingston Trio				1
12/01	3	22.	To Know Him, Is To Love Him	The Teddy Bears				3
12/22	4	23.	The Chipmunk Song	The Chipmunks				4

DATE	WKS		RECORD TITLE	ARTIST

1959

DATE	WKS		RECORD TITLE	ARTIST
1/19	3	1.	Smoke Gets In Your Eyes	The Platters
2/09	4	2.	Stagger Lee	Lloyd Price
3/09	5	3.	Venus	Frankie Avalon
4/13	4	4.	Come Softly To Me	Fleetwoods
5/11	1	5.	The Happy Organ	Dave "Baby" Cortez
5/18	2	6.	Kansas City	Wilbert Harrison
6/01	6	7.	The Battle Of New Orleans	Johnny Horton
7/13	4	8.	Lonely Boy	Paul Anka
8/10	2	9.	A Big Hunk O' Love	Elvis Presley
8/24	4	10.	The Three Bells	The Browns
9/21	2	11.	Sleep Walk	Santo & Johnny
10/05	9↕	12.	Mack The Knife	Bobby Darin
11/16	1	13.	Mr. Blue	The Fleetwoods
12/14	2	14.	Heartaches By The Number	Guy Mitchell
12/28	1	15.	Why	Frankie Avalon

DATE	WKS	RECORD TITLE		ARTIST

1960

DATE	WKS		RECORD TITLE	ARTIST
1/04	2	1.	El Paso	Marty Robbins
1/18	3	2.	Running Bear	Johnny Preston
2/08	2	3.	Teen Angel	Mark Dinning
2/22	9	4.	The Theme From "A Summer Place"	Percy Faith
4/25	4	5.	Stuck On You	Elvis Presley
5/23	5	6.	Cathy's Clown	The Everly Brothers
6/27	2	7.	Everybody's Somebody's Fool	Connie Francis
7/11	1	8.	Alley-Oop	Hollywood Argyles
7/18	3	9.	I'm Sorry	Brenda Lee
8/08	1	10.	Itsy Bitsy Teenie Weenie Yellow Polkadot Bikini	Brian Hyland
8/15	5	11.	It's Now Or Never	Elvis Presley
9/19	1	12.	The Twist	Chubby Checker
			RE-ENTERED #1 POSITION IN 1962 FOR 2 MORE WEEKS	
9/26	2	13.	My Heart Has A Mind Of Its Own	Connie Francis
10/10	1	14.	Mr. Custer	Larry Verne
10/17	3 ↕	15.	Save The Last Dance For Me	The Drifters
10/24	1	16.	I Want To Be Wanted	Brenda Lee
11/14	1	17.	Georgia On My Mind	Ray Charles
11/21	1	18.	Stay	Maurice Williams & The Zodiacs
11/28	6	19.	Are You Lonesome To-night?	Elvis Presley

1961

DATE	WKS		RECORD TITLE	ARTIST
1/09	3	1.	Wonderland By Night	Bert Kaempfert
1/30	2	2.	Will You Love Me Tomorrow	The Shirelles
2/13	2	3.	Calcutta	Lawrence Welk
2/27	3	4.	Pony Time	Chubby Checker
3/20	2	5.	Surrender	Elvis Presley
4/03	3	6.	Blue Moon	The Marcels
4/24	4	7.	Runaway	Del Shannon
5/22	1	8.	Mother-In-Law	Ernie K-Doe
5/29	2 ↕	9.	Travelin' Man	Ricky Nelson
6/05	1	10.	Running Scared	Roy Orbison
6/19	1	11.	Moody River	Pat Boone
6/26	2	12.	Quarter To Three	U.S. Bonds
7/10	7	13.	Tossin' And Turnin'	Bobby Lewis
8/28	1	14.	Wooden Heart	Joe Dowell
9/04	2	15.	Michael	The Highwaymen
9/18	3	16.	Take Good Care Of My Baby	Bobby Vee
10/09	2	17.	Hit The Road Jack	Ray Charles
10/23	2	18.	Runaround Sue	Dion
11/06	5	19.	Big Bad John	Jimmy Dean
12/11	1	20.	Please Mr. Postman	The Marvelettes
12/18	3	21.	The Lion Sleeps Tonight	The Tokens

1962

DATE	WKS		RECORD TITLE	ARTIST
1/13	2	1.	The Twist	Chubby Checker
			FIRST ENTERED #1 POSITION IN 1960 FOR 1 WEEK	

DATE	WKS		RECORD TITLE	ARTIST
1/27	3	2.	Peppermint Twist - Part I	Joey Dee & the Starliters
2/17	3	3.	Duke Of Earl	Gene Chandler
3/10	3	4.	Hey! Baby	Bruce Channel
3/31	1	5.	Don't Break The Heart That Loves You	Connie Francis
4/07	2	6.	Johnny Angel	Shelley Fabares
4/21	2	7.	Good Luck Charm	Elvis Presley
5/05	3	8.	Soldier Boy	The Shirelles
5/26	1	9.	Stranger On The Shore	Mr. Acker Bilk
6/02	5	10.	I Can't Stop Loving You	Ray Charles
7/07	1	11.	The Stripper	David Rose
7/14	4	12.	Roses Are Red (My Love)	Bobby Vinton
8/11	2	13.	Breaking Up Is Hard To Do	Neil Sedaka
8/25	1	14.	The Loco-Motion	Little Eva
9/01	2	15.	Sheila	Tommy Roe
9/15	5	16.	Sherry	The 4 Seasons
10/20	2	17.	Monster Mash	Bobby "Boris" Pickett & The Crypt-Kickers
11/03	2	18.	He's A Rebel	The Crystals
11/17	5	19.	Big Girls Don't Cry	The 4 Seasons
12/22	3	20.	Telstar	The Tornadoes

1963

DATE	WKS		RECORD TITLE	ARTIST
1/12	2	1.	Go Away Little Girl	Steve Lawrence
1/26	2	2.	Walk Right In	The Rooftop Singers
2/09	3	3.	Hey Paula	Paul & Paula
3/02	3	4.	Walk Like A Man	The 4 Seasons
3/23	1	5.	Our Day Will Come	Ruby & The Romantics
3/30	4	6.	He's So Fine	The Chiffons
4/27	3	7.	I Will Follow Him	Little Peggy March
5/18	2	8.	If You Wanna Be Happy	Jimmy Soul
6/01	2	9.	It's My Party	Lesley Gore
6/15	3	10.	Sukiyaki	Kyu Sakamoto
7/06	2	11.	Easier Said Than Done	The Essex
7/20	2	12.	Surf City	Jan & Dean
8/03	1	13.	So Much In Love	The Tymes
8/10	3	14.	Fingertips - Pt 2	Little Stevie Wonder
8/31	3	15.	My Boyfriend's Back	The Angels
9/21	3	16.	Blue Velvet	Bobby Vinton
10/12	5	17.	Sugar Shack	Jimmy Gilmer & The Fireballs
11/16	1	18.	Deep Purple	Nino Tempo & April Stevens
11/23	2	19.	I'm Leaving It Up To You	Dale & Grace
12/07	4	20.	Dominique	The Singing Nun

1964

DATE	WKS		RECORD TITLE	ARTIST
1/04	4	1.	There! I've Said It Again	Bobby Vinton
2/01	7	2.	I Want To Hold Your Hand	The Beatles
3/21	2	3.	She Loves You	The Beatles
4/04	5	4.	Can't Buy Me Love	The Beatles
5/09	1	5.	Hello, Dolly!	Louis Armstrong
5/16	2	6.	My Guy	Mary Wells
5/30	1	7.	Love Me Do	The Beatles
6/06	3	8.	Chapel Of Love	The Dixie Cups
6/27	1	9.	A World Without Love	Peter & Gordon
7/04	2	10.	I Get Around	The Beach Boys

DATE	WKS		RECORD TITLE	ARTIST
7/18	2	11.	Rag Doll	The 4 Seasons
8/01	2	12.	A Hard Day's Night	The Beatles
8/15	1	13.	Everybody Loves Somebody	Dean Martin
8/22	2	14.	Where Did Our Love Go	The Supremes
9/05	3	15.	The House Of The Rising Sun	The Animals
9/26	3	16.	Oh, Pretty Woman	Roy Orbison
10/17	2	17.	Do Wah Diddy Diddy	Manfred Mann
10/31	4	18.	Baby Love	The Supremes
11/28	1	19.	Leader Of The Pack	The Shangri-Las
12/05	1	20.	Ringo	Lorne Greene
12/12	1	21.	Mr. Lonely	Bobby Vinton
12/19	2 ↕	22.	Come See About Me	The Supremes
12/26	3	23.	I Feel Fine	The Beatles

1965

DATE	WKS		RECORD TITLE	ARTIST
1/23	2	1.	Downtown	Petula Clark
2/06	2	2.	You've Lost That Lovin' Feelin'	The Righteous Brothers
2/20	2	3.	This Diamond Ring	Gary Lewis & The Playboys
3/06	1	4.	My Girl	The Temptations
3/13	2	5.	Eight Days A Week	The Beatles
3/27	2	6.	Stop! In The Name Of Love	The Supremes
4/10	2	7.	I'm Telling You Now	Freddie & The Dreamers
4/24	1	8.	Game Of Love	Wayne Fontana & The Mindbenders
5/01	3	9.	Mrs. Brown You've Got A Lovely Daughter	Herman's Hermits
5/22	1	10.	Ticket To Ride	The Beatles
5/29	2	11.	Help Me, Rhonda	The Beach Boys
6/12	1	12.	Back In My Arms Again	The Supremes
6/19	2 ↕	13.	I Can't Help Myself	Four Tops
6/26	1	14.	Mr. Tambourine Man	The Byrds
7/10	4	15.	(I Can't Get No) Satisfaction	The Rolling Stones
8/07	1	16.	I'm Henry VIII, I Am	Herman's Hermits
8/14	3	17.	I Got You Babe	Sonny & Cher
9/04	3	18.	Help!	The Beatles
9/25	1	19.	Eve Of Destruction	Barry McGuire
10/02	1	20.	Hang On Sloopy	The McCoys
10/09	4	21.	Yesterday	The Beatles
11/06	2	22.	Get Off Of My Cloud	The Rolling Stones
11/20	2	23.	I Hear A Symphony	The Supremes
12/04	3	24.	Turn! Turn! Turn! (To Everything There Is A Season)	The Byrds
12/25	1	25.	Over And Over	The Dave Clark Five

1966

DATE	WKS		RECORD TITLE	ARTIST
1/01	2 ↕	1.	The Sounds Of Silence	Simon & Garfunkel
1/08	3 ↕	2.	We Can Work It Out	The Beatles
2/05	2	3.	My Love	Petula Clark
2/19	1	4.	Lightnin' Strikes	Lou Christie
2/26	1	5.	These Boots Are Made For Walkin'	Nancy Sinatra
3/05	5	6.	The Ballad Of The Green Berets	SSgt. Barry Sadler
4/09	3	7.	(You're My) Soul And Inspiration	The Righteous Brothers
4/30	1	8.	Good Lovin'	The Young Rascals
5/07	3	9.	Monday, Monday	The Mama's & The Papa's
5/28	2	10.	When A Man Loves A Woman	Percy Sledge
6/11	2	11.	Paint It, Black	The Rolling Stones

DATE	WKS		RECORD TITLE	ARTIST
6/25	2 ↕	12.	Paperback Writer	The Beatles
7/02	1	13.	Strangers In The Night	Frank Sinatra
7/16	2	14.	Hanky Panky	Tommy James & The Shondells
7/30	2	15.	Wild Thing	The Troggs
8/13	3	16.	Summer In The City	The Lovin' Spoonful
9/03	1	17.	Sunshine Superman	Donovan
9/10	2	18.	You Can't Hurry Love	The Supremes
9/24	3	19.	Cherish	The Association
10/15	2	20.	Reach Out I'll Be There	Four Tops
10/29	1	21.	96 Tears	? & The Mysterians
11/05	1	22.	Last Train To Clarksville	The Monkees
11/12	1	23.	Poor Side Of Town	Johnny Rivers
11/19	2	24.	You Keep Me Hangin' On	The Supremes
12/03	3 ↕	25.	Winchester Cathedral	The New Vaudeville Band
12/10	1	26.	Good Vibrations	The Beach Boys
12/31	7	27.	I'm A Believer	The Monkees

1967

DATE	WKS		RECORD TITLE	ARTIST
2/18	2	1.	Kind Of A Drag	The Buckinghams
3/04	1	2.	Ruby Tuesday	The Rolling Stones
3/11	1	3.	Love Is Here And Now You're Gone	The Supremes
3/18	1	4.	Penny Lane	The Beatles
3/25	3	5.	Happy Together	The Turtles
4/15	4	6.	Somethin' Stupid	Nancy Sinatra & Frank Sinatra
5/13	1	7.	The Happening	The Supremes
5/20	4 ↕	8.	Groovin'	The Young Rascals
6/03	2	9.	Respect	Aretha Franklin
7/01	4	10.	Windy	The Association
7/29	3	11.	Light My Fire	The Doors
8/19	1	12.	All You Need Is Love	The Beatles
8/26	4	13.	Ode To Billie Joe	Bobbie Gentry
9/23	4	14.	The Letter	The Box Tops
10/21	5	15.	To Sir With Love	Lulu
11/25	1	16.	Incense And Peppermints	Strawberry Alarm Clock
12/02	4	17.	Daydream Believer	The Monkees
12/30	3	18.	Hello Goodbye	The Beatles

1968

DATE	WKS		RECORD TITLE	ARTIST
1/20	2	1.	Judy In Disguise (With Glasses)	John Fred & His Playboy Band
2/03	1	2.	Green Tambourine	The Lemon Pipers
2/10	5	3.	Love Is Blue	Paul Mauriat
3/16	4	4.	(Sittin' On) The Dock Of The Bay	Otis Redding
4/13	5	5.	Honey	Bobby Goldsboro
5/18	2	6.	Tighten Up	Archie Bell & The Drells
6/01	3	7.	Mrs. Robinson	Simon & Garfunkel
6/22	4	8.	This Guy's In Love With You	Herb Alpert
7/20	2	9.	Grazing In The Grass	Hugh Masekela
8/03	2	10.	Hello, I Love You	The Doors
8/17	5	11.	People Got To Be Free	The Rascals
9/21	1	12.	Harper Valley P.T.A.	Jeannie C. Riley
9/28	9	13.	Hey Jude	The Beatles
11/30	2	14.	Love Child	Diana Ross & The Supremes
12/14	7	15.	I Heard It Through The Grapevine	Marvin Gaye

DATE	WKS	RECORD TITLE	ARTIST

1969

DATE	WKS	RECORD TITLE	ARTIST
2/01	2	1. Crimson And Clover	Tommy James & The Shondells
2/15	4	2. Everyday People	Sly & The Family Stone
3/15	4	3. Dizzy	Tommy Roe
4/12	6	4. Aquarius/Let The Sunshine In (The Flesh Failures)	The 5th Dimension
5/24	5	5. Get Back	The Beatles with Billy Preston
6/28	2	6. Love Theme From Romeo & Juliet	Henry Mancini
7/12	6	7. In The Year 2525 (Exordium & Terminus)	Zager & Evans
8/23	4	8. Honky Tonk Women	The Rolling Stones
9/20	4	9. Sugar, Sugar	The Archies
10/18	2	10. I Can't Get Next To You	The Temptations
11/01	1	11. Suspicious Minds	Elvis Presley
11/08	3	12. Wedding Bell Blues	The 5th Dimension
11/29	1	13. Come Together	The Beatles
12/06	2	14. Na Na Hey Hey Kiss Him Goodbye	Steam
12/20	1	15. Leaving On A Jet Plane	Peter, Paul & Mary
12/27	1	16. Someday We'll Be Together	Diana Ross & The Supremes

1970

DATE	WKS	RECORD TITLE	ARTIST
1/03	4	1. Raindrops Keep Fallin' On My Head	B.J. Thomas
1/31	1	2. I Want You Back	The Jackson 5
2/07	1	3. Venus	The Shocking Blue
2/14	2	4. Thank You (Falettinme Be Mice Elf Agin)	Sly & The Family Stone
2/28	6	5. Bridge Over Troubled Water	Simon & Garfunkel
4/11	2	6. Let It Be	The Beatles
4/25	2	7. ABC	The Jackson 5
5/09	3	8. American Woman	The Guess Who
5/30	2	9. Everything Is Beautiful	Ray Stevens
6/13	2	10. The Long And Winding Road	The Beatles
6/27	2	11. The Love You Save	The Jackson 5
7/11	2	12. Mama Told Me (Not To Come)	Three Dog Night
7/25	4	13. (They Long To Be) Close To You	Carpenters
8/22	1	14. Make It With You	Bread
8/29	3	15. War	Edwin Starr
9/19	3	16. Ain't No Mountain High Enough	Diana Ross
10/10	1	17. Cracklin' Rosie	Neil Diamond
10/17	5	18. I'll Be There	The Jackson 5
11/21	3	19. I Think I Love You	The Partridge Family
12/12	2	20. The Tears Of A Clown	Smokey Robinson & The Miracles
12/26	4	21. My Sweet Lord	George Harrison

1971

DATE	WKS	RECORD TITLE	ARTIST
1/23	3	1. Knock Three Times	Dawn
2/13	5	2. One Bad Apple	The Osmonds
3/20	2	3. Me And Bobby McGee	Janis Joplin
4/03	2	4. Just My Imagination (Running Away With Me)	The Temptations
4/17	6	5. Joy To The World	Three Dog Night
5/29	2	6. Brown Sugar	The Rolling Stones
6/12	1	7. Want Ads	The Honey Cone
6/19	5	8. It's Too Late	Carole King
7/24	1	9. Indian Reservation	Raiders
7/31	1	10. You've Got A Friend	James Taylor

DATE	WKS		RECORD TITLE	ARTIST
8/07	4	11.	How Can You Mend A Broken Heart	The Bee Gees
9/04	1	12.	Uncle Albert/Admiral Halsey	Paul & Linda McCartney
9/11	3	13.	Go Away Little Girl	Donny Osmond
10/02	5	14.	Maggie May	Rod Stewart
11/06	2	15.	Gypsys, Tramps & Thieves	Cher
11/20	2	16.	Theme From Shaft	Isaac Hayes
12/04	3	17.	Family Affair	Sly & The Family Stone
12/25	3	18.	Brand New Key	Melanie

1972

DATE	WKS		RECORD TITLE	ARTIST
1/15	4	1.	American Pie - Parts I & II	Don McLean
2/12	1	2.	Let's Stay Together	Al Green
2/19	4	3.	Without You	Nilsson
3/18	1	4.	Heart Of Gold	Neil Young
3/25	3	5.	A Horse With No Name	America
4/15	6	6.	The First Time Ever I Saw Your Face	Roberta Flack
5/27	1	7.	Oh Girl	Chi-Lites
6/03	1	8.	I'll Take You There	The Staple Singers
6/10	3	9.	The Candy Man	Sammy Davis, Jr.
7/01	1	10.	Song Sung Blue	Neil Diamond
7/08	3	11.	Lean On Me	Bill Withers
7/29	6 ↕	12.	Alone Again (Naturally)	Gilbert O'Sullivan
8/26	1	13.	Brandy (You're A Fine Girl)	Looking Glass
9/16	1	14.	Black & White	Three Dog Night
9/23	3	15.	Baby Don't Get Hooked On Me	Mac Davis
10/14	1	16.	Ben	Michael Jackson
10/21	2	17.	My Ding-A-Ling	Chuck Berry
11/04	4	18.	I Can See Clearly Now	Johnny Nash
12/02	1	19.	Papa Was A Rollin' Stone	The Temptations
12/09	1	20.	I Am Woman	Helen Reddy
12/16	3	21.	Me And Mrs. Jones	Billy Paul

1973

DATE	WKS		RECORD TITLE	ARTIST
1/06	3	1.	You're So Vain	Carly Simon
1/27	1	2.	Superstition	Stevie Wonder
2/03	3	3.	Crocodile Rock	Elton John
2/24	5 ↕	4.	Killing Me Softly With His Song	Roberta Flack
3/24	1	5.	Love Train	O'Jays
4/07	2	6.	The Night The Lights Went Out In Georgia	Vicki Lawrence
4/21	4	7.	Tie A Yellow Ribbon Round The Ole Oak Tree	Dawn Featuring Tony Orlando
5/19	1	8.	You Are The Sunshine Of My Life	Stevie Wonder
5/26	1	9.	Frankenstein	The Edgar Winter Group
6/02	4	10.	My Love	Paul McCartney & Wings
6/30	1	11.	Give Me Love - (Give Me Peace On Earth)	George Harrison
7/07	2	12.	Will It Go Round In Circles	Billy Preston
7/21	2	13.	Bad, Bad Leroy Brown	Jim Croce
8/04	2	14.	The Morning After	Maureen McGovern
8/18	1	15.	Touch Me In The Morning	Diana Ross
8/25	2	16.	Brother Louie	Stories
9/08	2 ↕	17.	Let's Get It On	Marvin Gaye
9/15	1	18.	Delta Dawn	Helen Reddy
9/29	1	19.	We're An American Band	Grand Funk
10/06	2	20.	Half-Breed	Cher
10/20	1	21.	Angie	The Rolling Stones

DATE	WKS		RECORD TITLE	ARTIST
10/27	2	22.	Midnight Train To Georgia	Gladys Knight & The Pips
11/10	2	23.	Keep On Truckin' (Part 1)	Eddie Kendricks
11/24	1	24.	Photograph	Ringo Starr
12/01	2	25.	Top Of The World	Carpenters
12/15	2	26.	The Most Beautiful Girl	Charlie Rich
12/29	2	27.	Time In A Bottle	Jim Croce

1974

DATE	WKS		RECORD TITLE	ARTIST
1/12	1	1.	The Joker	Steve Miller Band
1/19	1	2.	Show And Tell	Al Wilson
1/26	1	3.	You're Sixteen	Ringo Starr
2/02	3 ↕	4.	The Way We Were	Barbra Streisand
2/09	1	5.	Love's Theme	Love Unlimited Orchestra
3/02	3	6.	Seasons In The Sun	Terry Jacks
3/23	1	7.	Dark Lady	Cher
3/30	1	8.	Sunshine On My Shoulders	John Denver
4/06	1	9.	Hooked On A Feeling	Blue Swede
4/13	1	10.	Bennie And The Jets	Elton John
4/20	2	11.	TSOP (The Sound Of Philadelphia)	MFSB featuring The Three Degrees
5/04	2	12.	The Loco-Motion	Grand Funk
5/18	3	13.	The Streak	Ray Stevens
6/08	1	14.	Band On The Run	Paul McCartney & Wings
6/15	2	15.	Billy, Don't Be A Hero	Bo Donaldson & The Heywoods
6/29	1	16.	Sundown	Gordon Lightfoot
7/06	1	17.	Rock The Boat	The Hues Corporation
7/13	2	18.	Rock Your Baby	George McCrae
7/27	2	19.	Annie's Song	John Denver
8/10	1	20.	Feel Like Makin' Love	Roberta Flack
8/17	1	21.	The Night Chicago Died	Paper Lace
8/24	3	22.	(You're) Having My Baby	Paul Anka
9/14	1	23.	I Shot The Sheriff	Eric Clapton
9/21	1	24.	Can't Get Enough Of Your Love, Babe	Barry White
9/28	1	25.	Rock Me Gently	Andy Kim
10/05	2	26.	I Honestly Love You	Olivia Newton-John
10/19	1	27.	Nothing From Nothing	Billy Preston
10/26	1	28.	Then Came You	Dionne Warwicke & Spinners
11/02	1	29.	You Haven't Done Nothin	Stevie Wonder
11/09	1	30.	You Ain't Seen Nothing Yet	Bachman-Turner Overdrive
11/16	1	31.	Whatever Gets You Thru The Night	John Lennon/Plastic Ono Band
11/23	2	32.	I Can Help	Billy Swan
12/07	2	33.	Kung Fu Fighting	Carl Douglas
12/21	1	34.	Cat's In The Cradle	Harry Chapin
12/28	1	35.	Angie Baby	Helen Reddy

1975

DATE	WKS		RECORD TITLE	ARTIST
1/04	2	1.	Lucy In The Sky With Diamonds	Elton John
1/18	1	2.	Mandy	Barry Manilow
1/25	1	3.	Please Mr. Postman	Carpenters
2/01	1	4.	Laughter In The Rain	Neil Sedaka
2/08	1	5.	Fire	Ohio Players
2/15	1	6.	You're No Good	Linda Ronstadt
2/22	1	7.	Pick Up The Pieces	AWB
3/01	1	8.	Best Of My Love	Eagles
3/08	1	9.	Have You Never Been Mellow	Olivia Newton-John

DATE	WKS		RECORD TITLE	ARTIST
3/15	1	10.	Black Water	The Doobie Brothers
3/22	1	11.	My Eyes Adored You	Frankie Valli
3/29	1	12.	Lady Marmalade	LaBelle
4/05	1	13.	Lovin' You	Minnie Riperton
4/12	2	14.	Philadelphia Freedom	The Elton John Band
4/26	1	15.	(Hey Won't You Play) Another Somebody Done Somebody Wrong Song	B.J. Thomas
5/03	3	16.	He Don't Love You (Like I Love You)	Tony Orlando & Dawn
5/24	1	17.	Shining Star	Earth, Wind & Fire
5/31	1	18.	Before The Next Teardrop Falls	Freddy Fender
6/07	1	19.	Thank God I'm A Country Boy	John Denver
6/14	1	20.	Sister Golden Hair	America
6/21	4	21.	Love Will Keep Us Together	The Captain & Tennille
7/19	1	22.	Listen To What The Man Said	Wings
7/26	1	23.	The Hustle	Van McCoy/The Soul City Symphony
8/02	1	24.	One Of These Nights	Eagles
8/09	2	25.	Jive Talkin'	Bee Gees
8/23	1	26.	Fallin' In Love	Hamilton, Joe Frank & Reynolds
8/30	1	27.	Get Down Tonight	K.C. & The Sunshine Band
9/06	2	28.	Rhinestone Cowboy	Glen Campbell
9/20	2 ↕	29.	Fame	David Bowie
9/27	1	30.	I'm Sorry	John Denver
10/11	3	31.	Bad Blood	Neil Sedaka
11/01	3	32.	Island Girl	Elton John
11/22	2 ↕	33.	That's The Way (I Like It)	KC & The Sunshine Band
11/29	3	34.	Fly, Robin, Fly	Silver Convention
12/27	1	35.	Let's Do It Again	The Staple Singers

1976

DATE	WKS		RECORD TITLE	ARTIST
1/03	1	1.	Saturday Night	Bay City Rollers
1/10	1	2.	Convoy	C.W. McCall
1/17	1	3.	I Write The Songs	Barry Manilow
1/24	1	4.	Theme From Mahogany (Do You Know Where You're Going to)	Diana Ross
1/31	1	5.	Love Rollercoaster	Ohio Players
2/07	3	6.	50 Ways To Leave Your Lover	Paul Simon
2/28	1	7.	Theme From S.W.A.T.	Rhythm Heritage
3/06	1	8.	Love Machine (Part 1)	The Miracles
3/13	3	9.	December, 1963 (Oh, What a Night)	The Four Seasons
4/03	4	10.	Disco Lady	Johnnie Taylor
5/01	1	11.	Let Your Love Flow	Bellamy Brothers
5/08	1	12.	Welcome Back	John Sebastian
5/15	1	13.	Boogie Fever	Sylvers
5/22	5 ↕	14.	Silly Love Songs	Wings
5/29	2	15.	Love Hangover	Diana Ross
7/10	2	16.	Afternoon Delight	Starland Vocal Band
7/24	2	17.	Kiss And Say Goodbye	Manhattans
8/07	4	18.	Don't Go Breaking My Heart	Elton John & Kiki Dee
9/04	1	19.	You Should Be Dancing	Bee Gees
9/11	1	20.	(Shake, Shake, Shake) Shake Your Booty	KC & The Sunshine Band
9/18	3	21.	Play That Funky Music	Wild Cherry
10/09	1	22.	A Fifth Of Beethoven	Walter Murphy & The Big Apple Band
10/16	1	23.	Disco Duck (Part 1)	Rick Dees & His Cast Of Idiots

DATE	WKS		RECORD TITLE	ARTIST
10/23	2	24.	If You Leave Me Now	Chicago
11/06	1	25.	Rock'n Me	Steve Miller
11/13	8	26.	Tonight's The Night (Gonna Be Alright)	Rod Stewart

1977

DATE	WKS		RECORD TITLE	ARTIST
1/08	1	1.	You Don't Have To Be A Star (To Be In My Show)	Marilyn McCoo & Billy Davis, Jr.
1/15	1	2.	You Make Me Feel Like Dancing	Leo Sayer
1/22	1	3.	I Wish	Stevie Wonder
1/29	1	4.	Car Wash	Rose Royce
2/05	2	5.	Torn Between Two Lovers	Mary MacGregor
2/19	1	6.	Blinded By The Light	Manfred Mann's Earth Band
2/26	1	7.	New Kid In Town	Eagles
3/05	3	8.	Love Theme From "A Star Is Born" (Evergreen)	Barbra Streisand
3/26	2	9.	Rich Girl	Daryl Hall & John Oates
4/09	1	10.	Dancing Queen	Abba
4/16	1	11.	Don't Give Up On Us	David Soul
4/23	1	12.	Don't Leave Me This Way	Thelma Houston
4/30	1	13.	Southern Nights	Glen Campbell
5/07	1	14.	Hotel California	Eagles
5/14	1	15.	When I Need You	Leo Sayer
5/21	3	16.	Sir Duke	Stevie Wonder
6/11	1	17.	I'm Your Boogie Man	KC & The Sunshine Band
6/18	1	18.	Dreams	Fleetwood Mac
6/25	1	19.	Got To Give It Up (Pt. I)	Marvin Gaye
7/02	1	20.	Gonna Fly Now	Bill Conti
7/09	1	21.	Undercover Angel	Alan O'Day
7/16	1	22.	Da Doo Ron Ron	Shaun Cassidy
7/23	1	23.	Looks Like We Made It	Barry Manilow
7/30	4 ↕	24.	I Just Want To Be Your Everything	Andy Gibb
8/20	5 ↕	25.	Best Of My Love	Emotions
10/01	2	26.	Star Wars Theme/Cantina Band	Meco
10/15	10	27.	You Light Up My Life	Debby Boone
12/24	3	28.	How Deep Is Your Love	Bee Gees

1978

DATE	WKS		RECORD TITLE	ARTIST
1/14	3	1.	Baby Come Back	Player
2/04	4	2.	Stayin' Alive	Bee Gees
3/04	2	3.	(Love Is) Thicker Than Water	Andy Gibb
3/18	8	4.	Night Fever	Bee Gees
5/13	1	5.	If I Can't Have You	Yvonne Elliman
5/20	2	6.	With A Little Luck	Wings
6/03	1	7.	Too Much, Too Little, Too Late	Johnny Mathis/Deniece Williams
6/10	1	8.	You're The One That I Want	John Travolta & Olivia Newton-John
6/17	7	9.	Shadow Dancing	Andy Gibb
8/05	1	10.	Miss You	The Rolling Stones
8/12	2	11.	Three Times A Lady	Commodores
8/26	2	12.	Grease	Frankie Valli
9/09	3	13.	Boogie Oogie Oogie	A Taste Of Honey
9/30	4	14.	Kiss You All Over	Exile
10/28	1	15.	Hot Child In The City	Nick Gilder
11/04	1	16.	You Needed Me	Anne Murray
11/11	3	17.	MacArthur Park	Donna Summer
12/02	2 ↕	18.	You Don't Bring Me Flowers	Barbra Streisand & Neil Diamond
12/09	6 ↕	19.	Le Freak	Chic

DATE	WKS		RECORD TITLE	ARTIST

1979

DATE	WKS		RECORD TITLE	ARTIST
1/06	2	1.	Too Much Heaven	Bee Gees
2/10	4	2.	Da Ya Think I'm Sexy?	Rod Stewart
3/10	3 ↕	3.	I Will Survive	Gloria Gaynor
3/24	2	4.	Tragedy	Bee Gees
4/14	1	5.	What A Fool Believes	The Doobie Brothers
4/21	1	6.	Knock On Wood	Amii Stewart
4/28	1	7.	Heart Of Glass	Blondie
5/05	4	8.	Reunited	Peaches & Herb
6/02	3 ↕	9.	Hot Stuff	Donna Summer
6/09	1	10.	Love You Inside Out	Bee Gees
6/30	2	11.	Ring My Bell	Anita Ward
7/14	5	12.	Bad Girls	Donna Summer
8/18	1	13.	Good Times	Chic
8/25	6	14.	My Sharona	The Knack
10/06	1	15.	Sad Eyes	Robert John
10/13	1	16.	Don't Stop 'Til You Get Enough	Michael Jackson
10/20	2	17.	Rise	Herb Alpert
11/03	1	18.	Pop Muzik	M
11/10	1	19.	Heartache Tonight	Eagles
11/17	1	20.	Still	Commodores
11/24	2	21.	No More Tears (Enough Is Enough)	Barbra Streisand/Donna Summer
12/08	2	22.	Babe	Styx
12/22	3 ↕	23.	Escape (The Pina Colada Song)	Rupert Holmes

1980

DATE	WKS		RECORD TITLE	ARTIST
1/05	1	1.	Please Don't Go	K.C. & The Sunshine Band
1/19	4	2.	Rock With You	Michael Jackson
2/16	1	3.	Do That To Me One More Time	The Captain & Tennille
2/23	4	4.	Crazy Little Thing Called Love	Queen
3/22	4	5.	Another Brick In The Wall (Part II)	Pink Floyd
4/19	6	6.	Call Me	Blondie
5/31	4	7.	Funkytown	Lipps, Inc.
6/28	3	8.	Coming Up (Live at Glasgow)	Paul McCartney & Wings
7/19	2	9.	It's Still Rock And Roll To Me	Billy Joel
8/02	4	10.	Magic	Olivia Newton-John
8/30	1	11.	Sailing	Christopher Cross
9/06	4	12.	Upside Down	Diana Ross
10/04	3	13.	Another One Bites The Dust	Queen
10/25	3	14.	Woman In Love	Barbra Streisand
11/15	6	15.	Lady	Kenny Rogers
12/27	5	16.	(Just Like) Starting Over	John Lennon

1981

DATE	WKS		RECORD TITLE	ARTIST
1/31	1	1.	The Tide Is High	Blondie
2/07	2	2.	Celebration	Kool & The Gang
2/21	2 ↕	3.	9 To 5	Dolly Parton
2/28	2	4.	I Love A Rainy Night	Eddie Rabbitt
3/21	1	5.	Keep On Loving You	REO Speedwagon
3/28	2	6.	Rapture	Blondie
4/11	3	7.	Kiss On My List	Daryl Hall & John Oates
5/02	2	8.	Morning Train (Nine To Five)	Sheena Easton
5/16	9 ↕	9.	Bette Davis Eyes	Kim Carnes

DATE	WKS	RECORD TITLE	ARTIST
6/20	1	10. Medley	Stars on 45
7/25	1	11. The One That You Love	Air Supply
8/01	2	12. Jessie's Girl	Rick Springfield
8/15	9	13. Endless Love	Diana Ross & Lionel Richie
10/17	3	14. Arthur's Theme (Best That You Can Do)	Christopher Cross
11/07	2	15. Private Eyes	Daryl Hall & John Oates
11/21	10	16. Physical	Olivia Newton-John

1982

DATE	WKS	RECORD TITLE	ARTIST
1/30	1	1. I Can't Go For That (No Can Do)	Daryl Hall & John Oates
2/06	6	2. Centerfold	The J. Geils Band
3/20	7	3. I Love Rock 'N Roll	Joan Jett & The Blackhearts
5/08	1	4. Chariots Of Fire - Titles	Vangelis
5/15	7	5. Ebony And Ivory	Paul McCartney with Stevie Wonder
7/03	3	6. Don't You Want Me	The Human League
7/24	6	7. Eye Of The Tiger	Survivor
9/04	2 ↕	8. Abracadabra	The Steve Miller Band
9/11	2	9. Hard To Say I'm Sorry	Chicago
10/02	4	10. Jack & Diane	John Cougar
10/30	1	11. Who Can It Be Now?	Men At Work
11/06	3	12. Up Where We Belong	Joe Cocker & Jennifer Warnes
11/27	2	13. Truly	Lionel Richie
12/11	1	14. Mickey	Toni Basil
12/18	4	15. Maneater	Daryl Hall & John Oates

1983

DATE	WKS	RECORD TITLE	ARTIST
1/15	4 ↕	1. Down Under	Men At Work
2/05	1	2. Africa	Toto
2/19	2	3. Baby, Come To Me	Patti Austin with James Ingram
3/05	7	4. Billie Jean	Michael Jackson
4/23	1	5. Come On Eileen	Dexys Midnight Runners
4/30	3	6. Beat It	Michael Jackson
5/21	1	7. Let's Dance	David Bowie
5/28	6	8. Flashdance...What A Feeling	Irene Cara
7/09	8	9. Every Breath You Take	The Police
9/03	1	10. Sweet Dreams (Are Made of This)	Eurythmics
9/10	2	11. Maniac	Michael Sembello
9/24	1	12. Tell Her About It	Billy Joel
10/01	4	13. Total Eclipse Of The Heart	Bonnie Tyler
10/29	2	14. Islands In The Stream	Kenny Rogers with Dolly Parton
11/12	4	15. All Night Long (All Night)	Lionel Richie
12/10	6	16. Say Say Say	Paul McCartney & Michael Jackson

1984

DATE	WKS	RECORD TITLE	ARTIST
1/21	2	1. Owner Of A Lonely Heart	Yes
2/04	3	2. Karma Chameleon	Culture Club
2/25	5	3. Jump	Van Halen
3/31	3	4. Footloose	Kenny Loggins
4/21	3	5. Against All Odds (Take A Look At Me Now)	Phil Collins
5/12	2	6. Hello	Lionel Richie
5/26	2	7. Let's Hear It For The Boy	Deniece Williams
6/09	2	8. Time After Time	Cyndi Lauper

DATE	WKS		RECORD TITLE	ARTIST
6/23	2	9.	The Reflex	Duran Duran
7/07	5	10.	When Doves Cry	Prince
8/11	3	11.	Ghostbusters	Ray Parker Jr.
9/01	3	12.	What's Love Got To Do With It	Tina Turner
9/22	1	13.	Missing You	John Waite
9/29	2	14.	Let's Go Crazy	Prince & the Revolution
10/13	3	15.	I Just Called To Say I Love You	Stevie Wonder
11/03	2	16.	Caribbean Queen (No More Love On The Run)	Billy Ocean
11/17	3	17.	Wake Me Up Before You Go-Go	Wham!
12/08	2	18.	Out Of Touch	Daryl Hall & John Oates
12/22	6	19.	Like A Virgin	Madonna

1985

DATE	WKS		RECORD TITLE	ARTIST
2/02	2	1.	I Want To Know What Love Is	Foreigner
2/16	3	2.	Careless Whisper	Wham! Featuring George Michael
3/09	3	3.	Can't Fight This Feeling	REO Speedwagon
3/30	2	4.	One More Night	Phil Collins
4/13	4	5.	We Are The World	USA for Africa
5/11	1	6.	Crazy For You	Madonna
5/18	1	7.	Don't You (Forget About Me)	Simple Minds
5/25	2	8.	Everything She Wants	Wham!
6/08	2	9.	Everybody Wants To Rule The World	Tears For Fears
6/22	2	10.	Heaven	Bryan Adams
7/06	1	11.	Sussudio	Phil Collins
7/13	2	12.	A View To A Kill	Duran Duran
7/27	1	13.	Everytime You Go Away	Paul Young
8/03	3	14.	Shout	Tears For Fears
8/24	2	15.	The Power Of Love	Huey Lewis & the News
9/07	2	16.	St. Elmo's Fire (Man In Motion)	John Parr
9/21	3	17.	Money For Nothing	Dire Straits
10/12	1	18.	Oh Sheila	Ready For The World
10/19	1	19.	Take On Me	a-ha
10/26	1	20.	Saving All My Love For You	Whitney Houston
11/02	1	21.	Part-Time Lover	Stevie Wonder
11/09	1	22.	Miami Vice Theme	Jan Hammer
11/16	2	23.	We Built This City	Starship
11/30	1	24.	Separate Lives	Phil Collins & Marilyn Martin
12/07	2	25.	Broken Wings	Mr. Mister
12/21	4	26.	Say You, Say Me	Lionel Richie

1986

DATE	WKS		RECORD TITLE	ARTIST
1/18	4	1.	That's What Friends Are For	Dionne & Friends
2/15	2	2.	How Will I Know	Whitney Houston
3/01	2	3.	Kyrie	Mr. Mister
3/15	1	4.	Sara	Starship
3/22	1	5.	These Dreams	Heart
3/29	3	6.	Rock Me Amadeus	Falco
4/19	2	7.	Kiss	Prince & The Revolution
5/03	1	8.	Addicted To Love	Robert Palmer
5/10	1	9.	West End Girls	Pet Shop Boys
5/17	3	10.	Greatest Love Of All	Whitney Houston
6/07	1	11.	Live To Tell	Madonna
6/14	3	12.	On My Own	Patti LaBelle & Michael McDonald
7/05	1	13.	There'll Be Sad Songs (To Make You Cry)	Billy Ocean

DATE	WKS		RECORD TITLE	ARTIST
7/12	1	14.	Holding Back The Years	Simply Red
7/19	1	15.	Invisible Touch	Genesis
7/26	1	16.	Sledgehammer	Peter Gabriel
8/02	2	17.	Glory Of Love	Peter Cetera
8/16	2	18.	Papa Don't Preach	Madonna
8/30	1	19.	Higher Love	Steve Winwood
9/06	1	20.	Venus	Bananarama
9/13	1	21.	Take My Breath Away	Berlin
9/20	3	22.	Stuck With You	Huey Lewis & the News
10/11	2	23.	When I Think Of You	Janet Jackson
10/25	2	24.	True Colors	Cyndi Lauper
11/08	2	25.	Amanda	Boston
11/22	1	26.	Human	Human League
11/29	1	27.	You Give Love A Bad Name	Bon Jovi
12/06	1	28.	The Next Time I Fall	Peter Cetera w/Amy Grant
12/13	1	29.	The Way It Is	Bruce Hornsby & The Range
12/20	4	30.	Walk Like An Egyptian	Bangles

1987

DATE	WKS		RECORD TITLE	ARTIST
1/17	1	1.	Shake You Down	Gregory Abbott
1/24	2	2.	At This Moment	Billy Vera & The Beaters
2/07	1	3.	Open Your Heart	Madonna
2/14	4	4.	Livin' On A Prayer	Bon Jovi
3/14	1	5.	Jacob's Ladder	Huey Lewis & the News
3/21	2	6.	Lean On Me	Club Nouveau
4/04	2	7.	Nothing's Gonna Stop Us Now	Starship
4/18	2	8.	I Knew You Were Waiting (For Me)	Aretha Franklin & George Michael
5/02	2	9.	(I Just) Died In Your Arms	Cutting Crew
5/16	3	10.	With Or Without You	U2
6/06	1	11.	You Keep Me Hangin' On	Kim Wilde
6/13	1	12.	Always	Atlantic Starr
6/20	1	13.	Head To Toe	Lisa Lisa & Cult Jam
6/27	2	14.	I Wanna Dance With Somebody (Who Loves Me)	Whitney Houston
7/11	3	15.	Alone	Heart
8/01	1	16.	Shakedown	Bob Seger
8/08	2	17.	I Still Haven't Found What I'm Looking For	U2
8/22	1	18.	Who's That Girl	Madonna
8/29	3	19.	La Bamba	Los Lobos
9/19	1	20.	I Just Can't Stop Loving You	Michael Jackson
9/26	2	21.	Didn't We Almost Have It All	Whitney Houston
10/10	1	22.	Here I Go Again	Whitesnake
10/17	1	23.	Lost In Emotion	Lisa Lisa & Cult Jam
10/24	2	24.	Bad	Michael Jackson
11/07	2	25.	I Think We're Alone Now	Tiffany
11/21	1	26.	Mony Mony "Live"	Billy Idol
11/28	1	27.	(I've Had) The Time Of My Life	Bill Medley & Jennifer Warnes
12/05	1	28.	Heaven Is A Place On Earth	Belinda Carlisle
12/12	4	29.	Faith	George Michael

1988

DATE	WKS		RECORD TITLE	ARTIST
1/09	1	1.	So Emotional	Whitney Houston
1/16	1	2.	Got My Mind Set On You	George Harrison
1/23	1	3.	The Way You Make Me Feel	Michael Jackson

DATE	WKS		RECORD TITLE	ARTIST
1/30	1	4.	Need You Tonight	INXS
2/06	2	5.	Could've Been	Tiffany
2/20	1	6.	Seasons Change	Expose
2/27	2	7.	Father Figure	George Michael
3/12	2	8.	Never Gonna Give You Up	Rick Astley
3/26	2	9.	Man In The Mirror	Michael Jackson
4/09	2	10.	Get Outta My Dreams, Get Into My Car	Billy Ocean
4/23	2	11.	Where Do Broken Hearts Go	Whitney Houston
5/07	1	12.	Wishing Well	Terence Trent D'Arby
5/14	2	13.	Anything For You	Gloria Estefan & Miami Sound Machine
5/28	3	14.	One More Try	George Michael
6/18	1	15.	Together Forever	Rick Astley
6/25	1	16.	Foolish Beat	Debbie Gibson
7/02	1	17.	Dirty Diana	Michael Jackson
7/09	2	18.	The Flame	Cheap Trick
7/23	1	19.	Hold On To The Nights	Richard Marx
7/30	4	20.	Roll With It	Steve Winwood
8/27	2	21.	Monkey	George Michael
9/10	2	22.	Sweet Child O' Mine	Guns N' Roses
9/24	2	23.	Don't Worry Be Happy	Bobby McFerrin
10/08	1	24.	Love Bites	Def Leppard
10/15	1	25.	Red Red Wine	UB40
10/22	2	26.	Groovy Kind Of Love	Phil Collins
11/05	1	27.	Kokomo	The Beach Boys
11/12	1	28.	Wild, Wild West	The Escape Club
11/19	2	29.	Bad Medicine	Bon Jovi
12/03	1	30.	Baby, I Love Your Way/Freebird Medley (Free Baby)	Will To Power
12/10	2	31.	Look Away	Chicago
12/24	3	32.	Every Rose Has Its Thorn	Poison

1989

DATE	WKS		RECORD TITLE	ARTIST
1/14	1	1.	My Prerogative	Bobby Brown
1/21	2	2.	Two Hearts	Phil Collins
2/04	1	3.	When I'm With You	Sheriff
2/11	3	4.	Straight Up	Paula Abdul
3/04	3	5.	Lost In Your Eyes	Debbie Gibson
3/25	1	6.	The Living Years	Mike & The Mechanics
4/01	1	7.	Eternal Flame	Bangles
4/08	1	8.	The Look	Roxette
4/15	1	9.	She Drives Me Crazy	Fine Young Cannibals
4/22	3	10.	Like A Prayer	Madonna
5/13	1	11.	I'll Be There For You	Bon Jovi
5/20	2	12.	Forever Your Girl	Paula Abdul
6/03	1	13.	Rock On	Michael Damian
6/10	1	14.	Wind Beneath My Wings	Bette Midler
6/17	1	15.	I'll Be Loving You (Forever)	New Kids On The Block
6/24	1	16.	Satisfied	Richard Marx
7/01	1	17.	Baby Don't Forget My Number	Milli Vanilli
7/08	1	18.	Good Thing	Fine Young Cannibals
7/15	1	19.	If You Don't Know Me By Now	Simply Red
7/22	2	20.	Toy Soldiers	Martika

DATE	WKS		RECORD TITLE	ARTIST
8/05	1	21.	Batdance	Prince
8/12	3	22.	Right Here Waiting	Richard Marx
9/02	1	23.	Cold Hearted	Paula Abdul
9/09	1	24.	Hangin' Tough	New Kids On The Block
9/16	1	25.	Don't Wanna Lose You	Gloria Estefan
9/23	2	26.	Girl I'm Gonna Miss You	Milli Vanilli
10/07	4	27.	Miss You Much	Janet Jackson
11/04	1	28.	Listen To Your Heart	Roxette
11/11	2	29.	When I See You Smile	Bad English
11/25	2	30.	Blame It On The Rain	Milli Vanilli
12/09	2	31.	We Didn't Start The Fire	Billy Joel
12/23	4	32.	Another Day In Paradise	Phil Collins

1990

DATE	WKS		RECORD TITLE	ARTIST
1/20	3	1.	How Am I Supposed To Live Without You	Michael Bolton
2/10	3	2.	Opposites Attract	Paula Abdul with The Wild Pair
3/03	3	3.	Escapade	Janet Jackson
3/24	2	4.	Black Velvet	Alannah Myles
4/07	1	5.	Love Will Lead You Back	Taylor Dayne
4/14	1	6.	I'll Be Your Everything	Tommy Page
4/21	4	7.	Nothing Compares 2 U	Sinead O'Connor
5/19	3	8.	Vogue	Madonna
6/09	1	9.	Hold On	Wilson Phillips
6/16	2	10.	It Must Have Been Love	Roxette
6/30	3	11.	Step By Step	New Kids On The Block
7/21	2	12.	She Ain't Worth It	Glenn Medeiros Feat. Bobby Brown
8/04	4	13.	Vision Of Love	Mariah Carey
9/01	1	14.	If Wishes Came True	Sweet Sensation
9/08	1	15.	Blaze Of Glory	Jon Bon Jovi
9/15	2	16.	Release Me	Wilson Phillips
9/29	1	17.	(Can't Live Without Your) Love And Affection	Nelson
10/06	1	18.	Close To You	Maxi Priest
10/13	1	19.	Praying For Time	George Michael
10/20	1	20.	I Don't Have The Heart	James Ingram
10/27	1	21.	Black Cat	Janet Jackson
11/03	1	22.	Ice Ice Baby	Vanilla Ice
11/10	3	23.	Love Takes Time	Mariah Carey
12/01	1	24.	I'm Your Baby Tonight	Whitney Houston
12/08	4	25.	Because I Love You (The Postman Song)	Stevie B

1991

DATE	WKS		RECORD TITLE	ARTIST
1/05	2	1.	Justify My Love	Madonna
1/19	1	2.	Love Will Never Do (Without You)	Janet Jackson
1/26	2	3.	The First Time	Surface
2/09	2	4.	Gonna Make You Sweat (Everybody Dance Now)	C & C Music Factory Featuring Freedom Williams
2/23	2	5.	All The Man That I Need	Whitney Houston
3/09	2	6.	Someday	Mariah Carey
3/23	1	7.	One More Try	Timmy -T-
3/30	2	8.	Coming Out Of The Dark	Gloria Estefan
4/13	1	9.	I've Been Thinking About You	Londonbeat
4/20	1	10.	You're In Love	Wilson Phillips
4/27	2	11.	Baby Baby	Amy Grant

DATE	WKS		RECORD TITLE	ARTIST
5/11	1	12.	Joyride	Roxette
5/18	1	13.	I Like The Way (The Kissing Game)	Hi-Five
5/25	2	14.	I Don't Wanna Cry	Mariah Carey
6/08	1	15.	More Than Words	Extreme
6/15	5	16.	Rush, Rush	Paula Abdul
7/20	1	17.	Unbelievable	EMF
7/27	7	18.	(Everything I Do) I Do It For You	Bryan Adams
9/14	1	19.	The Promise Of A New Day	Paula Abdul
9/21	2	20.	I Adore Mi Amor	Color Me Badd
10/05	1	21.	Good Vibrations	Marky Mark & The Funky Bunch Featuring Loleatta Holloway
10/12	3	22.	Emotions	Mariah Carey
11/02	1	23.	Romantic	Karyn White
11/09	2	24.	Cream	Prince And The N.P.G.
11/23	1	25.	When A Man Loves A Woman	Michael Bolton

11/30/91: BILLBOARD BEGINS COMPILING "HOT 100" FROM DATA PROVIDED BY BDS AND SOUNDSCAN.

DATE	WKS		RECORD TITLE	ARTIST
11/30	1	26.	Set Adrift On Memory Bliss	PM Dawn
12/07	7	27.	Black Or White	Michael Jackson

1992

DATE	WKS		RECORD TITLE	ARTIST
1/25	1	1.	All 4 Love	Color Me Badd
2/01	1	2.	Don't Let The Sun Go Down On Me	George Michael/Elton John
2/08	3	3.	I'm Too Sexy	R*S*F (Right Said Fred)
2/29	3	4.	To Be With You	Mr. Big
3/21	5	5.	Save The Best For Last	Vanessa Williams
4/25	8	6.	Jump	Kris Kross
6/20	2	7.	I'll Be There	Mariah Carey
7/04	5	8.	Baby Got Back	Sir Mix-A-Lot
8/08	1	9.	This Used To Be My Playground	Madonna
8/15	13	10.	End of the Road	Boyz II Men
11/14	2	11.	How Do You Talk To An Angel	The Heights
11/28	14	12.	I Will Always Love You	Whitney Houston

1993

DATE	WKS		RECORD TITLE	ARTIST
3/06	1	1.	A Whole New World (Aladdin's Theme)	Peabo Bryson & Regina Belle
3/13	7	2.	Informer	Snow
5/01	2	3.	Freak Me	Silk
5/15	8	4.	That's The Way Love Goes	Janet Jackson
7/10	2	5.	Weak	SWV (Sisters With Voices)
7/24	7	6.	Can't Help Falling In Love	UB40
9/11	8	7.	Dreamlover	Mariah Carey
11/06	5	8.	I'd Do Anything For Love (But I Won't Do That)	Meat Loaf
12/11	2	9.	Again	Janet Jackson
12/25	4	10.	Hero	Mariah Carey

1994

DATE	WKS		RECORD TITLE	ARTIST
1/22	3	1.	All For Love	Bryan Adams/Rod Stewart/Sting
2/12	4	2.	The Power Of Love	Celine Dion
3/12	6 ↕	3.	The Sign	Ace Of Base
4/09	4	4.	Bump N' Grind	R. Kelly
5/21	11	5.	I Swear	All-4-One

DATE	WKS		RECORD TITLE	ARTIST
8/06	3	6.	Stay (I Missed You)	Lisa Loeb & Nine Stories
8/27	14	7.	I'll Make Love To You	Boyz II Men
12/03	6 ↕	8.	On Bended Knee	Boyz II Men
12/17	2	9.	Here Comes The Hotstepper	Ini Kamoze

1995

DATE	WKS		RECORD TITLE	ARTIST
1/28	4	1.	Creep	TLC
2/25	7	2.	Take A Bow	Madonna
4/15	7	3.	This Is How We Do It	Montell Jordan
6/03	5	4.	Have You Ever Really Loved Woman	Bryan Adams
7/08	7	5.	Waterfalls	TLC
8/26	1	6.	Kiss From A Rose	Seal
9/02	1	7.	You Are Not Alone	Michael Jackson
9/09	3	8.	Gangstas Paradise	Coolio Featuring L.V.
9/30	8	9.	Fantasy	Mariah Carey
11/25	1	10.	Exhale (Shoop Shoop)	Whitney Houston
12/02	16	11.	One Sweet Day	Mariah Carey & Boyz II Men

1996

DATE	WKS		RECORD TITLE	ARTIST
3/23	6	1.	Because You Loved Me	Celine Dion
5/04	2	2.	Always Be My Baby	Mariah Carey
5/18	8	3.	Tha Crossroads	Bones thugs-n-harmony
7/13	2	4.	How Do U Want It	2 Pac (featuring KC & JoJo)
7/27	1	5.	You're Makin' Me High	Toni Braxton
8/03	14	6.	Macarena (bayside boys mix)	Los Del rio
11/09	4	7.	No Diggity	BLACKstreet (Featuring Dr. Dre)
12/07	16 ᴬ	8.	Don't Speak	No Doubt
12/07	11	9.	Un-Break My Heart	Toni Braxton

1997

DATE	WKS		RECORD TITLE	ARTIST
2/22	4	1.	Wannabe	Spice Girls
3/22	6	2.	Can't Nobody Hold Me Down	Puff Daddy Featuring Mase
5/03	3	3.	Hypnotize	The Notorious B.I.G.
5/24	3	4.	MMMBop	Hanson
6/14	11	5.	I'll Be Missing You	Puff Daddy & Faith Evans (w/112)
8/09	4 ᴬ	6.	Men In Black	Will Smith
8/30	2	7.	Mo Money Mo Problems	The Notorious B.I.G. feat. Puff Daddy & Mase
9/13	3	8.	Honey	Mariah Carey
10/04	1	9.	4 Seasons Of Loneliness	Boyz II Men
10/11	14	10.	Candle In The Wind 1997/ Something About The Way You Look Tonight	Elton John
10/18	6 ᴬ	11.	Fly	Sugar Ray

1998

DATE	WKS		RECORD TITLE	ARTIST
1/17	2	1.	Truly Madly Deeply	Savage Garden
1/31	2	2.	Together Again	Janet Jackson
2/14	2	3.	Nice & Slow	Usher
2/28	2	4.	My Heart Will Go On (Love Theme From 'Titanic')	Celine Dion
3/14	3	5.	Gettin' Jiggy Wit It	Will Smith
4/04	3	6.	All My Life	K-Ci & JoJo
4/25	5 ↕	7.	Too Close	Next

DATE	WKS		RECORD TITLE	ARTIST
5/16	11 ^A	8.	Torn	Natalie Imbruglia
5/23	1	9.	My All	Mariah Carey
6/06	13	10.	The Boy Is Mine	Brandy & Monica
8/01	18 ^A	11.	Iris	Goo Goo Dolls
9/05	4	12.	I Don't Want To Miss A Thing	Aerosmith
10/03	5 ↕	13.	The First Night	Monica
10/17	1	14.	One Week	Barenaked Ladies
11/14	2	15.	Doo Wop (That Thing)	Lauryn Hill
11/28	1	16.	Lately	Divine
12/05	6	17.	I'm Your Angel	R. Kelly & Celine Dion

1999

DATE	WKS		RECORD TITLE	ARTIST
1/16	2	1.	Have You Ever?	Brandy
1/30	2	2.	…..Baby One More Time	Britney Spears
2/13	4	3.	Angel Of Mine	Monica
3/13	4	4.	Believe	Cher
4/10	4	5.	No Scrubs	TLC
5/08	5	6.	Livin' La Vida Loca	Ricky Martin
6/12	5	7.	If You Had My Love	Jennifer Lopez
7/17	1	8.	Bills, Bills, Bills	Destiny's Child
7/24	1	9.	Wild Wild West	Will Smith featuring Dru Hill & Kool Mo Dee
7/31	5	10.	Genie In A Bottle	Christina Aguilera
9/04	2	11.	Bailamos	Enrique Iglesias
9/18	3	12.	Unpretty	TLC
10/09	2	13.	Heartbreaker	Mariah Carey (Featuring Jay-Z)
10/23	12	14.	Smooth	Santana Feat. Rob Thomas

2000

DATE	WKS		RECORD TITLE	ARTIST
1/15	2	1.	What A Girl Wants	Christina Aguilera
1/29	4 ↕	2.	I Knew I Loved You	Savage Garden
2/19	1	3.	Thank God I Found You	Mariah (Carey) With Joe & 98°
3/04	2	4.	Amazed	Lonestar
3/18	3	5.	Say My Name	Destiny's Child
4/08	10	6.	Maria Maria	Santana Featuring The Product G&B
6/17	1	7.	Try Again	Aaliyah
6/24	3	8.	Be With You	Enrique Iglesias
7/15	1	9.	Everything You Want	Vertical Horizon
7/22	1	10.	Bent	Matchbox Twenty
7/29	2	11.	It's Gonna Be Me	*NSYNC
8/12	2	12.	Incomplete	Sisqó
8/26	3	13.	Doesn't Really Matter	Janet (Jackson)
9/16	4	14.	Music	Madonna
10/14	4	15.	Come On Over Baby (all I want is you)	Christina Aguilera
11/11	1	16.	With Arms Wide Open	Creed
11/18	11	17.	Independent Women Part I	Destiny's Child

2001

DATE	WKS		RECORD TITLE	ARTIST
2/03	2	1.	It Wasn't Me	Shaggy (Featuring Ricardo "RikRok" Ducent)
2/17	1	2.	Ms. Jackson	OutKast
2/24	4	3.	Stutter	Joe (featuring Mystikal)
3/24	2 ↕	4.	Butterfly	Crazy Town

DATE	WKS		RECORD TITLE	ARTIST
3/31	1	5.	Angel	Shaggy Featuring Rayvon
4/14	7	6.	All For You	Janet Jackson
6/02	5	7.	Lady Marmalade	Christina Aguilera, Lil' Kim, Mya and P!nk
7/07	4	8.	U Remind Me	Usher
8/04	1	9.	Bootylicious	Destiny's Child
8/18	6 ↕	10.	Fallin'	Alicia Keys
9/08	5 ↕	11.	I'm Real	Jennifer Lopez featuring Ja Rule
11/03	6	12.	Family Affair	Mary J. Blige
12/15	6 ↕	13.	U Got It Bad	Usher
12/22	4	14.	How You Remind Me	Nickelback

2002

DATE	WKS		RECORD TITLE	ARTIST
2/23	2	1.	Always On Time	Ja Rule (feat. Ashanti)
3/09	6	2.	Ain't It Funny	Jennifer Lopez featuring Ja Rule
4/20	10	3.	Foolish	Ashanti
6/29	7	4.	Hot In Herre	Nelly
8/17	10 ↕	5.	Dilemma	Nelly Featuring Kelly Rowland
10/05	2	6.	A Moment Like This	Kelly Clarkson
11/09	12	7.	Lose Yourself	Eminem

2003

DATE	WKS		RECORD TITLE	ARTIST
2/01	1	1.	Bump, Bump, Bump	B2K & P. Diddy
2/08	4	2.	All I Have	Jennifer Lopez Featuring LL Cool J
3/08	9	3.	In Da Club	50 Cent
5/10	3	4.	Get Busy	Sean Paul
5/31	4	5.	21 Questions	50 Cent Feat. Nate Dogg
6/28	2	6.	This Is The Night	Clay Aiken
7/12	8	7.	Crazy In Love	Beyoncé (Featuring Jay-Z)
9/06	4	8.	Shake Ya Tailfeather	Nelly/P. Diddy/Murphy Lee
10/04	9	9.	Baby Boy	Beyoncé (Featuring Sean Paul)
12/06	1	10.	Stand Up	Ludacris featuring Shawnna
12/13	9	11.	Hey Ya!	OutKast

THE CHARTS FROM TOP TO BOTTOM

WHEN THE TALK TURNS TO MUSIC, MORE PEOPLE TURN TO JOEL WHITBURN'S RECORD RESEARCH COLLECTION THAN TO ANY OTHER REFERENCE SOURCE.

That's because these are the **only** books that get right to the bottom of *Billboard's* major charts, with **complete, fully accurate chart data on every record ever charted.** So they're quoted with confidence by DJ's, music show hosts, program directors, collectors and other music enthusiasts worldwide.

Each book lists every record's significant chart data, such as peak position, debut date, peak date, weeks charted, label, record number and much more, all conveniently arranged for fast, easy reference. Most books also feature artist biographies, record notes, RIAA Platinum/Gold Record certifications, top artist and record achievements, all-time artist and record rankings, a chronological listing of all #1 hits, and additional in-depth chart information.

TOP POP SINGLES 1955-2002
Over 25,000 pop singles—every Hot 100 hit—arranged by artist. Features thousands of artist biographies and countless titles notes. Also includes the B-side title of every Hot 100 hit. 1,024 pages. Hardcover. $79.95.

POP ANNUAL 1955-1999
A year-by-year ranking, based on chart performance, of over 23,000 pop hits. Also includes, for the first time, the songwriters for every Hot 100 hit. 912 pages. $79.95 Hardcover / $69.95 Softcover.

HIT LIST 1955-1999
An accurate checklist of every title that appears in both our *Top Pop Singles 1955-1999* and *Pop Annual 1955-1999*. Features a check box for each record and picture sleeve (where applicable), debut year, and record label and number on an ample 11" x 8 1/2" page format. 304 pages. Spiral-bound softcover. $39.95.

POP HITS SINGLES & ALBUMS 1940-1954
Four big books in one: an artist-by-artist anthology of early pop classics, a year-by year ranking of pop's early hits, the complete story of the early pop albums and the top 10 singles charts of every *Billboard* Best Selling Singles chart. Filled with artist bios, title notes, and many special sections. 576 pages. Hardcover. $69.95.

POP MEMORIES 1890-1954
Unprecedented in depth and dimension. An artist-by-artist, title-by-title chronicle of the 65 formative years of recorded popular music. Fascinating facts and statistics on over 1,600 artists and 12,000 recordings, compiled directly from America's popular music charts, surveys and record listings. 660 pages. Hardcover. $59.95.

TOP POP ALBUMS 1955-2001
An artist-by-artist history of the over 22,000 albums that ever appeared on *Billboard's* pop albums charts, with a complete A-Z listing below each artist of tracks from every charted album by that artist. 1,208 pages. Hardcover. $99.95.

ALBUM CUTS 1955-2001
A companion guide to our *Top Pop Albums 1955-2001* book—an A-Z list of cut titles along with the artist name and chart debut year of the album on which the cut is first found. 720 pages. Hardcover. $44.95.

BILLBOARD HOT 100/POP SINGLES CHARTS:
THE NINETIES 1990-1999
THE EIGHTIES 1980-1989
THE SEVENTIES 1970-1979
THE SIXTIES 1960-1969
Four complete collections of the actual weekly Hot 100 charts from each decade; black-and-white reproductions at 70% of original size. Over 550 pages each. Deluxe Hardcover. $79.95 each.

POP CHARTS 1955-1959
Reproductions of every weekly pop singles chart *Billboard* published from 1955 through 1959 (Best Sellers, Jockeys, Juke Box, Top 100 and Hot 100). 496 pages. Deluxe Hardcover. $59.95.

BILLBOARD POP ALBUM CHARTS 1965-1969
The greatest of all album eras...straight off the pages of *Billboard!* Every weekly *Billboard* pop albums chart, shown in its entirety, from 1965 through 1969. Black-and-white reproductions at 70% of original size. 496 pages. Deluxe Hardcover. $59.95.

TOP ADULT CONTEMPORARY 1961-2001
Artist-by-artist listing of the nearly 8,000 singles and over 1,900 artists that appeared on *Billboard's* Easy Listening and Hot Adult Contemporary singles charts from July 17, 1961 through December 29, 2001. 352 pages. Hardcover. $44.95.

HOT DANCE/DISCO 1974-2003
First edition! Lists every one of the over 3,800 artists and over 8,000 hits that appeared on *Billboard's* national Dance/Disco Club Play chart from its inception. 368 pages. Hardcover. $49.95.

#1 POP PIX 1953-2003
A Record Research first! *Full-color* pictures of nearly 1,000 *Billboard* Pop/Hot 100 #1 hits of the past 51 years in chronological sequence. 112 pages. Softcover. $24.95.

#1 ALBUM PIX 1945-2004
A Record Research first! Full-color pictures of every *Billboard* Pop, Country and R&B #1 album in chronological sequence. 176 pages. Softcover. $29.95.

ROCK TRACKS 2002 Edition
Two separate artist-by-artist listings of of every title and artist that appeared on *Billboard's* Mainstream (Album)

Rock Tracks chart from March, 1981 through October, 2002 and every title and artist that appeared on *Billboard*'s Modern Rock Tracks chart from September, 1988, through October, 2002. 336 pages. Hardcover. $49.95.

TOP COUNTRY SINGLES 1944-2001
The complete history of the most genuine of American musical genres, with an artist-by-artist listing of every Country single ever charted. 608 pages. Hardcover. $69.95.

COUNTRY ANNUAL 1944-1997
A year-by-year ranking, based on chart performance, of over 16,000 Country hits. 704 pages. Hardcover. $64.95.

TOP COUNTRY ALBUMS 1964-1997
A music industry first and a Record Research exclusive—features an artist-by-artist listing of every album to appear on *Billboard*'s Top Country Albums chart from its first appearance in 1964 through September, 1997. Includes complete listings of all tracks from every Top 10 Country album. 304 pages. Hardcover. $49.95.

A CENTURY OF POP MUSIC
This unique book chronicles the biggest Pop hits of the past 100 years, in yearly rankings of the Top 40 songs of every year from 1900 through 1999. Includes complete artist and title sections, pictures of the top artists, top hits and top artists by decade, and more. 256 pages. Softcover. $39.95.

TOP R&B SINGLES 1942-1999
Revised edition of our R&B bestseller—loaded with new features! Every Soul, Black, Urban Contemporary and Rhythm & Blues charted single, listed by artist. 688 pages. Hardcover. $69.95.

TOP R&B ALBUMS 1965-1998
First edition! An artist-by-artist listing of each of the 2,177 artists and 6,940 albums to appear on *Billboard*'s Top R&B Albums chart. Includes complete listings of all tracks from every Top 10 R&B album. 360 pages. Hardcover. $49.95.

BUBBLING UNDER SINGLES AND ALBUMS 1998 Edition
All Bubbling Under The Hot 100 (1959-1997) and Bubbling Under The Top Pop Albums (1970-1985) charts covered in full and organized artist by artist. Also features a photo section of every EP that hit *Billboard*'s Best Selling Pop EP's chart (1957-1960). 416 pages. Softcover. $49.95.

BILLBOARD TOP 10 SINGLES CHARTS 1955-2000
A complete listing of each weekly Top 10 singles chart from *Billboard*'s Best Sellers chart (1955-July 28, 1958) and Hot 100 chart from its inception (August 4, 1958) through 2000. Each chart shows each single's current and previous week's positions, total weeks charted on the entire chart, original label & number, and more. 712 pages. Hardcover. $49.95.

BILLBOARD TOP 10 ALBUM CHARTS 1963-1998
This books contains more than 1,800 individual Top 10 charts from over 35 years of *Billboard*'s weekly Top Albums chart (currently titled The *Billboard* 200). Each chart shows each album's current and previous week's positions, total weeks charted on the entire Top Albums chart, original label & number, and more. 536 pages. Hardcover. $39.95.

BILLBOARD TOP 1000 x 5 1996 Edition
Includes five complete *separate* rankings—from #1 through #1000—of the all-time top charted hits of Pop & Hot 100 Singles 1955-1996, Pop Singles 1940-1954, Adult Contemporary Singles 1961-1996, R&B Singles 1942-1996, and Country Singles 1944-1996. 288 pages. Softcover. $29.95.

MUSIC YEARBOOKS 2003/2002/2001/2000/1999/1998/1997/1996/1995/1994/1993/1992/1991/1990
A complete review of each year's charted music—as well as a superb supplemental update of our Record Research Pop Singles and Albums, Country Singles, R&B Singles, Adult Contemporary Singles, and Bubbling Under Singles books. Various page lengths. Softcover. 1999 thru 2003 editions $39.95 each / 1995 thru 1998 editions $34.95 each / 1990 thru 1994 editions $29.95 each.

ORDER INFORMATION

Shipping/Handling Extra: If you do not order through our online Web site (see below), please contact us for shipping rates.

ORDER BY:

U.S. Toll-Free: 1-800-827-9810 (orders only please—Mon-Fri 8 AM-12 PM, 1 PM-5 PM CST)

Foreign Orders: 1-262-251-5408

Online at our Web site: www.recordresearch.com

Fax: 1-262-251-9452 (24 hours)

Mail to: Record Research Inc.
P.O. Box 200
Menomonee Falls, WI 53052-0200
U.S.A.

Questions?: 1-262-251-5408 or **Email:** books@recordresearch.com

U.S. orders are shipped **via UPS;** please allow **7-10 business days** for delivery. (If only a post office box number is given, it will be shipped 4th class media mail, which can lengthen the delivery time.)

Canadian and **foreign** orders are shipped **via surface mail;** please allow **8-12 weeks** for delivery. Orders must be paid in U.S. dollars and drawn on a U.S. bank.

For faster delivery, contact us for other shipping options/rates. We now offer **UPS Worldwide Express** service for Canadian and foreign orders as well as **airmail** service through the postal system.

Payment methods accepted: MasterCard, VISA, American Express, money order, or check (personal checks may be held up to 10 days for bank clearance).